S0-BDR-038

NetBEUI Networking . . . . .Chapter 13

NetWare Core OS . . . . .Chapter 11

Network Analyzers . . . . .Chapter 30

Network File System (NFS) . . . . .Chapter 3

Novell's LANalyzer . . . . .Chapter 31

OS/2 Based Networking . . . . . . .Chapter 15

OSI Reference Model . . . . .Chapter 2

Packet Switching . . . . .Chapter 6

Password Schemes . . . . .Chapter 27

Patch Panels . . . . .Chapter 35

Ping of Death . . . . .Chapter 28

Proxy Servers . . . . .Chapter 28

Punch-Down Panels . . . . .Chapter 8

Quick Logon . . . . .Chapter 17

RAID Systems . . . . .Chapter 33

RAS Server and Client
Installation . . . . .Chapter 22

Relay Switches . . . . .Chapter 5

Repeaters . . . . .Chapter 9

Ring Topology . . . . .Chapter 35

Routers .Chapter 9

Server Management . . . . .Chapter 37

Shiva LanRover E/T/Plus . . . . . . .Chapter 23

SMTP and SNMP . . . . .Chapter 3

Spoofing . . . . .Chapter 27

SSL and S-HTTP . . . . .Chapter 28

Stackable Hubs . . . . .Chapter 9

Star Topology . . . . .Chapter 35

Subnet Masks . . . . .Chapter 3

Switches . . . . .Chapter 9

TCP/IP .Chapter 3

Telecommuting . . . . .Chapter 22

Thick & Thin Ethernet . . . . .Chapter 35

Thinnet Cable . . . . .Chapter 7

Token Ring Topology . . . . .Chapter 35

Trend Analysis . . . . .Chapter 37

Troubleshooting Networks . . . . .Chapter 37

Tunneling . . . . .Chapter 22

Twisted-Pair Cable . . . . .Chapter 7

Unix . . . . .Chapter 22

Uplink Port Connection . . . . . . .Chapter 9

VINES/StreetTalk Naming
Convention . . . . .Chapter 15

Virtual Private Networks . . . . . .Chapter 21

VLAN Technology . . . . .Chapter 9

WAN Call Directory . . . . .Chapter 11

Web Servers . . . . .Chapter 18

Windows 95 & 98 . . . . .Chapter 17

Windows NT Server &
Workstation . . . . .Chapter 17

X.25 . . . . .Chapter 37

Zone names . . . . .Chapter 3

The Complete Network Upgrade & Maintenance Guide

The Complete Network Upgrade & Maintenance Guide

Mark Minasi
Jim Blaney
Chris Brenton

SYBEX®

San Francisco • Paris • Düsseldorf •Soest

Associate Publisher: Gary Masters
Contracts and Licensing Manager: Kristine Plachy
Acquisitions & Developmental Editor: Neil Edde
Editors: James A. Compton, Andy Carroll, Doug Robert
Project Editor: Emily K. Wolman
Technical Editor: Rima Regas
Book Designer: Kris Warrenburg
Graphic Illustrator: Tony Jonick
Electronic Publishing Specialists: Cyndy Johnsen, Nila Nichols, Koko Kaminski
Production Coordinators: Charles Mathews, Shannon Murphy
Indexer: Matthew Spence
Companion CD: Ginger Warner
Cover Designer: Archer Design
Cover Illustrator/Photographer: FPG International

Library of Congress Card Number: 98-86639
ISBN: 0-7821-2259-0

Manufactured in the United States of America

10 9 8 7 6 5 4 3 2 1

To Brian, Michael and Paul, Diane and Tônu, and
my little nephews Andy and Markus.
It's been too long since I've seen all of you.
Thanks for waiting for me.

—Jim Blaney

ACKNOWLEDGMENTS

Much credit must go to each of the following individuals, who contributed significantly to the material presented in this book:

Chris Brenton, for his substantial and well-written contributions to many parts of this book, including networking theory, networking hardware and software, and troubleshooting. His breadth of experience and grasp of networking issues are truly first-class.

Peter Loshin, for his detailed and very insightful presentation of extranets and WAN implementation and troubleshooting.

Logan G. Harbaugh, for his excellent coverage of the myriad issues involved in network troubleshooting, at both the hardware and software levels.

Many thanks also to Gary Govanus and Bill Heldman. These guys were both indispensable in writing some great chapters on a tough deadline after the project was already well under way. Good job, guys!

I also wish to thank all of the folks who helped out with this project at Sybex. To begin with, there's developmental and acquisitions editor Neil Edde, who first presented me with the idea for this project, and has ever since been helpful to me with his suggestions, encouragement, and behind-the-scenes help; Jim Compton led the editing team, which also included Andy Carroll, Doug Robert, and Kris Vanberg-Wolff. Emily Wolman, project editor for this book, did a super job of keeping me going. Her good-humored efforts to keep me running when the road ahead appeared long and winding were, thankfully, actually successful.

Thanks also to the Sybex production team: production coordinators Charles Mathews and Shannon Murphy, electronic publishing specialists Cyndy Johnsen, Koko Kaminski, and Nila Nichols, illustrator Tony Jonick, and last but not least, technical editor and Apple maven Rima Regas (who also deserves special thanks for contributing parts of several chapters). Without each of you, this book would just be a long string of ones and zeroes that happened to find their way across the Internet.

Sure hope I haven't left anyone out. To all of you involved in helping to make this project a success, my heartfelt thanks.

CONTENTS AT A GLANCE

Introduction   *xxxv*

PART I: **Network Communications Concepts**

Chapter 1:   Networking Overview   3

Chapter 2:   The OSI Model and Protocol Communication   29

Chapter 3:   Specific Networking Protocols   77

Chapter 4:   Ethernet Overview   171

Chapter 5:   Token Ring Overview   187

Chapter 6:   Network Topologies   207

PART II: **Network Hardware**

Chapter 7:   Transmission Media   269

Chapter 8:   Network Adapters and Punch-Down Panels   319

Chapter 9:   Repeaters, Hubs, Routers, and Bridges   335

Chapter 10: Workstations, Servers, and Additional Connectivity
             Hardware   383

PART III: **Network Server Software**

Chapter 11: Novell NetWare/IntraNetWare   403

Chapter 12: Windows NT Server   459

Chapter 13: Unix/Linux   501

Chapter 14: Lotus Notes   553

Chapter 15: OS/2 Warp, Banyan VINES/StreetTalk, and LANtastic   575

Chapter 16: AppleTalk and AppleShare   609

PART IV: Network Client Software

Chapter 17: Who Can Talk to Whom   633

PART V: Interconnecting Networks

Chapter 18: Adding Internet Access   707

Chapter 19: Building an Intranet   741

Chapter 20: Introduction to Extranets   771

Chapter 21: Extranet Infrastructure   805

PART VI: Accessing Networks Remotely

Chapter 22: Implementing an Effective Telecommuting System   837

Chapter 23: Remote Access Hardware   877

PART VII: Optimizing and Fine-Tuning for Performance

Chapter 24: Ways to Speed Up an Existing Server   901

Chapter 25: Creating and Using a Network Baseline   927

Chapter 26: Stress-Testing Techniques   949

PART VIII: Network Security Issues

Chapter 27: Top Ten Things You Can Do to Increase Security   963

Chapter 28: Internet-Related Security Issues   993

PART IX: Troubleshooting and Preventive Maintenance

Chapter 29: Basic Elements of Troubleshooting   1041

Chapter 30: Hardware Troubleshooting Tools   1059

Chapter 31: Software Troubleshooting Tools   1085

Chapter 32: Diagnosing Real-World Problems   1131

Chapter 33: Troubleshooting Servers   1155

Chapter 34: Troubleshooting Workstations   1213

Chapter 35: Troubleshooting the Physical Network   1277

Chapter 36: Troubleshooting Network Printing   1317

Chapter 37: Troubleshooting WANs   1357

Chapter 38: A Pound of Prevention   1393

Appendices

Appendix A: Information Resources   1425

Appendix B: Vendor Web Sites   1445

Appendix C: Manufacturer's Ethernet Identifiers   1455

Appendix D: Glossary   1463

Index   *1484*

TABLE OF CONTENTS

Introduction   *xxxv*

PART I   **Network Communications Concepts**   **1**

1   **Networking Overview**   **3**

Fundamental Networking Terms and Concepts   5
   Going Digital   5
   Basic Networking Conventions   6
A Tour of Networking Topics Covered   9
   Networking Theory and Concepts   9
   Network Hardware   12
   Server Software   16
   Client Software   19
   Interconnecting Networks   19
   Accessing Networks Remotely   21
   Optimizing and Fine-Tuning   22
   Security Issues   22
   Troubleshooting and Preventive Maintenance   24
Summary   27

2   **The OSI Model and Protocol Communication**   **29**

A Protocol's Job   31
   A Little Background   32
The OSI Model   33
   How the OSI Model Works   38
   More on the Network Layer   42
   Routers   43
Summary   75

3   **Specific Networking Protocols**   **77**

The Internet Protocol Suite (TCP/IP)   78
   IP Address Conventions   79

Standard Subnet Masks   80
Registered IP Addresses   83
Special Addresses   88
Reserved Address Ranges   93
Nonstandard Subnetting   94
Routing with IP   103
Transport Layer Services   110
IP Application Services   111
Internetwork Packet Exchange (IPX)   131
IPX Network Addressing   132
IPX Routing   134
Transport Layer Services   135
IPX Application Layer Services   147
Network Basic Input/Output System (NetBIOS)   148
NetBIOS Addressing   149
Routing with NetBIOS   153
Session and Transport Layer Support   156
NetBIOS Extended User Interface (NetBEUI)   157
AppleTalk   158
Address Space   159
Network Layer Services   162
AppleTalk Routing   163
Transport and Session Layer Services   164
Upper Layer Services   165
Summary   168

4   Ethernet Overview   171

The IEEE 802.*x* Standards   172
Ethernet Frames   173
Intro to CSMA/CD   175
How CSMA/CD Works: Transmitting   175
How CSMA/CD Works: Receiving   177
Ethernet Cabling Options   179
Thin and Thick Coax   180
Unshielded Twisted-Pair (UTP)   181
Advantages and Disadvantages of Ethernet   183
Summary   185

5   Token Ring Overview   187

How Token Ring Works   188
Token Ring Topology Basics   191
Token Ring Hardware Overview   191
   The Network Adapter   192
   The Cabling   192
   The Multi-Station Access Unit (MSAU)   192
   Connectors   193
   Relay Switches   193
Token Ring Stations   193
   Active Monitor (AM)   195
   Standby Monitor (SM)   197
   Ring Parameter Server (RPS)   197
   Ring Error Monitor (REM)   198
   Configuration Report Server (CRS)   198
Token Ring Processes   199
   Station Initialization   199
   Monitor Contention   200
   Ring Purge   200
   Ring Poll   200
   Beaconing   201
Advantages and Disadvantages of Token Ring   202
Summary   204

6   Network Topologies   207

Topology Basics   208
   Physical Topology   208
   Logical Topology   211
Connection Types   212
   Circuit Switching   212
   Message Switching   213
   Packet Switching   214
Ethernet Networks   216
   The Frame Header Section   218
Local Area Network Topologies   221
   10Mb Ethernet   221
   100Mb Ethernet   225
   1Gbps Ethernet   229
   100VG-AnyLAN   231

FDDI	235
ATM	242
Wide Area Network Topologies	246
Dial-Up Analog	249
ISDN	255
Leased Lines	258
T1	259
Frame Relay/X.25	261
SONET	264
Summary	265

PART II   Network Hardware   267

7   Transmission Media   269

Transmission Basics	270
Analog and Digital Transmissions	270
Sources of Noise	276
Communication Synchronization	278
Media Choices for Analog and Digital Transmissions	279
Thinnet Cable	282
Cable Properties	282
Connector Types	284
Advantages	286
Disadvantages	286
Appropriate Applications	288
Cable Specifications	288
Twisted-Pair Cable	289
Cable Properties	289
Full Duplex Support	292
Connector Types	293
Advantages	296
Disadvantages	297
Appropriate Applications	298
Cable Specifications	299
Fiber-Optic Cable	299
Cable Properties	299
Connector Types	305
Advantages	305
Disadvantages	307

Appropriate Applications   307
Cable Specifications   308
The Atmosphere   309
Light Transmissions   309
Radio Waves   310
Terrestrial Transmissions   310
Space-Based Transmissions   311
Network Design Examples   312
A Small Field Office   313
A Medium-Size Network   313
A Campus Network   314
Summary   316

8   Network Adapters and Punch-Down Panels   319

Network Interface Card   320
External Port Connection   321
PC Card Connection   322
Internal Network Card Connection   324
Topology and Wiring Support   326
Punch-Down Panels   328
Punching Down the Wire   328
Things to Consider   329
Labeling Schemes   330
Media Converters   330
Summary   333

9   Repeaters, Hubs, Routers, and Bridges   335

Repeaters   336
Why Use a Repeater?   337
Choosing a Repeater   337
Hubs   338
Chassis Hubs   338
Stackable Hubs   340
Splitting Up Networks   343
Bridges   345
A Bridge Example   345
Balancing Traffic Segmentation and Bridge Latency   348
Protocol Independence   349

The Spanning Tree Protocol   350
Use a Bridge to Segment Traffic   353
Monitoring Traffic in a Bridged Environment   358
Switches   359
Full-Duplex Operation   360
Cut-Through Mode   361
Store-and-Forward Mode   362
Avoiding Switch Overload   363
VLAN Technology   364
When to Deploy Switching   368
Routers   371
Protocols   371
A Routed Network Example   372
Protocol Specificity   374
Bridging and Routing Compared   375
Protocol Address Conventions   376
Switch Routers   379
When a Switch Router Is Useful   379
Brouters   380
Summary   380

**10   Workstations, Servers, and Additional
       Connectivity Hardware   383**

Workstations   384
The Workstation Image   385
From Boot PROMs to Thin Clients   386
Drawbacks   387
File Servers   388
Server Types   388
Workstation or Server?   391
Modems   393
Channel Binding   393
Codexes   394
ISDN Modems   395
Cable Modems   396
DSL   397
CSU/DSUs   398
DSU   398
CSU   399
Summary   399

PART III   Network Server Software   401

11   Novell NetWare/IntraNetWare   403

IntraNetWare Features   404
   IntraNetWare Setup   404
   NetWare Core OS   405
   File System   408
   Account Administration   410
   Security   411
   Networking   413
   IP Applications   414
Configuring IntraNetWare for Network Access   416
   Frame Types   416
   Configuring Networking from the Command Line 418
   Configuring Networking with INETCFG.NLM   426
IntraNetWare IP Applications   451
   Using SAMBA to Create Shares on IntraNetWare 451
NT 5, or the Future of IntraNetWare   455
Summary   456

12   Windows NT Server   459

Windows NT Features   460
   Windows NT Setup   460
   NT Core OS   462
   File System   464
   Account Administration   465
   Security   469
   Networking   470
   IP Applications   472
Configuring NT Server for Network Access   473
   System Identification   473
   Configuring Network Services   474
   Configuring Network Protocols   488
   Adapters   495
   Bindings   496
   Saving Your Changes   497
NT Server IP Applications   497
The Future of NT Server   498
Summary   499

13   Unix/Linux   **501**

So Many Flavors, So Few Pages   503
Linux History   504
  Linux Is Copyleft Software   505
Linux Features   505
  Linux Setup   506
Core OS   509
File System   514
Account Administration   516
Security   517
  Linux Security Tools   517
Networking   518
  OSI Layer 2 Support   519
  IP Networking Support   519
  Linux and NetWare   521
  NetBEUI Networking   522
  AppleTalk Networking   522
  Network Routing   522
IP Applications   523
Configuring Network Access   526
  To Make or Not to Make…   526
  Changing the Network Driver Settings   537
  Starting Network Services   538
  Configuring Routing   539
The SAMBA Suite   541
  Using SAMBA to Access Shares from Unix   541
  Using SAMBA to Create Shares from Unix   545
  Appropriate Uses for SAMBA   549
Configuring IP Services   549
The Future of Linux   550
Summary   550

14   Lotus Notes   **553**

Lotus Notes Features   555
Lotus Notes Setup   555
  Optimizing Windows NT for Lotus Notes   556
Core Features   557
  Replication   557
  The Client-Server Model   559
  Other OS Features   560
  Account Administration   561

Security   562
   The User ID File   562
   Certificates   563
   Encryption   564
   Access Control List (ACL)   565
Networking   567
Lotus Notes Client   568
Domino (Internet Services)   569
Configuring Network Access   570
Summary   573

15   OS/2 Warp, Banyan VINES/StreetTalk, and LANtastic   575
OS/2-Based Networking   576
   Installing and Configuring OS/2 Warp 4   578
   Sharing Resources Using OS/2 WARP   583
   Accessing Shared Resources Using OS/2 WARP   585
Banyan VINES and StreetTalk   586
   Installing StreetTalk for Windows NT   588
   Installing Banyan Enterprise Client   592
   Installing StreetTalk Explorer for Windows NT   594
   Using VINES   595
LANtastic (for Windows NT)   597
   Installing LANtastic on NT   597
   Configuring and Using LANtastic   599
   LANtastic Summary   605
Summary   606

16   AppleTalk and AppleShare   609
The AppleTalk Protocol   610
   LocalTalk   611
   EtherTalk   614
   TokenTalk   615
   Other AppleTalk Protocols   616
AppleShare: The Next Generation   619
   In the Beginning   619
   AppleShare and AppleShare IP   620
   ASIP 5 Features   620
Summary   628

PART IV   **Network Client Software**   **631**

17   Who Can Talk to Whom   **633**

Who Can Talk to Whom   634
Configuring Client Communications in a NetWare Environment   635
    The Novell Client Drivers for NetWare   635
    The Microsoft Client Drivers for NetWare   670
    Comparing Client32 and the Microsoft Client   673
    NetWare IP   681
Configuring Client Communications in a
    Windows NT Environment   683
    Installing the Microsoft Client on Windows 95/98   683
    Configuring the Microsoft Client on Windows 95/98   685
    Configuring NT Workstation   691
Using NFS to Access File Services between Unix Systems   692
Connectivity with Apple Computers   697
    Apple and NetWare   697
    Apple and NT   698
    Peer Networking with Apple, Windows 95/98, and NT   700
A Last Resort: Bridging the Gaps Using FTP   700
Summary   703

PART V   **Interconnecting Networks**   **705**

18   Adding Internet Access   **707**

Initial Considerations   709
    Firewalls and NAT   709
    Deciding on Throughput   712
    Additional Considerations   716
Web Servers   717
    NCSA Httpd   718
    Apache   718
    Microsoft Internet Information Server   719
    Netscape   719
Operating Systems   720
Choosing a Browser   721
    The Browser Wars—Internet Explorer vs. Communicator   721
    How They're Similar   722
    How They're Different   723

Which One Is Best?   723
Browser Administration   724
Plug-Ins and Companions   724
Best of the Rest   725
Getting Connected   726
Hardware   727
Other Charges   729
Rolling Out the Browser   730
Maintaining Your Connection   730
Internet Security   731
Starting to Secure Your Network   734
Browser Security   736
Summary   738

19   Building an Intranet   741

Needs Assessment   742
Benefits of an Intranet   743
Disadvantages of an Intranet   744
Intranet Considerations   746
Firewalls   747
Intranet Addressing Considerations   753
Assigning Addresses   763
Intranet Security   765
Selecting a Web Server   766
Adding and Maintaining Content   767
How Good Does It Get?   767
Summary   768

20   Introduction to Extranets   771

Technology Waves   772
A Very Brief History of Internetworking   774
The Internet Wave   777
The Intranet Wave   780
The Extranet Wave   781
The Next Waves   783
The Coming Wave: Extranets   786
A Logical Extension of Internetworking Technology   786
Extranet Application Architectures   787
External Intranets   787

Extended Intranets   790
    What Exactly Is an Extranet?   793
Extranets and Distributed Objects   794
Extending Internetworking Technologies   795
    Seamless Interoperability   796
    Platform Independence   796
Solving Real-World Problems   797
    Extending Intranet Functionality with Extranets   798
    Building Business Relationships with Extranets   800
    Fostering Internet Commerce with Extranets   800
    Adding Value with Extranets   801
Summary   802

21   Extranet Infrastructure   805

Interorganizational Internetworking   807
    A Very Big Extranet   807
    Extranet Topology Options   811
    The Private Extranet   812
    The Open Extranet   815
    The Hybrid Extranet   821
    Extranet Service Providers   821
Virtual Private Networks   823
    Tunnels and Gateways   823
    How the Virtual Private Network Works   824
    Virtual Private Network Security Issues   826
Extranet Design Structures   827
    Access Network Design Issues   829
    Extranet Structure and Backbones   830
Summary   832

PART VI   Accessing Networks Remotely   835

22   Implementing an Effective Telecommuting System   837

Telecommuting Basics   838
    When Is Telecommuting Appropriate?   839
    Advantages of Telecommuting   839
    Disadvantages of Telecommuting   844

Telecommuting via Remote Control   846
   Advantages of Remote Control   847
   Disadvantages of Remote Control   848
   Remote Control Options   849
Telecommuting via Remote Access   859
   Advantages of Remote Access   860
   Remote Access Options   860
   RAS Server and Client Installation   861
The Modem Connection   869
   Modem Basics   869
   Getting the Most from Your Modem   873
Higher-Speed Remote Access   874
   ISDN   874
   Tunneling   874
Summary   875

23   Remote Access Hardware   877
Network Operating System RAS   878
Multiport Serial Adapters   880
   Universal Asynchronous Receiver/Transmitter (UART) 883
   Installing the Multiport Serial Adapter   884
   Port Enumeration   886
   Cable Cluttering and Labeling   886
   Testing   887
   Integrated Services Digital Networks (ISDN) Lines 888
   Digital Subscriber Line (DSL)   888
Remote Access Servers   890
   The 3Com AccessBuilder 4000 Remote Access Server 891
   The Shiva LanRover E/T/Plus   894
   Costs   895
Technology Differences   895
Summary   896

PART VII   Optimizing and Fine-Tuning for Performance   899

24   Ways to Speed Up an Existing Server   901
Clones versus Name-Brand Servers   902
   The Microsoft Hardware Compatibility List (HCL)   904

Adding RAM 904
Improving Disk Performance 907
   Adding Another Hard Drive 907
   Adding RAID and Disk Striping 910
Making Ethernet Faster 914
   The Cable Plant 914
   Hubs 915
   Routers 920
Multiple Subnets 921
Profiling 922
Summary 923

25 Creating and Using a Network Baseline   **927**

Benefits of Baselining 929
When Should Baselining Be Performed? 930
How Is Baselining Performed? 931
   Baselining with Performance Monitor 932
   Selecting the Best Counters to Log 940
   Monitoring NetWare 3.x and 4.x Systems 941
   Using Utilities for Baseline Information 944
The Payoff: Applying Baseline Information 945
Summary 946

26 Stress-Testing Techniques   **949**

What Is Stress Testing? 950
Dumb vs. Intelligent Loads 950
   Dumb Loads 950
   Intelligent Loads 950
Benefits of Stress Testing 951
   Stress Testing and Planning for Upgrades 951
   Stress Testing and Security 952
When Should Stress Testing Be Performed? 953
How Is Stress Testing Performed? 954
Tools for Stress Testing 955
   Novell's GENLOAD and VARLOAD 955
   LoadRunner (Mercury Interactive) 956
   NetBench, ServerBench, and WebBench (Ziff-Davis) 956
   NetTester/1 (Phoenix Software) 957
   Chariot and Pegasus (Ganymede Software) 958
Summary 958

PART VIII   Network Security Issues   961

27   Top Ten Things You Can Do to Increase Security   963

Why Network Security?   964
Password Schemes   967
   Password Basics   967
Remove Default Accounts   969
Assigning User and Group Rights   970
   File System Rights   971
   Unique User Directories   974
Securing E-Mail   976
   E-Mail Basics   977
   Internal E-Mail Security   979
   External E-Mail Security   980
   Spamming Protection   982
   Spoofing   983
NT Workstation   984
   Advantages of NT Workstation (NTWS)   984
   Disadvantages of NTWS   985
Using Encryption   986
Separate Networks   987
Removable Disks and Drives   987
Monitoring Information Access   988
   Who Should Audit?   989
   What Should Be Audited?   989
Summary   990

28   Internet-Related Security Issues   993

Firewalls and Gateways   994
   Firewalls 101   994
   Types of Firewalls   996
   Application Gateways as Firewalls   999
   Firewall Issues   1000
Proxy Servers   1001
   Microsoft Proxy Server   1002
   Netscape Proxy Server   1003
   WinGate   1006

Peer-to-Peer File Sharing and the Internet 1007
    Security in an NT Environment 1008
User Authentication 1017
    SSL and S-HTTP 1017
Virtual Private Networks and Tunneling 1020
    How VPNs Work 1021
    Tunneling 1022
Browser Loopholes 1023
    Java and JavaScript 1023
    ActiveX 1025
Ping of Death, Denial-of-Service Attacks, and Other Threats 1026
    Ping of Death 1027
    Syn_Flooder 1027
    DNSKiller 1027
    arnudp100.c 1028
    cbcb.c 1028
Web Server Strategies 1028
    Access Logging 1028
    Directory-Level Access 1031
    Password Authentication 1035
    Client Certificate Authentication 1036
Summary 1037

PART IX   Troubleshooting and Preventive Maintenance   1039

29   Basic Elements of Troubleshooting   1041
An Approach to Troubleshooting 1043
    Breaking Down the Elements 1043
    Trying Different Solutions 1043
Troubleshooting New Systems and Additions to Existing Systems 1044
    Stripping Down to the Minimum 1045
    Keeping Track of Configuration Details 1045
Troubleshooting Existing Systems 1047
Attitude: The Most Important Troubleshooting Tool! 1048
Record Keeping 1049
Resources for Troubleshooters 1052
Aids for Troubleshooting 1053
    Fault Points for Identifying Problem Areas 1053
Summary 1056

30   Hardware Troubleshooting Tools   1059

Basic Cable Checkers   1060
   Topology Wiring Requirements   1062
Cable Testers   1063
   Testing Fiber Cable   1066
Handheld Diagnostic Tools   1066
Network Monitoring Tools   1067
Network Analyzers   1069
Monitoring through Network Hardware   1070
   Monitoring Features to Look For   1072
Summary   1082

31   Software Troubleshooting Tools   1085

Novell's LANalyzer   1086
   Dashboard   1086
   Capture Buffer   1087
   Alarms   1087
   Detailed Statistics and Trends   1088
   The Station Monitor   1090
IntraNetWare   1093
   Console Tools   1093
   Workstation Commands   1113
Windows NT Server   1114
   Command-Line Networking Tools   1114
   GUI Networking Tools   1121
Unix   1123
Summary   1129

32   Diagnosing Real-World Problems   1131

Ping Strangeness   1132
   Security   1133
   Bandwidth   1134
   Looking for Clues   1134
Duplicate IP Addresses   1136
Undeliverable Mail   1138
Connectivity Problems after a Server Upgrade   1143
Excessive Network Collisions   1150
   Diagnosing the Problem   1151
   Working through the Problem Logically   1151
Summary   1153

33 Troubleshooting Servers   **1155**

Snapshot: Troubleshooting Servers   1156
   NT Server Troubleshooting Snapshot   1156
   Novell NetWare Troubleshooting Snapshot   1160
A Brief History of NetWare   1162
Fault Points for Servers   1163
NetWare Version-Specific Information   1165
   NetWare 2.*x* Operation   1166
   NetWare 3.*x* Operation   1166
   NetWare 4.*x* Operation   1167
Troubleshooting New Servers   1169
   Hardware Problems in New Servers   1169
   Software Problems in New Servers   1178
Troubleshooting Existing Servers   1188
   Hardware Problems in Existing Servers   1189
   Software Problems in Existing Servers   1192
   Intermittent Problems with Servers   1194
Using Other Diagnostic Tools   1195
Managing the NetWare Binderies or NetWare Directory   1196
Upgrading NetWare   1197
Troubleshooting NetWare's NLM Problems   1197
Using System Fault Tolerance   1198
   Mirroring and Duplexing   1198
   RAID for Fault Tolerance   1199
   SFT Level III   1201
Real-Life Stories   1201
   Scenario One: Installing a New System   1202
   Scenario Two: Maintaining an Existing System   1207
Summary   1210

34 Troubleshooting Workstations   **1213**

Snapshot: Troubleshooting Workstations   1214
Fault Points for Workstations   1218
   Workstation-to-Network Connection Failures   1220
   PC Card, Motherboard, and BIOS Failures   1221
   Operating System and Network Driver Failures   1221
   User Failures   1224
Troubleshooting Workstations—The Basics   1224
   Checking Connections   1225

Checking for Changes 1226
Checking New Installations 1226
Troubleshooting PC-Compatible Stations 1226
Troubleshooting PC Hardware 1227
Troubleshooting PC Software 1233
Windows and Networks 1237
Windows 3 through Windows 3.11 1238
Windows 95/98 1240
Windows NT 1242
OS/2 Clients 1243
PS/2 (Micro Channel) Clients 1244
Macintosh Clients 1244
Macintosh Hardware and Software 1245
Understanding the Basics 1246
The Startup Sequence 1248
Mounting Remote Volumes 1258
Configuring Open Transport 1259
SCSI Devices for Macintoshes 1260
Macintosh Printing 1262
Unix Workstations 1262
Real-Life Stories 1263
Scenario One: Installing a New Workstation 1263
Scenario Two: Maintaining an Existing Workstation 1267
Scenario Three: Another Existing Workstation 1269
Scenario Four: An Existing Macintosh 1271
Summary 1274

35   Troubleshooting the Physical Network   1277

Snapshot: Troubleshooting the Physical Network 1278
Fault Points for the Physical Network 1280
Network Topologies 1282
Ring Topology 1284
Star Topology 1285
Linear Bus Topology 1285
Data Communication Protocols 1286
IPX/SPX 1287
IP (TCP/IP) 1287
NetBEUI 1288

NetBIOS   1288
AppleTalk   1288
OSI and the OSI Model   1288
An Overview of Hardware Standards   1290
Ethernet   1291
Token Ring   1292
LocalTalk   1294
ARCnet   1295
Tracking Down Cabling Plant Problems   1296
Cabling: Lengths, Termination, Grounds, Connectors, and Type   1297
Patch Panels, Repeaters, and Concentrators   1299
Routers, Bridges, and Gateways   1300
Documenting the Cabling Plant   1300
Real-Life Stories   1301
Scenario One: A New Cabling System   1301
Scenario Two: Part of an Existing Network Fails   1304
Scenario Three: An Existing Token Ring Network   1306
Scenario Four: Caring for a Growing Network   1308
Scenario Five: Fun with AppleTalk   1312
Summary   1315

36 Troubleshooting Network Printing   **1317**

Snapshot: Troubleshooting Network Printing   1318
Fault Points for Network Printing   1323
The Printing Process   1327
The "Shell"—(NetWare Printer Redirection)   1328
CAPTURE.EXE and Print Jobs—Printing Options   1329
The NetWare Print Queue   1330
PSERVER—Printing Controls   1331
The Print Server   1331
NetWare Configuration Files or Attributes   1332
Windows 9x/NT Client Printer Troubleshooting   1332
Serial and Parallel Interfaces   1334
The Printer   1335
Troubleshooting PostScript Printers   1336
Troubleshooting NetWare for Macintosh Printing   1337
Troubleshooting Unix Printing   1338
Real-Life Stories   1340
Scenario One: A New PostScript Printer   1340
Scenario Two: A Router As Print Server   1344

Scenario Three: Remote Printing with NetWare 4.*x*   1347
Scenario Four: A Single Workstation That Can't Print   1350
Scenario Five: Macintosh Printing Problems   1352
Summary   1354

37   Troubleshooting WANs   1357

How LANs Are Connected to Form WANs   1358
Connecting Multiple LANs at One Site   1359
Connecting LANs between Buildings   1361
Connecting LANs across Long Distances   1362
Connecting LANs around the World   1365
Additional Fault Points of WANs   1367
Troubleshooting WAN Hardware   1368
Dealing with Telecommunications Service Providers   1372
Troubleshooting WAN Software   1372
Network Management Tools   1375
What's Available   1376
Features to Look For   1376
Diagnostic Tools   1378
Hardware-Based Products   1379
Software-Only Products   1381
Managing without Diagnostic Equipment   1384
Services across WANs   1385
Printing on WANs   1385
Managing Multiple Logins   1386
Novell Directory Services and WANs   1386
The New Structure of NetWare 4.*x*   1387
NWADMIN: The New Management Tool   1390
Troubleshooting NDS   1390
Summary   1391

38   A Pound of Prevention   1393

Managing Backup Systems   1395
Evaluating Backup Systems   1396
Developing a Backup Plan   1400
Backing Up Workstation Data   1401
Managing Power Protection   1402
Evaluating Power Protection Systems   1402
Evaluating System Power Requirements   1404

The Quality of Your Equipment   1404
Preventive Maintenance and Other Precautions   1405
    Getting Rid of Dust and Other Contaminants   1406
    Checking Connections   1406
    Taking Anti-Static Precautions   1406
    Following Manufacturer's Directions   1407
    Maintaining a Return Path   1408
Maintaining Fault Tolerance   1409
Keeping Network Plans and Logs   1411
    Documenting the Network   1411
    Logging Network Events   1412
Training the Users   1413
Protecting Your Network against Viruses   1414
Elements of Network Security   1416
    Physical Security   1416
    Password and Login Security   1417
    Trustee and File Rights   1418
    Dial-In Access Security   1418
    Other Access Security   1419
Recovering from Disaster—in Advance   1419
    The Recovery Plan   1420
    Data Recovery in Advance   1420
    Recovery Services in Advance   1420
Summary   1421

Appendices   1423

A   Information Resources   1425
Books   1426
    Network Administration   1426
    Intranets   1428
    IntraNetWare/NetWare   1429
    Reference   1432
    Windows NT   1432
    Unix/Linux   1435
    Security   1435
Online Magazines   1435
Internet Newsgroups   1438

	Standards Organizations	1439
	Web Pages	1440
	Certification Programs	1442
	CNA, CNE	1442
	MCSE	1442
B	**Vendor Web Sites**	**1445**
	Hardware	1446
	Cables/Connectors	1451
	Software	1452
	Mail-Order Networking Equipment Suppliers	1452
C	**Manufacturer's Ethernet Identifiers**	**1455**
D	**Glossary**	**1463**
	Index	*1484*

INTRODUCTION

This is a book about communication—not just the networking technologies that allow computers to communicate, but also the communication between human beings that allows computer networks to operate effectively and meet their users' needs.

In the last half century, computers have steadily increased both their processing speed and their storage size, while software has played tag with each advance by increasing the level of sophistication achievable and at the same time demanding even greater speed and storage. Of course, these computers are not accomplishing their increasingly complex tasks one by one, in a vacuum. Just as communication enables human beings to accomplish far more together than they ever could singly, carrying this idea over to enable computers to intercommunicate with each other has brought incredible advances as well.

Networks are a more recent arrival than the computers, but much of what allows computers to intercommunicate is grounded in technology first developed to enable people to communicate. One of the first real "networks" was the US telephone network, with all its switches, hubs, and thousands of miles of connecting wires. Prior to that, we can trace the development backward to the telegraph; and it's not too much of a stretch to include smoke signals and the beating of drums.

Amazingly, one of the earliest implementations of computer networking was the precursor to the Transmission Control Protocol/Internet Protocol (TCP/IP). As discussed throughout this book, much of networking is simply the hashing out of standards, which when followed accurately allow for large networks to be put together relatively quickly. Decentralization, the use of distributed address directories, built-in redundancy, and automatic rerouting of packets—all of these aspects of TCP/IP are enabling an ongoing revolution in world-wide networking. Most important, the use of standards allows businesses and their networks to implement these changes with minimal down-time for needed repairs and upgrades.

Maintaining reliability is, or should be, a goal for all networks: Keep the network operational and dependable, even despite (and in the midst of) server failures, cable breaks, hub failures, and other types of problems.

Today, most networks consist of interdepartmental, interoffice, intercity, interagency, and, in some cases, international networks whose primary purpose is the rapid sharing of information. More and more, the limits of distance and geography are being transcended as the entire world is being "wired" with computer networks.

Where does this leave us? For one thing, it's pretty decent job security for anyone working with networks. There is one catch, though: The information that we as IP professionals need to implement current networking technologies efficiently and effectively is accumulating—and changing with challenging speed. Almost anyone can connect a few computers together with cable, but it takes quite a bit of knowledge and experience to develop and manage a larger network adequately.

Why This Book?

While there are plenty of networking books on the market, surprisingly few currently attempt to condense into one volume background theory, planning and troubleshooting theory, and plenty of actual experience as well. An important goal of this book has been to help you reinforce those areas you're already familiar with and fill in gaps in the areas where you may be lacking some knowledge. Most of all, we want you to learn from the mistakes and experiences of others. Seeing what has worked and what has not worked in similar situations may help you apply the networking theory and technical specifications to your own conditions.

In this book, heavy emphasis is given first to establishing how networks operate, in all their component pieces. First, we'll look at the theory, and then we'll move on to networking hardware components and server and client software. With this foundation, we'll move on to interconnecting smaller networks to create medium- and large-sized networks, including intranets, WANs, and extranets. A hefty section of this book then focuses on troubleshooting techniques—the equipment to use, the approaches to take, and plenty of details specific to particular types of networks or network components.

Throughout this book, we emphasize the importance of being and staying informed, and of preventing problems before they occur. Monitoring, benchmarking, stress testing and baselining are all explained, and many benefits to performing each of these functions are made clear. This may even help you justify additional budget or human resources allocations to address your network's needs.

Over the next few years, many exciting changes are coming for networking—computers and networks are both still in their beginning stages. By being properly informed now, we can be better equipped to assimilate whatever changes do occur. Certainly, we can look to the Internet as an example of where we're all headed: Networks will increasingly be interconnected to each other, information will become ever more accessible—not just quantitatively, but with hierarchical directories that will revolutionize the task of searching for new and related information. Within a very few years, satellite or other forms of communication may make networking so ubiquitous that networks may no longer be thought of primarily in terms of cabling. Not only that, but we'll also be talking to (and hearing from) our computers, and software for translating between human languages may even "go mainstream."

With any such changes, though, it will be necessary to get from here to there, and doing that will require many skilled network people who understand the current technology well and can address current networking problems effectively. While technology itself changes, the implementation and problem-solving concepts and strategies used to deploy these technologies largely do not change. That is why this book does not just encourage you to become familiar with technical gadgetry, it also tries to instill certain "frames of mind," concepts, and ideas that transcend particular technologies and can enable you to remain successful in keeping your network of computers running in top form, no matter what mix of technologies your network includes.

This book is intended to be a general-purpose, all-in-one-volume guide to networking. If you find yourself needing to upgrade the size or speed of your network, if you have strange or difficult network problems to track down, or if you are just wondering what more can be done to improve the overall efficiency and smooth operation of your network, you've come to the right book!

While we've attempted to make this a book anyone can pick up and start using, we've also not shied away from including networking theory and more technical details wherever these seemed likely to help and not simply belabor a point. Most professional LAN administrators should find something in here that is new, and anyone who digests all the material presented here should have a very thorough grounding not only in how networks work, but in how to improve them.

Who Should Read This Book?

Everyone whose livelihood depends upon a smoothly running network should read this book. This includes system administrators, network administrators, assistant network administrators, VARs, systems integrators, ISD folks, and anyone planning a new network or expanding an existing network—as well as just anyone else who is curious about how networks operate in top form (as well as how they operate at all).

Let's face it, a network is more than simply boxes with wires interconnecting them; it's a complex, constantly growing life form that we need to keep fed and happy, so that its users can work as productively as possible. Often, the only feedback network people like us receive is a terse message when something has gone wrong. A goal of this book is to encourage you to proactively root out the causes of these types of problems, using tried and tested troubleshooting techniques and good test equipment. Getting more information to those managing the network and encouraging the use of stress testing, benchmarking, baselining, and record-keeping are some other aspects we hope to assist with here.

The following section provides a brief glimpse of what we'll be covering, and Chapter 1 gives you a more detailed tour of the book. Hope you enjoy it!

What This Book Contains

You've probably often heard that the best way to deal with a complex issue or operation is to break it down into manageable steps. Nowhere is that principle more true than with computer networking, and we've applied it in organizing this wide-ranging book. Its 38 chapters are grouped into nine parts, each covering a broad component of the networking picture: concepts and theory, hardware, server software, client software, interconnecting networks, remote access, optimizing and fine tuning, security issues, and troubleshooting.

Part I: Network Communications Concepts

The chapters here introduce networking terminology and the OSI Reference Model and then delve into the various protocols. NetWare's IPX and SPX, Microsoft's NetBEUI, Apple's AppleTalk, and the Internet suite of protocols are all covered at length. We devote a chapter each to Ethernet and Token Ring, then move on to a closer look at network topologies.

A continual theme in this book is the need to compare and contrast. These chapters in particular point out strengths and weaknesses of the various approaches and technologies so you are better able to make informed choices.

Part II: Network Hardware

This section starts with a look at network cabling, covering all the standard types of transmission media, their characteristics, and tradeoffs. Thinnet, thicknet, the various categories of twisted-pair cable, fiber optic, and even wireless networking are discussed.

We spend a chapter each on the following hardware categories: punch panels and network adapters; repeaters, hubs, bridges, switches and routers; and finally other connectivity hardware, such as modems, ISDN, and cable modems.

Part III: Network Server Software

These chapters deal with the setup, configuration, and management of all main types of networking software. Chapters include coverage of NetWare/IntraNetWare, Windows NT Server, and Unix/Linux, as well as Lotus Notes, OS/2 Warp, Banyan's StreetTalk and VINES, LANtastic, and AppleTalk.

Again, comparisons are drawn where pertinent, to help you determine which NOS (network operating system) is appropriate for a given purpose.

Part IV: Network Client Software

The single chapter in this part discusses the client software needed to connect DOS, Windows 9x and NT Workstation, Unix, and Macintosh workstations to different types of servers. Both the Novell and Microsoft sets of drivers for NetWare are covered (and compared). We look at how to configure networking on Windows 9x and NT Workstation.

This chapter also includes a section describing how to configure Mac and Windows stations to talk to each other peacefully over the network.

Part V: Interconnecting Networks

Here we include chapters on building an intranet and setting up a Web server, and we spend two chapters explaining what an extranet is and how to set one up. You'll also learn about how to plan, implement, and manage very large networks. We discuss open and hybrid extranets, talk about virtual private networks using techniques such as tunneling and gateways, and look at some considerations involved when choosing WAN backbones.

Part VI: Accessing Networks Remotely

We start out this section with a chapter on effective telecommuting that compares the remote control and remote access methods and shows how to implement them. Modems, ISDN, and telecommuting via tunneling over the Internet are also covered.

The other chapter in this section shows how to soup up a network's remote-access capabilities for more users through the use of high-performance dedicated remote access hardware and multiport serial adapters.

Part VII: Optimizing and Fine-Tuning for Performance

First up for this section is a chapter on ways to speed up existing servers. RAM, disks drives, RAID and disk striping, fast(er) Ethernet, subnets, and profiling are discussed.

Next is a chapter on creating and using a network baseline. You'll learn exactly what a baseline is, what its advantages are, and how and when to create one.

A chapter on stress-testing techniques shows how to use dumb loads and intelligent loads to determine the bottleneck areas of your network and to discover some of those "strange" types of problems which only seem to resurface when it's Friday afternoon or the night before your vacation begins.

Part VIII: Network Security Issues

Here we deal with some very important things you should know, and practices you should make habitual, to beef up your network's security level to an adequate level. Almost every network has far worse security than most people realize, because of inadequate planning, lack of familiarity with technical details of the network's hardware and software, and/or inadequate security policies.

The first of this part's two chapters, entitled "Top Ten Things You Can Do to Increase Security," addresses general security issues that apply to all networks. The second chapter focuses exclusively on Internet-related security issues and the tools and techniques available for dealing with those issues.

Part IX: Troubleshooting and Preventive Maintenance

The last part of the book is the largest, with nine chapters devoted to different aspects of troubleshooting: basic strategies and techniques, specific hardware and software troubleshooting tools, diagnosing real-world problems, diagnosing servers, diagnosing workstations, troubleshooting the physical network and print servers, and troubleshooting WANs. The final chapter is perhaps the most important. It focuses on preventing problems before they occur: Power protection, preventive maintenance, fault tolerance, keeping network plans and logs, the importance of baselining, training your users, protecting against viruses, data-recovery options, and forming a disaster-recovery plan beforehand are among the topics covered.

A final tip: Books like this one *can* help you in an emergency, but are going to be more effective if you can digest the contents when things are relatively calm. Try keeping a copy near your work area, visible and available for those brief but welcome periods where you await the next network support incident…

Enjoy it!

PART I

Network Communications Concepts

■ CHAPTER 1: Networking Overview

■ CHAPTER 2: The OSI Model and Protocol Communication

■ CHAPTER 3: Specific Networking Protocols

■ CHAPTER 4: Ethernet Overview

■ CHAPTER 5: Token Ring Overview

■ CHAPTER 6: Network Topologies

CHAPTER

ONE

Networking Overview

- Fundamental networking terms and concepts

- Basic networking theory, hardware, and client/server software

- Interconnecting and remotely accessing networks

- Overview of fine-tuning, optimizing, and security issues

- Introduction to troubleshooting and preventive maintenance

It's amazing to think that only some 60 years have passed since the arrival of the first computers. From those first computers, which filled entire rooms and required staff on rollerskates to zip around replacing expired tubes, to the current desktop computer systems, an amazing amount of progress has been made. Great strides have been made, and not just in terms of reducing the size, increasing the power, and making computers affordable and approachable for the average user. Another way in which computers have made great strides is in their ability to *intercommunicate*—that is, for different types of networks and operating systems to communicate with each other—and in so doing, to enable their human operators also to intercommunicate more effectively, and collaborate on the whole range of endeavors that people find interesting.

Indeed, the latter half of this decade has seen explosive growth in "The" network, or the Internet, which itself comprises in its various parts most of the different networking technologies used by networks of any size, and is bringing in its wake changes that may exceed those brought about by the printing press, some 500 years ago.

Never before in history have people had the ability to share information and ideas in "real time," with anyone (or everyone) else, anywhere on the planet (or even off the planet, as with the space shuttle orbiters)—and moreover, to do so economically and effortlessly. Not all networks share such universal access, of course, but the amazing thing is that the potential to do so exists.

Even networks not directly connected to the Internet are sharing in the new hardware and software technologies being collectively opened up by the greater global enthusiasm towards networking.

Our goal in this book is an ambitious one: to provide, in a single volume, the information that administrators need in order to keep a network of any type commonly used today—newly installed or "legacy," single-platform or mixed—running efficiently and serving its users appropriately, and to make intelligent decisions about upgrading. We intend to show how to migrate from the very smallest networks to larger LANs, WANs, and extranets—covering along the way all the necessary hardware, software, and procedures you will need to upgrade, enhance, and maintain your network successfully and efficiently.

This chapter begins by introducing some essential concepts and terms that we will build upon in following chapters. The rest of the chapter will serve as a general overview to network upgrading and maintenance. It should help to clarify how the various chapters of this book interrelate, and how we'll progress to cover the breadth of material, all of which is geared towards helping you with installing, upgrading, and maintaining networks.

NOTE   For those seeking to shore up their knowledge of networking concepts and skills before planning a network upgrade/expansion, this chapter may help tie together the various hardware, software, concepts, strategies, and troubleshooting areas covered in future chapters. More experienced network administrators may prefer instead to dive right in to later chapters of particular interest.

Fundamental Networking Terms and Concepts

Throughout this book we make reference to many networking terms. These are all covered in detail in the various chapters, as well as the glossary in Appendix D. To jump-start our discussion of networking, though, we've selected a dozen or so of the most often-used terms in networking, which we'd like to review briefly here as a way to ease into the material we'll be covering in the coming chapters. This information is intended mainly to help those of you whose knowledge is more "hands-on" than theoretical fill in any conceptual gaps in your understanding.

Again, if you are thoroughly familiar with these concepts, feel free to jump ahead a few pages to the "Tour of Networking Topics Covered" section of this chapter. There we present a sort of blow-by-blow coverage of networking theory, hardware, software, network upgrading and expansion, and troubleshooting, in the order we will be covering all of these topics in this book. By the end of this chapter, you'll have not only a good idea of what all is in store for you in the pages ahead, but also a sense of how all these pieces fit together, effectively building upon each other.

First, though, some fundamentals…

Going Digital

The overwhelming majority of computers in use today are, of course, *digital* computers. The difference between digital and analog is roughly comparable to the difference between a TV channel switch and the tuning dial of a radio. Whereas analog covers a continuum, or a smooth unbroken range of values, the digital approach breaks up everything into discrete steps, or chunks—ultimately, into a long series of Yes and No, On and Off, True and False values. It turns out that storing and conveying a series of On or Off states is less prone to errors than it would be using an analog technology. It also turns out that the discrete, digital approach is quite efficiently supported by the silicon switches inside every transistor—millions of which now make up each computer CPU and memory chip. Computer memory is essentially one very long stream of on/off switches, and CPUs contain more such switches, plus circuitry which provides the ability to read and/or change the status of any of these switches in an extremely short period of time. Each switch of course is called a *bit*; eight such bits make up each *byte*, and with such relatively simple beginnings, it is quite amazing the volume and depth of information which can be stored and acted upon.

NOTE   If you're curious about what analog computing technology would consist of, you can find quite a few documents by searching the Web. However, you'll need a degree in electronics and/or mathematics to understand most of them.

Networking takes digital computing a step further by enabling many such systems to communicate with each other, sharing information itself as well as how that information is to be processed. What switches are for computers and computer memory, timed pulses accomplish for most networking equipment. That is, in order to convey the fact that a particular switch is in the "on" state, an agreed-upon pulse gets transmitted as a high or low voltage along a wire, or an intermittent beam of light is sent across a fiber-optic cable, or a microwave, infrared, or radio wave is modulated. All of these means, and more, are being used to convey information, or data, from one place to another.

Basic Networking Conventions

For each type of transmission *medium* that can be used for networking, there exist agreed-upon conventions, or standards, that specify what sort of signal will specify a bit, and how each group of eight bits (a byte) is to be sent. Building on this, such standards further specify what conventions will be used to tell the receiver when to receive, and the transmitter when to transmit, and when it is appropriate for the sender and receiver to exchange these roles. By convention, these standards go on to specify what constitutes a network frame.

As we'll discuss in coming chapters, a *network frame* is the fundamental block of information passed between network points. Each frame contains several bytes, including certain bytes that may specify the size of the frame and some redundant information used for error checking. Most importantly, each frame contains a group of bytes which together specify the address, called the *MAC* (or media access control) *address*, designating the destination where the frame is supposed to be transmitted. And, of course, frames also contain some space that can be filled with data that is to be transmitted.

Each stream of information being transmitted is first broken into smaller chunks which are transmitted separately, and this is what enables multiple streams of information to flow along the same network "simultaneously." Very much as multitasking on a single computer devotes a brief instant of time to each of many different processes, in a similar way network frames divvy up information into small enough pieces that no single piece takes up much time in transmission, and many different streams of data can appear to be moving through simultaneously. (These chunks of time are quite small—a few thousandths or even millionths of a second.)

Most types of networking build on the idea of frames by defining a slightly larger chunk of bytes (or a group of frames) to constitute what are referred to as *packets*. Different types of packet definitions exist, partly for historical reasons (early networks were proprietary), partly because different networks may need different amounts of information in each packet to designate the sender and recipient addresses and to provide different degrees of error checking or recovery, and also because different packet sizes may work better with one type of network media than another.

We've mentioned that multiple streams of information often flow across the same network transmission media. Because in most cases it is completely impractical to run a network connection from every computer on the network to every other computer on a network, a compromise is made which usually consists of groups of computers all interconnected in a single loop. Other types of connection configurations exist, and each such connection strategy is part of what is called a *network topology*.

Network topologies are dealt with at length in coming chapters. Different network topologies have their own cable types and requirements, and these differences make up one of the larger groups of considerations you will have to sort through and choose from when designing your own network's topology. Along with the nuts-and-bolts details of each topology, we'll summarize the pros and cons for each, because choosing a network topology is an essential part of defining any new (or newly upgraded) network.

Since most network topologies include transmission media segments that are used by multiple computers, a large part of creating an efficient network is in determining how to keep multiple stations on a segment sharing "fairly," and not exceeding the capacity of their segment. As we'll discuss, one of the major strategies for making networks run faster and more efficiently is to split them up, and then reconnect them where necessary using specialized hardware that keeps network traffic localized except when it is actually destined for a computer on a different segment.

Most networks use either of two general approaches to allow multiple stations to share the same network media. The first strategy allows any station to transmit whenever it doesn't hear any other station already transmitting (certain refinements of this head off "collisions" of two or more stations attempting to transmit simultaneously). The second approach is a more polite one, where a token, analogous to a relay baton or the "talking stick" of Native American tribal councils, is passed around in an orderly fashion; each station in turn "owns" the token and thus has the right to transmit. The former approach is used in most Ethernet networks; the latter approach is used in all Token Ring networks, as well as in some fiber networks.

In both approaches, all stations connected to the same network media typically "see" every network frame being transmitted on that segment. In other words, every frame passes through each station's network adapter interface on its way to the intended recipient. This explains why individual stations that are not actively transmitting network traffic can still be bogged down when their network segment is bearing a heavy traffic load. It's also a primary reason why splitting up networks into subnetworks can reduce overall traffic and increase the effective network throughput.

It may already be apparent to you that a major part of networking is simply adhering to the many standards that are already in place and cover virtually *all* aspects of networking. Network standards define everything from the underlying electrical characteristics of transmissions and the transmission media, to frame types and lower level protocols, to network adapter drivers, bridging and routing equipment, to higher level protocols, file, printer and application sharing services, and end-user application support for networking. The use of established standards makes it possible for these various parts to interoperate as expected. A large part of a network manager's job, then, is to become familiar with these standards, and by understanding their limitations and strengths, to work within them to improve a network's dependability and performance.

A Tour of Networking Topics Covered

To better acquaint you with the material being presented in this book, and to begin showing how it all fits together, the remainder of this chapter is a tour which breaks the book into each of its major sections, providing a sort of "fly-over" presentation of what is covered in the chapters of each section.

Networking Theory and Concepts

The six chapters in Part I of this book introduce the fundamentals of network protocols and topologies.

The OSI Seven-Layer Model

As networking products began to be implemented on a wide scale in the 1970s, one growing problem was the fact that most network vendors were selling proprietary solutions—there were competing "standards," with the unfortunate result that one system could not intercommunicate with another. In 1977, the ISO (International Standards Organization) developed a reference model for designing networking products in a modular, or layered, fashion. They looked at all the steps needed to implement networking, from the level of application software, all the way down to the physical level—how bits are conveyed over the network. They devised a model with seven distinct layers of functionality. The top-most layer is called the Application layer, the bottom-most is the Physical layer, and each layer in between is responsible for taking information passed to it from the layer above or below it and performing some necessary function before passing it along to the next layer in turn.

Because each layer's functionality is defined independently from the other layers, it becomes possible to replace a particular layer without necessarily impacting the functionality of any of the others. In other words, functionality for the different layers could be supplied from competing vendors, and these layers would still interoperate with each other, each layer fulfilling its specified role so that information flows as expected, up and down the seven OSI layers.

Surprisingly, this layer approach has actually worked well. The overwhelming majority of commercially available networking products (hardware and software) do adhere to this model.

Therefore, we start out this book (beginning in Chapter 2) with a detailed look at the OSI seven-layer model. If you understand how the model works, you are far along the way to understanding how all the different types of networking hardware and software interact with each other to bring about the goal of successful networking.

It is well worth the time for anyone serious about networking to memorize these seven layers and their respective functionality. Doing so will provide an effective framework you can advert to, in accumulating knowledge of networking. In planning new networks or upgrading existing ones, selecting and implementing appropriate hardware and software technology, and in effectively troubleshooting network problems, a grasp of what's going on "behind the scenes" will serve you really well. (OK, slight pun intended.)

Networking Protocols

While the seven OSI layers have helped to standardize networking, that is not to say that there is now only one standard. As you will find, networking is largely about standards—and there are lots of them.

For the most part, networking requires that all the information being sent around the network be broken into small, manageable pieces. In this way, information *packets* from multiple stations can be sent along a single wire one after the other, with apparent simultaneity. This also allows the network to respond quickly with corrective action when it detects that information packets are being successfully delivered.

Because there are different networking needs, transmission speeds, and types of transmission *media* (thick and thin coaxial cable, twisted-pair cable, fiber-optic, and even wireless technologies), there are also different packet types and sizes which are better suited to particular situations.

These various packets are specified according to different network *protocols*. In Chapter 3 we look at each of the major protocols being used in networking today. These include certainly TCP/IP (the protocols used on the Internet), as well as NetWare's IPX and SPX, Microsoft's NetBEUI, and Apple's AppleTalk. We'll be discussing each of these protocols in detail, covering how each one works, its peculiarities, and its specific strengths and weaknesses in comparison to the other protocols. Along the way we'll discuss related issues: for example, the difference between *routable* and *non-routable* protocols, different schemes for network addressing, and how packets are routed to their destination.

The Two Most Common Network Types— Ethernet and Token Ring

Still in the vein of networking theory, we next look at the two main types of networking being used today: Ethernet and Token Ring. These address, in different ways, the problem of moving data around on networks that have shared transmission media, where multiple stations must make use of the same cable circuit, without any one station using up more than its fair share of the bandwidth.

As you'll see in Chapter 4, *Ethernet* uses CSMA/CD (carrier sense multiple access with collision detection), a "brute-force" technique in which all stations listen for an available transmission spot, then transmit, listen for *collisions* (simultaneous transmissions from two or more stations), and if necessary, wait before retransmitting. This method is used in the majority of networks currently, although it does have some weaknesses which become more apparent as more stations are added. Chapter 4 looks closely at the actual processes of both transmitting and receiving using CSMA/CD, and points out a test procedure that can be used to verify that a given station is both transmitting and receiving correctly. Here again, an understanding of the theory of how Ethernet works is going to enhance your ability to plan Ethernet upgrades and expansions and to diagnose and resolve Ethernet-related problems.

The second most common type of networking, *Token Ring*, uses a somewhat more elegant approach to determine which stations transmit when. If Ethernet is somewhat akin to a classroom of schoolkids waving their hands to be called upon (and occasionally speaking out of turn), Token Ring is more a "take your turn, and we'll go around the room" approach. On a Token Ring network, a single networking frame, called a *token,* is passed around to each station in turn, and only when each station in turn is assigned the token does it get the right to transmit traffic.

Despite Ethernet's popularity, Token Ring has gained some followers in recent years. In part this may be due to the fact that a token passing scheme is used in fiber-optic network backbone connections. Also, generally speaking Token Ring is somewhat better suited than Ethernet is to efficiently convey larger packet sizes.

Thus in Chapter 5 we'll look at how Token Ring works. We'll also discuss its strengths and weaknesses vis-à-vis Ethernet, and we'll look at how the Token Ring topology differs from that of Ethernet.

Network Topologies

Networking *topology* refers to the layout and interconnection strategy used for transmission media, and includes, for example, the two most common topology types: the *ring* and the *bus* topology. A distinction is made also between physical and logical topology. What is physically a star topology, for example, may logically (or electrically) actually be a ring topology.

Related to topology is the set of physical characteristics exhibited by particular types of transmission media. The speed at which information can be conveyed and whether the data can be conveyed in only one or in both directions simultaneously (the latter being referred to as bidirectional or duplex behavior) are also important considerations in choosing and designing the network topology.

In our last chapter of this section, Chapter 6, we discuss these different types of topologies (both physical and logical). En route, we cover the different connection types—circuit, message, and packet-based switching—and then proceed to cover each of the major local area network (LAN) topology types and associated attributes. The various flavors of Ethernet (10Mb, 100Mb, and 1Gb Ethernet, 100VG Ethernet), as well as FDDI (Fiber Distributed Data Interface) and ATM (asynchronous transfer mode), are covered here. We then move on to a discussion of wide area network (WAN) topologies, including T1, Frame Relay/X.25 (leased lines), SONET (synchronous optical network), ISDN (Integrated Services Digital Network), and even dial-up modem connections.

The chapters in this first section are intended to provide you with a thorough grounding in the underlying theory and concepts that make networking work. In future sections, we'll focus more on the implementation details that all these concepts make possible—including, for example, the networking hardware, software, configuration, troubleshooting, and preventive maintenance techniques.

Network Hardware

Networking hardware includes myriad boxes, gadgets, computers, and cables. We sort all these out in Part II of the book.

Transmission Media

The choice of transmission media has a lot to do with the speed and distance over which a given network can communicate. Before jumping into the various types of transmission media and the properties and characteristics of each, a short discussion of digital vs. analog communications, and a comparison of their respective susceptibilities to interference, allow us to then point out some factors that affect most digital transmission media. These issues are all dealt with in Chapter 7.

Briefly, the two main sources of interference affecting most digital communications are *EMI* (electromagnetic interference) and *RFI* (radio frequency interference). EMI is the most common type of interference encountered on local area networks and can be produced by everything from fluorescent lights to network cables to certain types of heavy machinery. Some transmission media types are less susceptible to EMI, with optic fiber (FDDI) being exceptionally notable in this respect; it is not affected by EMI at all. Radio frequency interference (RFI) shows up on network cables as an unintended reflection of the transmitted signal, for example, on thinnet (thin coax) reflection is often caused by faulty termination at either end of a cable length. The terminator's job is to absorb any remaining signal from a transmission so that it is not echoed, or reflected, back toward where it came from.

Other issues we cover in Chapter 7 include transmission synchronization, factors affecting bandwidth, fault tolerance, and the cost of different transmission media.

A discussion of the transmission media choices available begins with *thinnet*, or thin Ethernet cable. This cable type is *coaxial*, having an inner conductor, separated by insulating material, and then electrically shielded with an outer wire braid (and outer layer of insulation). Very similar to the type of cable used by cable television, thinnet cable has some significant advantages: it's cheap, easier to work with than the larger, thicker sort of coax used in thick Ethernet (thicknet), and doesn't require any additional hardware to form a network outside of the network interface cards which are installed in each station. A characteristic of thin (and thick) Ethernet is that it connects in a bus topology—somewhat like Christmas tree lights, from one station to the next. This has its benefit in simplicity, but is bad news when a cable break occurs—a break anywhere on the cable length can bring down all stations on the entire segment, and because all the stations are down, this also adds to the difficulty of tracking down where the break occurred.

Although thinnet has the potential to carry more information (look at cable TV's use of it), for some reason its transmission speed of 10Mbps has not increased, and by current standards, with 100Mbps and faster becoming mainstream, this is another drawback to using it. Thinnet still is handy for small home-based networks or for networks that have to be taken down and re-setup frequently—for example, at trade shows.

Thicknet is similar to thinnet in its shortcomings. Thanks to its larger, thicker size, it is capable of carrying signals farther; its thickness also makes it much harder to work with and more expensive. Because of its greater usable distance, it sometimes is used as a backbone connector, with individual segments using thinnet cable for greater flexibility. Nowadays, however, thicknet is being replaced by faster and/or less expensive alternatives.

The most common type of cabling currently being installed is CAT5, or Category 5 unshielded twisted-pair (UTP) cable. This cable, which looks very similar to standard telephone cable, is rated for 100Mbps transmission speeds and is used extensively in twisted-pair Ethernet installations. Its higher throughput, lower cost, and ease of installation account for its popularity. Twisted-pair cable also avoids the "Christmas tree light" syndrome of impacting all stations when only one station has a cable break. It uses a *hub* (a physical star topology), which isolates the offending break and makes it much easier to determine the location of a cable break. Chapter 7 also looks at CAT3 cabling, which is only rated for 10Mbps.

Another cabling option, of course, is FDDI (fiber distributed digital interface), which for a higher cost brings several advantages: It's impervious to interference from EMI and RFI, has a very high bandwidth, and offers better security. One drawback is the difficulty of installing connectors at ends of cables—until this technology is improved upon, it takes a bit of effort and skill to polish the ends properly so the light beam is not impaired.

A final transmission medium discussed in Chapter 7 is *wireless*, an area likely to expand in importance in coming years. Especially interesting is the possibility of economical and ubiquitous satellite networking communications, which will at some point make Internet access available to even the most remote areas of the globe.

Network Connection Devices

Having discussed cables, we proceed to look at the most common items to which networking cables are connected. In Chapter 8, we discuss network adapters, punch-down panels, and media converters. Network adapters come in a variety of shapes and sizes, accommodating all bus types. Most common currently are PCI Ethernet network adapters and the PC Card adapters for laptops.

Punch-down panels provide an organized way of bringing all cable runs (segments) to a central location and connecting from there easily to hubs, routers, or other equipment. Media converters are handy gadgets that convert between different cable media—10BaseT and thinnet, for instance. These can very effectively allow older network segments to continue being used without risky alterations, while newer segments are installed using other transmission media.

Hardware for Enhancing Performance

Because all stations on a network segment add to the network traffic, network performance invariably decreases as more stations are added. Since there's only so much bandwidth available, some technology is needed to allow larger networks to function at usable speeds. This is the role filled by the hardware covered in Chapter 9.

Repeaters act as two-port signal amplifiers; they effectively double the maximum distance that can be spanned by a single cable run. Whatever signal is present on one port will be amplified and relayed to the second port. Repeaters simply relay whatever signal is present; they do not listen before (re)transmitting their signal, which means they are still subject to the overall maximum length for a given topology.

Hubs are one of the most common pieces of network hardware, after network adapters. Every UTP Ethernet network uses one or more hubs. Hubs are essentially multiport repeaters used as a central connecting point (thus their name) for a cluster of twisted-pair nodes. Various types are available, including chassis hubs, stackable, managed stackable, and unmanaged stackable hubs. Chassis hubs are large boxes designed to be mounted in an equipment rack. Each can typically support up to 24 nodes, or connections. Stackable hubs are free-standing, usually slim-line boxes which can be stacked one on top of the next. Unlike most chassis hubs, stackables are interchangeable between different manufacturers. One hub can be connected to the next via a special port called an *uplink port*.

Managed hubs can be remotely monitored, and in some models the ports can be reset remotely. Unmanaged hubs do not have this ability and use LEDs to indicate their status.

Before discussing bridges and routers, Chapter 9 next looks at why and how a network is split up into multiple segments. Segmenting a network is an essential strategy for obtaining adequate performance on any size network. Breaking a network into segments reduces the amount of traffic on each segment, as packets are only forwarded to other segments when their destination address specifically requires it.

While some network operating systems (NOSs) are capable of performing this routing function in software (NetWare, Unix, and Windows NT), it is more efficient to delegate routing to a piece of hardware called a router. Unlike a repeater or a hub, a *router* looks at each packet coming through and decides whether or not to forward it, based on the destination address.

A *bridge* is a similar piece of equipment which works a step below the packet level. It looks at frames to determine whether to forward a packet. Bridges communicate with each other to construct *bridge tables*, which allow each bridge to figure out how to forward packets that are more than one segment away. Chapter 9 looks at the important roles of bridges and routers, comparing and contrasting their functionality, and presenting as examples scenarios that call for one or the other (or both). Also covered in this chapter are switches and bridge/router hybrids called *brouters*.

Other Hardware

The final chapter in the networking hardware section is Chapter 10. Here we first describe workstations, servers, and thin clients, then survey additional connectivity hardware used to extend the reach of networks over wider distances. Such equipment includes the codex (short for coder/decoder), which is used to connect analog equipment such as faxes and modems to ISDN lines; the CSU/DSU (channel service unit/data service unit), which interconnects LANs by means of a 56K or faster leased line; ISDN "modems," ADSL/xDSL, and cable modems, all of which are increasingly being used to connect networks to the Internet and to other networks. We also look at standard modems and a method for greatly increasing the throughput on some types of connections, called channel binding.

Server Software

Having discussed networking concepts and networking hardware, we now shift the focus to networking software, beginning with Part III. In its six chapters, we cover the attributes, strengths and weaknesses, setup and configuration, and administration options of each leading brand of network server software.

NetWare

Chapter 11 focuses on what has been and continues to be a mainstay of the networking server industry: Novell's NetWare. NetWare, or IntraNetWare as it's now being called, has lost some of its market share in recent years to Windows NT, but still is a very capable and strong server contender, particularly for file and print services. NetWare's improved intranet and Internet support, including built-in FTP and Web services, allows existing networks to leverage the growing collection of TCP/IP software. Another unique feature IntraNetWare offers is TCP/IP support over IPX/SPX, which gives client stations the ability to access the Internet without using a real TCP/IP protocol stack.

Windows NT

In Chapter 12, we cover NetWare's chief competitor, Windows NT Server. Unlike IntraNetWare, NT has a GUI interface (and one which Windows 95 users are already very familiar with), the ability to run software as a workstation, and a simpler installation. On the negative side, NT does not scale to very large networks as well as IntraNetWare.

Account administration is one area that is arguably less intuitive on NT than it is on IntraNetWare. This is due to the security model NT uses, which separates different networks into domains and requires that domains have explicit trust relationships configured to permit users to access resources across domains.

NT and IntraNetWare both support the leading protocols: IP/IPX, AppleTalk, and TCP/IP. NT also supports Microsoft's non-routable NetBEUI protocol, useful mainly on smaller networks for its lower protocol overhead (and therefore somewhat faster throughput).

Besides discussing how to setup and configure NT for basic server functionality, Chapter 12 also covers setup of various services and protocols.

Unix and Linux

Next, in Chapter 13, we cover Unix and its "freeware" cousin, Linux. Unix may have a reputation as being hard to configure, and it has been hurt by a mix of competing standards. But with a dedicated support staff, Unix can be more customizable than anything else. Currently, Linux is increasing in popularity and is drawing renewed attention to Unix as a server platform.

Taking Red Hat Linux as a reference version, we look at how to install it, and then move on to issues such as the file system, account administration, security, and networking configuration. We also discuss free Linux software which provides NetWare, NT, and even AppleTalk interconnectivity.

Lotus Notes

While not exactly a network operating system in its own right, Lotus Notes has great strengths with its true client-server architecture which provides relational database services across multiple servers. In Chapter 14, we discuss Notes' abilities and how to configure and use it.

OS/2, Banyan VINES/StreetTalk, and LANtastic

In Chapter 15, we first look at the older LAN Manager software, then move on to OS/2 Warp Server software. While it doesn't get much publicity these days, Warp Server is a capable file and print server in its own right, and we discuss how to install, configure, and use it by itself as well as in a mixed network environment.

Lesser known but still around, Banyan VINES is another network server operating system. We discuss the VINES protocol called StreetTalk, which can be accessed from Windows 95 stations acting as clients. Also covered are VANGuard and issues relating to print management on a VINES network.

In a similar category, we have LANtastic. LANtastic is still appreciated by some for its ease of installation and use. Rather surprisingly, a version of LANtastic which can be installed on Windows 95 and NT is available as an add-on network package (through LANtastic). Chapter 15 concludes with a discussion on how to install and configure this networking software.

AppleTalk and AppleShare

Last but not least, in Chapter 16, we cover AppleTalk and the AppleShare protocol. AppleTalk over Ethernet makes the most sense, of course, for exclusively or primarily Apple networks. As a routable protocol, it is possible to build rather large networks with AppleTalk, although network resources are not organized in a hierarchical fashion as they are, for instance, with Novell's IntraNetWare. Given the degree to which software such as Microsoft Office now supports cross-platform document file formats, it is possible to have Macs and PCs get along rather well in a mixed network environment.

Client Software

With coverage of server software fresh in our memories, Chapter 17 explores ways of configuring client stations to talk to various server types.

We look at how to configure Windows 95 and NT Workstation to access both IntraNetWare and Windows networks. This can be done using either Microsoft's NetWare Client software or Novell's Client32 software (available for both Windows 95 and NT).

For Unix-to-Unix networking, we look at Unix's Network File System, or NFS, which allows server or peer-to-peer style networking between even different flavors of Unix.

For Mac clients, we discuss how to access NetWare and NT servers from the Macintosh. We first look at installing IPX on Macs (primarily used to access NetWare/IntraNetWare and also for cross-platform games). We also cover how to install Mac Services on NT Server. Finally, we look at installing the NT Client Login software on the Mac. While this software is not strictly needed once Apple Services are installed on NT, security-conscious network administrators may choose to use it, as it encrypts Apple login passwords before they are sent across the network.

Interconnecting Networks

After discussing ways of getting network clients and servers to communicate, Part V looks at ways of connecting servers to each other—in particular, connecting networks together over greater distances to form intranets, wide area networks (WANs), and extranets.

Connecting a Network to the Internet

Chapter 18 considers issues involving adding Internet access to a network. Connection approaches discussed include standard-modem, multiple-modem (using channel binding), ISDN, gateways, and intranets.

Browser issues covered include security, cost and support considerations, versioning, plug-ins, and ActiveX software. Almost weekly it seems new security holes are discovered (and almost as quickly, patched). Thanks to Java and ActiveX, software can be transparently downloaded and installed on a user's system just by browsing particular Web pages. This brings up a number of security concerns, which only partially are addressed by current browsing software.

Intranets

Intranets bring the TCP/IP-based tools developed for the Internet into internal networks. In Chapter 19, we look at intranet issues and discuss the benefits as well as the disadvantages of having an intranet. The primary benefit is much wider and more immediate access to information in a standard way. Primary drawbacks include the typical security concerns, time wasted by employees addicted to surfing, and the increase in networking traffic.

We also look at evaluating Web servers, as Web servers are not all alike. They differ greatly in ease of setup and use, sustained throughput speeds, security features, types of hooks to other software supported, and cost.

Other issues covered include proxy server and firewall considerations, and TCP/IP address ranges suitable for Internet-connected networks.

Extranets

An *extranet* is a type of network that crosses organizational boundaries, giving outsiders access to information and resources stored inside the organization's internal network. In Chapter 20, we define what extranets are, explore the difference between external and extended extranets, and discuss real-world problems that can be solved using them. We also look at extranet application architectures and the issue of distributed objects on extranets.

Two goals of extranet design are seamless interoperability and platform independence. Real-world problems addressed by extranets include extending intranet functionality, building business relationships with intranets, and fostering Internet commerce.

Extranet Infrastructure

We take a more detailed look at extranet infrastructure in Chapter 21, where we discuss very large extranets. Various extranet topologies are covered: the private, open, and hybrid topologies, as well as virtual private networks (VPNs).

Virtual private networks make use of tunneling protocols, which are encapsulated inside another protocol and usually include some sort of encryption. Configured properly, VPNs allow part or all of a network to be remotely accessible in a relatively secure fashion over a larger, unsecured network connection. Of course, special security precautions must be applied, and security risks must be assessed before choosing to use this technology.

Chapter 21 also looks at extranet structure and how extranet backbones are implemented.

Accessing Networks Remotely

Telecommuting is barely out of its infancy but promises to be an exciting trend in coming years. New software is appearing constantly, extending the range of work-related activities users can perform from remote locations. Home computers frequently surpass the speeds of the equipment available at work. As Internet connection speeds increase exponentially with new hardware (such as cable modems), look for fewer and fewer workers to be making the daily commute in to the office.

The two chapters in Part VI discuss remote access.

Telecommuting Issues

In Chapter 22, we explore the issues involved in accessing a corporate network remotely, either from home or while traveling. We discuss some telecommuting pros and cons. We compare remote control and remote access software (and their corresponding uses), and we compare some of the leading software solutions currently being used for both functions.

We also discuss ways to get the most throughput using your modem and look at approaches to telecommuting using the Internet.

Hardware for Remote Access

Companies with increasing numbers of telecommuters will want to read Chapter 23, wherein we discuss remote access hardware, including multiport modem products and multiport serial adapters. These devices multiply the number of dial-in connections which can be supported by each dial-in server.

We also look at other more specialized high-performance remote access hardware, which makes it feasible for even larger numbers of workers to telecommute.

Optimizing and Fine-Tuning

Having discussed in the first six parts of the book how to assemble networks of varying sizes and abilities, in Part VII we shift attention to ways of speeding up existing networks.

Optimizing Servers

In Chapter 24, various strategies are considered, including the first line of attack: adding more RAM and disk space. Another helpful strategy is to employ disk striping, and for increased dependability, some form of *RAID* (redundant arrays of independent disks). RAID is supported by Unix, IntraNetWare, and NT, and can be implemented in both software and hardware. The redundant storage used by some versions of RAID can enable you to literally remove an entire drive from a running server without causing a crash or any data to be lost. Unfortunately, some forms of RAID are not worth bothering with, so we'll point out the differences between various levels of RAID implementation.

Network Baselining

Part of keeping your network running at peak efficiency is knowing what its average efficiency and its peak efficiency look like. To find out what level of performance a particular server is capable of, we use a process called *baselining*. In Chapter 25, we look at how to perform network baselining. The chapter explains how and when a baseline should be created, and how it can be an important tool to analyze and increase the performance of your network.

Stress Testing

Another important procedure both for improving efficiency and for network disaster preparedness is stress testing. In Chapter 26, we explore techniques for stress testing your network by applying "dumb" loads or "intelligent" loads to mimic various levels of network usage. This is an effective technique for detecting lurking flaws, as well as for determining realistic expectations for existing networks.

Security Issues

Of course as networking becomes more and more ubiquitous, as more and more individual networks are interconnected, as the number of users increases, and as more information is placed online, so also does the need for network security increase. It is probably safe to say that most networks currently in use have less than adequate safeguards for controlling access to sensitive information. Confidentiality is not the only concern; perhaps equally important is the danger of damage to or destruction of data, either by accident or by malicious viruses or users—internal or external. The two chapters in Part VIII address these security issues.

A Network Security Top Ten List

In Chapter 27, we discuss a "top ten" list of things you can do to increase network security. First on this list is a discussion of password schemes, simple strategies for devising passwords that are neither too easy to guess on the one hand, or so difficult to remember that users write them down on scraps of paper left lying around their desk, thus defeating the purpose. Another important measure is looking for and removing default and inactive user accounts, as is making use of user and group rights to eliminate hard-to-find security exceptions. Other effective security measures to implement include using unique user directories, securing e-mail, and using NT Workstation's security features. More extreme measures include making use of encryption, using physically separate networks, removable disks and drives, and monitoring logins and information access.

Internet Security

Chapter 28 specifically focuses on Internet-related security issues. Firewalls, gateways, and proxy servers are revisited, as these are important lines of defense for networks which have to be connected in any fashion to the Internet. We compare some of the leading proxy servers available, including those by Microsoft and Netscape, as well as other third-party options.

Windows 95 offers some features worth considering carefully in the area of Internet security: peer file sharing, and peer Web and FTP servers. User authentication for file servers is essential, and for Web servers is a good idea. Malicious attacks including the so-called "Ping of Death," denial-of-service attacks, and other threats and strategies for dealing with them are discussed. Finally, the chapter looks at special tactics for Web servers, including access logging, directory level access, password authentication, Secure Sockets Layer (SSL), and obtaining and using authentication certificates.

Troubleshooting and Preventive Maintenance

The troubleshooting section of this book, Part IX, is the single largest, including ten detailed chapters devoted to all aspects of network troubleshooting.

Basic Troubleshooting

Chapter 29 looks at the important fundamental aspects of all troubleshooting. We start with a look at having the right attitude—being willing to play detective and apply analytical reasoning. The ability to take a situation and break it down into component pieces, each piece of which can be more easily tested to determine whether it is the actual problem area, is a crucial skill for successful troubleshooting.

Another important tool is accurate and thorough record keeping. As a network administrator, it is probably almost impossible to keep too many records—everything from cabling layouts to client station configurations to user group security access assignments and file and directory names and locations should be documented. Investing some time up front to keep such information available in case it's needed could save countless hours of trying to puzzle out the information later, at a time you'll be under pressure from users anxious to be back in operation, and perhaps less able to think clearly or otherwise reconstruct the missing information.

It should go without saying that printouts of important information are essential—it does no good to have the best records if they are rendered inaccessible because they're only stored on a network that has ceased to be operational.

As with each of the other chapters in this section, real-life examples are given to underscore the importance of certain points.

Hardware for Troubleshooting

Chapter 30 deals with various types of hardware troubleshooting tools. We start by discussing basic cable checkers, then we move on to cable testers, hand-held diagnostic tools, and hardware network analyzers. Each of these is discussed in detail, along with examples of where each would be needed. Even for smaller networks, it's worth reading this chapter, just to become familiar with what tools are available should you eventually need them. Even the simpler cable testers can be time savers when running new cables or checking existing ones for suspected problems.

Software for Troubleshooting

Chapter 31 looks at software troubleshooting utilities. In particular we focus on Novell's LANalyzer and NT's NetMon (network monitor). Both of these tools let you intercept individual packets to check for an excessive number of retransmitted, fragmented, or lost packets. We also look at various other console and command-line tools available on IntraNetWare and NT. Again, familiarizing yourself with the troubleshooting and diagnostic software that's available is very worthwhile, even if you don't think you'll need it right away.

Diagnosing Specific Problems

We carry the thread of problem diagnosing further with Chapter 32. Here we discuss specific real-world problems that happen all too frequently—for example, weird behaviors with Ping, duplicate IP address problems, undeliverable mail, excessive network collisions, and connectivity problems occurring after a server upgrade.

Troubleshooting Servers

Server troubleshooting is our emphasis in Chapter 33, where we concentrate on NetWare/IntraNetWare issues. We start with a series of snapshots, or fault points, where an error can occur. Does the server boot? Does it fail only for certain workstations? Or are the problems global but intermittent?

Covered next are version-specific problems and version upgrading issues. With NetWare, there's always the possibility of NLM problems.

Chapter 33 also discusses problems that can occur with SCSI adapters, how to prepare disks for server use, and issues involving supporting multiple protocols, account administration issues, and using system fault tolerance.

We conclude this chapter by analyzing two real-life examples of problem scenarios in order to illustrate server troubleshooting in action.

Troubleshooting Workstations

Conversely, in Chapter 34, we look at troubleshooting the other side of the network equation—workstations. Workstation troubleshooting issues range from BIOS and network adapter problems to various software problems caused by the operating system, drivers, and application software.

Specific attention is given to troubleshooting Windows and NT clients, as well as OS/2, Macintosh, and Unix workstation clients. Five real-world examples illustrate typical problems and how to resolve them.

Troubleshooting Network Connections and Cabling

Of course, problems may also occur with the physical network. Chapter 35 discusses issues and strategies appropriate to each of the different network topologies and major protocols.

The chapter also presents techniques for tracking down cable, connector, termination, and grounding-related problems, as well as problems with routing and bridging equipment. Five more real-life examples conclude this chapter.

Troubleshooting Printing Problems

Network printing, particularly as it is implemented on NetWare/IntraNetWare servers, deserves special attention. Chapter 36 first discusses NetWare printing issues, and then moves on to discuss printing problems with Windows NT, Unix, Macs, and postscript printers. Again, real-life scenarios illustrate network printing troubleshooting in action.

WAN Troubleshooting

The final chapter in this section, Chapter 37, looks at how to effectively troubleshoot WANs (wide area networks). Separation by distance poses additional problems in tracking down WAN problems. Problems posed simply by separation geographically complicate matters, particularly when more than a single WAN link is being used. Then too, WAN link problems can be related to or caused by problems outside your direct control—a backhoe clipping an underground cable, or your communications service provider having a part of their backbone link go down. Thus we discuss in this chapter techniques that can still be used to isolate problem areas and track down where faults occur in these larger networks.

Maintenance and Administration Issues

In our final chapter, Chapter 38, we stress the importance of heading off problems before they occur by using a "pound of prevention."

The necessity of implementing dependable backup systems is underscored. We also discuss power protection, preventive hardware maintenance, and various ways to achieve fault tolerance.

Other important topics of this chapter include the importance of keeping documentation, including cabling plans and event logs, monitoring servers for baselining purposes, the importance of training your users, strategies for protecting against viruses, and additional security issues.

A final section entitled "Recovering from Disaster in Advance" discusses ways you can minimize the damage caused by more serious network emergencies by preparing for them before they occur. Recovery plans, spare parts, and data recovery services are considered in this section.

Summary

If this chapter has achieved its purpose, you should now have a clear view of what lies in store for you in the coming chapters. Whether you are planning a new network, upgrading from peer to client/server, upgrading your server software, or adding more client stations, you'll find plenty of information here for planning and carrying out a trouble-free upgrade. If you are responsible for maintaining your network in top operating condition, or tracking down and fixing what ails your network, again you'll find plenty of both theoretical and practical information here to assist you.

CHAPTER

TWO

The OSI Model and Protocol Communication

- The purpose of a communications protocol

- The OSI model, its layers, and how it all works

- Network addresses

- Routing

- Connection-oriented and connectionless communications

- Network services

- Upper layer communications

This chapter is of key importance for understanding generally how networks operate. The information contained here will be referenced repeatedly from other chapters, so we encourage those of you inclined to skip the more theoretical sections to at least become somewhat familiar here with the seven layers of the OSI model, and then spend some time studying the discussion on protocol communications. It will pay off in the long run!

Briefly, before jumping into a discussion about network protocols, let's review some of the major points you should be familiar with from Chapter 1:

- All communications are either analog or digital in nature.

- Because of its resistance to interference, digital communication is the method of choice when transmitting information.

- Digital communications consist of pulses referred to as *bits*. A collection of eight bits is referred to as a *byte*, which represents one piece of information to be transferred.

- A *topology* defines how systems will be connected in order to communicate these bytes.

- Bytes are organized into logical *frames* when moving data along a specific topology.

- Most WAN topologies are designed to communicate point-to-point between two systems only.

- Most LAN topologies rely on shared media to allow multiple systems to communicate.

- When shared media are used, all systems see every frame transmitted.

- Devices such as bridges and switches can be used to regulate the flow of data by segmenting the network and restraining traffic to specific areas.

If any of these points do not seem clear to you, you may wish to go back and reread parts of the preceding chapter. Otherwise, let's begin.

A Protocol's Job

The points just listed constitute the baseline that all network communications have in common. How this baseline is implemented, however, depends on which protocol is used. For example, we'll see that when a system wants to transfer information to another system it does so by creating a frame with the target system's MAC (media access control) address in the destination field of the frame header. This method of communication is part of our topology's communication rules. This transmission raises the following questions:

- Should the transmitting system simply assume the frame was received in one piece?

- Should the destination system reply, saying, "We received your frame, thanks!"?

- If a reply should be sent, does each frame require its own acknowledgment, or is it okay to send just one for a group of frames?

- What if the destination system is not on the same local network?

- Even if the destination system is on the same local network, how do we find that system's MAC address?

- If the destination system is running e-mail, transferring a file, and browsing HTML Web pages on the source system, how does it know which application this data is for?

This is where a *protocol* comes in. A protocol's job is to answer each of the above questions as well as any others that may pop up in the course of the communication. When we talk about IP, IPX, AppleTalk, or NetBEUI, we are talking about protocols. So why are the specifications that characterize a protocol not simply defined by the topology? For the answer to this question we need to go back a few years to what was taking place in the 70s besides bellbottoms and disco.

A Little Background

In 1974 IBM released the System Network Architecture (SNA). This was the method used to communicate with its mainframe systems of the time. The specification defined everything from the method of communication to what type of connectors to use. Life was simple for a network administrator, as long as you didn't mind buying everything from IBM and their systems were capable of providing all the services your organization required.

In 1976 DEC released their Digital Network Architecture (DNA). This described every facet of communicating with a DEC system, specifying every wire and byte to be used. Again, life was simple, assuming that DEC could provide everything your organization required.

These systems are what is referred to as *proprietary*. The original vendor was typically the sole supplier of parts, updates, and software. While the specifications made sure that the vendor's systems were able to communicate together, they unfortunately did a pretty good job of ensuring that those computers could not interconnect with a system from another vendor. If your organization wanted to use a DEC machine for manufacturing and inventory control but liked the looks of the IBM system for corporate functions, you would be hard-pressed to communicate any information between the two systems.

Proprietary systems were the fad of the time. A vendor would sit in their own little bubble and define every aspect of the network. Besides the two companies mentioned above, there were many others that specified system communications from soup to nuts, and have, for that reason and others, gone the path of the Pet Rock.

A good analogy for proprietary systems is organized religion. Most organized religions are proprietary in that they have their own set of beliefs or specifications. Like vendors of the 70s, each has its own way of doing things which members believe to be most correct and can be a bit intolerant of other practices. A person who tries to incorporate the beliefs of two separate religious systems may be shunned by both. Shunning was pretty common in the computer industry as well, as each vendor fought to maintain market share from their true believers. The term "religious war" is still used quite frequently when describing the discussions between two proponents of a specific product or operating system.

The OSI Model

In 1977 the International Organization of Standards developed the *Open Systems Interconnection Reference Model* (*OSI model*) to help improve communications between different vendors' systems. The IOS was a committee represented by many different organizations whose goal was not to favor a specific method of communication but rather to develop a set of guidelines that would allow vendors to ensure that their products would interoperate.

The OSI model was created to simplify communications between systems. There are many events that need to take place in order to ensure that data first reaches the correct system, and is then passed along to the correct application in a usable format. A set of rules was required to break down the communication process into a simple set of building blocks.

An analogy to this would be the process used for building a house. While the final product may seem a complex piece of work, it is much easier to deal with when it is broken down into manageable sections.

A good house starts with a foundation. There are rules that define how wide the wall of the foundation should be as well as how far below the frost line it needs to sit. After that, the house is framed off, or *packaged*. Again, there are rules to define how thick the lumber needs to be as well as how long each piece of framing can span without support.

Once the house is framed, there is a defined process for putting on a roof, adding walls, and even connecting the electrical system and plumbing. By breaking this complicated process down into small, manageable sections, the process of building a house becomes easier. This breakdown also makes it easier to define who is responsible for which section. For example, when the electrical contractor shows up at the job site, they expect to be running wires and adding electrical outlets. They do not expect to show up and shingle the roof.

The entire structure becomes an interwoven tapestry with each piece relying on the others. For example, the frame of our house requires a solid foundation. Without it, the frame will eventually buckle and fall. The frame may also require that load-bearing walls be placed in certain areas of the house in order to ensure that the frame does not fall in on itself.

The OSI model strives to set up similar definitions and dependencies. Each portion of the communication process is broken out into separate building blocks. This makes it easier to determine what each portion of the communication process is required to do. It also helps to define how each piece will be connected together.

The OSI model is a set of seven layers. Each layer describes how its portion of the communication process should function, as well as how each will interface with the layers directly above it, below it, and adjacent to it on other systems. This allows a vendor to create a product that operates on a certain level and be sure it will operate in the widest range of applications. If the vendor's product follows a specific layer's guidelines, it should be able to communicate with products created by other vendors that operate at adjacent layers.

To return to our house analogy for a moment, let's assume we have a lumber yard that supplies main support beams used in house construction. So long as they follow the guidelines for thickness and material, they can expect their beams to function correctly in any house that has a proper foundation structure.

Figure 2.1 is a representation of the OSI model in all its glory. Lets take the layers one at a time to determine what functionality is expected of each.

Physical Layer

The *Physical* layer describes the specifications of our transmission media, connectors, and signal pulses. A repeater or a hub is a Physical layer device because it is "frame-stupid" and simply amplifies the electrical signal on the wire and passes it along.

FIGURE 2.1:

The OSI model

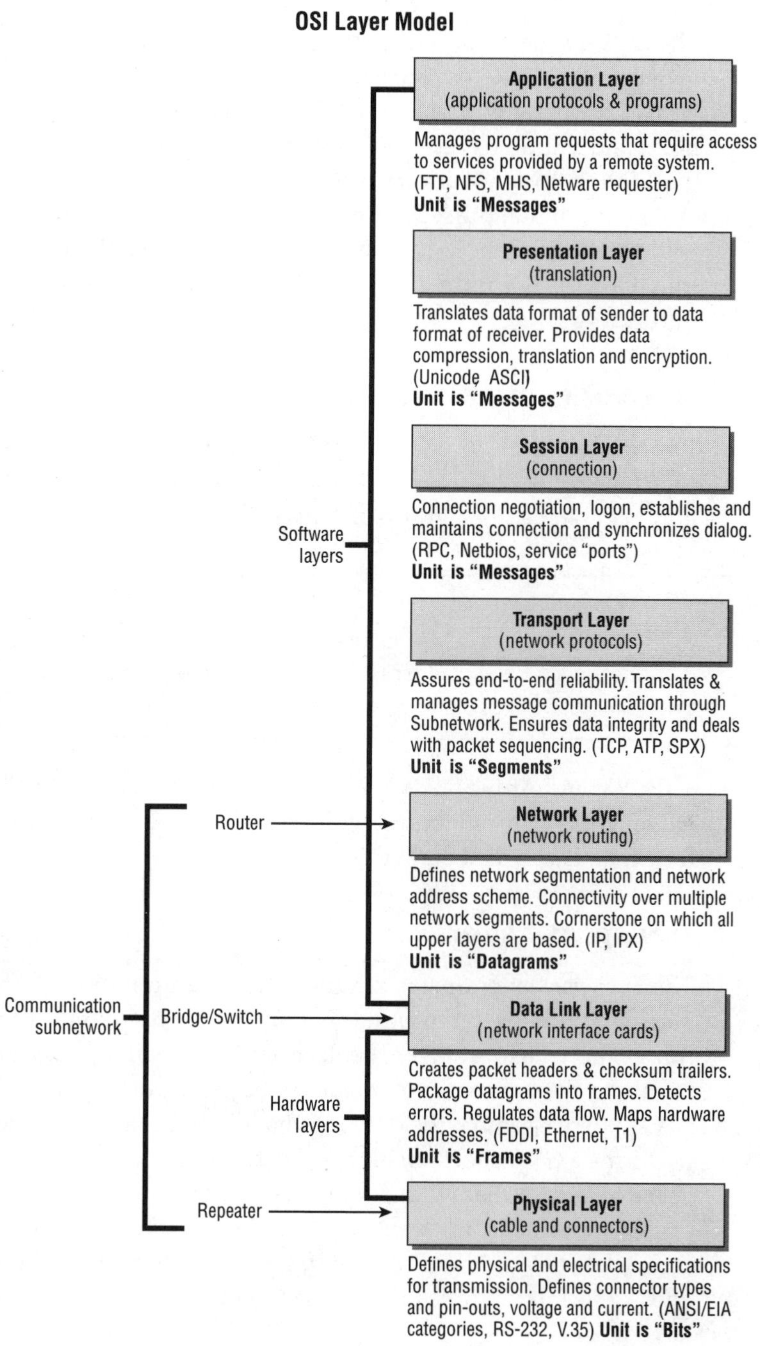

OSI Layer Model

Application Layer
(application protocols & programs)

Manages program requests that require access
to services provided by a remote system.
(FTP, NFS, MHS, Netware requester)
Unit is "Messages"

Presentation Layer
(translation)

Translates data format of sender to data
format of receiver. Provides data
compression, translation and encryption.
(Unicode ASCI)
Unit is "Messages"

Session Layer
(connection)

Connection negotiation, logon, establishes and
maintains connection and synchronizes dialog.
(RPC, Netbios, service "ports")
Unit is "Messages"

Transport Layer
(network protocols)

Assures end-to-end reliability. Translates &
manages message communication through
Subnetwork. Ensures data integrity and deals
with packet sequencing. (TCP, ATP, SPX)
Unit is "Segments"

Network Layer
(network routing)

Defines network segmentation and network
address scheme. Connectivity over multiple
network segments. Cornerstone on which all
upper layers are based. (IP, IPX)
Unit is "Datagrams"

Data Link Layer
(network interface cards)

Creates packet headers & checksum trailers.
Package datagrams into frames. Detects
errors. Regulates data flow. Maps hardware
addresses. (FDDI, Ethernet, T1)
Unit is "Frames"

Physical Layer
(cable and connectors)

Defines physical and electrical specifications
for transmission. Defines connector types
and pin-outs, voltage and current. (ANSI/EIA
categories, RS-232, V.35) **Unit is "Bits"**

Software layers

Communication subnetwork

Router

Bridge/Switch

Hardware layers

Repeater

Data Link Layer

The *Data Link* layer describes the specifications for topology and communication between local systems. Ethernet is a good example of a Data Link layer specification, as it works with multiple Physical layer specifications (twisted-pair cable, fiber) and multiple Network layer specifications (IPX, IP). The Data Link layer is the "door between worlds" as it connects the physical aspects of a network (the cables and digital pulses) with the abstract world of software and data streams. Bridges and switches are considered to be Data Link devices because they are frame-aware. Both use information specified in the frame header to regulate traffic.

Network Layer

The *Network* layer describes how systems on different network segments find each other; it also defines network addresses. A network address is a name or number assigned to a group of physically connected systems.

NOTE   The network address is assigned by the network administrator and should not be confused with the MAC address assigned to each network card. The purpose of a network address is to facilitate data delivery over long distances. Its functionality is similar to the zip code used when mailing a regular letter.

IP, IPX, and AppleTalk's Datagram Delivery Protocol (DDP) are all examples of Network layer functionality. Service and application availability are based on functionality prescribed at this level.

Transport Layer

The *Transport* layer deals with the actual manipulation of your data and prepares it for delivery through the network. If your data is too large for a single frame, the Transport layer breaks it up into smaller pieces and assigns sequence numbers. Sequence numbers allow the Transport layer on the other receiving system to reassemble the data into its original content. While the Data Link layer performs a CRC check on all frames, the Transport layer can act as a backup check to ensure that all the data was received and that it is usable. Examples of Transport layer functionality would be IP's Transmission Control Protocol (TCP), User Datagram Protocol (UDP), IPX's Sequence Packet Exchange (SPX), and AppleTalk's AppleTalk Transaction Protocol (ATP).

NOTE
To keep confusion from building up, keep in mind that *frame* and *packet* describe the same thing—a discreet group of data formatted to the network protocols specifications. There is no difference.

Session Layer

The *Session* layer deals with establishing and maintaining a connection between two or more systems. It is responsible for ensuring that a query for a specific type of service is made correctly. For example, if you try to access a system with your Web browser, the Session layers on both systems work together to ensure that you receive HTML pages and not e-mail. If a system is running multiple network applications, it is up to the Session layer to keep these communications orderly and ensure that incoming data is directed to the correct application.

Presentation Layer

The *Presentation* layer ensures that data is received in a format that applications running on the system can use. For example, if you are communicating over the Internet using encrypted communications, it would be the responsibility of the Presentation layer to encrypt and decrypt this information. Most Web browsers support this kind of functionality for performing financial transactions over the Internet. Data and language translation is also done at this level.

NOTE
Novell's *Unicode*, which ensures that multiple users of a specific server can view information in the language of their choice, would be considered a Presentation layer function.

Application Layer

The label "*Application* layer" is a bit misleading, as it does not describe the actual "program" that a user may be running on their system. Rather, this is the layer that is responsible for determining when access to network resources is required. For example, Microsoft Word does not function at the Application layer of the OSI model. If the user tries to retrieve a document from their home directory on a server, however, it is the Application layer network software that is responsible for delivering their request to the remote system.

NOTE   In geek lingo, the layers are numbered in the order described above. If we were to state that bridges function at layer 2 of the OSI model, you would interpret this to mean that bridges work within the guidelines provided by the Data Link layer of the OSI model.

How the OSI Model Works

Let's look at an example to see how these layers work together. Assume you're using your word processor program and trying to retrieve a file called RESUME.TXT from your home directory on a remote server. The networking software running on your system would react similarly to the following process.

Formulating a File Request

The **Application** layer would detect that you are requesting information from a remote file system. It would formulate a request to that system that RESUME.TXT should be read from disk. Once this request has been created, the Application layer would pass the request off to the presentation layer for further processing.

The **Presentation** layer would determine if it needs to encrypt this request or perform any type of data translation. Once this has been determined and completed, it would then add any information it needs to pass along to the Presentation layer on the remote system and forward the packet down to the Session layer.

The **Session** layer would check which application was requesting the information and verify what service was being requested from the remote system (file access). The Session layer would add information to the request to ensure that the remote system knows how to handle this request. Then it would pass all this information along to the Transport layer.

The **Transport** layer would ensure that it has a reliable connection to the remote system and begin the process of breaking down all the above information so that it can be packaged up into frames. If more than one frame is required, the information is split up and each block of information is assigned a sequence number. These sequenced chunks of information are passed one at a time down to the Network layer.

The **Network** layer receives the blocks of information from the above layer and adds the network address for both this and the remote system. This is done to each block before it is passed down to the Data Link layer.

At the **Data Link** layer the blocks are packaged up into individual frames. Notice in Figure 2.2 that all the information added by each of the above layers (as well as the actual file request) must be fit into the data field of the frame, 46 to 1,500 bytes. The Data Link layer would then add a frame header, consisting of the source and destination MAC addresses, and would use this information along with the contents of the data field to create a CRC trailer. The Data Link layer is then responsible for transmitting the frame according to the topology rules in use on the network. Depending on the topology, this could mean listening for a quiet moment on the network, waiting for a token, or waiting for a specific time division before transmitting the frame.

NOTE   Chapter 6 discusses MAC addresses in detail.

As the Data Link layer transmits the frame, it passes it along to the Physical layer (our network cables).

FIGURE 2.2:

The location of each layer's information within our frame

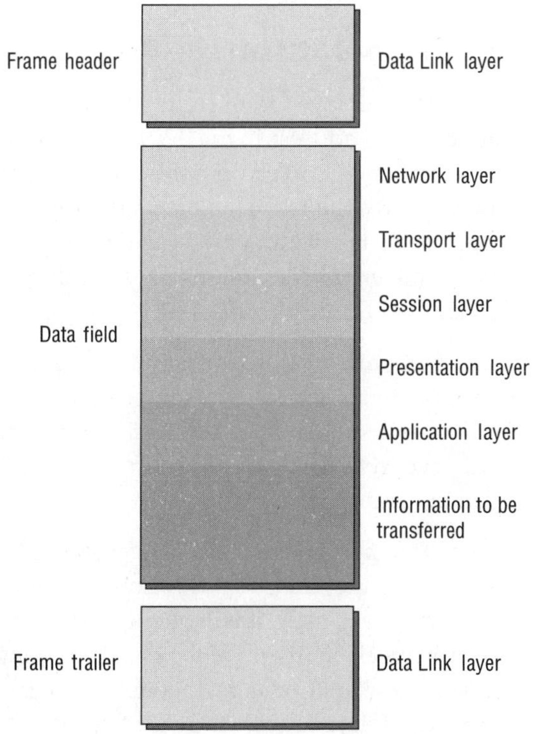

Frame header — Data Link layer

Data field — Network layer, Transport layer, Session layer, Presentation layer, Application layer, Information to be transferred

Frame trailer — Data Link layer

NOTE
As the amount of required layer information increases, the amount of available space within the data field goes down. This leaves us with less room to transmit the core information of our request. By minimizing the amount of space that each layer requires we can move our information using fewer frames. Fewer frames directly translates into a greater amount of available bandwidth for other transmissions. The Physical layer does not add any information to the frame.

The **Physical** layer is responsible for carrying the information from the source system to its destination. Because the Physical layer has no knowledge of frames, it is simply passing along the digital signal pulses transmitted by the Data Link layer. The Physical layer is the medium by which a connection is made between the two systems; it is responsible for carrying the signal to the Data Link layer on the remote system.

Our workstation has successfully formulated our data request ("Send me a copy of RESUME.TXT") and transmitted it to the remote system. At this point, the remote system follows a similar process, but in reverse.

Receiving Data on the Remote System

The **Data Link** layer on the remote system reads in the transmitted frame. It notes that the MAC address in the destination field of the header is its own and recognizes that it needs to process this request. It performs a CRC check on the frame and compares the results to the value stored in the frame trailer. If they match, it strips off the header and trailer and passes the data field up to the networking layer. If the value does not match, it sends a request to the source system asking that another frame be sent.

The **Network** layer on the remote system will analyze the information recorded by the Network layer on the source system. It will note the network address of the source system and record this information in a table. Once complete, the Network layer removes information related to this level and will pass the remainder up to the Transport layer.

The **Transport** layer receives the information and will analyze the information recorded by the Transport layer on the source system. If it finds that packet sequencing was used, it will queue any information it receives until all the data has been received. If any of the data is missing, the Transport layer will use the sequence information to formulate a reply to the source system, requesting that this piece of data be resent. Once all the data has been received, the Transport layer will strip out any transport information and pass the full request up to the Session layer.

The **Session** layer will receive the information and verify that it is from a valid connection and that the station requesting data has already passed the security check for the service it is requesting (login and password for file access). If the check is positive, the Session layer strips out any session information and passes the request up to the Presentation layer.

The **Presentation** layer receives the frame and analyzes the information recorded by the Presentation layer on the source system. It will then perform any translation or decryption required. Once this step is completed, it will strip out the Presentation layer information and pass the request up to the Application layer.

The **Application** layer ensures that the correct process running on the system receives the request for data. Because this is a file request, it is passed to whichever process is responsible for access to the file system.

This process would then read the requested file and pass the information back to the Application layer. At this point the entire process of passing the information through each of the layers, illustrated in Figure 2.3, would repeat. If you're amazed that the requested file can be retrieved in anything less than a standard coffee break, then you have a pretty good idea of the magnitude of what is taking place just to request a simple file.

FIGURE 2.3:

The OSI model in action

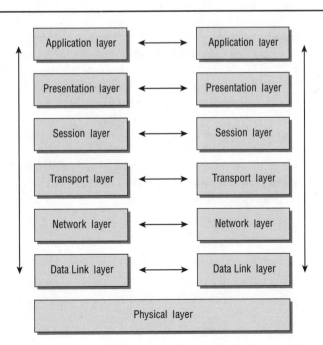

Each layer needs to communicate with the layers adjacent to it as well as with its counterpart on the remote system. While this all seems a bit complex, it's actually a good way to ensure that resources remain flexible and will interoperate with other products and technologies. For example, Ethernet is so adaptable to different protocols because it strictly adheres to the functionality outlined in layer 2 (Data Link) of the OSI model. This allows it to function seamlessly with a number of popular protocols like IP and IPX, which are designed to operate at layer 3 (Network). In contrast, ATM specifies not only layer 2 functionality, but layer 3 and above as well. The fact that it does not follow the OSI model has contributed greatly to its slow deployment and low acceptance because it is difficult to incorporate it into existing network infrastructures.

NOTE   The OSI model is simply a guideline—it is not a specification like Ethernet or the IP protocol. In this, it holds true to its original purpose of not favoring any specific way of providing network communications.

More on the Network Layer

As mentioned earlier, the Network layer is used for delivery of information between *logical networks*.

NOTE   A logical network is simply a group of systems assigned a common network address by the network administrator. These systems may be grouped together because they share a common geographical area or central point of wiring.

Network Addresses

The terminology used for *network addresses* is different depending on the protocol in use. If the protocol in use is IPX, the logical network is simply referred to as a network address. With IP it is a *subnet*, and when using AppleTalk it is referred to as a *zone*.

NOTE
Because NetBIOS and NetBEUI are non-routable protocols, they have no counter-part at this level. They do not use network numbers and do not have the ability to propagate information between logical network segments. A non-routable proto-col is a set of communication rules that expect all systems to be connected locally. They have no direct method of traveling between logical networks. A NetBIOS frame is incapable of crossing a router without some form of help.

Routers

Routers are used to connect logical networks, which is why they are sometimes incorrectly referred to in the IP world as *gateways*. Figure 2.4 shows the effect of adding a router to a network. Protocols on either side of the device must use a unique logical network address. Information destined for a non-local system must be routed to the logical network on which the system resides. The act of traversing a router from one logical network to another is referred to as a *hop*. When a proto-col hops a router, it must use a unique logical network address on both sides.

So how do systems on one logical network segment find out what other logical segments exist on the network? Routers use a special type of maintenance frame called the Router Information Protocol (RIP) to relay information about known networks. Routers use these frames to create a blueprint of the network known as a *routing table*.

NOTE
Routing tables tell the router which logical networks are available to deliver informa-tion to, and which routers are capable of forwarding information to that network.

The *Traceroute* Command

One example of how routing information is relayed is illustrated in Figure 2.5, which shows the output of running the `traceroute` command (renamed `tracert` on Windows 95 systems). The `traceroute` *command* is an IP protocol tool for docu-menting the subnets that must be traversed as a packet travels from one logical net-work to another. The left-hand column indicates the number of networks, so we must travel over 12 subnets to reach www.sun.com. If we subtract 1 from this we get our hop count because 12 subnets would require 11 routers to separate them.

FIGURE 2.4:

The effects of adding a router
to the network

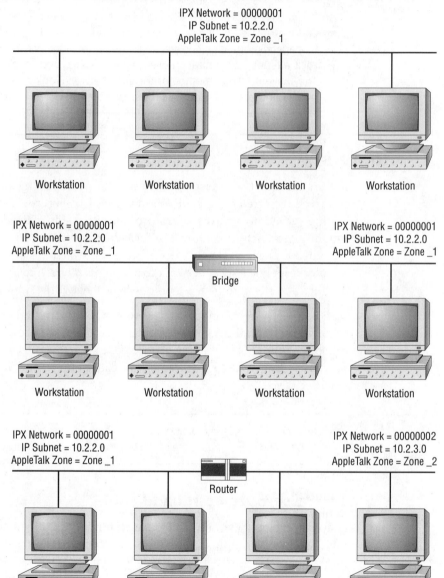

The next three columns measure the link speed for three consecutive tries. This is the amount of time it took our frame to travel from one router to the next. An asterisk (*) indicates that the attempt was not replied to in a reasonable time. Links that display high numbers or * for results are indications of a slow topology (such as a 28.8 dial-up connection) or heavy traffic. The final column identifies the name of the router we had to hop as well as its IP address.

FIGURE 2.5:

Output from running the traceroute command

```
C:\>tracert www.sun.com

Tracing route to www.sun.com [192.9.9.100]
over a maximum of 30 hops:

  1     *        *        *        Request timed out.
  2   197 ms   193 ms   195 ms    gis-gate.gis.net [206.42.64.1]
  3   204 ms   212 ms   204 ms    agis-gis.boston1.agis.net [206.185.153.25]
  4   209 ms   205 ms   207 ms    a2-0.1022.washington1.agis.net [206.185.153.210

  5   229 ms   222 ms   278 ms    maeeast-1.bbnplanet.net [192.41.177.1]
  6   258 ms   332 ms   252 ms    collegepk-br2.bbnplanet.net [4.0.1.17]
  7   364 ms   372 ms   360 ms    collegepk-br1.bbnplanet.net [128.167.253.5]
  8   290 ms   252 ms   256 ms    chicago2-br1.bbnplanet.net [4.0.1.5]
  9   317 ms   300 ms   307 ms    paloalto-br1.bbnplanet.net [4.0.1.1]
 10   329 ms   333 ms   305 ms    paloalto-cr5.bbnplanet.net [131.119.0.205]
 11   315 ms   285 ms   312 ms    sun2.bbnplanet.net [131.119.28.98]
 12   308 ms   306 ms   309 ms    www.sun.com [192.9.9.100]

Trace complete.

C:\>
```

Routing Tables

Do not confuse the output of the traceroute command with an actual routing table. The output is simply the path our data followed to get from Point A to Point B (Point B being www.sun.com). As an analogy, think of a routing table being like a road map. A road map shows all the streets in a local city or town in much the same way a router table keeps track of all the local networks. Now, think of the directions you may give a friend to get to your house based on this map (follow Oak Street to Pine and then take a left on Elm). These directions are synonymous with the output of the traceroute command. It does not show you the entire map, just how to get to a specific location.

Without having some method for each of these routers to communicate and let each other know who is connected where, this type of communication would be impossible.

There are three different methods used when routing information from one network to another—static, distance-vector, and link-state. While each protocol has its own ways of providing routing functionality, each implementation can be broken down into one of these three categories.

Static Routing

Static routing is the simplest method of getting information from one system to another. Used mostly in IP networks, a static route defines a specific router to be the point leading to a specific network. Static routing does not use RIP but relies on a configuration file that directs all traffic bound for a specific network to a particular router. This, of course, assumes that you can predefine all the logical networks you will wish to communicate with. When this is not feasible (for example, when communicating on the Internet) a single router may be designated as a default to receive all traffic destined for networks that have not been predefined. When static routing is used most workstations receive an entry for the default router only.

For example, let's assume we configure our system to have a default route that points to the router Galifrey. As our system passes information through the Network layer it will analyze the logical network of the destination system. If the system is located on the same logical network, the Data Link layer adds the MAC address of that system and transmits the frame onto the wire. If the system is located on some other logical network, the Data Link layer will use the MAC address for Galifrey and transmit the frame to it. Galifrey would then be responsible for ensuring that the frame makes it to its final destination.

The benefits of static routing are simplicity and low overhead. Our workstation is not required to know or care about what other logical networks may be available and how to get to them. It has only two possibilities to worry about—deliver locally or deliver to Galifrey. This can be useful when there is only one possible route to a final destination. For example, most organizations have only one Internet connection. Setting up a static route that points all IP traffic to the router that borders this connection may be the easiest way to ensure that all frames are delivered properly. Because all our routing information is configured at startup, our routers do not need to share route information with other routers. Each system is only concerned with forwarding information to their next default route. We do not need to have any RIP frames propagated through our network, because for each router we have preset where it should forward information.

This routing has a few obvious drawbacks, however. What happens if we have multiple routers connecting to our logical network segment and the traffic actually needs to traverse one of the other routers? As shown in Figure 2.6, the frame would still be delivered to Galifrey, which must then process the frame and pass it along to Tardis. Not only have we required Galifrey to process a frame that it did not need to see, but we have doubled our network traffic (one frame to Galifrey, one frame to Tardis). If this happens only occasionally, it would probably not be a problem. But if we typically see a large amount of traffic destined for the network on the other side of Tardis, we could potentially overload Galifrey. In the latter situation a single default route is definitely not recommended. Instead, we should use a more detailed static table or a routing method capable of advertising route information.

FIGURE 2.6:

When static routing is used, the default router must deliver all non-local frames.

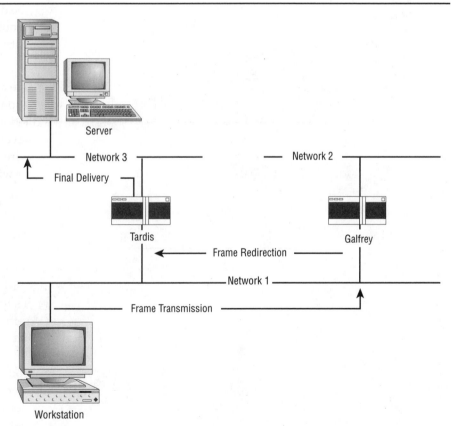

Server

Network 3

Final Delivery

Tardis

Network 2

Galfrey

Frame Redirection

Network 1

Frame Transmission

Workstation

NOTE   With static routing, the default router must deliver to all non-local frames even if the traffic must pass through a different, locally attached router.

Another problem with static routing is that it usually nullifies any attempts to add redundant routes. *Redundant routes* help to ensure that remote networks remain reachable when a single hardware device fails. For example, in Figure 2.7 we have two routers hooked up in parallel. The theory is that if one router dies, the other can continue to pass traffic to the remote network.

FIGURE 2.7:

Two parallel routers, Hermes and Bridgett

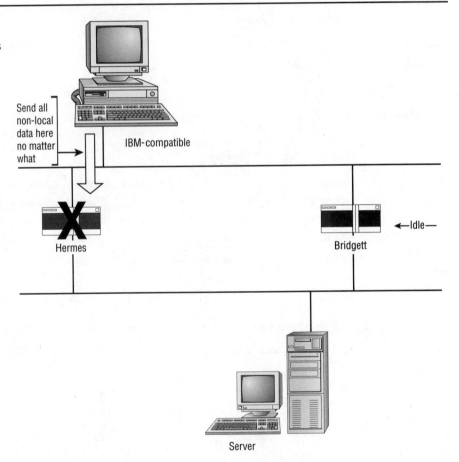

Send all non-local data here no matter what

IBM-compatible

Hermes

Bridgett   ←Idle—

Server

If we have set up Hermes as the default router and it drops offline, Bridgett will not be able to automatically step in. Because our systems are configured to send all non-local traffic to Hermes by default, they will not know that Bridgett is capable of supplying the same connectivity as Hermes. They will continue to attempt delivery to Hermes and eventually fail with a "Remote host unreachable" error. In order to let them know Bridgett supplied the same connectivity as Hermes, we would have to reconfigure each system by changing the default route to point at Bridgett instead of Hermes. Because manual intervention is needed to recover from a network failure, using static routes neutralizes any benefit provided by having redundant routes.

While static routing is easy to use, you can see that some major drawbacks severely limit its application. When redundant paths are provided or even when multiple routers are used on the same logical network, you should use some form of routing method that is capable of exchanging RIP packets. RIP allows routing tables to be developed on the fly which can compensate for hardware failures. Both distance-vector and link-state routing use RIP frames to ensure routing tables stay up to date.

Distance-Vector Routing

Distance-vector is the oldest and most popular form of creating routing tables. In fact, when someone says, "I'm using RIP to create our routing tables," they are referring to distance-vector. Distance-vector routing was the only dynamic routing option available for so long that people sometimes directly associate it with RIP.

Distance-vector routers build their tables based on secondhand information. A router will look at the tables being advertised by other routers and simply add 1 to the advertised hop values to create its own table. With distance-vector routing, every router will periodically broadcast its routing table (once per minute, for example).

Propagating Network Information with Distance-Vector Routing

Figure 2.8 shows how propagation of network information works with the distance-vector method.

FIGURE 2.8:

A routed network about
to build its routing tables
dynamically

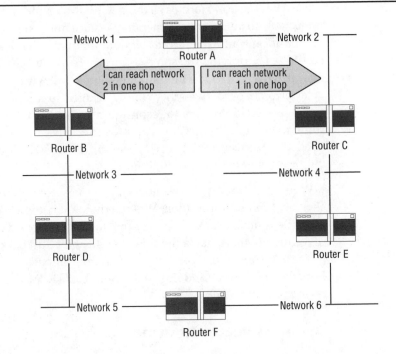

Router A has just come online. Because the two attached networks (1 and 2) have been programmed into it, it immediately adds these to its routing table, assigning a hop value of 1 to each. The hop value is 1 instead of 0 because this information is relative to other attached networks, not the router. For example, if the router is advertising the route to Network 1 on Network 2, then 1 hop is appropriate because any system sending information to Network 1 from Network 2 would have to travel 1 hop (the router itself) to get there. A router usually does not advertise routing information about a directly attached network on that network itself. This means that the router should not transmit a RIP frame stating, "We can reach Network 1 in one hop," on Network 1 itself.

So our router sends out two RIP packets, one on each network, to let any other devices know about the connectivity it can provide. When Routers B and C receive these packets, they reply with RIP packets of their own. Remember that the network was already up and running. This means that all the other routers have already had an opportunity to build their tables. From these other RIP packets Router A collects the following information:

Router	Network	Hops to Get There
B	3	1
B	5	2
B	6	3
B	4	4
B	2	5
C	4	1
C	6	2
C	5	3
C	3	4
C	1	5

Router A will then analyze this information, picking the lowest hop count to each network in order to build its own routing table. Routes that require a larger hop count are not discarded but rather are retained in case of a link failure, which would require an alternate route. These higher hop values are simply ignored during the normal operation of the router. Once complete, the table would look like the following:

Network	Hops to Get There	Next Router
1	1	Direct connection
2	1	Direct connection
3	2	B
4	2	C
5	3	B
6	3	C

All we've done is picked the lowest hop count to each network and added 1 to the advertised value. Once the table is complete, Router A will again broadcast two RIP packets, incorporating this new information.

Now that Routers B and C have noted that there is a new router on the network, they must reevaluate their routing tables as well. Prior to Router A coming online, the table for Router B would have been as follows:

Network	Hops to Get There	Next Router
1	1	Direct connection
2	5	D
3	1	Direct connection
4	4	D
5	2	D
6	3	D

Now that Router A is online, Router B would modify its table to reflect the following:

Network	Hops to Get There	Next Router
1	1	Direct connection
2	2	A
3	1	Direct connection
4	3	A
5	2	D
6	3	D

It takes us two RIPs on the same logical network to get to this point. The first time Router A sent a RIP to Router B it only knew about Network 2, as shown in Figure 2.8. It was not until Router C sent a reply RIP that Router A realized that it had a path to Networks 4, 6, 5, and 3 (in that order) through Router C. This required it to send a second RIP frame to Router B, incorporating this new information. The entire table above would be broadcast with only the direct common network information being removed (Network 1). This means that, while Router A was updating Router B with the information, it learned from Router C that it was also relaying back the route information originally sent to it by that router (Router B). The only difference is that Router A has increased each hop count reported by Router B by 1. Because the hop value is larger than what Router B currently has in its tables, it would simply ignore this information.

Router C would go through a similar process, adjusting its table according to the information it receives from Router A. Again it will require two RIP frames on the same logical network to yield a complete view of our entire network so that Router C can complete the changes to its tables.

These changes would then begin to propagate down through our network. Router B would update Router D when A first comes online and then again when it completes its tables. This activity will continue until all the routers have an accurate view of our new network layout. The amount of time that is required for all our routers to complete their table changes is known as the *convergence time*. The convergence time is important as our routing table is in a state of flux until all our routers become stabilized with their new tables.

WARNING   Keep in mind that in a large network, convergence time (the time needed for all routers to complete their routing table changes) can be quite long, as RIP updates are only sent approximately once or twice per minute.

Distance-Vector Routing Problems   It's important to note that this table has been built almost completely on secondhand information. Any route that a router reports with a hop count greater than 1 is based upon what it has learned from another router. When Router B tells Router A that it can reach Network 5 in 2 hops or Network 6 in 3, it is fully trusting the accuracy of the information it has received from Router D. If you have played the telephone game (where each person in a line tries to relay an identical message to the next) you quickly realize that secondhand information is not always as accurate as it appears to be.

Figure 2.9 is a pretty simple network layout. It consists of four logical networks separated by three routers. Once the point of convergence is reached, each router will have created a routing table as show in the diagram.

FIGURE 2.9:

Given the diagrammed net-
work, each router would
construct its own routing
table.

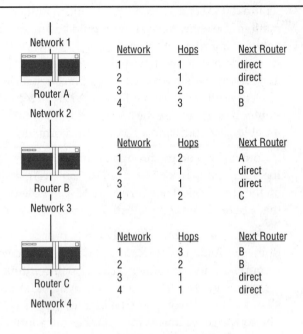

Network	Hops	Next Router
1	1	direct
2	1	direct
3	2	B
4	3	B

Network	Hops	Next Router
1	2	A
2	1	direct
3	1	direct
4	2	C

Network	Hops	Next Router
1	3	B
2	2	B
3	1	direct
4	1	direct

Now, let's assume that Router C dies a fiery death and drops offline. This will make Network 4 unreachable by all other network segments. Once Router B real- izes that Router C is offline it will review the RIP information it has received in the past, looking for an alternate route. This is where distance-vector routing starts to break down. Because Router A has been advertising that it can get to Network 4 in 3 hops, Router B simply adds 1 to this value and assumes it can now reach Network 4 through Router A. Relying on secondhand information causes problems because, of course, Router B can't reach Network 4 through Router A, now that router C is offline.

As shown in Figure 2.10, Router B would begin to advertise that it can now reach Network 4 in 4 hops. Remember that RIP frames do not identify *how* a router will get to a remote network, only that it *can* and how many hops it will take to get there. Without this information, Router B has no idea that Router A is basing its route information on the tables it originally received from Router B.

So Router A would receive a RIP update from Router B and realize that it has increased the hop count to Network 4 from 2 to 4. Router A would then adjust its table accordingly and begin to advertise that it will now take 5 hops to reach Net- work 4. It would again RIP, and Router B would again increase the hop count to Network 4 by 1.

FIGURE 2.10:

Router B incorrectly believes that it can now reach Network 4 through Router A and updates its tables accordingly.

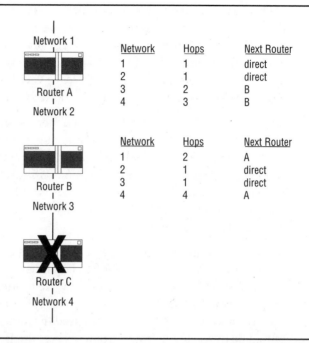

Network	Hops	Next Router
1	1	direct
2	1	direct
3	2	B
4	3	B

Network	Hops	Next Router
1	2	A
2	1	direct
3	1	direct
4	4	A

NOTE

This phenomenon is called *count to infinity* because both routers would continue to increase their hop counts forever. It is because of counting to infinity that distance-vector routing limits the maximum hop count to 12. Any route that is 16 or more hops away is considered unreachable and subsequently removed from the routing table. This allows our two routers to figure out in a reasonable amount of time that Network 4 can no longer be reached.

Reasonable is a subjective term, however. Remember that RIP updates are only sent out once or twice per minute. This means that it may be a minute or more before our routers realize that Network 4 is gone. With a technology that measures frame transmissions in the microsecond range, a minute or more is plenty of time to wreak havoc on our communications. For example, let's look at what is taking place on Network 2 while our routers are trying to converge.

Once Router C has dropped offline, Router B assumes that it has an alternate route to Network 4 through Router A. Any packets it receives are checked for errors and passed along to Router A. When Router A receives the frame, it performs an error check again. It then references its tables and realizes it needs to forward the frame to Router B in order to reach Network 4. Router B would again receive the frame and send it back to Router A.

This is what is referred to as a *routing loop*. Each router plays "hot potato" with the frame, assuming the other is responsible for its delivery, and passing it back and forth. While this is only one frame, imagine the amount of bandwidth lost if there is a considerable amount of traffic destined for Network 4. With all these frames looping between the two routers it would leave very little bandwidth available on Network 2 for any other systems that may need to transmit information.

Fortunately the Network layer has a method of eliminating this problem as well. As each router handles the frame, it is required to decrease a hop counter within the frame by 1. The hop counter is responsible for recording how many routers the information has crossed. As with RIP frames this counter has a maximum value of 15. As the information is handled for the 16th time (and the counter drops to zero) the router realizes that the information is undeliverable and simply drops the information.

While this 16-hop limitation is not a problem for the average corporate network, it can be a severe limitation in larger networks. For example, if you look back at Figure 2.5, you'll remember that we needed to hop 11 routers in order to reach Sun Microsystems' Web server. This is very close to our 15-hop maximum with distance-vectoring. If RIP was used throughout the Internet, many resources would be unreachable from certain areas of the Internet.

It was the combination of all the above mentioned limitations that spawned the development of link-state routing.

Link-State Routing

Link-state routers function in a similar fashion to distance-vector but with a few notable exceptions. Most importantly, link-state routers use only first hand information when developing their routing tables. Not only does this help to eliminate routing errors but it drops our time to convergence to nearly zero. Let's assume that our network from Figure 2.8 has been upgraded to use a link-state routing protocol. Now let's bring Router A online and watch what happens.

Propagating network information with link-state as Router A powers up, it sends out a type of RIP packet referred to as a *hello*. The hello packet is simply an introduction that states, "Greetings! I am a new router on this network, is there anybody out there?" This packet is transmitted on both of its ports and will be responded to by Routers B and C.

Once Router A receives a reply from Routers B and C it creates a Link-State Protocol (LSP) frame and transmits it to Routers B and C. An *LSP frame* is a routing maintenance frame that contains the following information:

- the router's name or identification

- the networks it is attached to

- the hop count or cost of getting to each network

- any other routers on each network that responded to its hello frame

Routers B and C would then make a copy of this frame and forward the information along through the network. Each router receiving the frame would then copy it and pass it along. With link-state routing, each router maintains a copy of every other router's LSP frame. This way, the router can use this information to diagram the network and thus build routing tables. Because each LSP frame contains only the route information that is local to each router that sent it, this network map is created strictly from firsthand information. A router will simply fit the LSP puzzle pieces together until its network picture is complete.

In our example, Router A would then make an LSP frame request from either Router B or C. Because each router has a copy of all LSP frames, either router is capable of supplying a copy from every router on the network. This avoids the necessity of Router A requesting this information from each router individually and thus saves bandwidth. Once an LSP network is up and running, updates are only transmitted every two hours or whenever a change takes place (such as a router going offline). This makes it an effective solution for networks that utilize *bandwidth on demand* WAN connections such as analog dial-up or ISDN. While a distance-vector network would require the link to be brought up once per minute in order to transfer route information, link-state would only need to bring this link up once every two hours.

Even in a non-WAN environment, link-state routing is a great way to save bandwidth. The RIP packets sent by a distance-vector router have a broadcast address in the destination MAC field. This means that once per minute every station is required to analyze every RIP packet, whether it needs the information or not. If the information is not required by the station, it will be dropped once it reaches the Network layer. However, this still means that the station is required to perform a CRC check, strip off the frame, and pass along the data field.

If you get the impression that the authors have a vendetta against broadcast traffic, then proceed to Go and collect $200. While broadcasts do have their place, they are the bandits of networking, robbing precious CPU time from all systems they encounter. Some broadcasts are necessary, such as our example above, for learning which networks are available for access. As you will see a little later on, however, some protocols have based all their communications around broadcasting frames instead of taking advantage of direct delivery. Not only does this type of connectivity not scale well, it can lead to dismal network performance.

Convergence Time with Link-State So our link-state network is up and running. Note that Routers B and C were not required to recompute their routing tables. They simply added the new piece from Router A and continued to pass traffic. This is why convergence time is nearly zero. The only change required of each router is to add the new piece to its table. Unlike distance-vector routing, link-state did not require updates in order to normalize the routing table. Router B did not need a second packet from Router A, telling it what networks where available through Router C. Router B simply added Router A's LSP information to its existing table and was already aware of the links.

Load Balancing This brings us to an interesting point. What if someone on Network 3 needs to send information to a system on Network 2? Network 3 would simply pass the information to Router B, which is reporting that it is only 2 hops away from Network 2. This is in contrast to Router D, which would require 4 hops.

Now let's say that Network 1 is a 300 baud analog dial-up connection (hey, it still works!) while Networks 2–6 are 1Gbps Ethernet. What would happen then? Unfortunately, with most routing protocols, Network 3 would still attempt to deliver the information through Router B. Because hop count is typically used as the sole means of selecting the best route, the link speed would not be taken into consideration. Thus the route with the lowest hop count gets the frame.

This is where *load balancing* comes in. Load balancing introduces the concepts of *link speed* and *segment congestion* to determine which route is best. A routing protocol that takes this information into consideration along with hop count is much better suited to make an informed decision about where to route traffic. The combination of link response time and hop count is referred to as *cost*. What's nice about load balancing is that it is dynamic. If a router notes that the cost along a certain path is increasing, it can divert traffic to a different path to avoid an overload. The cost of a certain path can (and does) change with traffic load. The more information passing along a specific logical network's segments, the higher the cost associated with using that link. Conversely, the faster the topology in use by a logical network segment, the lower the cost. For example, a 100Mbps Ethernet segment would have a lower cost value than an identical link operating at 10Mbps. Figure 2.11 shows a server performing load balancing over two network cards. Note that the outbound traffic count is nearly identical on both cards. The addition of a second card helps to ensure that the server is able to keep up with networks that experience a high frame rate.

FIGURE 2.11:

A NetWare server performing load balancing over two network cards

```
        3C5X9_E83 [3C5X9 port=300 int=A frame=ETHERNET_802.3]

    Version 4.20
    Node address: 0020AF13D29A
    Protocols:
       IPX
          Network address:   00008023

    Generic statistics
       Total packets sent:                            466,985
       Total packets received:                         83,336
       No ECB available count:                              0
       Send packet too big count:                           0
       Reserved:                                Not supported
       Receive packet overflow count:                       0
       Receive packet too big count:                        0
       Receive packet too small count:          Not supported
       Send packet miscellaneous errors:                    0
       Receive packet miscellaneous errors:                 0


        FD0_E83 [FD0490 port=340 int=5 frame=ETHERNET_802.3]

    Version 3.21
    Node address: 00C06C712979
    Protocols:
       IPX
          Network address:   00008023

    Generic statistics
       Total packets sent:                            467,275
       Total packets received:                            229
       No ECB available count:                              0
       Send packet too big count:                           0
       Reserved:                                Not supported
       Receive packet overflow count:                       0
       Receive packet too big count:                        0
       Receive packet too small count:          Not supported
       Send packet miscellaneous errors:                    0
       Receive packet miscellaneous errors:                 0

    Esc=Previous list   Alt+F10=Exit                    F1=Help
```

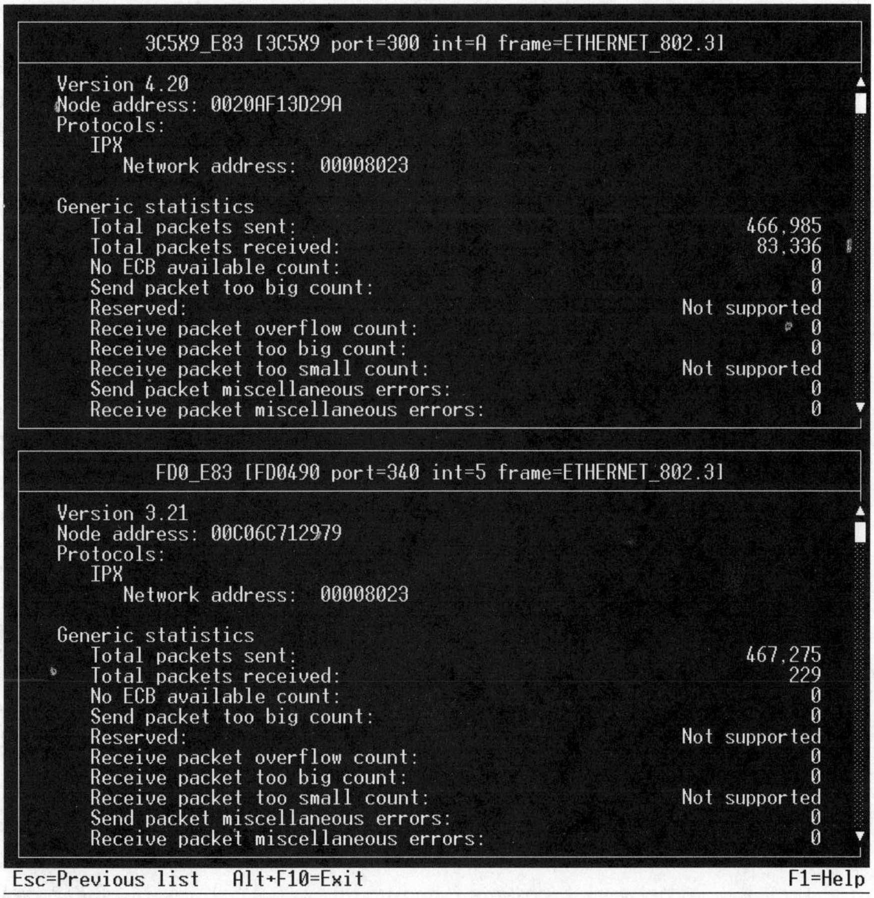

Because link-state routing has such a low convergence time, it is much better suited than is distance-vector to do load balancing. It is possible, however, to do

load balancing using either routing type. Load balancing is implementation specific. This means that it is the design of the routing protocol itself that determines whether load balancing is possible, not the fact that it may be distance-vector or link-state.

Typically, however, most routing protocols that are capable of performing load balancing operate as link-state. This is because the need to balance network traffic was not as much of an issue until network speeds started to rise. Because the latest releases of routing protocols are link-state, the ability to perform load balancing was built into them. As an example, NetWare supports two routing protocols: IPX RIP and Novell's Link-State Protocol (NLSP). RIP has been around longer, and because it predates the need for load balancing, it does not support it. NLSP, however, is a fairly new protocol and supports the use of cost when making routing decisions.

Recovering from a Router Failure in a Link-State Environment Finally, let's revisit Figure 2.9 to look at how link-state routing reacts when a router goes offline. Again, for the purpose of this example, let's assume that our routing protocol has been upgraded from distance-vector to link-state. Let's also assume that our routing tables have been created and that traffic is passing normally.

If Router C is shut down normally, it will transmit a maintenance frame (known as a dying gasp) to Router B informing it that it is about to go offline. Router B would then delete the copy of Router C's LSP frame that it has been maintaining and forward this information along to Router A. Both routers now have a valid copy of the new network layout and realize that Network 4 is no longer reachable. If Router C is not brought down gracefully and instead dies a fiery death, there would be a short delay before Router B realizes that Router C is no longer acknowledging packets that are being sent to it. At this point Router B would realize that Router C is offline. It would then delete Router C's LSP frame from its table and forward the change along to Router A. Again, both systems have a valid copy of the new network layout. Because we are dealing with strictly firsthand information, there are no pesky count-to-infinity problems as we experienced with distance-vector routing. Our router tables are accurate and our network is functioning with a minimum of updating. This allows link-state routing to traverse a larger number of network segments. The maximum is 127 hops, but it can be less depending on the implementation.

Connectionless and Connection-Oriented Communications

So we are now able to get our information from Point A to Point B, regardless of whether the systems are located on the same logical network. Once we get there, how do we carry on a proper conversation? This is where the Transport layer comes in.

The Transport layer is where we begin to set down the rules of communication etiquette. It's not enough that we can get this information from one system to another, we also have to ensure that both systems are operating at the same level of decorum.

As an analogy, let's say you pull up to the finest restaurant in the city in your GMC Pacer and proceed to the front door donning your best set of leather chaps, Harley jacket, and bandanna. Once inside, you greet the maitre d' by stating, "Yo wimp, gimme a table and some grub, NOW!" Surprisingly, you're escorted out of the restaurant at gunpoint. What went wrong? Why, improper etiquette was used, of course. Everyone knows the correct term is not "grub" but "escargot."

The above verbal breakdown, as well as those in network communications, can be avoided by ensuring that all parties involved are communicating at the same level of etiquette. The two forms of network communications etiquette are referred to as connectionless and connection-oriented communications.

Connection-oriented communication exchanges control information, referred to as a *handshake,* prior to transmitting data. The Transport layer uses the handshake to ensure that the destination system is ready to receive information. A connection-oriented exchange will also ensure that data is transmitted and received in its original order. Modems are heavy users of connection-oriented communications, as they need to negotiate a connection speed prior to sending any information. In networking, this functionality is accomplished through the use of a Transport layer field referred to as a *flag* in the IP and AppleTalk (AT) world, or as the *connection control* field under IPX. Only connection-oriented communications use these fields. When IP is the underlying routing protocol, TCP is used to create connection-oriented communications. IPX uses SPX, and AppleTalk uses AppleTalk Transport Protocol (ATP) to provide this functionality. As a communication session is started, the Application layer (not necessarily the program you are using) will specify if it needs to use a connection-oriented protocol. Telnet is just such an application. When a Telnet session is started, the Application layer will request TCP as its transport service in order to better ensure reliability of the connection. Let's look at how this session is established to see how a handshake works.

At your workstation (Windows 95/98, NT, or Unix), you type in **telnet thor .foobar.com** to establish a remote connection to that system. As the request is passed down through the Transport layer, TCP is selected to connect the two systems so that a connection-oriented communication can be established. The Transport layer sets the synchronization (SYN) flag to 1 and leaves all other flags at 0. IP uses multiple flag fields and uses the binary system to set values. This means that the only possible values of an IP flag are 1 and 0. IPX and AT use a hexadecimal value, as their frames only contain one flag field. This allows the one field to contain more than two values.

By setting SYN=1 and all other fields to 0, we let the system on the other end (thor.foobar.com) know that we wish to establish a new communication session with the system. This request would then be passed down the remaining layers, across the wire to the remote system, and then up through its OSI layers.

If the service is available on the remote system (more on services in a moment), the request is acknowledged and sent back down the stack until it reaches the Transport layer. The Transport layer would then set the SYN flag to 1, as did the originating system, but it will also set the acknowledgment (ACK) flag to 1 as well. This lets the originating system know that its transmission was received and that it's okay to send data. The request is then passed down the stack and over the wire back to the original system.

The original system would then set the SYN flag to 0 and the ACK flag to 1 and transfer this frame back to Thor. This lets Thor know, "I'm acknowledging your acknowledgment and I'm about to send data." At this point data would be transferred; and each system would be required to transmit an acknowledgment for each packet it receives. Figure 2.12 shows a Telnet session from the system Loki to the system Thor. Each line represents a different frame that has been transmitted from one system to the other. Source and destination systems are identified as well as some summary information about the frame. Note that the first three frames are identified as TCP frames, not Telnet, and that they perform the handshaking described above. Once TCP establishes the connection-oriented connection, then Telnet can step in to transfer the data required. The TCP frames that appear later in the conversation are for acknowledgment purposes. As stated, with a connection-oriented protocol, every frame must be acknowledged. If the frame was a request for information, the reply can be in the form of delivering the requested information. If a frame is sent that does not require a reply, however, the destination system is still required to acknowledge that the frame was received.

FIGURE 2.12:

An example of connection-oriented communication

No.	Siz	Source	Destination	Layer	Summary
1	64	LOKI.FOOBAR.COM	THOR.FOOBAR.COM	tcp	Port:1042 ---> TELNET SYN
2	64	THOR.FOOBAR.COM	LOKI.FOOBAR.COM	tcp	Port:TELNET ---> 1042 ACK SYN
3	64	LOKI.FOOBAR.COM	THOR.FOOBAR.COM	tcp	Port:1042 ---> TELNET ACK
4	82	LOKI.FOOBAR.COM	THOR.FOOBAR.COM	telnt	Cmd=Do; Code=Suppress Go Ahead; Cmd=Will; Code=Termin
5	64	THOR.FOOBAR.COM	LOKI.FOOBAR.COM	tcp	Port:TELNET ---> 1042 ACK
6	70	THOR.FOOBAR.COM	LOKI.FOOBAR.COM	telnt	Cmd=Do; Code=Terminal Type; Cmd=Do; Code=Terminal Spe
7	64	LOKI.FOOBAR.COM	THOR.FOOBAR.COM	telnt	Cmd=Won't; Code=; Cmd=Will; Code=Terminal Type;
8	73	THOR.FOOBAR.COM	LOKI.FOOBAR.COM	telnt	Cmd=Will; Code=Suppress Go Ahead; Cmd=Do; Code=; Cmd=
9	64	THOR.FOOBAR.COM	LOKI.FOOBAR.COM	tcp	Port:TELNET ---> 1042 ACK
10	67	LOKI.FOOBAR.COM	THOR.FOOBAR.COM	telnt	Cmd=Subnegotiation Begin; Code=; Data=..P....
11	76	THOR.FOOBAR.COM	LOKI.FOOBAR.COM	telnt	Cmd=Subnegotiation Begin; Code=Terminal Speed; Data= .....
12	64	LOKI.FOOBAR.COM	THOR.FOOBAR.COM	tcp	Port:1042 ---> TELNET ACK
13	64	THOR.FOOBAR.COM	LOKI.FOOBAR.COM	tcp	Port:TELNET ---> 1042 ACK
14	92	LOKI.FOOBAR.COM	THOR.FOOBAR.COM	telnt	Cmd=Subnegotiation Begin; Code=Terminal Speed; Data= .38
15	64	THOR.FOOBAR.COM	LOKI.FOOBAR.COM	telnt	Cmd=Do; Code=Echo;
16	64	LOKI.FOOBAR.COM	THOR.FOOBAR.COM	telnt	Cmd=Won't; Code=Echo;
17	129	THOR.FOOBAR.COM	LOKI.FOOBAR.COM	telnt	Cmd=Will; Code=Echo; Data=..Red Hat Linux release 4.1 (Var
18	64	LOKI.FOOBAR.COM	THOR.FOOBAR.COM	telnt	Cmd=Do; Code=Echo;
19	64	THOR.FOOBAR.COM	LOKI.FOOBAR.COM	tcp	Port:TELNET ---> 1042 ACK
20	65	THOR.FOOBAR.COM	LOKI.FOOBAR.COM	telnt	Data=login:
21	64	LOKI.FOOBAR.COM	THOR.FOOBAR.COM	tcp	Port:1042 ---> TELNET ACK

If you're still a bit fuzzy on handshaking and connection-oriented communications, let's look at an analogy. Let's say you call a friend to inform them you'll be having a network Quake party on Saturday night and that they should come by with their laptop. You follow these steps:

- You dial your friend's phone number. (SYN=1, ACK=0)

- Your friend answers the phone and says, "Hello?" (SYN=1, ACK=1)

- You reply by saying, "Hi Fred, this is Dave." (SYN=0, ACK=1)

You would then proceed to transfer your data about your upcoming party. Every time you pause, your friend would either transfer back information ("Yes, I'm free Saturday night!") or send some form of acknowledgment (ACK) to let you know they have not yet hung up.

When the conversation is complete, you would both *tear down* the connection by saying "goodbye," which is a handshake to let each other know that the conversation is complete and that it's okay to hang up the phone.

The purpose of connection-oriented communications is simple. It provides a reliable communication session when the underlying layers may be considered less than stable. By ensuring reliable connectivity at the Transport layer, it helps to speed up communication when data becomes lost. This is because the data does not have to be passed all the way up to the Application layer before a retransmission frame is created and sent. While this is important in modem communications, where a small amount of noise or a crossed line can kill a communication session, it is not as useful with network-based communication. TCP and SPX originate from the days when the Physical and Data Link layers could not always be relied on to successfully transmit information. These days this is less of a concern as reliability has increased dramatically from the earlier years of networking.

A *connectionless protocol* does not require an initial handshake or acknowledgments for every packet. When a connectionless transport is used, it makes its best effort to deliver the data, but relies on the stability of the underlying layers as well as Application layer acknowledgments to ensure that the data is delivered reliably. IP's User Datagram Protocol (UDP) and IPX's NetWare Core Protocol (NCP) are examples of connectionless transports. Both protocols rely on connectionless communications to transfer routing and server information as well. While AppleTalk does not utilize any connectionless communications for creating data sessions, it does use it when advertising servers with its Name Binding Protocol (NBP).

NOTE   Broadcasts are always transmitted using a connectionless transport.

As an example of connectionless communications, see the Network File System (NFS) session in Figure 2.13. NFS is a service that allows file sharing over IP. It uses UDP as its underlying transport protocol. Notice that all data acknowledgments are in the form of requests for additional information. The destination system (Thor) assumes that the last packet was received if the source system (Loki) requests additional information. Conversely, if Loki does not receive a reply from Thor for information it has requested, NFS takes care of requesting the information again. As long as we have a stable connection that does not require a large number of retransmissions, this is a very efficient method of communicating as it does not generate unnecessary acknowledgments.

NFS uses UDP to create a
connectionless session.

No.	Size	Source	Destination	Layer	Summary
1	198	LOKI.FOOBAR.COM	THOR.FOOBAR.COM	nfs	Call Lookup ???/games.tar.gz
2	174	THOR.FOOBAR.COM	LOKI.FOOBAR.COM	nfs	Reply Lookup for games.tar.gz
3	182	LOKI.FOOBAR.COM	THOR.FOOBAR.COM	nfs	Call Get File Attributes for games.tar.gz
4	142	THOR.FOOBAR.COM	LOKI.FOOBAR.COM	nfs	Reply Get File Attributes
5	194	LOKI.FOOBAR.COM	THOR.FOOBAR.COM	nfs	Call Read From File games.tar.gz; Offset 0; 1024 bytes
6	1,170	THOR.FOOBAR.COM	LOKI.FOOBAR.COM	nfs	Reply Read From File; 1024 bytes
7	194	LOKI.FOOBAR.COM	THOR.FOOBAR.COM	nfs	Call Read From File games.tar.gz; Offset 1024; 1024 bytes
8	1,170	THOR.FOOBAR.COM	LOKI.FOOBAR.COM	nfs	Reply Read From File; 1024 bytes
9	194	LOKI.FOOBAR.COM	THOR.FOOBAR.COM	nfs	Call Read From File games.tar.gz; Offset 2048; 1024 bytes
10	1,170	THOR.FOOBAR.COM	LOKI.FOOBAR.COM	nfs	Reply Read From File; 1024 bytes
11	194	LOKI.FOOBAR.COM	THOR.FOOBAR.COM	nfs	Call Read From File games.tar.gz; Offset 3072; 1024 bytes
12	1,170	THOR.FOOBAR.COM	LOKI.FOOBAR.COM	nfs	Reply Read From File; 1024 bytes
13	194	LOKI.FOOBAR.COM	THOR.FOOBAR.COM	nfs	Call Read From File games.tar.gz; Offset 4096; 1024 bytes
14	1,170	THOR.FOOBAR.COM	LOKI.FOOBAR.COM	nfs	Reply Read From File; 1024 bytes
15	194	LOKI.FOOBAR.COM	THOR.FOOBAR.COM	nfs	Call Read From File games.tar.gz; Offset 5120; 1024 bytes
16	1,170	THOR.FOOBAR.COM	LOKI.FOOBAR.COM	nfs	Reply Read From File; 1024 bytes
17	194	LOKI.FOOBAR.COM	THOR.FOOBAR.COM	nfs	Call Read From File games.tar.gz; Offset 6144; 1024 bytes
18	1,170	THOR.FOOBAR.COM	LOKI.FOOBAR.COM	nfs	Reply Read From File; 1024 bytes
19	194	LOKI.FOOBAR.COM	THOR.FOOBAR.COM	nfs	Call Read From File games.tar.gz; Offset 7168; 1024 bytes
20	1,170	THOR.FOOBAR.COM	LOKI.FOOBAR.COM	nfs	Reply Read From File; 1024 bytes
21	194	LOKI.FOOBAR.COM	THOR.FOOBAR.COM	nfs	Call Read From File games.tar.gz; Offset 8192; 1024 bytes
22	1,170	THOR.FOOBAR.COM	LOKI.FOOBAR.COM	nfs	Reply Read From File; 1024 bytes
23	194	LOKI.FOOBAR.COM	THOR.FOOBAR.COM	nfs	Call Read From File games.tar.gz; Offset 9216; 1024 bytes

Let's look at another analogy to see how this type of communication differs
from the connection-oriented one described earlier. Again, let's say you call a
friend to inform them you'll be having a network Quake party on Saturday night
and that they should come by with their laptop. You call their number but this
time get their answering machine. You leave a detailed message indicating when
the party will take place and what they are required to bring. Unlike the first
analogy you are now relying on:

- your ability to dial the correct phone number, as you did not reach your
  friend himself to confirm that this number was in fact his

- the fact that the phone company did not drop your phone connection in the
  middle of your leaving your friend the message (answering machines do
  not ACK, unless of course you talk until the beep, and it cuts you off)

You are also assuming that:

- the answering machine properly recorded the message and did not
  eat the tape

- your friend's cat does not mistake the tape for a ball of yarn

- the power did not go out, hiding the fact that your friend has a new message to listen to

- your friend is able to retrieve this message between now and the date of
  the party

As you can see, you have no real confirmation that your friend will actually receive the message. You are counting on none of the possible mishaps taking place so that your friend will receive the message in a timely manner. If you wanted to ensure the reliability of this data transmission you could send an Application layer acknowledgment request: "Please RSVP by Thursday." If you do not get a response by then you could try transmitting the data again.

The benefit of a connectionless protocol is that it allows for a bit more freedom when determining how nitpicky the systems must be to ensure proper data delivery. As we will find in our discussion on IPX, this can be leveraged, so that many frames of useful information can be sent before an acknowledgment of their receipt is required.

So which is a better transport to use? Unfortunately, the answer is "whichever one is specified by your Application layer." If Telnet wants TCP, you cannot force it to use UDP.

When a network program is initially coded, it is up to the programmers involved to choose which transport they will support. A majority of applications today use a connection-oriented transport, for a couple of reasons:

- The first is conditions at the time of development. Telnet has been around for so long that TCP was the appropriate transport at the time of development. Networking was still a very unstable animal back then. Trying to switch over to UDP now is possible but would cause a complete mess as some systems are upgraded before others.

- The other driving force is a misunderstanding as to when a connection-oriented protocol is required. A programmer who is faced with using a *reliable* or *unreliable* transport for moving their data will usually choose the former without regard for how inefficient this may make the communication session. They simply look at the term "unreliable" and shy away.

Some applications do require a connection-oriented session, even today. An example would be a network-based video conference program. Lost frames must be recovered immediately and the data must be received in the order it was sent to ensure that the resulting image does not appear choppy, or as if the person on the other end is moving in slow motion replay. This information is considered to be time-sensitive, as the information must be displayed as quickly as it is received in order to avoid delays.

Data transmissions that are not time-sensitive, such as e-mail or file transfers, are usually better left to a connectionless protocol. Because networks today are much more reliable than they were two decades ago, the number of times a retransmission is required now is minimal. As a result, this functionality can easily be provided by some upper layer. Also, receiving the data in its original order should not be a concern. The Transport layer has the ability to sequence data so that packets received out of order can be queued and assembled properly. While this may cause a brief delay before information is passed along to upper layers, this time is easily compensated for by streamlining communications and requiring fewer ACKs to maintain the data stream.

One technology that has made good use of the flag field of connection-oriented communications is firewalls. A firewall will use the information in the flag field to determine if a connection is inbound or outbound and based on its rule table either accept or deny the connection.

For example, let's say our firewall rules allow internal users access to the Internet but blocks external users from accessing internal systems. This is a pretty common security policy. How do we accomplish this?

We cannot simply block all inbound traffic, because this would prohibit our internal users from ever receiving a reply to their data requests. We need some method of allowing replies back in while denying external systems from being able to establish connections with internal systems. The secret to this is our TCP flags.

Remember that a TCP-based session needs to handshake prior to sending data. If we block all inbound frames that have the SYN field set to 1 and all other fields set to 0, we can prevent any external user from establishing a connection with our internal system. Because these settings are only used during the initial handshake and do not appear in any other part of the transmission, firewalls are an effective way of blocking external users. If external users cannot connect to an internal system, they cannot transmit or pull data from it.

Many firewalls will deny all UDP connections—UDP does not have a flag field, and most firewalls have no effective way of determining if the data is a connection request or a reply. This is what has made *dynamic packet filtering* firewalls so popular, as they monitor and remember all connection sessions. With dynamic packet filtering you can create a filter rule that accepts UDP packets from external hosts only when that host has been previously queried for information using UDP. This ensures that only UDP replies are allowed back in past the firewall. While a packet filter or some proxy firewalls can only effectively work with TCP connections, a dynamic packet filtering firewall can safely pass UDP as well.

Network Services

We can now find our remote system and can ensure that both systems are using the same level of communications. The question now is how to tell the server what we want. While computers are powerful tools—capable of processing many requests per second—they still have a problem with the phrase, "You know what I mean." This is why we require a method of letting a system know exactly what we want from it. It would be a real bummer to connect to a slick new Web site only to have the server start spewing e-mail or routing information at you because it had no idea what you were looking for.

To make sure the computer knows what we want from it, we need to look to the Session layer.

NOTE   You may remember from our discussion of the Session layer at the beginning of this chapter that it is responsible for ensuring that requests for service are formulated properly.

A *service* is a process or application which runs on a server and provides some form of benefit to a network user. E-mail is a good example of a value-added service. A system may queue your mail messages until you connect to the system with a mail client in order to read them. File and print sharing are two more common examples of network services.

Services are accessed by connecting to a specific port or socket. Think of ports as virtual mail slots on the system and you'll get the idea. A separate mail slot (port number) is designated for each service or application running on the system. When a user wishes to access a service, the Session layer is responsible for ensuring that the request reaches the correct mail slot or port number.

On a Windows 95/98, NT, or Unix system, IP port numbers are mapped to services in a file called (oddly enough) SERVICES. An abbreviated services file is listed on the following page. Note that the first column identifies the service by name while the second column identifies the port and transport to be used. The third column is a brief description of the functionality provided by the service. This is only a brief listing of IP services. More information can be found in request for comment (RFC) 1700, which is available through the World Wide Web Consortium site, www.W3C.org. Note that these port numbers are not operating-system–specific; any system using SMTP will connect to port 25.

```
ftp-data       20/tcp    #Used to transfer actual file information
ftp            21/tcp    #Used to transfer session commands
telnet         23/tcp    #Creates a remote session
smtp           25/tcp    #e-mail delivery
whois          43/tcp    #Internic domain name lookup
domain         53/tcp    #Domain name queries
domain         53/udp    #DNS zone transfers
bootps         67/udp    # bootp server
bootpc         68/udp    # bootp client
pop-3          110/tcp   # PostOffice V.3
nntp           119/tcp   # Network News Transfer
ntp            123/tcp   # Network Time Protocol
ntp            123/udp   # Network Time Protocol
netbios-ns     37/tcp    #nbns
netbios-ns     137/udp   #nbns
netbios-dgm    138/tcp   #nbdgm
netbios-dgm    138/udp   #nbdgm
netbios-ssn    139/tcp   #nbssn
snmp           161/udp   #Simple Network Management protocol
snmp-trap      162/udp   #Simple Network Management protocol
```

So according to the above file, any TCP request received on port 23 is assumed to be a Telnet session and is passed up to the application that handles remote access. If the requested port is 25, it is assumed that mail services are required and the session is passed up to the mail program.

The above file is used by a process called the Internet Daemon (inetd). inetd monitors each of the listed ports on a Unix system and is responsible for *waking up* the application that provides services to that port. This is an efficient means of managing the system for ports that are accessed infrequently. The process is only active and using system resources (memory, CPU time, and so on) when the service is actually needed. When the service is shut down, the process returns to a sleep mode, waiting for inetd to call on it again. Windows 95/98 and NT, on the other hand, typically monitor incoming port requests via the applications which service them.

Applications that receive heavy use should be left running in a constant listening mode—this is typically more efficient. For example, Web server access usually uses port 80. Note that it is not listed in the services file above as a process to be handled by inetd. This is because a Web server may be called upon to service many requests in the course of a day. It is more efficient to leave the process running all the time than to bother inetd every time you receive a page request.

All of the above mentioned port numbers are referred to as *well-known ports*. Well-known ports are de facto standards used to ensure that everyone is capable of accessing services on other machines without needing to guess which port number is used by the service. For example, there is nothing stopping you from setting up a Web server on port 573 provided that the port is not in use by some other service. The problem is that most users will expect the service to be available on port 80 and may be unable to find it. Sometimes, however, switching ports may be done on purpose—we will look at that in just a minute.

NOTE   *De facto standard* means that it is a standard by popularity; it is not a rule or law.

Ports 0–1023 are defined by the Internet Assigned Numbers Authority (IANA) for most well-known services. While ports have been assigned up to 7200, it is the ports below 1024 that make up the bulk of Internet communications. These assignments are not hard-and-fast rules, but rather guides to ensure that everyone offers public services on the same port. For example, if you want to access Microsoft's Web page you can assume they are offering the service on port 80 because this is the well-known port for that service.

When a system requests information, it not only specifies the port it wishes to access but also specifies which port should be used when returning the requested information. Port numbers for this task are selected from 1024 to 65535 and are referred to as *upper port numbers*.

To illustrate how this works, let's revisit our Telnet session in Figure 2.12. When Loki attempts to set up a Telnet session with Thor it will do so by accessing port 23 on that system (port 23 is the well-known service port for Telnet). If we look at frame number 2 we see that Thor is sending the acknowledgment (ACK) back on port 1042. This is because the session information in the original frame that Loki sent Thor specified a source port of 1042 and a destination port of 23. The destination port identified where the frame was going (port 23 on Thor), while the source port identified which port should be used when sending replies (port 1042 on Loki). Port 23 is our well-known service port, while port 1042 is our upper port number used for the reply.

Upper reply ports are assigned on the fly. It is nearly impossible to predict which upper port a system will request information to be received on, as the ports are assigned based on availability. It is for this reason that packet filters used for firewalling purposes are set up to leave ports above 1023 open all the time in order to accept replies.

This leads to one of the reasons why a port other than a well-known port may be used to offer a service. A savvy end user who realizes that a packet filter will block access to the Web server running on their system may assign the service to some upper port number like 8001. Because the connection will be made above port 1023 it may not be blocked. The result is that despite your corporate policy banning internal Web sites and a packet filter to help enforce it, this user can successfully advertise their Web site provided they supply the port number (8001) along with the *Uniform Resource Locator* (*URL*). The URL would look similar to the following:

```
http://thor.foobar.com:8001
```

The :8001 tells a Web browser to access the server using port 8001 instead of 80. Because most packet filters have poor logging facilities, the network administrator responsible for enforcing the above policy of "no internal Web sites" would probably never realize it exists unless they stumble across it.

TIP The next time your boss accuses you of wasting time by cruising the Web, correct him by stating, "I am performing a security audit by attempting to pursue links to renegade internal sites which do not conform to our corporate security policy. This activity is required due to inefficiencies in our firewalling mechanism." If they do not fire you on the spot, quickly submit a PO for a new firewall while the event is clear in their mind.

Speaking of switching port numbers, try to identify the session in Figure 2.14. While the session is identified as a Simple Mail Transfer Protocol (SMTP), it is actually a Telnet session redirected to port 25 (the well-known port for SMTP). We've fooled the analyzer recording this session into thinking that we simply have one mail system transferring mail to another. Most firewalls will be duped in the same fashion because they use the destination port to identify the session in progress—they do not look at the actual applications involved. This type of activity is usually analogous to someone spoofing or faking a mail message. Once connected to the remote mail system, the spoofer is free to pretend the message came from anywhere. Unless the routing information in the mail header is checked (most user-friendly mail programs simply discard this information), the actual origin of this information cannot be traced.

While this looks like a normal transfer of mail, it is actually someone spoofing a mail message to the destination system.

No.	Source	Destination	Layer	Summary	Size
1	0080C819F8DD	0080C82F9E9C	tcp	Port:1051 ---> SMTP SYN	64
2	0080C82F9E9C	0080C819F8DD	tcp	Port:SMTP ---> 1051 ACK SYN	64
3	0080C819F8DD	0080C82F9E9C	tcp	Port:1051 ---> SMTP ACK	64
4	0080C82F9E9C	0080C819F8DD	tcp	Port:SMTP ---> 1051 ACK PUSH	138
5	0080C819F8DD	0080C82F9E9C	tcp	Port:1051 ---> SMTP ACK	64
6	0080C819F8DD	0080C82F9E9C	tcp	Port:1051 ---> SMTP ACK PUSH	80
7	0080C82F9E9C	0080C819F8DD	tcp	Port:SMTP ---> 1051 ACK PUSH	134
8	0080C819F8DD	0080C82F9E9C	tcp	Port:1051 ---> SMTP ACK	64
9	0080C819F8DD	0080C82F9E9C	tcp	Port:1051 ---> SMTP ACK PUSH	91
10	0080C82F9E9C	0080C819F8DD	tcp	Port:SMTP ---> 1051 ACK	64
11	0080C82F9E9C	0080C819F8DD	tcp	Port:SMTP ---> 1051 ACK PUSH	97
12	0080C819F8DD	0080C82F9E9C	tcp	Port:1051 ---> SMTP ACK	64
15	0080C819F8DD	0080C82F9E9C	tcp	Port:1051 ---> SMTP ACK PUSH	93
16	0080C82F9E9C	0080C819F8DD	tcp	Port:SMTP ---> 1051 ACK	64
17	0080C82F9E9C	0080C819F8DD	tcp	Port:SMTP ---> 1051 ACK PUSH	104
18	0080C819F8DD	0080C82F9E9C	tcp	Port:1051 ---> SMTP ACK	64
19	0080C819F8DD	0080C82F9E9C	tcp	Port:1051 ---> SMTP ACK PUSH	64
20	0080C82F9E9C	0080C819F8DD	tcp	Port:SMTP ---> 1051 ACK PUSH	108
21	0080C819F8DD	0080C82F9E9C	tcp	Port:1051 ---> SMTP ACK	64
22	0080C819F8DD	0080C82F9E9C	tcp	Port:1051 ---> SMTP ACK PUSH	80
23	0080C82F9E9C	0080C819F8DD	tcp	Port:SMTP ---> 1051 ACK	64
24	0080C819F8DD	0080C82F9E9C	tcp	Port:1051 ---> SMTP ACK PUSH	122
25	0080C82F9E9C	0080C819F8DD	tcp	Port:SMTP ---> 1051 ACK	64
26	0080C819F8DD	0080C82F9E9C	tcp	Port:1051 ---> SMTP ACK PUSH	68
27	0080C82F9E9C	0080C819F8DD	tcp	Port:SMTP ---> 1051 ACK	64
28	0080C819F8DD	0080C82F9E9C	tcp	Port:1051 ---> SMTP ACK	64
29	0080C82F9E9C	0080C819F8DD	tcp	Port:SMTP ---> 1051 ACK	64
30	0080C82F9E9C	0080C819F8DD	tcp	Port:SMTP ---> 1051 ACK PUSH	102
31	0080C819F8DD	0080C82F9E9C	tcp	Port:1051 ---> SMTP ACK	64
32	0080C819F8DD	0080C82F9E9C	tcp	Port:1051 ---> SMTP ACK	64
33	0080C82F9E9C	0080C819F8DD	tcp	Port:SMTP ---> 1051 ACK PUSH	98
34	0080C82F9E9C	0080C819F8DD	tcp	Port:SMTP ---> 1051 ACK FIN	64

Figure 2.15 shows the final output of this spoofing session. Without the header information, we may actually believe this message came from bgates@ microsoft.com. The fact that the message was never touched by a mail system within the Microsoft domain indicates that it is a phony. We've used this example in the past while instructing Internet and security classes. Do not believe everything you read, especially if it comes from the Internet!

The output from our spoofed mail message

```
From bgates@microsoft.com  Wed Feb  5 16:42:21 1997
Return-Path: <bgates@microsoft.com>
Received: from loki.foobar.com (loki.foobar.com [10.2.2.20])
        by thor.foobar.com (8.8.4/8.8.4) with SMTP
        id QAA00887 for cbrenton@thor.foobar.com; Wed, 5 Feb 1997 16:41:04 -0500
Date: Wed, 5 Feb 1997 16:41:04 -0500
From: bgates@microsoft.com (Bill Gates)
Message-Id: <199702052141.QAA00887@thor.foobar.com>
Subject: Quake Party
Status: R

The party sounds cool! I'll bring the P5's and the cheeze wiz!

Later...
```

This type of redirection can also have its benefits. Let's assume that you already have a corporate Web server running on your system. Let's also assume that you pick up a product like Software.com's Post.Office. This product allows users to administer their post office protocol (POP) e-mail accounts using a friendly Web browser interface. The problem here is that port 80 is already in use by the company Web server. To resolve this conflict, simply set Post.Office to use some other port number for the Web browser interface than 80 and let your users know the correct URL to use when accessing this system. Using multiple port numbers allows you to have two separate Web servers running on the same system without conflict.

Port numbers are also used to distinctly identify similar sessions between systems. For example, let's build on Figure 2.12. We already have one Telnet session running from Loki to Thor. What happens if four or five more sessions are created? All sessions have the following information in common:

Source IP address: 10.2.2.20 (loki.foobar.com)

Destination IP address: 10.2.2.10 (thor.foobar.com)

Destination port: 23 (well-known port for Telnet)

The source ports remain distinctive in order to identify each individual session. Our first connection has already specified a source port of 1042 for its connection. Each sequential Telnet session that is established after that would be assigned some other upper port number to uniquely identify it. The actual numbers assigned would be based upon what was not currently being used by the source system. For example, ports 1118, 1398, 4023, and 6025 may be used as source ports for the next four sessions. The actual reply port number does not really matter, only that it can uniquely identify that specific session between the two systems. If we were to monitor a number of concurrent sessions taking place, the transaction would look similar to Figure 2.16. Now we see multiple reply ports in use to identify each session.

IP is not the only protocol to make use of ports. AppleTalk and IPX also use ports, only they are referred to as *sockets*. Unlike IP and AT, which use decimal numbers to identify different ports, IPX uses hexadecimal numbers. The functionality of well-known and upper ports is the same as for IP with these two protocols. The major difference is that there are not nearly as many different services defined. We will get into this in more detail when we cover each protocol individually.

FIGURE 2.16:

Multiple Telnet sessions in
progress between Loki
and Thor

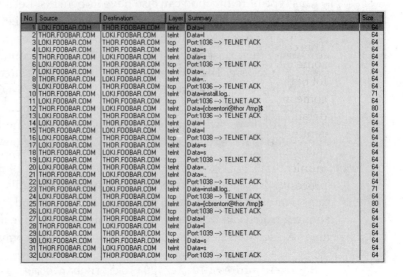

No.	Source	Destination	Layer	Summary	Size
1	LOKI.FOOBAR.COM	THOR.FOOBAR.COM	telnt	Data=l	64
2	THOR.FOOBAR.COM	LOKI.FOOBAR.COM	telnt	Data=l	64
3	LOKI.FOOBAR.COM	THOR.FOOBAR.COM	tcp	Port:1036 ---> TELNET ACK	64
4	LOKI.FOOBAR.COM	THOR.FOOBAR.COM	telnt	Data=s	64
5	THOR.FOOBAR.COM	LOKI.FOOBAR.COM	telnt	Data=s	64
6	LOKI.FOOBAR.COM	THOR.FOOBAR.COM	tcp	Port:1036 ---> TELNET ACK	64
7	LOKI.FOOBAR.COM	THOR.FOOBAR.COM	telnt	Data=.	64
8	THOR.FOOBAR.COM	LOKI.FOOBAR.COM	telnt	Data=.	64
9	LOKI.FOOBAR.COM	THOR.FOOBAR.COM	tcp	Port:1036 ---> TELNET ACK	64
10	THOR.FOOBAR.COM	LOKI.FOOBAR.COM	telnt	Data=install.log.	71
11	LOKI.FOOBAR.COM	THOR.FOOBAR.COM	tcp	Port:1036 ---> TELNET ACK	64
12	THOR.FOOBAR.COM	LOKI.FOOBAR.COM	telnt	Data=[cbrenton@thor /tmp]$	80
13	LOKI.FOOBAR.COM	THOR.FOOBAR.COM	tcp	Port:1036 ---> TELNET ACK	64
14	LOKI.FOOBAR.COM	THOR.FOOBAR.COM	telnt	Data=l	64
15	THOR.FOOBAR.COM	LOKI.FOOBAR.COM	telnt	Data=l	64
16	LOKI.FOOBAR.COM	THOR.FOOBAR.COM	tcp	Port:1038 ---> TELNET ACK	64
17	LOKI.FOOBAR.COM	THOR.FOOBAR.COM	telnt	Data=s	64
18	THOR.FOOBAR.COM	LOKI.FOOBAR.COM	telnt	Data=s	64
19	LOKI.FOOBAR.COM	THOR.FOOBAR.COM	tcp	Port:1038 ---> TELNET ACK	64
20	LOKI.FOOBAR.COM	THOR.FOOBAR.COM	telnt	Data=.	64
21	THOR.FOOBAR.COM	LOKI.FOOBAR.COM	telnt	Data=.	64
22	LOKI.FOOBAR.COM	THOR.FOOBAR.COM	tcp	Port:1038 ---> TELNET ACK	64
23	THOR.FOOBAR.COM	LOKI.FOOBAR.COM	telnt	Data=install.log.	71
24	LOKI.FOOBAR.COM	THOR.FOOBAR.COM	tcp	Port:1038 ---> TELNET ACK	64
25	THOR.FOOBAF.COM	LOKI.FOOBAR.COM	telnt	Data=[cbrenton@thor /tmp]$	80
26	LOKI.FOOBAR.COM	THOR.FOOBAR.COM	tcp	Port:1038 ---> TELNET ACK	64
27	LOKI.FOOBAR.COM	THOR.FOOBAR.COM	telnt	Data=l	64
28	THOR.FOOBAR.COM	LOKI.FOOBAR.COM	telnt	Data=l	64
29	LOKI.FOOBAR.COM	THOR.FOOBAR.COM	tcp	Port:1039 ---> TELNET ACK	64
30	LOKI.FOOBAR.COM	THOR.FOOBAR.COM	telnt	Data=s	64
31	THOR.FOOBAR.COM	LOKI.FOOBAR.COM	telnt	Data=s	64
32	LOKI.FOOBAR.COM	THOR.FOOBAR.COM	tcp	Port:1039 ---> TELNET ACK	64

Upper Layer Communications

Once we get above the Session layer, our communications become pretty specific
to the program in use. The responsibilities of the Presentation and Application
layers are more a function of the type of service requested than they are the
underlying protocol in use. Data translation and encryption are considered
portable features.

NOTE   *Portable* means that these features can be applied easily to different services without regard for the underlying protocol. It does not matter if you're using IP or IPX
to transfer your data; the ability to leverage these features will depend on the
application in use.

For example, IBM/Lotus Notes has the ability to encrypt mail messages prior
to transmission. This activity is performed at the Presentation layer of the program. It does not matter if you're connecting to your mail system via TCP, SPX,
or a modem. The encryption functionality is available with all three protocols
because the functionality is made available by the program itself. It is not dependent on the underlying protocol.

Summary

This concludes our general discussion of protocols and should help answer some questions about how two or more systems communicate. We've covered a lot of the terminology used in describing each portion of a transmission; this will come in handy during the next chapter when we cover each protocol in greater detail. Don't worry if you're still a bit fuzzy about how this all fits together. We'll continue to build upon our OSI-layer foundation when we specify the particular nuances of each individual protocol. There will be many more examples of communication sessions, so just stick with it. There is a lot of information here to process.

CHAPTER

THREE

Specific Networking Protocols

- The Internet protocol suite (TCP/IP)

- IP addressing conventions

- IP routing, Transport layer, and application services

- Internetwork Packet Exchange (IPX)

- IPX routing, Transport layer, and application services

- Network Basic Input/Output System (NetBIOS)

- NetBIOS addressing, routing, and the Session and Transport layers

- NetBIOS Extended User Interface (NetBEUI)

- AppleTalk and its services

In the last chapter we discussed protocol communications generally. We looked at the methods that can be used for discovering different networks as well as the processes used for accessing different services. It's now time to get specific and look at how each protocol implements these communication properties.

The Internet Protocol Suite (TCP/IP)

The *TCP/IP* (or just plain "IP") protocol suite has become a network administrator's tool kit. When dissimilar systems are used, administrators tend to turn to IP for providing connectivity. IP has its roots in the Unix operating system. It was this NOS that first leveraged the flexibility and diversity of services that IP can offer. This was a perfect match as both were designed to provide a plethora of services.

In the last several years, of course, the IP protocol suite has achieved much greater use, as the underlying protocol for the Internet. And because of this popularity, many more LANs have also adopted the IP protocol suite for internal use— even if they have no connection to the Internet.

WARNING   The IP protocol suite's versatility does not come without a price, however—it requires a higher level of administrator expertise and management to ensure that it is implemented correctly.

Figure 3.1 outlines how different portions of the IP suite match up to the OSI model. As you can see, it's not an exact match as the IP protocol predates the development of this model. As we continue through this chapter we will refer back to the OSI model to provide a quick reference to how the pieces in our communication puzzle fit together. If you do not recognize all the pieces outlined in the diagram, do not worry; we will cover them throughout this chapter.

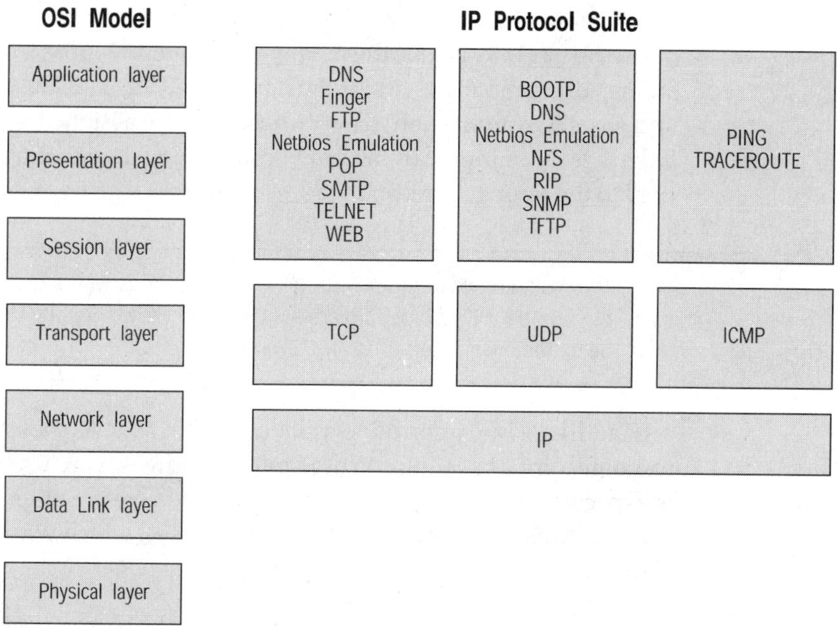

FIGURE 3.1:

The portions of the IP protocol suite and how they relate to the functionality outlined on the OSI model

OSI Model	IP Protocol Suite
Application layer	DNS / Finger / FTP / Netbios Emulation / POP / SMTP / TELNET / WEB — BOOTP / DNS / Netbios Emulation / NFS / RIP / SNMP / TFTP — PING / TRACEROUTE
Presentation layer	
Session layer	
Transport layer	TCP — UDP — ICMP
Network layer	IP
Data Link layer	
Physical layer	

IP Address Conventions

As mentioned in Chapter 2, IP logical network segments are referred to as *subnets*. A proper subnet address is made up of four blocks of numbers separated by periods. Each of these number blocks is referred to as a byte. Values for each of these bytes can range from 0 to 254. When writing a subnet address, trailing zeros are used to imply that an entire network segment is being referred to. For example, when we write 192.168.175.0, it is assumed that we are referring to the entire IP subnet whose address is 192.168.175. If we write 10.0.0.0, it is assumed that we are referring to the entire IP subnet whose address is 10.

When writing an IP address for a server or workstation (referred to as an IP *host*), the 0 field is replaced with a number to uniquely identify that system on the

IP subnet. Values for these numbers can range from 1 to 254. For example, given the IP subnet 192.168.175.0, the first system on this network may receive the address 192.168.175.1, the next may receive 192.168.175.2, and so on. In our subnet 10 example, the first IP host may be 10.1.1.1, the next may be 10.1.1.2, and so on. On an IP subnet, every host must be assigned a unique IP address. Otherwise, communications can become crossed, with information being delivered to the wrong system.

NOTE   The assigning of unique IP addresses is analogous to the assigning of social security numbers. If two people are assigned the same number, tax information would be extremely difficult to straighten out.

IP addresses are referred to as *unicast* addresses, as they are designed for point-to-point communications. When unicast addresses are used, only a single system is expected to receive and process the data. There are other types of addresses, referred to as *broadcast* and *multicast* addresses, which we will cover later in this chapter.

Standard Subnet Masks

So our IP address contains two parts—one that refers to the network segment and one that refers to the host. We now have a small problem. Simply looking at an IP host address, we can't easily determine which part of the address refers to the network and which portion refers to the host. For example, if we say that our IP address is 10.73.201.5, the following combinations are possible:

Network Portion of the Address	Host Portion of the Address
10	73.201.5
10.73	201.5
10.72.201	5

This is where the *subnet mask* is used. A subnet mask listed along with an address allows us to identify which portion of the host address identifies the network and which portion identifies the host. The subnet mask follows the same format as an IP host address consisting of four blocks of numbers separated by periods. In a standard subnet mask (we will talk about non-standard subnetting in a moment) the only values used are 255 and 0. A 255 denotes the network portion of the address while a 0 denotes the host portion. Some systems (such as a NetWare server) require the subnet mask to be entered in a hexadecimal format. In these cases we must convert our decimal value to its hexadecimal equivalent. A decimal 255 directly converts to a hexadecimal value of FF.

NOTE
Because decimal value is most prevalent, it will be used for all examples in this book. The reader should be aware, however, that sometimes a hexadecimal value will be required.

Given the above host address, our options would be as follows:

Decimal Subnet Mask	Hexadecimal Subnet Mask	Network Portion	Host Portion
255.0.0.0	FF.0.0.0	10	73.201.5
255.255.0.0	FF.FF.0.0	10.73	201.5
255.255.255.0	FF.FF.FF.0	10.73.201	5

Clearly if we are going to identify an IP host properly, we must know both the IP address and the subnet mask. It is important that a consistent subnet is used on all IP hosts to ensure that routing conflicts are not encountered. An IP host with an incorrect subnet mask may not be able to determine which other systems occupy the same logical network. Figure 3.2 shows a transmission decision table.

Transmission Decision Table

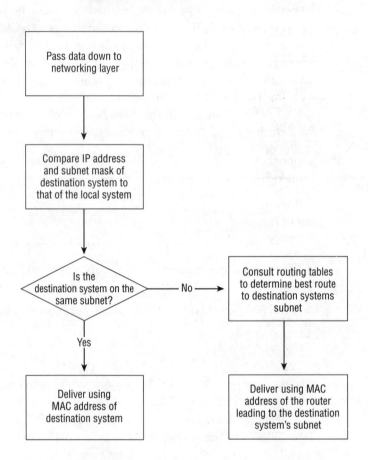

So why is subnetting used? Because every network has different requirements for the number of hosts that must be supported on any given network. By adjusting the subnet mask, we can increase or decrease the number of hosts supported on any given subnet by using up a portion of the network space. The table below shows how the maximum numbers of networks and subnet hosts change as the subnet mask is adjusted. The quantities reflect the segmentation of a single address. For example, 10.0.0.0, 11.0.0.0, 12.0.0.0, and so on.

Subnet Mask	Maximum Number of Networks	Maximum Number of Hosts
255.0.0.0	1	16,387,064
255.255.0.0	254	64,516
255.255.255.0	64,516	254

If we decide to use the address range of 10.0.0.0 for our IP addresses, we can use the subnet mask to customize the number of available hosts based upon our network requirements. If we have a small number of subnets with a large number of hosts on each, we may want to use a subnet mask of 255.255.0.0. This would support 254 subnets (10.1.1.0 through 10.254.0.0) with a maximum of 64,516 hosts on each.

If we are responsible for a large number of subnets that each have a small number of hosts, we may want to use a subnet mask of 255.255.255.0. This would support 64,516 subnets (10.1.1.0 through 10.254.254.0) with a maximum of 254 hosts on each. The choice is ours to make—however, keep in mind that you should always plan for growth. Changing the subnet mask on 250 or more hosts simply because you ran out of address space is a time-consuming chore at best.

WARNING   Technically, zero is considered a legal value when addressing an IP host. In other words, 10.0.0.113 is considered a valid IP address. It has been our experience, however, that networking devices from some vendors have difficulty dealing with host addresses that contain the character 0. While some systems will interpret 0 to be part of the network address, others will mistake it for a broadcast. We recommend that you do not use 0 in your address ranges if you have this option.

Registered IP Addresses

While you can select any random IP range to assign to your network, you may want to plan ahead for Internet connectivity and use a set of registered IP addresses. The *InterNIC* is the authority responsible for assigning and registering IP addresses when an organization wishes to communicate on the Internet. The

InterNIC tracks the assignment of IP addresses to ensure that there are no conflicts. If two organizations inadvertently try to use the same subnet numbers, routing errors will occur. If you assign random IP addresses to your network and later wish to connect to the Internet, you may find yourself reconfiguring your address range.

TIP   Rather than assigning a random IP range to your network, you may wish to use one of the actual IP address ranges specifically intended for this purpose. (See Table 3.3, under "Reserved Address Ranges," later in this chapter.)

Incidentally, if you do wish to go the random IP address route for now, you may wish to consider assigning your addresses from a special set of address ranges which have been set up for this purpose. The benefit to using these addresses is simply that packets originating from these addresses will not be forwarded outside your network to the Internet itself. Such addresses are "understood" by most Internet routing software to mean "do not forward/ internal use only." These addresses can be found in the table under "Reserved Address Ranges."

If you choose to connect your network to the Internet, you will need to obtain registered and unique address range from the InterNIC. You will also need to select an *Internet service provider* (*ISP*) through which you will connect your network to the Internet. Before you are connected through your Internet service provider, you may be required to fill out a number of forms documenting your current network configuration as well as the amount of network growth expected over the next five years. Based on this information, your ISP will assign one or more IP subnet numbers to your organization. Note that in most cases, when you work with an ISP, it will not be necessary for you to contact the InterNIC directly for address registration, as your ISP typically handles this for you.

The InterNIC has broken up the available IP subnets into different classes—*A*, *B*, and *C*. The class determines the size of your organization's address space. Table 3.1 defines these classes.

TABLE 3.1: InterNIC Subnet Class Definitions

Address Class	Address Range	Assumed Subnet Mask	Available Networks
A	1.0.0.0 - 126.0.0.0	255.0.0.0	64,516
B	128.0.0.0 - 191.0.0.0	255.255.0.0	254
C	192.0.0.0 - 223.0.0.0	255.255.255.0	1

For example, let's assume we are bringing a major telecommunications company onto the Internet for the first time. Our company has an extremely large world wide network. Given the size of our network, the InterNIC may see fit to assign a class A address. Let's say they assign us the address 10.0.0.0. This gives us control of the range of values between 10.1.1.0 and 10.254.254.254.

While the subnet mask 255.0.0.0 is assumed, we are actually free to break this range up any way we see fit. A class A subnet mask will only support a single logical subnet. If we have more than one logical subnet, we will need to change our subnet mask to accommodate the additional networks. Also, we may not be required to support up to 16,387,064 hosts on a single subnet. (If we do have that many hosts on a single subnet, we have much bigger problems than just assigning IP addresses!)

For example, we could choose to use a class B subnet mask of 255.255.0.0 to subnet the range assigned by the InterNIC. This would support 254 subnets, allowing us to use the values 10.1.0.0 through 10.254.0.0 for our subnet range. Each subnet would be capable of supporting 64,516 hosts.

In Figure 3.3 the subnet portion of the address changes whenever a router is crossed. Any given logical subnet is the area confined within our routers.

We could also choose to use a class C subnet mask of 255.255.255.0. This would support up to 64,516 subnets, allowing us to use the values 10.1.1.0 through 10.254.254.0 for our subnet range. Each subnet could have a maximum of 254 hosts. Figure 3.4 shows our network renumber for a class C subnet mask.

FIGURE 3.3:

A small section of what our telecommunications network may look like if a class B address is used

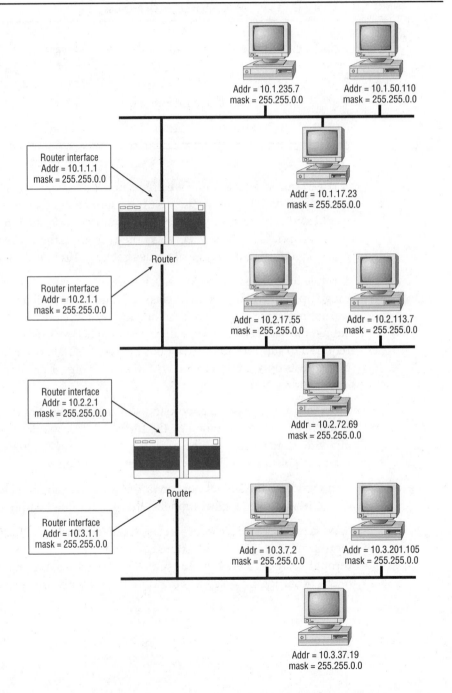

FIGURE 3.4:

Our network renumbered for
a class C subnet mask

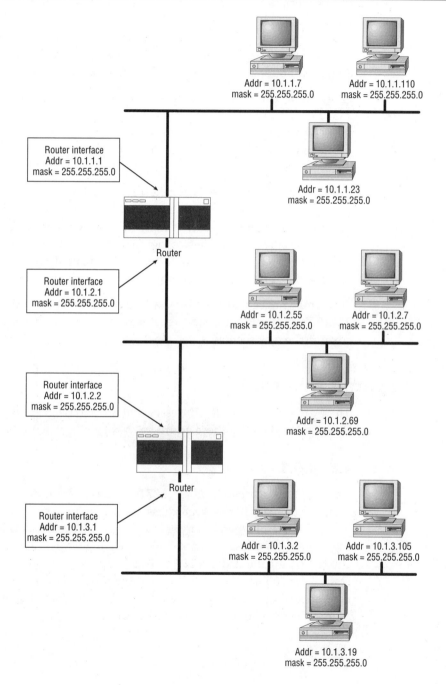

When a class B subnet is assigned, our choices are similar but somewhat more limited. Let's assume that our telecommunications company is really not quite so large. Perhaps it services only a specific continent or country. In this case, the InterNIC may assign a class B address instead. For our example, let's say they assign the address 172.25.0.0 to this organization.

Given this class B address, we can choose to use a class B subnet mask of 255.255.0.0, which would yield a single logical network with 64,516 hosts. If we need to support more than one logical subnet, we could opt to use a class C subnet mask of 255.255.255.0. This would support 254 networks with 254 hosts on each.

Finally, let's assume we are registering a small company with only 75 computers. In this case the ISP may issue a class C address such as 192.168.10.0. With this address we can only support a single network with up to 254 hosts. If this network is actually made up of two logical subnets we may have to request a second address from our ISP. This address may be sequential (for example, 192.168.11.0), or it could end up being in a completely different address range.

You may notice that the class C address range stops at 223.0.0.0 instead of 254.0.0.0. This range of addresses is reserved for a special purpose that we will cover in the next section.

Special Addresses

There are some special IP addresses that are not assigned by the InterNIC for regular use. We'll look at those addresses next.

127.0.0.1

Referred to as a *loopback address*, 127.0.0.1 is a test address automatically assigned to every IP host regardless of the operating system it is loaded on. This address is useful when ensuring that the IP protocol stack is loaded and functioning properly. If a system is not communicating with other network systems, we can try to ping the address 127.0.0.1. If this is successful we know that our IP stack is functioning properly and that the problem may be related to our network card or cabling. If the attempt is unsuccessful we know that our problem is software related and that the protocol stack is at fault.

Typically, the easier-to-remember text string localhost is mapped for you already to the loopback address 127.0.0.1. Thus, rather than pinging 127.0.0.1, you can simply ping localhost with the same effect.

TIP

To ping from a Windows 95/98 or NT workstation (or a Unix workstation for that matter), simply open a command prompt window and type **ping *address***, where *address* is any IP address or domain name. Graphical ping utilities also exist, including some that you can download from the Internet as shareware or freeware.

Broadcast Address

In the above examples we noted that 255 was not a valid IP host address value. This is because the address is reserved for network broadcasts. If we send information to the address 192.168.11.255, we are effectively sending information to every host on the network 192.168.11.0. Broadcasts are useful when a system needs to convey information but it is unsure of the destination system's address. For example, when a router sends a RIP packet, it will address it to the broadcast address to ensure that all routers located on the network segment will receive the information.

NOTE

A simple broadcast is local to the subnet and is not propagated by any routers.

There is a special type of broadcast referred to as an *all network broadcast* that always has the destination address of 255.255.255.255. This type of broadcast is used when a system does not know the local IP subnet address. For example, there is a process that allows systems to learn which IP address they should use during startup by querying a server. Upon initial boot, the system may have no idea what its IP address may be (or what the local subnet address is for that matter). The 255.255.255.255 broadcast allows this systems to send out a request for an IP address without knowing anything about the current IP addressing.

Multicast Addresses

There is a fourth address type, not mentioned above, referred to as the class D or *multicast address* range. This class includes IP addresses in the range of 224.0.0.0 through 239.255.255.0. Multicast is a special type of information delivery that is designed to let one IP host efficiently deliver information to multiple recipients on remote networks. It is based upon configuring the routers on the network with address mapping tables. These tables tell the router which unicast address to forward information to, based upon the transmission to a specific multicast address. When a host transmits to a multicast address, routers on the local subnet pick up the transmission and search their mapping tables for a match to this address. If a match is found, the router will forward the information to all the destination hosts listed in the table. Let's look at an example to see how this works.

Let's say we are designing a network for a large commercial television organization. This organization would like to develop a special service for delivering time-sensitive news to all of its affiliates. The organization would like to have the following criteria worked into the design:

- All information should be transmittable from a single system.

- There are well over 3000 nodes that will require the delivery of the news feeds.

- The delivery should be as quick as possible, as the information is timely and is updated frequently.

- A minimal amount of bandwidth should be used, because most links (currently) are frame-relay operating at only 56Kbps.

Figure 3.5 shows a small portion of how our network might look. (This figure represents only a small portion of the network as there are over 3000 end stations.)

Let's review our two other types of communications to see the effect they would have on this network.

FIGURE 3.5:

Our commercial television
station's wide area network

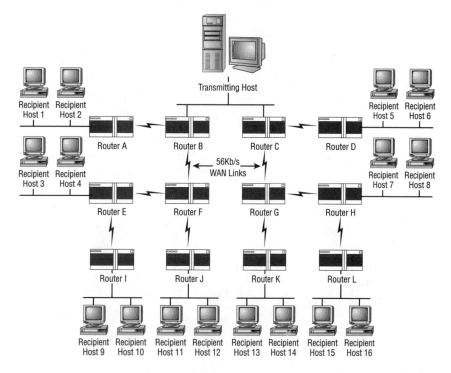

Unicast   *Unicast* is our regular point-to-point communication. It would require our transmitting host to establish an individual communication session with each recipient host. This immediately raises two problems. The first is traffic. If our transmitting host is required to set up a communication session with 3000 receiving hosts (including transmissions and acknowledgments), the amount of traffic generated would quickly saturate the network. The second problem is time. It will take our transmitting host a certain amount of time to run through all 3000 hosts when delivering information. If there are frequent news updates, it is possible that the delivery time may make it difficult for the host to keep up.

Broadcast   *Broadcasts* are delivered either to all hosts located on the same local subnet or to all hosts on the entire network (if the router is configured to forward broadcasts). Again, we have two problems. The first is performance. Given our network design we would need to use all network broadcasts. This would produce dismal network performance because the network would be saturated with broadcasts. The second problem is security. Because our broadcasts will be propagated to all networks indiscriminately, there is the potential that our news information could find itself on networks where it does not belong.

Given the above descriptions, *multicasting* would be our most efficient means of transmitting our news feeds along this network. Let's apply some multicast tables to our routers to see how this would work.

According to Table 3.2, when Router B receives a packet to the destination multicast address of 224.10.10.5, it knows to forward the information to Routers A and F. When Router A receives the packet, it looks up the source address in its table which tells it to forward the information to hosts 1 and 2. This type of propagation continues down through the network until all the hosts have received the information.

TABLE 3.2: A Network Routing Table

Router	Destination Address	Forward to
A	224.10.10.5	Hosts 1 & 2
B	224.10.10.5	Routers A & F
C	224.10.10.5	Routers D & G
D	224.10.10.5	Hosts 5 & 6
E	224.10.10.5	Hosts 3 & 4
F	224.10.10.5	Routers E & J
G	224.10.10.5	Routers H & K
H	224.10.10.5	Hosts 7 & 8
I	224.10.10.5	Hosts 9 & 10
J	224.10.10.5	Hosts 11 & 12
K	224.10.10.5	Hosts 13 & 14
L	224.10.10.5	Hosts 15 & 16

There are a couple of points worth noting with this type of communication. First, our single source host is able to communicate efficiently with a large number of recipients. It is only required to transmit the data once; the tables on the routers take care of propagating the information as required. This spreads out the overhead required to communicate with each of our 3000 recipient systems.

A second benefit to this type of communication is that we are creating very little traffic along our WAN links. For example, Router B is only required to generate a single communication session along each of its 56Kbps connections. If a retransmission is required, the request can go back to the previous router in the chain. The request is not required to return all the way back to the source system. Again, this cuts down on the amount of traffic along our slow links.

Because of the one-shot data transmission and light network traffic, we can deliver information in a timely manner. No single network device is required to communicate with all systems on the network. This overhead is spread out over multiple routers and network connections. This means that our source system is immediately free to transmit new information as required.

There are some drawbacks to this type of communication, however, that make it applicable in only specific situations. First, in order for multicasting to work properly, our routers must be reconfigured so they know what information needs to be forwarded where. If the destination is dynamic or random it will be nearly impossible to keep up with the table changes.

Second, multicast communication goes in a single direction only. The destination systems cannot relay information back up to the source system. This means that software such as Web browsers or FTP clients will not work.

Reserved Address Ranges

There are certain IP addresses that the InterNIC has reserved for general use; their use does not need InterNIC approval. While these addresses may be used freely by any organization, they are not allowed to be used for Internet communications. They will never be assigned to an organization by the InterNIC and thus may be used by anyone for internal use only. Table 3.3 shows which IP address ranges are considered reserved.

TABLE 3.3: Reserved Address Ranges

Starting Address	Ending Address
10.0.0.0	10.254.254.0
172.16.0.0	172.31.254.0
192.168.0.0	192.168.254.0

The use of reserved addresses has come about as a result of the depletion of registered addresses. As more and more organizations connect to the Internet, the pool of *legal* IP addresses available for Internet connectivity has shrunk dramatically. Reserved addresses are available for use when an IP subnet does not need Internet connectivity or when a network address translation (NAT) device will be used.

An NAT device is a network system capable of changing packets from one IP address to another. For example, a large network that requires a class A address could use the reserved address range of 10.0.0.0 when assigning IP addresses to internal hosts. When Internet access is required, an NAT device would then intercept these communications and map these addresses to a legal class C subnet address. If multiple class A addresses are mapped to a single class C host address, port numbers are used by the NAT device to keep the communication sessions orderly. This allows a large number of hosts to be easily supported by a small legal address range. Because the NAT device must sit between the internal network and the Internet, its functionality has been incorporated into many of the top firewall products.

Nonstandard Subnetting

All of our IP examples up until now have used standard subnet masks. By standard, we mean that the mask has had two possible values, 0 or 255. While this is fine in most situations, sometimes a little more control over our address range is required.

For example, let's say that you administer a very busy 80-node network and as part of traffic control you have created two separate subnets with a router in between. Let's also assume that your organization has decided to connect to the Internet but does not want to use address translation because of performance concerns. You want every internal host to receive a valid IP address. You find an ISP and file all the required paperwork with them in order to get connected. Our example network is shown in Figure 3.6. Because of traffic concerns, the network is split into two separate subnets with a single router. The IP address information reflects what was in place prior to connecting to the Internet.

FIGURE 3.6:

Our small 80-node network

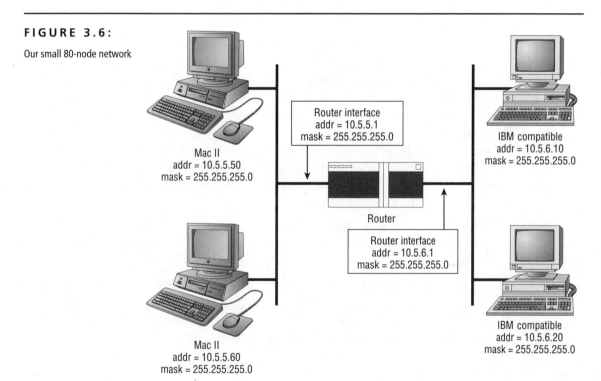

Mac II
addr = 10.5.5.50
mask = 255.255.255.0

Router interface
addr = 10.5.5.1
mask = 255.255.255.0

IBM compatible
addr = 10.5.6.10
mask = 255.255.255.0

Router

Router interface
addr = 10.5.6.1
mask = 255.255.255.0

Mac II
addr = 10.5.5.60
mask = 255.255.255.0

IBM compatible
addr = 10.5.6.20
mask = 255.255.255.0

You find, however, that because your network is considered quite small, your ISP is only willing to give you one valid class C address. This leaves you with four options:

- Find another ISP that will give you two valid addresses.

- Only allow one of your subnets to have Internet access.

- Combine your two logical subnets into one and live with the performance degradation.

- Apply a nonstandard subnet mask.

A *nonstandard subnet mask* lets you take a single network address and break it up into multiple subnets. This is done by using some other value for the mask's bytes besides 0 or 255. A value of 255 designates that the corresponding section of the IP address should be considered part of the network address. A value of 0 denotes that the number is unique to one specific host. By using some value between 0 and 255 for the final byte in the mask we can set a portion of it aside as being part of the network address and a portion as belonging to the host. Sound confusing? It can be. Nonstandard subnetting is considered to be one of the most difficult theories to grasp in IP networking. Let's continue with our example to help clarify the above statements.

Let's assume that the address assigned to us is 192.168.50.0. If we use a standard subnet mask of 255.255.255.0, we can configure a single subnet with 254 hosts.

If we change our subnet mask to 255.255.255.128, we have effectively split our network in half. Each of our two new networks can use roughly half the host addresses available between 1 and 254. Table 3.4 shows our new configuration. Figure 3.7 shows this configuration applied to our network.

TABLE 3.4: The Network Split in Half

Network	Subnet Mask	First Host Address	Last Host Address	Broadcast Address
192.168.50.0	255.255.255.128	192.168.50.1	192.168.50.126	192.168.50.127
192.168.50.128	255.255.255.128	192.168.50.129	192.168.50.254	192.168.50.255

A couple of changes are worth noting here. Because of our nonstandard subnet mask, 127 is now considered to be the broadcast address for our first subnet. Also, 128 is now considered a valid network address number just like 0. This reinforces our earlier comment that an IP address is really meaningless unless you know the subnet mask as well. With a standard subnet, 127 and 128 would signify specific hosts. Here they indicate a broadcast address and our entire second network, respectively.

FIGURE 3.7:

Our network example with a nonstandard subnet mask applied

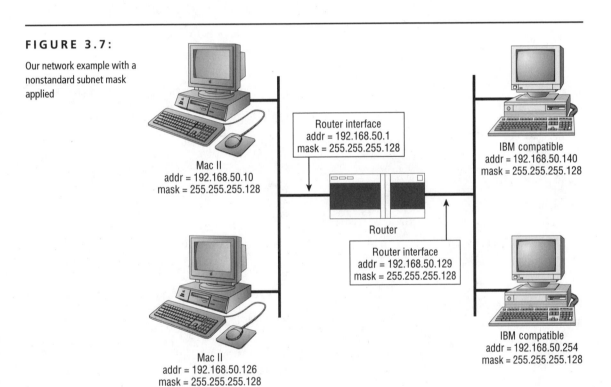

Router interface
addr = 192.168.50.1
mask = 255.255.255.128

Mac II
addr = 192.168.50.10
mask = 255.255.255.128

IBM compatible
addr = 192.168.50.140
mask = 255.255.255.128

Router

Router interface
addr = 192.168.50.129
mask = 255.255.255.128

Mac II
addr = 192.168.50.126
mask = 255.255.255.128

IBM compatible
addr = 192.168.50.254
mask = 255.255.255.128

Table 3.5 depicts some potential nonstandard subnet masks as well as their effect on an IP address range. Masks that create more than four subnets have been abbreviated in the interest of saving space. Only the first three subnets and the last are defined here. Given this information, it should be a simple matter for the reader to calculate the values for the subnets not listed. All address values are for the final byte in an IP address because this is the only value that changes.

TABLE 3.5: Some Potential Nonstandard Subnet Masks

Mask	Number of Subnets	Hosts per Subnet	Available Host Address Ranges	Network Address Value	Broadcast Address Value
255.255.255.0	1	254	1 – 254	0	255
255.255.255.128	2	126	1 – 126	0	127
			129 – 254	128	255
255.255.255.192	4	62	1 – 62	0	63
			65 – 126	64	127
			129 – 190	128	191
			193 – 254	192	255
255.255.255.224	8	30	1 – 30	0	31
			33 – 62	32	63
			65 – 94	64	95
			225 –254	224	255
255.255.255.240	16	14	1 – 14	0	15
			17 – 30	16	31
			33 – 46	32	47
			241 – 254	240	255
255.255.255.248	32	6	1 – 6	0	7
			9 – 14	8	15
			17 – 22	16	23
			249 – 254	248	255
255.255.255.252	64	2	1 – 2	0	3
			5 – 6	4	7
			9 – 10	8	11
			253 – 254	252	255
255.255.255.254	128	0	0	0	0

Our first table entry is our standard class C subnet mask. This creates only one logical subnet. Our final nonstandard mask, 255.255.255.254, creates 128 subnets, but none are able to support any hosts. This means our largest *useful* subnet mask is 255.255.255.252. Because only two hosts are supported, this mask is typically used on WAN links where the only devices that are on the segment are the routers at both ends of the link.

It is also possible to mix and match different subnet masks within the same IP address range. For example, let's say that we have a single subnet with approximately 100 hosts and four other subnets with 20 hosts on each. This gives a total of five subnets to address. Our closest match in the above table is 255.255.255.224, which will yield eight subnets. The problem is that this mask is only capable of supporting 30 hosts per subnet.

The answer is to use a 255.255.255.128 subnet for half our address range, and 255.255.255.224 for the other half. This will allow us to break up our range into a total of five subnets. The mask of 255.255.255.128 could be used to reserve the first half of our available host addresses for the 100 host segment. The remaining half of our address range could be broken up using a mask of 255.255.255.224 to create four additional segments supporting 30 hosts each.

Table 3.6 shows how the address range would be broken down using these masks. Let's assume that the class C address we are subnetting is 192.168.200.0.

TABLE 3.6: Address Range Breakdown

Mask	Network Address	First Host Address	Last Host Address	Broadcast Address
255.255.255.128	192.168.200.0	192.168.200.1	192.168.200.126	192.168.200.127
255.255.255.224	192.168.200.128	192.168.200.129	192.168.200.158	192.168.200.159
255.255.255.224	192.168.200.160	192.168.200.161	192.168.200.190	192.168.200.191
255.255.255.224	192.168.200.192	192.168.200.193	192.168.200.222	192.168.200.223
255.255.255.224	192.168.200.224	192.168.200.225	192.168.200.254	192.168.200.255

Figure 3.8 shows this address scheme applied to a network. By mixing our subnet masks we can achieve the most efficient use of a single address range.

FIGURE 3.8:

A mixture of subnet masks used to support multiple subnets with a varying number of hosts

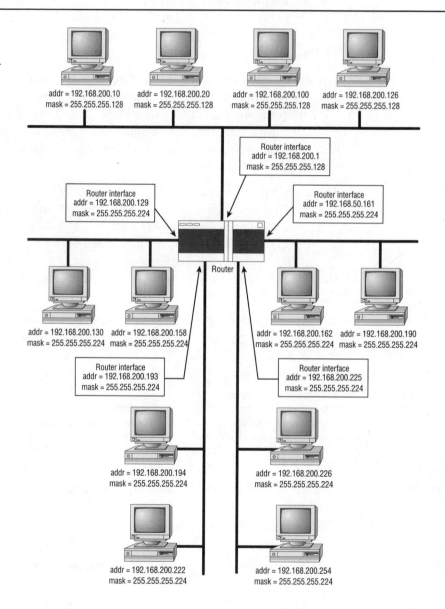

Lost Address Space

As Table 3.5 shows, each time we further subnet our address the number of hosts we can support decreases. For example, while a class C subnet will support 254 hosts, a nonstandard subnet mask of 255.255.255.248 will only support 192 (32 subnets of 6 hosts each). This is because each time we further divide our address, we lose two potential host numbers—one to identify the network address and one to identify the broadcast address.

Also, the Request for Comments documents (RFCs) that define how the IP protocol will operate require that the first and last subnet created by a nonstandard subnet mask be ignored. Therefore, while a mask of 255.255.255.248 will create 32 subnets, only 30 of them are really legal. This drops the number of supported hosts to 180 (30 legal subnets with 6 hosts each).

With this in mind, our network in Figure 3.7 would actually be considered illegal. In order to bring it into full compliance we would need to use a mask of 255.255.255.192, which will create four subnets. This will allow us to ignore the first and last subnets while still having two subnets available for our network. Our revised network appears in Figure 3.9.

> **NOTE**
>
> Figure 3.8 would be considered illegal as well because we are using the entire address range—we do not have the luxury of ignoring the first and last subnet.

In an age where IP addresses are at a premium, many have questioned the practice of ignoring the first and last subnet range created by a nonstandard mask. Problems appeared when nonstandard subnetting first began to be used. Many network devices would assume that a last byte value of 0 or 255 would apply to all local hosts. This would occur in part because the subnet mask was not being referenced properly. In fact, some vendors would specifically configure their IP stack to reject outer range values. NetWare 3.1x is a good example.

Today, these limitations are rarely experienced. Most (if not all) modern network operating systems will accept and communicate within these outer address ranges. While doing so means that your network does not fully meet RFC specifications, it does have the benefit of providing additional address space.

FIGURE 3.9:

Because of the requirement that the first and last subnet range created by a nonstandard subnet mask must be ignored, we must further divide our network address.

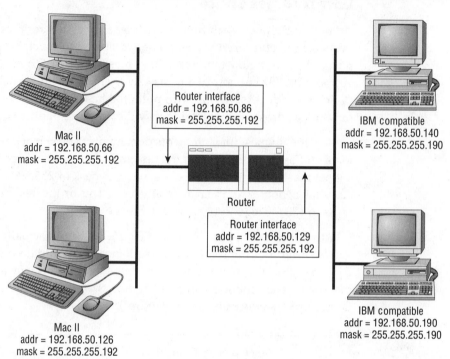

Mac II
addr = 192.168.50.66
mask = 255.255.255.192

Router interface
addr = 192.168.50.86
mask = 255.255.255.192

IBM compatible
addr = 192.168.50.140
mask = 255.255.255.190

Router

Router interface
addr = 192.168.50.129
mask = 255.255.255.192

Mac II
addr = 192.168.50.126
mask = 255.255.255.192

IBM compatible
addr = 192.168.50.190
mask = 255.255.255.190

Address Discovery

IP uses the *Address Resolution Protocol* (*ARP*) when it needs to deliver data. All local delivery is performed using the destination system's media access control (MAC) number. ARP is used by a transmitting system to map the destination system's IP address to its MAC address.

For example, let's say you are using your favorite Web browser, and enter the URL:

```
http://www.sun.com
```

Your system will first use *Domain Name Service* (*DNS*) (see the description of DNS later in this section) to map the host www.sun.com to an IP address. Your system would then compare this IP address to its own to see if the system is located on the same subnet or not. At this point, one of two things will happen:

- If the system is local, your computer will ARP (send an Address Resolution Protocol packet) for the destination system's MAC address.

- If the system is on another subnet, your computer will ARP for the MAC address of the local router.

ARP is simply a local broadcast frame that says, "If you are using this IP address, please reply." The frame contains the IP address for which it needs to find a MAC address. The Ethernet portion of the frame header will contain your system's MAC address in the source field and a broadcast address of FFFFFFFFFFFF in the destination field.

When the system using the IP address replies, saying "I'm here," the frame it sends you will contain the system's MAC address in the Ethernet source field. Now your system can associate the IP address with a MAC address and perform a local delivery. Your system will also cache this information in its *ARP table*. This way if you need to send this system more information, it already knows the local address.

ARP can also be used to avoid IP address conflicts. Most modern network operating systems now use ARP during startup to ensure that there are no address conflicts with other systems. Before assuming it can use a specific IP address, the machine will ARP for the address on the local subnet. If it does not receive a reply, it assumes the address is free to use. If it does receive a reply, it will display an error message and disable IP networking. This process helps to ensure that no two machines try to share the same IP address.

Routing with IP

IP supports both static and dynamic routing between subnets. These may be used exclusively or in combination on any given network. When dynamic routing is used, both distance-vector and link-state options are available. We covered the differences between these routing methods in Chapter 2. Let's now look at how each method is implemented when communicating with IP.

Static Routing

In *static routing*, the path from one subnet to another is programmed into a networking device. This is done by defining the router that a data stream must pass through when traveling to a remote subnet. The entry may be manually entered by an administrator or the device may be configured to reset the static path during startup. With the exception of NetWare, this is normally performed with the `route` command. While the `route` command varies slightly from platform to platform, the common syntax is as follows:

```
route switch subnet mask subnet-mask router
```

Valid switches are `add`, `delete`, `change`, and `print`. Here is an example:

```
route add 10.3.3.0 mask 255.255.255.0 10.2.50.5
```

The above command line would add an entry to a system's routing table that states, "When communicating with any system on the subnet 10.3.3.0, forward all packets through the router located at 10.2.50.5." The command assumes that the router located at 10.2.50.5 is on the local subnet and will know how to reach the network 10.3.3.0. While the `mask` switch is optional, the `route` command will assign a subnet mask based on the class of the IP subnet address. In the above example, `route` would have assigned a class A mask of 255.0.0.0 (because 10.3.3.0 falls between 1.0.0.0 and 126.0.0.0), which would be incorrect. Figure 3.10 shows the above example applied to a workstation. In the figure, our first entry is a default route, any subnet that does not have a route entry will be reached through the router at this address. The entry we added appears four lines down. The "interface" column lists the IP address that the workstation is using.

TIP

If you are adding a route to Windows NT, make sure you use the -p switch so the route entry will be "permanent." This automatically adds the route back in when the system is rebooted.

FIGURE 3.10:

Static routes used to define connectivity between different subnets

When route is used with the delete switch, an existing entry may be removed from the local routing table. The following would delete the routing entry created with the above add command:

```
route delete 10.3.3.0 mask 255.255.255.0 10.2.50.5
```

The switch change is used to modify the routing table entry so that a different router is used. For example:

```
route change 10.3.3.0 mask 255.255.255.0 10.2.50.10
```

would change the border router used when communicating with a system on the subnet 10.3.3.0 from 10.2.50.5 to 10.2.50.10.

Finally, the print switch displays all matching router entries. For example:

```
route print 10.3.3.0
```

will produce a list of routers used when communicating with that subnet. Given our above example, the only entry would be 10.2.50.5.

The route command also allows for the definition of a *default route*. A default route tells a system to forward all traffic bound for any remote subnet to a specific router. Depending on the operating system, the command would appear similar to one of the following:

```
route add 0.0.0.0 10.2.50.1
route add default 10.2.50.1
```

NOTE   The route command, like other IP tools, is platform-specific. It is not considered to be an IP protocol command per se. There is nothing in the IP protocol suite that defines the route command, only a definition of how static routing should be implemented. The developers of the NOS can choose whether to implement the command or give it another name.

Note that NetWare does not use the route command, but instead uses additional switches with the bind command, to provide the same functionality. Another example of routing configuration is Microsoft's tracert command; it provides the same functionality as Unix's traceroute command, but the name was shortened to meet DOS's *eight.three* file-naming convention.

Usually, however, the command names for IP tools used on Unix are adopted on other NOSes to maintain consistency. For example, the command `ping` was first used on Unix. A command with the same name has been developed for nearly every platform that supports IP, most of which provide nearly the same functionality.

Static routing is the most common configuration used for workstation configurations. It frees up the local system from having to maintain dynamic tables and relies on the network routers to keep track of the best routes. Static routing generates the least amount of traffic as it does not require that routing updates be propagated throughout the network. It also requires the greatest amount of administration, because each system must be configured manually with its own routing table.

Static routing is supported by all network operating systems that support IP.

Dynamic Routing

Dynamic routing allows a network to *learn* which subnets are available and how to reach them. This is particularly useful when more than one path is available between subnets. The ability of a network to deal with routing changes is highly dependent on the routing protocol in use.

Routing Information Protocol (RIP)   RIP was first developed in 1980 by Xerox for use with their Xerox Network System (XNS) protocol. It saw its first use with IP in 1982 when it was adapted and shipped with BSD Unix. After 1982, different Unix vendors began shipping slightly different versions of RIP which caused incompatibility problems. This was all tied together in 1988 with the release of RFC 1058, which defined a common structure for RIP. While RIP is the oldest IP routing protocol, it is still widely used today.

RIP is a distance-vector protocol, which gives it a slow convergence time and makes it prone to routing errors. It can route information for no more than 16 hops and bases its routing decisions strictly on hop count. It cannot intelligently load-balance traffic by using such variables as link speed and traffic load.

RIP is also one of the easiest routing protocols to use and configure. Simply enable RIP and the protocol will propagate route information through the use of

RIP broadcasts. While it is a somewhat noisy protocol, sending routing updates every 60 seconds, this amount of traffic is usually negligible on a small network.

RIP is best suited for small networks (10–15 subnets or less) or in networking environments where redundant routes are not used. In larger environments RIP can cause broadcast storms as each router attempts to propagate its table information throughout the network. When redundant routes are available, RIP cannot make use of the multiple paths for load balancing. Secondary routes are only used when the primary route fails. In each of these situations it is better to use one of the link state protocols described below.

RIP is supported by all flavors of Unix and NetWare 3.1x and 4.x. Windows NT has added support for RIP as of version 4.0.

Exterior Gateway Protocol (EGP)   EGP is another distance-vector protocol that was developed in the mid-1980s as the Internet began to grow beyond the bounds of what could be easily supported by RIP. EGP introduced the concept of *autonomous systems* (*AS*) as a way to reduce the amount of routing information propagated between networks.

NOTE

> An AS is a collection of subnets which are all administrated by the same group or organization. Typically this would be an entire domain but can be divided even further for larger networks. By "domains" we are referring to the domain names issued by the InterNIC, not to Microsoft NT domains.

EGP reduces the amount of information propagated by advertising *reachability* information only. Instead of advertising hop information, an EGP router will simply list all the networks it is responsible for within its autonomous system. In Figure 3.11 we see three AS groups connected by a backbone. Each EGP router transmits reachability information only along the backbone. This tells the other EGP routers, "If you need to send information to one of these subnets, forward the frame to me and I'll take care of delivery." This reduces the amount of information that must be propagated along the backbone. Because a single router is responsible for delivery to any given subnet, hop counts do not need to be calculated during a failure. Either the subnet is reachable or it is not. This limitation on the information being sent helps to eliminate convergence problems along the backbone.

FIGURE 3.11:

EGP used to propagate information between autonomous systems

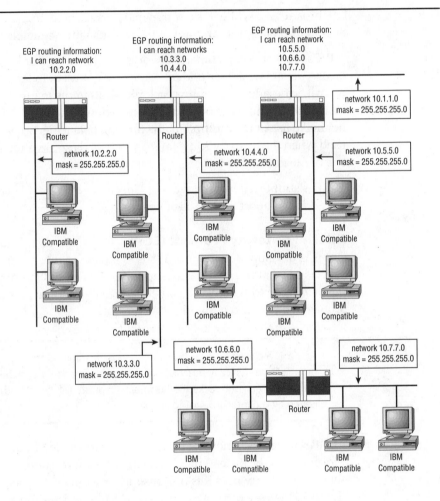

Inside each AS, another routing protocol such as RIP can be used to ensure delivery and provide secondary routing paths as required. EGP simply eliminates the need to send this RIP information along the backbone.

The biggest drawback of EGP is that it relies on a hierarchical design with all traffic passing through a single point. Not only does this create a single point of failure, it also eliminates the ability to perform load balancing through alternate links. EGP routers also need to be configured to reflect which subnets they are responsible for.

NOTE   While EGP was extremely useful in its prime, the explosive growth of the Internet has caused it to become a bit dated. Use of EGP has been on the decline now that more advanced link-state protocols are available.

EGP is typically supported only by hardware routing devices. Because EGP is an external routing protocol, most vendors have not seen a need to include it with their network operating systems.

Open Shortest Path First (OSPF)   OSPF was the first protocol to integrate both internal and external autonomous system updates into a single IP routing protocol. Like EGP, it can be configured to exchange only reachability information along a network backbone. Unlike EGP, however, it can also be configured to provide full routing table information within each autonomous system. This eliminates the need to run two separate routing protocols, one for inside the AS and one for outside.

OSPF also brings authentication to the table, requiring routers to supply a password in order to participate in routing updates. This helps to ensure that a rogue system cannot propagate information that can either corrupt the current routing table or breach network security.

As a link-state protocol, OSPF makes internal AS routing decisions based upon such measurements as link speed and traffic load. It is not limited to using only hop count information when selecting the best route. Its ability to support load balancing as well as a hierarchical network structure has lead to OSPF's wide acceptance.

OSPF is supported by NetWare 4.1 and many flavors of Unix. Windows NT has not yet added support for OSPF or any other link-state routing protocol.

Border Gateway Protocol (BGP)   BGP is designed to be used both inside and between autonomous systems. The brainchild of Cisco Systems, BGP is the routing protocol that glues most of the Internet's backbone together. BGP comes in two flavors, Internal Border Gateway Protocol (IBGP) and External Border Gateway Protocol (EBGP). IBGP is used when two routers that are part of the same autonomous system need to exchange information. EBGP is used between routers of different autonomous systems.

On a BGP network, each autonomous system is assigned a unique group number. Each router must be configured with a table defining its neighbors' IP addresses and autonomous system group numbers. A router will assume that any neighbor that has the same group number is part of the same autonomous system and thus responsible for the same group of subnets. This allows for the use of multiple paths and provides a greater degree of flexibility over EGP or OSPF in backbone areas. Neighboring routers communicate using unicast TCP connections instead of simply broadcasting table information.

As a link-state protocol, BGP can leverage these multiple paths by providing load balancing based on link speed, Internetwork delay, and available bandwidth. This allows for the most efficient use of network resources when multiple paths are available along a backbone connection.

No network operating systems currently support BGP. Like EGP, it has been implemented on hardware routing devices only.

Transport Layer Services

IP's Transport layer services were described in great detail in Chapter 2, so we will add only a simple review here.

Transmission Control Protocol (TCP)

TCP is IP's connection-oriented transport protocol. It is used when an application wants the Transport layer to ensure that all packets have been received by the destination system correctly. In a TCP transmission, the receiving system is required to acknowledge every packet it receives.

User Datagram Protocol (UDP)

UDP is IP's connectionless transport protocol. UDP is used when an application is capable of ensuring that all packets have been received by the destination system. If a packet is missed, it is the application, not UDP, that is responsible for first detecting that a packet was missed and then retransmitting the data. Thanks to its reduced overhead, UDP has the potential to transmit more information with fewer packets than TCP.

IP Application Services

There are many application services designed to use IP as a transport. Some were created to aid the end user in transferring information, while others support the functionality of IP itself. Some of the most common services are outlined below. Where applicable, you'll see the transport used for data delivery and the well-known port number assigned to the service.

Boot Protocol (bootp) and
Dynamic Host Configuration Protocol (DHCP)

There are three methods of assigning IP addresses to host systems:

> **Manual**　Manually configure an IP host to use a specific address
>
> **Automatic**　Have a server automatically assign a specific address to a host during startup
>
> **Dynamic**　Have a server dynamically assign free addresses from a pool to hosts during startup

The manual method is the most time-consuming, but is also the most fault-tolerant. It requires that each IP host be configured with all the information the system requires to communicate using IP. Manual is the most appropriate method to use for systems that need to maintain the same IP address or systems that need to be accessible even when the IP address server may be down. Web servers, mail servers, and any other servers providing IP services are usually manually configured for IP communications.

Bootp supports automatic address assignment. A table is maintained on the bootp server, listing each host's MAC number. Each entry also contains the IP address to be used by the system. When the bootp server receives a request for an IP address, it looks in its table for the sending system's MAC number. It then returns the appropriate IP address for that system. While this makes management a little simpler because all administration can be performed from a central system, the process is still time consuming because each MAC address must be recorded. It also does nothing to free up IP address space that may not be in use.

DHCP supports both automatic and dynamic IP address assignments. When addresses are dynamically assigned, IP addresses are issued by the server to host systems from a pool of available numbers. The benefit of a dynamic assignment over an automatic is that only the hosts that require an IP address have one assigned. Once complete, the IP addresses can be returned to the pool to be issued to another host. The amount of time a host retains a specific IP address is referred to as the *lease period*. A short lease period ensures that only systems that require an IP address have one assigned. When IP is only occasionally used, a small pool of addresses can be used to support a large number of hosts.

The other benefit of DHCP is that the server can send more than just address information. The remote host can also be configured with its host name, default router, domain name, local DNS server, etc. This allows an administrator to remotely configure IP services on a large number of hosts with a minimum of work. A single DHCP server is capable of servicing multiple subnets.

The only drawbacks with DHCP are increased broadcast traffic (clients send an all-networks broadcast when they need an address) and address space instability if the DHCP server is shut down. On many systems the tables that track address assignments are saved in memory only. When the network goes down, this table is lost. When the network is restarted, it's possible that an IP address already leased to one host (workstation) prior to the shutdown may be assigned to another host. If this occurs, you may need to renew the lease on all hosts or wait until the lease time expires.

NOTE   Both bootp and DHCP use UDP as their communication transport. Clients transmit address requests from a source port of 68 to a destination port of 67.

Domain Name Service (DNS)

DNS is responsible for mapping host names to IP addresses and vice versa. It is the service that allows you to connect to Novell's Web server by entering www.novell.com instead of having to remember the system's IP address. All IP routing is done with addresses, not names. While IP systems do not use names when transferring information, names are easier for people to remember. It is for this reason that DNS was developed to make reaching remote systems easier. It allows a person to enter an easy-to-remember name while allowing the computer to translate this into the address information it needs to route the requested data.

DNS follows a hierarchical, distributed structure. No single DNS server is responsible for keeping track of every host name on the Internet. Each system is responsible for only a portion of the framework.

Figure 3.12 is an example of how DNS is structured. Visually it resembles a number of trees strapped to a pole and hanging upside down. (The *pole* is not meant to represent the backbone of the Internet, it simply indicates that there is DNS connectivity between the different domains.) The systems located just below the pole are referred to as the *root name servers*. Each root name server is responsible for one or more top-level domains. The top-level domains are the .com, .edu, .org, .mil, or .gov found at the end of a domain name. Every domain that ends in .com is said to be part of the same top-level domain.

FIGURE 3.12:

A visual representation of the hierarchical structure of DNS

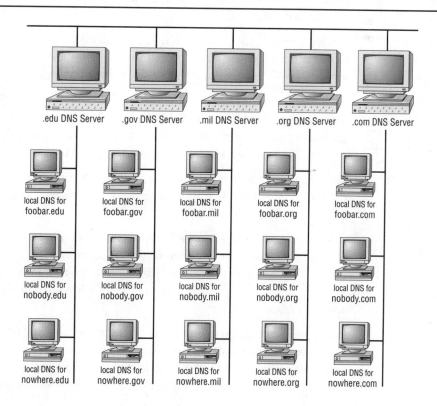

The root name servers are responsible for keeping track of the DNS servers for each subdomain within a top-level domain. They do not know about individual systems within each subdomain, only the DNS servers that are responsible for them.

Each subdomain DNS server is responsible for tracking the IP addresses for all the hosts within its domain.

Let's walk through an example to see how it works. Let's assume you're part of the foobar.com domain. Let's also assume that you are running a Web browser and have entered the following URL:

```
http://www.sun.com
```

Your system will first check its DNS cache (if it has one) to see if it knows the IP address for www.sun.com. If it does not, it forms a DNS query (a DNS query is simply a request for IP information) and asks one of the DNS servers within the foobar.com domain for the address. Let's assume the system it queries is ns.foobar.com.

If ns.foobar.com does not have this information cached, it also forms a DNS query and forwards the request to the root name server responsible for the top-level domain .com, because this is where the Sun domain is located.

The root name server will consult its tables and form a reply similar to the following: "I do not know the IP address for www.sun.com. I do, however, know that ns.sun.com is responsible for all the hosts within the sun.com domain. Its IP address is 10.5.5.1. Please forward your query to that system."

ns.foobar.com now knows that if it needs to find a system with the sun.com domain, it needs to ask ns.sun.com. It caches this information and forwards the request to ns.sun.com.

ns.sun.com will then in turn consult its tables and look up the IP address for www.sun.com. It would then forward this information to ns.foobar.com. ns.foobar.com will then cache this information and forward the answer to your system. Your system would now use this IP address information to reach the remote Web server.

If it appears that there is a whole lot of querying going on, then you have a good understanding of the process. The additional traffic is highly preferable, however, to the amount of overhead that would be required to allow a single system to maintain the DNS information for every system on the Internet.

As you may have noticed, DNS makes effective use of caching information during queries. This helps to reduce traffic when looking up popular sites. For example, if someone else within foobar.com now attempts to reach www.sun.com, the IP address for this system has been cached by ns.foobar.com. It is now able to answer this query directly.

The amount of time that ns.foobar.com remembers this information is determined by the time to live (TTL) set for this address. The TTL is set by the administrator responsible for managing the remote name server (in this case ns.sun.com). If www.sun.com is a stable system, this value may be set at a high value such as 30 days. If it is expected that the IP address for www.sun.com is likely to change frequently, the TTL may be set to a lower value such as a few hours.

A further example will illustrate why this is important. Let's say the mail relay for foobar.com is run from the system mail.foobar.com. Let's also assume that a high TTL value of 30 days has been set in order to reduce the number of DNS queries entering the network from the Internet. Now let's also assume that our network has changed ISPs and we have been assigned a new set of IP numbers to use when communicating with the Internet.

The network is readdressed, and the changeover takes place. Immediately, users begin to receive phone calls from people saying that mail sent to their address is being returned with a delivery failure notice. The failure is intermittent—some mail gets through while other messages fail.

What went wrong? Since the TTL value has been set for 30 days, remote DNS servers will remember the old IP address until the TTL expires. If someone sent mail to the foobar.com domain the day before the changeover, it may be 30 days before their DNS server creates another query and realizes that the IP address has changed! Unfortunately the domains most likely to be affected by this change are the ones you exchange mail with the most. There are two ways to resolve this failure:

1. Ignore it and hide under your desk. Once the TTL expires, mail delivery will return to normal.

2. Contact the DNS administrator for each domain you exchange mail with and ask them to reset their DNS cache. This will force the remote system to again look up the address the next time a mail message must be sent. This option is not only embarrassing but may be impossible when dealing with large domains such as AOL or CompuServe.

Avoiding this type of failure takes some fundamental planning. Simply turn down the TTL value to an extremely short period of time (like one hour) at least 30 days prior to the changeover. This forces remote systems to cache the information for only a brief amount of time. Once the changeover is complete, the TTL can be adjusted back up to 30 days to help reduce traffic. 30 days is a good TTL value for systems that are not expected to change their host name or address.

NOTE   DNS uses TCP and UDP transports when communicating. Both use a destination port of 53.

File Transfer Protocol (FTP)

FTP is used to transfer file information from one system to another. FTP uses TCP as its transport and utilizes ports 20 and 21 for communication. Port 21 is used to transfer session information (user name, password, commands), while port 20 is referred to as the *data port* and is used to transfer the actual file.

Figure 3.13 shows an FTP command session between two systems (Loki is connecting to Thor). At the beginning of the session, notice the three-packet TCP exchange, which was described in Chapter 2. All communications are using port 21, which is simply referred to as the FTP port. Port 1038 is the random upper port used by Loki when receiving replies. This connection was initiated by Loki at port 1038 to Thor at port 21.

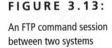

FIGURE 3.13:

An FTP command session between two systems

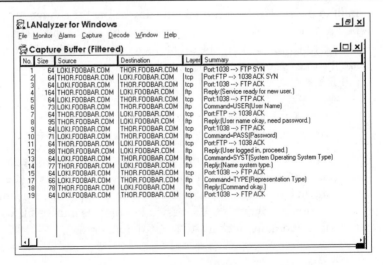

Figure 3.14 shows Loki initiating a file transfer from Thor. Lines 7, 8, and 9 show the TCP three-packet handshake we discussed in Chapter 2. Lines 10 through 24 show the actual data transfer.

FIGURE 3.14:

An FTP data session

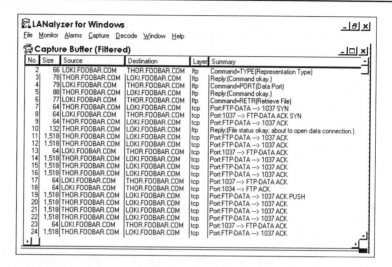

This is where things get a bit weird. Loki and Thor still have an active session on ports 1038 and 21 as indicated in Figure 3.13. Figure 3.14 shows a second, separate session running parallel to the one shown in Figure 3.13. This second session is initiated in order to transfer the actual file or data.

There is also something else a bit odd about this connection. Look closely at line 7. Thor is actually initiating the TCP three-packet handshake in order to transfer the file information, not Loki. This means that in order to support FTP sessions to the Internet, we must allow connections to be established from the Internet to our internal network on port 20.

This type of configuration can be a problem when firewalls or packet filters are used. The two systems must be able to initiate a communication session using both ports in order to transfer data. Also, it needs to be possible for the second session to be established from the Internet to our internal network. Proxy firewalls are usually configured with a specific application just for dealing with FTP's special requirements.

There is a second type of FTP transfer, known as *Passive FTP* (*PASV FTP*). Passive FTP is identical to standard FTP in that it sends commands over port 21. The difference lies in how the data session is initiated. This is the mode supported by most Web browsers.

Prior to transferring data, a client can request PASV mode transmission. If the FTP server acknowledges this request, the client is allowed to initiate the TCP three-packet handshake, instead of the server. The client still uses an upper port number (like 1037) and the server still uses port 20; the only difference is that the client is initiating the session.

This fixes one problem but causes another. Since the client initiates the session, we can now close inbound access from port 20. This lets us tighten up our inbound security policy a bit. Note that to initiate this passive session, however, the client uses a random upper port number. This mean that the port the client will use to transfer data can and will change from session to session. Therefore, in order to support PASV FTP, we must allow outbound sessions to be established *on all ports above 1023*. Not a very good security stance if you want to control outbound Internet access (such as a policy stating that Internet Quake games are not allowed).

As if all of the above was not enough to deal with, administrators can run into another problem with FTP when they use a firewall or NAT device. The problem revolves around the fact that FTP uses two separate sessions.

While we are transferring a large file over the Internet (let's say the latest 40MB patch file from Microsoft), our control session to port 21 stays quiet. This session is not required to transmit any information during a file transfer until the transfer is complete. Once it is complete, the systems acknowledge over the control session that the file was in fact received in its entirety.

If it has taken a long time to transfer the file (say, over an hour), the firewall or NAT device may assume that the control session is no longer valid. Since it has seen no data pass between the two systems for a long period of time, it assumes that the connection is gone and purges the session entry from its tables. This is a bad thing as once the file transfer is complete, the systems have no means to handshake to insure that the file was received. The typical symptom of this is that the client transferring or receiving the file hangs at 99% complete.

Luckily, most vendors make this setting adjustable. If you are experiencing the symptoms just described, check your firewall or NAT device to see if it has a "TCP time-out" setting. If so, simply increase the listed value.

NOTE   FTP uses the TCP transport for all communications. Commands are sent over port 21 while data uses port 20.

Gopher

Gopher is a powerful, yet simple, file-retrieval tool. Its functionality lies somewhere between FTP and a Web browser. It has a very simple menu interface that can be used to browse directories and retrieve files.

Like Web servers, Gopher servers can be linked together. This allows a user to search for file information across multiple systems transparently. Like a Web browser, a Gopher client can distinguish between different file types and respond appropriately. For example, if the file being retrieved is text, the Gopher client will display it on the screen. If it is a binary file, it will transfer it to the local system in a similar fashion to FTP.

Gopher does not support the more advanced features of HTTP such as displaying graphics or playing sounds or video. It is for this reason that Gopher clients are now quite rarely used. When the typical user accesses Gopher services, it is through a Web browser interface when file searching capability is required.

NOTE   Gopher uses TCP as a transport for all communications. Gopher requests are sent to a destination port of 70.

Hypertext Transfer Protocol (HTTP)

HTTP is used in communications between Web browsers and Web servers. It differs from most services in that it does not create and maintain a single session while a user is retrieving information from a server. Every request for information, whether it is text, graphics, or sound, creates a separate session which is terminated once that request is completed. A Web page with lots of graphics needs to have multiple simultaneous connections created in order to be loaded onto a browser.

Since version 1.0, HTTP has included Multimedia Internet Mail Extensions (MIME) to support the negotiation of data types. This has helped HTTP to become a true cross-platform service, as it allows the Web browser to tell the server which file formats it can support. It also allows the server to alert the Web browser about the type of data it is about to receive. This allows the browser to select the correct platform-specific viewing or playing software for the data it is about to receive.

NOTE   HTTP uses the TCP transport and a destination port of 80.

Internet Message Access Protocol, Version 4 (IMAP4)

IMAP is designed to be the next evolutionary step from the post office protocol (see below for a description of POP). While it has the same features as POP, it includes many more that allow it to scale more easily in a workgroup environment.

As in POP3, users have the option to either leave their messages up on the server and view them remotely (referred to as "online mail") or download the messages to the local system and read them offline (referred to as "offline mail"). IMAP, however, supports a third connection mode, referred to as "disconnected."

In online mode, all messages are stored on the IMAP server. While it can be time-consuming to start up a POP mail client in online mode if many messages are involved, IMAP avoids this problem through the use of *flags*.

When connecting to a POP server, a POP client will simply authenticate and begin to download messages. All messages on the server are considered to be new and unread. This means that the user's entire inbox must be transferred before messages can be viewed or read. When an IMAP client connects to a IMAP server, however, it authenticates and checks the flag status on existing messages. Flagging allows a message to be marked as "seen," "deleted," or "answered." This means that an IMAP client can be configured to collect only messages that have not been seen and avoid the transfer of the entire mailbox.

In offline mode, connection time can be reduced through the use of "previewing." Previewing allows the user to scan the header information of all new messages without actually transferring them to their local system. This way, if the user is looking to remotely retrieve only a specific message, they can choose which messages to receive and which messages to leave on the server as unread. It also allows the user to delete messages based upon the header information or file size without having to transfer them to the local system first. This can be a real time-saver if you usually retrieve your mail remotely and receive a lot of unsolicited advertisements.

IMAP includes a third connection mode, not supported by POP, referred to as *disconnected*. (Someone *certainly* had a twisted sense of humor when they called it that—you can just see the poor technical writers and support people pulling their hair out over this one. "I disconnected my computer just like the instructions said, so how come I can't see my mail?") When a remote IMAP client is operating in disconnected mode, it retrieves only a copy of all new messages. The originals are left up on the IMAP server. The next time the client connects to the system the server is synchronized with any changes made to the cached information. This mode has a few major benefits:

- Connection time is minimized, reducing network traffic or dial-in time.

- Messages are centrally located so they can be backed up easily.

- Because all messages are server-based, mail can be retrieved from multiple clients and/or multiple computers.

The last benefit is extremely useful in an environment where people do not always work from the same computer. For example, an engineer who works from home a few days a week can easily keep his or her mail synchronized between home and work computers. When working in offline mode as most POP clients do, mail retrieved by the engineer's work system would not be viewable on their home system. An IMAP client does not have this limitation.

Another improvement over POP is that IMAP supports the writing of messages up to the server. This allows a user to have server-based folders instead of just local ones. These folders can be synchronized in disconnect mode as well.

Group folders are also supported. This allows mail users to have *bulletin board* areas where messages can be posted and viewed by multiple people. This functionality is similar to the News service under NNTP (see the "Network News Transfer Protocol" section later in this chapter for a description of NNTP and News). Group folders provide an excellent means of sharing information. For example, the human resources department could set up a group folder for corporate policy information. This would reduce the need to create printed manuals.

TIP   If you are using IMAP or if your current e-mail system supports group folders, create one entitled `computer support` or something similar. In it you can post messages providing support for some of your most common support calls. This can help reduce the number of support calls received and provide the user with written directions about how to work through their problem. You can even add screen captures to make resolving the problem easier.

IMAP has been designed to integrate with the *Application Configuration Access Protocol (ACAP)*. ACAP is an independent service that allows a client to access configuration information and preferences from a central location. Support for ACAP enhances the portability of IMAP even further.

For example, our engineer who works from home a few days a week could also store their personal address book and configuration information up on the server as well. If they are at work and add a new name and e-mail address to their address book, that name would be available when using their home system as well. This would not be true with POP as each client would have a separate address book saved on each local system. Any configuration changes would also take effect on both systems as well.

ACAP also provides mail administrators some control to set up corporate standards for users when accessing mail. For example, the administrator can set up a global address book which would be accessible by everyone.

NOTE   IMAP uses TCP as a transport with a destination port of 143.

Network File System (NFS)

NFS provides access to remote file systems. The user is able to access the remote file system as if the files are located on the local system. NFS provides file access only. This means that other functionality such as processor time or printing must be provided by the local system.

NFS requires configuration changes on both the server and the client. On the server, the file system to be shared must first be "exported." This is done by defining which files are to be made sharable. This can be a single directory or an entire disk. Who has access to this file system must also be defined.

On the client side, the system must be configured to "mount" the remote file system. On a Unix machine this is done by creating an entry in the system's /ETC/FSTAB file, indicating the name of the remote system, the file system to be mounted, and where it should be placed on the local system. In the Unix world this is typically a directory structure located under a directory. In the DOS world, the remote file system may be assigned a unique drive letter. DOS, Windows 3.*x*, Windows 95, and the Mac OS require third-party software in order to use NFS.

While a convenient way to share files, NFS suffers from a number of functional deficiencies. File transfer times are comparatively slow when compared to FTP or when using NetWare's NCP protocol. NFS has no file-locking capability to ensure that more than one user does not attempt to write to a file. As if this was not bad enough, NFS makes no assurances that the information has been received intact. I've seen situations where entire directories have been copied to a remote system using NFS and have become corrupted in transit. Because NFS does not check data integrity, the errors were not found until the files were processed.

NOTE   NFS uses the UDP transport and communicates using port 2049.

Network News Transfer Protocol (NNTP)

NNTP is used in the delivery of *news*. News is very similar in functionality to e-mail except messages are delivered to *newsgroups*, not end users. Each of these newsgroups is a storage area for messages that follow a common thread or subject. Instead of a mail client, a News client is used to read messages that have been posted to different subject areas.

For example, let's say you are having trouble configuring networking on your NetWare server. You could check out the messages that have been posted to `comp.os.netware.connectivity` to see if anyone else has had the same problem and found a way to resolve it. There are literally tens of thousands of newsgroups on a wide range of subjects. The author's personal favorites are:

```
comp.protocols
alt.clueless
alt.barney.dinosaur.die.die.die
```

In order to read News postings, you must have access to a News server. News servers exchange messages by relaying any new messages they receive to other servers. The process is a bit slow as it can take three to five days for a new message to be circulated to every News server.

News is very resource-intensive. It's not uncommon for a News server to receive several gigabits of information per week. The processes required to send, receive, and clean up old messages can eat up a lot of CPU time as well.

News has dwindled in appeal over the last few years due to an activity known as *spamming*. Spamming is the activity of posting unsolicited or off-subject postings. For example, at the time of this writing the connectivity newsgroup mentioned above contains 383 messages. Of these, 11% are advertisements for get-rich-quick schemes, 8% are ads for computer-related hardware or services, 6% are postings describing the sender's opinion on someone or something using many superlatives, and another 23% are NetWare related but have nothing to do with connectivity. This means that slightly more than half the postings are actually on-topic. For some groups the percentages are even worse.

NOTE   NNTP uses TCP as a transport and port 119 for all communications.

NetBIOS over IP

NetBIOS over IP is not a service *per se*, but it does add Session-layer support to enable the encapsulation of NetBIOS or NetBEUI traffic within an IP packet. This is required when using Windows NT or SAMBA, which use NetBIOS for file sharing. If IP is the only protocol bound to an NT server, it is still using NetBIOS for file sharing via encapsulation.

SAMBA is a suite of programs which allow Unix file systems and printers to be accessed as shares from an NT network. In effect, this makes the Unix system appear to be an NT server. Clients can be other Unix systems (running the SAMBA client) or Windows 95 and NT systems. The Windows clients do not require any additional software because they use the same configuration as when they are communicating with an NT server.

The source code for SAMBA is available as freeware on the Internet. Over 15 different flavors of Unix are supported. For further information on configuring and using SAMBA, see Chapter 13, on Unix/Linux.

We will discuss the functionality of NetBIOS and NetBEUI later in this chapter.

NOTE   When NetBIOS is encapsulated within IP, both TCP and UDP are used as a transport. All communications are conducted on ports 137 through 139.

Post Office Protocol (POP)

The *post office protocol* is used when retrieving mail from a Unix shell account. It allows users to read their mail without creating a Telnet connection to the system.

When a Unix user receives an e-mail message, it is typically stored in the /var/spool/mail directory. Normally this message could be retrieved remotely by Telnetting to the system and running the `mail` command. While it's a useful utility, `mail` does not have much of a user interface. To the inexperienced user the commands can appear to be cryptic and hard to remember.

POP allows a user to connect to the system and retrieve their mail using their user name and password. POP does not provide shell access, it simply retrieves any mail messages the user may have pending on the system.

There are a variety of mail clients available that support POP (POP3 being the latest version) so you as administrator are free to choose the e-mail client that works best for your users. Popular POP/POP3 e-mail clients include Pegasus, Eudora, Netscape's browser-integrated e-mail, and Microsoft's Exchange.

When using POP3, users can either leave their messages up on the POP server and view them remotely (*online mail*) or download the messages to the local system and read them offline (*offline mail*). Leaving the messages on the server allows the system administrator to centrally back up everyone's mail when they back up the server. The drawback, however, is that if the user never deletes their messages (I've seen mailboxes with over 12,000 messages), the load time for the client can be excruciatingly long. Because a copy of all messages is left up on the server, they must be downloaded every time the client connects.

The benefit of using the POP client in offline mode is that local folders can be created to organize old messages. Because messages are stored locally, the load time when many messages are involved is relatively short. This can provide a dramatic improvement in speed when the POP server is accessed over a dial-up connection. Note that only local folders can be used. POP3 does not support the use of global or shared folders. The downside to offline mode is that each local system must be backed up to ensure recovery in the event of a drive failure. Most POP clients operate in offline mode.

One of POP3's biggest drawbacks is that it does not support the automatic creation of global address books. Only personal address books can be used. For example, if your organization is using a POP3 mail system, you have no way of automatically viewing the addresses of other users on the system. This leaves you with two options:

- Manually discover the other addresses through some other means and add them to your personal address book.

- Require that the system administrator generate a list of e-mail addresses on the system and e-mail this list to all users. The users can then use the file to update their personal address books.

NOTE   Although they are outside the scope of this book, scripting tools such as ActiveX, VB, and AppleScript, as well as the cross-platform scripting environment Frontier, can be used to automate address book replication and distribute the results to end users rather seamlessly.

Neither one of these options is particularly appealing, so POP is best suited for the home Internet user who does not have a need for sharable address books or folders. For business use, the IMAP4 protocol described above is more appropriate.

NOTE   POP3 does support commands that can provide some IMAP-like features, such as TOP (fetching headers and a user-defined number of body lines) and UIDL (assigning a message a unique ID number for storage and state flagging). The APOP command enhances the authentication process, though it is still not as good as IMAP4. The majority of mail servers support these optional commands, as well as most POP3 clients.

When a message is delivered by a POP3 client, the client either forwards the message back to the POP server or sends it on to a central mail relay. Which is performed depends on how the POP client is configured. In either case the POP client uses Simple Mail Transfer Protocol (SMTP) when delivering new messages or replies. It is this forwarding system, not the POP client, that is ultimately responsible for the delivery of the message.

By using a forwarding mail relay, the POP client can disconnect from the network before the message is delivered to its final destination. While most SMTP messages are delivered very quickly (in less than 1 second), a busy mail system can take 10 minutes or more to accept a message. Using a forwarding system helps to reduce the amount of time a remote POP client is required to remain dialed in.

If the mail relay encounters a problem (such as a typo in the recipient's e-mail address) and the message cannot be delivered, the POP client will receive a delivery failure notice the next time it connects to the POP server.

NOTE   POP uses TCP as a transport and communicates using a destination port of 110.

Simple Mail Transfer Protocol (SMTP)

SMTP is used to transfer mail messages between systems. SMTP uses a message-switched type of connection, as each mail message is processed in its entirety before the session between two systems is terminated. If more than one message must be transferred, a separate session must be established for each mail message.

SMTP is capable of transferring ASCII text only. It does not have the ability to support rich text or transfer binary files and attachments. When these types of transfers are required, an external program is needed to first translate the attachment into an ASCII format.

The original programs used to provide this functionality were uuencode and uudecode. A binary file would first be processed by uuencode to translate it into an ASCII format. The file could then be attached to a mail message and sent to its intended recipient. Once received, the file would be processed through uudecode to return it to its original binary format.

Uuencode/uudecode has been replaced by the use of MIME. While MIME performs the same translational duties, it also compresses the resulting ASCII information. The result is smaller attachments which produce faster message transfers with reduced overhead. Apple computers use an application called Binhex which has the same functionality as MIME. MIME is now supported by most Unix and PC mail systems.

Uuencode/uudecode, Binhex, and MIME are not compatible. If you can exchange text messages with a remote mail system, but attachments end up unusable, then you are probably using different translation formats. Many modern mail gateways provide support for both uuencode/uudecode and MIME to eliminate these types of communication problems. Some even include support for Binhex.

NOTE   SMTP uses the TCP transport and destination port 25 when creating a communication session.

Simple Network Management Protocol (SNMP)

SNMP is used both to monitor and control network devices. The monitoring or controlling station is referred to as the *SNMP management station*. The network devices to be controlled are required to run *SNMP agents*. The agents and the management station work together to give the network administrator a central point of control over the network.

The SNMP agent provides the link into the networking device. The device can be a manageable hub, a router, or even a server. The agent uses both static and dynamic information when reporting to the management station.

The static information is data stored within the device in order to identify it uniquely. For example, the administrator may choose to store the device's physical location and serial number as part of the SNMP static information. This makes it easier to identify which device you're working with from the SNMP management station.

The dynamic information is data that pertains to the current state of the device. For example, port status on a hub would be considered dynamic information as the port may be enabled or disabled, depending on whether it is functioning properly.

The SNMP management station is the central console used to control all network devices that have SNMP agents. The management station first learns about a network device through the use of a Management Information Base (MIB). The MIB is a piece of software supplied by the network device vendor, usually on floppy disk. When the MIB is added to the management station, the MIB teaches it about the network device. This helps to ensure that SNMP management stations created by one vendor will operate properly with network devices produced by another.

Information is usually collected by the SNMP management station through polling. The SNMP management station will issue queries at predetermined intervals in order to check the status of each network device. SNMP only supports two commands for collecting information, `get` and `getnext`. The `get` command allows the management station to retrieve information on a specific operating parameter. For example, it may query a router to report on the current status of one of its ports. The `getnext` command is used when a complete status will be collected from a device. Instead of forcing the SNMP management station to issue a series of specific `get` commands, `getnext` can be used to sequentially retrieve each piece of information a device is capable of reporting on.

SNMP also allows for the controlling of network devices through the `set` command. This command can be used to alter some of the operational parameters on a network device. For example, if our above `get` command reported that port 2 on the router was disabled, we could issue a `set` command to the router to enable the port.

SNMP typically does not offer the same range of control as a network device's management utility. For example, while we may be able to turn ports on and off on our router, we would probably be unable to initialize IP networking and assign an IP address to the port. How much control is available through SNMP is limited by which commands are included in the vendor's MIB as well as the command structure of SNMP itself. The operative word in SNMP is "simple." SNMP provides only a minimal amount of control over network devices.

While most reporting is done by having the SNMP management station poll network devices, SNMP does allow network devices to report critical events immediately back to the management station. These messages are referred to as *traps*. Traps are sent when an event occurs that is important enough to not wait until the device is again polled. For example, our router may send a trap to the SNMP management console if it has just been power cycled. Because this event will have a grave impact on network connectivity, it is reported to the SNMP management station immediately instead of waiting until the device is again polled.

NOTE   SNMP uses the UDP transport and destination ports 161 and 162 when communicating.

Telnet

Telnet is used when a remote communication session is required with some other system on the network. Its functionality is similar to a mainframe terminal or remote control session. The local system becomes little more than a dumb terminal providing system updates only. The remote system supplies the file system and all processing time required when running programs.

NOTE   Telnet uses the TCP transport and destination port 23 when creating a communication session.

WHOIS

WHOIS is a utility used to gathering information about a specific domain. The utility usually connects to the system `rs.internic.net` and displays administrative contact information as well as the root servers for a domain.

This is useful when you wish to find out what organization is using a particular domain name. For example, typing the command:

```
whois sun.com
```

will produce the following information regarding the domain:

```
Sun Microsystems Inc. (SUN) SUN.COM        192.9.9.1
Sun Microsystems, Inc. (SUN-DOM)           SUN.COM
```

If we performed a further search by entering the command:

```
whois sun-dom
```

the following additional information would be produced:

```
Sun Microsystems Inc. (SUN)
      2550 Garcia Avenue
      Building 1, Room 235
      Mountain View, CA 94043

Hostname: SUN.COM
Address: 192.9.9.1
System: SUN-3/160 running SUNOS

Coordinator:
      Finn, Huch (HF00) Huch.Finn@EBAY.SUN.COM
      408-555-1212

      domain server

Record last updated on 23-Aug-96.

Database last updated on 25-Apr-98 04:08:18 EDT.
```

NOTE whois can be an extremely powerful troubleshooting tool as it enables us to know who is responsible for maintaining the domain, how to contact them, and which systems are considered to be primary name servers. We could then use a DNS tool such as nslookup to find the IP addresses of Sun's mail systems or even their Web server. WHOIS uses the TCP transport and destination port 43 when creating a communication session.

Although there is no command-line version of whois for Windows or Mac users (at least included with the OS), there are whois gateways you can point your Web browser to. Here is one such current URL: www.martinet.com/~tadman/whois/.

Internetwork Packet Exchange (IPX)

In 1986 Novell released NetWare 2.0, and with it, the *IPX* protocol. Based upon Xerox's Xerox Network System (XNS) protocol, IPX is highly optimized and designed to provide efficient network communications. With the release of such enhancements as Large Internet Protocol (LIP) and burst mode, IPX has arguably become the most effective protocol in use today. Figure 3.15 is a graphic representation of how the pieces of the IPX protocol suite match up to the OSI model.

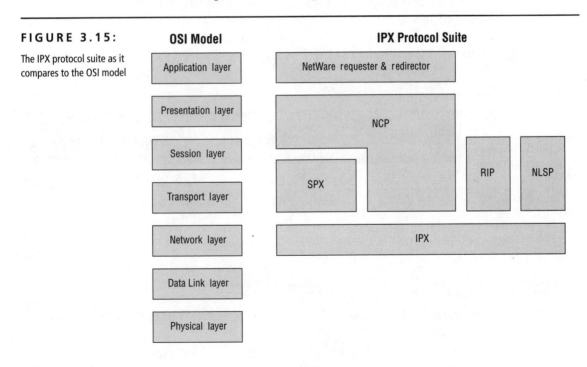

FIGURE 3.15:

The IPX protocol suite as it compares to the OSI model

IPX Network Addressing

If IP addressing has left you a bit confused, than you'll love the simplicity of IPX. IPX uses an 8-bit hexadecimal network address, which means that any value in the range 0–9 and A–F are valid. The only exceptions are 00000000 and FFFFFFFF, the former because it is a null value and the latter because it is considered an all-networks broadcast address.

Devices on the network which will be performing routing services (including NetWare servers even if they have only one NIC) must be manually configured with their network address. All other devices are capable of autoconfiguring their network address during startup.

Figure 3.16 shows the initial packet sent by an IPX workstation in order to discover the local network address. In this case the workstation sends an SAP (NetWare Service Advertising Protocol, discussed later in this chapter) packet, but some client software (such as Microsoft's) may use RIP instead. In either case the handshake is similar. If you look closely you'll see that the source and destination network address is set to zero. This is because the workstation does not yet know where it is located.

FIGURE 3.16:

A Windows 95 workstation with Client32 attempting to discover what IPX network segment it is on

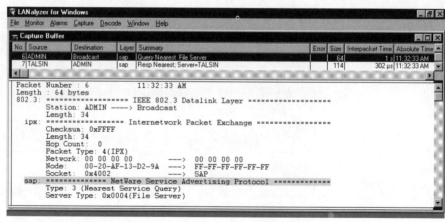

Figure 3.17 shows the server's response to the client. Note that the address values are now filled in. Our workstation will record the value in the destination network address field and use it during all future communications.

FIGURE 3.17:

The server Talsin's response to the SAP packet

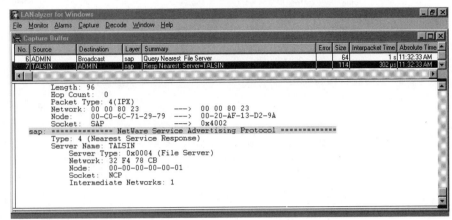

Figure 3.18 shows the very next packet sent by the Admin workstation. Note that the address field is filled in and our workstation now knows the local network address (00008023) and will use it during all future communications. With a simple exchange of only two frames, our workstation is now ready to communicate on the network.

FIGURE 3.18:

The Admin workstation has now learned the address for the local network.

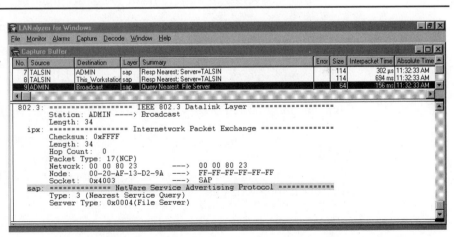

You may remember from our discussion of IP that each station requires a unique network address to avoid communication conflicts. The same is true with IPX. Our Admin workstation will simply append its MAC address to the end of the local network number. Its full address will become 00008023:0020AF13D29A. Because every network device is required to have a unique MAC number, there should be no possibility of this address conflicting with another system.

IPX Routing

IPX supports static, distance-vector, and link-state routing. Unlike IP with its plethora of dynamic routing choices, IPX only has one routing protocol for each. Distance-vector routing is supported with RIP, and link-state routing is provided by the NetWare Link State Protocol (NLSP).

RIP

As it is under the IP protocol suite, RIP under IPX is based upon the distance-vector routing information protocol developed for XNS. This is why it is prone to the same problems and limitations as its IP counterpart. In summary, these are:

- Routing tables are built on secondhand information.
- The time to convergence is long because of slow propagation.
- During convergence the routing table is susceptible to errors and loops.
- The maximum hop count is limited to 15 in order to counteract the count-to-infinity problem.

All 3.*x* and 4.*x* versions of NetWare support IPX RIP. It is also supported by Windows NT as of version 4 and many Unix systems—Linux, SUN, and SCO being the most popular.

NLSP

NetWare's link-state protocol is a vast improvement over RIP. Like most link-state protocols, it sports the following features:

- Only firsthand information is used to build routing tables.
- Minimal convergence time means a reduced chance of routing errors.
- Less network traffic is required to keep routing tables up-to-date.
- Most communications are unicast, not broadcast.

- Traffic load balancing is based upon utilization and link speed.

- The maximum hop count is 128.

NLSP routers retain backward compatibility by transmitting RIP as well as NLSP packets on segments where RIP-only devices are detected. If they did not, a RIP device would see the server during its initialization and add it to its routing table. It would then remove the entry three minutes later as NLSP routing information is not broadcast once per minute but rather every two hours or when a change takes place. This would cause the RIP-only device to assume that the NLSP system is no longer available.

NetWare servers perform load balancing when two or more NIC cards are attached to the same logical segment and NLSP is used (glance back at Figure 2.11 for an example). Load balancing simply means equalizing the quantity of traffic sent over two or more paths. This can be an excellent performance-enhancing feature because it nearly doubles the communication speed of the server. Take care that the disk subsystem does not become overloaded now that the server is able to receive more read and write requests per second.

When load balancing is performed, traffic is switched between the cards on a per-message basis, not per-packet. In other words, if the server transfers a file that requires six frames to a workstation, and two cards are performing load balancing, all six frames will travel through the same network interface card. It will not send three over one and three over another. The very next file request by that same workstation may very well use the second card, depending on the current load.

While this message switching may appear to greatly diminish the effectiveness of load balancing, it actually does not. Remember that a busy server is required to process many read and write requests per second. The server will have many opportunities to simultaneously send two separate replies, one to each card.

NetWare is the only network operating system that supports NLSP. It is, however, supported by many router hardware vendors.

Transport Layer Services

IPX uses three separate transports when sending and receiving data. They are IPX, Sequence Packet Exchange (SPX and SPX II), and NetWare Core Protocol (NCP). Each has its own responsibilities when conducting IPX communications.

IPX

The *IPX* protocol is the foundation of the NetWare IPX/SPX protocol suite. All communications take place on top of IPX. Each frame contains a 30-byte section following the frame header which contains all the information required to route and identify the frame.

IPX is a connectionless protocol, meaning that it does not require a handshake prior to data transmission. It also does not require packet acknowledgments. This means that it has no way to guarantee the final delivery of data. Also, IPX does not guarantee sequential delivery, which means that packets can be received in any order.

Sound like a pretty poor protocol? Actually, it is quite the opposite. IPX is specifically designed to do only one thing well—route information. It does not concern itself with things like acknowledgments and packet sequencing, but rather leaves this to the upper layers to deal with. By leaving the scope of IPX fairly loose, the door is left open to optimize communications.

For example, burst mode (discussed later in this section) allows for the sending of multiple frames before an acknowledgment is sent. If IPX had been designed to require an acknowledgment after each frame, burst mode would not be possible without revamping the entire protocol suite from the ground up. This would of course lead to backward-compatibility problems because it would be difficult to keep the new and old specifications compatible.

Because IPX is a loose specification and acknowledgments are handled at a higher communication layer, IPX did not need to change when burst mode was introduced. This allowed older systems to continue to function as they always did while the newer software was deployed on the same network.

The only drawback to this type of design is that acknowledgments need to be passed further up the stack in order to be verified. Because this means that additional communication layers become involved during a retransmission of a frame, the system uses more resources and takes longer to send a replacement. Figure 3.19 shows why this occurs. If a protocol requires an acknowledgment of successful frames at the Network layer, as in Protocol A, it can respond with a replacement frame quickly using a minimal amount of CPU time. If acknowledgments are handled at a higher layer as in Protocol B, the replacement frame requires more processing than it did with Protocol A because it needs to be handled by additional layers.

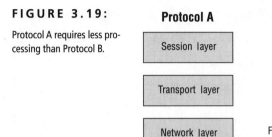

FIGURE 3.19:

Protocol A requires less processing than Protocol B.

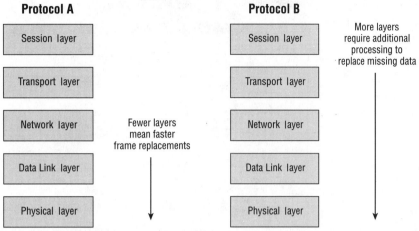

How much effect this has depends on the stability of the network. If errors are few and far between, the ratio of retransmissions to the amount of data that is moved becomes negligible. Today's networks can be very stable when designed and installed properly.

IPX supports both unicast and broadcast frames. Multicast is not supported at this time.

A *raw* IPX packet (one where no other transport is used) will have an IPX type-field value of zero or four. Note that this field is different than the type field used by some frame headers. The IPX type field is located in the data portion of the frame, not the frame header.

SPX

SPX is the connection-oriented portion of the IPX protocol suite. SPX does not replace IPX, but rather communicates just above it. All SPX frames still include an IPX header section. As shown in Figure 3.20, the SPX header follows the IPX header within the data portion of a frame. SPX packets are identified by an IPX packet type value of five. Note that we have an Ethernet section (identified as 802.3), an IPX section, an SPX section, and then the text "Data." Because our Ethernet frame has a fixed header length, which includes the information required for local delivery, the IPX and SPX fields are stored in the data section of the frame.

FIGURE 3.20:

A packet decode of an SPX frame

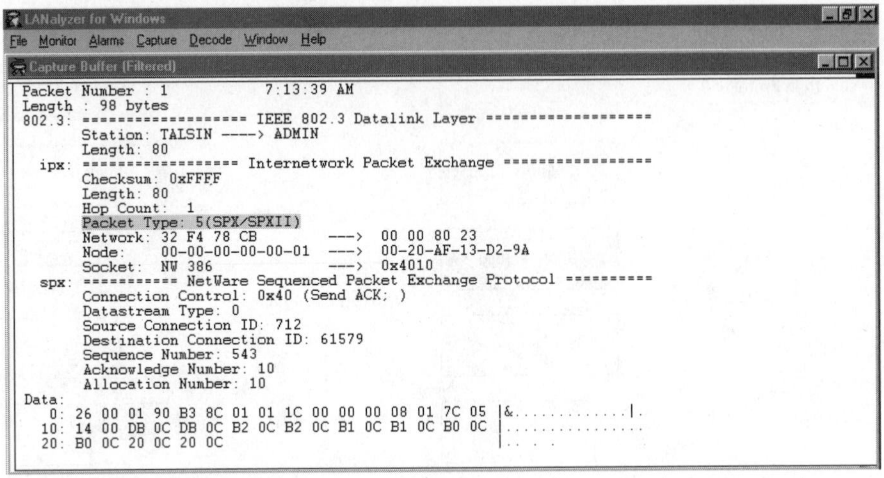

```
LANalyzer for Windows                                              _ 8 X
File  Monitor  Alarms  Capture  Decode  Window  Help
Capture Buffer (Filtered)                                         _ □ X
Packet Number : 1              7:13:39 AM
Length : 98 bytes
802.3: =================== IEEE 802.3 Datalink Layer ===================
       Station: TALSIN ----> ADMIN
       Length: 80
  ipx: =================== Internetwork Packet Exchange =================
       Checksum: 0xFFFF
       Length: 80
       Hop Count: 1
       Packet Type: 5(SPX/SPXII)
       Network: 32 F4 78 CB        ---> 00 00 80 23
       Node:    00-00-00-00-00-01  ---> 00-20-AF-13-D2-9A
       Socket:  NW 386             ---> 0x4010
  spx: =========== NetWare Sequenced Packet Exchange Protocol ===========
       Connection Control: 0x40 (Send ACK; )
       Datastream Type: 0
       Source Connection ID: 712
       Destination Connection ID: 61579
       Sequence Number: 543
       Acknowledge Number: 10
       Allocation Number: 10
Data:
   0: 26 00 01 90 B3 8C 01 01 1C 00 00 00 08 01 7C 05 |&............|.
  10: 14 00 DB 0C DB 0C B2 0C B2 0C B1 0C B1 0C B0 0C |................
  20: B0 0C 20 0C 20 0C                               |. . .
```

SPX communications handshake prior to the data transmission and require an acknowledgment for each frame of data sent. SPX sequences transmitted frames (note the sequence number in the SPX section of Figure 3.20) and ensures that they are received in the proper order. Because it is connection-oriented, SPX supports unicast communications only.

Figure 3.21 shows an SPX session in progress. This is an Rconsole connection between a workstation and a server. Rconsole is a NetWare utility that allows a remote control session to be set up from the workstation to the server. All information that is shown on the server's monitor is also displayed through the Rconsole session window. In our example, the session has been idle long enough for the server's screen blanker to be activated. The screen blanker is simply a blank screen with an ASCII character snake moving randomly around the screen. The busier the server's CPU, the longer the tail is on the snake.

NOTE   Have a look at the "ping pong" effect between data transmission and acknowledgments (ACK). We are transmitting four frames per second just watching the snake move around the screen! To avoid unnecessary traffic, Rconsole sessions should be shut down when not in use.

FIGURE 3.21:

An SPX session in progress

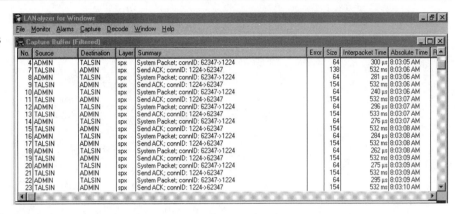

There are actually two separate versions of SPX—SPX and SPX II. The above descriptions apply to both specifications. The original SPX has been available since NetWare version 2.0. SPX II was introduced with NetWare 4.0.

SPX I

The original SPX protocol, *SPX I* uses 12 bytes within the data field and has a maximum frame size of 576 bytes. If you refer to Figure 3.22, you'll see that this only leaves 516 bytes free to carry actual data. Combine this with SPX's requirement for an acknowledgment after each frame transmission, and we have a horribly inefficient means of communication.

So why all the overhead and the smaller packet size? The overhead is used to ensure proper delivery of every single frame. SPX was not designed for everyday communications; it is reserved for those special situations when a stable connection is preferable to speed. For example, when the above-described rconsole session is created, stability while controlling the server is far more important than speed. SPX was spawned in the days of thinnet and thicknet wiring as well as 1200bps modems with minimal error correction. This is why it is so uptight about ensuring that all the data is received in one piece. In the old days, the Physical layer of networks was not as stable as it is today. In situations where the stability of the circuit between the two communicating systems is questionable, SPX is the best method available to ensure that the data is sent in one piece.

FIGURE 3.22:

Only 516 bytes are available
to carry data.

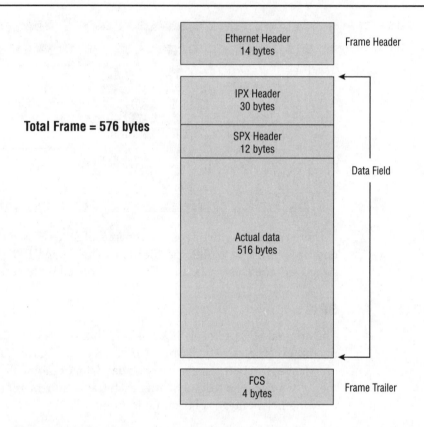

Total Frame = 576 bytes

As for its puny frame size, prior to 1992 IPX would negotiate a frame size of 576 bytes if the server and client were not on the same logical network. Fixing the SPX frame at 576 bytes avoided the need for this negotiation. The size limit was overcome when Novell released LIP, which is described later in this section.

Because of the above-noted issues, SPX should be avoided in stable network environments whenever possible. Its small frame size (size *does* matter in networking) and connection-oriented nature can generate an excessive number of frames in medium to large environments. The following is a list of common software known to use SPX:

- Rconsole
- Pserver

- Lotus Notes when IPX is selected as the transport

- SAA Gateway when IPX is selected as the transport

- Many client/server database programs

In many cases the administrator has the option of not using SPX. For example, Notes can be run over IP as well and operates much more efficiently. Sometimes, however, SPX may be the only transport supported by the software. Rconsole is a good example of a program that only runs over SPX. If SPX must be used, an administrator's only recourse is to limit its effect on the rest of the network.

SPX II

SPX II fixed many of the problems with SPX while still maintaining a connection-oriented session. The packet size was increased to support the maximum allow-able frame size per the topology in use. In the case of Ethernet, this means that a frame could be as large as 1518 bytes.

SPX II also assumes that the Physical layer connecting the two systems is a bit more stable than it used to be. With this in mind, SPX II supports a method of communication known as *windowing*. With SPX, a frame must be acknowledged before the next one can be sent. SPX II allows for multiple frames to be outstand-ing without receiving an acknowledgment. The window size is negotiated using the allocation number field within the SPX II header, but it is not allowed to exceed 10 outstanding packets at any given time.

SPX II will use the sequence numbers and negative acknowledgments (NAK) to recover lost frames during a communication session. When a frame is lost, the receiving system will send a NAK to the transmitting system identifying the sequence number of the missing frame. This allows the transmitting system to resend just the missing piece of information.

SPX II is a big improvement in communication efficiency over SPX. Some backup software vendors have developed *push agents,* which allow their software to use SPX II during server-to-server backups. Cheyenne's ARCServe and Sea-gate's Backup Exec are two popular examples.

NCP

The *NetWare Core Protocol* is appropriately named, as it is the transport responsi-ble for a majority of IPX communications. NCP defines the structure of requests and responses as they apply to most NetWare communications. The packet type field with the IPX header section has a value of 17 when NCP is used. The NCP header follows the IPX header as well as the SPX header if one is required.

NCP uses a type field to identify the purpose of the information contained within the data field of the frame. Because a NetWare environment uses mutually exclusive definitions of a "client" and a "server" (for example, you cannot sit at the server console and access files located on a logged-in client), the type field is labeled according to what kind of system originated the information. If the frame originates from a client, the field is referred to as *request type*. If the frame comes from a server, the field is called *reply type*. Tables 3.7 and 3.8 list the most common NCP communication types.

TABLE 3.7: Client Request Types

Type Value	Description
1111	Used prior to authentication to request a server connection.
2222	Manipulation or information request. Most commonly used during directory listings, path searches, file and directory creation or deletion, or when trustee right information is required or must be set.
5555	Destroy connection. Most commonly used when the server that replies to the initial "Get nearest server" request is not the server the client wishes to authenticate with. This removes the client's connection and frees it up for another client. Connections identified as being "not logged in" are clients that have not yet sent a type 5555 request.

TABLE 3.8: Server Reply Types

Type Value	Description
3333	Information reply. A type 3333 reply is always preceded by a client sending a type 2222 request.
9999	Request pending, no ECB time out. A type 9999 reply is a server's way of saying "She can't take any more speed, Captain! The emergency bypass control of the matter, anti-matter integrator is going to fuse!" When a server replies with a type 9999 NCP frame, it is telling the client that its buffer for accepting inbound requests is currently full. It needs to process the pending requests before it can accept any more from the client.

There is a single NCP type that is used by both the client and the server. An NCP type 7777 is used during all packet burst communications. This includes requests, acknowledgments, and actual data transfers.

In addition to NCP types, other fields are used to further identify the purpose of a frame. All NCP frames include a *function code* and *subfunction code* field as well. Novell has specified a number of codes to provide more granularity in identifying a frame's purpose beyond that provided by the NCP type field.

For example, Figure 3.23 shows a decoding of the NCP portion of a frame. The request type is 2222, so we know it is a client requesting manipulation or information regarding a file or directory. If we look at the value of the data field it is identified as *temp*. So what is temp and what do we want to do with it?

FIGURE 3.23:

A decoding of the NCP portion of a frame

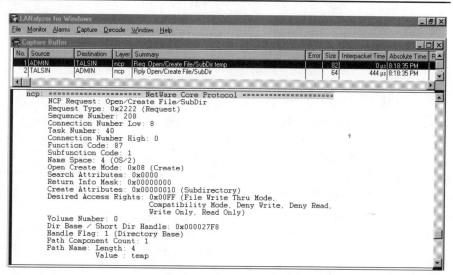

This is where our function code and subfunction code fields come in handy. Novell has defined a request type of 2222, with a function code of 87 and a subfunction code of 1, as a request to open or create a file or directory.

So now we know we need to open or create a file or directory named TEMP. While we're a bit closer, we still don't know the precise action our workstation is requesting of the server. While all NCP frames contain a function code and a subfunction code, other fields are used only as required.

This particular frame has an Open Create Mode field, which identifies whether we want to open or create the value in the data field (TEMP). A value of 8 tells us we wish to create it. There is also a Create Attributes field, which identifies with a value of 10 that TEMP is a directory.

Through the use of these five fields, we now know that TEMP is a directory we wish to create at our current location. While they are cryptic even for the average network geek to read, control fields are an efficient, space-saving means of relaying information. In most situations only the type, function, and subfunction fields are required. When this is true, only eight bytes of frame space are needed to identify the requested service. Novell has categorized over 350 services using these three fields.

Large Internet Protocol (LIP)   LIP was added to the functionality of NCP in 1992. Prior to that time, a client would limit the size of its frames to 576 bytes when it detected a router between itself and the server. LIP allows a client to communicate with the server using the maximum allowable frame size (1518 bytes for Ethernet), even when the hop count field indicates there are one or more routers in between.

Burst Mode   Burst mode is arguably the single biggest improvement Novell has made to the NCP transport. It allows a system using NCP to send multiple frames of data without having to acknowledge the receipt of each one. It also allows the communicating systems to adjust the wait time between frame transmissions, known as the *interpacket gap*.

Figure 3.24 shows burst mode in action. In frame 112, the client Admin is requesting 28,720 bytes of file information from the server Talsin. In frames 113 through 133, Talsin is replying with the requested file information. Notice that the only required acknowledgment occurs when Admin requests another 29,084 bytes in frame number 134. What would normally require 42 frames to transfer (between data transfers and acknowledgments), is completed in just 22 frames. This is approximately a 50% reduction in network traffic!

When a client and a server are both capable of burst-mode communications, they will negotiate how many packets to transfer between acknowledgments (the *burst packet count*), and how long to wait between transmissions (the *interpacket gap*). During the course of their communication these values will be adjusted as required. For example, in Figure 3.24 we see that our server is able to successfully transfer 28,720 bytes to our client in burst mode. When our client requested additional file information in frame number 134, it pushed the envelope a bit and requested 29,084 bytes. This would continue until an error occurs or the maximum burst-mode size is reached.

FIGURE 3.24:

A NCP client and server communicating in burst mode. Note that an acknowledgment is not required until all the requested file information is transferred.

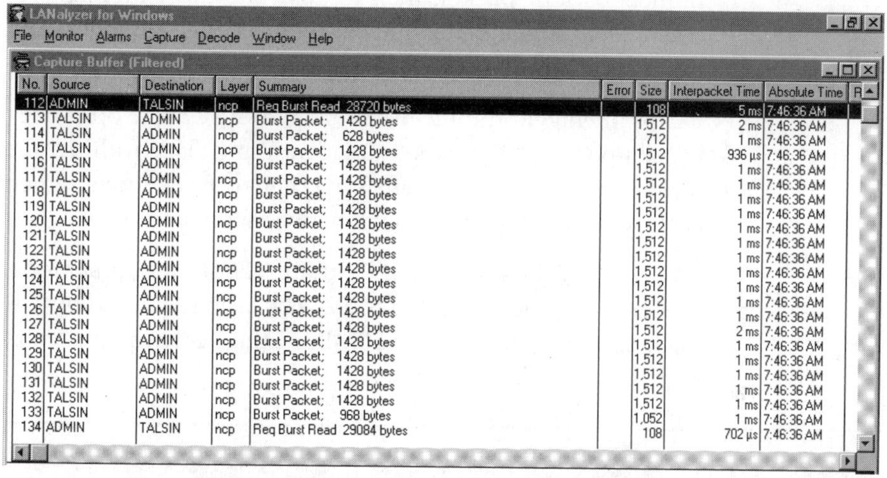

No.	Source	Destination	Layer	Summary	Error	Size	Interpacket Time	Absolute Time
112	ADMIN	TALSIN	ncp	Req Burst Read 28720 bytes		108	5 ms	7:46:36 AM
113	TALSIN	ADMIN	ncp	Burst Packet; 1428 bytes		1,512	2 ms	7:46:36 AM
114	TALSIN	ADMIN	ncp	Burst Packet; 628 bytes		712	1 ms	7:46:36 AM
115	TALSIN	ADMIN	ncp	Burst Packet; 1428 bytes		1,512	936 µs	7:46:36 AM
116	TALSIN	ADMIN	ncp	Burst Packet; 1428 bytes		1,512	1 ms	7:46:36 AM
117	TALSIN	ADMIN	ncp	Burst Packet; 1428 bytes		1,512	1 ms	7:46:36 AM
118	TALSIN	ADMIN	ncp	Burst Packet; 1428 bytes		1,512	1 ms	7:46:36 AM
119	TALSIN	ADMIN	ncp	Burst Packet; 1428 bytes		1,512	1 ms	7:46:36 AM
120	TALSIN	ADMIN	ncp	Burst Packet; 1428 bytes		1,512	1 ms	7:46:36 AM
121	TALSIN	ADMIN	ncp	Burst Packet; 1428 bytes		1,512	1 ms	7:46:36 AM
122	TALSIN	ADMIN	ncp	Burst Packet; 1428 bytes		1,512	1 ms	7:46:36 AM
123	TALSIN	ADMIN	ncp	Burst Packet; 1428 bytes		1,512	1 ms	7:46:36 AM
124	TALSIN	ADMIN	ncp	Burst Packet; 1428 bytes		1,512	1 ms	7:46:36 AM
125	TALSIN	ADMIN	ncp	Burst Packet; 1428 bytes		1,512	1 ms	7:46:36 AM
126	TALSIN	ADMIN	ncp	Burst Packet; 1428 bytes		1,512	1 ms	7:46:36 AM
127	TALSIN	ADMIN	ncp	Burst Packet; 1428 bytes		1,512	2 ms	7:46:36 AM
128	TALSIN	ADMIN	ncp	Burst Packet; 1428 bytes		1,512	1 ms	7:46:36 AM
129	TALSIN	ADMIN	ncp	Burst Packet; 1428 bytes		1,512	1 ms	7:46:36 AM
130	TALSIN	ADMIN	ncp	Burst Packet; 1428 bytes		1,512	1 ms	7:46:36 AM
131	TALSIN	ADMIN	ncp	Burst Packet; 1428 bytes		1,512	1 ms	7:46:36 AM
132	TALSIN	ADMIN	ncp	Burst Packet; 1428 bytes		1,512	1 ms	7:46:36 AM
133	TALSIN	ADMIN	ncp	Burst Packet; 968 bytes		1,052	1 ms	7:46:36 AM
134	ADMIN	TALSIN	ncp	Req Burst Read 29084 bytes		108	702 µs	7:46:36 AM

Figure 3.25 shows what happens when a burst mode session is not successful. In frame 185, the client Admin is notifying the server Talsin that it missed 4284 bytes worth of information. In frames 186 through 189, the server replies with the requested information. Notice that these four frames total 4284 bytes exactly.

FIGURE 3.25:

A burst mode communication recovering from a transmission error. Only the missing data needs to be retransmitted.

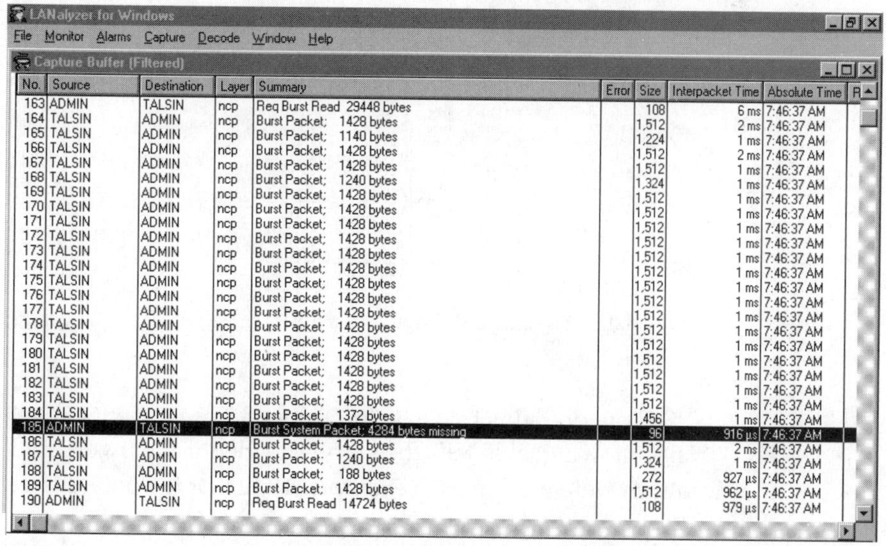

No.	Source	Destination	Layer	Summary	Error	Size	Interpacket Time	Absolute Time
163	ADMIN	TALSIN	ncp	Req Burst Read 29448 bytes		108	6 ms	7:46:37 AM
164	TALSIN	ADMIN	ncp	Burst Packet; 1428 bytes		1,512	2 ms	7:46:37 AM
165	TALSIN	ADMIN	ncp	Burst Packet; 1140 bytes		1,224	1 ms	7:46:37 AM
166	TALSIN	ADMIN	ncp	Burst Packet; 1428 bytes		1,512	2 ms	7:46:37 AM
167	TALSIN	ADMIN	ncp	Burst Packet; 1428 bytes		1,512	1 ms	7:46:37 AM
168	TALSIN	ADMIN	ncp	Burst Packet; 1240 bytes		1,324	1 ms	7:46:37 AM
169	TALSIN	ADMIN	ncp	Burst Packet; 1428 bytes		1,512	1 ms	7:46:37 AM
170	TALSIN	ADMIN	ncp	Burst Packet; 1428 bytes		1,512	1 ms	7:46:37 AM
171	TALSIN	ADMIN	ncp	Burst Packet; 1428 bytes		1,512	1 ms	7:46:37 AM
172	TALSIN	ADMIN	ncp	Burst Packet; 1428 bytes		1,512	1 ms	7:46:37 AM
173	TALSIN	ADMIN	ncp	Burst Packet; 1428 bytes		1,512	1 ms	7:46:37 AM
174	TALSIN	ADMIN	ncp	Burst Packet; 1428 bytes		1,512	1 ms	7:46:37 AM
175	TALSIN	ADMIN	ncp	Burst Packet; 1428 bytes		1,512	1 ms	7:46:37 AM
176	TALSIN	ADMIN	ncp	Burst Packet; 1428 bytes		1,512	1 ms	7:46:37 AM
177	TALSIN	ADMIN	ncp	Burst Packet; 1428 bytes		1,512	1 ms	7:46:37 AM
178	TALSIN	ADMIN	ncp	Burst Packet; 1428 bytes		1,512	1 ms	7:46:37 AM
179	TALSIN	ADMIN	ncp	Burst Packet; 1428 bytes		1,512	1 ms	7:46:37 AM
180	TALSIN	ADMIN	ncp	Burst Packet; 1428 bytes		1,512	1 ms	7:46:37 AM
181	TALSIN	ADMIN	ncp	Burst Packet; 1428 bytes		1,512	1 ms	7:46:37 AM
182	TALSIN	ADMIN	ncp	Burst Packet; 1428 bytes		1,512	1 ms	7:46:37 AM
183	TALSIN	ADMIN	ncp	Burst Packet; 1428 bytes		1,512	1 ms	7:46:37 AM
184	TALSIN	ADMIN	ncp	Burst Packet; 1372 bytes		1,456	1 ms	7:46:37 AM
185	ADMIN	TALSIN	ncp	Burst System Packet: 4284 bytes missing		96	916 µs	7:46:37 AM
186	TALSIN	ADMIN	ncp	Burst Packet; 1428 bytes		1,512	2 ms	7:46:37 AM
187	TALSIN	ADMIN	ncp	Burst Packet; 1240 bytes		1,324	1 ms	7:46:37 AM
188	TALSIN	ADMIN	ncp	Burst Packet; 188 bytes		272	927 µs	7:46:37 AM
189	TALSIN	ADMIN	ncp	Burst Packet; 1428 bytes		1,512	962 µs	7:46:37 AM
190	ADMIN	TALSIN	ncp	Req Burst Read 14724 bytes		108	979 µs	7:46:37 AM

What is extremely interesting (if you are a wire geek, that is) is Admin's next request for data in frame 190. The client is only requesting 14,724 bytes of information. This is exactly half the amount of file information it requested in frame 163. Since an error was encountered, the client has decided to back off on the number of burst packets in order to avoid future problems. If this transfer is successful, it may again negotiate a slightly larger number of burst packets until it finds the maximum number of frames that can be transferred without error.

This intelligent tuning allows the two systems to optimize their communication based upon the current network conditions. The healthier the network, the more information that can be transferred between acknowledgments and the less time each system is required to wait between transmissions.

So just how fast can you go? Figure 3.26 shows burst mode pushed just about to its limits. A write request of 65,024 has been requested by the client with an interpacket gap of 2ms. This is a 10MBps Ethernet segment. A faster pipe will be able to produce a lower gap time.

FIGURE 3.26:

Burst mode pushed to the max. A total of 45 burst packets will be transmitted before an acknowledgment is required.

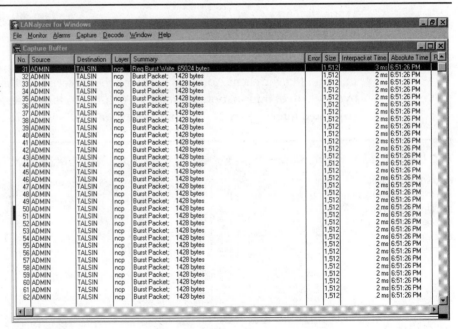

So how does this translate into actual improvements in network performance? The following table tells the story. The identical network and computer configurations were used in each example. Note that the only difference is whether burst mode was turned on or off. The data in question is a 5MB .ZIP file. This test simply measures the raw transfer rate of a file; your mileage may vary.

Connection Mode	File Transfer Time	Number of Frames Required
burst mode enabled	6 seconds	3946
burst mode disabled	12 seconds	7790

As you can see, burst mode can have a dramatic effect on the time and number of frames it takes to transfer a file. Since regular network usage is a mixture of file transfers and other activities, the net effect of enabling burst mode on a network is usually quite a bit less than the factor-of-two improvement seen here. Still, it's hard to beat free bandwidth.

IPX Application Layer Services

IPX uses the term *sockets* instead of ports to identify Application-layer services. While they are not nearly as diverse as IP, there are a few commonly used socket numbers worth noting. These are listed in Table 3.9. IPX socket numbers are identified in a hex format.

TABLE 3.9: Commonly Used IPX Socket Numbers

Socket	Service	Description
0451	NCP	NetWare Core Protocol
0452	SAP	Service Advertising Protocol
0453	RIP	Routing Information Protocol
0455	NetBIOS	NetBIOS over IPX
0456	Diag. Packet	Server diagnostic packet
0457	Serial # check	License serial number check between servers
4000–8000	reply	Upper reply socket randomly assigned by client
5100	Descent	Default for multi-player updates
869C	Id games	Default for doom2, heretic, etc.
26000	Quake	Default for multi-player updates

SAP frames are used to advertise what services are available from each IPX system on the network. The NetWare "display servers" command will list each server on the network, once for each service it provides. This is why some NetWare servers may appear multiple times within a server list. Table 3.10 lists the most common services available on an IPX network. SAP types are identified in hex format.

TABLE 3.10: The Most Common Services Available on an IPX Network

SAP Type	Service
0004	File Server
0047	Print Server
0278	NDS Server
026B	Time Sync Server

Network Basic Input/Output System (NetBIOS)

Developed by IBM for their PC Network LAN, *NetBIOS* was created to be an application program interface (API). NetBIOS is designed to be a *front end* for carrying out interapplication communications. NetBIOS defines the interface to the network protocol, not the protocol itself. At the time of development it was assumed that the application accessing NetBIOS would assume responsibility for defining the protocols required for transmitting the information.

Figure 3.27 is a graphic representation of NetBIOS and some of its related components, as they compare to the OSI model. NetBIOS provides Transport-layer and Session-layer services only. It does not provide networking services, which means that NetBIOS is a non-routable protocol. If a network is broken up by one or more routers, NetBIOS does not have the ability to reach nodes located on remote segments.

NetBIOS has a very loose specification for the Presentation and Application layers. There is no standard structure or format specified. This has lead to NetBIOS being paired with other protocols, such as NetBEUI, that can provide a precise specification. It has also lead to incompatibility problems as vendors were left to create proprietary implementations. Artisoft's LANtastic is a good example of a system which communicates using a proprietary NetBIOS implementation and is unable to communicate with other NetBIOS systems.

FIGURE 3.27:

NetBIOS as it compares to the OSI model

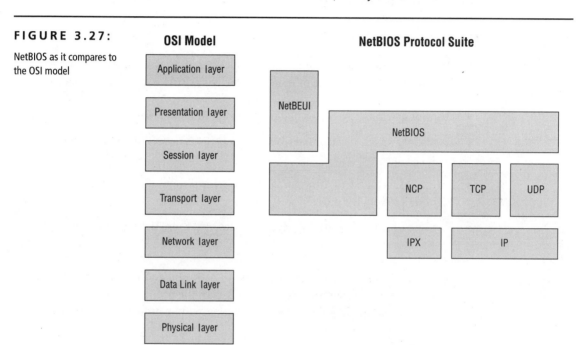

NetBIOS is designed to allow all nodes on a network to communicate on an equal basis. This is also known as *peer-to-peer networking*. All NetBIOS systems are able to both share local files and access shared files on remote systems. This model is the exact opposite of that discussed under IPX and NCP.

NetBIOS Addressing

Each machine on a NetBIOS network receives a unique name. This name can be up to 16 characters long but must not start with an asterisk (*). NetBIOS uses this name to discover a system's MAC number. Once the MAC address is known, all local transmissions will take place using this address. A system's NetBIOS name is very similar in purpose to a system's host name under IP. In a mixed protocol environment, these two names are usually kept the same.

When a NetBIOS system first initializes on a network, it is required to register its NetBIOS name. How the registration process takes place depends upon the node type of the system.

Node Types

NetBIOS identifies four different node types. The node types are categorized based upon how they resolve names on the network. The four types of nodes are:

- b-nodes, which use broadcast communications to resolve names

- p-nodes, which use point-to-point communications with a name server to resolve names

- m-nodes, which first function as b-nodes and then, if necessary, function as p-nodes to resolve names

- h-nodes, which first function as p-nodes and then, if necessary, function as b-nodes to resolve names

A *b-node* system uses broadcasts for name registration and resolution. Figure 3.28 shows a b-node system named Fenrus, which is in the process of powering up. When NetBIOS is initialized, the system broadcasts the name it wishes to use.

FIGURE 3.28:

A b-node NetBIOS system registering the name it wishes to use

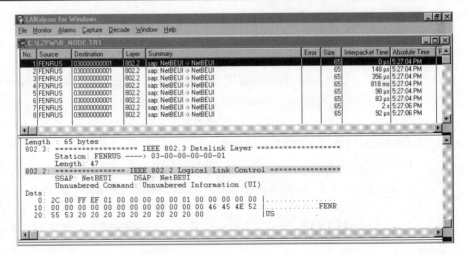

If no response is received, the station assumes the name is not in use and will begin identifying itself as Fenrus. If the name is in use by another system, the station will receive a name challenge. A name challenge lets the broadcasting system know that the name is already in use. Names are registered on a first come, first served basis. Because NetBIOS names must be unique, a system should never register a NetBIOS name for which it has received a challenge.

WARNING It is possible to force a workstation into registering a name even after it has received a challenge. This should never be done in a production environment as it will affect connectivity to the system that originally registered the name.

A b-node system will also broadcast when it is performing a discovery. A *discovery* is performed when one system wishes to connect to another but does not know its network address. The system will broadcast a discovery message asking the destination system to reply with its address. Once a b-node system finds the address of the system it wishes to contact, it will begin communicating in a unicast mode.

Returning to Figure 3.28, note the destination broadcast address. This is not the typical broadcast address of FFFFFFFFFFFF that we normally see. The address 030000000001 is actually a multicast address used only by NetBIOS systems operating in broadcast mode. There are two major benefits to this mode of operation:

1. Non-NetBIOS systems are not required to process this multicast. It will be viewed as a unicast frame to other systems.

2. The only systems that will interpret this frame as a broadcast are the ones that need to process it anyway. All b-node systems need to be involved in each name registration and discovery message.

So while b-node communications say they are broadcast-based, they are actually multicast-based and are not as inefficient as the typical network broadcast. Still, if we can remove our workstations from the registration and discovery process, it will free up bandwidth and CPU cycles to perform other functions.

When *p-nodes* are used, a central system referred to as a NetBIOS Name Server (NBNS) tracks the registration of NetBIOS names. A p-node system does not need to broadcast during startup; it simply sends a unicast query to the NBNS to find out if the name it wishes to register is already in use.

Likewise, when the system needs to discover another system, it will again contact the NBNS with a unicast query. This communication method eliminates the need for network broadcasts during registration and discovery and prevents all systems from being involved in each of these queries.

The drawback to using p-nodes is that each system needs to be preconfigured with the network address of the NBNS. It also relies on the NBNS being online and functional to support all NetBIOS communications. If the NBNS goes down, discovery is no longer possible. Another problem with the NBNS crashing is that it could lose all p-node table information regarding systems that had been registered prior to the crash. If this occurs, a second system could conceivably register a name that is already in use.

Note that b-node and p-node systems are not compatible. A b-node system will not register or discover through a NBNS, and a p-node system will ignore any NetBIOS broadcasts it receives from a b-node system. To get around some of the problems with both p-node and b-node systems, *m-node* and *h-node* systems provide a mixture of the functionality supported by each.

An m-node system will broadcast when performing registration and discovery. If the discovery should happen to fail, the m-node will then act like a p-node and query the local NBNS. While adding a bit of versatility, this does not really address many of the problems noted with b-node and p-node operation.

An h-node system will first register and discover through an NBNS in the same manner that a p-node does. If either of these two processes fail, it will drop back to b-node and use broadcasts to perform registration and discovery.

This mode of operation offers the best of both worlds. The h-node will first communicate using unicast transmissions. This helps to limit the number of broadcasts being transmitted on our network. If this should fail (for example, if the NBNS is offline), the system is able to recover by communicating in broadcast mode.

When Microsoft's DHCP services are used, the node operation of Windows systems can be configured as desired. Operating as a b-node is the default for Microsoft Windows systems as well as SAMBA. When NetBIOS is run over IP and Windows Internet Name Service (WINS) is used, the Microsoft Windows default changes to h-node. WINS is Microsoft's implementation of a NBNS. We will discuss WINS further as we get into the dilemma of trying to pass NetBIOS traffic over a router.

Routing with NetBIOS

When routers must be crossed, NetBIOS needs to be run on top of IPX or IP. Only when a NetBIOS packet is encapsulated within an IPX or IP packet can it traverse routers. This inadequacy can severely limit NetBIOS's ability to scale in larger networks. NetBIOS was originally designed to operate on single segment LANs with 200 or less nodes.

NetBIOS over IPX

IPX supports the encapsulation of NetBIOS messages. When a NetBIOS message is contained within an IPX packet, the type field is set to a hexadecimal value of 14 and uses a socket of 0455. When NetBIOS is encapsulated within IPX and it is passed across a router, it is commonly referred to as *type 20 propagation*. This is because the type field value of 14 converts to a decimal value of 20.

Figure 3.29 shows a NetBIOS name claim (registration) encapsulated with an IPX packet. The NetBIOS header follows the IPX header within the data portion of the frame. Our IPX header has not only identified our IPX network number (8023), but it has correctly flagged the packet type as being NetBIOS (Packet Type 20).

FIGURE 3.29:

A NetBIOS message encapsulated within an IPX packet

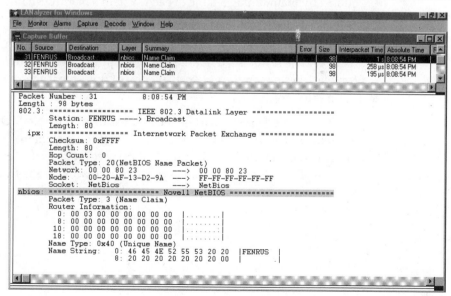

Our IPX header has also converted our NetBIOS broadcast to a standard network broadcast. This means that our NetBIOS message will now have to be processed by every system on the local network.

Now that our NetBIOS message is contained with an IPX packet, it is capable of traversing a maximum of eight hops. Most routers will require the additional step of enabling type 20 propagation over IPX on each port that must pass this packet. As the packet is passing the router, the hop value will be decreased by one, and the packet will be propagated until the hop count value reaches zero.

NetBIOS over IP

IP also supports the encapsulation of NetBIOS messages. UDP is used to support broadcast messages, while TCP takes care of unicast transmissions. Ports 137 through 139 are used for all communications. The NetBIOS header information immediately follows the TCP or UDP header within the frame.

With IP as the underlying transport, p-node systems can be supported for communications across a router. A good example of this type of functionality is Microsoft's WINS. Figure 3.30 shows an example of a WINS implementation. Each WINS server acts as an NBNS for each of the p-node systems on its local subnet by maintaining a table of each system's NetBIOS name. In addition to this, however, it also stores each system's IP address.

Each WINS server periodically updates the other WINS servers with a copy of its table. The result is a dynamic listing mapping NetBIOS names to IP addresses for every system on the network. A copy of the table is then stored on each of the three WINS systems.

When a p-node system needs the address of another NetBIOS system, it sends a discovery packet to its local WINS server. If the system in question happens to be located on a remote subnet, the WINS server returns the remote system's IP address. This allows the remote system to be discovered without propagating broadcast frames throughout the network. When h-nodes are used, the functionality is identical.

FIGURE 3.30:

Our example network with
three WINS servers, one
located on each subnet

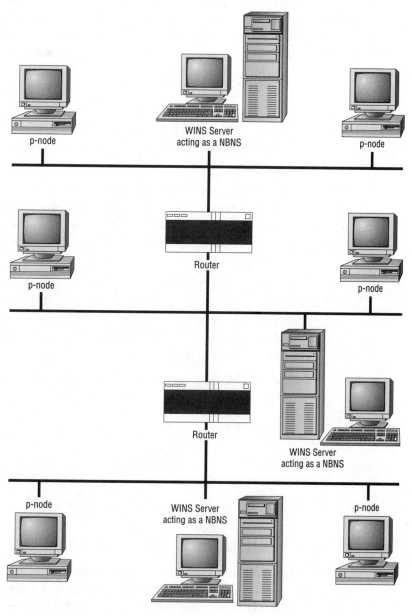

When NetBIOS is run over IP, a NetBIOS scope can be used to group systems together. A NetBIOS scope is a group of computers along which a registered NetBIOS name is known. A system's NetBIOS name must be unique within a specific scope. WINS server will propagate name information within a specific scope. A scope identifier is a unique character string by which the scope is known.

The scope identifier is very similar in functionality to the domain name used with DNS under IP. If the scope identifier is set to the same name as the IP domain name (for example, foobar.com), then the NetBIOS and IP fully qualified domain names will be identical.

As with DNS, this feature can also be used to increase the available name space. For example, a large company could use two scopes, one called corp.foobar.com and the other eng.foobar.com. This would double the available name space, as two systems would be allowed to share the same name provided they are part of two separate scopes.

If WINS is not used, Windows-based systems allow you to use a special file called LMHOSTS. This file is similar to the standard HOSTS file except it is referenced by NetBIOS over IP when it is looking for remote systems. Since NetBIOS-over-IP broadcasts are not propagated by routers, this is the only method available to our client to find remote systems if WINS is not used.

The format of this file is identical to the HOSTS file, except that it allows you to specify an entry as being a domain controller. A typical entry may appear as followed:

```
192.168.1.10        Fritz          PRE:domain_name
```

NetBIOS over IP is outlined in great detail in request for comments (RFCs) 1001 and 1002. RFC 1001 provides an overview of the functionality while 1002 offers greater detail.

Session and Transport Layer Support

NetBIOS supports three types of communication services: name, datagram, and session. The name services have been explained in detail. These services are used when a NetBIOS system needs to register or discover a name.

Datagram is NetBIOS's connectionless service for data delivery. While it is arguably faster than session, it provides no error correction and no guarantee of final delivery. If the receiving system is offline or busy, any data sent is lost. Datagram supports both unicast and broadcast-based communications.

Datagram supports the following four API calls:

Send   Send message using unicast communications

Send Broadcast   Send message using broadcast communications

Receive   Receive unicast message

Receive Broadcast   Receive broadcast message

Session is NetBIOS's connection-oriented data delivery service. It handshakes prior to transmitting data but provides no flow control. Session provides error correction but can only guarantee delivery on the first 64KB of a message. All session communications are unicast.

Session supports the following API calls:

Call   Initialize a session with a listening system

Listen   Accept sessions attempting a "call"

Hangup   Normal session termination

Send   Transmit one message up to 131,071 bytes in length

Receive   Receive message

Session Status   Report on all current sessions

NetBIOS Extended User Interface (NetBEUI)

Designed by IBM for LANManager in 1985, *NetBEUI* formalizes the transport framework left a bit vague by NetBIOS. NetBEUI specifies how the upper-layer software should send and receive messages when NetBIOS is the transport.

Like NetBIOS, NetBEUI is not routable. It is optimized for the same single-segment networks with 200 nodes or less. The current version of NetBEUI is 3.0, which fixes the problems encountered by earlier versions in the following ways:

- 254 sessions limit over a single NIC can be exceeded

- better memory optimization

- self tuning to optimize local communications

- slightly better WAN performance

Except for a few missing API calls, NetBEUI 3.0 is fully compatible with NetBIOS 3.0.

Despite the limitation that it's not a routable protocol, NetBEUI has been implemented on a number of platforms. It is supported by all of Microsoft's Windows operating systems, LANManager, IBM's OS/2 WARP, and Pathworks.

TIP   When installing NetBEUI on an NT system with multiple protocols, set NetBEUI first. This will cause NT to use raw NetBEUI for all local communications. Encapsulation will only be used when communicating with remote networks.

AppleTalk

AppleTalk was developed by Apple Computer in 1984 as a means of connecting their Mac and Apple II computers on an Ethernet network. AppleTalk should not be confused with LocalTalk, which was also developed by Apple but was a Data Link layer protocol designed to run on a proprietary bus topology (i.e. not Ethernet). The two protocols are separate. While the original AppleTalk included support for various flavors of Unix, DEC VAX, and even DOS systems, it was primarily used to provide connectivity for the Mac. With the introduction of AppleShare IP 5.0, Apple amended the AppleTalk protocol to version 2.2, adding improved server and volume reporting features.

In 1989 Apple released AppleTalk Phase II, version 2.2 of which is the current revision in use today. AFP 2.2 offers solutions to a number of problems that occurred with Phase I and also enhances AFP 2.1:

- It increases the number of supported hosts beyond 254 per network segment.

- It allows for more than one Zone Name to be used per network.

- It improves coexistence when other protocols are used on the same network.

- It includes support for ring topologies.

- It adds support for the TCP/IP suite of protocols.

- It offers enhanced server reporting methods.

Figure 3.31 is a graphic representation of the AppleTalk protocol suite and how it compares to the OSI model.

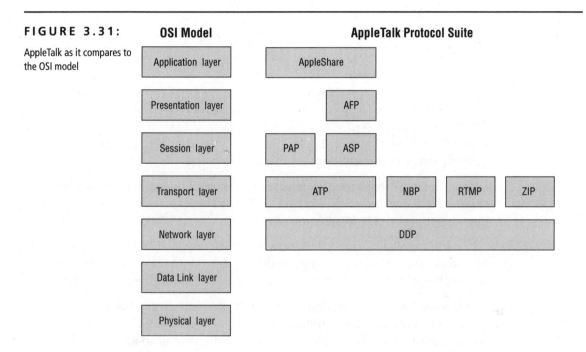

FIGURE 3.31:

AppleTalk as it compares to the OSI model

Address Space

AppleTalk Phase II supports the use of extended network numbers. Numbers can range from 1 through 65,279. Network addresses are assigned in ranges, so a starting and stopping value must be specified. AppleTalk hosts are dynamically assigned a node address within the specified range. Valid node addresses are 1 through 254. Table 3.11 shows some potential numbering schemes:

TABLE 3.11: AppleTalk Potential Numbering Ranges

Network Range	First Node Addresses	Last Node Address	Number of Hosts Supported
1 - 1	1.1	1.254	254
200 - 201	200.1	201.254	508
65100 - 65200	65100.1	65200.254	50,800

AppleTalk, unlike IP, does not use address classes or subnet masks. This gives the administrator the freedom to adjust the network range values as required for a growing network. If you need to support an additional 254 hosts, simply increase the network range. AppleTalk nodes will automatically (after rebooting) take advantage of the additional address space.

There are two categories of AppleTalk nodes, seeding and nonseeding. Seeding systems have their network range preconfigured and are responsible for advertising this network range to other systems.

Nonseeding systems have their network range set to 0-0, which tells them to discover the real network range during startup. Once the network range is known, the system will attempt to register a valid node address within the range.

This setup has a few major advantages. The first is that only one system (usually a router) needs to be configured with the network range. This saves the administrator a lot of leg work, as each system does not need to be touched prior to communicating on the network. Because a majority of the users on the system can learn their address dynamically, administration is minimized.

AppleTalk has shortened the discovery process by allowing a nonseeding host to remember its last node address. When the system initializes, it first ensures that the network range has not changed. If it has not (which is usually the case), it tries to use its old node address. If it receives a challenge from another node using this address it will then go back through the discovery process to find a free address.

The big drawback to AppleTalk addressing is that it does not accept changes very easily. If a network address range is changed, other systems on the network will challenge this new address stating that the old range is the correct one. It is for this reason that *all* AppleTalk devices (hosts, servers, printers, etc.) must be shut down while the change takes place. Once the devices power up they will accept the new address range and all will be happy.

Needless to say this does not bode well for large environments. If you have 1000 or more AppleTalk hosts it may be nearly impossible to shut down every system. A coauthor of this book was once in a situation where his team needed to make AppleTalk network changes on a 250-node network. The changes had to be completed by the end of the weekend. While they thought they had powered down every AppleTalk device within the building, it became apparent that they had not. The new network ranges were not being accepted. A walk through the building confirmed that there were some inaccessible areas, which probably had AppleTalk devices. The team did, however, have access to all the hub closets and quickly identified which hub ports were still active. The solution? They unplugged every connection that still had a link light. This disconnected the remaining AppleTalk systems from the network, which allowed them to success-fully make their changes. On Monday morning when they again had access to these locked areas, they simply shut down the remaining systems and recon-nected them back into the network.

Local Frame Delivery

Just like the other protocols we have discussed, AppleTalk uses a network card's MAC address when delivering frames to systems located on the same network range. AppleTalk uses the AppleTalk Address Resolution Protocol (AARP) to dis-cover these addresses.

AARP functions in the same fashion as IP's ARP protocol. AARP will send out a network broadcast containing the node address of the system it needs to send information to. When the system replies, the value in the Ethernet source address field can now be used for local delivery.

AARP will cache this information in its Address Mapping Table (AMT). The AMT serves the same purpose as IP's ARP cache, mapping MAC addresses to node addresses. This allows the system to reference the table instead of issuing another AARP when it again needs to send this system data.

Zone Names

Zone names allow for the assignment of a useful name to a specified network range. Zone assignments are made as part of the seeding system's configuration. Every AppleTalk network range must be assigned at least one zone name, which is known as the *primary zone*. Secondary zones may be assigned to the network range as required.

Through the use of zones, resources can be logically grouped for easier access. For example, let's assume that we have a large network with many remote sites. The office located in Boston, MA, could be assigned the primary zone name Boston. If a user is looking for a network resource (server, printer, etc.) located at the Boston office, they can logically assume that they need to look in the Boston zone.

Secondary zones could also be assigned to provide even greater resolution. For example, let's assume we create secondary zones under Boston called HR, Sales, and Dilbert. If a Human Resources person needs to print a document, they can probably assume that the closest printer to their location is located in the HR zone. Sales people's resources could be located in the Sales zone and upper management would keep their resources in the Dilbert zone (don't worry, they probably wouldn't get it anyway).

The Zone Information Protocol (ZIP) is used when a network address needs to be mapped to a zone name. The Name Binding Protocol (NBP) is used when a zone name must be mapped to a network address. It is also used to translate host names into node addresses.

Network Layer Services

Network layer services are provided by the Datagram Delivery Protocol (DDP). DDP is similar to IPX in that it is the foundation on which all AppleTalk communications travel. The DDP header appears at the front of the data portion of the frame.

DDP is a connectionless protocol, which performs no handshaking and requires no acknowledgments. Like IPX, it is happy to deliver information, but it makes no guarantee that it will arrive at its final destination. These responsibilities are left to the upper layers.

DDP does not support packet sequencing. As such it can make no guarantee that frames will be delivered in order. Again, this is left to the upper-layer protocols.

AppleTalk Routing

AppleTalk supports static and only a single dynamic routing protocol. The Routing Table Maintenance Protocol (RTMP) is a distance-vector protocol used to maintain the network address tables. Figure 3.32 is a packet decoding of an RTMP frame.

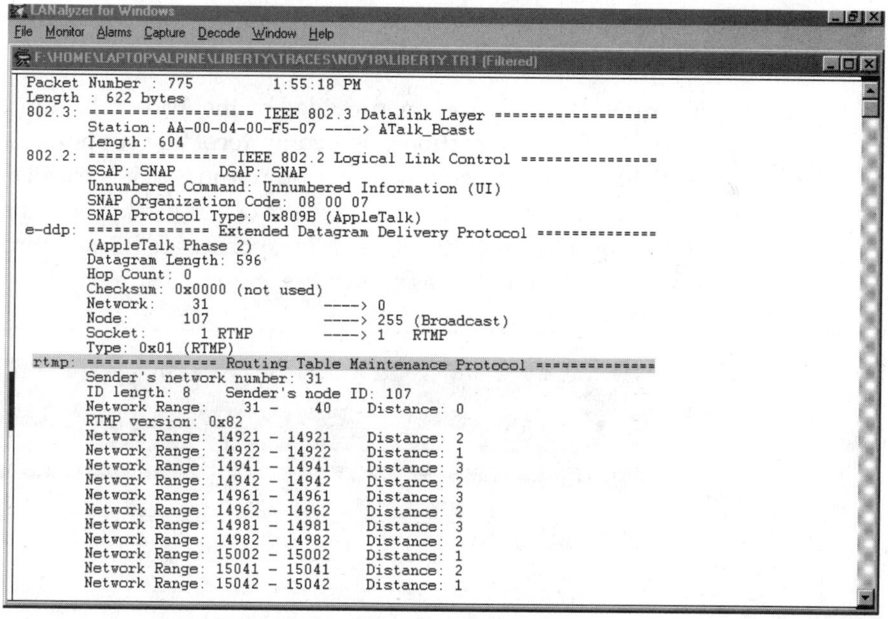

FIGURE 3.32:

A router using RTMP to broadcast its known routes

```
LANalyzer for Windows                                                    _ 8 X
File  Monitor  Alarms  Capture  Decode  Window  Help
F:\HOME\LAPTOP\ALPINE\LIBERTY\TRACES\NOV18\LIBERTY.TR1 [Filtered]        _ □ X
Packet Number : 775          1:55:18 PM
Length : 622 bytes
802.3: =================== IEEE 802.3 Datalink Layer ==================
       Station: AA-00-04-00-F5-07 ----> ATalk_Bcast
       Length: 604
802.2: ================= IEEE 802.2 Logical Link Control ================
       SSAP: SNAP     DSAP: SNAP
       Unnumbered Command: Unnumbered Information (UI)
       SNAP Organization Code: 08 00 07
       SNAP Protocol Type: 0x809B (AppleTalk)
e-ddp: ============== Extended Datagram Delivery Protocol =============
       (AppleTalk Phase 2)
       Datagram Length: 596
       Hop Count: 0
       Checksum: 0x0000 (not used)
       Network:      31        ----> 0
       Node:        107        ----> 255 (Broadcast)
       Socket:        1 RTMP   ----> 1    RTMP
       Type: 0x01 (RTMP)
rtmp:  ============== Routing Table Maintenance Protocol ==============
       Sender's network number: 31
       ID length: 8    Sender's node ID: 107
       Network Range:    31 -    40    Distance: 0
       RTMP version: 0x82
       Network Range: 14921 - 14921    Distance: 2
       Network Range: 14922 - 14922    Distance: 1
       Network Range: 14941 - 14941    Distance: 3
       Network Range: 14942 - 14942    Distance: 2
       Network Range: 14961 - 14961    Distance: 3
       Network Range: 14962 - 14962    Distance: 2
       Network Range: 14981 - 14981    Distance: 3
       Network Range: 14982 - 14982    Distance: 2
       Network Range: 15002 - 15002    Distance: 1
       Network Range: 15041 - 15041    Distance: 2
       Network Range: 15042 - 15042    Distance: 1
```

Notice the RTMP information listed at the bottom of the screen. It contains the telltale signs of a router handing out secondhand information and thus using a distance-vector protocol. In a link-state routing protocol, we would not require a "distance" value, since link-state routers only report firsthand information.

As a distance-vector routing protocol, RTMP is susceptible to all the previously mentioned problems encountered when using secondhand routing information. The only difference is that RTMP broadcast routing updates every 30 seconds instead of once per minute. While this gives it a faster convergence time, it also makes it twice as noisy as most distance-vector routing protocols.

At the time of this writing, Apple has not announced any plans to update AppleTalk to include link-state routing.

Transport and Session Layer Services

AppleTalk uses a number of different protocols to maintain transport and session communications. The most important is the AppleTalk Transaction Protocol, which is used by all file and print sharing.

AppleTalk Transaction Protocol

Transport layer services are provided by the AppleTalk Transaction Protocol (ATP). ATP is a connection-oriented protocol that supports packet sequencing. ATP differs from most transport protocols in that it is based on transactions, not on byte streams. A transaction consists of a request by a client followed by a response by a server. Requests and responses are tracked through the use of a transaction ID number, as shown in Figure 3.33.

FIGURE 3.33:

A packet decoding of an ATP frame

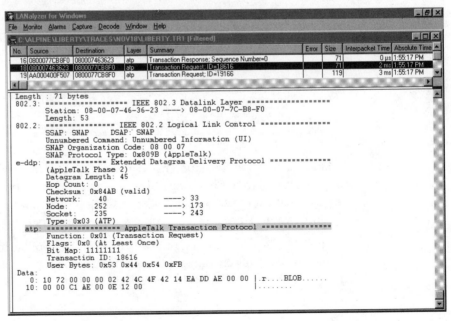

ATP also takes care of packet fragmentation and reassembly. In order to ensure that each transaction can be tracked properly, messages are limited to eight frames. Each frame can contain no more than 578 bytes of data. This means the maximum frame size with header information is limited to 625 bytes.

AppleTalk Session Protocol

The AppleTalk Session Protocol (ASP) is a client of ATP and works with it to provide connectivity for file share access. As a Session layer protocol, it is responsible for negotiating a connection when a client wishes to access files on a server. This is not to say that it takes care of authentication. It is simply responsible for establishing the connection between the two systems. The upper layers are actually responsible for the authentication process.

ASP is also responsible for maintaining the connection once it is established. It makes sure that queries and command sets are in an acceptable format for the upper layer service. ASP is also responsible for properly terminating a connection when the session is complete.

Printer Access Protocol

The Printer Access Protocol (PAP) performs services identical to those of ASP, except that it is responsible for printer access. It takes care of sessions between printers located directly in the network as well as printers that are being shared by host systems.

Upper Layer Services

AppleTalk supports two upper layer services: the AppleTalk Filing Protocol, which takes care of file requests on both clients and servers; and AppleShare, which provides remote file and printer services to network clients.

AppleTalk Filing Protocol

The AppleTalk Filing Protocol (AFP) provides transparent access to both local and remote file systems. It is designed to make dealing with remote file systems just as easy as dealing with the files on the local drive. AFP also takes care of authentication when remote file systems are requested.

When a file access command is issued, AFP determines if the request involves local or remote file access. If the access is local, the request is passed along to the local operating system (usually some version of MacOS System 7; common today are versions 7.5.5, 7.6.1, and 8.*x*, with 7.5.5 being the predominant workstation OS). If remote file access is requested, AFP passes the request down through ASP and across the network to the server. AFP on the server accepts the request (if authentication is accepted) and passes it along to AppleShare.

If the remote file system is not compatible (System 7 and later versions use a special file system that requires a resource fork file and a data fork file for each piece of information; though Apple has updated HFS to HFS+, there has been no change to the fork/data arrangement), AFP takes care of translating the two file formats if it can. AFP then takes care of returning the information to the requesting client.

With the advent of AppleShare IP 5.0 and the soon-to-be-released 6.0, there have been some modifications to the AFP specification to allow for TCP/IP transactions, primarily in enhanced or, in one case, added server reporting. The additional information will enhance your troubleshooting capabilities in an AppleTalk-based networking environment.

Server Polling   Clients that can retrieve more detailed information about a server on a network will work well with AFP 2.*x* operations (not to worry, this includes just about any MacOS-compatible application there is). The enhancements allow for greater access and control over remote systems/users/nodes and the like.

When the client makes a connection to a server that is running AppleShare IP (ASIP) it requests specific information about that server. The client uses this information to maintain, regain, and modify the connection to the server. The data returned from the polled server is as follows:

- Machine type

- AFP versions

- UAM strings (User Authentication Method)

- Volume icon and mask (optional; an offset of 0 indicates no icon/mask, and default icons will be supplied by the workstation)

- Flags word

- Padded server name (to an even boundry)

- Server signature (optional)

- IP numbers (optional; required for AFP over TCP)

NOTE   The server can pack the fields in any order it chooses, with the exception of the signature field, which always follows the Flags field. Make no assumptions and you will make fewer networking mistakes.

This simple enhancement to AFP makes possible many of the TCP/IP-related activities that are provided by ASIP 5.0. Let's look at the other major revision that appears in AFP 2.2.

Remote Volumes   AFP 2.2 can now request extensive information from remote volumes. The important data returned by the request are as follows (returned values are expressed in a bitmap format):

- Volume attributes

- Volume signature

- Creation date

- Modification date

- Backup date

- Volume ID

- Bytes free

- Bytes total

- Volume name

- Extended bytes free

- Extended bytes total

The last two bits in the bitmap allow for volumes larger than 4 gigabytes, a great boon as large servers typically use volumes of much greater capacity.

AppleShare IP

AppleShare IP is the roof that sits on top of the AppleTalk protocol suite. It is the application that coordinates Internet, file, mail, and printer access through the lower layers. AppleShare has four major components—AppleShare Web & File Server, AppleShare Print Server, AppleShare Mail Server, and COPSTalk.

AppleShare Web & File Server works with AFP and/or TCP/IP to allow users to remotely access and save their files in a LAN, WAN, WAIS, or via the Internet. AppleShare IP is responsible for registering users and mapping them to their appropriate volumes and directories.

AppleShare Print Server works with NBP and PAP to allow users to remotely access printers. When a printer is selected, NBP is used to find the remote printer's node address and PAP is used to send it data. AppleShare is responsible for spooling the print job prior to sending it to the printer. AppleShare uses the PostScript command set when communicating with a printer, so there is no native support for non-PostScript printers.

AppleShare Mail Server is a standards-based e-mail server. It supports SMTP, POP3, IMAP, APOP, PASS, Finger, and Notify Mail, making it an excellent choice for a multiplatform mail server. The server also supports network aliases which allow users to represent themselves using an unrestricted name for LAN access and a username-type alias for e-mail services outside the LAN. This allows for uncomplicated support across all platforms, including Unix.

Apple has licensed COPSTalk from COPS, Inc., an AppleShare client for Windows 95/98 and NT 4.0 that allows a network client using a DOS-based file system to access and exchange files with a Macintosh server. AppleShare takes care of all the conversion requirements between the two dissimilar file systems, while COPSTalk provides an easy-to-use interface familiar to Windows users.

Summary

This completes our discussion of the major protocol suites. Hopefully at this point your eyes are not too bloodshot; there is a lot of information to digest in this chapter. Our focus here was on how the various protocols define the details of their tasks. This discussion was, by necessity, somewhat abstract and condensed. If you prefer a more hands-on approach, feel free to try out protocol configuration on one or more operating systems, as discussed in later chapters, and then refer back to this chapter as needed.

In the next chapter we will look at the most common networking standard in use today: Ethernet. As we'll discuss, Ethernet is not tied to any one protocol, and in fact can carry multiple procotols on a network simultaneously.

CHAPTER

FOUR

Ethernet Overview

- The IEEE 802.*x* standards

- How CSMA/CD works

- Thicknet and thinnet coax cable

- Unshielded twisted-pair (UTP) cable

- Advantages and disadvantages of Ethernet

In Chapter 1 we noted that Ethernet is still the most common type of network in use today. Chapter 6 will continue our discussion of Ethernet, looking at its various "flavors" in the context of networking topologies. In this chapter, we'll first look at the IEEE 802.*x* standards that defined Ethernet. Then we'll move on to a discussion of CSMA/CD (carrier sense multiple access with collision detection), Ethernet's solution to the problem of moving data around on networks that have shared transmission media—what it is and how it works in both transmitting and receiving modes.

Note that by gaining an understanding of how CSMA/CD works, you'll be better equipped to troubleshoot Ethernet network communications problems and better able to determine when it's time to subdivide your network into more networks for increased performance.

Following our discussion of CSMA/CD, we'll look at both the coax (thin and thicknet) and UTP (unshielded twisted-pair) cabling systems used with Ethernet, and compare the benefits and drawbacks of each.

Wrapping up the chapter, we'll review the main advantages and disadvantages of using Ethernet as a networking type.

The IEEE 802.*x* Standards

In Chapter 2, we looked at the seven-layer reference model devised by the ISO (International Standards Organization), to which almost all commercial networking hardware and software systems adhere.

Another standards body, the IEEE (Institute of Electrical and Electronic Engineers), first met in February 1980 (incidentally, the year and month numbers are where the number 802 was taken from) to further specify how networking operations should operate at the lower levels of the OSI model.

What the 802 Project came up with was a total of 12 standards covering network interface cards, network topologies, and connection types. Some of the more significant standards put forward include:

> **802.2:**   This standard divided the OSI model's Data Link layer (DLC) into two sublayers: the Logical Link Control (LLC) layer and the Media Access Control (MAC) layer.

802.3: This standard defined Ethernet's method of allowing multiple stations to share common sections of network transmission media. This standard is called carrier sense multiple access with collision detection (CSMA/CD), and we'll be looking at it in more detail in the following section of this chapter. The original 802.3 standard specifies a 10Mbps transmission speed. As computers have gotten faster, the need has arisen for faster network technologies. The 802.3u specification defines 100Mbps Ethernet, and the new 802.3z standard will define 1Gbps Ethernet. These and other Ethernet flavors are described in Chapter 6.

802.5: This standard defined Token Ring's method of handling shared media, which we'll delve into in the next chapter.

Other standards defined in this series include 10Base2, 10BaseT, Token Bus, and FDDI (Fiber Distributed Digital Interface).

As we mentioned in Chapter 1, for practical reasons most networks rely on common sections of cable to interconnect multiple stations. Because there are several stations sharing the same transmission media, a system needed to be devised to determine how these stations could effectively take turns transmitting and receiving on the same lengths of cable. Part of the answer lies in the concept of *frames*, the basic units of information transmitted on an Ethernet network. Let's quickly summarize what a frame consists of.

Ethernet Frames

An Ethernet frame is a set of digital pulses (bits) transmitted onto the transmission media in order to convey information. An Ethernet frame can be anywhere from 64 to 1518 bytes in size and is organized into four sections: the preamble, the header, the data, and the frame check sequence (FCS).

Preamble

A *preamble* is a defined series of communication pulses that tells all receiving stations, "Get ready—I've got something to say." The standard preamble is eight bytes long.

NOTE   Because the preamble is considered part of the communication process and not part of the actual information being transferred, it is not usually included when measuring a frame's size.

Header

A *header* always contains information about who sent the frame and where they are trying to send it. It may also contain other information, such as how many bytes the frame contains; this is referred to as the *length field* and is used for error correction. If the receiving station measures the frame to be a different size than indicated in the length field, it asks the transmitting system to send a new frame. If the length field is not used, the header may instead contain a *type field* that describes what type of Ethernet frame it is.

The header size is always 14 bytes.

In Chapter 6 we'll take a closer look at how the frame header helps data get where it's going.

Data

The *data* section of the frame contains the actual data the station needs to transmit. It can be anywhere from 46 to 1500 bytes in size. If a station has more than 1500 bytes of information to transfer, it will break up the information over multiple frames and identify the proper order by using sequence numbers. Sequence numbers identify the order in which the destination system should reassemble the data. If the frame does not have 46 bytes of information to convey, the station pads the end of this section by filling it in with ones (remember that digital connections use binary numbers). Depending on the frame type, this section may also contain additional information describing what protocol or method of communication the systems are using.

NOTE   Protocols are covered in detail in Chapters 2 and 3.

Frame Check Sequence (FCS)

The *frame check sequence* is used to ensure that the data received is actually the data sent. The transmitting system processes the FCS portion of the frame through an algorithm called a *cyclic redundancy check,* or *CRC*. This CRC takes the values of the fields described above and creates a 4-byte number. When the destination system receives the frame, it runs the same CRC and compares it to the value within this field. If the destination system finds a match, it assumes the frame is free from errors and processes the information. If the comparison fails, the destination station assumes that something happened to the frame in its travels and requests that another copy of the frame be sent by the transmitting system.

Intro to CSMA/CD

Again, the basic problem Ethernet was designed to solve is how stations on a network can take turns transmitting and receiving on the same lengths of cable. Ethernet's solution is called *CSMA/CD (carrier sense multiple access with collision detection)*, and it essentially combines two strategies: First, a station listens for an opportunity to begin transmitting; then, during transmission, it listens for other stations attempting a transmission at the same time. If there are any, it backs off for a random period of time before retrying.

The random period of time helps prevent repeated simultaneous attempts by multiple stations to transmit. When two or more stations attempt to transmit at the same time, it's called a collision.

Lets see now how CSMA/CD works in greater detail.

How CSMA/CD Works: Transmitting

When a station on an Ethernet network determines that it needs to transmit data, the data is handed down through a series of software processes (corresponding to the OSI layers), which prepare it for transmission. Data is broken up into packets (according to the protocol being used), and then into frames. These frames are queued for transmission. At this point, the Ethernet transceiver (which is typically part of the network adapter card) begins a series of steps intended to successfully transmit each frame to its intended recipient.

Figure 4.1 is a flowchart illustrating the transmission process. Let's walk through the steps.

Before transmitting, the transceiver listens on the transmission medium (that is, the cable) for a carrier signal, which would indicate that the medium is not currently being used. If the carrier is sensed, transmission begins; otherwise the transceiver continues listening for an opportunity to transmit.

FIGURE 4.1:

The CSMA/CD logic for transmitting a frame

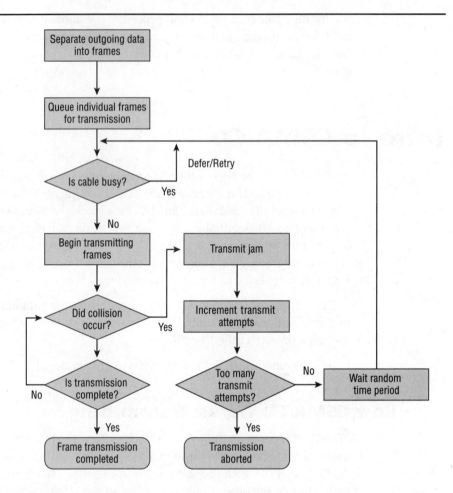

Even though all stations (transceivers) on the segment are listening, it is possible that two or more of them may have frames to transmit and, sensing the carrier, simultaneously begin transmitting. Actually, simultaneous transmissions over the same line are not possible and are referred to as a *collision*.

For this reason, once a frame transmission begins, the station's transceiver continues monitoring the line in order to detect whether a collision occurs before it has finished transmitting.

If a collision does occur, all stations transmitting should sense this and stop. A special "jam" signal is transmitted, and all stations involved in the collision begin "evasive action." The evasive action consists of waiting a random period of time before again listening and attempting to transmit. The random period of time (each transceiver arriving at its own random amount) helps decrease the likelihood of a repeat collision, although this isn't guaranteed. If another collision does occur, the stations will once more each wait another (and usually longer) random time period before once more attempting to transmit.

Each time a transceiver attempts transmission, it increments an internal transmission counter. If this counter reaches a preset maximum retries value, the transmission will be aborted, and a transmission error will be propagated back up through the transmission layers where it may either result in another attempt at transmission or be brought eventually to the attention of the Application layer (and probably the user). Most often what happens is that a transmission finally will succeed after repeated tries, but the user may still notice a slowed or sluggish response time.

This listen-and-retry strategy works quite well—at first. As the number of stations on the network segment increases, so does the likelihood of collisions. Once a collision does occur, it can also increase the chances of further collisions because in the intervening time period more stations will now have data to transmit, which causes a backlog of transmissions. This is why Ethernet segments sometimes become noticeably sluggish long before their maximum throughput rate has been reached.

The general solution to excess frame collisions and most other types of throughput problems on an Ethernet segment is to divide the segment. We'll discuss this more in coming chapters, particularly in Chapter 9, where we'll be covering the various types of hardware used to separate and more efficiently rejoin multiple network segments.

Now, let's look at how CSMA works in receiving mode.

How CSMA/CD Works: Receiving

We've seen how the transmitting process works. Recall that when a frame is transmitted, it is sent throughout the local segment. Each station on the segment sees every frame on the wire, regardless of which station the frame is addressed to.

Each station on the segment must view incoming frames and check for fragments. A *fragment*, or partial frame, is an indication of a collision or a faulty transmission for some other reason. Each station also checks the MAC address to see whether it is the intended recipient of the frame. If so, it processes the packet.

Let's look at these steps in a more detailed fashion, following the flowchart in Figure 4.2.

FIGURE 4.2:

CSMA/CD logic in receiving mode

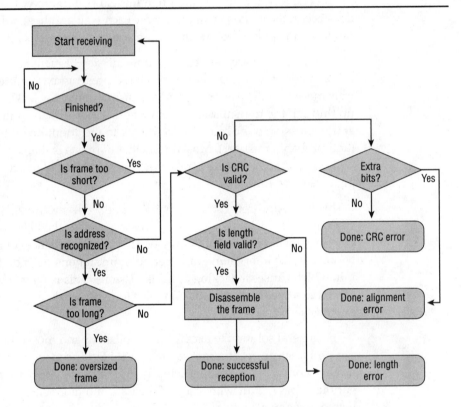

As we've already alluded to, the first step in receiving a frame is to determine whether the frame is long enough to be valid. Valid Ethernet frames must have a minimum of 64 bytes. If a frame is shorter than this, it is assumed to be a fragment caused by a collision and is not processed further. If the frame passes the minimum length test, the frame's MAC address is checked. The frame is processed further if the MAC address matches that of the listening station, or if it is either a broadcast transmission (sent to all stations on the segment) or a multicast transmission (sent to all devices in a particular category).

NOTE   Keep in mind that a station can actually have more than one MAC address if it has multiple network adapters installed.

The next step the station must take is to verify that the frame is properly formed. It does this through a series of checks of various elements in the frame. Ethernet frame length, first of all, cannot exceed 1518 bytes, so if the frame exceeds this it is a considered a faulty frame. Next, the station needs to verify that the information in the frame matches what was sent. It does this by running the frame's bits through a CRC formula and comparing the resulting CRC value with the CRC value placed in the frame by the transmitting station.

Next, the receiving station checks to see whether the frame contains extra bits at the end. Since frames are composed of bytes, a frame that does not have an even multiple of eight bits will fail this check. This check is called a byte alignment test.

If a frame passes all these tests—i.e., it is not too short, nor too long, nor misaligned, nor containing faulty data (determined via the CRC check)—it is considered a valid, well-formed frame. At this point, the frame's data would be copied to a frame buffer or otherwise temporarily saved in order to be recombined with the data from other incoming frames. Then it would be forwarded up the networking software layers (as the layers are implemented in the network driver and one or more protocol drivers), where additional processing would be done, such as converting the frames back into one or more packets and then into the larger chunks of the original data. Finally, if the higher levels do not detect any higher-level errors (protocol-specific errors, for example), the incoming data is delivered to the Application layer. Note that in some cases, depending on the protocol being used, an error found at the Data Link layer (for example) might result in a transmission back to the sending station, requesting a retransmission of that packet.

Ethernet Cabling Options

Now that we've seen how Ethernet frames are sent and received, let's look at the types of cabling used to connect Ethernet stations to form network segments. The two main categories used are coaxial cable and unshielded twisted-pair (UTP) cable. We'll have more to say about these and other cable types in Chapter 7, so for now we'll limit our remarks to general observations about how these cable types are used in Ethernet networks.

Thin and Thick Coax

Thin and thick Ethernet cable, sometimes also called *thinnet* and *thicknet* cable, respectively, are both types of coaxial cable. *Coaxial cable*, or *coax*, is made up of a solid or stranded inner conductor, surrounded by insulation, then an outer wire braid or foil, which is in turn covered by vinyl insulation. The inner conductor is used to convey a signal, while the outer wire braid or foil's purpose is to help shield the inner conductor from interference, and to provide an electrical ground. (Glance ahead to Figure 7.6 for an illustration of thinnet coaxial cable.)

Thinnet cable is about 0.25" in diameter, quite flexible, and relatively easy to work with. Thicknet cable, on the other hand, is about 0.5" in diameter and is quite difficult to work with—its stiffness makes it awkward to route around corners, for example.

The key point about coax to remember for this chapter is that stations interconnected using coax are connected in a bus style, which means each station is connected to the next one in turn. Like most things, this has a good side and a bad side. On the good side, coax (thinnet in particular) can be quite easy and inexpensive to use to connect several stations, if the stations to be connected are positioned so that running a cable from one to the next is practical. On the bad side, connecting several stations together like Christmas-tree lights has the very undesirable drawback of usually causing all stations on the segment to lose their network connection when the connection is broken anywhere along the line.

In some cases, if the break occurs partway down a cable length, the stations that are still physically connected to the server may continue working. This isn't dependable, though, because when a cable breaks, the *terminator* at the far end of the cable length is now disconnected, which means the remaining stations attached to the server on this segment are at least likely to be subject to network errors due to reflected signal transmissions along the cable. The terminator, or terminating resistor, which is normally attached at both ends of each coax segment, plays the important role of absorbing any excess signal once it has reached the end of the cable, preventing it from being reflected back. A reflected signal, remember, is going to produce extra unwanted frames, which are likely to cause all sorts of errors and instability in those remaining stations.

Figure 4.3 shows a typical coaxial Ethernet segment. Note that although thicknet typically has an obvious backbone look to it, with individual stations connecting to it with short lengths of cable, thinnet mirrors this connection style in miniature, with each station's network adapter connecting to the thinnet cable via a very short gadget called a *T-connector*.

FIGURE 4.3:

A coaxial Ethernet segment
(bus topology)

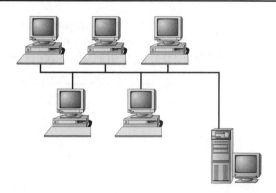

One drawback to using coax is that no new higher-speed Ethernet technologies have come out that run on coax. Thus, if you stick with using coax, you're limited to the 10Mbps speed that is currently supported. It is likely that greater bandwidth could be achieved using coax; however, it is unclear at this point whether the industry will move in that direction any time soon.

Unshielded Twisted-Pair (UTP)

The other, and currently more popular, type of cable used in Ethernet networks is *UTP* cable. (There is also shielded twisted-pair, but it isn't used as much.) The primary point I wish to make about UTP cable in this chapter is that it uses a different connection pattern than coax—instead of using a bus, it connects clusters of stations together in a star formation, or like spokes radiating from a wheel. The "hub" of each wheel is a multiport box called, fittingly enough, a *hub*. And multiple hubs can usually be connected one to the next, if desired, allowing multiple hubs to form part of a single network segment.

A significant advantage over thinnet and thicknet is that UTP reduces the point of failure to what is most often a single station (if the cable breaks between the hub and that station). If the cable between the hub and the server breaks (or if the hub itself fails), all stations connected to that hub will lose their connection. Although this would lead to a significant loss of productivity, it has some diagnostic value; it points to the cable segment running between the hub and server as being at fault. A different hub can be swapped in temporarily to rule out the possibility of the hub itself having a problem.

Figure 4.4 shows a typical Ethernet cable using UTP, with a second hub connecting off the first hub. A better approach (in terms of reducing network traffic) is depicted in Figure 4.5, where each of the two hubs is connected back to the network server directly, each to a different network adapter. This causes traffic on one segment to be relayed (or routed) to the other segment only when the destination address of such traffic refers to the other segment.

FIGURE 4.4:

Two hubs interconnected to form one segment

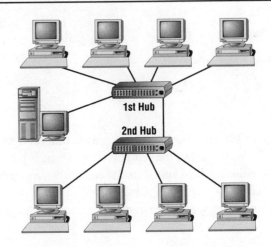

FIGURE 4.5:

Two Ethernet segments connected to a single server

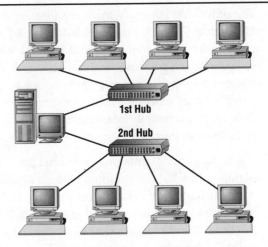

This is perhaps the simplest form of network segmentation to improve performance. If the two segments in fact never needed to communicate with each other, an even more efficient result could be achieved by connecting each segment to a different server (effectively forming two separate networks).

Advantages and Disadvantages of Ethernet

Chapter 6 will continue our look at the nuts and bolts of Ethernet technologies, exploring in particular the different varieties defined by 802.3 specifications. For now, we'll conclude our overview by considering the advantages and disadvantages of Ethernet.

Widespread use: Ethernet has a lot going for it, but perhaps above all else is the fact that it is used in the majority of networks currently in existence, and therefore is a very proven and familiar set of technologies.

Low cost: Then too, Ethernet adapters, hubs, and related devices are very economical (and growing less expensive all the time). Currently 100BaseT (100Mb Ethernet) cards are at the price standard 10BaseT cards were at just a few years ago. Perhaps in a few more years we'll be able to make a similar statement about 1Gb. In any case, Ethernet hardware is already ubiquitous and inexpensive, and provided you stick to dependable manufacturers, there are really no surprises with Ethernet—unless of course you really expect to achieve full theoretical bandwidth on each of your network segments. (More on that when we look at the disadvantages.)

Flexible wiring options: Another advantage is the choice of wiring configurations—for quick and simple networks, thinnet coax may fit the bill. For added flexibility and greater dependability, there's UTP and hubs.

Diagnostic ease: A related advantage, too, is the ease of tracking down cable problems when using UTP cable and hubs. True, long cable runs still can be a pain to replace, but when one or more stations goes down, you immediately have important clues as to which length of cable is faulty (and as we said earlier, swapping in a different hub easily shows whether the hub itself is at fault).

Continuing technological development: Finally, perhaps because Ethernet is already very widely used, it seems to be where the focus is for new higher bandwidth technologies—in particular, the technologies that have the greatest likelihood of becoming mainstream any time soon. In comparison to ATM (asynchronous transfer mode), which has lots of promise but not yet a significantly sized installed base, Ethernet benefits by its adherence to the OSI layers, which makes integrating it with other existing networking technology easier. Duplex 100BaseT (which is simply 100Mb simultaneously in two directions) has been available now for more than a year, and at the time of this writing, the standard for 1Gb Ethernet is right on the verge of being released.

Given Ethernet's popularity, various connection options, and the availability of a wide variety of inexpensive adapter cards and hubs, there don't seem to be many disadvantages. But there are a few we should highlight:

Limited packet size: In comparison with Token Ring (which we'll look at next, in Chapter 5), Ethernet is handicapped by a smaller maximum packet size (which means more work to send the same amount of data, which means less efficiency, which means slower throughput).

Poor scalability: Another disadvantage to Ethernet is that it has a problem with scaling gracefully as you exceed about 50% bandwidth utilization. This number will vary somewhat because of different usage patterns in individual networks, but the fact remains that it is difficult to ever reach the theoretical upper bandwidth limit (of 10Mbps or 100Mbps, depending on your equipment), because long before you reach that point, the number of stations on the network segment will tend to drag down the performance. Of course, if your network consists of only two stations, you can ignore this limitation, but in most real networks, the Ethernet scalability factor is something to be considered. In practical terms, this may simply mean that you need to plan on further segmenting your networks whenever you see they're reaching approximately 50% bandwidth utilization on a regular basis.

Difficult cable troubleshooting: The difficulty of troubleshooting thick and thin coax problems can also be considered a disadvantage of Ethernet. However, the availability of UTP as an alternative mitigates this disadvantage. In a large network that is already using thick and/or thin coax, replacing a lot of cable at once is, of course, impractical; administrators and users must live with this scenario for the time being. Unless a new higher-speed standard for Ethernet on coax appears, it is difficult to ignore the speed benefit UTP has over coax when it is used for 100BaseT networking.

Summary

In this chapter we've taken a first look at Ethernet technology and its pros and cons. We started out looking at the IEEE 802 Project, noting that 802.3 in particular is what defined the CSMA/CD approach used in all Ethernet networks to achieve shared usage of network media by multiple interconnected stations.

We looked at thicknet and thinnet coax cable as they are used in Ethernet networks, and observed that while thinnet is easy to use for connecting several stations in a row, it takes a back seat now to the other type of Ethernet cabling—UTP—because of its greater susceptibility to catastrophic cable failure and the greater difficulty in determining where cable breaks or faults have occurred. Unfortunately, coax Ethernet is also still limited to 10Mbps speeds, although this is still quite adequate for smaller networks or networks that need to be put up quickly.

In a nutshell, Ethernet is a proven technology, relatively inexpensive, widely used, relatively easy to implement, and with well-documented and well-adhered-to standards.

In the next chapter, we'll look at the second most common network type, Token Ring. In the last several years, Token Ring's rather elegant token-passing scheme has been gaining more support.

As we'll also see in the next chapter, Token Ring is used in some of the fastest networks available (using fiber), and has certain advantages which make it better optimized to run at higher speeds and with greater throughput.

CHAPTER

FIVE

Token Ring Overview

- Token Ring operation and topology

- Token Ring hardware: network adapters, cabling, multi-station access units (MSAUs), and other devices

- Functional roles of Token Ring stations: active monitor, standby monitor, ring parameter server, ring error monitor, and configuration report server

- Token Ring processes: station initialization, contention monitoring, ring polling, ring purging, and beaconing

- Advantages and disadvantages of Token Ring

In the last chapter, we briefly discussed the IEEE 802 Project, which produced a set of standards defining implementation details for the lower levels of the OSI networking model. These standards cover network interface cards, network topologies, and connection types. In this chapter we will be looking exclusively at the Token Ring networking model, initially developed by IBM and further standardized by the IEEE 802.5 standard for Token Ring.

We'll start out with an overview of how Token Ring works and then look at the Token Ring topology and its unique cabling strategy. We'll look at the various types of hardware needed to implement Token Ring, and finally, we'll discuss the various advantages Token Ring has over other types of networking (such as Ethernet), as well as its disadvantages.

How Token Ring Works

Unlike Ethernet, Token Ring does not allow stations to transmit whenever they find the transmission medium is not being used. Instead, like relay runners passing a baton, the stations on a Token Ring network do not transmit until each receives in its turn a special bit pattern, called a *token*. The token can be thought of as an empty frame that, when seen (or "captured") by a station, can be filled with data. Only the station that currently "owns" the token is allowed to transmit, and then only until it either reaches a time limit (10 milliseconds by default) or has completed sending its data.

As Figure 5.1 shows, stations on a Token Ring are (electrically) connected to each other in a ring. Each station has two pairs of wire, one pair for transmitting, the other for receiving. The transmit pair is connected through a hub to the next station in line, and the receive pair is connected to the preceding station. Note that each connection requires a pair of wires because both transmit and receive are separate circuits. In Token Ring parlance, each station has an *upstream* neighbor and a *downstream* neighbor. Upstream is the station it receives from, and downstream is the station it transmits to.

Each station then effectively functions as a repeater, passing the filled-in token (now a frame of data) around the ring until it reaches its destination.

FIGURE 5.1:

Stations on a Token Ring are electrically a ring topology, but are physically connected in a star, with a Token Ring hub in the center.

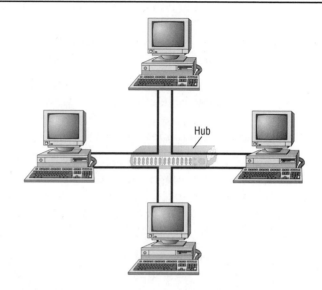

Let's break down the transmitting process into the following four steps:

1. A station "captures" a token.

2. It transmits its queued data.

3. It discards its own already transmitted frames.

4. It transmits a new token.

Note that each of these steps is performed at the Physical and Transport layers (the OSI model again), which are implemented by the Token Ring adapter logic (typically embedded in a chip on the card). Let's look at each of these steps in turn.

As we've mentioned, before a station can transmit, it must first receive the special bit pattern referred to as a token. Receiving the token is referred to as "capturing the token" and designates the station as having the opportunity to transmit until it is finished or else reaches the maximum time period for a transmission.

Once a station has captured the token, it immediately begins sending a frame. This frame may contain valid data, or if the station is not quite ready, the frame may contain an empty, or idling, bit pattern. Frames queued for transmission are now sent, as the transmitting station watches for the transmit time limit to expire.

As soon as the station has transmitted all of its pending frames or has reached the time limit, it stops transmitting. The frames it has transmitted make their way around the ring, each station checking the address in each frame to see whether it is the intended recipient.

One job performed by each station in turn is to examine incoming frames for errors. If an error is detected, a flag is set within the frame, indicating that an error has been detected. This eliminates the need for the following stations on the ring to check that frame for errors.

When the address in a frame matches the current station's address, that station sets the "address recognized" indicator flag in the frame. If the station has available frame buffer space, it also copies the frame for processing and it sets the "frame copied" indicator in the frame. The station then forwards the frame along to its next upstream neighbor.

When a frame has gone full-circuit, it arrives back at the originating station. Each frame also has a "frame copied" flag and an error indicator flag. When the error indicator flag is set, it indicates that some upstream station detected an error within the frame. If the "frame copied" flag is also on, however, this indicates that the frame was copied successfully by the intended recipient, but the frame became corrupted somewhere along the way, after it was successfully received. Frames containing the "address recognized" indicator but without the "frame copied" indicator signal the transmitting station that the intended receiver had insufficient space to accept the frame. Frames returning without the "address recognized" flag set indicate that the receiving station is offline or otherwise unavailable. Software at levels above the Physical and Transport layers will then typically handle the decision of whether to retransmit frames or alert the user.

An important responsibility of the originating station is to recognize its own frames as they return, and to not forward them further. Not forwarding a frame is referred to as *stripping* it.

The final step made by the transmitting station is to transmit a new empty token. This relinquishes control, giving the next station the opportunity to transmit.

Note the orderly way in which every station on a Token Ring network is given an equal opportunity to transmit, one at a time and each in turn. The maximum time period each station can transmit is also identical (by default, although this can be reconfigured), so that it is possible to calculate, for a given time frame, how much transmit time will be available to any station on a Token Ring.

Token Ring Topology Basics

We've mentioned that electrically, stations on a Token Ring are connected one to the next in a ring. As you saw in Figure 5.1, however, this ring physically resembles a star pattern. In this respect, Token Ring is quite similar to the layout of UTP Ethernet, with individual stations connected to a central hub, much like the spokes of a wagon wheel.

The central connector, or hub, for Token Ring is called a *multi-station access unit*, or *MSAU*. Each MSAU typically supports eight Token Ring stations, although MSAUs with fewer or more ports are available.

An MSAU performs the important role of providing fault tolerance and maintaining the ring's electrical integrity. In the event of a cable break on either the receiving or transmitting cable pair, an electrically activated switch in the MSAU called a *relay switch* disconnects the offending station from the ring.

As with Ethernet hubs, MSAUs help to consolidate the connections running to the various workstations, providing a central access point in case something goes wrong. This centralized arrangement greatly simplifies the troubleshooting of cable and hardware problems, and allows other stations on the ring to continue operating when a station is taken offline in order to be repaired.

Token Ring Hardware Overview

As you can see in Figure 5.2, the hardware needed for a minimal Token Ring network is not unlike that which is needed for twisted-pair Ethernet. Let's briefly look at each component.

FIGURE 5.2:

Hardware needed for a Token Ring

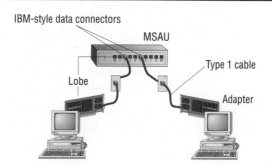

The Network Adapter

Network adapters of course must be Token Ring network adapters. These tend to be noticeably more expensive than Ethernet adapters. The chip set in the adapter is what implements the Token Ring frame processing described in the previous section. Typical Token Ring chip sets include IBM's LANStreamer or Tropic chip set, used on IBM adapters, and the Texas Instruments chip set used on third-party adapters. As with Ethernet, Token Ring adapter cards are available in various bus types: ISA, PCI, and PC Card versions are all currently on the market.

Initially Token Ring was limited to 4Mbps. The current maximum speed is 16Mbps. Most Token Ring network adapters now on the market auto-sense the speed being used on the ring, and run at either speed, as dictated by the slowest equipment on the ring.

The Cabling

The cable run from each network adapter to the MSAU is called a *lobe*. This can be either shielded or unshielded twisted-pair cable. Recall that four wires are used: two for transmit and two for receive. Type 1 or fiber cable is needed for 16Mbps Token Ring. Type 3 cable is sufficient for 4Mbps connections.

The Multi-Station Access Unit (MSAU)

MSAUs come in various sizes, supporting anywhere from four to 16 or more ports, and multiple MSAUs can be chained together to add more stations to a ring. Like the uplink and downlink ports on an Ethernet hub, MSAUs are connected to each other's ring-in and ring-out ports.

Each ring can have up to 33 MSAUs, with a maximum station count of 260 on IBM's standard, or 255 on the ISO standard. With type 3 cable, however, the maximum goes down to 72 stations.

Fancier MSAUs support remote management features and are called *controlled access units* (*CAUs*). A CAU uses devices called *lobe attachment modules* (*LAMs*) to which the ring stations are connected. LAMs typically support 20 station connections, and each CAU can support up to four LAMs. A benefit of CAUs is that they support a management agent which can allow the network administrator to remotely monitor and manage individual connections to the LAM.

Connectors

The connectors used on Token Ring networks include the nine-pin DB-style connector, which is used to connect a 4Mbps Token Ring adapter to a lobe. IBM-style connectors are used on 4Mbps Token Ring to connect two lengths of cable to each other and to MSAUs. For 16Mbps Token Ring, RJ-45 jacks and connectors are used, just as with UTP Ethernet.

Relay Switches

Just because a lobe is connected to an MSAU (or CAU) does not necessarily mean the station connected to it is electrically connected into the ring. This is because inside the MSAU or CAU there are relay switches that can switch individual stations/lobes into and out of the ring. When switched out of the ring, a lobe's transmit and receive wire pairs are connected to each other. This is referred to as *loopback mode*. The use of relay switches also allows stations that are turned off (and therefore do not have power supplied to their adapter cards) to be switched out of the ring automatically. When powered back on, the adapter applies an electrical charge, called a *phantom charge*, to the lobe, causing the relay in the MSAU to switch the lobe back into the ring circuit.

NOTE   If you follow the recommended cabling scheme for interconnecting two or more MSAUs together, the ring-in and ring-out ports are both interconnected between the MSAUs, and this provides MSAU connection redundancy: If one patch cable becomes disconnected, it is cut out of the ring circuit and the second cable alone is used.

Token Ring Stations

One area where Token Ring really differs from Ethernet is in its assignment of specific roles or functions to stations in the ring. These roles assist the Token Ring in performing "housekeeping" or management chores. Some of them are essential in enabling the ring to work at all; other tasks are optional but can provide very helpful information for network administrators wishing to keep tabs on the "health" of the Token Ring.

Figure 5.3 shows the five different station assignments for Token Ring stations. The first two, the active and standby monitors, are required. The last three—the ring parameter server, ring error monitor, and configuration report server—are all optional. Let's look at the functions performed by each of these.

FIGURE 5.3:

Token Ring functional
station assignments

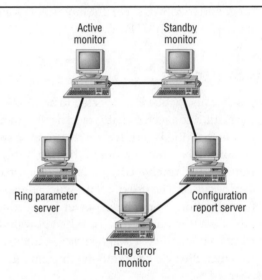

In addition to the normal address assigned to each node on a Token Ring network, a special address called a *functional address* is assigned to each functional station. This allows other stations to address frames generically to "the active monitor," for example (whoever this currently is).

These functional addresses are standard, logical addresses, using the following values:

Functional Station	Functional Address
Active monitor	C0 00 00 00 00 01
Standby monitor	(see text)
Ring parameter server	C0 00 00 00 00 02
Ring error monitor	C0 00 00 00 00 08
Configuration report server	C0 00 00 00 00 10

As you see, standby monitors are an exception—they are not assigned a functional address because there are multiple standby monitors on a ring. As we'll explain shortly, every station that is not an active monitor takes on the role of a standby monitor.

Active Monitor (AM)

When a Token Ring initializes, all Token Ring adapters on the ring perform an "election," via a process called *monitor contention*, to designate one adapter as the *active monitor* (*AM*). This role is absolutely essential for the Token Ring to operate. The functionality for performing the role of active monitor is built right into each Token Ring adapter; no additional software is required.

An AM has several duties. It starts the ring polling process, verifies correct token protocol operation, restarts the ring after any interruption of the token protocol, supplies a clock signal to the ring, and ensures that a latency delay is enforced on the ring. We'll cover each of these separately.

Starts Ring Poll Sequence

The ring poll sequence is a ritual undertaken every seven seconds on a Token Ring. Through this process, newly active stations are made part of the ring, and each active station in turn learns the identity of its current next upstream neighbor. This process, of course, also enables newly inactive stations to be gracefully dropped out of the ring—as in the game "red rover," the stations on either side of the inactive station "join hands" (electrically speaking), becoming upstream/downstream neighbors, until the inactive station eventually rejoins the ring. The AM gets the ring poll started, on the dot, every seven seconds, as long as there is an active ring (two or more stations).

Monitors Token Protocol

The AM monitors the operation of the Token Ring protocol on the ring, primarily checking that there's always either a token or a frame being placed on the ring within the specified time limit (the default is every 10 milliseconds).

Restarts the Token

When the token timer elapses without the active monitor detecting either a valid frame or a token on the ring, it sends out a new token to get the ring started again.

Synchronizes Ring Operations

Unlike an Ethernet segment, which can have traffic appear sporadically and therefore requires a string of bits to be sent to synchronize adapters, Token Ring operates on a strict schedule, imposed by the "master clock," which is a timing signal placed on the ring continuously by the active monitor station. The Token Ring adapters of all active stations are therefore always synchronized with each other just by monitoring this clock signal. This way, each adapter knows exactly when to expect a token or frame to appear on the ring, and synchronization bits don't need to be transmitted before each transmission.

Adds Necessary Latency to Ring

The token on a token ring travels very fast. Whether using electricity or light, the signal travels at a speed approaching the speed of light in a vacuum (approximately 186,000 miles per second). This presents a challenge to Token Ring networks, which usually measure only some number of feet in diameter/length. Since a token (or longer yet, a frame) is made up of sequential bits transmitted one after another, the entire token has a certain length to it. That is, it takes a certain amount of time for each bit to be sent out; this time may actually be longer than it takes for a single bit to traverse the ring. How can we guarantee that the entire token or frame will fit on the ring at once, without the tail overlapping the head (or vice-versa)? It wouldn't do to have a station that is still transmitting a frame suddenly be interrupted by the arrival of the start of that same frame, before the end of the frame was even finished transmitting. Such a situation, illustrated in Figure 5.4, would make it impossible for complete frames to be transmitted at all, as they would constantly be interrupted in the process of being transmitted.

The solution to this problem is to have the active monitor ensure that there's always a *delay* of 24 bits transmit-time on the ring. Why 24 bits? Because this is exactly the time needed to send an empty frame (a token). The delay is created by the Token Ring adapter temporarily holding the incoming token or frame in a special buffer on the adapter, then releasing it back onto the ring after the 24-bit delay has elapsed.

FIGURE 5.4:

A token that took longer to transmit than to travel around the ring would run into itself.

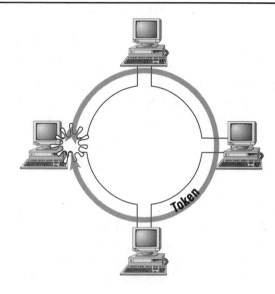

Standby Monitor (SM)

Every active station on a ring, except for the designated active monitor, is automatically designated a *standby monitor* (*SM*). This functionality also is essential, and therefore is built into the chip set on every Token Ring adapter. The duty of the SM(s) is simply to monitor the active monitor, and whenever a frame or token is not detected within the token time-out period specified (again, the default for this is 10 milliseconds), a new monitor contention process is instigated, so that a new active monitor is elected, or designated.

Ring Parameter Server (RPS)

The *ring parameter server* (*RPS*) is the first of three *optional* Token Ring station roles. RPS functionality is implemented in software that, when an RPS is needed, is loaded on some station attached to the ring. The purpose of this station is to allow the network administrator to specify optional parameters for all the ring stations to use, and these settings are communicated to each ring station via the RPS. As each station first initializes, it queries for the existence of an RPS, and if one is found, queries it for the values for each parameter setting. If an RPS is not found on the ring, then default values are used.

Among the parameters which can be specified in this way are the following: the local ring number, physical drop number, allowed access priority, soft error report timer, and authorized environment.

Ring Error Monitor (REM)

The role of the (optional) *ring error monitor (REM)* is to simply monitor the ring for any errors which are reported by the other ring stations and keep a running list of them. To be an REM, a station must have REM software installed and running on it. The collected errors can then be viewed at a later point by the network administrator, who can view the errors on the REM station, or (depending on the REM software) query the station from elsewhere for the list of errors.

Error monitoring is not the same as the error detection and recovery process that is part of the basic token ring operation. A ring error monitor simply saves all the errors it detects in a list for retrieval by the network administrator.

The error list, of course, lets the network administrator see whether bad frames are being detected, not arriving at their destination, or recipient stations are not responding, etc. Needless to say, viewing the error listing collected by the REM station gives a good indication of how well the ring is functioning over a period of time.

Configuration Report Server (CRS)

A *configuration report server* (another optional server, set up by running CRS software on an active station) provides network administrators with a means of setting various ring parameters, logging ring events (for example, a change in active monitor status, changes in upstream neighbor addresses, active monitor errors, or ring poll failure), and adding and removing stations from the ring.

This should give you a good idea of what each ring station's role and features are. However, the features and functionality of the last three stations are not fixed, and are provided by various ring station software implementations, so the exact feature set supported can differ from one product to the next.

Token Ring Processes

The various procedures that are part of Token Ring behavior, and keep a ring operating reliably, are referred to as Token Ring *processes*. These processes follow a predictable and fixed behavior, written into the firmware programming of every Token Ring network adapter card. The fact that these instructions are stored on the adapter cards means that no additional software need be loaded on a station for these basic Token Ring operations to be performed.

Station Initialization

When a running station is attached to a ring, or when the network driver is first initialized, the station must go through a six-step procedure in order to become an active ring participant.

This procedure goes as follows:

1. First, the station's network adapter sets its configurable parameters to their default values.

2. It performs a lobe test. Because the transmit/receive cables initially are connected to each other via the relay in the MSAU, the cable test can simply consist of transmitting out on the transmit cable, and listening for the same signal back on the receiving cable. This type of test, by the way, is called a *loopback test*.

3. Next, assuming the loopback test didn't fail, the adapter places current (called *phantom current*) onto the cable, which causes the relay to switch this lobe into the ring.

4. The adapter now checks to be sure its hardware address is not already in use by any station on the ring. It does this by sending a special Duplicate Address Check MAC frame. If no station sets an indicator flag in this frame, the station assumes its address is unique (otherwise, it removes itself from the ring until someone can reconfigure its network address).

5. Within seven seconds, a ring poll (described below) will occur, during which the station will note the address of its next upstream neighbor and become a "member" of the ring.

6. Finally, the ring station sends a Request Initialization MAC frame to query whether a Ring Parameter server is operational, and if so, queries this server for the configuration values to use in configuring its various settings.

At this point, the station is a full-fledged member of its Token Ring.

Monitor Contention

In describing the role of active monitor, we mentioned the *monitor contention* process, by which a new active monitor is chosen whenever the standby monitors discover that a new active monitor is needed.

Monitor contention is initiated by whichever station first notices that the duties of an AM are no longer being performed. Typically this will be the next downstream neighbor to the failed AM. A station initiates the monitor contention process by transmitting a special frame called a Claim Token MAC frame, repeating this every 20 milliseconds. Other stations follow suit, and the station having the highest Token Ring address becomes the new designated monitor. A station transmitting claim tokens stops doing so as soon as it receives any other claim token with a higher originating address than its own. Also, if the initiating station receives three of its own claim tokens back again (which implies that no higher address stations are contending for the job), then it becomes the AM. As the new active monitor, its first job is to perform the ring purge process, described next.

Ring Purge

Ring purging is the process of removing a defective token and restoring normal token operation to a ring. This process is performed by the AM, both when it first becomes the active monitor, and then whenever it detects that the ring's token has been lost or corrupted. Basically, the active monitor sends out a ring purge MAC frame until it successfully receives one valid ring purge MAC frame back again. At this point, the AM simply sends out a new token, and the ring is back in operation again.

Ring Poll

We stated earlier that *ring polling* occurs every seven seconds, and that by this process each station becomes aware of its next upstream neighbor. This allows a network administrator to query the ring for a list of stations, which can assist in troubleshooting by identifying which station is not communicating on the ring (and possibly why). Ring polling also lets all stations on the ring see that the ring has an active monitor present, and that the ring is functioning as it should.

Beaconing

Beaconing is a last-resort process initiated by the ring when a hardware error occurs, in an attempt to get the ring back into operation. If the beaconing process succeeds, offending stations are removed from the ring by the process, and the ring picks back up again. The way this happens is rather fascinating.

When a station does not receive a signal from its upstream neighbor within the normal maximum time frame, it creates a MAC frame called a *beacon frame*. Inside this frame it lists its upstream neighbor as a suspect for having the hardware problem, and this frame is then transmitted to the next downstream neighbor. Every 20 milliseconds, this station continues to send out another (identical) beacon frame. Each other station, as it receives a beacon frame, immediately stops anything else it was doing and begins repeating each beacon frame as it arrives. When the station listed as the "problem suspect" in the beacon frame has received eight such beacon frames, it temporarily takes itself offline (disconnects from the ring) and performs a loopback test of its lobe. If this test succeeds, it reenters the ring; otherwise, this station keeps itself disconnected from the ring until it is reset by the network administrator (or an impatient user).

Meanwhile, the station that sent out the beacon station is waiting to see whether its upstream neighbor will rejoin the ring. If the time limit for performing a lobe self-test elapses, and the station is still receiving its own beacon frame back, this indicates the former upstream neighbor found itself at fault and will not be rejoining the ring anytime soon. The beacon station in this case immediately ceases sending beacon frames and initiates the AM contention process (which is described above).

If the upstream neighbor passes its self-test and rejoins the ring, the beacon station notices it hasn't received its own beacon frame back again within the time-out period (16 seconds), and realizes this means its upstream neighbor has rejoined the ring. The beaconing station itself now goes off the ring to perform its own self-test. As this happens, its downstream neighbor notices that beacon frames have stopped coming, so it begins sending beacon frames itself, although at a lower priority level than the last ones. After the 16-second time-out, either the initial beacon station will pass its self-test and rejoin the ring, or it will find a problem with itself and not rejoin. If it rejoins the ring, then its next downstream neighbor will detect that this has happened (in the same way the beaconing station itself previously detected its upstream neighbor rejoining), and now this station will take itself off the ring to perform a self-test. On the other hand, if the initial beaconing station does not rejoin the ring, then its downstream neighbor will detect this and initiate a new monitor contention process, which should succeed in electing a new AM, restoring the ring to normal operating order.

At this point, hopefully either the original beaconing station (which detected a cable problem to begin with) or one of its two neighbors will have found itself to have a problem, and will have removed itself from the ring until further notice.

If none of the three stations (the initiating station nor either of its neighbors) fails the self-test, however, then the first station will continue beaconing until the network administrator steps in to correct the problem.

Even in this case, however, the administrator is provided an indication of where the problem occurred: Inside any beacon frame still traversing the ring is the address of the originating beacon station, plus the address of its (suspect) upstream neighbor.

NOTE   Frames and packets can be viewed using network monitoring hardware and/or software. Two such examples are NT's NetMonitor and Novell's LANalyzer, which we cover in Chapter 31.

The administrator therefore knows that the problem is (or at least was) occurring somewhere between those two stations. By a process of elimination, it should be relatively easy to determine whether the problem lies with either of the lobes, with a connector, or with one of the network adapters (or a driver).

As you can see, Token Ring uses a variety of interesting strategies to self-correct errors (when it can), and can supply a good deal of information about what has occurred on the ring, assisting the attentive network administrator a great deal in keeping the Token Ring operational.

Advantages and Disadvantages of Token Ring

As we did with Ethernet, we can usefully summarize the advantages and disadvantages of Token Ring as a network technology. First, let's consider the advantages:

Self-correction: As we've just seen, one advantage Token Ring certainly has is its ability to self-correct some problems which occur (cable or connector failure for example), and to provide network administrators with a collection of useful current and historical information about the operating state of the ring.

Frame size and throughput: Another benefit of Token Ring is that it isn't limited to a relatively small frame size, as Ethernet is. This means a Token Ring network is capable of conveying more information with less over-head, which translates into higher effective throughput.

Guaranteed access: Also an advantage of Token Ring is the fact that each station is guaranteed a known quantity of transmission time. This is an important consideration in networks where data must be conveyed in "real time"—unlike Ethernet, Token Ring can guarantee that (barring other hardware problems) any station will have its opportunity to transmit a given amount of information in a given time slot. (With Ethernet, on the other hand, transmission is hit or miss, as the transmission media simply may not be free at all in a given time frame.)

Of course, some of the Token Ring features we've examined in this chapter can also be considered disadvantages:

Cost: One definite disadvantage of Token ring is its cost. Unfortunately, all Token Ring hardware seems to cost measurably more than the counter-part Ethernet components. (For example, one national vendor is currently selling Ethernet adapters for as little as $20 each, while the least expensive Token Ring adapter cards from the same vendor are priced at $200 to $300 each!)

Difficulty of installation: Another disadvantage of Token Ring is the fact that installation is always at least somewhat more complicated than it would be for a comparable Ethernet network. Token Ring standards are more numerous and more stringent, and therefore there are more things that can go wrong.

Administration: Moreover, the ability of Token Ring to self-correct vari-ous problems can itself turn into a disadvantage for the inattentive net-work administrator. The ring can take some corrective action, but in doing so, can cause hardware problems to go unnoticed for longer periods of time, resulting perhaps in more serious problems down the line. If you have a Token Ring network, it pays to use the monitoring features and be attentive to any errors that are reported.

Summary

This completes our overview of Token Ring networks. We started by explaining the way tokens and frames are passed around a Token Ring: A token is captured, frames are transmitted, returning frames are stripped, and a new token is then sent for the next station to begin transmitting. We discussed the physical (star) and electrical (ring) topology, looked at the required hardware for a Token Ring, and next began a discussion of the various ring stations and their roles and functionality.

We then explained the various Token Ring processes which initialize and maintain the token passing behavior, even to the point of attempting to auto-correct various hardware errors.

In the next chapter, we're going to explore network topologies in more detail, revisiting the ring and star, and some other topologies as well.

CHAPTER

SIX

6

Network Topologies

- Physical and logical topologies

- Types of connections: circuit-switching, message-switching, and packet-switching

- The Ethernet frame header

- Ethernet topologies: 10Mbps, 100Mbps, and 1Gbps

- Other LAN topologies: 100VG-AnyLAN, Fiber Distributed Data Interface (FDDI), and asynchronous transfer mode (ATM)

- WAN topologies: ISDN, T1, X.25/Frame Relay, and others

Our discussions of Ethernet and Token Ring technologies in the two preceding chapters touched lightly on the notion of network topologies. You will recall that Ethernet typically uses either a bus or a star (physical) topology, while Token Ring uses a (physical) ring topology. In this chapter we will look more closely at how different network topologies convey network traffic, discuss the tradeoffs inherent in these various approaches, and then look at each of the major LAN and WAN topologies—including the various Ethernet flavors (10Mbps, 100Mbps, 100VG, 1Gbps) Fiber Distributed Data Interface (FDDI), asynchronous transfer mode (ATM), ISDN, T1, modem dial-up, leased lines, Frame Relay/X.25, and SONET (Synchronous Optical Network). By the end of this chapter, you should have a clear understanding of the range of connection options that are available, and you should be able to evaluate these different options for their suitability for interconnecting your own network or networks.

Topology Basics

The *topology* of a network is the set of rules for physically connecting and communicating on a given network medium. When you decide on a particular topology for connecting your network servers, workstations, and other devices, you will need to follow a number of specifications that tell you how these machines need to be wired together, what type of connectors to use, and even how these systems must speak to each other on the wire.

Topology is broken down into two categories, physical and logical.

Physical Topology

Physical topology refers to how the transmission media are wired together. The three types of physical topology are *bus*, *star*, and *ring*.

Bus Topology

The *bus topology* is the common configuration for thinnet wiring. Systems attached to the bus are connected in a series type of connection. All systems are connected via a single long cable run and tap in via T-connectors. A bus topology can also be used to directly connect two systems. Figure 6.1 shows an example of a bus topology.

FIGURE 6.1:

An example of a bus topology

All systems connect to the same logical cable length

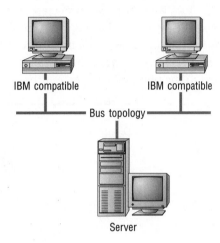

Star Topology

The *star topology* is the common configuration of twisted-pair wiring. Each system is connected to a central device, such as a hub or a switch. Only two stations are ever connected to each physical wire, and they branch out from the central device like a starburst. These hubs and switches can then be linked together to form larger networks. Figure 6.2 shows an example of a star topology.

FIGURE 6.2:

An example of a star topology

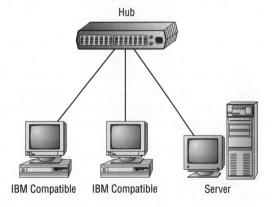

Ring Topology

The *ring topology* is the common configuration for fiber cable. The output data port (Tx for "transmit") is connected to the input data port (Rx for "receive") of the next station along the ring. This continues until the last station connects its output data port to the input data port of the first station, forming a complete ring. Figure 6.3 is an example of ring topology. Systems are connected in a similar fashion to the bus topology, except that the two ends of the bus are tied together.

FIGURE 6.3:

An example of a ring topology

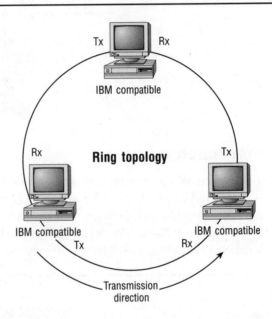

NOTE   The transmission media is separate from the physical topology. Some media can be used with more than one topology, and vice-versa. The examples just given show the combinations you will commonly find in the field, but these are not hard-and-fast rules. For example, even though fiber is commonly used in a ring topology, you can use it in a star or even a bus topology. We'll cover this in greater detail later in the chapter.

Each of these physical topologies has its own inherent strengths and weaknesses. In order to determine which physical topology best fits your environment, you must first decide on which logical topology you will use.

Logical Topology

A *logical topology* describes the communication rules each station should use when communicating on a network. For example, the specifications of the logical topology describe how each station should determine if it's okay to transmit data, and what a station should do if it tries to transmit data at the same time as another station. The logical topology's job is to ensure that information gets transferred as quickly and as error-free as possible. Think of a discussion group moderator and you'll get the idea. The moderator ensures that each person in the group gets a turn to speak. They also ensure that if two individuals try to speak at the same time, one gets priority and the other waits their turn.

So how are physical and logical topologies related? Any given logical topology will operate on only specific physical topologies. For example, the Ethernet specification will operate on a bus or a star physical topology but will not work on a ring; FDDI will function on a ring or a star topology but not on a bus. Once you have determined which logical topology you will use, you can then go about selecting your physical topology.

Logical topologies are defined by the Institute of Electrical and Electronics Engineers (IEEE). The IEEE is a not-for-profit organization that consists of an assembly of companies and private individuals within the networking industry. The members of the IEEE work together to define specifications, preventing any single company from claiming ownership of the technology and helping to ensure that products from multiple vendors will interoperate successfully in a network.

The most common network specifications are:

Specification	Defines
IEEE 802.3	10Mb Ethernet
IEEE 802.3u	100Mb Ethernet
IEEE 802.3x	Full Duplex Ethernet
IEEE 802.3z	1Gbps Ethernet
IEEE 802.5	Token Ring
IEEE 802.11	Wireless LANs
IEEE 802.12	100VG-AnyLAN
IEEE 802.14	Cable Modem

Note that 802.3z is still under development, and its final spec is not due until late 1998.

Now let's explore the rules involved in each of our logical topologies. The logical topology of a large network can contain multiple paths to the same destination. This is usually done for *redundancy* (if one link dies, another can be used) or for *load balancing* (spreading the load over multiple links).

When data is transmitted onto a network, it is broken up into smaller pieces referred to as frames (you'll learn more about frames when we cover Ethernet later in this chapter). Each frame is stamped with a *sequence number* to identify the order in which the data was split up. By looking at these sequence numbers, a station receiving these frames knows in what order to place them to reassemble the data correctly.

Connection Types

Every logical topology uses one of three methods for creating the connections between end stations. These are referred to as *circuit switching*, *message switching*, and *packet switching*.

Circuit Switching

Circuit switching means that when data needs to be transferred from one node to another, a dedicated connection is created between the two systems. Bandwidth is dedicated to this communication session and remains available until the connection is no longer required. A regular phone call uses circuit switching. When you place a call, a connection is set up between your phone and the one you are calling. This connection remains in effect until you finish your call and hang up. Figure 6.4 illustrates a circuit-switched network. The best route is selected, and bandwidth is dedicated to this communication session the entire length of the circuit and remains in place until no longer needed. All data follows the same path.

FIGURE 6.4:

An example of a circuit-
switched network

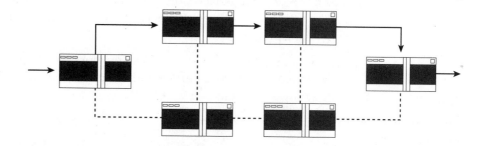

Circuit-switched networks are useful for delivering information that must be received in the order it was sent—for example, applications such as real-time audio and video cannot tolerate the delays incurred in reassembling the data in the correct order. While circuit switching ensures that data is delivered as quickly as possible by dedicating a connection to the task, it can also be wasteful compared to other types of connections because the circuit will remain active even if the end stations are not currently transmitting.

Examples of circuit-switched networks include:

- asynchronous transfer mode (ATM)
- analog dial-up line (public telephone network)
- ISDN
- leased line
- T1

Message Switching

Message switching means that a *store-and-forward* type of connection is set up between connectivity devices along the message path. The first device creates a connection to the next and transmits the entire message. Once this is complete, the connection is torn down, and the second device repeats the process if required.

Delivery of e-mail is a good example of message switching. As you type in your e-mail message, your computer queues the information until you are done. When you hit the Send button, your system delivers your message in its entirety to your local post office, which again queues the message. Your post office then contacts the post office of the person to whom you have addressed the message. Again, the message is delivered in its entirety and queued by the receiving system. Finally the remote post office delivers your message to its intended recipient using the same process.

Figure 6.5 illustrates a message-switched network. While all the data still follows the same path, only one portion of the network is dedicated to delivering this data at any given time.

FIGURE 6.5:

An example of a message-switched network

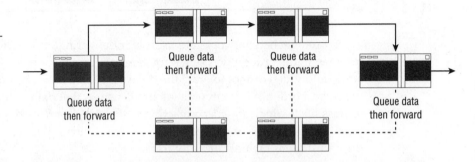

NOTE   Besides e-mail, HTTP (Web access) is another example of a message-switching technology. Above the topology level, HTTP creates a separate session for each piece of information that needs to be transferred. For example, a page with text and two graphics would create three separate message-switched sessions. These sessions will remain active until the information is completely transferred. Once transfer is complete, the session is then closed. Any new requests will create new sessions.

None of the logical topologies covered in this book utilize message switching for the delivery of data.

Message switching increases the memory and processing requirements on interim hardware in order to store the information prior to delivery.

Packet Switching

The final method for connecting end stations is *packet switching*. This method is by far the most widely used in current networking topologies. Within a packet-switching network, each individual frame can follow a different path to its final destination. Because each frame may follow a different path, frames may or may not be received in the same order they were transmitted, so the receiving station uses the sequence numbers on the frames to reassemble the data in the correct order.

Note the operative phrase "can follow a different path." As you'll see later in the chapter, there are other factors besides the logical topology that play a part in determining whether this feature is exploited. For now, it is enough to realize that in a packet-switched network all the data may not follow the same path.

Figure 6.6 illustrates a packet-switched network. Data is allowed to follow any path to its destination. Packet switching does not require that any bandwidth be reserved for this transmission.

FIGURE 6.6:

An example of a packet-switched network

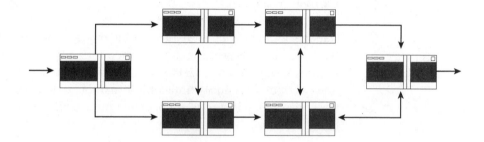

Packet-switched networks are useful for transmitting regular network data. This includes storing files, printing, or cruising the Web. In short, all the activities you would normally associate with network usage will run fine in a packet-switched network. While packet switching is a poor choice for the delivery of live audio and video, it is extremely efficient for delivering information that is not time sensitive, because it does not require dedicating bandwidth to the delivery of information. Other nodes are capable of sharing the available bandwidth as required.

Examples of packet-switched networks include:

- all Ethernet topologies
- 100VG-AnyLAN
- FDDI
- Frame Relay and X.25

Ethernet Networks

We looked at Ethernet in Chapter 4, so here we will just summarize the important points for comparison with other network topologies. Ethernet is by far the most popular networking topology. Its ability to support a wide range of cable types, low-cost hardware, and Plug-and-Play connectivity has caused it to find its way into more corporate (as well as home) networks than any other topology.

Ethernet's communication rules are called *carrier sense multiple access with collision detection (CSMA/CD)*. This is a mouthful, but it's simple enough to interpret when you break it down:

- **Carrier sense** means that all Ethernet stations are required to listen to the wire if they are not currently transmitting. By "listen," we mean that the station should be constantly monitoring the network to see if any other stations are currently sending data. By monitoring the transmissions of other stations, a station can tell if the network is open or in use. This way, the station does not just blindly transfer information and interfere with other stations; also, being in a constant listening mode means that the station is ready when another station wants to send it data.

- **Multiple access** simply means that more than two stations can be connected to the same network, and that all stations are allowed to transmit whenever the network is free. As we discussed in Chapter 3, it is far more efficient to allow stations to transmit only when they need to than it is to assign each system a time block in which it is allowed to transmit. Multiple access is also much easier to scale as you add more stations to the network.

- **Collision detection** answers the question, "What happens if two systems think the circuit is free and try to transmit data at the same time?" When two stations transmit simultaneously, a *collision* takes place. A collision is similar to RFI interference, and the resulting transmission becomes mangled and useless for carrying data. As a station transmits data, it watches for this condition; if it detected such a condition, the workstation assumes that a collision has taken place. This causes the station to back off, wait for a random period of time, and then retransmit.

Each station is responsible for determining its own random waiting period before retransmission. This helps to ensure that each station is waiting for a different period of time so that another collision does not take place. In the unlikely event that a second collision does occur (the station backs off but is again involved in a collision), each station is required to double its waiting period before trying again. When two or more collisions take place at the same time, it is referred to as a *multiple collision*.

While collisions are a normal part of Ethernet communications and are expected to happen from time to time, multiple collisions can be a sign that there is a problem with the network (for example, that there is a bad network card or that the network is carrying too much traffic). If a station is involved in 15 consecutive collisions, it will give up, returning an error to the application that was attempting to transmit data. We'll discuss multiple collisions in more detail in the troubleshooting section of the book.

If you were to chart CSMA/CD, it would look something like Figure 6.7.

FIGURE 6.7:

Flowchart of Ethernet communication rules

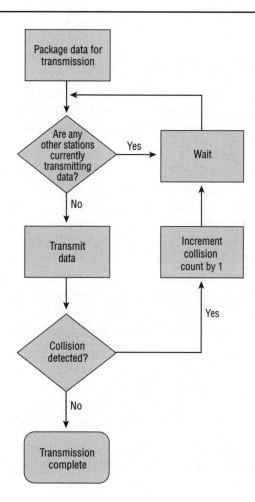

An integral part of Ethernet communications is that each system is constantly monitoring the transmissions of all the other stations on the wire. It is possible to configure a workstation to read all of this information it receives. This is commonly referred to as a *promiscuous mode* system. Operating in promiscuous mode is what allows most network analyzers to function; and a network administrator can take advantage of it to monitor a network from one central station, so that errors and network statistics can be gathered.

Unfortunately, the existence of promiscuous mode also means that a not-so-honest person may be able to eavesdrop on the communications of their coworkers. This has increased the popularity of security and encryption products.

So how does a station determine if it should read the data being transmitted or ignore it? The answer lies in the Ethernet frame header.

The Frame Header Section

Chapter 4 outlined the components of an Ethernet frame. The information in the header frame section is what is ultimately responsible for identifying who sent the data and where they wanted it to go.

The header contains two fields to identify the source and destination of the transmission. These are the node addresses of both the source and destination systems. The node address is also referred to as the *media access control (MAC)* address. The *node address* is a unique number that serializes the network devices (like network cards or networking hardware) and is a unique identifier that distinguishes each device from any other networking device in the world. No two networking devices should ever be assigned the same number. Think of this number as being the equivalent of a telephone number. Every home with a telephone has a unique phone number so that the phone company knows where to direct the call. In this same fashion, a networked computer will use the destination system's MAC address to send the frame to the proper device.

NOTE   The MAC address has nothing to do with Apple computers and is always capitalized. It is the number used by all systems attached to the network (PCs and Macs included) to uniquely identify themselves.

This six-byte, 12-digit hexadecimal number consists of two parts. The first half of the address is the manufacturer's identifier. A manufacturer is assigned a range of MAC addresses to use when serializing their devices. Some of the more predominant MAC addresses are:

First Six Bytes of MAC Address	Manufacturer
00000C	Cisco
0000A2	Bay Networks
0080D3	Shiva
00AA00	Intel
02608C	3Com
080009	Hewlett-Packard
080020	Sun
08005A	IBM

TIP The first six bytes of the MAC address can be a good troubleshooting aid. If you are investigating a problem, try to determine the source MAC address. Knowing who made the device may put you a little closer to determining which system is causing the problem. For example, if the first six bytes are **0000A2**, you know you need to focus your attention on any Bay Networks device on your network.

The second half of the MAC address is the serial number the manufacturer has assigned to the device. Figure 6.8 shows some examples of decoded addresses. The first denotes all digits that constitute the full address. The second assumes the leading "0" is always implied and ignores them.

One address worthy of note is FF-FF-FF-FF-FF-FF. This is referred to as a *broadcast address*. A broadcast address is special in that it means all systems receiving this packet should read the included data. If a system sees a frame that has been sent to the broadcast address, it will read the frame and process the data if it can.

NOTE You should never encounter a frame that has a broadcast address in the source node field.

FIGURE 6.8:

Two forms of formatting are commonly used when writing a MAC address.

Two examples of the same node address

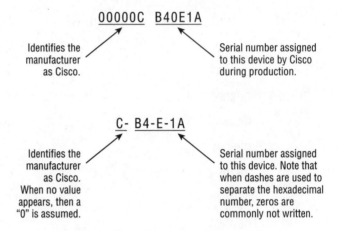

00000C B40E1A

Identifies the manufacturer as Cisco.

Serial number assigned to this device by Cisco during production.

C- B4-E-1A

Identifies the manufacturer as Cisco. When no value appears, then a "0" is assumed.

Serial number assigned to this device. Note that when dashes are used to separate the hexadecimal number, zeros are commonly not written.

How do we find out what the destination node address is in order to send data to a system? After all, network cards do not ship with phone books. This is done with a special frame referred to as an *address resolution protocol* frame, or *ARP* frame. ARP functions differently depending on which protocol you're using (IPX, IP, or NetBEUI, for example). We looked at ARP in greater detail in Chapter 3, where we discussed networking protocols. The important fact to keep in mind here is that on an Ethernet network, systems have a method of automatically discovering each other. No initial setup is required by the network administrator.

A quick point about Ethernet frame size. We mentioned that each frame contains a 14-byte header and a four-byte FCS. These field lengths are fixed and never change. The sum of the two is 18 bytes. The data field, however, is allowed to vary from 46 to 1500 bytes. This is where our minimum and maximum frame sizes come from.

46 + 18 = 64 bytes (minimum frame size)

1500 + 18 = 1518 bytes (maximum frame size)

Remember that every system on our Ethernet segment sees every packet and needs to look at that packet to see if it is addressed to it or not. If you are using a PC that only speaks IPX to a NetWare server, and somewhere on your network are two Apple computers speaking AppleTalk, your workstation still sees those

AppleTalk frames and needs to look at every one of them to determine if it needs to read the data within the frame or not. The fact that your system speaks a different protocol makes no difference—the CSMA/CD communication rules of Ethernet require every computer on the segment to look at every packet.

NOTE   That a computer must dedicate some CPU time to analyzing frames on a network may seem a minor point, but it isn't: If the network is busy, a workstation can appear to respond sluggishly, even though it is not intentionally transmitting or receiving network data.

Ethernet communications fall into a number of different categories. While most use identical means of communication, they differ in their rate of data transmission. Let's take a look at each category now.

Local Area Network Topologies

Local area network (LAN) topologies are network configurations that are confined to a small area such as a single floor or a building. LAN topologies are focused on delivering data to many systems within a small geographical area.

10Mb Ethernet

10Mb Ethernet is the oldest member of the Ethernet family. Developed in the late 1970s by Xerox, it later evolved into the IEEE specification 802.3 (pronounced *eight oh two dot three*). Its flexibility, high transmission rate (at the time anyway), and nonproprietary nature quickly made it the networking topology of choice for many network administrators.

10Mb refers to the transmission speed of 10 megabits per second (Mbps). This means that 10Mb Ethernet is capable of transferring 10,000,000 bits (or 1,250,000 bytes) from one network station to another in a one-second period of time. This is under ideal conditions, however, and your mileage will vary. Again note that 10Mb does not translate into a 10-megabyte (MB) transfer rate but rather 1.25 megabytes per second (MBps). This confusion arises from the fact that some people refer to this topology as *10 Meg Ethernet*, which makes it sound as though the phrase refers to 10MB instead of 10Mb.

The CSMA/CD nature of Ethernet means that most networks will begin to show a degradation in performance at 40–50 percent (4,000,000 to 5,000,000 bits per second) of maximum throughput. By the time 90 percent utilization is reached, response time is usually so slow that applications begin to time out.

The percentage of maximum throughput is referred to as the *utilization rate*. For example, if you were to take a measurement and note that 7,500,000 bits of data were passing by on the network, you could refer to this as a 75 percent utilization rate (7,500,000/10,000,000 × 100).

High utilization can be a bad thing. Every station needs to monitor the network for traffic prior to transmitting. The more traffic on the network, the longer a station has to wait before it is allowed to transmit its frame. This can make network response appear to be sluggish. Also, because more stations are trying to get their information out, there is an increased chance of collision. While collisions are a normal part of Ethernet transmissions, they slow down the transfer of information even more.

Another common measurement of throughput is *frame rate*, the number of frames that pass from one station to another in one second (frames per second, or *fps*). The relationship between frame rate and utilization is directly related to the size of the frames.

As we mentioned earlier, a legal Ethernet frame can be anywhere from 64 to 1518 bytes in length. This means that a 10Mbps Ethernet segment that is experiencing 100 percent utilization of 1518 byte frames would have a frame rate of approximately 813 fps. Written out mathematically it would look something like this:

$$(10,000,000/8)/(1518 + 8 + 12) = 813 \text{ fps}$$

- The (10,000,000/8) portion converts the maximum transfer rate in bits to bytes. This way the unit of measure is consistent throughout the formula, because our frame size is in bytes as well.

- The value 1518 is the size of the frame as stated in our example.

- We add 8 to this because of the preamble. As mentioned earlier in this chapter, the preamble is technically not considered part of the frame, but it does use up bandwidth on our media.

- The 12 represents station listening time. As mentioned earlier, CSMA/CD requires each station to monitor the network for other transmitting stations before sending data.

The preamble and the listening time would be considered overhead on this circuit. It represents 20 bytes of bandwidth that is lost every time a packet is transmitted. A breakdown of maximum fps based on frame size would be as follows:

Frame Size in Bytes	Number of Frames at 100% Utilization
64	14,881
256	4529
512	2350
1024	1193
1518	813

This breakdown brings up an interesting question—which is more efficient, many small frames or fewer larger ones? As you saw earlier, transmitting Ethernet frames carries with it a certain amount of overhead due to listening time and the preamble. If we multiply the size of the data field (frame size minus the header and FCS) by the number of frames transmitted, we can get a rough idea of what our potential throughput of raw data would be:

Data Field Size Times Frame Rate	Bytes of Data per Second
$46 \times 14{,}881$	684,526
238×4529	1,077,902
494×2350	1,160,900
1006×1193	1,200,158
1500×813	1,219,500

As you can see, the frame size can make a dramatic difference in the amount of information the network is capable of transferring.

Using the largest possible frame size, we can move 1.2 megabytes per second of data along the network. At the smallest frame size, this transfer rate is cut almost in half to 685 kilobytes per second (KBps).

Some of the factors that go into controlling a network's average frame size are protocol selection and regulating the amount of broadcast traffic (broadcast frames tend to be small in size). Chapters 33 and 34 discuss these options.

So which is a better measure of network health, frame rate or utilization? While both are important, utilization is the meter that tells you how much of your bandwidth is currently in use, and the percentage of bandwidth in use dictates whether a network responds quickly to requests or appears to slow down application speed. The key is the frame size. We've seen networks running at 1100 fps that appear to crawl while others sustain 3000 or more fps with no noticeable performance degradation. When utilization levels consistently range from 30 percent to 50 percent, it may be time to look at load balancing the network with more efficient protocols or faster topologies like 100Mbps Ethernet.

Appropriate Applications

10Mbps Ethernet is appropriate for the following applications:

- **Small office environments:** If your environment is, say, a small law office or accounting firm, then 10Mbps Ethernet may be all you need. The average workstation bus is only capable of processing data at a rate of 1.5Mbps to 5.0Mbps, so in light-traffic environments the network is definitely not the performance gate.

The *performance gate* of a system is considered to be that portion of the configuration that supports the lowest level of throughput. For example, if you have two computers that can process data at 20Mb, and they are connected by a network that supports only 10Mb communications, the 10Mb network link would be the performance gate because it is capable of processing the least amount of data.

- **Workstation connections:** If you have a large environment (100 or more nodes), 10Mb Ethernet may still be sufficient for workstation connection. There are devices available that allow you to run your servers on one topology (such as 100Mb Ethernet) and your workstations on another. This type of configuration is usually sufficient when you are dealing with simple word processing and spreadsheet files but there are more nodes doing it. If you have a few workstations with higher data transfer needs (such as graphics development), they can be placed on the faster topology as well.

Topology Rules

Table 6.1 summarizes the topology rules for 10Mb Ethernet.

TABLE 6.1: Topology Rules for 10Mb Ethernet

Item	Rules
Maximum cable lengths	Thinnet: 600 ft
	Twisted-pair: 325 ft
	Fiber: 3000 ft
Minimum cable lengths	Thinnet: 1.5 ft
Maximum number of stations per cable	Thinnet: 30
	Twisted-pair: 2
	Fiber: 2
Maximum number of stations per logical network	1024
Maximum number of segments	5 segments, only three of which are populated
Maximum overall length of logical network	3000 ft

100Mb Ethernet

100Mb Ethernet is the natural progression from 10Mb Ethernet. Communication is still CSMA/CD, only faster. The time between digital pulses is condensed, and the time a system is required to wait and listen is shorter. The result is a tenfold increase in throughput. Because 100Mb Ethernet is an extension of 10Mb Ethernet, the IEEE simply extended the original Ethernet specification and dubbed this topology IEEE 802.3u. The "u" is used for revision control and indicates that this specification has simply been appended to the original 802.3 specification.

There are currently two implementations of 100Mb Ethernet: 100Tx and 100T4. 100Tx is the older of the two and by far the more widely used. 100T4 has the additional benefit of working with Category 3 (CAT3) twisted-pair cabling, while 100Tx requires Category 5 (CAT5) cable.

WARNING 100Tx and 100T4 are not directly compatible: For example, you cannot use 100T4 network cards with a 100Tx hub and expect them to work. When purchasing hardware for a 100Mb Ethernet network, make sure you know what you're getting.

The improvements that 100Mb Ethernet offers do not come without a price, however. The shorter transmission times means that the overall cable lengths for 100Mb Ethernet must be shorter than for 10Mb Ethernet.

Just as electronics engineers must increasingly be concerned with switching time—the delay experienced when an electrical circuit tries to change state from one voltage level to another—network engineers must deal with a similar phenomenon referred to as *propagation delay*. Propagation delay is the period of time it takes for a signal change to travel from one end of a cable to the other.

As an analogy, think of a very long and skinny fish tank. If you start to quickly fill the tank from one end, the water will eventually work its way throughout the tank and will attempt to remain level. The side of the tank that you're filling from, however, will always contain just a little more water because the forces of gravity and friction will be resisting the water's movement to seek its own level. At any given time, there will be a delay between when the side you're filling reaches a certain level and the opposite end reaches that same level. This is, in effect, propagation delay. Figure 6.9 is an example of propagation delay. As station A transmits its data, there will be a brief delay before the electrical signal reaches station B and then station C. This is because the wire is resisting the change in voltage of the signal.

FIGURE 6.9:

An example of propagation
delay

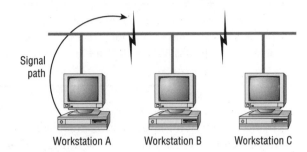

Signal path

Workstation A   Workstation B   Workstation C

As another example, let's say you have a very long length of cable similar to that in Figure 6.9. Let's also assume that workstation A sends a digital pulse onto the network cable as it begins to transmit an Ethernet frame to workstation B. Recalling our fish tank analogy, the forces resisting this change in voltage level would be the resistance in the wire and electromagnetic radiation. Therefore, there would be a difference in voltage level at each end of the wire as the signal moves down the network cable.

Now let's also assume that workstation C needs to transmit data to workstation B, but it is currently in a listening mode. If the cable length is long enough, the propagation delay (measured in seconds) from one end of the cable to the other could be longer than the time it takes a station to completely transmit a frame. This means that station A may be able to complete the transmission of a frame before the first digital pulse of that frame reaches station C.

The result would be a collision that made both frames unusable. While collisions are normal in an Ethernet network, this particular situation has a unique spin. Workstation A (and possibly workstation C as well) completed frame transmission before the collision took place. As far as workstation A is concerned, it was not involved in the collision and does not need to retransmit the data! Depending on the upper-level protocol used on the network, either the data would be lost or workstation A would eventually time out waiting for a receipt acknowledgment from workstation B and would retransmit the data. But this time-out is typically far longer than the time it would normally take to retransmit after a collision.

NOTE Propagation delay is not as much of an issue with fiber cable, because the delays are almost unmeasurable for your average network cable run. Recall that light in a vacuum travels at 186,000 miles per second—along a cable it doesn't do too shabby, either.

Propagation delay is the reason why maintaining specified cable lengths is so important, and why cable lengths must be shortened for 100Mb Ethernet. The shorter transmission times when sending frames means that there is less toleration for propagation delay.

Appropriate Applications

The appropriate applications for 100Mb Ethernet are the following:

- **High-end workstations:** If your environment includes end users who process large graphics files or compile code over the network, 100Mb Ethernet may be just the trick to improve performance. These stations usually have a high-performance bus that allows them to process data at a rate of 10Mbps to 20Mbps. While these data rates would overwhelm 10Mb Ethernet, 100Mb gives a bit more breathing room. The additional bandwidth may be just the thing to improve network response time. A word of caution, however: Some of the newer desktop machines utilize the same technology as server-class machines. A busy 100Mb segment can easily move the performance gate from the network to the server itself. The result is that the server is unable to keep up with the rate of file requests and responds by crashing or losing data. You will need to ensure that your server is up to the task of servicing a 100Mb network. RAID level 5 (RAID is short for *redundant array of independent/inexpensive disks*) and other *go fast* technologies will go a long way towards ensuring that a server will remain stable at these higher data rates.

- **Backbones and server connections:** As we mentioned in the section on 10Mb Ethernet, a larger environment (100 or more nodes) may benefit from leaving the user community at 10Mb but upgrading the servers to 100Mb. Busy but non-populated segments that connect office floors or departments could benefit from the 100Mb performance increase as well.

Topology Rules

Table 6.2 shows the topology rules for 100Mb Ethernet.

TABLE 6.2: Topology Rules for 100Mb Ethernet

Item	Rules
Maximum cable lengths	Twisted-pair: 325 ft
	Fiber: 650 ft
Minimum cable lengths	None
Maximum number of stations per cable	Twisted-pair: 2
	Fiber: 2
Maximum number of stations per logical network	1024
Maximum number of segments	2
Maximum overall length of logical network	650 ft

1Gbps Ethernet

Network transmission speeds are definitely on the rise. It was not until June of 1995 that the IEEE gave their full blessing to the final specification of 100Mb Ethernet. By July of 1996, they were back in committee appointing a task force to create specifications for *1Gbps Ethernet*. This task force has been dubbed 802.3z, as the specification is expected to simply be a natural progression from the original Ethernet standards. This new specification has received phenomenal support, with more than 80 organizations having joined the Gigabit Ethernet Alliance as of this writing. While a final specification is not due till the summer of 1998, some vendors have already begun shipping 1Gbps Ethernet products. Truly the "need for speed" has taken hold in full force.

The 1Gbps Ethernet specification is meant to compete directly with asynchronous transfer mode (ATM) as a topology for local-area networks. ATM, discussed later in this chapter, has been in development for a number of years and currently has the potential of supporting data rates up to 622Mbps. Lack of agreement between vendors has delayed approval of final specifications for ATM, so it appears that 1Gbps Ethernet may become a fully recognized topology before ATM.

Even though 1Gbps Ethernet appears to be following in the footsteps of its predecessors, there is one change of focus. While 10Mb and 100Mb Ethernet have been implemented mostly on twisted-pair cabling, 1Gbps Ethernet is made to run over fiber. Concessions will be made to leverage existing twisted-pair cable runs from wiring closets out to the desktop, but the majority of the cabling will need to be fiber. At this writing, it appears that 1Gbps Ethernet over CAT5 twisted-pair will be limited to approximately 80 feet. Any lengths greater than that will require fiber cable.

The reasoning is twofold:

- First, the current specification has adopted the communication properties of Fiber Channel, which was developed for fiber-optic cable.

- Second, propagation delay is a big factor. 1Gbps Ethernet represents a 100X increase in transmission speed over 10Mb Ethernet. This means that only a minimal amount of propagation delay can be tolerated. Fiber is a perfect mate for this technology, as its propagation delay is very close to zero.

Appropriate Applications

At the time of this writing, the best fit for 1Gbps Ethernet is a server or backbone connection where the desktop systems are already running at 100Mbps. Our earlier cautions about ensuring that servers are up to handling this high rate of data apply even more with 1Gbps transmission speeds. Only a top-of-the-line server specifically designed for this rate of data processing can ever hope to keep up in a busy 1Gbps environment.

Topology Rules

These rules are somewhat speculative. Because a final specification has not yet been drafted, it is based on early published notes from the 802.3z Task Force.

Table 6.3 shows the topology rules for Gigabit Ethernet.

TABLE 6.3: Topology Rules for Gigabit Ethernet

Item	Rules
Maximum cable lengths	Fiber: 1640 ft
	Twisted-pair: currently 82 ft, possibly increasing to 325 ft later
Minimum cable lengths	None
Maximum number of stations per cable	Twisted-pair: 2
	Fiber: 2
Maximum number of stations per logical network	Still under development, should be 1024
Maximum number of segments	Still under development, should be 1 or 2
Maximum overall length of logical network	Will be media dependent

This concludes our discussion of purely Ethernet-based topologies. Next, we will explore what other options besides CSMA/CD are available for constructing a network topology.

100VG-AnyLAN

100VG-AnyLAN was developed by Hewlett-Packard (HP) in parallel to the development of 100Tx. The *VG* portion of the name stands for *voice grade*, implying that the technology can be utilized on voice-grade wiring (100VG supports CAT3 twisted-pair cabling).

While HP worked hard to have its specification considered as the successor to 10Mb Ethernet, it has a few additional features that prompted the IEEE to give it a specification all its own. The specification 802.12 was incorporated to cover 100VG, while 100Tx was incorporated as 802.3u, thus becoming the successor to the Ethernet legacy.

Demand Priority

As a communication scheme, 100VG does away with CSMA/CD. Instead, it utilizes a feature called *demand priority*. Demand priority is an attempt to take some of the best features of Ethernet and ATM and mix them together. It's designed to have the ease of setup that Ethernet enjoys along with the quality of service supported by ATM.

TIP

Quality of service is the ability to allocate bandwidth to support real-time audio and video. While normal network data is robust enough to deal with short delays and frames received out of order, real-time audio and video are not. Quality of service ensures that these less tolerant applications receive the bandwidth required to function properly when it is needed.

In a true Ethernet environment, a hub is a "dumb" multiport amplifier. When a frame is received on a specific port, it is immediately amplified and transmitted on all other ports of the hub. The hub does not care if it receives a proper frame or a noisy signal; it simply boosts the voltage level and passes it along. The first frame it receives is the one amplified and sent along its merry way.

In a 100VG environment, however, a hub is an intelligent device; it is a central control unit with functionality that recalls the old days of the mainframe. While the 100VG hub still amplifies network signals the same way an Ethernet hub does, it determines which frames get transmitted first by scanning its ports in order. Workstations are allowed to set a priority level to their data—either normal or high. As the hub scans its ports, it gives a larger slice of the bandwidth pie to this high-priority data. High-priority data is considered to be data that cannot tolerate delays—for example, real time audio and video. If a video conference does not receive all the bandwidth it requires to immediately send information back and forth, the images received may be choppy or the audio may be unrecognizable. Demand priority attempts to allocate the bandwidth these applications require to function smoothly.

In Favor of 100VG

There are some strong arguments for 100VG technology over regular Ethernet. First, 100VG does make some concessions for quality of service. While 100VG is capable of allotting additional bandwidth to applications like video conferencing, Ethernet would handle these frames like any other data on the wire.

Second, bandwidth becomes a bit more predictable on a 100VG network. Because the hub systematically scans its ports to look for pending transmissions, it is a bit easier to predict what the available bandwidth is for each workstation.

For example, on an Ethernet network, the amount of bandwidth available to any given station depends on how much information the other stations are trying to send. If the other stations are transmitting many large files, it is harder for our station to find a moment of free network time to transmit its frame. If the other stations only need to transmit occasionally, there are more windows of opportunity for frame transmission.

Because 100VG scans each of the ports and will accept one frame transmission at a time, every station has an equal opportunity to transmit its information.

100VG Drawbacks

Unfortunately, at this writing, 100VG suffers from more drawbacks than benefits. The first drawback is performance. Even though it was designed from the ground up to support high utilization rates, 100VG has slightly less usable bandwidth than 100Tx networks with no priority data. This is mostly due to the overhead involved in port scanning. 100VG stations must wait until the hub tells them that it is okay to transmit. Even then, if the data has normal priority, the hub will only accept one data frame before moving on to the next port. Ethernet does not have this problem, as any station can transmit when it is ready, provided the circuit is free.

Another drawback of 100VG is that demand priority has no allowance for supporting full-duplex communications. Full duplex allows a station to effectively double the amount of available bandwidth. This allows a network using 100Tx to reach nearly a 200Mbps data transfer rate. Demand priority does not have this ability.

Third, 100VG has also suffered from poor vendor support. While everyone seems to be shipping 100Tx products, there are very few 100VG vendors besides HP. This syndrome is similar to what happened to IBM's Token Ring topology. With limited product sources, some potential end users went with Ethernet because there was a much larger vendor base to choose from. Limited vendor support also helps to drive up the cost, which makes the technology even less appealing.

Probably the biggest drawback of 100VG is the way demand priority determines whether a station needs to send normal or high-priority data. Hewlett-Packard originally hoped that application developers would support the technology. Software that needed to send time-sensitive data could send a request to the hub requesting a high-priority channel. When this type of support was not developed (it requires that the software be written specifically for 100VG networks), hardware vendors started adding the support to their network card drivers. The problem is that it is very easy for any savvy end user to enable this feature, setting all their network communications to high priority. The result is that this one user can suck up nearly all available bandwidth and bring a network to its knees.

CAT3 Operation

As we mentioned a little earlier, 100VG has another interesting feature: the ability to operate over CAT3 (Category 3) cabling. We will cover cable types in the following chapter, but CAT3 cabling is only rated for 10Mb operation. 100VG circumvents this limitation by transmitting and receiving over all four wire pairs. Each pair sustains a 30Mb transmission rate, with approximately 5Mb on each going to communication overhead. The result is (30–5) x 4 or 100Mbps worth of throughput.

Despite all its drawbacks, 100VG does bring some interesting technology to the table. Using multiple wire pairs to transmit data goes a long way towards extending the life of twisted-pair cabling. Don't be surprised if you see this functionality utilized in other topologies down the road. Also, demand priority is a wonderful first pass at providing quality of service on a topology other than ATM. It is rumored that Hewlett-Packard may extend 802.12 to include transmission rates of up to 1Gbps. It's possible that if the 100VG specifications are revised, improvements may be made to some of the current inadequacies of demand priority. While it appears to be a dead-end technology, 100VG-AnyLAN deserves some credit for the innovations it has produced.

Appropriate Applications

Given 100VG's advantages and disadvantages, its most appropriate application at present is leveraging old network wiring. If you find yourself administering a network made up of CAT3 wiring, and it is unlikely that funding will be made available to upgrade the cabling to CAT5, 100VG-AnyLAN may be a good fit. Keep in mind that you must have all four pairs of cable available. Some installations have split their cabling so that two pairs are used for networking and two pairs are used for the phone system.

If your network meets all of the above criteria, 100VG may be just the thing to breathe new life into it.

Topology Rules

Table 6.4 shows the topology rules for 100VG-AnyLAN.

TABLE 6.4: Topology Rules for 100VG-AnyLAN

Item	Rules
Maximum cable lengths	CAT3 twisted-pair: 325 ft
	CAT5 twisted-pair: 700 ft
	Fiber: 1640 ft
Minimum cable lengths	None
Maximum number of stations per cable	Twisted-pair: 2
	Fiber: 2
Maximum number of stations per logical network	1024
Maximum number of segments	5
Maximum overall length of logical network	Twisted-pair: 4200 ft
	Fiber: 1.2 miles

FDDI

Fiber Distributed Data Interface (FDDI) was the first of the popular networking topologies to reach 100Mbps throughput. For a number of years, if you needed 100Mb performance, FDDI was the only way to go. While other topologies have caught up in raw throughput, FDDI has benefits in network stability and fault-tolerance that still make it a good choice. While the transmission media of choice for FDDI is fiber, the specification also makes concessions for running CAT5 out to the desktop.

FDDI supports two physical topologies, ring and star. Ring is far more widely implemented than star because it allows the use of FDDI's fault-tolerant features. FDDI's ring topology is similar to IBM's legacy Token Ring topology, but with an additional ring that has been added for redundancy. This second ring is normally dormant and is only used if a failure occurs in the primary ring.

Figure 6.10 shows FDDI networks with star and ring physical topologies. As a ring, FDDI can recover from a cable failure by activating the secondary ring. This redundancy is lost when FDDI is implemented in a star topology.

FIGURE 6.10:

An example of an FDDI network, including star and ring physical topologies

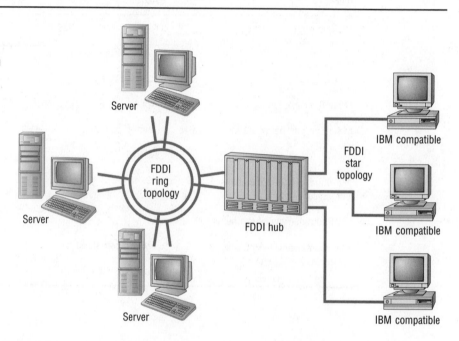

FDDI has also borrowed Token Ring's method of data transmission. A single frame referred to as a *token* is passed around the ring from station to station. When a station has data to transmit, it grabs the token and transmits a frame of data in its place. This frame then travels around the ring until it is received by the destination node it was addressed to. The destination station then makes a copy of the frame and continues to forward it along the ring, setting the Frame Copied Indicator (FCI) bit. When the station that originally transmitted the frame receives the frame back and sees that the FCI bit has been set, it assumes the transmission has been successful. It then removes the frame from the ring and transmits the token in its place. The next station wishing to transmit data will then grab the token and repeat the process.

Token communications have some inherent advantages over Ethernet. The first is the ability to support a larger frame size of 4096 bytes. If you remember our discussion about frame size versus network utilization, you will remember that the larger the average frame size, the more data that can be transmitted in a given period of time, thanks to reduced overhead.

Token passing is also a bit more orderly than Ethernet's CSMA/CD method of communication. It tends to perform better as higher utilization levels are achieved. This makes it an ideal choice when you are expecting to move very large data files over the network.

You'll remember from our discussion on fiber media that fiber stations get their output data port (Tx) connected to the input data port (Rx) of their downstream neighbor. This continues around the ring until the last station connects its Tx port to the Rx port of the first station.

This still applies to FDDI topology as well, except that an FDDI station will have a second set of transmit-and-receive ports for the second ring. On the second ring, the Rx port of a station connects to the Tx port of its downstream neighbor. This dual set of transmit-and-receive ports is why these stations are referred to as *dual-attach stations (DAS)*. To avoid confusion these ports are grouped by destination and labeled A and B. This yields four wires (two sets) to deal with instead of eight (four sets).

NOTE   When connecting DAS systems, you attach connection A to connection B of its downstream neighbor. This simplifies wiring and avoids cross-connecting the rings.

Figure 6.11 illustrates FDDI dual-attach stations. Note that each node connects to both rings in case of a failure.

The reason that stations are connected in this fashion is to guard against cable or hardware failure. Let's assume that we have a cable failure between two of the routers shown in Figure 6.11. When this cable failure occurs, the station immediately downstream from the failure will quickly realize it is no longer receiving data. It then begins to send out a special maintenance packet called a *beacon*. A beacon is the method used by a token station to let other systems around the ring know it has detected a problem. A beacon frame is a system's way of saying,

"Hey, I think there is a problem between me and my upstream neighbor because I am no longer receiving data from her." The station would then initialize its connection on the secondary ring so that it would now send and receive data on connector A.

FIGURE 6.11:

An example of FDDI dual-attach stations

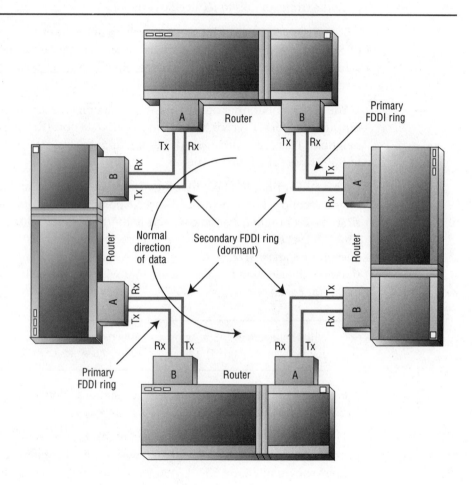

The beacon packet would continue to be forwarded until it reached the beaconing system's upstream neighbor. This upstream neighbor would then initialize its connection to the secondary ring by sending and receiving on connector B. This in effect isolates the problem area and returns normal connectivity. When the beaconing station begins to receive its own beacons, it ceases transmission, and ring operation returns to normal. The final transmission path would resemble the network shown in Figure 6.12. By using beacon frames, the systems on the network can determine the failure area and isolate it by activating the secondary ring.

FIGURE 6.12:

How FDDI DASs recover from a cable failure

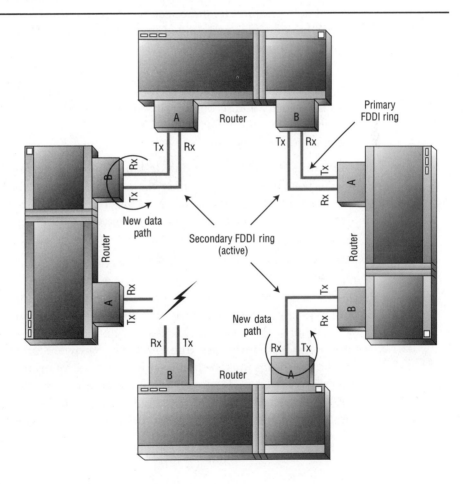

If this had in fact been a hardware failure caused by a fault in the upstream neighbor and that system was unable to initialize the secondary ring, the faulty system's upstream neighbor would have detected this and stepped in to close the ring. This would isolate the problem hardware but allow the rest of the network to continue to function.

The DASs would continue to monitor the faulty links until it appears that connectivity has been restored. If the link passes an integrity test, the primary ring returns to full operation, and the secondary ring again goes dormant. This type of network fault tolerance can be deemed critical in environments where connectivity must be maintained seven days a week, 24 hours a day (referred to as "7 by 24 operation"). This functionality is what still makes FDDI the most fault-tolerant networking topology available today for local area networks.

If fault tolerance is not required, most FDDI hardware will allow you to activate both the primary and secondary ring simultaneously. This provides full-duplex communication with a potential of 200Mb throughput. The trade-off, of course, is that fault tolerance is lost.

One drawback of this dual ring design is that distance specifications are half of what is usually supported by fiber cable. This is because when a ring fails, the effective ring size can double (because the effective ring size is the primary ring size plus the secondary ring size). However, given the exceptional distance specification of fiber cable, this is rarely a problem.

FDDI also supports a star topology for connecting systems that do not require this level of fault tolerance. Devices called dual-attach concentrators (DACs) are connected to the ring topology, providing multiple single-attach station (SAS) connections. SAS connections are typically used for end user workstations. These stations are usually not deemed critical and can endure short periods of down time due to cable or hardware failures. While DAS and DAC connections must be made with fiber, SAS connections can be fiber or category 5 twisted-pair. Figure 6.13 shows a network using a mixture of DAS, DAC, and SAS connections. The ring topology is deployed in the area requiring fault tolerance (server connections) while the less critical workstations are connected as a star.

FDDI DAC connecting SAS
systems to the ring

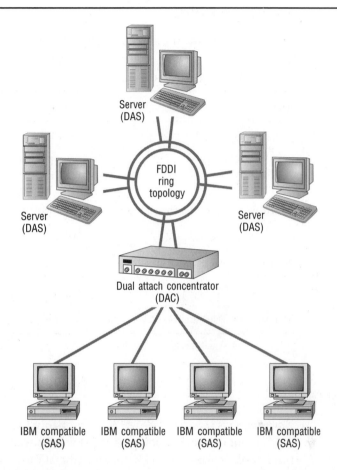

Appropriate Applications

The most appropriate applications for FDDI are servers and backbones. Because of its high level of fault tolerance, FDDI is a wonderful fit for server rooms and connecting workgroup clusters. Its resistance to cable and hardware failures makes for a stable environment.

FDDI has been around for a while, so finding hardware vendors and support is not very difficult. Because it is a more efficient topology than Ethernet, it can keep up when connected to multiple 100Tx segments.

Topology Rules

Table 6.5 shows the topology rules for FDDI.

TABLE 6.5: Topology Rules for FDDI

Item	Rules
Maximum cable lengths	CAT5 twisted-pair: 325 ft
	Fiber: 1.2 miles
Minimum cable lengths	None
Maximum number of stations per cable	Ring topology: 500
	Star: 2
Maximum number of stations per logical network	500
Maximum number of segments	Gated by performance
Maximum overall length of logical network	62 miles

ATM

Asynchronous transfer mode (ATM) is probably the most elusive and least understood of all network topologies. ATM was conceived in 1983 by AT&T Bell Labs, but it took nearly 10 years before an official forum was created to mature this technology into a production-quality topology. It then took the ATM forum another four years (until June 1995) just to release its first specification for ATM LAN emulation (LANE). In November 1996, the much anticipated LANE 2.0 was released, only to be found lacking in much-needed features such as scalability and multiprotocol support. To add insult to injury, some LANE 1-compliant hardware was incapable of supporting LANE 2. Pioneers of this new technology found themselves replacing some very expensive hardware just to stay current.

With this history, why has ATM captured so much attention? Because ATM has the potential to provide high data rates and quality of service, and to blur the lines between LANs and WANs.

ATM represents a significant change in network design. To start, it does not vary its frame size like Ethernet or token-based topologies. Instead, ATM uses a fixed packet size of 48 bytes (referred to as a *cell*) for all communications. This fixed size allows for a more predictable traffic rate than networks with variable-length packets. By regulating the number of packets that flow between connections, ATM can accurately predict and closely control bandwidth utilization. The drawback to this fixed packet size, of course, is increased overhead. As we found in our discussion of 10Mb Ethernet, smaller packets mean a less efficient data transfer and more network bottlenecks. An ATM cell is roughly three percent the size of a full Ethernet frame and one percent the size of a Token Ring or 100VG-AnyLAN frame.

To quantify this loss in performance, when 155Mb ATM is deployed on a LAN to handle normal network traffic (file access and printing, for example), it provides less throughput than 100Mb Ethernet. While some of this loss is due to protocol translation (described below), much of it is due to the smaller frame size.

Another significant difference is how ATM stations communicate with each other. While other topologies rely on upper-layer protocols like IPX and IP to route information between logical networks, ATM uses permanent virtual connections (PVCs) and switched virtual connections (SVCs) between communicating stations. Virtual connections (VCs) are logical communication channels between end stations—logical because this circuit is created along shared media that may also contain other virtual connections providing a circuit between other end stations. While the circuits must share available bandwidth along the media, communications are kept separate from each other through the use of connection identifiers. This is the complete opposite of Ethernet, where every station shares a single circuit along the media and is required to listen to packet transmissions between other stations. Figure 6.14 shows an example of virtual circuit and virtual path switching.

ATM is a connection-oriented topology. This means that a connection or VC circuit must be established between the source and destination stations before data transfer. Again, this is in contrast to other topologies like Ethernet, which simply transmit the data onto the wire and rely on networking hardware to route the information to its destination network. With ATM connectivity, devices on the network called ATM switches maintain tables with the identifications of all end stations. When a station needs to transmit data, it issues a maintenance packet

FIGURE 6.14:

Virtual circuit and virtual path
switching

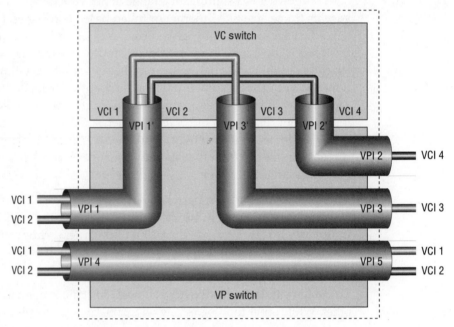

called a virtual path identifier (VPI) that propagates out into the network, setting up a virtual connection between the two systems. The purpose of the VPI is to create a circuit-switched connection between the two systems and ensure that each portion of the path along the way has enough available bandwidth to carry the signal. Once this circuit is complete, data transmission may begin.

A big plus to this type of connectivity is quality of service. If the bandwidth demands of the application can be identified before setting up the virtual connection, the VPI can reserve the required bandwidth and only pick routes that can support the required transmission rate. In effect, this a form of automatic load balancing of the network.

This type of connectivity is nearly identical to the connectivity of the public telephone network (PTN). When you dial a phone number, a signal similar to a VPI goes out over the network, setting up a connection between your phone and the phone at the number you just dialed. This is accomplished in that brief period of time between when you dial the number and when you hear that first ring. If there is a problem in a direct line connection between you and the destination number (for example, if there is a broken connection or if there is currently heavy usage), the network will switch you to an alternate circuit path that is free. When the circuit is complete, your call goes through, and the phone rings on the other end. When your call is complete, the circuit is torn down and the bandwidth is made available to other users.

Because ATM functions in a similar fashion to the PTN, it is an ideal candidate for large networks. ATM is able to leverage the largest existing network in the world (PTN) by integrating without translation or modification. A connection can be made from LAN to WAN to LAN using strictly ATM. The PTN becomes a seamless extension of the local network, as no translation is required.

Let's say we have two Ethernet LANs connected by a Frame Relay WAN. Let's also assume we wish to send a frame of data from one Ethernet network to the other. With this configuration, our network will require additional hardware at both ends of the WAN to translate between the two topologies. Our frame will undergo translation as it enters the WAN, and then again when it leaves it to be transmitted onto the other Ethernet segment. If we replace this configuration with ATM, no translation is required because ATM can be supported on both the LAN and the WAN.

ATM Drawbacks

Currently there are some problems with this configuration. To start, ATM wants to handle all of the end-to-end connections. This is the same type of functionality provided by existing upper-layer protocols like IPX and IP. Methods for incorporating these existing protocols with ATM have met with a number of delays. For example, LANE 2 was supposed to include changes to the frame header to support multiple protocols, but this feature was dropped from the specification by the time it was released. Such configuration problems are not an issue in an ATM-only environment, but they can make incorporating ATM functionality into an existing network infrastructure difficult at best.

Another issue with ATM is the *node maps* maintained by ATM switches. These node maps are what allow VPIs to create paths from one end station to another. There is currently no auto-discovery method for creating these tables in PVC circuits; these tables must be maintained manually. This can make maintaining a network with many nodes a real nightmare. While SVCs do not have this limitation, there is no guarantee that the circuit will be able to allocate the full bandwidth required by the end station if a WAN connection is required. If you have ever tried to make a phone call during peak hours and received a busy circuit signal, you have experienced this phenomenon. If the connection is not permanent, there is no guarantee it will be there 100 percent of the time. In some environments (such as money transfers or credit checks), this type of unpredictability can be unacceptable.

As if all of this were not confusing enough, a number of ATM vendors have grown weary of waiting for specification drafts to add functionality to their networking hardware. To compensate, they have developed proprietary implementations of this functionality that may or may not work with equipment from other vendors. In effect, you could end up locked into a single vendor for all your ATM needs. This has created a real "buyer beware" environment when purchasing network components. As an example, when LANE 2.0 was released, some ATM vendors were able to provide the additional functionality it supported with a simple software upgrade to existing hardware; other vendors, however, were unable to provide this level of support, and customers found themselves in the position of needing to replace some very expensive hardware to gain the additional functionality.

Appropriate Applications

ATM specifications are still in a state of flux. While the technology shows great promise, it is difficult to recommend it for any application at this time. There are still a number of bugs that need to be shaken out of this technology. With the recent hype over 1Gbps Ethernet, it is questionable if ATM will receive the resources and attention it so desperately needs to be molded into a stable production topology.

Most network managers have decided to err on the side of caution by letting others ride out ATM's bumpy road ahead and adopting a wait-and-see policy. ATM's greatest benefits will be in backbone implementations, which is the last place a seasoned network person wants to introduce a metamorphosing technology.

Wide Area Network Topologies

Wide area network (WAN) topologies are network configurations that are designed to carry data over a great distance. Unlike LANs, which are designed to deliver data between many systems, WAN topologies are usually point-to-point. *Point-to-point* means that the technology was developed to support only two nodes sending and receiving data. It is expected that if multiple nodes need access to the WAN, a LAN will be placed behind it to accommodate this functionality.

Figure 6.15 displays this type of connectivity. The only devices communicating directly on the WAN are the two routers. The routers provide connectivity from one single point to another. Any other devices that need to use the WAN must communicate through the two routers.

FIGURE 6.15:

There are only two devices (routers) that are directly communicating on the WAN.

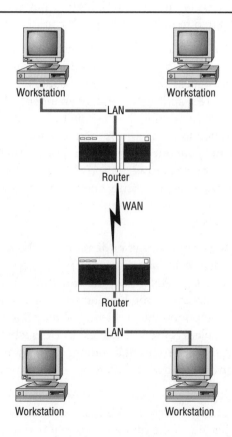

NOTE   We will explore the best ways to interconnect LANs and WANs when we discuss networking hardware.

Local Exchange Carriers

In Chapters 20 and 21, we'll discuss means for setting up private networks—known as *extranets*—and transmitting data over wide geographical areas. But sometimes it is more cost effective to take advantage of the services provided by a local exchange carrier. Most local exchange carriers can provide WAN connectivity from 56K to 45Mb. If your bandwidth demands are minimal (less than 10Mb) and the distance between nodes is great, leasing services from your local carrier may make more sense than setting up a private network. While the raw long-term costs can seem to be higher, they can easily be offset because you are not required to maintain the WAN communication equipment.

If an exchange carrier will be handling your WAN needs, you first need to get the carrier your data. This is done by running a connection between you and the closest local exchange carrier facility—typically one of the baby Bells created by the AT&T split-up in 1984, or an independent. The local exchange carrier will take care of connecting their facility to yours. Somewhere within your facility is a point referred to as the *demarc* (demarcation point). This is the point to which the local carrier guarantees service. You want to make sure that this point is as close to your networking hardware as possible, as it identifies the point where the local exchange carrier's responsibility ends. If the connection is active up to the demarc, but you're still having connectivity problems, most local exchange carriers will be of little help.

For example, if your demarc is in the same room as your servers and network hardware, it's a straightforward process to isolate a connectivity problem (it's either the WAN link or the hardware). If your demarc is in another building or 20 floors away, you have an additional length of cable to add into the equation. To compound the problem, you may find that no one wishes to take ownership of a problem caused by that cable. Does it belong to the exchange carrier? The building owner? Your organization? By locating the demarc in the same room as your network hardware, you remove this gray area.

If you are establishing a WAN that connects to a local geographical location, all that may be required is to have the same local exchange carrier wire up to the other site. If the connection is required to span a large distance, however, you will probably need to involve a long-distance carrier, as illustrated in Figure 6.16. Long-distance carriers like AT&T, Sprint, and MCI connect to the local carrier at a location called the *point of presence* (*POP*). A POP is simply telephone-speak for the point where the networks for the local exchange carrier and the long distance carrier meet. Most towns will have at least one POP. Major cities will have quite a few.

FIGURE 6.16:

Responsibilities of both local exchange and long distance carriers

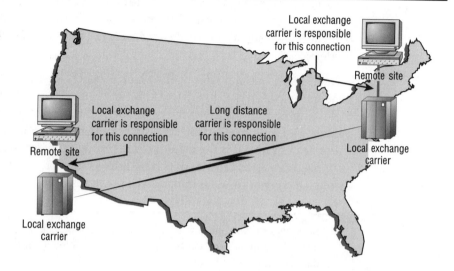

If all this sounds a bit complex—well, it can be. But most long distance carriers have revamped their service departments and are willing to take care of the setup for you. They will take care of contacting all local exchange carriers involved and schedule the wiring and testing for you.

Dial-Up Analog

Dial-up analog connections use the same PTN (public telephone network) to create end-to-end connections that your telephone uses. In data communications, this type of connection is most commonly made through a modem (short for modulator/demodulator) to dial up the phone number you wish to contact.

Unfortunately, the public telephone network was originally designed to carry voice, which does not require a large amount of bandwidth. This is why modem connections are in the kilobit range instead of the megabit range. Because it was easier to service voice with an analog connection, the telephone network was originally designed to be analog, not digital. These analog lines are referred to as *plain old telephone service (POTS)*.

A modem takes the digital signals from a computer and converts them to analog. This analog signal is then transmitted over the dial-up line to the POP, where it is converted back to a digital signal. Even though analog is still used to connect to people's homes, most of the connections between POPs have been upgraded to digital.

So our modem's signal has been returned to a digital format. It travels over the backbone to the destination POP where it is again translated into an analog signal. The analog signal travels down the POTS on the other side to the receiving modem.

Analog transmission rates peak around 9600bps. Despite this limitation, modem vendors have been able to push raw throughput to 28.8K, 33.6K, and even 56Kbps by leveraging technologies such as frequency shifting or phase shifting. If you include data compression, this rate can be as high as 115Kbps. 115Kbps is not the true transfer rate—it is the effective rate through the use of compression. For example, a 33.6Kbps modem may be able to achieve a throughput rate of 115Kbps through the use of compression, but the raw transfer rate is still 33.6Kbps.

NOTE   *Frequency shifting* and *phase shifting* involve using more than one carrier wave to transmit a signal. *Compression* involves removing redundant characters from the data prior to transmission.

Limiting the speed of a modem is the noise created when the signal is translated between the digital and analog formats. The faster a connection, the more susceptible it becomes to errors from noise interference. Modem manufacturers must walk the line between making modem transfer data as fast as possible, but not so fast that noise begins to generate errors. 56K modems get around this noise problem by eliminating some of these translations, and thus reducing the amount of noise generated on the circuit.

56K modems function under the principle that converting information from digital to analog creates more noise than translating it from analog to digital. In order for a 56K modem to work properly, the signal cannot go through any digital-to-analog conversions once it leaves the modem. The theory is that if the destination system has a digital connection to their local POP, no digital-to-analog conversions are required (besides the modem itself).

For example, let's assume you are using a 56K modem to call your Internet service provider (ISP). This ISP maintains a T1 digital connection to their local POP for dial-in access. This connection leads directly into their network, which is also digital.

When the signal leaves your modem, it is converted from digital to analog. The signal then travels down the POTS to the POP, where it is converted back to a digital signal. This signal then travels down a digital backbone to the ISP's POP. Up to this point, the functionality has been identical to a regular modem connection. Once the signal leaves the ISP's POP, however, it does not need to be converted. Because the ISP maintains a digital connection, the signal can remain digital from your POP all the way into the ISP's network. This eliminates the need to perform any digital-to-analog conversions once the signal has left the modem.

There are a few caveats with this type of connection. First, you cannot put two 56K modems on each end and expect a 56K connection. Doing so would require the use of POTS on each end and thus a digital-to-analog conversion by the destination POP. Special hardware is required on the receiving end to accommodate a digital connection to the POP (such as the T1 mentioned above).

NOTE   When two 56K modems are connected to each other via "normal" phone lines (POTS), the connection speed will not exceed 33.6 and could even be slower, depending on line conditions.

The second issue is that this connection speed assumes that near-perfect phone conditions and wiring exist, which is rarely the case. Even if the receiving station is outfitted for a digital connection, expect a 56K modem to connect between 45K to 53K.

In a business environment, dial-up analog is good for load-balancing; you can also use it as a backup connection to some other WAN topology. Many wide-area network devices include circuitry to switch over to a secondary means of connection if the primary means of connection fails. For example, a company may rely on a Frame Relay circuit to connect a remote office site, but have an analog dial-up connection configured in case the Frame Relay fails.

Dial-up connections may also be required when users need remote access to the local network. The users dial in to some form of remote connectivity device and receive access to network resources, typically either via remote node or via remote control.

Remote Control

A *remote control* dial-in connection involves dedicating a computer with a modem as the *host* and running remote-control software (such as Symantec's pcANYWHERE) on it. Note that usually one dedicated computer is required for each concurrent connection being supported. The user also runs a version of the remote-control software and dials in to the host computer. When the user authenticates (usually by entering a user name and password), they gain control of the host located on the network. The user can now run applications located on that host and access network resources.

NOTE In remote control, the remote client becomes the equivalent of a dumb terminal. All processing, disk activity, and network access are being provided by the host system. This means that special steps must be taken to print and copy files to the remote client. If you are in a remote session and simply click the Print button, it will be the host system that prints, not the remote client.

The benefit to this type of connection is speed. The only information that travels the analog line is screen updates. Response time is much faster than remote node (described below). The down side to this type of connectivity is that a single computer must be dedicated to each concurrent connection. All required software must be loaded on the machine or available over the network. Special considerations must be taken with programs such as e-mail that expect the same user to always be using the same client. Also, two licensed copies of the remote-control software may be required—one for the host and one for the client.

Remote Node

A *remote node* connection allows the user to dial in to the network and have their computer attach to the network as if it were physically located in the office. Examples of remote-node devices are Shiva's LanRover and NetModems, or Microsoft's Remote Access Service (RAS). The remote user dials in to the modem pool and is authenticated by the device. Once this is complete, the user is able to access network resources the same way they normally do, albeit slower.

The benefit to this type of connection is flexibility and lower cost. If you dial in to a remote control system and need access to a Unix system, but the host only supports IPX, you're out of luck. With a remote node connection, you simply have to make sure that the computer dialing in supports IP. The cost factor comes into play in that a remote node connection does not require a fully configured PC loaded with software on the network end. Additionally, most types of remote-node server software can support multiple users dialing into a single machine.

NOTE
Most remote node devices will allow you to additionally (and simultaneously) use network-based remote control software, if you later wish to locate hosts on your network or decide to provide both types of connectivity.

The downside to remote node connections is speed. If you think a 10Mb network is slow, response time can absolutely crawl when squeezed through a 28.8Kb connection. It is not unheard of for it to take five minutes or more just to log in to a NetWare server. Clearly if remote node is to be used effectively, preparation is required. Plan on running as many applications as possible from the remote system and only use the dial-up connection to transfer needed data files.

Creating Hunt Groups for Modem Pools

Whether you are using remote control or remote node, modem pools can be made easier to use by creating *hunt groups*. A hunt group allows you to assign a single dial-in number that can scan multiple phone lines looking for a connection that is free. For example, let's say you have four telephone numbers—555-1212, 555-1313, 555-1414, and 555-1515—each connected to a modem providing remote connectivity to your network. Normally your remote users would have to remember all four separate numbers in case the first one they try is busy. With a hunt group, you could point the 555-1212 number at each of the three remaining numbers, so that if 1212 is busy, the call is directed to 1313. If this line is free, the number will ring, and the user will connect without even knowing their call was redirected. If 1313 is also busy, the connection will be directed to 1414 and so on. This will continue until the last number is reached (1515 in this example). If all the numbers were in use, the user would then receive a busy signal.

We've seen this work quite well, except for one flaw. Sometimes when a user abnormally disconnects (for example, if they break the connection by shutting off their modem), the modem on the network side can become hung and drop off auto-answer. (Auto-answer is what tells the modem to answer the phone when it rings.) If auto-answer becomes disabled, the modem will not answer the phone when it rings. Because the hunt group only looks for a free line, it will direct users to this modem, and they will not be able to connect.

Given the above hunt group, let's assume that 1313 drops off of auto-answer. The first user to call in is directed to 1212, and connects to the network. The next user calls in and is hunted to 1313 because 1212 is busy. 1313 then proceeds to ring off the hook because the modem is no longer answering the phone. When this user gets tired of listening to the phone ring and the next user calls in, they are hunted to 1313 and receive the same response. Even though there is only one "functionally challenged" modem, we still have only one operational phone line. 1414 and 1515 are not used unless someone else happens to call in while someone is sitting listening to 1313 ring without answer. What makes this problem even more dramatic is that it appears to be intermittent. Some users will be able to connect while others will not (depending on whether the first line is free or not).

To troubleshoot a hung modem in a hunt group, you must start at the end of your hunt group (1515) and work backward until you find the modem that will not pick up. Usually you need to *power cycle* the modem—switch it off and then back on—to clear the problem.

NOTE   Some remote access devices that use internal modems provide the capability to dial in on a free line and reboot the device remotely, which power cycles the modems. This is a last resort, because rebooting the device will disconnect anyone else who is currently dialed in.

WARNING   We've seen hunt groups set up as described here but with the additional criterion that all numbers also hunt to the first (for example, calling 1313, 1414, or 1515 causes 1212 to ring first). This can be a very bad thing: If you have a bad modem line, you have no easy way to isolate it.

Hunt groups can be set up through your local telephone company. Simply contact your customer representative, and they'll point you in the right direction. Hunt group charges vary but are usually pretty reasonable.

Use Regular Analog Lines for Remote Access

When setting up remote network access, use straight analog lines. Many businesses will try to run their modem pool through their PBX in order to save on phone costs. The problem is that most PBXs are made to support voice, not data, and fall apart at connection speeds above 9600 baud. A good indication that this is occurring is if users have problems establishing connections or if the connection is frequently dropped while in use.

NOTE   If the line requires you to dial a 9 or an 8 to call outside of your office, it may be connected through your PBX. When in doubt, consult your company's phone technician—unless of course you happen to wear that hat as well!

Dial-up analog can be an effective solution for creating remote connectivity. The cost breakpoint occurs when you are using dial-up analog to connect the same two locations for more than four or five hours a day. At this point, it may be more cost effective to use some other form of WAN connectivity that creates a permanent connection and bills on a flat-rate basis.

Appropriate Applications

The following are appropriate applications for dial-up analog:

- home access to the Internet
- home access to the corporate network
- corporate access to the Internet when only a few users need access
- backup connectivity for other WAN services

ISDN

Integrated Services Digital Network (*ISDN*) is the digital alternative to the analog PTN. There are two levels of service available: basic rate ISDN (BRI) and primary rate ISDN (PRI).

Basic rate ISDN is two 64Kb channels referred to as B channels (*bearer* channels) and one 16Kb channel referred to as a D channel (*data* channel). The two B channels are used for transmitting data. The D channel is used for overhead to maintain the connection. Primary rate ISDN includes 23 B channels and one D channel, and has the effective throughput of a T1 connection (1.544Mb).

An ISDN line uses separate phone numbers for each channel the same way an analog dial-up connection does for each line. For example, a BRI connection would have two separate phone numbers, one for each B channel. Because the two channels are completely separate, ISDN can load-balance a connection by using the second line only when required or by leaving it open for other communications.

For example, let's say you're using your ISDN connection to cruise the Internet. You're buzzing around from Web page to Web page. At this point, you most likely only have one B channel active, for an effective throughput rate of 64Kb. You then run across a site that has every Dilbert comic for the last three years located in a single 450-meg zip file. Interested in cubicle art, you click on the link and start downloading the file. At some predetermined point in the communication, the second B channel will kick in, increasing the transfer rate to 128Kb. This effectively cuts the time it would take to download the file by nearly half. When the large file transfer is complete, the second B channel drops and your effective throughput rate returns to 64Kb.

As mentioned, this second channel can also be used for completely separate communications as well, both inbound and outbound. While cruising the Web on the first B channel, you could also be carrying on a telephone conversation or sending (or receiving) a fax on the second B channel.

Because ISDN uses digital transmissions, it is typically a more stable connection than analog. Connectivity is provided by an ISDN card that fits in your PC or by a piece of hardware you can connect to your network. The network version allows anyone on the network to open an ISDN connection through the device. Connection times are near instantaneous. This is a good thing, as a connection can easily be established before a network connection can time out. The delays imposed in setting up an analog modem connection makes this type of connectivity impractical if not impossible. In effect, ISDN can serve up *bandwidth on demand*, leaving the connection closed when not in use.

Unfortunately this has led to some abuses of ISDN. Small companies have been sucked in by the glamour of ISDN hoping that a pay-as-you-go structure would be more economical than a full-time connection, only to get burned when they receive the phone bill.

As mentioned, ISDN is capable of doing load balancing by bringing up the second B channel when needed. This is usually configured as a balance between time and current throughput. We want the second line to kick in under heavy traffic loads, but not so quickly that it responds to small files and is used for a few seconds and then not at all. Conversely, we do not want it to kick in too late, because it would then do very little to improve file transfer time.

At the other end of the transmission we want to tear that second connection down as quickly as possible when it is no longer needed. We do not want to tear it down too quickly, however, as the user may have a number of files to transfer, which would cause the line to be brought back up again immediately.

The above is somewhat true for the initial B channel as well. Initialization is easy; you bring up the channel when it is needed. But when do you tear it down? In the Web example above, if you tear the connection down too quickly you will end up bringing the link back up every time the user clicks on a new link.

Here's the kicker. ISDN costs anywhere from two to four times what you would pay for an analog line. This varies with your local exchange carrier, but should get you in the ball park of what ISDN will cost. Like an analog call, the first minute of an ISDN call is typically far more expensive than the minutes that follow. The result is that if you are tearing down and bringing up lines continuously, you could end up paying as much as $1 or more per minute. We know of a few companies that have been shocked to receive a first-month phone bill over $4,500. This is over twice what they would have paid for a T1 with 1.544Mb bandwidth!

Also, if you are using ISDN for Internet connectivity, keep in mind that the connection can only be established from your end. While this is not a problem if you are connecting from a single system and rely on your provider for services such as mail, it can cause problems if you are trying to connect your company's network to the Internet. Services such as mail and DNS need to be able to create connections bidirectionally. If someone on the Internet needs to send your company mail, your mail system needs to be constantly reachable. Because ISDN connections are constantly brought up and torn down, your mail system may or may not be reachable. This can cause mail to be delayed or, even worse, undeliverable.

If your ISP offers ISDN network connections, make sure they can host your Web server, reply to any DNS requests for you, and can queue your mail until your connection is brought back up online. You should also make sure that their method of transferring your mail to your local site is supported by your mail gateway. For example, some ISPs expect your mail system to use the `finger` command to trigger mail delivery. This command is supported by very few mail gateways.

This type of one-way connectivity can also cause problems if you are using ISDN to connect a remote office. Keep in mind that you must specifically design the circuit so that it can be initiated from either side (possibly by using two dial-up numbers). Otherwise, your home office may not be able to contact the remote network unless the connection has already been initiated by the remote office.

Another misconception is that a firewall or some other form of network protection is not required with an ISDN connection to the Internet. In fact, when an ISDN connection is active, a network is just as susceptible to attack as if it was linked to the Internet with a full-time connection.

Because ISDN is digital, it is not directly compatible with devices such as analog phones and faxes. These devices must be replaced with their digital counterparts or run through a coder/decoder (codec). A codec converts the analog signal from these devices to digital.

Appropriate Applications

These are the most appropriate applications for ISDN:

- home access to the Internet

- home access to the corporate network

- corporate access to the Internet when only a few users need access

- backup connectivity for other WAN services

- connectivity of remote office sites

Leased Lines

Leased lines are dedicated analog or digital circuits that are paid for on a flat-rate basis. This means that whether you use the circuit or not, you are paying a fixed monthly fee. Leased lines are point-to-point connections—they are used to connect one geographical location to another. You cannot dial a phone number and point the connection to a new destination.

There are two common way leased lines are deployed:

- The leased line constitutes the entire length of the connection between the two geographic locations.

- The leased line is used for the connection from each location to its local exchange carrier. Connectivity between the two exchange carriers is then provided by some other technology like Frame Relay (discussed later in this chapter).

Analog leased lines are conditioned to facilitate a lower error rate than would normally be achieved with a dial-up line. Conditioning helps to remove noise from the circuit which allows the connection to be used with less overhead for error correction. Digital leased lines are also referred to as *digital data service lines* and are available with bandwidths up to 56K. With analog leased lines a modem may still be used. Digital data service lines require a channel service unit/data service unit, or CSU/DSU (discussed further in Chapter 10). They also require some form of data terminating equipment (DTE)—typically, a router—to regulate traffic flow across the line. The DTE connects to the CSU/DSU via an RS232 serial connector, or possibly an RS449 connector for 56K connections. Digital data services are full duplexed, meaning that data transmissions are bidirectional, flowing in both directions at the same time.

Analog leased lines are used very little today. They were popular back in the mainframe days when they were used for connecting dumb-terminal users at remote sites. Digital leased lines are usually sufficient for connecting small companies to the Internet or providing connectivity for remote offices.

NOTE   A leased line is not expandable. To provide more bandwidth, you have to replace the line with a T1 (discussed in the next section).

Appropriate Applications

The following are appropriate applications for leased lines:

- connecting remote sites to the corporate office when bandwidth requirements are small

- Internet connectivity for small offices

- carrying voice or data

T1

A *T1* is a full-duplex signal over two-pair wire cabling. This wire pair terminates in a receptacle that resembles the square phone jacks used in older homes. T1s are used for dedicated point-to-point connections in the same way that leased lines are. Bandwidth on a T1 is available in increments from 64Kb up to 1.544Mb.

T1s use time division to break the two wire pairs up into 24 separate channels. *Time division* is the allotment of available bandwidth based on time increments. In the case of a T1 circuit, each channel is allowed to transmit for 5.2 microseconds (µs). This is the amount of time a T1 requires to transmit 8 bits (or 1 byte) of information. At the end of 5.2 µs, the channel must stop transmitting and relinquish control of the circuit to the next channel. If the channel has additional information to transmit, it must wait 119.8 µs—the amount of time it takes to cycle through the other 23 channels so that it is again that channel's turn to transmit.

To determine the available bandwidth on each channel, we must first determine the *sample rate*. The sample rate is the number of times each channel is allowed to transmit in a one-second period of time. Because each channel is allowed to transmit for 5.2 µs before releasing control to the next channel, we can determine the number of transmissions per second by using the following calculation:

1 (second) /.0000052 (transmit time per channel) = 192,398 transmissions per second

This is the total number of transmissions possible in a one-second period of time along a T1 line. These 192,398 transmissions are then broken up equally over the 24 channels:

192,398 (transmissions) / 24 (the number of channels) = 8000

Each of the 24 channels is allowed to transmit 8000 times per second. This is our sample rate—the number of times per second that each channel is sampled or checked to see if it needs to transmit data.

To determine the available bandwidth per channel, we multiply the sample rate by the amount of data we can transmit each sample period:

8 bits × 8000 samples per second = 64Kbps

The short answer to all this number-crunching is that each of the 24 channels on a T1 line is capable of moving 64Kb worth of data per second.

With 24 active channels, the full bandwidth available on a T1 is:

64Kbps × 24 = 1.536Mbps

NOTE   You'll notice that there are 8Kbps unaccounted for from the 1.544Mbps bandwidth stated in the first paragraph (1544Kbps – 1536Kbps = 8Kbps). This 8Kbps is overhead that goes towards managing the connections. So while a T1 is able to move 1.544Mb of information per second, only 1.536Mb can be actual data.

The nice thing about this setup is that an exchange carrier will lease you individual channels of this T1 based on your bandwidth requirements. This is called *fractional T1*. If you only need 512Kb, then you only need to lease eight channels. In the long term, this can save a considerable amount of money over leasing a full T1. This can be an ideal solution for a company that only needs 64 or 128Kb now but may want to upgrade to a larger pipe later. By initially connecting via a fractional T1 instead of a leased line, you will not need to rewire—you can simply turn on additional channels.

These 24 channels can also be broken up and dedicated to different services. For example, three channels can be dedicated to data with one channel being dedicated to voice. In this way, a single connection can provide connectivity for multiple services. By combining these services over a single T1, an organization can achieve a lower communication cost than if separate wiring was used for each.

The cost of a T1 is based on bandwidth requirements and the distance to your local exchange carrier. The typical cost for a T1 can be anywhere from $500 to $1,500 per month. Consult your local exchange carrier for their price structure.

Appropriate Applications

The following are appropriate applications for T1 lines:

- connecting remote sites to the corporate office when a large amount of bandwidth is required

- Internet connectivity for all but the largest offices

- carrying multiple voice and data lines to reduce cost

Frame Relay/X.25

Frame Relay and *X.25* are packet-switched technologies. Because data on a packet-switched network is capable of following any available circuit path, such networks are often represented by clouds in graphical presentations such as Figure 6.17.

FIGURE 6.17:

A WAN Frame Relay cloud connecting three networks

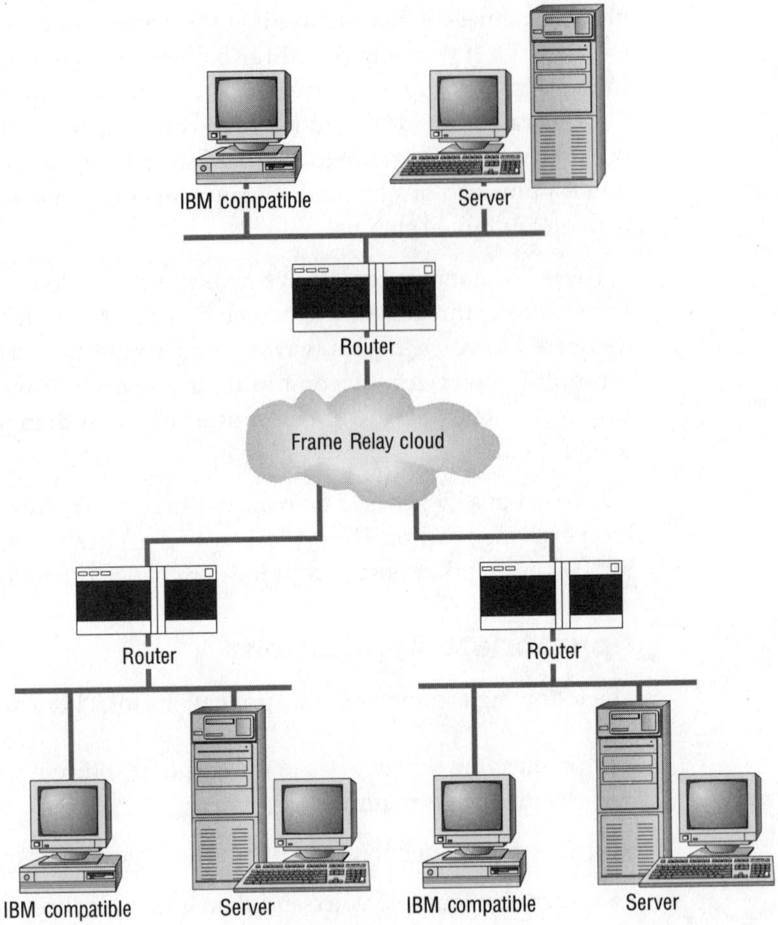

Both topologies must be configured as *permanent virtual circuits* (PVCs), meaning that all data entering the cloud at point A is automatically forwarded to point B. These end points are defined at the time the service is leased.

Note that the packet-switched network is a shared medium. Your exchange carrier uses the same network for all PVCs they lease out. In effect, you are sharing available bandwidth with every one of their clients. While this does not provide the truly private connection supplied by a leased line, it does help to keep down the costs of available bandwidth.

Frame Relay supports data transmission rates of 56K to 1.544Mb. Frame Relay is identical to and built upon the original X.25 specification, except that X.25 is analog, whereas Frame Relay is digital. As a digital transmission, Frame Relay requires less overhead for error correction and thus supports higher bandwidths than X.25 (X.25 only supports 56Kb). These topologies are an excellent example of how more usable bandwidth can be achieved by simply switching from analog to digital communications.

When ordering Frame Relay, the amount of bandwidth you purchase is based on a *committed information rate* (*CIR*). The CIR is the minimum amount of bandwidth your exchange carrier will guarantee as being available at any given time. Many carriers will allow you to burst above that rate depending on how much traffic is currently being passed through the cloud.

For example, let's say that you order a Frame Relay circuit with a CIR of 128Kb. If traffic is light within the Frame Relay cloud, you may be able to achieve momentary burst rates of 150Kb to 190Kb. Because Frame Relay has become popular, however, it has become more difficult to find windows where these higher transfer rates are available.

NOTE While many warn that the Internet may be headed for a meltdown, Frame Relay may already be experiencing a meltdown of its own. As a packet-switched network, each permanent virtual connection shares available bandwidth with other PVCs. It is not uncommon during peak utilization hours for a connection's effective throughput to fall below the CIR rate. If your bandwidth demands cannot endure momentary lapses, go for a higher CIR rate or stick with leased line.

For large WAN environments, Frame Relay can be far more cost effective than dedicated circuits. This is because you can run multiple PVCs through a single WAN connection.

For example, let's say we have four remote sites that require a 56Kb connection to the home office. If we were to construct this network out of dedicated circuits, it would require a 56Kb connection at each of the remote sites as well as four 56Kb connections running into the main office.

With Frame Relay, however, we could replace the four dedicated connections at the main office with one fractional T1 connection and simply activate four channels of the T1 circuit to accept the data. By requiring only a single circuit at the main site, we can reduce WAN costs.

In fact, there is nothing that says the CIR at the main office must equal the CIR value of all our remote sites. For example, let's assume that the connections to our remote site are used strictly for transferring e-mail. If bandwidth requirements are low, we may be able to drop the CIR at the main office from 256Kb to 128Kb. So long as the combined traffic to our four remote sites never exceeds 128Kb, our users would not even notice a drop in performance. This would reduce WAN costs even further.

X.25 is a mature technology with connectivity worldwide. Frame Relay is a bit newer and, as such, not as widely deployed. Most implementations should be able to utilize the benefits of Frame Relay. If you're running a truly global network, however, you may be stuck with X.25 in some areas.

> **NOTE** To connect to a Frame Relay or X.25 network, you must have a leased line or T1 wired between your organization and your local exchange carrier. From there, the circuit enters the cloud instead of following a dedicated path.

Appropriate Applications

The following are appropriate applications for Frame Relay and X.25:

- connecting remote sites to the corporate office, when only data connectivity is required

- carrying data that is not time sensitive (not voice or video)

SONET

SONET, or *synchronous optical network*, is available in bandwidths from 64Kb to 2.4Gbps (yes, Gb is "gigabit"). SONET uses time division (the same as a T1) over fiber and is being billed as the next-generation replacement to T1. SONET has some additional benefits that certainly make this a possibility.

The first benefit that SONET offers is direct support of the ATM topology. If ATM technology should ever take off on the LAN, SONET will be poised to extend the boundaries of ATM LAN networks by providing transparent support over the WAN. This, in effect, helps to blur the lines between LAN and WAN by utilizing similar communication rules across the entire transmission domain. If ATM has been deployed on the LAN, SONET is the ideal medium to utilize ATM over the WAN as well. This removes the usual requirement of translating between LAN and WAN topologies.

SONET is also in a much better position to support global networks. One drawback of T1 is that it is deployed in North America only. Most countries follow Conference and European Posts and Telecommunications Standards, which specify an E1 carrier that is not directly compatible with a T1 carrier. SONET is a much closer match to the European optical WAN specification called Synchronous Digital Hierarchy. When you're implementing a large global network, you may encounter many problems between the services offered by U.S. and European carriers. SONET is an approach to try and close some of these gaps.

SONET supports private virtual channels and will transmit ATM as well as ISDN natively; this removes the translation requirement between LAN and WAN topologies.

Appropriate Applications

The following are appropriate applications for SONET:

- connecting large metropolitan networks together
- Internet connectivity for large global companies
- network backbones for Internet service providers
- carrying voice and data via ATM from LAN to WAN to LAN

Summary

In this chapter, we looked at the difference between logical and physical topologies, discussed frames and switching types, and then looked at each of the existing network topologies, discussing the pros and cons and appropriate applications for each.

In the next chapter, we move on down to the network *media*, the wires and cables that physically interconnect computers and networks to build LANs and WANs.

PART II

Network Hardware

- CHAPTER 7: Transmission Media
- CHAPTER 8: Network Adapters and Punch-Down Panels
- CHAPTER 9: Repeaters, Hubs, Routers, and Bridges
- CHAPTER 10: Workstations, Servers, and Additional Connectivity Hardware

CHAPTER
SEVEN

7

Transmission Media

- Analog vs. digital transmissions

- Electromagnetic interference (EMI) and radio frequency interference (RFI)

- Thinnet cabling

- Twisted-pair cabling

- Fiber-optic cabling

- Radio transmissions and other atmospheric media

- Examples of network cabling design

The foundation of any network is the *transmission media*, or cables and circuitry used to interconnect and carry network signals between computer systems. In this chapter we will first cover digital and analog transmission basics, noise sources, synchronization, and fault tolerance, and then discuss cable and connector types. We'll finish by going through some examples of how to choose the appropriate cabling (media) for different situations.

To begin with, let's define transmission media. The network transmission medium (*media* in the plural) is what provides the path through which data travels on its way from one computer (or network) to another. The most commonly used transmission media are:

- copper cable, which carries electrical signals

- fiber-optic cable, which carries light

- the atmosphere, which can transmit light or radio waves

As we'll see, each of these media types has certain properties making it useful for transmitting data, yet also has certain limitations which require creativity to overcome. These three media types happen to have sufficiently different yet complimentary combinations of cost, efficiency, and range of transmission that none of them are likely to become obsolete in the foreseeable future. Our efficiency in using all three will likely improve significantly, though, in the years ahead.

Transmission Basics

Regardless of the medium used, we need some method of transmitting information from one place to another. These transmissions can take two forms—analog or digital.

Analog and Digital Transmissions

An *analog* transmission is a signal that can vary either in power level (known as *amplitude*) or in the number of times this power level changes in a fixed time period (known as *frequency*). An analog transmission can have a nearly infinite number of permissible values over a given range. For example, think of how we communicate verbally. Our vocal cords vibrate the air at different frequencies and amplitudes. These vibrations are received by the eardrum and interpreted into words. Subtle changes in tone or volume can dramatically change the meaning of what we say. Figure 7.1 shows an example of an analog transmission.

FIGURE 7.1:

An example of an analog transmission plotted over time

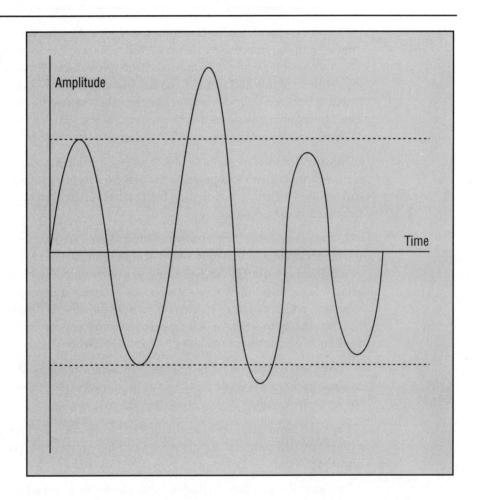

Notice the different amplitude each time the waveform peaks. Each of the three amplitude levels could be used to convey different information (like alphanumeric characters). This makes for a very efficient way to communicate information, as each wave cycle can be used to convey additional information. In a perfect world, this might be the ideal way to convey information.

NOTE   Frequency is measured in cycles per second, or hertz (Hz). If Figure 7.1 was measured over a period of one second, it would be identified as a frequency of three cycles per second, or 3Hz.

The problem with analog transmissions is that they are very susceptible to "noise" or interference. *Noise* is the addition of unwanted signal information. Think of having a conversation in a crowded room with lots of people conversing. With all of this background "noise" going on, it now becomes difficult to distinguish between your discussion and the others taking place within the room. This can result in a number of data retransmissions, signaled by phrases such as "What?" and "What did you say?"; this slows down the rate of information transfer.

Figure 7.2 shows an example of an analog signal in a noisy circuit. Note that it is now more difficult to determine the precise amplitude of each waveform. This can result in incorrect information being transmitted or in requiring the correct information to be resent.

To the rescue come *digital* transmissions. Digital communications are based on the binary system in that only two pieces of information are ever transmitted, a 1 or a 0. In an electrical circuit, a 0 is usually represented by a voltage of zero volts and a 1 is represented by five volts. This is radically different from analog transmissions, which can have an infinite number of possible values. These 1s and 0s are then strung together in certain patterns to convey information. For example, the binary equivalent of the letter "A" is 01000001.

The byte is considered to be the base unit when dealing with digital communications. Each byte is expected to relay one complete piece of information (such as the letter "A").

Digital communication is analogous to Morse code or the early telegraph system; certain patterns of pulses are used to represent different letters of the alphabet.

In Figure 7.3, you can see that our waveform has changed shape. It is no longer a free-flowing series of arcs but follows a rigid and predictable format.

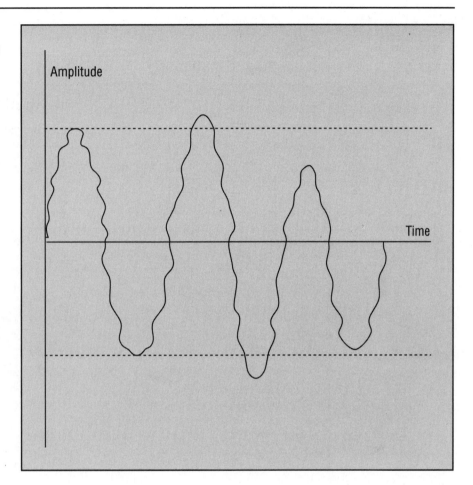

Because this waveform is so predictable and the variation between acceptable
values is so great, it is now much easier to determine what is being transmitted.
As shown in Figure 7.4, even when there is noise in the circuit, you can still see
which part of the signal is a binary 1 and which is a 0.

FIGURE 7.3:

A digital transmission plotted over time

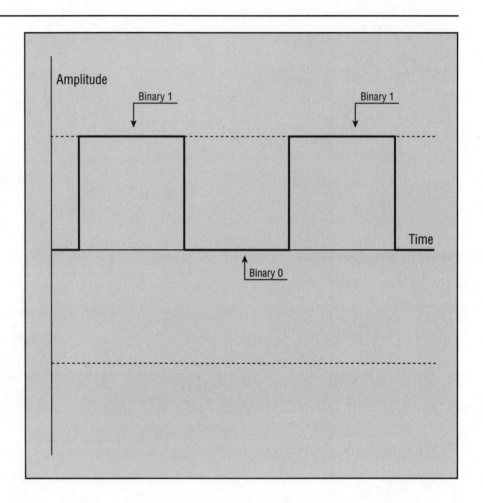

This simple format that allows digital communications to be so noise resistant can also be its biggest drawback. The information for the ASCII character A can be transmitted with a single analog wave or vibration, but transmitting the binary or digital equivalent requires eight separate waves or vibrations (to transmit 01000001). Despite this inherent drawback, it is usually much more efficient to use digital communication whenever possible. Analog circuits require a larger amount of overhead in order to detect and correct noisy transmissions. As we will discuss in later chapters, particularly when we cover wide area network (WAN) options, you can get greater bandwidth by simply converting a circuit from analog to digital communications.

FIGURE 7.4:

A digital transmission on a noisy circuit

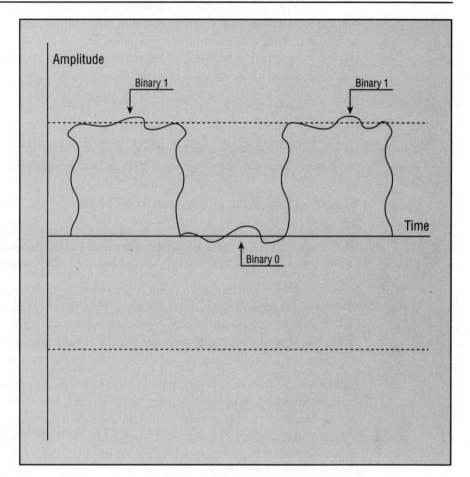

> **NOTE**
>
> *Overhead* is the amount of additional information that must be transmitted on a circuit to ensure that the receiving system gets the correct data and that the data is free of errors. Typically, when a circuit requires more overhead, less bandwidth is available to transmit the actual data. This is like the packaging used when something is shipped to you in a box. You didn't want hundreds of little Styrofoam acorns, but they're there in the box taking up space to ensure that your item is delivered safely.

Another big plus for digital communications is that computers process information in digital format. If you use analog communications to transfer information from one computer to another, you need some form of converter (such as a modem or a codex) at each end of the circuit to translate the information from digital to analog and then back to digital again.

Sources of Noise

So where does (electrical) noise come from? This noise can be broken down into two categories, *electromagnetic interference* (*EMI*) and *radio frequency interference* (*RFI*).

Electromagnetic Interference (EMI)

EMI is produced by circuits that use an alternating signal (referred to as an *alternating current* or an *AC circuit*). EMI is not produced by circuits that contain a consistent power level (referred to as a *direct current* or a *DC circuit*).

For example, if you could slice one of the wires coming from a car battery and watch the electrons moving down the wire (kids: don't try this at home!), you would see a steady stream of power moving evenly and uniformly down the cable. The power level would never change: It would stay at a constant 12 volts. A battery is an example of a DC circuit because the power level remains stable.

Now, let's say you could slice the wire to a household lamp and try the same experiment (kids: *definitely* do not try this at home!). You would now see that depending on the point in time when you measured the voltage on the wire it would read anywhere between −120 volts and +120 volts. The voltage level of the circuit is constantly changing. Plotted over time, the voltage level would resemble the analog signal shown in Figure 7.1.

If you watched the flow of electrons now in the AC wire, you would notice something very interesting. As the voltage changes and the current flows down the wire, the electrons tend to ride predominantly on the surface of the wire. The center point of the wire would show almost no electron movement at all. If you increased the frequency of the power cycle, more and more of the electrons would travel on the surface of the wire instead of at the core. This effect is somewhat similar to what happens to a water skier—the faster the boat travels, the closer to the top of the water the skier rides.

As the frequency of the power cycle increases, energy begins to radiate at a 90-degree angle to the flow of current. The same way water will ripple out when a rock breaks its surface, so too will energy move out from the center core of the wire. This radiation is in a direct relationship with the signal on the wire, such that if the voltage level or the frequency is increased, the amount of energy radiated will also increase (see Figure 7.5).

FIGURE 7.5:

A conductor carrying an AC signal radiating EMI

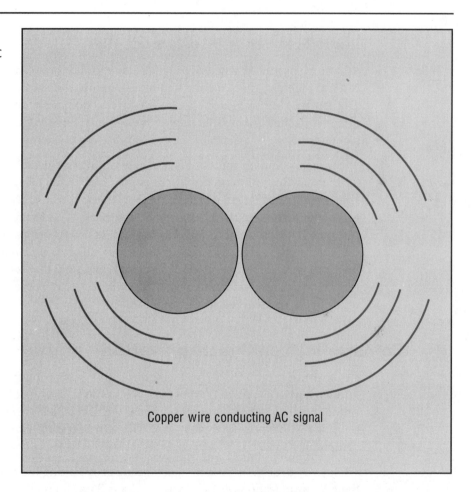

Copper wire conducting AC signal

This energy has magnetic properties and is the basis of how electromagnets and transformers operate. The downside to all of this is that the electromagnetic radiation can introduce an electrical signal into another wire if one is nearby. This interference either adds to or subtracts from the existing signal and is considered to be noise. EMI is the most common type of interference encountered on local area networks and can be produced by everything from fluorescent lights to network cables to heavy machinery. EMI also causes signal loss. Any energy that is dissipated as EMI is energy that can no longer be used to carry the signal down the wire.

Radio Frequency Interference (RFI)

RFI can be produced when two signals have similar properties. The waveforms can join together, changing the frequency or amplitude of the resulting signal. This is why geographically close radio stations do not transmit on adjacent frequencies. If they did, a radio might not be able to receive the weaker of the two stations.

The most common source of RFI in networking is caused by a condition known as *reflection*. Reflection occurs when a signal is reflected back upon itself by some component along its connection path. For example, thinnet cabling (described in greater detail later in this chapter) requires the use of a terminator at each end of the cable. The terminator's job is to "terminate" or absorb any electrical signal that reaches the end of the cable. If the terminator is faulty, it may not be able to fully absorb all of the signal. The portion of the signal that is not absorbed will be reflected back up the thinnet cable. This will distort any other signals that are currently being transmitted onto the wire.

Communication Synchronization

Another important property in communications is letting the receiving system know when to expect data transmissions. If the beginning of a transmission cannot be determined, a receiving system may mistake the beginning of a transmission for the middle or vice versa. This is true for both analog and digital communications.

One way to achieve proper signal timing is by having the systems synchronize their communications so that each transmits data at a predetermined time. For example, the two systems may agree to take turns, transmitting for one second each and then passing control over to the other system (similar to a human conversation). While this type of negotiation is simple and straightforward, it has a number of inherent flaws. First, if a station has nothing to say, its time slice will be wasted while the second station sits by idle, waiting to transmit additional information. Also, if the stations' clocks are slightly different, the two systems will eventually fall out of sync and smother each other's communication. Finally, consider what happens when further stations are plugged into the same circuit and also have something to say—the time slices could be renegotiated, but this will severely diminish the amount of data that could be transmitted on this circuit in a timely fashion.

To resolve these issues, communications typically use a *preamble*—a defined series of communication pulses that tell all receiving stations, "Get ready—I've got something to say." The preamble ensures that all stations are able to "sync up" and receive the data in the same time measure that it was sent. This is like a singer or drummer "counting off" the beat to begin a song, to make sure all band members start the first note at exactly the same time and are in sync with each other. A station sends a preamble only when it needs to transmit data, thus eliminating "dead air" time by leaving the circuit open for systems that need it. Also, if the data transmission bursts are kept fairly small, the preamble method resolves the issue of systems falling out of sync due to time variations, because the stations can resynchronize their times during each data delivery.

Media Choices for Analog and Digital Transmissions

So which transmission medium will work with either analog or digital communications? The short answer is that *all* media are capable of carrying either analog or digital signals. The circuit design determines which type of communication is most appropriate.

For example, copper wire was originally used for telegraphs, which were a type of digital communication. This was because the telegraph used an electromagnet that interpreted the electrical signals as a series of long and short audible clicks.

Now, change the circuit by replacing the telegraph hardware with two telephones, and that same copper wire can be used for telephone communications, which are a type of analog signal. Information is transferred by a nearly infinite number of frequency and amplitude changes.

So how does one go about choosing which transmission media is most appropriate for their networking application? Typically, a number of different factors play a role in this choice.

NOTE   Don't worry about the terminology or specifics of the following issues just yet. They're simply meant to get you looking at the big picture as we explore the technology in greater detail later in the book.

User and Application Bandwidth Demands

If you have a small number of users who will only need to share a printer and maybe exchange a few spreadsheet files, a medium that supports relatively slow communications—for example, Category 3 copper cable—may be sufficient. But if you have a large number of users who will be sharing large graphic files or compiling common source code, stick with a medium that will support faster transmission rates (for example, fiber).

Future Growth

Future growth is always one of the toughest variables to determine. For example, Category 3 cable is all that the small office mentioned above needs—for now. But if this small office has the potential to grow to hundreds of users, it may be wiser to start wiring with Category 5 cable from day one, so you do not need to go back and rewire your network later when the office needs greater bandwidth.

TIP   One of the most difficult and time-consuming tasks an administrator can undertake is to rewire a network. When in doubt, overestimate growth and bandwidth demands.

For example, the added cost of installing Category 5 instead of Category 3 is minimal. Removing that Category 3 cable in order to update to Category 5 later is far more expensive than doing it right the first time (remember to factor in such things as labor and downtime). If you are debating Category 5 versus fiber, consider pulling the fiber cable at the same time as the Category 5 but leaving it unused until needed. Unfortunately, there is no real rule of thumb for determining network growth. This can only be determined by evaluating your company's needs and intended expansion.

Distances between Computer Systems

All forms of transmission media have some form of distance limitation. This is why most larger networks incorporate a mixture of media types. Typically, for short runs, copper is sufficient, while longer distances may require fiber or satellite communications.

Geographic Environment

Location can quickly limit the number of available options. If the distance between the systems you're connecting is a matter of miles rather than meters, your choices will be limited to satellite or leased line communications.

Required Fault Tolerance

Fault tolerance is the ability of a network to remain functional despite a critical failure (such as a cable failure). While fault tolerance is more a function of the overlying topology or circuit design, keep it in mind when choosing media, as some topologies only support certain types of media. For example, the dual-ring design of the FDDI topology only supports fiber-optic cable.

Environment

Locations that contain devices that produce EMI or RFI noise will require transmission media that are not susceptible to this type of interference. For example, if the network will be used in a machine-shop environment, media such as shielded coax or fiber would be better choices than twisted-pair cable because of their superior resistance to EMI interference.

Cost

As with most things in life, the media a company implements usually comes down to what it can ultimately afford. Typically, the better the media, the higher the cost. When justifying a media choice, add in such factors as lost productivity due to network slowdowns or full-blown outages. Also weigh the cost of upgrading at a later date. The cost of superior transmission media and connection hardware can suddenly look much more reasonable when you factor in circumstances such as downtime and additional administration. It's always cheaper to do it right the first time.

Now let's take a closer look at what media options are available.

NOTE   There really is no consistent formula to determine which form of cable media is more cost-effective beyond estimating the footage required for each.

Thinnet Cable

Thinnet cable is somewhat of an enigma. While it has the potential to support high data transfer rates, it is currently not supported by any technology faster than 10Mbps. Its tough outer sheathing makes the inner cabling difficult to damage, and yet its physical topology allows any single failure to bring down an entire network. Finally, while thinnet cable is very easy to install, it can be extremely difficult to troubleshoot when a problem occurs.

Cable Properties

Thinnet coaxial is cable that consists of a copper center core encased in a dielectric material. This dielectric is then encased in a braided shielding that in turn is covered in a protective plastic skin. The term *thinnet* comes from the fact that the overall wire diameter is .18" thick. The cable is termed *coaxial* because the cable uses two conductors that center around the same axis (the copper wire and the braided shielding). Figure 7.6 illustrates thinnet cable.

The center copper core carries the electrical signal along the media. This is the conductor on which the AC signal travels from station to station.

The dielectric is typically a ceramic/plastic mix that helps to reduce the amount of EMI produced by the copper core during data transmission. The dielectric resists the creation of the EMI waves, thus reducing noise and signal loss.

The braided cable serves two functions, one as a conductor, the other as a shield. All electrical circuits need a complete path to transmit energy. The braided cable acts as the return path or "ground" of the circuit. The braided cable's job is to maintain a voltage of zero volts. If this seems odd, think of the properties of an AC signal. The waveform is in a constant state of flux, changing from one voltage level to another. Without some form of reference, it is impossible to determine what the actual voltage level is on the circuit at any given time.

FIGURE 7.6:

A stripped-back thinnet cable and one with connectors

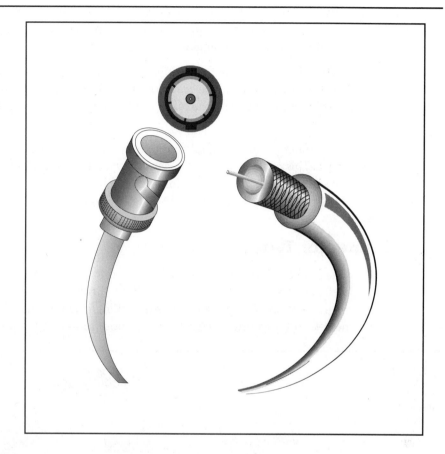

This is similar to driving down the road and passing a car traveling in the opposite direction. If you use a radar gun to measure the speed of the other car and find it reads 100 miles per hour, you really have no idea how fast the other car is traveling, because the radar gun assumes you're stationary, which you are not. Without a point of reference, this measurement is meaningless. You also need to know how fast you're moving to properly compensate for the radar gun's measurement. For example, if you are traveling at 55 mph, you can calculate that the other car must be moving at 45 mph (100 – 55 = 45). If you're traveling at 120 mph, you would know that the other car is actually backing up at 20 mph (100 – 120 = –20).

By keeping the braided cable at zero volts, we now have a known factor or reference to measure the copper core against and thus accurately determine the amplitude level of our signal.

The other function of the braided cable is to provide protection against EMI and RFI noise. Because the braided cable is kept at zero volts, it can shunt any interference received by the cable and keep it from affecting the signal on the copper core.

The outer coating is simply a tough skin to protect the cable from physical abuse. This coating (referred to as a *jacket*) is made from PVC or Plenum. PVC is the same material used for plumbing only much thinner. Plenum is a similar material, but it is much more fire resistant.

Connector Types

Coax cable connectors are usually referred to as *BNC connectors* (short for Bayonet Neill-Concelman—also sometimes called "British Naval Connectors"). These connectors use a set pin with an interlocking ring design so they may be connected and disconnected easily and without tools (see Figure 7.7).

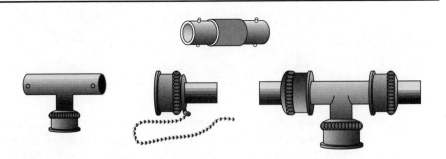

The wiring design of a thinnet network is referred to as a *bus topology* and resembles a series type of connection: A single cable snakes from system to system, connecting them all in a row. Wherever a station is connected to the circuit, the cable is split and a BNC "T" connector is installed. The "T" connector contains two couplers for connecting the two pieces of cable and a third coupler designed to connect a computer's network interface card (NIC). The end of the circuit is capped off with a *terminator* that shunts all electrical signals to ground to ensure that the signal is not reflected back down the wire. A reflected signal can introduce RFI noise into the circuit. A good terminator should measure 50 Ohms, +/− 1 Ohm, on a multimeter. Figure 7.8 shows thinnet wire used to form a bus topology.

FIGURE 7.8:

Example of thinnet wire used to form a bus topology

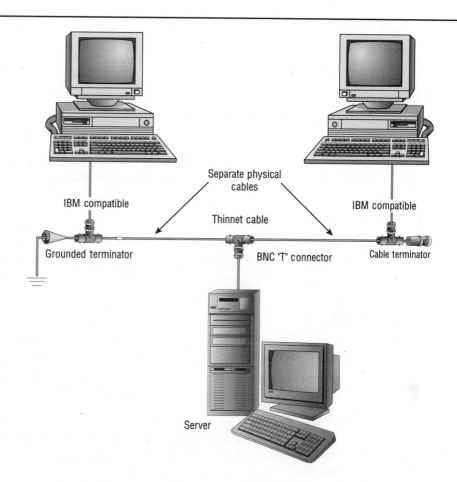

Note that in the above example one end of the thinnet circuit is grounded. Thinnet terminators come in two types: regular terminators and those with short beaded chains attached. The latter should be used on one end (and only one end) of the circuit. This beaded chain should be attached to a known ground, such as one of the screws in a metal computer chassis. This ensures that the voltage on the braided cabling remains at zero, and that electrical "noise" can therefore be shunted effectively.

Advantages

Thinnet cable has the following advantages:

- resistance to noise
- tough shielding
- relatively low cost

Resistance to Noise

Because of its braided shielding, thinnet cable is highly resistant (although not impervious) to electromagnetic interference and radio frequency interference. This can make it a good fit for manufacturing or other noisy environments.

Tough Shielding

Because of its tough outer skin and braided shielding, thinnet can be more resistant to physical and environmental abuse than other cable options, such as twisted-pair.

Cost

Thinnet is relatively inexpensive. At $.15 to $.50 a foot (without connectors), it is more expensive than twisted-pair cable but far less expensive than fiber. The cost of hardware that will use thinnet (NIC cards, repeaters, and so on) is on a par with twisted-pair cable and substantially less than fiber.

NOTE   If the cable is to be run in ceiling or wall areas, check your local building codes. While PVC coated thinnet is dramatically cheaper than Plenum, the latter is usually required to conform to fire and safety codes.

Disadvantages

Thinnet cable has the following disadvantages:

- bulky design
- poor scalability

- low fault resistance

- topology support is limited to 10Mbps Ethernet

Bulky Design

Because of its thick sheathing and large connectors, thinnet can be a real bear to wire. It is not nearly as flexible as twisted-pair cable, which can make it difficult to route through tight areas.

Scalability

Because each station is connected in series, thinnet does not lend itself to attaching and removing stations on the fly. If you need to add a station to a segment of cable that does not have an existing "T" connector, you need to shut down the network and splice the cable to add one. Needless to say, shutting down the network is completely unacceptable during working hours in most networking environments.

The other problem with scalability is the old "where does that cable go again?" syndrome. With twisted-pair, all cables are typically wired back to a central location. This makes determining a wire path pretty straightforward. Because thinnet is run from station to station, it can be difficult to keep track of where individual wire runs go as additional stations are added to the network. These runs may not follow straight lines between users but rather snake in and out of different office areas as connections are required. Unfortunately, these wire runs may go undocumented as the urgency is placed on getting the users connected to the network, not in planning the installation in case of future failure. This can also make ensuring that your cable lengths remain within specification difficult at best. Troubleshooting a cable problem under these conditions can become an absolute nightmare.

Fault Resistance

Thinnet scores low in fault resistance, because the series connectivity comes back to haunt it. Because everyone is connected to the same logical segment of cable, a failure at any point in that cabling can cause the entire segment to go down. This could be due to anything from a faulty connector to a user who incorrectly disconnects their system from the network. Because a failure can affect a group of users, it becomes much more difficult to isolate the specific failure area.

NOTE
One of coauthor Chris Brenton's worst days was spent troubleshooting a segment failure that was being intermittently caused by someone running over a thinnet cable with their chair. As the user moved their chair in and out, it would either cause or fix the failure. Unfortunately this user had impeccable timing, as they were doing this while Chris was swapping out connectors at some other point on the cable. Needless to say, each time Chris thought the problem was resolved, the user would again trigger the failure mode. As Chris would again begin to swap out additional suspect connectors and cables, the user would move their chair again, thus causing the cable to function properly again. While thinnet cable is quite rugged, you should still take appropriate steps to ensure it does not become damaged.

Topology Support

Thinnet is currently supported by 10Mbps Ethernet only. There is currently no specification to utilize thinnet cabling at 100Mbps operation. Partly because of the ever-widening speed gap between thinnet and twisted-pair cabling, the number of thinnet installations has fallen off dramatically. Because of the significant drawbacks listed above, network administrators have started to look to other media for their connectivity needs.

Appropriate Applications

These are the appropriate applications for thinnet cable:

- areas of light to medium EMI and RFI interference, such as machine shops or manufacturing environments

- connection of non-workstation hardware like hubs and servers where 10Mbps throughput is sufficient

- very small networks (such as home networks)

- medium-length cable runs where twisted-pair specifications would be exceeded, such as between multiple floors of a building

Cable Specifications

Table 7.1 shows the specifications for thinnet.

TABLE 7.1:   Thinnet Cable Specifications

Item	Specifications
Transmission source	Electrical
Topologies supported	10Mbps Ethernet
Maximum cable length	600 ft (185 M)
Minimum cable length	1.5 ft (.5 M)
Maximum number of stations	30 per cable segment
Maximum number of segments	For 10Mbps Ethernet, five repeated segments with only three populated by stations
Maximum overall segment length	For 10Mbps Ethernet, 3000 ft (925 M)

NOTE   A repeated segment consists of two lengths of cable connected by an amplification device. A populated segment is a cable run that consists of end user workstations or servers. An unpopulated segment is a cable run that consists of only two repeaters. Unpopulated segments are used to connect populated segments that are separated geographically.

Twisted-Pair Cable

Used for both voice and data lines, *twisted-pair* cable can span a reasonable distance without a repeater, is somewhat resistant to outside noise, and is relatively easy to work with. Twisted-pair cable enjoys a wide acceptance, as it is supported by nearly all local area network topologies. Combine this with a fairly robust wiring scheme, and it is easy to see why twisted-pair cable has become the cabling of choice for most organizations.

Cable Properties

Twisted-pair cable consists of four pairs (eight individual wires) of 24-gauge wire. This wire can be single or multi-stranded. Each wire is covered by a uniquely color-coded plastic sheath which allows the wires to be distinguished from one another. Each wire pair is twisted together to provide a small amount of insulation from outside interference (thus the name twisted-pair). All of the wires are then encapsulated in a plastic sheath covering. Figure 7.9 shows a twisted-pair cable.

FIGURE 7.9:

A stripped back twisted-pair cable

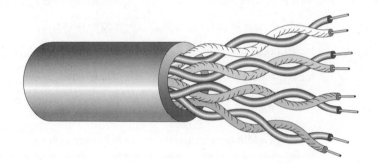

If you will be running strictly 10Mbps Ethernet, only two of the four pairs are actually required. This is similar to how most modern homes are wired, with three pairs of twisted cable—only one of the pairs is actually used, with the second set available for adding an additional phone line. We know of a few savvy individuals who have taken advantage of this setup to wire up an Ethernet network in their home using their existing phone cabling. For business applications, however, it is usually good practice to keep the phone and data lines separate and wire all four pairs for data use. If bandwidth limitations require the network to be pushed up to a faster speed later, you may need to put those additional wire pairs into use.

ANSI/EIA (American National Standards Institute/Electronic Industries Association) standard 568 calls out a number of categories (the singular is commonly referred to as "CAT") to specify the fastest data transfer rates that can be supported by a particular cable construction. These specifications cover everything from the material of the cables themselves to the types of connectors and junction blocks the cables use. These categories are:

Category	Description
CAT1 & CAT2	voice and low-speed data (like modem connections)
CAT3	voice and data rates up to 10Mbps
CAT4	voice and data rates up to 16Mbps
CAT5	voice and data rates up to 100Mbps

NOTE CAT5 has been approved for use in the 1Gbps Ethernet specification, for distances up to 100 meters. While most 1Gbps Ethernet networks are expected to run on fiber, the goal is to leverage the CAT5 wiring most organizations currently use for connections out to the desktop.

The two most popular specifications are Categories 3 and 5. While the two cables may look physically identical, CAT3 has a lower specification that can cause errors if pushed to a faster transmission rates.

NOTE Always certify your cables with a tester that will check them at the transmission speed you will be using. We've seen quite a few wire runs that test fine at 10Mbps but fall apart when the transmission rate is pushed to 100Mbps.

You should examine every link in the chain while trying to maintain a certain category of wiring. More than one organization has ended up in a bind by investing heavily in CAT5 cabling only to cut corners later and purchase CAT3 punch-down blocks (a punch-down block is a device used for organizing wires at central locations such as wiring closets or server rooms). Your network is only as good as its weakest link.

Twisted-pair networks are commonly wired in a *star topology*, as shown in Figure 7.10. In a small environment, all systems will connect back to a central device known as a *hub* or a *switch*. These devices can then be linked together to form larger networks. This linkage makes for a very robust environment, as the failure of one cable will typically affect only one system (unless, of course, that one system happens to be your server, in which case your entire environment is affected as its resources become unreachable).

Linking devices together also makes fault isolation far easier than dealing with thinnet's series connection. Because each office drop is its own circuit, a single user cannot bring down the whole network by incorrectly disconnecting their system.

NOTE We'll cover punch-down blocks, along with hubs and switches, in Chapters 8 and 9.

FIGURE 7.10:

An example of twisted-pair cable being used in a star LAN topology

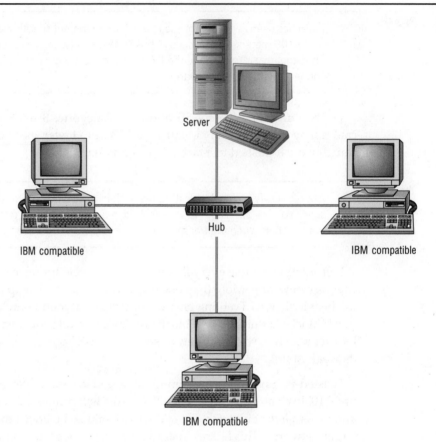

Full Duplex Support

One interesting property of twisted-pair cable is its ability to support *full duplex* communications. Most network communications take place in a half duplex mode. This means that while any one system is transmitting data, every other system must be in a listening mode. This is like Citizen Band (CB) radio communications—whenever one person is communicating, they in effect "own" the channel. If another individual tries to transmit at the same time, the two signals will interfere with each other. In order for a conversation to take place, everyone must communicate in an orderly fashion by taking turns. Only one person can be transmitting at any given time.

Full duplex allows communications to take place in both directions simultaneously. A telephone conversation is an example of a full duplex communication. Both parties are allowed to send information at the same time (though the louder person's information usually comes through clearer). The catch to full duplex is that only two systems can be attached to any one logical segment. Still, full duplex can double the amount of data a system can process. With full duplex, a server with a 10Mbps Ethernet connection would have the potential to process 20 megs of information (transmitting 10Mbps and receiving 10Mbps). I'll cover this in greater detail later in this book.

NOTE   Two quick notes here: First, while full duplex communication is possible with other cable types, it involves running two sets of cables rather than the one set that twisted-pair cable requires. Second, full duplex is topology-dependent—some topologies (for example, 100VG-AnyLAN) do not support full duplex communications.

Connector Types

Connector types commonly used for twisted-pair cabling are RJ-11 and RJ-45 connectors, shown in Figure 7.11. These connectors are crimp-ons; each requires a different size crimping tool. RJ-11 is the smaller six-pin jack that is commonly used for telephone connections. RJ-45 is the larger of the two, has eight pins, and is the one most commonly used for data connections.

As mentioned before, each of the individual wires is encased in a color-coded sheath for easy identification. Unfortunately, the sequence in which these color codes get attached to a connector is not as standard as the rest of this cable's specifications. To date, there are at least five standards in use. The most common standard, AT&T 258A, is used by most cable installation companies, but you'll also run into the EIA Preferred Commercial Building Specification and the IEEE's 10BaseT specification from time to time.

If you view a twisted-pair connector from the bottom (the opposite side from the connector catch) and have the end that the cable plugs into facing down, the pins are numbered 1–8 from left to right, as shown in Figure 7.12.

FIGURE 7.11:

Twisted-pair cables with
RJ-11 and RJ-45 connectors

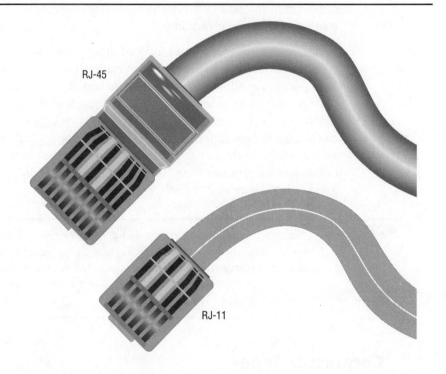

RJ-45

RJ-11

The color codes are listed in Table 7.2.

TABLE 7.2: Pin Numbers for an RJ-45 Connector (Using the AT&T 258A Specification)

Pin #	Ethernet Usage	AT&T	EIA	IEEE
1	+ transmit	white/orange	white/green	white/orange
2	– transmit	orange/white	green/white	orange/white
3	+ receive	white/green	white/orange	white/green
4		blue/white	blue/white	not used
5		white/blue	white/blue	not used
6	– receive	green/white	orange/white	green/white
7		white/brown	white/brown	not used
8		brown/white	brown/white	not used

FIGURE 7.12:

Pins 1 through 8 of a
twisted-pair connector
(from the bottom)

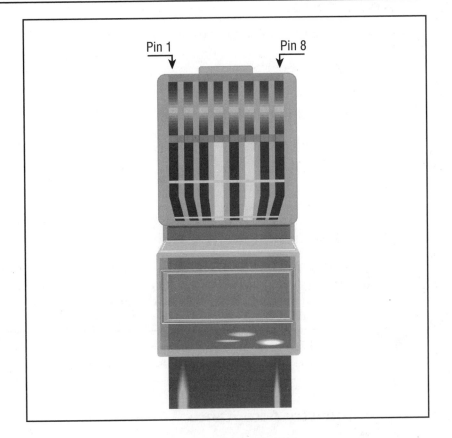

Which color coding should you use? If you're given a choice, stay clear of the IEEE specification. If a different topology is required later, you may find yourself retrofitting or repulling cables. There is no electrical benefit between the AT&T specification and the EIA specification, but the AT&T specification is more widely used and supported. More important, though, is to remain consistent with the color codes currently in place if your building contains existing wiring.

NOTE Incidentally, the color codes listed in Table 7.2 are for straight-through cabling. At some point, you may need to create a *cross cable* that has the transmit and receive pairs switched. These cables are commonly used for attaching hubs that do not have an uplink port (we discuss uplink ports in Chapter 9) or for connecting two (but no more) network computers. If you need to create a cross cable, the color codes for pins 1 and 3 and for 2 and 6 should be swapped on one end (and one end only) of the patch cable. **It's good practice to label cross cables as such to avoid mistaking them for straight-through cables.**

Advantages

Twisted-pair cable has the following advantages:

- wide deployment
- industry acceptance
- ease of installation
- fault tolerance
- bandwidth
- low cost

Wide Deployment

Twisted-pair cable is by far the most popular transmission medium. Your building may well already be wired for twisted-pair cable. If so, you can save a lot of time and money by utilizing the existing wiring.

NOTE   Always have your cabling certified by a professional cable installer or by using a cable tester (we'll cover cable testers in Chapter 32).

Industry Acceptance

Because of its popularity, twisted-pair cable has been incorporated into more LAN topology specifications than any other transmission media. Standardizing on twisted-pair cable ensures that you will have an upgrade path to faster topologies.

Easy Installation

Of the three cable media covered in this book, twisted-pair cable is by far the easiest to install. Its flexible design makes it easy to route through tight areas. The crimp connector design means that connectors can be installed with inexpensive tools (though as always, you will need to test all cables before using them).

Fault Tolerance

The star configuration used by most topologies specifies that only two systems are ever connected to each cable. This means that a single cable fault usually affects only a single system, making troubleshooting straightforward.

Bandwidth

As we mentioned earlier, twisted-pair cable is the only cable medium that allows upgrading from half duplex to full duplex communications without the need to rewire (although you may have to replace network hardware).

> **NOTE** If you're stuck with legacy CAT3 cabling, moving your servers to full duplex communications may be just the thing to squeeze a little more bandwidth out of your existing wiring.

Low Cost

Twisted-pair cable is the cheapest network cable on the market. Four-pair CAT3 cable runs between $.01 and $.15 a foot. CAT5 typically runs between $.15 and $.40 a foot without connectors. As with thinnet, check local building and safety codes to see if the more expensive Plenum sheathing is required over the cheaper PVC.

> **NOTE** Plenum cable, by the way, is cable that uses a plastic insulating sheath which remains non-toxic even when melted or burned (as in a fire). This type of cable is commonly used in the *plenum*, which is the area between the floors of a building (typical with drop-ceilings).

Disadvantages

Twisted-pair cable has two main disadvantages: its *length limit* and poor *noise resistance*.

Length Limit

Twisted-pair cable is limited to 325 feet under most topologies. For most networking environments, this length limitation won't be a problem, but for a large facility, you may need to set up multiple wiring closets. Also, because twisted-pair cable requires a separate connection to each desktop system, it may require far more wire than thinnet cable would. This can make the cost comparison between the two a bit deceiving.

Noise Resistance

Twisted-pair cable is more susceptible to electromagnetic and radio frequency interference than thinnet or fiber. I've seen some strange network problems resolved by simply moving ceiling cables away from fluorescent lighting.

NOTE   If you're pulling twisted-pair cable, make sure the runs are as far away as possible from all noise sources, such as fluorescent lights. A few feet is usually sufficient, depending on the strength of the noise source.

Items to be avoided are:

- fluorescent lights
- power transformers
- devices with motors
- devices that transmit a signal like radio station antennas

Appropriate Applications

These are the appropriate applications for twisted-pair cable:

- areas of little to no EMI or RFI noise such as a standard office building
- relatively short cable runs
- connections out to users' desktops
- server connections that don't require 100% fault tolerance

Cable Specifications

Table 7.3 shows the specifications for twisted-pair cable.

TABLE 7.3:   Twisted-Pair Cable Specifications

Item	Specification
Transmission source	Electrical
Topologies supported	10Mbps, 100Mbps and 1Gbps Ethernet, FDDI, ATM
Maximum cable length	325 ft (100 M)
Minimum cable length	None
Maximum number of stations	2 per cable; 1024 per logical segment
Maximum number of segments	Dependent on topology: for 10Mbps Ethernet, five repeated segments with only three populated; for 100Tx and 100T4, only two repeated segments; for 100VG-AnyLAN, five repeated segments, all of which may be populated; for 1000BaseX (4Gbps Ethernet), two repeated segments.
Maximum overall segment length	Dependent on topology: for 10Mbps Ethernet and 100V-AnyLAN, 3000 ft (925 M); for 100Tx and 100T4, 650 ft (200 M); for 1Gbps Ethernet, currently 325 feet (100 M).

Fiber-Optic Cable

Fiber is expected to be the medium of the twenty-first century. While attaching connectors to *fiber-optic cable* is currently a difficult chore, fiber's ability to support extremely high data rates makes it worth the additional effort. Today, fiber is found mostly on high-speed network backbones, but expect to see it work its way out to the desktop over the next 10 years as bandwidth requirements increase and the process for adding connectors becomes easier.

Cable Properties

Fiber-optic cable consists of a cylindrical glass thread center core 62.5 microns in diameter wrapped in cladding that protects the center core and reflects the light back into the glass conductor. This is then encapsulated in a tough Kevlar jacket.

The whole thing is then sheathed in PVC or Plenum. The diameter of this outer sheath is 125 microns. The diameter measurements are why this cabling is sometimes referred to as 62.5/125 cable. While the glass core is breakable, the Kevlar jacket helps fiber-optic cable stand up to a fair amount of abuse. Figure 7.13 shows a fiber-optic cable.

NOTE   Kevlar is the same material that bulletproof vests are made of—talk about a bulletproof network!

FIGURE 7.13:

A stripped-back fiber-optic cable

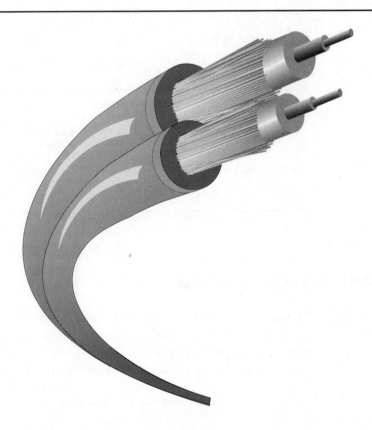

Unlike twisted-pair cable and thinnet cable, fiber uses a light source for data transmission. This light source is typically a light-emitting diode (LED) that produces a signal in the visible infrared range. On the other end of the cable is another diode that receives the LED signals. The type of light transmissions can take one of two forms, single mode or multimode.

Never look into the beam of an active fiber-optic cable. **The light intensity is strong enough to cause permanent blindness**. If you must visually inspect a cable, first make sure that it is completely disconnected from the network. Just because a cable is dark for a moment does not mean it is inactive. The risk of blindness or visual "dead spots" is high enough that it's just not worth it unless you know the cable is completely disconnected.

Single-mode fiber consists of an LED that produces a single frequency of light. This single frequency is pulsed in a digital format to transmit data from one end of the cable to another. The benefit of single-mode fiber over multimode is that it is faster and will travel longer distances (in the range of miles). The drawbacks are that the hardware is extremely expensive and installation can be tedious at best. Unless your company name ends with the word "Telephone," single-mode fiber would be overkill for any application, so I'll focus on multimode fiber.

Multimode transmissions consist of multiple light frequencies. Because the light range does not need to be quite so precise as single-mode, the hardware costs for multimode are dramatically less than for single-mode. The drawback of multi-mode fiber is *light dispersion*, the tendency of light rays to spread out as they travel. You'll see light dispersion if you shine a flashlight against a nearby wall: The light pattern on the wall will have a larger diameter than the flashlight lens. If you hold two flashlights together and shine them both against the wall, you'll get a fuzzy area in the middle where it's difficult to determine which light source is responsible for which portion of the illumination. The further away from the wall you move, the larger this fuzzy area gets. This is, in effect, what limits the distance on multimode fiber (that is, if you can call 1.2 miles a "distance limita-tion" for a single cable run). As the length of the cable increases, it becomes more difficult for the diode on the receiving end to distinguish between the different light frequencies.

NOTE

Because multimode transmissions are light-based instead of electrical, fiber bene-fits from being completely immune to all types of EMI and RFI noise.

Multimode transmission makes an extremely good candidate for high-noise environments. Fluorescent lights, transformers, and heavy machinery have no effect on these signal transmissions.

Fiber is also capable of handling extremely high bandwidths. As twisted-pair cable and other transmission media struggle to break the 100Mbps barrier, fiber is already enjoying throughputs of 655Mbps with ATM and even 1Gbps under the new Ethernet specifications. If you remember that twisted-pair cable started out at 1Mbps and has currently grown by a factor of 100, it's safe to say that we have not even begun to scratch the surface of what fiber-optic cable will handle.

The secret lies in its transmission properties. As discussed earlier in this chapter, EMI radiates out from an electrical cable whenever the voltage or frequency changes. Another property of EMI is that as the voltage level drops, the EMI field collapses and will actually put some of the energy back into the circuit. The result is that instead of the circuit immediately returning to zero volts, it slowly declines in voltage. The same is true during power-up. EMI will resist the increase in voltage, causing the power to ramp up instead of immediately hitting full signal strength.

This transmission is like driving your car. If you step on the gas, you do not immediately jump to 65 mph but rather slowly increase in velocity until this speed is reached. This is because friction (like EMI in an electrical circuit) is resisting your change in speed. It takes you less time to move from a standing stop to 30 mph than it does to get to 70 mph.

Taking into account the EMI forces, our nice clean digital signal actually looks more like Figure 7.14.

This delay is referred to as *switching time* and limits just how quickly information can be pushed down the wire. If the signal changes are faster than a circuit's switching time, the circuit will not have the opportunity to finish changing voltage levels before the next transmission is sent. To return to the car analogy, you can go from zero to 30 mph and back to zero faster than you can go from zero to 70 mph and back to zero. Slower speeds are easier to achieve.

Because light does not produce EMI, it does not suffer this shortcoming of electrical circuits. As the light pulses on and off, it has no real resistance to these changes in state. This allows the light to be pulsated very quickly, supporting very large data transfer rates (the more the light pulses in a given time period, the more information that can be transferred). The limiting factor is the switching time of the sending and receiving diodes, which are, alas, electrical devices.

FIGURE 7.14:

EMI effect on a digital electrical signal

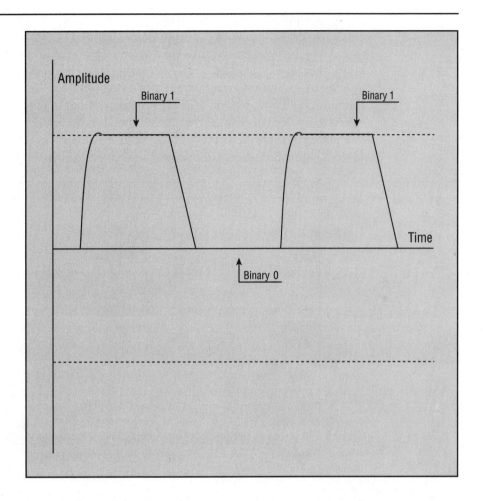

One minor inconvenience of fiber circuits is that all communications can take place in one direction only. The send and receive diodes are specific to their tasks and cannot accept data in the opposite direction. So fiber-optic cables are usually run in pairs, one cable to carry the data in each direction. Connections are usually labeled as Tx (for "transmit") and Rx (for "receive"). When connecting systems together, make sure the connections run from Tx on one system to Rx on the other. Because two channels are used, fiber connections are usually "full duplex" in nature. The exceptions to this are 100VG-AnyLAN, ATM, and FDDI (when properly configured for fault-tolerant operation).

Wiring topology for fiber networks can be configured as a bus (similar to thin-net) when only two stations are used, a star (similar to twisted-pair cable), or a ring. Think of a bus topology twisted around into a circle and you get the idea of how a ring topology is laid out. The circuit follows a complete path with stations tapping in around the circumference. In a ring topology, the Tx port of a station is connected to the Rx port of its downstream neighbor (a fancy way of saying the next station along the ring). This station then has its Tx port connected to the next downstream neighbor. This continues until the circuit loops back to the original station. Figure 7.15 shows fiber-optic cable creating a ring topology.

FIGURE 7.15:

Fiber-optic cable used to create a ring topology

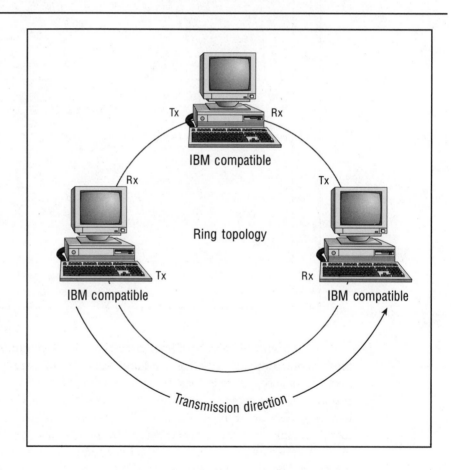

NOTE   Fiber is supported by a number of different communication protocols. The existence of fiber-optic cable does not automatically mean you are running FDDI (or even operating at 100Mbps, for that matter). We've run into a number of network administrators who have assumed their backbone was operating at 100Mbps because they were using fiber, only to find out it was a normal 10Mbps Ethernet circuit. When in doubt, check the specifications on your hardware and be very specific when purchasing from your vendor.

Connector Types

There are a number of different connector types used with fiber. The most popular are SMA and FDDI connectors. Plan on buying all of your cabling with the connectors already installed or having a qualified professional install the connectors for you. Attaching fiber connectors is a precise art that must be done in a near–clean-room environment, because a single speck of dust can destroy the transmission characteristics of a fiber-optic cable. This will become less of an issue over time as the tools to both connect and test fiber-optic cables become cheaper and more readily available. While dirt and dust will always be a problem, it will be much easier to determine if a connector has been attached properly. Figure 7.16 shows common fiber-optic cable connectors.

NOTE   FDDI connectors are only used when connecting systems to an FDDI ring. SMA connectors make up a majority of other connection requirements.

Advantages

Fiber-optic cable has the following advantages:

- strong resistance to noise
- better security
- very high bandwidth
- wide industry acceptance

Common fiber-optic cable connectors include FDDI and SMA.

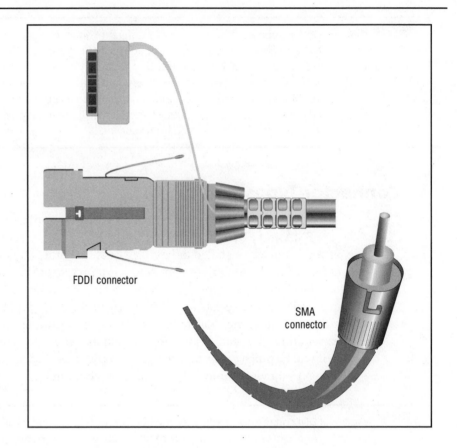

FDDI connector

SMA connector

Resistance to Noise

Because fiber uses light as its transmission source, it is impervious to EMI and RFI noise.

Better Security

Because light sources do not generate EMI fields, it is impossible to capture information traveling on the fiber-optic cable without breaking the circuit.

High Bandwidth

Fiber has the ability to transfer data at extremely high rates. It is faster than any other type of cabling.

Industry Acceptance

Because of its high bandwidth potential, fiber is guaranteed a place in all upcoming LAN topology specifications. Standardizing on fiber ensures that you will have an upgrade path to faster topologies later.

Disadvantages

Fiber-optic cable has two main disadvantages: difficulty of installation and cost.

Installation

Fiber-optic cable is light and flexible, which makes it easy to route in tight areas, but the difficulty in adding connectors makes it cumbersome to work with. Fiber-optic cable is sold preconnected in standard lengths. But if the standard length is one foot shy of what you need, you could be looking at custom-length cables, which tend to be expensive.

NOTE   It's a good idea always to overestimate your requirements for cable runs. Very rarely can you run your cables in a straight line from point "A" to point "B". There are almost always obstacles that you will need to route your cables around. **Never install a cable so that it is taut.** Tension between the cable and the connector can lead to premature failure.

Cost

Fiber is the most expensive of the three cable media. Much of the expense comes from the work required to install the connectors: While a three-foot cable will run in the neighborhood of $50–$60, a ten-foot cable will usually be only a few dollars more ($60–$70).

Appropriate Applications

These are the appropriate applications for fiber:

- areas of medium to high EMI or RFI noise, such as machine shops or power plants

- extremely long cable runs, for example, in high-rise office buildings

- environments with sensitive data or where security is an issue, such as financial, military, or government contractor facilities

- high-speed backbone connectivity

- server connections where 100% fault tolerance is required

NOTE   Fiber is required to support FDDI's dual ring design, as discussed in greater detail in the preceding chapter.

Cable Specifications

Table 7.4 shows the specifications for fiber.

TABLE 7.4: Fiber Cable Specifications

Item	Specification
Transmission source	Infrared LED
Topologies supported	10Mbps, 100Mbps and 1Gbps Ethernet, FDDI, ATM
Maximum cable length	1.2 miles (2 KM)
Minimum cable length	none
Maximum number of stations	Dependent on topology: for Ethernet, 1024 per logical segment; for FDDI, 500 stations
Maximum number of segments	Dependent on topology: for 10Mbps Ethernet, five repeated segments with only three being populated; 100Tx, two repeated segments; for 100T4, two repeated segments; for 100VG-AnyLAN, five repeated segments, all of which may be populated; for FDDI, dependent on configuration; for 1Gbps Ethernet, under development, possibly two repeated segments
Maximum overall segment length	Dependent on topology: for 10Mbps Ethernet, 3000 ft (925 M); for 100VG-AnyLAN, 3000 ft (925 M); for 100Tx, 650 ft (100 M); for 100T4: 650 ft (100 M) FDDI, maximum ring size of 3280 ft (1 KM) ; for 1Gbps Ethernet: under development, possibly 3280 ft (1 KM)

The Atmosphere

The atmosphere is what is referred to as an *unbound* medium—a circuit with no formal boundaries. It has no constraints to force a signal to flow within a certain path. Coax, twisted-pair cable, and fiber-optic cable are all examples of *bounded* media as they restrain the signal to within the wire. An unbounded transmission is free to travel anywhere.

The atmosphere is capable of transmitting a variety of signal types. The most commonly used are light and radio waves. Each of these transmission types has its own strengths and weaknesses that make it most appropriate for only specific applications.

Light Transmissions

Light transmissions use lasers. These devices operate in a very similar fashion to a fiber cable circuit, except without the glass media. Because laser transmissions are directional, they require a clear line of sight and precise alignment between the devices. This helps to enhance system security, but it limits the light transmissions' effective distance. They are also sensitive to environmental conditions—a heavy mist or snowfall can interfere with their transmission properties. Still, the use of light as a transmission medium makes high bandwidths easy to achieve.

Advantages

Light transmissions have the following advantages:

- They require no FCC approval.
- They have the potential for high bandwidth (10Mbps or more).
- They require no cabling between systems.

Disadvantages

Light transmissions have the following disadvantages:

- They provide short effective distances.
- They are sensitive to environmental changes.
- Maintaining alignment between devices can be a nuisance.

Appropriate Applications

Light transmissions are especially useful in campus networks where running network cables between buildings is impossible due to zoning or physical obstructions.

Radio Waves

Radio waves used for networking purposes are typically transmitted in the 1–20GHz range and are referred to as *microwave* signals. These signals can be fixed-frequency or spread-spectrum.

A *fixed-frequency* signal is a single frequency used as a *carrier wave* for the information you wish to transmit. A radio station is a good example of a single frequency transmission. When you tune in to a station's carrier wave frequency on your FM dial, you can hear the signal that is riding on it.

A carrier wave is a signal that is used to carry other information. This information is superimposed onto the signal (much the same way as noise), and the resultant wave is transmitted out into the atmosphere. This signal is then received by a device called a "demodulator" (in effect your car radio is a demodulator that can be set for different frequencies), which removes the carrier signal and passes along the remaining information. A carrier wave is used to boost a signal's power and extend the receiving range of the signal.

A *spread-spectrum* signal is identical to a fixed-frequency, except that multiple frequencies are transmitted. This is done to reduce interference caused by noise. Spread spectrum is a technology that came out of wartime, when an enemy would transmit on an identical frequency and jam a fixed-frequency signal. Because spread spectrum uses multiple frequencies, it is less prone to interference.

There are two methods that can be used to transmit both fixed-frequency and spread-spectrum signals. These are referred to as terrestrial and space-based transmissions.

Terrestrial Transmissions

Terrestrial transmissions are radio signals that are completely land-based in nature. The sending stations are typically transmission towers located on the top of mountains or tall buildings. The range of these systems is usually line of sight, although an unobstructed view is not required. Depending on the signal strength,

50 miles is about the maximum range achievable with a terrestrial satellite system. Local TV and radio stations are good examples of industries that rely on terrestrial-based broadcasts. Their signal can only be received locally.

Advantages

Terrestrial transmissions have the following advantages:

- They require no FCC approval on spread-spectrum signals under 1 watt.
- Terrestrial transmissions are less affected than laser transmissions by environmental changes.
- Terrestrial transmissions have a longer range than laser transmissions.
- Long-term costs can be cheaper than using a local exchange carrier.

Disadvantages

Terrestrial transmissions have the following disadvantages:

- They require FCC approval for most configurations.
- Security is a concern, as the signal can be easily snooped.

Appropriate Applications

There are two main applications for terrestrial transmissions:

- metropolitan area networks (MANs)
- small mobile networks

Space-Based Transmissions

Space-based transmissions are signals that originate from a land-based system but are then bounced off one or more satellites that orbit the earth in the upper atmosphere. The greatest benefit of space-based communications is range. Signals can be received from almost every corner of the world. The space-based satellites can be tuned to increase or decrease the effective broadcast area.

NOTE   Unless you're charged with managing the backbone of a Fortune 500 company, or you're in the broadcasting business, space-based transmissions are probably overkill.

Advantages

Space-based transmissions have the following advantages:

- Transmission distances are greater than with any other technology.
- They are less affected by environmental changes.
- They are capable of supporting a fully portable network.

Disadvantages

Space-based transmissions have two main disadvantages:

- They are expensive to set up and maintain.
- FCC and foreign licensing are required prior to installation.

Appropriate Applications

The most appropriate application for space-based transmissions is as backbones of very large organizations.

Network Design Examples

Let's look at three network examples and try to determine which medium or media would be the best fit for each one's network wiring. Because network topologies and network operating systems are covered elsewhere in this book, we will not factor these in as part of our discussion here—we will only be focusing on the criteria covered in this chapter.

A Small Field Office

Let's assume we have been charged with networking a small remote office that consists of four salespeople. The office space is a single room and is not expected to grow over the next five years. Most sales activity takes place back at the corporate office. These individuals are located here in this office space as a convenience to some of the organization's larger customers. This group's bandwidth requirements are minimal.

There are three key points to pull out of this description:

- small number of users (four)
- no expected growth
- minimal bandwidth requirements

Based on these factors, our best choice would probably be thinnet wiring. Wiring would be laid out as a bus topology. Because all of our users are located in a single room, keeping track of which computer is directly connected to which other computer should not be a problem. The benefits would be an easy and inexpensive installation.

A Medium-Size Network

In our next example, we need to develop the wiring scheme for a 250-user network. There are multiple servers providing a central storage area for all files. Bandwidth demands are high, as many users are graphic artists who are rendering large images across the network.

The key points of this description are:

- 250 users
- high bandwidth demands

Clearly thinnet would not be a good choice in this situation. Its susceptibility to causing a major network outage has the potential of affecting too many users. Also, its ability to support no more than a 10Mbps throughput rate makes it a poor choice.

Because of the bandwidth demands, we need to attack this network as two separate halves. The first portion is the user connectivity. While all users need to push large amounts of information, it is doubtful that they will need more than the 100Mbps supported by twisted-pair cable. In fact, depending upon the performance level of their computers, 10Mbps may even be sufficient. Each user could be connected to the network using CAT5 twisted-pair cable in a star topology.

The server portion of the equation has a much higher bandwidth requirement. Because we have many end users who will be attempting to transfer information with only a few servers, these servers will require "fatter pipes" in order to keep up with the data rate. The server may need to communicate with the network at 100Mbps or possibly even 1Gbps. With this in mind, fiber-optic cables may be our best choice.

For now, do not worry about the technology required to connect these systems running at different speeds, or even connecting dissimilar cabling types.

NOTE   We cover the hardware required to accomplish these tasks in Chapters 9 and 10.

A Campus Network

Finally, we are required to design the wiring for a multi-building organization. There are two buildings, each 16 stories high. Users on each floor require network access. While each building will contain its own data center, users will still need access to networking resources in the other building.

The twist is that the buildings are 300 yards apart and separated by a set of railroad tracks. The railroad company that owns the tracks will not grant permission to dig underneath them for the purpose of running cable. The local exchange carrier (telephone) will allow you to use their poles for cable routing, but only at a high monthly service rate.

Our key points are:

- There are two 16-story buildings.
- Each building has a data center but connectivity is required between the buildings.
- Options for cabling between buildings are expensive because of obstructions.

Again, let's break our network up into manageable groups. We have three separate areas to focus on:

- connecting the end users
- connecting the floors of each building together
- connectivity between the two buildings

As in our last example, our users on each floor could be connected via twisted-pair cabling in a star topology. While no bandwidth requirements were given, it may be best to wire CAT5 cabling just in case a high level of throughput is required now or in the future.

Our next problem is providing connectivity between the different floors of each building. While no precise distances were given, it is probably safe to assume that there is a distance of 200 ft to 300 ft between the first floor and the sixteenth floor. This could be connected as well with twisted-pair cable as it is below our maximum length of 325 ft. To be safe we could even add a repeater, which would extend our maximum distance to 650 ft.

What's also missing from this description, however, is the space available for running the cabling between floors. It is not uncommon for the network wiring to be run alongside the power cables that provide electricity to the upper levels. In fact it may also be possible that some of the rooms the network backbone passes through will contain large transformer units.

With this in mind, we may be better off connecting our floors using fiber-optic cable. Its resistance to electromagnetic fields will leave it completely unaffected in these environments.

Our final problem is how to connect the two buildings. Our choices here will depend upon the annual climate and how well outages can be tolerated.

If the prevailing weather is temperate and brief outages due to inclement weather can be tolerated, using lasers may be the best option. The laser hardware could be set up on each roof and aligned to provide network connectivity between the two buildings.

If the climate tends to be a bit more hostile, with frequent bouts of fog and snow, or if connectivity between the two building must be operational at all times, then terrestrial radio transmissions may be the way to go. While more expensive than the laser solution, radio is a much more robust option.

Summary

There are a number of choices available when selecting a transmission medium. Each has its own inherent strengths and weaknesses and is most appropriate for only certain applications. There is no single "killer medium" that can combine low cost, high noise resistance, easy installation, long cable runs, and high bandwidth. It's important to analyze your environment and choose media wisely. Out of all the pieces that go into making up a network, transmission media is the most difficult to upgrade later.

In the next chapter, we'll discuss the items to which our network cables are most often connected: punch-down panels and network adapter cards.

8

Network Adapters and Punch-Down Panels

- Network interface cards (NICs)

- External port connections

- PC card connections

- Internal NIC connections

- Punch-down panels

- Media converters

In this chapter, we'll focus on the immediate endpoints to which you will most frequently be connecting networking cable. The first is the network adapter itself, the second is the patch panel or punch-down panel (not needed for small networks), and finally, we'll look at a gadget called a media converter, which performs the handy function of letting you connect different types of network media together. (We'll cover more sophisticated network endpoints and interconnectors such as network hubs, routers, and bridges in the next chapter.)

As always, we will outline the pros and cons (where appropriate) of each device type, and also give examples of how each item is used properly.

Network Interface Card

A *network interface card* (NIC) is, of course, the essential piece of equipment used to connect a computer to the network. It includes two interfaces—one to connect to the network and one to connect to the computer itself. The NIC is the "brains" of the network connection, containing its own processor chip; this helps to take some of the load off the computer's central processing unit (CPU). The more efficient the NIC card's circuitry is, the less load it will place on the system. While this load is not usually a significant issue on a workstation, it can be much more important in a server, which may contain multiple NICs. When choosing a server network card, make sure you stick with a vendor that is known to produce high-performance cards. This consideration cannot be stressed enough.

> **NOTE**   Buy dependable, brand-name cards. NICs are one place you can easily waste tremendous amounts of time troubleshooting, and when something goes wrong, they are the most cumbersome part of the network to get at and diagnose.

There are several varieties of NIC cards. The first thing to look at is how the card interfaces with the computer. There are three types of NIC card interfaces:

- The card can be connected to an external port on the computer such as the parallel port.

- In a laptop, it may be installed internally in a PC card slot (formerly known as a Peripheral Component Interconnect Mezzanine/Computer Interface Adapter—PCMCIA—slot.

- It may be installed internally within the system and connected directly to the computer bus.

External Port Connection

An external port interface is probably the easiest to use but yields the poorest performance. An *external port* is typically an oval device that fits in the palm of your hand. On one side is a male 25-pin connector that attaches directly to the parallel port of the computer. This is why these network cards are commonly referred to as *parallel port network cards*.

On the other side is a 10BT, a coaxial connector, or both for connecting to the network. Most of these devices also require power and need to be plugged into an AC outlet or the PS/2 port of the computer. The software drivers used are identical to standard (internal) network card drivers except that they direct all network traffic through the parallel port. If you use one of these cards, you cannot use the parallel port for local printing (although you can still print to a network printer).

The benefit of a parallel port connection is ease of use. It was originally intended to connect laptop systems which did not have a bus or PC slot available. If you have an older laptop, this may be your only means of connecting it to a network.

NOTE While they haven't yet become mainstream, external network adapters that connect via the USB port could eliminate the performance penalty and become one of the easiest types of network adapters to connect—to both laptops and desktops. This remains to be seen, however. Apple has recently announced the iMac, which uses USB exclusively (connecting the mouse, keyboard, and possibly a Zip drive).

The downside to external ports is that their performance (so far) is quite poor. Because typically everything runs through the parallel port, these network cards become saturated at about 1300 frames per second (fps). Still, this may be ample for someone who simply wants to share a few files or print. The other drawback is that such adapters are usually limited to the 10Mbps Ethernet topology. Don't expect to see expanded support for these devices, because of their poor performance and the popularity of PC cards. One final thing to be sure of is that the parallel port supports bidirectional communications. A standard parallel port only supports one-way (outbound) communications—as it was designed to send data to a printer without expecting a reply back. While bidirectional parallel ports are pretty common these days, the older systems that could most benefit from this type of network connection are the ones that were outfitted with the one-way ports.

Figure 8.1 shows a parallel port network adapter card.

A parallel port network adapter card. The knobs on each side of the unit attach it securely to the parallel port.

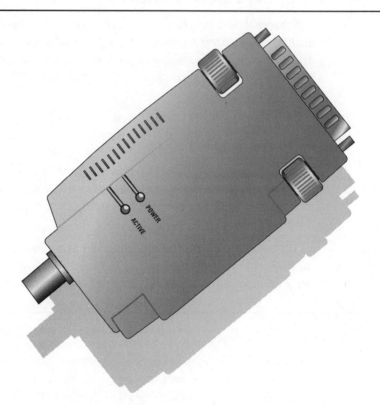

PC Card Connection

PC-card connections are pretty common these days and are typically used for connecting a laptop to a network. These cards are about the size of a credit card and only 3 or 4 times thicker. The card slides into a PC card slot on the computer and usually has some type of special cable that allows the card to connect to standard network wiring.

The upside to PC cards is increased performance. The average user will not notice a performance difference between a PC slot network card and one that plugs directly into the bus. A PC card is the preferred method of connecting a laptop to a network when possible.

One major drawback of these devices is that configuration can be difficult. If you're using a Plug-and-Play computer and operating system, setup is usually pretty easy (it's *almost* Plug-and-Play).

If you're using a non–Plug-and-Play operating system like DOS (I wouldn't recommend trying this!), the configuration can be a real nightmare for even a seasoned PC support specialist. In this case, most cards will require about half a dozen drivers to be loaded prior to loading the network drivers. Even if you are successful in configuring the system and are able to log in to the network, there is no guarantee you will still have enough conventional memory left on your system to run any of your programs.

Figure 8.2 shows a PCMCIA or PC card network adapter. Notice the special cable used to connect this card to a standard RJ-45 connector.

FIGURE 8.2:

A PCMCIA or PC card network adapter

Internal Network Card Connection

Internal network cards are by far the most popular variety of connection. They are internal cards that plug directly into the computer's bus through a free expansion slot in the back of the system, as shown in Figure 8.3. The circuit board plug at the bottom of the card plugs into the expansion slot of the computer.

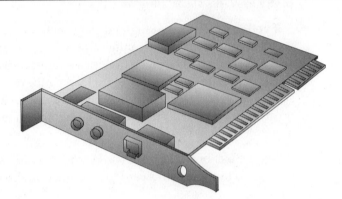

Internal network cards support the largest diversity of network topologies. There are vendors making internal network cards for every topology we cover in this book. One important consideration is to determine what kind of bus your computer uses. The most common are:

ISA (Industry Standard Architecture) The 8-bit version of the ISA bus was developed in 1979 for the IBM PC/XT and was the foundation for later architectures implemented in all PC-compatible systems to date. The 16-bit version of ISA was introduced by IBM in 1984 with the AT class computers and is what people normally refer to when they use the term "ISA bus." ISA is the slowest bus architecture available for the PC, typically running at only 8MHz. This is fine, however, for a low-end work-station connecting to a 10Mbps network to do simple file and printer sharing. The average ISA NIC can push a 10Mbps network to about a 35% utilization rate if it is tuned properly. While there are 100Mbps ISA cards available, their performance is pretty dismal. The bus is just too slow to take advantage of the additional bandwidth that 100Mbps provides. This is definitely not the bus to use in a server!

NOTE   If you are faced with having to reconfigure an old jumper-style ISA network card, our advice is: *don't*. Unless you have the documentation (which even then can be incorrect), futzing with these little jumpers repeatedly to try to solve an IRQ conflict is really not worth it anymore. You can buy the newer style "auto-configuration" ISA network adapters for $25 and save yourself a major headache.

EISA (Extended Industry Standard Architecture)   Developed in 1987 to provide 32-bit throughput using the standard ISA architecture, this is the next generation to the ISA bus. Because EISA can easily keep up with wire speed traffic (100% utilization) on a 10Mbps network, it makes a good fit for server class machines. When the bandwidth jumps to 100Mbps, however, they have trouble keeping up. While there are some decent 100Mbps cards available they are best limited to workstation use only at these speeds. Keep in mind that your server needs to process information from multiple network clients. Therefore it is always a good idea to maintain it as the fastest system on the network.

Micro Channel   Developed in 1987 to provide a proprietary 32-bit alternative to ISA, this was IBM's next generation to the ISA bus. Performance is on par with EISA but the fact that it is only supported by IBM makes for a minimal number of card options.

NU-Bus   Developed by Texas Instruments in 1984, this architecture relies on one proprietary processor slot, the Processor Direct Slot. This is a legacy bus architecture used by Apple for the Macintosh computers. All Power-Mac computers now use PCI bus slots.

VESA Bus   The Video Electronics Standards Association standard is an enhanced EISA design that provides a dedicated 32-bit line directly from the VESA slot to the processor. This is known as local bus technology and is ten times faster than ISA.

S-Bus   SUN's bus architecture for the SPARC station.

PCI (Peripheral Component Interconnect)   Developed by Intel, this is now the bus architecture of choice and certainly the fastest of the bunch. To top it off, it is also cheaper to implement than all of the buses listed above with the exception of ISA. Most newer PC systems will contain a minimum of two PCI slots with the rest being made up of some other architecture. PCI has not only found its way into PC compatibles but into Macs as well. All 100Mbps and faster cards should be plugged into a free PCI slot when possible. If the server's PCI slots are at a premium, you may want to check out some of the multi-port cards that have hit the market. These are specifically designed for servers that need to connect to more than one network segment. Each card contains two or four RJ-45 connections.

In the old days, workstations used ISA NICs and servers used EISA. Because the server had the faster bus, it was in a better position to handle data requests from multiple clients. The result was a built-in *check valve* to control the flow of network traffic. Life was good and traffic flowed smoothly.

PCI has brought an interesting spin to network design. Because it is so inexpensive, it is also widely implemented, finding its way into both servers and workstation-class machines. This means that many of the new workstations are able to crank out data just as fast as the server (maybe even faster, if the server has not been upgraded to PCI over the last few years). The result is that the server's NIC card is pushed into saturation, receiving more traffic than it can handle. While this is rare on 10Mbps networks, it can be quite common when speeds are pushed up to 100Mbps. PCI is currently the fastest thing around, but it still has trouble with a 100Mbps or faster network pushed to full speed. This needs to be taken under careful consideration when you're planning network upgrades. We've seen servers that have run stably for months roll over and play dead when upgraded to 100Mbps pipes because the bus has become saturated from the increase in traffic it receives.

Topology and Wiring Support

The final consideration in choosing a network card is to ensure that it supports the topology and the wiring you are using. If your topology is 100VG-AnyLAN, then you need a 100VG card. A 100Mbps Ethernet card will not work. Many vendors are now shipping cards that support multiple topologies. If you are currently running 10Mbps Ethernet but have your eye on 100Mbps Ethernet for the future, you can purchase 10/100 cards that support both topologies. The card will work in your current environment and be ready for when you upgrade later. Most of these include an *auto sensing* feature, which will detect the network speed you are running at. This is a great feature in that when the upgrade does take place you will not have to configure any of the workstations. Simply power cycle them and they will connect at the faster speed.

Also make sure the NIC's connector is correct for your cabling. If you're using thinnet, the card should have a BNC connector. For twisted-pair, it should be an RJ-45. While media converters are available to connect dissimilar media types, it is always a good idea to limit the number of connectors used. An excessive number of connectors can introduce noise or signal loss to the circuit. Many vendors have had multiple-port cards (referred to as *combo cards*) available for a number of years that will connect to a variety of media types. They contain an RJ-45, a BNC, and an AUI (attachment unit interface) connector. An AUI connector is a type of generic connection that requires a transceiver to connect to your cabling. A *transceiver* is a type of media converter that allows you to attach the network card to any type of cabling that your topology allows. Figure 8.4 shows a transceiver.

FIGURE 8.4:

Transceivers—these devices connect a generic networking port called an AUI to any type of cable media supported by the device.

Punch-Down Panels

Use a *punch-down panel* to connect hardware located in wiring closets or server rooms to the cabling that runs out to the users' workstations. A punch-down panel is a panel the width of a network rack (a rack with a 19"-wide frame used to hold networking equipment) and contains female RJ-45, RJ-11 (for twisted-pair), or SMA (for fiber) connectors in the front and *punch-down blocks* in the back. Panels with RJ-11 connectors are typically used for phone connections, while RJ-45 is used with networking.

> **NOTE**
> Check the ANSI/EIA category standards (these are listed in Chapter 7) to see what level of bandwidth a particular punch-down panel supports. While CAT3 is sufficient for phone use, you will usually want CAT5 for any panels used to support network communications. Don't skimp here, either!

Punching Down the Wire

The punch-down blocks on a twisted-pair panel (CAT3 or CAT5) for data use a set of eight bare metal teeth, which consist of two blades each. The separation between the two blades is such that a single wire from a standard twisted-pair cable can be pushed in between them and the cable insulation will be cut back, allowing the blades to make an electrical connection with the conductor.

> **NOTE**
> The act of connecting a cable is referred to as *punching down the wire*. Note that while fiber does not use metal teeth (instead it's a standard buffed and polished fiber connection) the term is still used for consistency.

Punch-down panels are extremely useful for keeping your wiring organized. Typically these panels are wall- or rack-mounted. The punched-down wire will lead back to a wall connector in an office area or to another central wiring point. This allows you to plug a cable into the front connector on the panel and either connect the *drop* to a device within the room (like a hub) or route it to another drop area.

> **NOTE**
> A drop is a wire run from one geographical location to another.

Using punch-down panels is greatly preferred over simply putting a connector on the wiring-room side of the drop cable, as it increases the flexibility of the wiring plan. A cable with a connector on the end cannot be as easily rerouted to another drop area and it cannot be extended in length if you need to move equipment around the room.

WARNING   You *cannot* extend a twisted-pair cable by splicing in more wire with the old twist and tape method. Don't even *think* about it. Spliced cable is too susceptible to signal loss and outside noise. If you need a longer cable you must replace the entire length.

Things to Consider

Consider the following items when deciding to use a punch-down panel:

- Use a punch-down panel that supports your wiring specification. For example, *do not use a CAT3 punch-down panel with CAT5 cable*. The result is a network that only meets CAT3 specification.

- Choose the location of your punch-down panel wisely. Once it's in place, it can be a real bear to move.

- Ensure that wherever you locate the punch-down panel there is some means of supporting the weight of all the cables that will be running to it (both in the front and in the back). It always helps to think big and plan on having two or three times as many wires as you think you will ever need. While you may initially be wiring only a few drops this number can grow quickly. Wire runs that hang or droop prior to being punched down will cause stress on the punch-down block. It's not uncommon for wires to pull themselves loose in these situations. Use a wiring ladder or fasteners to carry the weight of the wires.

- Label your network drops on the front of the panel. Someday you *will* have a problem that can only be resolved by tracing the cables. If drops are not labeled, you're in for a long night. A label can simply be some form of a unique alphanumeric identifier that indicates where the cable drop goes. Make sure you label the wall plate on the other end with this same identifier.

Labeling Schemes

Among the many labeling schemes we have encountered, one in particular seems to be pretty efficient. It focuses on the location to which the user's drop is wired back. It has six characters, but can be modified for smaller environments. Wire drops are labeled as follows:

- A number indicating to which floor the drop connects
- A letter indicating to which wire or server room the drop connects
- A number indicating to which rack the drop connects
- A letter indicating to which patch panel on the rack the drop connects
- A number indicating to which connector on the panel the drop connects

Let's say a user calls the help desk line and states that they cannot connect to the network. After questioning them you feel that their system may be okay, but you want to check their network connection. You ask them to read the label on their network wall plate and they reply, "4A3B23." You now know you need to go to the fourth floor, Room A. Within the room this user's network drop is wired to the third rack on the patch panel labeled B. Their connection would be number 23 on that panel. For smaller environments you could simply drop the floor and room identifiers. Figure 8.5 shows a set of patch panels mounted in a standard network rack.

Most of the other numbering systems we've seen require you to look up the user's location in some form of matrix and cross reference this information to find the drop's location. This can be a pain if the user catches you in the hall or in some other location where you cannot quickly access this information.

Media Converters

Media converters are devices used to connect two dissimilar cable types. They are usually palm-size boxes with mating connectors on either end. Converters are available to connect twisted-pair, coax, and fiber in any possible combination. Depending on the application, they may or may not require an external power source.

FIGURE 8.5:

A set of patch panels mounted in a standard network rack

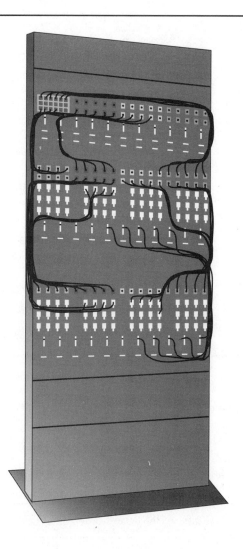

NOTE   Because it is not always practical to upgrade all network devices when a media change occurs, media converters can be lifesavers in a pinch.

Saved by a Media Converter

Here's an example from coauthor Chris Brenton's casebook. Chris and his team were upgrading an operations center from thinnet to twisted-pair. The center contained a good mixture of Banyan VINES, NetWare, Sun, and Lotus Notes systems. In the process of the upgrade they discovered that a NetWare 2.2 and two Banyan 4.0 servers did not have combo cards as they had thought. The network cards were of an unknown vendor and contained only a BNC connector. All three systems were scheduled to be replaced over the next few months but were currently critical to the company's day-to-day operations. Rather than scheduling additional down time to replace the network cards and taking the chance that these dinosaurs might never come back up again, the team instead installed a media converter.

The systems were connected together with a short run of thinnet cable. They terminated and grounded one end, and on the other installed a media converter. The media converter was then connected to a twisted-pair cable, which in turn connected to a brand new switch (more on switches in the next chapter).

The result? The systems were back online and functional, and the team avoided dedicating another Sunday or more to the project.

When using a media converter, you must pay close attention to the maximum distances of your cables. Keep the combined distance to the smallest specification of the two cables to avoid difficulty. For example, in the situation described in the sidebar, you would want to keep your cable distance to 325 feet because this is the maximum for twisted-pair cabling. A converter introduces latency, so it is a good idea to stay well below the maximum.

NOTE   *Latency* is the delay incurred on a circuit when the signal must undergo processing.

The act of amplifying the signal takes a small amount of time which can be measured as the time from when the repeater receives the signal to when it transmits it on its other port. If too much latency is added to a network, connections may time out prematurely. We'll discuss this further when we cover troubleshooting later in the book.

Summary

That wraps up our discussion of network adapters (NICs), punch-down panels, and media converters. In the next chapter we'll look at more sophisticated tools for interconnecting network segments in order to build larger local area networks (LANs) or wide area networks (WANs).

CHAPTER
NINE

Repeaters, Hubs, Routers, and Bridges

- Repeaters and hubs

- Bridges

- Latency, protocol independence, and other bridging issues

- Switches and their modes of operation

- VLAN technology

- Routers, protocol addressing, and brouters

In this chapter, we will look at the important category of networking hardware that makes it possible to interconnect multiple smaller networks to form larger ones—essential in building medium-sized and larger LANs and WANs.

If your concern is with setting up or upgrading a relatively small network of a dozen or fewer users, two sections of this chapter are especially worth noting. The first is the discussion of repeaters and hubs, since any network that uses 10BaseT or 100BaseT, no matter how small, will at least need a hub and possibly a repeater as well. The second section, which can benefit both smaller and larger networks, is the discussion of how splitting your network into two or more segments can allow network traffic on each portion to flow faster and more efficiently.

The remaining parts of this chapter survey the various standard types of networking hardware that enable different network segments to be joined together intelligently. These devices act more or less like smart traffic cops or switchboard operators—switching or routing network traffic efficiently across segments, and without permitting all network traffic to travel on every segment indiscriminately.

For each type of gadget, we'll discuss the pros and cons, and we'll provide examples of where the device would (and would not) be helpful to you.

Repeaters

Repeaters are simple two-port signal amplifiers. They are used in a bus topology to extend the maximum distance that can be spanned on a cable run. The strength of the signal is boosted as it travels down the wire. A repeater will receive a digital signal on one of its ports, amplify it, and transmit it out the other side.

A repeater is like a typical home stereo amplifier. The amp takes the signal it receives from the CD, tape deck, etc., amplifies the signal, and sends it on its way to the speakers. If the signal is a brand-new Alanis Morisette CD, recorded with sparkling digital clarity, it simply boosts the signal and sends it on its way. If it's an old Grateful Dead concert tape, barely audible through the background hiss, the amp happily boosts this signal as well and sends it on its way.

In a similar way, repeaters simply boost whatever they receive and send it again on its way. Because they are indiscriminate about what they amplify, the signal they amplify could be a bad frame of data, or even background noise. Unfortunately, a repeater does not discern data quality; it simply looks at each of the individual digital pulses and amplifies them.

Why Use a Repeater?

A repeater is a cheap, effective way of extending your cable lengths. For example, the maximum allowable distance for thinnet cable is 600 feet. Using a repeater can extend this distance to 1200 feet. Using multiple repeaters, we can further extend this distance until the maximum *overall* length specification of the topology is reached. For example, 10Mbps Ethernet allows a maximum of 3000 feet, so no more than five thinnet repeaters could be used.

A repeater does not follow Ethernet's CSMA/CD rules of listening before transmitting. If another station is partially through a frame transmission, a repeater will still blindly transmit, thereby causing a collision. This is why the overall maximum topology length must still be adhered to with a repeater: Stations at either end still need to be able to monitor the entire length of the network correctly prior to transmission.

Choosing a Repeater

When choosing a repeater, be sure it has transmit and jam lights for each of its ports. These lights are LED indicators that monitor the repeater's operation. The transmit lights let you know when traffic is detected on each of the ports. The jam lights let you know if a collision or a cable problem occurs along an individual length of cable. If a jam light blinks quickly, then two frames have collided. If the light turns on and stays on, then you probably have a failure somewhere along the length of cable. These indicators can be invaluable troubleshooting tools when you are trying to diagnose a connectivity problem. Figure 9.1 shows a common network repeater. The front indicator lights quickly verify the operation of the device.

FIGURE 9.1:

A common network repeater

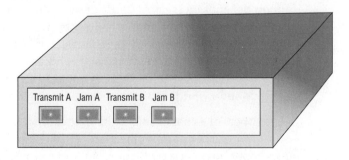

Hubs

Hubs are probably the most common piece of network hardware after network interface cards. Physically they are boxes of varying sizes that have multiple female RJ-45 connectors. Each connector is designed to accept one twisted-pair cable outfitted with a male RJ-45 connector. This twisted-pair cable is then used to connect a single server or workstation to the hub. Hubs are essential in any Ethernet network using UTP (unshielded twisted-pair) cable; a hub is the point that interconnects stations with each other and with the server(s).

Think of hubs as multiport repeaters that support twisted-pair cables in a star topology. Each node communicates with the hub, which in turn amplifies the signal and transmits it on its remaining ports. As with a repeater, hubs work at the electrical level.

NOTE   Because hubs have no way to determine if a frame is good or bad, you may consider them as functionally equivalent to repeaters—and you can use them in that capacity when expanding or upgrading your network.

Chassis Hubs

Hubs come in two categories, chassis and stackable. A *chassis hub* is a large box (typically one or two feet tall and the width of a network rack) that is made to mount into a network rack. The chassis has slots somewhat similar to the expansion card slots in the back of a standard PC. These are usually designed so that you can slide a card directly in from the front without disassembling the device. On the front of the card are multiple RJ-45 connectors. The number of stations a hub can support depends on the *port density* of each card and how many such cards are installed. Cards typically support anywhere from four to 24 connections. The number of cards supported by the chassis varies from model to model. Typically one slot is lost to some form of management card that is used to configure and monitor the remaining cards. Besides hub cards, a chassis hub may also support cards that supply bridge, switch, or even routing functionality.

The appeal of a chassis hub is that it is compact. There are chassis hubs that will support 200 or more connections. If you have a large number of users to support but do not have a lot of room for networking equipment, a chassis hub may be your best bet. Also alluring is the ability to monitor all these ports through a single point of management. A chassis hub management card will usually allow you to monitor every port, allowing you to determine which ones are in use.

Unfortunately, chassis hubs also have many drawbacks, the first of which is that they present a single point of failure. If you support 150 users through a single chassis hub and it goes down, then your entire network is offline. Another drawback is that many of the denser hub cards do away with the RJ-45 connectors and use a single proprietary connector with separate twisted-pair cables attached to it. This is the only way to fit 24 or more connections onto a single card; it increases the number of connections a single card can handle, but it can also make it difficult to trace wires. While you will be able to determine which card the drop connects to, you may be hard-pressed to determine which of the card's ports it is using. Also, if one cable is just a bit too short, you cannot just replace it with a standard twisted-pair patch cord. You will need to replace the entire assembly with a longer proprietary unit, if one is even available. These longer units are proprietary in that they do not use connectors commonly deployed with network wiring, so they must be specially made and are not considered an off-the-shelf item like a standard twisted-pair patch cord, which is available from most computer stores and mail order catalogs.

Another major drawback of chassis hubs is the lack of indicator lights. LEDs that indicate port status are removed in order to connect more users. Link status and transmit indicators for each port on a hub are convenient visual aids when trying to diagnose a problem. The link status light will come on when a system is connected and correctly wired to the hub port. The transmit light will flash whenever that station sends data. While most chassis hubs have the ability to monitor a port's health through some form of management software, the loss of visual indicators can greatly inhibit the troubleshooting process.

Chassis hubs are also not very flexible. If you fill a 200-port chassis hub, you many end up with so much traffic on your network that end users are constantly complaining about poor network performance. While most vendors will sell you an optional card to segment the chassis into multiple *virtual hubs*, you can usually only create three or four of them. Again, with 200 users you would still have 50 or more people contending for bandwidth. In a busy environment this may still be grossly inadequate. While the argument can be made that an administrator should refrain from putting so many users on a single chassis hub, doing so would limit a chassis hub's greatest appeal, which is that it supports many users within a small enclosure.

As if all this was not enough, chassis hubs also tend to cost more than their stackable counterparts. With management and segmentation modules, the per-port cost can easily be two to three times or more what you would pay for the equivalent number of ports using stackable hubs.

Stackable Hubs

Stackable hubs are slim-line boxes that usually contain between six and 24 ports. Most have link and transmit lights to help monitor the health of each port. Stackables are so named because, as your port requirements grow, you can simply buy another hub and stack it on top of the first. Stackables can also be rack-mounted or flush-mounted to a wall.

Stackables have a lot going for them, and they've become the hub of choice. The first reason is cost. If you have a small network, purchase a cheap four-, six-, or eight-port hub and you're off and networking. As your needs grow you can purchase larger hubs or link smaller ones together.

One of the nice things about stackables is that, if you're using more than one, you do not have a central point of failure. If a hub fails, you can simply move your important users (your boss, her boss, the secretary who brings you cookies every day, etc.) to the hub that is still functioning until a replacement can be found. Note that you can usually mix and match stackable hubs from different vendors, so in a real pinch you may be able to run down to your local computer store and purchase a replacement.

NOTE The mix-and-match nature of stackable hubs is in contrast to chassis hubs, which are proprietary; replacements can usually only be purchased through the manufacturer or one of their *value added resellers*.

Managed Stackable Hubs

Stackables come in two varieties, managed and unmanaged. A *managed hub* (sometimes referred to as an *intelligent* hub) runs some form of software that allows you to communicate with the device (either over the network or from a directly attached terminal) and check operating parameters like port status (up or down). This communication is useful if you have an extremely large environment and it is impractical to walk over to the hub and check the indicator lights.

NOTE This capacity to check operating parameters is identical to what you get with a chassis hub. Some vendors are even including backbone connectors that allow you to connect multiple hubs and manage them as if they were one device.

It is also possible to have an intelligent hub send out alerts to a management station; however, this may not be as useful as it sounds because these alerts occur only when the hub has been rebooted or a port goes down. You should be less concerned with a hub's rebooting and more concerned with it going offline initially. Unfortunately, an offline hub has no way of sending an alert. Also, a port will technically go down every time a user shuts off his workstation. Clearly, intelligent hubs are not quite as clever as their name implies. Their usefulness is tailored to very specific environments. Unless you know that you will definitely use additional functionality, they may not be worth the additional cost.

Unmanaged Stackable Hubs

An *unmanaged hub* has no management or monitoring software. The only indication of its status is the supplied LEDs. We have seen hubs that have locked up, and even though they appear operational at first glance, they will not transmit any data. In such a case, the online LED will be lit as will be the link lights for each of the attached stations. If you watch the transmit lights, however, you will see no activity.

Clearly, it is essential that you only use hubs with indicator lights. Another LED to look for is a collision indicator. Because a hub is a dumb amplifier, it only needs a single collision light for all of its ports. A collision light can be an early warning signal that something is not right with the network. If this light is turned on solid, it's time to break out a network analyzer (discussed in Chapter 30) and find out what is going on.

Backbone Connection

Stackable hubs can be connected in either of two ways—through a backbone connection (if one is supplied) or through an uplink port. A *backbone connection* is a separate connector designed to be attached to hubs; it is usually implemented as a BNC connector in 10Mbps hubs and connects the hubs with a short run of thinnet cable.

NOTE Some vendors use a proprietary cable to connect their hubs together for management purposes. In this case, these cables will supply the required network connection between the hubs as well.

Uplink Port Connection

An *uplink port* is a special port that reverses the transmit-and-receive pair of a twisted-pair cable. An uplink port can look like any other hub port, so you should be careful not to use it inadvertently. An uplink port is required because if you wired two hubs together directly, the wire pairs would be connected transmit-to-transmit and receive-to-receive; wired this way the hubs would be unable to communicate with each other. Some uplink ports have a switch that allows you to select their mode of operation. If you have a small network and do not need to connect your hub to another, you can usually throw the switch and use it to connect an extra workstation. Note that only one hub needs to be uplinked. If you use the uplink port on both sides, the hubs will again be unable to communicate.

TIP	If you need to connect two hubs together and neither one has an uplink port, you can connect them together with a cross (or crossover) cable. A cross cable is a twisted-pair wire that has the transmit-and-receive pairs switched at one end; this provides the same functionality as an uplink port. (Chapter 7 describes how to make one.) Also, make sure cross cables are labeled as such so they are not confused with regular cables.

The hub can have its RJ-45 connectors on either the front or the back of the unit. Select a unit that fits your wiring scheme. For example, if the hub will be rack mounted, it may make more sense to purchase a hub with the connectors in the back. This cuts down on cable clutter, giving the front of the rack a cleaner look.

Figure 9.2 shows three stackable hubs of various port densities. Note the lack of front indicator lights.

FIGURE 9.2:

Three stackable hubs of various port densities

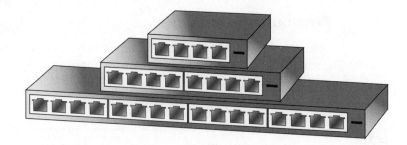

Splitting Up Networks

Before we talk about bridges and routers, let's look for a moment at why and when it makes sense to split networks up into two or more pieces.

As mentioned at the start of this chapter, even small networks can often benefit by being split into different parts. These sections or parts are referred to as network *segments*. A segment refers to one physical string of computers, whether they're connected together by a star, a bus, or a ring.

To appreciate the benefit that comes from splitting up, or segmenting, a network, consider for a moment what would happen if we just kept adding more stations onto the same physical network. Eventually, of course, we would run into the maximum station limit (also referred to as the *node limit*), which could be anywhere from 30 (with 10Base2) to 1000 or more (10- or 100BaseT). But usually long before this happens, the addition of more and more stations will cause network traffic to slow to an apparent crawl. This is because each additional station increases the amount of broadcast traffic on the segment, in addition to the amount of data traffic. As you may recall from earlier chapters, every network frame (regardless of type) also must be looked at and forwarded by every station in turn, as each passes all traffic not intended for itself down the line to the next station.

Even worse, if you recall the basic distinction between Token Ring and Ethernet networks, there is yet another way that adding stations (nodes) to a network segment adversely impacts network throughput. Recall that Ethernet networks use CSMA/CD (carrier sense multiple access with collision detection) to determine when to transmit. This means that any station needing to transmit frames will listen for an open time, then transmit, backing off for a random period of time whenever it detects that another station has beat it to the wire. It is easy to see that by adding stations, we increase the number of participants in this game of "listen and chatter," which reduces the time available to any one station to transmit. It also increases the probability of two or more stations trying to talk simultaneously (collisions)—more time that will be unavailable for any station to use. Token Ring escapes this latter problem, but unavoidably also suffers decreased throughput when more stations are added.

One solution to this is simply to cut a network into two or more networks—separate the stations into two or more groups, assign a separate server to each, and since now the groups (segments) are no longer connected with each other, traffic on each network is reduced to whatever is generated by that segment alone. While this works, it has (in most cases) the undesirable effect of isolating each network segment completely, so that no station on one segment can communicate with a station on any other segment. It *will* speed up network throughput on each segment, however.

An inexpensive alternative to separate physical networks is to split the stations into separate groups, but rather than connect each segment to a separate server, instead connect each segment to a different network interface card in the *same* server. While this doesn't normally reduce the *server's* workload any, it does reduce the traffic on each segment. Additionally, with multiple network cards in your server, you have two options: You can keep the traffic on each segment isolated from the other segments (as you would using completely separate servers), or (and probably more desirable) you can have the server forward frames (or packets) between segments. This still reduces network traffic on each segment, as the server will not forward frames from one segment to another unless the sender and recipient actually are on separate segments. This latter strategy is very commonly used, and it usually provides noticeable improvement in throughput compared to using just a single network card per server.

NOTE   Splitting your network into multiple parts by installing multiple network cards in your server essentially gives you the benefits of a *router*, albeit not quite as fast or efficient as a "real" router would be. (More on routers shortly.)

So how many stations does a network segment need to have before it makes sense to subdivide it into additional segments? Well, if you have fewer than ten stations, splitting will probably not buy you much. But with ten to twelve or more stations, start thinking about splitting into two segments. It also makes sense to assign any station that generates an especially large volume of traffic to its own segment. Some example candidates for this would include high-speed image scanners, a high-volume send/receive fax server, or a high-performance graphics workstation. Of course there's a limit to how many network cards you can add to a single server—four is common—and you will have even better results if you also add separate servers to handle the different segments.

But how to make different network segments then talk to each other? That is the topic of the next sections, which discuss the hardware that excels in this role—namely, bridges, switches, routers, and brouters.

Bridges

A *bridge* looks a lot like a repeater; it is a small box with two network connectors that attach to two separate portions of the network. A bridge incorporates the functionality of a repeater (signal amplification), but it actually looks at the frames of data, which is a great benefit. A common bridge is nearly identical to a repeater except for the indicator lights, as shown in Figure 9.3. A *forward* light flashes whenever the bridge needs to pass traffic from one collision domain to another.

FIGURE 9.3:

A common bridge

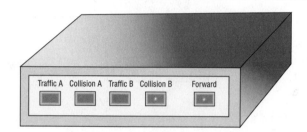

In our discussion of Ethernet in Chapter 4, we reviewed the concept of a data frame and described the information contained within the frame header. Bridges put this header information to use by monitoring the source and destination MAC address on each frame of data. By monitoring the source address, the bridge will learn where all the network systems are located. It will construct a table, listing which MAC addresses are directly accessible by each of its ports. It will then use that information to play traffic cop and regulate the flow of data on the network. Let's look at an example.

A Bridge Example

Given the network in Figure 9.4, Betty needs to send data to the server Thoth. Because everyone on the network is required to monitor the network, Betty (that is, her NIC) first listens for the transmissions of other stations. If the wire is free, Betty will then transmit a frame of data. The bridge is also watching for traffic, and it will look at the source address in the header of Betty's frame. Because it is unsure of which port the system with MAC address 00C08BBE0052 (Thoth) is connected to, it amplifies the signal and retransmits it out port B. Note that up until now, the bridge functionality is very similar to that of a repeater. The bridge does a little extra, however; it has learned that Betty is attached to port A and creates a table entry with her MAC address.

FIGURE 9.4:

Betty transmits data to the server Thoth by putting Thoth's MAC address into the destination field of the frame.

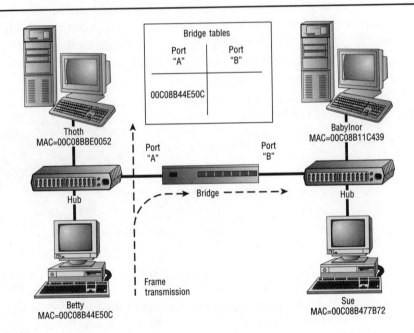

When Thoth replies to Betty's request, as shown in Figure 9.5, the bridge will look at the destination address in the frame of data again. This time, however, it finds a match in its table, noting that Betty is also attached to port A. Because it knows Betty can receive this information directly, it drops the frame and blocks it from being transmitted out of port B. It will also make a new table entry for Thoth, recording the MAC address as being off port A.

The benefit is that, for as long as the bridge remembers each station's MAC address, all communications between Betty and Thoth will be isolated from Sue and Babylnor.

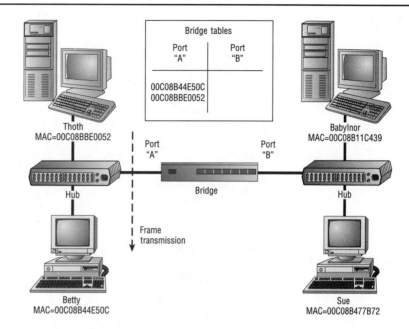

NOTE   Traffic isolation is a powerful feature because it means that systems on both side of the bridge can be carrying on conversations at the same time, effectively doubling the available bandwidth.

The bridge ensures that communications on both sides stay isolated, as if they were not even connected together. Because stations cannot see transmissions on the other side of the bridge, they assume the network is free and send their data.

Each system only needs to contend for bandwidth with systems on its own segment. This means that there is no way for a station to have a collision outside of its segment. Thus these segments are referred to as *collision domains*, as shown in Figure 9.6. Note that one port on each side of the bridge is part of each collision domain. This is because each of its ports will contend for bandwidth with the systems it is directly connected to. Because the bridge isolates traffic within each collision domain, there is no way for separated systems to collide their signals. The effect is a doubling of potential bandwidth.

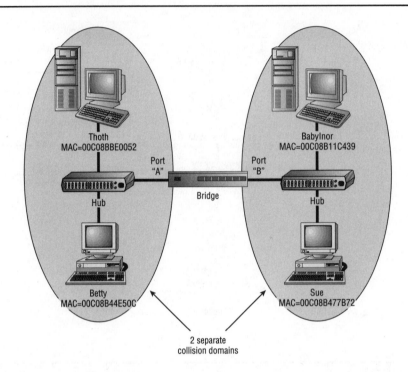

2 separate
collision domains

So what happens when traffic needs to traverse the bridge? As stated above, when a bridge is unsure of the location of a system, it will always pass the packet along just in case. Once the bridge learns that the system is in fact located off its other port, it will continue to pass the frame along as required.

As we mentioned in our discussion of Ethernet frames, there is a special destination address referred to as a broadcast address. Broadcasts contain information required by multiple stations on the network. Broadcast frames are typically used by upper-layer protocols like IPX and IP to relay network and server information. For this reason a bridge will always pass a broadcast frame and will not bother making a table entry for it.

Balancing Traffic Segmentation and Bridge Latency

There is an old bridging rule that states that 80 percent of your traffic should be directly connected, with only 20 percent or less being bridged. This rule is a general guideline to ensure that you keep a good balance between traffic segmentation and *bridge latency*. A bridge will introduce a bit more latency than a repeater or a hub; this is because it actually needs to look at the frame information and respond depending on the destination MAC address.

> **NOTE** In short, if your users frequently access a particular server, do not put a bridge in between them and that server.

Bridge latency refers to the theory that a full 100 percent utilization can never be achieved through the device because the signal is being delayed en route. While that's true, the delay is rarely noticeable. From the testing we've performed, it appears that the average bridge is able to keep up with a 90 percent utilization level. While the 10 percent loss may seem quite large, remember that an Ethernet network starts to degrade in performance by the time it reaches 50 percent utilization. A 90 percent utilization level on Ethernet feels downright dismal. So, to the average end user, the bridge should show no noticeable performance hit if they need to access systems on the other side of it. In fact, if the bridge is implemented properly it should improve performance because it would regulate traffic flow and hopefully bring the utilization down to a more reasonable level.

> **NOTE** Bridges reset the maximum spans for a topology. The maximum span for an Ethernet network is 3000 feet. But if we attach a bridge to the end of it, we could add another 3000 feet to our overall network length; this is because a bridge listens to the network prior to transmitting, just like any other intelligent network device. Hubs and repeaters do not do this because they function at the electrical level only.

Protocol Independence

Bridges are *protocol independent*. This means that it does not matter if you're running AppleTalk, IPX, IP, NetBEUI or any other 802.3-compliant means of communicating. All a bridge cares about are the source and destination MAC addresses present in any valid Ethernet frame. Protocol independence can come in handy if you're using a protocol that receives limited hardware support like Banyan's VINES IP (discussed in Chapter 15). Note that many of these protocols operate by having the administrator assign a *network address* for them to use. Because bridges do not look at the upper layer protocol, this number would be the same on both sides of the bridge.

NOTE   We'll talk a little more about protocols and network addresses when we cover routers.

Some bridges can analyze the frame check sequence (FCS) located in the trailer of the frame. The FCS contains the cyclic redundancy check (CRC), which is an algorithm used to determine if the frame is intact or has become damaged during transmission. If FCS checking is enabled, the bridge will perform its own CRC check on the frame and compare the value to what is contained in the FCS field of each frame before forwarding the frame along. If a frame is found to fail the CRC comparison, then the bridge contacts the transmitting system and asks it to send a new copy of the frame.

If you commonly have a lot of CRC errors on your network, this check feature may be useful, as it keeps the frame from being passed to the destination system, which would then find the CRC failure and need to request a new frame itself. By letting the bridge do it, you cut down on the bandwidth used by the bad frame and the resulting request to only a single collision domain.

If you do not see a lot of error you may want to keep this feature disabled, as it does require some additional overhead on the bridge. If you do see a lot of errors (if, say, one percent of your traffic is bad CRC frames), enable this feature. Then set out to determine their cause and eliminate it.

NOTE   Excessive CRC failures are usually caused by a bad network interface card.

The Spanning Tree Protocol

Bridges are capable of communicating with each other via a set of rules called the *Spanning Tree protocol*. The Spanning Tree protocol is used to configure default paths dynamically when two or more bridges are connected in parallel to each other.

Bridge Looping Causes Problems

The Spanning Tree protocol helps to avoid a situation called *bridge looping*. To get an idea of how bridge looping works, let's look at an example.

Given a network layout similar to our last example, you decide to add a second bridge for redundancy. This way, if someone spills coffee on the first bridge and it quickly dies in a shower of sparks, the second bridge can continue to provide connectivity between the two collision domains. The configuration would look something like Figure 9.7.

FIGURE 9.7:

Two bridges connected parallel to each other create a redundant link between the two collision domains.

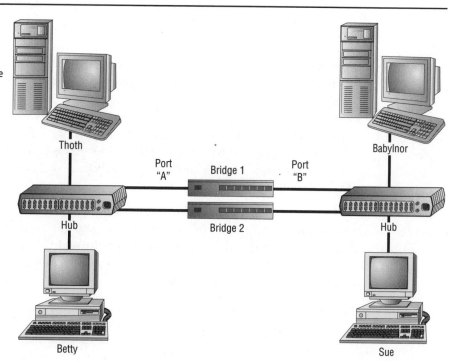

If both bridges are active, a curious behavior occurs. Given a situation where Betty sends a frame of data to Thoth, both bridges would detect the frame and be unsure where Thoth is located, so they would both transmit the data to the other segment and make an entry for Betty in their tables, placing her off port A.

NOTE When both bridges detect the frame and transmit the data to the other segment, two separate copies of the frame have been transmitted onto the other collision domain (off port B).

As each bridge detects the frame sent by the other on the port B collision domain, they would assume that this is a new attempt by Betty to send Thoth a frame of data. Because both bridges would still be unsure where Thoth is located, they would pass the frame back to the collision domain off port A. Each bridge will also assume that Betty has now moved to the other collision domain and would incorrectly list the system as being off port B.

We have a couple of problems at this point. First we have three identical frames (one from Betty and one from each of the bridges) floating around off port A, when there should only be one. Instead of improving our traffic pattern, the bridges have tripled our frame rate on this segment. Also, because Betty is now incorrectly listed as being off port B, any data transmitted to Betty by Babylnor and Sue would be blocked by both bridges because they now incorrectly assume that Betty is on the same local segment as Babylnor and Sue. The result is that Betty is unable to receive any data sent to her from stations off port B, because neither bridge will forward the information.

At this point the entire situation repeats itself. Both bridges detect the frame transmission of the other off port A. They retransmit the frame onto the segment attached to port B and move the entry for Betty's MAC address back to port A again. At this point Betty is able to receive data across the bridge, but only until the tables are incorrectly reset again.

NOTE This looping effect is referred to as *counting to infinity*.

The bridges will continue to pass the frame back and forth until the end of time or until the bridge's power plug is pulled, whichever comes first. This happens because a bridge has no way of identifying duplicate frames. When the frame is analyzed, the bridge only looks at the source and destination MAC addresses. Performing some form of a check to determine if it has seen a particular frame before is beyond the scope of a bridge's functionality; it would also severely degrade a bridge's performance, causing it to become a bottleneck on the network.

Now, take this situation with Betty's system and multiply it by a network full of systems. It's easy to see how two misconfigured bridges could easily bring an entire network to its knees.

Eliminating Bridging Loops with the Spanning Tree Protocol

To the rescue comes the Spanning Tree protocol. This protocol allows bridges to communicate with each other and learn where they are in relation to one another. If a bridge is configured to use the Spanning Tree protocol, it will transmit a maintenance frame on startup, called a Bridge Protocol Data Unit (BPDU). This frame contains an ID number for the bridge and is transmitted on all the bridge's ports. This ID number is a combination of a number preset by the network administrator and the device's MAC address.

If the Spanning Tree protocol is used in the above example, both bridges would transmit BPDUs from each of their ports. Each bridge would receive a BPDU from the other bridge on both of its ports and realize that the two devices are hooked up in parallel. They would then compare their BPDUs to see which bridge has the lowest ID number. The bridge with the lower ID number would become active, while the other would enter a standby mode. The second bridge would remain in standby mode until it detects that the first bridge is no longer passing packets. If the first bridge drops offline, the second bridge would step in to supply connectivity. Because there is only one active path for the frames to follow, bridge looping is eliminated.

TIP

A bridge's ID is prefixed by a number that you can assign. If you prefer to use one particular bridge for performance reasons, you can assign it a lower number (like 01) to ensure that it initiates as the active bridge.

About the only drawback of the Spanning Tree protocol is that the switchover occurs so quickly that you will probably never know the bridge has failed unless you are monitoring the devices.

Use a Bridge to Segment Traffic

Let's look at three sample networks and determine which environment would benefit the most by the use of bridging. Note that we're focusing on the network infrastructure, not on the actual operating systems or the functionality of the protocols being used. As you read each example, see if (and why) you think bridging would be a good idea before reading on.

Example 1

The first example is a group of 25 software engineers using SGI Unix workstations. They use their machines to write code and create images for computer games. As part of the software development process, the engineers need to exchange file information with each other. They are not organized into defined workgroups, as all development is a collaborative effort. Each engineer may need to share files with any one of the other engineers at any given time. The data transfers between systems can also be quite intensive, as large graphic files are used and source code is compiled over the network. Figure 9.8 depicts our first example.

FIGURE 9.8:

Our first example network consists of 25 (eight shown here) engineers who need to share file information between their workstations.

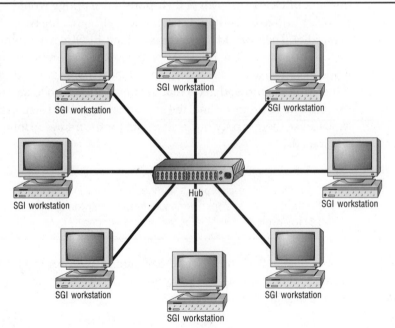

SGI workstation

SGI workstation

SGI workstation

SGI workstation

Hub

SGI workstation

SGI workstation

SGI workstation

SGI workstation

Example 2

The second example is a small advertising firm with approximately 50 employees. They have three servers—one NetWare, one Mac, and one Unix. Fifteen of the 50 use Mac workstations to do graphic design work that involves moving some average-size image files. All files are stored on the Mac server using Apple's native AppleTalk protocol. The remaining 35 users perform mostly administrative tasks and connect with the NetWare system via the IPX protocol for file and print services. All users run IP as well to connect to the Unix system for mail and Internet access. Figure 9.9 illustrates our second scenario.

FIGURE 9.9:

Our second example net-
work, with multiple server
types and protocols

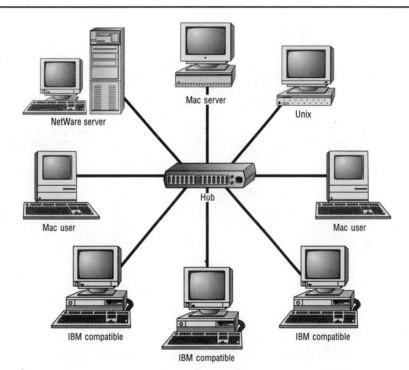

Example 3

Finally, the third example is a network of 100 users with three NT servers. Fifty of the users use one of the servers for file and print services. The remaining 50 use the second server for the same services. A third system runs the company's mail program and needs to be accessed by everyone. NetBEUI is used to access all servers. Figure 9.10 shows our third example.

FIGURE 9.10:

Our third example network, with users neatly broken up by workgroup and everyone needing access to mail

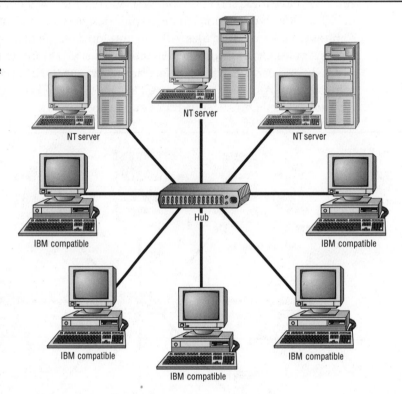

In all three examples the users are complaining about slow network response time. As always, cost is a factor and any hardware purchases will need to be justified.

While the task of redesigning each of these networks may seem a bit over-whelming, think of what we have learned about a bridge's functionality and try to apply its traffic isolation features to each of the above examples. Move systems around as required if you think it will help improve performance.

TIP   Feel free to stop for a moment before reading on. A large part of being a success-ful network engineer is having good problem solving skills and learning to be ana-lytical. Learning the theory of how network systems work is the easy part. Applying it on a daily basis is the real challenge.

The first example is clearly not a good choice for implementing a bridge. Because everyone shares files with everyone else, there is no way to maintain our "directly connect 80 percent and bridge no more than 20 percent" rule. Bridging would be of very little use in this environment.

The second example shows a bit more potential. Users are loosely grouped into workgroups, as administration mostly uses the NetWare server and graphic design mostly accesses the Mac server. We may very well be able to meet our 80/20 rule in this environment. If we were to separate these work groups with bridges, putting the Unix system in the middle, as shown in Figure 9.11, we might be able to isolate enough traffic to improve network performance.

FIGURE 9.11:

A potential network design for our advertising firm

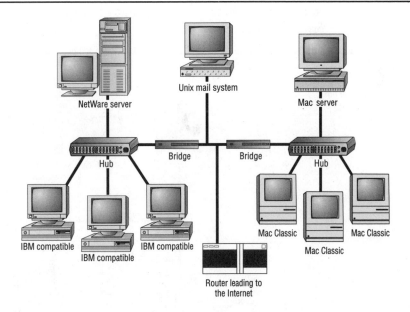

The only caveat to this is that we have three different protocols in use. As mentioned previously, protocols make use of the broadcast address to relay information concerning servers and networks. Also, as we discussed in the section on Ethernet, all stations are required to process a frame that contains a broadcast address in the MAC destination field, whether it is currently using the protocol that sent it or not. Of course, if it is not, the frame is discarded because the information has no relevance. However, it still takes time and CPU cycles for the system to determine that it did not actually need this information.

Clearly, if we can isolate the protocols from the stations that do not need to see them, we may well be able to increase overall performance even more. Because bridging is protocol-stupid and cannot provide this functionality, we may be better off waiting to see if another technology would be a better fit. Unfortunately, we cannot simply disconnect them from each other because they still need to share the Unix system for mail, and they still need access to the Internet.

The third example looks like a good fit. It has a similar layout to the second example, but without having multiple protocols to worry about. Users are in two distinct workgroups but have a common need to share mail. If we install two bridges, as shown in Figure 9.12, we set up three distinct collision domains. This isolates the work groups from each other and even isolates file and print traffic from the mail server. Overall, bridging looks like a good fit for improving performance on this network.

FIGURE 9.12:

A bridging design for our third network example

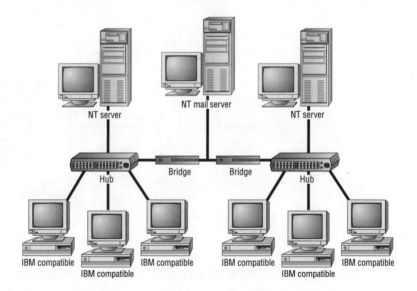

Monitoring Traffic in a Bridged Environment

While bridges have many benefits, they do have one minor drawback. If you are trying to monitor your network's health with some form of network analyzer, a bridge will block you from ever seeing a full picture. An analyzer relies on being able to detect each frame in order to collect statistics. When you use a bridge, your view is limited to the collision domain you are connected to. If you have a single bridge installed and want to monitor all traffic on your network, you will need to purchase a second analyzer and keep one hooked up to each collision domain.

Switches

Switches are the marriage of hub and bridge technology. They resemble stackable hubs in appearance, having multiple RJ-45 connectors for connecting network systems. Instead of being dumb amplifiers like hubs, however, switches function as though they have a little miniature bridge built into each port. A switch will keep track of the MAC addresses attached to each of its ports and route traffic destined for a certain address only to the appropriate port.

Figure 9.13 shows a switched environment in which the device will learn the position of each station once a single frame transmission occurs (identical to a bridge). Assuming that this has already happened, we now find that at exactly the same instant Station 1 needs to send data to Server 1, Station 2 needs to send data to Server 2, and Station 3 needs to send data to Server 3.

There are some interesting things about this situation. The first is that each wire run involves only the switch and the station attached to it. This means that each collision domain is limited to only these two devices because each port of the switch is acting like a bridge. The only traffic seen by the workstations and servers consists of frames specifically sent to them or the broadcast address. The result is that all three stations will see very little network traffic and will be able to transmit immediately. This is a powerful feature that goes a long way towards increasing potential bandwidth.

NOTE   Given our example, if this is a 10Mbps topology, the potential throughput has just increased by a factor of 3. This is because all three sets of systems are able to carry on their conversation simultaneously as the switch isolates them from each other. While it is still technically 10Mbps Ethernet, potential throughput has increased to 30Mbps.

A switch installation showing three workstations and
three servers that need to
communicate

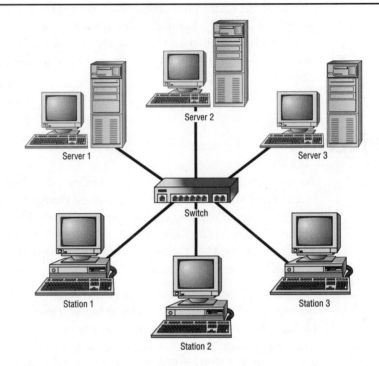

Because each collision domain is limited to only two devices (the switch and
the system attached) we could completely eliminate the chance of any collisions if
we can come up with some way to keep these two systems from stepping on each
other's transmissions.

Full-Duplex Operation

This is where *full-duplex operation* comes into play. Full-duplex under Ethernet
changes the communication rules by telling a system it is okay if it receives different data than what it is currently transmitting. Each of the two systems has exclusive access to a pair of wires in order to transmit data. The result is that each
system can transmit data without having to worry about pesky collisions. A system can continually transmit 10Mbps on one wire pair while receiving 10Mbps
on the other.

NOTE   Applying this to the above mentioned network, our potential throughput has just jumped from 30Mbps to 60Mbps!

Our topology has not changed—we are achieving these bandwidth potentials using standard 10Mbps Ethernet hardware.

Note the operative word "potential." It would be an extremely rare situation for these six systems to transmit this much data simultaneously. Still, having exclusive wire access is a great way to ensure that a system can transmit whenever it needs to. If applied only to servers, full-duplex operation gives these systems a bit of an edge in keeping up with requests from multiple clients. The result is a governing effect, allocating more bandwidth to the server than the workstations. This will help the server keep up with the additional frames it will see now that each workstation has its own 10Mbps pipe.

NOTE   Some network cards have a feature that allows them to *auto-detect* when full-duplex operation may be used. This feature should be **disabled** and the card should be specifically configured for the correct mode of operation (full or half duplex).

We have seen situations where the first computer booted on the network will assume it has exclusive access to a collision domain and switch to full-duplex mode. It will not realize it is connected through a shared hub. This works fine until the rest of the network's systems begin to power up. The result is that one station will be attempting to transmit and receive data simultaneously. This will cause the entire network to crawl to a halt, as each system that's not full-duplex assumes multiple collisions are taking place. This also can be a difficult problem to diagnose. The only clue is that the collision light will be lit up like a Christmas tree.

Cut-Through Mode

Switches have two modes of operation—cut-through and store-and-forward. In *cut-through mode*, the switch receives only the first 14 bytes of the frame (just the header) and will immediately begin to decide where the frame should be sent. In this mode, a switch has the ability to begin transmitting the frame on the destination port before it receives it in its entirety; resulting in extremely fast switching times, with a minimal amount of latency added to the circuit. The greatest benefits of cut-through mode are seen in quiet or full-duplex environments where it is unlikely the switch will need to pause prior to transmission.

NOTE   The benefits of cut-through mode diminish as traffic levels increase.

If utilization is high, it is unlikely that the switch will ever be able to transmit the frame onto a collision domain prior to receiving it in its entirety anyway. In these cases store-and-forward mode can be just as effective.

Store-and-Forward Mode

Store-and-forward mode requires the switch to read the entire frame into memory prior to transmission. While reading the entire frame adds a bit of a delay, the store-and-forward mode definitely has its advantages. Like a bridge, a switch in store-and-forward mode has the ability to check the FCS field for CRC errors; this ensures that bad frames are not propagated across the network. Another cool feature is that store-and-forward mode gives the switch the ability to support multiple topologies. A server could be connected to a 100Mbps port while all the workstations are connected to 10Mbps ports; this would allow the server to keep up with data requests from multiple workstations easily, and it would speed up overall network performance.

NOTE   Store-and-forward switching is always used with mixed topologies because it ensures that the switch has the entire frame available prior to attempting a transmission.

Because in cut-through mode a switch can begin transmitting a frame prior to receiving it in its entirety, problems may arise in a mixed-speed situation. Let's say a frame is received on a 10Mbps port and it is addressed to a system on the 100Mbps port. In cut-through mode the switch would immediately begin delivery on the faster segment. This can be a problem because there is the potential for the switch to transmit all the frame information it has received on the faster segment and then have to pause and wait for the delivery of the rest of the frame information. Obviously this would cause communication problems on the faster segment.

Avoiding Switch Overload

Take care not to overload the switch with excessive traffic. Let's look at an extreme example of how *switch overload* can occur.

Assume you have an old 386 server running NetWare 2.15. Because the system has continued to function, it has been pretty much ignored over the years. Your users are a different story, however, complaining about how slow their workstations are and claiming they require dual processor Pentium II machines with PCI buses and every go-fast computer part you can think of (insert a Tim Allen grunt here).

You decide to upgrade your network infrastructure by replacing your old hub with a brand-new switch. You swap in the new device, connect all systems but the server in full-duplex mode (the server has an old card that does not support this feature), and wait for your users to begin working. A curious thing occurs— network performance actually gets worse! Why did this happen? To answer this, let's look at what was probably going on prior to the switch installation.

On a repeated network (remember that your hub is just a multiport repeater), all systems are in direct communication with each other. This means that the maximum amount of information that can be transmitted at any given time is limited by the topology speed. The nice thing about this situation is that it is self-regulating. To be sure, network performance can be a bit sluggish, but it helps to keep any one system from becoming overloaded (although this can still occur).

Now, let's drop our switch back in and see what happened. In full-duplex mode each workstation assumed it had full bandwidth available and would transmit information whenever it needed to. Because each workstation never has to contend for bandwidth, it is capable of sending more information in a given period of time than it could before the switch was installed. The switch would then attempt to deliver these frames of data to the server.

As the pipe leading to the server begins to become overloaded (we have multiple 10Mbps full-duplex connections trying to send data to a half-duplex 10Mbps connection), the switch begins to queue up packets sent by the workstations. If the server's pipe cannot eventually catch up with the frames stored in the switch's queue (a very likely situation given our example), the frames will eventually fill up the switch's memory pool. Once this occurs, any new frames transmitted to the switch have nowhere to be stored and subsequently are ignored. In short, the switch is throwing away information because it has nowhere to store it.

To make matters even worse, the workstations will eventually time out waiting for a reply to the frames the switch threw away; this causes them to transmit the same information again, compounding the bottleneck.

This is a good example of why it is important to maintain a balance on your network and make sure you know the impact of any hardware you install. While this example may seem a bit extreme, it is not too far off from a real-life network situation one of the authors had to diagnose.

Some switches handle queued frames better than others. There are even some high-end switches that could handle the above example without dropping a single frame.

> **TIP** It is a good idea to verify a vendor's performance claims through some impartial review, prior to purchasing any equipment.

VLAN Technology

Switching introduces a new technology referred to as the *virtual local area network* (*VLAN*). Software running on the switch allows you to set up connectivity parameters for connecting systems by workgroup, instead of by geographical location. The switch's administrator is allowed to organize port transmissions logically so that connectivity is grouped according to each user's requirements. The "virtual" part of it is that these workgroups can span over multiple physical network segments. By assigning all switch ports that connect to PCs used by accounting personnel to the same workgroup, for example, a virtual accounting network can be created.

Let's look at a more detailed example to see how this works.

A VLAN Example

Say we have two groups of users who work exclusively with each other and a particular server. We could create two VLANs, isolating the traffic so that all communications remain within the group. While a switch will do this anyway for point-to-point communications, the addition of the VLANs will block broadcast traffic as well. This isolation will help to reduce unnecessary traffic even further.

The added bonus is security, as users from one VLAN will be unable to connect to the server in the other VLAN. This extra security may be useful in a higher-security environment.

There may be a problem with this setup, however. What if the two servers are running NetWare 4.11 and need to exchange NDS information with each other? The solution is to add a third VLAN that includes only the servers. VLANs are allowed to overlap as circumstances require. This overlap allows server broadcasts to reach all members of the workgroup as well as the other server. Workstations located in the other workgroup would not see these broadcasts and would thus be safeguarded from this additional traffic. Our network would look something like Figure 9.14.

FIGURE 9.14:

VLAN implementation in a small networking environment

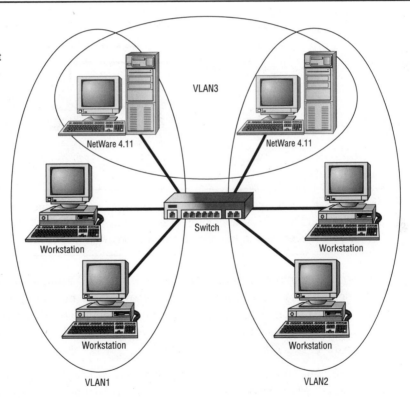

While the true benefits of VLANs may not be apparent immediately, let's increase the scale of our network and watch what happens. Figure 9.15 shows an organization that occupies a number of floors in a building. If each department is confined to a single floor, then our network design may be fine as is.

A large network using switches to connect to the backbone

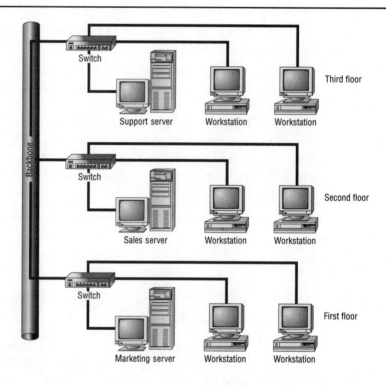

NOTE A *backbone* is a network segment used to connect other segments that contain end users. It usually runs a faster topology than the populated segments in order to keep up with the larger bandwidth demands it may experience.

Unfortunately, this is rarely the case, and workgroups can find themselves spread out over a wide geographical area. If the marketing server is located on the first floor, then any marketing personnel who need to access it will find themselves traversing the backbone on a regular basis. Let's assume this situation is true for other departments as well.

Because there is no way to organize our workgroups geographically, network broadcasts must be propagated to every corner of the network as valid users could be located anywhere; this can make for a very busy network.

Now let's create some virtual networks and see what happens. If VLANs are used to segment, our network traffic can be confined to each individual workgroup, even though they are spread throughout the building. This confinement would give us better traffic isolation and thus better network performance. Figure 9.16 shows how these users could be grouped.

FIGURE 9.16:

A large network using VLANs to better isolate network traffic

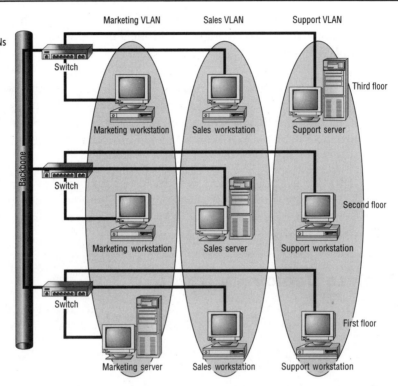

While we may be able to wire each user's station directly to the same floor where their server is located, this could be impractical. Ignoring the fact that this kind of wiring could create a spaghetti nightmare, what happens when a user moves down the hall? Then you would have to rewire their new office space to connect to their server location, and you might also have to rewire their old office if a user from another department moves in. With a VLAN, this type of relocation would mean a simple configuration change through the switch's management software.

VLAN Drawbacks

VLANs do have a few drawbacks. The first is that the scalability just described is usually vendor specific. There are a number of different ways virtual LANs are created. You may find that some vendor implementations will not work with others. While this discrepancy should correct itself over the next few years, you will need to be conscious of this limitation for now.

Also, segmentation is very specific. Each user is completely confined to working only within their workgroup. While this was acceptable in the scenarios we looked at, what if all users need to share access to multiple servers or require access to the Internet? In these situations, the usefulness of VLAN can begin to fall apart as routers would be required to connect separate VLANs. As with any technology, make sure you know exactly how you plan to use it and that it does in fact support this use before you make any hardware purchases. To take poetic liberty with an old carpenter's saying, research twice and purchase once.

One final drawback of VLANs is that they can be very high-maintenance items. If you have a large network with each user connected to a single switch port, it will take some time to get all the ports configured correctly and it will require you to make changes whenever a user is moved. Plan on gaining an intimate knowledge of the VLAN administration software.

When to Deploy Switching

When is it a good idea to deploy switching? Let's revisit our three example networks, shown in Figures 9.8–9.10, to see where it makes sense.

With 25 Engineers

Our group of 25 engineers would be a great fit for switching technology. Let's say we gave each engineer their own port connection. When they share files with another engineer, the traffic generated would stay isolated from the remaining systems. If each system is outfitted with a 100Mbps card, the potential bandwidth would be in the 1.2Gbps range. In fact, because we have only one system per port, we could utilize full-duplex connections and raise the potential bandwidth to the 2.4Gbps range.

NOTE   Increasing the potential bandwidth to the 2.4Gbps range could yield up to a 2400 percent improvement in available bandwidth. Not bad for replacing a single piece of hardware!

With Multiple Servers and Protocols

There are two potential network layouts for our second network example. The first is to use VLANs and segregate traffic by workgroup. Each virtual LAN would include the users and their server. The Unix system and the Internet connection would be overlapped by both VLANs, as shared access is required for both. Our network design might look similar to Figure 9.17.

FIGURE 9.17:

A potential network design for our advertising firm's network using VLANs

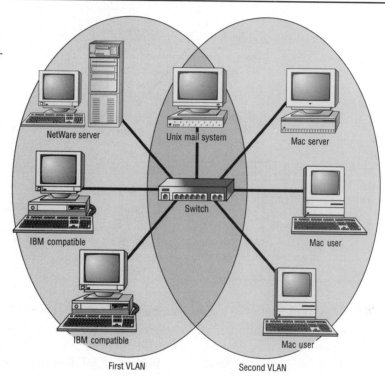

While this design would yield an increase in network performance, it does have a few minor drawbacks. The first is that switches with VLAN support are expensive, running between $200 to $400 per port. This cost could be considered excessive by an organization this small. The fact that bandwidth requirements would not be considered excessive would make this cost outlay even more difficult to justify. Also, networks this small generally have poor network support. Even if they do staff a LAN administrator, that person is usually focused on supporting the end users. The added task of supporting VLAN tables may be beyond their skill set.

Our second option would be to use the switch as the network backbone with hubs cascaded off it to support small user groups. Servers could receive a dedicated connection and be connected in full-duplex mode. Our potential design appears in Figure 9.18.

FIGURE 9.18:

Another potential design for our advertising network

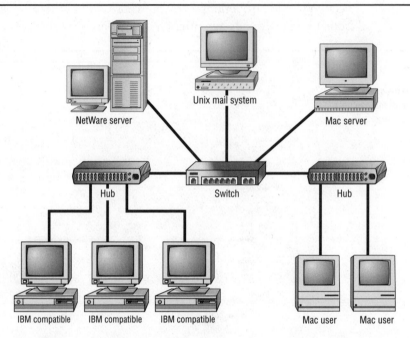

This option may be more desirable because it can be supported by a switch with a minimal number of ports, and thus reduce the cost. It also reduces the maintenance requirements, as we did not need to create any VLANs. The only real drawback is that we have no broadcast isolation between different protocols.

NOTE   This option would not be able to help with our protocol broadcast issue.

With Three NT Servers

Our final example network would benefit in much the same way. If we gave each of the three NT servers its own port and cascaded hubs off the switch for the user community, we would strike the best balance between cost and performance. A switch would cost a bit more than the bridge solution we discussed earlier, but it would allow for greater flexibility. When we bridged the network, each collision domain consisted of 50 users each. There was no easy way to further segment the users. With a switch, we could simply cascade an additional hub off a free hub port and migrate some of the users over to it.

Also, as we've discussed in an earlier chapter, NetBEUI is a nonroutable protocol. This means that while NetBEUI can cross a bridge or a switch, it cannot cross a router.

Routers

A *router* is a multiport device that makes decisions on how to handle a frame, based on protocol and network address. To fully understand what this means you should understand what a protocol is and how it works (covered in Chapters 2 and 3).

Up until now we've been happily communicating using the media access control (MAC) address assigned to our networking devices. Our systems have used this number to contact other systems and transmit information as required.

The problem with this scheme is that it does not scale very well. For example, what if a network has 2000 systems that need to communicate with each other? Even employing switching and virtual networking, the network will eventually reach a point where performance degrades and no more systems can be added. This is where protocols come in.

Protocols

As discussed in earlier chapters, a *protocol* is a set of communication rules that provide the means for networking systems to be grouped by geographical area and common wiring. To indicate that they are part of a specific group, systems are assigned protocol network addresses with a common prefix.

Network addresses are rather like zip codes. Let's assume someone mails a letter and the front of the envelope simply reads:

Amber Apple

7 Spring Rd.

In a very small town, this letter would probably get through (as if you used a MAC address on a LAN).

If the letter was mailed in a city like Boston or New York, however, the post office where it lands would have no clue where to send it (although they would probably get a good laugh). Without a zip code, they might not even attempt delivery. The zip code provides a way to specify the general area where this letter needs to be delivered. The postal worker processing the letter is not required to know exactly where Spring Rd. is located. They simply look at the zip code and forward the letter to the post office responsible for that code. It is up to the local post office to know where Spring Rd. is located and use this information to ensure that the letter reaches its destination address.

Protocol network addresses operate in a similar fashion. A protocol-aware device will add the network address of the device it wishes to reach to the data field of a frame. It will also record its own network address in case the remote system needs to send a reply.

This is where a router comes in. A router will maintain a table of all known networks. It will use these tables to help forward information to its final destination. Let's walk through an example to see how a routed network operates.

A Routed Network Example

Lets assume we have a network similar to that shown in Figure 9.19 and that system B needs to transmit information to system F.

FIGURE 9.19:

An example of a routed network

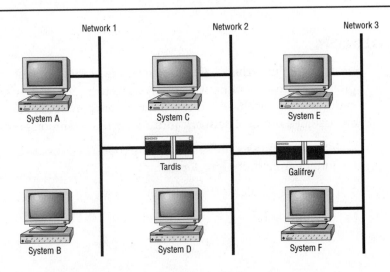

System B will begin by comparing its network address to that of System F. If there is a match it will assume the system is local and attempt to deliver the information directly. If the network addresses are different (as they are in our example), it will broadcast a *route request* query to see if any other systems on its network segment (Network 1) know how to get to the destination system's network (Network 3). A route request is essentially a request for directions. It's a networked system's way of asking, "How do I get there from here?"

Because Tardis is a router, it maintains tables of all known networks. Tardis knows it can get to Network 3 by delivering information to Galifrey. Tardis would then send this information to System B as a reply to its routing request. Because this is the only reply System B receives to its route request, it assumes that Tardis is the only route. System B would then add the delivery information for System F (its network and MAC addresses) to the data and create a frame using Tardis's MAC address as the destination. It does this because Tardis indicated that it knew the way to Network 3 in its reply. Station B is sending the frame to Tardis because it assumes that Tardis will take care of forwarding it to the destination network.

Once Tardis receives the frame it performs a CRC check to ensure the integrity of the data. If the frame checks out, it will then completely strip off the header and trailer. It would then create a new frame around the data by creating a new CRC, adding its MAC address to the source address field and putting Galifrey's MAC address in the destination field.

NOTE Remember that routers are placed at the **borders** of a network segment. The CRC check is performed to ensure that bad frames are not propagated throughout the network.

While all this stripping and re-creating seems like a lot of work, it is a necessary part of this type of communication. The header information is stripped away because it is only applicable on Network 1. When Tardis goes to transmit the frame on Network 2, the original source and destination MAC addresses have no meaning. This is why it must replace these values with ones that are valid for Network 2. Because most (12 of the 14 bytes) of the header needs to be replaced anyway, it is easier to simply strip it completely away and create it from scratch. As for stripping off the trailer, once the source and destination MAC addresses change, the original CRC value is no longer valid. This is why the router must strip it off and create a new one. By the way, a data field that contains protocol information is referred to as a *packet*. While this term is sometimes used interchangeably with the term *frame*, it in fact only describes a portion of the frame.

So Tardis has created a new frame around the packet and is ready to transmit it. Tardis looks at the destination and has no idea who System F is, but it does know it can get to Network 3 by delivering the frame to Galifrey. It then transmits the frame out onto Network 2. Galifrey then receives the frame and processes it in a similar fashion to Tardis. It checks the CRC and strips off the header and trailer.

At this point, however, Galifrey realizes that it has a local connection to system F, because they are both connected to Network 3. It builds a new frame around the packet and, instead of needing to reference a table, it simply delivers the frame directly.

Protocol Specificity

In order for a router to provide this type of functionality, it needs to understand the rules for the protocol being used. This means that a router is *protocol specific*. Unlike a bridge, which will handle any valid topology traffic you throw at it, a router has to be specifically designed to support both the topology and the protocol being used. For example, if your network contains Banyan VINES systems, make sure that your router supports VINES IP.

WARNING   All of this functionality comes at a cost. Routers are typically poor performers when compared to bridges and switches because of the overhead involved with removing and re-creating the frame. While a router can be a valuable tool, it should be used wisely.

Routers can be a powerful tool for controlling the flow of traffic on your network. If you have a network segment that is using IPX and IP but only IP is approved for use on the company backbone, simply enable IP support only on your router. Any IPX traffic the router receives will be ignored.

A wonderful feature of routers is their ability to block broadcasts. As mentioned earlier, broadcasts are frames that contain all F's for the destination MAC address. Because any point on the other side of the router is a new network, these frames are blocked.

NOTE There is a counterpart to this called an *all networks broadcast* that contains all F's in both the network and MAC address fields. These frames are used to broadcast to local networks, when the network address is not known. Most routers will still block these all-network broadcasts by default (but can be configured to forward them).

Most routers also have the ability to filter out certain traffic. For example, let's say your company enters a partnership with another organization. You need to access services on this new network but do not want to allow them to access your servers. To accomplish this, simply install a router between the two networks and configure it to filter out any network information that would normally be propagated from your network to theirs, as well as any inbound sessions. Without this connectivity information, they have no way of accessing servers on your network.

Bridging and Routing Compared

Here's a quick summary of the differences between bridging and routing.

A Bridge	A Router
Uses the same network address off all ports	Uses different network addresses off all ports
Builds tables based on MAC address	Builds tables based on network addresses
Forwards broadcast traffic	Blocks broadcast traffic
Forwards traffic to unknown addresses	Blocks traffic to unknown addresses
Does not modify frame	Creates a new header and trailer
Can forward traffic based on the frame header	Must always queue traffic before forwarding

Protocol Address Conventions

Different protocols use different address conventions. While we've covered this in greater detail in Chapters 2 and 3, it's useful to recap those conventions here:

IP   Four blocks of numbers in the range 1–255, separated by periods, such as 10.254.11.105

IPX   An eight-digit hexadecimal number, such as BA5EBA11

AppleTalk   Any combination of alphanumeric characters, such as Manufacturing

NetBEUI and NetBIOS do not have network addresses and are referred to as non-routable protocols. While it is still possible for them to exchange traffic across a router, it is not by design. Without a network address to evaluate, a router cannot determine where to send the frame.

> **NOTE**   Many network servers have the ability to accept multiple network cards and therefore function as routers.

Server routing varies from simply providing connectivity to providing advanced features like full-blown filter tables. In either case, a hardware router should always outperform its server-based counterpart. A hardware router is dedicated to this type of functionality. A server-based solution needs to share CPU and bandwidth with all the other processes running on the system.

Now let's revisit our three network examples to see if any of them could benefit from the addition of routing.

With 25 Engineers

Our first example is clearly a "no go." Because traffic flow is unpredictable, a router would be of very little use.

With Multiple Servers and Protocols

Our second network shows more promise. It has two of the main ingredients that make routing an interesting choice, multiple protocols and the need for traffic isolation. If we were to configure our network as shown in Figure 9.20, we would have gained the following:

- The ability to isolate IPX and AppleTalk traffic by simply not passing them across the router

- The ability to support IP traffic throughout the network while still isolating each workgroup from the traffic generated by the other

- The ability to add a second line of defense between our internal systems and the Internet

Routing holds some interesting possibilities in this configuration.

FIGURE 9.20:

Our accounting network is segmented with a router.

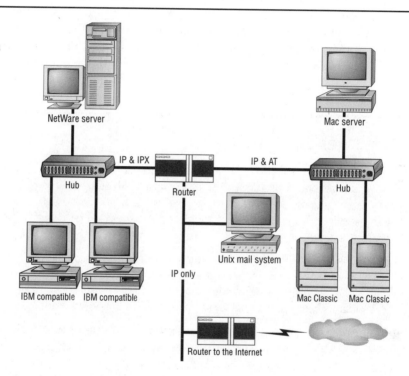

With Three NT Servers

As for our third example, we could configure it in a similar fashion to the second. Each workgroup could be located off a router port along with its NT server. The mail system could be installed off a third port to isolate users communicating to it from the other workgroup. This configuration would provide the traffic isolation we need as well as continued shared access to the mail server. As we will discuss later, however, NetBEUI is a non-routable protocol. This means that it has no way to traverse any routers installed in our network. The use of routers would completely isolate each of the network segments created.

Variations

You may have noticed that two of the three examples had multiple solutions. We did not even get into the possibilities of mixing and matching different technologies! This is because we are trying to make a judgment based on a very limited amount of information. While some of these examples appear to be toss-ups in terms of which technology is the best fit, if you dig deep enough you may find some little tidbit that will tip the scales in one direction or the other. For example, we never considered whether all employees use the network at the same time or if they are broken up over different daily shifts. This could dramatically change the traffic patterns and thus our network requirements. Do not take anything for granted.

Consider Everything

Chris Brenton had an experience a few years back that really drove home how important it is to consider all factors. He was working as a LAN administrator for a company that made network print servers. Part of his long job description included helping out with second line Tech Support. If a service engineer got in over their head, they would conference him in to give them a hand.

One day an engineer called and asked if Chris could help him with a customer. He had spent the last hour and a half on the phone with her and was unable to get the print server working. He was confused because this was a small single NetWare server environment. There was nothing out of the ordinary in the environment from what he could tell.

Chris listened in as the engineer walked the customer through setting up a print queue and print server in Pconsole. Usually once this is complete you can simply plug in the device and it works. At the end of the process he asked her to try a test print. She stated that the print server still didn't work. Frustrated, but still willing to give it another shot, he sent her back into Pconsole to delete the last configuration and create it from scratch. As they were creating the print server entry yet again, Chris realized that he was not hearing the usual background noises of someone wrestling with a phone or using a speakerphone. On a hunch he spoke up and asked her to read what was on the screen:

"C-colon-backslash-D-O-S."

The engineer spoke up and said, "You mean you're not in Pconsole?"

To which the client replied, "What's that? You mean you expect me to type all this stuff?"

Never assume!

Switch Routers

Switch routers are fairly new to the networking world. These devices provide all the functionality of a switch and include some of the benefits of a router when VLANs are implemented.

As discussed, normal switches are protocol-stupid. When a VLAN is created it restricts all communications to within itself. There is no way to tell a VLAN to react differently depending on protocol. Segmentation is done by port selection or by analyzing the system's MAC address.

Switch routers provide the ability to route differently based on protocol types. Let's look at how this can be useful.

When a Switch Router Is Useful

Let's assume we have a network of 75 users. These users are divided into groups of 25, each with its own NetWare server. The users communicate only with their own server and use the IPX protocol. So far we have a good application for a regular switch. We could create three VLANs and segregate traffic as we did in earlier examples.

Now let's throw in a twist and assume that all the workstations are providing file sharing via IP to all other workstations on the network. With a regular switch, our VLANs would immediately become useless. This is because every workstation requires the ability to communicate with every other workstation on the network, and our switch VLANs would block this connectivity.

This is where a switch router comes in handy. In this situation a switch router could be configured to restrict IPX traffic to the VLANs we defined while allowing IP traffic to flow freely throughout the network. The switch router provides an additional level of fine tuning when isolating traffic on the network.

Switch routing is a new technology, and so its features and design advantages are still under development. As people become more familiar with switch routers, expect to see additional features added and new applications discovered.

NOTE Switch routers are still quite expensive and will need to come down in price before they become widely implemented.

Brouters

There is one other variation on the theme of a router or a bridge, and that is called a *brouter*. Just as it sounds, a brouter combines the functionality of a bridge and a router in one box.

Recall that a bridge works at the network frame level, using the MAC address which is stored in every frame (regardless of protocol), to decide whether to forward the frame to the other segment. Routers operate at the somewhat higher protocol level and can read the addressing information stored in each packet to determine where to it should be forwarded.

A brouter checks incoming packets first to determine whether they are from a routable protocol. Protocols such as TCP/IP can be routed, for example, whereas Microsoft's NetBEUI protocol cannot. If the router determines the packet is routable, it uses its routing tables just as a router would, to determine where to route the packet. If, on the other hand, the packet is from a non-routable protocol, then the brouter looks at the MAC address stored within the frames being sent and uses its bridging tables to determine the proper recipient.

As you can see, a brouter has to maintain both a routing table and a bridging table, and it has the ability to function both at the Data Link layer (when it looks at frames) and at the Network layer (when it looks at packets).

Summary

We began this chapter by talking about the ability of repeaters and hubs to amplify and extend the effective length between LAN connections. We looked at the three types of hubs: chassis, stackable, and managed stackable. We saw that hubs can be interconnected by an uplink port, or on some models by a backbone connection.

Next we discussed how splitting networks into segments reduces traffic and thereby increases the effective throughput on each segment. We went on to look at routers, bridges, switches, and brouters, discussing the abilities each of these has to join network segments. Routers forward traffic at the packet level, whereas bridges and switches forward at the frame level. Brouters, finally, function at both levels.

This equipment has become indispensible to networking because it enables networks to divide up the responsibility of forwarding information, keeping as much traffic as possible on a local level, and therefore avoiding unnecessarily burdening other servers with an extra workload. This is a key step toward enabling mid- to larger-sized networks to operate effectively, and is a major portion of what enables very large networks, such as the Internet itself, to exist at all.

In the next chapter we'll continue this thread by looking at additional types of hardware used to interconnect networks and workstations.

CHAPTER

TEN

Workstations, Servers, and Additional Connectivity Hardware

- ■ Workstations and thin clients

- ■ File servers, print servers, and application servers

- ■ Blurring the line between workstation and server

- ■ Modems and channel binding

- ■ ISDN modems and cable modems

- ■ Digital subscriber lines

In previous chapters, we've looked at how networks collaborate and share information by breaking it down into frames and packets. We looked specifically at how Token Ring and Ethernet accomplish this, discussed various types of transmission media in great detail, and in the preceding chapter, discussed the various types of hardware that enable us to split networks into subnetworks, or segments.

In this chapter, we continue on the subject of networking hardware, beginning with a look at what constitutes a workstation, a server, and a thin client. Then, we'll shift our focus to enumerate the various types of hardware used to make the more far-flung connections—those between an office and remote workstations, between two LANs separated geographically, and between a workstation or LAN and the Internet itself. In future chapters we will look further at the software that enables these disparate pieces of hardware to collaborate to form networks.

Workstations

A *workstation* is simply a regular desktop computer system outfitted with a network card. It contains a central processor unit (CPU), memory, and usually a hard drive. This hardware allows the system to run programs either across the network or off the local drive as required. Except for the network card, these systems can be identical to the computers purchased for home use.

Common operating systems are Microsoft's Windows 95/98, NT Workstation, or Apple's System 7.x and System 8 (used on the Mac). If the operating system does not have built-in support for a particular network protocol, such as NetBEUI or IPX, then additional software that allows the system to communicate on the network will be required. Most network operating systems ship with all the software required to allow a workstation to communicate with the server.

In a commercial environment, a workstation is usually configured with all the user's required applications loaded on the local drive. Having the user's word processor, spreadsheet program, and so on loaded on the hard drive reduces network traffic because users don't need to load these applications across the network. As features have been added over the years, desktop applications have become quite large.

As an example, just the main executable file for Microsoft Excel (EXCEL.EXE) has a file size of 4.7MB. This means that for a single workstation to load this one file (not including all the required support files) over a 10Mbps network would require four to 10 seconds (depending on frame size). Not only does this greatly increase the amount of time it will take to load the application, but this large data request will reduce the amount of bandwidth available to other stations while the data transfer is taking place. While this would probably not be an issue with only one workstation, consider what the effect may be if you have 10–15 accountants popping in and out of Excel frequently in the course of the day.

Data files created by these programs are then saved out to a network server so that they can be protected by a nightly backup system. Each user is typically given a directory area on the server to save their files as required.

The Workstation Image

If users are not saving work files on their local computers, recovery from system crashes becomes much easier. Most administrators will create what is referred to as a *workstation image*. This image is simply a copy of a fully configured workstation including all corporate applications. If a user's system crashes, it is a simple matter of using this image to create a new system quickly. A workstation image is also useful when configuring new hardware before releasing it to the end user community. Let's see how this may work.

Suppose your company has a standard workstation configuration that includes Microsoft Office, cc:Mail, and Novell's software for connecting to a NetWare server. Each user has these software packages loaded on their system as a minimum. To create a workstation image, you would simply take a single workstation and load each of the above applications. Each piece of software would be installed using the package's installation routine (usually a matter of running *setup* or *install*). Up to this point the process is identical to the way you might configure an individual system, except that information specific to an individual user is omitted (such as their NetWare or cc:Mail login name).

Once you have loaded all the necessary applications, simply copy all files and directories up to a local server. Now, whenever a new workstation must be configured, simply boot and format the workstation with a floppy disk and copy this directory structure to the workstation's local drive. The new workstation will contain all the applications required by the end user. Because you are simply copying files and not running setup programs, the time it takes to create a usable workstation is greatly reduced. Also, because the file copying does not require user interaction, it is possible to configure many workstations simultaneously. We've seen people configure 20–30 workstations an hour using this method.

If your corporate workstations are running a more "advanced" operating system such as Windows 95/98 or NT, then a simple directory copy may not suffice. One reason for this is that there are various hidden files required by the operating system which may not get copied. Another reason is that extensions to the operating system (DLLs and ActiveX controls, for example) may be located elsewhere on the drive. In these cases, look to third-party administration software that can create a disk image for you. Two such programs are Picture Taker (Lanovation) and Ghost (Binary Research International). The additional benefit of these programs is that they will compress the image as it is stored so that it uses up less space on your server.

Because workstations make up the largest portion of your network, it is a good idea to have a solid handle on their administration. Reducing the time you spend solving user problems will greatly increase the amount of time you can dedicate to maintaining your network infrastructure.

From Boot PROMs to Thin Clients

Thin clients are a good example of dusting off an old idea and packaging it with a new face. A *thin client* is simply a computer without any drives. The hype about these systems has mostly involved the promise of reduced support. Without any local drives, the system cannot be used to store information locally. This prevents users from customizing their setup or potentially making changes to their configuration that could make their operating system unstable.

In the early days of networking, NIC card vendors would outfit their network cards with a chip called a *boot PROM*. A boot PROM allowed a workstation to receive all the information it required to boot from a local server. The benefit of this was that the workstation did not require its own hard drive or even a floppy. When the system was powered up, the boot PROM would seek out the local server and pull the operating system and all supporting files it needed over the network.

This configuration made a lot of sense at the time. Applications were relatively small, so that the need to load all software off of the server did not greatly affect network traffic. Also, hard drives were extremely expensive at the time. The average cost of hard drive storage was $8 to $10 per megabyte (compared to $ 0.05 today). Finally, except for the missing floppy drive, this configuration looked the same to the end user as any standalone computer. The system would still boot up using DOS, and all the applications they'd grown to know and love could still be used.

Drawbacks

Unfortunately, at the time of this writing, despite increased publicity, thin clients still seem to have more drawbacks than benefits. One feature not shared with their predecessors is that these systems tend to be proprietary. A special server must be used when working with these systems. If you want to use Sun's thin clients, then you must purchase a Sun server. Want to use IBM clients? Then you will need to purchase an IBM server. The systems will not interoperate with each other.

The same goes for the operating system as well. Applications such as Lotus 1-2-3, WordPerfect, and Access do not run on those operating systems. The hope is that third parties will create comparable products for these operating systems in order to fill in the missing gaps. Unfortunately, this software has been slow in coming. If your users have been spoiled by Windows 95's highly customizable interface, Unix's wide berth of tools, or even the many available features of applications like Word, then running a thin client will feel like a step into the stone age. The applications available for these platforms usually contain only the most rudimentary features.

The exception to this is Citrix's WinFrame product. WinFrame turns a Windows NT server into a multiterminal device. Clients run a software component that allows them to connect to the WinFrame over the network and have their own unique desktop on the NT server. This allows users to run all the Windows NT-compatible applications that they have grown accustomed to—without conflicting with other users. Since the client is effectively a dumb terminal presenting a view to the NT server, its requirements are minimal. An older 386 system with floppy drive and 4MB of RAM is more than sufficient to run the full Microsoft Office suite. The only visual drawback of this product is that it still uses the old Program Manager interface since Microsoft has refused to license the newer NT 4.0 toolbar code to Citrix.

Probably the largest drawback of any thin-client configuration is that it creates a central point of failure. If a server that supports a number of thin clients drops off line, then all users relying on that server are dead in the water. While workstation users would be free to continue running their local programs during a server failure, a thin client has no means of accessing the software it requires to keep its user productive. Thus the financial impact that can be caused by a major server outage while using thin clients can easily offset the cost of providing support under a workstation/server configuration for many years.

File Servers

A *server*, simply put, is a networked computer that offers some kind of service to other computers on the network. These systems are typically identical to the average workstation except they may contain more memory, a faster processor, and larger hard drives. For software, they need to run some form of network operating system (NOS) that provides connectivity for many users. While a workstation only needs to interface with one user at a time, a server may be expected to take care of multiple users and offer multiple services.

NOTE   A *service* is some form of value-added process that can benefit from allowing multiple users to have access to it.

Server Types

There are three main types of servers:

File servers provide a common area for users to share and use files.

Print servers provide a common printer that networked users can access.

Application servers provide a software program for common user access.

File Servers

A *file server* is the most common type of server. Disk space is allocated on a networked system that users can access to store and retrieve files. Permissions can be set such that one user may have exclusive access to these files, or the files may be shared with other networked users. Security is provided by requiring the user to enter a username and password prior to file access. If the user passes this security check they are allowed access to their files.

How this file system appears varies depending on the workstation. If the user is running DOS, the file system on the server would appear as additional drive letters. The user is not required to know anything about the network beyond, "If I save to the F drive, I'm saving to the server."

On a Unix workstation the server's file system would appear as a simple extension to one of the workstation's directories. For example, the command

```
cd /mount/mars/home
```

may bring you to your home directory on the remote server MARS. The act of adding this remote file system to a workstation is referred to as *mounting* the directory.

An Apple Mac system mounts file systems as well, except that it appears as an icon on the desktop. Clicking this icon opens the remote file system. While this is not quite as invisible to the end user as a Unix mount, it is sufficient to provide access to the remote file system.

Windows-based systems use two methods for incorporating remote file systems. The first is identical to a DOS system, allocating drive letters that point to remote file areas located on the server. The second is by using a *share*, also known as a universal naming convention or UNC. A UNC is a pointer that can be retrieved on the fly and specifies a remote file system location. For example, a shared file area may have a UNC of \\talsin\share. The benefit of this type of connection is that you are not limited by the number of letters in the alphabet. If you start mapping network drives in a DOS environment at F, you will have 21 pointers available to remote file areas (F–Z). While this may sound like a lot, they can be used up quickly in an environment with many file servers. Using UNCs instead of drive mappings, you can have as many pointers as you require.

Print Servers

A *print server* provides a central point for network users to share a printing device. When a user needs to print, the output is directed to a central holding area called a queue. This can be done by using *network aware applications* that can communicate directly with a network print queue or by using redirection software that captures all information sent to a printer port. While your application thinks it's printing to a printer directly attached to the system, the redirector diverts the print job to the network queue.

A *network print queue* is a holding area for print jobs. The queue is typically located on a file server and is used to stage the print jobs prior to printing. Because a computer can transmit data faster than the typical printer is capable of putting this information to paper, a staging area is required in case someone tries to print while the printer is servicing another user. If this occurs, the second print job will be retained in the print queue until the first job is completed.

The print server provides the processing power required to poll the queue and determine if there is a job that needs to be printed. If one is found, the print server takes care of feeding the print job to the printer.

Application Servers

The final type of server is an *application server*, software that runs on an NOS and provides direct connectivity to a software program. Application servers usually require that a portion of the software be running on both the client and the server at the same time. For example, a backup server would be a type of application server that provides system backup services to clients on the network. A backup server would require that software be running on the NOS to collect the remote file information and write it to tape. It may also require that a portion of its software be running on the workstation so that the server can access the file system to back it up.

Application servers are sometimes confused with file servers that happen to hold software that users can run from their network drive. For example, if Microsoft Word is located on the server and is accessed by multiple network users, this would not be considered an application server. The server in this case simply provides disk space to store the program. It does not provide any of the processing power required to execute the program. When you run Word from the network, all necessary processing power is provided by your local workstation.

An application server usually employs some form of client/server technology to connect the *front end* running on the client with the application running on the server; this *back end* is doing the actual work. Lotus Notes is an example of one kind of application server. It is a database system that includes a server portion, which maintains the data files and security access to the server. It also includes a workstation portion referred to as a *client,* which is used to access and manipulate information stored in the remote Notes server.

A large benefit of application servers over their file-based counterparts is reduced network traffic. For example, cc:Mail is a file-based mail system. The post office (PO) resides on a file server and all application processing is provided by the clients that connect to this file server. While this setup is fine for a small office, it does not scale very well. For example, let's assume we have a medium-size network with five remote sites all connected by 56Kb lines. In order to reduce WAN traffic, we house a cc:Mail PO at each of the remote sites.

The problem occurs when we try to exchange mail between each of the POs. Since the server does not provide any of the processing (the PO is a file-based system), a workstation must be set up to "poll" each PO to see if there is any mail in queue for delivery to another PO. This means that the workstation must log on to each file server that houses a PO and periodically scan each one looking for queued mail. If a message is in queue, the workstation pulls down the message and forwards it to the appropriate PO for final delivery.

All this scanning can create an excessive amount of network traffic. The default is to have the workstation scan each PO every one or two minutes (the mail must get through, after all); this sucks up an exorbitant amount of bandwidth on our WAN to effectively do nothing if there are no waiting messages.

With an application-based mail system (like Lotus Notes or Microsoft Exchange), this does not occur. The application server is capable of checking its own database for queued messages. There is no workstation scanning required. When a queued message is found, the mail server is capable of forwarding the message to the remote system. This way, the only network bandwidth that is used is in actual message delivery.

Workstation or Server?

With the increased deployment of 32-bit Windows operating systems, as well as the long-established use of Unix machines, the definition of which systems should be considered *servers* has become blurred. It is becoming more common these days to find a computer that is doing double duty as both a workstation and a server.

Back in the old DOS/NetWare days, there was a distinct line between workstations and servers. Because DOS was designed to be a single-user interface, it was never very good at providing services to network users. It was a true workstation system in the sense that it provided an interface for only a single user to work. The NetWare server, because it provided both file and printer sharing, was considered to be the network server. In this configuration, security was pretty straightforward. Guard the NetWare system and you can sleep well knowing your network is secure.

Blurring the Line between a Workstation and a Server

Now, since the release of Windows 95 and NT, it is fairly common for the same user's workstation to be not only accessing a NetWare server but also offering file, print, and even application services of its own. While this multiuser environment has been available for many years in Unix (which was designed from the beginning to support multiuser environments) and even Mac systems, it was not quite as extensive as it is now for two reasons:

- The first is simply that DOS and its Windows successors are much more widespread in the business community than Unix or the Mac OS.

- The second reason is that networks have become larger and more accessible from remote locations. With the growth of the Internet and remote network access, many LANs are no longer isolated when the doors are locked at night.

WARNING   These days, multiuser environments can make for some administrative nightmares. While you may do an extensive job of locking down your network and systems that are considered servers in the conventional sense, it does not help if one of your users running NT has a modem attached and decides to enable the remote access server and hand out the number to their friends, so they can access the Internet. While this may sound far-fetched, we've seen it happen—and have even seen people lose their jobs over it.

In short, just about any modern operating system these days is capable of functioning as a server. Part of the job of a network administrator is to identify these systems and ensure that they meet the security policies set forth by your organization. What's that? Your company does not have any network security policies? As network administrator, it may very well be your job to develop these policies as well.

Modems

While most people are familiar with modems, they are worth a brief mention here. A *modem* is a device used for converting a digital signal into an analog transmission that is capable of traversing plain old telephone service (POTS) lines.

There are two distinct measurements used when describing modems, *bits per second* and *baud*. A bit is simply a single digital pulse or transmission. With POTS communications, these pulses are in the form of tones. The term *bit* refers to the amount of digital information the device is capable of converting into an analog signal, such as 28,800 bits per second (bps).

Why is the bit rate so low compared to a LAN? When POTS was first conceived, it was designed to carry voice communications only. Because the average human voice will only produce sounds between 300 and 3,300 cycles per second, this was all the bandwidth that was supported. Modems are required to operate within these limited constraints. They do not have the benefit of being designed from the ground up to relay digital information. This is sort of like trying to fit a round peg into a square hole. It will fit, provided you whack it with a hammer a few times.

Baud refers to an individual signal event along the POTS line. This can be any change in frequency, amplitude, or phase of the analog signal being transmitted. Baud and byte are not directly comparable. The baud rate usually lags behind the bit rate in value as modem manufacturers attempt to squeeze every bit of bandwidth they can out of the phone lines.

The modem industry can appear at times to be a little bit like Scotty from Star Trek. With each new release of modem speeds, a claim is made that we've reached the maximum bit rate for POTS lines, and "she can't take any more, Captain!" This has been occurring since the 9600 bps modems were released. At the time of this writing, 56,000bps modems are finally settling on a single 56K standard.

The reason for this is simple—technology continues to evolve. Just as computers that used to take up entire rooms will now fit in your shirt pocket, so too have communication engineers continued to find new ways to push larger quantities of information through this same tiny pipe.

Channel Binding

One interesting development in the area of using modems to interconnect workstations and networks (or one network to another) is the introduction of channel binding. *Channel binding* combines multiple data channels into a single "virtual channel," such that a wider (and therefore faster) path is made available for network traffic. While this idea has been around on Unix stations for some time, it is now available on Windows 95/98 and NT. This means that many more users now have the ability to speed up their modem throughput by double, triple, or more, using multiple modems simultaneously communicating between their system and a remote one.

The main drawback to modem channel binding is that multiple phone lines and pairs of modems are required to effect such links. But this can still be more cost-effective than ISDN, for example, especially where rates for (local) ISDN connections are still being charged by the minute, as opposed to the far less expensive flat rates of normal POTS connections.

NOTE   Incidentally, the way Microsoft has implemented channel binding also works with multiple ISDN or other types of connection hardware! This is something to keep in mind when the cost of jumping to the next plateau of connection speed technology exceeds your current connection costs by more than double, because you can always use channel binding to achieve approximately double the speed for no more than double the cost of a single channel.

Codexes

A codex (or codec) is the opposite of a modem. Short for coder/decoder, a *codex* is used for converting an analog signal into a digital transmission. Physically, it is a small box, or a computer expansion card, with multiple RJ-11 connectors. If it is an external unit, a connector is also provided to connect a digital device such as a computer.

With the popularity of ISDN comes a problem—what do we do with all the analog devices we have for communicating over a dial-up network?

A codex is a type of converter that allows you to plug a standard telephone, fax, or even modem into one side and communicate digitally with an ISDN line on the other. While there are digital equivalents to the standard phone and fax, these devices are rather new to the market and are still quite expensive. In fact, a single digital phone can cost as much as a codex providing multiple analog connections. Of course, the drawback of using a converter is lost bandwidth. An analog phone run through a codex is incapable of leveraging the additional available bandwidth. Then again, if you are using the phone for voice communications, do you really need the additional bandwidth?

ISDN Modems

Although often referred to as modems, ISDN adapters are actually not modems, because the whole idea of a modem is to convert between analog and digital signals, whereas ISDN conveys digital signals directly. Technically, ISDN "modems" are more properly referred to as *TUs*, or terminal units. (They are sometimes also called terminal adapters.)

ISDN, which stands for *Integrated Services Digital Network*, is actually an older telephone technology, which arguably has not been promoted as actively as it should have been earlier on, and currently is still overpriced in most areas of the US, particularly considering the recent arrival of Digital Subscriber Line (DSL) and cable modem technologies.

ISDN divides a phone line into three digital channels—two "B" channels, which carry data, and one "D" channel, which is used for behind-the-scenes communication overhead (such as setting up and disconnecting calls and communicating with the phone network). Each of the two data channels can convey either 56Kbps or 64Kbps (depending on your phone company), and at any time you have the option of using one or both channels—the two channels can be used for two simultaneous but separate calls, or for one "bonded" connection. Thus the maximum throughput ISDN offers is either 112Kbps or 128Kbps, again depending on your phone company's configuration.

Because ISDN is simply an enhanced version of a normal telephone connection, you can also use it to place normal voice calls and to send and receive faxes. Because the two channels can operate independently, you could be speaking on one channel while surfing the Web on the other. Thus, if you happen to be in one of those areas where only a flat rate is charged for ISDN use, it may be worthwhile canceling your normal voice line in favor of an ISDN line.

ISDN has caught on much more in certain other countries, such as Germany, where the cost to the consumer for ISDN is hardly any different than POTS service.

The ISDN adapter is available in internal and external models, and uses either an S/T or U interface. The "S/T" (subscriber/termination) interface uses four wires and is normally used to extend the ISDN connection to four-wire jacks inside a building. The two-wire U interface is used to convey an ISDN connection over longer distances. Depending on which interface your equipment supports, you may also need a device called an NT-1 (network terminator 1), which converts between the S/T and U interfaces.

An ISDN adapter can be connected either to a single computer or to a network. It is usually connected to a computer using a serial port (for external ISDN adapters) or by plugging the ISDN adapter into the computer's bus (for internal ISDN adapters). The external units tend to be more expensive and sometimes harder to use. Moreover, in order to take full advantage of ISDN throughput using an external adapter, you will probably need to add a special high-speed serial port, as the ports supplied with most computers peak at around 115Kbps—less than what ISDN is capable of providing. If you get an internal ISDN adapter, this problem doesn't exist because the adapter exchanges data directly on the system bus.

Connecting ISDN to a network typically requires an ISDN router or an ISDN bridge. These function just like any normal router or bridge, but are scaled down somewhat to only handle ISDN, and for that reason are less expensive.

It is also possible to connect ISDN to a single station, and then use a software-only routing solution to supply the ISDN connection to other stations on the network. Windows NT, for example, has software routing functionality built-in, and programs such as proxy servers (which we cover in coming chapters) can offer this ability in addition to providing a somewhat higher degree of security.

Cable Modems

Cable modems are just starting to become widespread, as various cable TV companies get into the business of supplying high-speed Internet connections to their customers. We believe they will become one of the preferred means of connecting to the Internet, as their typical cost (a flat rate of $30 to $50/month) vs. throughput (8 to 10 Mbps or faster) is vastly better than other alternatives right now.

Cable modems come in two main types right now: receive-only (unidirectional) and send-receive (bidirectional). The receive-only types require the user to still have a modem connection in order to send data back out—the high speed cable connection only delivers incoming data. By contrast, the send-receive, or bidirectional, cable modems both send and receive at the higher speed, and are far preferable for this reason.

Unidirectional cable modems will be around for a while, however, at least in certain regions of the country, because they are easier for cable companies to install using existing cabling. Many cable companies may opt for this route initially, thinking they'll upgrade to bidirectional modems if sufficient interest is generated with the unidirectional modems.

Cable modems really are not modems per se, but receivers (or transceivers) that connect an incoming coaxial cable from the cable company to your computer. The most common means of connecting this unit to your computer is via an Ethernet transceiver, which requires that you have an Ethernet adapter card installed in your computer. You then simply connect the unit to your computer using a standard Ethernet patch cable.

The biggest advantages of this type of connection are the attractive flat rate (as opposed to per-minute fees for services like ISDN!) and the fact that it can be rolled out to already-wired cable customers without significant additional labor costs.

Although cable modems show great potential as a "no-brainer" consumer replacement for modems, it remains to be seen whether cable companies are going to make the commitment to obtain sufficient back-end throughput to support these vastly higher speeds for all of their users. It's possible that limits may be placed on the peak throughput available to each user, making the 10Mbps a combined neighborhood limit, or a "street limit." In any case the back-end connections will need to increase throughput exponentially in coming years.

DSL

DSL stands for "Digital Subscriber Line." DSL is the phone company's equivalent of cable TV's cable modems, as it uses existing phone wiring to convey data at much higher speeds, through the use of a transceiver unit at the customer's site, paired with a corresponding transceiver module at the phone company.

There now are several variations of DSL: ADSL (Asymmetric DSL), HDSL (High-speed DSL), SDSL (Symmetric DSL), VDSL (Very high rate DSL), WDSL (Wavelet DSL), and so on. Collectively, these technologies are all often referred to as *x*DSL. There are many different variants of DSL because there are right now many competing DSL standards, many standards actually being single-company offerings at this point. What they all have in common is their use of advanced signal processing techniques to greatly increase the rate of data throughput over standard phone company wiring. Typically these technologies offer connection speeds of 6Kbps, 8Kbps, 10Kbps, or faster, and they connect to a computer (or a network) via a standard Ethernet adapter.

Two drawbacks to the DSL approach are the short distances it can support between the phone company and a user's connection, typically around three miles, and the requirement for a pair of devices, one at either end, for every DSL connection being used. These are mainly problems for the phone companies to work out, but they account for the difficulty phone companies are having in making this technology available to enough people, quickly enough, to be cost effective. Within the distances allowed, and aside from the labor and equipment investments needed to provide the connections, this is a good technology and shows great promise.

Expect cable modems and variations on DSL technology to be the chief competitors for higher-speed network connections in the new few years.

CSU/DSUs

A *CSU/DSU* is a device that combines the functionality of a channel service unit (CSU) and a data service unit (DSU). These devices are used to connect a LAN to a WAN by means of the faster connection services offered by phone companies, and they take care of all the translation required to convert a data stream between these two methods of communication. Figure 10.1 shows a 56K leased-line DSU. The indicator lights on the front of the unit let you monitor its operational status.

FIGURE 10.1:

A 56K leased-line DSU

DSU

A *DSU* provides all the handshaking and error correction required to maintain a connection across a wide-area link. In this aspect it is similar to a modem or codex in functionality. The DSU will accept a serial data stream from a device on the LAN and translate it into a data stream the digital WAN network can work with. For example, if the WAN link is a T1 connection, the DSU would break the information up into a time-division format acceptable for use on this circuit. It would also take care of converting any inbound data streams from the WAN back to serial communication.

CSU

A *CSU* is similar to a DSU except it does not have the ability to provide handshaking or error correction. It is strictly an interface between the LAN and the WAN and relies on some other device to provide handshaking and error correction.

The network device of choice to combine with a CSU is a router. While it is possible to use a bridge or a switch with these devices, a router is more appropriate as it is better able to isolate traffic and keep unwanted packets from traversing the WAN. Because bandwidth is at a premium over a wide area link, the more unnecessary traffic that can be kept off it, the better. The combination of a CSU with a router has become so common that there is currently a trend to incorporate the functionality of the CSU directly into the router itself.

CSU/DSUs differ in the type of wide area links and amount of bandwidth they will support. If you currently have a digital leased line and you're thinking of upgrading to a full T1, expect to replace this hardware.

Summary

This chapter wraps up our extended discussion of the types of hardware needed for networking. In this chapter, we first looked at the definitions of a workstation, a thin client, and a server (and saw how these distinctions are becoming less clear-cut). We looked at various server services, including file, print, and application services. We then discussed the various types of hardware being used to interconnect workstations and servers over greater distances: modems, codexes, ISDN modems, cable modems, ADSL/xDSL, and CSU/DSUs.

In the next series of chapters (Part III), we'll be focusing on the network server software, which is used to harness all this hardware to provide various network services.

PART III

Network Server Software

■ CHAPTER 11: Novell NetWare/IntraNetWare

■ CHAPTER 12: Windows NT Server

■ CHAPTER 13: Unix/Linux

■ CHAPTER 14: Lotus Notes

■ CHAPTER 15: Other Networks: OS/2 Warp, Banyan
        VINES/StreetTalk, and LANtastic

■ CHAPTER 16: AppleTalk and AppleShare

Novell NetWare/IntraNetWare

- ■ The core operating system

- ■ The file system

- ■ Security features

- ■ IP support and other intranet features

- ■ Configuring IntraNetWare via the command line

- ■ Configuring IntraNetWare with INETCFG.NLM

- ■ SAMBA and IntraNetWare

- ■ A first look at NetWare 5

Released in 1983, Novell's NetWare has been the mainstay for a majority of networks in providing file and print services. As of version 4.11, the product includes a number of IP applications designed to facilitate the construction of an internal Internet, known as an *intranet*. Later chapters will discuss intranet concepts at length; briefly, they provide many of the connectivity options usually associated with the Internet (HTTP, FTP, etc.), except that access to these resources is usually restricted to internal personnel only.

IntraNetWare Features

With the addition of Web, Internet/intranet, and FTP support, the NetWare product was renamed IntraNetWare. For this reason, in this chapter, we'll cover NetWare and IntraNetWare combined. However, note that as of this writing, it appears Novell is leaning toward releasing NetWare 5 as a separate product. Near the end of the chapter, we will provide an overview of the new features slated to ship with NetWare 5.

IntraNetWare Setup

The IntraNetWare setup utility now supports hardware auto-detection. That is, it can detect the configuration of the server on which the software is being installed. This is a real time-saver for the novice administrator who may not be familiar with the model numbers of each piece of hardware installed in their server.

Protocol configuration has also been enhanced. If the server is attached to a network during configuration, the installation program will detect which protocols are in use along with their appropriate network and zone numbers.

The biggest weakness with the IntraNetWare installation is that it does not automatically include all the server's features. There are separate procedures for installing the online help, FTP server, and multiprotocol router. While the CD case is clearly marked as to how to install these products, it would be nice if they where directly integrated into the installation process.

IntraNetWare now includes a stripped-down version of the DSMigrate utility. DSMigrate is a Windows-based utility that simplifies the upgrade process from NetWare 3.*x* to IntraNetWare. It has the ability to read the old bindery databases used by NetWare 3.*x* to track user logon and group information. It can also read the file system trustee rights, which define who has access to which directories. Once it has gathered this account information from the older server, it can manipulate it into the hierarchical structure of NetWare Directory Services (described in greater detail later in this chapter), which is used by IntraNetWare.

All of this is done offline so that if an NDS tree already exists, it is not affected during the development process. Once you have completed your additions, it is a simple matter to set these changes by incorporating them into an existing tree or creating a new one from scratch. Once the account information has been moved, the NetWare file manager takes care of moving the file information from the old server onto the new one.

NOTE The only real drawback with the DSMigrate process is that password information is not migrated. This means that after a migration users will have either no password or one that was chosen by the administrator. This makes the migration process a bit less transparent to your users.

NetWare Core OS

The core of IntraNetWare is a 32-bit, multitasking, multithreaded kernel. Symmetrical multiprocessor support is now included with the core OS. This means that multiple processors are supported right out of the box. Additional software and licensing is no longer required as it was in earlier versions.

The Kernel

The kernel is designed to be modular. This means that applications and support drivers can be loaded and unloaded on the fly. It also means that a majority of the changes can be made without rebooting the system. Need to change an IP address? This can be done with two commands at the command prompt and takes effect immediately. This can be a lifesaver for environments that cannot afford to reboot a server every time a change has been made.

Memory

IntraNetWare is designed to run entirely within the physical memory installed on the server; it does not use swap space or virtual memory. This means that the total memory available to the system is what is physically installed on the server. IntraNetWare cannot partition a portion of the disk as alternate memory, as most network operating systems can.

By using only physical memory, IntraNetWare dramatically reduces system response time. Accessing information from disk takes approximately 100 times longer than accessing the same information from memory. This factor is what made disk caching software so popular and why it has such a dramatic effect on system performance.

Memory never goes to waste on an IntraNetWare server. Any memory that remains after the core OS, supporting applications, and drivers have been loaded goes to caching frequently accessed files. The more available memory, the more files can be cached. This means that when a user requests a commonly used file, the server can access the information from faster memory instead of disk. When additional memory is required by the operating system, it takes it from the file caching pool.

With falling memory prices and ever-growing network sizes, it is not uncommon for servers to have 256 or 512MB of RAM. Some network administrators use a standard multiplier to estimate the amount of RAM needed for a given number of stations (1 to 2 megs per station, for example), but memory needs can vary widely depending on the type of applications being used, as well as the number of files being accessed and the size of each. A safer way to determine whether enough RAM is installed is to watch for symptoms of the server becoming disk-bound (its hard drive light constantly lit, or decreased throughput without great bandwidth utilization, for example). Adding memory is most often the single most effective way to achieve greater network performance, and as we've already mentioned, any amount of RAM you add to a server will be used.

So by running applications only within physical memory, the core OS is able to access files much quicker. The limitation is that programs must be written efficiently so they use as small a portion of memory as possible. This is why the IntraNetWare server still uses an archaic prompt and ASCII menus instead of a full graphical user interface.

Improved ABEND Handling

Novell has also improved recovery from critical system errors, known as an *abnormal ends* or *ABENDs*. In previous versions of NetWare, an ABEND would cause a server to stop all processing. The only way to recover was to restart the server either through the online debugger or by hitting the power switch.

IntraNetWare now has the ability to isolate or reset the offending process. This allows the server to continue running so that it can be reset during non-work hours. Figure 11.1 shows a typical error message. Note that the server continues to function after the error, and the command prompt is returned.

> **NOTE**   The fact that you don't have to reboot a server immediately when an ABEND occurs is a major improvement over earlier versions of NetWare.

FIGURE 11.1

An IntraNetWare server recovering from an ABEND

```
Abend: Page Fault Processor Exception (Error code 00000000)
      OS version: Novell NetWare 4.11  August 22, 1996
      Running Process: Server 05 Process
      Stack: 3F 58 23 F1 5C 18 02 F8 D8 3A E2 01 40 64 B4 01
             00 00 00 00 00 17 03 FB 73 73 73 73 0C CC 65 F0
             00 30 00 00 A0 46 03 00 78 56 34 12 46 72 65 65

Additional Information:
      The CPU encountered a problem executing code in IPXRTR.NLM.  The
      problem may be in that module or in data passed to that module
      by a process owned by SERVER.NLM.

The running process will be returned to a safe state.


 5-14-97  11:23:26 am:    SERVER-4.11-4631
      WARNING! Server TALSIN experienced a critical error.  The offending
      process was suspended or recovered.  However, services hosted by this
      server may have been effected.

|TALSIN <1>:
```

IntraNetWare also has the ability to restart the server after a predetermined period of time if an ABEND occurs. It is also possible to select what kind of an ABEND causes a server restart. For example, the server can be set to simply recover from application ABENDs but to perform a system restart if the failure mode is hardware related.

Improved "Garbage Collection"

IntraNetWare also includes a *garbage collection* setting. While this will not stop by your cubicle and empty your trash, it can recover server memory from unloaded processes.

With earlier versions of NetWare, if a poorly coded application was unloaded from memory, it might not return all the memory it was using to the free memory pool. This can be a problem if the application is loaded and unloaded a number of times, because the amount of available memory would slowly become unusable. The garbage collection process scans for these memory areas that are no longer in use. When they are found, the pointers are deleted and the space is returned to the free memory pool so that it can be used by other applications.

New features have been added to ensure that applications do not tie up the processor(s) for an excessive amount of time. IntraNetWare includes a "relinquish control alert" setting that produces an error message when an application refuses to play fair and share the available CPU cycles. There is also a *CPU hog time out* setting, which allows the system to automatically kill any process that is monopolizing all of the server's processor time.

File System

IntraNetWare includes a high performance file system that supports DOS, Macintosh, Unix, OS/2, and Windows long file names. The file allocation table has been enhanced so that it does not require a disk optimization utility for file fragmentation.

TIP   Long file name support used to be provided by the OS2.NAM driver. As of IntraNetWare, this has been renamed LONG.NAM.

The system excels as a file server, thanks to a number of features designed to enhance the system's performance. Along with the file caching mentioned above, there are settings that allow for the optimizing of file storage.

Disk Suballocation

IntraNetWare includes *disk suballocation*. This feature allows the system to reduce the number of sectors required to store a specific file. This provides additional free space on the system for file storage.

Compression

File system *compression* is also supported. This reduces the amount of space needed to save a file to disk and extends the storage capacity of the system. For example, it is not uncommon to have a 500MB hard disk store over 1GB worth of information.

Compression is performed on a per-file basis similar to Pkzip, rather than the per-volume basis used by such utilities as Microsoft's Drive Space. This allows files to be compressed selectively, instead of simply compressing the entire file system. Where Novell's compression differs from Pkzip is that the compression is completely invisible to the end user. File extensions remain unchanged and the system automatically decompresses the file during access.

The administrator can tune compression by specifiying which files can be compressed and how long a file must go unaccessed before compression is performed. With these settings, you can make sure that only infrequently used files are reduced in size. Compression slows down file access time slightly, so this setting helps to ensure that heavily used files will not have to be decompressed during access.

The administrator can also specify the compression gain that must be achievable before the system will compress a file. For example, you may decide not to bother compressing any files that will not yield at least a 10 percent reduction in storage space. Again, this helps to improve file access time.

Data Migration

IntraNetWare also supports file migration. *Migration* is the process of moving older files to media with a larger capacity but slower access time, while the files still appear to reside in their original directory. For example, an accounting firm processes financial and tax information for a number of clients. Information that is over three years old is rarely used but is still required to be online in case a client calls in with a question.

Data migration would allow the system administrator to move all client records over three years old from the server's hard drives to an optical jukebox. An optical jukebox is a storage device with a capacity in the tens of gigabytes, but a slower file access time equivalent to a CD-ROM drive. By moving these files to the jukebox, more hard drive space is made available for storing recent client files.

When migration is used, the directory where the file was originally located contains a "shortcut" to the file in its new location on the jukebox. To the end user, this shortcut is identical to the file itself and as far as they know the file is still located in its original directory. This allows them to continue accessing this older information in the same manner they always have. The difference is that file access is noticeably slower. Still, it beats having the administrator search through old backup tapes.

Account Administration

As mentioned, IntraNetWare uses Novell Directory Services (NDS) for tracking user access to network resources. NDS is hierarchical, meaning that all administration can be done from a central point and that access to network resources can be specified on a granular scale.

It is even possible to assign subadministrators who only have supervisor privileges for a small portion of the tree. NDS scales extremely well because it allows a large organization to have administrators who can only manage the resources for their specific group, while allowing full management rights to the people responsible for the entire network.

Network access is also centralized. When a user logs in to the network they are authenticating to the entire NDS tree, not just a specific server or portion of the tree. This means that they automatically receive access to all network resources that have been assigned to them, even if that resource exists on a remote portion of the tree (such as a printer in a remote field office).

NDS is not just for assigning user access rights. NDS can be used to create an online "phone book" of all network users. This information can include the person's full name, e-mail address, phone extension, department, etc. It is even possible to extend the available fields (known as the scheme) to include additional information.

For example, when the IntraNetWare Web server is installed, the scheme is extended to include a graphic file for each user. If the Web server is configured to allow browsing of the NDS account information, a photo of each user can be included as well. This creates an online company directory that not only provides a mailing address and phone number for each user, but a picture for identification as well.

Novell's Application Launcher

Also included with IntraNetWare is Novell's Application Launcher (NAL). NAL extends NDS to record information for network applications. Network programs become their own objects with the NDS tree. The benefit of associating users with application objects instead of simply giving them access to the application's directory is fault tolerance. If the program is located on multiple servers, and one of those servers goes offline, NAL will ensure that all users attempting to access the program will be pointed to the servers that are still in operation.

NAL also allows for the creation of standard desktops. Administrators can assign program groups to individual users or to groups of users. When a user logs in, they are presented with a program group that contains all the software they have access to. This information is associated with the user's logon ID, not their computer. This means that if the user walks down the hall and logs in, they will be presented with the same program group.

When ManageWise is used (Novell's network management product), NAL can include setup scripts for local software installation. For example, if a company decides to upgrade the version of the word processing software they are using, NAL and ManageWise can work together to add a *setup* icon to each user's program group. The user simply runs the setup script, which automatically installs and configures the new software.

NAL supports Windows 3.*x*, Windows 95, and Windows NT workstation. (Novell may release a specific Windows 98 upgrade shortly, but the current Windows 95 version apparently runs on Windows 98 without problems.)

Security

NetWare (and thus IntraNetWare) is the only distributed network operating system to receive C2 certification as a trusted *network* component from the National Computer Security Center (NCSC). While Windows NT is also C2 certified, at the time of this writing it is not approved as a trusted network, only as an operating system. (Even then, it is only certified when used as a stand-alone workstation with no removable media or network connection.)

IntraNetWare is also being evaluated for Electronic Data's E2 rating. E2 is the European counterpart to C2. The specifications of each are very similar.

Inherent Rights Mask

As mentioned above, file system access can be tuned down to the file level. Normally, file access rights trickle down through directories. This means that if a user is given read access to directories at a certain level, they will also have read access to any subdirectories below that level. IntraNetWare provides an *inherent rights mask* that allows these rights to be masked out as they attempt to trickle down. This allows the system administrator to assign the precise rights required at any level.

Packet Signature

IntraNetWare also has a *packet-signature* option, designed to combat a type of system attack known as *connection jumping*. This occurs when someone on the network sends information to a server and pretends that the data is actually coming from an administrator who is currently logged in. The attacker can send commands to the server, and the server will accept them, thinking they are coming from the system administrator.

The packet signature technique is useful in deterring these types of attacks. It requires both the server and the workstation to "sign" each frame prior to transmission. The signature is determined dynamically and changes from frame to frame. The server will only accept commands from a station that is properly signing frames.

In practice, if an attacker sends commands to the server pretending to be the administrator, the server will reject and log all frames received without a valid signature. Since the correct signature is changing constantly, it is extremely difficult for an attacker to determine what to use for a signature. This feature helps to protect an administrator's connection during daily maintenance. The feature can also be enabled for all users.

Auditcon

IntraNetWare also includes *Auditcon*, Novell's system auditing utility. Auditcon allows the system administrator or someone they designate to monitor server events. Events range from user logons to password changes to specific file access. Over 70 events can be monitored. The benefit of Auditcon being a separate utility is that the administrator can designate a regular user to monitor events.

Auditcon is an excellent solution for large organizations where the person administrating the network is not the same person who is monitoring security. An auditor can be designated to monitor system events without being given any other type of administration privileges.

Tightening Server Security

IntraNetWare includes a script called SECURE.NCF. When run during server startup, it automatically enables many of IntraNetWare's security features, thus enhancing the security of the server.

Networking

IntraNetWare includes support for IPX, IP, and AppleTalk. All three protocols can be used when accessing file and print services. IP is supported via encapsulation. The client and server still create an IPX packet; however, the packet is encased inside an IP frame. This is similar to how NetBIOS is supported over IP. When IP is used for IntraNetWare file and print services, UDP ports 43981 and 43982 are used for transferring data, and port 396 (both TCP and UDP) is used for SAP and RIP broadcasts.

IntraNetWare includes support for Ethernet, Token Ring, ATM, FDDI, PPP, X.25, ISDN, and Frame Relay. Monitoring and diagnostic consoles are provided for each of the WAN topologies to aid in their setup and maintenance.

Built-In Routing

IntraNetWare also includes Novell's multiprotocol router. If a server has two or more network cards (either LAN or WAN), the server can act as a bridge or a router between the connected segments. Consoles are provided to both monitor traffic and configure filtering for each of the three supported protocols.

When acting as a router, an IntraNetWare server supports the following routing protocols:

IPX: RIP, NLSP

IP: RIP, EGP, OSPF

AppleTalk: RTMP

NOTE   Both a distance-vector and a link-state routing protocol are supported for both IPX and IP. AppleTalk, however, only supports distance-vector routing.

TCP/IP over IPX

IntraNetWare also includes an IPX-to-IP gateway. This allows a client communicating with IPX to access Internet and intranet resources. The WINSOCK.DLL file on the client's system must be replaced with one that supports IPX as a transport. Once complete, the gateway takes care of translating all packets into IP and delivering them to their intended destination.

The gateway can be configured to allow only certain users or certain groups access to IP resources. The gateway also logs each session so that the administrator can keep track of which sites are being visited. This can even be combined with the filtering portion of the multiprotocol router to block out certain sites.

There are two important benefits when using the IPX-to-IP gateway. First, all internal users can be hidden behind a single IP address. This means that an extremely large site can communicate using a single class C address or even just a portion of one. The second benefit is that the server automatically functions as a firewall. Because internal systems are not using IP to communicate, it is harder for a would-be attacker to reach these systems.

The downside is that a gateway does add a sizable delay to all communication sessions. Access to IP resources is noticeably slower than when a direct connection is established. This can cause problems if a slow WAN link is used. For example, if a server is configured to use both the gateway and a 28.8K PPP dial-up connection, users may find that their software "times out" before a session can be established.

IP Applications

Most of IntraNetWare's IP applications have been available for a number of years but as separate add-on products. IntraNetWare is the first release that includes them free of charge with the core OS.

Some applications are "maintenance related" in that their function is to aid client systems in accessing IP resources. DHCP and DNS are good examples.

DHCP Server

The DHCP server is capable of dynamically assigning clients their IP address, domain and host name, default router, and the address of the DNS server. Bootp is also supported; however, care should be taken if both bootp and DNCP are to be serviced from the same server. Remember that a bootp client assumes it can keep the IP address assigned to it while DHCP expects addresses to be returned upon the expiration of the lease period.

WARNING Bootp and DHCP can conflict with each other when run from the same server. If you need to service both types of clients, either statically assign addresses to one of them or divide the services over two separate servers.

The DNS server can act as a primary or secondary domain name server. This can be run on the same system as DHCP or from a separate server. The DNS server can also act as a Network Information Server (NIS). NIS is used by Sun-SPARC systems to share host, group, and user information.

FTP Server

An FTP server is also included. The FTP server can be configured to allow anonymous logons, or to only accept connections from certain IntraNetWare users. When users connect to the FTP server, they simply use their regular password.

Web Server

The included Web server supports the Common Gateway Interface (CGI), Perl 5.0, Java, and NetBasic. NetBasic is an easy-to-use programming language that is similar in structure to regular Basic. The Web server also supports Secure Sockets Layer (SSL), a public/private key encryption system that allows for secure HTTP sessions. SSL is by far the most popular Web encryption system and is supported by major browsers such as Netscape.

Novell's Web server also supports multihoming. *Multihoming* provides the ability to support multiple domains on the same Web server. For example, let's say our company has two subdivisions, each with its own domain name. The first is foobar.com and the second is nowhere.com. Each wishes to host its own Web site and have the server appear within its domain.

With multihoming, both Web servers could be housed on the same IntraNet-Ware server under two separate directory trees. When a user enters the address `www.foobar.com` the server will automatically point them to the directory tree with `foobar`'s files. If the user enters the address `www.nowhere.com`, they will be pointed to `nowhere`'s files instead. The fact that these two Web sites are being hosted on the same server is completely transparent to the user.

NOTE   IntraNetWare also ships with a slightly modified version of Netscape's Web browser.

Configuring IntraNetWare for Network Access

There are two methods for providing connectivity to an IntraNetWare server. The first is via the command line. This is the same method used to configure networking on NetWare 3.*x* systems. These commands can be saved in the `AUTOEXEC.NCF` file so they are executed automatically on server startup. The second method is to use a graphical utility called `INETCFG`. This utility walks the administrator through the configuration of the network interfaces and automatically generates the commands necessary to enable networking.

Regardless of which method you choose, you will still be required to select an appropriate frame type.

Frame Types

IntraNetWare provides multiple frame formats in order to natively support each of the above mentioned protocols. For example, while IPX, IP, and AppleTalk will all communicate over an Ethernet topology, each requires that the Ethernet frame contain certain information fields. By selecting the correct frame format, you ensure connectivity with devices from other manufacturers. Table 11.1 is a quick reference list of the frame types supported by IntraNetWare.

TABLE 11.1: Frame Types Supported by IntraNetWare

Topology	Frame Type	Protocols Supported	Distinguishing Fields
Ethernet	802.3	IPX	Header includes length field. No fields contained in the data portion of the frame.
Ethernet	802.2	IPX	Header includes length field. The data portion of the frame contains two service access point fields to identify the encapsulated protocol.
Ethernet	Ethernet_SNAP	IPX, IP AT Phase II	Identical to 802.2 frame except that the data portion also includes control, type, and organizational code fields.
Ethernet	Ethernet_II	IPX, IP AT Phase I	Header includes a type field to identify encapsulated protocol. No fields contained in the data portion of the frame.
Token	Token_Ring	IPX	Similar to 802.2.
Token	Token_SNAP	IPX, IP, AT Phase II	Similar to Ethernet_SNAP.

A couple of qualifiers for the above table. The statement "No fields contained in the data portion of the frame" means that there are no Ethernet (OSI layer 2) fields. Each protocol (OSI layer 3) still stores header information within the data portion of the frame, as described in Chapter 2. The topology "Token" refers to all physical topologies that use a token passing method of communication. This includes FDDI, 100VG-AnyLAN, as well as the older Token Ring specification.

When selecting a frame type, ensure that it supports the protocol you wish to use for communication. Multiple protocols can be supported by a single or multiple frame types. For example, let's assume that an IntraNetWare server needs to speak IPX, IP, and AppleTalk Phase II. Let's also assume that the server is connected to an Ethernet network. We could choose to:

- Support all three protocols through Ethernet SNAP

- Support IPX with Ethernet 802.2, IP with Ethernet II, and AppleTalk with Ethernet SNAP

It is up to you to decide which configuration to use. Using a single frame type does reduce server overhead by a slight margin. If you are running a mixed NetWare environment, and you have 3.x servers to support as well, you may want to use the second option. NetWare 3.x does not support the use of a single frame for multiple protocols. Only a single protocol is allowed per frame type. Option two would allow you to remain consistent from server to server.

You must ensure that your clients are configured to use the same frame type as your IntraNetWare server. For example, if the server is using an 802.2 frame for IPX (the default for IntraNetWare) and your clients are configured to use 802.3 with IPX, the systems will be unable to communicate.

Configuring Networking from the Command Line

Enabling networking from the command line requires the execution of three steps:

- Load protocol support files (required for IP and AppleTalk only).
- Load the network driver and select a frame type.
- Bind the appropriate protocol to the network driver.

If you are using IP, the protocol support module needed is TCPIP.NLM. If you are using AppleTalk, the protocol support module is APPLETLK.NLM (note the missing letter "a"). IPX does not require an additional protocol support module. These support modules must be loaded prior to binding the protocol to the network driver.

Loading the Support Module

Table 11.2 identifies the switches supported by TCPIP.NLM.

TABLE 11.2: Switches Supported by TCPIP.NLM

Switch	Description
forward=yes/no	Enables (y) or disables (n) the forwarding of IP traffic. If two or more network cards are installed in the server, this switch determines if it will act as a router and forward packets from one segment to another.

Continued on next page

TABLE 11.2 CONTINUED: Switches Supported by TCPIP.NLM

Switch	Description
rip=*yes/no*	Enables (y) or disables (n) the processing of RIP packets. When this switch is set to "no" the server will not create or process RIP packets. This value should be "yes" if the server will be routing IP traffic between two network cards or "no" if it has a single card and will be acting as an end node.
trap=*address*	Identifies the host to receive SNMP trap messages. The address can be either an IP address or a host name (if the server is capable of resolving the name to an IP address). The default is to use the loop-back address.

An example of loading TCP/IP support would be:

```
load tcpip forward=yes rip=no trap=10.5.7.3
```

Reading from left to right, the server would interpret this command to mean, "Load the support driver for the IP protocol. When it is loaded, allow the server to forward IP packets, thus acting as a router. Do not use RIP to advertise or learn routing information. If a critical error occurs, send a trap message to the SNMP management station located at IP address 10.5.7.3."

Table 11.3 identifies the switches supported by APPLETLK.NLM.

TABLE 11.3: Switches Supported by APPLETALK.NLM

Switch	Description
phase1=*yes/no*	Defines whether AppleTalk networking will comply with Phase 1 (y) or Phase 2 (n) addressing rules. It is preferable to use Phase 2 when possible as it supports extended addressing.
checksum=*yes/no*	Enables (y) or disables (n) the use of the DDP checksum field. The Datagram Delivery Protocol provides a checksum field in addition to the FCS field provided by the layer 2 topology for additional data verification. This is normally left off, as it adds overhead and provides very little additional insurance that the data is received intact.
routing=*yes/no*	Enables (y) or disables (n) AppleTalk routing. When enabled, the server can pass AppleTalk frames between multiple network cards. It also allows for an additional zone to be defined just for AppleTalk services provided by the server. When disabled, the server appears as a end node within the defined zone.

Continued on next page

TABLE 11.3 CONTINUED: Switches Supported by APPLETALK.NLM

Switch	Description
Internal_net_mode=*yes/no*	Enables (y) or disables (n) the use of an internal AppleTalk network. If routing is disabled, this switch is not valid. If routing is enabled, it determines if the server will use its own zone and network number for the AppleTalk services it provides or if it will appear as a end node within the defined zone.
zfiles=*yes/no*	Defines whether zone names will be defined in the file ATZONES.CFG, located in the sys:\system directory (y), or if zones will be defined on the command line (n). The default is yes.
net=*start addr-end addr*	If Internal_net_mode=yes, then this command defines the network range for the internal AppleTalk network. Typically the start and end address are the same value because this provides 254 node addresses, which is more than sufficient for a server (only two to five are ever used).
zone={"*zone name*"}	If zfiles=no and Internal_net_mode=yes, this command defines the zone name to use on the internal network. All AppleTalk services provided by the server will appear in this zone. The zone name must appear within braces and quotes.

An example of loading AppleTalk support would be:

```
load appletlk phase1=no checksum=no routing=yes zfiles=no
Internal_net_mode=yes net=10000-10000 zone={"Dilbert"}
```

Reading from left to right, the server would interpret this command to mean, "Load support for the AppleTalk protocol. When it is loaded, do not enable support for older Phase 1 networks. Do not use the checksum field within the Apple-Talk header to perform additional CRC checking. Allow this system to act as an AppleTalk router using DDP to learn and propagate AppleTalk network information. Do not use the ATZONES.CFG file for zone name information; all zones will be specified on the command line. Allow this server to operate its own internal AppleTalk network which has a network address range of 10000–10000 and a zone name of Dilbert."

TIP

If the server will be providing file services to AppleTalk workstations, you can customize the description of the server's volumes. If a Macintosh computer mounts the server's SYS volume, the icon created on its desktop is identified as *server_name*.SYS. All subsequent volumes, however, are only identified with the volume name. This can make determining file locations difficult if your servers follow a naming convention such as vol1, vol2, etc. The Macintosh user has no way of knowing where the volume is located. You can edit the hidden text file SYS:\SYSTEM\VOLNAME.AFP to add descriptions for the additional volumes. The syntax is: volume_name=*aliases*.

Loading the LAN Driver

Next you need to load the network driver and select a frame type. Table 11.4 shows a list of valid switches when loading the driver.

TABLE 11.4: Valid Switches to Use When Loading the Driver

Switch	Description
Driver Name	The name of the driver supplied by the driver manufacturer for supporting IntraNetWare with their NIC.
port=*addr*	The input/output port address in use by the NIC.
int=*addr*	The interrupt address used by the NIC.
mem=*addr*	The memory address used by the NIC.
DMA=*addr*	The direct memory access channel used by the NIC.
slot=*number*	The slot number in which the NIC is installed.
frame=	The frame type being associate with the NIC.
name=	The name used to describe the NIC/frame type association.
retries=*number*	The maximum number of times this card should retry a failed frame transmission. When the retry count is reached, the card assumes it cannot reach the destination system.
node=*addr*	The 12-byte node address to be used by this card. Every card has a node address assigned to it by the manufacturer. This switch allows that address to be overridden.

An example of loading LAN driver support would be:

```
load 3c5x9 slot=3 frame=Ethernet_802.2 name=board1 retries=3
```

Reading from left to right, the server would interpret this command to mean, "Load LAN driver support for a 3COM Etherlink_III network card. The LAN card is located in expansion slot number 3. Load support for the 802.2 frame type and name this LAN driver/frame type combination board1. When this LAN card transmits a frame to which it does not receive a reply, it should retry the transmission three times."

The name parameter identifies the combination of this frame type associated with this particular LAN card. If multiple frame types were associated with this card, each would receive a different name so that the combination can be easily identified.

To identify the network card, the slot it is installed in may be used when the server has an EISA or PCI bus. If the network card is in a ISA slot, the DMA, PORT, INT, and MEM switches are used. Most ISA NIC cards do not require all four parameters, only two or three. Which parameters are required is specified by the manufacturer of the network card.

Binding Protocols to the LAN Card

The final command starts up networking on the card. Valid switches for all protocols are identified in Table 11.5.

TABLE 11.5: Valid Switches for All Protocols

Switch	Description
Protocol	Defines the protocol to be bound to the NIC/frame combination.
Board Name	Defines the name of the board used to identify the NIC/frame combination.

Table 11.6 defines the only additional switch when IPX is the protocol being bound.

TABLE 11.6: Additional Switch for IPX

Switch	Description
net=addr	Defines the attached network address. All IPX servers attached to the same segment and using the same frame type must also use the same network address.

An example of binding the IPX protocol would be:

```
bind IPX to board1 net=ba5eba11
```

From left to right, this command reads, "Bind IPX to board1 (the LAN card and frame type combination defined in the load statement). The IPX network attached to the card has a network address of ba5eba11."

Table 11.7 defines additional switches when AppleTalk is the protocol being bound.

TABLE 11.7: Additional Switches for AppleTalk

Switch	Description
net=*addr-addr*	If the protocol is AppleTalk, defines the network address range to use on the attached segment. A value of "0-0" defines the interface as *non-seeding*. This means that some other device on the segment is acting as a seed router and that it is broadcasting the network address range. If any other value than "0-0" is used, it is assumed that this device is the seed router responsible for setting the network address range. Each network can only have one seed router.
zone={"*zone name*"}	Defines the zone name of the attached segment. If the server does not have an internal address, this is the zone in which the server will appear. Note that if zfiles=yes was defined during the loading of the AppleTalk support module, the system will retrieve the zone name from the file SYS:\SYSTEM\ATZONES.CFG.

An example of binding the AppleTalk protocol would be:

```
bind appletlk to board1 net=100-101 zone={"Combat"}
```

From left to right, the server would interpret this command to mean, "Bind the AppleTalk protocol to the LAN driver/frame type combination that has been named "board1." This interface will act as the seed router for this network segment and should assign a network address range of 100–101. The interface should also assign the default Zone name of "Combat" (without quotes) to this network segment."

Table 11.8 defines additional switches when IP is the protocol being bound.

TABLE 11.8: Additional Switches for IP

Switch	Description
arp=*yes/no*	Enables (y) or disables (n) the use of ARP for resolving IP addresses to media access control numbers. If you disable ARP, the host portion of the IP address is mapped directly to the local hardware address. The default is yes.
addr=	Specifies the IP address to be assigned to this interface.
mask=	Defines the subnet mask for the specified IP address. If a mask is not specified, it is assigned based upon the class of the address assigned.
bcast=	Defines the broadcast address for this interface. If not defined, the all-network broadcast address is used.
gate=	Defines the default router on the local subnet. If not defined, the server will only use the routers it learns about through RIP.
defroute=*yes/no*	When set to yes, the server announces itself as the default router through RIP. The default is no.
cost=	Specifies the cost value added to a packet that crosses the server. Cost can be used to control traffic patterns. The default value is 1.
poisonn=*yes/no*	Enables (y) or disables (n) the broadcasting of routing information back onto the subnet on which it was receive. To prevent routing loops, routing information is normally not broadcast back onto the subnet from which it was received. This switch allows that functionality to be overridden. The default is no.

An example of binding the IP protocol would be:

```
bind tcpip to board1 addr=10.5.5.100 mask=255.255.255.0 gate=10.5.5.1
```

Reading from left to right, the server would interpret this command to mean, "Bind the IP protocol to the LAN driver/frame type combination named board1. Assign an IP address to this interface of 10.5.5.100, overriding the default subnet mask and setting it to 255.255.255.0. The default router to use when transmitting non-local traffic is at IP address 10.5.5.1."

Enabling Networking during System Startup

Each of the above commands can be run from the server command line to immediately initialize networking. They can also be saved within the AUTOEXEC.NCF file so that networking is enabled during system startup. Figure 11.2 shows a portion of a server's AUTOEXEC.NCF file.

FIGURE 11.2:

A server using the
AUTOEXEC.NCF file
to initialize networking

The second and third lines of the displayed portion of the file add support for IP and AppleTalk, respectively. Notice that AppleTalk has internal routing enabled but a zone name is not specified. This is because the `zfiles` switch defaults to yes when it is not specified. Zone names will be retrieved from the file SYS:\SYSTEM\ATZONES.CFG instead of specified on the command line.

The three `load` commands define three separate frame types for use on our server. We can tell this is an ISA LAN card, because a port and an interrupt value are specified. While this is fine for a test server, production servers should always use PCI network cards for optimal performance.

The three `bind` statements assign a protocol to be used with each NIC/frame combination. The board name allows us to specify which NIC/frame combination each protocol should be bound to. Note that the first `bind` statement has the word T0 after the protocol while the other two do not. Either syntax is correct. Using the word T0 makes the line easier for people to read while leaving it out saves a bit of typing.

TIP   If the network card is initialized prior to the mounting of all network volumes, users who attempt to log on while the server is starting up may receive only some of their drive mappings. To prevent this, place the `mount all` statement earlier in the AUTOEXEC.NCF file so that it is executed prior to initialization of the networking card.

Configuring Networking with INETCFG.NLM

The INETCFG utility was originally used to configure Novell's Multiprotocol router. As of NetWare version 4.0, it is the default method of configuring networking on Novell servers. While you can use the AUTOEXEC.NCF file to configure networking on a NetWare 4.*x* server, if you later run INETCFG.NLM it will attempt to remove these commands.

INETCFG provides an ASCII graphical interface and is designed to simplify the processes of configuring protocols on the server. Figure 11.3 is the opening screen for INETCFG. Note the context-sensitive help displayed at the bottom of the screen. More help can be found by pressing the F1 key.

FIGURE 11.3:

The initial screen for INETCFG

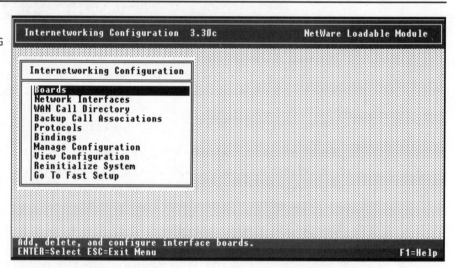

If this is the first time you are configuring networking, INETCFG will ask if you wish to import all networking commands located in the AUTOEXEC.NCF file. You should answer "yes" so that all networking commands are located in one area. The existing AUTOEXEC.NCF network commands will be commented out and the statement SYS:\ETC\INITSYS.NCF will be added. This makes a call to the script file INITSYS to initialize networking.

To configure networking, you will first define the LAN card under Boards, then select which protocols you wish to use under Protocols, and finally define which protocols to enable on which cards under Bindings.

Boards

When the Boards menu option is selected, the Configured Boards window will appear, listing all defined boards. If no boards are defined, the list will simply contain the value <Empty List>, as shown in Figure 11.4.

FIGURE 11.4:

The Configured Boards window

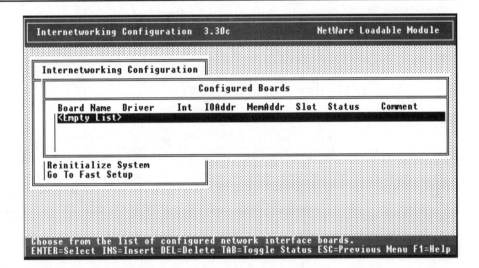

By pressing the Insert key, we can begin to configure our first board. This brings up a list of known LAN drivers in alphabetical order by driver name. If the driver you wish to install is not listed, you can again press the Insert key and define the path to where the driver is located. This will add the driver to the list. We can then select the driver and move on to configuration.

TIP

To scroll through the driver list quickly, begin typing the name of the driver. The list is *hot keyed*. You can simply begin typing the driver name, and the selection bar will jump to the appropriate selection. Hot keys are available on most configuration menus.

We are next presented with the Board Configuration screen as shown in Figure 11. 5. First we are asked to name the board. This is not the LAN card/frame name as discussed in the last section; it is simply a unique name to be used when identifying this specific card. A name that includes the type of card and the bus slot it is installed in helps to simplify troubleshooting. Later, when we define bindings, we will associate protocols and network numbers with these names. By naming the cards with their slot number, we have an easy reference to which network numbers are used by each card.

FIGURE 11.5:

Once a LAN driver is selected, it is configured in the Board Configuration window.

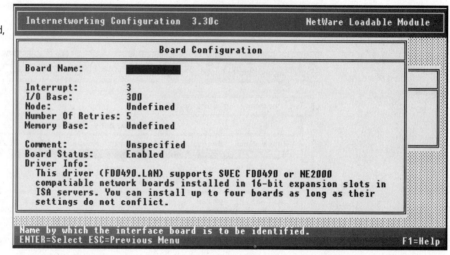

The next set of menu options is dependent on the driver we have selected. Because the driver in our example is for a 16-bit ISA card, the configuration options reflect the setting used by this card. If this had been an EISA card, Interrupt and I/O Base would have been replaced by Slot Number.

The values shown are the default factory settings for the card. By pressing Enter on the settings for Interrupt, I/O Base, and Memory Base, you receive a menu of available values. Scroll through the list to select the desired value.

Not all available values may be listed. For example, you may have configured a card to use interrupt 7, but this value may not be available from this menu. If this occurs you will need to edit the driver configuration file associated with the LAN driver. This is a text file with the same name as the driver but a file extension of .LDI. Simply edit the file with a text editor to add the values you require. The following is an example LDI file for the driver FD0490:

```
;Driver Description
VER:    1.00
SYN:    1.00
DR FD0490
{

        DES:    $DES
        HELP:   $HELP
```

```
PAR:    1.00
FILE:   FD0490.LAN
OF:     MSM.NLM, ETHERTSM.NLM

PR INT REQ
{
        VAL:    2, 3, 4, 5, B, C
        DEF:    3
}

PR PORT REQ
{
        VAL:    300, 320, 340, 360
        DEF:    300
        RES:    20
}
```

The section entitled PR INT REQ defines our interrupt setting. VAL defines which interrupts are available for selection, while DEF: defines the default value. To add a configuration value, simply follow the formatting and inset it into the proper section. For example, if we want interrupt seven to be available for selection, we would add 7, between the values 5 and B.

The next section, entitled PR PORT REQ, is similar except it applies to the port address. Edit this section in the same manner. The rest of the Board Configuration values are optional; you may complete them only if you require them. A brief description of each is listed in Table 11.8.

TABLE 11.8: Board Configuration Options

Menu Option	Description
Node	Overrides the 12-byte node address assigned to the card.
Number of Retries	The number of times to retry a failed transmission. When the retry count is reached, the card will assume the destination system is unreachable.
Comment	Allows you to add a brief description or comment for this card.
Board Status	Defines whether this board will be enabled or disabled during startup. The Disable option is useful if you wish to define the required parameters for the card, but do not need to enable networking on it at this time. If you later need to use the card, its required configuration parameters will be known. The Force option automatically causes all frame types to be loaded for this driver. This command should not be required as frame types are selectively loaded when protocols are selected.

Once you're finished, press Escape and select Yes to save changes. There will now be an entry for the card on the `Configured Boards` list. Repeat the procedure for each network card installed in the server.

Network Interface

The Network Interface option is used for assigning network interfaces to board names. By default, LAN cards receive a single network interface and are not configurable through this menu option. For WAN cards, the number of available interfaces depends on the type of card in use. Figure 11.6 shows the Network Interfaces list with WAN boards supporting `DIALUP` and an `ISDN PRI`. Note that even though LAN cards are listed as well, no configuration options are available. The ISDN card has 23 interfaces listed, one to support each PRI channel.

FIGURE 11.6:

The Network Interfaces list for configuring WAN cards

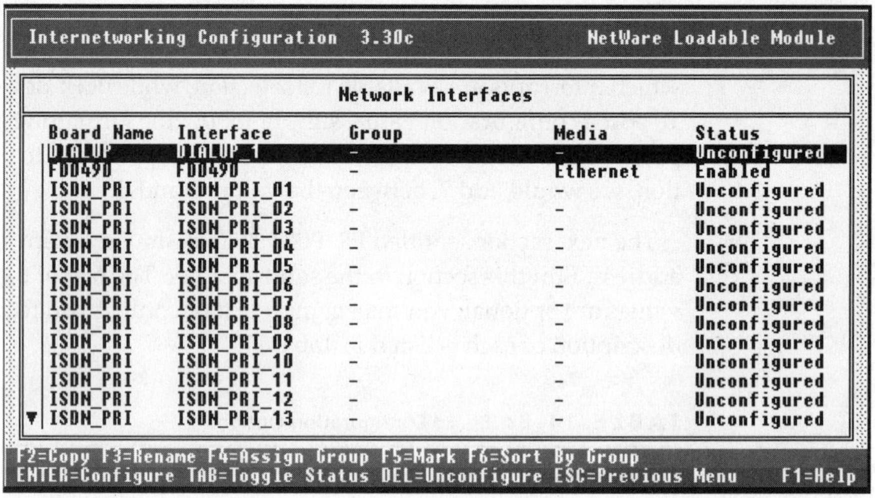

```
Internetworking Configuration  3.30c              NetWare Loadable Module

                              Network Interfaces

    Board Name    Interface        Group          Media        Status
    DIALUP        DIALUP_1         -              -            Unconfigured
    FD049D        FD049D           -              Ethernet     Enabled
    ISDN_PRI      ISDN_PRI_01      -              -            Unconfigured
    ISDN_PRI      ISDN_PRI_02      -              -            Unconfigured
    ISDN_PRI      ISDN_PRI_03      -              -            Unconfigured
    ISDN_PRI      ISDN_PRI_04      -              -            Unconfigured
    ISDN_PRI      ISDN_PRI_05      -              -            Unconfigured
    ISDN_PRI      ISDN_PRI_06      -              -            Unconfigured
    ISDN_PRI      ISDN_PRI_07      -              -            Unconfigured
    ISDN_PRI      ISDN_PRI_08      -              -            Unconfigured
    ISDN_PRI      ISDN_PRI_09      -              -            Unconfigured
    ISDN_PRI      ISDN_PRI_10      -              -            Unconfigured
    ISDN_PRI      ISDN_PRI_11      -              -            Unconfigured
    ISDN_PRI      ISDN_PRI_12      -              -            Unconfigured
  ▼ ISDN_PRI      ISDN_PRI_13      -              -            Unconfigured

  F2=Copy F3=Rename F4=Assign Group F5=Mark F6=Sort By Group
  ENTER=Configure TAB=Toggle Status DEL=Unconfigure ESC=Previous Menu   F1=Help
```

If we select the dial-up board (which uses Novell's AIO driver), we are presented with a menu to select a medium. Because this is an *on demand* connection, our only option is *PPP*. Had this been a full-time connection, we would have received options for Frame Relay or X.25 as well. After selecting the medium, we are presented with the configuration screen shown in Figure 11.7.

FIGURE 11.7:

The PPP Network Interface Configuration window

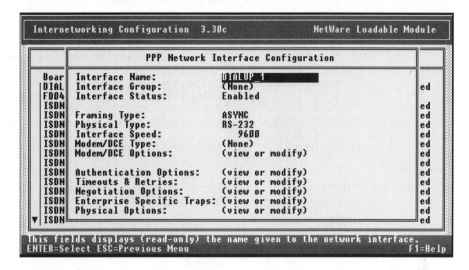

The PPP Network Configuration window displays general options as well as those that are specific to using a PPP connection. A brief description of each option is listed in Table 11.9.

TABLE 11.9: PPP Network Configuration Options

Menu Option	Description
Interface Name	Name given to this particular interface on the board.
Interface Group	Allows us to associate this and other PPP interfaces with a group name. This allows WAN calls to be associated with a group instead of a specific interface. When a call is placed, the first available interface within the group is used.
Interface Status	Defines whether this interface is initialized during system startup.
Framing Type	Defines whether this connection is synchronous or asynchronous. If the server's serial ports are used, this value must be asynchronous.
Physical Type	Defines the type of serial connector. RS-232 is the default.
Interface Speed	Specifies the clock rate of the serial interface. The interface speed is not set automatically based on your modem selection. You must manually configure this option.

Continued on next page

TABLE 11.9 CONTINUED: PPP Network Configuration Options

Menu Option	Description
Modem/DCE Type	Select the brand of modem attached to this interface.
Modem/DCE Options	Allows you to define attention (AT) commands for use with the above-specified modem.
Authentication Options	Allows you to define security parameters for inbound PPP sessions.
Timeouts & Retries	Allows you to customize communication recovery when transmission failures occur.
Negotiation Options	Allows you to customize communication properties associated with PPP sessions on this interface.
Enterprise Specific Traps	Allows you to set logging options for session diagnostics and monitoring.
Physical Options	Allows you to customize communication options between the serial port and the modem.

Once our configuration is complete, we can press Escape and select Yes to save changes. Our dial-up connection will now appear in the Network Interfaces list as being configured.

WAN Call Directory

The WAN call directory allows us to associate WAN network interfaces with specific destinations. Let's walk through the configuration of our above PPP network interface so that we can connect to a local ISP and receive Internet access.

When the WAN call directory option is selected, we are presented with the Configured WAN Call Destinations list. At this point, the list is empty. Press the Insert key to configure our ISP connection.

We are prompted to name the destination. This is an alphanumeric name to describe the specific connection. For the sake of our example, we will name the destination INTERNET. We are then asked to select a wide area medium. Because this is a dial-up connection we select PPP. This brings us to the PPP Call Destination Configuration window, shown in Figure 11.8.

FIGURE 11.8:

The PPP Call Destination
Configuration window

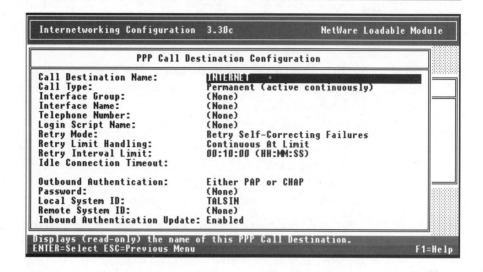

Setting the Call Type We are first asked to define the Call Type. Our options are Permanent or On Demand. Permanent keeps the WAN connection up as long as the server is active. On Demand only brings up the connection if the server needs to route data over the WAN link. Because we are using an analog modem, we will probably want to configure a permanent connection.

It takes 30 seconds or so for a modem to listen for a carrier (a dial tone), dial the phone number, and authenticate on the remote system. This means that if the server waits until data is received before initializing the call, it will take 30 seconds before it can pass this data along the link. Unfortunately, this is more than sufficient to time out an application wishing to send data across the link.

If ISDN is used, you can safely specify the connection as on-demand because a much lower connection time is required. An ISDN circuit can begin passing data in as little as one second.

Hunting to Available Network Interfaces We are then asked to assign this destination to an Interface Group. Pressing Enter on this field will bring up a menu of any interface groups defined while configuring the network interfaces. Defining a group allows us to hunt to an available network interface—that is, to search for the interface, validate it, and connect to it, all in a single operation.

If a group is selected, the Interface Name field becomes grayed out. If we did not select a group, we can use this field to select a specific interface to use when placing the call.

Setting the Destination Options The Telephone Number field allows us to configure the number to call when bringing up the WAN link. If you need to dial a 9 for an outside line, make sure it is specified here. A comma can be used to add a one-second delay between numbers.

The Login Script Name field is used when the destination requires authentication prior to establishing a PPP connection. The sample script provided has fields to pass along a logon name and password during authentication. The sample script should be sufficient for most applications.

Retry Mode defines how the server should react when it encounters a problem. While all errors are logged to the call manager (the utility that monitors WAN sessions), this defines what additional action should be taken.

The server can be told not to retry on failures, to retry regardless of the failure mode, or to retry only on self-correcting failures. The self-correcting option allows the server to recover from the failures it can and stop on the failures it cannot. For example, a busy signal would be considered a self-correcting failure and the server would simply continue to try the number. If the modem cannot detect a carrier (no dial tone), the server has no hope of correcting this failure mode and will simply stop.

Retry Limit Handling and Retry Interval Limit work together to determine how long the system should spend trying to establish the PPP connection. If the retry limit is set for Continuous at Limit, the value in the retry interval field is how often the server will attempt to establish a connection. The server will retry the connection forever at the interval specified.

If Retry Limit is set for Stop at Limit, the server will retry the connection for the amount of time specified in the Retry Interval field. The frequency of the retry varies. The first retry will take place after eight seconds. The pause before each subsequent retry will increase exponentially until the retry interval value is reached.

Idle Time Connection Timeout defines how long the server should wait after the last packet of data has crossed the WAN link before bringing the link down. This allows the link to be shut down when not in use. If a permanent connection type has been selected, this option is grayed out.

Outbound Authentication allows you to choose the authentication method used to establish the link. Password Authentication Protocol (PAP) and Challenge Handshake Authentication Protocol (CHAP) are supported. The default of PAP Or CHAP will try both methods. The method selected needs to match the authentication protocol in use by the destination system. The next field, Password, defines the outbound authentication password to use with PAP or CHAP. Authentication also uses the Local System ID to identify this system during authentication. For ISP authentication, this value should match the logon name specified in the sample script.

Remote System ID is used to define which remote systems are allowed to connect to this interface. If this field is left blank, the interface will only allow outbound calls to be established. Because we are configuring this interface for outbound use only, the Inbound Authentication Update field is not required.

Once our configuration is complete, we can press Escape and select Yes to save changes. If the authentication name and logon name do not match, you will receive an error message stating this is the case. The system will not change either value; you must go back into the configuration screen and change the appropriate value.

Backup Call Association

The backup call association allows us to define an alternate method of creating our WAN if the primary connection fails. When the server detects a failure in the primary connection (caused by lost carrier or failed data transmissions), it can automatically enable a secondary connection for use in its place.

For example, let's say we have a Frame Relay WAN connection that is used to connect to a remote site in Boston. We have gone through the process of configuring the board and network interface for this connection. The link has been tested and found to be operational.

Let's also assume that we wish to configure a backup solution in case this Frame Relay link fails. This is where the backup call association option comes in. It allows us to define another interface for creating an alternate method of communication. If the Frame Relay link fails, this alternate solution will be brought up in its place.

A secondary board has been defined to create a dial-up PPP link if the Frame Relay connection fails. While PPP supports a much slower transmission speed than Frame Relay, it is usually sufficient to bridge the brief outages experienced on the primary link. It is also a far less expensive solution than using ISDN.

The configuration process for our secondary PPP link is similar to the ISP connection detailed above, except the board is left disabled until it is needed. Once both interfaces are configured, we can associate them with each other.

Figure 11.9 shows the configuration screen for backup association. The call destination for our Frame Relay link has been named BOSTON. This is the primary destination that will be monitored in case of failure. The backup destination, Boston_ALT, is our PPP call destination. This is the link that will be enabled if the primary fails.

FIGURE 11.9:

The Backup Association Configuration window

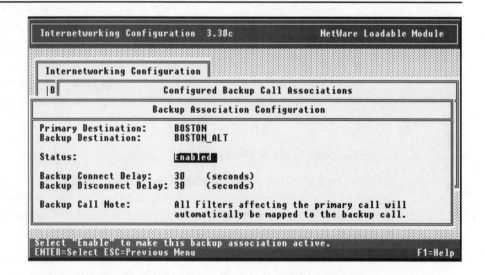

```
Internetworking Configuration  3.30c              NetWare Loadable Module

  ┌ Internetworking Configuration ┐
  │B│              Configured Backup Call Associations
  ├──────────────────────────────────────────────────────────────┤
  │                  Backup Association Configuration              │
  │                                                                │
  │  Primary Destination:      BOSTON                              │
  │  Backup Destination:       BOSTON_ALT                          │
  │                                                                │
  │  Status:                   Enabled                             │
  │                                                                │
  │  Backup Connect Delay:     30    (seconds)                     │
  │  Backup Disconnect Delay:  30    (seconds)                     │
  │                                                                │
  │  Backup Call Note:         All Filters affecting the primary call will
  │                            automatically be mapped to the backup call. │
  └────────────────────────────────────────────────────────────────┘
  Select "Enable" to make this backup association active.
  ENTER=Select ESC=Previous Menu                            F1=Help
```

The Backup Connect Delay is the amount of time to wait after the failure of the primary link before bringing up the secondary. This value should be set high enough to give the primary link time to recover from a failure.

The Backup Disconnect Delay is the amount of time the primary link should be active before the secondary is brought down and the primary is again used for providing connectivity. This delay should be long enough to ensure that the primary link has returned and is stable.

Once our configuration is complete, we can press Escape and select Yes to save changes. Our backup link is now defined to step in when the primary link fails.

Protocols

Our next menu option allows us to configure which protocols will be used on the server. We will not yet define information specific to each interface, but rather the general information required by the server to use each of the protocols we wish to support. Figure 11.10 shows the initial Protocol Configuration screen.

NOTE   By default, IPX must always be enabled.

FIGURE 11.10:

The Protocol Configuration window

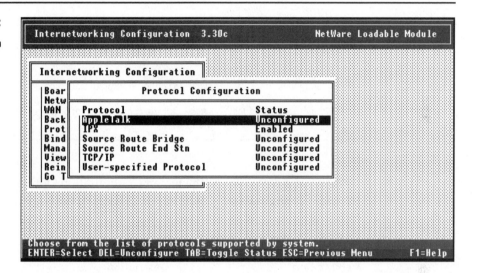

Configuring the IPX Protocol   Pressing Enter on the IPX menu option brings up the configuration menu for the IPX protocol. The available menu options are listed in Table 11.10.

TABLE 11.10: Menu Options for IPX Configuration

Menu Option	Description
Packet Forwarding	Enables or disables IPX router functionality on the server. This option must be enabled for the server to pass IPX traffic from one network interface to another.
Routing Protocol	Selects the IPX routing protocol. NLSP or RIP/SAP may be selected.

Continued on next page

TABLE 11.10 CONTINUED: Menu Options for IPX Configuration

Menu Option	Description
Tunnel IPX through IP	This option is used to pass IPX traffic through an IP-only link. The IPX packets are encapsulated within an IP frame prior to transmission.
Tunnel Configuration	Allows the IP address of the server on the remote end of the tunnel to be defined. The remote server must be configured to support tunneling as well.
Mobile IPX Support	Enables or disables the mobile IPX home router support used for remote LAN connectivity.
Mobile IPX Configuration	Used to configure parameters for mobile communications.
Filtering Support	When enabled, tells the server to filter out RIP and SAP information as defined through the `FILTCFG` utility.
IPX/SPX Parameters	Used to configure communication parameters and time-outs.
Expert Configuration Options	Allows for the configuration of advanced features as defined in Table 11.11.

When you press Enter on the Expert Configuration Options field, a submenu of advanced configuration options appears. These options are defined in Table 11.11.

TABLE 11.11: Advanced Options for Configuration

Menu Option	Description
Get Nearest Server Requests	Defines whether the server should respond to "get nearest server" requests. Requests are accepted by default but should be disabled on test servers or servers with a low connection license.
Override Nearest Server	Allows the server to respond to a "get nearest server" request with another server's name. This method is preferable to simply ignoring the request, as it allows the workstation to find a server that much quicker.
Nearest Server	Grayed out unless Override Nearest Server is enabled. This field contains the name to use when replying as another server.
Advanced Packet Type 20 Flooding	When disabled, NetBIOS frames are indiscriminately propagated to all interfaces. When enabled, reverse-path forwarding is used to insure that the frame is not propagated to a network segment more than once.

Continued on next page

TABLE 11.11 CONTINUED: Advanced Options for Configuration

Menu Option	Description
Hop Count Limit	The maximum number of routers a packet can cross before it is discarded. This should be set to reflect the diameter of your network to reduce traffic load during convergence.
Maximum Number of Path Splits	Used for load balancing. This value should reflect the number of network cards attached to the same logical network segment. This option is only available if NLSP was selected as the routing protocol on the previous screen.
Load Balance NCP Packets	Used for load balancing. When enabled, frame transmissions to clients will be equally split on a per session basis between each card connected to the same logical network segment. This option is only available if NLSP was selected as the routing protocol on the previous screen.
LSP Size	Used by NLSP to tune convergence. The size should reflect the smallest frame size used on your network minus the space used by the IPX header. The default value is sufficient for most networks. This option is only available if NLSP was selected as the routing protocol on the previous screen.
NLSP Local Area Addresses	Allows you to define which IPX networks this NLSP router should exchange information with. If an update is received from an undefined network, it is ignored. The default is to accept information from all networks. This option is only available if NLSP was selected as the routing protocol on the previous screen.
Override NLSP System ID	Disables NLSP's ability to dynamically assign a unique ID to this router. When enabled, the "NLSP System Identification" field becomes active, requiring you to manually assign an ID to this system. This option is only available if NLSP was selected as the routing protocol on the previous screen.
NLSP Convergence Rate	Set the rate of convergence when network changes occur. Changing this value to Fast improves recovery time but increases network traffic. Setting this field to Manual allows you to manually configure the convergence parameters. This option is only available if NLSP was selected as the routing protocol on the previous screen.
NLSP Convergence Rate Configuration	This submenu contains read-only information unless Manual was selected under Convergence Rate. The menu provides configuration parameters for NLSP timing. This option is only available if NLSP was selected as the routing protocol on the previous screen.

Once our configuration is complete, we can press Escape and select Yes to save changes. The IPX protocol is now configured. We are ready to assign IPX information that is specific to each interface.

Configuring the AppleTalk Protocol Pressing Enter on the AppleTalk menu option on the main Protocol Configuration screen brings up the configuration menu for the AppleTalk protocol. The available menu options are listed in Table 11.12.

TABLE 11.12: Menu Options for AppleTalk

Menu Option	Description
AppleTalk Status	When enabled, AppleTalk is initialized during system startup.
Packet Forwarding	When enabled, the server acts as an AppleTalk router. When disabled, the server acts as an end-node.
Type of Packet Forwarding	Defines whether the AppleTalk network is Phase 2 and extended network numbers can be used or if Phase 1 numbering must be used for backward-compatibility. This option is only available if packet forwarding is enabled.
DDP Checksum	The Datagram Delivery Protocol provides a checksum field in addition to the FCS field provided by the layer two topology for additional data verification. This is normally left off as it adds overhead and provides very little additional insurance that the data is received intact.
Tunnel AppleTalk through IP	This option is used to pass AppleTalk traffic through an IP-only link. The AppleTalk packets are encapsulated within an IP frame prior to transmission. This option is only available if packet forwarding is enabled.
AURP Configuration	Allows the IP address of the server on the remote end of the tunnel to be defined. The remote server must be configured to support tunneling as well. This option is only available if Packet Forwarding and Tunnel AppleTalk through IP are enabled.
Filtering Support	When enabled, tells the server to filter out device and network address information as defined through the FILTCFG utility. This option is only available if Packet Forwarding is enabled.
Internal Network	Enables the use of an internal network address and zone name. This option is only available if Packet Forwarding is enabled.
Network Number	Allows an internal network number to be defined if Packet Forwarding and Internal Network are enabled. A single address is specified instead of a start and end address because it is assumed the values are the same.

Continued on next page

TABLE 11.12 CONTINUED: Menu Options for AppleTalk

Menu Option	Description
Network Zone list	Assigns one or more zone names to the internal network number. This option is only available if Packet Forwarding and Internal Network are enabled.
Static Routes for on Demand Calls	Enables or disables the use of static routing for WAN links. This option is only available if Packet Forwarding is enabled.
Expert Configuration Options	When WAN links are used, this option allows for the definition of the remote hardware so that compatibility may be maintained. This option is only available if Packet Forwarding is enabled.

Once our configuration is complete, we can press Escape and select Yes to save changes. The AppleTalk protocol is now configured. We are ready to assign AppleTalk information that is specific to each interface.

Configuring the IP Protocol Pressing Enter on the TCP/IP menu option on the main Protocol Configuration screen brings up the configuration menu for the IP protocol. The available menu options are listed in Table 11.13.

TABLE 11.13: Menu Options for IP

Menu Option	Description
TCP/IP Status	When enabled, AppleTalk is initialized during system startup.
IP Packet Forwarding	When enabled, the server acts as an AppleTalk router. When disabled, the server acts as an end-node.
RIP	Enables or disables the use of RIP.
OSPF	Enables or disables the use of OSPF.
OSPF Configuration	When OSPF is enabled, this option allows the operational parameters for OSPF routing to be configured.
Static Routing	Enables or disables the use of static routing.
Static Routing Table	When Static Routing is enabled, this option allows routes to be configured. A static route can define the next hop when traveling to a network, or a specific IP host. A single default route entry may be created as well.

Continued on next page

TABLE 11.13 CONTINUED: Menu Options for IP

Menu Option	Description
SNMP Management Table	Defines the hosts to receive SNMP trap messages.
IPX/IP Gateway	When selected, displays a submenu with options to enable or disable the gateway, enable client logging, and enable the use of an access control list.
Filter Support	When enabled, tells the server to filter out packets based upon source address, destination address, and port number as defined through the FILTCFG utility.
Expert Configuration Options	Allows for the advanced configuration of IP broadcast traffic.

Once our configuration is complete, we can press Escape and select Yes to save changes. The IP protocol is now configured. We are ready to assign IP information that is specific to each interface.

Bindings

The Bindings menu option allows us to configure protocol information that is specific to each interface. For example, if we enabled IP under Protocols, this option allows us to assign IP addresses to each of our interfaces.

When the Bindings option is selected, we are presented with the Protocol To Interface/Group Bindings list. To add protocol support, press the Insert key. This will bring up a list of protocols that were configured under the Protocol menu option. Highlight the protocol you wish to configure and press Enter.

The next menu will ask if you wish to bind the protocol to a specific network interface or to a WAN group that was defined under the Network Interface menu option. If you select an interface, the values you configure apply to that interface only. If you select a group, the values apply to whichever interface is selected to create the WAN connection defined under the WAN Call Directory menu option.

Depending on your selection, an appropriate list of choices will be presented. If you selected a network interface, you will see a list of interfaces that have not been assigned to a group. If you selected Group from the Bind To menu, you will be presented with a list of valid group names.

Configuring a LAN Interface to Use IPX   When you select to configure IPX on a LAN interface, the Binding IPX To A LAN Interface menu appears. The available options are defined in Table 11.14.

TABLE 11.14: Menu Options for IPX

Menu Option	Description
IPX Network Number	Defines a hexadecimal network address to assign to this interface.
Frame Type	Selects a frame type to use with the above assigned address. If multiple frames using IPX are required, you must create separate entries for each frame assigning each a unique network address.
Expert Bind Options	Configures routing and SAP communication values for this interface. The default values are sufficient for most networks.

Once you're finished, press Escape and select Yes to save changes. The IPX protocol is now configured for this interface.

Configuring a LAN Interface to Use AppleTalk When you choose to configure AppleTalk on a LAN interface, the Binding NetWare AppleTalk To A LAN Interface menu appears. The available options are defined in Table 11.15.

TABLE 11.15: Menu Options for AppleTalk on a LAN Interface

Menu Option	Description
Network Range and Zone Configuration	Defines whether this interface will seed the network address and zone names for this network segment (seed) or will learn this information from another router on the network (non-seed). This option is only available if Packet Forwarding was enabled under the protocol configuration.
AppleTalk Network Type	Defines whether the attached network is an extended (Phase 2) or non-extended (Phase 1) network.
Network Range	If Packet Forwarding was enabled under the protocol configuration and this interface is configured to seed, this field defines the network range to use on this interface.
Zone List	If packet forwarding was enabled under the protocol configuration and this interface is configured to seed, this field defines the zone names to be assigned to the attached interface. Pressing the Insert key allows you to define a new zone name.
Provide Applications on this Interface	If no internal network address or zone is defined, this setting identifies whether the AppleTalk server applications (such as file and print) appear within the zone and network address defined for this interface.

Continued on next page

TABLE 11.15 CONTINUED: Menu Options for AppleTalk on a LAN Interface

Menu Option	Description
Application Zone Name	Selects which zone assigned to this interface server applications should be located in. This option is only available if Provide Applications on this Interface is set to Yes.

Once you're finished, press Escape and select Yes to save changes. The Apple-Talk protocol is now configured for this interface.

Configuring a LAN Interface to Use IP   When you select to configure IP on a LAN interface, the Binding TCP/IP to a LAN Interface menu appears. The available options are defined in table 11.16.

TABLE 11.16: Menu Options for IP on a LAN Interface

Menu Option	Description
Local IP Address	Assigns an IP address to this interface. If multiple addresses are required, then a separate binding must be completed for each.
Subnet Mask	Assigns a subnet mask for the attached network. The default value is based upon the class of the address assigned.
RIP Bind Options	Activates a submenu that allows you to configure the interface cost. You can also specify whether this interface advertises itself as a default route, you can set timing updates for RIP traffic.
OSPF Bind Options	Activates a submenu that allows the configuration of the interface cost, the area address range, and timing updates for OSPF traffic.
Expert TCP/IP Bind Options	Activates a submenu thta allows a frame type to be selected, the use of ARP to be enabled, and a broadcast address to be specified.

Once you're finished, press Escape and select Yes to save changes. The IP protocol is now configured for this interface.

Configuring a WAN Group to Use IP   The WAN group configuration is very similar to the LAN interface configuration. As an example, we will walk through the setup of a WAN group which will be bound to the IP protocol. When TCP/IP is selected from the list of configured protocols, we would then select to bind to each interface in a group rather than a specific interface.

Selecting to bind IP to a group activates the Binding TCP/IP To A WAN Interface configuration menu. The available options are defined in Table 11.17.

TABLE 11.17: Menu Options for IP on a WAN

Menu Option	Description
Interface Group	Identifies the WAN Group selected for configuration.
WAN Network Mode	Identifies if one or more destinations will be used and if an IP address is required by the remote systems.
Local IP Address	Assigns an IP address to the WAN group. Whichever interface creates the WAN connection will use this as its IP address.
Subnet Mask	Assigns a subnet mask to the WAN link. The default value is based upon the class of the address assigned.
WAN Call Destination	Defines the entry created under the WAN Call Directory menu option to use with this configuration. This configuration defines the connection type as well as the phone number to be dialed.

All remaining configuration options (RIP, OSPF, and Expert) are identical to their LAN counterparts. We can now press Escape and select Yes to save changes. The IP protocol is now configured for use with our WAN group. Figure 11.11 shows our completed set of bindings as they are displayed in the Protocol to Interface/Group Bindings list.

FIGURE 11.11:

Our list of configured interfaces and groups

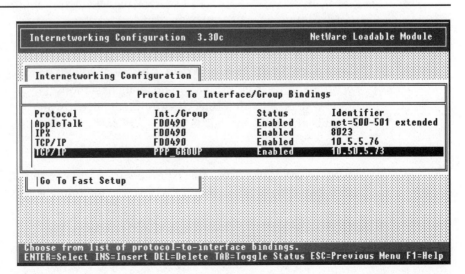

Manage Configuration

The Manage Configuration option allows us to define system management parameters. From here we can configure SNMP information, import or export our network configuration, and configure remote access to the server. Figure 11.12 shows the Manage Configuration window.

FIGURE 11.12:

Configuration management is performed from the Manage Configuration window.

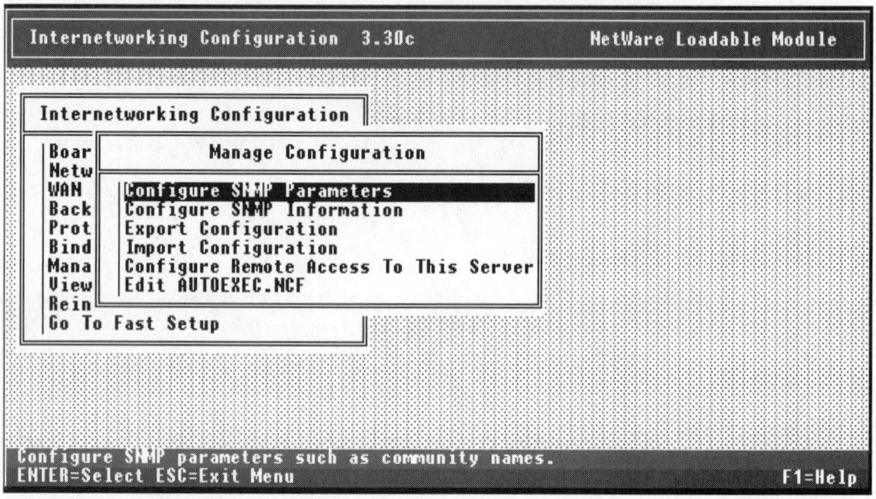

```
Internetworking Configuration   3.30c              NetWare Loadable Module


   Internetworking Configuration

   Boar          Manage Configuration
   Netw
   WAN     Configure SNMP Parameters
   Back    Configure SNMP Information
   Prot    Export Configuration
   Bind    Import Configuration
   Mana    Configure Remote Access To This Server
   View    Edit AUTOEXEC.NCF
   Rein
   Go To Fast Setup



Configure SNMP parameters such as community names.
ENTER=Select ESC=Exit Menu                              F1=Help
```

Configure SNMP Parameters From this menu option we can configure SNMP access to this server from SNMP management stations. We can configure which communities (if any) have read and set access, as well as how traps are handled.

Configure SNMP Information This menu allows us to configure how this server identifies itself to SNMP management stations. We can configure the name of the system, provide a brief description of its hardware, and identify where the server is physically located as well as who to contact if the server is generating trap errors.

Export Configuration The export configuration option allows us to save our networking configuration to an external medium, usually a floppy disk. By default, all local interface information is saved. We can also selectively save X.25 profiles, WAN call destinations, and authentication files.

The purpose of the export file is disaster recovery. If the network configuration is changed or becomes corrupt, the exported file can be used to return our networking configuration to a known working state.

Import Configuration The import configuration allows us to import the backup file created through the export menu option. All configuration information is restored. You can then go back through the other menu options and customize the configuration as required.

Configure Remote Access to This Server The Remote Access menu allows us to define which methods can be used to access the server remotely, beyond the normal logon process. These options should be enabled with care because most provide access to the server console. Figure 11.13 shows the Configure Remote Access To This Server window.

FIGURE 11.13:

The Configure Remote Access To This Server window

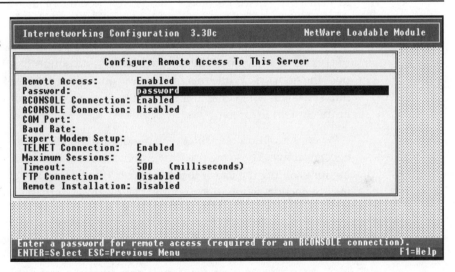

The remote access field enables or disables remote access to the server. When this field is disabled, all other fields are grayed out. The only console access is then from the console itself. Enabling this option allows for an alternate means of connecting to the server console.

The password field contains the value of the challenge string presented to the user when they attempt to remotely access the server. When remote access is enabled, this is the only form of authentication used. You are not prompted for a valid user logon, just the remote access password. This password should be guarded carefully because some methods of remote connection (such as Telnet and Remote Installation) are not logged.

The RCONSOLE field enables or disables the use of Rconsole as a remote means of console access. Rconsole uses SPX to provide in-band console access over the network. When a user connects using Rconsole, their network and MAC address are recorded in the System Error log and displayed on the server.

NOTE   "In-band" means "over the network." You do not need a separate cable connection to support an in-band management session.

The ACONSOLE field enables or disables remote access to the console via a dial-up connection. When this option is enabled, the COM Port, BAUD Rate, and Modem Setup fields become active as well. Aconsole allows out-of-band remote access to the server without requiring a network connection.

The Telnet connection field enables or disables Telnet and XWindows access to the server. IP must be enabled on the server, and connectivity is provided in-band over the network. While this provides a convenient means of console access, care must be taken when enabling this option as sessions are not logged to the console or the System Error log.

When this option is enabled, the Maximum Sessions and Timeout fields become active. These are used to limit the number of sessions and to set the timing for enabling the use of the Escape key (the Escape key character is used during connection negotiation and must be disabled until the session is established).

TIP   The FILTCFG utility can be used to restrict Telnet access to the server from only certain IP addresses.

The FTP Connection field does not enable a fully functional FTP server. It simply allows single session FTP access. Authentication is through the remote password specified above. This option should rarely be needed and should be left off unless absolutely required.

The Remote Installation field enables or disables the ability to install software from a remote server. It is possible to access software located on other servers from the console prompt. Remote Installation allows NetWare Loadable Modules (NLMs) to be loaded from remote systems.

Remote Installation can be a potential security breach and should only be enabled as required. If a potential attacker is able to gain console access, they may be able to load NLM software located on a remote system that they have already cracked. Remote Installation could aid them in gaining access to this server.

Of course, the argument can be made that if the attacker has console access, they have sufficient access to simply load the support modules required for remote software installation. Even if this option is left disabled, they can enable it because they have access to the console. This only enforces the statement that the remote access password should be well safeguarded and changed often.

Edit AUTOEXEC.NCF This menu option provides a convenient means of editing the startup file, AUTOEXEC.NCF. It allows you to view or change any modifications made by the INETCFG utility.

Once you have completed your changes to the Manage Configuration menu, simply press Escape to return to the main INETCFG screen.

View Configuration

The View Configuration menu allows you to view all of the networking changes you have made so far using the INETCFG utility or just certain portions of those changes. If you are an "old salt" accustomed to configuring networking on the command line, this is a good place to review your changes to ensure they are correct. Figure 11.14 shows a small portion of the commands generated by the INETCFG utility. If any of our selections require support modules, they are automatically added to the network startup script. This file is read-only and cannot be edited. If you need to make changes, you must do it through the menu options described above.

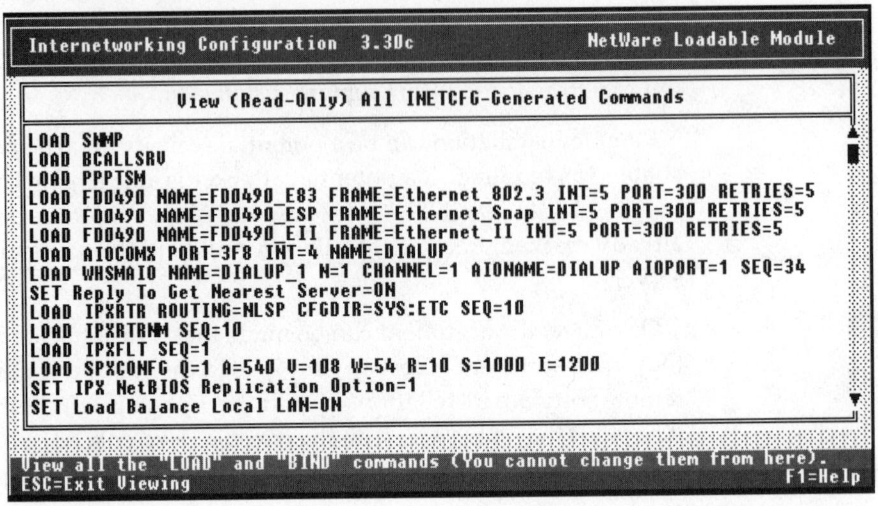

FIGURE 11.14:

A sample set of commands generated by INETCFG

```
Internetworking Configuration   3.30c              NetWare Loadable Module

              View (Read-Only) All INETCFG-Generated Commands

LOAD SNMP
LOAD BCALLSRV
LOAD PPPTSM
LOAD FD0490 NAME=FD0490_E83 FRAME=Ethernet_802.3 INT=5 PORT=300 RETRIES=5
LOAD FD0490 NAME=FD0490_ESP FRAME=Ethernet_Snap INT=5 PORT=300 RETRIES=5
LOAD FD0490 NAME=FD0490_EII FRAME=Ethernet_II INT=5 PORT=300 RETRIES=5
LOAD AIOCOMX PORT=3F8 INT=4 NAME=DIALUP
LOAD WHSMAIO NAME=DIALUP_1 N=1 CHANNEL=1 AIONAME=DIALUP AIOPORT=1 SEQ=34
SET Reply To Get Nearest Server=ON
LOAD IPXRTR ROUTING=NLSP CFGDIR=SYS:ETC SEQ=10
LOAD IPXRTRNM SEQ=10
LOAD IPXFLT SEQ=1
LOAD SPXCONFG Q=1 A=540 V=108 W=54 R=10 S=1000 I=1200
SET IPX NetBIOS Replication Option=1
SET Load Balance Local LAN=ON

View all the "LOAD" and "BIND" commands (You cannot change them from here).
ESC=Exit Viewing                                                    F1=Help
```

The displayed networking commands are updated dynamically. The configuration files are not updated when you exit the INETCFG utility, but rather each time you finish configuration of a specific menu option.

Also from this menu you can review the log created by the CONSOLE.NLM utility. CONSOLE.NLM logs all messages that are displayed on the console screen. It is typically used during system startup to record module information. This is helpful, as messages typically scroll past the screen at a faster rate than most people can read. The console log is a good place to troubleshoot connectivity problems if you think a LAN driver is not loading properly or a bind command is incorrect.

Reinitialize System

The Reinitialize System option restarts *networking* on the server; it does not restart the server itself. This option should not be used during normal working hours as it may interrupt user connectivity to the server. When using this option, do so from the server console, not a remote session. Once activated, Reinitialize System will cause you to lose your remote connection to the server.

If you've made a few minor changes and need them to take effect during working hours, manually enter the commands at the server command line. This will enable the new networking commands without affecting user connectivity.

For example, if your users connect to the server using IPX, you could manually enter the required commands to initialize IP connectivity without affecting any user connections. You can later (during off hours) reinitialize the server to insure that your saved changes are correct. While this method creates a little extra work, it allows your changes to take effect immediately without effecting normal server operation.

Go to Fast Setup

Fast Setup allows you to review the changes you have made with the above menu options and edit them as required. It also allows you to configure new boards and bindings. The option is prompt-driven and is designed to ease setup through a series of questions. This makes configuring network parameters easier if you are not familiar with the INETCFG utility.

By making networking simpler, however, many of the advanced options are not available. For example, you cannot configure AppleTalk or access the expert options for any of the protocols. Still, if you have a small environment and your networking requirements are simple, the fast setup is a simplified method of getting your server up and running.

IntraNetWare IP Applications

Describing the configuration and administration of all of IntraNetWare's new IP applications is beyond the scope of this book. For setup and configuration of the new IP applications that have been added to IntraNetWare, see Morgan Stern and Tom Rasmussen's book *Building Intranets on NT, NetWare, and Solaris* (Sybex, 1997). It is an excellent reference on how to set up and administer these newly added features. Development tools are also covered.

Using SAMBA to Create Shares on IntraNetWare

The SAMBA suite is a set of client and server tools for both accessing and advertising file and printer shares. Shares are used by Windows NT, Windows 95, LAN Manager, and OS/2 when exchanging information. Connectivity is supplied by the NetBIOS and NetBEUI protocols, including encapsulation of NetBIOS over IP.

There is even a version of SAMBA for IntraNetWare. This was developed by Novell Consulting Services as a tool for migrating to IntraNetWare from NT or LAN Manager. While it is still considered beta code at the time of this writing, it does allow a 4.1 or later NetWare server to advertise file and printer shares just like an NT server. While its original intent was to ease the migration path from LAN Manager or Windows NT to a NetWare environment, it can be used even if you do not plan on migrating services to a new platform.

At this writing, the IntraNetWare SAMBA tools are still considered beta code and can be a bit unstable. For example, the simple act of unloading SAMBA.NLM will cause it to refuse to release some memory resources. Also, if you load NBNS.NLM without the -G switch (even though it does not actually use it), NBNS.NLM will cause a race condition and use up 100 percent of the processor's time.

If you are using IntraNetWare, both of these conditions are recoverable. The garbage collection will eventually return the memory resources to the pool and the race condition will be stopped after a minute of hogging the processor. If you are still using 4.1, however, the race condition will bring the server to its knees.

Bearing in mind the above disclaimer, let's look at how to install and configure SAMBA for use with an IntraNetWare system.

Retrieving the SAMBA Files for IntraNetWare

The SAMBA files for IntraNetWare are available from the Novell Web site (www.novell.com). If you perform a search on the key word SAMBA, you will be linked to a document which will let you retrieve the archive. The archive should include:

- SAMBA.NLM   The equivalent of smbd for IntraNetWare

- NWGLUE.NLM   API layer to allow NetBIOS based access to the server

- NBNS.NLM   The equivalent of nmbd for IntraNetWare

- NETBEUI.NLM   Support for the NetBEUI protocol

- TCPBEUI.NLM   Support for NetBEUI over IP

- SMB.CFG   The equivalent of SMB.CONF for IntraNetWare

Preparing the IntraNetWare System

There are a number of steps to preparing an IntraNetWare server for use with the SAMBA.NLM. Do not simply load it and hope for the best. There is little (if any) documentation included with the above archive. With this in mind, we will step through the exact process required to install the files.

Preparing the Directory Structure

SAMBA for IntraNetWare is hard coded to use a specific directory structure. If you do not duplicate this structure exactly, it can become very upset and retaliate by causing a server ABEND.

With this in mind, you will want to create a SAMBA directory named SAMBA directly off the root of sys. Within this new directory, create another directory called locks. You will also need to create a directory named tmp off of the root of sys.

Modifying Needed Support Files

In the sys:\etc directory, you will want to check your hosts file to ensure that it has an entry for the loopback address, as well as for the system itself. The entries would appear similar to the following:

```
127.0.0.1     loopback localhost lb     #loopback address

10.1.1.10     hostname                   #IP address of this system
```

The format of the hosts file is to list IP addresses in the first column, host names in the second, and comments in the third. Columns should be separated by tabs, not spaces. The comment field should begin with the pound sign (#).

You should replace the entry 10.1.1.10 with the IP address of your server. Also, replace the hostname entry with the name of your server.

You will also need to create two empty files in the sys:\SAMBA directory. Name these files LOG.NMB and LOG.SMB. These files will be used to record any run time messages or errors.

Placing the Files in Their Correct Locations

Copy the following files to the sys:\system directory:

- NWGLUE.NLM
- NBNS.NLM
- NETBEUI.NLM
- TCPBEUI.NLM

Copy the following two files to the sys:\SAMBA directory:

- SAMBA.NLM
- SMB.CFG

If your archive file did not contain an SMB.CFG file (which ours did not), you can create one by using the parameters described above for the SMB.CONF file. In fact, the easiest way to create it would be to obtain a SMB.CONF file from a Unix system and modify the settings as you require.

Starting up SAMBA for IntraNetWare

Load the support files in the exact order listed below:

- NWGLUE.NLM
- NBNS.NLM –G workgroup
- SAMBA.NLM
- NETBEUI.NLM
- TCPBEUI.NLM

nbns should be loaded with the workgroup switch, even though nbns appears not to use it. Setting this switch seemed to resolve race conditions with the NLM. This problem should be fixed in later releases. We still had to use the workgroup= switch under global settings in the SMB.CFG file. nbns appears to support many of the same switches as nmbd.

Once the support files are loaded, you should now be able to advertise file and printer shares located on the IntraNetWare server. Figure 11.15 shows the IntraNetWare server Talsin advertising shares the same as an NT server, or a Unix system running SAMBA would do.

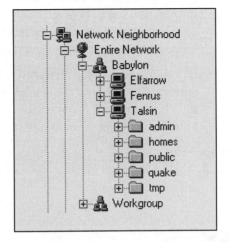

NT 5, or the Future of IntraNetWare

At the time of this writing, Novell has released beta 3 of the successor to NetWare/
IntraNetWare, code named MOAB. MOAB/NT 5 builds upon the foundation created by IntraNetWare and should include the following new features:

Portable NCP: NCP will be broken off from IPX so that it is supported by
other protocols. This will bring connectivity features of NCP to other protocols such as IP. This will also create native support for other protocols so
that communications are no longer IPX dependent.

Process Prioritization: Processes running on a server will be able to be
prioritized by the system administrator. This is a similar functionality as to
what is currently supported by Unix. The administrator can decide which
server applications are deemed most important and give them a larger
percentage of the available CPU cycles.

Virtual Memory: The administrator will be allowed to set up a portion of
disk space as virtual memory. Processes that are not currently active can be
moved from physical memory to disk. This allows for the creation of larger
applications than would normally be supported by the amount of physical
memory installed in the server.

Java Virtual Machine: MOAB will support network client machines through the use of Java applications. The network client is not required to save any applications locally. It can access all required applications from the server using a browser interface.

IP Version 6:   As registered address space becomes limited, work is being performed to expand the available address range through a new version of IP. While version 6 is not backwards compatible, MOAB will release support for this version for organizations that wish to begin testing.

Enhancements to file storage, replication, and printing services will also be included when the final version of MOAB is released.

Summary

This completes our discussion of configuring network communications on NetWare/IntraNetWare. You should now have a good understanding of how to provide connectivity to an IntraNetWare server. You should also have a good understanding of the features and services provided by this NOS.

In the following chapter, we will take a similar look at Microsoft's NT Server. We will look at its supported features as well as how to configure it for network communications.

CHAPTER
TWELVE

12

Windows NT Server

■ Setup features

■ The core operating system and the file system

■ Account administration and security features

■ Networking and protocol support

■ Basic configuration

■ Configuring network services

■ Configuring network protocols

■ A quick preview of NT Server 5.0

Released in 1993, Windows NT Server was arguably the first network operating system to focus on ease of use and administration. Its initial release used the same interface as the then-popular Windows 3.1. For administrators who were familiar with this desktop system, it was not a far stretch to set up and administer an NT system using this same familiar interface.

The current release of Windows NT Server, version 4.0, follows in its predecessor's footprints by utilizing the Windows 95 interface. If you are familiar with Windows 95, you'll feel right at home using NT. The NT Server interface is identical to Windows 95. The differences lie in the additional features supported by NT Server and in the core operating system itself.

Windows NT Features

Let's first cover some of the features of Windows NT in order to give you a good feel for the operating system. As is apparent from its connectivity options, Windows NT is designed for a slightly different market group than NetWare/IntraNetWare or Unix. NT has been targeted so far at small to mid-sized networks, offering easier GUI-based configuration and administration tools. While exact ease-of-use levels are somewhat subjective, it does seem to have at least an edge over both Unix and NetWare in this regard. Microsoft is adding features to NT to start positioning it for much larger networks. (At the same time, of course, Novell and the various Unix publishers will continue to add enhancements to their own products.) NT 5, in beta release at the time this book goes to press, will bring 64-bit memory accessing and (possibly) fault-tolerant clusters of servers (allowing a failed server's functionality to be replaced on the fly with another server).

Windows NT Setup

NT Server provides a full GUI interface during most of the server configuration. Curiously, the setup runs in two passes. The first copies some (but not all) of the files needed for installation to the hard drive. During the second pass, the installation is actually performed. While space is normally not a problem, you should ensure that you have an additional 100MB of free disk space over and above what the OS will require. These temporary files are cleaned up during the final stages of the installation.

While NT supports hardware auto-detection, it does not support Plug and Play like Windows 95. This simply means that each hardware component must be pre-set with interrupts and memory addresses it needs. For the seasoned administrator, this is usually not a problem.

The network configuration requires a bit more work than IntraNetWare. NT Server does not detect which protocols are currently running on your network. It simply presents the administrator with the usual defaults for providing file and print services. This is usually not a problem because NT relies on NetBEUI for these services. Unlike IPX, NetBEUI has no Network layer support, so entering the correct network address number is not a concern.

NT is also a bit lacking in the infrastructure department. While IntraNetWare will detect which NDS trees are available on the network and walk the administrator through the process of grafting the server onto an existing tree, NT is unable to detect existing domains. The administrator must know which server and domains are available. While most administrators are aware of their network environment, an auto-detect feature like IntraNetWare's would simplify this step and prevent misspellings.

NOTE   We will discuss domains in greater detail later in this chapter.

To its credit, NT has fully integrated all available server options into its installation process, something that IntraNetWare has yet to do. For example, the administrator help files must be installed separately under IntraNetWare but are part of the standard installation with NT Server. To be fair, however, the NT Server help files are not nearly as thorough or complete as IntraNetWare's.

As for performing server migrations, NT Server provides an easy-to-use utility for environments upgrading from NetWare 2.2x or 3.1x. NetWare 4.x or IntraNetWare is not supported. The utility first documents the existing server and all account information. This information can then be migrated from one platform to another over the network. The only things lost during the migration are trustee rights for file access; these must be re-created manually.

Curiously, there is no migration utility for upgrading from NT Server 3.x. The only supported upgrade method is to overwrite the existing server. This process is a bit buggy as some files will still identify the OS version as 3.5x. Another problem is that overwriting the old server does not allow for the complete upgrade of the server platform; and of course, it doesn't allow you to keep the old server on standby in case there is a problem. Once a same-server migration is started, the only way back is by restoring the old system from backup tape—not a happy alternative if the problem is found during working hours. To do a server-to-server migration, you will have to move files and set permissions manually.

NOTE   One other option you may want to consider when upgrading NT is to do a new install to a different directory. While this uses more disk space and does not migrate any settings, it does give you the option of leaving your NT 3.*x* version intact. This way, you have the ability to choose either installed NT version at boot time—something that may come in handy if you need an interim server while finalizing NT 4 settings.

NT Server can support both Intel and RISC processors. This increases the number of platforms supported by this NOS. Not all NT applications will run if a RISC processor is used, however. If you are investigating the use of a RISC-based server, make sure the platform will support all your required applications. Disappointingly, Microsoft has announced it will discontinue support of NT for PowerPC processors after NT 4. It appears in fact that DEC's Alpha is the only remaining non-Intel compatible processor that NT will continue to support.

NT Core OS

The core operating system of NT Server is 32-bit. While this creates some backward-compatibility problems with 16-bit applications, it ensures that the OS kernel remains stable. Unlike IntraNetWare, NT is both multitasking and multithreaded. This helps to prevent any single process from monopolizing all available CPU time.

NT Server uses the same Windows 32 application programming interface as NT Workstation and Windows 95 (note that 95 actually supports only a subset of Win32). This ensures a familiar programming environment, which theoretically allows a programmer to write a more stable application.

For example, a programmer who is familiar with writing Windows desktop applications will find programming for NT Server very similar, as both use the Win32 interface. This is in contrast to the NetWare Loadable Module (NLM) technology used by an IntraNetWare server. A programmer writing code for an IntraNetWare server must be specifically aware of the NLM environment.

Because the server uses the same Win32 interface as Windows workstations, most desktop applications are supported. This can be a real money-saver for smaller businesses that cannot afford to dedicate a system to server activities. Unlike IntraNetWare, which requires you to dedicate a system as a server, NT Server can perform double duty as a user workstation as well.

Unfortunately, NT also lacks the remote-control features of IntraNetWare's Rconsole. While there are tools available from Microsoft's Web site (`www.microsoft.com`) and from their Resource Kits to manage some server functions remotely, you cannot remotely add or remove protocols, launch applications, or access the NT Server desktop from a remote location. Third-party remote-control software such as pcANYWHERE is needed to provide this functionality.

NT Server supports memory isolation of all applications running on the system. This is similar to Novell's core OS rings, except that once an application has been found to be stable it can never be promoted to having direct access to the core OS. While increasing server stability, it does so at a cost of application execution speed.

Out of the box, NT Server provides support for up to four processors. With hardware support, this can be increased to 32. The benefit of additional processors is that more CPU time can be made available to applications running on the server.

NT Server supports the use of *virtual memory*. This allows the server to utilize more memory than is physically installed in the system. The benefit is that applications are free to use more memory to add additional features. The drawback is that virtual memory is stored to disk, which has a slower access time than physical memory by a factor of 100. But again, this can be a real cost-saver to a small environment that cannot afford to outfit a server with a lot of physical memory.

Additionally, virtual memory is important because NT's minimum memory requirements are four times higher than for IntraNetWare. For a minimal server providing basic file, HTTP, and WINS services, plan on installing at least from 96MB to 128MB of physical memory.

Tracking down which applications are loaded into memory and which processes are using CPU time can also be a bit of a chore. To determine what is running, you must check the Services dialog box, the Device dialog box, and the Task Manager (both the Application and Processes tabs). By contrast, IntraNetWare requires you to look in only two places (the process monitor and the `modules` command), and Unix requires only one check (the Process ID or `pid` command).

File System

NT Server 4 supports two file systems: FAT and the NT file system (NTFS). While both support long file names, FAT is optimized for drives up to 500MB while NTFS is designed for drives of 500MB and larger. Neither format supports Macintosh files in their native format (although NTFS does provide support for Mac file storage). NTFS is the preferred file system for storing applications and user files.

While file compression is supported under NTFS, there is no method to have the server automatically compress files at a preset time or selectively perform compression based upon compression gains as there is with IntraNetWare. Files must be manually compressed through Explorer or can be processed through batch files. You can, however, set desired directories/folders as compressed, which will cause all files in these folders to be transparently compressed and uncompressed as needed.

TIP

If you are going to use NTFS drive partitions larger than 2048MB and you wish to use compression, use the command-line **format** command to force the cluster size to 4KB when formatting the drive. NT Server does not support compression when clusters are larger than 4KB. After 2048MB, the cluster size increases to 8KB.

Unlike IntraNetWare, NT Server does not support disk suballocation. The configured cluster size is the only size available for storing files. This means that you should carefully analyze what type of data will be stored on each of your NTFS drives. If your applications create large files (database, graphics, and so on), then a larger cluster size should be used to decrease the number of required reads when accessing a file. This will speed up file access.

If you will be storing small files (text, HTML, and so on), then use a small cluster size to avoid wasting disk space. When a file is written to disk, it is stored in one or more clusters. If the file does not completely fill a cluster, the remainder goes to waste. A small cluster size ensures that the minimal amount of disk space goes unused.

For example, if you have an 11K file that you write to a disk with 2KB clusters, the file is saved in six separate clusters with 1KB unused and going to waste. If you save the file to a disk with 16KB clusters, it only takes one cluster to save the file (and only one cluster needs to be read for file access), but you are wasting 5KB worth of potential storage space.

This is why it is important to determine in advance what type of files will be saved to the drive. Preplanning ensures that you strike a good balance between space conservation and disk access speed.

NT Server supports directory replication. This allows entire directories to be exported to other servers or even NT workstations. Any changes are updated immediately. This can be extremely useful when it is not practical to always use the server for access to these files.

For example, let's say you are using an NT server to provide services to a number of programmers. The programmers use a common set of tools and code extensions while compiling their code. They do not wish to run their compilation jobs over the network, because of the amount of traffic this creates.

The solution would be to create a master copy of these files on the server and export them to each user's NT workstation. This allows them to store their tools locally so that their compile jobs do not have to be run over the network. Because the replication option will immediately export any changes, the programmers can be sure they are always using the latest tools.

Deleted files can be recovered only under the FAT file system. NT provides no tools for recovering files deleted from an NTFS drive (with the exception of files deleted locally, using the recycle bin). Also missing is a defragment utility for NTFS. Applications such as Microsoft Exchange are constantly creating and deleting files; and this tends to fragment the file system over time. If you are running a file-intensive application, pick up a third-party defragment utility. Without such a utility, you must back up the file system, delete and re-create the drive, and then restore your files to return them to an unfragmented state.

Account Administration

NT Server uses the Windows NT Directory Services for user and group management. This is not, as the name implies, a fully hierarchical directory service like IntraNetWare's NDS. It is a flat security structure based upon the use of domains. Domains can be extended to support NetWare 2.2x and 3.1x servers. At the time of this writing, 4.x is not supported. Note that Novell is now shipping a version of NDS for NT Server, which adds enhanced browsing and management services, as well as the ability to access Novell NDS resources transparently.

A *domain* is a group of workstations and servers associated by a single security policy. A user can perform a single logon and gain access to every server within the domain; they do not need to perform separate logons for each server. To emulate a hierarchical structure, domains can be configured to be *trusting*. When a domain trusts another domain, it allows users of that trusted domain to retain the same level of access they have in the trusted domain.

For example, domain A trusts domain B. This means that everyone that has domain user rights to domain B (trusted domain) will be allowed the same level of access to domain A (trusting domain). While it's fine for a small environment, this model does not scale very well. For example, you cannot administer each domain from a single user manager. You must connect to each domain you wish to work with one at a time.

The other problem is, what if you want only some of the users to have access to the other domain? With IntraNetWare you can simply create an aliases object in each container where you wish the user to have access. With NT Server, this can still be done, but it's more complicated. In addition to setting a trust relationship, you must either create a similar account on the remote station for each user, or define user groups to include or exclude individual users. Finally, you cannot check your trust relationships from a central location. You must go to each primary server in each domain to see what trust relationships have been set up. If it is a large environment, you may have to put pen to paper to ensure that you have not set up any trust loops that unintentionally give access to users who shouldn't have access. With IntraNetWare, a simple scan of the NDS tree will identify who has access and where.

Domain information is stored on *domain controllers*. Each domain has a single *primary domain controller* (*PDC*). The PDC contains the master record of all domain information. Any other NT server can be set up as a *backup domain controller* (*BDC*). The BDC receives updates from the PDC so that there is a backup copy of the domain information. When a user logs in, they can authenticate with either the PDC or any one of the BDCs.

This brings a degree of server-centric dependency to the whole domain model. To ensure that changes stay synchronized, all user administration must be performed on the PDC. Any user information that is not specific to the domain must be manually updated out to the BDCs if they will be performing logon authentication.

For example, if the PDC contains a logon script to connect users to network resources, a copy of this logon script must be provided on each BDC. If the logon script on the PDC is changed, the change must be synchronized with each of the BDC servers. This is in contrast to NDS, where the user logs on to a container instead of a server—regardless of which system replies, the same logon script is available to them.

There is also no way to optimize network performance by specifying which users authenticate with which servers. For example, NDS allows you to place partitions of the NDS tree on only certain servers, so that authentication traffic can be better balanced. In an NT domain, the user authenticates with the first server that replies.

Curiously, systems can be promoted within a domain but not demoted. In other words, you can make a regular server a BDC, or a BDC a PDC. No other combinations are available.

For example, let's say you buy a new server with all the go-fast bells and whistles and connect this system to a full-duplex switch port running at 100Mbps. You add this system to the domain and make it a BDC.

Later, you decide that the existing PDC is getting a bit old. While it is still functional, you would like to move the PDC functionality to the other server in order to improve performance. You also want to demote the PDC to a BDC so that it can still be used for file and printer sharing.

You promote the BDC to a PDC; this part of the process goes without incident. You then turn your attention to the old PDC. Because of the limitations described above, you cannot simply demote this system to a BDC. You must in fact do a complete reinstall (not just an upgrade), reinstall all patches and hot-fixes, and then reintegrate it into the domain. Needless to say, this is not quite as smooth as the NDS model.

NT Server supports the use of *policies* to help enforce a standard desktop. Policies can be set up for users, groups, or systems. There are 30 different policies that can be configured for a user or a group of users. These allow customization ranging from the selection of a standard wallpaper to the removal of the Run command from the Start menu. There are also 30 system policies, which range from specifying the logon banner to limiting the number of authentication retries.

NT policies are not like NAL under IntraNetWare. Policies are mainly designed to customize the look and feel of the interface and to remove available options. Policies do not include some of the higher-level features that NAL has, such as standard network program groups or software distribution and setup. Also, policies are only supported by NT, while NAL includes support for Windows 3.1*x* and Windows 95. These features are typically utilized by only large organizations. A small network environment may not even use these features.

NT has an *Administrative Wizard* for administrators who are new to the NT environment or are just unsure of how to perform certain operations. Figure 12.1 shows the main window for the Administrative Wizard.

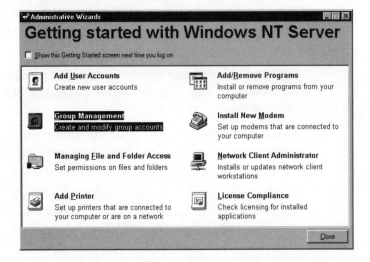

The Administrative Wizard is question-and-answer based, so the administrator is walked through all necessary configuration steps. Figure 12.2 is an example of one of the Wizard windows for adding a new user. There are also Wizards for administrating groups, printers, and program licenses, as well as for installing new modems or software.

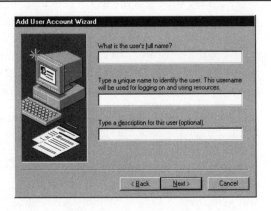

Security

Windows NT has been C2 certified by the National Computer Security Center (NCSC) for stand-alone use. It has not yet received approval as a trusted network. This means that to comply with the C2 approval, the NT system cannot have any means of remote connection (no NIC card or modem). Because this defeats the purpose of a server, you cannot run NT as a server and comply with its C2 certification.

Users are assigned their access rights based on association with predefined groups. A user who is part of a group receives all the access rights associated with that group. NT supplies eight local and three domain groups with which users can be associated for varying levels of access.

For example, a Backup Operator group provides read access to the entire server for the purpose of performing backups. There is also a Print Operator group, which allows its members to manage printers and print queues.

While this is fine for small environments with simple security requirements, it does not scale very well. For example, assume you have fifteen NT servers. Thirteen of them provide file and print services, one runs Lotus Notes, and the other runs a Web server. You wish to give the Notes administrator full, unrestricted access to the Notes server and the Webmaster the same level of access to the Web server. You want both of these users to have regular user rights on the remaining thirteen servers.

Under the single-domain model, this is not possible. As soon as you give them administrator access to their respective systems, they have the same level of access throughout the domain.

In order to work around this problem you would need to set up three separate domains—one for the thirteen file and print servers and one for each of the two remaining systems. If you later bring in a mail server under the same conditions, you are now looking at adding a fourth domain. Because in a typical small network the same person or group of people is responsible for all aspects of the network, this problem is rarely an issue.

NT Server supports auditing of user activity and system events. Seven events can be monitored in all. While this number pales in comparison to IntraNetWare's ability to monitor 70, it is usually sufficient for the auditing requirements of a smaller environment.

These seven events are not very customizable, however. For example, while you can monitor when people log on and log off the server, you cannot select a specific account to monitor (such as Administrator). Also, while you can log who accesses a file, you cannot specify which files to watch or even what type of access is performed (read, delete, copy, and so on).

NT Server allows trustee rights to be assigned to directories on NTFS drives. This regulates who is permitted to access the files and what they are allowed to do with them. For example, some users may be allowed to delete and change files while others have only read access.

There are a few drawbacks with this system. First, all users are given full access by default. It is up to the administrator to go back and restrict access to only those users who require it. Also, trustee rights cannot be assigned through the same utility where users and groups are created. This means the administrator must check in two separate areas to identify what type of access a user has to a server.

Windows NT has also been plagued with a high number of security flaws. At the time of this writing, there are well over two dozen security-related hot-fixes that must be installed in addition to the service packs in order to insure that the system is not compromised. To their credit, Microsoft has been very responsive in developing hot-fixes once a security flaw has gone public. The problem is that the security flaw may be exploited for weeks or even months before it is publicly recognized. This also increases the need for network administrators to keep up to date on installing such fixes, if ensuring security is an objective.

Networking

NT Server includes protocol support for NetBEUI, IP, IPX, AppleTalk, and DLC. NetBEUI, IP, and AppleTalk can be used when accessing file and print services. IP support is via NetBEUI encapsulation.

NT Server includes support for Ethernet, Token Ring, ATM, FDDI, PPP, ISDN, and Frame Relay. Monitoring of all LAN topologies is performed through a single network monitoring tool. The network monitor is covered in Chapter 31.

When two or more networking cards are installed, NT Server has the ability to act as a router. For outbound connectivity (LAN to WAN), only full-time WAN links are supported. For inbound (WAN to LAN), both full-time and bandwidth-on-demand connections are supported.

Inbound dial-up connections are handled by the *Remote Access Service* (*RAS*) component. RAS provides authentication based upon NT account information. Users can dial in via PPP or ISDN using the same logon name and password they use while on the LAN. The administrator has the ability to grant rights selectively on a user-by-user basis. Callback options are even available for enhanced security. Once authentication is complete, the user has access to all IP, IPX, and NetBEUI services on the network, not just the NT server itself. This is an extremely cost-effective feature for environments that cannot afford the additional cost of a modem pool.

RAS supports multilink channel aggregation. *Channel aggregation* allows a dial-in user to utilize more than one phone line for network access. For example, a user with two 28.8K modems can dial in on two separate lines to receive an effective throughput of 57.6K. At the time of this writing, only NT Workstation and Server can leverage this capability with anything but ISDN.

NT Server also supports the *Point-to-Point Tunneling Protocol* (*PPTP*). This service allows users to access the NT server from any place out on the Internet, which means that an administrator is not required to run a modem pool to allow home users to access the internal network. Users can dial in to their regular ISP account and use the Internet as a transport when accessing the organization's network resources.

As a router, NT Server supports static routing under IP and distance vector for IP, IPX, and AppleTalk. Link-state routing is not supported for any protocol. Because NT's primary focus has been the smaller network environment, this is usually not a problem.

When IPX is used, NT has the ability to auto-detect (during startup) which frame types and network numbers are being used. It will also perform a test ARP during startup to ensure that no other systems are using the server's IP address. These two features help to greatly simplify administration.

Unlike IntraNetWare, NT Server does not support any packet filtering for IPX or AppleTalk, and it does not support a full set of tools for IP. While it will filter IP based on port number, there are a number of drawbacks with this minimal configuration.

First, it will not selectively pass traffic based upon source and destination address. This makes it ineffective as a packet filter for Internet use. Also, filtering is performed on the NIC as the traffic comes into the server. You cannot filter traffic as it is exiting the server through the NIC.

For example, if you want to set up the NT server as a Web server on one of its ports and hide what type of system the Web server is running on (in order to minimize the chance of an attack), you have no way of shutting off the NetBIOS broadcast on that port—a broadcast that in effect says, "Hi, I'm an NT server, come and get me!" This is the Internet equivalent of walking around with your money roll pinned to your sleeve. Once an attacker knows what you have, it's easier for them to figure out how to violate it.

The one extremely annoying peculiarity of NT networking is that any change, no matter how minor, requires a reboot of the machine to initialize the changes. Want to point to a new DNS server? The machine must be rebooted. Want to add a new protocol? Again, the machine must be rebooted. This is usually not a problem in small environments where server availability is only required from 8 A.M. to 5 P.M. It can be completely unacceptable in a larger shop that requires "7×24" server access (7 days a week, 24 hours a day).

TIP   If you have just rebooted an NT server and receive the error message, "The service database is currently locked" when working with the network configuration, have a cup of coffee and try again later. Being able to log on to an NT server does not mean it has finished initializing. How long the initialization process will take depends on how many services it is required to start.

IP Applications

NT Server ships with a full set of IP applications. About the only things missing are an IPX-to-IP gateway (or even a NetBEUI-to-IP gateway) and a decent set of packet filters or a firewall. (Microsoft does sell a proxy server as an add-on product.) With this in mind it is better to keep an NT server inside the protection of a firewall.

NT Server includes the *Internet Information Server* (*IIS*). IIS installs servers for Web, FTP, and Gopher services. The Web server sports an access speed that is nearly twice as fast as its predecessor, which ran on NT version 3.51 (although the access speed is not quite up to par with IntraNetWare or Unix). For Web development, CGI, WINCGI, Visual Basic, and Perl are supported. The Web server also supports *secure sockets layer* (SSL) for secure transactions (IIS 4.0 now supports SSL version 3.0t) and the new HTTP 1.1 Host Header standard, which allows multiple distinct Web sites on a single Web server to share a single IP address.

Microsoft has also made an index server available for download, free of charge. The index server is capable of accepting advanced queries and searching text, HTML, or Microsoft Office documents for instances of the search string. The index server is an easy way to add document retrieval to the list of features supported by your Web server.

NT Server also supports DNCP, IP printing, DNS, and WINS. When DNS is configured to refer to WINS for host information, the two are capable of exchanging information. When a NetBIOS-based system registers itself with the WINS server, that information is conveyed to the DNS server. This allows a system to be known by the same name under NetBIOS and IP. It also allows the administrator to keep the DNS host name table up to date with a minimal amount of administration.

Configuring NT Server for Network Access

All network connectivity is installed through the Network Properties window. This can be accessed by right-clicking on Network Neighborhood and selecting Properties or by selecting the Networking icon under the Control Panel.

System Identification

Figure 12.3 shows the Identification tab for the Network Properties window. This server is identified as using the NetBIOS name Talsin and belonging to the domain Brenton. Under the identification description it states, "You may change the name of this computer or the name of the domain that it manages." This lets you know that this machine is a PDC.

While an NT server can be promoted from a regular server to a BDC and from a BDC to a PDC, once a system has become a PDC the operating system must be reinstalled to make it anything else. This is in contrast to NDS on IntraNetWare, which allows you to promote or demote any server on-the-fly.

If you click the Change button, you are presented with the dialog box shown in Figure 12.4. Because this system is already a PDC, you are not allowed to make it a BDC or join another domain. Your only options are to change the server's name or the name of the domain it is responsible for. If you change your domain name, you will also be required to reconfigure your BDC servers.

FIGURE 12.3:

The Identification tab for this NT server identifies its Net-BIOS name, the domain, and the fact that it is a PDC.

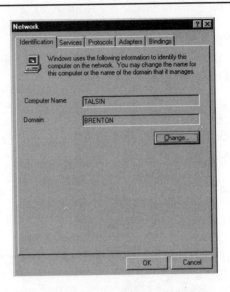

FIGURE 12.4:

Because this system is already a PDC, the only options are to change its name or to change the domain name.

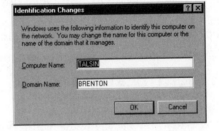

Once your changes are complete you can continue through the remaining tabs or reboot the server to initialize your changes.

Configuring Network Services

Your next option is to configure network services. *Services* are the applications you can make available to your clients using the protocols you will configure in the next step. For example, if you will be running IP on your network, you can install the IIS server to provide Web, FTP, and Gopher access to this system. Figure 12.5 is a sample Network Services tab with a number of supported services installed.

FIGURE 12.5:

A sample Network Services tab—this is where you will install the network applications and connectivity options that you will make available to your clients.

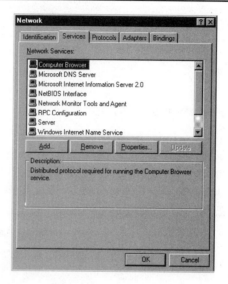

By clicking the Add or Remove buttons, you can selectively choose which services to run on the server. The Properties button is only available for some services. For example, Figure 12.6 is the configurable properties for the Server services. These options allow the server to be optimized based upon your system requirements.

> **NOTE**
> Pay close attention to your configuration when you are adding and removing services. NT does not always track the relationship between installed services and protocols. For example, if you remove IP as a protocol from the system, it will not automatically remove support for any IP applications (DNCP, DNS, and so on). In fact you may find yourself *reinstalling* the protocol just to remove the services. For example, let's assume you no longer require IP services on the system and so you remove IP from the list of protocols. Later, you realize that you forgot to remove the IIS server as well. When you attempt to remove it, NT will require you to reinstall IP prior to removing the IIS service.

FIGURE 12.6:

Server properties under the Services tab—these settings allow the server to be tuned based upon its intended use.

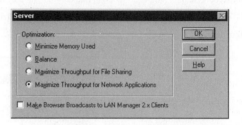

Available Services

The following is a list of available services that come with NT Server and a brief description of each. Figure 12.7 shows the menu for adding additional services. The listed services are those that ship with NT Server. The Have Disk option can be used for adding services created by third-party developers.

FIGURE 12.7:

The menu for adding additional services to the NT server

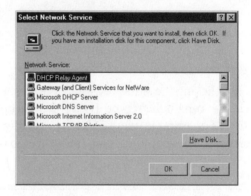

Computer Browser   When NetBIOS and NetBEUI are used, the Computer Browser creates and maintains a list of system names on the network. It also provides this list to applications running on the system such as the Network Neighborhood. The Computer Browser properties allow you to add additional domains to be checked for system names.

DHCP Relay Agent   When a DHCP client and server exist on two separate network segments, the DCHP Relay Agent acts as a proxy between the two systems.

The DHCP Relay Agent ensures that the client's DHCP requests are passed along to the segment where the DHCP server resides. In turn, it also ensures that the replies sent by the server make it back to the client. The benefit of a DHCP Relay Agent is that it removes the necessity of having a separate DHCP server on each logical network. The relay agent can be located on the same network segment as the client or at the border between the client's and the DHCP server's network segments (acting as a router).

The DHCP Relay Agent requires the IP protocol to be installed. It also requires the IP address of at least one DHCP server.

Gateway (and Client) Services for NetWare   This service allows an NT server to access file and print services on a NetWare server. The client portion of the services allows the server to log on to the NetWare server in a fashion similar to any NetWare client. The logon script can be processed, and the NT server is allowed to map drive letters pointing to the file system on the NetWare server.

The gateway portion of the service allows users running only NetBEUI to access files on the NetWare server through the NT server. The gateway has a separate authentication configuration from that used by the client. Once the gateway has authenticated and mapped drive letters to the NetWare server, it can make these drives available as shares.

The gateway allows the NT server to create share names for each of the drive letters mapped to the NetWare server. From the user's perspective, these shares appear to be located on the NT server, not the NetWare server. Figure 12.8 shows how this share may be configured. The NT server Loki logs on to the NetWare server Athena using IPX, just like any other client. As part of the logon process, Loki maps drive G: to the apps directory on VOL1 of Athena.

The gateway allows Loki to share drive G: as \\Loki\apps. The NT clients can then direct file requests to Loki using NetBEUI. Any requests received by Loki are translated to IPX and passed along to Athena. When a reply is received, Loki translates the response to NetBEUI and passes it along to the client. As far as Loki clients are concerned, the shared files reside on Loki.

While the gateway service is a good way to bridge the gap between NT and NetWare, the translation does reduce file access speed. The gateway is designed to be a migration aid or to provide occasional access to files on the NetWare server. When heavy NetWare file access is required (such as compiling code or database searches), direct access should be used.

FIGURE 12.8:

The NT client and gateway services for NetWare allow an NT server to share files located on a NetWare server.

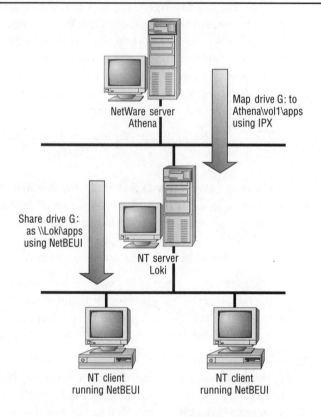

NetWare server
Athena

Map drive G: to
Athena\vol1\apps
using IPX

Share drive G:
as \\Loki\apps
using NetBEUI

NT server
Loki

NT client
running NetBEUI

NT client
running NetBEUI

Once the gateway service is installed, a new button called Network Access Order appears at the bottom of the Services tab. Clicking this button produces the window shown in Figure 12.9. The Network Access Order dialog box allows you to configure the order in which the NT server attempts to find resources.

FIGURE 12.9:

The Network Access Order dialog box allows you to select the order in which the NT server should search for resources.

With the configuration shown in Figure 12.9, the NT server will look for Net-Ware resources (IPX) before it will look for Windows resources (NetBEUI). For example, if you tell the NT server to search for a specific computer name, it will first attempt to access the resource via IPX. If the name is not found, it then looks for the name using NetBEUI.

TIP

If the NT server will be authenticating during startup to all the NetWare servers it needs access to, change the network access order so that "Microsoft Windows Network" precedes the "NetWare or Compatible Network." This will allow the NT server to discover other Windows systems (such as Windows 95 machines with file sharing enabled) faster.

The NetWare client and gateway services require that the NwLink IPX/SPX-compatible transport protocol be installed. The client portion creates an icon on the Control Panel (labeled GSNW) so that a preferred server or tree may be selected. There is a Enable Gateway button in the Configure Gateway dialog box, shown in Figure 12.10, which allows for the gateway portion of the services to be enabled and configured. The Configure Gateway dialog box also accepts the account information required to connect with the NetWare server and to share information for each of the drives.

FIGURE 12.10:

The Configure Gateway dialog box allows you to enable or disable the NetWare gateway and enter account information.

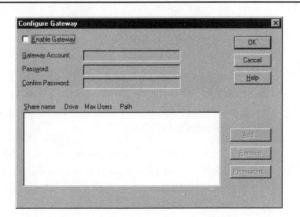

Microsoft DHCP Server   The DHCP server allows the NT server to provide IP address information to network clients automatically. When a client sends out a DHCP request, it can receive all the information required to communicate on an IP network, including an IP address, subnet mask, domain name, and DNS server.

The DHCP server requires that the IP protocol be installed. When the DHCP server is installed, it automatically adds a menu option for the DHCP manager to the Administrative Tools menu.

Microsoft DNS Server   The Microsoft DNS server allows the NT server to respond to clients and other DNS servers with IP domain name information. When the DNS server is configured to use WINS resolution, host name information is provided by WINS, based upon NetBIOS system names.

A DNS server normally requires that host name information be manually maintained in a set of text files. If a machine changes its IP address, the DNS tables must be updated to reflect this change. If DHCP is used to provide IP address information, DNS has no way of knowing which host name will be assigned to which IP address.

By using WINS resolution, the DNS server can query the WINS server for host information. The DNS server passes the query along to WINS, which uses its Net-BIOS table to match an IP address to a host name. The WINS server then returns this information to the DNS server. To a client querying a DNS server, the transaction is transparent. As far as the client is concerned, the DNS server is solely responsible for responding to the request. The two services do not need to be configured on the same NT server.

The DNS server requires that the IP protocol be installed. When the DNS server is installed, it automatically adds a menu option for the DNS manager to the Administrative Tools menu.

Microsoft Internet Information Server (IIS) 4.0   The Microsoft Internet Information Server adds Web, FTP, and Gopher functionality to NT Server. Once it is installed, clients can access HTML pages, transfer files via FTP, and perform Gopher searches for files.

By default, the installation creates the directory `InetPub` and places four directories inside it. The first three are the root directories for each of the three servers. All files and directories for each of the three services are to be placed under their respective root directory.

The fourth directory is for scripts. Web applications developed with CGI, WINCGI, Visual Basic, or Perl can be stored in this directory. It also contains some sample scripts as well as a few development tools.

The IIS requires that IP be installed. During IIS installation, a menu folder called Microsoft Internet Server is created for the management tools required for these services.

Microsoft TCP/IP Printing   Microsoft's TCP/IP printing allows an NT server to support Unix printing, referred to as line printer daemon (lpd). TCP/IP printing allows the NT server to print to a print server that supports lpd, or to a Unix system that has a directly connected printer.

IP printing also allows the NT server to act as a printing gateway for Microsoft clients. The NT server connects to lpd via IP, and it can advertise this printer as a shared resource on NetBEUI. Microsoft clients using only NetBEUI can send print jobs to this advertised share. The NT server then forwards these jobs on to the lpd printer.

Microsoft TCP/IP printing requires that the IP protocol be installed. During installation, it adds a new printer port type called LPR, as shown in Figure 12.11. LPR is *Line Printer Remote,* which provides remote access to lpd printers.

FIGURE 12.11:

Installing IP printing adds an additional printer port, called the LPR port, through which an NT server can access Unix printers.

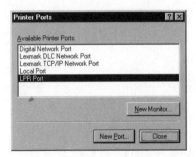

NetBIOS Interface   The NetBIOS interface provides backward compatibility with LAN MAN systems that do not use the NetBEUI protocol for communications.

Network Monitor Agent   The Network Monitor agent allows the NT server to be remotely accessed and monitored by systems running the NT Server Network Monitoring Tools.

Network Monitor Tools and Agent   Network Monitor installs a network analyzer similar to Novell's LANalyzer or Network General's Sniffer, except that it can only capture broadcast frames or traffic from or to the NT server. This network monitoring tool allows the server to capture and decode network frames for the purpose of analysis. Figure 12.12 shows a typical packet capture with the Network Monitor. The tool displays the source and destination address of each system, as well as the protocol in use.

FIGURE 12.12:

The network monitoring tool can capture network traffic so that it can be decoded and analyzed.

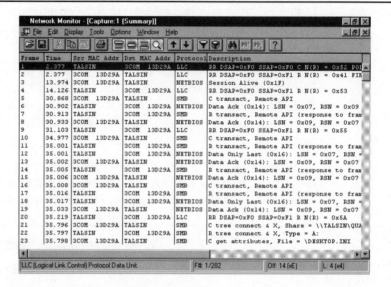

Network Monitor is a great tool for diagnosing problems or analyzing traffic patterns on the network. It is a bit limited, however, in that it can only monitor server-centric traffic.

Remote Access Service (RAS) The Remote Access Service allows the NT server to provide dial-in access to the server and other network resources. Clients can dial in to RAS and authenticate using their standard Microsoft username and password.

The Remote Access Setup dialog box, shown in Figure 12.13, allows you to select which of the modems that are attached to the server to dedicate to RAS use. If you attempt to install RAS without any modems configured, it will warn you and offer to start the modem configuration utility. This box also allows you to select which modems RAS should monitor for dial-in activity.

FIGURE 12.13:

The Remote Access Setup
dialog box

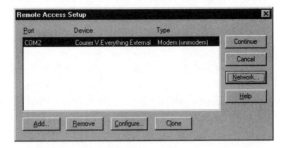

RAS allows you to select whether dial-in users will be allowed to access just the RAS server or will be granted full network access. If network access is allowed, RAS lets you select which protocols are acceptable for dial-in access.

For example, if you wish to give dial-in users access to your NT and NetWare servers, but do not wish to give them access to the Internet, simply disable the IP protocol. The only drawback is that this is a global setting; it is not configurable on a user-by-user basis. A network administrator who wants to enable IP services just for their own account, say for network diagnostic purposes (for example, to ensure that the Dilbert site and Subspace arena servers are still accessible), will need to find some other method of accessing the network remotely. Figure 12.14 shows the Network Configuration dialog box.

FIGURE 12.14:

The Network Configuration
dialog box allows the administrator to select which protocols are available during
dial-in access.

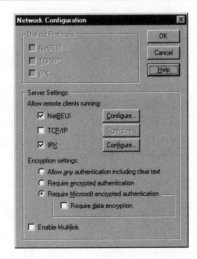

RAS requires that the NetBIOS interface service be installed. During RAS installation, a menu option for the Remote Access Manager is added to the Administrative Tools menu.

Remoteboot Service   The Remoteboot service allows the NT server to boot DOS, Windows 3.1, and Windows 95 workstations remotely. Windows for Workgroup clients are not supported. This allows the use of network clients that do not have any means of internal storage (no floppy or hard drive). The client's network card must have a *boot PROM* installed in order to access its required initialization files on the NT server. 3COM-, AMD-, Intel SMC-, and NE2000-compatible network cards are supported.

When a diskless client first powers up, the boot PROM sends out a network broadcast requesting the system's startup files. When Remoteboot is installed on the NT server, it allows the server to reply to these requests with the initialization files that the client requires.

Remoteboot Manager allows the NT administrator to configure the type of startup information the client receives. The NT administrator first creates a workstation profile, which describes what type of network cards will be used in the workstation, as well as which operating system they will be running. Figure 12.15 shows the New Profile dialog box. Enter the operating system in the Description text box and select the type of network card to be used by the client. This combination can be given a profile name in the Profile Name text box for later use when the individual workstations are configured.

FIGURE 12.15:

The New Profile dialog box

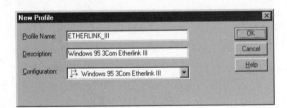

Once a profile is created, each individual workstation can be configured. Figure 12.16 shows the New Remoteboot Workstation dialog box. The Adapter ID field requires the MAC address for the workstation to be configured. This address is used by the workstation when it queries the server for its configuration information. The remoteboot service can provide the workstation with a unique system name, IP address (if DHCP is not used), and all the files required to initialize the operating system. These files are stored as system images on the NT server.

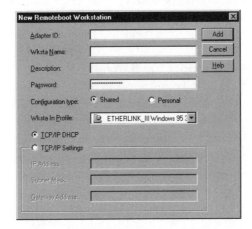

The Remoteboot service requires that the DLC protocol be installed. During Remoteboot installation, a menu option for the Remoteboot Manager is added to the Administrative Tools menu. Remoteboot does not automatically initialize during system startup. It must be manually started as a service or have its startup changed from manual to automatic.

RIP for Internet Protocol   The RIP for Internet Protocol service allows the NT server to use and propagate routing information broadcasts for the IP protocol. RIP is the only dynamic routing protocol supported for IP. NT Server does not support any IP border gateway or link-state routing protocols.

RIP for Internet Protocol requires that the IP protocol be installed.

RIP for NWLink IPX/SPX-Compatible Transport   The RIP for NWLink service allows the NT server to propagate routing information broadcasts for the IPX protocol. This service is typically enabled when the NT server will be acting as a router and needs to propagate IPX network information. NT Server supports only RIP routing with the IPX protocol. Link-state routing is not supported. If the NT server is to coexist on a network with IntraNetWare servers, the IntraNetWare servers must have backward compatibility with RIP enabled.

There are no properties for NWLink RIP, only a dialog box that prompts you to enable or disable the forwarding of NetBIOS over IPX frames (referred to as type 20 propagation). RIP for NWLink requires that the NwLink IPX/SPX-Compatible Transport protocol be installed.

RPC Configuration   The RPC Configuration service enables NT Server support for Remote Procedure Call (RPC). RPC is used by some applications to exchange information and functionality at a peer-to-peer level.

RPC Support for Banyan   RPC Support for Banyan allows RPC-enabled applications running on an NT server to exchange information with their counterpart applications operating on a Banyan VINES server.

SAP Agent   The SAP agent allows an NT server to propagate IPX Service Advertising Protocol (SAP) broadcasts. This service is typically used when the NT server will be acting as a router and needs to propagate IPX service information.

The SAP agent requires that the NWLink IPX/SPX-Compatible Transport protocol be installed.

Server   The Server service is what allows the NT server to offer file and print services to network clients. This service is installed by default and allows clients to communicate to the server via NetBEUI. Without the Server service, the NT system can only offer application services.

The Server service requires that the NetBEUI protocol be installed.

Services for Macintosh   Services for Macintosh installs all the required software components to allow Macintosh computers to exchange files on an NT server.

The Microsoft AppleTalk Protocol Properties dialog box allows the administrator to choose which zone the NT server will reside in. The administrator can also configure whether the NT will act as a "soft" seed and discover the local network addresses or act as a router and seed the network. When the server acts as a seed, zone names can also be assigned and at least one zone name must be specified. Figure 12.17 shows the Routing tab of the Microsoft AppleTalk Protocol Properties dialog box.

Services for Macintosh requires that at least one NT Server drive be configured as an NTFS partition. Software translation, along with NTFS's support for extended files, is used to allow a connected Mac system to save and retrieve file information. Because Services for Macintosh installs all the required software, no additional protocol loading is required.

When Services for Macintosh are installed, the NT server can learn the network address range by acting as a soft seed, or it can define the network range by acting as the seed router.

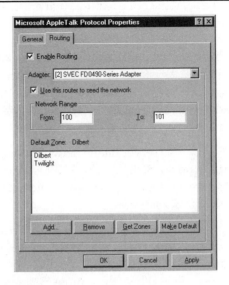

Simple TCP/IP Services   Simple TCP/IP Services installs support for some fun but little-used IP applications such as Echo and Quote of the Day. The quote of the day can serve up such selections as, "We want a few mad people now. See where the sane ones have landed us!" by George Bernard Shaw (1856-1950).

The Simple TCP/IP Services requires that the IP protocol be installed.

SNMP Service   The SNMP service allows the NT server to be monitored by an SNMP management station. It also allows the performance monitor on the NT server to monitor IP statistics as well as statistics for IP applications (DNS, WINS, and so on).

When the SNMP service is installed, the NT server can send configuration and performance information to an SNMP management station such as Hewlett-Packard's HP Openview. This allows the status of the NT server, as well as other SNMP devices, to be monitored from a central location. Monitoring can be performed over the IP or IPX protocol.

The SNMP service also adds functionality to the NT Performance Monitor. For example, it allows you to monitor the number of IP packets with errors or the number of WINS queries the server has received. Both SNMP and the applicable service must be installed for these features to be added to Performance Monitor.

The SNMP service requires that either the IP or IPX protocol be installed for station monitoring.

Windows Internet Name Service (WINS) A WINS server allows NetBIOS or NetBEUI systems to communicate across a router using IP encapsulation of NetBIOS. The WINS server acts as a NetBIOS Name Server (NBNS) for p-node and h-node systems located on the NT server's local subnet. WINS stores the system's NetBIOS name and its IP address.

Each WINS server on the network periodically updates the other WINS servers with a copy of its table. The result is a dynamic list, mapping NetBIOS names to IP addresses for every system on the network. A copy of the list is then stored on each WINS server.

When a p-node system needs the address of another NetBIOS system, it sends a discovery packet to its local WINS server. If the system in question happens to be located on a remote subnet, the WINS server returns the remote system's IP address. This allows the remote system to be discovered without propagating broadcast frames throughout the network. When h-nodes are used, the functionality is identical.

WINS requires that the IP protocol be installed. During WINS installation, a menu option for the WINS Manager is added to the Administrative Tools menu.

Workstation The Workstation service is the counterpart to the Server service. It allows the NT server to access file and printer shares on other computers acting as a client. The Workstation service requires that the NetBEUI protocol be installed.

Once you have completed configuring the services, you can continue through the remaining tabs or reboot the server to initialize your changes.

Configuring Network Protocols

Your next option is to configure network protocols. Protocols provide the means of communication required to support the applications reviewed in the last section. For example, if you decided to install the DNS services, you must ensure that the IP protocol is installed and configured. Figure 12.18 shows a sample Protocols tab.

FIGURE 12.18:

All the protocols needed to support your required services can be installed from the Protocols tab of the Network window.

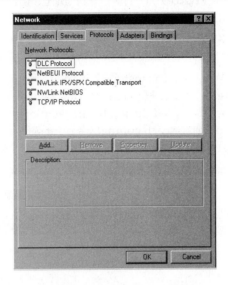

The Add and Remove buttons allow you to choose which protocols you require. The Properties button allows you to configure any protocol parameters, if required. Figure 12.19 shows the list of available protocols when the Add button is selected. The Have Disk button is used to add third-party protocol support.

FIGURE 12.19:

The Select Network Protocol dialog box

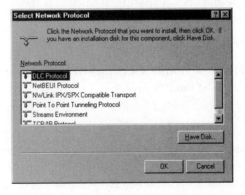

Available Protocols

The following is a list of available protocols that come with NT Server and a brief description of each.

DLC Protocol   The Data Link Control (DLC) protocol provides applications with hardware-level communications (using MAC addresses). It provides local segment communications only. DLC is used by IBM mainframes as well as print server manufacturers such as HP.

When DLC is installed, it adds additional printer port drivers, as shown in Figure 12.20. The Hewlett-Packard Network Port and the Lexmark DLC Network Port are added during the installation of the DLC protocol. This adds print server support for each company's print server products. The DLC protocol has no configurable properties.

FIGURE 12.20:

The Printer Ports dialog box

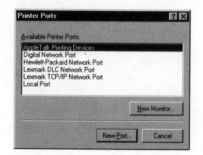

NetBEUI Protocol   The NetBEUI protocol provides support for NT Server file and printer sharing. If Microsoft clients will be accessing the NT server for file and print services, this protocol should be installed. NetBEUI has no configurable properties.

NWLink IPX/SPX-Compatible Transport   NWLink is Microsoft's implementation of the IPX protocol. This protocol is required if the NT server needs to communicate with a NetWare server (either as a client or as a gateway).

When NWLink is installed, the NT server can be assigned an internal IPX network number just like an IntraNetWare server, or this field can be left blank. The internal IPX number is used when you wish to have the NT server transmit SAP frames and emulate a NetWare server. This functionality requires the SAP agent to be installed as well.

NT Server can also be configured either to auto-detect network cards or to manually assign an IPX network address to each one. Figure 12.21 shows the General tab of the NWLink IPX/SPX Properties window. When the Manual Frame Type

Detection button is selected, you must specify which NetWare frame type and what IPX network number to use for the selected network card. If the NT server is the only IPX server or router on a particular network segment, the frame type and address should be configured manually.

FIGURE 12.21:

The General tab of the NWLink IPX/SPX Properties window

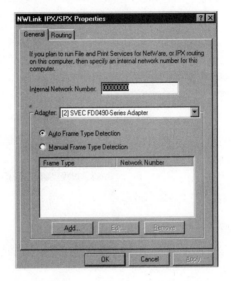

NWLink NetBIOS   NWLink NetBIOS is Microsoft's implementation of NetBIOS over IPX (referred to as type 20 IPX packets). Enabling the NWLink NetBIOS protocol allows the NT server to exchange type 20 IPX packets with other network devices.

If the server is acting as a router, RIP for NWLink must have type 20 propagation enabled in order for an NT server to forward these packets from one network segment to another.

NWLink for NetBIOS has no configurable properties.

Point-to-Point Tunneling Protocol (PPTP)   The PPTP protocol allows a user to access an RAS server over an insecure network such as the Internet. PPTP sets up a virtual private network (VPN) between the client and the RAS server.

The PPTP Configuration dialog box, shown in Figure 12.22, allows the administrator to configure how many VPN sessions may be set up to the server. Once this value is set, you will be prompted to install and configure the RAS server as well.

FIGURE 12.22:

Configure how many VPN sessions will be supported by the server in the PPTP Configuration dialog box.

As part of the RAS server configuration, you can define the VPN sessions as potential ports for users to use when connecting to the RAS server. The Remote Access Setup dialog box is shown in Figure 12.23 with one VPN port available for network sessions.

FIGURE 12.23:

Once you have defined the number of available VPN sessions, you can assign them as available connection ports for the RAS server to monitor.

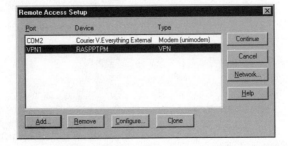

In order to connect to the RAS server over a VPN, the client must have an additional WAN driver that supports PPTP installed in their dial-up networking. Windows NT (both Server and Workstation) ships with a PPTP driver. A Windows 95 driver is available for download at Microsoft's Web site (www.microsoft.com).

The client can then connect to their ISP as they would for regular network access. Once they have complete the authentication process with the ISP, they can use the PPTP driver to access the RAS server. The authentication process uses the same logon name and password that the user enters when they are on the network.

Once a session is established, the user is provided services based upon the RAS server configuration as described above. The user can be limited to accessing just the RAS server or they can connect to other network resources. PPTP supports the tunneling of NetBEUI, IP, and IPX, so any resource using these protocols can be accessed.

When PPTP is used, the RAS server can be configured to accept only PPTP traffic, by selecting the Enable PPTP Filtering button. This is a good security feature because it permits only PPTP traffic to access the server. Used in combination with a good firewall, this feature can help ensure that "undesirables" do not access your NT server from the Internet. If the NT server will be providing Web or FTP services to the Internet as well, leave PPTP filtering disabled. PPTP filtering is configured under the Advanced IP Addressing dialog box, as shown in Figure 12.24.

FIGURE 12.24:

PPTP filtering can be enabled from the Advanced IP Addressing dialog box.

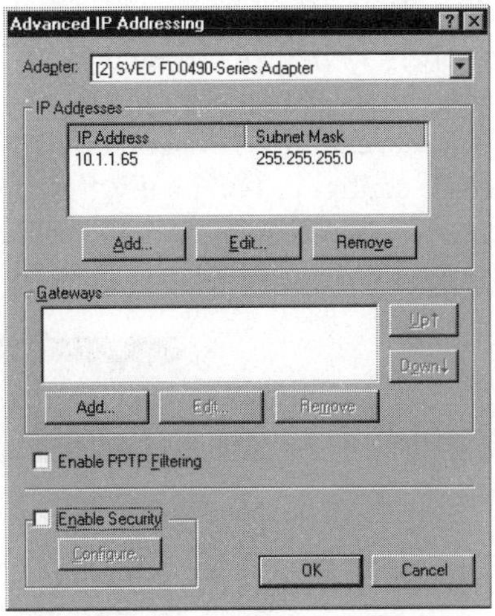

PPTP uses the Password Authentication Protocol (PAP) and Challenge Handshake Authentication Protocol (CHAP) as defined in Request For Comment (RFC) 1334 for performing session authentication. These authentication methods were designed for the Point-to-Point (PPP) protocol, which is normally used over a dial-up link. With this in mind, security is not exactly *bulletproof*. PAP sends passwords as clear text, and CHAP only occasionally verifies that the remote system is authentic.

Through RAS, PPTP supports bulk data encryption with a 40-bit session key that is negotiated once authentication is complete. This means that the encryption key is transmitted between the two systems during the remote session. While this is in no way as secure as a public-private encryption key scheme, it is certainly more secure than using Telnet or FTP to access network resources.

Streams   Streams provide encapsulation of other network protocols such as IPX or IP. By wrapping around the transport protocol, they can provide a common interface to applications as well as Data Link layer drivers. Streaming is not a true protocol per se, as it relies on the encapsulated protocol to provide transport services.

Streaming is primarily for the use of third-party protocols. It allows developers to port other transports to NT using streams as a common interface. The Streams option has no configurable properties.

TCP/IP   TCP/IP adds support for the IP protocol. Figure 12.25 shows the Microsoft TCP/IP Properties window. This window allows the administrator to configure an IP address for each interface or receive the address automatically from a DHCP server. If this NT server will be running the DHCP service, IP addresses should be configured manually. If more than one IP address is required on a given interface, configure it in the Advanced Addressing dialog box (see Figure 12.24).

FIGURE 12.25:

The IP Address tab of the Microsoft TCP/IP Properties window

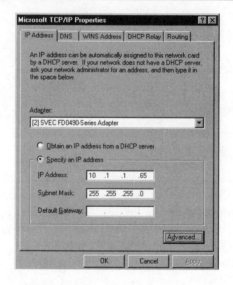

As you look at Figure 12.25, note that a default gateway has not been set. This server must have the RIP for Internet Protocol service installed if it needs to communicate with unknown subnets. Known subnets can be configured with the IPCONFIG command-line utility.

If the DNS tab is selected, an IP host name and domain can be set. The host name should match the server's NetBIOS machine name for consistency. The DNS servers this machine should use when resolving IP host names can also be configured in this dialog box. Multiple DNS servers can be specified for redundancy. If the first DNS server does not respond to queries, the system can redirect them to the second DNS server listed.

When the WINS Address tab is selected, the IP address of the local WINS servers can be identified. The WINS server is the system to be referenced when the NT server needs to resolve a NetBIOS name to an address. The *scope ID* allows the server to be identified as part of a specific group of NetBIOS machines. The scope ID follows a hierarchical structure similar to DNS. Refer to the NetBIOS section of Chapter 6 for more information on scope IDs.

On the DHCP Relay tab, you can enter the IP address for the DHCP server that is responsible for the local subnet. When an IP address is entered, the NT server will forward any bootp or DHCP requests it receives to the DHCP server. It is expected that the DHCP server is not located on the local subnet, as it would then be able to receive and reply to DHCP requests directly. This parameter is only used when the DHCP server is not located on the same network as the NT server.

The Routing tab allows IP routing to be enabled or disabled. This option is only needed when there are two or more network cards in the server. Selecting the check box allows the NT server to route IP packets from one network interface to another.

Once you have completed changes to your protocols you can continue through the remaining tabs or reboot the server to initialize your changes.

Adapters

The Adapters tab in the Network window, shown in Figure 12.26, allows you to install and configure NICs in the NT server. From here you can add and remove network adapters. When a newer revision driver is required, simply select the appropriate card and press the Update button. You will be prompted to install the disk with the updated Microsoft NT driver.

The Properties button allows you to configure operation parameters. If your network card requires an interrupt or an I/O port setting, you will be prompted for these values under Properties. Windows NT does not support Plug and Play, so all configuration parameters must be set manually if they cannot be detected.

FIGURE 12.26:

The Network Adapters tab

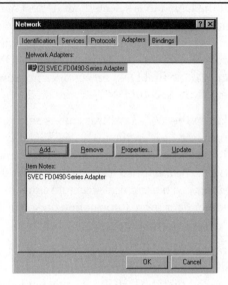

Once you have completed changes to your Adapter tab you can move on to Bindings or reboot the server to initialize your changes.

Bindings

The Bindings tab allows you to configure the order in which the NT server should utilize the installed protocols. This order should reflect the communication characteristics of your network. Separate orders can be defined for the NetBIOS interface, server connectivity, and workstation connectivity. The Network Monitor Tools and Agent object defines which protocols will be available for decoding. Figure 12.27 shows the Bindings tab.

For example, assume your workstation bindings list the NetBEUI protocol and then WINS Client (TCP/IP). You launch Explorer and tell it to search for the computer Phoenix, which is not currently listed in your network neighborhood. Because of the workstation bindings order, the NT server will first attempt to find this system using NetBEUI. If this fails, it will then use WINS.

Set the protocol binding order to reflect which communication protocols your system will use the most. For example, if most of the resources you are likely to access are NetBEUI systems located on a remote network, set WINS at the top of the workstation binding order.

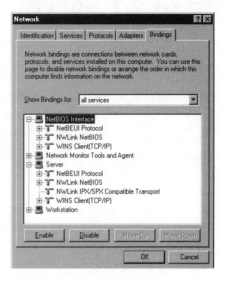

FIGURE 12.27:

The Bindings tab of the
Network window

Saving Your Changes

Once your network configuration is complete, select the OK button and reboot
the system to initialize your changes. If you accidentally add the wrong protocol
or service during the installation process, you may have to reboot the server anyway before the server will let you remove it. Once the reboot is complete and the
service database is unlocked, you can remove the unneeded service or protocol.
You will then have to reboot the system one last time to finalize the configuration.

NT Server IP Applications

Describing the setup and administration of all of NT Server's IP applications is
beyond the scope of this book. For configuration of NT Server's IP applications,
see Morgan Stern and Tom Rasmussen's *Building Intranets on NT, NetWare, and
Solaris* (Sybex, 1997). Stern and Rasmussen's book is an excellent reference on
how to set up and administer these IP applications. The book also covers development tools such as FrontPage.

The Future of NT Server

The next version of NT Server (5.0) is being touted by Microsoft as the greatest thing since sliced bread. While the expected feature list is more than impressive, many doubt that all the features will make it into the final product. This is certainly plausible, as in the past Microsoft has sometimes failed to implement all the features they have promised for a specific revision. They have even been known to retract features included in beta versions prior to final release.

At the time of this writing, the following features have been advertised for NT Server 5.0:

- Active Directory, a domain system that mimics Novell's NDS by allowing domains to be tied together without needing to create trust relationship. Active Directory also provides a central point of management for all account administration.

- Clustering, which allows multiple servers to share the load as if they were one physical system. Clustering also adds fault tolerance in case of a system failure.

- Support for disk quotas and file system encryption.

- Distributed security services.

- Distributed File System (DFS) support, which allows NT Server to use a distributed file system similar to the Network File System (NFS) protocol.

- Microsoft Management Console, which provides a central point of management for all NT servers.

- Support for Quality of Service (QoS) over TCP/IP.

- A scheduler similar to Unix's `cron`.

- An automatic application installer, which allows the system administrator to push applications out to the user's desktop.

- Terminal server ability, which integrates WinFrame functionality into the base operating system.

- Security improvements such as direct support for the Kerberos authentication system, public encryption key certificate services, IPSEC support and support for smart cards.

Summary

You should now have a good understanding of how to configure NT Server for network communications. You should also be familiar with the applications and features provided by this NOS.

In Chapter 13 we will look at Unix, the granddaddy of NOSs. We will discuss why it has remained popular after so many years, as well as the features it can provide that no other NOS has been able to fully replicate.

CHAPTER
THIRTEEN

Unix/Linux

- Flavors of Unix

- A brief history of Linux

- The Linux core OS and file system

- Account administration and security features

- Linux networking, connectivity, and protocol support

- IP applications in Linux

- Linux configuration and MAKE files

- The SAMBA suite

- The future of Linux

Developed in 1969 at Bell Labs, Unix is by far the oldest distributed NOS in use today. Its creation is credited to Ken Thompson, who was working at that time for Bell Labs on the Multiplex Information Computing System (MULTICS) for a General Electric mainframe. Bell Labs eventually dropped the project, and with it went a very important piece of software, a game called Space Travel.

It is rumored that Ken set out to create a new operating system to which the game could be ported. MULTICS assembly code was rewritten for an available DEC PDP-7, and the new operating system was named UNICS (I'm sure the emasculation reference was not intentional).

Bell Labs eventually took interest in UNICS once additional functionality was added (beyond the game Space Travel) which gave the operating system some commercial appeal. By 1972 it was named Unix and had an installed base of 10 computers. In 1973 Thompson and Dennis Richie rewrote the kernel in C, which made the operating system much more portable.

In 1974 the IP protocol was developed and integrated into the Unix operating system. No longer were multiple terminals required to access a single Unix system. A shared medium called Ethernet could be used to access the system. Unix had become a true NOS.

In the mid-70s Bell Labs started releasing Unix to universities. Since Ma Bell was still regulated at the time, they were not allowed to profit from Unix's sales. For this reason, only a minimal fee was charged for the Unix source code, which helped to make it widely available.

Once Unix hit the universities, its development expanded through the (figurative) injection of fresh blood. Students began improving the code and adding features. So dramatic were these changes at the University of California at Berkeley that Berkeley began distributing their own flavor of Unix called the Berkeley Software distribution (BSD). The Unix version that continued to be developed by Bell Labs is known as System V(5).

Many versions of Unix exist today, including AIX, BSDI, Digital UNIX, FreeBSD, HP-UX, IRIX, NetBSD, OpenBSD, Pyramid, SCO, Solaris, SunOS BSD, and Linux. Most of these are based on either System 5 release 4.x or BSD Unix. Linux is sometimes described as a "Unix clone" or "based on Unix," but aside from the fact it uses a completely rewritten kernel, Linux is for all practical purposes another Unix variant.

In 1983 TCP/IP, or just IP as it's now called, became the official protocol of the Internet. Around this same time, none other than Microsoft released the first PC-compatible version of Unix.

So Many Flavors, So Few Pages

While all Unix implementations are similar, each has its own particular feel. Commands and their uses are fairly consistent between different flavors. The difference is that vendors may choose different locations to store particular executables or startup scripts. Some versions may even include a few extra commands that others do not.

The latter is rarely a problem if you understand C code. Most Unix utilities are available as source code which can be compiled to run on your specific Unix platform. For example, if you would like to send and receive Internet mail but do not have a copy of Sendmail on your system, you can obtain the source files for free from a number of FTP sites on the Internet. Then you simply adjust the MAKE file to fit your operating system and run the source through your compiler.

NOTE   A MAKE file is a plain text file that customizes the source code as it is compiled into an executable. Usually, modifying this file is a simple matter of un-commenting the lines that pertain to your implementation of Unix.

It is beyond the scope of this book to pay appropriate attention to every flavor of Unix. Entire books can be written—and have been—on any given specific implementation. This is why we will focus on just a single flavor. As mentioned above, most Unix applications are portable, so what we discuss for one particular version can usually be applied to any other.

We have chosen to focus on the Linux implementation of Unix for a number of reasons. The first is that it holds true to the roots of Unix in being a collaborative effort. Linux has been developed over the Internet on a mostly volunteer basis. The second is that it is free software and accessible to all who wish to use it.

The fact that Linux has been and continues to be developed by a worldwide group of mainly volunteer programmers should not necessarily discourage its consideration for serious use in business. As of this writing, Linux running the

Apache Web server is the most popular Web server configuration for Internet service providers. At least as a server platform, it's worth considering because it can support a mix of Apple, Windows, and Unix clients, and has plenty of Internet server software choices. While the initial cost is not necessarily what you should base your choice of a server on, Linux costs either nothing (if downloaded from the Internet) or no more than $50 for the set of installation files and utilities on CD-ROM. Provided you run a "stable release" of Linux, it is quite stable indeed (many users report uninterrupted up time of months, or even years).

When downloading Linux installation files, be sure to look for a "stable release" rather than a "developer release" version. "Developer release" versions are incremental updates that may have problems. Each developer release is followed eventually by a stable release, which helps ensure that the latest set of updates and revisions are in synch with each other. The CD-ROM sets available in software shops and in some bookstores typically contain the more stable release versions.

Linux History

Linux (pronounced in the US as Lih' nux) was first developed in 1991 by Linus Torvalds, a Finnish student. He developed a minimal Unix operating system and posted a message to an Internet newsgroup, asking if anyone would be interested in helping to develop it.

What followed shows the true power of the Internet as a method of collaboration. First tens, then hundreds of individuals began dedicating their free time to developing Linux. Now the number of volunteers has grown into the thousands. Individuals volunteer their time to perform such tasks as kernel debugging, quality control, and writing documentation. The forum for this development has been the Free Software Foundation's GNU (GNU's Not Unix!) project.

NOTE   You can learn more about GNU at the project's Web site: **www.gnu.org**.

The result is a production-class operating system that rivals, and even arguably exceeds, commercial releases of Unix available today. Its stability and breadth of features has captured the attention of network administrators who have deployed Linux for file, print, and Web servers. Linux has even been recognized by *InfoWorld* magazine, who named it their desktop operating system of the year in 1996.

In April 1997 Linux even made it onto the space shuttle to be used in monitoring hydroponics experiments. Who could have guessed that this small band of loosely knit hackers would create an operating system that would literally reach for the stars?

Linux Is Copyleft Software

Linux is not shareware or public domain freeware. It has been copyrighted by Linus through the Free Software Foundation's GNU General Public License (GPL). This is sometimes referred to as "copyleft" as it does not prevent you from freely distributing the software.

The GPL states that you are allowed to distribute the Linux software, provided:

- you do not attempt to further restrict or copyright your modification
- you make the source code available as part of the distribution

In effect, this means that you could create a 1000-node network using only Linux and not pay a dime in software charges.

The GPL does allow a software manufacturer to recoup some of their costs if they distribute the software to the public market. For example, you could decide to go into production selling CD-ROM releases of Linux without having to pay a royalty charge. You would, however:

- not be able to restrict usage of the software. If an individual wishes to purchase a single copy to load on 1000 machines, it is their right
- have to make the source code available as part of the distribution

All this has been done to ensure that Linux remains freely available to all who wish to use it.

Linux Features

As we discuss Linux, we will look specifically at a release developed by a company called Red Hat. There are many releases of Linux available. All provide the same core OS and are capable of running the same applications. The differences usually lie in the setup and configuration program as well as which applications are included.

Red Hat has made a name for itself by providing an extensive list of applications as well as an easy to use installation program. While you can purchase a CD-ROM copy of their Linux bundle for a minimal fee, they have also made their distribution freely available over the Internet via FTP.

> **NOTE** Unless you have a T1 connection to the Internet, you will probably want to purchase a copy of Linux on CD-ROM. The NOS has many features and can literally take days to install over a slow link. Purchasing Linux on CD-ROM is extremely reasonable when compared to other NOSs. Once you have installed the base operating system from CD-ROM, you can use your Internet connection to retrieve free updates.

Linux Setup

No matter how you choose to install Red Hat Linux (from CD-ROM, FTP, and so on), the installation processes are almost identical. If you purchase the CD-ROM, it is supplied with a single boot disk for initializing a minimal Linux kernel to perform the install. If you are installing over the Internet, you must first retrieve an image of the floppy from Red Hat's FTP site and create a boot disk using *rawwrite*.

> **NOTE** Rawwrite is a DOS-based utility that allows you to create floppy disks from disk image files. This allows the utility to use DOS while creating Unix-based floppies.

Once you have a bootable floppy (which can also be used for disaster recovery), simply boot the system and follow the prompts. As shown in Figure 13.1, you will be asked if you wish to install Linux from CD-ROM, hard drive, FTP, an NT or SAMBA share, or NFS. If you select CD-ROM, you simply identify the drive as either an IDE or a SCSI unit, and the device is automatically configured. If you select SAMBA, FTP, or NFS, you are walked through your network card configuration and will need to supply the name or IP address of a host where the installation files can be found.

From here on, the setup process is identical for both methods. While the installation program is ASCII-based and not a true GUI, it is sufficient for installing the software.

FIGURE 13.1:

Red Hat Linux allows you to decide which method of installation you would like to perform.

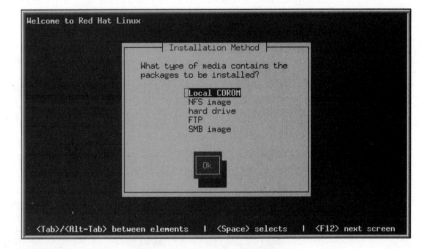

```
Welcome to Red Hat Linux

              ┤ Installation Method ├

          What type of media contains the
          packages to be installed?

              Local CDROM
              NFS image
              hard drive
              FTP
              SMB image


                    Ok


  <Tab>/<Alt-Tab> between elements  |  <Space> selects  |  <F12> next screen
```

One feature of the Red Hat installation is that it performs a dependency check for all the Linux components (packages) you've chosen to install. Unix uses programs and libraries that can be accessed by multiple applications. The benefit of this is a reduction in the amount of required disk space. Instead of each application requiring a full set of support files, they can share one or more sets of common routines. This reduces the amount of required storage space and makes upgrades far easier.

The Red Hat installation will verify the dependencies of each program you have selected to install. If a required program or library is missing, you will be informed and offered the opportunity to include it as part of the installation. This can be extremely helpful if you are doing a selective installation in order to save disk space.

Installation programs for Linux vary in the number of setup options offered. Fortunately, most of the current distributions include at least some hardware detection ability, which certainly helps to simplify the installation process. Be prepared, though, to answer a list of questions about any and all hardware installed in your system, including mouse and keyboard type, video adapter, IDE and SCSI hard drive controllers, and network adapters. If hardware detection isn't completely successful, you may need to supply IRQ, DMA, and I/O memory addresses for various pieces of hardware. For example, Figure 13.2 shows two applications that require the installation of XFree86 in order to run.

Because XFree86 was not selected as one of the packages to install, the dependency check is warning that these two programs will not run without it.

Two Linux packages that require the installation of another package, XFree86, in order to run

```
Red Hat Linux (C) 1997 Red Hat Software              Choose packages to install
                    ┌───────────── Unresolved Dependencies ─────────────┐
                    │ Some of the packages you have selected to          │
                    │ install require packages you have not              │
                    │ selected. If you just select Ok all of those       │
                    │ required packages will be installed.               │
                    │                                                    │
                    │   Package              Requirement                 │
                    │   Xconfigurator        XFree86                  #  │
                    │   mkxauth              XFree86                     │
                    │                                                    │
                    │                                                    │
                    │        [*] Install packages to satisfy dependencies│
                    │                                                    │
                    │         ┌────┐              ┌────────┐             │
                    │         │ Ok │              │ Cancel │             │
                    │         └────┘              └────────┘             │
                    └────────────────────────────────────────────────────┘
    <Tab>/<Alt-Tab> between elements   |   <Space> selects   |   <F12> next screen
```

NOTE   The term *Linux* technically applies only to the kernel, but by convention usually is taken to mean any of the several entire Linux distributions with all their supporting files. Some applications installed during the initial setup might more properly be called *system tools*. Note that a C compiler (and other programming tools) are also considered part of the Linux distribution, and in certain cases adding hardware support for some devices may involve running the kernel source code through the supplied compiler to produce a new kernel.

The rest of the setup walks the administrator through the required steps to get the system running and communicating on the network (such as creating user accounts and configuring IP networking). All selected network applications are set up to initialize during system startup (when applicable), but are not configured as part of the initial setup process.

For example, if the administrator chooses to install bind, Unix's DNS application, bind will be set up to initialize once its main configuration file, /ETC/ NAMED.BOOT, has been created. The install process will not, however, walk the administrator through the procedure of creating NAMED.BOOT, but rather will leave that to be accomplished once the installation is complete. For the novice

Unix administrator, this can prove a bit frustrating as the installation process gives no indication that the NAMED.BOOT file is required. Once the system is operational, however, there is extensive help available in text, HTML, and Post-Script format.

A minimal installation can be performed in about 40MB worth of disk space. A Linux system with only network-related tools (Web server, FTP, NFS, and so on) will require closer to 150MB. A full installation also includes a client-server relational database, desktop publishing tools, programming tools for six languages, games, and so on—over 800 software packages in all—and requires closer to 500MB of space.

Core OS

Linux is a fully preemptive, multitasking, multithreaded, and multiuser *Unix-like* environment. We say "Unix-like" because, while it includes extensions for System V and BSD, it utilizes a different software base.

Linux strives to meet the IEEE "Portable Operating System Interface for Computing Environments" (POSIX) specification. POSIX defines the application programming interface (API) between C language applications and the underlying operating system. POSIX's purpose is to ensure that compliant applications developed for one POSIX environment can be easily ported to another.

Linux is certainly one of the most "equal opportunity" operating systems when it comes to hardware selection. There are versions of Linux that will run on PC, Mac, SUN, DEC Alpha, PowerPC, MIPS, and even Amiga and Atari hardware platforms. Linux is not run on top of the original operating system, but rather replaces it. When an Intel or SUN SPARC is used, symmetrical multiple processors are supported.

NOTE   As mentioned, Linux is a work in progress by many volunteers. As such, the kernel is constantly under development. A standard has been created for identifying which kernels are considered *production* and which are considered *development*. When the character in the tenths place of the version number is even, the kernel is a stable release. If it is odd, it is considered work in progress. For example, 2.0, 2.4.5, and 3.6 would all be considered production. 2.1, 2.5.4, and 3.7 would all be considered development kernels.

Linux supports virtual memory. This means that like NT, Linux can execute programs larger than the available physical memory size. Linux also fully supports memory paging. Memory paging allows the system to selectively move portions of an executable to virtual memory, instead of the entire file. This allows infrequently accessed sections of the program's code to be placed in virtual memory while the heavier used sections are executed in faster physical memory. The result is quicker application speed and less delay from *memory shuffle*.

Like IntraNetWare, Linux supports a unified memory pool. This means that free memory does not go to waste. If a portion of physical memory is not currently in use, the system allocates it for file caching. When an application needs additional memory, the memory is allocated from the file caching pool as required. Since cached files are read from physical memory instead of from disk, file caching can make a dramatic difference in file access time.

Linux also uses demand loading of executables. This means that only the required portion of an application's file is read into memory. For example, if the main executable for your Web server application is 2MB in size, but only 100KB of that code is required to monitor incoming connections, Linux will only use 100KB of memory until a connection is established. This can substantially reduce the memory requirements of a system that must run multiple processes.

While Linux supports memory protection between processes so that no single application can bring down the entire system, it also supports *shared copy on write* pages. This allows two applications to use the same memory space. If one of the applications attempts to write to the memory area, the required code is moved elsewhere. The benefits of shared copy on write is that it reduces system memory requirements, which will increase performance by decreasing the number of required memory swaps.

Linux supports a command-line interface (similar to DOS) and a graphical user interface called X-Windows (similar to Microsoft's Windows). The Red Hat installation even includes extensions for X-Windows to give it the same look and feel as a Windows 95 machine. X-Windows even supports GUI connections to remote systems, which Microsoft's Windows does not (although Citrix's WinFrame does). For example, think of using your Windows 95 or NT interface but to be actually working on, and controlling, a remote machine, without the need of setting up shares. With X-Windows, this is possible for multiple simultaneous users.

Linux is a true multiuser system. All tasks that can be performed at the console can also be performed through a remote connection (either dial-up or over the network). By contrast, NT Server provides no remote console ability or shared execution space; IntraNetWare dedicates the server console only to administration of the operating system.

For example, let's assume we are working for a company called Foobar which employs over a thousand people. Foobar has three separate network groups, one to manage servers, one to manage the routers and WAN links to remote offices, and a third to manage infrastructure hardware such as hubs and switches. Foobar decides to purchase an SNMP management system to control and monitor all their network hardware. We need to decide whether to run the management system on NT Server or Unix.

In a Unix environment, only one SNMP management station would be required. Each group could simply attach to this system through a separate Telnet or X-Windows session. From this session, they could manage the hardware their group is responsible for. Only one SNMP management license would be required because it is all running from a single system.

Because NT Server does not support remote sessions, multiple SNMP management stations, and thus licenses, would be required. Each group would need direct access to the SNMP management system in order to view the network hardware they are responsible for.

Even if a remote console product such as pcANYWHERE were used, there would still be problems, as this does not provide separate sessions. Each group would end up controlling the same desktop and may require a different network view to work with their pertinent network hardware.

The result is that Unix's multisession ability allows all three groups to retrieve the information they need from a single system. This reduces both hardware and licenses cost. In fact, if the Unix system being used is Linux, the supplied CMU SNMP tools can be used to create a custom SNMP management station.

Another useful feature of Linux is its ability to initiate background processes. When a command is followed by an ampersand (&), it is assigned a process ID (PID) and allocated as a background function. This frees up the workspace to continue working on something else. When the process is complete, a message is sent to the console session.

Figure 13.3 shows an example of this functionality. Our first command begins a search for files larger than 2MB. The command also states that the output should be redirected to the file LARGEFILE.TXT, which is to be created in the /home/cbrenton directory. The & at the end tells the system to run this command in the background. On the second line, the system informs us that it has assigned a PID of 552 to this command.

FIGURE 13.3:

The ampersand (&) can be used to run commands or applications in the background.

```
[cbrenton@toby /usr]$ find . -size 2000k >/home/cbrenton/largefile.txt &
[1] 552
[cbrenton@toby /usr]$ ls
X11           dict           i486-linuxaout  libexec      sbin
X11R6         doc            include         local        share
X386          etc            info            man          src
bin           games          lib             openwin      tmp
[cbrenton@toby /usr]$
[1]+  Done                   find . -size 2000k >/home/cbrenton/largefile.txt
[cbrenton@toby /usr]$
```

The third line shows our command line being returned to us so that we are free to go off and perform other activities. In this case we have simply listed the contents of the current directory. The second-to-last line is the system letting us know that it has completed the background task.

While similar functionality can be achieved by simply opening multiple windows in a GUI environment, this feature allows us to perform multiple activities without the additional overhead of a GUI environment. It also allows us to perform multiple activities through a single Telnet session.

All running applications and processes can be monitored from a single command, ps. Figure 13.4 shows the output of the ps command. The first column identifies the PID number assigned to the process. This is useful in case we need to manipulate it or shut it down. Because a process can be executed multiple times—for example if accepting multiple FTP or mail connections—it cannot be identified just by name. The PID ensures that each process can be uniquely identified.

The second column identifies which terminal session created the process. A question mark (?) usually indicates that the process was started during system initialization or that the process does not require a terminal session (such as transferring e-mail). A number identifies which server console session is using the process. If the number is preceded by a p, it indicates a remote connection.

For example, we have three processes listed that are running on TTY (terminal) 1. PID 389 shows us that the root user is logged on and using the first local console. PID 421 identifies the environment shell that root is using (bash), and PID 851 shows that root is currently running the find command.

We also have three processes identified with a TTY of p1. First, PID 715 identifies that this is a remote user coming from the IP address 10.1.1.150. Second, PID 721 tells us that this user is also using the bash shell; and, third, 855 shows that they are running the ps-ax command.

FIGURE 13.4:

Output of the ps command

```
[cbrenton@toby cbrenton]$ ps -ax
 PID TTY STAT  TIME COMMAND
   1  ?  S     0:05 init [3]
   2  ?  SW    0:00 (kflushd)
   3  ?  SW<   0:00 (kswapd)
  21  ?  S     0:00 /sbin/kerneld
 101  ?  S     0:00 syslogd
 110  ?  S     0:00 klogd
 121  ?  S     0:00 crond
 144  ?  S     0:00 inetd
 320  ?  S     0:00 sendmail: accepting connections on port 25
 389  1  S     0:00 /bin/login -- root
 390  2  S     0:00 /sbin/mingetty tty2
 391  3  S     0:00 /sbin/mingetty tty3
 397  ?  S     0:00 update (bdflush)
 421  1  S     0:00 -bash
 655  ?  S     0:00 in.telnetd
 801  6  S     0:00 /sbin/mingetty tty6
 803  5  S     0:00 /sbin/mingetty tty5
 804  4  S     0:00 /sbin/mingetty tty4
 851  1  R     0:03 find . -size 2000
 132  ?  S     0:00 portmap
 715 p1  S     0:00 login -h 10.1.1.150 -p
 721 p1  S     0:00 -bash
 855 p1  R     0:00 ps -ax
[cbrenton@toby cbrenton]$
```

The STAT column shows the current status of each process. If it is identified as an S, the process is sleeping and is not currently performing any work. An R indicates that the process is in a running state.

The TIME column identifies how much of the CPU clock time is being used by this process. It is a percentage based upon the number of cycles used since the process was initiated. A higher number means that the process is extremely busy.

Finally, the COMMAND column identifies the name of the process being identified. The ps command provides a lot of useful information about the state of our processes and who is responsible for them. Other ps switches would even allow you to monitor memory utilization of each process. This gives us a single command to monitor all core server activities.

This single-command management is in contrast to other operating systems that separate processes into separate categories and require different procedures to manage them. For example, in an NT environment, you would use Task Manager to monitor and stop any process that was started through the GUI interface.

If the application was started as a service, however, you would need to administer it from the Service Manager. If you needed to monitor the memory or process usage of a running service, you would then need to use a third utility called Performance Monitor.

Unix (and Linux) have been developed to provide "7×24" availability. We have worked with Unix machines that have been operational for over two years without a crash or being rebooted. This is the biggest reason why Unix has been accepted into environments where system availability is considered critical.

Linux will also coexist with other operating systems on the same machine. For example, you can use the Linux boot manager (LILO) to start the machine as Linux, NetWare, or Windows 95/98, for example. Linux can even read files created in another operating system, as described below.

File System

Linux provides a POSIX-compliant file system that accepts file names up to 254 characters. Names are case-sensitive, so `Myfile.txt` and `myfile.txt` would be considered two separate files. It is a high-performance file system which helps to reduce the amount of file fragmentation. A file defragmentation utility is provided for systems where files are created and deleted frequently.

Linux supplies some unique tools for maintaining the file system. The first is a revision control utility, which can be used to monitor and track file changes. This can be used to maintain older copies of files. If required, a file or a set of files can be rolled back to a certain date or revision.

Like NT Server, Linux also supports file system replication. This helps to maintain an identical set of files over multiple systems.

Linux will also natively support a wide range of file systems. Figure 13.5 shows the output of the `fdisk` command, which lists the file systems supported by Linux. This is not remote support but support for drives that are local to the system. For example, you can read a floppy disk created by a DOS or OS/2 file system. You could also mount a volume created by NetWare. This functionality can be invaluable in a mixed system environment or when the machine can be multi-booted between different operating systems.

FIGURE 13.5:

A list of file systems supported by Linux

```
Command (m for help):
   0  Empty            9  AIX bootable   75  PC/IX          b7  BSDI fs
   1  DOS 12-bit FAT   a  OS/2 Boot Manag 80  Old MINIX     b8  BSDI swap
   2  XENIX root       40  Venix 80286    81  Linux/MINIX    c7  Syrinx
   3  XENIX usr        51  Novell?        82  Linux swap     db  CP/M
   4  DOS 16-bit <32M  52  Microport      83  Linux native   e1  DOS access
   5  Extended         63  GNU HURD       93  Amoeba         e3  DOS R/O
   6  DOS 16-bit >=32  64  Novell Netware 94  Amoeba BBT     f2  DOS secondary
   7  OS/2 HPFS        65  Novell Netware a5  BSD/386        ff  BBT
   8  AIX

Command (m for help):
```

Unfortunately, Linux does not support online file or disk compression, nor can it read other file systems that use compression (such as DOS, Windows 95/98, or NT). There is, however, software available for reading FAT and even NTFS partitions.

Unix uses mount points instead of drive letters when additional disks are added. A *mount point* is simply a point in the directory structure where the storage of the additional disk has been added. This provides a cleaner feel to the file structure and helps to consolidate information.

For example, let's assume we have two drives that we plan to use for creating a Unix machine. We want to dedicate the first drive to the operating system and use the second drive for our users' home directories.

Instead of installing the OS on C: and putting the users' home directories on D:, it's better to simply assign the second drive for storage of all files under the /home directory. This would store all files on the primary drive except for those located under the home directory.

There are a few benefits to this. First, it allows the addition of extra drives to be transparent. If you are looking for a file and have no idea where it is located, you can simply go to the root and perform a single search. You are not required to repeat the search for each additional drive because they have been woven into the fabric of the directory structure.

Using mount points also helps to reduce the risk of a system-wide failure caused by a crashed drive. For example, if our second disk were to fail, we would lose only the users' home directories, not the entire system. This is in contrast to NetWare, which requires you to span the entire volume structure over both disks. If one of those drives fails, none of the files on the volume can be accessed.

Account Administration

With Linux you can administrate user and group accounts for each server independently, or manage all the servers centrally through Network Information Services (NIS), informally known as the Yellow Pages (YP).

NIS is a flat database system designed to share user and group information across multiple systems. A collection of systems sharing NIS information is referred to as a *domain*. To give a user access to the domain, an administrator simply needs to add their account to the master NIS server. The master then takes care of propagating this information out to the other NIS systems on the network.

NIS shares the same drawbacks as NT's domain structure because neither are hierarchical. Because Unix provides many additional services over NT, this problem is a bit more compounded. As you will see when we discuss security, file permissions under Unix can be a bit loose. This combined with NIS can provide some additional loopholes for a potential attacker to wiggle through.

All versions of Linux provide command-line tools for administering users and groups. Red Hat Linux also provides a GUI user administration utility. While the GUI can be a bit slower if multiple accounts need to be configured, it provides a simple interface for the novice Unix administrator. Figure 13.6 shows Red Hat's GUI interface for managing users and groups. This interface also tells you which accounts have passwords and which ones do not. The application runs under X-Windows.

FIGURE 13.6:

The Red Hat user and group manager can be used to add and delete accounts.

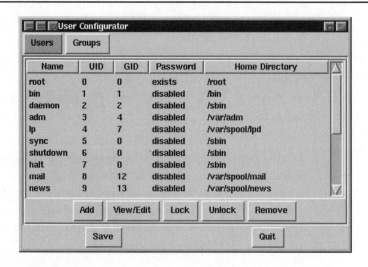

Name	UID	GID	Password	Home Directory
root	0	0	exists	/root
bin	1	1	disabled	/bin
daemon	2	2	disabled	/sbin
adm	3	4	disabled	/var/adm
lp	4	7	disabled	/var/spool/lpd
sync	5	0	disabled	/sbin
shutdown	6	0	disabled	/sbin
halt	7	0	disabled	/sbin
mail	8	12	disabled	/var/spool/mail
news	9	13	disabled	/var/spool/news

Security

Most Unix administrators have a love/hate relationship when it comes to implementing security on a Unix system. Its flexibility allows it to be configured as an extremely secure system, or incorrectly configured to give attackers an open door. Think of Unix as a finely tuned Ferrari. In the hands of a professional driver, the car is capable of amazing speed. In the hands of a novice, it will most likely end up being a bow tie on the first oak tree it sees.

Linux Security Tools

Linux provides the administrator with some wonderful tools for safeguarding the system. Cracker is a program that allows the administrator to verify the integrity of user passwords. Passwords can be checked against known words to ensure that they cannot be easily broken.

TCP Wrapper is a program that allows an administrator to monitor and control the access of services to a machine. For example, a computer could be configured to allow Telnet access from a specific network or host and reject connections from other sources. There is even a verification program to check the configuration of the wrapper and suggest appropriate changes.

Linux supports *shadow passwords*. These allow the encrypted password information to be stored in a different location than the user information. This helps to keep the encrypted passwords away from prying eyes.

As with most things in life, these features are only useful if they are actually implemented. TCP Wrapper cannot help to protect your system if you do not configure system access appropriately and check the logs for suspect connection attempts.

Some of these tools can even be used against the administrator if they are not carefully guarded. For example, Cracker can be used to break passwords as easily as it can be used to verify them. It is a wise system administrator who checks their system with these tools instead of letting an attacker do it for them. This is true for any environment, as tools similar to Cracker are available for NT and older NetWare versions as well.

If Unix has one major security weakness, it is its file permission settings. Permissions are set by three distinct classes—owner, group, and nobody. File owners can set specific permissions for when they access a file, when anyone in their group accesses a file, or when anyone else on the system accesses the file.

For example, let's assume you have a file called SERVERPASSWORDS.TXT in your home directory (yes, that's a bad idea, but this is *only* an example). Let's also assume that you are part of a group called Admin. You can set permissions on this file so that you can read and write to it, members of the Admin group have read-only access, and everyone else on the system has no access.

There are a few problems with this setup. First of all, even though "everyone else" has no access, they can still see that the file exists. This may prompt them to take further steps to try and access the file now that they know it is there.

Another problem is that permissions are too general. You cannot say, "Give read and write access of this file to Sean and Deb from the Admin group, but give all other members read-only access." Unix was spawned out of a much simpler time when complicated file access was not required. In fact, for many years the focus was on making system access easier, not more difficult.

The system can be configured so that a root logon is not possible except from the server console. This way, users connecting to the system remotely must use their regular username and password. Once connected, they can assume the privileges of root. These connections can be logged to see who is accessing the root account and when. The system can be configured to only give certain users the ability to assume root.

Why all these restrictions? Think of it this way—if you have a group of 10 NetWare or NT administrators, how many of them know the administrator password? Half? All 10 maybe? If something becomes broken by the administrator account, how do you determine who many have caused the problem?

Because in a Unix environment each user would be required to assume the privileges of root from their own account, there will be a log entry tracking this event.

Networking

Linux may very well be the undisputed king of networking. It provides connectivity through more protocols and offers more services than any other network operating system.

OSI Layer 2 Support

At OSI layer 2, Linux supports Ethernet, Token Ring, FDDI, ATM, Frame Relay, T1 cards, PPP, SLIP, ISDN, and spread-spectrum wireless LANs. It can even support dumb terminals. Clearly, whatever kind of connectivity you're using, Linux can support it.

Linux is frequently found hanging out at the borders of LANs and WANs. It is an extremely popular product for providing a link to an ISP as well as running the connectivity services at the ISP itself. In fact, there is an entire how-to manual dedicated to describing how to use Linux to provide ISP services. (Again, Linux is widely used to host commercial Web sites. If you have a Web site hosted on an ISP's server, it could very well be served from a Linux system.)

If you will be using a dial-up connection to create your link to your ISP, then PPP load balancing may come in handy. Linux's PPP load balancing allows you to create your Internet connection with more than one dial-up line. This is true for POTS as well as ISDN connectivity. The only real drawback is that the additional lines are not "on demand." With PPP load balancing over POTS, there is no method of monitoring traffic to see if the second line is required for providing greater bandwidth. ISDN, on the other hand, allows for dynamic adding or removal of ISDN channels to match fluctuating bandwidth needs. (Note that most, but not all, ISDN "modems" or terminal units support this feature.)

As for networking protocols, Linux supports IP, NetBIOS over IP, IPX, AppleTalk, and even DECNET. Again, whatever type of connectivity you may require is probably already supported.

IP Networking Support

Unix was the original platform for the IP protocol, so it should be no surprise that Linux has embraced this protocol by supporting every available feature.

Linux provides support for some of the higher-level IP methods of connectivity. Along with the typical unicast and broadcast communications, Linux also supports multicasting, IP encapsulation in IP, mobile IP, IP masquerading, a transparent proxy, and even firewalling.

While encapsulating IP packets within IP packets may seem like a strange thing to do, it can actually be quite useful. Some amateur radio communications are now taking place across the Internet. IP encapsulation of IP provides the transport needed to move these transmissions. It also provides the baseline for mobile IP, which allows a system to use a fixed IP address and communicate from any point on the Internet. Along with auto-routing, this provides a means for a mobile user to connect to the Internet from any location and appear to be communicating from their home base network.

When Linux is used as a router, IP masquerading allows many IP addresses to be hidden behind a single address. For example, let's assume we have the network diagrammed in Figure 13.7. If the Linux system is using IP masquerading, all internal traffic that goes out to the Internet will appear to be originating from the Linux machine's external interface. This allows our internal network to communicate using a reserved address range, which improves security since a reserved address cannot be easily reached from the Internet. It also means that the address of the external interface of the Linux system is the only legal address that can be specified for incoming traffic.

FIGURE 13.7:

IP masquerading allows us to hide an entire network behind a single, legal IP address.

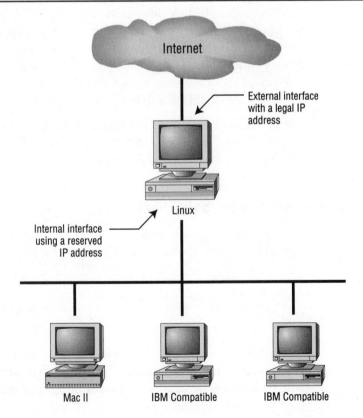

When IP masquerading is combined with the transparent proxy, a powerful combination is formed for protecting your internal network. The transparent proxy allows the Linux system to redirect requests for certain services to an internal machine.

For example, let's assume that the Mac II in Figure 13.7 is running a HTTP server. Using a transparent proxy, we could advertise the IP address on the external interface of the Linux machine as being the address of our HTTP server. When an Internet user attempts to connect to this address, the Linux machine transparently passes the request on to the Mac. As the reply is returned, the Linux machine again rewrites the IP header so that it appears that the reply originated from the Linux machine.

The benefits here are twofold—first, while the Linux machine could easily house any IP services we wish to offer, this allows the load to be balanced over multiple machines. We could be using separate computers for mail, HTTP, and FTP services, but the transparent proxy would make it appear to Internet users that all these services share the same IP address. The side benefit of this is that we have hidden the real IP address of these machines, making it more difficult to launch a direct attack against them. The only service that a would-be attacker can connect to is the service for which we have explicitly created a proxy.

Firewalling can be added to make our Internet connection even more secure. Linux ships with a packet filter firewall that is integrated directly with the kernel. The benefit of direct integration over a separate application is that if the firewall is broken by a would-be attacker, it is extremely likely that the kernel will break as well, causing all processing to stop. This in effect shuts down the connection, not allowing any traffic to pass.

If you feel more comfortable with a proxy-type firewall instead of a packet filter, Trusted Information Systems (TIS) provides a proxy toolkit as free software for Linux and other Unix platforms. While not as comprehensive as their commercial product, it has been used successfully to protect many internal networks and is one of the most popular firewalling methods available.

Linux and NetWare

Linux includes a set of NCP tools that allow it to both emulate and connect to a NetWare server. In emulation mode, the system advertises itself as a NetWare 3.1x network server. Users can log on to the system and print or map drives as they would any NetWare server. The only catch is that Linux does not supply the files typically found in NetWare public and login directories. These files must be copied over from a NetWare server. Also, Linux cannot be integrated into an NDS tree. Despite these drawbacks, the ability to emulate a NetWare server and provide connectivity to IPX-only workstations can be a valuable feature.

The NCP tools also allow a Linux user to connect to a NetWare server. This is useful for transferring files or providing additional storage on the NetWare system. The client NCP tools provide functionality similar to NFS. NetWare volumes can be mounted anywhere with the Linux directory structure. The only two drawbacks are that Linux will not process a logon script and it requires a bindery or bindery emulation to connect to a NetWare server.

NetBEUI Networking

Linux can also emulate or connect to an NT server via NetBEUI or NetBIOS over IP. Linux ships with SAMBA, a set of tools that allows the Linux system to advertise shares (both file and printers) just like an NT server. It also includes client tools so that a Linux user may log on to an NT server. At the end of this chapter, you'll find a whole discussion of the SAMBA suite of client and server tools.

As with IntraNetWare, the only drawback of using SAMBA is that it does not allow a Linux system to join a domain and share account information with other NT servers.

AppleTalk Networking

Linux's AppleTalk support allows it to function only in server mode. Linux can offer print or file services to Macintosh machines, including the saving of files in their native fork format. When routing, Linux can act as a seed or a soft seed router.

Network Routing

Routing support is a bit weaker when Linux is compared to IntraNetWare. Distance-vector routing is supported for all protocols except NetBEUI (which is non-routable). The only link-state routing protocol supported is IP's OSPF.

IP Applications

Linux includes many IP applications. Here are a few of the more popular ones, to give you an idea of what is included. If a service you require is not on the list, chances are someone has already ported it to Linux. You can check one of the many Linux archives to see if it exists.

bootp Server   Linux provides a bootp server for providing bootp and DHCP services to network clients. DHCP and bootp clients can be serviced independently or in a mixed environment. There is also a bootp client so that the Linux system may remotely access its IP address information if a server already exists.

DNS Server   Red Hat Linux ships with the latest version of bind. Bind is the original utility used to exchange domain name information on the Internet, and still the most popular. A bind server can be configured to provide primary, secondary, or caching-only domain name services.

Finger Server   Finger is one of those services that are extremely useful but receive very little attention. Essentially, it allows you to test an account by name and see if the person is online. Linux provides both client and server finger services. As a finger server, the Linux server can host files of information about users or computers located on its network. An administrator can set up finger to provide information about all or selected accounts on the network. The information finger can provide isn't limited to a summary of whether the user is connected. For example, students at various universities have wired up their local soft-drink machines as finger accounts, so that Internet users anywhere in the world can see what flavors are available, as well as how many cans of each.

While this has apparently endless entertainment value, finger can also provide useful business services as well. For example, a site that has dial-up network access to its ISP may be able to use Finger to let the ISP's mail server know when it's back on line. When the mail server is fingered, it begins to transfer any mail messages sent to your organization while your connection was inactive.

FTP Server   Linux provides FTP services, including the ability to service anonymous FTP requests. A directory structure is set up under /home/ftp for anonymous file access. Directories set up under this structure can allow anonymous users to receive read-only or read-write access to files.

The administrator can optionally disable the ability to connect to the server with the root user account; this is done as a security precaution. Red Hat Linux has this functionality enabled by default.

Gopher Server   Although it's not as widely used since the rise of the Web, Gopher is a useful tool for searching documents, and Linux still provides a Gopher server. The Web has largely replaced Gopher in popularity, as it can provide the user with a graphical interface when searching for documents. Still, Gopher is a quick way to perform keyword searches when your are rummaging through a large number of files looking for a specific piece of information.

HTTP Server   Linux ships with Apache to provide Web server access. Apache is one of the more popular Unix Web servers and supports advanced features such as Java scripting and multihoming. *Multihoming* is the ability to host multiple domain names on the same Web server. Apache looks at the destination Web server address and directs the query to the appropriate directory structure for that domain.

Linux also provides both graphic and text-only Web browsers for accessing HTTP services. Red Hat Linux ships with a set of help files formatted for Web browser viewing.

IMAP and POP3 Servers   Linux supports remote mail retrieval using both POP3 and IMAP. POP3 is the older standard and is supported by most remote mail clients. IMAP has more features than POP3 but is just starting to become popular. With Linux as your mail server you can use POP3 today, and later migrate to IMAP as clients become available for your specific platform.

Internet Relay Chat (IRC)   Linux provides both a client and a server for communicating using Internet Relay Chat. When an IRC client connects to an IRC server, the client can select from any of the available *channels* on which they wish to communicate. Once a channel is selected, the IRC client user can relay text messages in real time to other IRC client users. Communications can be private between two users or part of a large group.

Mail Server   Red Hat Linux always ships with the latest version of Sendmail to provide connectivity for SMTP messages. Sendmail is the most widely used mail program on the Internet. Linux also provides at least a half dozen local mail clients for users to send, receive, and read their mail. The user simply Telnets to the Linux system and runs their mail utility of choice.

News Server   Linux provides the InterNetNews daemon (INND) for news server connectivity. When a Linux news server is provided with an appropriate feed, remote users can connect to the server to read and post news articles. If no feed is available, the server can be used for Intranet discussion groups.

NFS Server   Linux can use NFS either to export portions of the server's file system to NFS clients, or act as an NFS client itself and mount remote file systems. NFS functionality is similar to that provided by NetWare, where you would map a drive letter to a section of the remote file system; or NT Server, where you would map to a share. The remote NFS file system can be mounted to any point in Linux's file system.

SNMP Manager   Linux ships with tools for creating an SNMP management station. SNMP allows the management station to both monitor and control SNMP devices on the network. Linux can provide information to other SNMP management stations or house the management station itself.

Talk   Linux also supports `talk`, which is similar to IRC. `Talk` does not require a server, as a connection is established directly between two users. You establish a connection by typing:

```
talk user@host.domain
```

The recipient can either accept or reject the connection. Once a connection is established, the screen is split so that each user may be typing a message at the same time.

Time Server   Linux can use the network time protocol (NTP) to both send and receive time synchronization updates. Typically, one system on the network is set up as a time reference server. This server synchronizes its time with one of the many available time servers on the Internet. Other systems on the network then check with the reference time server to ensure that their system time remains accurate.

Telnet Server   Linux can accept Telnet requests to provide remote console access to the server. Clients connecting to the system through Telnet have the same abilities as if they were sitting in front of the server console.

The administrator can optionally disable the ability to connect to the server with the root user account. This is done as a security precaution. Red Hat Linux has this functionality enabled by default.

Configuring Network Access

Most network administration of Red Hat Linux can be done either from the command line or through a graphical utility in X-Windows. Because the command line uses less overhead, it is usually faster for the experienced user. If you are new to Linux, you may find the GUI utilities a bit easier to use.

There are two basic steps to configuring network support on Linux. The first is adding driver and protocol support to the kernel. This is referred to as *making the kernel* because you will use a utility called make to compile the kernel, in effect turning the kernel source code into an executable C program (take a deep breath, it's not as tough as it sounds). If you are using Red Hat Linux, this may not be required. The default kernel provides support for many popular networking cards, and the more popular protocols and topologies are already enabled.

Once you have customized your kernel, you will then need to start your required services. Again, Red Hat Linux ships with the more popular services enabled. You may, however, wish to disable the ones you have installed but do not plan to use immediately.

To Make or Not to Make…

The Red Hat Linux installation adds support for a single network card. If the system will be acting as a server, this is probably all you will ever need. If you need to add support for another card, however, it may be time to rebuild the kernel.

Even if you do not need to add a second network card, there are other reasons why you may wish to customize the modules used by the kernel:

- To enable support for other required features

- To disable support for unneeded features

- To tune memory utilization

- Because it's cool…

The standard Linux kernel is configured using the lowest common denominators. While this allows it to run on the widest range of systems, it is probably not optimized for your specific configuration. For example, the kernel is configured to support a 386 without a math coprocessor (requiring coprocessor emulation). If you are running a 486, Pentium, or higher, you can optimize the system's performance and save memory by changing these settings.

There are five commands used in making the kernel. They are:

- `make config`, or `make menuconfig`, or `make xconfig`
- `make dep`
- `make clean`
- `make zImage`
- `make zlilo`

Only one of the three commands in the first bullet needs to be used. The differences are explained below. Note that `make clean` is no longer a required command, but it will not hurt to run it. All five commands should be executed from the /usr/src/linux directory.

Configuring the Kernel

Always back up your kernel before you start. That way, if something embarrassing happens, you can always fall back to your original configuration. The kernel file is /VMLINUZ. Simply copy (do not move!) the file to /VMLINUZ.OLD. There are three command choices when it comes to selecting the configuration parameters of the kernel. They are:

- `make config`
- `make menuconfig`
- `make xconfig`

The command `make config` is the oldest and the most familiar command to experienced Linux administrators. The `make config` interface is completely command-line driven. While this is not very pretty, it provides default settings that should be fine if left alone. If you do not understand a prompt, do not change it. You can access online help by typing a question mark in the prompt answer field. The biggest drawback is that you pretty much have to walk through each and every prompt. With the menu utilities, you can jump in and just change what you need to. Figure 13.8 shows the typical output when a `make config` is performed.

FIGURE 13.8:

Output of a make config

```
[root@toby linux]# make config
rm -f include/asm
( cd include ; ln -sf asm-i386 asm)
/bin/sh scripts/Configure arch/i386/config.in
#
# Using defaults found in arch/i386/defconfig
#
*
* Code maturity level options
*
Prompt for development and/or incomplete code/drivers (CONFIG_EXPERIMENTAL) [N/y/?]
*
* Loadable module support
*
Enable loadable module support (CONFIG_MODULES) [Y/n/?]
Set version information on all symbols for modules (CONFIG_MODVERSIONS) [Y/n/?]
Kernel daemon support (e.g. autoload of modules) (CONFIG_KERNELD) [Y/n/?]
*
* General setup
*
Kernel math emulation (CONFIG_MATH_EMULATION) [Y/n/?]
Networking support (CONFIG_NET) [Y/n/?]
```

Typing **make menuconfig** enables the ASCII character interface shown in Figure 13.9. Using the arrow keys, you can navigate between menu options. Selecting **y** while an option is highlighted enables support, and pressing **n** disables support. Some menu items allow you to select **m** for modular support. This allows the driver to be loaded or unloaded as required while the system is running. Pressing **h** brings up a brief help menu.

The command make xconfig is intended to be run from a shell within X-Windows. It is similar to menuconfig, but it's a lot prettier. It is also a bit easier to navigate around. Figure 13.10 shows the network section of the xconfig utility.

Configuration Options   Regardless of which method you choose, you will need to select which features you wish to enable or disable. A brief description of features related to networking are listed here. For a more complete list see the online help and how-to files.

> **Networking Support?**   Enables networking. If you do not answer yes to this prompt, you will not receive any of the other networking prompts. The default is yes.

FIGURE 13.9:

The menu-based kernel configuration screen

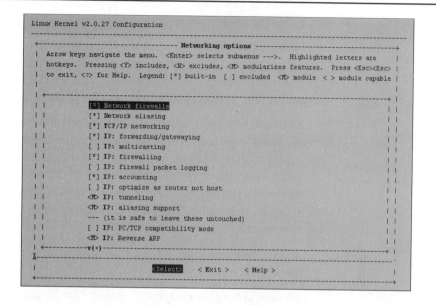

```
Linux Kernel v2.0.27 Configuration
--------------------------------------------------------------------
+------------------------ Networking options ------------------------+
| Arrow keys navigate the menu.  <Enter> selects submenus --->.  Highlighted letters are  |
| hotkeys.  Pressing <Y> includes, <N> excludes, <M> modularizes features.  Press <Esc><Esc> |
| to exit, <?> for Help.  Legend: [*] built-in  [ ] excluded  <M> module  < > module capable |
|                                                                    |
| +----------------------------------------------------------------+ |
| |         [*] Network firewalls                                  | |
| |         [*] Network aliasing                                   | |
| |         [*] TCP/IP networking                                  | |
| |         [*] IP: forwarding/gatewaying                          | |
| |         [ ] IP: multicasting                                   | |
| |         [*] IP: firewalling                                    | |
| |         [ ] IP: firewall packet logging                        | |
| |         [*] IP: accounting                                     | |
| |         [ ] IP: optimize as router not host                    | |
| |         <M> IP: tunneling                                      | |
| |         <M> IP: aliasing support                               | |
| |         --- (it is safe to leave these untouched)             | |
| |         [ ] IP: PC/TCP compatibility mode                      | |
| |         <M> IP: Reverse ARP                                    | |
| +----------v(+)--------------------------------------------------+ |
|                                                                    |
|              <Select>     < Exit >    < Help >                     |
+--------------------------------------------------------------------+
```

FIGURE 13.10:

The X-Windows–based kernel configuration screen

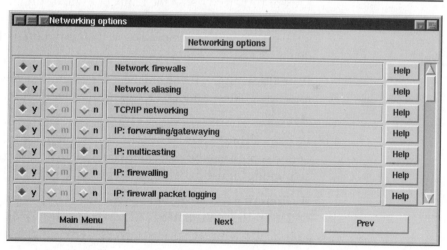

Limit memory to low 16MB?   Provided for older systems that have trouble addressing memory above 16MB. Most systems do not need this support. The default is no.

PCI BIOS support?   Provides support for systems with one or more PCI bus slots. Most newer systems support PCI. The default is yes.

Network firewall?   Allows the Linux system to act as a firewall. This option enables firewalling in general although firewalling for IP is the only protocol supported at this time. This option also needs to be enabled if you wish to do IP masquerading. The default is yes.

Network aliasing?   Allows multiple network addresses to be assigned to the same interface. Currently, the only supported protocol is IP. This is useful if you need to route two logical networks on the same physical segment. This option should be enabled if you plan to use the Apache Web server in a multihomed capacity. Apache can use the different IP addresses assigned to the interface to direct HTTP requests to different Web sites running on the machine. The default is yes.

TCP/IP networking?   Enables or disables IP networking. If you wish to use IP to communicate, this option should be enabled. The default is yes.

IP: forwarding/gatewaying?   Allows the Linux system to forward IP traffic from one interface to another acting as a router. This can be LAN to LAN or LAN to WAN. If the Linux box will be providing firewall services, this option should be disabled. If you will be using IP masquerading (even if the system will be a firewall as well), this option should be enabled. The default is yes.

IP: multicasting?   If you will be using IP multicasting or transmitting routing updates using OSPF, this option should be enabled. The default is no.

IP: firewalling?   Enables the firewall support for the IP protocol. This option should also be enabled if you wish to do IP masquerading, traffic accounting, or use the transparent proxy. The default answer is yes.

IP: firewall packet logging?   When the system is used as a firewall, this option creates a file that logs all passing traffic. It also records what the firewall did with each packet (accept, deny). Logging is a good way to keep an eye on who may be knocking at the front door. We usually enable this option. That way if you do not need the information you can simply clean it out from time to time. The default is no.

IP: accounting?   When the system acts as a firewall or gateway, this option logs all passing traffic. If Linux will be routing on the internal network, you may want to disable this option as the log can get quite large. If Linux will be routing to a WAN connection, or firewalling one, you may want to enable this option to keep track of WAN utilization. The default is yes.

IP: optimize as router not host?   If the Linux box will be acting strictly as a router, firewall, or proxy, you should enable this option. If the system will be hosting HTTP, FTP, DNS, or any other type of service, this option should be disabled. The default is no.

IP: tunneling?   Enables support for IP encapsulation of IP packets. This is useful for amateur radio or mobile IP. The default is modular support, which means you can load it while the system is active if you need it.

IP: aliasing support?   This option allows you to assign two or more IP addresses to the same interface. Network Aliasing must also be enabled. The default is modular support.

IP: PC/TCP compatibility mode?   PC/TCP is a DOS-based IP protocol stack. There are some compatibility issues, as older versions do not quite follow the same set of communication rules as everyone else. If you have trouble connecting to a Linux system from a host running PC/TCP, then enable this option. Otherwise, this option should be disabled. The default is no.

IP: Reverse ARP?   Typically used by diskless workstations to discover their IP address. Enabling this option allows the Linux system to reply to these requests. If you plan on running bootp services, you may want to enable this option in case you need it (now or later). If the Linux system will not be providing bootp or DHCP services, this option can be disabled. The default is modular support.

IP: Disable Path MTU Discovery?   Maximum Transfer Unit (MTU) allows a system to discover the largest packet size it may use when communicating with a remote machine. When MTU is disabled, the system assumes it must always use the smallest packet size for a given transmission. Because this option can greatly affect communication speed, MTU should be used unless you run into a compatibility problem. The default is no, which enables MTU discovery.

IP: Drop source routed frames?   Source routing allows a transmitting station to specify the network path along which replies should be sent. This forces the system replying to the request to transmit along the specified path instead of the one defined by the local routing table.

WARNING   There is a type of attack where a potential attacker can use source-routed frames to pretend to be communicating from a host inside your network when they are actually located out on the Internet. Source routing is used to direct the frame back out to the Internet instead of toward the network where the host claims to be located. When source routing is used for this purpose it is referred to as *IP spoofing*.

Some network topologies such as Token Ring and FDDI use source routing as part of their regular communications. If the Linux box is connected to one of these token-based topologies, source routing should be left enabled. If you are not using these topologies to communicate, this option should be disabled to increase security. The default is yes, which will drop all source-routed frames.

IP: Allow large windows?   This option increases the transmission buffer pool to allow a greater number of frames to be *in transit* without a reply. This is useful when the Linux box is directly connected to a high-speed WAN link (multiple T1 lines or faster) that connects two sites separated by an extremely long distance (for example, from coast to coast). The additional buffer space does require additional memory, so this option should only be enabled on systems that meet the above criteria and have at least 16MB of physical memory. The default is yes.

The IPX Protocol?   This option enables support for the IPX protocol. You must answer yes to this prompt in order to configure any IPX services. The default is modular support.

Full internal IPX network?   NetWare servers use an internal IPX network in order to communicate between the core OS and different subsystems. This option takes IPX one step further by making the internal IPX network a regular network capable of supporting *virtual hosts*. This is more for development than anything else right now as it allows a single Linux system to appear to be multiple NetWare servers. Unless you are doing development work, this option should be disabled. The default is no.

AppleTalk DDP?   This option enables support for the AppleTalk protocol. When used with the Netatalk package (Linux support for AppleTalk), the Linux system can provide file and printer services to Mac clients. The default is modular support.

Amateur Radio AX.25 Level 2?   This option is used to support amateur radio communications. These communications can be either point-to-point or through IP encapsulation of IP. The default is no.

Kernel/User network link driver?   This option enables communications between the kernel and user processes designed to support it. As of this writing, the drive is still experimental and is not required on a production server. The default is no.

Network device support?   This option enables driver-level support for network communications. You must answer yes to this prompt in order to enable support for network cards and WAN communications. The default is yes.

Dummy net driver support?   This option enables the use of a loop back address. Most IP systems understand that transmitting to the IP address 127.0.0.1 will direct the traffic flow back at the system itself. This option should be enabled because some applications do use it. The default is modular support.

EQL (serial line load balancing) support?   This option allows Linux to balance network load over two dial-up links. For example, you may be able to call your ISP on two separate lines, doubling your available bandwidth. The default is modular support.

PLIP (parallel port) support?   This option enables support for communication between two systems using a null printer cable. Both systems must use bi-directional parallel ports in order for communications to be successful. This is similar to connecting two systems via the serial ports with a null modem cable, but it supports faster communications. The default is modular support.

PPP (point-to-point) support?   This option allows the Linux system to create or accept PPP WAN connections. This should be enabled if you plan on using your Linux system to create dial-up connections. The default is modular support.

SLIP (serial line) support?   SLIP is the predecessor to PPP. It provides IP connectivity between two systems. Its most popular use is for transferring mail. Because of the additional features provided by PPP, SLIP is used very little. The default is to provide modular support.

Radio network interfaces? This option allows the Linux system to support spread spectrum communications. Spread spectrum is most commonly used for wireless LAN communications. You must answer yes to this prompt in order to receive prompts to configure the radio interface. The default is no.

Ethernet (10 or 100Mbps)? This option allows the Linux system to communicate using Ethernet network cards. You must answer yes to this prompt to later select an Ethernet driver. The default answer is yes.

3Com cards? This option allows you to select from a list of supported 3Com network cards. If you answer no, you will not be prompted with any 3Com card options. If you select yes, you will receive further prompts allowing you to selectively enable support for each 3Com card that is supported by Linux.

Upon startup, Linux will attempt to find and auto-detect the setting used on each network card. The accuracy rate is pretty good, although it sometimes misses ISA cards. When you reboot the system, watch the configuration parameters it selects for the card. If they are correct, you're all set. If they are wrong, you will need to change either the card settings or the configuration parameters. The card is set through the configuration utility that ships with it. The startup settings can be changed through the Red Hat control panel's Kernel Daemon Configuration option. The default answer for this prompt is yes.

AMD LANCE and PCnet (AT1500 and NE2100)? Similar to the 3COM prompt, this option will enable support for AMD and PCnet network cards. The default is yes.

Western Digital/SMC cards? Similar to the 3COM prompt, this option will enable support for Western Digital and SMC network cards. The default is yes.

Other ISA cards? Similar to the 3COM prompt, except this option enables support for some of the more obscure network cards such as Cabletron's E21 series or HP's 100VG PCLAN. If you select yes, you will receive further prompts allowing you to selectively enable support for a variety of network cards that are supported by Linux. The default is yes.

NE2000/NE1000 support? This is the generic Ethernet network card support. If your card has not been specifically listed in any of the above prompts, then enable this option. Most Ethernet network cards are "NE2000 compatible" so this prompt is a bit of a catch-all. The default is modular support.

EISA, VLB, PCI and on board controllers?   There are a number of network cards built directly into the motherboard. If you select yes, you will receive further prompts allowing you to selectively enable support for a variety of built-in network cards that are supported by Linux. The default answer is yes.

Pocket and portable adapters?   Linux also supports parallel port network adapters. If you select yes, you will receive further prompts allowing you to selectively enable support for a variety of parallel port network adapters that are supported by Linux. The default answer is yes.

Token Ring driver support?   Linux supports a collection of Token Ring network adapters. If you select yes, you will receive further prompts allowing you to selectively enable support for a variety of Token Ring network adapters that are supported by Linux. The default answer is yes.

FDDI driver support?   Linux supports a few FDDI network adapters. If you select yes, you will receive further prompts allowing you to selectively enable support for different FDDI network cards that are supported by Linux. The default answer is no.

ARCnet support?   ARCnet is an old token-based network topology that is used very little today. If you select yes, you will receive further prompts allowing you to selectively enable support for different FDDI network cards that are supported by Linux. The default support is modular.

ISDN support?   This option enables support for ISDN WAN cards. If you plan on using ISDN, you should also enable the PPP support listed above. The default support is modular.

Support synchronous PPP?   This option provides support for synchronous communications over an ISDN line. Some ISDN devices require this to be enabled and will negotiate its use during connection. If you plan on using ISDN, you should enable this option in case you need it. The default is yes.

Use VJ-compression with synchronous PPP?   This option enables header compression when synchronous PPP is used. The default is yes.

Support generic MP (RFC 1717)? When synchronous PPP is used, this option allows communications to take place over multiple ISDN lines. Since this is a new specification and not yet widely supported, the default answer is no.

Support audio via ISDN? When supported by the ISDN card, this option allows the Linux system to accept incoming voice calls and act as an answering machine. The default answer is no.

NFS file system support? This option enables support for mounting and exporting file systems using NFS. NFS is most frequently used when sharing files between Unix systems; however, it is supported by other platforms as well. The default answer is yes.

SMB file system support? This option enables support for NetBIOS/NetBEUI shares. This is most frequently used between Microsoft Windows systems for sharing files and printers. The default answer is yes.

SMB Win95 bug work-around? This option fixes some connectivity problems when the Linux system attempts to retrieve directory information from a Windows 95 system that is sharing files. If you use file sharing for Windows 95, you should enable this option. The default is no.

NCP file system support? This option allows the Linux system to connect to NetWare servers. Once connected, the Linux system can mount file systems located on the NetWare server. The default support is modular.

Dependency Check

Once you have finished the configuration, it is now time to run make dep. This command performs a dependency check, as described earlier, to ensure that all required files are present before compiling the kernel. Depending on your system speed, this command could take one to 15 minutes to run. While it is not quite as thrilling as watching grass grow, you should keep an eye on the dependency check to ensure that there are no errors. Errors are usually in the form of missing files. If you note what is missing, you can go back and see where you may have lost it.

Cleaning Up the Work Space

Next you can run a make clean to ensure that any object files get removed. This is typically not required with the latest revision kernels, but it does not hurt to run it just in case. This command usually takes less than one minute to execute.

Compiling the Kernel

Up until now we have not changed the active system. All our changes have been to configuration files. Our next command, `make zImage` will create a kernel with the configuration parameters we selected and replace the one we are currently using. Notice the capital I in `zImage`. This is important because characters are case sensitive.

How long this command will take to run depends on your processor speed and the amount of physical memory that is installed in the system. A 200MHz Pentium with 32MB of RAM should take eight to 10 minutes to create a new kernel. The first Linux kernel one author ever configured was version .97, which was a bit smaller than the current release. The machine was a 16MHz 386SX with 4MB of memory. It took about 12 hours to create a new kernel. Your mileage may vary but you can use these two configurations as a guide.

Configuring the Boot Manager

Our last step is to tell Linux's boot manager LILO that it needs to set pointers for a new image. This is done with the command `make zlilo`. The command should take a minute or less to execute. Once complete you can take a look in the root directory to compare your old and new kernels. If all went well, the time stamp for the new image should be more recent than the /VMLINUZ.OLD file that we created. If we got real lucky, our new kernel should even be a little smaller. This is usually the case, but may not be true if you enabled support on many of the options.

We can now restart the system and boot from the new kernel. You should not notice any new errors during system startup. If you do or the system refuses to boot altogether, you can use the original boot disk as an emergency recovery disk. This will let you onto the drive so you can copy back the original image until you can figure out what went wrong.

Changing the Network Driver Settings

As mentioned above, you may need to change the network driver setting if auto-probe fails to configure it properly. This can be done through the Red Hat control panel using the Kernel Daemon Configuration option. Figure 13.11 shows the Kernel Configurator window, in which you can add or remove device drivers or change their settings.

FIGURE 13.11:

The Kernel Configurator

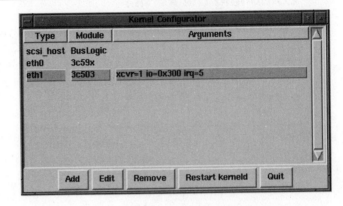

When you highlight a specific driver and select Edit, you will see the Set Module Options dialog box, shown in Figure 13.12. This allows you to change the configuration parameters that Linux uses to initialize your network card. Once the changes are complete, you can select Restart Kernel to have these changes take effect.

FIGURE 13.12:

The Set Module Options window allows you to change the startup parameters for a specific driver.

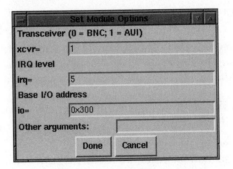

Starting Network Services

The startup scripts for most of the networking services can be found in the /etc/rc.d/init.d directory. Most of these services are configured to initialize once their main configuration file has been created. The following is a representative list of some services and their corresponding configuration files. These configuration files must exist in order for a service to start. A complete list of all services available in a particular Linux installation can be retrieved via the online help (called man, for manual).

Service	Daemon	Main Configuration File
lpd	lpd	/ETC/PRINTCAP
DNS	named	/ETC/NAMED.BOOT
news	innd	/ETC/RC.D/NEWS
NFS	rpc.nfsd & rpc.mountd	/ETC/EXPORTS

If you need to disable one of the services from starting during bootup, simply rename its initialization file temporarily. For example, the initialization script for Sendmail is SENDMAIL.INIT. If you rename this file SENDMAIL.INIT.OLD, Sendmail will no longer initialize during system startup.

With Red Hat Linux, you can also use Red Hat's runtime editor, located on the control panel, to load, unload, or prevent a service from initializing.

Configuring Routing

The Network Configurator option on the Red Hat control panel allows you to add and delete interfaces as well as set up aliasing. You can also configure routing.

NOTE   *Aliasing* is an important feature for anyone wishing to host multiple Web sites from the same server. Multiple IP addresses can be configured to point to the same physical station, with each "virtual address" accessing a different set of Web pages.

Figure 13.13 shows the properties for a network interface alias. We can tell it is an alias because of the :0 designation in the interface name. Aliasing allows us to set up multiple IP addresses to the same interface.

The Routing button allows us to configure static routing. Figure 13.14 shows an example of how this is configured. The default gateway defines where to send traffic when the network address is not defined in the lower table. Selecting the Add button brings up the Edit Static Route window, shown in the foreground. This allows us to create entries for specific networks. We only need to do this if the IP address of the next hop router is different than the IP address of the default gateway. In this case, the specific entries have been added because the next hop router is at a different IP address than the default gateway. Without these entries, traffic destined for 10.1.2.0–10.1.4.0 would first go to the default gateway address before being forwarded to 10.1.1.254.

FIGURE 13.13:

The Network Configurator window. This is where we can configure our alias options.

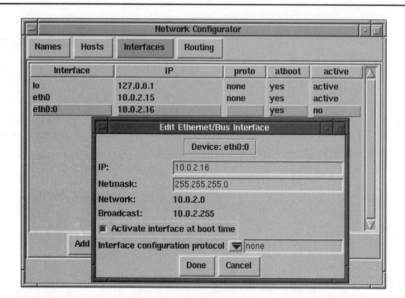

FIGURE 13.14:

Our static routing definitions

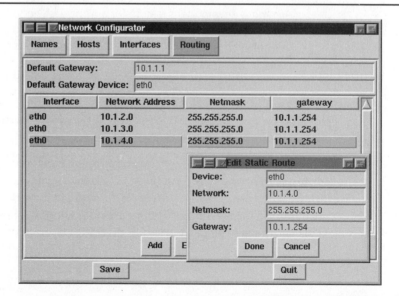

The SAMBA Suite

The SAMBA suite is a set of client and server tools for both accessing and advertising file and printer shares. Shares are used by Windows NT, Windows 95/98, LAN Manager, and OS/2 when exchanging information. Connectivity is supplied by the NetBIOS and NetBEUI protocols, including encapsulation of NetBIOS over IP.

The SAMBA suite is public domain and directly supports over a dozen different flavors of Unix. If you are using the Red Hat version of Linux, SAMBA is already loaded with a minimal configuration. If you do not have a pre-installed version of SAMBA, you can retrieve it from a number of different FTP and Web sites on the Internet. You will then have to tune the MAKE file for your specific flavor of Unix and compile the source code.

There is even a version of SAMBA for IntraNetWare. This was developed by Novell Consulting Services as a tool for migrating to IntranetWare from NT or LAN Manager. While it is still considered beta code at the time of this writing, it does allow a 4.1 or later NetWare server to advertise file and printer shares just like an NT server.

Through SAMBA, we can provide both file and printer sharing to all of our NOSs using a common protocol and service.

Using SAMBA to Access Shares from Unix

There are a number of SAMBA tools specifically designed to allow a Unix system to access file shares located on a remote server. The remote server can be Windows NT, Windows 95/98, or even another Unix system. If the remote server is advertising shares, the SAMBA client tools allow a Unix system to access them.

smbclient

The smbclient is used to access remote file shares. Once you are authenticated, the interface looks very similar to FTP. A command-line interface is provided for transferring files between the two systems. While not as elegant as the smbmount command, it is functional nonetheless.

You may need to play with the syntax for the share name in order to successfully connect to a remote system. For example, given the share name:

```
\\server\share
```

we found that in order to successfully access an NT system (workstation or server), we needed to enter the file share as:

```
\\\\server\\share
```

Keep this difference in syntax in mind while using this utility. In this example, we will use the syntax that is normally associated with a share name (the first version). You may need to modify the examples accordingly.

Available smbclient switches:

sharename	complete share name path such as \\server\share
-U *username*	logon username
password	logon password
-L	list all known servers and shares

If you are performing a logon to a system that configures share-level passwords (such as Windows 95/98), use the *password* switch. If you are performing a logon to a system that uses logon accounts (such as Windows NT), use the -U switch.

For example, if you wanted to connect to the NT server Talsin to access the share notes, you would enter the command string:

```
smbclient \\talsin\\notes -U cbrenton
```

This command string will prompt me for a password and then present me with the smb command prompt. If you omit the *username* switch, your user logon name for the Linux system is passed along in its place. If your password is "bovine," you can pass this along in the command string by typing:

```
smbclient \\talsin\\notes -U cbrenton%bovine
```

The percent sign after the logon name is required to let the system know that the remainder of the line is the password. There is no other switch to indicate this.

Some systems that are advertising shares require that the logon name, password, or both be entered in full capitalization. Play with these values to see what works best in your particular environment.

If you wanted to connect to the Windows 95 system ElfArrow and access the share named quake, which has a file system password of "tombstone," you would enter:

```
smbclient \\elfarrow\quake%tombstone
```

Our final switch, -L, will query a server as to what shares it has available. It will also query the system's browser to see what other shares the server has discovered out on the network. For example, the command string:

```
smbclient -L talsin
```

would produce the following output:

```
Domain=[BABYLON] OS=[Windows NT 4.0] Server=[NT LAN Manager 4.0]

Server=[TALSIN] User=[] Workgroup=[BABYLON] Domain=[]

        Sharename       Type       Comment
        -----           --         ----
        ADMIN$          Disk       Remote Admin
        C$              Disk       Default share
        IPC$            IPC        Remote IPC
        notes           Disk
        TEMP            Disk

This machine has a browse list:

        Server                  Comment
        -----                   ----
        ELFARROW                CHRIS BRENTON
        FENRUS                  CHRIS BRENTON
        TANGNEY                 TEST1
        TALSIN
        THOTH                   TEST2
        TUTTLE                  TEST3
This machine has a workgroup list:

        Workgroup               Master
        -----                   ----
        BABYLON                 TALSIN
```

From this list, you can see what shares the server Talsin has available. You can also see what other servers are on the network advertising shares and can query each one of them directly.

NOTE   The Comment field is the equivalent of the Computer Description on Windows 95.

---

smbmount

While the smbclient allows you to transfer files between the Unix system and systems offering file shares, it does not exactly provide transparent access to the file system. For this type of access we need to use the smbmount utility. The smbmount utility is functionally identical to the ncpmount utility, but the switches are slightly different.

Available smbmount switches:

share name	A share entered in the format *//server/share*
mount point	The directory to which we wish to attach the fileshare
-I *server*	The server where the share is located
-U *username*	The username to use during logon
-P *password*	The password to use during logon
-n	The logon name has no password, do not prompt for one
-h	Print a simple help message listing available switches

For example, if you wish to mount the file share \\talsin\notes to the directory /mnt/talsin using a logon name of "cbrenton" and a password of "bovine," you would enter the command:

```
smbmount //talsin/notes /mnt/talsin -I talsin -U cbrenton -P bovine
```

Notice that the command expects the share slashes to face in the opposite direction. The command also requires the -I switch, even though the server name is specified as part of the share.

smbumount

The smbumount utility is used to remove file shares accessed with smbmount. It is functionally identical to the ncpumount command. The only required switch is the mount point where the share is located. For example, to remove the mounted share created in the last example, you would type:

```
smbumount /mnt/talsin
```

Using SAMBA to Create Shares from Unix

In addition to client services, SAMBA can allow a Unix system to advertise both file and printer shares as well. There are three files that provide this connectivity. They are:

- nmbd
- smbd
- smb.conf

nmbd

The nmbd utility controls the NetBIOS communication of the system. It is run as a daemon and is responsible for listening on the NetBIOS port for name service requests. When a name service request is received, nmbd responds with the system's IP address. It is also responsible for maintaining the browser informing which catalogs NetBIOS names within a given workgroup.

Available nmbd switches:

-D	Tells nmbd to run as a daemon.
-H *lmhost_file*	Path and name of the NetBIOS host name file.
-d *number*	Tells nmbd to run in the debug level specified by *number*. Levels 0–5 are valid.
-l *log_file_base*	Specifies the base name for the log file.
-n *NetBIOS_name*	Specifies the NetBIOS name for this system if the host name should not be used.
-p *port_number*	Changes the default port number to listen on.
-s *config_file*	Specifies the location of smb.conf if it is not located in /etc.

smbd

The smbd utility is the daemon responsible for all file and printer share services. Once a client locates a SAMBA server through nmbd, it is smbd that takes care of servicing the clients file and printer requests.

While smbd will retrieve most of its configuration information from the file /etc/smbd.conf, it does have a few switches available to override the setting in that file.

Available smbd switches:

-D	Tells nmbd to run as a daemon.
-O *socket_option*	Tunes communication parameters.
-a	Overwrites the log files. The default is to append.
-d *number*	Tells smbd to run at the debug level specified by *number*. Levels 0–5 are valid.
-l *log_file_base*	Specifies the base name for the log file.
-p *port_number*	Changes the default port number to listen on.
-s *config_file*	Specifies the location of smb.conf if it is not located in /etc.

smb.conf

smb.conf is used to configure nmbd and smbd during initialization. You should configure this file before loading the two daemons. If you make changes to this file during server operation, you must send a signup to both of the daemons. This will force them to reread the configuration file.

smb.conf supports too many switch options to list here. The man page documentation for this file runs over 50 pages. Instead, we will look at only the most commonly used commands. Consult the man pages for a complete description. On a Red Hat Linux system, you can also review the documentation in the directory /usr/doc/samba-*revision*, where *revision* is the revision number of the version of SAMBA you are using.

Global Settings Global settings are used to configure the overall SAMBA environment as opposed to configuring a specific share. Global settings are listed with the SMB.CONF file under the section heading [global].

load printers = yes/no Specifies whether the printcap files should be read and whether printers available through lpd should be advertised as printer shares.

guest account = username   Allows you to specify the valid guest account to use when browsing the shares. This must be a valid account name and should only have minimal system rights. Usually setting this to ftp will allow shares to be accessed.

workgroup = Workgroup   Allows you to specify the name of the workgroup that this system should join. Workgroups are similar to domains in that they represent a collection of NetBIOS systems. Workgroups differ from domains in that there is no central account administration—all logon names and passwords are managed by each individual system.

Home Directories   When a user authenticates to SAMBA, you have the option to allow them to access their home directory as a share. The directory location is retrieved from the /ETC/PASSWD file, which is used system-wide to define logon names and passwords. Home directory settings are listed with the SMB.CONF file under the section heading [homes].

Other Shares   You can create shares to any portion of the file system that you wish. When creating a share, begin the section with a share name enclosed in brackets, like this: [public]. After the share name, specify any parameters you want to have applied to that share, with one command listed per line.

Share Settings   The following is a brief list of some of the commands that can be used to manipulate a share.

browseable = yes/no   Indicates whether the share is visible to a client which is browsing or can only be accessed by using the Universal Naming Convention (UNC). For example, to access the share named public, which has browsing disabled, you must access it by entering UNC\\SERVER\ public. It will not show up in a browse list.

create mode = number   Allows you to assign default permissions to files when they are created on the SAMBA share. The value for this field uses the same numeric format as the chmod command. See the man pages for more information.

only guest = yes   Specifies that users accessing this share will have guest-level access only. If the file permissions are set correctly, this can be used so that users can see the files in a directory, but they do not have read or write access.

path = share directory path   Defines the directory that will be accessed when a user accesses the advertised share name. For example, if you create a share named public, and you set the path statement equal to /usr/expenses/template, then accessing the share public will put you directly into the template directory. You are not allowed to navigate up the directory structure, only down.

public = yes/no   Defines whether a share is open to public access. When this value is set to yes, users who do not have an account on the system will receive access based on the attributes of the defined guest account.

valid users = username   Specifies that only users with the specified logon name can access the share. Multiple logon names can be specified, separated by spaces.

writable = yes/no   Defines whether a share can be accessed with read/write permissions or the file system should instead be considered read-only. What defines the level of access a user receives is a combination of this setting and the permissions assigned to the user's Unix account, whichever is lower. For example, if a user accesses a share marked as writable, but their Unix account has read-only permissions, the user will receive read-only access to the share.

Figure 13.15 shows an example smb.conf file with heading and settings put into place. This file sets some global settings, and advertises two shares—home and public. When a user sees their home directory in the browser list, it will be identified with their logon name. This is a minimal configuration. There are many other options available for configuring the system.

FIGURE 13.15:

A sample SMB.CONF file

```
;A Sample smb.conf file with
;only a few configured options
[global]
    workgroup = Support
    guest account = ftp

[homes]
    browseable = yes
    writable = yes
    create mode = 0750

[public]
    path = /home/samba
    public = yes
    writable = yes
```

Appropriate Uses for SAMBA

SAMBA appears to be our best bet for supporting IntraNetWare, Windows NT, and Unix, using a single protocol and a single set of services. Through SAMBA, we are able to gain access to file and print services on all of our NOSs, including many flavors of Unix.

This is not without its drawbacks, however. First, we standardized on IP for a networking protocol. While IP is extremely efficient, it is not nearly as efficient for providing file services as IPX and NCP. If our network relies on heavy NetWare use, we may actually increase traffic by losing the use of packet burst.

Also, SAMBA is still beta code on the NetWare platform and is not the most stable software available. There is a very real possibility that it would conflict with NLMs produced by third-party manufacturers. For example, if you are running a server-based backup program and use it to back up workstations or other servers, SAMBA may not be able to use NetBEUI to communicate with these systems. SAMBA may expect to be able to use IPX because this is the default protocol on all NetWare servers.

So when would using SAMBA be a good idea? Clearly it would have to be an environment that does not rely heavily on NetWare servers. If you are running a mixed NT and Unix environment, or an environment that only has one or two NetWare systems that receive only a peripheral amount of traffic, SAMBA may be just the thing to standardize your network on a single protocol and service.

Configuring IP Services

There are a number of wonderful resources available for configuring services on Linux and Unix in general. Some of these are:

The Linux HOW-TO and FAQ guides (written by a wide range of authors), available at `www.redhat.com/manual`

TCP/IP Network Administration
by Craig Hunt
(O'Reilly and Associates, 1992)

Managing Internet Information Services
by Cricket Liu, Jerry Peek, Russ Jones, Bryan Buus, & Adrian Nye
(O'Reilly and Associates, 1994)

The Future of Linux

It is difficult to predict the future of Linux or what additional features may be added in the future. Support for a given technology is added almost as quickly as it is released or discovered. While Linux is a solid production system, it is also a playground. Features are not added based upon market studies, or investment to sales ratios. There is no one attempting to control product cost, or worrying about "target markets."

Features are added to Linux because its developers love the technology and think the innovations are cool. It's pretty amazing what can be accomplished when the money factor is pulled out of the statement, "Can we get it to work and will it sell?"

Of one thing there is no doubt—Linux will remain on the cutting edge of technology for many years to come.

Summary

This completes our discussion of the features and services provided by Linux. You should now have a good understanding of how to configure the kernel as well as enable protocols and services.

In Chapter 14, we will look at Lotus Notes. While not a true NOS, it has a wide implementation and supports a number of network protocols.

Later in Chapters 33, 36, and 38, we'll revisit Linux and look at options for troubleshooting and optimizing network communications. We will also have the opportunity to evaluate the network monitoring and connectivity tools it provides.

CHAPTER
FOURTEEN

Lotus Notes

- Optimizing NT for Lotus Notes

- The core feature set

- Account administration and security

- Configuring Lotus Notes for networking

- The Lotus Notes client

- Lotus Domino and Internet access

Released in 1989, Lotus Notes set the standard for groupware and collaboration products before these terms even became buzzwords. In short, it has revolutionized the way organizations can do business and share information.

NOTE   If you are considering installing Lotus Notes for the first time, you may be well advised to take a training class on setting up and configuring it beforehand. Certain aspects of Notes installation seem to take for granted more familiarity than is likely the first time around.

At its core, Lotus Notes is a database—not a relational database designed to work with tables containing uniquely keyed single-line records, but a "semi-structured" database designed to store the the kinds of moderately structured data and documents that make up the bulk of an organization's internal information and communications. Examples of such information include e-mail messages, electronic documents such as Word or Excel files and index information about them, and a company's HTML-based employee timesheets, to name but a few. Notes proponents suggest that its greatest strength lies in providing an organizational framework for that information and moving it through an organization for modification, approval, and comment.

When multiple Notes servers are used, these document databases can be linked together and synchronized across multiple servers. This can be a powerful feature in a large networking environment. Linked databases allow users accessing information to retrieve all their data from a local Notes server. They do not need to tie up WAN links accessing information located on remote networks.

If Lotus Notes is not itself a network operating system, why include it in a book dedicated to networks and operating systems? There are two reasons:

- The popularity of the product
- It's a model for other client-server applications

Notes has enjoyed wide deployment. It is found on many networks and is a good example of the connectivity requirements of the typical client-server application. Many of the tuning and optimization tricks that we will use on Lotus Notes can be directly applied to other client-server applications.

Lotus Notes Features

Because Lotus Notes is not a true NOS, you must have an operating system installed on the server before installing Notes. The server component of Lotus Notes supports Windows 95, Windows 98, Windows NT, OS/2, NetWare (including IntraNetWare), Solaris, HP-UX, and IBM's AIX. While OS/2 was originally the Notes platform of choice, as of the spring of 1997, Lotus announced that Windows NT is the preferred platform for running Notes—a surprising announcement considering that IBM, which owns OS/2, also owns Lotus.

With this in mind, all the following examples for Lotus Notes assume an installation on a Windows NT server, version 4.0. Many of the configuration options, however, are applicable to every supported platform.

Lotus Notes Setup

As mentioned, Lotus Notes requires that an NOS be installed and operational prior to its installation. This includes enabling any protocols that Notes may require to conduct communications with clients and other servers. (The "Networking" section later in this chapter discusses the general procedure for protocol configuration in Notes.)

The installation utility does little more than install the required files on the server. There is no prompt to name the Lotus Notes server, enable certain network protocols, or even create a server certification key. This lack of guidance can be a bit disheartening for the network administrator who has not had the opportunity to receive formal Lotus Notes training. Before setting up a Notes server for the first time, you should consider getting Notes training to help increase your chances of a smooth installation.

The server is initially configured by running the Lotus Notes client on it. Once the client has been launched, you are prompted to name the server, assign an administrator, and select a default network protocol. The First Server Setup window is shown in Figure 14.1. Note that you can only configure one protocol and serial port. This initial configuration allows you to set up the bare minimums required to get your server communicating.

FIGURE 14.1:

The First Server Setup
window

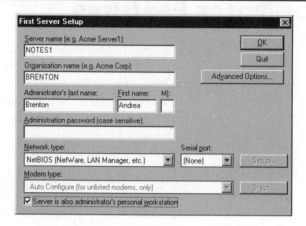

NOTE   If you are running the Lotus Notes client on the server for the first time and it does not prompt you to configure the server, check the settings in the NOTES.INI file. It should include the line KitType=2. This tells the system that a server will be installed on the machine. KitType=1 is used for workstation-only installations.

Optimizing Windows NT for Lotus Notes

There are two Windows NT settings you will want to optimize when running Lotus Notes—both are accessible from the Control Panel.

The first is located through the System icon. Click on the Performance tab in the System Properties window and change the Boost setting in the Application Performance window to None. This ensures that if the Lotus Notes server is not within the currently active window or is set up as a service, it will not suffer a performance degradation. This setting is shown in Figure 14.2.

The second setting to optimize is located through the Network icon. Select the Services tab and select Properties for the Server service. You will want to ensure that Maximize Throughput for Network Applications is selected. This tunes the system to pay more attention to network communications instead of file or printer sharing. The Server window was shown in Figure 12.6, as part of our discussion of NT Server.

Once your settings are complete, you should reboot the NT server to make your changes take effect.

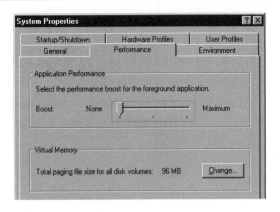

FIGURE 14.2:

Optimizing application boost
for use with Lotus Notes

Core Features

As of the time of this writing, the latest release of Lotus Notes is version 4.6. As mentioned in the introduction to this chapter, Lotus Notes is a database that can be linked across multiple servers.

Replication

With Lotus Notes, database information can be shared between servers using a process called *replication*. Replication allows two servers to synchronize the contents of one or more databases to ensure that each contains identical information. Replication can be performed on a predetermined schedule, or whenever a relevant event takes place (such as when a new Notes server is added).

Lotus Notes servers can connect to each other over a LAN or WAN using pretty much any networking protocol (except nonroutable protocols like NetBEUI, of course). They can also connect to each other directly via modem to exchange information.

As an example of this functionality, consider Figure 14.3. Three networks are connected by two 56Kbps leased-line WAN connections. The fourth site has no network connection to the other three and is an isolated network. Let's assume the organization has corporate policies and procedures that apply to each of the four locations. They want to provide access to a Notes database system containing this information. There are employees at each of the four sites who will need access to this information.

FIGURE 14.3:

A geographically separated
network that needs to share
a database

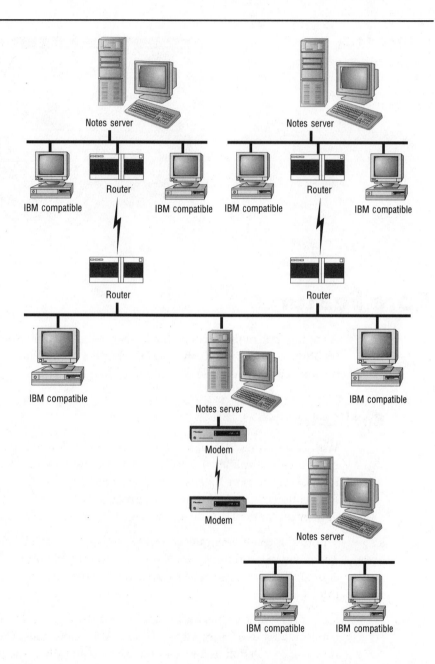

With a standard database program such as Access or dBase, all files would have
to be located on a central server in order to avoid having to connect (in this case via
a slow link) to each server. Employees at each of the two remote sites connected by

the leased line would need to access the database over the WAN. The more people accessing the database, the less bandwidth is available on the WAN for other services.

Also, the isolated network would have no way of accessing this central database. A modem pool would have to be created with enough modems to support the number of employees that may need to dial in simultaneously. Multiple modems would require multiple phone lines and software to connect to the network where the database is located.

If we were to replace the standard database model with one that uses Lotus Notes, the three Lotus Notes servers connected via WAN could exchange database updates over the WAN itself. Traffic would be kept to a minimum, as only database changes would need to traverse the WAN. Because each server would contain the same information once replication is complete, employees could view the database directly from their local server. This would not only reduce WAN traffic, it would also decrease the time required to view the database, because the connection would not need to traverse the slower WAN link.

As for the isolated site, two Lotus Notes servers could be configured to connect via modem. This would require only one phone line at each site and no special software. Each Lotus Notes server could call the other whenever it needed to relay database changes. Once the changes were sent, the dial-up link could then be terminated.

All of these information exchanges could be controlled on a per-server and a per-database level by adjusting the database properties. For example, we could configure replication so that our main server would accept document deletions from one server (and remove the appropriate documents from its own database) but reject attempts to delete records from the other two servers.

Replication is a powerful feature that made Lotus Notes a unique product for quite a few years. While there are currently other products hitting the market that can provide the same type of functionality, they do not yet have the maturity that makes Lotus Notes a stable product (of course, "stable" is a relative term when you are talking about software).

The Client-Server Model

Lotus Notes is a true client-server application: Some of the processing used to manipulate a database file is provided by the local workstation, while some of it is provided by the server itself.

For example, if you need to compress a database file (optimize it by removing unused space), you do not need to perform this function from your client workstation. You can simply use your client to create the request and submit it to the server, which will carry out the task. This frees up your desktop system to perform other functions.

The purpose of the client-server model is to isolate processes, locating each one on the system that can best carry it out. In the above example, it is more efficient to have the server perform the compression, as this is where the database is located. Performing the compression from your client would require that every byte of data contained within the database files be transmitted over the network to your workstation. The client would then have to transmit this information back to the server as it optimizes the file. Clearly, this could dramatically increase the amount of traffic on the network. By having the server carry out the task, you create less of a traffic impact on the entire network.

Other OS Features

Along with text, Lotus Notes database entries, referred to as *documents*, can contain embedded images, sound, video, applications, and even scripts. For example, you can create a Java or ActiveX script that users can execute by simply clicking on an icon. Such scripting can perform validation checks on user-supplied data, dynamically chart a set of data points on the screen, or connect to a remote ActiveX component and trigger remote processing of any kind. (If you can think of it, you can probably do it, using scripting and remote objects.) This makes Lotus Notes a powerful tool for sharing any kind of information.

Along with Java and ActiveX, Lotus Notes supports Lotus Script, a scripting language similar to Basic that can be used for filtering information or carrying out certain tasks. While Lotus Script will only function with Lotus Notes, it is directly portable to any platform that Lotus Notes may be running on. For example, a Lotus Script created for Lotus Notes running on NT will operate unmodified on a Lotus Notes system running on Solaris.

Lotus Notes also supplies e-mail capability. Each user gets their own personal database file for storing their e-mail messages. When a message is received, it is stored in a user's database file. When servers replicate database information, they can also exchange e-mail messages at the same time.

As of version 4.0, Lotus has integrated the interface of cc:Mail with Notes. This interface is simpler and yet more powerful than the original interface Lotus Notes used for e-mail. It supports advanced features, such as automatic message categorization through scripting as well as personal folders. Also included with 4.0 and later is a mail gateway, which allows the Lotus Notes server to exchange messages with other mail systems using SMTP.

As part of Lotus Notes' e-mail security and management, a central address book of all users is maintained. As of the latest Lotus Notes version, this address book has been expanded to include contact management and scheduling information. Through Lotus Notes, you can now schedule other users and resources (such as conference rooms) for meetings. The user is allowed to see unscheduled time periods for the people they wish to invite. This helps to ensure that there are no scheduling conflicts. The potential attendee has the ability to accept or reject the meeting invitation, as well as attempt to schedule it for another time.

Lotus Notes also offers tight integration with most major office suites. For example, a user can choose to change the default mail editor to use their favorite word processor program. A user who has Office 97 installed can choose to use the Word interface when creating e-mail messages.

Account Administration

Lotus Notes maintains a tight integration with NT Server. User account information can be synchronized between the two so that account additions or deletions are propagated across both systems. Passwords can be synchronized between Lotus Notes and the NT domain so that only a single logon is required for access to both network resources. This is done by checking the Add NT User Account(s) box in the Register Person window, shown in Figure 14.4.

FIGURE 14.4:

You can automatically add NT accounts when creating Notes accounts.

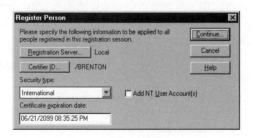

Lotus Notes can even use the NT server's event viewer for reporting operational events. The event viewer provides the administrator with a single point of reference to check the health of both Lotus Notes and the underlying operating system.

Security

Lotus Notes is arguably one of the most secure methods of exchanging information over a network. Its support for certifying user access and encrypting document information helps to ensure that the system remains secure.

When a user first logs on to a Lotus Notes server, they are challenged for a user name and password. This type of security is common with most networking systems. Lotus Notes takes this one step further, however, by requiring that the user have a valid User ID file.

The User ID File

A *User ID* is an encrypted identification number that uniquely identifies each user. This information is saved in a file format containing an .ID extension and must be made available during database access.

For example, let's assume you are away from your desk and realize that you need to access a particular Lotus Notes database. You sit down in front of the closest workstation and attempt to log on. Although you have entered the correct username and password, you find that the system will not allow you to access the required database.

This is because you also need to have your User ID file in order to prove you are actually who you say you are. While a snooping employee may be able to look over your shoulder and see your password as you type it in, if you protect your User ID file they will still be unable to access the Lotus Notes server using your account. How can you protect your User ID? One way would be to store it on a floppy and wear it around your neck as the latest in fashion accessories. Seriously, this information is normally stored on the user's local drive, in the notes\data directory.

The User ID file is made up of six components:

1. The user's name as recorded in the server's address book

2. The Lotus Notes license number assigned to the User ID during creation

3. The user's public and private authentication keys

4. The encryption keys used for encrypting fields within documents

5. Certificates, which grant the user access to specific servers

6. The user's password

The combination of these six items makes every User ID unique. If a user loses their User ID file and needs to have a new one created, any documents encrypted with the old key will be unreadable. This is because, even though the same user name and password may be assigned, the license and authentication keys would be different for the new ID file.

To ensure that a new key does not have to be generated when a user loses their User ID file, you should maintain a backup copy of every user's User ID file in a secure location.

WARNING There is no way to remove or clear a password from a User ID file without knowing the existing password. Do not forget what you assign for a password or you will need to create a new ID file!

Lotus Notes servers also use ID files, which are referred to as Server IDs. The files are identical except that a server name is used instead of a user name. A disadvantage of this type of security is that maintaining such data in a file that is openly accessible makes it vulnerable to hackers.

Certificates

Certificates are used on a Lotus Notes server to regulate who can gain access to it. This not only includes users, but also other Lotus Notes servers during replication. When a user or Lotus Notes server becomes certified, they are allowed access to the system. The kind of access to be received is governed by the Access Control List (ACL), which we will discuss later in this section. A certificate simply regulates who is allowed through the front door. A server's certification file is named CERT.ID and is located in the Lotus Notes program directory.

When a user first needs access to a Lotus Notes server, they must provide the Lotus Notes Administrator with a *safe copy* of their User ID file. A safe copy can be generated through the Lotus Notes client, which produces a copy of the User ID that can be certified but not used for Lotus Notes server access—yet. Once the Lotus Notes Administrator receives the safe copy of the User ID, they can use the server's CERT.ID file to *stamp* it. This stamp becomes part of the User ID code and provides the authentication required to allow the user to access the Lotus Notes server.

Once the safe copy of the User ID has been stamped, the user must merge the copy back into their real ID file (a one-time operation). Once the merge process has taken place, the user can gain access to the Lotus Notes server simply by logging on.

The process is nearly identical when certifying two Lotus Notes servers for replication. The differences are:

- A safe copy of the Server ID file is used instead of a User ID file.

- The process must be performed twice, once for each server. This is referred to as *cross-certification* and allows either server to initiate a connection with the other.

Certification helps to ensure that users or servers attempting to access the Lotus Notes server are in fact who they claim to be. It adds an additional level of protection to ensure that the data remains secure.

Lotus Notes security can be configured to follow either a flat or hierarchical model. Hierarchical is the preferred method of configuration, as it increases the amount of control the Lotus Notes Administrator has over the Lotus Notes domain.

Encryption

Lotus Notes uses RSA Corporation's Message Digest 2 (MD2) when performing encryption. Notes will encrypt the following:

- mail messages

- fields within a document

- communications with the server (either from a workstation or another server)

This is to help ensure that even when your information is being moved off of the server, it remains secure. Lotus Notes uses two separate encryption key lengths: a 64-bit key with the International version of their software, and a 128-bit key for the US version. The larger the key, the harder it is for an attacker to break the encryption code and gain access to your data.

The International key is smaller due to US federal regulation. During WWII, encryption was designated as a type of munitions and a threat to national security. Because of this, it is (still) heavily regulated. Messages sent outside of the US are limited to an encryption key length of 40 bits. Despite the efforts of many individuals and organizations to increase the acceptable key length, no progress has been made in doing so.

NOTE Lotus Notes gets around this 40-bit key limitation by using 24 bits of a special government RSA key. This means that while most people would have to decrypt 64 bits, the US government only has to decrypt 40 bits (64 – 24 = 40); thus, this configuration meets the maximum encryption export guidelines.

The US government reserves the right to decrypt any message they feel may be illegal or a threat to national security. As the key length increases, the difficulty in breaking the key increases exponentially. The current record for decrypting a 40-bit encrypted message by a private citizen is eight days. With the computing power resources of the US government, they could probably do this in even less time.

If your organization is global and requires encrypted connectivity from the US to any outside country, you should use the International version of Lotus Notes.

Access Control List (ACL)

The *ACL* controls the tasks that users are allowed to perform on a specific database as well as what information other servers are allowed to replicate. Each database has its own ACL to control access. The following sections cover the different levels of access.

Manager

Users with Manager access can modify ACL settings, encrypt a database for local security, modify replication settings, and delete a database. In addition, Managers can perform all tasks allowed by each of the lower access levels. Manager is the highest level of access that can be assigned to a user account. Lotus Notes requires each database to have at least one Manager. It's best to assign two people Manager access to a database in case one of them is absent.

Designer

Users with Designer access can modify all database design elements (fields, forms, views, and so on), as well as modify replication formulas and create a full text index. Designers can also perform all tasks allowed by lower access levels. Assign Designer access to the original designer of a database or to a user responsible for updating the design.

Editor

Users assigned Editor access can create documents and edit all documents, including those created by other users. Editors can also perform all tasks allowed by lower access levels. Assign Editor access to a user responsible for maintaining all data in a database.

Author

Users assigned Author access can create documents and edit documents they create. They cannot, however, edit documents created by other users. Authors can also perform all tasks allowed by lower access levels.

Reader

Users assigned Reader access can read documents in a database, but cannot create or edit documents. For example, you could create a Technical Support database describing helpful tips for resolving some of the more common problems your users encounter. You could then assign it Reader access to all of your users so they can reference the information prior to calling you on the phone. (Hey, it could happen…)

Depositor

Users assigned Depositor access can create documents but are not allowed to view any documents, even the ones they create. Once a depositor saves a document, it is removed from their view and cannot be retrieved. This setting can also be applied to other servers during replication when you wish to accept additions but not changes or deletions.

No Access

The name says it all. Users assigned No Access cannot access the database.

The various ACLs just listed allow the Lotus Notes Administrator to secure access to the databases as well as delegate tasks to other individuals. For example, we could assign Manager access to one of our Technical Support employees so they can maintain the support database mentioned above. This would allow the Lotus Notes Administrator to delegate the responsibility of administrating this specific database to another individual so they are free to perform other tasks (such as performing security audits by attempting to purge links to renegade internal Web sites that do not conform to the corporate security policy).

Networking

As mentioned, Lotus Notes requires that networking be enabled on the underlying NOS. Any protocols that you wish to use for Lotus Notes communications must first be enabled and functioning correctly on the operating system itself. For example, if you wish to use IP for Lotus Notes communications, NT must be configured with a valid IP address and a default route when applicable; also, it must have access to a DNS server or hosts file.

Once the underlying NOS is properly configured, Lotus Notes will support NetBIOS, NetBIOS encapsulated in IPX, IPX/SPX, VinesIP (Banyan VINES' communication protocol), AppleTalk, and IP. When IP is used, Lotus Notes uses the TCP transport and a destination port of 1352 for all communications. This includes all client-to-server and server-to-server communications.

TIP

If you will be connecting to your Lotus Notes server over the Internet for either client access or replication, you will want to make sure that TCP port 1352 is open on your firewall and/or packet filtering router.

Curiously, Lotus Notes must also be redundantly configured to use the same protocols configured on the NOS. It has no method of detecting which protocols the NOS is using in order to configure itself appropriately. While this is not a really big deal, as networking protocols are rarely changed once a server is in operation, it can be a bit of a hassle as Lotus Notes has its own unique way of configuring networking services. This method is very different than the configuration process used on any of the NOSs covered so far. We discuss the configuration of network protocols in the "Configuring Network Access" section of this chapter.

Lotus Notes also supports remote dial-up connections. Remote dial-up connections can be used to replicate information between servers. They can also be used to allow users to access databases remotely, from home or on the road.

For example, let's assume a traveling salesperson needs to periodically check in for e-mail. She would also like to keep her client database up to date with the latest contact information. Changes to the client database may originate back at the corporate office, but it is also likely that she may need to generate them while on site with a client.

With Lotus Notes this is a fairly elementary process. She simply places a copy of her mail file and the client database on her laptop computer. If she is at a client site and needs to update a record, she can edit the local copy located on her hard drive. (She does not need to connect to the corporate network to perform this task.) Then, when it is convenient, she can call the Lotus Notes server with her laptop and replicate the two databases (client and mail) with the originals located on the corporate Lotus Notes server. This keeps all the databases synchronized so they contain identical information.

Changes are not the only information replicated. For example, let's assume that while out on the road our sales rep receives a number of technical specifications on the product line from Engineering. Having no use for these documents, she deletes them from the mail file located on her laptop's hard drive. The next time she replicates, these deletions are replicated as well and the documents are removed from her mail file located on the Lotus Notes server. This way, she does not have to delete them again the next time she is in the office. The replication process ensures that her mail file remains identical on both the Lotus Notes server and her laptop.

As with networking protocols, the modem has to be properly installed within the NOS in order for Lotus Notes to utilize it.

Lotus Notes Client

The Lotus Notes client is designed to run on Windows 3.1, Windows 95/98, Windows NT, Mac System 7.x and 8.x, Solaris, HP-UX, OS/2, and AIX. Along with allowing a client to remotely access the Lotus Notes server, the client is also typically run on the server as well in order to configure it. For example, if you need to add a protocol to a Lotus Notes server running on NT, you will need to launch the Lotus Notes client in order to configure it. With this in mind, configuring communications on either a client or a server is identical.

TIP   Care should be taken to secure the Lotus Notes server console. If a client is launched from the server and databases are accessed as "Local," all ACL security can be circumvented for any database that is not encrypted.

The Lotus Notes client also contains an integrated Web browser. This provides a single user interface for Web, mail, and database access. The Web browser has the ability to monitor specified pages to see if they have been changed. If a change is detected, the Web browser can retrieve a copy of the page for later offline viewing. This can be a real timesaver if you frequent Web sites that contain many graphic files, such as the comics page on the United Media site.

Domino (Internet Services)

Beginning with version 4.0 and later, Notes includes Domino, Lotus's answer to Internet services. Domino includes some interesting features which make it an attractive fit for some networking environments.

Domino includes a Web server with support for CGI, Java, and ActiveX. While this type of functionality has become pretty common, Domino has the unique ability to integrate directly with one or more Lotus Notes databases.

One of the most difficult processes in developing a Web server is adding solid database support. It can be difficult at best for an administrator to link in basic services such as document searches and retrieval. It can be an outright scripting nightmare if you need to link in real-time services such as a discussion database.

NOTE   Domino lets you Web-enable Notes databases in record time.

Because Domino directly integrates with Lotus Notes, it leverages the ability of Lotus Notes to provide this type of functionality and focuses on simply organizing the data when it is presented to the Web browser. Domino includes an easy-to-use question-and-answer configuration utility. Simply fill in the fields describing which database you wish to link to, and what type of views you wish to present, and Domino does the rest. This can dramatically reduce the time required to develop a Web site with document search capability.

Domino also allows Lotus Notes users to access their mail from outside, using the POP3 protocol. This is useful if you have users who occasionally need to check their mail from their ISP. Of course, by using POP3 you lose all the replication and security benefits normally associated with Lotus Notes mail. Still, POP3 can be an engaging solution given the right set of requirements.

Domino can even support newsgroups and allow users to connect to the system using a newsreader. This is useful if you have a small number of actual Lotus Notes users but wish to create discussion forums that are accessible to all. News postings are saved to a database in the typical document format. Postings can then be viewed by either the Lotus Notes client or by any available newsreader.

Configuring Network Access

To configure networking on a Lotus Notes server, you must first shut down the server and launch the Lotus Notes client. From the client, select File ➢ Tools ➢ User Preferences. This will display the User Preferences dialog box. Select the Ports icon on the left-hand side of the screen. The User Preferences dialog box should appear as it does in Figure 14.5.

FIGURE 14.5:

The Communication Ports list of the User Preferences window

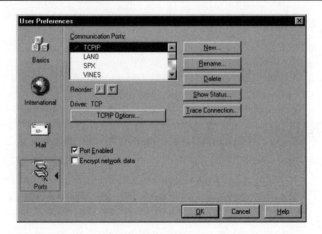

The Communications Ports list allows you to select which protocols and serial ports the server should use for communication. All active ports have a check mark next to them along with a check mark in the Port Enabled check box. The Reorder arrow buttons are only useful when configuring communications for the Lotus Notes client itself (not the server). This option sets up the order in which Lotus Notes will utilize each protocol as it attempts to find a service. Because a server monitors each protocol equally, this setting has no effect.

The New button allows you to set up a new communications port. Because Lotus Notes comes with a configuration for each supported protocol, you usually do not need this button unless you accidentally delete a port.

The Rename button allows you to assign a new name to the selected communication port. For example, we could rename the port TCPIP to be IP_PORT if we found this name to be more descriptive.

The Delete button allows us to remove a port from the Communications Ports list. This button is usually not required, as Lotus Notes will ignore any ports that are disabled. You do not need to remove them from the list.

The Show Status button displays the current state of the selected port. For example, our TCPIP port would show a status of being active and using TCP as a transport. Any of the deactivated ports would simply display "No Port information available."

TIP   If you activate a port, but the status display states that port information is not available, remember to stop and restart the server.

If the server is running while the Show Status button is selected, the status display will indicate any active sessions with the server. Figure 14.6 shows the status of an IP port with one active session. Notes session 03730001 is a session in progress from IP address 10.1.1.100. The status also indicates that the server is using port 1055 when sending replies. Notes session 03720002 is a session originating from the current client. This session is using a reply port of 1352.

FIGURE 14.6:

The TCPIP Port Status dialog box displaying session information regarding the IP port

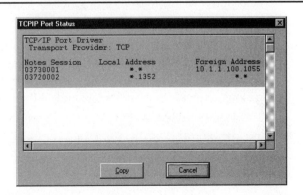

The Trace Connection button in the User Preferences window gives us a connectivity tool when diagnosing communication problems. We simply enter the name of the server we are looking for, and the client will report diagnostic information as it attempts to contact the server. The following is an example of a successful trace of the IP port for a Lotus Notes server named Notes1:

```
Determining path to server notes1
Checking normal priority connection records only...
Checking for notes1 at last known address 'notes1' on TCPIP...
notes1 is available on TCPIP
Connecting to notes1 over TCPIP
Using address '10.1.1.232' on TCPIP
Connected to server notes1
```

The following is an example trace to a server that is currently offline. The line numbers have been added for annotation purposes only:

```
1 Determining path to server notes1
2 Checking normal priority connection records only...
3 Checking for notes1 at last known address 'notes1' on TCPIP...
4 No answer at last known address
5 Performing extended search... (CTRL+BREAK to cancel)
6 Allowing wild card connection records...
7 Enabling name service requests and probes...
8 Checking for notes1 on TCPIP using address 'notes1'
9 Checking low and normal priority connection records...
10 Allowing wild card connection records...
11 Enabling name service requests and probes...
12 No default passthru server defined
13 Unable to find any path to notes1
14 Local Error: Unable to find path to server
```

Lines 1–3 show the initial attempt to contact the server Notes1. At line 4 this connection fails. Lines 5–11 represent two more subsequent attempts to contact the server using expanded pattern matching.

In line 12, the client attempts to look for another Lotus Notes server that may accept data destined for this system. For example, if Notes1 were located on a remote network, one of the servers on our network may be responsible for passing along requests to it. In lines 13 and 14 the trace gives up, determining that the server is unreachable.

Trace Connection can be used when verifying the connectivity between a workstation and the server, or from one server to another.

The TCPIP Options button is protocol-dependent and will change to reflect the selected protocol. The available configuration options will change as well. For example, when TCPIP is selected, this option lets us change the communication timeout value. When SPX is selected, the name of this button changes to SPX Options and you can select whether Lotus Notes should look for NetWare servers using DNS, Bindery services, or both.

The Encrypt Network Data option specifies that any data sent through this port should be transmitted in an encrypted format. This is useful when data may be traversing an insecure network such as the Internet. The systems at both ends of the connection must have encryption enabled.

Once your changes are complete, you can exit the client and restart the Lotus Notes server. During Lotus Notes server initialization, you should watch the Lotus Notes server screen to ensure that it does not report any errors with the newly added protocols.

Summary

This completes our discussion of Lotus Notes. In the next chapter, we'll return to the focus of network operating systems, with a discussion of IBM's Warp Server (known previously as OS/2 with LAN Manager), along with some other less commonly used network operating systems, including Banyan VINES and LANtastic.

CHAPTER

FIFTEEN

OS/2 Warp, Banyan VINES/StreetTalk, and LANtastic

- Configuring and using OS/2-based networking

- Configuring and using Banyan VINES, StreetTalk, and StreetTalk Explorer

- Configuring and using LANtastic

The previous chapters in Part III have each examined individual network server operating systems or environments in some detail: Novell NetWare/IntraNetWare, Microsoft Windows NT, Unix (and particularly the Red Hat implementation of Linux), and Lotus Notes. While those systems account for the great majority of NOS installations in use today, they are by no means the only ones. For instance, there's the whole topic of networking Apple computers (we'll discuss that topic in Chapter 16, where we cover AppleTalk and AppleShare). There are also plenty of existing networks that are using older, less favored technology. This chapter takes a brief look at three of the most important older systems: IBM's OS/2 Warp, Banyan Systems' VINES (and its offspring StreetTalk and StreetTalk Explorer), and Artisoft's LANtastic, focusing on installation and configuration. Although these networking tools have all lost market share over the last few years, they each have individual strengths as server software, and each of them is worth a look.

OS/2-Based Networking

Some readers may recall a time in the mid-eighties when Microsoft and IBM were jointly working on OS/2. During this time, they also produced a network operating system called LAN Manager. LAN Manager provided file- and print-sharing capabilities and ran on top of OS/2. After the two companies parted ways, each continued developing its own network operating system. In IBM's case, the name was changed to LAN Server, and at Microsoft, their product retained the name LAN Manager.

LAN Manager included some interesting features that have since become commonplace. To start with, it used the client/server architecture. The server software provided the file, print, and security services; the client software included a redirector, which would forward requests for networked resources to the correct LAN Manager server. Also, multiple LAN Manager servers could be configured to appear as a single server, so that a client station could log on using only a single user ID and password to access resources on multiple servers. Additionally, LAN Manager came with a variety of helpful administration tools, including a network monitor and tools for performing remote network administration from a client station. LAN Manager could provide the network administrator with an audit log of all accesses of network resources.

Surprisingly, LAN Manager could receive a shutdown signal from an uninterruptible power supply, offered AppleTalk connectivity for network services for Apple Macintosh computers, supported TCP/IP, and also came with a set of tools to allow easy configuration for internetworking with Novell Netware servers.

As Microsoft began developing the first version of Windows NT, they merged the functionality of LAN Manager into NT and, with NT's release, began phasing out LAN Manager. Interestingly, some vestiges of LAN Manager still remain in NT. It is possible to internetwork between NT and LAN Manager, for example. Also, parts of the networking APIs used by programmers on NT still include a number of LAN Manager functions, which also work on NT.

For IBM's part, they continued developing and supporting LAN Server. When IBM changed the name OS/2 to OS/2 Warp, LAN Server changed its name to become OS/2 Warp Server. IBM also added networking functionality to the OS/2 Warp client operating system, giving it integrated access to both Windows and Netware networks, as well as its own peer networking services. The peer services, like those in Windows 9x, allow one client station to share drives, folders, and printers with other client (and server) stations on the network, and they can do so in a way that is compatible with Windows networks. Thus both OS/2 Warp Server and the OS/2 Warp client can make files or printers accessible to Windows 9x and NT stations.

IBM also uses domains for administering multiple servers more easily and for handling security. An OS/2 domain, however, is more like a Windows 9x (or NT Workstation) workgroup than an NT domain in the way multiple OS/2 domains can be configured to share information.

OS/2 Warp and OS/2 Warp Server have taken a back seat in recent years because of Windows NT's growing popularity. Perhaps the main disadvantage now to using the OS/2 Warp products is simply that they are not able to run programs developed for NT. Aside from that, OS/2 Warp and OS/2 Warp Server are surprisingly stable platforms, capable of fitting in gracefully in a mixed network environment of Netware or NT servers. Because OS/2 Warp is an IBM product, and IBM's business includes mainframes, one benefit of using OS/2 Warp is that a good variety of mainframe gateway software is available, which enables OS/2 Warp to interconnect quite well with many types of mainframes.

Installing and Configuring OS/2 Warp 4

Because the OS/2 Warp client has networking support similar to that of OS/2 Warp Server, and because it is more likely to be installed in mixed network environments, the following procedure focuses on installing the OS/2 Warp client with the networking options needed to connect to Netware and Windows networks. Keep in mind that OS/2 Warp Server also provides these options, in addition to supporting OS/2 domains, and offers greater network management capabilities.

NOTE If you are installing OS/2 Warp for the first time, be aware that some machines will require it to be be installed on the first 512MB or the first 1023 cylinders of the first partition of the first drive in the system. The Warp Boot Manager program must itself be installed in this area in any case; however, some of the newer BIOSes allow you to install OS/2 Warp to other partitions or drives. If you cannot get the installation to work because no partition options appear where you can install the operating system, the problem is most likely due to this limitation. To get around it, you will need to adjust your first drive's partitioning (utilities such as Partition Magic or PartitionIt are invaluable for resizing and shifting partitions without destroying any existing data).

1. Insert the OS/2 Warp installation diskette (you may want to also insert the OS/2 Warp installation CD-ROM at this point).

2. Reboot the system.

3. A blue screen with IBM in white letters will appear, prompting you to insert Disk 1. Insert Disk 1 and press Enter.

4. After a few moments you will be prompted for Disk 2. Insert this and press Enter.

5. Next, you will be prompted to insert the OS/2 Warp Installation CD-ROM. If you have not already done this, insert the CD-ROM. (If you happen to have more than one CD-ROM drive, you may use whichever one you prefer, as the setup program will search all attached CD-ROM drives for the disc.) Press Enter to continue.

6. A Welcome screen will next appear, congratulating you on installing OS/2 Warp. Press Enter to continue.

7. Next, you will be requested to choose between Easy and Advanced installation options. The Advanced option lets you choose individual options to install. For the sake of starting with a standard set of options, we recommend starting with the Easy option. Note that you can always add or even remove options later, once the initial installation is complete.

8. A message saying *Loading system files* will appear. Eventually, a text-mode progress bar graph will appear, tracking the percentage of files copied. Be patient, as this is the longest part of the installation process.

9. Finally, you'll be prompted to remove any floppy disk from the drive. Do this, and press Enter to continue.

10. The system will now reboot, and after some files are loaded, the System Configuration screen will appear. If the indicated hardware and country choices are correct, click Next, otherwise, click the icon next to the individual option that needs to be changed. Following are the individual options you can change on this screen:

- Locale, Country

- Keyboard Type/Keyboard Layout

- Mouse/Pointing Device Type

- Primary Display Type

- Secondary Display Type

- Serial Device Support (i.e., the COM ports)

- CD-ROM Device Support

- Printer Support

- Multimedia Device

- SCSI Adapter Support

Again, to change any of these options, simply click its icon, and you will be presented with a list of choices. For certain types of hardware, such as multimedia adapters, you may wish to postpone making a selection now, as you can always add support for these devices later. Similarly, if your particular hardware does not appear on the list of available choices, just skip it for now. Once OS/2 Warp is up and running, you may be able to locate an

OS/2 driver for the device. (Try looking on the Internet, or phone or e-mail the company that supplied your hardware.)

Once these options are configured as desired, click the Next button to continue.

11. Another configuration screen will appear, containing more installation choices, most of which pertain to portable computers. You can change any of the following:

   - Advanced Power Management

   - SCSI II/Optical Drive Support

   - External Disk Drive Support

   - Infrared Port Support

   - PCMCIA/PC Card Support

   - Docking Station Support

   - Ultrabay Device Swapping Support

   Again, once these options are configured as desired, click Next to continue.

12. Next, you have the option of selecting a specific printer driver and a printer port. You can do this now or add printers at any time once OS/2 Warp is installed and running. Click the OK button to continue.

13. The next screen presents a number of optional items you may wish to install. Clicking on the check box for a category enables you to select individual items:

   - Assistance Center (Warp Tutorial, Command Reference, REX Information, Warp Graphical User Interface Guide, User Interface Agent).

   - Fonts (Courier, Helvetica, etc.). Generally you will want all fonts installed, which is the default setting.

   - Optional System Utilities (Backup, Change File Attributes, Display Directory Tree, Disk Partition Management, Disk Label utility, Link Object Modules). The last two items are needed only if you are a programmer and will be using this station to write OS/2 Warp software.

- Serviceability and Diagnostic Aids (Picture Viewer, PMREXX, File Recovery, Backup Restoring utility, Sort filter, Client installation utilities, Create Utility Diskettes).

- Optional System Componenents (OpenDoc, VoiceType, Security, Dedicated DOS/Windows session, HPFS). Generally you will want to install at least the HPFS (High Performance Disk System) option.

- Bonus Pack (CompuServe, HyperAccess Lite, IBMWorks, FaxWorks, Video In for OS/2, AskPSP, Remote OS/2 Support).

- More Printer Options (Printer Utilities, HP JetAdmin, JetAdmin Port Driver, MarkVision for OS/2, MarkNet Port Driver).

- Tools and Games (Enhanced Editor, Search and Scan Tool, Open GL 3-D Graphics, Optional Bitmaps, Solitaire Klondike, Pulse, Chess, Mahjongg Solitaire).

- Advanced Configuration (OS/2 DOS Support, DPMI, VEMM Expanded Memory Support, VEMS Extended Memory Support).

- Windows OS/2 Support (Destination Drive to use, Readme files, Accessories, Screen Savers, Sound).

- Win-OS/2 Desktop Configuration (Automatic or Advanced Configuration).

- Multimedia Software Support (Destination Drive to use, Base Multimedia support, Multimedia OpenDoc Support, Software Motion Video Support).

Once you've selected the desired options from these choices, click the Next button to continue.

14. A screen will appear (see Figure 15.1), listing Type of Activities options to choose from. These options are as follows:

- Access the Internet
- Connect directly to a LAN
- Connect to a LAN remotely using a modem
- Let me choose from all the services

FIGURE 15.1:

Installing Warp (OS/2)
Networking

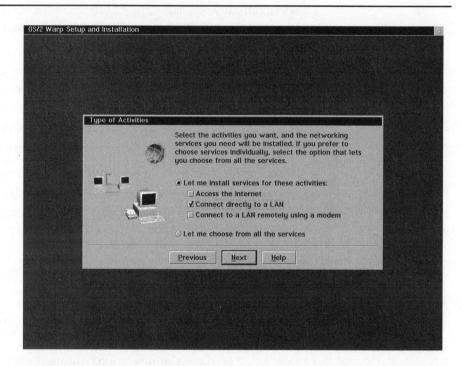

The last option lets you individually choose from all the drivers and modules. Because you can always add or remove options later, it is generally safer to choose from the first three options for now, letting OS/2 Warp select the corresponding software modules for each choice.

For our purposes, assuming you already have a network adapter installed in the computer, choose the first two options (Internet and direct connection to a LAN). If you envision needing to connect to a LAN over a modem dial-up connection, also choose the third option. Click Next to continue.

15. The next choice you are prompted for is whether to install File and Print Client. Note that this is a necessary component if you plan to access network files or printers located on an NT or Windows 9x system. Later steps in this procedure will assume that this option is installed.

16. Also select the File and Printer Sharing check box, unless you are certain you will not want to share files or printers from this system. Note that this option is what enables your OS/2 Warp system to act like a file and print server. Again, later steps will assume this option is installed.

17. Next, you must specify the workstation name, and type a description for your workstation. The main thing here is to be sure you select a workstation name that is not used elsewhere on your network. Click Next to continue.

18. On the OS/2 Domain Name screen, you must enter the name of an OS/2 domain to be used for login purposes. This corresponds more or less to a Workgroup in Windows 9x or NT Workstation. The default domain is OS2GROUP. Click Next to continue.

19. Now you will be prompted to enter a unique User ID and Password. The password needs to be entered a second time, for verification. Be sure to remember what you select as your password. You are not permitted to choose a blank password, so pay attention to what you choose for the password, as you will need it later to log in. Click Next to continue.

20. On the next screen, you will be asked whether you wish to install the Novell Netware Client. If not, choose No to continue, and skip to step 22. If you do wish to install Netware support, click Yes.

21. Assuming you answered Yes, you will next be prompted for a Netware Name Context and a Netware Preferred Server, to be used when logging in. Enter these (or you will need to do so later), and click Next.

22. If all went well, and OS/2 detected a network adapter installed in your system, this adapter will appear as the selected network adapter, for which driver support will be installed. If you need to, click on the adapter listed to select a different network adapter driver. If your network adapter is not listed, you may be able to use the NE2000 driver. Click Next to continue.

23. A confirmation screen will appear, showing you which network options are about to be installed, based on your choices. If need be, you can go back and make changes to your earlier choices at this point. When you are ready, click the Install button.

After copying some files, the system will reboot. Once OS/2 Warp has booted, you will be able to begin using or further configuring OS/2 Warp.

Sharing Resources Using OS/2 WARP

There are several ways to share a drive, folder, or printer under OS/2 Warp, so that it becomes available on the network for others to use.

To start with, you must have File and Print Sharing installed (as described in the previous section) and enabled.

The following procedure can be used to share any drive or printer:

1. With File and Print Sharing enabled, simply right-click on any drive or printer icon, and then select Properties from the pop-up menu.

2. Click on the Shares tab to display the Shares property sheet. Figure 15.2 shows an example of what you should see on the Shares tab.

3. On the Shares property sheet, you can change the description associated with this shared resource, specify a maximum number of simultaneous connections to this resource, and specify whether sharing of this resource should begin automatically upon booting.

4. To set or change the share name (which appears in browse listings for this resource), click the Manage Access button.

5. Be sure to click Save after making your changes.

FIGURE 15.2:

Sharing a printer in
Warp (OS/2)

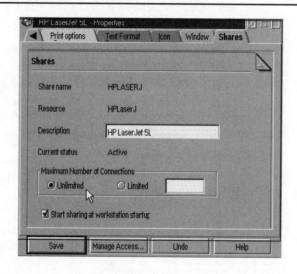

Resources shared in this way can be accessed from Windows 95 or Windows 98 and Windows NT, as well as other OS/2 Warp systems. If you cannot browse shared folders or printers from Windows 9x or NT stations, make sure you have NetBEUI (NetBIOS) or at least one other protocol installed on both the OS/2 Warp and the Windows machines.

There are at least two other ways of specifying shares or changing the properties of shares: You can open the Shared Resources applet, which lets you manage all the shares on your system from one central location; alternatively, you can specify shares via either the command line or a script, by invoking the NET SHARE command. The syntax for this is:

```
NET SHARE sharename=drive:path
```

To end a share from a command line, you can use the following syntax:

```
NET SHARE sharename /DELETE
```

Accessing Shared Resources Using OS/2 WARP

Once sharing has been set up for a drive, folder, or printer, there are several ways other stations on the network can access the shared network resource in OS/2 Warp. One graphical way to do this is as follows:

1. Open the Connections folder (typically located right on your desktop).

2. Open the File and Print Client Resource Browser.

3. This should display all machines on the network that have shared resources you can browse. Select a machine and double-click to view its shared resource(s).

4. From here, you can simply select any shared resource you see, double-clicking on it to open and access it. Files can be dragged to or from any shared drive or folder, and files can be printed to shared printers, provided you first install an appropriate printer driver that matches the shared printer.

5. To map a drive letter to a shared drive or folder, simply right-click on the resource, and select Assign Drive to assign it a drive. Note that once you've assigned a drive letter, the Assign option on this pop-up menu toggles to Unassign Drive, so you can easily unassign the mapped drive letter when you're finished with it.

Another way to access shared resources on an OS/2 Warp system is to use the command prompt or a script and invoke the NET USE command. The syntax is as follows:

```
NET USE driveletter: sharename
```

That is, you type **NET USE**, a space, a drive letter and colon, then another space, followed by the UNC (Universal Naming Convention) name of the shared resource. To remove a share in this manner, simply type:

```
NET USE driveletter: /DELETE
```

You might ask, Don't we need to include the sharename here, too? Wouldn't this example just delete the whole drive? Well, no, this doesn't delete the drive, it just deletes the net use mapping to that drive letter.

As you can see, file and printer sharing on OS/2 Warp is very similar to sharing files or printers on Windows 9x or NT: The same protocols can be used on both, and both allow you to share a resource via a context (right-click) menu command. Once a resource is shared, it can be browsed in a Windows 9x or NT Network Neighborhood just like any other network resource. In a similar way, resources shared via Windows 9x peer networking, or on Windows NT, can be browsed and accessed via Warp's File/Print Client Resource Browser applet or from the command line.

For businesses that use OS/2 Warp clients, or Warp Server as a server platform, Warp's network connectivity options are stable, easy to set up and configure, and best of all, can be accessed transparently from other types of client systems.

Incidentally, before OS/2 Warp became so network-friendly, one common approach to creating a network was to use LANtastic software, as LANtastic is very simple to set up and use, it works across different platforms, and it has been available in the various platform versions for several years.

In the next section, we'll look at using Banyan's networking products (VINES and StreetTalk), and then finish with a section on installing and using Artisoft's LANtastic.

Banyan VINES and StreetTalk

Banyan Systems has long been a pioneer in the network business. There was a time when 15 percent to 20 percent of all network seats were connected using VINES software. In recent years, however, its market share has been in the single digits.

One thing Banyan had going for it early on was its directory services architecture, called StreetTalk, which simplified the management of very large networks.

In this respect, Banyan was years ahead of Windows NT and even NetWare, but an indifferent marketing effort, combined with a number of limitations in early versions, have perhaps held back Banyan networking from really becoming mainstream.

It wasn't until version 7.5, for instance, that StreetTalk had client support for Winsock (which is necessary for running Windows Internet applications). Prior to this, it used a proprietary version of TCP/IP and required at least one VINES server residing on the same network.

The Varieties of VINES

Banyan's product names need a word of explanation. *VINES* itself is Banyan's full-blown, flagship network OS, which it still sells. VINES will install on Intel-compatible systems and offers the Banyan network server services. *StreetTalk* is the name of Banyan's directory services—the part that allows even very large networks to be managed from one network directory "tree." This is one of the primary remaining benefits of Banyan's network offerings, which is interesting, since they've been around since before NetWare (which now has NetWare Directory Services), and long before Windows NT (which is only now adding enterprise-wide directory services, slated for the next version of NT).

Not to confuse matters, but Banyan's most recent product offering, called *StreetTalk for Windows NT*, actually provides much more than its name implies. In other words, it doesn't just provide StreetTalk directory services on NT, rather, it brings almost all the features of a standard VINES server, *with* StreetTalk, to any NT system. Thus it actually deserves to be called "VINES on NT," or perhaps "VINES Lite." In fact, StreetTalk for NT will run very well even on NT Workstation, an option which may be worth looking at for the value it offers to small networks needing to maintain VINES compatibility. (NT Workstation's licensing prohibits more than 10 simultaneous connections. StreetTalk has no problem doing this, although the documentation warns you to observe your licensing agreements.)

At the time of this writing, VINES version 8.5 is shipping, and includes Year 2000 support, larger file systems (up to 16GB file systems and 2GB file sizes) and long filename support, increased file and print services per server, a larger communications buffer (up to 4MB in size), and remote management from NT systems, via the NT StreetTalk Explorer software.

What is particularly interesting now is Banyan's newest offering: the version of StreetTalk that runs on Windows NT. This, combined with the StreetTalk Explorer for NT, means you can both provide and access most VINES networking services right from any NT system.

For companies needing to support existing VINES networks, or looking at options for directory services conducive to managing larger networks, StreetTalk on NT provides a great way to set up a VINES server using all the networking hardware and other hardware drivers already provided for and configured by NT, and it also provides the added benefit of allowing the same machine to access both VINES and NT Server shared resources simultaneously.

In the following discussion, we'll look at installing and configuring StreetTalk for NT (version 8.5 is the shipping version at the time of this writing), together with StreetTalk Explorer (the current version of StreetTalk Explorer for NT is version 2.1).

Installing StreetTalk for Windows NT

Here are the steps for installing StreetTalk version 8.5 on a Windows NT system:

1. Locate and start the Setup program, which should be located in the Install folder on your CD-ROM. This will bring up the initial setup screen. (Note that it may seem to take a while before this initial screen appears.)

2. The initial screen prompts you for a language choice (English, French, German, Spanish, or Japanese). Select one and click Next.

3. The Welcome to StreetTalk screen will appear. Click Next to continue.

4. The Software License Agreement screen appears. Click Next to continue.

5. Now, you'll be asked for the Server Code and the Server Enabler Code, both of which can be found on a sheet of paper which should have come with your StreetTalk package. Enter these and click Next.

6. You'll now be prompted for the StreetTalk Admin Account password, as shown in Figure 15.3. Enter this twice and click Next. Important: note the name of the StreetTalk user shown at the top of this dialog; you will need to log in using this exact username in order to gain access to the system after setup!

7. Setup next asks for which setup type you want: Typical, Compact, or Custom. You also have the option of changing the destination directory. For this procedure, let's choose Typical (the default), and the default program location, which is [Server Root]:\Program Files\Banyan.

FIGURE 15.3:

Entering the password for StreetTalk's Admin account during setup—don't misplace this password!

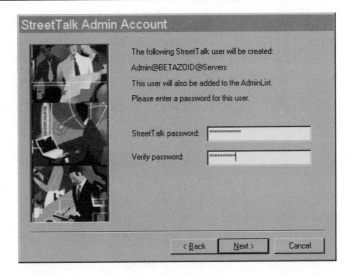

StreetTalk Admin Account

The following StreetTalk user will be created:

Admin@BETAZOID@Servers

This user will also be added to the AdminList.

Please enter a password for this user.

StreetTalk password: ***********

Verify password: *********

< Back   Next >   Cancel

8. The next screen prompts you for the directory for installing VINES files. (As mentioned before, StreetTalk/NT could really be considered "VINES lite.") Again, we'll choose the default, which is the same directory as step 7.

9. You are prompted now for which VINES client files to install: DOS, OS/2, or Win32. For this, we'll choose the two defaults of DOS and Win32. Click Next to continue.

10. The next prompt is for which Program Folder to install the Start menu shortcut into. Let's choose the default of StreetTalk for Windows NT.

11. The next screen is a review of all choices you have made, allowing you to back up and make changes if anything doesn't look right. When ready, click Next to continue.

12. This starts the file copying process, which may take a few minutes.

13. Now you'll be prompted for the Client Components Suite CD-ROM. Insert this and click OK to continue.

14. The Network Communications dialog box will appear next (see Figure 15.4). This screen has a number of different options, so I'll go over each one in turn.

FIGURE 15.4:

Configuring StreetTalk's
network options

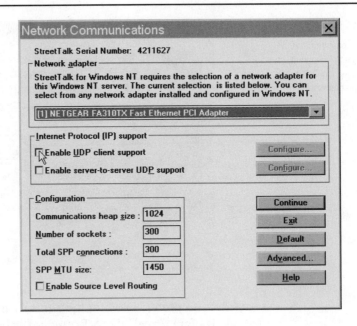

Network Adapter First you are asked to select a network adapter to use, from the one or more installed NICs on your system. Because you can only choose from cards already installed, this option is pretty straightforward— simply choose the card you've decided will be used for connecting VINES/StreetTalk clients to the server.

Enable UDP Client Support (Y/N) This option enables StreetTalk to transmit UDP packets in addition to VINES IP packets (which it will transmit in either case). Using UDP allows different StreetTalk servers to communicate over the Internet-standard UDP protocol; to do this, however, you must already have Microsoft TCP/IP installed, and your TCP/IP routing tables must be configured so that your Windows NT server is able to send and receive packets successfully with other NT servers running TCP/IP. We'll leave this option OFF for now.

Communications Heap Size The heap size must be large enough to handle the total simultaneous SPP connections and opened sockets, plus the data being transmitted by those connections and sockets. If your server only has 16MB of RAM, you cannot set this value any higher than the default of 1024, but with 32MB or more installed, you should be able to set this to 4096 or higher. Since you can increase this later as needed, go with the default value for now.

SPP stands for *Sequenced Packet Protocol*, which is a transport-level protocol that enables faster transmission of larger blocks of data as a single entity.

Number of Sockets   Each running program using network resources will use a minimum of one socket. Each socket uses between 70 and 80 bytes of space, so memory isn't much of a factor for this option. We'll stick with the default value, 300.

Total SPP Connections   Each session communicating with a StreetTalk server will generally use one SPP connection. SPP connections have a low memory cost also (between 80 and 100 bytes). Keep the default value (300) here also.

SPP MTU Size   MTU, which stands for maximum transmitted unit, refers to the maximum size of the SPP data that can be sent in an Ethernet, Token Ring, or FDDI packet. For now, we'll leave this setting also at the default value, 1450.

If your NT server is also configured for IP routing, you must decrease the MTU size to avoid fragmentation of the VINES IP packets. Packet fragmentation is undesirable as it impairs performance; however, the MTU value you select will affect all SPP connections to the server, so that should also be taken into account when selecting a size.

Enable Source Level Routing (Y/N)   This option should only be enabled when your server will be transmitting and receiving over IBM Token Ring bridges, and the Token Ring LAN your server is connected to itself has no other servers with source-level routing enabled. Leave this disabled as well.

Advanced   Also on the Network Configuration screen is an Advanced button. Clicking this button displays a warning that you should only tamper with these settings if you know what you're doing and need to. Since we're describing the most common settings during this install, we'll leave these settings as is.

To continue with Setup, click the Continue button.

15. You'll now be prompted for a StreetTalk name for this station to use. The name you specify must belong to a StreetTalk group for which the logged-on user is a StreetTalk administrator. Also on this screen, you can enter the name(s) of other StreetTalk groups to be searched for in locating other StreetTalk client stations on the network. These names can be identical to the Windows NT station names. To identify this station for this example, we'll choose the name MainStreet. When you're ready, click the Continue button.

16. At this point, you're almost done. A Setup Complete dialog appears, asking if you want to read the ReadMe file. To finish setting up, click the Finish button.

17. You'll now be prompted to restart your NT system so that setup can complete. Choose Yes and click the Finish button to do this.

18. Windows NT should boot back up, and the Banyan folder will already be opened on the desktop.

This completes the installation of StreetTalk itself. However, to create and manage StreetTalk's File and Print Services (that is, to use StreetTalk for the first time), you must also install the StreetTalk Explorer. StreetTalk Explorer can be installed on the same and/or a different NT station, giving you a good deal of flexibility in terms of where you manage your StreetTalk server from.

We'll cover the installation of StreetTalk Explorer shortly, but first we need to install the Banyan Enterprise Client software, which is required when installing StreetTalk Explorer.

Installing Banyan Enterprise Client

Banyan Enterprise Client is the name of Banyan's client software. This software, which is supplied in versions for DOS, Windows 3.x, Windows 9x, Windows NT, OS/2 Warp, and the Macintosh, allows these systems to act as clients, accessing Banyan shared files and printers. This client software must also be installed on a system as a prerequisite in order to use Banyan's remote network administration utilities, or StreetTalk Explorer (which is described shortly).

1. Insert the Banyan Client Component Suite CD-ROM if it is not already in your drive.

2. Start the Setup program, which is located in the \WINNT folder on this CD-ROM.

3. A Banyan Enterprise Client Installation and Setup dialog box should appear. Click the Install button to begin.

4. You'll be prompted for the directory to install the Banyan Enterprise Client software to. We'll keep the default location for this procedure. Click the Continue button.

5. On the Banyan Enterprise Client dialog, you're asked to enter up to three StreetTalk groups, which will be appended to your username whenever you forget to specify your group or organization while logging in. If your StreetTalk name is John Smith, then by entering GroupName@Organization-Name, you will only need to enter John Smith each time you log in, and the rest (the group name and organization name) will be appended to your username. There are three other options on this screen:

   - **Load Banyan Client Software at System Start**—This defaults to enabled.

   - **Use Windows NT Login for Banyan Client Login**—This defaults to disabled, but we recommend enabling it.

   - **Timeout Login Status Dialog Box**—The login status dialog is set to automatically close after six seconds, so this option lets you change this value. This option should be left as is.

   Click the Continue button when ready.

6. The next screen asks whether a common program group containing Banyan Client applications should be created. Go with the default of Yes, with the default location of VINES. A second question asks whether you want DOS and Windows 3.1 support to automatically load a DOS TSR (terminate and stay resident) program when such programs are started. If you run any older Windows programs, you may want this; otherwise, you can disable the option. Click on Continue.

7. The next screen asks you to enter a preferred and alternate revision range of VINES files. Just go with the default here, as this will include all Banyan revisions going back to version 5 or earlier. Click the Continue button.

8. The last screen asks if you're ready to restart NT. Click the Restart button when ready.

9. When NT starts up again, you should be able to log in as the StreetTalk administrator for this server.

Installing StreetTalk Explorer for Windows NT

StreetTalk Explorer is an application that offers browsing access and remote VINES configuration functionality. This program requires that Banyan Enterprise Client software for NT be installed first. (Installing in reverse order is not recommended—you'll get error messages both during the install and at login time.) Here's how to go about installing StreetTalk Explorer:

1. If it's not already in your drive from the preceding setup, insert the Banyan Client Components Suite CD-ROM into the drive and start the StreetTalk Explorer Setup program. It should be located in the STEXP folder on your CD-ROM. (It may be that you can find this and other setup programs in a USA folder inside STEXP.)

2. After some temporary files have copied, you'll see a Welcome screen. Click the Next button to continue.

3. This brings you to the Software License Agreement screen. If you agree with the terms stated, click Yes to continue.

4. On the Setup Type screen, you can choose from three options: Typical, Compact, and Custom. For now, let's choose Typical, which is the default choice. This screen also lets you modify the destination drive/directory where files will be installed. Click Browse to change this directory if you wish, and click Next to continue.

5. On the Select Program Folder screen, you can change the folder that will be used to contain the StreetTalk Explorer shortcut on the Start/Program menu. Change this, or keep the default of Banyan. Click Next to continue.

6. You will now see the Start Copying Files dialog, which gives you one last chance to view all the options you've selected (and back up to make changes if necessary). If everything looks correct, click Next to begin the file copying.

Once the file-copying process finishes, you'll be prompted to restart NT. Click Yes to restart. When NT comes back up, you should be able to log in using the Admin password you entered back when you were first installing StreetTalk.

Using VINES

Earlier versions of VINES were not quite so easy to install as StreetTalk for NT. Once StreetTalk, StreetTalk Explorer, and VINES Client software are installed, actually using VINES is remarkably straightforward.

The VINES/StreetTalk Naming Convention

For those new to VINES and StreetTalk, their naming convention may seem slightly unusual. Whereas the Internet expects periods to be used to separate parts of a subdomain from a main domain, VINES instead uses an @ symbol between each segment. Examples of VINES user addresses would be the following:

```
MaryRodgers@Graphics@MTINet
JohnClark@RainbowSix@milnet
```

This may be particularly confusing to users just getting accustomed to Internet e-mail addresses, which, although they also use an @ symbol, use only one of them, to separate the username from the domain name. The VINES naming convention, together with the underlying technology which supports it, is what has enabled VINES users to create very large networks consisting of many systems, within an orderly hierarchy of users, groups, and organizations, all easily accessible from the browser or Explorer client software. For example, Figure 15.5 shows Banyan VINES appearing in Network Neighborhood. Note the StreetTalk-style global network name showing in the foreground.

FIGURE 15.5:

Banyan VINES networking is accessible from Windows 9x and NT's Network Neighborhood.

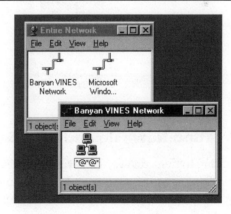

Logging In to VINES

To log in to VINES, click the Start menu and choose Programs ➤ VINES ➤ Login. This brings up a dialog for entering your user ID and password. Remember, you can also use a common NT logon once you've set up a VINES username that corresponds to the username you log in to NT with. With a common login, you'll only need to enter your user ID and password once to be logged in to both NT and VINES.

Creating New Users, Groups, and Organizations

Once you've successfully logged in to VINES, you'll be able to start up StreetTalk Explorer and use it to create additional users, groups, and organizations. Doing so requires simply clicking the StreetTalk main menu option, then New, then selecting either User, Group, or Organization to create each, respectively, as shown in Figure 15.6. Of course you must be logged in with Admin (administrator) rights before you'll be able to access all create options within an organization or group.

FIGURE 15.6:

StreetTalk Explorer running on NT

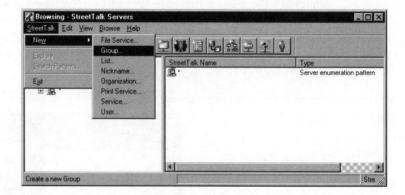

Creating New File and Print Services

Sharing folders, drives, and printers is also simple. Once again, using the StreetTalk Explorer, you can just go to the main menu, select StreetTalk ➤ New, and then choose either File Service or Print Service to share either drives/folders or printers.

Once a service has been created, you'll be able to access it from other client stations that have the VINES client software installed and are logged in with a valid username.

LANtastic (for Windows NT)

Artisoft's LANtastic has been a favorite of smaller businesses that need network services but don't want or need a full-fledged network with a full-time network administrator to go with it. Until recently, LANtastic was looking like it was really on the way out, but the new offering (version 8), which runs on NT, breathes new life into it. Like Banyan's StreetTalk, this software allows networks that have begun standardizing on NT to continue to support their other network clients, even from the same servers. In fact, it is actually possible to install both LANtastic for NT and Banyan's StreetTalk on the same NT Server machine, so that you can then access the same server from either StreetTalk or from LANtastic clients—and the client needn't have NT, Netware, or other client software installed, either.

Installing LANtastic on NT

While installing LANtastic on NT may seem really redundant in terms of providing networking services, recall that this allows any existing LANtastic client stations (running DOS, OS/2 Warp, Windows 3.x, Windows 9x, or NT) to then be able to access shared resources on the NT server (or NT workstation). Moreover, as with StreetTalk for NT, this gives you the capability of having a single physical server providing network services for a variety of different clients. NT clients and LANtastic clients, for example, can access the same shared drives, folders, or printers.

1. Start the Setup program from your LANtastic setup CD-ROM (or the self-extracting setup file from the downloadable trial version).

2. A Welcome to LANtastic screen will appear, with the option of immediately opening the setup readme.

3. A License Agreement dialog will display. If this looks acceptable to you, click Yes to continue.

4. You'll now need to enter your LANtastic serial number and verification key (which is located on your registration card). After doing this, click Next.

5. The next screen prompts you for a server name. This can be identical to your Windows NT machine name, or you can choose something different. Note that this name will be used by both the client and server parts of LANtastic on this machine. Another option on this screen is a check box to enable the sharing of drives and printer(s) on this machine. Presumably you want to enable this, so check this box (you can always change share options after the installation is complete). Click Next.

6. Now you'll be prompted for the installation directory. Click the Browse button if you to specify a directory other than the default. Again, click Next.

7. Next is the option to change the program folder name for the LANtastic programs on the Start menu. Enter a name or choose the default, and click Next.

8. A dialog box will now appear, advising you that several more dialogs will briefly appear in succession, as various components are being installed. Click the OK button and sit back as this happens.

9. The standard NT Network configuration applet will appear, now showing LANtastic Client and LANtastic Server as two new entries on the Services tab. The LANtastic NetBIOS Protocol appears on the Protocols tab. You may view the settings for these, or just click OK to clear this dialog.

10. A message will appear, explaining that you need to shut down and restart NT to complete the setup. Click the Restart button to initiate this process.

11. When NT restarts (and after you've logged on), a LANtastic dialog will appear, asking whether you want to add resources that will allow you to share your drives and printer(s). Clicking Yes here causes a brief flurry of activity, as various messages appear and disappear as each drive and printer on your system has an entry created for it.

12. Finally, you'll see an opened instance of the LANtastic Custom Control Panel. Amazingly, this single application contains all the configuration options needed to manage your LANtastic network. In the next section, we'll look at performing some of the more common tasks for Administering LANtastic networking using this program.

Configuring and Using LANtastic

As we've mentioned, all configuration of LANtastic networking services can be accomplished using the LANtastic Custom Control Panel program. If this is not already open on your desktop, you can get to it from going to the Start menu and choosing Programs ➢ Lantastic ➢ Lantastic. You should see the application as shown in Figure 15.7.

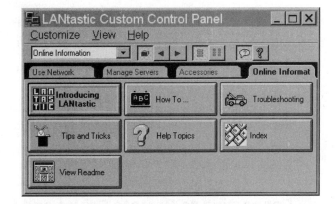

Initially, you'll see the Online Information tab. You may want to browse some of the information available here before proceeding, or return to it later. The other three tabs are labeled Use Network, Manage Servers, and Accessories.

Connecting to Computers

Before you can access remote drives and printers on the network, you will need to set up a connection to each computer that has resources you want to access. To do this, select the Use Network tab and click the Connect to Computers button. This will display a configuration dialog like that shown in Figure 15.8. Simply select the desired computer from the tree display in the upper left panel and click the Connect button. If you need to specify a different username and/or password (other than your default), check the Ask For User Name/Password First check box. (Entering a different name/password would be necessary if each computer is not configured to use the same login account information. Otherwise, leave it blank.) The drop-down list below the Connect button allows for easy selection of any of the most recently connected computers.

FIGURE 15.8:

Use the LANtastic
Connections window to
configure network
connections.

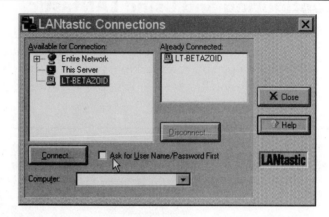

The grayed-out Disconnect button becomes visible whenever a currently connected computer is selected, allowing you to remove the connection.

Once you've specified one or more computer connections, you're ready to access remote drives and printers.

Connecting to Remote Drives and Printers

To use a networked resource shared from another station on the network, click on the Use Network tab, then click the Assign Drives or Assign Printers button. This will display a dialog like that shown in Figure 15.9.

FIGURE 15.9:

Use the Assign Drives
window to connect to a
remote drive.

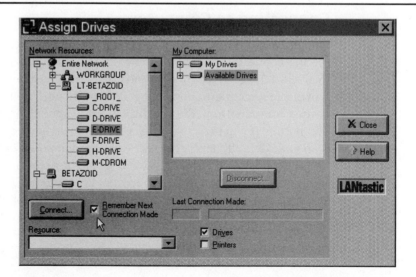

Scroll through the tree list of servers and their resources displayed in the left panel (Network Resources). Select the drive (or printer) you wish to access. If you want this connection to be reestablished automatically the next time you log in, place a check in the Remember Next Connection Made check box.

LANtastic will pick out the next available drive letter (for drives); however, you may select any particular drive letter via the My Computer panel. Simply choose a drive from either My Drives (for already designated drives), or the Available Drives (which shows all the unused drive letters).

After selecting both the network resource and its drive letter, simply click the Connect button to establish the connection. Immediately, this new connection will appear in your My Computer folder on your Desktop, using the designated drive letter.

Printer connections are made in a very similar fashion. Just by clicking the Printers check box on this dialog, you can create both printer and drive connections from the same screen. Select a network printer from the Network Resources list, and then select the desired printer port to connect to it from the Available Printer Ports listing in the right panel (see Figure 15.10). As soon as you click Connect, the selected network printer will appear in your Printers folder, which is located in your My Computer folder on the desktop (as well as in NT's Control Panel).

FIGURE 15.10:

Clicking the Printers check box allows you to assign both drives and printers from the same screen.

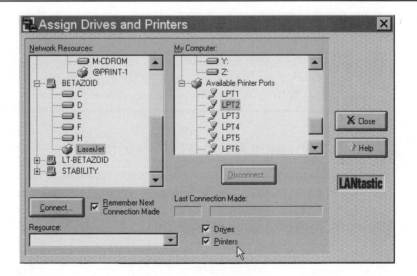

When you no longer need a connection, simply return to this window, select the connection, and click the Disconnect button.

That's all there is to creating and removing connections to shared network resources.

Preferred Servers

The Use Network tab also has a Preferred Servers button. Use this to designate which servers you want to appear in Network Neighborhood. This is a nice feature, as it lets you eliminate servers you rarely or never need to access, thereby keeping your Network Neighborhood less cluttered. You can still browse for these other servers by opening Entire Network and then opening the LANtastic icon.

Sharing Drives and Printers

We've looked at how you access resources shared on other machines; now let's look at how local drives and printers can be shared to other machines on the network. On the Manage Servers tab, click the Share Drives and Printers button. This displays a dialog from which you can add a new share, just by clicking the Add button and then specifying the resource and the share name you wish to use. You can also delete or modify any existing shared resource by simply highlighting its name on the list and clicking the Delete or Modify button.

NOTE
Before you're permitted to make changes to security-related settings, you'll need to log in using a supervisor-level username and password. The initial Supervisor account uses supervisor as both the username and the password. (See the "Connecting to Computers" section preceding this one for a description of connecting to a computer with a username and password.)

Managing Accounts (Security)

To add, remove, or modify user or group accounts for a server, click the Manage Servers tab and then click the Manage Accounts button. You should see a dialog like the one shown in Figure 15.11.

FIGURE 15.11:

You can manage accounts and account groups on both local and remote servers from this dialog.

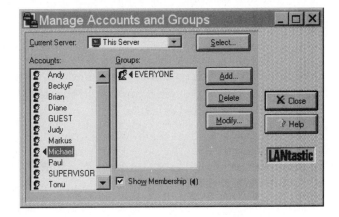

To add a new account, click the Add button; or to modify an existing account, highlight that account and click the Modify button. You'll see an Add or Modify dialog like that shown in Figure 15.12.

FIGURE 15.12:

LANtastic allows you to set individual permissions, password expiration, and other account information via this dialog.

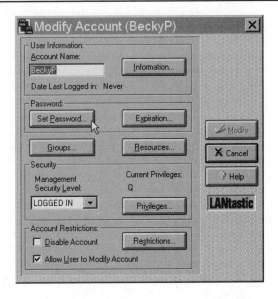

The Information button lets you enter phone number, address, and other information about the user. The Set Password and Expiration buttons allow you to specify the password and an expiration date or interval before which the password will expire.

The Groups button allows you to designate the groups this account is a member of, and the Resources button lets you select which network resources this account is permitted to access.

The Privileges button allows you to specify access privileges, including the following:

Super Access   Grants the account holder complete access to every shared resource, regardless of other settings.

Super File   Grants the account holder complete access to every shared file and folder, regardless of other settings.

Super Disk   Grants the account holder complete access to any disk drive, regardless of any security restrictions in place for the drive(s).

Super Queue   Allows the account holder to manage (view, cancel, pause, and restart) all items in the print queue, regardless of who placed them there. (Without this privilige, an account holder can only modify his or her own print jobs.)

Create Audit   Allows the account holder to make a user audit entry into the server's audit log file.

Notice the check box at the very bottom, which specifies whether the user is permitted to modify their account.

The Restrictions button allows you to specify the maximum number of concurrent logins, specify when the account expires, and even specify time periods (by as little as a half hour) and days of the week when the user may or may not be permitted to log in.

Adjusting LANtastic Server Performance

From the Manage Servers tab, clicking on the Server Control Panel button brings up a dialog that allows you to specify the server's relative priority in terms of the system's processing time. As you can see in Figure 15.13, a slider bar allows you to adjust the server's performance to favor either application performance or server performance. (The default setting is right in the middle.)

FIGURE 15.13:

The Server Control Panel

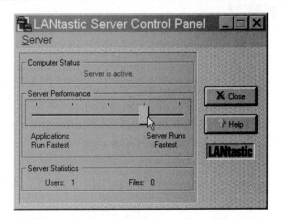

FIGURE 15.13:

The Server Control Panel

The bottom portion of this dialog also displays the number of users currently connected to this server and the number of opened (shared) files. This helps you get some sense of what the current demand is for server processing, which you can take into account when setting the server's relative performance level.

Here's another handy feature of this dialog, and one that you might easily overlook: under the Server menu on this dialog, there's a Server Summary option. Selecting this displays a list of server statistics, including the maximum allowed logins, maximum opened files, maximum threads, whether auditing is currently enabled, and other helpful information.

LANtastic Summary

As you can see, LANtastic provides a good deal of networking functionality in an easy-to-use package. LANtastic is still a favorite among home users and smaller offices. Although we've only been focusing on LANtastic for NT, there are also versions for Windows 9x, OS/2 Warp, and other operating systems, and all versions can communicate with each other.

LANtastic would not be a good choice for running a large network with lots of servers, because it lacks the global directory services that have become standard in other network operating environments, which are offering more and more now out of necessity. Even so, LANtastic is a great choice for smaller networks that don't want or need a dedicated network administrator to manage the network.

Summary

In this chapter, we've covered quite a bit of ground, looking at three quite different network operating systems, each with certain trade-offs in terms of ease of use, functionality, and cross-platform support.

OS/2 Warp is most like Windows 9x's peer-to-peer networking, and Warp Server provides very solid network performance on a variety of network protocols. It can simultaneously support both Warp client workstations and Windows clients.

Banyan's StreetTalk for Windows NT, and the companion StreetTalk Explorer for NT, breath new life into StreetTalk and VINES, by making the VINES services available on top of any NT server or workstation. In this way, VINES clients can continue to be quite easily supported within an environment that consists of NT servers.

LANtastic is somewhat limited compared to the other two networking tools, but despite its simplicity in installation and configuring, it offers a surprising degree of flexibility for smaller networks.

In our next chapter, we'll look at yet another type of networking: Apple networking via AppleTalk and AppleShare IP.

CHAPTER

SIXTEEN

16

AppleTalk and AppleShare

- The AppleTalk Protocol

- LocalTalk

- EtherTalk

- TokenTalk

- AppleShare

- AppleShare IP Version 5

Many people don't realize it, but the concept of peer-to-peer networking was introduced to consumers by Apple Corporation, when it incorporated AppleTalk into the Macintosh operating system. The ability to network Mac computers really helped Macs to rise in popularity, as it allowed an entire group of users to access such relatively expensive items as, for instance, a larger hard drive or a high-quality printer. Peer-to-peer networking (or networking generally) was also of course a boon to workgroup productivity, as files of any size could be copied from one station to another with a simple drag of the mouse.

In this chapter, we'll first look at some of the technical aspects of the AppleTalk protocol (which is actually a group of protocols), and see how AppleTalk and its underlying protocols support user-friendly file and print services for networks of Apple computers.

Then we'll look at Apple's server product, called AppleShare IP, which allows a Mac to not only behave as a file and print server for other Macs, but (as of version 5) also brings with it the ability to offer Web and FTP services. At the time of this writing, AppleShare IP 6.0 is still in beta, but if the release version contains all the features currently planned, it will introduce a long-awaited and much-needed feature: support for Windows networks.

The AppleTalk Protocol

Just as TCP/IP (or just IP) really refers to an entire suite of protocols that together make up the Internet protocol suite, *AppleTalk* actually comprises many specialized protocols, each of which performs one or more roles in making AppleTalk a seamless networking experience for Apple users. In Figure 16.1, you can see each of these protocols, as well as the layer in the OSI model to which each protocol corresponds.

AppleTalk also supports a variety of transmission media, including Apple's own original networking hardware, plus Ethernet and Token Ring. As you can see in Figure 16.1, the different hardware types—LocalTalk, EtherTalk, and TokenTalk—are served by their corresponding Data Link layer protocols.

FIGURE 16.1:

AppleTalk's various protocols as they map to the OSI reference model

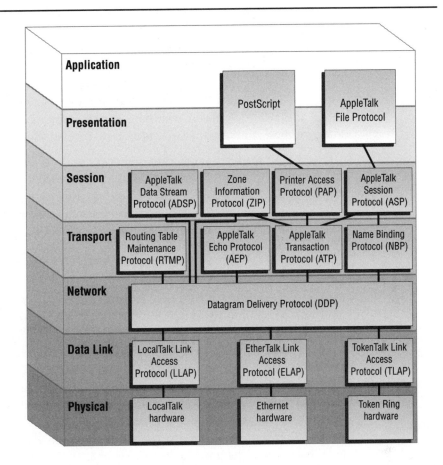

LocalTalk

LocalTalk was the name given to AppleTalk running on Apple's low-cost proprietary networking hardware. LocalTalk hardware consisted of (in most cases) a built-in transceiver together with twisted-pair cabling, and provided 230.4Kbps throughput. While not fast by today's networking standards, 230Kbps is still faster than either parallel or serial connections on PCs (which can also support low-speed networking via Windows' Direct Cable Connection), and LocalTalk works on even the oldest Macs.

LocalTalk Link Access Protocol (LLAP)   LocalTalk makes use of the *LocalTalk Link Access Protocol* (*LLAP*). The LLAP protocol is responsible for regulating shared access to the network medium (determining who gets to talk next), encapsulating data into packets for transmission, and specifying the destination node address for each packet. Although LLAP also checks for and discards any corrupted packets (which it detects using a CRC, or cyclic redundancy check code), LLAP does not guarantee that each packet arrives at its destination. Thanks to the integrity check, though, any packets that *are* received should contain accurate data.

Over time, other companies have come out with Apple networking solutions that use LLAP but use different types of physical media. One such product that is still available is PhoneNET, from Netopia (formerly Farallon Computing). PhoneNET uses standard twisted-pair cabling and is connected in a star topology, using a central hub. Given the ever-decreasing cost of standard Ethernet adapters and hubs, however, unless you're on a shoestring budget, it generally makes more sense to use Ethernet or even Token Ring.

Carrier Sense Multiple Access with Collision Avoidance (CSMA/CA)
One innovation introduced by LLAP is the approach it uses to manage shared access to the transmission medium. This approach, which is unique to Apple networking, is called *CSMA/CA*, or *carrier sense multiple access with collision avoidance*. This is similar, but not identical, to Ethernet's CSMA/CD (whose last two letters, you will recall, stand for *collision detection*). The CSMA part functions like standard Ethernet—each transceiver monitors the transmission medium to see if it is available before attempting to transmit—but in addition, the first thing an AppleTalk transmitting station does is transmit a small handshaking packet to tell other stations the line is in use. Once other stations see this packet, they will refrain from transmitting. Even with this technique, it is still possible that two or more stations may send their initial handshaking packet simultaneously. When this happens, the collision avoidance strategy kicks in: Both stations wait a random period of time before attempting to send again.

The effect of this difference from standard Ethernet's CSMA/CD is that collisions during transmission of larger data frames are reduced, because if a collision is going to occur, it will happen during the initial handshaking stage. Thus, the advantage to this approach is that fewer time-wasting collisions occur on the network segment. The disadvantage is that the initial handshaking packets themselves take up bandwidth on the segment. Overall, this is not such a big problem for small networks, but it does cause a noticeable decrease in usable bandwidth on large networks.

Although CSMA/CA was initially designed for use with LocalTalk (using LocalTalk transmission media), it is also used on Apple's EtherTalk implementation, which is much faster in comparison.

Dynamic Node Assignment   Another innovation of LLAP is the way network node addresses are assigned. Recall that with other protocols, network addresses are specified either in hardware (a ROM chip on the network adapter for example) or in software (a locally specified TCP/IP address for example), or are assigned via a server (with DHCP for example). LLAP assigns network addresses at boot time, without requiring a centralized address server. (DHCP provides a similar benefit.) Note that this LLAP-assigned address is a Protocol-level address. Apple networking hardware also has and makes use of the network adapter's unique hardware address at the Physical and Data Link levels, but users are not required to know or care what the physical address is. The Protocol-level address uniquely identifies a particular Apple protocol stack, and is used to identify particular peer nodes on an AppleTalk network.

The way this works is as follows:

1. Each station on the network, as it is booting and initializing its protocol stack, chooses either a random number or its last used address (which it retrieves from nonvolatile memory).

2. AppleTalk Address Resolution Protocol (AARP) compares this number or address with addresses of other known stations (stored on each station in a list called the Address Mapping Table—AMT). If it is already in use, the process is repeated from step 1.

3. If the selected number/address is not already in use, AARP then attempts to *make sure* the address is not already in use anywhere else on the network, by sending a series of broadcast packets that contain the proposed address number. These packets are called *AARP probe packets*.

4. Other nodes' AARP layers watch for incoming probe packets and check the proposed address number to see if it matches their own address.

    - If it matches, the station sends back a response packet to the originating station. When the probing node receives this acknowledgment to its probe packet, it drops the tentative address and selects another candidate (that is, it repeats the process from step 1).

- If no acknowledgment is received, the originating station interprets this to mean that the selected address is available to be used. Once it makes this determination, the originating station can claim the address, and other stations' AARPs will then add that station's new address to their AMTs.

NOTE   LLAP uses only an 8-bit network addressing scheme, and is therefore limited to a maximum of 254 nodes.

EtherTalk

EtherTalk, as its name implies, is Apple's implementation of Ethernet. Like standard Ethernet, EtherTalk supports thick or thin coax as well as twisted-pair Ethernet. Twisted-pair cabling is generally the preferred transmission medium now, given the widespread availability of 100Mbps PCI networking adapters, which Apple happily supports.

EtherTalk is essentially an Ethernet variation of LLAP. Being a link-access protocol like LLAP, it too operates at the Data Link layer, and it performs duties similar to LLAP. The *EtherTalk Link Access Protocol*, or *ELAP*, incorporates both CSMA/CA and dynamic node addressing. It has some differences from LLAP to handle the faster Ethernet transmission speeds and cabling, and, as of Phase 2 AppleTalk (which has been available now for several years), it can make use of a larger addressing range, allowing the creation of larger networks.

NOTE   In addition to being able to use EtherTalk, Macs are capable of being configured to use Netware's IPX or TCP/IP over Ethernet as well. With the release of AppleShare IP 6.0, it appears they will also gain the ability to communicate with Windows stations using Microsoft's NetBEUI implementation.

Zones   With AppleTalk, a group of Macs can be designated as part of a *zone*. Essentially, a zone is just a name tied to a number, and allows for convenient grouping of Macs by work area or other designation within a larger physical network. Whereas LocalTalk networks consist entirely of one zone, EtherTalk and TokenTalk networks can comprise many interconnected zones. A special protocol called the Zone Information Protocol (ZIP) handles zone name and member lookups. Typically, ZIP works in conjunction with the Name Binding Protocol (NBP) to match network node names with node addresses.

Non-Etended vs. Extended Networks   Earlier we stated that LocalTalk is limited to 254 nodes, because it uses eight-bit addressing. Such a network is referred to as a *non-extended network*. Fortunately, Macs can also use an *extended network* addressing scheme, where each node is designated by both a node number and a network number. The combination of network and node numbers permits a theoretical maximum of some 16 million concurrently active nodes.

Another aspect of extended networks is their ability to support multiple zone names. As we've mentioned, this makes for a more convenient partitioning of networked nodes; it reduces, for instance, the number of nodes visible at any one time in the Chooser panel (when connecting to networked resources). This allows Macs to be grouped according to function, and is somewhat analogous to the workgroup concept used by Windows 95/98 (and earlier by Windows for Workgroups).

While extended networks create the possibility for larger networks (actually networks of networks), and zones provide some grouping ability, zones by themselves are nowhere near as convenient or scalable as Novell's NetWare Directory Services (NDS) when managing larger networks. On the other hand, zones are far simpler to administer than multiple NT domains, for instance, albeit with less flexibility (and less security).

TokenTalk

Like EtherTalk, *TokenTalk* maps hardware network addresses to AppleTalk protocol node numbers, and it encapsulates the AppleTalk-specific networking information into an AppleTalk datagram, which is then transmitted by the Data Link layer. *TLAP (TokenTalk Link Address Protocol)* works in conjunction with the underlying Token Ring Data Link layer, applying AppleTalk-specific packet packaging and AppleTalk-friendly node addressing over an otherwise standard Token Ring network. Because it uses standard Token Ring hardware and cabling, TokenTalk can coexist with other Token Ring stations on a Token Ring network.

Other AppleTalk Protocols

We've already mentioned the Zone Information Protocol (ZIP) and Name Binding Protocol (NBP), as well as the Link Access protocols for LocalTalk, EtherTalk, and TokenTalk (LLAP, ELAP, and TLAP, respectively). Referring back to Figure 16.1, there are a number of other protocols that provide AppleTalk services at the various Session layers. We'll look at each of the rest of these in turn.

Datagram Delivery Protocol

Datagram Delivery Protocol operates just above the Link Access protocols, at the Network layer. Its job is to forward packets, or datagrams, to a destination address. Incoming datagrams that are damaged (as detected via a CRC) are dropped, which ensures that all packets that are received are error free. DDP does not however, guarantee that all datagrams that are sent are actually received. This function is performed by a higher-level protocol.

AppleTalk Session Protocol

The *AppleTalk Session Protocol* (*ASP*) is a higher-level protocol whose purpose is to allow workstations to establish an ongoing dialog with a server for the purpose of fulfilling a set of requested functions. ASP communications are typically lopsided—that is, the workstation typically sends multiple requests to the server, and the server may reply only periodically, or in any case, less frequently, using the session number that was uniquely assigned to the session. This protocol allows workstations to request server status information, and it allows servers to send an "attention" command back to the workstation when needed, to alert the workstation of the status of an earlier request.

AppleTalk Data Stream Protocol

The *AppleTalk Data Stream Protocol* (*ADSP*) is a connection-oriented (two-way) protocol that makes possible a bidirectional data flow between two nodes. As a higher-level protocol, ADSP abstracts network communications to act like a pipe or channel, which, once established between two nodes, allows the sending node to dump data into the pipe without concern for synchronization or acknowledgment. A receiving stream can also be used to simultaneously perform the reverse function, allowing the receiving node to transmit back to the original node whenever it needs to. Streaming protocols are popular with programmers because they make sending data across the network rather like copying a file—data can be sent in an ad-hoc manner, in varying amounts, and whenever needed.

AppleTalk Transaction Protocol

AppleTalk Transaction Protocol, or *ATP*, provides the important function of enabling network nodes to verify the success of a transmission. ATP packets include a packet sequencing number, a retry timeout value, the number of reply packets expected, and space for data. The sequencing number helps the receiving node to resequence incoming packets in the event they happen to arrive out of order. (This is something that cannot happen on a simple non-extended network, but it can happen where multiple segments and routing are taking place.) The timeout value allows the receiving station to determine the longest time the receiving station should wait before acknowledging that packet. Depending on how many packets are being sent, some number of reply packets will be expected back; and unless the sending station receives all of them in a timely manner, it will attempt a retransmission or finally report a network error.

ATP can be viewed as a two-way dialog that ensures safe delivery. This type of communication is sometimes referred to as a connection-oriented delivery (as opposed to a connectionless delivery, which is what occurs at the lower Data Link level).

Routing Table Maintenance Protocol

The *Routing Table Maintenance Protocol* (*RTMP*) is used by AppleTalk routers to establish and maintain the routing tables, which are lists of network and node numbers needed to direct the flow of datagrams between stations residing on different networks.

RTMP allows multiple routers to periodically exchange routing information. This is what allows each router to know where to route packets whose destinations are more than one "hop" away. As each station's router receives additional routing information from the other stations, it accumulates any new information and thereby adds to the range of stations it knows how to forward packets to.

AppleTalk Echo Protocol

The function of the *AppleTalk Echo Protocol* (*AEP*) is simply to send back to the originating station an exact copy of the data portion of the echo packet. When first being transmitted, an echo packet is called an Echo Request packet. When it is received, the destination station changes the function field in the packet to turn it into an Echo Reply packet, and then returns it to the originating station.

The echo protocol provides much the same service as pinging on an IP network. The originating station can set the data portion of the echo packet to a unique set of values, and then check the data values of incoming Echo Reply packets to determine which packet is which, and whether the packet was retransmitted accurately. Essentially, AEP's role is to provide a means of testing both the transmitting and receiving functions between any two nodes on an AppleTalk network.

Printer Access Protocol

The *AppleTalk Printer Access Protocol*, or *PAP*, has a somewhat misleading name. The word "printer" remains only for historical reasons, as this protocol was initially designed specifically for communication with print servers. The protocol itself, however, has nothing internal that would prevent its being used in a variety of other workstation-server communications. A PAP-based server is designed to handle some preset maximum number of jobs from multiple workstations, with an open connection between workstation and server being maintained for each job during the entire server request function. This allows each workstation to monitor its server request for successful completion. One interesting aspect to the server-side implementation of PAP is that it keeps track of which stations were most recently serviced, and it attempts to service new station requests prior to serving "repeat customers" (our term, not PAP's). This has the effect of giving all stations an equal share of access (over time) to the server's services or resources.

AppleTalk Filing Protocol

The *AppleTalk Filing Protocol* (*AFP*) performs many communications functions necessary to sharing and accessing files across the network. It allows a program running on a workstation to access files on a server using the same file manipulation functions used for accessing local files. A translation layer converts these file system commands into AFP commands, which are then sent across the network to the node containing the desired resource. AFP permits remote accessing of all of the following file-related entities: file servers, file volumes (drives), folders, files, file and folder names, file type information, and individual file forks (recall that data and resources for a given file are kept in separate parts, called forks). AFP also handles the login functionality required for files that require user authentication in order to be accessed.

AppleShare: The Next Generation

In addition to standard peer-to-peer networking over AppleTalk, Macs running software called *AppleShare* can function as dedicated file and print servers. While AppleShare runs on the top of the Mac OS (which does not yet support full memory protection, thread management, and secure data flow [I/O]), it is still possible to use AppleShare to create a very functional and stable networking solution. In our experience, AppleShare server stability varies widely, and behind the more stable AppleShare installations you will typically find more experienced Apple-savvy administrators. We've heard of cases of AppleShare servers running several months without rebooting, but we've also seen cases where AppleShare servers needed rebooting practically every morning due to hangs or crashes.

Most AppleShare stability problems stem from one of three sources:

- Running with a defective version of the operating system. (Several 7.*x* series releases had notorious networking bugs.)

- Running other software on the server simultaneously. (This should work, but it's not recommended, for reasons of speed and stability.)

- Having a conflict with one or more loaded extensions. (You should eliminate all extensions that aren't really needed.)

In what follows, we'll look briefly at the history of AppleShare, then survey the most recent version of AppleShare (ASIP version 5), occasionally pointing out new features in the forthcoming version (version 6.0, currently in beta).

In the Beginning

In 1986 Apple introduced AppleTalk, a networking protocol that brought networking to the masses. And at that time, Apple *was* the masses. Apple was the market leader. Most people who did consider owning a personal computer owned an Apple; the IBM PC was for business users.

Before Apple wowed their users with AppleTalk, they wowed the world with the Macintosh, a tiny little computer with a flair for making the previously complicated easy. The Macintosh integrated a lot of the features that weren't available with other kinds of computers without purchasing and adding extra equipment (if such equipment was even available for that other computer).

After a period of what has seemed like several years of relatively little innovation and dwindling market share, it appears that Apple's Macs are making a comeback. With Steve Jobs at the helm, and tapping what are currently the fastest consumer processors on the market, Apple's products deserve renewed interest.

AppleShare and AppleShare IP

Early versions of AppleShare offered an upper-level networking solution for the Macintosh. Initially it offered file and print services over AppleTalk networks. DOS and Unix stations were supported only in the sense that an AppleTalk network adapter was made available to be installed in these machines. By 1995, however, some time after the Internet had started to become something more than a lark, AppleShare was no longer able to handle the traffic that network administrators were looking for, and it was clear that Apple needed a new networking solution if it wanted to stay in the game. Longtime Apple-oriented companies were turning to Unix, NetWare, Windows NT, and early implementations of Apple TCP/IP to upgrade their solutions.

Apple delivered *ASIP* (*AppleShare IP*) in 1995, incorporating many of the features that users had been looking for in an Apple networking solution. Most importantly, ASIP offered full support for TCP/IP. Even the AppleTalk protocol itself was modified, to facilitate TCP/IP-related server polling within the AppleTalk Filing Protocol specifications. At the time of this writing (mid-1998), the currently shipping version of ASIP is version 5.0. For the rest of this chapter we'll take a close look at what's available with this version, with a few comments on what you can expect in ASIP 6.0.

ASIP 5 Features

AppleShare 5.0 includes the following features:

- Full integration of TCP/IP-based services

- Improved file services and 250-stream Web server

- Complete HTTP 1.0 and FTP services

- Support for MIME (Multipurpose Internet Mail Extensions)

- Four-port "multihoming"

- Remote application serving

- 2TB (terabyte) volume capacity

- Full support for SMTP, POP3, IMAP, APOP, PASS, Finger, and Notify Mail

- PostScript printer support

- Support for up to 500 queued print jobs on up to 30 printers

TCP/IP over AFP

TCP/IP enables the server to serve files and give users access to files stored on the server in an Internet Protocol format, such as Web pages or FTP directories. With ASIP's "TCP/IP over AFP" feature, these actions can be performed in either the traditional AFP or by using TCP/IP. The server and the client work well in this aspect. If the latest version of the AppleShare client is installed on your Apple workstations, then the client can determine the fastest and most efficient protocol to use.

You may be interested to know that the TCP/IP frame is not modified when inserted into an AFP frame. AFP merely acts as a facilitator to the protocol and delivers it to the requesting client (most likely a browser or FTP client). ASIP is extremely talented at making the network connection as seamless as possible, and this is just one example of that.

Web and FTP Services

ASIP 5's *Web and File Server* provides complete Internet services via an integrated HTTP 1.0 and FTP server. These services are not just available over a LAN, but can serve any user connecting from anywhere. The AS client, which is available in the Chooser, allows connection to an ASIP server via a network interface or by having the user enter an IP address.

Once connected, the mapped drive appears on the workstation's desktop like any other drive, and is navigable as such. This is an extremely attractive feature for network administrators or Web masters, since very little additional user training is required. If the user knows how to use a system based on the Mac OS, they know how to use AppleShare. If the user chooses to access the files on the server using an FTP client application, like Fetch 3.0.*x*, then the files will appear in a standard FTP format. All this makes the end-user environment very accessible.

As mentioned, ASIP 5 also provides standards-based HTTP 1.0 file-serving services. ASIP places a folder called "Web Folder" at the root of the server's drive. This is the folder from which the server serves pages. The home page defaults to

DEFAULT.HTML, which is also placed in the folder by ASIP, but any HTML file structure can be served from this folder. All of these services are available to any user who is granted access to the server. An ASIP server can even be used as a Web server for general Internet access—you will have to purchase a different license from Apple to implement ASIP on a Web server, however.

WARNING Even though ASIP 5 can be used to serve Web pages over the Internet, this is not its intended purpose. ASIP is optimized for deployment in a workgroup environment and integrates tools for this specific task. If the target for your solution is Internet or corporate Internet/intranet file services, you should use Apple Internet Server Solution (AISS).

TIP ASIP 5's *Alias Sharing* feature enables you to make an alias of a drive, server, file, or folder and send it to your colleagues. When they open the alias it will connect to the respective drive, server, file, or folder automatically. The alias contains all the path information to make the connection possible.

Administration and Security

Administration in ASIP 5 was improved with the introduction of AppleShare Registry API. This API stores user and group information in a centrally accessible file, which provides privilege and access information for all users and groups to all of the servers (with the exception of the print server).

The improved usability was also evident throughout the administration setup process. Administrators could make changes, additions, or removals from the central location and all servers would be updated. This was also a boon for security, since the administrator no longer had to chase down all instances of a defunct user.

Another powerful security tool in ASIP 5 was actually a part of the way the Web server operates on the host machine: Unlike most other Web server applications, an ASIP 5 server serves its Web Folder as the *root* of the drive. The Web Folder is thus the lowest section of the drive a Web surfer can ever attain. This prevents Web users from accessing other directories on the drive.

NOTE   The Users & Groups access privileges also filter down to the Web server level. This greatly lessens the amount of time an administrator has to spend on maintaining security.

CGI Support

CGI, or *Common Gateway Interface,* is a simple way of transmitting unsecure data to a server for parsing. This information could be of a database query or personal information for delivery to a server-located application, and usually results in a Web page being returned to the user. You commonly see CGIs in use on Web search engines. You enter the term in the field, click the Search button, and watch as a load of barely identifiable characters get shuffled into the Address Field of your browser. In return you receive a list of "hits." ASIP 5 supports CGIs that perform tasks like the one just described.

Logging

ASIP 5 also supports HTTP *logging,* which can show an administrator exactly which pages are getting the hits and which aren't. This data is useful since an administrator can use it to determine which pages and files are most helpful and which ones are not. It is often quite difficult to get such information out of users simply by asking.

Mail Server

The ASIP 5 mail server is much like any other mail server you may have come across lately. Its job is to send and receive e-mail and enclosures or attachments and route them to the proper user. This is achieved by assigning each user a unique "address." An example address is `user@sub-domain.domain`. In an ASIP environment, the e-mail would most likely be workgroup-related.

The mail server is compatible with all SMTP/POP3-compliant mail clients and can be accessed from any platform. This eliminates the need to distribute compatible mail clients and the related training costs. Of course, the server is not limited to serving only over TCP/IP. If that were so, it would be much less desirable. Needless to say, it is also ready to use with an AppleTalk LAN. In this case, the users would need a client that is AppleTalk-compatible, most commonly Claris Em@iler (which is available for both Mac OS and Windows 95/98/NT platforms), but any AppleTalk client can be used.

As with all the other servers (with the exception of the print server as previously mentioned), the mail server uses the AppleShare Registry API to access the common Users & Groups files for uniform access privileges. Also, users of the mail server can have two names: one Users & Groups name and one Internet alias. The U&G name can contain any legal Macintosh character, but the Internet alias is limited to the ASCII character set to allow compatibility with other Internet-based systems.

The mail server also supports SMTP routing, DNS, and Mail Exchange (MX). Users can also choose to encrypt their passwords via APOP or just let them flap in the wind. (The former, of course, is always preferable.) Also, if the user's address gets moved, the administrator can simply set the previous address as a forwarder. In this case, the mail will be forwarded to the new address automatically.

IMAP

Without a doubt, *IMAP* was one of the more exciting technologies to be added to the ASIP mail server. Many services that were previously unavailable without specialty programs before ASIP 5 were made available via ASIP 5's IMAP support. (Actually, though, many commercial mail clients had already implemented services like IMAP through clever manipulation of POP3 capabilities.) IMAP added these features in earnest, eliminating the often sketchy results of even the most seasoned e-mail clients.

IMAP offers many capabilities that make managing a workgroup's mail much easier and allows remote users greater access and control to their mail. First of all, mail is not deleted from the server when it is requested by the user. The user can determine, after they have reviewed the message, whether to have the server delete it or not. Likewise, IMAP does not download the entire message when it is requested. Instead, IMAP allows clients to receive the headers of the messages only if they wish, giving the user the option to download large attachments at a later time.

NOTE   Despite their capabilities, the POP3-only clients cannot download only headers using POP3. POP3 *does* have commands for copying a message to the client and other management tricks, but remember, it's not real IMAP.

Print Server

The print server is a rather interesting animal. The print services do not reside entirely within the server. Instead, the server merely provides the facilities for workstations to locate and use printers attached to the network. The printing is actually handled by the workstations' own local drivers. The main driver in this rather slim arsenal is called Apple LaserWriter 8 (ALW8).

Conveniently, ALW8 (which comes with Mac OS 8.1) provides complete support for PostScript versions up to 3, and it provides a slew of options most of us will never need. ALW8 can print to a real printer or a file, convert to a PDF (if Acrobat Pro is installed), print a file at a predefined time, use ColorSync printer profiles, define printer layouts, and more. And all that is in the Print dialog! And the great thing is, most of these services are available to *all* applications that print.

Considering this, it's easy to see why the ASIP print server is one of the easiest to administer. Since the administrator merely maps printers to groups and gives them recognizable names, there's not much left to do. With the print server, a help desk call might go like this:

Support: Hello, can I help you?

User: Uh, yes. I forgot which button to click when I'm done.

Support: Oh. Could you read me the options, please?

User: Cancel and OK.

Though ridiculous, this mock dialog is quite illustrative. There are few if any things that could cause catastrophic problems using the print server. But that's not all. (Do you hear the sound of Ginsu knives, too?) Serving speed was improved through the use of Open Transport (OT) and Threading support since System 7.5.*x*, and is native in Mac OS 8.*x*.

Open Transport is a faster network interface than the interface offered by ASIP 4, and is quite an improvement over other schemes that are supported by the Mac OS (with the clear exception of IPX/SPX). Using OT, the ALW8 driver sends a Printer Page Description (PPD) file to the server, which determines the queue it is intended for, then reroutes it. If there is more than one printer on the queue, the print server will balance the load by sorting the file to the shortest queue. This sorting is dynamic, so if a printer becomes free, the oldest file will be re-sorted for the next print job on that printer.

Administration

Before the advent of ASIP 5 there was little to administer, and the job was a cinch since the administration applications made it so. ASIP 5 continued that ease-of-use concept with another streamlined collection of server management tools. Not only does each server have a configuration application, but there is a central application that manages all of the configuration utilities. This application, called AppleShare IP Manager, gives the administrator instant access to server status without having to open each application one at a time.

To OpenDoc or Not to OpenDoc?

Whether to use OpenDoc or not is not really a valid question if you're using ASIP, because OpenDoc version 1.2.1 or later *must* be installed on the server host for AppleShare IP Manager and other configuration utilities to run. This requirement raises many interesting questions considering the current lack of OpenDoc (OD) development activity on the part of Apple. Without getting into that too much before we even understand OD, let's move on to more pertinent information.

There are a few things that should be cleared up regarding OpenDoc and its future (or lack thereof). OpenDoc is an application environment that serves the interface in a document-centric manner. Each interface is a document; objects, which are called OD Parts, can be placed into this, removed from it, or modified. In the case of the ASIP Manager application, each button is an OpenDoc Part.

The confusing part of all this is that the document is not an application in and of itself. There is an application called OpenDoc that resides in the Extensions folder, but it is a faceless app that ties the OD Parts and Editors together. The general idea is that all of the application-like components are contained in the OpenDoc software that is installed as an addition to the Mac OS system software.

Let's say a developer wanted to add, in relation to AppleShare, a service handled by the OpenDoc Manager. They would simply code the part into the OD framework and compile it. The compiled OD Part would then be inserted into the document like, say, a graphic in a Word document. This is a great, object-oriented way to program, as each OD Part is a discrete object and can be installed or removed from the target document at any time. The developer could even drag the part to the document window to install it.

Continued on next page

The only problem is that Apple officially killed OpenDoc. The result is that, even though OD is still distributed by Apple, still required by ASIP 5 and even 6.0, and supported by a small band of dedicated third-party developers, it will never be upgraded, improved, or integrated into future releases of the Mac OS.

(Or will it...? AppleShare IP 6.0 seems quite a major upgrade to go wasting a *dead* technology on.)

Vicom Internet Gateway

The *Internet Gateway* is a rather interesting piece of software that is included with the ASIP 5 package. Vicom bills it as a software router that allows several users to use one Internet connection simultaneously. This setup allows the users to access the same account while using a single IP address.

Each connected system receives its own IP number, which can be dynamically assigned. When the gateway is installed, the automatic configuration wizard, humorously named Darko (a little wizard guy in a star-bedecked pointy hat), locates all workstations on the LAN and assigns them an IP number that it writes to a simple routing table.

Let's say, for example, that the gateway Enterprise (205.100.100.1) is instructed to get a page from Starfleet (192.100.100.1) by Kirk (192.100.100.1), Spock (192.100.100.2), and Bones (192.100.100.3). The Enterprise logs the request for the page from Kirk, Spock, and Bones and sends the request to Starfleet. Starfleet returns the three requested (in this case identical) pages back to Enterprise. Upon receipt, Enterprise examines the header to determine who gets the file. Based on its own logs, it distributes the file to Kirk, Spock, and Bones.

Simply stated, this means you can set up a single Macintosh as a router to handle all of your LAN's Internet data. The Gateway can also be used as a firewall for LAN security: As we'll cover in later chapters, a firewall acts as a one-way filter, allowing stations inside the firewall to access Internet resources located outside the firewall, but restricting stations outside the firewall from initiating contact with stations inside the firewall.

Summary

We started this chapter by pointing out that peer-to-peer networking was really introduced by Apple when they released AppleTalk and corresponding built-in LocalTalk hardware.

We discussed the LocalTalk Link Access Protocol (LLAP), and its Ethernet and Token Ring counterparts (EtherTalk Link Access Protocol and TokenTalk Link Access Protocol), and compared AppleTalk's CSMA/CA methodology to Ethernet's CSMA/CD. AppleTalk's collision avoidance approach reduces the number of lengthy network collisions at the cost of more handshaking overhead in order to avoid collisions.

We then discussed dynamic node address assignment, zones, and the difference between non-extended and extended networks.

We then moved on to a discussion of AppleShare server software, in particular the latest released version of AppleShare IP (currently version 5). We saw that ASIP brings many Internet-related services to Mac servers including FTP and Web services (including logging and CGI support), an IMAP-compliant e-mail server, and the Vicom Internet Gateway and firewall. It also provides a centralized AppleShare Registry and improved administration tools.

AppleShare IP 6.0, yet to be released but already in the trade journals, promises support for Microsoft-compatible internetworking. If this feature makes it into the 6.0 release, it could make AppleShare an intriguing option in mixed Mac/PC network settings.

In the next chapter, we'll look at the various network client software solutions available for enabling client stations to access shared network resources. The end of the next chapter includes a discussion of various Apple client software options for internetworking with server systems such as NetWare (IntraNetWare) and Windows NT.

PART IV

Network Client Software

■ CHAPTER 17: Who Can Talk to Whom

CHAPTER
SEVENTEEN

Who Can Talk to Whom

- Which client operating systems can connect to which networks?

- Configuring client communications in a NetWare environment

- Configuring client communications in a Windows NT environment

- Using NFS to access file services between Unix systems

- Connectivity with Apple computers

We have reviewed each of our server-based operating systems and covered how to get them communicating on the network. It is now time to look at the client side of the equation to determine how to best optimize this end of the connection.

Who Can Talk to Whom

First, let's establish a baseline. We need to determine which client operating systems are capable of communicating with each server. If we look at native support or client support that is shipped with the server software, our connectivity matrix would appear as shown in Table 17.1.

TABLE 17.1: The Connectivity Matrix

Client OS	NetWare	NT Server	Lotus Notes	Unix Running NFS
DOS/Windows 3.1x	X	X	Win 3.1x only	*
Windows 95/98	X	X	X	*
NT Workstation	X	X	X	*
Mac	X	**	X	*
Unix			X	X

* Requires third-party software
** Requires that AppleTalk be enabled on the server

We now begin to see a few patterns. The first is that Lotus Notes supports all listed platforms except DOS. This may be a bit misleading in terms of Unix, however, because the only flavors of Unix that Lotus Notes supports are Solaris, HP-UX, and AIX. Lotus Notes does not support Linux, FreeBSD, SGI, or a host of other Unix flavors.

After Lotus Notes, NetWare and NT provide the best connectivity support. NetWare has a bit of an edge, as it supplies both IPX and AppleTalk connectivity to Mac clients; this allows you to consolidate both PC and Mac clients on a single protocol (IPX). Windows NT provides support for the Mac only through the AppleTalk protocol. Because PC clients will use NetBEUI or NetBIOS over IP to connect to resources, a minimum of two protocols is required.

NFS appears to be the most difficult remote file system to support, as all operating systems except for Unix require additional third-party tools in order to provide connectivity; this increases both the cost and complexity of our network configuration.

Now that we know which client operating systems can connect to each of our servers, it is time to look at the configuration process required to get each of our clients connected. In the interest of brevity, we will eliminate portions of the matrix with the poorest showing. Because NFS is only natively supported between Unix systems, we will discuss this configuration only. Although the Mac does not natively support half our listed servers (a limitation that Apple really should remedy), in the last section of this chapter we will look at the best options available for integrating Macs with NetWare and NT servers.

Configuring Client Communications in a NetWare Environment

The client software used to connect to a NetWare server can come from one of two sources. The first is Novell, which supplies a set of client drivers when you purchase the IntraNetWare operating system. Windows 95/98 and Windows NT Workstation ship with a set of NetWare client drivers, but they are manufactured by Microsoft. If you are using Windows 95/98 or NT Workstation, you can choose which client (Novell's or Microsoft's) you wish to use.

The Novell Client Drivers for NetWare

Novell's client drivers for NetWare, referred to as *Client32*, have the greatest number of configurable options, and have been independently tested to provide the fastest connectivity. There are clients available for supporting DOS, Windows 95/98, Windows NT, OS/2, and the Mac OS. Windows 3.1x is supported through the DOS client.

Legacy Clients

Novell's older clients directly supported the Open Datalink Interface (ODI). This is a fairly open programming interface (although Novell owns the trademark) that supports the use of multiple protocol stacks. For example, by using the ODI interface, a workstation can communicate using IPX and IP to access resources using either protocol.

There are two major drawbacks to the legacy drivers. First, they operated in 16-bit real mode, which means that the software is capable of crashing the entire workstation if it fails. Because real mode does not afford any kind of memory protection between programs, crashing is a common problem with any real mode software. Also, ODI has not been as widely accepted as Novell hoped it would be. For example, Microsoft opted to focus on the Network Driver Interface Specification (NDIS) instead of ODI.

During a Client32 install, you still have the option of installing the legacy 16-bit drivers, which directly support ODI. However, you should definitely use the new 32-bit drivers unless you run into compatibility problems or you are using older NIC cards that do not support the new client software.

Client32

Since the advent of Client32, Novell has incorporated into the workstation the communication technology it has used on its servers for many years. Client32 drivers are very similar to the LAN and NLM modules used to enable networking on the server. While it still uses ODI technology, Novell has created a thin programming layer that allows LAN and NLM drivers to be used on other operating systems besides a NetWare server.

There are a few immediate benefits to using LAN and NLM drivers. The first is that the drivers operate in 32-bit protected mode. Besides being faster than their 16-bit counterparts, they are also more stable.

Client32 drivers are modular and dynamic. They are modular in that the driver software is not just one large program but is made up of many smaller pieces. Dynamic means that Client32 can load and unload these pieces as required. This means that the memory footprint can be kept to a minimum by dynamically accessing support modules as required. The benefit is that while legacy 16-bit drivers may require 45KB–75KB to load, Client32 only requires 4KB of conventional or upper memory. Memory management for all drivers is provided by the NetWare I/O Subsystem (NIOS).

Client32 even has benefits for NIC manufacturers. Because the workstation now uses LAN drivers similar to those on the server, the amount of effort required to develop NIC card drivers is reduced. The NIC manufacturer is only required to write code for one type of driver (LAN); it no longer needs to develop a separate legacy ODI driver to support workstation communications.

Installing Client32 for DOS/Windows 3.1x

If you still have stations needing to run DOS or Windows 3.1, the client drivers for DOS/Windows 3.1x can be found in the SYS:\public\client\doswin32 directory of a NetWare server. The latest version of the drivers can also be obtained from the Novell Web site. At the time of this writing, the URL for downloading all NetWare client software is www.novell.com/download. Note that DOS/Windows 3.1 drivers are simply referred to as "DOS/Windows client" software.

To install the drivers, go to the Client32 subdirectory (that is, SYS:\public\client\client32 if you are using a NetWare/IntraNetWare server). If you are installing from DOS, execute the file inst or install, depending on which version of the Client32 for DOS you are using. If you are installing from Windows 3.1x, execute the file setup. Regardless of the method you choose, you can install support for both DOS and Windows 3.1x.

NOTE   Curiously, there is no online help during the installation. While the prompts are very descriptive, it would be nice if some additional help was included, in case the administrator is uncertain about some of the options.

Figure 17.1 shows the opening screen for the DOS-based installation utility. You can choose to install support for DOS or Windows 3.1x. By default, the installation program assumes you will be using IPX to communicate with the server. If you choose to install the NetWare IP stack, you can install NetWare IP as well. We will discuss NetWare IP later in this chapter.

You are also allowed to install support for SNMP, which will allow the workstation to be polled by and controlled from an SNMP management station. The final option, NetWare TSA for SMS, allows you to install the Target Service Agent (TSA) for Storage Management Services (SMS). SMS allows the NetWare backup utility to reach out from the server and back up files from the workstation. Once you have selected the options you wish to install, press the F10 key to continue the installation.

FIGURE 17.1:

The Client32 DOS-based installation utility

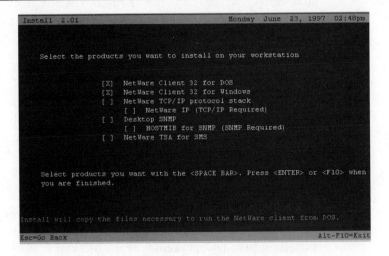

If you have opted for Windows support, you will be asked if you require support for multiple country codes. Usually, the answer to this question is no. Unless your workstation is on a global WAN and will need to access servers in multiple countries, single support should be fine. You will also be asked if you will be using a shared network copy of Windows. If you load Windows off of your local hard drive, the answer to this is no. If you access Windows through a shared directory out on the server, the answer is yes. When you have finished, press F10.

Next, you are asked if you wish to install support for 16-bit or 32-bit drivers. As mentioned previously, you should install 32-bit support unless you know for sure that this will cause problems. Regardless of your choice, you are presented next with a list of available network drivers. If the NIC you are using is not listed, you will need to obtain the drivers from the manufacturer. Once you have the drivers you need, press the Insert key and enter the full path to the drivers' location. Press F10 when you have finished.

You are next prompted to configure your NIC driver settings. You must enter the frame type you wish to use, as well as any interrupt or I/O port settings you are prompted for. You can select support for multiple frame types by pressing Enter on the field and using the F5 key to select the ones you want. Once you have finished, press F10.

If you are upgrading your network drivers and have a **net.cfg** file, the installation program will use the settings from this file to determine the correct frame type. The **net.cfg** file is described later in this chapter.

The next screen asks you if you want the installation utility to make the required changes to your `config.sys` and `autoexec.bat` files. The changes it will make are as follows:

16-Bit Drivers

- Add the line `lastdrive=z` to the `config.sys` file.

- Add the location of the network drivers to the `path` statement in `autoexec.bat`.

- Add the command `call startnet.bat` to the end of `autoexec.bat` to initialize networking.

32-Bit Drivers

- Remove the line `lastdrive=z` if it exists in the `config.sys` file.

- Add the location of the network drivers to the `path` statement in `autoexec.bat`.

- Add the command `call startnet.bat` to the end of `autoexec.bat` to initialize networking.

The `startnet.bat` file contains different commands to initialize 16-bit and 32-bit networking. We will look at the contents of this file later in this section.

You are also prompted to input where you would like to have the network drivers installed. Unless you really need to put them elsewhere (such as on drive D instead of C because of space concerns), the default should be fine. The files to be installed take up 2.3MB of space for DOS only, and 5MB if Windows support is installed as well.

Finally, you are shown one last time whether you selected to install 16-bit or 32-bit drivers, as well as the driver name. This is your last chance to change these settings before the installation utility begins copying files. If you are happy with your selection, press the F10 key to begin copying files.

If you are rerunning the setup utility because you have swapped in a new network card and need to install support for it, you will need to edit the `startnet.bat` file once the installation is complete. The install utility will not remove the `load` statement for the old network card driver; you will have to do this manually.

Once the installation is complete, you will be prompted to reboot your computer. This should initialize networking, and you should now be able to log on to a NetWare server.

The startnet.bat File   Depending on whether you choose a 16-bit or 32-bit installation, the `startnet.bat` file will contain the commands shown in Table 17.2 and Table 17.3.

TABLE 17.2: Commands for 16-Bit Installation

Command	Description
`set nwlanguage=english`	Sets the default language to English.
`lsl.com`	Loads Link Support Layer (LSL) support. This is the interface between the network card driver and the ODI driver.
`nic_driver.com`	Loads network driver support. `nic_driver` is usually replaced with a descriptive name for the network card. For example, the driver name for an Eagle NE200 network card is `ne2000.com`.
`ipxodi.com`	Loads legacy ODI support for the IPX protocol. There may be a TCPODI driver as well, if support for IP was installed.
`vlm.exe`	Loads support for Novell's Virtual Loadable Modules (VLM). This is the legacy DOS requester, which is responsible for monitoring application requests for file and print services and redirecting them to the network server when required.

TABLE 17.3:   Commands for 32-Bit Installation

Command	Description
set nwlanguage=english	Sets the default language to English.
nios.exe	Loads the NetWare I/O Subsystem driver. This is the interface between DOS and the 32-bit LAN and NLM environment.
load lslc32.nlm	Loads the Link Support Layer (LSL) driver for Client32.
load cmsm.nlm	The Client32 media support module (CMSM). This driver acts as an interface between the LSLC32 driver and the LAN driver.
load ethertsm.nlm	Loads Ethernet topology support. This driver will be replaced with tokentsm.nlm for Token Ring environments and fdditsm.nlm when the FDDI topology is used.
load nic_driver.lan	Loads network driver support. nic_driver is usually replaced with a descriptive name for the network card. For example, the driver name for an Eagle NE2000 network card is ne2000.lan. There are also command-line switches for selecting the protocol and setting the correct port and interrupt. Refer to the "Configuring Networking from the Command Line" section of Chapter 11 for these parameters.
load ipx.nlm	Loads support for the IPX protocol. The tcpip.nlm will also be installed if you selected support for that protocol.
load client32.nlm	Loads the Client32 requester. This driver is responsible for monitoring application requests for file and print services and redirecting them to the network server when required.

If you are using the 16-bit drivers, it may be beneficial to copy the listed drivers from the startnet.bat file and load them directly from the autoexec.bat file. This will allow your memory manager to include these files when it optimizes memory usage. Because the 32-bit drivers use very little memory, there is not much of a benefit to optimizing these files.

Note that the 32-bit startnet.bat file uses the load command when initializing support drivers. This is not a DOS-based command but rather a command used on NetWare servers. The NIOS sets up the API interface which makes load a valid command.

Configuring Networking with the NET.CFG File   The net.cfg file is used by Client32 to configure the networking environment. As each driver is loaded, the net.cfg file is referenced to see if the driver requires any special configuration parameters.

With Client32, a basic net.cfg file would contain the following:

```
NetWare DOS Requester
     FIRST NETWORK DRIVE F
     NETWARE PROTOCOL NDS BIND

Protocol IPX
     IPX SOCKETS 40
```

The lines that are not indented here are section titles that identify which driver is to be configured. For example, commands under the NetWare DOS Requester are commands used by either vlm.exe or client32.nlm. The lines we've indented are commands used to configure that specific driver. (These commands can be indented using the Tab key or spaces.)

A net.cfg file used with 16-bit drivers would include an additional section title:

```
Link driver nic_driver
```

with *nic_driver* being replaced with the actual name of the network card driver. Commands under this section are used to select the appropriate frame type and specify the correct interrupt and port number to use with the card. Because the LAN driver used with Client32 specifies these settings on the command line, this section is not required.

Because the available configuration options used in the net.cfg file are nearly identical to the settings used to configure Client32 on Windows 95/98 and NT, we will cover all the valid settings at the end of this section.

Installing Client32 for Windows 95/98

Installing Client32 for Windows 95/98 is a straightforward process. The installation program is located in the sys:\public\client\win95 (or \win98) directory of the IntraNetWare server. The latest version can also be downloaded from Novell's Web site. Currently you can find all NetWare client software, including the Windows 95/Windows 98 clients, at www.novell.com/download/. In either case, execute the file setup.exe.

Figure 17.2 shows the initial configuration screen for Client32 for Windows 95. Thankfully, this installation has online help in case you need it. The utility also attempts to be helpful by replacing native NDIS drivers with ODI drivers. If you will only be running NetWare, this should not be a problem. If you need to support other protocol stacks, such as NetBEUI or Microsoft's TCP/IP, replacing NDIS drivers with ODI drivers means that you will also need to install ODIN-SUP. ODINSUP is ODI's support driver, which allows it to communicate with NDIS stacks. This just adds an additional layer of complexity if you later need to diagnose a communication problem. If you will be using other protocol stacks, you may wish to disable the replacement of your existing drivers. In either case, select Start to begin the installation.

FIGURE 17.2:

The initial banner screen for the Client32 Installation utility

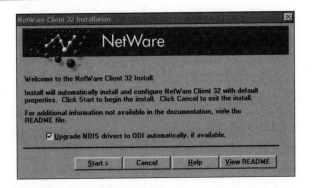

Once you select Start, the utility will begin to install files and configure your system. It will display summary information to inform you of its progress. The first thing you will notice is that even if you tell it not to replace your NDIS drivers, it will display the message replacing existing drivers. Don't worry, if you instructed the utility not to replace the drivers, it will not. This is a generic prompt.

Once the file copy is complete, you are prompted to set a default tree or server. If your network is using Novell Directory Services (NDS), set a default NDS tree. If your network consists of older bindery-based servers (version 3.12 and prior), set a default server. Once you are finished, select the OK button to continue.

You are then asked if you wish to reboot the computer, return to Windows, or customize the settings. You should choose to reboot the computer unless there are other programs running in the background that you wish to shut down first. In this case, return to Windows, shut down the programs, and then reboot.

WARNING   While it is tempting to customize the settings at this time, you should first restart the system to ensure that the new client is working properly. If you change the advanced settings now and then have a connectivity problem during startup, you cannot be sure if it is a driver problem or something you configured incorrectly.

During the installation process, Client32 creates the following log file:

```
c:\Novell\client32\install\net2reg.log
```

If you encounter problems with your newly installed client, you can check this log to see if the installation program had any difficulties while modifying the Windows 95 Registry. For example, as part of the installation process, the Registry is modified so that the Primary Network Logon under Networking Properties is changed to Novell NetWare Client 32.

Configuring Client32 for Windows 95/98

Once you are satisfied that your client software is working, you can proceed to the Network Configuration tab to customize the settings. Figure 17.3 shows this tab with the Novell NetWare Client 32 client highlighted. Select the Properties button to configure the client for Client32.

FIGURE 17.3:

The Windows 95 Network Configuration tab

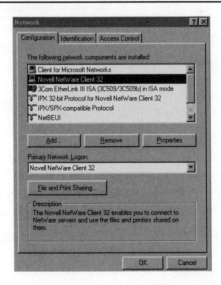

The Client 32 Tab Figure 17.4 shows the Client 32 tab in the NetWare Client 32 Properties window. This tab is used for setting a preferred server or NDS tree, just as you were prompted to do during the client installation. You should not need to use this tab unless you need to make changes, such as when you have a new server or NDS tree.

FIGURE 17.4:

The Client 32 tab under Net-Ware Client 32 Properties

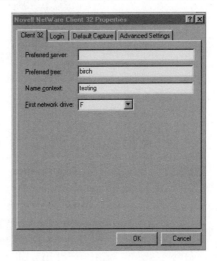

The Login Tab Figure 17.5 shows the Login tab in the NetWare Client 32 Properties window. The Display Connection Page prompt changes the banner screen during initial logon. When this setting is not checked, you are presented with the server or tree options selected under the Client 32 tab and cannot change them. When this setting is checked, the options are displayed in an editable format so that you can change them. This is useful for a network administrator who may be required to log on to different trees or servers.

Checking Display Connection Page sets up a second page to the logon banner that allows the user to switch between performing a logon to a tree and performing a logon to a server. If Log In To Server is selected, you have the option of choosing a bindery-based logon. The final option in this section, Clear Current Connections, is used if you are performing a logon from a system that is already authenticated to NetWare services. Enabling this setting logs you out of these services prior to performing the new logon.

The Login tab of the NetWare
Client 32 Properties window

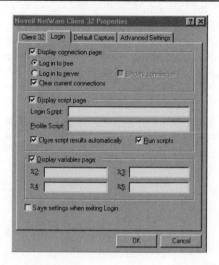

The Display Script Page check box enables or disables the use of an alternate logon script and profile during authentication. The logon script is used to set up the workstation's network environment by mapping drives, capturing printers, and even launching applications. By default, users authenticating to the network process the system logon script in a bindery environment, and the container logon script in an NDS environment. The Login Script field allows an alternate file to be processed as the logon script.

Profiles are used to set up user access and even process additional logon commands. With NetWare 3.1*x*, security access and the processing of additional script commands were typically accomplished through the use of *groups*. A user would be assigned to a group and the group would be given access to certain files and directories. The group name may even be referenced to process certain commands within the logon script. By using profiles, trustee access and logon commands can be maintained in a central place. The Profile Script prompt allows you to specify a profile to be used during network authentication.

The Display Variables Page check box is used to pass variable information on to `login.exe` during authentication. Under DOS, variables can be used during the logon process using the syntax `login %2 %3 %4 %5`. In Windows 95, the fields under the Display Variables Page check box allow you to pass along this information.

The Save Settings When Exiting Login check box allows you to specify if your default settings can be changed during network logon. For example, let's assume you have defined the default tree of Birch. One day while performing a network logon, you realize that there is information you need to retrieve that is located on the tree Oak. You change your preferred tree and perform authentication. If Save Settings When Exiting Login is checked, the next time you perform a logon you will be asked to authenticate to the tree Oak. If the box is not checked, you will be asked to authenticate to the tree Birch. The setting Save Settings When Exiting Login determines if your defaults are absolute, or if they should be customizable from the logon banner screen.

The Default Capture Tab   Figure 17.6 shows the Default Capture tab of the NetWare Client 32 Properties window. This tab is used to configure the printing environment. Number of Copies specifies how many copies of each print job should be sent to the printer. While it is usually easier to select the number of required copies from the application that is producing the print job, this setting is useful when you consistently need to print out a certain number of copies, regardless of what is being printed. For example, if you always print in triplicate, setting this field to three will keep you from having to select three copies from your application every time you print.

FIGURE 17.6:

The Default Capture tab of the NetWare Client 32 Properties window

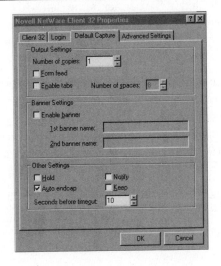

The Form Feed setting allows you to specify whether a form feed should be sent to the printer after every print job. This setting is useful if you have a dot matrix printer that you have to advance in order to remove your print job from the printer. It is also useful if you are using a laser printer with applications that do not send an end-of-job sequence: If you've noticed that your laser printer will not print the last page unless you hit the form feed button or another print job comes through, the application is probably not ending the print job properly. The problem with the Form Feed setting is that when you are using applications that do send a correct end-of-job sequence, the printer will print a blank page after each job.

The Enable Tabs check box allows you to customize how tabs look on your printed document. Enabling this setting replaces any tab characters with the number of specified spaces. This setting is somewhat of a holdover from the old days when different DOS applications defined tabs differently. Some defined a tab as five spaces, some as eight, and some as many as ten. This setting allowed all these applications to produce printed output that followed the same tab spacing format. You should not need to use this setting if you are printing through Windows.

The Banner Settings allow you to produce a cover page at the beginning of each print job. The page will display the name of the file printed as well as the name indicated in the banner name fields (usually the name of the user). This setting is useful in a large environment when many people are using the same printer. By enabling the banner page, it becomes easier to identify which print job belongs to whom.

Under Other Settings, the Hold check box allows you to send your print job to the print queue, but holds all your jobs in the queue until you okay them for printing. This is useful if you typically send many print jobs to the printer, but do not want to spend the whole day walking back and forth retrieving print jobs. When you are ready to print, you can use the Pconsole utility to change the status of all the jobs from Hold to Ready. This will cause them all to be printed out at the same time.

Auto Endcap is used for controlling the printing on older DOS-based applications. Enabling Auto Endcap causes all printing sent to the queue by an application to be printed when the application is exited. This setting has no effect on applications that send an end-of-job sequence at the end of every print job.

When the Notify box is checked, a dialog box pops up on the screen to notify you when your print job has been sent to the printer. This is useful in environments where many people share the same printer or when a printer usually receives large print jobs. By notifying you when your print job is being processed, it prevents you from having to stand around and wait while other jobs are printing.

When the Keep box is checked, a print job will remain in the print queue even after it has been printed. This is useful if you wish to print a test copy of a document prior to printing many copies. Once you are satisfied that the test printout looks okay, you can then use Pconsole to increase the number of copies to print and release the job from the print queue.

The Seconds Before Timeout setting is useful for those pesky programs that will not send an end-of-job sequence. Once an application has stopped sending data to the print queue, the client will wait the specified amount of time and then send an end-of-job sequence. This method of dealing with these older applications is preferred over the form-feed method as it will not produce an extra page on print jobs that are ended correctly.

The Advanced Settings Tab Figure 17.7 shows the Advanced Settings tab of the NetWare Client 32 Properties window. This tab is used to configure communication parameters for the network drivers. The Parameter Groups menu will display certain configuration parameters based on the selected group. For example, selecting the group Printing displays the three advanced settings that deal with customizing printing. The default group is All, which is typically the easiest group to work with because all configuration parameters are listed in alphabetical order.

FIGURE 17.7:

The Advanced Settings tab in the NetWare Client 32 Properties window

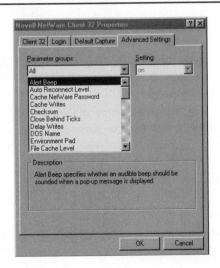

The Setting menu displays the available parameters for the highlighted configuration option. For example, in Figure 17.7 the Alert Beep configuration option is highlighted—it has two available settings, On and Off.

The advanced settings are similar to the net.cfg settings used with Client32 for DOS. For this reason, they are covered together at the end of this section.

Installing the IntraNetWare Client for Windows NT

The IntraNetWare client (Client32) for NT may be used on an NT workstation or server. It is functionally identical to Client32 for Windows 95/98 except in appearance and in having fewer advanced settings to configure. The NT client does not ship with IntraNetWare as of this writing. You must retrieve it from the Novell Web site (www.novell.com). Once you have uncompressed the files, execute the setup.exe file to begin the installation utility.

Figure 17.8 shows the initial banner screen for the IntraNetWare client for NT. You'll notice that it does not prompt you to upgrade any existing drivers. From this screen you can review the readme file for any last-minute changes and then continue with the installation by selecting the Continue button.

FIGURE 17.8:

The IntraNetWare Client Installation window

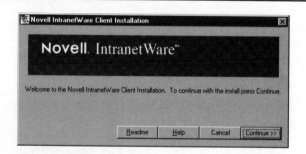

If you have the Microsoft Gateway (client) services for NetWare installed, the IntraNetWare client will inform you that it must be removed in order to continue with the installation. While you can still share NetWare files through the NT system, you will not be able to manage account security as you can with the Microsoft client. This prohibits the use of the IntraNetWare client in some networking situations where this type of file sharing is required. It is Novell's way of ensuring that only one user takes advantage of each NetWare connection—a point that is well justified in light of the license agreement. The dialog box for gateway removal is shown in Figure 17.9.

The installation utility will then begin to copy all required files and make modifications to the Registry. Once complete, it will prompt you to reboot the system. During system logon, you will notice that the logon window has been changed to include the IntraNetWare banner. This logon window is similar to the Windows 95 window except it allows a different name to be used for IntraNetWare and NT authentication. For example, you can log on to NetWare with the username Admin, and log on to NT using the logon name Administrator. If different logon names are used, different passwords may be used as well.

Configuring the IntraNetWare Client for Windows NT

The IntraNetWare client makes a few changes to the desktop. Along with a new IntraNetWare program group, the context menu produced by right-clicking the Network Neighborhood has two additional options, as shown in Figure 17.10. From this menu, we can log on to an NDS tree or bindery server, as well as check to see which system we are currently authenticated on.

FIGURE 17.10:

Additional properties have
been added to the Network
Neighborhood context menu.

The IntraNetWare client can be configured by going to Network Properties and looking under the Services tab. The client is identified as Novell IntraNetWare Client for Windows NT. Highlight the entry and select the Properties button to configure it.

The Client Tab   The Client tab of the IntraNetWare Client Services Configuration window is similar to the Client 32 tab under the client properties for Windows 95. As shown in Figure 17.11, the only real difference is that the NT client window allows you to configure multiple servers and NDS trees to authenticate to. By filling out the preferred server or preferred tree fields and selecting the Add button, you can authenticate on multiple systems simultaneously. This assumes that you have the same username and password on each NetWare system.

FIGURE 17.11:

The Client tab for the IntraNetWare client properties window

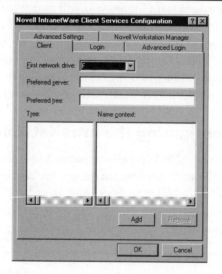

The Login Tab   The Login tab for the IntraNetWare client is identical to the Login tab under Client32 properties for Windows 95. All the features are the same.

The Advanced Login Tab   The Advanced Login tab, as shown in Figure 17.12, is Novell's way of taking a Microsoft concept and making it even easier to administer. The Policy Path and Filename is used to define a path to the configuration file that defines which desktop resources will be available to users when they log on to the workstation. For example, the policy can state that the user is restricted to a specific program group and is not allowed to execute programs through the Run command or through Explorer. What makes using policies easier in an IntraNetWare environment than in an NT environment is the hierarchical nature of NDS.

FIGURE 17.12:

The Advanced Login tab for
the IntraNetWare client properties screen

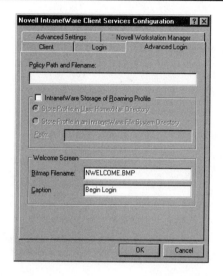

FIGURE 17.12:

The Advanced Login tab for
the IntraNetWare client properties screen

In an NT environment, policy files must be synchronized between the PDC and
every single BDC. This is because the logon is server-specific. The policy file must
be available on the server to which the user authenticates.

In an NDS environment, users log on to a tree, not a server. With this in mind,
policy files do not need to be synchronized across every single NDS server. Once
users are authenticated to a tree, they can retrieve their policy file from any server
they have access to. This allows the administrator to create a single point of management for policy files.

The Profile field is similar to the policy file, except control is user-specific. As
with the policy files, IntraNetWare allows a single point of management for profile files. They do not need to be synchronized across multiple servers.

The Welcome Screen settings allow the administrator to customize how the
logon banner appears to the user. The Bitmap Filename field allows you to select
a background while the Caption field allows you to add a text message to the
welcome header.

The Novell Workstation Manager Tab   The Novell Workstation Manager
tab, shown in Figure 17.13, allows NetWare administrators to manage the NT
workstation through IntraNetWare's NDS. This is a powerful tool that goes
beyond the functionality provided in a pure NT domain.

FIGURE 17.13:

The Novell Workstation Manager tab for the IntraNetWare client properties screen

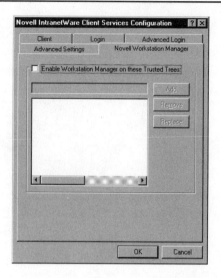

In an NT domain, the network administrator is required to create both a domain account and a workstation account for each user. This is required because workstation security is maintained separately from domain security. This means that the administrator must configure every workstation that the user may need to use. This can be extremely time consuming in a large or shared workstation environment, as the administrator may be required to configure many systems.

By selecting Enable Workstation Manager On These Trusted Trees, you can add NDS trees that are allowed to manage this NT workstation. As the NDS administrator uses the NWADMIN tool to manage the NDS tree, they can also manage this NT workstation. This means that user account information created on the NDS tree can be propagated out to the NT workstation. This propagation can be configured to occur automatically as soon as the user performs a logon at the system. These changes can even be configured to be permanent, becoming part of the NT security accounts manager, or to be deleted as soon as the user logs off the system. The benefit is that the network administrator is not required to manage the NT workstation as a separate system.

The Advanced Settings Tab   The Advanced Settings tab for the IntraNetWare client is identical to the Advanced Settings tab under Client32 properties for Windows 95. All the features are the same.

Advanced Settings and Configuring the net.cfg File

As mentioned previously, the available settings for each of the available clients are nearly identical. The differences are that settings under DOS are changed by adding lines to the `net.cfg` file, while Windows 95/98 and NT allow these settings to be changed through the Advanced Settings tab on the client's properties dialog box. Under DOS, if a parameter is not configured in the `net.cfg` file, the default setting is used.

Following is a list of available settings. Listed are each setting's name, description, and default value. Also listed is the syntax to use when adding the setting to the `net.cfg` file. Unless otherwise specified, all commands should be added under the NETWARE DOS REQUESTOR heading within the `net.cfg` file.

Alert Beep   The Alert Beep option enables a warning sound through the computer speaker when a pop-up message is displayed. The default is On.

Supported platforms: DOS, Windows 95/98. This parameter is added under the NIOS heading within the `net.cfg` file.

Syntax: `alert beep = on | off`

Auto Reconnect Level   This setting determines which connection attributes are restored when a connection to the server is lost and then reestablished. The levels are:

0	Do not reconnect to the server.
1	Remap drive and reconnect to printers.
2	Same as 1 but includes files opened for read access only.
3	Same as 1 and 2 but opens all files including those opened for write access and restores file locks.
4	Same as 1, 2, and 3, but adds file write data recovery guarantee.
5	Not yet used. If set to this level, the setting will revert to level 4.

The default level is 3.

Supported platforms: DOS, Windows 95/98

Syntax: `auto reconnect level = number`

Burst Mode This is the Windows NT counterpart for the Packet Burst setting described later in this list. It allows packet burst to be enabled or disabled. The default is On.

Supported platform: Windows NT

Syntax: `burst mode = on | off`

Cache NetWare Password This setting determines if the password entered during initial logon should be saved to memory and used to authenticate to additional NetWare resources. The default is On.

Supported platform: Windows 95/98

Syntax: `cache netware password = on | off`

Cache Writes This setting enables or disables the caching of information on the workstation that is destined to be written to the NetWare server. Caching improves performance, as many small blocks of information that need to be saved to the server can be transmitted simultaneously, thus reducing traffic. The drawback is that if the workstation crashes before this transmission takes place, the data will be lost. The default is On.

Supported platforms: DOS, Windows 95/98

Syntax: `cache writes = on | off`

Checksum Checksum determines if the checksum field within the NCP header should be used. This field can produce a redundant CRC check added to the field included in the frame trailer. This produces a slight increase in data integrity at the cost of overall performance. This option should only be used if you know you are having data integrity problems. The options are:

0   Disabled.

1   Only enable checksum if the server insists on it.

2   Perform a checksum if the server is capable.

3   Require a checksum. Do not communicate with servers that cannot perform a checksum.

Servers have a similar checksum setting, which is why some servers may perform a checksum, while others will not. The default level is 1.

Supported platforms: DOS, Windows 95/98

Syntax: `checksum = number`

Close Behind Ticks   Close Behind Ticks determines how long a client should wait to close a network file when an application has requested that it do so. This is useful for applications that frequently open and close the same files. For example, let's say we set this setting to five seconds. Our desktop application then sends a request to close a file that it has been using. Because of our Close Behind Ticks setting, the client will wait five seconds before it actually sends the close request to the server. Now let's assume the same client requests that the same file be opened three seconds later. Because the client has not yet closed the file on the server, it can access the file from local memory instead of having to create a network request. The benefits are faster application response time and less network traffic. The value for this field is set in ticks, which are equal to 1/18 of a second. To set this value to five seconds, then, we'd use a setting of 90. (A tick is roughly the time it takes to traverse one hop on a 10Mbps Ethernet network.) The default is 0, which closes files immediately upon request.

Supported platforms: DOS, Windows 95/98

Syntax: `close behind ticks = number`

Delay Writes   When Close Behind Ticks is set to some other value besides zero, Delay Writes determines if the close delay applies to read-only files, or files you have changed by writing to them as well. Enabling this feature improves application performance because they do not have to wait for write acknowledgments. The drawback is that if the client crashes before the close is performed, any data changes may be lost. The default is Off.

Supported platforms: DOS, Windows 95/98

Syntax: `delay writes = on | off`

DOS Name   The DOS Name setting defines the value to use for this system in the variable %OS. By correctly identifying this field, the system administrator can customize the logon script to be dependent on the operating system in use. For example, the logon script could analyze the contents of this variable to determine which virus checker version should be used. The default name for DOS is DOS, the default name for Windows 95 is WIN95, and the default for Windows NT is WINNT.

Supported platforms: DOS, Windows 95/98, Windows NT

Syntax: `DOS name = OS_name`

Environment Pad   Environment Pad increases the available DOS environment space by the indicated amount whenever a DOS-based application is run. The DOS environment is a small portion of memory set up by `command.com` for storing variables. Typing the command **set** at a DOS prompt yields some of the variables stored in environment memory. If a large enough environment space is not configured during system startup, some DOS-based applications will fail. This option allows an additional portion of memory to be set aside for each DOS program that is executed. The default is 24 bytes.

Supported platforms: DOS, Windows 95/98

Syntax: `environment pad = number`

File Cache Level   This setting determines what type of caching should be performed on network files. The available options are:

0	Do not perform file caching.
1	Use read-ahead and write-behind caching. With read-ahead caching, the client will read an entire block of information instead of reading only the information requested. This can increase performance during sequential file reads, as the client can retrieve the data before it is even requested to do so by the application. Write-behind is similar, except it applies when writing data to the server. The client will send write requests in blocks instead of smaller portions.
2	Use short-lived caching as well as the features from option 1. Short-lived caching allows the system to cache file information until the time the file is closed (closure time is set by Close Behind Ticks).
3	Use long-lived caching as well as the features from option 1. Long-lived caching allows the client to continue caching a file even after it is closed. If another open request for the same file is received from an application, the client checks with the server to ensure that the file has not changed since the last time the file

was opened. If the file has not changed, the file is read from local cache instead of from the server.

4   Not currently in use

The default value is 2 (short-lived cache). This option is disabled if True Commit is set to On or if Cache Writes is set to Off.

Supported platforms: DOS, Windows 95/98

Syntax: `file cache level = number`

Force First Network Drive   When enabled, this setting sets the login directory to the first available network drive (usually F) once the user logs off of the server. When this setting is disabled, the login directory is set to whichever network drive was last used. This setting is more useful in a DOS environment because Windows hides the network drive used to authenticate with the network. The default is On.

Supported platforms: DOS, Windows 95/98

Syntax: `force first network drive = on | off`

Handle Net Error   This setting determines whether the client software or the application in use will handle network errors, such as a server no longer responding. When set to On, the client software handles the error. When set to Off, the client generates an INT 24 and passes this along to the application. The default is On.

Supported platforms: DOS, Windows 95/98

Syntax: `handle net errors = on | off`

Hold Files   If a program opens a file using File Control Blocks (FCB_IO), this setting determines if the file is held open until the program exits. Some programs that are not network-aware need this setting enabled. The default is Off.

Supported platforms: DOS, Windows 95/98

Syntax: `hold = on | off`

Ignore Below 16meg Memory Allocate Flag   When allocating additional memory for network drivers, this setting determines if additional memory should only be allocated from the first 16MB, or if all available memory should be used. When enabled, all memory is used. When disabled, only memory from the first 16MB is allocated. If there is no memory free below 16MB, the request fails. Many LAN drivers have difficulties if they are moved above the 16MB area. You should leave this setting Off unless it is absolutely required. The default is Off.

Supported platforms: DOS. This parameter is added under the NIOS heading within the net.cfg file.

Syntax: `ignore below 16meg memory allocate flag = on | off`

Large Internet Packets   This setting enables or disables the use of LIP for packet size negotiations across network routers. The default is On.

Supported platforms: DOS, Windows 95/98, Windows NT

Syntax: `large internet packets = on | off`

Large Internet Packet Start Size   When LIP is enabled, this setting sets the size in bytes to use when negotiating large Internet packets. The client and server will negotiate down from this size until a usable value is achieved. Setting this value to the largest packet size supported by your topology will reduce negotiation time. The default is 65,535 bytes.

Supported platforms: DOS, Windows 95/98, Windows NT

Syntax: `lip start size = number`

Link Support Layer Max Buffer Size   Sets the buffer size, in bytes, that the client should use to queue inbound and outbound frames. This setting needs to be at least as large as the maximum frame size supported by the topology. Adjusting this setting to a value larger than the maximum frame size can waste memory because the difference will go unused. Adjusting this setting too low can cause communication problems because the workstation will be unable to receive frames larger than the specified size. The default is 4736 bytes.

Supported platforms: DOS, Windows 95/98, Windows NT. This parameter is added under the LINK SUPPORT heading within the net.cfg file.

Syntax: `max buffer size = number`

Lock Delay   When an application receives a sharing error and is unable to achieve exclusive access to a file, the lock delay determines how long in ticks the client should wait before attempting to lock the file again. The default is 1 tick.

Supported platforms: DOS, Windows 95/98

Syntax: `lock delay = number`

Lock Retries This setting determines the number of retries to be performed after a sharing error is received. Each retry is separated by the amount of time specified in the Lock Delay setting. The default is 5.

Supported platforms: DOS, Windows 95/98

Syntax: `lock retries = number`

Log File This setting specifies the location and name of a log file to be created during initialization of the network drivers. The log is typically used for diagnostic purposes only. The default is blank, which means a log file is not created.

Supported platforms: DOS, Windows 95/98. This parameter is added under the NIOS heading within the `net.cfg` file.

Syntax: `log file=c:\novell\client32\log.txt`

Log File Size When a log file is created, this setting specifies in bytes the maximum size the log file is allowed to grow to. The default is 64KB.

Supported platforms: DOS, Windows 95/98. This parameter is added under the NIOS heading within the `net.cfg` file.

Syntax: `log file size = number`

Long Machine Type This setting defines the value to use for this system in the variable %MACHINE. By correctly identifying this field, the system administrator can customize the logon script to be dependent on the computer type or manufacturer. The default is IBM_PC.

Supported platforms: DOS, Windows 95/98, Windows NT

Syntax: `long machine type = name`

Max Cache Size This setting determines the amount of memory in kilobytes to be used by NetWare for caching purposes. When this value is set to 0, the client, during initialization, sets aside 25 percent of the available free memory for NetWare caching. Any other value fixes the cache size to the value specified. This fixed setting cannot be larger than 75 percent of available memory. If it is, the client will adjust the cache size so that it is no larger than 75 percent. The default is 0.

Supported platforms: DOS, Windows 95/98

Syntax: `max cache size = number`

Max Cur Dir Length This setting sets the maximum length of the DOS command line. The value specified is the maximum number of characters that can be entered at the DOS prompt. Any characters entered beyond this maximum are ignored. The default is 64 characters, which is the default for DOS as well.

Supported platforms: DOS, Windows 95/98

Syntax: `max cur dir length = number`

Max Read Burst Size This sets the maximum number of bytes the workstation can negotiate during a packet burst read. This setting is NT-specific and differs from the Packet Burst Read Window Size used on the DOS and Windows 95/98 client in that it specifies the number of bytes that can be read, not the number of packets that can be negotiated. The default is 36,000 bytes.

Supported platforms: Windows NT

Syntax: `max read burst size = number (in bytes)`

Max Write Burst Size This sets the maximum number of bytes the workstation can negotiate during a packet burst write. This setting is NT-specific and differs from the Packet Burst Write Window Size used on the DOS and Windows 95/98 client in that it specifies the number of bytes that can be written, not the number of packets that can be negotiated. The default is 15,000 bytes.

Supported platforms: Windows NT

Syntax: `max write burst size = number (in bytes)`

Mem Pool Size This setting specifies the amount of memory in kilobytes that Client32 can allocate for special use. This pool is used when drivers are called from Windows or when no additional extended memory can be allocated to module loading. The memory pool is disabled if a value of 31KB or less is set. The default is 128KB.

Supported platforms: DOS. This parameter is added under the NIOS heading within the `net.cfg` file.

Syntax: `mem pool size = number`

Message Timeout If the client receives a network broadcast message, the Message Timeout value indicates how long in ticks the client should wait before automatically clearing the broadcast message from the screen. A value of 0 specifies that the messages should not automatically be cleared, but that the message should be displayed until it is cleared by the user. The default is 0.

Supported platforms: DOS, Windows 95/98

Syntax: `message timeout = number`

Minimum Time To Net This value allows you to increase the amount of time in milliseconds that the system should wait for a response before deciding that the transmission failed. This setting is useful for large networks that span one or more WAN links in a bridged environment. If the client is having trouble connecting with a remote resource, try increasing this setting. The default is 0.

Supported platforms: DOS, Windows 95/98, Windows NT

Syntax: `minimum time to net = number`

Name Context This setting specifies the context of the NDS tree where the user wishes to authenticate. This is usually the section of the tree that contains the user's user ID object. There is no default for this setting.

Supported platforms: DOS (set elsewhere in Windows 95/98 and NT)

Syntax: `name context = name_context`

NCP Max Timeout This setting specifies the amount of time (in seconds) that the client should continue retrying a failed resource before determining that the resource is no longer reachable. The default is 30.

Supported platforms: DOS, Windows 95/98

Syntax: `ncp max timeout = number`

NetWare Protocol Determines the search order that the client should use when locating resources. If you have a pure NDS (NetWare 4.x) or bindery (NetWare 3.1x) environment, changing this setting can speed up the authentication process. The default is to use NDS first, and then bindery.

Supported platforms: DOS, Windows 95/98

Syntax: `netware protocol=bind nds | nds bind | nds | bind`

Net Status Busy Timeout When a client receives a type 9999 reply (system busy, try again later) from a server, this setting determines how long in seconds the client should continue issuing the request while still receiving a busy response. After the specified amount of time, the transmission fails. A type 9999 response is indicative of a server that is overloaded. The default is 20 seconds.

Supported platforms: DOS, Windows 95/98

Syntax: `net status busy timeout = ` *number*

Net Status Timeout This setting specifies the amount of time in seconds the client should wait without receiving a response before determining that a network error has occurred. The actual amount of time a client waits will be either the value set in this field, or four times the amount of time it takes for a packet to travel the round trip between the client and the server, whichever is larger.

For example, if this value is set to five seconds, but the client determines that it takes two seconds for a packet to travel to the server and back, the client would wait eight seconds (2×4) before generating an error. If this setting was changed to 10 seconds, the client would wait 10 seconds before generating an error ($10 > 2 \times 4$). The default is 10 seconds.

Supported platforms: DOS, Windows 95/98

Syntax: `net status timeout = ` *number* .

Network Printers When printing in a NetWare environment, print jobs sent to the local printer port (referred to as an LPT port) are redirected by the client out to a network printer. The number of network printers that a user can simultaneously access (access without changing their configuration) is determined by how many LPT ports are specified. This setting adjusts the number of LPT ports recognized by NetWare. The default is 3, which is the maximum number supported by DOS.

Supported platforms: DOS, Windows 95/98

Syntax: `network printers = ` *number*

NWLanguage This setting determines which language should be used for NetWare help files and utilities. The default is English.

Supported platforms: DOS, Windows 95/98, Windows NT. DOS does not have a `net.cfg` setting for this parameter. It is set through the use of the `set` command in the `startnet.bat` file.

Syntax: `set nwlanguage = english`

Opportunistic Locking Enabling Opportunistic Locking allows the client to auto-detect opportunities to gain exclusive access to files. This setting only affects access to files that may be in use by one or more users. The default for this setting is Off, as it has been known to cause problems in some database environments.

Supported platforms: DOS, Windows NT

Syntax: `opportunistic locking = on | off`

Packet Burst This setting enables or disables the use of Packet Burst. In previous DOS-based NetWare clients, the PB Buffers parameter specified the number of Packet Burst buffers. Client32 uses the Packet Burst Read Window Size and Packet Burst Write Window Size to specify the number of buffers to use. To accommodate this change, Client32 interprets a Packet Burst value of 0 to signify that Packet Burst is Off. A value in this field numbering from 1 to 10 signifies that Packet Burst is On. The default is On.

Supported platforms: DOS, Windows 95/98

Syntax: `pb buffers = number`

Packet Burst Read Window Size This specifies the maximum number of packets that can be buffered during a packet burst read. The number of packets specified, times the negotiated frame size, cannot exceed 65,535 bytes. For example, let's say you are operating on an Ethernet network and your client has negotiated a packet size of 1500 bytes. You have also set the Packet Burst Read Window Size to a value of 100. The client will automatically adjust this setting down to 43 during packet burst read negotiations because $43 \times 1500 = 64,500$ bytes, which is just below our maximum of 65,535 bytes. The default is 24.

Supported platforms: DOS, Windows 95/98

Syntax: `pburst read window size = number`

Packet Burst Write Window Size This specifies the maximum number of packets that can be buffered during a packet burst write. Like the Packet Burst Read Window Size, the buffer is limited to 65,535 bytes worth of frames. The default is 10.

Supported platforms: DOS, Windows 95/98

Syntax: `pburst write window size = number`

Preferred Server This setting specifies the name of the NetWare server the client attaches to for authentication purposes when `client32.nlm` loads. There is no default for this setting.

Supported platforms: DOS (set elsewhere in Windows 95/98 and NT)

Syntax: `preferred server = server_name`

Preferred Tree This setting specifies the name of the NetWare NDS tree the client wishes to authenticate to. There is no default for this setting.

Supported platforms: DOS (set elsewhere in Windows 95/98 and NT)

Syntax: `preferred tree = tree_name`

Print Header Print Header sets the size of the print head buffer in bytes. This buffer is used to hold printer initialization information. This setting may need to be adjusted upward if you print complex print jobs or are using PostScript. The default is 64 bytes.

Supported platforms: DOS, Windows 95/98

Syntax: `print header = number`

Print Tail This sets the size of the print tail buffer in bytes. This buffer is used to hold the necessary commands to reset the printer once your print job is complete. The default is 16 bytes.

Supported platforms: DOS, Windows 95/98

Syntax: `print tail = number`

Read Only Compatibility This setting determines whether a read/write call can be used to open a read-only file. Some applications, such as older versions of Microsoft Office, will attempt to open all files with read/write access. If this setting is set to Off, these applications will fail and be unable to open files to which you have been given read-only access. When this setting is set to On, the application opens the file using a read/write call. The application still receives read-only access, however, because file access security is still maintained. The default is Off.

Supported platforms: DOS, Windows 95/98

Syntax: `read only compatibility on | off`

Search Dirs First Sets the display order when the `dir` command is used. When this setting is Off, network files are listed before directories. When this setting is On, directories are listed first, then files. Note that the environment setting `set dircmd =` will override the value set in this parameter. The default is Off.

Supported platforms: DOS, Windows 95/98

Syntax: `search dir first = on | off`

Search Mode Search mode alters the method for finding support files when a program file is executed. The search mode is only referenced when the support file is not located in the same directory as the program file. This setting is useful if a program is set up to be shared over a network when it was not designed to do so. Available settings are:

0	No search instructions. This is the default value for executable files.
1	If a directory path is specified in the executable file, the executable file searches only that path. If a path is not specified, the executable file searches the default directory and network search drives.
2	The executable file searches only the default directory or the path specified.
3	If a directory path is specified in the executable file, the executable file searches only that path. If a path is not specified and the executable file opens data files flagged Read Only, the executable file searches the default directory and search drives.
4	Reserved.
5	The executable file searches the default directory and NetWare search drives whether or not the path is specified. If a search mode is set, the shell allows searches for any files with .xxx extension; otherwise the executable file searches only for .exe, .com, and .bat files.
6	Reserved.
7	If the executable file opens data files flagged Read Only, the executable file searches the default directory and search drives whether or not the path is specified in the executable file.

The default setting is 1.

Supported platforms: DOS, Windows 95/98

Syntax: `search mode = ` *`number`*

Set Station Time   This setting determines whether the workstation's time and date should be synchronized with the NetWare server. The default is On.

Supported platforms: DOS, Windows 95/98

Syntax: `set station time = on | off`

Short Machine Type   Similar to Long Machine Type except the variable is %SMACHINE. The default is `IBM`.

Supported platforms: DOS, Windows 95/98, Windows NT

Syntax: `short machine type = ` *`name`*

Show Dots   This setting allows . and .. to be displayed at the top of a directory listing when NetWare directories are viewed. Many DOS-based programs use these entries when changing directories. The default is Off.

Supported platforms: DOS, Windows 95/98

Syntax: `show dots = on | off`

NOTE   These dots, by the way, are a carryover from Unix. The single dot is a reference to the current directory, while the double-dot refers to the parent directory. (Thus, double-clicking in Explorer on the double-dots is one way to jump up a level to the parent directory.)

Signature Level   Signature Level enables the use of a security token so that both systems can verify the source of a transmission. This token changes with each data exchange between a client and a server. Packet Signature helps to prevent a type of attack known as *connection hijacking*. For example, let's assume that Packet Signature is in use between a client and a server. Each time the two systems communicate, the token is changed. Next, let's assume that the server receives a packet of data that appears to be from the client because it has the correct source MAC address and session number. Let's also assume that the value of the signature token is not correct. In this case, the server will assume that the transmission is in fact not from the client and ignores any data it contains. It will also display an error message on the server console.

Connection hijacking is a very real danger on a NetWare network. In the role of a security auditor, coauthor Chris Brenton used connection hijacking to gain full server access in less than a minute to some very prestigious networks that were thought to be secure. If your account has administrator or supervisor access, you should ensure that Packet Signature is enabled.

The available settings for Signature Level are:

0	Packet Signature disabled.
1	Only enable Packet Signature if the server requires it.
2	Use Packet Signature if the server supports it.
3	Only communicate using Packet Signature. Do not communicate with servers that do not support it.

The default is 1.

Supported platforms: DOS, Windows 95/98, Windows NT

Syntax: `signature level` = *number*

True Commit True Commit overrides all performance settings to ensure that data is immediately written to disk. If any file-write caching is enabled, this setting takes precedence. The default is Off.

Supported platforms: DOS, Windows 95/98

Syntax: `true commit = on | off`

Use Video BIOS This setting specifies whether the client should use direct video memory access or video BIOS calls for displaying pop-up windows. Using video BIOS is slower but can add stability on some systems. The default is Off, meaning that direct video memory access is used.

Supported platforms: DOS, Windows 95/98. This parameter is added under the NIOS heading within the `net.cfg` file.

Syntax: `use video bios = on | off`

The Microsoft Client Drivers for NetWare

Microsoft only supplies NetWare client drivers for the Windows 95/98 and NT platforms. The NT client only supports bindery services at the time of this writing. If you will be using Microsoft's NT client in an IntraNetWare environment, you will need to enable bindery services on each of the servers the client will need access to.

The latest version of Windows 95 includes the Microsoft Service for NetWare Directory Services. This allows the Microsoft NetWare client for Windows 95 to become NDS-aware. If you are running an older version of Windows 95 that does not include this service, you can retrieve it from the Microsoft Web site.

We covered NT's NetWare Client and Gateway Services in great detail back in Chapter 12, so reviewing it again here would be redundant. Instead, we will focus on the Windows 95/98 client and NDS service.

Installing the Microsoft Client for NetWare

To install the NetWare client that ships with Windows 95/98, enter the network properties screen through the Control Panel icon called Network, or by right-clicking the Network Neighborhood and selecting Properties. The Configuration tab of the Network window is shown in Figure 17.14. To begin installing the client, click the Add button.

FIGURE 17.14:

The Windows 95 Configuration tab of the Network window

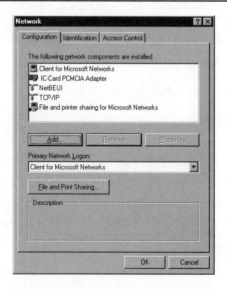

The next dialog box is the Select Network Component Type dialog box. Highlight Client, which is the first option, and click the Add button.

The next window is the Select Network Client window, shown in Figure 17.15. Highlight Microsoft in the Manufacturers column, and select the Client for NetWare Networks in the Network Clients column. Now click the OK button.

FIGURE 17.15:

The Windows 95 Select Network Client window

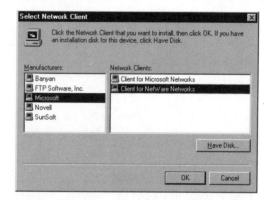

The installer will now begin to install the required software and may request that you load the Windows 95 CD. Once installation is complete, you can configure the Microsoft NetWare Client for your specific environment. Simply highlight the client driver and click the Properties button.

We also need the IPX/SPX protocol in order to communicate with a NetWare server. This protocol is automatically installed during client installation.

Configuring the Microsoft Client for NetWare

Figure 17.16 shows the General tab of the Microsoft Client for NetWare Networks Properties window. The available options are pretty basic. You can configure which server you wish to log on to in the Preferred Server field. You can also select which drive letter you would like to use as your first network drive, and whether the logon script should be processed during authentication. If you do not process the logon script, you should set up permanent mapping to all required file systems and print queues. This will prevent you from having to navigate the Network Neighborhood every time you need to access a NetWare resource.

FIGURE 17.16:

The General tab of the
Microsoft Client for NetWare
Networks Properties window

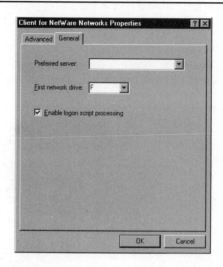

Unlike Client32, with its abundance of configuration options, the Advanced tab of the Microsoft Client for NetWare Networks Properties window has but a single option. The Preserve Case setting can be set to a value of either Yes or No. This determines if files saved to the NetWare server should conform to the DOS convention of creating file names that are fully capitalized. When this setting is set to Yes (which is the default), you can choose to use uppercase or lowercase characters.

Once your configuration is complete, select the OK button on both the Client for NetWare dialog box as well as the Network Properties dialog box. You will then be prompted to reboot your computer. After you do so, you will have access to NetWare bindery servers and services.

Installing the Microsoft NDS Service

To install the Microsoft NDS client, go to the Network Properties screen as you did when installing the Microsoft client for NetWare. Again click the Add button, but this time select the option for installing a service.

The Select Network Service window is shown in Figure 17.17. In the Manufacturers column, highlight Microsoft. You should now see the Service for NetWare Directory Services. If you do not, you have an older version of Windows 95 and will have to click the Have Disk button and enter a path to the extracted NDS files that you retrieved from the Microsoft Web site. Once you do this you will see the Service for NetWare Directory Services. From here, the installation is identical using either version.

FIGURE 17.17:

The Select Network Service window

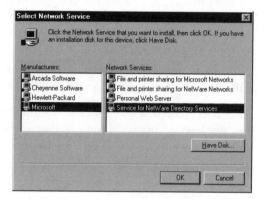

Highlight the Service for NetWare Directory Services option and click the OK button. All required services files will be copied to your system. Once this is completed, you will be returned to the Configuration tab of the Network window. The new service should be one of the last network components listed. From here, you can click OK to complete the installation and reboot your computer, or you can move on to configuring the service.

Configuring the Microsoft NDS Service

Like the Microsoft Client for NetWare, the Microsoft NDS service has very few configurable options. By highlighting the service from the Network Component list and clicking the Properties button, you can configure a preferred tree setting as well as a default context.

Once you are done, select OK from the Service for NetWare Directory Services Properties dialog box, as well as in the Network Properties dialog box. This will initiate an additional file copy of required support files and add statements to the autoexec.bat file to delete any older NetWare drivers you may have on your system. Once this process is complete, you will also be prompted to reboot your computer.

Comparing Client32 and the Microsoft Client

So how do Client32 and the Microsoft client for Windows 95/98 compare? The results may surprise you.

Certainly Client32 has more configuration options. This makes it far easier to customize the client for your specific networking needs. If the main concern is data integrity, you can tune Client32 to commit files to disk immediately and even perform an additional CRC check. If raw throughput is your main goal, you can take advantage of file caching and increase the number of available packet burst buffers until your client is running like a 69 Boss Mustang bored .03 over.

There is something to be said for simplicity, however. While the Microsoft client may not have all the fancy buttons that are included with Client32, this also means that your users have fewer settings to play with and ultimately less chance to incorrectly configure their systems. By keeping it simple, you keep the number of support calls incurred to a minimum.

Of course, the big question is which client can move data while creating the lowest network utilization impact. As an unscientific test, we took three Windows 95 workstations and loaded up Client32 so they could connect to our IntraNetWare server. The clients were tested both in default form and after tuning many of the performance settings covered in the last section. These same workstations then had Client32 removed and the Microsoft client installed. The identical NIC drivers were used on both configurations.

In both cases, we took a 5MB compressed file and measured the results as it was copied back and forth between the workstation and the IntraNetWare server. During the test, we varied the amount of background traffic traveling on our 10Mbps Ethernet segment from 0 to 200 frames per second (fps). The background traffic did not contain any broadcast frames and we made sure that the destination MAC addresses used in the background traffic did not belong to any of our test systems. The idea was to simulate various levels of background traffic that the clients would normally have to contend with in a real-world environment. By ensuring that none of the background traffic was ever addressed to our test systems, we helped to ensure that all their processing was focused on the measured test.

At least ten passes were made of each test. While this testing method is not precise, it will at least put us in the ballpark as to how these clients perform.

The result was that Client32 averaged approximately 4500 frames to move the data, while the Microsoft client required only 4150. This makes the Microsoft client approximately eight percent more efficient when transferring large files.

The difference is how the two clients react to delayed or missing frame retransmissions. Missing frame retransmissions occur when a recipient system either does not receive a frame of data, or receives it in an unusable format (such as with a bad CRC). When this happens, the receiving system will request that the sender retransmit the data.

In Figure 17.18 you can see a normal Client32 packet burst transaction. In frame number 223, the workstation Fenrus requests that the server Talsin send 26,212 bytes of data. Talsin then transmits this data in frames 224 through 242. Because no errors occurred, Fenrus requests another 26,576 bytes of data in frame 243, a quantity just slightly more than it had requested the last time.

No.	Source	Destination	Layer	Summary	Error	Size	Interpacket Time	Absolute Time
223	FENRUS	TALSIN	ncp	Req Burst Read 26212 bytes		108	6 ms	3:00:20 PM
224	TALSIN	FENRUS	ncp	Burst Packet; 1428 bytes		1,512	2 ms	3:00:20 PM
225	TALSIN	FENRUS	ncp	Burst Packet; 628 bytes		712	577 µs	3:00:20 PM
226	TALSIN	FENRUS	ncp	Burst Packet; 1428 bytes		1,512	1 ms	3:00:20 PM
227	TALSIN	FENRUS	ncp	Burst Packet; 1428 bytes		1,512	1 ms	3:00:20 PM
228	TALSIN	FENRUS	ncp	Burst Packet; 1428 bytes		1,512	1 ms	3:00:20 PM
229	TALSIN	FENRUS	ncp	Burst Packet; 1428 bytes		1,512	1 ms	3:00:20 PM
230	TALSIN	FENRUS	ncp	Burst Packet; 1428 bytes		1,512	1 ms	3:00:20 PM
231	TALSIN	FENRUS	ncp	Burst Packet; 1428 bytes		1,512	1 ms	3:00:20 PM
232	TALSIN	FENRUS	ncp	Burst Packet; 1428 bytes		1,512	1 ms	3:00:20 PM
233	TALSIN	FENRUS	ncp	Burst Packet; 1428 bytes		1,512	1 ms	3:00:20 PM
234	TALSIN	FENRUS	ncp	Burst Packet; 1428 bytes		1,512	1 ms	3:00:20 PM
235	TALSIN	FENRUS	ncp	Burst Packet; 1428 bytes		1,512	1 ms	3:00:20 PM
236	TALSIN	FENRUS	ncp	Burst Packet; 1428 bytes		1,512	1 ms	3:00:20 PM
237	TALSIN	FENRUS	ncp	Burst Packet; 1428 bytes		1,512	1 ms	3:00:20 PM
238	TALSIN	FENRUS	ncp	Burst Packet; 1428 bytes		1,512	1 ms	3:00:20 PM
239	TALSIN	FENRUS	ncp	Burst Packet; 1428 bytes		1,512	1 ms	3:00:20 PM
240	TALSIN	FENRUS	ncp	Burst Packet; 1428 bytes		1,512	1 ms	3:00:20 PM
241	TALSIN	FENRUS	ncp	Burst Packet; 1428 bytes		1,512	1 ms	3:00:20 PM
242	TALSIN	FENRUS	ncp	Burst Packet; 1316 bytes		1,400	1 ms	3:00:20 PM
243	FENRUS	TALSIN	ncp	Req Burst Read 26576 bytes		108	568 µs	3:00:20 PM

Figure 17.19 shows the results of the Client32 packet burst transaction initiated in frame number 243. Talsin replies in frames 244 through 263 with the requested information. A curious thing happens, however—frame 245 shows that it was not transmitted to Fenrus for 2 ms. It is normal for there to be some delay in the first and last frame of a packet burst transfer. This is because the transmitting system needs to open and then close the requested information. It is abnormal, however, to experience a large delay during any of the middle packet burst transmissions. The transmitting system should already have the information sitting in queue and waiting to be pushed out onto the wire once the prior packet has been transmitted.

The only logical explanation is that something occurred on the network that delayed delivery. This could have been an error or even a normal frame transmission by another station. Regardless of what caused it, what is interesting is how Client32 deals with the increase in the interpacket gap. If you look at frame 264, you'll see that it is now requesting a packet burst transaction that is roughly half the size of the last one. The result is that less data will be moved before the next acknowledgment, thus increasing our total frame count. If the packet burst transaction initiated by frame 264 does not detect any further problems, it will respond in a similar manner to frame 243 by slightly increasing the quantity of information requested in the next packet burst negotiation.

FIGURE 17.19:

A delay in one of our frame transmissions

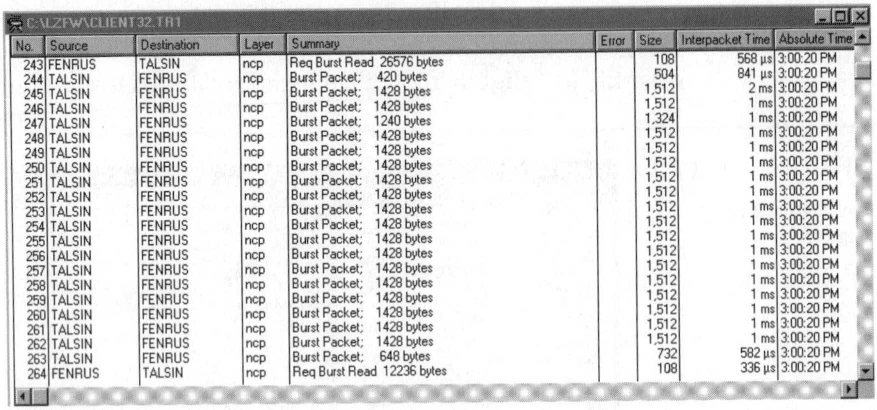

No.	Source	Destination	Layer	Summary	Error	Size	Interpacket Time	Absolute Time
243	FENRUS	TALSIN	ncp	Req Burst Read 26576 bytes		108	568 µs	3:00:20 PM
244	TALSIN	FENRUS	ncp	Burst Packet; 420 bytes		504	841 µs	3:00:20 PM
245	TALSIN	FENRUS	ncp	Burst Packet; 1428 bytes		1,512	2 ms	3:00:20 PM
246	TALSIN	FENRUS	ncp	Burst Packet; 1428 bytes		1,512	1 ms	3:00:20 PM
247	TALSIN	FENRUS	ncp	Burst Packet; 1240 bytes		1,324	1 ms	3:00:20 PM
248	TALSIN	FENRUS	ncp	Burst Packet; 1428 bytes		1,512	1 ms	3:00:20 PM
249	TALSIN	FENRUS	ncp	Burst Packet; 1428 bytes		1,512	1 ms	3:00:20 PM
250	TALSIN	FENRUS	ncp	Burst Packet; 1428 bytes		1,512	1 ms	3:00:20 PM
251	TALSIN	FENRUS	ncp	Burst Packet; 1428 bytes		1,512	1 ms	3:00:20 PM
252	TALSIN	FENRUS	ncp	Burst Packet; 1428 bytes		1,512	1 ms	3:00:20 PM
253	TALSIN	FENRUS	ncp	Burst Packet; 1428 bytes		1,512	1 ms	3:00:20 PM
254	TALSIN	FENRUS	ncp	Burst Packet; 1428 bytes		1,512	1 ms	3:00:20 PM
255	TALSIN	FENRUS	ncp	Burst Packet; 1428 bytes		1,512	1 ms	3:00:20 PM
256	TALSIN	FENRUS	ncp	Burst Packet; 1428 bytes		1,512	1 ms	3:00:20 PM
257	TALSIN	FENRUS	ncp	Burst Packet; 1428 bytes		1,512	1 ms	3:00:20 PM
258	TALSIN	FENRUS	ncp	Burst Packet; 1428 bytes		1,512	1 ms	3:00:20 PM
259	TALSIN	FENRUS	ncp	Burst Packet; 1428 bytes		1,512	1 ms	3:00:20 PM
260	TALSIN	FENRUS	ncp	Burst Packet; 1428 bytes		1,512	1 ms	3:00:20 PM
261	TALSIN	FENRUS	ncp	Burst Packet; 1428 bytes		1,512	1 ms	3:00:20 PM
262	TALSIN	FENRUS	ncp	Burst Packet; 1428 bytes		1,512	1 ms	3:00:20 PM
263	TALSIN	FENRUS	ncp	Burst Packet; 648 bytes		732	582 µs	3:00:20 PM
264	FENRUS	TALSIN	ncp	Req Burst Read 12236 bytes		108	336 µs	3:00:20 PM

Now let's look at how the Microsoft client deals with a similar problem. Figure 17.20 shows an initial packet burst request for 20,992 bytes of data in frame number 184. The server Talsin then transmits this data in frames 185 through 199. If you look at the reply sent by Fenrus in frame 200, you will see that not all of the transmitted data was received. Fenrus is stating that there were 4296 bytes it either did not receive or could not process. Frame 200 is a request that this data be re-sent.

So Talsin re-sends the missing data in frames 201 through 204. Frame 205 is another burst request for a small amount of data, and frames 206 and 207 are the replies.

Frame 208 is where things get interesting. Despite the earlier errors, the Microsoft client is back to asking for 20,992 bytes of data, the exact number it asked for when the error occurred! Unlike Client32, which reduced the requested number of bytes to be read after an error and then slowly increased the value, the Microsoft client jumps right back in requesting the same amount of data.

This is why the Microsoft client was able to move our test file with a fewer number of frames. Because it did not negotiate a smaller packet burst read, it required fewer acknowledgments when moving data. The fewer the number of acknowledgments, the lower the overall frame count.

FIGURE 17.20:

The Microsoft client recovering from an error

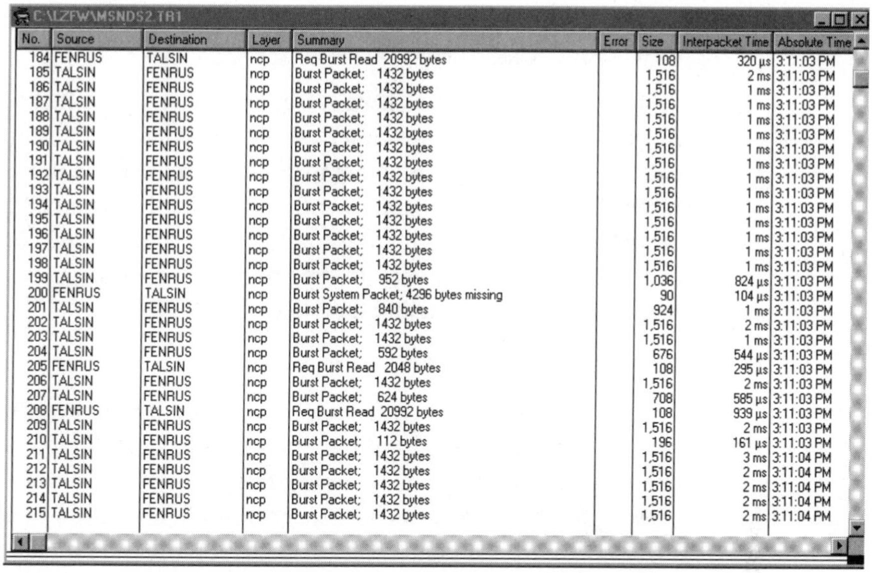

No.	Source	Destination	Layer	Summary	Error	Size	Interpacket Time	Absolute Time
184	FENRUS	TALSIN	ncp	Req Burst Read 20992 bytes		108	320 μs	3:11:03 PM
185	TALSIN	FENRUS	ncp	Burst Packet; 1432 bytes		1,516	2 ms	3:11:03 PM
186	TALSIN	FENRUS	ncp	Burst Packet; 1432 bytes		1,516	1 ms	3:11:03 PM
187	TALSIN	FENRUS	ncp	Burst Packet; 1432 bytes		1,516	1 ms	3:11:03 PM
188	TALSIN	FENRUS	ncp	Burst Packet; 1432 bytes		1,516	1 ms	3:11:03 PM
189	TALSIN	FENRUS	ncp	Burst Packet; 1432 bytes		1,516	1 ms	3:11:03 PM
190	TALSIN	FENRUS	ncp	Burst Packet; 1432 bytes		1,516	1 ms	3:11:03 PM
191	TALSIN	FENRUS	ncp	Burst Packet; 1432 bytes		1,516	1 ms	3:11:03 PM
192	TALSIN	FENRUS	ncp	Burst Packet; 1432 bytes		1,516	1 ms	3:11:03 PM
193	TALSIN	FENRUS	ncp	Burst Packet; 1432 bytes		1,516	1 ms	3:11:03 PM
194	TALSIN	FENRUS	ncp	Burst Packet; 1432 bytes		1,516	1 ms	3:11:03 PM
195	TALSIN	FENRUS	ncp	Burst Packet; 1432 bytes		1,516	1 ms	3:11:03 PM
196	TALSIN	FENRUS	ncp	Burst Packet; 1432 bytes		1,516	1 ms	3:11:03 PM
197	TALSIN	FENRUS	ncp	Burst Packet; 1432 bytes		1,516	1 ms	3:11:03 PM
198	TALSIN	FENRUS	ncp	Burst Packet; 1432 bytes		1,516	1 ms	3:11:03 PM
199	TALSIN	FENRUS	ncp	Burst Packet; 952 bytes		1,036	824 μs	3:11:03 PM
200	FENRUS	TALSIN	ncp	Burst System Packet; 4296 bytes missing		90	104 μs	3:11:03 PM
201	TALSIN	FENRUS	ncp	Burst Packet; 840 bytes		924	1 ms	3:11:03 PM
202	TALSIN	FENRUS	ncp	Burst Packet; 1432 bytes		1,516	2 ms	3:11:03 PM
203	TALSIN	FENRUS	ncp	Burst Packet; 1432 bytes		1,516	1 ms	3:11:03 PM
204	TALSIN	FENRUS	ncp	Burst Packet; 592 bytes		676	544 μs	3:11:03 PM
205	FENRUS	TALSIN	ncp	Req Burst Read 2048 bytes		108	295 μs	3:11:03 PM
206	TALSIN	FENRUS	ncp	Burst Packet; 1432 bytes		1,516	2 ms	3:11:03 PM
207	TALSIN	FENRUS	ncp	Burst Packet; 624 bytes		708	585 μs	3:11:03 PM
208	FENRUS	TALSIN	ncp	Req Burst Read 20992 bytes		108	939 μs	3:11:03 PM
209	TALSIN	FENRUS	ncp	Burst Packet; 1432 bytes		1,516	2 ms	3:11:03 PM
210	TALSIN	FENRUS	ncp	Burst Packet; 112 bytes		196	161 μs	3:11:03 PM
211	TALSIN	FENRUS	ncp	Burst Packet; 1432 bytes		1,516	3 ms	3:11:04 PM
212	TALSIN	FENRUS	ncp	Burst Packet; 1432 bytes		1,516	2 ms	3:11:04 PM
213	TALSIN	FENRUS	ncp	Burst Packet; 1432 bytes		1,516	2 ms	3:11:04 PM
214	TALSIN	FENRUS	ncp	Burst Packet; 1432 bytes		1,516	2 ms	3:11:04 PM
215	TALSIN	FENRUS	ncp	Burst Packet; 1432 bytes		1,516	2 ms	3:11:04 PM

So the Microsoft client is more efficient than Client32, right?

Not quite. Look at frames 208 through 215 in Figure 17.20. While the Microsoft client requested the same amount of data during the packet burst read, it also increased the interpacket gap from 1 ms to 2 ms. The interpacket gap is the delay between frame transmission. The larger the gap, the longer a station waits before transmitting the next packet burst frame. If we increase our interpacket gap from 1 ms to 2 ms, it is going to take us twice as long to move our data from one system to another.

This gap becomes evident in the overall transfer times. While Client32 was consistently able to move our 5MB file in roughly 10 seconds, the Microsoft client averaged 17 seconds. This is roughly a 70 percent increase in overall transfer time. So while the Microsoft client was using fewer frames, it was taking far longer to move the data from one system to another.

So Client32 is more efficient than the Microsoft client, right?

Again, not quite. In order to measure network performance with the Microsoft client, we had to continually change the file name as it was moved back and forth between the workstation and the server. The reason? When the Microsoft client detected that it was working with a file that had been recently moved, it would generate just enough traffic to ensure that the version on the server matched the copy in memory. If this proved to be true, the file was pulled from memory instead of over the network.

This is referred to as a cache hit, and when it occurs it can substantially reduce the number of frames generated, as well as the total transfer time, because the file can be retrieved from local memory. How much of a difference? During a cache hit, the Microsoft client consistently generated less than 80 frames of data to verify the file and closed the transfer in under two seconds. This means that if a client consistently works with the same set of files, it can realize a dramatic performance increase by using the Microsoft client.

So the Microsoft client is more efficient than Client32, right?

Do I have to say it? Our test file was 5MB, a bit on the large size for the average networking environment. While this large size helped to maximize the number of packet burst frames that would be negotiated, it does not present a real-world view of the number of packet burst frames that would be negotiated in the typical networking environment. The average would be somewhat smaller than we encountered during our testing.

So we need to take into account how efficiently each client reacts to many small file requests. With this in mind we took a look at how many frames were exchanged to both open and close a file for packet burst transfer.

Figure 17.21 shows the exchange required by Client32 in order to find a file and initiate a packet burst transfer. In this case it took 16 frames to initiate the file transfer, which was consistent throughout our testing. It was also consistent in terminating the transfer using eight frames.

FIGURE 17.21:

Client32 initiating a file transfer

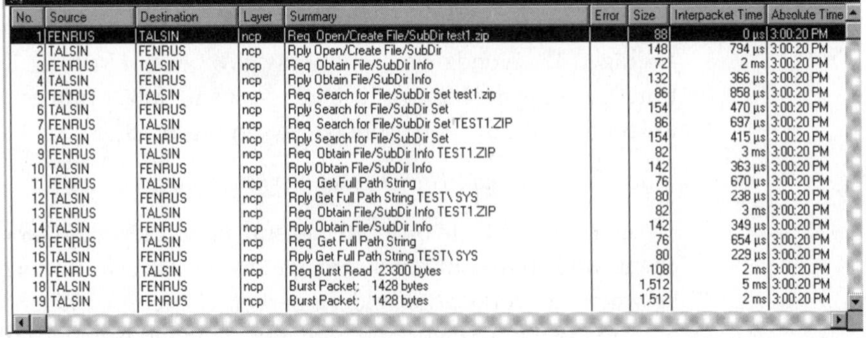

No.	Source	Destination	Layer	Summary	Error	Size	Interpacket Time	Absolute Time
1	FENRUS	TALSIN	ncp	Req Open/Create File/SubDir test1.zip		88	0 µs	3:00:20 PM
2	TALSIN	FENRUS	ncp	Rply Open/Create File/SubDir		148	794 µs	3:00:20 PM
3	FENRUS	TALSIN	ncp	Req Obtain File/SubDir Info		72	2 ms	3:00:20 PM
4	TALSIN	FENRUS	ncp	Rply Obtain File/SubDir Info		132	366 µs	3:00:20 PM
5	FENRUS	TALSIN	ncp	Req Search for File/SubDir Set test1.zip		86	858 µs	3:00:20 PM
6	TALSIN	FENRUS	ncp	Rply Search for File/SubDir Set		154	470 µs	3:00:20 PM
7	FENRUS	TALSIN	ncp	Req Search for File/SubDir Set TEST1.ZIP		86	697 µs	3:00:20 PM
8	TALSIN	FENRUS	ncp	Rply Search for File/SubDir Set		154	415 µs	3:00:20 PM
9	FENRUS	TALSIN	ncp	Req Obtain File/SubDir Info TEST1.ZIP		82	3 ms	3:00:20 PM
10	TALSIN	FENRUS	ncp	Rply Obtain File/SubDir Info		142	363 µs	3:00:20 PM
11	FENRUS	TALSIN	ncp	Req Get Full Path String		76	670 µs	3:00:20 PM
12	TALSIN	FENRUS	ncp	Rply Get Full Path String TEST\ SYS		80	238 µs	3:00:20 PM
13	FENRUS	TALSIN	ncp	Req Obtain File/SubDir Info TEST1.ZIP		82	3 ms	3:00:20 PM
14	TALSIN	FENRUS	ncp	Rply Obtain File/SubDir Info		142	349 µs	3:00:20 PM
15	FENRUS	TALSIN	ncp	Req Get Full Path String		76	654 µs	3:00:20 PM
16	TALSIN	FENRUS	ncp	Rply Get Full Path String TEST\ SYS		80	229 µs	3:00:20 PM
17	FENRUS	TALSIN	ncp	Req Burst Read 23300 bytes		108	2 ms	3:00:20 PM
18	TALSIN	FENRUS	ncp	Burst Packet; 1428 bytes		1,512	5 ms	3:00:20 PM
19	TALSIN	FENRUS	ncp	Burst Packet; 1428 bytes		1,512	2 ms	3:00:20 PM

C:\LZFW\CLIENT32.TR1

Figure 17.22 shows the exchange required by the Microsoft client in order to find a file and initiate a packet burst transfer. Notice that in this case we are using 26 frames in order to initiate a transfer. When closing the file, the Microsoft client used 10 frames.

No.	Source	Destination	Layer	Summary	Error	Size	Interpacket Time	Absolute Time
1	FENRUS	TALSIN	ncp	Req Open File TEST\TEST1.ZIP		73	0 µs	3:11:03 PM
2	TALSIN	FENRUS	ncp	Rply Open File TEST1.ZIP		92	645 µs	3:11:03 PM
3	FENRUS	TALSIN	ncp	Req Close File TEST1.ZIP		64	898 µs	3:11:03 PM
4	TALSIN	FENRUS	ncp	Rply Close File		64	534 µs	3:11:03 PM
5	FENRUS	TALSIN	ncp	Req Allocate Short Dir Handle TEST		72	856 µs	3:11:03 PM
6	TALSIN	FENRUS	ncp	Rply Allocate Short Dir Handle		64	249 µs	3:11:03 PM
7	FENRUS	TALSIN	ncp	Req Set Dir Handle		64	415 µs	3:11:03 PM
8	TALSIN	FENRUS	ncp	Rply Set Dir Handle		64	200 µs	3:11:03 PM
9	FENRUS	TALSIN	ncp	Req Initialize Search		65	376 µs	3:11:03 PM
10	TALSIN	FENRUS	ncp	Rply Initialize Search		66	197 µs	3:11:03 PM
11	FENRUS	TALSIN	ncp	Req Deallocate Directory Handle		64	383 µs	3:11:03 PM
12	TALSIN	FENRUS	ncp	Rply Deallocate Directory Handle		64	175 µs	3:11:03 PM
13	FENRUS	TALSIN	ncp	Req Search for File/SubDir TEST1.ZIP		83	430 µs	3:11:03 PM
14	TALSIN	FENRUS	ncp	Rply Search for File/SubDir		152	377 µs	3:11:03 PM
15	FENRUS	TALSIN	ncp	Req Get Name Space Directory Entry		64	476 µs	3:11:03 PM
16	TALSIN	FENRUS	ncp	Rply Get Name Space Directory Entry		188	445 µs	3:11:03 PM
17	FENRUS	TALSIN	ncp	Req Obtain File/SubDir Info TEST		76	3 ms	3:11:03 PM
18	TALSIN	FENRUS	ncp	Rply Obtain File/SubDir Info		138	365 µs	3:11:03 PM
19	FENRUS	TALSIN	ncp	Req Obtain File/SubDir Info TEST\ TEST1.ZIP		86	457 µs	3:11:03 PM
20	TALSIN	FENRUS	ncp	Rply Obtain File/SubDir Info		142	399 µs	3:11:03 PM
21	FENRUS	TALSIN	ncp	Req Obtain File/SubDir Info TEST		76	2 ms	3:11:03 PM
22	TALSIN	FENRUS	ncp	Rply Obtain File/SubDir Info		138	364 µs	3:11:03 PM
23	FENRUS	TALSIN	ncp	Req Obtain File/SubDir Info TEST\ TEST1.ZIP		86	368 µs	3:11:03 PM
24	TALSIN	FENRUS	ncp	Rply Obtain File/SubDir Info		142	397 µs	3:11:03 PM
25	FENRUS	TALSIN	ncp	Req Open File TEST\TEST1.ZIP		73	895 µs	3:11:03 PM
26	TALSIN	FENRUS	ncp	Rply Open File TEST1.ZIP		92	347 µs	3:11:03 PM
27	FENRUS	TALSIN	ncp	Req Burst Read 20992 bytes		108	2 ms	3:11:03 PM
28	TALSIN	FENRUS	ncp	Burst Packet: 1432 bytes		1,516	14 ms	3:11:03 PM
29	TALSIN	FENRUS	ncp	Burst Packet: 1432 bytes		1,516	2 ms	3:11:03 PM

This means that each time a file transfer is initiated and closed (regardless of the file size), the Microsoft client uses 12 frames more than Client32 as transfer overhead. While this difference is negligible during large file transfers (as we found out in our testing), it will begin to have an increasing effect on transmission efficiency as the size of the files we are using decreases.

One of the points we have yet to touch on is the bandwidth used by each client during the file transfer. During our testing, Client32 achieved an average transfer rate of approximately 450 fps, slightly more than a 50 percent utilization level on our 10Mbps Ethernet network. The Microsoft client, on the other hand, only averaged 230 fps, roughly a 28 percent utilization level. The lower utilization level of the Microsoft client is caused by its use of a longer interpacket gap.

Deciding which transfer rate is preferable is like trying to decide how to best remove a Band-Aid. You can rip it off quickly, which is very painful but is over almost immediately, or you can choose to peel it off slowly, which does not cause nearly as much pain but the pain it does cause lasts for the duration.

With Client32, file transfers can be performed much faster, but two workstations theoretically have the ability to use up all the available bandwidth on the network. With the Microsoft client, the file transfers take place more slowly, but it would require more workstations performing file transfers to use up all the available bandwidth.

So which client is better? The answer is, it depends on your networking environment. If your network neatly meets one or more of the following criteria, then Client32 may be the way to go:

- Predominantly small files are transferred.

- Collision domain contains very few computers.

- Backbone utilizes switching technology.

- Servers are connected to a faster topology than the clients are.

- Users can access most of their resources locally (same logical network segment).

In short, if your network is well-optimized for efficient communications, Client32 will be an effective means of transferring data. Its ability to move data quickly in shorter bursts will have a positive impact on the above-listed environments.

If your network more closely meets one or more of the following criteria, you may be better off using the Microsoft client for NetWare:

- There is heavy use of applications that frequently open the same files, such as databases.

- Collision domains consist of many computers (50 or more).

- Users frequently traverse routers to access network resources.

- Servers connect at the same topology speed as the clients.

- Clients do not need to connect to resources over a WAN.

Because the Microsoft client has a lower transfer rate, we can use this to our advantage by throttling the clients that connect to networks which may already be on the verge of overloading. By dropping the raw transfer rates of the clients, we help to limit the amount of data that can be pushed out onto the network at any given time.

Of course, the real test is to set up an analyzer and measure the average network utilization. If the average utilization is high (40 percent or more), go with the Microsoft client to help reduce the overall network traffic. If the average utilization is low (30 percent or less), then Client32 will add some punch to your network access time by reducing the amount of time it takes to transfer files.

Sometimes you do not have a choice as to which client to use. For example, Novell's network analyzer, LANalyzer, *requires* that Client32 be used. This is also true for the administration utilities NWADMN95 and NWADMN3X. If you will be administrating IntraNetWare servers, you need to use the client created by Novell (Client32). This makes the choice of which client to use a bit more straightforward.

While this example applies specifically to IPX and the differences between Client32 and the Microsoft NetWare client, the communication characteristics of these two clients and their effects on network utilization can be applied to any protocol.

NetWare IP

NetWare IP is a Novell client tool that allows you to connect to a NetWare server using the IP protocol. It does this by encapsulating a full IPX packet within an IP frame. Figure 17.23 shows a frame decode of a NetWare IP frame. As you can see in the figure, the frame contains the following headers:

- Ethernet
- IP
- UDP
- IPX
- NCP

All of these but the Ethernet header are located in the data field of the frame. The space used by these headers is no longer available for transferring data. This means that a NetWare IP frame that is exactly the same length as an IPX frame will not be able to carry as much data. This also means that it may require that more NetWare IP frames be transmitted in order to transfer all the required information from one system to another.

```
Packet Number : 227          1:55:17 PM
Length : 121 bytes
ether: ==================== Ethernet Datalink Layer ====================
       Station: AA-00-04-00-F5-07 ----> 00-80-5F-08-FA-CD
       Type: 0x0800 (IP)
   ip: ==================== Internet Protocol ====================
       Station:136.184.11.147 ---->136.184.2.48
       Protocol: UDP
       Version: 4
       Header Length (32 bit words): 5
       Precedence: Routine
             Normal Delay, Normal Throughput, Normal Reliability
       Total length: 103
       Identification: 44836
       Fragmentation allowed, Last fragment
       Fragment Offset: 0
       Time to Live: 31  seconds
       Checksum: 0xCD2E(Valid)
  udp: ==================== User Datagram Protocol ====================
       Source Port: 43981
       Destination Port: 43981
       Length = 83
       Checksum: 0x6B40(Valid)
  ipx: ==================== Internetwork Packet Exchange ====================
       Checksum: 0xFFFF
       Length: 75
       Hop Count:  0
       Packet Type: 17(NCP)
       Network: 05 52 00 17        ---> 05 52 01 06
       Node:    7E-00-88-B8-0B-93  ---> 00-00-00-00-00-01
       Socket:  0x401C             ---> NCP
  ncp: ==================== NetWare Core Protocol ====================
       NCP Request: Open/Create File/SubDir
       Request Type: 0x2222 (Request)
       Sequence Number: 139
       Connection Number Low: 69
```

If you look at Figure 17.24 you'll see something else that is a bit strange: We are
no longer using packet burst to communicate with the server! Each request for
data is followed by an acknowledgment that the data was received. The result is
that this transaction will require approximately twice as many frames to transfer
the information than if IPX were used as the communication protocol.

No.	Source	Destination	Layer	Summary	Error	Size	Interpacket Time	Absolute Time
227	AA0C0400F507	C0805F08FACD	ncp	Req Open/Create File/SubDir CCDATA\ CLANDATA		121	3 ms	1:55:17 PM
220	00005FC0FACD	AA000400F507	ncp	Rply Open/Create File/SubDir		170	1 ms	1:55:17 PM
229	AA0C0400F507	C0805F08FACD	ncp	Req Log Physical Record; Handle C000FB490000		100	8 ms	1:55:17 PM
230	00805FC8FACD	AA000400F507	ncp	Rply Log Physical Record		84	562 μs	1:55:17 PM
231	AA0C0400F507	C0805F08FACD	ncp	Req Read; Handle 0000FB490000; 512 bytes		96	5 ms	1:55:17 PM
232	00805F08FACD	AA0J0400F507	ncp	Rply Read; 512 bytes		598	1 ms	1:55:17 PM
237	AA0C0400F507	C0805F08FACD	ncp	Req Read; Handle 0000FB490000; 512 bytes		96	2 ms	1:55:17 PM
239	00805FC8FACD	AA000400F507	ncp	Rply Read; 512 bytes		598	768 μs	1:55:17 PM
248	AA0C0400F507	C0805F08FACD	ncp	Req Read; Handle 0000FB490000; 512 bytes		96	4 ms	1:55:17 PM
250	00805FC8FACD	AA000400F507	ncp	Rply Read; 512 bytes		598	1 ms	1:55:17 PM
252	AA0C0400F507	C0805F08FACD	ncp	Req Read; Handle 0000FB490000; 512 bytes		96	3 ms	1:55:17 PM
253	00805FC8FACD	AA000400F507	ncp	Rply Read; 512 bytes		598	579 μs	1:55:17 PM
254	AA0C0400F507	C0805F08FACD	ncp	Req Read; Handle 0000FD490000; 512 bytes		0C	3 ms	1:55:17 PM
255	00805FC8FACD	AA000400F507	ncp	Rply Read; 512 bytes		598	586 μs	1:55:17 PM
256	AA0C0400F507	C0805F08FACD	ncp	Req Read; Handle 0000FB490000; 512 bytes		96	7 ms	1:55:17 PM
257	00805FC8FACD	AA000400F507	ncp	Rply Read; 512 bytes		598	538 μs	1:55:17 PM
260	AA0LC400F507	C0805F08FACD	ncp	Req Read; Handle 0000FB490000; 512 bytes		96	2 ms	1:55:17 PM
261	00805F08FACD	AA000400F507	ncp	Rply Read; 512 bytes		598	716 μs	1:55:17 PM
267	AA0C0400F507	C0805F08FACD	ncp	Req Read; Handle 0000FB490000; 512 bytes		96	3 ms	1:55:17 PM
266	00805FC8FACD	AA000400F507	ncp	Rply Read; 512 bytes		598	1 ms	1:55:17 PM
271	AA0C0400F507	C0805F08FACD	ncp	Req Read; Handle 0000FB490000; 512 bytes		96	2 ms	1:55:17 PM
273	00805FC8FACD	AA000400F507	ncp	Rply Read; 512 bytes		598	593 μs	1:55:17 PM
274	AA0C0400F507	C0805F08FACD	ncp	Req Read; Handle 0000FB490000; 512 bytes		96	2 ms	1:55:17 PM
275	00805FC8FACD	AA000400F507	ncp	Rply Read; 512 bytes		598	620 μs	1:55:17 PM
276	AA0C0400F507	C0805F08FACD	ncp	Req Read; Handle 0000FB490000; 512 bytes		96	2 ms	1:55:17 PM
277	00805FC8FACD	AA000400F507	ncp	Rply Read; 512 bytes		598	633 μs	1:55:17 PM

This does not mean that NetWare IP cannot be an extremely valuable connectivity tool. For example, if you need to traverse a WAN link that only supports the IP protocol, NetWare IP is the perfect solution for filling this need.

It does mean that you need to analyze where and when to use NetWare IP. It is not designed to be a drop-in replacement for IPX communications, and it can produce a reduction in performance if it is used in this manner.

The setup and configuration of NetWare IP is nearly identical to the Client32 installation. The only real difference is that you must assign an IP address to the system or supply the address of a bootp server.

NOTE   When communicating, NetWare IP uses ports 43981 and 43982 as both the source and destination ports. RIP/SAP broadcasts are transmitted on port 396.

Configuring Client Communications in a Windows NT Environment

When selecting a client to communicate with an NT server, your options are a bit more limited than when you are setting up a NetWare client. Microsoft is the only supplier of client software when connecting to Windows Networking-based servers. The necessary client software is installed by default if the installation utility detects that a network card is installed.

Installing the Microsoft Client on Windows 95/98

Installing Microsoft's client support for Windows NT is very similar to the process we used when installing the Microsoft client support for NetWare. To begin the installation, we must go to the Network Properties dialog box and click the Add button.

From the Select Network Component Type dialog box, highlight the option for adding a client and click the Add button. This will bring up the Select Network Client dialog box.

When the Select Network Client window is displayed (you can refer back to Figure 17.15 to see this window), highlight Microsoft in the Manufacturers column, and select the Client for Microsoft Networks in the Network Clients column. Now click the OK button.

You will be returned to the Network window where you should now see the Microsoft client listed at the top of the list. The installation should also have installed the NetBEUI protocol. If all your NT communications will take place on the same logical network, you are finished with the installation. If you will be communicating over a router, you will want to install the IP protocol.

Installing IP Support

To install IP, again click the Add button in the Network window. This time, when the Select Network Component Type window appears, select Protocol and click the Add button. The Select Network Protocol window is shown in Figure 17.25. When this window appears, highlight Microsoft under Manufacturers and select TCP/IP under Network Protocols. Then click the OK button.

FIGURE 17.25:

The Select Network Protocol window

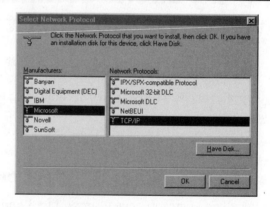

When IP is installed on Windows 95/98, the default is to obtain all required IP information from a DHCP server. If you are not using a DHCP server, you will need to manually configure each required IP parameter.

Once the installation process is complete, you can either configure each of these network components or select the OK button to copy any required files and to reboot the computer.

Configuring the Microsoft Client on Windows 95/98

To configure the client for Microsoft networks, highlight its entry in the Network Components field of the Configuration tab in the Network window, and click the Properties button.

This will bring up the General tab of the Client for Microsoft Networks Properties window, shown in Figure 17.26. We have only a few options that can be configured.

FIGURE 17.26:

The Client for Microsoft Networks Properties window

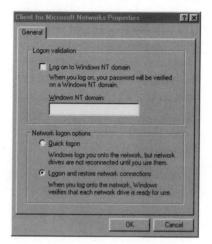

Windows NT Domain

Our first configurable option under Logon Validation is to select whether we will be performing a logon to a Windows NT domain. If we select this box, our logon name will be authenticated on the domain as well as the local system. If we choose to authenticate to a domain, we should also specify which domain to authenticate to in the Windows NT Domain field.

Quick Logon

Under Network Logon Options, we can choose between performing a quick logon, or a logon that verifies all network connections.

During a quick logon, you are authenticated to the domain, and any permanent share mappings, or mappings that are set up as part of a logon script, are mapped and configured on your system. Access to each of these shares is not verified until you actually try to use the share resource.

For example, let's say that you have found a share on your NT domain named Quake. You map a drive letter to it for easy reference, and access it during nonworking hours (when your boss is in a meeting, for instance). This works fine for you, for a couple of weeks. One day, however, when you log on to the NT domain, you may find that you are denied access to the Quake share, even though all the shares are mapped as they normally are. This, in effect, is how a quick logon functions: If security rights to a share have been changed, you won't *realize* that you no longer have access to those files until you actually try to access them.

This, in effect, is how a quick logon functions.

NOTE   Quick logon displays the potential path to resources without regard as to whether you can actually reach those resources.

The Logon and Restore Network Connections option actually verifies each of the share connections. If you cannot access a mapped share during authentication, an error message is produced. This lets you know right away that one of your resources is not available.

Once the configuration is complete, select the OK button. You can now select OK from the Network Properties dialog box to reboot and implement your changes, or you can go on to configure another network component.

Configuring the TCP/IP Protocol

To configure Windows 95/98 to use the IP protocol, highlight TCP/IP in the Network Components field and click the Properties button. This will display the TCP/IP Properties dialog box.

The IP Address Tab   The IP Address tab of the TCP/IP Properties window is shown in Figure 17.27. The default is to obtain all required IP information from a DHCP server. If you are using DHCP, it may be that no additional IP configuration is required. If you do not have a DHCP server, you will need to configure all required IP parameters manually.

FIGURE 17.27:

The IP Address tab of the
TCP/IP Properties window

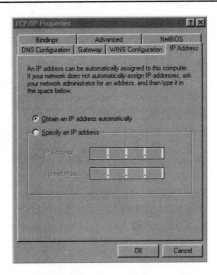

To set an IP address manually, click the Specify an IP Address button. This will activate the IP Address and Subnet Mask fields. Fill in appropriate values for each, depending on your network configuration.

The DNS Configuration Tab   The DNS Configuration tab of the TCP/IP Properties window, shown in Figure 17.28, is used to configure domain name information. If DNS is disabled, no other field on this tab requires configuration. By selecting the Enable DNS button, we can configure each of the displayed fields.

> **Host**   The Host field specifies the unique DNS name used to identify this system. Entering a host name in this field does not automatically register this name through DNS. The DNS administrator must do this manually from the DNS server. You should make sure that the host name you enter here matches the DNS entry for your system. You should also make sure that this name matches the entry listed under the Machine Name field of the Identification tab. The Identification tab can be accessed directly from the Network window (see Figure 17.14).
>
> **Domain**   Our next configurable field is Domain. This field is used to identify the domain name where this system will be located. Only fill in the domain name, not the fully qualified domain name (FQDN) for this

machine. For example, if our host name is Fenrus and we are located in the domain foobar.com, we would enter the domain as foobar.com, not Fenrus.foobar.com.

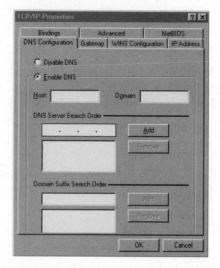

DNS Server Search Order   The DNS Server Search Order field is used to identify the IP address of the domain name servers this system should use when resolving host addresses to IP address. For fault tolerance, the IP address of multiple servers may be entered. If the host is unable to contact the first server on the list, it will direct all DNS queries to the second listed IP address.

Domain Suffix Search Order   The Domain Suffix Search Order field is used to define other domain names to search, besides the one where this system is located, when only a host name is presented in a DNS query. For example, let's assume we have a system whose FQDN is fire.testing .foobar.com. From this system, we wish to access our local Web server located at www.foobar.com. If we enter just the Web server's host name www, our DNS query will fail. This is because our system assumes that we are trying to access a system within the same domain. This means that our system thinks we are looking for the IP address of the system www.testing .foobar.com, which does not exist. The Domain Suffix Search Order allows us to define additional domains to search when we enter just a host name for IP address resolution. If we were to add the domain `foobar.com` to the search order list, the address would now be resolved correctly. This is because once the DNS lookup on `www.testing.foobar.com` failed, the search order list would be referenced and a new query would be sent looking for the IP address for `www.foobar.com`.

The Gateway Tab   The Gateway tab has a single option—to configure the IP address of the local routers. The first address listed is considered the default router or gateway and will be used for all nonlocal network communications. If we need to transmit information to a system that is not on our local network, we will forward it to the first listed IP address and let that system figure out how to best deliver the information.

If a second IP address is listed, traffic will be forwarded to the second address if the router located at the first IP address fails to respond. This provides some fault tolerance in case our first router should fail.

The NetBIOS Tab   The NetBIOS tab also has a single option. We can choose to enable or disable the use of NetBIOS over IP. When this box is checked, the system can take advantage of encapsulating NetBIOS traffic within IP frames in order to communicate with systems that are not located on the same logical network.

The WINS Configuration Tab   The WINS Configuration tab, shown in Figure 17.29, allows us to identify the IP address of the WINS servers located on our local network. WINS servers are used to propagate NetBIOS system names between logical networks. When our system needs to find another NetBIOS- or NetBEUI-based system, it references the WINS server to obtain the system's IP address. It can then use this address to communicate with the remote system by encapsulating the traffic within IP frames.

We are allowed to enter the IP address of two WINS servers. This provides some fault tolerance in case one of them is not available. The Scope ID identifies the scope under which this system's name is considered unique. Scope IDs are similar to domain names and often share the same name or value. Unless you are part of an extremely large network, it is safe to leave the Scope ID blank.

FIGURE 17.29:

The WINS Configuration tab
of the TCP/IP Properties
window

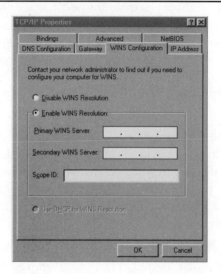

There is an option at the bottom of the dialog box that we are not allowed to select—the Use DHCP for WINS Resolution button. This option is only active when you select Obtain an IP Address Automatically from the IP Address tab. When the Use DHCP for WINS Resolution button is selected, it tells the system to retrieve WINS server information from the DHCP server when DHCP is queried for an IP address.

The Bindings Tab   The Bindings tab identifies which clients should use the IP protocol. If you want to enable IP, but you do not want to use IP when accessing network shares, deselect the option labeled Client for Microsoft Networks.

If you have file sharing enabled on your system, and you want to make sure that only local clients can access your file shares, make sure the option for File and Printer Sharing for Microsoft Networks is deselected.

TIP

Besides security, there are also performance gains to disabling services that do not require the IP protocol. Whenever you perform a search for a network resource, your system attempts to find it, using all available protocols. By deselecting protocols that do not provide a path to any network resources, you expedite the search process.

The Advanced Tab The Advanced tab has a single option—you can choose to set IP as the default protocol. The default protocol is the first protocol used by the Microsoft client when searching for network resources. If the resource is not located using the default protocol, any other protocols the Microsoft client is bound to will be used.

If you deselect the binding of the Microsoft client to the IP protocol, you should not (even though you can) set IP as the default protocol.

Once you are satisfied with your changes, click the OK button to close the TCP/IP Properties window and click OK again to close the Network Properties dialog box. The system will now reboot so your changes will take effect.

Configuring NT Workstation

NT Workstation does not use a Microsoft client. Instead, it uses a service called Workstation when accessing NT resources. Configuring NT services, including the Workstation service, was covered at length in Chapter 12.

There is one additional step to using an NT workstation on a Microsoft domain, beyond configuring the proper services and protocols: You must also register the system with the domain controllers. The registration process ensures that users performing a logon from this system should be allowed access to domain resources. The user is still required to use a valid logon name and password; the registration process simply verifies that this system is acceptable to use for domain access.

Figure 12.3 showed the Identification Tab of the Network window. By clicking the Change button, we were able to rename our server or domain. When this same button is selected on an NT workstation or an NT server that is not a domain controller, the Identification Changes dialog box, shown in Figure 17.30, appears.

From this dialog box, we can enter the name of the domain we wish to join in the domain field. If we select the Create a Computer Account in the Domain button, the two fields directly below it become active. These fields allow us to enter the logon name and password of a domain administrator (such as Administrator). When we click the OK button, the name and password entered are verified by one of the domain controllers. If this combination is accepted, the NT workstation is allowed access to the domain.

FIGURE 17.30:

The Identification Changes
dialog box

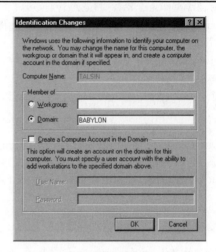

Using NFS to Access File Services between Unix Systems

The *Network File System* (*NFS*) protocol can be used to share files and directories between Unix systems. It is functionally similar to the file shares or drive mappings, except that remote file systems are mounted to some point in the existing directory structure.

While the mainstay of NFS use is Unix, there are third-party tools available for every major platform to support NFS. This allows other operating systems to access NFS servers, and many of them, such as IntraNetWare, are able to *act* as NFS servers as well.

There are two parts to configuring NFS:

- The server system must export the files to be shared.
- The client system must mount the shared files.

Configuring the NFS Server

The first step in configuring an NFS server is to decide which file systems to export and who should have access to them. File systems are exported at the directory level and are recursive, so if we export the directory /usr/games, we export all files within the games directory as well as subdirectories located below this.

While Linux allows you to export a parent directory as well as one of its child directories, many Unix flavors, such as Solaris, will not allow you to do this. The second export attempt will fail. For example, if we wish to set up /usr/games and /usr/games/doom as two separate exports, Linux will allow us to do this while Solaris would fail on the second entry.

Exporting file systems can only be performed by the root user. This is to help ensure that someone does not accidentally make public a private section of the directory structure.

Who is allowed to access each exported file system is determined at the host level. You can set access permissions on a per-system basis and have a small amount of control over file access once the connection is established.

NFS assumes that the user ID and group ID are synchronized between the two systems. It uses the IDs to determine file access rights instead of using the logon name. For example, let's assume you are currently logged on to the Unix system Mars. Your logon name is user1, and both your user ID and group ID are set to 150.

If you mount a file system on Mars that is being exported from the Unix system Venus, your user ID and group ID would be used to determine which files you have access to. If your account on Venus was also set to use a user ID and a group ID of 150, life is happy and you should have no problems accessing your files. If this ID number belongs to another user, or your ID is set to some other value, you will not have the same level of file access that you would normally receive when you Telnet directly to Venus. Since the ID numbers do not match, the exporting system (Venus) cannot correctly identify who you are.

Configuring NFS Exports   To configure the file systems you wish to export, make sure you are logged on as the root user. You can use Red Hat's graphical Control Panel tool (accessed through XWindows) or you can directly edit the /etc/exports file. The Control Panel tool is by far the easiest method and is self-explanatory once you understand how the exports file is used. With this in mind we will look at what is involved with editing the exports file directly.

Editing the Exports File   The exports file consists of two columns separated by either tabs or spaces. In the first column is the name of the directory you wish to export. The second column lists the security criteria that must be passed in order to access the listed file system. Some valid security parameters are listed in Table 17.4.

TABLE 17.4: Security Parameters

Parameter	Description
ro	Provide read-only access to the file system.
rw	Provide read/write access to the file system.
host	Only allow access from the specified *host*.
domain	Only allow access from the specified *domain*.
*	Only allow access from hosts that meet the wildcard criteria.
IP Subnet	Only allow access from hosts on the specified *IP subnet*.
root_squash	File access requests that originate from the root user on the remote file system are handled as if they were from an anonymous user.
all_squash	Handle all file access requests as if they originated from an anonymous user.

> **NOTE**   In Unix, the anonymous user is the equivalent of the guest user under NetWare or Windows NT. Typically, this account is provided with little to no file-system access.

If you were to implement these parameters, an example export file could look something like this:

```
# Sample /etc/exports file
/home/cbrenton        fenrus(rw)
/home/ftp/pub         *.foobar.com(ro,root_squash)
/data/testing         sean(rw) test*.foobar.com(ro,all_squash)
/data/salary          10.5.7.0(r,w)
```

The first line is simply a comment to identify the file. The second line exports the contents of /home/cbrenton for read/write access, but only from the system fenrus.

The third line exports the contents of /home/ftp/pub to everyone in the foobar.com domain. Access is restricted to read only, and if a root user attempts to access files, they are given the same level of access as the anonymous user.

The fourth line exports the contents of /data/testing. Read/write access is provided to the system sean. Access is also provided to any host that meets the naming criteria test*.foobar.com. For example, if the systems test1, test2, and testing are part of the foobar.com domain, they are allowed access to this export. Access is at a read-only level, and all user file access rights are handled as if they originated from an anonymous user.

Our final line exports the contents of /data/salary to every system on the IP subnet 10.5.7.0. All systems on this subnet are allowed read/write access.

Exporting File Systems   Once we have finished editing our /etc/exports file, we must start up the services that will make these file systems available on the network. First we must ensure that the NFS daemon is running. This may be named nfsd, or rpc.nfsd, depending on the operating system you are using. You can see if one of these processes is running by typing the commands:

```
ps -ax|grep nfsd
ps -ax|grep rpc.nfsd
```

The command ps -ax generates a list of all running processes. We then take the output from this command and pipe it through grep, which searches for the specified character string. You will see one instance of the command for the grep process itself (remember we are listing out all processes, including the process which is looking for other processes); if you see a second instance, then the NFS daemon is already running. If it is not running, you can start the daemon directly from the command line. Look in the /usr/sbin directory to see which version of the daemon you are using and simply type in its name at the command line.

Once the daemon is running, enter the command:

```
exportfs -a
```

This will cause the daemon to read the /etc/exports file and make all listed file systems available for network access.

Configuring the NFS Client

The NFS client configuration follows a similar process to the server configuration. We must edit the configuration file, start the required daemon, and execute the required command to initiate the process. The file we need to edit is /etc/fstab.

Configuring the fstab File The fstab file is used by the operating system to identify each of the different file systems that it has to interact with. Figure 17.31 shows a sample fstab file from a system named Sean. In order for Sean to be able to mount the exported files from the system that we configured in the last section (which we'll name Toby), Sean's fstab file needs to have an entry for these exported file systems.

FIGURE 17.31:

Sean's fstab file

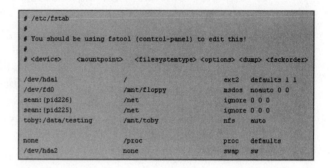

```
# /etc/fstab
#
# You should be using fstool (control-panel) to edit this!
#
# <device>      <mountpoint>    <filesystemtype> <options> <dump> <fsckorder>

/dev/hda1                   /                       ext2    defaults 1 1
/dev/fd0                    /mnt/floppy             msdos   noauto 0 0
sean:(pid226)               /net                    ignore 0 0 0
sean:(pid225)               /net                    ignore 0 0 0
toby:/data/testing          /mnt/toby               nfs     auto

none                        /proc                   proc    defaults
/dev/hda2                   none                    swap    sw
```

If you look down the first column, you'll see an entry that begins `toby:/data/testing`. This tells Sean that the file system we wish to mount is located on the system Toby. This entry also tells the system that out of all the file systems being exported, the one we're interested in is `/data/testing`.

The second column indicates where Sean should locate Toby's exported file system. According to the entry, we asked that the file system be placed under the `/mnt/toby` directory. Once the mount is complete, a directory listing on Sean under `/mnt/toby` will produce the same information as a directory listing on Toby under `/data/testing`.

The third column identifies what type of file system will be attached to this mount point. Whenever we perform an NFS mount, we always identify the file system as being NFS, regardless of the source operating system.

The final column identifies how the operating system should handle this file system. The `auto` switch tells the operating system that it should try to restore this connection whenever the machine is rebooted. This way Sean will automatically mount Toby's directory during system startup. No user intervention will be required to restore this connection.

Mounting the Remote File System Once we have finished editing our fstab file, we can start up the required services to mount the remote file system.

To perform an NFS mount, the `mountd` daemon must be running on the system. We can check to see if it's running by typing the command

```
ps -ax|grep mountd
```

If two entries for `mountd` are printed, we know our service is running. If it is not currently running as a process, we can start it from the command line. Once `mountd` is running, we can use the command `mount` to attach to the remote file system. We do this by typing

```
mount /mnt/toby
```

The switch tells mount to reference the fstab file and mount the file system associated with the mount point /mnt/toby. If we need to make multiple mounts, we can enter them one by one, specifying the mount point of each, or by entering the command

```
mount -a
```

The -a switch tells mount to initialize all mount points that have `auto` specified as one of their options. This is the command that is executed during system startup to restore the connections to our remote file systems.

Connectivity with Apple Computers

Toward the start of this chapter we observed that Apple's Mac OS does not provide much built-in support for non-AppleTalk networks. Perhaps this will be remedied by Apple's upcoming OS X or Rhapsody operating systems. In the meantime, however, there are enough Mac users out there needing to connect to non-Apple network resources that we'd like to present some options here that are currently available to address this need.

Apple and NetWare

Shortly before this book went to press, Novell signed an agreement with ProSoft Engineering for Mac OS/NetWare development. The agreement reportedly will provide:

1. A new NetWare client to address long-standing issues

2. Native-IP NetWare client

3. Additional products, including AppleTalk NLM updates

4. Updates to IPX SDK

It should be interesting to see what transpires from this.

Apple and NT

Windows NT Server includes a version of the AppleTalk protocol, as well as Services for Macintosh, which provides both file and print sharing services for Mac clients. Unfortunately this does not mean you can use NT as a *client* to browse Apple shared files. As a server, however, it performs exactly as you would expect, emulating Apple's dual-fork file system and allowing both Macs and PCs to access the same shared folders (if desired).

NT's file sharing service for Macs allows you to share any folders on an NTFS (not FAT) partition, such that Mac OS clients can access these via the Apple Chooser, just as if NT Server were another Mac offering peer file sharing services. NT includes transparent support for Apple's dual-fork file scheme. (Transparent for Macs that is—PCs will be able to see the resource fork as a separate file if they have "Show all files" enabled in their folder options.)

This file sharing causes an interesting situation with file naming conventions. DOS has a file name limitation of eight characters plus three for the file extension, Macs have a file name limitation of 33 characters, and Windows NT and Windows 95/98 can have file names up to 254 characters in length. Therefore, NT automatically truncates displayed client versions of file names down (when necessary) to fit the maximum length supported by the client operating system. That is, the actual file name (whatever its length) is retained on NT, but the Mac client is given a copy of the file name that is shortened to 33 characters.

Most mixed Mac and PC network environments will, for this reason, implement a policy of keeping file names to 32 characters or less, at least on partitions or folders that are visible to the Mac clients. This allows all users to see files with one consistent set of file names.

File extensions also become more of an issue when you have Mac network clients. Because on a Mac the file type information is stored in the resource fork, files can have any name whatsoever, and are not required to carry a file extension designating the file type. This can cause problems for Windows users who attempt to access files created by Mac users; without the file extension, Windows clients will not know which software to use to open the file.

The solution again is to implement a policy of requiring file extensions to indicate the type of file. (This is not necessary, however, if the file area being shared by the Mac clients will not need to be accessed by Windows (or DOS) clients.)

One interesting feature of NT's printer sharing for Macs is that it actually allows Macs to print over the network even to non-PostScript printers. NT is able to accomplish this because it includes PostScript emulator software that allows non-PostScript printers to appear as Apple LaserWriter printers. Note, however, that this built-in PostScript software currently supports black-and-white printing only (color PostScript is converted to black-and-white), and unfortunately Microsoft has not announced plans to support PostScript printing (using this emulator) in color.

Installing AppleTalk and Apple Services on an NT Server is reasonably straightforward.

To Install AppleTalk on NT:

1. Open the Control Panel (from the Start menu or My Computer).

2. Open the Network applet in Control Panel.

3. Click on the Protocols tab in the Network window.

4. Click Add, select Microsoft ➢ AppleTalk Protocol, and click OK.

5. Select the now installed AppleTalk entry, and click on Properties to choose an AppleTalk zone.

6. Click the Services tab, select Microsoft ➢ Services for Macintosh, and click OK.

With Apple Services (and AppleTalk) installed, two new applets will appear in your Control Panel: File Server for Macintosh (also called MacFile), which allows you to share files and folders on any NTFS volume; and Print Server for Macintosh (a.k.a. MacPrint), which lets you share any printers connected to NT as networked printers accessible to Macs.

When sharing files with Mac clients, MacFile gives you the ability to restrict file permissions. Rather than the "normal" NT file permissions, these are limited to See Files, See Folders, and Make Changes. You can also control whether directories can be replaced, as well as whether files can be moved, renamed, or deleted.

Peer Networking with Apple, Windows 95/98, and NT

Windows 95/98/NT systems can, of course, share files and printers with each other using Microsoft's built-in file sharing. Apple systems can also share files and printers with each other using built-in AppleTalk. Did you know, however, that you have the ability to set up peer networking between Mac OS and Windows clients (even without the help of NT's Mac OS support)?

At the time of this writing, a new version of AppleShare IP is in beta testing, and it will allow Macs to browse and access files and printers shared via Windows peer networking (or NT).

Another solution that has been available for more than a few years is Miramar's MacLan product. This software, when installed on a Windows 95/98 or NT system, essentially adds AppleTalk protocol support directly to Windows.

Moreover, MacLan provides AppleTalk browsing support seamlessly to the Windows Network Neighborhood, and without adding any software on the Mac side, allows Mac clients to access files and printers shared on the Windows stations (provided they're shared using the Miramar file- or printer-sharing applets). The first time we tried this product, we were delighted to see Mac OS computers appear when we opened Network Neighborhood. We could drag and drop files to and from the Macs and browse folders just as easily as on another PC. It is also nice to have Windows 95 or Windows 98 function as a server to a group of Macs. If you have a mixed PC/Mac environment, you should definitely check out this product. Miramar's Web site can be found at www.miramarsys.com.

A Last Resort: Bridging the Gaps Using FTP

Wherever you have several dissimilar computers that are all able to run TCP/IP, it's just a matter of setting up an FTP or Web server on one system (and FTP or Web client software on the others) to enable files to be both uploaded and downloaded between the various systems.

You don't have an FTP or Web server? Just use your FTP client or Web browser to download one of many programs available on the Internet. All platforms mentioned in this book each have at least a few such server applications available, including decent freeware, shareware, and try-before-you-buy-ware options, which work well in a pinch.

Here are a few tips for each platform to get you started.

Mac OS

On earlier Mac systems, you can run into a sort of "chicken and egg" dilemma, trying to get Internet client software on a Mac that doesn't already have any Internet client software. This is no problem at all if you have a second Mac, or a friend with a Mac, and can transfer software via floppy. One of your first goals should be to get a copy of Stuffit or some similar decompression utility installed, as most Mac software on the Internet is compressed using Stuffit or MacBinary.

> **NOTE**   If you happen to have Stuffit installed, you could even download Mac software using a friend's PC, transferring it to the Mac on a PC floppy using Apple's built-in PC File Exchange. (This works best with Stuffit files, although we've also transferred MacBinary files this way.)

However, if you have Mac OS 8 or later, things have been made a lot easier for you. Mac OS 8 includes a personal Web server. If you install Cyberdog, you also get a Web browser and FTP client. Also, Microsoft offers a free Mac version of their "lite" Web server, called Personal Web Server, as an optional download with Internet Explorer 4 for the Mac. Popular Mac shareware software includes: Anarchie (an FTP and Archie client), Fetch (a popular FTP client), and Download Deputy (another good FTP client supporting batch downloads). The leading browsers are of course available (including Netscape's Navigator and Communicator, and Microsoft's Internet Explorer). For further software download choices, be sure to check out the TUCOWS (www.tucows.com) Web site.

Windows 3.1

One of my favorite FTP clients, called CuteFTP, is also available for Windows 3.1. It lets you drag/drop, do batch copies, save default local and remote paths, and create catalogs of frequently accessed FTP sites. Another nice feature is support for resuming downloads after interruption. Other FTP clients include WS-FTP LE and WS-FTP Pro, WholeSite FTP, Integrated Internet FTP (both client and server in one package), and Drag and File. For Web browsers, there's Netscape's Navigator and Communicator, Microsoft's Internet Explorer, and lesser known browsers, such as BeConn (which doesn't support Java, but has a very simple-to-use interface and built-in e-mail and FTP capabilities.

Windows 95/98/NT Workstation 4.0

Quite conveniently, all of these operating systems come with built-in FTP and Telnet clients—install the TCP/IP protocol and you also have FTP access added automatically. While the FTP client program uses a command-line interface (very much like its Unix counterparts), it at least is sufficient to use to download more full-featured Internet software. On a system that has no browser or other client installed, it sure is helpful to be able to count on the built-in FTP client as a way to get out on the Internet (or an intranet) and transfer files.

Except for the original "A" version of Windows 95, all the later OSs also include Microsoft's Peer/Personal Web, Gopher, and FTP servers built in. You do need to install these (via the Network applet in Control Panel—click on Services, and add MS Peer Web Services) and then enable them before they're available for use. Enabling/disabling and configuring is done via a Web browser interface (this is also accessible via the Control Panel).

In fact, all the software mentioned in the previous section for Windows 3.1 is also available in 32-bit versions for Windows 95 and later.

Windows NT Server

Everything mentioned previously for Windows 95 and later also applies to NT Server, except that NT Server 4.0 and later include Microsoft's full-blown Web server (Internet Information Server). Basically, this is a faster and more robust Web server that includes advanced configuration and security features, plus support for technologies such as Active Server Pages and various types of server-side scripting. We should also mention Netscape's and O'Reilly's great Web server offerings, plus the great Apache freeware server, all of which are supported on NT.

For more such software, search the Internet for "Winsock" and "FTP server" to bring up more links than you'll need.

TIP   For lots of Internet related shareware and freeware, try the TUCOWS download Web site, mentioned earlier, which has a large and attractively arranged selection of Internet (and other) software available for download, for both Macs and PCs.

Unix (Including Linux)

You need to ask? Unix is what started the TCP/IP "revolution." Almost every Unix variant has an FTP server daemon built in. For those that don't, just grab some C source code off the Web and compile it. The most popular (and free) Web server for Linux/Unix is called Apache, and is available from many places on the Web. The Apache project Web site is currently located at `sunsite.doc.ic.ac.uk/packages/apache/`.

Both Netscape's Navigator and Communicator, as well as Microsoft's Internet Explorer, are available for Unix. (Netscape's programs support Linux and more versions of Unix than Internet Explorer does.) Plenty of other Internet software (in many cases including source code) is available as well.

TIP

Remember: Any two computers, no matter how dissimilar, can transfer files between them using FTP (or Web) software. All that's needed is the TCP/IP protocol, plus FTP server software on one system, and FTP client software on the other system. Not only is FTP much faster than trying to transfer files by floppy or removable disks, it also automatically avoids the problem of different file systems.

Summary

This concludes our discussion on client software and how to connect workstations to various network services. You should now have a good understanding of how to get a workstation communicating with some of the more popular network operating systems.

In the next chapter, we will take a look at ways of connecting networks to the Internet. We'll discuss different hardware access methods, then take a look at browser and server issues (including Web servers, security, and supporting add-in software such as plug-ins and ActiveX controls).

PART V

Interconnecting Networks

- CHAPTER 18: Adding Internet Access

- CHAPTER 19: Building an Intranet

- CHAPTER 20: Introduction to Extranets

- CHAPTER 21: Extranet Infrastructure

CHAPTER

EIGHTEEN

Adding Internet Access

- Choosing a firewall and network address translations

- Selecting an operating system

- Selecting a Web server

- Choosing a browser

- Connecting the hardware

- Considering security

It usually starts out something like this: Over the years, your network has grown and grown. Because there were some applications that worked best using TCP/IP, TCP/IP was installed on all of the gazillion workstations within the company. This was no big deal; since the company was not connected to the outside world, any old IP addressing scheme would do. You just grabbed the nearest Class A address and went to town.

Meanwhile on Mahogany Row, some CEO goes to lunch with friends, and some other suits mention how great it is to have Internet access. With Internet access they can sit at their desks and watch their portfolios grow! This is a great thing, and it also gives them something to do with the fancy computers sitting on their desks. So, the CEO comes back and tells you that it's time to get out to that Internet place; your company really needs to connect and make all that vital information available. And just to make your life really interesting, the technology-aware executive group wants to make sure that the Internet connection is *really fast* and also *really cheap*.

After this conversation, you start to panic. All those IP addresses are going to need to be changed and someone is going to have to decide on things like an Internet service provider (ISP) and routers and gateways and bridges and e-mail gateways or connectors—and life just got a whole lot more complicated, right? Wrong! While this is going to involve some work on your part, look at it this way: Internet access is becoming more and more a corporate way of life. Everybody has got to have it.

This can be one of the great projects of your career. After all, it is the really visible projects with immediate results that get noticed. What could possibly be more noticeable than a connection to the Internet? One day it simply shows up on the desktop, and when it does, it works!

In order to make sure this is one of the great projects of your career, let's try to eliminate all the possible problems before they occur. After all, proper planning prevents poor performance.

Initial Considerations

Before you begin to hook up to the outside world, let's take an inventory of what you currently have and what needs to be done before the great day arrives. First of all, it has been determined that you have a gazillion workstations currently assigned IP addresses. These workstations, no matter which desktop operating system they are running, can communicate with one another running IP. That is a definite addition to the plus side of the ledger. To offset that entry, there is the fact that each one of these systems is using a bogus IP address that is probably assigned to some great powerful corporation that will take a very dim view of you messing up its network by using some of its IP addresses.

First of all, don't let this concern you too much. No matter how new you are to the networking world, you have probably heard of the terms "firewall" and "gateway." A *gateway* is a device configured to provide access to the outside world. It will be your actual connection to the Internet. A *firewall* is a device that you configure to act as the guard dog to your gateway, and it works this way: Whenever a packet is addressed to a system on your network from somewhere on the Internet, it needs to clear the firewall to get through. Whenever a packet from inside your network wants to get out, it has to go through the firewall. In either direction, the firewall can either let the packet pass through, or it can discard the packet. The firewall acts as the guardian to the network.

What, you are thinking, does all this have to do with a gazillion IP addresses? Simple. One of the functions that many firewalls provide is to mask the IP addresses of the hosts on the company side of the firewall. This is called *Network Address Translation (NAT)*.

Firewalls and NAT

The design of the firewall and NAT is extremely simple. You start with a file server that has at least two network cards in it. Each network card connects to a separate concentrator. One card is the "public" card, and the other links the system to the "private" or company network. Look at Figure 18.1 to see the appropriate layout.

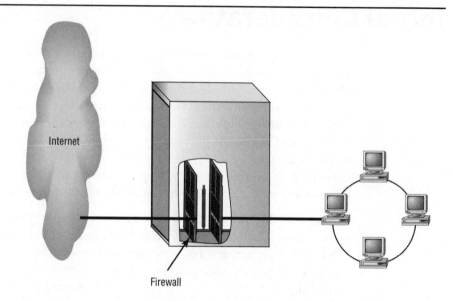

Firewall

As you can see, the Internet connects to a public card. Because this is a *public* card, the IP address assigned to the card must have a legitimate IP address. There are several ways to obtain these, the simplest being to rent an IP address from your ISP.

Your server will be running some kind of NAT/Firewall software. Because of the NAT/Firewall software, everything on the private side of the network is hidden from the outside world, including all the IP addresses that you made up as you went along. So, if all these gazillion addresses are hidden from the outside world, that means they don't have to be InterNIC-assigned addresses, which means they won't have to be changed.

Like most good things, this comes with a cost. The cost usually depends on the functionality of the firewall and the number of connections that will be going through it. More connections means more money. However, there are ways of cost-justifying the firewall. Try these arguments on for size—they have all worked at least once somewhere.

- **Security:** Every officer of every company is concerned with one thing, keeping the corporate data safe and away from prying eyes. A firewall will help to protect your network from people trying to hack into your network from the outside. If you work for a normal, run-of-the-mill company, putting up a firewall may be a sufficient deterrent to keep hackers out. The hacker may recognize that you have a firewall, and figure that the stuff on the other side just isn't worth the effort to hack into. If you are not a run-of-the-mill company, firewalls are one piece in the security plan. The cost-justification you make to management starts out something like, "How much is the data on our network worth? If I can provide a first level of security for $$$$, would that be worth it?"

NOTE   The level of management commitment usually has a price. The really important stuff that is stored on your server really does have a dollars-and-cents price. Protecting the data on the server is worth $X. At $X+1, to heck with it, they can hack the data. You have to try and keep the price below $X.

- **Labor Costs:** Another way of cost-justifying this system is to figure out the labor costs of changing each IP address, or reconfiguring the network to use DHCP. If your network relies on workstations with static addresses, you can approach management by saying, "In order to process your request for Internet connectivity, we will have to touch each workstation to change an address. This process, while not costly or time-consuming on a small scale, can prove to be somewhat prohibitive when we start dealing with a gazillion workstations. On average, it will take a technician approximately ten minutes per workstation to change and test a new IP address. At an average labor cost of $20 per hour, that is a cost of approximately $3.00 per workstation. As you can see, our cost in labor will be approximately 3 gazillion dollars. In order to lower this cost, I have found a product that will make it unnecessary to touch every workstation, and the cost of this product is $$$$$." Make sure you keep talking after you say $3 gazillion; don't even breathe. This would be an ideal point for the manager to say to heck with the project.

- **Added Benefits:** Firewalls do come with added benefits that might not be immediately apparent. For example, not only do they keep the bad, unwanted packets out, but they can also be used to keep some bad, unwanted packets in! Most firewalls will let you limit who can access what services. You may not want anyone in the Accounting Department to access the Internet for anything other than e-mail. In that case, you can set the firewall to prohibit IP requests going to ports other than the Simple Mail Transport Protocol (SMTP) port from the range of addresses that serves the Accounting Department. Some firewalls are even sophisticated enough to limit communications by time of day. In this case, the Accounting Department could not browse the Web during business hours, but after 5:30 pm, it would be okay.

- **Sexual Harassment:** One of the very difficult and serious issues facing management today is the issue of sexual harassment. The issue starts with the definition of sexual harassment. One proven type of sexual harassment is the display of pornographic material in the workplace. Many firewalls have technology built in that will prohibit packets from exiting the network bound for known pornographic sites. The lists of these sites are updated regularly. If nothing else, having a firewall in place that acts as a censor helps to show that the company is concerned about the issue and is making an attempt to protect employees.

> **TIP** This book is not designed to discuss First Amendment rights. Each company has to make its own decisions about what should or should not be allowed in the workplace. This technology can even be too restrictive. For example, if an employee went to the Internet to do a search for information on breast cancer, the search might be denied because "breast" might be a restricted word.

- **The Real Thing:** If you have a techno-savvy manager (there are at least three out there!) you can tell the manager exactly why you need the firewall and NAT, and they will agree because they will already know all the other stuff we mentioned above.

Deciding on Throughput

Once you have figured out how to handle the IP addressing problem, a very large load will be removed from your shoulders, and everything else will seem to be easy. The next decisions that must be made are how fast is fast and how much you can spend to get fast access.

Speed is a relative term, and relativity never had so many factors as it does on the Internet. The connection between a computer on your network and a Web site is only as fast as the slowest segment. Here is an example: Your company could invest in the fastest possible connection to the Internet. Your Internet provider may invest in the fastest possible connection to the Internet trunk line. The Internet provider of the Web site may invest in the fastest possible connection to the Internet trunk, but your connection will only be as fast as the ISDN connection from the target ISP to the computer hosting the Web site you want to access. Everything is just screaming along until the last possible connection, where it slows down considerably. The connection can also be slowed by the type of computer hosting the Web page. As you will see in the next chapter, it really doesn't require much to host a Web site. If you are using only a 486/100 as a Web server, though, and you have a popular Web site, the response time may be affected by the hardware.

There are several methods of connecting to the Internet, and, unfortunately, all of them involve renting lines from a local utility. The local utility is almost always a telephone company. In some areas of the country, other utilities may be providing Internet access services—these utilities may be cable television outlets or even the local power company. Even though the rental agreement for your line may come through your local ISP, there is always another utility involved here somewhere.

You will have to decide what type of connection your company needs to facilitate Internet access. Internet access can be configured with a simple modem at each workstation, or through a direct fiber link to the Internet backbone. Each hookup comes with associated hardware and rental costs. A good rule of thumb to follow is that faster is *always* more expensive. A faster link is more expensive to establish and more expensive to maintain on a monthly basis.

There are a variety of different hookup methods available. Which hookup is best for your company depends on a variety of factors, including things like:

- How many people are going to have Internet access?

- How do you anticipate the Internet being used? A gateway hookup for e-mail use is going to require less bandwidth than a group of 1000 researchers constantly accessing the Internet for information.

- Will the connection need to be constant, or can you dial in?

- Will the connection need to be open 24 hours a day?

- How much file transfer is going to be done?

Before going much further, let's take a look at the types of hookups that are available from some Internet providers. The types of hookups, and the speed and cost of each will vary by ISP, so it is best to do some serious research before signing a contract.

The types of hookups generally used are summarized in Table 18.1.

TABLE 18.1: Internet Connection Technologies

Types of Service	Description	Speed
Switched and Leased Analog Lines	Dial-up connection to a local ISP	Under ideal dial-up conditions using compression, speeds in excess of 115.2Kbps can be attained
Digital Links	ISDN has two main types of service. The Basic Rate Interface (BRI) is designed for homes and small businesses. BRI provides two 64Kbps channels known as bearer or B-channels, and one 16Kbps D-channel for out-of-band signaling and link management. B-channels can carry voice, data, or image communication. The channels can be multiplexed into a single 128Kbps channel. The second service, intended for larger installations, is called Primary Rate Interface (PRI). It comprises 23 B-channels and 1 D-channel, also 64Kbps. This corresponds to the T1 rate of 1.544Mbps.	56Kbps to 1.544Mbps
X.25 and Frame Relay	X.25 is a mature, stable technology offered by ISPs around the world. Because it is connection-oriented, guaranteed delivery, X.25 requires an overhead to manage the connection. This causes speed and throughput to suffer, with 56Kbps being the maximum available bandwidth. Frame Relay is one of the "new" fast packet technologies that take advantage of higher bandwidth transmission mediums. Fast packet switching is a simplified form of packet switching, giving the benefits of reduced protocol processing, which equates to a more efficient use of the bandwidth provided. Frame Relay is similar to X.25, but Frame Relay does not have the added connection-oriented overhead. Frame Relay is connection oriented but is not reliable. It uses a permanent virtual circuit (PVC), and as a result, a point-to-point virtual circuit must be established at the time the service is ordered.	X.25 offers speeds up to 56Kbps Frame Relay speeds vary from 56Kbps to 1.536Mbps

Continued on next page

TABLE 18.1 CONTINUED: Internet Connection Technologies

Types of Service	Description	Speed
SMDS and ATM Cell Switching	Switched Multimegabit Data Service (SMDS) was developed by Bellcore. SMDS provides a connectionless service that supports variable length data units. SMDS is the first broadband ISDN (BISDN) offering and it is a precursor to ATM. It also includes built-in security and management.	SMDS speed ranges from 56Kbps to 44.736Mbps ATM offers speeds of 1.5Mbps to 622Mbps
	The Bellcore standard specifies how Customer Premise Equipment (CPE) can access an SMDS switch using twisted-pair at the T1 rate or optical fiber (SONET) at the T3 rate and higher. SMDS uses a dual-ring technology.	
WAN Technologies	The T1 facility—the basic technology upon which all T-carrier facilities are based—uses a full-duplex digital signal over two wire pairs.	1.544Mbps
	Using time division multiplexing (TDM), T1 splits 1.544Mbps bandwidth into 24 channels plus one bit that is used for synchronization. In this way, 24 conversations can be transmitted over two wire pairs at the same time.	
	T1 connections can be purchased in fractions, referred to as a fractional T1.	
	T3 connections operate off of microwave communications or fiber optics.	45Mbps

You will notice there is no cost column in Table 18.1. When we started designing the table, we thought we would add a column for cost, but it did not take long to realize that costs vary widely. Checking the Internet by searching on ISP and the name of the state provided a wide variety of rates for what appears to be the same service—rates varying by hundreds of dollars a month at the high end. You can bypass the ISP and contract directly with the local telephone company for your line, if you so choose. You may be able to save a few bucks here, but you need to weigh the savings against the difficulties coordinating installations and configurations. Depending on the speed of the line and the location of your ISP's point of presence (the office or a connection site), this can be a very healthy charge.

NOTE The Winter 1998 *Quarterly Directory of Internet Service Providers*, published by Boardwatch Magazine, reported that the 1.544Mbps T1 monthly charge from nationwide ISPs ranged from a low of $1,199 for Exodus to a high of $3,000 for IBM. Local ISPs may be less expensive than the nationwide providers. Prices vary substantially, based on the level of service.

To make sure that you get the most bang for the corporate buck, be sure to interview several ISPs. Tell them the size of your company, the type of network infrastructure you have, the network operating system you are using, and what you expect out of your Internet connection. Take careful notes, or get written proposals. When you are all done, compare companies, and then interview the ISP's customers. Find out if the ISP will do as promised. Check to make sure the speed ratings match what real customers are experiencing and be sure to check on the skill of the ISP technical support department. You want to make sure you get what you pay for. What you pay for is called the port charge. This is the monthly charge that connects you to the ISP router and gives you an Internet connection. It is not the only charge you will incur, however.

Additional Considerations

The line coming into the building isn't the only thing that is going to show up on your initial bill. Besides the monthly charge for service, most ISPs will charge you an installation fee. This fee is a one time hit, and the fee will vary with the services provided. Your ISP may provide all the equipment you need to hook into the ISP as part of the setup fee, or just use the setup fees to buy the equipment necessary for their end of the connection.

Intranets

Now that the subject of Web sites has been broached, we can also look at something called an *intranet*.

Unless your recent neighbors have been the Skipper and Gilligan, you are familiar with the Internet. Even if your company does not have a connection, most people reading this book have probably paid for their own dial-up Internet connection. You are familiar with the way the Internet works and the vast amount of information that is available on the Web. An intranet is really just the World Wide Web scaled down to a corporate environment.

Continued on next page

The computer desktop is becoming more and more browser-like. All the major desktop and network operating system vendors seem to agree on one thing (a miracle in itself), and that is that the reliance on the Internet and intranets will continue to increase in the workplace. Each vendor is working hard to make sure its products are at the forefront of this venture.

An intranet brings information to the masses, just like the Internet. The difference is that an intranet is *corporate-centric*. With a properly designed intranet, your end users will be able to browse to the IS department's home page to find out the status of the rollout of the new desktops. This can be done just as easily as they will be able to browse to the NFL Web site to find out who is the latest owner of the Minnesota Vikings. The potential is staggering.

An intranet sounds complicated (read expensive) to create. Really, it's not. The corporate intranet starts with a Web server, and some of the most popular Web servers are free! Even the hardware to host a Web server may be in your computer room right now. Web servers are designed to work with the three most popular network operating systems, Novell, Unix, and Windows NT. If you currently have a server that is not being overworked, chances are it can host your intranet.

For more information on creating and working with intranets, see Chapter 19.

Web Servers

Whether you are talking about a presence on the Internet that revolves around a locally hosted Web page or an intranet, the process starts with a Web server. Part of your planning process will involve selecting which Web server is going to make your piece of the World Wide Web go round.

Whenever people see the word "server," they tend to think of hardware. The mention of hardware tends to bring groans from the corporate bigwigs in Accounting. In the case of the Web server, though, neither vision may be accurate. First of all, the Web server is not hardware at all; it is a suite of software products that run on an existing operating system. The history of Web servers is rich. Some of the early Web servers are still in use today, and one of the derivatives of the early Web servers is the most popular system used.

NCSA Httpd

NCSA httpd was one of the first Web servers written. It came from The National Center for Supercomputing Applications (NCSA) at the University of Illinois at Champaign-Urbana. Httpd runs on the Unix operating system.

Because it is a Unix application, httpd has no fancy wizards to guide you through installation and configuration. Configuration of NCSA httpd is done through editing configuration files. Woe be to the administrator who is not up on Unix commands, because there is no graphical interface for administration.

Security at NCSA Web sites is rather sparse. NCSA supports only the most basic security, authenticating users by password. As far as some of the other things Netizens of the 90s take for granted, NCSA httpd is basic. It supports the common gateway interface (CGI), but it has no application programming interface (API) for running database searches or other CGI scripts normally considered part of a powerful Web server. Httpd is no longer a supported product, and the University of Illinois at Champaign-Urbana is referring users to the next generation of httpd: Apache.

> **NOTE**   Back in the early days of the Internet, before there was a Netscape Communicator and an Internet Explorer, people used another NCSA product—the original graphical Web browser called Mosaic.

Apache

Apache is a Unix Web server that is available for the cost of the download. Apache is a flexible, HTTP 1.1-compliant Web server that works with the latest protocols. It is highly configurable and extensible with third-party modules, including modules that provide Secured Socket Layer (SSL) capabilities. For those users who would rather write it than download it, Apache provides full source code and the keys to the API. In June, 1998, Apache announced a Web server that would run on Windows.

For security, Apache allows the Webmaster to set up password-protected Web pages. The database authentication method allows hundreds of authorized users to access the Web page without slowing the response to the rest of the server. Apache also can automatically provide clients with the right document for their particular Web browser.

According to a June 1998 Web survey compiled by Netcraft (`www.netcraft.com/survey`), Apache was the most-used Web server. The complete survey results are shown in Table 18.2.

TABLE 18.2: June 1998 Web Server Survey

Server	May 98	Percent	June 98	Percent	Change
Apache	1,114,153	48.26	1,182,142	49.05	0.79
Microsoft-IIS	492,558	21.34	529,267	21.96	0.62
Netscape-Enterprise	119,925	5.19	121,321	5.03	-0.16
NCSA	66,505	2.88	64,310	2.67	-0.21

Source: Netcraft (`http://www.netcraft.com/survey`)

Microsoft Internet Information Server

As you can see, there are other popular Web servers. Microsoft has Internet Information Server (IIS), which is included with Windows NT. IIS is a graphical Web server that integrates well with Microsoft BackOffice and SQL Server. As is the case with most Microsoft products, IIS is NT-based and is not available for any other operating system.

Netscape

The figures for *Netscape* encompass all versions of their Web server products, from FastTrack to Enterprise. Netscape is the only real cross-platform product in the list. It has Web servers that run on Windows NT, Unix, and NetWare products. Both Netscape and IIS support SSL. Netscape FastTrack is available with NetWare 5. All other Netscape products are a "cost" item. FastTrack starts at around $300 and the Enterprise server can cost over $1300.

Operating Systems

When choosing a Web server, there are several things to look at, the most important being the *operating system* (OS) that the Web server will run on. The OS provides the Web server with

- **Security:** Your intranet or your Internet Web site can contain vital information, placed in areas that only certain people should have access to. It is up to the operating system to provide this security. Preventing users from accessing areas they are not supposed to be in means they cannot accidentally or maliciously destroy information.

- **Multitasking:** A busy Web server should be able to handle multiple hits at the same time. Depending on the design of the Web pages, a single user can trigger several different processes at the same time. The operating system must be able to handle this level of activity.

- **Reliability:** An Internet Web site is not a sometimes thing. It is available to users 24 hours a day, 7 days a week. If you have spent much time on the Internet, you know how frustrating it can be to be told that a Web site cannot be found. If your site is a commercial site, having an operating system that crashes often or stops responding means lost sales, and even worse, customers may simply stop looking for the site, because it is "never there."

Table 18.3 shows some of the OSs that popular Web servers operate on.

TABLE 18.3:   Popular Web Servers and Their Operating Systems

Web Server	Operating System	Vendor	Cost
AOLServer	Unix, Windows	America Online	Free
Apache	Unix, Windows, OS/2, Amiga	Apache	Free
Cisco MicroWeb Server	Proprietary	Cisco	~$995
IBM Internet Connection Secure Server	Windows, Unix, and OS/2	IBM	~$295
Internet Genie	Windows	Frontier	~$2740 for five licensed connections.

Continued on next page

TABLE 18.3 CONTINUED: Popular Web Servers and Their Operating Systems

Web Server	Operating System	Vendor	Cost
JAVA Web Server	Unix, Windows, OS/2	Javasoft/SUN	~$295
MacHTTP	Mac OS	Quarterdeck	~$95
Microsoft Internet Information Server	Windows NT	Microsoft	Comes with Windows NT
Netscape	Unix, Windows, OS/2, NetWare	Netscape	Depends on product

Once you have picked out your Web server, the next thing you should take a look at is the official corporate Web browser.

Choosing a Browser

This may come as a shock, but there are more browsers available than the latest versions of Netscape Communicator and Microsoft Internet Explorer. In this section, we will take a look at the advantages and disadvantages of the Big Two, and also explore some of the alternative browsers.

We will look at customizing browsers by adding various plug-ins and other supporting software. We will also look at security issues associated with browsers. But first, we will look at the effects of the ever-evolving browser wars. What version of which browser are you using? If you got your browser yesterday, it is probably out-of-date today.

The Browser Wars— Internet Explorer vs. Communicator

There have been dozens of articles written on the differences between Microsoft Internet Explorer and Netscape Communicator. You would think that since both software packages are designed to do basically the same thing, the two packages would in fact be getting more and more similar. In fact, the opposite is the case. Both packages are diverging in several ways. To make matters worse, Web page designers are starting to take sides. You may find some Web pages that look really spiffy and work really well with one product, but if you go back to the same Web page with the other browser, you will be lucky if you recognize the page. It is becoming more and more common to see users with *both* browsers on their computers. They are both free—all you are giving up is *lots* of disk space. If the browser manufacturers could just agree on a common way to handle bookmarks/favorites and e-mail address books, life would be very good indeed.

NOTE   Any discussion of browsers needs to be time-stamped. Browser versions change almost monthly, so any topics covered in this book will be outdated by the time you read them. We will try to point out some Web sites where you can go for browser information, although most of these will also go out-of-date. At this writing, Communicator is at version 4.5 and Internet Explorer is at version 4.01.

How They're Similar

Internet Explorer and Communicator do have a lot in common. Both of the browsers give the user the opportunity to customize their work area. In Communicator, your work area is the program suite. Internet Explorer will take over your entire desktop if you let it, providing all sorts of links to other sites trying to get you to buy stuff.

In both browsers you can customize the toolbars. For the power user, this can be a godsend. Both browsers provide "hot buttons" to the most popular search engines. Further, both let you set a default search engine, if you so choose, rather than taking a chance on search engine roulette.

Both browsers will point you toward their particular home pages, where there are a variety of different things to play with. You can customize your system so you get your news sent to you each morning, covering only the topics you are interested in. You can configure each home page to deliver stock quotes on the companies or mutual funds in your portfolio, as well as provide you with all the news you need to know about each business.

Each browser comes with a set of similar tools, like an offline Network News Transport Protocol (NNTP) reader. The e-mail clients are small and robust, and they both utilize the latest in e-mail standards like IMAP4 and POP3. Both e-mail packages will recognize HTML code in an e-mail message and display it accordingly.

Little things mean a lot—things like drag-and-drop support, automatic completion of URLs, and last, but definitely not least, the ability to automatically update the software from within the Web browser. Since these packages are tweaked almost weekly, this part of the package serves as a constant reminder to check on the latest release.

How They're Different

Microsoft and Netscape have two completely different views of the desktop. This is not surprising. If you have used Internet Explorer 4 or Windows 98, you know that Microsoft has completely embedded the Web browser into the operating system. Internet Explorer 4 has the ability to *be* your desktop, providing links to the Internet through subscriptions to various sites. Internet Explorer 4 is very Microsoft-centric; it works on Windows 9x systems and on Windows NT systems. If you use a Mac, you have your choice of IE 4 or Netscape. For Unix, you are pretty much a Netscape or an alternative browser user.

Netscape views its role as a client for accessing information. Netscape wants to work with whatever operating system is in place in your enterprise, so it will run on at least 15 different platforms.

Internet Explorer has basically one product with a bunch of plug-in applications. Netscape has a bunch of product levels, each with more features than the last. Netscape Communicator Pro even has a group-scheduling application and a Java-based terminal emulator. Netscape offers Java support, and Internet Explorer says it offers Java support. Netscape says it offers ActiveX support, and Internet Explorer offers ActiveX support.

Which One Is Best?

Andrew Tannebaum, a computer science professor and author, once wrote, "The nice thing about standards is that there are so many of them to choose from." There seem to be standards, and then Microsoft implementations of those standards. In this world of Microsoft-dominated desktops, you could say there are Microsoft standards and there are the other standards. This divergence of standards makes it difficult for the corporation or network administrator to make a decision about which browser to roll out to the desktop. It becomes a coin flip. Where you want to go with your browser will determine which will give you the best service. When in doubt, pick one and stick with it. Or just use both!

Browser Administration

Both Microsoft and Netscape have tools available to help the administrator roll the browser out to the desktop. Netscape has a suite of tools called Mission Control, and Microsoft offers the Internet Explorer Administration Kit (IEAK). Microsoft will also provide ISPs and other third party vendors the ability to customize the installation of Internet Explorer 4.

In the tools war, Microsoft wins. The IEAK has one big thing going for it—it's free. The Netscape Mission Control kit has a list price of around $1,300.

Netscape's tools are mostly designed to use HTML, Java, and JavaScript code. Some of the tools are even command-line driven. The configuration editor will allow you to set certain preferences for your users, including server names. The system will also let you configure the software to check a central location for any upgrades to the configuration or software.

IEAK uses a wizard to design a custom implementation of Internet Explorer 4. It will take you through the design process step by step, letting you configure the parameters that are important to your company and disabling the ones that aren't. Just like Mission Control, you can specify a location for common configuration or upgrade files.

Plug-Ins and Companions

Plug-ins, or Active X components in the case of IE 4, provide the opportunity to customize your browser to take advantage of some of the cooler things on the Internet—things like full motion video and sounds. Now it is possible to sit in a hotel room where the television doesn't work and listen to the broadcast of a championship basketball game right from the Internet. You even get to pick your announcers!

There are a variety of plug-ins for each of the major browsers. Plug-ins will enhance the way your browser will react to the Internet's special effects. You can play music, watch video clips, read articles formatted in a particular fashion, or even listen to the radio, all from your computer. Links are provided from the browser's home page. Some of the plug-ins are free, and some aren't. As a network administrator, it will be up to you to determine which of the plug-ins to make available to your users.

Companions will enhance the way the browser works with the infrastructure of the Internet. A companion will help you speed up your browser, provide a more robust handling of bookmarks, prohibit the browser from opening certain Web sites, or help locate Web sites that provide specific types of information.

NOTE   There are two Web sites that provide a lot of information on browsers, plug-ins, and companions. The URLs are `www.download.com/browsers` and `www.cnet.com`.

Best of the Rest

Internet Explorer and Communicator are not the only browsers that work with the Web; they're just the best known. There may be any number of reasons that you have decided you want to look at other browsers. You may be anti-Microsoft. You may still be using DOS. You may not have a computer powerful enough to handle the new 32-bit operating systems.

When you start looking for an alternative browser, you'll want to find something that closely resembles Communicator and Internet Explorer. After all, both of those do work and work well with a variety of different protocols and features provided by the Internet. Make sure your new browser supports the latest level of HTML code and JavaScript. These are the things that will give you all the basics of the Internet without all the fluff.

Some of the alternative browsers are:

- **Amaya:** Designed to be used as a testing tool by Web developers, Amaya does not have some of the niceties of Communicator or Internet Explorer. Amaya was developed by the same people who maintain the HTML standards—the World Wide Web Consortium (W3C). Amaya, naturally, supports all levels of HTML code, including forms and tables. It is not ready for prime time because it will not display frames and JavaScript well, and these are becoming mainstays of today's Web development. This browser is free from the World Wide Web Consortium.

- **Cyberdog:** Mac users want to play on the Internet, too! Cyberdog will display frames, forms, and tables. It is as fast as the big boys, and while it can't handle all the stuff that is put into pages specifically for Internet Explorer and Communicator, the stuff it doesn't handle does not come out looking too weird. Cyberdog will support many plug-ins and will support Java with a Virtual Machine installed. Cyberdog even has a full e-mail package, a newsreader, and FTP support incorporated. Cyberdog is available from

Apple for free. However, all good things must come to an end, and Cyberdog is no longer in development.

- **HotJava:** Just from looking at the name, would you bet it could handle Java? You would be right. HotJava was developed by Sun from and for Java. HotJava is platform-independent, and can run on just about anything. It has some built-in security that supports Java 1.1 applets, SSL-encrypted secure transactions, and cookies. HotJava does not support JavaScript. It is available for free from Sun Microsystems.

- **Mosaic:** This is the antique of Web browsers; NCSA has stopped development of Mosaic. Because this is one of the first browsers created and it is no longer supported, it has some shortcomings. It doesn't do Java or scripting or tables. Mosaic is included in this discussion simply because it is the best known of the alternative browsers. It may still be available for free from NCSA.

- **Opera:** Of all the alternatives, this is probably the coolest. It is small, fast, and stable. Opera is about 1.2MB, so you won't get a lot of the fluff that is inherent in Communicator and Internet Explorer. Some of the fluff that is left out includes things like videoconferencing, VRML clients, and Java support. It does display forms, frames, and tables. Opera does not include full e-mail support, but you can send mail. Opera does support plug-ins like Macromedia Flash and Adobe Acrobat. Opera is available for Win 3.x, 95, 98, NT 3.5.1, NT 4.0 and soon for Amiga OS, Mac OS, Linux, BeOS, and others. The upcoming version, Opera 3.5, will support Java. Here is a list of other things it can do: full graphics support, inline AVI, MPEG, and MIDI, support for Netscape plug-ins, SSL 2.0 and 3.0, TLS 1.0, client-side ISMAP, client pull, server push, secure NNTP, SMTP support, and contextual menus. Opera is available for $35 from Opera software.

Getting Connected

Now that all of the decisions are made, it is time to install the communication channel and make the thing work. The channel installation involves hardware, and a very specialized breed of hardware it is.

Hardware

Besides the physical line coming into the building, you will also need some sort of terminal equipment at your end of the connection. This equipment can take the shape of a modem, a router, a channel service unit (CSU)/digital service unit (DSU), or more commonly, a combination of some of the above.

To start, let's look at a simple dial-up connection between your computer and the Internet. From the big picture, you know that the CPU processes a request to dial the phone. That request is passed to the *modem*, which, through a series of commands, dials the number and then negotiates with the modem on the other side to determine how these two systems are going to communicate. Things like speed, data flow, error checking, and the agreement on how many bits will be sent in each transmission must all be agreed upon before communication can be successful.

When it is time for the conversation to end, one modem must signal the other that the conversation is in fact over. This allows the circuit to be closed properly and made available to another caller. Anyone who has ever worked in a company that makes use of asynchronous gateways will have some experience in resetting modems after an improper disconnect.

If the communication is important when one workstation is involved, imagine how important it is when there is one line handling several hundred connections to the Internet. In this case, a stable connection to the ISP is mandatory. These connections are made through CSU/DSUs. A CSU/DSU is the "modem" that connects your network to the ISP; the other end of the CSU/DSU is connected to a router. CSU/DSUs come in a variety of shapes and sizes with varying features, but the one feature you are most concerned about is the speed of the unit. The speed of the CSU/DSU must be compatible with the speed of the line coming into your company.

A router works in conjunction with the CSU/DSU and a connection to your network. The *router* is responsible for routing data packets from one location to another. It is up to the router to determine the appropriate path from your computer to the packet's destination, say www.microsoft.com. The router will re-address the communication packet and send it to another router, until the packet reaches its destination. A router is a Network layer device.

The layout of a connection to the Internet is shown in Figure 18.2.

FIGURE 18.2:

Connecting a LAN/WAN to
the Internet

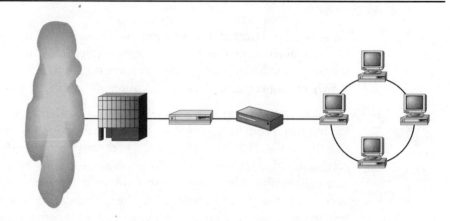

When you talk with your potential ISP, be sure to ask if the ISP will provide the equipment on your end of the connection. The ISP is not going to do this from the goodness of its corporate heart, but the charge may be well worth the cost. Whenever you establish a WAN connection, there are going to be times when small problems occur. If the ISP is installing the equipment, the installers are familiar with the installation and have probably handled most of the gotchas in the past. This means a smoother installation for you.

There are other points in favor of using the ISP's equipment. In most cases, if the ISP owns it, it is up to the ISP to maintain it. If something breaks, you don't have to fix it. When you are dealing with high-level communication equipment that the average LAN/WAN person does not work with on a daily basis, being able to push this responsibility off to someone else can pay for itself quickly.

Finally, by using the ISP's equipment, you can avoid the finger pointing sessions whenever there is a problem. You must be familiar with the scenario: There is a problem on your network. You call the vendor that installed the network, and the vendor tells you it is up to the hardware vendor to provide tech support. You call the hardware vendor, and the tech support people tell you it is not their problem; it is the problem of the software people. You call the software people, and they tell you it is not their problem because it is obviously a hardware flaw. Every vendor points a finger at another vendor, and meanwhile your network doesn't work. If you use the ISP's equipment, you just call the ISP and say, "Fix it."

NOTE   The charge for the hardware may be a monthly rental or a one-time setup charge.

Other Charges

Connecting to the Internet is a very personal thing. It is a unique experience, and most ISPs will tailor the services they provide to the requirements of your company. The charges we have discussed are not the only costs you may incur. Some other common examples include:

- Registering and hosting your domain name—If you would like to have an Internet presence that represents your particular company, your ISP can apply for a Domain Name Service (DNS) name. The registration fee will be at least $100 to register it for the first two years, and then at least $50 after that. These figures are minimums, because that is what InterNIC charges for the service. Your ISP may put a charge on top of that to handle the paperwork.

NOTE   The DNS name you want may be already taken. If you would like to check and you have some form of Internet connection, go to `rs.internic.net/cgi-bin/whois` and try typing in the names you would like for your company. You may need to be really creative to get a unique name.

- Hosting POP3 e-mail accounts—If you have a small company, it may not pay to have a grand and glorious, fully robust e-mail system for your company. Any one of dozens of small e-mail clients may work just fine for your system. In this case, all e-mail may be sent over the Internet using POP3 e-mail accounts. If your ISP hosts these accounts, there will be a monthly charge.

- Hosting your corporate Web page—What would an Internet presence be without a Web page? After all, there are probably thousands of your customers waiting to be able to go out to www.yourcompany.com and send in hundreds of orders. Well, maybe not, but the Internet helps to level the playing field. How are your customers going to know that the Web page at www.yourcompany.com does not represent a Fortune 500 company, even if the company is housed in your basement? If your ISP hosts your Web page, there may or may not be a charge. Some ISPs provide you with 5MB of disk space for your Web page at no charge. Others don't.

Rolling Out the Browser

In the "Browser Administration" section earlier in this chapter, we discussed the tools available for both Microsoft Internet Explorer and Netscape Communicator to administrate the rollout of the browser to the desktop. Netscape's tools are called Mission Control, and Microsoft offers the Internet Explorer Administration Kit (IEAK). Microsoft will also provide ISPs and other third-party vendors the ability to customize the installation of Internet Explorer 4.

To recap, Netscape's tools are mostly designed to use HTML, Java, and JavaScript code. Some of the tools are even command-line driven. The configuration editor will allow you to set certain preferences for your users, including server names. The system will also let you configure the software to check a central location for any upgrades to the configuration or software.

IEAK uses a wizard to design a custom implementation of Internet Explorer 4. It will take you through the design process step by step, letting you configure the parameters that are important to your company and disabling the ones that aren't. Just like Mission Control, you can specify a location for common configuration or upgrade files.

> **NOTE** Make sure you plan ahead for version upgrades. Designate a location where these upgrades will be made available and make sure each browser knows the location of the upgrade files. Browser versions and patches are released far too frequently.

Maintaining Your Connection

Once the system has been connected and the browsers have been installed, then it comes time to maintain the connection. In a properly installed system, maintaining the connection from a hardware standpoint should not be difficult. It may revolve around resetting a router occasionally to make sure the router remembers where the rest of the world is. Maintaining your connection from interference, either from outside the company or inside the company, is a completely different matter. Now you are getting into very serious topics.

Internet Security

Some years ago there was a memorable advertisement for the forgettable movie *Jaws II*. It started out something like, "Just when you thought it was safe to go back in the water." When you start talking about security on the Internet, you are looking down the maw of that giant shark, and it is not a pretty sight.

The Scary Truth

Did you know that every year there is a convention of hackers who are just trying to come up with ways of breaking into your server? It's true. If your reaction to this is normal, you'll be wondering indignantly, "Why don't the police put a stop to this?" According to someone who has been there, the police do try to put a stop to it, by going in undercover to see what these people are up to. The people at the convention know they are being watched, and the watchers know the watchees know they are being watched, so there is a game created called "Spot the Fed." If an officer is identified, the person doing the identification gets a tee shirt that says something really creative like "I spotted the Fed."

Just to confuse the issue even more, in some companies you not only have to protect the information on the inside from the people outside, but you have to limit what users on the inside can see of the outside. After all, you do not necessarily want the CEO's administrative assistant in a board meeting to inadvertently run across a site depicting semi-clothed people engaging in unnatural acts, would you? It could happen, and probably has.

There are many levels of Internet security, and they multiply depending on how you are using the Internet. For example, if you have a home page that is hosted on your local ISP's server, and that page is an informational page that doesn't sell anything, or gather information, the security risks are pretty minimal. The "worst" thing that can happen is someone can break into your home page and rewrite the code so the corporate logo is now the dancing baby (or something worse). This would not necessarily make your day, but given enough time, you might end up seeing the humor in it.

Compare this security problem with having the Web site hosted on a Web server in your own computer complex. This server houses not only your corporate Web page but also the company intranet as well. In addition, your company makes the finest widgets in the whole wide world, and you are using the Internet to sell these widgets for $9.95 to anyone with Visa, MasterCard, or American Express. Your system now has all sorts of personal and credit information from hundreds of people. This server also connects indirectly to every other computer in the organization, including payroll, engineering, research and development, advertising, and design. All the other widget makers who want to know your secrets would just love to get into your network, and by hooking that one server up to the Internet and to your internal network, the window has been left unlocked.

Before we get too far into this discussion of security, it should probably be mentioned that there really is no such thing as a *completely* secure environment. You may think your system is secure, but reevaluate your stance the next time you see one of your users with their password posted on the monitor with a sticky note. Think about how insecure your network is the next time you hear a user give someone (even you!) their password. This is not designed to scare you, but... well, yes, actually we are trying to scare you. Fear usually is a great motivator, and security is something that should be enforced.

NOTE   For more information on security, see Chapters 27 and 28.

Network security is like any other type of security. If someone wants to break into your system badly enough, and they have the skill and the time, they will probably be successful. Your job is to make it so difficult for them to break into the system that they figure there must be easier systems to attack. Hopefully, at that point, they will go and play somewhere else.

A lot of this has to do with what you are protecting. Now, let's face it, even if your company makes the greatest widgets in the world, the number of people interested in widget secrets pales in comparison to the number of hackers that would just love to get into the computers at the Federal Reserve, the CIA, the House of Commons, the Pentagon, Scotland Yard, and the FBI. Security at these *cool* places needs to be much more refined than at the average company.

When we start talking about security, there are several problems inherent in the corporate world that start jumping right out at you. The first problem is a lack of understanding. People just don't believe that "their" network is subject to attack, from either the inside or the outside. Companies find it particularly troubling to think that their employees might want to harm the company in some way. Let's look at a real life example that is really scary.

Several years ago, a consultant was called to work at a small financial institution in an upper Midwestern town. The goals for this project were to:

- Install a new NetWare 3.12 file server

- Move the data and applications from the old NetWare 2.2 server to the new server and test the installation

- Do whatever was necessary to prepare for a major corporate expansion, taking the company from approximately 25 people to 250 people in a year

On the initial tour of the company, the consultant entered the computer room and decided to see what type of naming standards were currently in place. The consultant accessed the monitor screen and checked active connections to find that all 25 people were currently logged into the server; 24 of those users were logged in as Supervisor, giving them unrestricted rights to anything on the server, including all client information. The 25th person had a "real" login name. She was the one giving the tour, so she was asked why she was not logged in as Supervisor. She pointed out that she had been given an account that was the equivalent of Supervisor, so it really didn't matter.

In a meeting later that afternoon with the chief financial officer, it was pointed out to him that some time should be allotted in order to implement a security plan for the network. The CFO started out by recapping why the company didn't need a security plan; everyone was "like a family" and had worked for the company for years and they were all trusted, valued employees. In the X number of years the company had been in business, they had never had a disgruntled employee. After he went on for about five minutes, the CFO was asked about the young lady sitting at the receptionist desk. It was pointed out that it seemed odd no one knew this family member's name. He said, "Oh, she is just a temp," and his face paled. It wasn't necessary to point out that temp had access to literally millions of dollars of assets, if she (or anyone else) knew how to take advantage of the situation. In this case, the company was lucky; no one did take advantage of the situation. It could have been a lot worse.

A very good friend of ours likes to say that he can tell how good a network administrator is by the person's level of paranoia. As a *very* good network administrator, therefore, you should be *very* paranoid. Assume someone is going to try to steal the information stored on your network, and consider it a personal challenge to keep it safe.

It's a tough job. The first thing that a security-conscious administrator has to overcome is management apathy. Senior management tends to have more important things to worry about than a little thing called data. It is the network administrator's job to make management understand that losing all the research data on the company's newest product is not good for the bottom line. If a hacker gets into your network and finds that information, you may find out about the security breach when you see your research spread out over the Internet. It's really bad news for the network administrator when an intrusion happens.

Starting to Secure Your Network

First off all, let's take a look at some of the really simple things you can do to start securing your network.

- Sell senior management on the fact that the network needs to be secure, both from attack on the inside and from attack on the outside. Make sure senior management is really sold on the idea, because some of the steps you are going to have to take to secure the network may lead to employee complaints. Someone has to back you.

- For protection from the internal attack, use common-sense security procedures. Have individual user login names. Make sure each user has a password made up of letters and numbers. Make sure each user changes that password once a month, at least. Make sure users do not share their passwords and login names with anyone else, inside or outside the company. Make sure users know sharing passwords with anyone is grounds for slow, painful torture.

- Education is the key. Make sure the network administrators are trained in all forms of security issues for all operating systems on the network. Make sure network administrators are trained to look for hacker attacks. And, as we mentioned earlier, make sure end users know the dangers of giving out login names and passwords.

- Make sure appropriate file system rights are established and in place.

- Make sure user accounts are deleted, renamed, or expired when a user leaves the company. Do not leave any old accounts on the network.

- Make sure whichever network operating system you are using is totally patched. Unix was originally designed to be an open system with very lax security. It has been tightened, but there are still holes known to hackers everywhere. These holes have been patched, but unless you apply the system patches, the holes remain. Windows NT is notoriously porous. There are lots of security patches for NT—apply them. NetWare has several patches. Make sure they are applied, no matter which version of the OS you are using.

- Never attach a server to the Internet without a firewall. Ever.

- Find, buy, beg, borrow, or download from the Internet any of the auditing programs that will watch your network for signs of attack. Use the auditing software and actually check the logs. If you are unsure which package to buy, take a trip to your favorite geek book store and look for books on security. Most come with CDs, and most of the CDs have sample auditing programs. Some of these are even free.

- Have an attack plan in place. After you have taken the security training, put a plan in place to make sure that when an attack has been detected, you close the door and check the level of incursion. Most hackers, once into a system, will create back doors so they can get in again even if you shut off the current point of access. Don't think that clearing the connection and disabling the offending user is going to protect the system. Assume the hacker has created back doors into the system and try to find them.

- Make sure everyone in the company, from the CEO on down, knows what to do in case of an attack. This revolves around who to call and what to document. Taking the appropriate steps early in the discovery may make the difference between tracking the hacker and frustration.

- Make sure senior management knows they are the most susceptible to hacking. Think about it...who has access to more valuable information, a clerk or the CEO? Whose name is in the public, either through news reports, press releases, or the annual report—the clerk or the CEO?

- Don't stop at the servers. With many of today's networks depending on IP communications, every workstation or host on the network is open season.

- Beware of trust relationships between servers or hosts. While a trust relationship may make your administrative job easier, it will also make the job of the hacker that much easier.

- Lose the "It can't happen here" attitude. It can, it might, and if it does, it can be devastating.

- Lose the "It's not my job" attitude. If you work for the company, it is your job. If you work in Information Services, think about what will happen when you apply for your next job. The question always comes up: "Why did you leave your last job?" How are you going to sugarcoat the fact that someone broke into the network and stole/destroyed valuable information? The "It wasn't my job" approach just isn't going to cut it.

As you read through this list, you're probably thinking about how much time this will all take, and all the budget that isn't available to do it. But if you work in Information Services, your main job is to work with information, and information is data. Everything you do revolves around data. Add a new user to the network? Why? To access or generate more data. Add more hardware? Why? To make the storage or access of data easier or safer. Everything you do revolves around the data. It makes a lot of sense to protect the stuff your job revolves around. It is tough to protect data once they have been destroyed.

Browser Security

Here is another area where the two warring factions are just making life miserable for the administrator. Both Communicator and Internet Explorer 4 will do many of the same things, but they will do them in completely different ways. For example, you may have heard of the problems Java and ActiveX applets can cause. Since both of these features are downloaded off the Net as part of a Web page, you have no control over what is coming to your computer. When the applet has been downloaded, it runs in your computer's memory space with access to your computer's local hardware. If the developer of the applet had any evil intent, you would have little to say about it.

Both Internet Explorer and Communicator give digitally-signed Java applets limited access to your computer. That is a good thing. Unfortunately, neither supports the other's security algorithm. This means if you go to www.*something*.com while running Communicator and download an applet, you will get a message asking if it is okay to run this applet. If you say yes, you can decide to accept all applets from that site. In this case, you will never be asked to accept those applets again, unless you switch browsers. If you switch over to Internet Explorer 4 and go back to the same site to access the same Web page, it will make you go through the same administrative overhead. After a while this can become somewhat tiresome.

From the administrator's point of view, Internet Explorer offers more choices for administration. You can select all sorts of options and make all sorts of choices to decide exactly how your users will be working with resources. With Netscape, it is a more simplistic, all-or-nothing approach.

Microsoft divides the world into zones. There is the Internet zone, the Local Intranet, Trusted sites, and Restricted sites. Trusted sites and Restricted sites are added manually and can reside in the Internet zone or the Local Intranet. When an administrator defines security, it can be specified that Internet Explorer can only run unsigned ActiveX applets if the applet comes from within the Local Intranet. Security options can be set for each zone, including allowing or prohibiting file downloads or saving Web content locally.

The Microsoft plan is exceptionally functional and flexible, except when it comes to Java. With Java you are given the choice for High, Medium, or Low security for Java applets, but there is no documentation to indicate what each choice will or will not allow. You can also disable Java scripts. These options are only available with IEAK.

Communicator takes the all-or-nothing approach. You can configure the browser to run all Java applets, or none at all. There are also fewer choices to make. File downloading cannot be prohibited in Communicator. While Communicator gives you fewer choices, that is not necessarily a bad thing. Microsoft tends to get very granular with all of its products. You can customize just about everything. While this provides tremendous amounts of flexibility, it also provides opportunities for overlaps. You may be experiencing problems because of security settings at another level. The policy can become very complicated, very quickly.

NOTE   Each of the two most popular browsers has had security holes widely reported. The holes in Internet Explorer are very well known. Make sure the browser you use is patched regularly to close any security loopholes before they are compromised.

Summary

Getting your network hooked up to the Internet does not have to be a daunting task. Consider the following points when planning such a project:

- What will your Internet presence consist of?
- What Internet connection speed will you need?
- Who will provide the hardware?
- Who will be in charge of security?
- Will you need a firewall?
- Which browser will be the corporate standard, and how will it be rolled out?

Once you actually start to set up the connection, keep the following tips in mind:

- Implement your addressing strategy and security plans before the connection is made to the Internet.
- Choose an Internet provider and make arrangements for the installation of the connection and appropriate hardware.
- Roll the browser out to desktops.
- Establish a Web site or an e-mail solution.
- Monitor Internet performance to ensure the connection is appropriate to the task.
- Monitor and audit the network to ensure against breaches of security.
- Make sure the browser versions are kept up-to-date with the appropriate patches.
- Make sure the network is up-to-date with the appropriate patches.

CHAPTER
NINETEEN

Building an Intranet

- Planning your intranet

- Designing your intranet

- Choosing a firewall

- Setting up IP addressing

- Choosing a Web server

- Publishing to the intranet

Browsers are taking over the world! It won't be long before the desktop operating system will be a thing of the past, and no one will care if you are using Windows 02 (have you ever wondered what will happen to the Windows naming convention after the year 2000?), OS/2, Windows NT, Linux, or anything else. All that people will care about is the browser you are using.

In the information age, quick, reliable, and easy to access information has become the standard by which things are measured. The new operating systems (OSs) are incorporating browsing into the desktop. Network administration for Windows NT and for Novell NetWare will be done using browsers rather than specific utilities. It is definitely becoming a browser world. Even the next version of the Mac OS (8.5 or Allegro) is using Apple's V-Twin search engine technology to search everything—inside documents, even the Internet, returning results in its own window. (Look Mom! No browser!!) And early tests make it 20 times faster than the previous albatross, Find File.

How does this information revolution affect the average end user on your network? In the last chapter, we took a look at how to hook your network up to the Internet. Sooner or later, some suit somewhere on Mahogany Row is going to wonder why users on the network can't have the same kind of access to internal information as they have to external information. And for once the suits have a really good question! Why not?

Your users can have access to the same kind of capability internally as they do externally. As a matter of fact, your users do not even need access to the Internet to have that kind of internal capability. Instead of the Internet, this is called an *intranet*.

Needs Assessment

Before we do a benefit analysis of an intranet, we should define what exactly an intranet really is. One definition of an intranet is that it is a smaller, private version of the Internet. It uses TCP/IP, HTTP, and other Internet protocols to create an enterprise-wide network that may consist of interconnected local area networks. An intranet may or may not include a connection to the Internet. The main purpose of an intranet is to share information and resources among employees.

Benefits of an Intranet

Computer networks are designed so that people connected to the network can share information. The network makes the storage of information easy; the gathering and dissemination of the information is the hard part. The intranet can simplify the process and put the information in the hands of the people who need it.

Let's take a common example. If you have ever worked for a company that has over 25 or 30 people, you have come in contact with a Human Resources Department. Now, the HR Department serves many useful purposes, not the least of which is generating the offer of employment letter that you accepted to get your job. The HR Department is where many company policies are generated, and this is a task that most HR professionals excel at. There are personnel policies, hiring policies, firing policies, vacation policies, insurance policies, Internet access policies, etc. You name it, there is a policy for it.

For the sake of this example, let's look more closely at one policy near and dear to every employee's heart, the vacation policy. Every company has one; it usually says something like five vacation days after one year, 10 vacation days after three years, 15 vacation days after 10 years, and 20 vacation days the day before you retire. The question here is not how the policy is generated, but rather how the policy is circulated.

In the pre-intranet days, there were several circulation methods. Once the policy had been written and approved, the policy was usually typed up on official company policy paper and then taken to the copy room. In the copy room, the clerk in charge of copying is given an order to make a copy of the new vacation policy for each employee within the firm. Once the copy has been made, the copies are forwarded to the mail room where the clerk in charge of interoffice mail is presented with the stack of copies and told to prepare an interoffice mail envelope for each employee and put a copy of the new policy in the envelope. Once the clerk in charge of interoffice mail has finished, the stack of several hundred envelopes is then passed to the clerk in charge of delivering interoffice mail.

So, the clerk comes by your cubicle and drops off the interoffice envelope with the new vacation policy. You open the envelope, glance at the policy for approximately 10 seconds, and then either trash it or place it in the official Human Resources Policy Binder under the tab that says Vacation. The binder goes back in your bookcase, where it continues to gather dust until the next time you have to figure out how many vacation days you have left. Think of the hours spent copying and distributing that policy! Think of the number of trees that have been lost just to the annual change in any policy of any company! We could reforest the rain forest. Surely there has to be a better way.

Suppose the person who typed the original policy saved it to the corporate intranet, instead of printing it. When the document is saved in the Vacation area, using the Save As an HTML document, all of a sudden the policy is available immediately for everyone within the company. No printing, no copying, no distributing, no interoffice mail envelopes, no binders, no filing—it is just there!

The policy is now accessible to anyone with a Web browser—the same Web browser that is used to access the Internet. This time it is used to access the intranet. This is not just for HR policies anymore; the latest Technical Information documents, the company phone book, the pictures of the last company picnic, and even the company Mission Statement can be stored on the intranet.

An intranet offers tremendous flexibility. Besides the general area of the intranet that is accessible to everyone, you can also have secured areas. For example, the Research and Development team working on the top secret Widget-2000 project can have an area that only they can access. The IS department can have an area where they can share all sorts of the latest technical information, and no one outside of the IS department can access it.

Using one of the protocols that make up the TCP/IP protocol suite, you can even have a File Transfer Protocol (FTP) area. Think of it: The latest patch to the latest feature of the latest software product could be saved in an area where anyone in the company could access it. The help desk could talk people through the process of downloading and installing the patch themselves without you having to go and stand over them. People could use the intranet to share the latest copies of drawings, help files, utilities, anything!

Disadvantages of an Intranet

While the corporate intranet has great potential, there is also a downside. Someone is going to have to manage this thing.

Most computer networks have a "shared" area. You are probably familiar with the area—it is the informational black hole of the network. It is the area where information can be shared across departmental boundaries, the area where just about anyone who logs on can put stuff to be accessed by just about anyone else who logs on. Most information that gets saved to the shared area is never removed. If you check the shared area of your network, you probably have files out there dating from years ago. If you ask the owner of the file if it is actually necessary that it be maintained, the owner will contend that the entire company would cease to exist if that file were removed. Think about what would happen to the intranet if all this information were suddenly published? Who would make the decisions about where they would go? Would someone have to go through each and every file to determine where it was supposed to be placed? Surely, this is a nightmare just waiting to happen. Who is going to be responsible for policing this area and for removing things when they are no longer vital?

What about publishing information to the intranet? Who is going to teach users how to publish a document to the intranet? Now, we know that publishing documents to the intranet is as simple as changing a setting in Save As, but someone has got to tell users that this is how it's done. Think of the can of worms this is going to open. Not only are you going to have to teach end users how to save documents as HTML code, but you are going to have to introduce them to new places to save information. Most end users have a difficult time remembering the subtle differences between their user home directory and shared network areas. Now you are going to expect them to remember how to save something to the intranet.

There is another potential problem. Once users get the hang of working with the intranet, some of them are going to realize that they could create really cool Web pages on the intranet using ActiveX or Java or Perl or anything else. Who gets the pleasure of training these users?

And once you have created this growing population of aspiring Webmasters, decisions must be made as to what is appropriate material for the intranet and what is inappropriate material for the Web page. This kicks off another spate of meetings, leading to more policies to be published to the intranet.

That is the soft problem. What about the hard issues involved in the dissemination of this information? What about hardware? Where is this growing intranet going to be housed? Do you have some kind of computer capable of running a Web server and accepting all these hits? Are you going to need just one computer, or, if you work in a large company, will you need several computers to act as Web servers? How are your users going to access these Web servers?

Access is a key point. In the beginning, an assumption was made. If you want a Web server, you are going to have to be running some form of TCP/IP on the server hosting the Web site and on the client accessing the site. This seems like a small thing, but as anyone who has ever managed an IP network knows, address management can be a nightmare. As soon as the decision is made to attach the intranet to the Internet, and you need official, registered IP addresses, things may get even trickier.

When your company makes the decision to go with an intranet, make sure the powers that be understand that money will be involved. Creating an intranet is easy; managing it and policing it can be somewhat challenging. Is it worth it? It is your call, but let us assume that you decide it is. Now the task breaks down into planning, implementation, and maintenance.

Intranet Considerations

Any time you start planning a project, it is always good to have a goal in sight. In this case, the goal will look like the network map in Figure 19.1.

FIGURE 19.1:

A network map

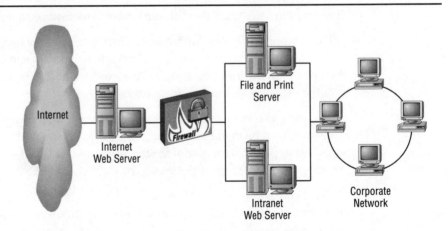

You will notice that some assumptions have been made here. For example, one assumption was that your network would need to hook up to the Internet. Internet access is becoming more and more a fact of business life, and part of this chapter will deal with firewalls, which make Internet connections relatively safe.

You will also notice that on the private side of the firewall there are two servers, one for file and print services and one to act as your intranet Web server. This may be the way your network will eventually look, so the plan should be able to accommodate it.

Chapter 18 covered the topic of connecting your network to the Internet. To continue the discussion of intranets, we will move from the outside in, and start with firewalls.

Firewalls

When a building contractor thinks of a firewall, what comes to mind is a wall built from foundation to roof, front to back, made from a completely fire retardant material like brick. The purpose of the firewall is to prevent a fire from spreading from one area of the building to another. It is designed to protect parts of the building from disaster.

A firewall for a network serves exactly the same purpose, except the definition of fire is somewhat different. In the case of computer networks, a *firewall* protects the private network from attacks from the public side of the equation.

The easiest way to imagine a firewall is to picture a server or a router with two cards in it. Take a look at Figure 19.2, which shows such a system.

FIGURE 19.2:

Firewall

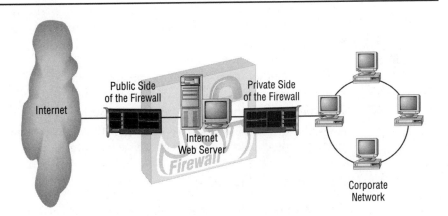

As you can see, one side of the network goes out to the Internet. This is the public side of the network. The other side is hooked into the corporate network, so it is the private side of the wall. The system in between, a software program running on one of several possible operating systems, is the firewall. Basically, a firewall is simply a merging of hardware and software that protects your network from users on the Internet.

Firewall Basics

Firewalls not only protect your network from outside dangers; they can protect the Internet from your network. A firewall can watch both inbound traffic and outbound traffic, and either allow or prevent access based on a set of specific criteria. For example, a firewall can:

- Allow a salesperson sitting in a hotel room hundreds of miles away from the corporate network to access the system and upload the orders generated that day.

- Restrict a user within the company office from accessing a site that has been determined to be pornographic.

- Allow users throughout the network to send e-mail, while prohibiting anyone using the computer in the reception area from accessing protected portions of the corporate intranet.

- Block a user who is trying to hack a way into the network.

- Hide the identities of both the internal users and the network itself. This is done so that no one can "eavesdrop" and pick up IP addresses or user information.

There are other things a firewall can accomplish. An effective firewall should provide some sort of alarm system to warn if unauthorized or unexpected access is encountered. If there is an attempt at unauthorized access, there should be accurate logs of incoming and outgoing traffic. There should also be some type of backup protection if part or all of the system goes down.

Choosing a Firewall

There are hundreds of different firewalls that run on different platforms: firewalls that work with NetWare, firewalls that help Windows NT security, firewalls that are Unix-based. If you are looking for a firewall, one place to start is the latest copy of the *Firewall Buyers Guide*, published by the National Computer Security Association (NCSA, `www.ncsa.com`). The NCSA is an independent, for-profit organization composed of a group of vendors, technology experts, and the NCSA staff.

The Buyers Guide is sponsored by a long list of some of the biggest names in the computing industry, including Novell, Cisco, Ascend, Digital, and Computer Associates.

As a rule, firewalls are available in a variety of configurations. Some of these are covered below.

Packet-Filtering Routers   *Packet filtering* means that the router examines each communication packet as it passes through, and routes the packet based not only on destination address, but on the type of protocol it is using. For example, a Simple Mail Transfer Protocol (SMTP) packet may be routed to a different gateway than a packet using File Transfer Protocol (FTP). Other things that can be used to filter packets include the source IP address of the packet, the destination IP address of the packet, the TCP/UDP source port, and the TCP/UDP destination port.

NOTE   This filtering is done according to a specific set of rules, and these rules are configured by the network administrator. These rules should be included in the Network Security Policy and Procedures Manual.

Packet filtering can also be used to block connections from or to specific hosts or sites, and can even block connections to specific TCP/IP ports. This would come in handy if you wanted to block network access to your main competition's employment Web page, or to other sites that were deemed unacceptable for one reason or another. You may also decide to block connections to any external addresses except from a specific TCP/UDP port, such as the SMTP port. People do get upset when you block them from receiving e-mail.

Using TCP or UDP port filtering and IP address filtering gives the network administrator a great deal of flexibility. As mentioned before, there are default ports used for a variety of services on the Internet. Each of these ports is a listening point or a security hole into your network. An understanding of these ports and how they operate will allow the administrator to block or allow access to certain network services, as well as to certain network sites. The policy of who you will let go where can be very specific. One employee may be able to establish a Telnet session with a remote Unix host, while another cannot. The user that can't use Telnet may be able to copy files to and from FTP servers. Finally, a third employee may be able to use both Telnet and FTP, as long as the packets are coming from that employee's regular computer.

Packet-filtering routers are not perfect. Traditionally, configuring a packet-filtering router has been as user-friendly as a root canal without Novocain. The GUI age has changed this, but don't expect a stroll in the park. Any time you add more specific restrictions, you are increasing complexity. Increased complexity flies in the face of the KISS (Keep It Simple, Stupid) rule, though it does increase security.

The problem with implementing a packet-filtering rule lies in the fact that usually there is no testing facility for verifying that the rules work. Once the rule has been applied, the only way to check it is by trial and error, by hand. If you are applying the rule to the one "helpful" person on your staff who is constantly applying the wrong patch, this is not a big problem. Testing and applying specific rules at a Technical College with a student body of 10,000 might become a little tiresome.

Other shortcomings of packet-filtering routers include the lack of a logging capability. Without a logging function, you may not realize that a router's rules still let "bad" packets through until you have been hacked. If you decide that packet filtering is the way to go, look for a router that offers extensive logging, simplified setup, and some form of rule checking.

You don't have to work in computing for very long to realize that for every rule there is an exception. Exceptions to filtering rules grant certain types of access that may be blocked for other users. These exceptions contribute to making the filtering rules so complex that they are unworkable. For example, it is relatively straightforward to specify a rule that blocks all inbound connections to port 23 (the Telnet server), but some sites make exceptions so that certain specified systems can accept Telnet connections directly. To do this, the administrator must add a rule for each system. Again, if you have a small number of employees, this may not be a problem. When you are working in a large organization, granting too many exceptions may defeat the actual purpose of the packet-filtering router.

Proxy Servers/Application Gateways   Proxy servers, in a traditional sense, can act as a mini-Internet, caching frequently requested information. For example, if a proxy server was protecting a network where there were frequent requests to the www.ferblitzer.com Web site, the page would be cached (stored in memory) at the proxy server. The administrator could determine how often the proxy server checks for changes, but in most cases, it would be one system checking, not multiple systems. Whenever a request was made from a host inside the firewall for the page at www.ferblitzer.com, the page returned would be from the cache at the proxy server and not from the actual Web site. This speeds access for end users.

In this section, we are going to look at other ways a proxy server can be used on your network. When talking about firewalls and proxy servers, another term is frequently mentioned: application gateway. The differences between application gateways and proxy servers are like the differences between the host and the operating system it runs. The software that provides the service is referred to as a proxy server, while the machine running the software is referred to as an application gateway.

Proxy servers or application gateways were designed to offset some of the shortcomings of packet-filtering routers. These software applications are designed to forward and filter connections for services such as Telnet and FTP.

A proxy server can work alongside a packet-filtering router to provide higher levels of security and greater flexibility than either standalone system could. Proxy servers work by allowing through only those services for which there is a proxy. In other words, if an application gateway contains proxies for HTTP and Telnet, then only HTTP and Telnet may be allowed into the protected subnet, and all other services will be blocked.

Application gateways offer a number of advantages over other types of firewalls. These advantages include:

- Masking of network information—The names of hosts on the private network are not known to DNS or to outside systems. The application gateway can be the only host whose name is known to the outside world.

- Better logging and authentication—The gateway can validate traffic before it reaches the internal host. The traffic can then be logged more effectively than with standard logging.

- Cost—Third-party software or hardware for authentication or logging need be located only at the application gateway.

- Ease of filtering—The rules at the packet-filtering router will be less complex because the packet-filtering router does not have to handle application-level filtering. The packet-filtering router allows application traffic to find its way to the application gateway and discards any other traffic.

You are probably saying to yourself, it can't be this simple, and in this case, you are right. Problems arise when you begin to use client-server protocols like Telnet. In the case of Telnet, application gateways need two steps to establish either an inbound or outbound connection. This may not seem like a big deal, but it does require the end user to connect (but not log in) to the firewall instead of connecting directly to the host, which means a little extra training for users.

You can also explore other options. For example, a different type of Telnet client could make the firewall transparent to users and permit them to specify the destination system in the Telnet command. In this case, the firewall would serve as the route to the remote host and intercept the connection. Once the firewall controlled the connection, it could then perform whatever additional steps were necessary to complete the connection. These steps might include asking for a password. The advantage to this solution would be that end users would not need to change their behavior, but you would have to install this new client on all the hosts.

In addition to Telnet, application gateways can accommodate FTP and e-mail, as well as other services. The e-mail gateway acts as a collection and distribution point for corporate e-mail. To anyone outside the company, all corporate users have e-mail addresses of the form *user@company.com* where *company.com* points to the e-mail gateway. The gateway accepts mail from outsiders and forwards it to internal systems. Internal system users can send e-mail directly from their desktops, or to the application gateway, which then forwards the mail to the outside world.

Packet Inspection   Some firewalls combine the packet-filtering and application-gateway features, offering the best of both worlds. For the network administrator, this allows a very high level of control. But although control is usually a good thing, there may be problems with how easy the firewall is to penetrate. While you do not want outside (or even inside) hackers to penetrate the firewall, you do want your end users to be able to get out. Another issue with this type of system is the cost. As usual, when you get bigger, better, and more flexible, you also get increased cost, increased management, and more extensive education needed to operate the system.

Another approach that's gaining acceptance is to *inspect* packets rather than just filtering them; that is, to consider their contents as well as their addresses. Firewalls of this type employ an inspection module. Some of these "inspection firewalls" take into account the state of the connections they handle. In this case, a packet coming into the network can be matched with the outbound request, and the inbound packet will be allowed in. If an incoming packet is trying to act like a response to a nonexistent outbound request, that packet can be discarded.

All of the Above   Finally, there is the firewall that does it all, combining a variety of techniques to give you the most bang for your buck. Since the firewall industry, like the rest of the computer industry, is changing rapidly, a product that started life as a packet-filtering firewall may since have been reworked with smart filtering to work at the application level. You should read the information provided by vendors for more details of how particular products are designed.

The summaries for certified firewalls can be found at the NCSA Web site (www.ncsa.com). When the NCSA certifies a firewall, it has passed the same set of tests, regardless of the product type. Unless you are a firewall expert, you may not be entirely sure what you are getting in a firewall, and whether the firewall actually does what it says it is going to do. NCSA certification can give you an indication that you are buying a product that will perform the advertised functions.

Intranet Addressing Considerations

Once you get past the firewall, you are faced with a dilemma. Whether you are on the Internet or just a local intranet, you are not going to be able to get away from *IP addressing*. Each computer on your network has to have a valid IP address. Whether this IP address is registered or not, each host must have a valid IP address. This means that you must know enough to be able to determine things like:

- How many subnets will you need?

- Once you have an address and a subnet mask, how many subnets are possible?

- Given an address and a subnet mask, how many hosts can reside on each subnet?

- Given an address and a subnet mask, which host addresses belong on which network?

- Given an address and a subnet mask, which is the host address and what is the network address?

This section will spend some time showing you how to manually do some of these things. If you are not a math whiz, don't panic; there are several great freeware subnet calculators available on the Web. All it takes is a little searching.

NOTE   Much of the discussion on subnets revolves around the conversion of binary numbers into decimal equivalents and decimals back to binary. If you are uncomfortable with doing this manually, any good scientific calculator should be able to provide this functionality.

Addressing Basics

Communication at any level revolves around a sender and a receiver. For the communication to carry on for any period of time, the sender will become the receiver and the receiver will become the sender. In each case, both parties must have a way of finding each other.

Computer communication is very similar to postal service. When someone sends you a letter, they have your name, address, city, state, and zip code. When the letter is picked up from the sender, the city, state, and zip code are checked to find out if the letter is to be delivered locally or if it is to go out of the local postal zone. If the letter is destined out of the local postal zone, the letter is forwarded to a regional center, which forwards it to another regional center, which sends it to a local center, which delivers the letter.

In IP communications, the process works this way: Assume that your computer wants to request some information from an FTP server. You type in the appropriate IP address for the FTP server and press Enter. What happens behind the scenes? The sending computer formats the data to be sent in a *packet* or *datagram*. This packet has a source address (the sender) and a destination address (the recipient), as does your envelope. When your computer is ready to send out the packet, it looks at the destination address to determine if the packet is destined for the local network or somewhere else. If the packet is destined for the local network, the computer sends it on its way. If it is destined for somewhere else, the computer sends the packet to the designated gateway and lets the gateway handle it.

The packet IP addresses are a little more cryptic than a familiar mailing address, but just as your mailing address is made up of several parts, so is an IP address. Your address consists of a street address to identify your house, and a city, state, and zip code. An IP address consists of the network address the host resides on and a host address to identify the computer on the network.

IP Addressing

Network addresses are interesting things. If you have a network that is not connected to the Internet, it really doesn't matter what network address you give each network segment. Just make sure that everything is unique. This is referred to as the 1.2.3.4 method of network addressing. You start numbering the first machine at 1.2.3.4 and slowly increment by one for each new host you install on the subnet.

Things become a little more complicated when you decide to hook your system to the Internet. Every computer on a network must have a unique address. It doesn't matter if the network is the three-workstation configuration at the corner insurance office or the world-wide Internet. Everything has to be unique. At the Internet level, you cannot just pick yourself a block of addresses and go. You or your company must be assigned addresses by the Internet Network Information Center, commonly known as InterNIC. It is up to InterNIC to determine what address block you can use. There are four ways to apply. You can go to the Inter-NIC Web site at `www.internic.net`, you can call Network Solutions at 703-742-4777, you can send e-mail to `hostmaster@internic.net`, or you can send them an application at the following address:

Network Solutions
InterNIC Registration Services
505 Huntmar Park Drive
Herndon, VA 22070

Applications are available from the Web site.

NOTE Actually, depending on the size of your organization, you can also ask your Internet service provider to cut through the paperwork for you. The ISP may have a block of addresses you can rent. The problem with renting a block of addresses from an ISP is that the ISP owns the addresses. If you decide to change ISPs, you have to reconfigure your entire network addressing scheme.

When you receive your assignment, it will be in the form of an IP address. The typical IP address looks like 205.46.15.198. This address uniquely identifies a host on a network.

The IP address is made up of four bytes. Because each byte is made up of eight bits, each byte is also referred to as an *octet*. Each octet is expressed as the decimal representation of a binary number. To translate a decimal number to a binary number, we need some kind of translation table. The number we are going to translate is the first number of the octet, 205. Look closely at Table 19.1 to see how to translate this number from binary to decimal.

TABLE 19.1: Binary to Decimal Translation of Decimal 205

	Bit 8	Bit 7	Bit 6	Bit 5	Bit 4	Bit 3	Bit 2	Bit 1
Decimal value	$2^7 = 128$	$2^6 = 64$	$2^5 = 32$	$2^4 = 16$	$2^3 = 8$	$2^2 = 4$	$2^1 = 2$	$2^0 = 1$
Binary value of byte	1	1	0	0	1	1	0	1
Decimal conversion	128	64	0	0	8	4	0	1

To figure out the decimal value of the binary number, just add up the decimal values of the bits that are set to 1. In this example, 11001101 in binary translates to $128 + 64 + 8 + 4 + 1 = 205$. To us, it is 205; to your computer it is 11001101.

If all the bits are set to 1, you have a maximum value of 255. There are some rules to IP addressing, and one of those rules states that an address cannot have all the bits set to all 1s or all 0s. That means there are no network (or host) addresses of 255 or 0. In addition, there is a reserved address, 127.0.0.1, which is called a *loopback address*. A loopback address is an address used for testing the local machine.

InterNIC has divided IP network addresses into five classes. Microsoft TCP/IP recognizes the first three classes, so those are what we will concentrate on, but you should know about all five. Table 19.2 gives you a breakdown of the classes.

TABLE 19.2: InterNIC Address Classes

Class	Value of First Byte	Binary Range	Decimal Range
A	First bit must be 0.	00000001-01111111 Note: A value of 0 for the network address is not permitted.	1 to 127 Note: 127 is reserved for testing.
B	First two bits must be 10.	10000000-10111111	128 to 191
C	First 3 bits must be 110.	11000000-11011111	192 to 223
D Note: This range of network addresses is reserved for multicasts and is not available for host addressing.	First 4 bits must be 1110.	11100000-11101111	224-239
E Note: This range of addresses is reserved for experimental purposes and is not available for host addressing.	First 5 bits must be 11110.	11110000-11110111	240-247

Because the Class D and Class E network addresses are reserved, we will ignore them.

The IP addressing scheme takes into account that some networks are very large, some are medium sized, and some are small. A *Class A* address uses the first octet to represent the network address and the last three octets to represent hosts. Looking at the chart above, with only 127 numbers available for Class A addresses, there aren't many given out. They were designed for large organizations with lots of hosts.

A *Class B* address fulfills the needs of a medium-sized organization. The first two octets designate the network, and the last two octets designate the number of hosts. A *Class C* address uses the first three octets to designate the network and the last octet to designate the host. There is a formula to determine the number of networks or the number of hosts. The formula is 2 raised to the number of bits for varying minus 2. You subtract 2 to take into account that you cannot use 0 or 255. So, in the case of a Class A address, 1 bit is used to designate the network and 7 bits are left for "varying" in the first octet. Applying the formula, 27- 2 = 126 networks. Table 19.3 shows how the addresses break down.

TABLE 19.3: IP Addressing Scheme

Class	IP Address	Number of Networks	Number of Hosts
A	NET.host.host.host	126 Network = 7 bits $2^7 - 2 = 126$	16,777,214 Hosts = 24 bits $2^{24} - 2 = 16,777,214$
B	NET.NET.host.host	16,384 Network = 14 bits $2^{14} - 2 = 16,384$	65,534 Hosts = 16 bits $2^{16} - 2 = 65,534$
C	NET.NET.NET.host	2,097,152 Network = 21 bits $2^{21} - 2 = 2,097,152$	254 Hosts = 8 bits $2^8 - 2 = 254$

So, if you just pinged Microsoft, you received an IP address of 207.46.130.17. From the information you have seen so far, you should be able to determine that this is a Class C address because the first octet is greater than 191 and less than 224. Because it is a Class C address, you know that this host is on network number 207.46.130.0 and the unique host number is 0.0.0.17. You also know that this is one host out of a possible 254.

Subnets and Subnetting

Suppose you applied to InterNIC for your IP address, and you were returned a number like 207.46.130.0 and a subnet mask of 255.255.255.0. You were told that you could have 254 different hosts on that network. At this point, it is very important to understand the term network. It is often used casually and has different meanings depending on its context. If you look in your testing lab, you may see a server hooked up to a couple of workstations, and that is a network. Or, a major corporation could have a nationwide network. In terms of this section of the book, a network should really be defined as a network segment. Each server that has a network card in it has a network number assigned to that card. Each network card may define its own network segment.

As you look at the structure of your network, you will see that you have multiple network segments. Depending on the type of network you have (Ethernet versus Token Ring), you may only have 50 hosts on any network segment. Does this mean that you will have to apply for a separate IP address for each network segment? After all, each network must have its own unique address. That would be really wasteful. You would have an address that could use up to 254 hosts and you are applying it to a segment that has only 50 hosts, wasting 204 addresses. With the explosive growth of the Internet, everybody wants an IP address, so they are in short supply. Wasting them like that would be criminal. But there is a better way—it's called *subnetting*.

NOTE   With the popularity of the Internet increasing, there is a shortage of IP addresses. A new IP addressing scheme is in the works, called IP version 6, or *IPv6*. In keeping with the current fads, it is also called IPng, for IP Next Generation. The new IP is going to be incompatible with the old IP. In addition, the next generation will have a 128-bit source and destination address. A valid IP address in the future will look something like 1543:B24E:9853:574C:3336:43C7:4B3E:7C36. Rumor has it that given the 128-bit addressing scheme, there will be five IP addresses available for every square meter on earth.

When we take an IP address and subnet it, we take an address that is designed for one unique network with 254 hosts (in the case of a Class C network) and give ourselves more unique network numbers with a fewer number of hosts per network segment.

This is how it works. In a Class C network, we know the first three octets are destined for the network number and the last octet is determined to be the host. So, in binary, it would look something like this, with 1s determining the network and 0s determining the host:

11111111.11111111.11111111.00000000

That would give us the default Class C subnet of 255.255.255.0.

NOTE   Each class has its own default subnet; for Class A it is 255.0.0.0, for Class B it is 255.255.0.0, and for Class C it is 255.255.255.0.

To give us the opportunity to have more networks and fewer hosts, IP will let us "borrow" bits from the host address to use as a network address. We can use the formula of 2^x-2, where x is the number of borrowed bits, to determine the number of networks. Using 2^x-2 with the number of remaining bits will give you the number of hosts per segment.

Before, our subnet in binary was 11111111.11111111.11111111.00000000. Let's change that to 11111111.11111111.11111111.11110000. To figure out what our new custom subnet mask would be, take the numbers we used earlier and plug them into the chart. The conversion of this subnet is shown in Table 19.4.

To convert this back to decimal, we add 128 + 64 + 32 + 16 = 240, so our new subnet mask is 255.255.255.240. Using the formula, we see that we have 24 - 2 = 14 subnets available and also 14 hosts available per subnet for this Class C address.

If our subnet had been 11111111.11111111.11111111.11100000, our subnet mask would have been 255.255.255.224, and we would have had the ability to have six subnets with 30 hosts each. To keep you from having to do the math and conversions each time, look at the tables below to see what the subnet mask is and how many subnets and hosts you can get for each subnet. Table 19.5 will show Class C addresses.

TABLE 19.4: Subnet Conversion

	Bit 8	Bit 7	Bit 6	Bit 5	Bit 4	Bit 3	Bit 2	Bit 1
Decimal value	$2^7 = 128$	$2^6 = 64$	$2^5 = 32$	$2^4 = 16$	$2^3 = 8$	$2^2 = 4$	$2^1 = 2$	$2^0 = 1$
Binary value of byte	1	1	1	1	0	0	0	0
Decimal conversion	128	64	32	16	0	0	0	0

TABLE 19.5 Summary of Subnet Mask Effects on a Class C Address

Number of Bits Used in the Subnet	Subnet Mask	Number of Networks	Number of Hosts
2	255.255.255.192	2	62
3	255.255.255.224	6	30
4	255.255.255.240	14	14

Continued on next page

TABLE 19.5 CONTINUED: Summary of Subnet Mask Effects on a Class C Address

Number of Bits Used in the Subnet	Subnet Mask	Number of Networks	Number of Hosts
5	255.255.255.248	30	6
6	255.255.255.252	62	2
7	255.255.255.254	Not allowed	Not allowed
8	255.255.255.255	Not allowed	Not allowed

Determining Network and Host Addresses

Once you have determined the appropriate subnet mask to provide you with the number of network addresses and host addresses you want, the host addresses must be assigned to the appropriate network address; otherwise, systems on the subnet will not be able to communicate. The next step in the process is to take the network address assigned, with the appropriate subnet mask applied, and break it down into subnets and host addresses.

The sample address from Microsoft was 205.46.15.76. Because this is a Class C address, if the default subnet mask of 255.255.255.0 were used, the network address would be 205.46.15.0 and the host address would be .0.0.0.76. Let's assume that when Microsoft was assigned this address, they were going to use it on a network with four subnets and 25 hosts on each subnet. Looking at Table 19.5, we find that the subnet mask that meets all of those criteria is 255.255.255.224, using the first three bits of the last octets for a network address and the remaining five bits for host addresses.

Using the three bits of the last octet gives us six choices for the network number. These would be the binary choices:

- 00000000—Invalid address because the network portion contains all 0s.
- 00100000 = 32
- 01000000 = 64
- 01100000 = 96
- 10000000 = 128
- 10100000 = 160

- 11000000 = 192

- 11100000—Invalid address because the network portion contains all 1s.

To convert the binary choices to decimal, remember that we are dealing with only three bits from the octet. The conversion chart shows us the first three bits have values 128, 64, and 32.

Using the original network address of 205.46.15.0 and applying a subnet mask of 255.255.255.224 produces the following network numbers:

- 205.46.15.32

- 205.46.15.64

- 205.46.15.96

- 205.46.15.128

- 205.46.15.160

- 205.46.15.192

Now that we have determined the network numbers, we must determine the host addresses by applying the last five bits of the octet. Using the binary representation for the first network, our range of host addresses would be between 00100001 and 00111110. Converting those binary numbers to decimal, we find the network 205.46.15.32 has hosts ranging from 205.46.15.33 to 205.46.15.62. Applying the same principal to the next subnet, we would have addresses ranging from 01000001 to 01011110. Remember, the first three positions are the network address and the last five are the host address. Network number 205.46.15.64 would be made up of hosts 205.46.15.65 to 205.46.15.126. You can use the same procedure to find the host addresses on any subnet, using any subnet mask. Just use the binary method to define the network portion of the address, and then use the binary method to determine the host portion of the address.

You can use the same method to back-engineer an IP address. For example, given the sample address of 205.46.15.198 and a subnet mask of 255.255.255.224, what is the network address and what is the host address? In looking at the information above, we know that the highest available network address is 205.46.15.192. This host must reside on that network. If the network address is 192, the host address must be 0.0.0.6.

Assigning Addresses

Now that you know how to apply for your network address and how to subnet it once you get it, the discussion comes down to how you assign all those addresses to all those workstations. Two of the greatest time-savers for administrators who use TCP/IP have been Microsoft's 32-bit operating systems and *Dynamic Host Control Protocol* (*DHCP*).

Prior to Windows NT and Windows 95, configuring a DOS-based computer or a Unix-based system to run a TCP/IP stack was not a job for the faint of heart. Manually configuring workstations with IP addresses and tracking those addresses to prevent duplication was a nightmare. DHCP has certainly relieved much of that strain.

DHCP Basics

There are two ways of assigning IP addresses: manually and dynamically. Using the dynamic approach, you can configure one server on a subnet to "lease" IP addresses to any host that needs one. You can specify the range of IP addresses the server can assign and reserve certain addresses for particular computers. You can even make sure the hosts receive other information, such as gateway and subnetting addresses. When a host is done with an address, it returns the address to the server. The next time the host comes up, it will ask for and receive an IP address. It may not be the same address the host had before shutting down, but in most cases that doesn't matter.

The choice between manual and dynamic assignments is not an either/or solution. You can, and probably will, do both. Some systems do not work well getting their addresses from a DHCP server. For example, if you want to host an intranet, it will make sense for the host server to have a static IP address that will never change.

How does DHCP work? The process is really quite simple. You configure a system to be a DHCP server. You then provide the DHCP server with a *scope*, or list, of valid IP addresses. You also configure the DHCP server to pass out all that other information you want the systems to know about—things such as the IP address of the gateway and the IP address of the DNS servers you use. You then set the lease period so that it can loan addresses out for a period of time. By default, the IP lease is three days.

The placement of a DHCP server can be important. If your network uses routers, check to make sure the routers comply with Request for Comment (RFC) 1542. If the router complies with RFC 1542, it will pass requests for DHCP assignments from one subnet to another. If the router does not meet those specifications, there should be a DHCP server on each network segment. Check the documentation for the DHCP system you use.

Now that the server is configured, what about the client? When a workstation has been configured to use DHCP and it is turned on, it recognizes the need for an IP address. At this point, the workstation broadcasts a lease request, called a DHCPDISCOVER message. The client has no idea about the IP address of the DHCP server. This means the DHCPDISCOVER message is a *broadcast message*, so every client on the subnet will receive the packet. If nothing responds to the request, the workstation will send the lease request four more times, at nine seconds, 13 seconds, 16 seconds, and then at a random number of seconds. If the client still doesn't get an answer, it will continue to issue lease requests every five minutes.

When a DHCP server receives a lease request, it answers by sending back an IP lease offer or a DHCPOFFER packet. The offer packet is also sent as a broadcast message because, at this point, the client does not have an IP address. The DHCP offer will contain an IP address and subnet mask, the hardware address of the DHCP client, the IP address of the DHCP server, and the duration of the lease. Back at the client side, the client receives the DHCPOFFER packet. If you have multiple DHCP servers on a subnet, the client may receive multiple offers. The client accepts the first offer it receives by sending back a packet called the DHCPREQUEST packet, which tells the successful DHCP server that the workstation is taking it up on its offer. All the other servers realize the IP addresses they offered can be returned to the scope to be used by another workstation.

The process has not been completed. The DHCP server still needs to verify the successful lease. The server sends back an acknowledgment in the form of a packet known as a DHCPACK. This confirms the address and other configuration information. Once the client receives the DHCPACK, the client can initialize TCP/IP and the communications begin.

What if the client is unsuccessful in its lease or it is trying to renew a lease that has expired and the number has been reassigned? In that case, the DHCP server will send out a DHCPNACK. When a client gets a DHCPNACK, it knows it is back to square one and it starts the process over again.

Once the client has acknowledged the configuration information, it can keep that address until the system shuts down or the address is released manually. Like all leases, this one does have to be renewed. The default lease period is three days. After 50 percent of the time is up, the client will attempt to renew its lease. If the DHCP server is up and working, the client gets a new lease on the address. However, if the DHCP server is down, the client can still keep using the address because the lease will not expire for another 36 hours. DHCP clients also attempt to renew their leases on startup by broadcasting their last leased IP address. If the address hasn't been given out, it will be reassigned.

Intranet Security

Now that IP addresses are assigned and hosts can communicate with one another, security becomes an issue. You thought you didn't really have to worry about security since the intranet is an internal device? Well, depending on how you lay the intranet out, and what you are going to use it for, security on the intranet is just as important as setting up file system security on a file and print server, or protecting the network from hackers outside the company.

When a company decides to go with an intranet, it doesn't take long for everyone to want to get into the act. You can start out with the Human Resources (HR) Department wanting to publish the policies and procedures manual so that everyone can see it. Once they see how many hits the HR Web site gets, the decision is made to expand it and include a listing of new or open positions within the company. Now everyone can see what jobs are open and apply online.

Soon, the Research and Development Department wants to get in the act. It has pages of information that it needs to share, but its needs are different from the HR Department. The HR Department wants everyone in the company to see its information. The R&D Department wants its information shared with just a select few. This can be done, but it must be done carefully.

As we mentioned in the last chapter, there really is no such thing as a completely secure environment. You may think your system is secure, but re-evaluate your stance the next time you see one of your users with their password posted on the monitor with a sticky note.

NOTE   For more information on security, see Chapters 27 and 28.

Intranet security is like any other type of security. If someone wants to break into your system badly enough, and they have the skill, they will probably be successful. Your job is to make it too difficult to be worth their time.

Another issue of the intranet is file transfer. Earlier in this chapter, under the section "Benefits of an Intranet," we mentioned that using FTP will allow users to access and exchange files. Most implementations of FTP have a robust security scheme in place, allowing the administrator to specify who can have access to which areas. Each user can have their access levels set to the directory level, and even to the file level, but FTP will also allow for anonymous access using just the word "anonymous" as a login name and an e-mail address as the password. Some administrators take the easy way out and just allow this type of access. When you design your FTP site, make full use of the anonymous access principles for public files, but make sure each area has its own FTP site with security in place.

Selecting a Web Server

At this point the foundation has been laid, and it is time to start publishing information to the intranet and making it accessible to end users throughout the company. This is done with the use of a Web server.

It is difficult to project if you will need a separate server or even several separate servers for an intranet. One of the things you will have to do before you install your intranet is project how much it will actually be used. This puts you into the magician's role, because there really is no way of accurately predicting how many hits an area will actually receive before it is put in place. If you anticipate that the intranet will be actively used, you may want to create a new host just to host the intranet. This way, the intranet will not be slowing down the main file, print, and e-mail servers, and your users will receive faster response time.

There are several other reasons for keeping the intranet on its own host. Security comes to mind. You are going to be granting large numbers of people access to this server, and it will have its own security plan. However, it may still be a good idea to segregate some information or divisions onto another server.

Another reason to put the intranet on a separate server is to aid in troubleshooting. How many times have you solved a computer-related problem by simply rebooting the computer? The same can happen with a system hosting the intranet. If you need to reboot the Web server, at least you will not be kicking everyone off the file, print, and e-mail servers as well.

System minimums fall into the "it depends" category. There are several popular Web servers, and they run on a variety of different operating systems. Certainly the operating system's minimum requirements will come into play when you are planning how you will outfit the intranet. When it comes to installing new hardware, get the most server processor you can buy, and when in doubt, add more memory. Most Web servers rely heavily on caching information to reduce response time. In this case, there is no such thing as "too much memory."

What about disk space? This is a tough question. If you look at the "average" Web page, even with Java or ActiveX scripts, graphics, and all the rest, chances are it takes up less than 10MB of storage. If you decide to allocate 10MB per department just for the departmental Web page, you should be fine. However, when they start exchanging files and placing large spreadsheets on the intranet, the requirements may change drastically. Fortunately, disk space is currently relatively inexpensive and getting cheaper all the time. Add as much as you can afford while keeping in mind Murphy's Law of disk space that states that data will always grow to exceed the amount of available disk space.

Adding and Maintaining Content

Once your intranet has been configured and your Web server selected and installed, all that remains is to put information onto the server so people can access it. Adding and maintaining content on your intranet is not as difficult as it sounds. As a matter of fact, most word processing programs can take a document and save it using HTML code. This means that if your end users can use Word or WordPerfect, they can create Web pages.

How Good Does It Get?

The Web pages that will appear on your intranet will only be as good as the people creating them. Some information can be saved as simple HTML code from a word processing program so that the document will look just like a corporate memo. Other people may want to get a bit more creative and come up with a home page for their department. In that case, some special Web development tools may come in handy.

Web development tools can be as simple or as complex as you want them to be, or as you can afford. Some of these tools may already be at your fingertips. If you or your end users have Windows 98 installed, the stripped-down version of Microsoft FrontPage is already included. FrontPage will allow you to develop a home page by using the GUI method of point and click. The full version of Front-Page 98 sells for around $100, with upgrades going for about half that.

There are also authoring tools that are available as shareware or freeware on the Web. Some of the best known include HotDog, HoTMetaL Pro, Macromedia's Dreamweaver, and NetObject's Fusion. In addition, AOL and Netscape both provide Web authoring tools.

At this point, the sky is the limit and your company should have the corporate intranet up and running.

Summary

As you begin to plan your corporate intranet, remember that this is going to be one of the most visible projects you will ever work on. Each and every day, each and every employee may have an opportunity to sample your handy work. Be sure to:

- Plan it well.
- Protect it from outside attacks.
- Make sure you have a valid IP addressing scheme.
- Secure the network from internal attacks.
- Choose the right hardware and software to host the intranet.
- And finally, when in doubt, add more RAM.

CHAPTER

TWENTY

Introduction to Extranets

- A brief history of internetworking

- Extranets as a logical extension of internetworking technology

- Extranet application architectures

- Extranets and distributed objects

- Solving real-world problems

This chapter introduces the concept of extranets by explaining the waves of internetworking technology and showing how extranets fit into the historical development of internetworking. This chapter defines these technologies in the context of actual business problems, and you'll see examples of extranets and their applications. Extranets are an important option that is becoming available to companies planning network upgrades, one of the underlying themes of this book.

What Is an Extranet?

In the simplest terms possible, an *extranet* is a type of network that crosses organizational boundaries, giving outsiders access to information and resources stored inside the organization's internal network. For a simple example, an online catalog that displays product information dynamically retrieved from the vendor's own internal product database gives potential customers access to the most current information possible. When the product description, price, or availability change, the page display changes too. Explaining how this process works is what this chapter and the next are all about.

Technology Waves

Tracking the progress of how we integrate a new technology into our daily lives is difficult, especially from a distance of many years. Television, telecommunications, the internal combustion engine, steam power, and air travel are all examples of technologies that have taken decades to change the world. Businesses and individuals had many years to get used to these newfangled technologies, to plan for them, save for them, and slowly try them out. The leisurely pace suits us—it is manageable, and our lives change slowly. We still speak of "dialing" a phone number, even though we actually push buttons on a keypad and rotary dial telephones are fast becoming collectors' pieces. Likewise, we still speak of "cranking" a car engine, even though we actually use electronically controlled ignitions to start our cars.

The rate of change has been accelerating over the last half century. As the 1960s turned into the 1970s and the first man stepped onto the moon, the dual seeds of today's internetworking revolution were being planted. Research that would ultimately result in the precursors of today's Internet was starting in 1969 and 1970, and the first microprocessors were rolling off assembly lines by 1971. Moore's Law, which stipulates the doubling of microprocessing power every 18 months, and an Internet that has been roughly doubling in size annually for almost 20 years, have combined to produce a business world with ubiquitous desktop systems capable of computing feats far beyond the abilities of yesterday's million-dollar mainframes. And these desktop systems are all connected (or soon will be connected) through robust open networks.

The rapid growth of technology deployment means that businesses no longer have the luxury of waiting a few years to see how new technologies work out for the early adopters. Early adopters may be only a year—or even just a few months—ahead of the rest of the pack, and waiting two years to implement a new technology may be enough to brand a company as old-fashioned.

New technologies, such as computing, networking, and the Internet, have life cycles. They begin in universities and research labs as ideas, and if the creators can find sponsors, the ideas and concepts eventually find a more concrete expression in projects and experiments. Again, if they succeed at this stage in demonstrating the kernel of a useful product, they may be developed into prototypes and perfected through trial and error. Successful prototypes that find financial backing eventually appear in the market as products, and successful products spawn imitators and competitors. This continuous buildup is like the surging of a wave, building in intensity until it breaks as it meets the shore—the market. Many waves fizzle out with relatively little impact; under certain circumstances they may alter the structure of the beach on which they land—but in all cases, they are followed by more waves.

The parallel developments of the microprocessor and internetworking technologies have generated those special circumstances in which large waves of new technologies wash over us in rapid succession. Businesses and people who understood the implications of the Internet in the early 90s and moved quickly to take business advantage of those implications have benefited. Businesses and people who understood the implications of intranets in the mid-90s and moved to take business advantage of those implications have also benefited. Similarly, at the end of the 90s, businesses and people who understand the implications of extranets and take business advantage of those implications will also benefit.

Understanding a new technology—what it is, how it works, and what it can do for your organization—is a key step to using the technology to achieve your organization's goals and is an absolute prerequisite to deploying that technology. This chapter will help you achieve the goal of understanding this new thing called an *extranet*.

NOTE   The terms *internetwork, Internet,* and *extranet* are used throughout this book and defined in its glossary, Appendix D. For the purpose of clarity, this chapter refers to any network running TCP/IP as an *internetwork*. Within this framework, *internetwork* includes the Internet, intranets, and extranets.

A Very Brief History of Internetworking

For their first 25 years, the history of internetworking and the history of the Internet were essentially the same. Although a detailed historical account of the origins of the Internet protocols is beyond the scope of this book, a very brief overview will lay the groundwork for the topics at hand.

A very successful data communications network was well in place by the late 60s, with terminals in almost every home and office in North America. Those terminals—also known as telephones—can connect people (or computers) virtually anywhere, as long as the copper, fiber, microwave, or satellite links are in place. At the height of the cold war, the U.S. government decided that telecommunications links, especially those used for command and control of strategic weapons systems, were vulnerable to attack. Telecommunications switches offered enemies attractive targets, being single points of failure that could bring a network to its knees or worse. Figure 20.1 shows how such a single point of failure would sever communications between the eastern and western parts of the United States.

FIGURE 20.1:

A switched network with a single point of failure is highly vulnerable to disastrous failure.

Chicago, IL

Portland, OR

Boston, MA

San Francisco, CA

New York, NY

San Diego, CA

Washington, DC

In the late 60s, the U.S. Department of Defense (DoD) Advanced Research Projects Agency (ARPA) began funding research into ways to protect strategic networks from nuclear attacks that could destroy large parts of the networks. The basic idea, as shown in Figure 20.2, was to create a network of networks, or an *internetwork*, with multiple links between each network. Failure on any given link between any two networks would not necessarily break the rest of the internetwork. If a link failed, data would be intelligently rerouted to its destination over some other link or combination of links.

FIGURE 20.2:

With multiple links and no single point of failure, an internetwork can withstand considerable damage without losing connectivity.

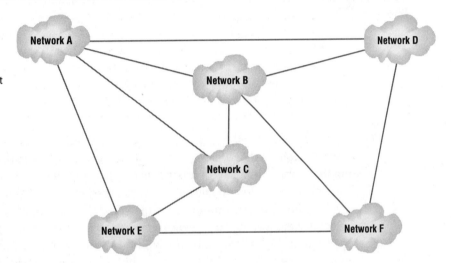

The very interesting saga of how this idea became a reality is best told elsewhere—what interests us here is how this experiment grew into a global infrastructure. The heart of the problem was not so much a technical issue as it was an issue of the big messy world we live in.

Robust internetworking would, of course, be easiest in the best of all possible worlds—where all connected systems are compatible, where all systems are connected with the same type of network medium, and where a central authority manages all the systems connected to the internetwork. Programmers could easily write software for that single platform—software that could deliver data, efficiently and quickly, between any two connected systems, using the centrally administered directory. Broken links and failed networks could be managed elegantly and simply, and performance would always be excellent.

The problem is that such a world is not only impossible to achieve but would also be destined to experience overwhelming systemic failure within a few years (and probably much sooner), due to ever-expanding scalability needs. This closed static system would very likely prohibit any significant innovation improving scalability, so any significant increase in the number of systems or networks connected to the internetwork would soon doom it. One possible solution to scalability problems is the introduction of new technologies in the form of hardware, software, or network media capable of handling more traffic, but this avenue is closed, since it would require all systems, networks, and hardware to be updated simultaneously. Any bug, error, or miscalculation would quickly strand all users.

> **NOTE**
> As discussed throughout this book, *scalability* is the degree to which any networking product used by more than one user at a time is able to handle ever-increasing numbers of concurrent users. Network wiring, network server hardware, and network server software will usually have some implicit limits on the number of concurrent users, and the ability of a networking product to gracefully handle increasing loads determines how *scalable* the product is.

The potential number of hardware, software, and local area network combinations on systems that we might like to link together is virtually limitless. By defining the problem in terms of linking disparate computers and running unknown software over unimaginable networks, the research task was more challenging than trying to link similar computers running on uniform networks, but ultimately the rewards were well worth the effort. The result is technology that allows us to create applications that operate globally without knowing anything about the systems on which they will run, the networks that will carry the data, or the systems and software used to store, process, and deliver the results.

Engineers and programmers needed more than 20 years to develop internetworking into a commercial technology, capable of supporting seamless interoperability within heterogeneous networks. As those technologies are developed into products, they enable the technology consumers to achieve their organizational goals by making information systems work for the organization, rather than against it.

The new internetworking technologies have obviously not developed all at once, but have broken upon the market sequentially, very much like waves. These waves have each brought profound changes in the way people think about working with computers, working with networks, and working with each other. The waves relevant to this discussion are

- The Internet wave
- The intranet wave

- The extranet wave

- The next waves

The Internet Wave

In the late 1980s most large U.S. colleges and universities had begun to offer their staff and students access to e-mail and other Internet applications. For the first time a large population of students had access to a far more powerful tool than most corporate computer users: global e-mail. By the early 90s the U.S. government started pulling out of the business of running the Internet, and corporations started to notice the potential benefits of getting connected.

The user population aware of the Internet was reaching a critical mass, but actually getting connected to the Internet and using standard applications like e-mail was still difficult. A few commercial software vendors were selling often inadequate (and usually hard to install and use) TCP/IP implementations, and most major hardware, networking, and operating system companies were still looking at TCP/IP as competition for their proprietary network solutions.

The World Wide Web was the fuse that ignited that critical mass of potential Internet users. The Web provided a single consistent user interface, giving access to text, graphics, and virtually any other kind of data file, as well as offering an easy-to-use front end for the more esoteric Internet applications, such as File Transfer Protocol (FTP) and Telnet (terminal emulation). The Web's graphical user interface replaced the Unix-like command syntax of most then-current Internet applications and made Internet resources accessible to a much wider audience.

The new products and companies doing Internet work washed over the marketplace in a virtual wave, as vendors like Microsoft, IBM, Novell, Apple, DEC, and others adjusted their product strategies to accommodate this new technology, some with more success than others.

Despite all the hype about the Internet as a new information resource, the World Wide Web was most useful as a resource for information *about* the Internet and the World Wide Web itself during its first few years—if you were interested in other topics, relatively little information was initially available.

NOTE An exception to this is the substantial amount of academic information which was already available via Gopher and Archie servers, although these sites too have since grown tremendously in quantity and coverage—and have largely been ported to HTML (Web) format now.

This situation is not surprising; most of the people connected to the Web at first were those involved in building and testing the technologies, and the most logical first application was to provide information about the Web on the Web.

The first important Internet application was global e-mail, enabling people to communicate easily and cheaply across any organizational boundary; the Web did not become a significant research resource for several more years, and it continues to be a mixed blessing.

NOTE   Unquestionably, the Web now provides a vital and immediate communication medium that carries news, technical information, and commerce, but at the same time, as an open medium, it carries gigabytes of paranoid rants and misinformed lecturing, lurid and lewd entertainment material, jokes, and pranks, and untold numbers of personal home pages with pictures of the owners' cats. Accessibility "for the masses" to the means of publication is a good thing for society, as long as accessibility does not threaten the medium itself.

The companies that succeeded best in this wave were companies that made the Internet accessible. Internet service providers (ISPs) quickly moved in to fill the void the U.S. government created when it stopped subsidizing access. Software publishers selling products that helped individuals get connected, like browser programs, did particularly well. Software publishers selling products that helped companies get their messages online, like Internet servers, did well, as did companies selling tools for creating, managing, and updating Internet content. Web site publishers able to deliver mass audiences, particularly those providing the important service of Web indexing, also did well through the sales of advertisements. Hardware vendors manufacturing the routers, gateways, and other networking devices necessary to keep the corporate Internet systems up and running also prospered.

The Internet wave was mostly about building an infrastructure for users of the new technology; the creative use of the technology to achieve business goals would have to wait until enough systems were online and enough people knew how to use them. As shown in Figure 20.3, Internet applications are built on a client/server model. The end user uses a piece of client software running on a local system, which connects to another piece of software, running on another computer connected to the Internet somewhere else.

FIGURE 20.3:

Hosts running the appropriate client software can connect across the Internet to hosts running the correct server software.

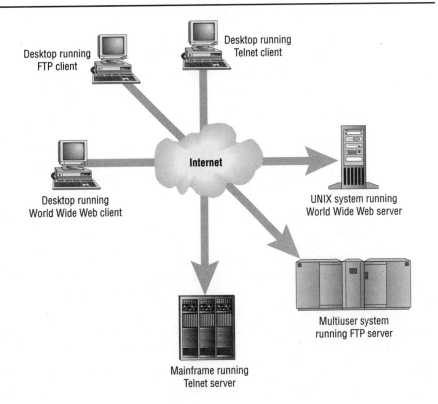

The key to the Internet, as well as part of the limitation of it, is an explicit, though virtual, link between the client and the server, which is never far from the end user's consciousness. The idea of using an Internet application like FTP or Telnet always involved the user's question, "What and where is the system to which I am going to be connecting?" An explicit interaction between the client software and the user *always* begins each session. The software asks the user, "What system do you want to connect with?" and the user responds with the name or address of the remote system. This interaction is only slightly less explicit with the World Wide Web, where the user can specify a home page (or accept the default home page) and use Web hyperlinks to navigate from system to system.

The Intranet Wave

The idea of building an organizational internetwork is not new: Research labs, universities, and corporations had been doing so for almost as long as the Internet and its predecessors had been around. The idea of having a single set of protocols for all networking, running on all computer platforms, is compelling. For example, a single set of protocols can:

- Eliminate (some) problems of software compatibility and data accessibility

- Cost less than proprietary commercial solutions offered by hardware and software vendors

- Accommodate growth, mergers, and downsizing easily

However, most corporations tended to avoid even considering alternatives to their proprietary LANs for data communication. The TCP/IP alternative may have been more elegant, robust, and appealing, but the costs of replacing their Novell NetWare, IBM SNA, and Digital DECnet networks did not seem to generate any appreciable benefits in terms of increasing network usability or deploying any significant productivity applications.

The World Wide Web changed the networking picture. Information professionals soon realized that putting the friendly Web front end on their corporate systems would make computing easier not only for the end users but also for the MIS and systems support staffs. A further benefit was the ease with which they could deploy multiplatform support for new systems. Any system capable of running a TCP/IP stack and a Web browser could access corporate resources over any internetwork—the Internet or an intranet.

Intranets are simply smaller versions of the Internet. They operate as self-contained internetworks, as shown in Figure 20.4. The Internet "cloud" is separated from the intranet cloud only by a gateway; network clouds simplify the representation of an internetwork, since they show that some kind of connectivity exists within the cloud, but the exact structure of the cloud is immaterial. An intranet may be linked to the Internet through a plain gateway, but it more often connects through a firewall to stem the undesired flow of data in or out of the organizational intranet.

Some of the same companies that benefited from the Internet wave also benefited from the intranet wave, particularly those selling the internal corporate infrastructure components, which turn out to be almost exactly the same as components of the Internet infrastructure: publishers of browser and server software and manufacturers of routers and gateways. Internet software and hardware companies soon realized that the market for Internet products was relatively limited in comparison to the market for internal organizational inter-networks. The most successful vendors continued to sell their products for use on the Internet but began to concentrate on positioning their products as intranet solutions. Witness the campaigns by Lotus, Microsoft, and Netscape to position their Web servers as corporate resources within intranets rather than as World Wide Web servers. At the same time, the leading browsers have been expanded from mere World Wide Web clients to include e-mail and network news clients, scheduling and calendaring features, and collaborative computing tools, all to lure in the corporate customer. Likewise, Digital's AltaVista software division developed an outstanding Web site search engine, which, when marketed strictly as a World Wide Web server tool also had a limited market. However, by expanding its scope as an intranet tool, and even as a desktop search tool, the AltaVista search engine has a considerably wider audience.

FIGURE 20.4:

An organizational intranet can be the functional equivalent of the Internet, only on a much smaller scale.

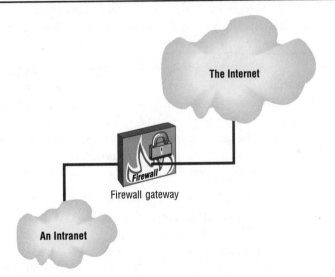

The Extranet Wave

The creation of the predecessors to the global Internet through the 1970s and early 1980s solved an important problem at the time: how to allow access to scarce resources from anywhere in the world. Mainframes and supercomputers were the scarce resources, and the applications were terminal emulation and file transfer. After all, a session with a supercomputer will always take place over some sort of terminal, so why not extend that application to make it accessible to anyone with any type of terminal—including a virtual terminal through an Internet connection?

As the 1990s brought ever–more-powerful systems to the average desktop, and as supercomputer manufacturers hit hard times, users were interested in access to a different kind of scarce resource. As high-performance computers became increasingly plentiful, the really important commodity became seamless and instant access to timely information.

Information stored on a legacy mainframe system connected to the Internet or to an intranet is accessible to users as long as they are able to run a terminal emulation program on their desktop systems, and as long as they have a valid user ID and password, *and* as long as they are able to use the legacy software running the mainframe application. Users needing this information may in fact have access to it, particularly if they are employees with workstations inside the corporate firewall. Unfortunately, employees working outside the firewall, corporate business partners, or customers are far less likely to have access to this information, even though it may be in the organization's interest to provide them with at least partial access to some of this information.

The current wave of internetworking technologies creates a level of abstraction that rises above the network and addresses the underlying information. The ability to assemble information and make it available to those who need it (and are authorized to have it) is the basic concept underlying the *extranet*. Defining applications and data to be independent of any underlying platform means that end users can access the information they need seamlessly, across any intervening networks, and in a manner appropriate to the platform they choose to use.

Figure 20.5 shows how the extranet overlays corporate boundaries and the Internet. Relevant information is pulled or pushed onto the individual desktop from whatever sources are required. Whether the data resides on legacy systems, on a corporate mainframe on the user's intranet, on some other organization's legacy system on a remote intranet, or on public or semipublic servers on the Internet, the extranet desktop aggregates the information and presents it in a useful form to the end user.

The companies that will profit most (and are already profiting) from this wave sell the software components that make extranets happen—in particular, tools for creating distributed-object frameworks for accessing organizational information, and the tools for securing private transmission channels that traverse open networks like the Internet. The first group includes makers of Java and other platform-independent software and software development tools: advanced e-mail, Web, and other types of Internet client and server software; middleware for accessing and publishing data from legacy systems; and sophisticated network management and administration tools. The second group includes hardware and software vendors building firewall systems, secure gateways and routers, and tools for encrypting and digitally signing the data, applets, and applications that are transmitted across open networks.

FIGURE 20.5:

An extranet can connect users of separate intranets using the Internet as a communications channel.

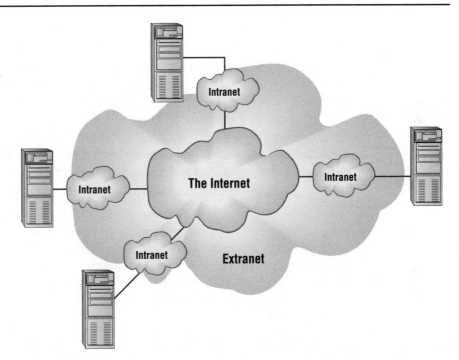

The Next Waves

One way to predict future internetworking waves is simply to look at the technologies and products that academic and industry researchers are working on today. These coming waves are best followed by perusing the latest issues of computer magazines, or the Web, but a brief mention of the next three obvious waves is in order here.

Ubiquitous High-Speed Internet Access

As of mid-1998, most Internet access is either through a corporate connection (for most organizations) or through a dial-up connection with a modem over POTS (plain old telephone service) lines. Many corporate links run over high-speed, high-bandwidth connections like ISDN, T1, and T3 telecommunications links, which support high-bandwidth applications like audio and video, although bottle-necks to Internet connectivity performance are still common. Dial-up links, on the other hand, are currently limited to a maximum modem transmission rate of 56Kbps, and users of typical modems are limited by modem speeds as low as 28.8Kbps or less. These links tend to be adequate for relatively low-bandwidth applications like e-mail and still-image graphical browsing but tend to be insuffi-cient to support audio, let alone video, transmissions.

Bandwidth is a term that describes the frequency characteristics of a data trans-mission medium; in practice, the higher the bandwidth of a data transmission medium, the more data can be transmitted over it in a given unit of time. If you imagine the network medium as a pipeline carrying physical bits of information, higher-bandwidth pipes would appear much fatter than lower-bandwidth pipes, which can carry less traffic. Links using the publicly switched telephone network (PSTN) are generally limited to a bandwidth of no greater than 56Kbps; 10BaseT Ethernet can support 10Mbps; gigabit Ethernets can support up to 1Gbps of data.

The bandwidth problem is this: how to get all those many megabytes of inter-esting audio or video to your desktop when your modem can only handle 28.8Kbps or even 56Kbps? Some solutions are starting to appear which address this problem: satellite downlinks (high download speed at moderate cost), ADSL (very high download speed and high upload speed, available in limited areas), and cable modems (very high download and in some cases also very high upload speeds).

Consumers and mobile workforces are only beginning to tap the potential of these higher-speed connections. In part, cable modems and *x*DSL technologies are only available in limited areas, and satellite hasn't caught on in mainstream usage (probably mostly due to it's needing a modem uplink connection). These types of access will spawn an entirely new class of Internet services, starting with audio and video conferencing and the delivery of other types of video and audio content.

Market Acceptance of Digital Commerce

Despite a promising start, the market is far from granting general acceptance to digital commerce. Transactions over the Internet are rapidly increasing, scores of companies are offering Internet commerce services, and specifications for secure electronic transactions have been drawn and agreed upon by the major players, including Visa and MasterCard. And yet, it will take some time before buying over the Internet is as widely accepted as buying through a catalog or over the telephone. Two of the most important reasons for the public's slow acceptance of Internet commerce are that, so far, too few consumers and too few full-service merchants are connected to the Internet.

Merely transferring a telephone- or mail-order operation to the Internet will not be sufficient to lure consumers away from known and trusted methods of shopping. As merchants add value to draw new customers, however, those customers will find that online shopping may be less expensive and more convenient than traditional trips to the mall.

Merchants who add the most value to the online shopping experience will tend to do best, as will companies selling merchant services and companies manufacturing products that can be delivered digitally.

HomeNet and BodyNet

Microprocessors continue to get faster, smaller, and cheaper. As this trend continues, it makes more sense to embed computers into what used to be very simple devices and to expand the capabilities of existing embedded microprocessors. *HomeNet* and *BodyNet* refer to networks that intelligently link intelligent devices used within the home and worn on the body, respectively.

Special-purpose computers have long been integrated into products as diverse as automobiles, toasters, telephones, and thermostats. Increasingly, people are carrying an array of electronic equipment wherever they go, including pagers, personal digital assistants, cellular phones, digital watches, and even global positioning systems. As all these computers gain new capabilities, the next logical step will be to link them together.

The current upgrade to the Internet Protocol, IPv6, expands the available address space so that there is enough space to assign a fairly large personal network to each person on Earth with plenty of room to spare for other networking purposes. Extending internetworking technologies to our homes and to our personal lives opens up many interesting possibilities, as well as many risks.

The Coming Wave: Extranets

Extranets are already being deployed, and some have been in use for years throughout the Internet and within private networks linking groups of business partners. The extranet wave should peak sometime in the next year or so as organizations quickly move to make their information accessible to those who need it, over whatever internetwork they choose for the task.

A Logical Extension of Internetworking Technology

Internetworks enable *seamless interoperability*, which simply means the ability to interoperate across networks, hardware platforms, and software architectures as if the communicating systems were directly connected. Seamless interoperability is closely tied to another function of internetworking, *platform independence*. The ability to connect any two systems seamlessly frees the end user—and the application developer—from dependence on any single platform.

The next logical step in this progression is to create a system in which information resources are *portable*. Separating information from the application with which it was created, and from the system on which it resides, extends the benefit of highly networked systems. With portable resources, the individual can enjoy rapid access to information from various sources, all controlled by the individual rather than by systems managers, application developers, and database administrators. The user can control what information is retrieved from where, how frequently, and how it is displayed and used.

To illustrate, consider one of the new features found on browsers released in the last year or so: the ability to drag and drop content resources that are published on a Web site onto the end user's desktop. In Microsoft's Internet Explorer 4.0, for example, a software component displays a stock ticker, with data drawn from an online stock quote service. The user can grab the control with the mouse pointer, drop it onto the desktop, and have stock quotes incorporated into his or her Windows desktop. The software component includes options for adding and removing stocks from the ticker, as well as for searching for a stock symbol. All the information functions are performed remotely through the content provider, but the user controls how the information is displayed.

Early demos of Netscape's Constellation technology included a similar function, showing how any Web service could be piped through the system and displayed on the desktop. For example, the user could request that as news stories about extranets came in from a news provider, the stories would be pulled down and made available in some form (on a pull-down menu, in a ticker, or somewhere on a live section of the desktop). A compelling example of this technology is a system that links the user's desktop to online package-tracking services, like that pioneered by Federal Express. The software component could take tracking numbers from the mail room over an organizational intranet, periodically check on their status with the delivery company over the Internet, and notify the end user of the delivery with an alarm.

The concept of an extranet is no newer than the concept of the intranet was in 1994. Intranets, in the form of organizational internetworks, have been common in research and educational circles since the late 1980s. However, corporations could not justify the large investment in upgrading existing LAN-oriented networks until a killer app appeared in the form of the World Wide Web.

An extranet extends the concept of the organizational network beyond the boundaries of the organization. Extranets imply an opening up of the organization's resources to those who need access from outside the firewall. Extranets also legitimize the use of resources external to the organization to support internal business objectives.

Extranet Application Architectures

The boundaries and topology of an extranet will vary from one instance to the next. (Extranet topologies are discussed in greater detail in Chapter 21.) However, an organization that attempts to implement an extranet topology without implementing an appropriate application architecture will not reap the complete benefits. Access to extranet systems without the proper distributed-object application tools limits the portability and utility of extranet resources. The next two sections discuss how extranets might appear as networks, ignoring (for the moment) the issues of application architecture.

External Intranets

On first hearing, the concept of an *external intranet* is very clearly an oxymoron. After all, *intra* means "internal," and the word *intranet* originally meant an "internal internetwork." *Intranets* are often defined as organizational TCP/IP internetworks that operate within a single organization, behind the organizational firewall, and that deny access to everyone outside the organization. The very idea that an intranet can be external to the sponsoring organization seems as ridiculous as saying that a television station that accepts paid advertisements is "noncommercial," or as illogical as starting a "private" club that is open to all.

A moment's thought will explain the paradox. Even though an intranet belongs to a single organization, the organization is not necessarily a monolithic entity. Large, modern organizations have any number of different departments, subsidiaries, joint ventures, and business partners. They operate out of huge skyscrapers, suburban office campuses, branch offices, and home offices; and their employees include top-level executives, bonded security officers, managers, professionals, temporary-agency clerks, consultants, and contractors.

Restricting access to an organizational intranet, in the traditional sense of allowing only employees of an organization working at the organization's physical plant, severely limits the intranet's usefulness. A corporate intranet that can be accessed from inside as well as from outside the confines of the corporation becomes much more useful to those who

- Travel on behalf of the organization
- Work from home or the road
- Consult for the organization
- Work from branch or satellite offices

Safely constructing an external intranet, one that permits access from outside the boundaries at which firewalls protect the internal intranet, can substantially increase the usefulness of the intranet. The simple example in Figure 20.6 shows one approach to the external intranet. Users at branch offices can access the corporate headquarters' intranet by tunneling encrypted data streams across the Internet, and users at headquarters can access branch-office intranets the same way. In other words, users connected to the headquarters' intranet or any of the branch offices' intranets have access to the same resources, whereas anyone else is denied access to these systems. Furthermore, while the traffic passes across the Internet, it is encrypted to protect against interception; in addition, it is digitally signed to protect against fraudulent transmissions. The result is sometimes referred to as a *virtual private network* (*VPN*) because it allows organizations to use public networks (i.e., the Internet) to carry private traffic securely.

Figure 20.7 shows how the users of this extranet view its structure. It is simply a big intranet connecting all the branches of the organization, as well as its headquarters. The effect is similar whenever an organization extends the means by which users outside the corporate firewall can access the organizational intranet.

FIGURE 20.6:

Encrypting data streams allows use of the Internet to create a virtual private network.

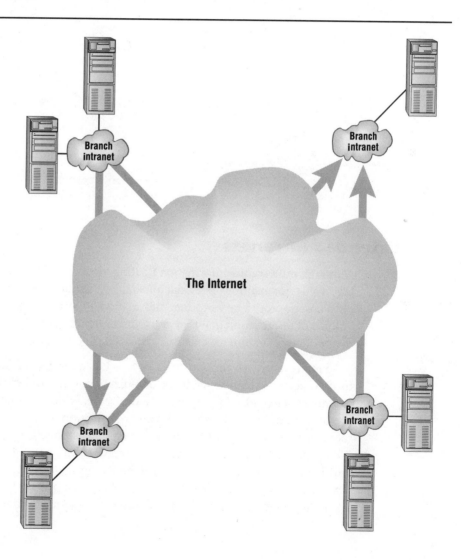

FIGURE 20.7:

One objective of the extranet is to make access to remote hosts (and data) transparent.

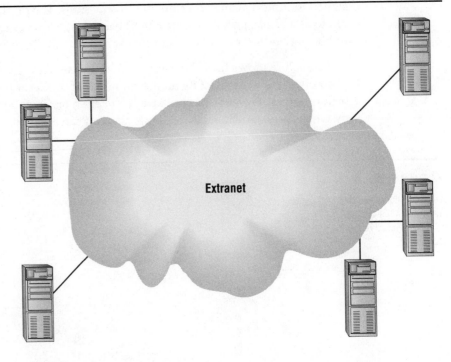

Extended Intranets

Although much of the information floating around inside any given organization is private—for example, personal information about employees, long-range strategic plans, or proprietary product information—most organizations have a sizable volume of information that they must disseminate publicly or semipublicly to their potential customers, existing customers, and trading partners.

Again, you can use various methods to achieve the goal of extending an intranet to allow access to those outside the organization. Here, we will outline two extreme examples of extended intranets. The first type, which has already been widely implemented, is usually set up by an organization that maintains a large customer service department to handle incoming customer queries. Federal Express, which built an interface between the corporate database of package deliveries and the World Wide Web, is an excellent example of this type of organization. Any customer seeking the status of a package can bypass the human customer service representative and directly send what amounts to a database query to the

Federal Express corporate database through the World Wide Web. A graphical representation of this approach appears in Figure 20.8.

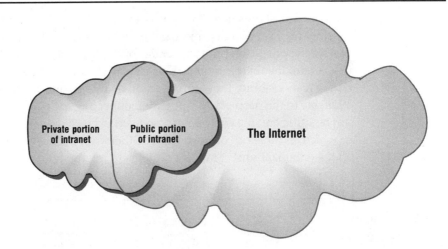

Private portion of intranet   Public portion of intranet   The Internet

For the purposes of package tracking, virtually anyone connected to the Internet has the potential of connecting to this organization's extended intranet and accessing a subset of the data contained in the organization's databases. The rest of the organizational database, which may very well contain proprietary information such as customer lists and billing information, remains inside the corporate intranet.

Some critics dismiss this type of extranet as simply an extension of the function of the Internet and the use of simple tools that give companies a mechanism for publishing information stored in legacy systems. However, as user applications become more sophisticated, this type of service becomes much more interesting. For instance, application software capable of using shipping information retrieved from the delivery companies' extranets could be valuable to any company whose business depends on shipping goods promptly.

Although this approach is obviously useful for companies with broad customer bases, at the other extreme are companies that do business with a handful of business partners. The larger the amount of money involved in any particular sale, the more likely that a high level of communication between the vendor and the customer is necessary. For example, the Air Force doesn't just call up Ace Aircraft Company, order 200 fighter jets, and give a credit card number—a huge amount of interaction occurs as the buyer and seller agree on specifications and prices for the jets, as the manufacturer designs and builds the planes, and as the finished goods are delivered and serviced.

Figure 20.9 shows how this type of extranet might look for three firms working together on a very large project. All three firms share the same objective of completing the project on time and under budget, which justifies the possible security risks of linking their intranets. This risk can be minimized by each organization taking responsibility for securing its own systems and making shared resources available to the partners. Simply interconnecting the companies' intranets will not be sufficient; the companies also need to create a higher-level data abstraction to which all three can communicate. Otherwise, the astronomical costs of getting all the organizations' computer systems to interoperate could easily exceed any savings.

FIGURE 20.9:

Connecting private intranets, with no external connectivity, creates a private extranet.

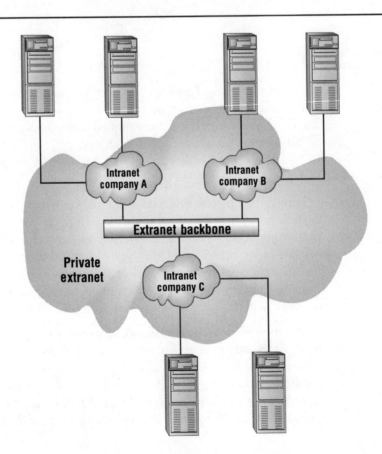

Organizations whose information is extremely valuable, or vulnerable to attack, may consider creating this type of extranet. Electronic Data Interchange (EDI) companies have been running value-added networks (VANs) for some time with a similar architecture, though with much greater focus. Banks, electronic merchants, brokers, and other financial institutions, as well as defense contractors, government units, and law enforcement agencies, might consider this approach.

What Exactly Is an Extranet?

As this discussion makes clear, an extranet, whether it is an extended intranet, an external intranet, or something else, goes beyond conventional internetworking as deployed in the Internet or on organizational intranets. At the moment, we do not have a single, universally accepted definition of exactly what differentiates an extranet from other types of internetworks.

Extranets must provide information in a form that any extranet-connected system can transparently use. This requirement means taking interoperability to a higher level than TCP/IP provides (see the Note on the following page). The degree to which an application can support interactions with other applications varies with its degree of connectivity:

- A system that is not connected to a network at all may support interaction only between applications running on the same system.

- A system connected to a LAN can access services running on other systems connected to the same LAN as long as they are all using the same (or compatible) LAN software.

- A system connected to the Internet can interoperate, through its client software, with any other system connected to the Internet through its counterpart server software.

The extranet usually adds one more layer of abstraction on top of the whole stew, by making *objects*—that is, individual bits of function connected with information—accessible to other authorized objects living anywhere else on the network.

NOTE   The TCP/IP protocols (described in more detail in Chapter 3) provide a set of rules that enable any kind of computer connected to any kind of network to interoperate with any other kind of computer connected to any other kind of network—as long as some level of connectivity exists between the two networks. *Interoperability* means that each system can exchange data and requests for data without having to know anything about the other system or the networks through which they are both connected.

Although the concepts of object-oriented systems are not new, their application to internetworking is. A detailed discussion of objects, Object Request Brokers (ORBs), and distributed objects is beyond the scope of this book, but these elements are integral to any discussion of extranetworking. The next section provides a brief introduction to these concepts.

Extranets and Distributed Objects

Very simply, objects combine function with data in a way that allows other objects to use them. This level of interoperability goes well beyond the interoperability available with a browser interface to a legacy database. For example, you can use a distributed-object architecture to embed object front-end access to legacy systems into a Web page—making the data living in those systems accessible to any authorized user (person, program, or object). Another feature of some object architectures is that the objects can be self-describing. In addition, the interaction between objects does not necessarily have to be explicitly spelled out ahead of time but can depend on the contents of the interacting objects.

Consequently, client front-end software can navigate through a network searching for objects that meet a user's criteria, and it can present the results in the desired format. In comparison, when using intranets or the Internet, the end user must have the correct client for the remote resource. Even when legacy system resources are available through a GUI or Web browser front end, the information remains stored in a single system; an object architecture enables a single front end to accumulate information from various resources and present it as a unified result.

The success of TCP/IP as an internetworking standard has much to do with its global acceptance as a nonproprietary standard. Without this acceptance, TCP/IP would be just another set of protocols that might have gained limited implementation in certain organizations or industries—and a proprietary solution almost certainly would not have achieved the same degree of success in the market. A similar drive to a single set of standards for distributed objects is occurring now. With so many sets of standards, organizations are unwilling to commit to any one for fear of committing to the wrong one. However, as of 1998 the options appear to have been narrowed down to two: Microsoft versus the rest of the world, with Microsoft's solutions increasingly being put forward as another, more attractive (according to Microsoft) set of open standards.

Microsoft's Object Linking and Embedding (OLE), which is built on the Common Object Model (COM) and Distributed Common Object Model (DCOM), is one model that Microsoft (for obvious reasons) would very much like to become the object architecture of choice, as it will encourage the use of Microsoft products. The alternative is being developed by the Object Management Group (OMG), a project in which more than 700 organizations are participating. The result is called the *Common Object Request Broker Architecture* (*CORBA*), and it has been revised and expanded to provide cross-platform (and cross-object architecture) interoperability with the Internet Inter-ORB Protocol (IIOP).

Many other companies have joined Netscape Communications in backing CORBA as the appropriate architecture for the future of internetworking. Although the so-called browser war, which started between Netscape and Microsoft in 1996, has captured the lion's share of media attention, the battle for the extranet object architecture is significantly more vital to these two companies, as well as to anyone interested in the future direction of internetworking.

Although a single, universally supported object architecture is the ideal, it does appear that for now we will have to deal with two: Microsoft's OLE/COM/DCOM and OMG's CORBA/IIOP.

Extending Internetworking Technologies

Extranets are more than merely extended intranets, or external intranets. Essentially, they provide a superset of the functions provided by standard TCP/IP internetworking. TCP/IP internetworks can be characterized as seamlessly interoperable and platform independent; extranets add resource portability through object architecture. The result is to further the goal of submerging the network into the background while making the information resources on the network even more accessible.

Seamless Interoperability

In TCP/IP internetworks, any connected device running a protocol-compliant client program can use the services of any other connected device running a protocol-compliant server. The only requirement is that both client and server conform to the same protocol. Neither device needs to know anything about the other except for TCP/IP addressing information. The brand of TCP/IP software, hardware platform, or local area network medium is irrelevant. Likewise, neither device needs to have any information about where the other is on the internetwork, what routers lie between the devices, or what route the actual data takes to arrive at its destination.

Seamless interoperability made it possible to create applications like the World Wide Web, which simplify the task of accessing remote (and separated) internetworked resources through a single client. Extranets can extend this seamless interoperability with object architecture. Objects can interact in predefined ways to gather information or to complete transactions; they can also interact in unexpected ways to complete relatively complex tasks. Objects can be published within an extranet for public or private consumption; customers may pay for their use, or publishers may make them available at no cost. In any case the ultimate use to which the objects may be put cannot be predicted or predefined, but is ultimately limited only by the imagination and ingenuity of the user.

Platform Independence

That any computer running TCP/IP can interoperate with any other computer running TCP/IP may not seem so miraculous anymore, particularly if you have forgotten (or never had to deal with) the many competing and totally incompatible computer systems vendors produced in an effort to differentiate their systems and lock corporate customers into their unique architectures. The resulting Babel of operating systems (*and* data representation schemes) meant that in the 1980s the desks of some information workers held as many as four CRTs, each with its own special cable: a VT-100 terminal connected to a serial cable, next to an IBM mainframe terminal hooked up to a terminal server, next to an Intel-processor PC on the office LAN, and possibly even a Macintosh connected to an AppleTalk wire for good measure.

A TCP/IP intranet consolidates all those monitors and cables, since a single workstation can be used to connect to all resources. Although eliminating extra hardware and cabling is a good thing, the true benefit of internetworking goes well beyond hardware savings. All those separate systems and terminals prevent organizations from making the best use of their information and computing resources. Information that is stored on the mainframe, and put into a mainframe file by a mainframe application using the mainframe EBCDIC character set, is not accessible to anyone not using the mainframe. Even if there were a simple way for the PC and the mainframe to exchange files, the file format, character set, and application prevent the PC from using the mainframe file for any useful purpose.

TCP/IP protocols eliminate these platform incompatibilities and allow a single workstation to act as a terminal to all remote hosts. The same workstation can also download data transparently from remote hosts, or upload data to those hosts, without having to worry about how the remote host stores its data.

This platform independence supports seamless interoperability in TCP/IP networks. Extranets extend the concept of platform independence to the data itself, not just the representation of the data. Data living within an object is no longer tied to some particular application on some particular host, but can now be distributed to any other connected host independent of the software, hardware, and network platform.

Solving Real-World Problems

Connectivity for the sake of connectivity is not a sufficient reason to allocate the time, money, and resources necessary to upgrade a corporate LAN system to an intranet. The return on investment must be greater than the savings from shared hardware; in fact, the potential return from these upgrades is vast and extends to many areas. For example, certain internal documents, such as human resources handbooks, telephone directories, and operating instructions, can be expensive to publish as hard-copy publications. They must also be continually, and expensively, updated. Using the organizational intranet to publish these documents may result in an immediate and significant cost savings, often large enough to justify the cost of the entire exercise.

Less concrete savings, such as productivity gains, often follow these initial savings when an intranet is installed. Using e-mail and workgroup applications to replace paper mail and decades-old work flows can result in incredible increases in productivity as digital communications can expedite processes that were previously bound by lengthy paper delivery times. Formal intranet work-flow systems and tighter integration with legacy systems eventually result in platform-independent legacy system data entry and retrieval.

The speed with which businesses have embraced intranets is no less astonishing than the value those intranets bring. Extranets will likely be embraced at least as quickly, as businesses discover that this technology will not only reduce costs but also generate additional revenue.

Extending Intranet Functionality with Extranets

As the concept of the extranet matures, extranets will be more easily differentiated from intranets, but for now, an extranet will look very much like an extended, expanded, or external intranet. Many of the examples of extranets may appear to be nothing more than intranets whose boundaries have been extended or Internet Web sites whose functions have been expanded, but as distributed objects are increasingly deployed to solve business problems, extranets will be more easily identified as an entirely different animal.

NOTE Of course, the fact that extranets are difficult for users to distinguish from intranets points to another benefit: The standardization of technologies and interfaces allows greater functionality over greater distances, but without requiring additional user training. Admittedly, the distinction between extranets and more local types of networks is primarily relevant to technical people and to those needing to cost-justify the added expenses involved. For others, extranets will continue to be easily confused with intranets.

An intranet's function, in the broadest terms possible, is to enable information resource sharing within an organization. As the boundary of the intranet is stretched to accommodate the extranet, the borders at which the organization is defined are stretched by the expanded function of the extranet: to enable information resource sharing within the organization and within the groups of parties interacting with the organization. In its simplest form, an extranet simply extends intranet access outside the confines of the organization. Opening an intranet resource to customers, suppliers, or business partners need not require any technological changes in the intranet.

Another important application of the extranet is to replace costly and inefficient dedicated and dial-up connections and to take advantage of the Internet to carry intranet traffic securely and efficiently. Replacing these links with less expensive Internet connections not only saves money but also simplifies matters for end users who no longer need to use different sets of tools for intranet and Internet tasks.

Distributed objects will be one of the distinguishing marks of the mature extranet because they will make possible applications like these:

- Procurement departments will be able to deploy internal catalogs of office products, extracting product descriptions, illustrations, specifications, and pricing from a range of suppliers' databases—dynamically displaying current stock levels, shipping options, and availability, and even automatically replacing primary approved products with secondary suppliers' products depending on availability.

- Engineering firms will be able to process designs and modifications in minutes or hours instead of days or weeks, as design work is submitted electronically to approvers, and approvals (or requests for modifications) can be processed immediately.

- Manufacturers can automate ordering procedures through suppliers, linking them together through warehouse and workshop inventory systems.

- Individuals will be able to reliably conduct complicated, conditional transactions with Internet merchants. Travelers may be able to specify sets of alternative-yet-dependent itinerary options, for example, booking airline tickets, rental cars, and overnight accommodations in a single step.

Extranets will extend intranet functionality in two directions:

- Expanding the borders of the intranet
- Expanding the possibilities of what may be done with information resources

Expanding borders means allowing public or semipublic access to an intranet resource through the Internet; it can also mean simply linking one intranet to another intranet, or building a private network of intranets. With distributed-object technologies running across extranets, the functional possibilities just explode, because all sorts of applications that were formerly difficult to program (or even conceive of) become much easier, and quite practical to implement. For example, complicated transactions requiring access to information on legacy databases can be implemented more easily when existing, proven components can be readily adapted to interface with those databases. Extranets *can* be deployed without object technologies, but extranet applications will be much easier to create and maintain using objects rather than using more traditional client/server programming techniques.

Building Business Relationships with Extranets

An intranet, by definition, is strictly about and within the organization. If it is connected to the Internet at all, it is guarded by a firewall gateway to keep intruders outside and keep organizational inmates inside. An intranet may cut costs and improve efficiency, but it has no direct effect on an organization's customers, suppliers, or partners. Although intranets do link individuals, groups, and units within the organization and help foster relationships among those entities, all the relationships remain entirely within the organization.

Extranets, on the other hand, are intended to foster relationships between organizations, as well as between the organization and its customers, suppliers, and partners. By opening up organizations to other organizations and individuals, extranets add value for their users. This corporate *glasnost* requires careful implementation to avoid security problems, but new extranet risks are unlikely to overtake the disgruntled or greedy employee as a source of security breach.

Fostering Internet Commerce with Extranets

The most popular type of business relationship is the one between buyer and seller. Any mechanism that encourages or enhances relationships with businesses cannot fail to foster commerce. Extranets, with distributed objects, will certainly propel Internet commerce from a cumbersome novelty to a mainstream market channel. Even though the Secure Electronic Transaction (SET) specification should bring some order to a disorderly world of digital commerce, it is only the first step toward making Internet commerce a viable way to do business.

Although SET offers a mechanism by which credit (and charge and debit) card transactions can be consummated across the Internet, many other steps occur in the process of making a sale. Before the sale is completed, the buyer and seller may need to negotiate pricing, specifications, delivery, and options; after the sale is complete, the buyer and seller must continue their relationship as products are assembled, delivered, and serviced—and payment settlement is completed. Extranets will provide not only the infrastructure upon which buyers and sellers can transact their business but also a framework upon which complex financial transactions can be consummated to the satisfaction of all concerned parties.

Adding Value with Extranets

Just as some businesses are more successful than others at building sales through catalogs, direct mail, telemarketing, or retail outlets, some businesses have been more successful than others at using the Internet to achieve their business goals. Businesses whose Web sites are little more than brochure servers don't get the full benefit of their connectivity investment. On the other hand, businesses whose Web sites provide customers with enough information about their products to make a buying decision, in an attractive and easy-to-use format, and who enable online transactions, are more likely to see a payoff. However, merely turning a Web site into an order server in most cases provides neither competitive advantages to the merchant nor added value to the consumer.

Creating a Web site that simply replicates a more standard buying process— for example, duplicating a catalog purchase experience—offers the buyer no compelling reason to switch. In fact, online catalog shopping is often a less-than-satisfactory experience when bandwidth to download product images is at a premium or when product colors are poorly reproduced on the consumer's monitor. Internet merchants who use the Internet to add value, however, can more easily attract new customers—for example, merchants who not only accept orders 24 hours a day, seven days a week, but also process and ship all orders immediately, rather than waiting for the next business day (as some Internet merchants do); merchants who provide a single source for complete specialty product lines; and merchants who offer digital delivery of their software or other digital products.

Extranets will offer even more opportunities for sellers to add value for their customers. One very early example is the Federal Express Internet package-tracking page described earlier in this chapter. As these extranets start deploying distributed-object technologies, and the customer's organization integrates desktop information systems with internal shipping systems and with the delivery of company extranets, the process of package and order tracking will be further streamlined and simplified. End users may even opt to be notified at their desktops as soon as their package arrives.

Summary

In this chapter, we've attempted to give a clear picture of what extranets are, despite the fact that they take many forms, and really have yet to be assigned a solid and universally accepted definition. We started by looking at the development of networks, the Internet, and intranets, and how by extending the concept further we get extranets. Whereas intranets seek to leverage Internet technology to make information more accessible to people throughout an entire organization, extranets seek to also make some information accessible outside the organization, to other individuals and organizations who share some kind of commercial or collaborative relationship and whose effectiveness and helpfulness would be enhanced by more timely or convenient access to the information.

Next, the discussion moved to external intranets, which enable access to an intranet outside the physical confines of that intranet, and extended intranets, which export some of the intranet's information or functionality to the public or to a group of users outside the intranet. These are two types of extranets, although an extranet may actually be a mixture of both of these, or may take other forms.

The extranet "wave" hasn't crested yet, even as new technology waves prepare to hurtle toward us. In the next few years, ubiquitous and very high-speed inter-network access will qualitatively change the types of information that are sent across networks, as well as the range of things networks are used for. Standards for transacting online commerce and the ever-increasing role of networked object programming technology will also have an impact on how networks are used. Extranets are about finding new ways of accomplishing more by making more information available to more people, in increasingly useful formats.

In the next chapter, we'll look at specific issues that must be addressed for the successful planning and implementation of extranets.

CHAPTER

TWENTY-ONE

Extranet Infrastructure

- The Internet 2 project as an example

- Extranet topology options

- Private extranets

- Open extranets

- Hybrid extranets

- Virtual private networks

- Extranet design structures

All networks require some sort of infrastructure across which data flows. Infrastructure issues for internal networks are discussed throughout this book, yet extranets can have particularly interesting (that is, complicated) infrastructures because they can span so many different boundaries. Extranet topologies may be modeled on traditional internetworking structures, or they may cross and overlap intranet and Internet boundaries. Finally, even though we have only a handful of basic models upon which to build extranets, each specific implementation will be different in some way from every other extranet.

This chapter introduces basic extranet *topologies,* or the forms extranets take as they relate to existing internal and external networks. Among the basic building blocks that designers use to build extranets are backbones and virtual private networks (VPNs); neither is a prerequisite, and both are discussed in this chapter. Firewall gateways are also important extranet components; they are discussed below and in Chapter 28.

Extranets have many other physical components, such as routers and servers, but these are well documented in the sections covering intranet and Internet implementation issues, and their use does not change significantly when deployed in extranets or in other internetworks. Likewise, although this chapter includes a brief survey of backbone design, the specific technical details are best documented in data networking design texts. One good introduction is Darren Spohn's *Data Network Design, 2nd edition* (McGraw-Hill, 1997).

Although every extranet does not require a private backbone, organizations seeking some degree of security from external attack will at least consider this approach. This chapter discusses how to approach the task of building a private backbone for an extranet linking two or more organizations' intranets. Extranet backbone design is discussed in the context of backbone topologies used for internetworks designed for local, regional, and national internetworks.

Virtual private networks can function as supplements to or replacements for extranets. This chapter introduces virtual private networks, and it explains what they are, how they work, and how they are built.

Interorganizational Internetworking

From a networking perspective, extranets can be considered *interorganizational internetworks*. Consequently, extranet designers and administrators can draw on their experience working with other types of internetworks: intranets and the Internet. Seen in this light, designing and implementing an extranet should be no more (and no less) difficult than building an intranet. In fact, however, extranets require considerable attention to issues like security and sharing network administration duties across organizational boundaries.

A Very Big Extranet

To get an idea of what is involved in building an interorganizational internetwork, consider the Internet 2 project. In 1996 representatives of 40 educational institutions announced this project: to create a high-performance internetwork linking universities and related research organizations. As of mid-1998 the total count reached over 120 charter member institutions (primarily universities), and more than 30 partner and affiliate member organizations.

Their objective is to create a high-performance, broadband internetwork to link their organizations and to foster the use of applications suited to such networks. For example:

- Multimedia, multicasting applications required for distance learning and remote classroom applications

- Virtual access to national laboratories and supercomputing facilities

- Access to large bodies of simulation or observed data of the type required for astronomical, geophysical, or meteorological research

- Remote medical consultations and diagnoses for research purposes

- Access to large volumes of financial and commercial transactions for real-time economics analysis

The Internet 2 project includes the following design specifications:

- Support for high-bandwidth networking applications

- Use of IP version 6 (but with backward compatibility to IP version 4)

- A high degree of interoperability by providing access to a wide range of client devices

More to the point, Internet 2 will be interoperable with the existing Internet, use object brokering services and software components to foster interoperability across a large population of users, and connect as many as 100 or more educational and related organizations from its start.

NOTE   Although its purpose is to provide faster, more reliable internetworking to its members, Internet 2 is not intended as a replacement for the Internet. Member institutions will still use Internet access, but Internet 2 services will supplement the Internet applications already in use. Internet 2 applications will go beyond those possible on the Internet, supporting applications like remote learning and helping develop new applications that require high bandwidth and reliability, such as distance medicine.

In other words, the Internet 2 project is very much a model for extranet designers. Internet 2 is being designed to support a largely new set of applications to be deployed within the research community. However, the intention is not to build a computer science research test bed (as was the original Internet for much of its existence), but to develop a practical tool for conducting research in a wide range of fields. In other words, the Internet 2 is a production extranet.

NOTE   The Internet 2 project maintains a Web site at www.internet2.edu/. Full details of the project, as well as the latest news about the project, are published here.

The rest of this section will refer to some aspects of this project as it relates to the development of more modest extranets.

Design Principles

In the Internet 2 project preliminary engineering report, the following principles were presented as having come out of the Engineering Working Group's initial deliberations:

- Use available, well-supported, and reliable technologies instead of creating new ones, wherever possible.

- Use open standards instead of proprietary solutions and generally maintain the network as openly as possible. This principle includes sharing performance information with other members.

- Build the network as reliably as possible through redundancy. The objective is to avoid any single point of failure that might result from reliance on any single service provider, hardware manufacturer, or software publisher by building in backup routes and using alternative vendors to the greatest extent possible.

- Build the basic network functions (as defined in the project specifications) before adding more-advanced functions. The project is sufficiently complex that it would be counterproductive to start adding advanced new features before implementing the base set of features.

- Become a production network, not an experimental research test bed. Although technical innovation may be impossible to avoid, the network is an engineering project, not a computer science project.

- Complement, not compete against, commercial networks. Any Internet 2 services provided by, for example, commercial Internet service providers must remain separate from access to commercial networks like the Internet.

These principles are well worth following for almost any networking project, but particularly when planning a project that will affect more than 100 very large participating organizations. Extranet designers would be well served by at least considering these principles when formulating their guidelines for new extranets.

Linking Organizations

Building Internet 2 requires the cooperation of many organizations. For the Internet 2 project, charter members were required to make commitments that included, but were not limited to, financial support of the project. According to the Internet 2 project Web page, estimates of the cost for member institutions could be as high as $500,000 per year for the first few years of the project (although some of that cost may be covered by existing budgets for networking), with a commitment of as much as $25,000 per year to cover administrative and support expenses.

However, participation goes beyond a simple economic commitment. Charter members must also commit to these additional tasks:

- Providing executive-level support to the project management effort

- Helping to build application-development and network-services project teams to support the Internet 2 project

- Implementing end-to-end broadband Internet access so that project developers can build, test, and use Internet 2 applications

The Internet 2 project is huge and requires significant allocation of resources. In the tradition of Internet development, much of this activity is delegated to member organizations through a steering committee. The project has working groups for applications development and for engineering, and member organizations can participate in various project meetings, depending on membership level.

An Overview of Internet 2 Architecture

As of the project's start in 1997, the Internet 2 architecture looked something like what is shown in Figure 21.1. A connectivity cloud provided some yet-to-be-determined high-speed, high-bandwidth data communication service. Access to the connectivity cloud is through "gigapops" (gigabit-capacity points of presence) that serve Internet 2 members within the same region. Each member organization installs a high-speed circuit to link itself to the local gigapop, and the gigapops provide access to other member organizations using other gigapops across the connectivity cloud.

If the architecture for this huge project appears to be a bit vague, that impression is deliberate. Rather than attempt to specify all the details before determining the best architecture, technology, data communication media, and protocols, the Internet 2 planners have begun instead by specifying the objectives of their project in the most basic and general terms of functionality. By first specifying the network's functions, the designers will be able to make the best choices for implementation technologies. This approach avoids the problem of choosing technologies first and later finding that the project is tied to an inappropriate design that will be incapable of achieving the project's goals.

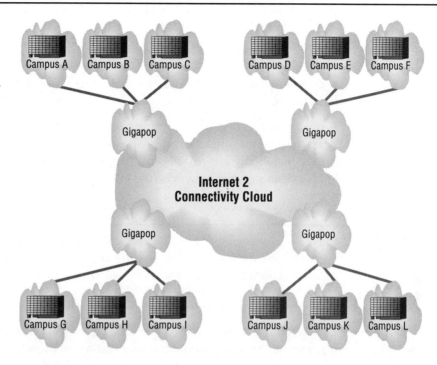

FIGURE 21.1:

The Internet 2 project architecture uses high-speed, high-bandwidth gigapops to link campuses to a connectivity cloud.

Extranet Topology Options

Building any kind of network requires making many decisions that will affect the network topology: what kind of LAN medium to use (Ethernet or Token Ring; 10Mbps or 100Mbps Ethernet), and how to connect those LANs (with repeaters, bridges, routers, simple backbone, or collapsed backbone). In practice, these decisions are rarely irrevocable and often must be revised from time to time as needs change: departments expand or contract, organizations merge or spin off subsidiaries.

Moving across a continuum of extranet implementations produces the following general types of extranets in the space between private and public:

- Private extranet, for members only

- Hybrid extranet, using the public extranet as a channel for private data

- Extranet service provider, offering customer organizations extranet services over their own infrastructure

- Public extranet, open to all users

The details of extranet implementation are much like the details of other internetworks.

However, two very different approaches to the overall extranet structure are of interest to us here. As mentioned in Chapter 20, an extranet can be entirely private, completely disconnected from any other networks. A public extranet, on the other hand, uses public networks (the Internet) and provides resource access to any user.

NOTE   The Internet 2 project can be considered a *private extranet* (of a sort). Even though its users will probably be able to access it from the Internet, and access the Internet through it, the project is an entirely separate network entity that is open to its members and to authorized users only.

Between these two extremes is an entire rainbow of intermediate options, all with more or less restrictive policies depending on the needs of the sponsoring organizations.

Another option, the *hybrid extranet*, is based on a virtual private network, which is a network that uses encrypted channels across a public network to connect physically separated parts of an extranet.

One last option for organizations wishing to create extranets, but without the resources or expertise to do so, is to purchase extranetworking services from a network service provider. These vendors may be networking providers, with extensive private data communications networks of their own, who are able to sell their excess bandwidth to other organizations. Network service providers may also operate as consultants, setting up leased lines to create a private extranet for each client and using their own staff to maintain and manage all their clients' extranets.

The Private Extranet

Figure 21.2 shows a typical private extranet. Its structure resembles the structure of the Internet: a central cloud of connectivity across which users within connected organizations can communicate. A private extranet and the Internet are functionally identical: Both link organizations across heterogeneous data communications networks using open networking protocols.

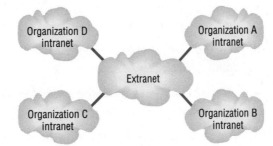

The primary difference between a private extranet and the Internet is a matter of scale and exclusivity. The private extranet links member organizations; for example, the educational and research member organizations of the Internet 2 project. On the other hand, the Internet is a global and inclusive network. Most organizations belonging to a private extranet will likely have some link to the Internet. However, the Venn diagram in Figure 21.3 shows that Internet connectivity is not a prerequisite for private extranet connectivity. Although most organizations either are connected or are planning to connect to the Internet, those organizations that have been reticent to date may prefer to join private extranets to meet their interorganizational data communications needs.

FIGURE 21.3:

Many, but not all, organizations connected to a private extranet will also be connected to the Internet.

All organizations connected to the Internet

All organizations connected to a private extranet

Why Build a Private Extranet?

Building a closed-system, private extranet provides the following advantages to the participants:

- Greater protection from unauthorized uses of the extranet because there is no "public entrance" (via the Internet, for example) to the private extranet

- Greater control over performance variables, including end-to-end performance, throughput, and latency

- Greater confidence in sharing sensitive or proprietary information with business partners across a nonpublic network

- Improved protection against denial-of-service attacks that can be relatively easy to perpetrate when a network or system is exposed to the Internet or other public networks

The number of organizations that share the need for the same or similar applications limits the size of the private extranet.

WARNING   As the number of organizations sharing a private extranet increases, the expectation of security implicit in keeping the network private must decrease.

The Internet 2 extranet brings together a relatively large number of organizations sharing the same goals for educational applications, but all participants will continue to maintain their own security programs. There is little or no expectation that Internet 2 will be a totally private and inaccessible network. The potential for vastly improved network performance is the driving force behind the project.

NOTE   A word of warning to organizations considering buying extranet services from Internet service providers. As with all products and services, things change (and change rapidly) in the world of internetworking, so you must be very much aware of what service you are buying and monitor that service closely for any changes. AT&T's Worldnet Intranet Connect Service (AWICS) was originally designed to be a "secure" Internet for company-to-company communications. However, that goal has since mutated somewhat, and a number of subscribers were surprised to learn that AT&T connected the Internet to the AWICS cloud with no provision for security, other than that which the subscriber may (or may not) already have in place.

Implementing a Private Extranet

The Internet 2 project is worth examining as an example of how to approach the creation of any extranet, but particularly an extranet providing services only to member organizations. The high cost in money, networking resources, and network personnel of such an endeavor makes it imperative for all participants to believe that they are getting their money's worth. Building an advisory committee with representatives from all member organizations, or at least a representative sampling for larger extranets, is an excellent first step. Likewise, the sponsor must get full corporate support for this type of project from all participants, because a long-term, infrastructure-building project could easily be viewed as dispensable unless it has high-level backing.

Disadvantages of the Private Extranet

Although private extranets provide the potential for great control over the performance characteristics of the network, this advantage comes at a price: Members of the extranet must build—and pay for—this control. Designing, provisioning, deploying, and managing a high-performance, high-traffic extranet backbone can be dizzyingly expensive. Without a strong organizational resolve to participate, the private extranet is unlikely to be a good option for most extranets.

Another potential drawback for some organizations is that membership in a private extranet may bind the organization to a group from which it can be difficult to extricate itself. This shortcoming will be particularly true for companies in fast-moving industries where today's business partner may be tomorrow's competitor.

The Open Extranet

As the number of organizations and individuals connected to the Internet continues to grow, so does the incentive for organizations wishing to link to many other entities to create an open extranet. You might, for example, wish to build a private telecommunications network, if you and your associates desired to maintain complete control over who can use the network, how they can use it, how it works, and who pays for it—this is much like building a private extranet. On the other hand, if you prefer to talk to anyone, even people you don't know—and allow them to contact you—then you would call your local telephone company and have them connect you to the global telecommunication network.

The same goes for extranets: If you prefer to be exclusive and need to retain control, you would build a private extranet. If you prefer to be as inclusive as possible and don't mind using public networks, you would build an *open extranet*. Figure 21.4 shows how the open extranet works. The open extranet itself is simply an intranet (offering some form of a distributed application, of course) that has been connected to the Internet. (It may or may not have a firewall gateway, even though firewall gateways are strongly recommended for all networks connected to the Internet.) Any client that is connected to the Internet, whether directly (through a dial-up link, for example) or indirectly (through an intranet connected to the Internet by a firewall gateway, for example), is able to access extranet resources.

FIGURE 21.4:

Open extranets use open networks like the Internet as a communication medium to link users and extranet resources.

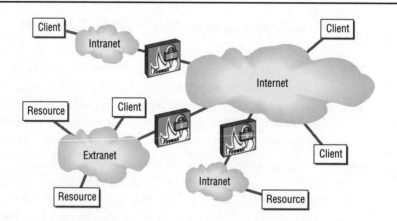

Another feature of an open extranet is that clients and resources connected to it may use resources outside the boundaries of the designated extranet; for example, a client connected to the extranet might use resources resident on an intranet, another extranet, or the Internet. Furthermore, resources connected to the extranet may point to other resources at other organizations or on other networks.

The diagram in Figure 21.5 shows that open extranets tend to be inclusive rather than exclusive. Almost all organizations that are connected to the Internet could potentially connect to an open extranet. Exceptions might be those that do not permit use of extranet applications across a firewall, those that do not permit use of external applications at all, and those that exclude access to the networks or hosts on which the extranet resources are stored. (Also see Chapter 28 for more information about how firewalls can exclude access in these ways.) For the most part, the open extranet is open to all users.

FIGURE 21.5:

All open extranet users will be connected to the Internet, and almost all users connected to the Internet at least have the potential to connect to an open extranet.

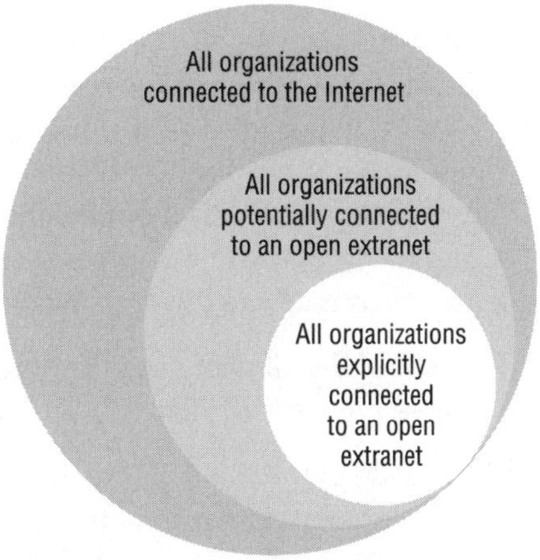

All organizations connected to the Internet

All organizations potentially connected to an open extranet

All organizations explicitly connected to an open extranet

Extranet Technology on the Internet

One of the most important applications of extranet technologies is Internet commerce. By definition (at least, when it is done correctly), Internet commerce invites outsiders into an organization's network resources to make modifications: preferably, to cause an order system to generate fulfillment orders and an accounting system to note an increase in income due to a sale.

Implementation of an extranet largely addresses the problems of Internet commerce, even if not always explicitly. Among Internet commerce problems that extranets solve are the following:

- How to keep customer payment information secure (especially credit card numbers and personal information)

- How to handle complicated transactions with multiple participants (like those involving credit card payments)

- How to speed up the completion of a sale (integrating the Internet commerce stream directly into the order processing stream)

- How to streamline customer service operations (putting the customer directly in touch with account, ordering, and support information)

Why Build an Open Extranet

Whereas *control* is the key to most of the reasons for building a private extranet, *openness* is the key to most of the reasons for building an open extranet. Here are some reasons that organizations build open extranets:

- The widest possible body of business partners (customers or suppliers) are accessible to extranet resources (very important to companies wishing to sell to mass markets through a value-added extranet).

- The cost of distributing applications to the widest possible body of potential business partners is relatively small.

- Changes in extranet structure, including improvements and additions to services or expansions in network access performance, are relatively easy.

- Availability of alternative and complementary resources through the Internet enhances the value of the services provided.

Examples of open extranets are many and varied, though the details of implementation may not always be available. For instance, in 1995, Federal Express began offering its customers access to package-tracking services through its Web site. Any user with access to the Internet and a browser could enter a package-tracking number and other shipping information, and be rewarded, practically instantly, with the status and location of the package. The functional diagram in Figure 21.6 shows how a delivery company might reproduce this service (which, in fact, other delivery companies did quickly imitate).

FIGURE 21.6:

A delivery company gathers information from drivers and other staff and then makes that information available to customers through the World Wide Web.

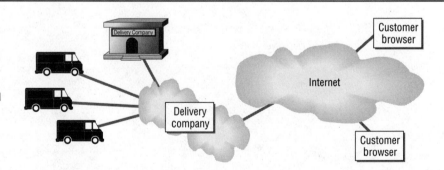

Delivery information generated in the field, as packages are picked up, moved, and finally delivered, is sent directly to the delivery company. This data may include everything from shipper and recipient information to accounting and billing data and the name and employee number of the driver of the delivery truck. Some of the information will be made available to customers through the Web page. The delivery company is shown in this figure with clouds connecting it both to the field, from which it gathers data, and to the Internet, over which it distributes data.

The exact mechanisms by which these functions are completed can vary. In one approach, the field data is transmitted directly to a large mainframe database that is connected directly to the Internet, with all customer queries handled directly through SQL queries. Alternatively, the field data could be transmitted to the mainframe database, which periodically replicates only relevant data (removing billing, accounting, and human resources information) to a system accessible only by the Web server.

You can find somewhat more complicated examples at many online stores. The most sophisticated stores can be linked to various corporate systems, including inventory (to indicate the availability of products on sale), fulfillment (to initiate shipments immediately upon receiving the electronic order), accounting, billing, accounts receivable, marketing, and sales.

Implementing an Open Extranet

The simplest, and least desirable, way to implement an open extranet is to simply build a Web site with links to extranet resources and plug it all directly into the Internet. This process would open the organization to an entire universe of trouble. Criminals could break into sensitive corporate systems, vandals could "edit" product descriptions (or write their own), and other evil-doers could shut down services, systems, and even whole networks. At the very least, some form of firewall protection is absolutely necessary.

Developing an extranet application that permits outsiders to access organizational resources is a basic requirement for building an extranet, but it is not the only prerequisite for an extranet. At least as important as building the application is building in security for the application. Also important is security through constant vigilance (in the form of monitoring log files for suspicious activities) coupled with intelligent deployment of systems. Protecting sensitive systems while still providing access to some of the information on those systems through application servers is the goal of the successful extranet.

Disadvantages of the Open Extranet

Anything that relies on an open or public network is always at the mercy of that network. The telecommunications networks in some less-developed nations are neither sufficiently reliable nor sufficiently widespread for working people to use them to perform their jobs. Likewise, the public transportation networks in some American cities are neither sufficiently reliable nor sufficiently widespread for working people to be able to use them to commute to and from work.

Whether or not the Internet is sufficiently reliable for companies to base their businesses on its availability depends on a multitude of factors, but the answer to this question underlies the basic disadvantage of implementing an open extranet. Undoubtedly, Internet service will eventually improve, perhaps to the point at which it is as reliable as the North American telephone system. However, until that day, businesses may not be able to afford to rely on the Internet too much.

Who Controls Your Extranet?

One of the biggest problems with using the Internet for mission-critical extranet applications is that you have direct control over (at most) only those parts of the extranet that are internal to your organization (or that are under the control of the central extranet committee). You have indirect control, through your Internet service provider, over only those links connecting your extranet to the Internet.

Who actually handles the rest of the network can vary from moment to moment. There is no certain way to predict the path your data may be taking, and there is no way to hold any single entity responsible for that path.

The result is that your provider may be doing a wonderful job of providing service, but when a backhoe severs a backbone circuit maintained by some regional, national, or global operator halfway across town or halfway around the world, it may stop your extranet dead in its tracks—without there being anything you or your Internet service provider can do to fix it.

The Hybrid Extranet

At this point, it should be obvious that no extranet is likely to be purely open or purely private. Private extranets may offer some services to outsiders, through gateways, and almost all open extranets will use some form of exclusionary device, like a firewall system, to keep out undesirables. Likewise, private extranets may permit or even encourage Internet connectivity for members, while open extranets may use private data communication conduits for backup, or to provide parallel services to key extranet users—preferred customers and business partners, for example.

Extranets, just like other networks, must be designed around the requirements of their users, rather than around a technology. This approach gives the extranet designer full latitude to choose the most appropriate method of deploying services to fulfill application requirements as they relate to security, availability, and functionality.

Extranet Service Providers

Organizations offering extranet services fall into three categories:

- Consulting firms offering intranet and Internet connectivity services in addition to extranet services

- Communications firms that sell connectivity, such as America Online, which offers private networking services

- Value-added network (VAN) services, such as those offered by EDI and other special-purpose networking organizations

The services these companies offer can be invaluable, although no organization should delegate *all* its extranet tasks to outsiders. Even if outside consultants are called in to build the corporate extranet, the organization should also create its own team to be responsible for managing and coordinating its extranet development.

Electronic Data Interchange

Electronic Data Interchange, or EDI, is an application for business-to-business digital commerce. Its basic premise is that the primary barrier to electronically transacting business is the incompatibility of formats used to represent information in purchase orders and sales orders. In other words, the buying organization uses its own formats for representing the important information about a purchase it wishes to make, including special items like department numbers and special chargeback information, while the selling organization has its own set of information that relates to each sale. Many of these data items overlap (e.g., quantity, price, item number, and description), but even these items may be stored in incompatible formats.

Solving this problem is increasingly important, as the actual cost of processing a purchase order for many companies has risen to as high as $100 or more for every purchase made by the organization. There are similar costs to the selling organization.

The EDI solution uses special software that helps each participant link its internal data items to a set of universal data items. Each participant then translates its proprietary information into the universal standard and exchanges that data. When the buyer submits a purchase order through an EDI system, the seller can immediately process the order automatically.

One major sticking point for EDI is building a framework for transmitting this information between organizations. Companies that buy from only one vendor and sell to only one customer can solve the problem with a pair of dial-up lines. In the real world, however, that solution probably won't work. Most organizations either have many suppliers, many customers, or both. The result has been the value-added network (VAN), a private network linking all the organizations that subscribe to that network.

A VAN is very much like a private extranet. However, another problem that arises is that there are several very large VANs and not all your trading partners will belong to the same VAN as you do. The result is a need for multiple VAN memberships.

Increasingly EDI vendors are making their software and services available over the Internet, usually by providing a secure channel over the Internet that links their users to their EDI servers.

Virtual Private Networks

A *virtual private network* (*VPN*) uses strong encryption and authentication to secure a private channel across a public network like the Internet. These private channels, as shown in Figure 21.7, can link two remote networks or connect a host to a remote network. When linking two networks, a virtual private network provides a channel that can carry all traffic between the two networks. VPNs usually operate by encapsulating regular IP traffic inside an encrypted IP channel. The virtual private network host or gateway transmits the encrypted, encapsulated packets directly to the remote virtual private network gateway, which decrypts the datagrams and forwards them to their final destinations on the remote segment of the virtual private network.

FIGURE 21.7:

Virtual private networks can link networks and individual hosts using encrypted channels transmitted across the Internet.

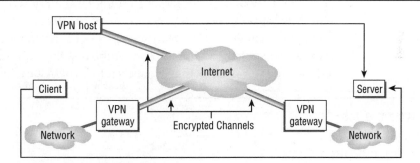

Tunnels and Gateways

VPN products come in two flavors: those delivered as part of a firewall gateway and those delivered as stand-alone tunneling solutions. In either case, remote access to the main network is possible either from a satellite network (e.g., a branch office or a business partner) or from an individual host (e.g., a telecommuting employee's home PC or a traveling employee's laptop).

AltaVista Tunnel (from AltaVista Internet Software) is one tunnel solution for virtual private networks. It operates independent of any firewall gateway and supports connections between two networks or between a host and a network.

The rest of this section discusses the AltaVista Tunnel implementation of virtual private networks. A list of some other virtual private network software products is included within Appendix B.

How the Virtual Private Network Works

Under normal, non-tunneled circumstances, a host can connect to a remote network through the Internet without any special arrangements, as long as both ends support TCP/IP. (See Chapter 3 for more details about the TCP/IP protocol suite.) Data is simply packaged into IP datagrams (also sometimes known as packets), which are sent in the clear (i.e., without encryption) across the Internet for delivery to the remote network. The same arrangement is in place for two networks. Any data that one network's router is willing to forward to the other network's router will pass through the Internet. Delivery is based on IP addresses, with each network connection getting a unique IP address. For example, each router shown in Figure 21.8 has two network connections. Therefore, each will have two separate IP addresses: one for the link that connects it to the Internet and the other for the link that connects it to its own local intranet.

FIGURE 21.8:

Non-tunneling IP connectivity across the Internet is simple, but not secure.

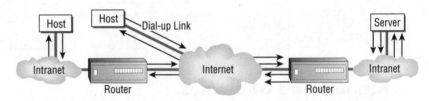

IP addresses can normally be assigned only where a corresponding network link exists, whether it is a point-to-point dial-up link, an Ethernet adapter connecting to a LAN, or a connection to an ATM network. This attribute of IP addresses comes about because they are ordinarily used to bind a logical (Network layer) host address to a physical (link layer) address, enabling the IP network software to transmit data across a physical medium.

To create a virtual private network, however, AltaVista Tunnel creates a software-only pseudonetwork adapter that uses its own IP address while the tunnel is in operation. The tunnel server also uses a pseudonetwork adapter, with another IP address, to serve as the other end of the tunnel. When the remote user wants to connect to the network securely through the tunnel, the upper layers (Application and TCP) send their data streams to the tunnel IP address's TCP/IP network protocol stack for processing.

Sending the datagrams to a pseudonetwork adapter on the same host is functionally equivalent to sending those datagrams to some other host. In both cases an entirely different set of programs will process the datagrams, encrypt them, and forward them to the other end of the tunnel.

Once the datagrams arrive at the pseudonetwork adapter's protocol stack, the tunnel software encrypts them and forwards them to the other end of the tunnel through the real, physically connected TCP/IP network protocol stack. Remember that each datagram has two sets of endpoints; the originating host's tunnel IP address and the destination host's normal IP address are both associated with the unencrypted datagram. They are encrypted and encapsulated inside a datagram that is addressed from the real IP address of the tunneling workstation to the real IP address of the tunnel server. Figure 21.9 shows how the tunneling effect is achieved.

FIGURE 21.9:

A datagram being sent through a virtual private network tunnel is encrypted before being sent over the Internet.

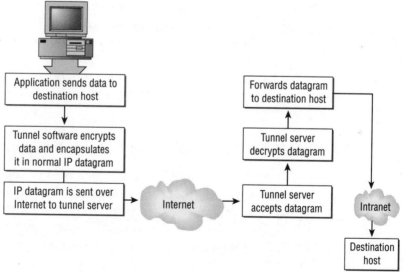

The originating host generates a datagram using the tunnel IP address as the source address and the destination host's IP address as the destination address. This datagram is encrypted and can be treated as if it were the output of any other network application process on the host. It is packaged into other datagrams, which are sent out to the Internet with the originating host's hardware-linked IP address as the source and the tunnel server's IP address as the destination. Once the tunnel server receives this datagram, it strips off the protocol headers to reveal the encrypted datagram, which in turn is decrypted to reveal the original datagram, intended for a host local to the tunnel server. The tunnel server then forwards that datagram to its destination.

When the destination host responds to the originating host, it addresses its datagrams to the originating host's tunnel IP address. These datagrams will be routed to the tunnel server, which encrypts them and encapsulates them into datagrams addressed to the remote host. The process is reversed when the remote host receives these datagrams. (The remote host performs the same decryption functions as the tunnel server.)

The tunnel server behaves like an IP router, accepting datagrams intended for the other end of the tunnel, packaging them, and forwarding them. Although the example above shows how the tunnel works for an individual host connecting into a remote network through a tunnel server, the principles are the same for network-to-network tunneling. Each network has its own tunnel server, and hosts on either network communicate with hosts on the other network by forwarding all packets to the local tunnel server, which encrypts and encapsulates those packets into datagrams to be delivered to the remote tunnel server. When the datagrams arrive at the remote tunnel server, the outer IP headers are stripped away, the encapsulated datagrams are decrypted, and those datagrams are forwarded to their destination host on the remote network.

Microsoft Point-to-Point Tunneling Protocol (PPTP)

Starting with Windows NT version 4.0, Microsoft began shipping its own tunneling protocol, the Point-to-Point Tunneling Protocol (PPTP). The goal of this protocol is to protect data streams passing between hosts connected using the Point-to-Point Protocol (PPP) for remote network access. PPTP simply uses the facilities inherent in PPP for authentication, and it encrypts and encapsulates the resulting data stream between the systems.

Virtual Private Network Security Issues

A recent National Computer Security Association (NCSA) report indicates that virtual private networks may provide sufficient encryption and authentication protection for most uses. However, just as high-security, high-profile systems, such as those maintained by the government, military, or telecommunications industry, often attract attackers because of their perceived inaccessibility, virtual private networks may attract intruders. Their vulnerability increases as large volumes of encrypted data begin flowing across the Internet.

Another, more disturbing, potential problem for virtual private networks is the *denial-of-service* attack. (For a description of some of the most common denial-of-service attacks, including SYN flooding and the Ping of Death, see Chapter 28.) Organizations wishing to deploy production applications across a virtual private network must be very careful in considering the consequences of an intermediate network outage or a denial-of-service attack against virtual private network nodes, both of which can bring an extranet down for hours or even days. Although most firewalls now available have been enhanced to deal with the most typical denial-of-service attacks—which are also the easiest to launch—you will very likely always be somewhat vulnerable to such attacks as long as you are connected to a public network.

Extranet Design Structures

Although you could build a very simple extranet from a pair of routers linking two organizations' intranets over a modem connection, the result would be far from robust, scalable, or reliable. More serious interorganizational internetworking—that is, linking more organizations with better performance and more traffic—over a private extranet requires a very significant resolve from all parties to commit time, money, and resources to the effort. Private extranets, being special cases of large-scale data communications networks, are usually approached in three sections:

- End-user or application section
- Network access section
- Backbone section

The end-user or application section is the part of the network with which the user interacts. It has three components: the personal computer, workstation, or terminal; the network interface card; and all the supporting network software and LAN media that carry data to and from the user.

The network access section defines the interface between the Application layer of the network and the backbone layer of the network—the part of the network that passes data between an intranet and the extranet, for example.

The backbone section is the part that passes data between different network access points. Backbone section usually refers to a very high-performance network that can handle a lot of bandwidth. Figure 21.10 shows how the three sections fit into the typical private extranet.

FIGURE 21.10:

The backbone part of a data network connects network access points, which act as entry points to the extranet for its end users.

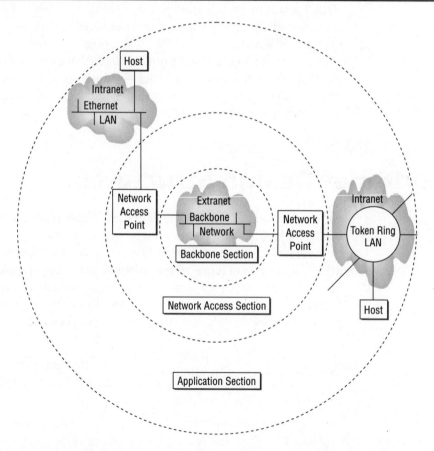

The extranet designer does not necessarily have to be concerned with the specifics of the underlying network structures of the component intranets, since these will likely be the domain of their respective organizations and are also likely to already be in place and operational. The network access design, linking the intranets to the backbone, is very much part of the extranet design. The Internet 2 project pays considerable attention to the network access portion of the program, for example.

Finally, the backbone gives the private extranet its structure and makes it useful, carrying all interorganizational traffic. Should the backbone fail, be unreliable, or be unable to handle all extranet traffic, the extranet itself will fail.

If network backbone design could be explained completely in a single book (let alone chapter), demand for experienced extranet designers would very likely plummet. The rest of this section introduces some of the issues and options available to extranet designers. For more in-depth coverage of these topics, a book like Spohn's *Data Network Design, 2nd edition* (McGraw-Hill, 1997) is a good place to start.

Access Network Design Issues

This piece of the puzzle provides the interface from the LAN to the wide area network (WAN). The network access points of any extranet (or intranet, or the Internet) need to accept data generated by users and the processes they run, and then forward the data to the network backbone for delivery across the internetwork. Access networks have the following components:

- Routers to pass IP datagrams
- Switches and other network transmission devices to move the bits across wires
- Protocols to properly package all the data being transmitted

The access network design solves all the issues involved in moving IP datagrams off LAN media, encapsulating them into the right data transmission units for the backbone network, and transmitting them onto a high-speed backbone medium.

Determining how network access works means analyzing the extranet requirements, with special attention to these issues:

- The volume of data expected
- The routes the data takes to get from desktops to network access points

- Network and application performance criteria
- Budgetary considerations
- The structure of the network backbone

Extranet Structure and Backbones

Simple extranets don't necessarily require backbones. Linking two intranets with a point-to-point link (preferably a monitored leased-line solution) is one alternative. Linking all participating intranets with point-to-point links is an acceptable solution in certain situations. This approach, which results in a *full-mesh* network, is illustrated in Figure 21.11. The full-mesh approach provides reliability because it connects every participating network directly with every other participating network. If one network goes down, no other network will be affected by its failure.

The full-mesh network approach is not very scalable—each participating network must build and maintain a separate point-to-point link for every other network. Therefore, with three participants, each network must manage two links; with 10 participants, 44 point-to-point links are required.

FIGURE 21.11:

The full-mesh network uses direct links between every participating network.

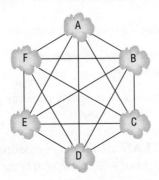

You can achieve some of the benefits of the full-mesh approach, like the ability to withstand circuit failures without affecting interconnectivity, at much lower cost with partial-mesh solutions. As shown in Figure 21.12, a six-network routing extranet can easily operate with nine point-to-point circuits instead of the 15 of a full-mesh network. Traffic going from network A to network B, D, or F is transmitted directly; traffic from A to C or E is routed by B or F, respectively. And if the A-to-B link failed, traffic between the two networks could still be carried by routing it through network F.

The partial-mesh network reduces the number of point-to-point links without significantly impairing connectivity.

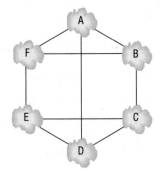

The partial-mesh network is somewhat more scalable than the full-mesh approach, but as the number of networks attached increases, the amount of traffic that must be routed by intermediate networks also increases. This increased traffic burden limits the degree to which these networks can expand. Likewise, as the number of networks increases, the number of point-to-point links will also increase to an unacceptable level (albeit more slowly than with the full-mesh network).

The solution is to build a backbone—a high-speed network where all participating networks are equidistant, at least conceptually, as shown in Figure 21.13. Every network in this extranet is a single hop away from any other network, and the member networks are not burdened with routing traffic between two or more other networks.

A backbone network helps eliminate bottlenecks and can improve efficiency.

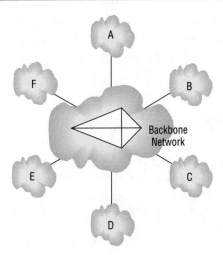

The actual configuration of the backbone network will vary depending on a variety of factors, including

- The geographic distribution of member networks
- What type of network medium is required to meet bandwidth needs
- The number of member networks
- Application performance criteria
- Budgetary considerations

Whether the backbone is deployed as a set of high-speed, point-to-point links, to whose endpoints member networks connect (resembling a bus network), or as a collapsed backplane to which all members connect (producing a sort of star structure), or as some other configuration, will vary from extranet to extranet.

Private backbones solve many of the problems of running a mission-critical application over the extranet, but they pose a new one: The backbone itself becomes a single point of failure for the extranet. When using the Internet as the backbone, you can bypass most failures within the network cloud by routing within the Internet. You can resolve problems with Internet service providers by maintaining a backup or parallel link with another provider, but when the extranet backbone goes down, the entire extranet goes with it. Another drawback to the private extranet backbone is the expense. The backbone usually calls for a significant outlay of capital to build it, as well as the ongoing expense associated with hiring the necessary technical expertise to keep it running.

Ultimately, most extranets won't fit precisely into these categories, but will be implemented with some blend of technologies—mostly because no single solution is applicable to every extranet problem.

Summary

In this chapter, we've focused on important considerations necessary for successfully designing and implementing extranets. While the hardware used is identical to that used in intranets and other types of networks, extranets do present some new challenges. We've borrowed the Internet 2 project in this chapter as a good example of a very large extranet—both in terms of what it hopes to accomplish, and in the guiding principles it is using in the process.

These principles or guidelines include the following: Wherever possible, use widely available, well supported, and reliable technology rather than simply the latest (less tried and true) technology; adopt open standards rather than proprietary ones wherever possible; achieve maximal redundancy by ensuring that there is no single software or hardware product, vendor, or service provider being depended upon exclusively; and focus on establishing basic networking functionality before adding the more advanced functionality.

We also discussed private extranets (which provide greater control and more privacy at greater expense) and public extranets (which provide greater interconnectivity options with less expense, but at the cost of far less control and greater threats to security). We concluded that the majority of extranets will be some form of hybrid, using elements of both private and public extranets.

Two enabling technologies we looked at for extranets are high-speed backbones for interconnecting LANs and tunneling protocols that allow the creation of virtual private networks by adding some form of encryption to encapsulated network packets.

It bears restating that extranets will often depend on people and technology outside your organization, and will require patience and good planning to be successful. Extranets also often require a large capital and resource investment (particularly where redundant WAN connections or high-speed backbones are needed), and successful implementation in these cases depends on a firm commitment by upper management both to the expenses and the human resources required to provide dependable ongoing support to the extranet infrastructure.

In the next group of chapters, Part VI, we'll look at a more scaled-back approach to networking over distances, primarily useful for mobile employees and for the ever-growing ranks of employees who are working from home.

PART VI

Accessing Networks Remotely

■ CHAPTER 22: Implementing an Effective Telecommuting System

■ CHAPTER 23: Remote Access Hardware

CHAPTER
TWENTY-TWO

Implementing an Effective Telecommuting System

- Every administrator's dream—a network without local users

- Help users be productive while working from home

- Remote control and remote access

- Using pcANYWHERE or Carbon Copy

- A quick guide to modems

- ISDN line basics

- Using parts of the Internet to build your own tunnel

Are you really tired of dealing with people who hate to get up in the morning? Don't you wish you could tell them to just go back to bed and call you when they can be civil? Telecommuting might be the answer to your dreams.

Maybe *you* are one of those people who have trouble waking up in the morning. Does the sight of really chipper people make you want to crawl back into the computer room and not come out until noon? Do you sometimes wish that those people could just be locked in a room all by themselves? If these people fit the telecommuting profile, you just might get your wish!

Are there people in your company who don't really have to be in the office? You know the type. First there are the sales people who are out making calls. Their job is on the street; why do they need a desk and an office? What about other people who work with you? Does a telephone technical support person need to have a desk in the corporate headquarters? Is it necessary for an accounting clerk to be taking up office space? What about technical writers, programmers, editors, marketing people, the advertising department, the art department, the travel department or some engineers? Any number of people who work for your company don't really have to be in the office every day. Let's work with management to get rid of them!

Telecommuting Basics

Telecommuting is the fine art of moving end users out of expensive office space, but still helping them get their work done. It helps to open up whole new worlds of office space management. For example, now instead of having multiple empty cubicles for a sales force that is out on the street, you can "hotel" sales people. Create one or two cubicles with a phone and a network connection, and let the sales people share space. Management will love this idea, and so will Building Services.

Telecommuting is the ability to configure a computer network so that someone else can do a job from a remote location, but still have complete access to all the services the company has to offer. Telecommuting may not be the answer to every need, but in more and more companies it is an option that is being explored by those managers who truly think "out of the box."

When Is Telecommuting Appropriate?

Telecommuting is not for everyone, and it is not appropriate for every situation. Even if a position requires flexibility, telecommuting may not be the best option.

Telecommuting involves setting up an office in an employee's home or some other off-campus location. It means having to set up communication channels so users can still communicate with the office, even if it is hundreds of miles away. Telecommuting *may* be right for members of your corporate staff who are disciplined self-starters, able to get up and walk into what used to be a bedroom and put in eight to ten hours of work without being disturbed. The more such users you can find from the corporate employee pool, the more users can be working from home.

Even if all the employees at a company are disciplined self-starters, there may be other factors that affect the decision to implement a telecommuter program. You must have sympathetic managers who understand the concept, are comfortable without being able to see everyone's smiling face every day, and who can quantify the amount of work telecommuters are getting done. Telecommuting can be a wonderful thing, or it can lead to increased levels of stress and extreme feelings of guilt.

Another factor is resource usage. A job that requires high utilization of the corporate network is not a good candidate for telecommuting, even if the individual and their manager are emotionally suited to working that way. For example, consider an accounting clerk who is constantly accessing the large accounting database or a CAD/CAM operator who is frequently printing out large drawings on a plotter. In each of these cases, the bandwidth taken up to accomplish these tasks would be beyond the capabilities of a simple dial-up connection.

Advantages of Telecommuting

Let's look at some of the advantages of telecommuting. Since this subject is necessarily a two-way street, we will examine it from both the employer's and the employee's perspective.

Benefits for the Employer

As this book is being written, the American economy is going along great guns. Each month, extremely low unemployment rates are being reported. You can hardly go into a business, store, or restaurant without seeing signs indicating that the place is hiring. It is a tough world out there trying to recruit quality people. One of the benefits that Human Resources can offer job candidates is the ability to work from home. Now the potential employee can save on child (or even parent) care. Even the ability to work a flexible schedule can make the difference between having a candidate accept or reject a job offer.

With the expanding economy and the favorable business climate, companies are also trying to expand. As they do, they find that the "corporate headquarters" may be stretched a little thin with office space. "Well," some managers think, "that's OK; we have needed a new location for a long time anyway." So the search for a new home begins, and in many locations, so does the frustration. With many businesses expanding, everyone has the same idea. Office space is at a premium and there are multiple companies bidding for the same space. This is great for landlords, but not so great for tenants. The laws of supply and demand kick in. Economics 101 taught that when supplies were low and demand was high, the price went up. Depending on what city you live in, office space usually starts renting from about $1.25 per square foot per month. (And at that low rate, you will not usually get much in the way of amenities!) So what is an employer to do?

One of the methods of solving this problem is to get rid of some of the employees you already have on-site. Don't get the wrong idea—I don't mean terminate them; after all, the company is in an expansion mode. I mean get them the heck out of the building. The first question that any manager has to ask is, "Is it really necessary that this person be in the building all day, every day?" If the answer to the question is no, perhaps telecommuting and flexible scheduling could be the answer.

Reduced Hard Dollar Costs   A hard dollar cost is something that you can quantify. It is a cost where an actual check is cut to meet the expense. Here is an example. Suppose you have a worker, named Fred, who does research off the Internet for a variety of reasons, helping the marketing department, the sales department, senior management, and everyone else within the company. Fred sits at a desk all day and is paid relatively big bucks to surf the Internet, compile statistics, gather information, and pass that information along to the powers that be. Currently he has a 12' × 12' cubicle with a computer, a desk, a phone, and an e-mail connection. Fred is a dedicated employee who is always at work early and stays late when necessary, but he has been complaining lately about the length of the commute, the inability to be home when the kids are sick, and the hassle of parking downtown.

A manager may take a look at Fred and determine that there is absolutely no reason why he has to be in the office every day. The work is portable and can be done wherever there is an Internet connection. Assume the company is spending about $3.00 per square foot for the office space Fred is using. With 144 square feet of office space, it costs over $400 a month just to "put a seat in a seat." If office space is tight, why not move Fred to an office in his home, invest some of that $400 a month in a new phone line (maybe even an ISDN line), a modem, and even a raise for "loaning" part of their house to the organization? Again, decisions about resources would have to depend on the type of job a person does, and the amount of information they are transmitting back to the corporate network. Assuming the hardware implications can be worked out, now you have a productive employee who has all the resources of the office at his fingertips, but works out of his home.

The company saves money on new office space, and has just removed two factors that might cause the employee to look for a job somewhere else.

Increased Employee Productivity   There are some old-school management types who firmly believe that employment is location-dependent. Can't you just hear them now, screaming about the lack of control and saying things like, "How can we be sure they are actually working when they are at home?" As we'll see, that's actually a reasonable question. But the answer can be measured in productivity. The United States National Institute of Health (NIH), Office of Telecommunications Management reports that productivity climbs an average of 20 percent when individuals telecommute.

Improved Corporate Citizenship   Meanwhile, encouraging telecommuting also helps the planet. According to a study done in 1992 by Arthur D. Little, entitled "Can Telecommuting Help Solve America's Transportation Problems?" with a 10 to 20 percent substitution of telecommunications for transportation the following can be attained:

- Elimination of 1.8 million tons of pollutants produced by vehicles

- Savings of 2.5 billion gallons of gasoline

- Freeing up of 3.1 billion hours of personal time (not spent in traffic congestion)

- Savings of $5 million in annual infrastructure maintenance

Just think how those figures will look in the annual report!

Corporate Expansion with Reduced Cost and Exposure   A popular corporate catchphrase lately has been a desire to "grow the business." In management-speak, growing the business usually translates into selling more stuff to customers. Telecommuting will help your company grow by extending the size of its marketplace. Now, the company can put sales people in the far-flung reaches of the world. The company may not even have to establish a "regional office," just a phone line and a modem may do the trick. Now, instead of having to dictate orders over the phone, or enter, print and fax, the sales person can access the corporate network and enter orders just as if sitting at a desk.

Expanded Employee Recruitment   If your company has an effective telecommuting policy, it doesn't take long for Human Resources to realize that its recruitment efforts do not have to tied down to a single location. If an employee is communicating using the telephone, the fax machine and e-mail, what difference does it make if the employee is 10 miles away or 10,000 miles away?

Insurance Reductions   While most of what we have discussed so far has been common sense, there are some less obvious benefits. The NIH reports that historically, companies with telecommuting policies report a reduction in sickness and disability expenses as some employees with chronic illnesses or other conditions may be able to work at home even when they cannot get into the office. And with a cold, flu, or other minor illness, an employee who does not feel well enough to commute to the office may still be able to put in at least part of a working day at home with a PC.

Disaster Recovery   Another often overlooked benefit to telecommuting involves disaster recovery, both major and minor. For a few days every year or so, floods, blizzards, or even earthquakes can make simply getting to the office a nightmare. The computer network may be up and working (assuming electricity is available), but no one can get to it. And on a "snow day," even those employees who made it in to work are not going to be very productive. When they finally arrive, there will be a water cooler/printer/fax machine de facto meeting to share war stories about how long it took to get into work. Once the meeting breaks up, everyone is thinking about how early they have to leave to beat the traffic. On days like this, telecommuters can be happily working away at home.

Decreased Absenteeism from Other Causes   Telecommuting can also reduce absenteeism caused by transportation problems. The telecommuter is going to have a real hard time convincing the boss that they can't go to work in their home office because the car won't start!

Benefits for the Employee

Much of the impetus for telecommuting has come from users. Let's consider why they find it attractive.

Flexible Scheduling   If you have users who are not "morning people" but instead are at peak efficiency at 7 P.M., they can design a workday around that schedule.

Other users may be the opposite. If you substitute 7 A.M. for 7 P.M., that is when they are at their best. There is no mandate that says that a telecommuter's work-day has to run on a traditional 9 to 5 schedule. Many very effective people work *really* odd hours, but the bottom line is that the work gets done, no matter if it is at 10 in the morning or 10 at night. If the deadline is met and the work is complete, does management care when it's done, as long as it *is* done? Probably not. (On the other hand, if the bottom line is that the work needs to be done for a 10 A.M. meeting, then having it arrive at 10 P.M. could be a disaster.)

Improved Employee Morale   For parents of small children, telecommuting can have all sorts of benefits. Everyone knows personally, or has heard, about the high cost of child care. With a telecommuting arrangement, this cost can be cut drastically. Dad or Mom can be home with the kids when they get home from school, and by careful arranging of the work schedule, still get the work done. It happens every day.

Employees are the ones who really benefit from some of those figures quoted in the Little study. It is the employee who is not going to have to sit in traffic, wasting their lives, when they could be at home working. It is the employee who may get an immediate raise, simply by not having to pay for parking, buy a bus pass, pay for gas, or pay higher insurance rates because they drive their car so many miles each year.

Employee Tax Benefits   Depending on the structure of the employment agreement, there may also be some income tax benefits to an employee for using a room of their home as an office. Only a good tax advisor can tell if the home office will qualify, but your coworkers may be able to deduct a percentage of the cost of their house as depreciation. That may even make the difference between getting a tax refund and signing a check to the IRS. (Just be sure to consult a qualified tax advisor before you do anything.)

Disadvantages of Telecommuting

Before entering into a telecommuting program, both the employees and management need to consider the disadvantages as well as the benefits we've just looked at.

Issues for the Employer

There are some very real concerns that any employer planning on implementing a telecommuter program should consider before committing to the project.

Increased Management Tasks   For the supervisor, overseeing an employee who telecommutes can be a challenging experience. After all, the manager does not "see" the employee every day; all they see is the finished product. Some supervisors are able to carry this off without a hitch. For others, it is a serious issue. They need to "know" their employees. It is not to say that one style of management is better or worse than another, it is just important for the manager to recognize their strengths and weaknesses.

Increased Support Costs   One of the nice things about having most employees on-site is that support costs can be kept in check. Because the IS department controls installations and configurations, there is a set of standards that are adhered to. In addition, when problems do arise, they tend to be somewhat repetitive. It is always easier to solve a problem the second time. When you move people off campus, they will be using a variety of equipment that may or may not meet the corporate standards. In addition, it is awfully difficult to sit down at someone's desk when that desk is 300 miles away.

Issues for the Employee

For the telecommuter, there are several things that can cause problems. The first is discipline. It sounds great to be able to wake up in the morning and throw on some sweats, go to the kitchen and make coffee, and then walk to the basement or extra bedroom to start work. It sounds great, but it can be really hard! You would be surprised by the number of distractions there are for the telecommuter on the way to work, especially if the task at hand is one that we would all just as soon put off. Getting the intestinal fortitude to do those nasty tasks is difficult enough when you are sitting at your desk at work and your boss is giving you the fish-eye.

As a telecommuter, you start to "go to the office" and discover that the baby needs changing, the dog needs walking, the dishes need to be done, the bed needs to be made, you have to run to the bank, there are office supplies you really need right now, and there is something really important happening on your favorite soap or talk show. Then, of course, it is lunch time. After lunch, you finish up all those tasks you didn't complete in the morning, including vacuuming under the bed, trimming the dog's claws, cleaning out traps in sinks, sweeping the garage, and washing the car. It is amazing how the day can get away from you.

In order to be a successful telecommuter, the employee needs the ability to shut out other distractions, walk into the office, and stay there until the "workday" is done.

Lack of Team Spirit   Another problem regularly cited is the feeling of isolation. Working from home removes the sense of teamwork and camaraderie that exists in office settings. This can take various forms, including just sensing a lack of positive reinforcement when a project is completed, or the ability to "vent" to a coworker when things are not going well.

Dr. Jekyll and Mr. Hyde   While the lack of separation between the work and home environment can be considered a plus, it is also a negative. It is *too* easy to go work. We have all had nights lying awake thinking of what has to be done in the morning. When an employee telecommutes, it is really easy just to decide to go into the office—that is, the spare bedroom—and finish those things up. Since the list of things to do is never finished, it is very easy to become a workaholic. Also, weekends lose all meaning. It is just another day at the office! If the telecommuter has a family, these nocturnal wanderings can impact every member of the family.

Domestic Strife   Telecommuting can have an effect on an employee's personal relationships. For example, a telecommuter who is locked in the home office all day sees only the mail carrier or pizza delivery person. By the time the significant other (SO) returns from a traditional job, the telecommuter wants to see *people*. But if the SO has had a day full of people, the last thing she or he may want is to go out of the house. You can almost hear the argument brewing: "We never go out anymore!"

At the other extreme, some telecommuters report a reduced motivation to leave the house. Because it has become the center of their universe, why leave? Without the social interaction of other people daily, you also lose the after hours events that make up the life of the average office worker. It is difficult to get together Friday night at a local watering hole to wish someone well in their new job when you are not sure what that person looks like and the local watering hole is 500 miles away.

Telecommuting via Remote Control

Now that we've considered some of the "why" and "what-for" issues with telecommuting, it's time to look at the "how-to" issues. Technically, there are two basic models involved: remote control and remote access. We'll examine remote control first.

Remote control requires two computers for every network connection. One computer will be set up at the remote site (the end user's home office), complete with a modem and a phone line. The other computer will be in the central office, also with a modem and a dedicated phone line. The remote site computer will dial in and connect to the computer at the office. The remote site will then "take over" the office computer, and any command issued at the remote site will actually be run from the office computer. The remote user can log in to the network, execute applications running on network servers, download and upload files, and do most things that a user in the office can do.

When you set up someone to work from home using remote control, you are in effect having that person dial in and take over a workstation at the office. They then use that workstation to do their work. Figure 22.1 illustrates this concept.

FIGURE 22.1

Remote control access

Laptop or other computer equipped with a modem dials in from a remote site and connects to a remote host. After the connection has been authenticated, the user "takes over" control of the remote host.

Host at the office configured with a modem, a dedicated phone line, and a network connection. This is the system that is used to execute all network commands.

Network server providing file and print services.

Company network

Remote control access is not a capability provided with your average desktop operating system. It is a special implementation that must be designed and installed from both the host site (usually the central office) and the remote site (usually the home office). Remote control software has been around for a while, so the technology has stabilized, and most software packages are offering many of the same features. Besides the obvious "dial in and take over features," most programs will let users upload and download files and print either remotely or locally.

For the administrator who is charged with supporting the system, one benefit of the software is the built-in chat feature. If you are at the office and a user is dialed in and having trouble, the administrator can start running the keyboard on the host computer, or can open up a chat window to "talk" the end user through the problem. We will be looking at various software packages later in the chapter.

Advantages of Remote Control

This access method has some very large pluses for the administrator. First, it is a relatively simple solution to set up. At the central location, you install a workstation with a connection to the network and a dedicated phone line plugged into its modem. You install one of several software programs that allows the system to be taken over and you are pretty much in business. Setup is not a difficult task. The system that is going to be used at the remote office just needs to have the client piece of the software installed, and it needs to be told the phone number to dial and the password needed to access the remote system.

NOTE   Netopia's Timbuktu Pro uses a copy of itself on all workstations, instead of having a thin client on the target workstations. In reality, you can remove all the peripheral, user-oriented software from the workstation and leave only the components used to facilitate connection and to access the systems that need to be checked.

Since this technology has been around for a while, the various vendors have designed the client end to be rather straightforward. That means it is user-friendly. Once the dial-up connection is established, the end user just needs to know a remote login name and password. After authentication is accomplished, the system is menu-driven. Your end user can take over the remote computer and act like they were in the office. It is important to point out that this connection is operating over a modem and a phone line. If you are using an analog modem, you are going to have somewhat longer connection times. If, however, you have an ISDN or better connection between the office and the remote site, performance may take a hit, but it will not be as significant.

If there is any kind of special task that needs to be done, the menus are laid out in a manner that most people can figure them out. About the toughest part of your job will be explaining the differences between uploading a file and downloading a file. Another explanation that will be necessary is printing. Users printing to a remote printer probably won't see output. This may confuse them, until you point out the job printed out just perfectly at the office—or explain to them that it didn't print, because it was formatted for a different paper size than the printer expected.

Disadvantages of Remote Control

In spite of its benefits, remote control has a number of disadvantages. We'll examine these below.

Security

One of the drawbacks of remote control telecommuting is that security is compromised. The remote user needs a login name and a password to access the network, but by the time you publish it to every user who needs to dial in, it might as well be an open connection. In addition, once the information has been published, changing it may not be impossible, but it is darn close. There are just too many people with the old information who would need to have their systems reconfigured to make it a simple task.

Cost Factor

Another factor is cost. For one connection to the network, you have now dedicated two PCs, two phone lines, and two modems—one at the remote site and one on the local network. You also have dedicated one of your precious telephone lines to a communication channel that will be used for a very small part of the day. If you have a large traveling staff and you need multiple connections, figure two computers, a phone line and a modem for every connection, another network connection, extra power, extra space, extra cooling—you get the picture. It can get pricey in a big hurry.

Usability

Finally there is the usability factor. Any time you get this many computers talking to each other using this many different protocols or communication methods, you have the potential for problems. If just one system in the string decides to freeze up, it can put a damper on the whole process. Now the MIS staff has to get involved to reset the host computer. This usually requires still another phone call. The remote control process does require some extra management on behalf of the MIS staff.

Remote Control Options

If you decide to go with the remote-control approach, there are a few software programs that you will want to take a look at. We're not endorsing any of these packages; they are simply listed in alphabetical order.

Compaq's Carbon Copy

One of the old reliable software packages for remote connections is Carbon Copy. Carbon Copy was one of the first remote-control programs, and, according to many sources, it has always been one of the best. One of the biggest changes for the software package is that it's now from Compaq rather than Microcom because Compaq recently acquired Microcom. Carbon Copy 32 sells at a manufacturer's estimated price of around $140 for a two-system license. On the whole, it lives up to its legacy.

Operating System Support   During its long history, Carbon Copy has seen a lot of different operating systems come and go. Because of this it has a high compatibility rating among different operating systems. The latest version runs on Windows 98, Windows 95, and Windows NT 3.51 and 4.0; the same package includes versions for Windows 3.x and Windows CE. A DOS version is available separately. OS/2 and the Mac are not supported.

Installation   Installing and using Carbon Copy is very straightforward. To install the program, simply run the setup program from the CD and define the connections for the host and guest. Defining connections for either a local area network (LAN) or a modem is also very intuitive.

End User Interface   Carbon Copy is also very user-friendly. The program offers five communication modes: remote control, file transfer, remote clipboard, remote printing, and chat. When the administrator defines a profile, any or all of these modes to launch can start with the connection. Different modes can also be loaded or closed as needed during a session.

The default for remote control is for the guest to show the host screen in a window, with scroll bars if the screen doesn't fit in the window. If the remote user views the image full screen and the host has a higher resolution than the guest, you can scan the image by moving the mouse to the edge of the screen. The screen-update speed for remote control is surprisingly fast. Now, remember, we are talking modem connections here, so the term *fast* is subjective. You are not going to be seeing screen refreshes like you were on a gigabit Ethernet segment, but fast for the world of modem communications.

NOTE   One of the major drawbacks of any remote-access solution will be the speed of the connection. If your connection is using a modem and a telephone line, the connection is going to be much slower than a standard LAN connection. There is no way to bypass this problem.

The file-transfer mode is also user-friendly. It shows two windows—one each for guest and host—with a directory tree and list of files in each. You can copy or move files between systems using all the standard Windows methods: by dragging and dropping, or by Copy, Cut, and Paste commands.

The chat feature is standard with this type of software. A user on the guest and a user at the host can communicate, which is a great method for administrators to be able to troubleshoot and solve problems. Carbon Copy provides voice chat as well as keyboard chat. What if you don't have a microphone installed in your computer? Well, Compaq takes care of everything, even including a microphone to plug into your sound card. The conversations do suffer somewhat for being over a modem.

pcANYWHERE

Another longtime standard from the PC side is Symantec's pcANYWHERE. The latest iteration is pcANYWHERE32, which sells for around $150.

Operating System Support   pcANYWHERE32 is also platform-independent. It can support all major Intel platform operating systems for two computers, called, in this case, the host and the remote.

Installation   When you install pcANYWHERE32, the program CD includes versions for DOS 3.3 and later, Windows 3.x, Windows 95/98, and Windows NT 3.51 and 4.0. As with Carbon Copy, you are not limited to just a modem connection; there is network support available, including CA-Unicenter, and network connections can be made via the Internet, ISDN, Microsoft BackOffice, Novell NetWare, TCP/IP, and RAS connections. The program is backward-compatible with earlier versions of pcANYWHERE32 and pcANYWHERE CE.

Installation requires two computers. You have to install the host software on one computer and the remote software on the other. The computers that we'll use in this example are a Windows NT 4.0 server for the host and a Windows 98 laptop for the remote.

NOTE   Our intention is simply to give you a brief description of how to install the software and not show you each page of the configuration information.

Host Installation

When you put the CD into the reader, it will autostart the pcANYWHERE32 Version 8 Installation. To install the host software:

1. From the pcANYWHERE splash screen, click on Install Software.

2. Click Next to bypass the welcome screen.

3. This brings up the standard User Information screen. Enter the name of the installer and the name of the company, and click Next.

4. Click Yes to agree to the license screen.

5. Set the destination directory for the software; the default is C:\Program Files\pcANYWHERE. Click Next to accept the folder.

6. Check the Setup Review screen and click Next to continue. This triggers the file copying.

7. Click your way through a series of Symantec and Microsoft marketing windows until you reach the registration instructions.

8. Follow the on-screen instructions over several windows to register the software.

9. Click No to bypass the README file, and click Finish to restart the computer.

10. Once the computer restarts, you can configure the host by clicking Start ➤ Programs ➤ pcANYWHERE32.

11. Now the system setup starts to get interesting. Figure 22.2 shows the opening screen of the Smart Setup Wizard. In this case, the software has checked for an installed modem and found a Zoom V.34X. Notice that if you have not installed a modem, there is an Add Modem button that will start the Modem Installation Wizard. Click Next to continue.

12. The next screen allows you to choose the protocols necessary to communicate with the remote system. Figure 22.3 shows the available settings. Notice that pcANYWHERE can use TCP/IP, the default, or Sequenced Packet Exchange (SPX) for NetWare, NetBIOS for a Windows network, and Banyan VINES. Click Next after making your selection.

13. The next screen gives you the opportunity to choose a serial port for a direct cable connection. Click Finish to close the Wizard.

14. Once the Wizard has been closed, you'll see the pcANYWHERE main screen for configuring the system (Figure 22.4). From this screen we will choose Quick Start ➤ Add Be a Host PC Item.

15. From the next window, type in a host connection name. Click Next to continue.

FIGURE 22.3:

Choosing a protocol in the Smart Setup Wizard

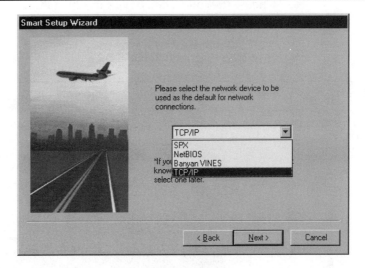

FIGURE 22.4:

The pcANYWHERE main screen

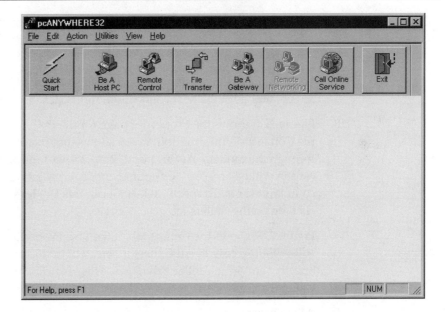

16. Choose the connection device this host PC will use; in this case, it will be the modem. Clicking Next brings up the Be a Host PC Wizard closing screen shown in Figure 22.5, which tells you how to configure the individual caller privileges. Click on Finish.

FIGURE 22.5:

Completing the host configuration

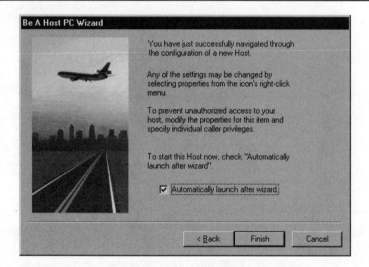

17. To set up individual user information, from the pcANYWHERE32 main screen, highlight the host connection, right-click, and select Properties.

18. Figure 22.6 shows the Properties page for the PSC host. You will notice that the Connection Information screen shows that the connection will be made through the modem. At this point, you can start the service and anyone who calls in will be accepted. Of course, that's not what a security-conscious company wants. To specify who can call this PC, let's create a sales caller by clicking on the Callers tab.

19. Figure 22.7 shows the Callers tab of the PSC Properties page. By default, Allow Full Access To All Callers is selected. In this case, we have chosen Specify Individual Caller Privileges. This also allows us to click the Add Caller icon.

20. After clicking the Add Caller icon, you are prompted to name the caller and click Next. In this case, we will name the caller Sales.

FIGURE 22.6:

The Connection Info tab of the PSC Properties page

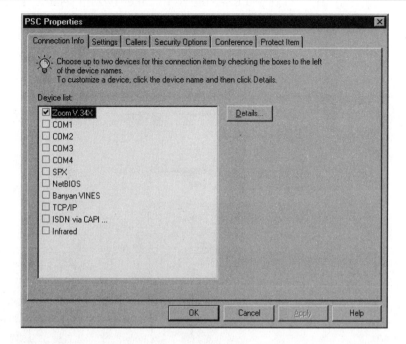

FIGURE 22.7:

Adding a caller in the Callers tab

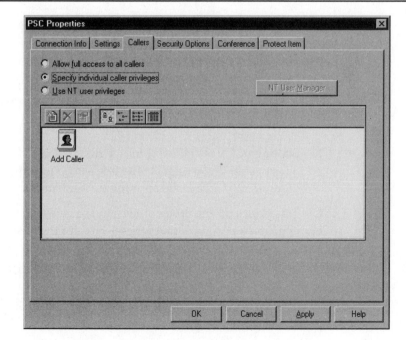

21. Next you'll see the New Caller Wizard security screen (Figure 22.8). Notice that by default we have a login name but no password yet. Add and confirm the password. Make a note of it because you will need it for the client configuration. Click Next and then Finish to complete the caller configuration. Click OK to close the PSC Properties window.

FIGURE 22.8:

The New Caller Wizard
security screen

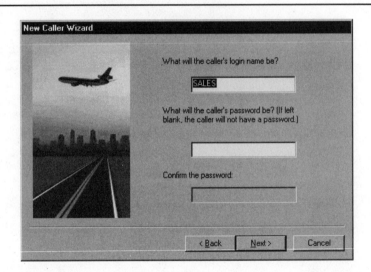

To start the host, click on the host name from the pcANYWHERE main screen.

Remote Client Installation

To prepare a remote client to call the local host, install the pcANYWHERE32 software as covered in steps 1 to 10. After the program has been installed, start pcANYWHERE32 by clicking Start ➤ Programs ➤ pcANYWHERE32.

1. Starting pcANYWHERE32 for the first time on the remote client starts the Smart Setup Wizard again. The first screen prompts for the modem. (See Figure 22.2.) Choose the appropriate modem and click Next.

2. This brings up the protocol selection screen. (See Figure 22.3.) Select the appropriate protocol that was selected for the host and click Next.

3. You are now presented with the port for the direct cable connection. Make the selection appropriate for this computer and click Finish.

4. You are now brought back to the pcANYWHERE32 main screen. To institute a remote connection, go to Remote Control ➤ Modem. Figure 22.9 shows

the pcANYWHERE Waiting screen, waiting for the phone number to be entered.

FIGURE 22.9:

The pcANYWHERE Waiting screen

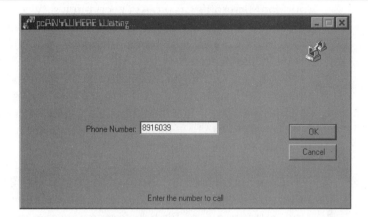

5. Once the other phone line answers, you know you have success when you see the main screen of the computer you are connecting to, as in Figure 22.10.

FIGURE 22.10 :

Once the connection is made, the remote user will see the host computer's main screen.

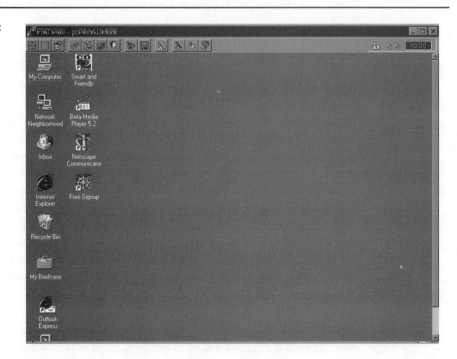

pcANYWHERE Features   pcANYWHERE has several advanced features that allow it to be used for more than just modem-to-modem communication. For environments where security is a major concern, pcANYWHERE provides support for Microsoft's Crypto API encryption services, a technology that allows up to 128-bit security-key lengths. For large installations, pcANYWHERE32 also has Host Multi-Connect conferencing support for up to 256 users. Now the telecommuter does not even have to come into the office for meetings—pcANYWHERE will bring the meeting to the telecommuter! (Depending on your point of view, that may or may not be a good thing.) White Pine's CU-SeeMe Internet and intranet software is included for video teleconferencing, presentations, training, and support, or to hold meetings from remote locations with both face-to-face video and whiteboarding.

End User Interface   Symantec's pcANYWHERE32 has not forgotten its roots. It is also easy to use for those remote control sessions, providing access to files and system resources, file transfers, remote operations, or even checking e-mail. As with other Symantec software, pcANYWHERE32 includes the Live Update feature for fast checking and updating of program files. This option on the Help menu will dial the Symantec Web site, compare your software and file versions with the newest ones at the site, and give you the option of downloading updates.

Timbuktu Pro

Timbuktu Pro was originally designed primarily to work in Macintosh systems. Netopia has expanded its line to include Windows and Mac OS administration tools. Now an administrator can manage either a Windows machine or a Mac from the same workstation—imagine being able to graphically operate both Windows and Mac OS-based systems from a Macintosh computer!

Operating System Support   Timbuktu Pro does for both Windows and Mac OS-based networks what Carbon Copy and pcANYWHERE do for the PC, only it is more expensive. Timbuktu Pro is priced around $140 for Windows-based systems and $190 for Mac OS-based systems. Besides the normal remote-to-host communication, the latest version of TP has added audioconferencing, file synchronization, Apple-events scripting support, and a vastly improved and faster file-transfer facility.

Installation   Since Timbuktu Pro is available for Mac or Windows, it can be used to provide cross-platform remote control in either direction.

The program's simple interface allows you to easily configure host and client machines to communicate over AppleTalk, IPX, or TCP/IP networks, or via a direct modem connection, and now, over the Internet using IP addressing. Once connected, you have the option of taking full control of a remote machine or simply observing the remote computer's screen in a window on your local monitor. This can be a great troubleshooting tool.

Like the other packages we have looked at, TP includes a text-based chat window for communicating with remote users and an intercom feature for real-time audioconferencing. Depending on the speed of your connection, you can use the intercom to talk to a remote user while observing or controlling their computer. However, when you are using the intercom mode over a direct phone connection between two modems, do not expect crystal-clear communication. That only comes with a network connection with a lot of bandwidth.

End User Interface   Timbuktu, like all of these products, includes a standard file transfer interface; you can drag and drop files between the host and remote machines, and use a special Exchange window to copy and delete files to and from either the host or the client machine.

One feature the time-challenged will appreciate is the ability to use an automated remote control process. You can write control scripts or record them through Apple-events scripting, more commonly known as AppleScript. Although you can't use scripts to control the remote machine, you can automate tasks for your local instance of Timbuktu. For example, you can easily create scripts that establish a connection with a remote machine and synchronize or copy files late at night, allowing you more time to do your real job during the day.

Telecommuting via Remote Access

With *remote access*, your home will still need a computer and some type of dial-in connection to the network. The difference from remote control is that instead of dialing in and taking over a computer physically located at the office, the home user will dial in and establish a session with the server, just as if they were logging in from the local area network. By using remote access, you are, in effect, eliminating the middle computer, and the home system is actually executing all the commands.

Figure 22.11 illustrates a basic remote access setup.

Remote access

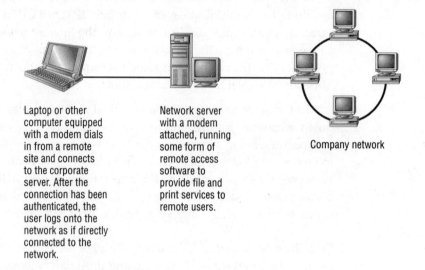

Laptop or other computer equipped with a modem dials in from a remote site and connects to the corporate server. After the connection has been authenticated, the user logs onto the network as if directly connected to the network.

Network server with a modem attached, running some form of remote access software to provide file and print services to remote users.

Company network

Advantages of Remote Access

Depending on the operating system you are running on the remote computers and the operating system you are running on the network communications servers, telecommuting via remote access makes a great deal of sense. Unlike remote control, this approach does not require an extra computer at the central office for each remote connection. This eliminates extra cost. Second, it eliminates another computer to reset if things go wrong. On *your* network, of course, things never go wrong. But across the country people have reported that some end users forget the right way to terminate a session, or they get impatient while downloading a 100MB file and just reboot the local machine, and wonder why the remote connection is goofed up.

Remote Access Options

Remote access means that a user can dial in to a communications server and log in to the network just as if they were sitting at a desk in the office. There are several different types of remote access, from the Telnet utility in Unix to NetWare Connect to Windows NT Remote Access Service (RAS).

The choice of which tool to use pretty much depends on the network operating system, which (as discussed elsewhere in this book) is often a matter of "religion." In a mixed network, however, the choice is not automatic.

Unix

As far as dial-in capability goes, we can probably rule out Unix for the majority of companies, simply because of the difficulty of user training. Most network administrators have a difficult time teaching their users how to use Windows or a Mac; trying to teach a sales weenie how to navigate with Unix is not a job that most of us would embrace without a *very* large raise.

Novell vs. Microsoft

That leaves NetWare and RAS. If you have a single-NOS network, your decision is made for you. If your network has both systems running side by side, you may have to make a difficult decision. On the whole, we prefer Microsoft's RAS, but it's worth discussing both. We'll start with NetWare Connect.

Most people who have installed and configured NetWare Connect sing its praises, but only *after* it has been installed and configured. *While* it is being installed and configured, most first-time (or even second-time) NetWare Connect users are singing, but it is usually not the praises of the product. NetWare is not as user-unfriendly as Unix, but it does tend to offer you choices that are not obvious.

RAS, on the other hand, has a rather straightforward installation routine. Once the product is installed, you can configure remote systems to dial in, and the setup is finished. While not entirely without challenges, the Windows NT Installation Wizard is certainly a blessing compared to other installation routines.

RAS Server and Client Installation

Telecommunications is a two-way street. In this example, we will look at installing both the server side and the client side of the Windows NT 4.0 RAS connection.

Configuring RAS Communications

RAS is an NT network service and is installed like most of the other network services, from the Network icon in Control Panel. Before beginning to install RAS, or any network service, be sure to have the NT Installation CD handy, or at least have access to the files it contains. To install and configure RAS:

1. Log on to the computer as Administrator.

2. Open Control Panel by choosing Start ➤ Settings ➤ Control Panel.

3. Double-click on the Network icon.

4. Open the Services tab by clicking on it.

5. Since RAS is not installed, click Add.

6. Clicking Add will open the Select Network Service window. This is a selection of all the services available but not currently installed on your server. Scroll down to Remote Access Service, highlight it with a single click, and then click OK.

7. By clicking OK, you have opened the Windows NT setup screen, which is looking for the location of the NT setup files. Provide the appropriate location and click the Continue button. At this point, the Installation Wizard copies the necessary files.

8. The next window you are presented lists all the RAS-capable devices attached to the server. If you have more than one modem attached to the server, the drop-down menu will allow you to select the device for RAS communications. If you haven't installed a modem, you can choose Install Modem or Install X.25 Pad from this screen. Once you have chosen a device, click OK.

NOTE   RAS is selfish. The communication channel must be dedicated to RAS. If you want to use the channel for something else, you will have to stop RAS and restart it when you are finished.

---

9. At this juncture, you should see the Remote Access Setup screen, shown in Figure 22.12. Instead of continuing at this time, click on Configure.

FIGURE 22.12:

The Remote Access Setup screen

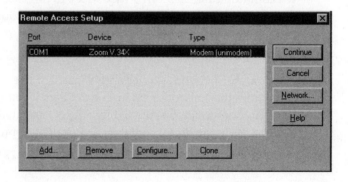

10. Clicking Configure opens the Configure Port Usage screen. This allows you to specify how you want the port used. Make your selection from the choices below and click OK to return to the Remote Access Setup Screen.

Dial Out Only: The appropriate selection if you are configuring this server to dial in to another RAS connection and you only want this machine to dial out.

Receive Calls Only: The default selection; appropriate if your RAS connection will not be dialing in to other servers.

Dial Out and Receive Calls: This selection provides two-way communication.

11. You should now be back at the Remote Access Setup screen. Click on Continue to open the RAS Server NetBEUI Configuration window.

Configuring RAS Protocols

The first protocol that is configured is for the simplest and most basic of network protocols, NetBEUI. You will also be prompted to provide information about TCP/IP and NWLink. Enough theory—let's continue the installation and see where it takes us.

12. The RAS Server NetBEUI Configuration window allows you to choose how far your NetBEUI clients can go. Do you want them to access the entire network, or just this particular computer? Make your choice by selecting the appropriate radio button and then click OK.

13. The next screen is the RAS Server TCP/IP Configuration screen. As you can see in Figure 22.13, this screen is a little more complicated than the NetBEUI screen. There are several decisions you will have to make before continuing on.

- The first choice is whether the TCP/IP client will be allowed access to the Entire Network or to This Computer Only.

Things now begin to get interesting. You are going to have to make some decisions about TCP/IP addressing.

- Choosing Use Static Address Pool will let this service decide which of the IP addresses to assign to each connecting device.

- The check box at the bottom of the screen allows the remote client to request a predetermined IP address. After making the appropriate selections, click OK.

FIGURE 22.13:

The TCP/IP Configuration
screen

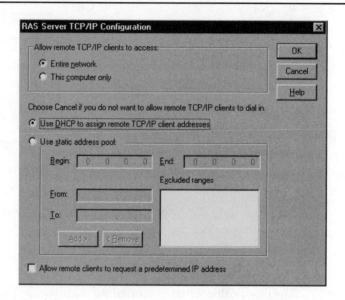

NOTE

Notice that further selections need to be made if you choose to use a static
address pool. For a more complete discussion of TCP/IP addressing, see *MCSE:
TCP/IP Study Guide*, by Todd Lammle with Monica Lammle and James Chellis
(Sybex, 1997).

14. The next screen brings up the last protocol to configure, IPX. As you can see
in Figure 22.14, there are several decisions to be made in the RAS Server IPX
configuration window:

- The top selection of radio buttons allows you to choose to let the IPX
client use the entire network or just this computer.

- The next selection of radio buttons lets you allocate network numbers
either automatically or by specifying a range.

- The bottom of the screen provides two check boxes. Checking the first
will give the same network segment number to all IPX clients. Selecting
the second check box will allow the client computer to select its own
node address.

15. Click OK to close the RAS Installation Wizard.

FIGURE 22.14:

Configuring IPX on the RAS server

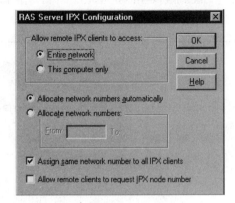

FIGURE 22.14:

Configuring IPX on the RAS server

16. Agree to allow NetBIOS broadcasts for IPX clients.

17. Click Close to close the Network Configuration window.

18. Finally, select Yes to restart the computer.

Configuring RAS Security

RAS Security is configured using both the Remote Access Admin tool and the Network Configuration window from the Remote Access Setup screen. Using the Admin tool, you'll grant dial-up access rights to the server and select the level of call-back support. Encryption information and selections are made through the Network Configuration tool.

To provide dial-up access:

1. Start the Remote Access Administration utility by selecting Start ➤ Programs ➤ Administrative Tools (Common) ➤ Remote Access Admin.

2. From the Remote Access Administrative screen, click on Users to show the list of users who currently have access to this server.

   - To provide access to users from another domain or another server, click on Server, select Domain or Server, and choose the Domain you would like to administer.

   - To actually select the domain, double-click on the domain name in the Select Domain window. Once this has been accomplished, the users in the other domain will show up in the Remote Access Administrative screen.

3. Click on Permissions to display the Remote Access Permissions screen, shown in Figure 22.15.

FIGURE 22.15:

Setting RAS Permissions

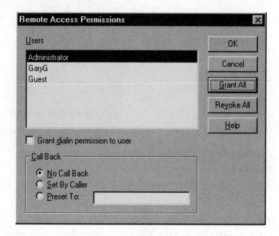

4. The Remote Access Permissions window will list the users associated with this system. By using the selection buttons to the right, you can Grant All access to dial-up networking or Revoke All access from dial-up networking. To grant individual users the right to dial in, highlight the user's name and check in the Grant Dialin Permission to User box at the bottom of the window.

5. You can also use this screen to provide three levels of Call Back support. By filling the appropriate radio button you can select:

   No Call Back: The call-back feature is disabled.

   Set By Caller: The caller will be prompted for a phone number for the return call.

   Preset To: The system will only call back the preset number.

   To change the default encryption scheme for passwords and data:

6. From the NT Server desktop, right-click on the Network Neighborhood icon.

7. Click on Properties.

8. Click on the Services tab and highlight Remote Access Services.

9. Click on the Properties button to bring up the Remote Access Setup screen.

10. Next, click on the Network button. This brings up the Network Configuration window, shown in Figure 22.16.

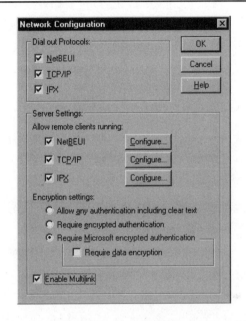

11. The default encryption setting is Require Microsoft Encrypted Authentication. This provides for MS-CHAP. Filling the check button to Require Data Encryption will encrypt not only the password but any data flowing between the RAS server and the client.

- Select Require Encrypted Authentication if you are providing access to non-Microsoft operating systems, like Unix. This provides for CHAP-based encryption.

- Select Allow Any Authentication Including Clear Text for no encryption.

12. Close the Wizard and restart the computer.

Configuring Dial-Up Networking Clients

On a Windows NT computer, before you can connect to the RAS server, you must have RAS services installed. Once RAS has been installed, you must configure a dial-out connection in the RAS phone book. To configure the dial-out connection:

1. Double-click on the My Computer icon on the Desktop.

2. Double-click on the Dial-Up Networking icon.

3. If this is the first entry in your phone book, you will get an NT "nag screen" that says the Phone Book is empty. Click OK.

4. Click New to start the New Phonebook Entry Wizard.

5. Type in the name of the phone book entry, check the I Know All About Phonebook Entries box, and then click on the Finish button.

6. You need to enter a name for the dial-up entry you are creating. Use the receiving server name.

7. Select the modem to use.

8. Click the Use Telephony dialing properties option.

9. Enter the area code and phone number of your RAS server on the Phone Number input lines.

10. Does your RAS server have more than one phone number? If so, you can check the Alternate button and add in any other phone numbers to call.

11. Click the Server tab. Select the protocol that your RAS server uses. The protocols must match between the client and the server for communication to take place.

12. Next, the security must also be the same, so click the Security tab. Since this is a "non-secure" network, let's check "Allow any encryption including clear text."

13. Click OK to save the settings, and click Close.

14. Restart your computer.

Things to Look For with RAS

RAS does have a downside. If you are going to run multiple remote connections off the same server, you probably do not want this to be a primary or backup domain controller. Those servers have an awful lot to do already, without dedicating CPU cycles to a remote session. If you shouldn't install it on the primary domain controller or backup domain controller, that means the possibility of another NT server. As we all know, the minimum hardware requirements for a usable NT server are rather steep. Break out the checkbook, folks, you are about to make a computer sales person somewhere very happy!

The Modem Connection

One of the fundamental components of the telecommuting model is the modem connection. Modems were discussed along with other networking hardware in Chapter 10, but it's worth summarizing the basic elements here. Feel free to skip this section if the information is already familiar to you.

Modem Basics

You probably know that the word *modem* is a contraction of *Modulator/Demodulator*. Modulating and demodulating essentially mean translating a digital signal from a computer to an analog signal that a phone line can understand and vice versa.

When you set out to buy a modem, you will hear the terms *baud*, *bps* (bits per second), and *cps* (characters per second) as speed measurements. Confusingly, these terms are often used as if they were interchangeable; in fact, they mean different things.

The term *baud* comes from the name of the 19th century French inventor Baudot and originally referred to the speed a telegrapher could send Morse code. It later came to mean the number of shifts or switches made on a line every second.

We all know that a *bit* is a single piece of data, a binary 0 or 1 represented on a computer or transmission medium by the presence or absence of power, basically a shift between a high voltage state and a low voltage state. So if baud rate and bits both represent state shifts, it would seem intuitively obvious that the terms are synonymous. The reason they are not is that rather than just using state shifts, modern high-speed modems compress the data they are sending by using a variety of symbols, each of which can signify one of many bit patterns. For example, V.34 modems use symbols which can transmit about nine bits each, and thus can achieve a data rate of 28,800 bits per second. This transfer rate is achieved even though the modem is using a much lower symbol rate of about 3200 symbols per second.

NOTE   When discussing modem speed, the term "smoke and mirrors" comes to mind. Modems are rated for speed, but the rated speed is usually never attained. A modem that is rated at 56K will only provide that throughput if connected to another modem of the same type that uses the same compression algorithms over a perfect phone line.

The proper term to use when talking about modems is *bps* (bits per second), not baud. While a normal byte is made up of eight bits, each byte also contains start and stop bits. These bits are added by the sending serial port's UART and removed by the receiving UART.

NOTE   When data is sent to a modem, it is sent through one of the four (normally) serial ports the computer can address. The process is accomplished within a chip called the Universal Asynchronous Receiver/Transmitter, or UART. UARTs include a serial port and baud rate generator which controls when, what, and how fast data is sent from the serial port. Internal modems normally have built-in UARTs to handle the serial port data movement. The newest version of the UART, the 16550AFN, has a first-in, first-out (FIFO) buffer storage; this cuts down on lost data.

Anyone who works in the computer industry knows that just about everything has some kind of standard associated with it. Modems are no different. With modems the standards are called the "V dot" standards. For example, if you have a modem that operates at 28.8 or 33.6 kilobits per second (Kbps) you are working with a V.34 standard modem.

The 56Kbps modems utilize one of two V.90 standards, the X2 or the K56 standard. When the V.90 standards were proposed, there were basically two ways of accomplishing the task of communicating at 56Kbps. Rather than taking sides, the standards agency more or less determined to let the market decide, and told modem manufacturers to go for it. This left users in a lurch. You may have an X2 modem that connects to a K56 modem, and though both are supposed to communicate at 56Kbps, there is no way that is going to happen with this configuration.

Configuring the Modem

Once you have purchased a modem, the next step is to configure it in the communications program. This involves entering the correct parameters to identify. While each communication program is different in its setup, nearly all require knowledge of the modem brand name, whether or not it is "Hayes-compatible"—the modem speed, the computer serial/com port, and the interrupt (IRQ). In addition, some modems require you set the "flow control."

Before we get too deep into a discussion of modems, let's be sure we have one installed. As we look at installing a modem, we will again use NT as the operating system.

Installing a Modem

Start by physically installing the modem. If you have a problem with your internal modem, check the interrupt and COM port setting. COM1 and COM3 share an interrupt, COM2 and COM4 share an interrupt, and interrupt 3 is a common choice among network cards. Keep the peace, no conflicts. When in doubt, read the manual.

Since we are dealing with NT, which is not plug-and-play compatible, we will have to manually install the modem.

1. Open Control Panel.

2. Select Modems.

3. If this is the first modem in the system, the Installation Wizard will kick off. The Installation Wizard will go out and search for the modem and return the brand and type of the modem. If the brand and type it displays don't match what you have, there is a Change button, and a drop-down menu with a long list of modem manufacturers and models. Choose the one that matches your needs. If your modem still does not show up, check the modem documentation for a compatible model.

4. Once the hardware is recognized, you will be presented with a Modem Properties screen. This screen lists the modems installed. Highlighting a specific modem and choosing Properties brings up a screen whose options depend on the modem you install. The General tab allows you to select how

loud you want the modem speaker to be and the speed of the modem. Anyone who has ever dialed an Internet provider late at night from a hotel room with the volume turned all the way up can appreciate how hard it is to find this setting in a hurry!

5. The Connection tab will allow you to change the connection preferences, if necessary, and determine how to handle outgoing calls. You can choose whether to wait for a dial tone before dialing, cancel the call if not connected within a specified time, and so on.

6. The interesting options come when you select the Advanced button on the Connection tab. The Advanced Connection Settings screen (Figure 22.17) allows the administrator to choose how to handle error control and to set the type of flow control and the type of modulation. For error control, you can require error control to connect, you can choose to compress data, and you can use the cellular protocol for users dialing in using cell phones.

FIGURE 22.17:

The Advanced Connection Settings window

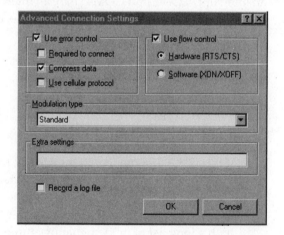

7. Use Flow Control tells the modem how to determine how fast or slow to send data. Your two choices are Hardware and Software.

Unless you have a specific reason to do otherwise, keeping modems set to the defaults is good practice. The basic rule of telecommunications between computing devices is that both modems must agree on certain parameters. If these parameters don't match, there will be no communication. Modem speed is usually not an issue. The modems will negotiate a common speed. Flow control, or "handshaking," establishes which modem talks and when it talks. Modems negotiate to determine at which speed they will communicate. The negotiations also include how the two modems will indicate that they are finished talking. This prevents both modems from trying to transmit at the same time. The RS-232 serial port standard supports two forms of flow control, "software handshaking" and "hardware handshaking." Software handshaking, as the name implies, involves sending a signal within the data stream to indicate when the transmission is complete. Hardware handshaking involves sending these signals via a separate channel.

Additionally, there is another type of flow control, called "end-to-end," that dictates the type of handshaking between the two modems. End-to-end flow control is usually determined automatically by the error-control standards defined by the modem manufacturer or by the file-control protocol used by the communication program.

Fortunately, once you've made all these settings on the local network modem, you can communicate them to your telecommuting end users, who will each need to match the settings on their remote side of the connection.

Getting the Most from Your Modem

Once you have decided which modem (or modems, if you are implementing remote control) to buy for the company, how do you get the most out of it?

With at least one telecommuter using the modem, possibly every day, it is a good idea to have a dedicated telephone line for each modem. When you order the separate phone line, make sure the phone jack is put in an accessible place.

If possible, both the remote telecommuters and the local network hosts should use the same type of modem. Especially with the K56 standards, having the same type of modem on both ends of the system can really pay off. Modems have proprietary methods of data compression. If both modems are working with the same data compression system, faster speeds will result.

Pay attention to the communication software you are using. Again, it's easiest if both sides of the connection are using the same program. But if both the local and remote modems are using standard programs, like those discussed in this chapter, chances are that they will get along. If either side uses a specialized program, read the "fine" manual. There may be some gotchas that you need to look out for. One of these may be data compression. Some proprietary programs compress the data before sending it through the modem. Once the compressed data gets to the modem, the modem tries to compress it again, and data corruption can occur. In this case, turning off data compression at both modems can work to solve the problem.

Higher-Speed Remote Access

In telecommuting, as usual in computing, faster is better. Faster is usually more expensive, too, but speed is worth it. The telephone line is not the only way to go!

ISDN

The first way to speed up the telecommuting process is to bypass the usual dial-up analog phone line and go digital. After all, computers speak digital, so it just makes sense that a digital connection is faster. Integrated Service Digital Network (ISDN) is the most common type of digital phone service currently available.

ISDN has two main types of service. The Basic Rate Interface (BRI) is designed for homes and small businesses. BRI provides two 64Kbps channels known as bearer or B-channels, and one 16Kbps D-channel for out-of-band signaling and link management. B-channels can carry voice, data, or image communication. The channels can be multiplexed into a single 128Kbps channel.

The second service, intended for larger installations, is called Primary Rate Interface (PRI). It comprises 23 B-channels and one D-channel, also 64Kbps. This corresponds to the T1 rate of 1.544Mbps.

Before getting your heart set on ISDN, make sure that your local phone company offers ISDN service to your area. Pricing and equipment may vary; expect to pay more than you are for a local telephone service.

NOTE   An emerging alternative to ISDN for high-speed remote access is Asynchronous Digital Subscriber Line (ADSL), discussed in Chapter 23.

Tunneling

Once there is an on-demand connection to the Internet using a technology like ISDN, other vistas open up for the telecommuter. Now, instead of using remote control or remote access technology, you can "use" part of the Internet infrastructure to make your connection to the home office. This is called tunneling.

Tunneling is the process that establishes a connection with the home office using the Internet as your network medium. Your software program will then use the

Internet to create a virtual private network, or VPN. Once the VPN is established, you have access to the corporate network, as if you were sitting in the office without the hassle of using a dial-up connection. The response time is usually quicker than with dial-up, and the communication is usually encrypted and compressed, so it is a more secure environment. See Chapter 21 for more information about VPNs, tunneling, and extranets.

Summary

There are many advantages and disadvantages to telecommuting, but the bottom line is that it can save your company money, and you can have more productive long-term employees using telecommuting.

The two major ways of accessing the office from a remote environment are remote control and remote access. Remote control involves having more equipment available for your remote users. Remote access involves having a more powerful communication subsystem. As alternatives, evolving technologies using the Internet make it possible to use part of the Internet infrastructure as the communication links.

CHAPTER
TWENTY-THREE

Remote Access Hardware

- Remote Access Service (RAS)

- Multiport serial adapters

- Remote access servers

Chapter 22 covered effective telecommuting—the idea that users on a network can dial in to a server from home and function just as though they were connected to the network with a network interface card (NIC) rather than a phone line and modem. There are all kinds of users who could benefit from such a scenario:

- Salespeople

- Executives who have to travel or work from home

- Employees who need to stay home frequently but who could work if they had some method of dialing in

- Working mothers on maternity leave

Having established that there is a reasonable business need, the task now is to figure out the best way to implement the system. There are several methods of setting up a system for remote access:

- You can choose a network operating system (NOS) that allows you to set up remote access.

- You can also choose hardware methods that work interactively with the NOS.

- You can choose hardware methods that work without (necessarily) needing NOS intervention.

- You can select an Internet access method.

Network Operating System RAS

The major network operating systems allow you to set up some form of telecommuting, either right out of the box or through third-party solutions. Windows NT Server, for example, allows you to set up what is termed *Remote Access Service* (*RAS*) using conventional asynchronous telephone lines, ISDN, or X.25 connections.

Although it is possible, most of the users you'll be supporting will not have ISDN lines running into their houses. The ISDN RAS feature of NT has a dual purpose—it can be used by users dialing in from home or by WAN connections. The X.25 feature is for WAN connectivity.

Windows NT RAS is designed to support the telecommuting features that users need and allow servers that have no WAN connection with each another to communicate using RAS.

Additionally, a new feature of the leading NOSs is that they have the ability to support access to servers via the Internet using the Point-to-Point Tunneling Protocol (PPTP, discussed in Chapter 22) and Virtual Private Networks (VPNs). This method allows users to dial in to their Internet service providers (ISPs) and then connect through the Internet to the company's servers as though they were on the local network. This is a brand-new area of networking called *extranets,* and hardware vendors are just now coming to the fore with products that are extranet-aware.

You could, with standard operating system features, simply plug a modem or two into the back of a server, set up the RAS service, and you'd be in business to offer your users telecommuting. The problem with this is that you're essentially limited to two modems. What if you have a lot of users that need this service, and a two-modem setup just won't handle the load? Do you install NT RAS on several servers and pass out all the servers' phone numbers? Intuitively, this scenario could get pretty cumbersome.

NOTE   Phone companies and most PBX vendors allow you to set up a functionality where users can call one phone number even though there are several modems hooked up to a system. All of the phone numbers are tied together, and when the user calls in, if the first modem is busy, the next vacant one is selected. The phone number that the user calls is termed a *hunt number.*

There are other hardware solutions that provide expandability to your telecommuting needs by either cooperating and interacting with the NOS or acting as independent devices on the network. This chapter covers two such alternatives: multiport serial adapters and remote access servers.

Multiport Serial Adapters

If budget dollars are a concern or you don't want the hassle of a dedicated remote access device, a *multiport serial adapter* is just what the doctor ordered. They're called:

- *multiport* because you can hang several modems, or other serial devices such as Point of Sale (POS) terminals, off of them

- *serial* because they have serial ports similar to the serial ports on the back of your server (the difference being that typically the server will have DB-9 ports for its serial ports and the multiport serial adapters typically use DB-25 connectors, as shown in Figure 23.1 below)

- *adapters* because they usually come in the form of a card that you have to plug into the bus on the server

FIGURE 23.1:

A DB-9 and a DB-25 connector

The multiport serial adapter is a hardware device that allows you to install multiple modems on a computer. Usually these devices come equipped with four, eight, or sixteen serial ports and thus can support the same number of connected modems. You can double the number of modems supported simply by buying a card that supports more modems or by doubling up on the cards in your system. The number of supported modems for any one computer depends on the company through which you're buying the cards—the typical maximum is thirty-two modems, although you can go much higher with certain vendors.

The typical multiport serial adapter comes in two flavors: non-intelligent and intelligent. There are two basic differences between the intelligent adapters and the non-intelligent adapters. An intelligent multiport serial adapter has a processor on it that manages requests to and from the modems, thus offloading the work of the CPU. Also, the intelligent adapter doesn't require that you assign an IRQ, but the non-intelligent adapter does. As you might imagine, an intelligent multiport serial adapter is more expensive (by about one-third to one-half) but it has the advantage that your server won't bog down when it is trying to do normal server duties and talk to the modems at the same time. Non-intelligent multiport serial adapters, of course, don't have the processor, and so they cost significantly less.

You can get multiport serial adapters in two different configurations. In the first configuration, you get the adapter card that goes into the server and a cable that is called an octopus (because it looks like an octopus with one head and eight tentacles). The octopus cable has only one socket to plug into the card, but eight cables can run out of it to eight modems. Figure 23.2 shows such a card—one from Digiboard International called a PC/X (see www.digiboard.com for Digiboard's Web site). This is a non-intelligent multiport serial adapter. Digiboard has been a leader in the multiport serial adapter remote access industry for a long time and the quality of their products and services is outstanding. There are, of course, other companies that have multiport serial adapter offerings.

FIGURE 23.2:

A Digiboard PC/X card with octopus cable

In another configuration, you get the adapter card and then you get one thick cable that leads to a box that has the serial ports on it. This box is referred to as a DB-25 I/O box. Figure 23.3 shows this configuration in a product from Comtrol Corporation called the Hostessi (see Comtrol's Web site at www.comtrol.com).

Comtrol offers a wide variety of advanced remote access computing solutions using intelligent and non-intelligent multiport serial adapters.

FIGURE 23.3:

A Comtrol Hostessi intelligent multiport serial adapter with serial box

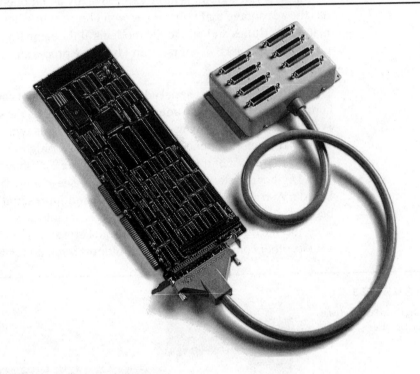

The cable choice—octopus or DB-25 I/O box—is your decision regardless of the intelligence or lack thereof of the adapter.

You can purchase the adapters in the standard variety of bus architectures: ISA, EISA, PCI, and MCA. You decide which type of connecting cable you want: the octopus cable or the I/O box. You can also choose, with some models, to purchase the 16550 UART and get advanced FIFO features, but this is extra money and if you have a limited budget, you can stick with the 16450 UART (see the discussion of UARTs in the next section of this chapter). When you purchase one of these adapters, you'll get the adapter, cable, software and drivers, instruction booklet, and loopback adapter. If you get an I/O box type cable, some vendors allow you to purchase add-on cards for the boxes so that you can expand DB-25 ports when needed.

NOTE The loopback adapter is handy for testing the adapter to make sure it's working correctly. Hang on to the loopback adapter. You'll need it if you have to call technical support. If you didn't get a loopback adapter with the product, request one.

In addition to the multiport serial adapter, you'll need two other things:

- The modems themselves—it is recommended that you choose modems that are alike and not mix and match modem types and speeds. Although you certainly can mix the modems, administration will be easier if you standardize on a certain brand. It's also wise to pay attention to compression standards. For example, some modems have problems connecting to modems that have V.42 compression.

- The phone lines that the modems will plug into—either your company's PBX, which may require intervention with your company telephone people, or private lines that have been installed by the phone company for modem usage.

NOTE Older PBX equipment doesn't support very high baud rates. If you work for a company that has an older PBX and you're considering installing telecommuting, you may be wise to have the local phone company provide some new private lines for your system. This way you can give your users the maximum baud rates that today's modems can use.

Universal Asynchronous Receiver/Transmitter (UART)

The *UART* is responsible for receiving data coming into the computer (serial communications—bits all in a line) and spreading them out in parallel (bits side-by-side in 4s, 8s, or 16s) or vice-versa. This is analogous to 4, 8, or 16 lanes of traffic going down a highway and being forced into one lane, one car after the other. The better the UART, the faster this activity, the translating of parallel to serial or serial to parallel, can be done.

There have essentially been three versions of the UART: 8250, 16450, and 16550. The 16550 introduced the concept of "first in—first out," or *FIFO buffering*. The idea here is that if the computer's CPU can't keep up with the data streaming in from an incoming connection or, conversely, the connection can't keep up with the outgoing stream, there could be a potential for overruns and lost bits. A FIFO buffer gives the data a place to live while the system catches up. There were some problems in the early days of the 16550 UART and FIFO buffering, but they've been worked out and buffering is a valuable feature to have in today's UARTs.

The UART comes as part of an internal modem but not as part of an external modem. Thus, the serial ports on your computer have a UART to accommodate external modems. You can find out the type of UART the COM ports have by checking the Microsoft Diagnostics (MSD) program or your system documentation. Often now a UART is supplied on the motherboard of the computer rather than on the serial ports. For more information on UARTs, visit `www.pcwebopaedia.com/UART.htm`.

In the realm of using multiport serial adapters for remote access, you don't really care about internally supplied UARTs and are more concerned about the UARTs that come with the adapter.

Installing the Multiport Serial Adapter

You've selected the vendor for your adapter, decided whether to get an intelligent or non-intelligent card, and determined the UART that will ship with the card. You've received the box containing the goodies and now you're ready to install. The multiport serial adapter vendors have done a marvelous job of making things very simple. Let's walk through the steps of installing one of these adapters:

1. First and foremost, read all documentation thoroughly. Be sure to pay attention to any separately included addendum, corrections, or deletions to the documentation (called release notes) as well.

2. When perusing the documentation, make sure that the adapter you're going to install includes the software drivers for the type of NOS you're going to be using with this card. It is always a good idea to check the vendor's Web, BBS, or FTP sites for the latest and greatest driver updates.

3. If you're using a non-intelligent ISA card, ascertain the IRQs and I/O addresses currently in use on the computer you're installing the adapter on. Write them down.

4. After performing an orderly shutdown of the computer, unplug all cables and open the computer up. Be sure to wear some form of grounding strap when working with computer cards! You don't want a stray electrostatic surge to wipe out part of the card or your computer. Better safe than sorry.

5. If the card is an ISA non-intelligent card and jumper-configurable, select an open IRQ.

6. Reconnect all cables, including the new cable that came with the adapter, and power up the computer.

7. Connect the modems. Note that you don't have to physically fill all the serial ports on the adapter. You can use just one modem if you like, or more as needed. Be sure to connect the phone lines up and power on the modems.

8. Add the appropriate software driver and configure it accordingly.

9. Using the NOS software, add the modem and RAS software as needed.

10. Test it.

NOTE   If you're using the Windows NT software, the modems will have to be set up through the modem wizard. The process of installing RAS launches this program for you, but you can also choose to detect the modems first and then install RAS.

You shouldn't have to troubleshoot the adapter unless you're having a problem with it. These adapters are very well-built and will run quite well, so you shouldn't have to use any of the supplied troubleshooting software to make sure the adapter's working okay, unless you're absolutely sure you've got a hardware problem with the adapter itself. Nine times out of ten it's a configuration or IRQ problem and not the adapter's fault.

Port Enumeration

When setting up multiport serial adapters, you may have the ability to change the name of the ports being used. For example, in normal parlance the serial ports on a computer are called COM1, COM2, COM3, and COM4. You can choose, when setting up the adapter, to name the ports on the adapter something other than COM. For example, you could call them RAS1, RAS2, and so forth. This would give you the ability to differentiate between the COM ports on the computer and the serial ports on the adapter.

Usually the adapter will suggest using the COM verbiage and automatically name its ports starting with the number after the last COM port on your system. For example, if you have two COM ports on your system, COM1 and COM2, you can allow your adapter to name its ports COM3 through COM10 (for an eight-port adapter). Or you can name the ports something different. If, for example, you chose to name the ports RAS but kept auto-enumeration on, the ports would show up as RAS1, RAS2, etc. This automatic numbering process is called *auto enumerating*. You can choose to turn auto enumerating off and assign any name and number you want to each of the ports.

Cable Cluttering and Labeling

If you ordered an octopus cable and you're only using a few modems, you'll have a cable clutter problem that you'll want to handle with nylon ties or something. Otherwise the loose cables will have a tendency to be in your way all the time. It's a good idea to label each of the DB-25 inputs on the octopus cable with the appropriate COM port ID and label the corresponding modem as well. Label the modem with the phone number it's using. These tricks will help you in troubleshooting problems later.

With an I/O DB-25 box it's a good idea to label each serial port with the COM port ID you've assigned. Also, if using fewer modems than the number of ports you have, leave the dust covers on the serial ports on the box.

Testing

The best method for testing the setup of the system and making sure all the pieces are working okay is to stop any RAS services that the NOS is currently running and then use a standard communications software package to test the COM ports. You have to stop the RAS service first, because the service has the COM ports tied up and they are inaccessible to other communications programs.

A wonderfully inexpensive way of doing this when using Windows-type software is to use either the older Terminal or the new Hyperterminal program. You simply launch the Terminal or Hyperterminal program, select the port you want to dial out on, and then dial a test number to make sure communications are working. If you're familiar with the AT command set that modems use, you can do everything from the command line, as follows (the modems you purchase will include in their operating manual the commands that they'll recognize):

1. You type **ATH**. (This clears any usage of the port by hanging up, and gets the system ready.) The computer responds: OK.

2. You type **ATDT <phone number>**. The computer responds by dialing the number and putting the appropriate connection verbiage onscreen.

3. You could test connecting to a fax machine, another RAS server somewhere, a BBS, or even another RAS port on the adapter. The important question to ask yourself here is, did the computer have any difficulty using the port you selected when dialing out?

4. Next, test dialing into the computer. This tests the modem and makes sure the answer string is set correctly.

5. When you're sure the multiport serial adapter card is communicating correctly with the modems and vice-versa, turn the RAS service back on and you're ready to test the RAS service itself.

6. From another computer on the network equipped with a modem, perhaps a laptop, dial in to the RAS server and make sure you can connect okay. Test by logging on, copying files, running an executable, and doing any other things you might do as a user connected to the system.

Once you've tested the adapter, modems, and RAS software and made sure everything's working correctly, you can put it into production use.

Integrated Services Digital Networks (ISDN) Lines

ISDN is a phone service that you can purchase from your local phone company. It provides two 64KB *bearer* lines for data and one digital line for synchronization. Thus it's commonly called 2B+D. The 64KB bandwidth of each of the bearer lines provides for high speed connections. The phone company has to run a separate phone cable for it and it requires a special setup. You can purchase ISDN telephone sets and modems. You can't usually call an asynchronous phone or modem using ISDN. Instead, you must plan on calling another ISDN device. The ISDN service is billed a flat fee per month and then a usage fee for time online.

Some of your power users may want to have the phone company install an ISDN line into their houses and then telecommute using the high speed of ISDN. This requires, on their end, an ISDN modem of some kind, an example of which might be a Motorola BitSurfr. The modem will come with Windows drivers for the modem, and it'll be fully compatible, just like a conventional asynchronous modem would be.

To support this user you would have to do the following things:

- Request a Basic Rate Interface (BRI) ISDN phone installed in your company.

- Purchase an ISDN modem that is compatible with your user's modem.

or

- Purchase a multiport serial adapter that can support both asynchronous modems and ISDN modems at the same time.

or

- Purchase an internal ISDN adapter for the server.

You will find that getting the ISDN line from the phone company and then setting up and testing the line will be the most time-consuming part of this endeavor. But once set up, ISDN is very fast and reliable. If you have users that want this service, don't be afraid of checking into it.

Digital Subscriber Line (DSL)

A brand new high-speed asynchronous phone line that is just now becoming available is called the *Digital Subscriber Line*, or *DSL*. Incredibly high speeds, beyond the 1 megabyte per second limits, are promised, and all this over conventional copper phone lines. The idea behind DSL is that for over one hundred years, your phone has had the ability to utilize a huge quantity of frequency bandwidth, from the kilohertz (KHz) to the megahertz (MHz) range. But, up until now, every phone has only utilized the 4KHz range. Until the information age dawned, the need to transport huge quantities of data over phone lines just wasn't there. But now the phone companies have simply figured out a way to allow you to use what you already have! You'll require a phone company to supply a DSL modem on your end. You can choose to have the DSL service attached to just one line, or DSL can feed the entire house so that any device connecting to a phone line anywhere in the house can connect.

There are several different ways of doing DSL, the most common of which is called Asynchronous DSL, or *ADSL*. With some telephone companies you may also have a choice of speeds that you can connect with. The general start-up speed is 256K. DSL prices run around $60–70 a month for standard service and, as you might expect, escalate from there. In a recent demonstration I saw, the US West 56K analog service was pitted against their DSL service. Hands-down there was no contest—the DSL was significantly faster and a pleasure to watch as it flew through the Web sites.

The DSL line has become the vogue among telephony engineers and large telecommunications companies because of the slow speed of standard phone/modem circuits when using the Internet. For the Internet to grow in usage, bandwidth has to be increased. The DSL line is a potential answer to this problem.

Currently there are some rules about who may obtain DSL; in particular, there are geographic limitations involving the distance between the subscriber and the phone company's central office (CO). With some phone companies the distance limitation is two miles from the CO. Phone companies know that there is a distance limitation and they are working hard to install DSL "repeaters" (DSLAMS) that will allow people further from the CO to connect, but this takes time and money, and the telephone companies want to make sure there is a vested interest before they invest in costly gear such as this. Thus it's a waiting game.

To date there are no DSL multiport serial adapters available but, as DSL becomes more popular, you are bound to find vendors bundling DSL support into their adapters.

Interested purchasers of multiport serial adapters need do nothing more than perform a simple query on the Web for "Multiport Serial Adapters". You'll find more information than you can possibly handle, including computer equipment companies that can sell you the gear straight off of the Web.

NOTE Multiport serial adapters run anywhere between $400 and $2000. Modems run between $80 and $500.

Remote Access Servers

Multiport serial adapters have a couple of problems. First, they require some interaction with the CPU of the computer they're attached to, even if they're intelligent adapters. You may find that this function is using up too much of the computer's horsepower to do other things efficiently. Similarly, the user isn't getting the fastest connection possible by using one of these devices.

Second, maybe not all of your users are, say, Windows NT users. Maybe you have some AppleTalk, Banyan VINES, or Unix users as well and want to provide them with telecommuting services. While you may be able to accomplish this with some articulate stacking of protocols on the server, perhaps you'd be better off trying to find a device that could support these users natively, without having to go through extra steps.

You've now reached the level where you'll want to begin investigating remote access servers—devices especially made for telecommuting.

These devices are available from a wide variety of vendors: Cisco, 3Com, Shiva, MultiTech, and others. Devices such as these are essentially comprised of a computer with a RISC processor, operating system software that runs the device, and open bays for you to provide various telephony or WAN cards. You can purchase asynchronous, ISDN, or other cards and mix and match them. The number of ports (phone lines) you want to support determines the size of the remote access server you need to purchase and the number of cards you'll need to add.

Upon purchasing the telecommuting device, you'll also receive client software that may need to be installed at each client workstation that is going to make use of the device.

These devices have high-speed serial ports and, coupled with an on-board microprocessor and security databases, provide much faster throughput than conventional multiport serial adapter RAS.

The 3Com AccessBuilder 4000 Remote Access Server

One company manufacturing remote access servers is 3Com Corporation. You can get a product sheet from their Web site at www.3com.com/products/dsheets/400212a.html#4000.

Figure 23.4 shows a picture of 3Com's AccessBuilder 4000 remote access server. The box is not very big—about the size of a small attaché case—and doesn't have many controls. The front of the box gives you some LED lights so you can check activity. The back of the box is where you plug in the various cables.

FIGURE 23.4:

The 3Com AccessBuilder 4000 remote access server

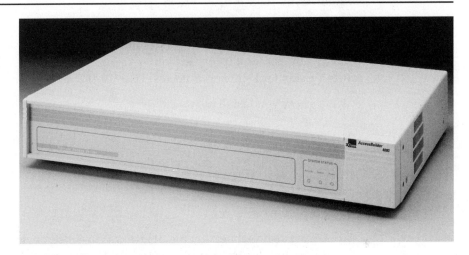

The 3Com Corporation has engineered hubs, switches, routers, remote access servers, and other network devices that stack and can function together in a homogeneous networking environment. The AccessBuilder 4000 is a mid-level remote access server with some servers classed above it in performance and capacity and others classed below it (such as the AccessBuilder 2000 and the OfficeConnect Remote Access Server 1000). Their newest entries are the Super-Stack II 1500 and SuperStack II 3000 remote access servers.

The AccessBuilder 4000 has a modular design and allows you to intermix telephony modules. One bay can be ISDN and the other asynchronous. Since you have two bays and either four ISDN or eight asynchronous ports per bay, you can have up to eight ISDN or sixteen asynchronous connections. You can select token ring or Ethernet, and if you purchase an Ethernet server you can toggle between AUI, RJ-45, or BNC connections. Included is a serial management port for connecting a PC directly to the server when configuring it. Connecting a PC to the management port on the device isn't necessary—you can choose to configure it using software supplied with the server.

When you purchase the AccessBuilder 4000, you get the server, the manuals, software for managing the device, and cables (RJ-45 to DB-25) for the modems. You'll have to purchase the telephony cards and any special software that you require for the device.

The device is rack-mountable or can be fitted with rubber feet for stacking. You'll need an open Ethernet port to connect it to the network and a dedicated TCP/IP number for it (provided you're using TCP/IP—the AccessBuilder supports the standard suite of protocols, TCP/IP, IPX, and AppleTalk).

Here's how you install it:

1. Install the device in a rack or stack.

2. Hook the Ethernet cable up to the server.

3. Hook up the modems to the server and to the phone lines coming in.

4. Power the server on.

5. On the same subnet that the device was installed on, install the Transcend AccessBuilder Manager (TABM) software that came with the server. (When TABM starts up, it will use bootp to locate the server and bootp won't cross routers, so you'll want to have TABM on the same subnet.)

6. Upon starting TABM, it will search the network for new devices. Once it has found your device you can configure it with the appropriate IP number, tell it what modems are hooked to it, set up security, and apply other special settings as needed.

TABM can be used later on to reboot the server or make modifications as needed. Figure 23.5 shows a picture of the TABM screen showing a production AccessBuilder 4000 with ports 3 and 4 in use.

If you opt to go with the manual configuration method and not use TABM, then you'll be forced to learn the AccessBuilder's command language and set up everything from its command prompt. While this is not an overwhelming thing to do, it's better if you use TABM for everything.

TABM Management Screen showing an active Access-Builder 4000. Ports 3 and 4 are in use as indicated by the darker color.

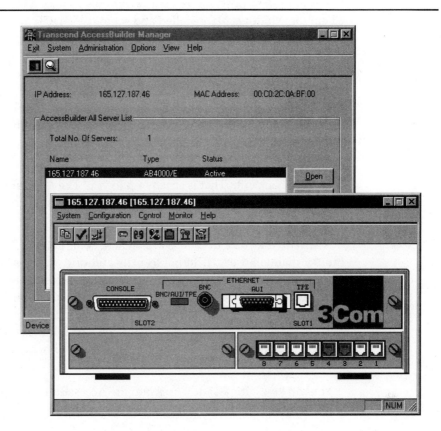

Client Authentication Software

The remote access server typically comes with the ability to set up a user database that is known to the server itself. In other words, you have the ability to key in the names of users who will be allowed to dial in to the server. The remote access server, and not your regular network servers, thus handles *authentication*. This may be the way that you want to go, because you can tightly restrict who is and who is not allowed to dial in to the server. The advantage to this kind of setup is that when a user dials in, at authentication time the protocol stack on the user's PC and network clients that the user has loaded will operate just as though he or she is connected to the network and will find the servers the user needs to log on to.

The AccessBuilder validates the user as a legitimate user by checking its internal database, and after that the user is validated by the servers used for logon. For example, suppose you're using Windows 95 to dial in, and you have the Client for Windows NT installed and set to use DHCP. You dial in to the AccessBuilder and supply your credentials. Then you are passed to validating servers. If your username and password in the AccessBuilder match your NT username and password, you'll be validated and treated just like a LAN node. If not, you'll be presented with a user authentication credentials box and required to fill in your NT username and password before proceeding. You would want to use this kind of authentication (internal database) if your users had a protocol that the AccessBuilder didn't support, such as the VINES protocol.

The main problem with the internal database method is that it may or may not be easy to hack into. That is strictly up to you. The AccessBuilder's administrative account is named Admin, by default, and if you're not careful with passwords, you'll have a large security hole.

Alternatively you can choose to purchase some extra software for the AccessBuilder that will use an external security authority, such as Windows NT's security system or Novell NetWare's NDS or bindery systems (among others). This method is nice because the user keys in one username and password, and after the modem handshake, the user's credentials are passed to validating servers and the user is authenticated by the servers rather than the AccessBuilder. The problem with this method is that the user must wait for the AccessBuilder to pass the credentials to a validating server and then get logon authority back.

You can key static IP addresses into the AccessBuilder or it can use DHCP. You can also use IPX or AppleTalk. NetBEUI is *not* supported by the AccessBuilder.

WARNING   In the NT world, users have to have log on locally-advanced user rights to use the AccessBuilder equipped with the NT authentication package. You can set up a local group with this right and then populate it with users who are going to RAS-in using the AccessBuilder.

The Shiva LanRover E/T/Plus

Shiva Corporation has been in the remote access business for a long time. They are highly respected in the industry and can provide a wide array of products that will fit your remote computing needs.

NOTE Both Shiva and 3Com (among others) have recently come out with products (both hardware and client software) that support virtual private networking. Look for this technology to be the next big event in remote computing.

You can visit Shiva's Web site and get more information on the LanRover at `www.shiva.com/lanrover`.

Shiva's product is essentially the same as the AccessBuilder product. The supported clients and protocols are basically the same. Both units support ISDN or asynchronous ports and you can mix and match on the LanRover as you can on the AccessBuilder. The LanRover Plus has integrated Shiva v.34 modems that can be configured mix and match with BRI ISDN ports.

There are some minor differences: separate authentication and enhancement packages called *power kits* are available for the LanRover. These kits allow the LanRover to be used to dial out and to be used as a fax server.

A centralized management power kit is available that allows you to monitor the usage of your LanRover(s). Another kit provides support for NetBEUI and LAN to LAN communications.

NOTE You can have multiple Shiva LanRovers that communicate with one another. The AccessBuilders do not have this functionality.

Costs

Costs for remote access servers are much higher than multiport serial adapters. The servers are between $2500 and $10,000, not including add-in authentication packages or telephony boards. The authentication packages are between $500 and $1500. Boards range in the few hundreds of dollars.

Technology Differences

The question before you now is whether to go forward with multiport serial adapters or to launch into a dedicated server for telecommuting purposes. Table 23.1 will help to illustrate the differences in the two technologies.

TABLE 23.1: Differences Between Multiport Serial Adapters and Remote Access Servers

Device	Multiport serial adapters	Remote access servers
Cost	Not a budget-breaker.	Could get pretty expensive, especially if you add authentication software.
Implementation	Fairly easy. Making sure IRQs are correct and testing are the most difficult parts.	Fairly straightforward. Could be confusing using bootp to get an IP address. Console work is very confusing.
Speed	Good, depending on the modem and whether you purchase an intelligent adapter or not. Remember that the server's CPU will be handling lots of the load.	Excellent.
Advanced Features	Add-on modules for adding additional serial ports.	Add-on software kits for extending the power of the devices. SNMP-ready. VPN support available.
Caveats	No VPN support (yet).	Not for the networking beginner! Also, internal databases may not be desirable, given your security model.

Summary

When the decision is made to move from standard NOS-based remote access to a more robust solution, as in the case when your telecommuting users begin to outnumber the ports you can offer, it's time to investigate hardware solutions. There are two intelligent choices that you can make when investigating telecommuting hardware:

- Multiport serial adapters
- Remote access servers

The multiport serial adapter consists of a card and either an octopus cable or DB-25 I/O cable. The octopus cable has one plug that goes to the card and multiple DB-25 cables that plug into modems. The DB-25 I/O box has one thick cable that plugs into the card and multiple serial ports that the modems plug into. You'll have to supply your own modem cables if you purchase a DB-25 I/O box, but you'll also have less cable clutter and the box will be more durable.

The adapters can be purchased as intelligent or non-intelligent. Intelligent adapters have their own processor for offloading work from the host computer CPU and don't require an IRQ. Non-intelligent adapters rely on the host computer's CPU to do all processing. Non-PCI non-intelligent adapters may need to have their IRQ set.

Several good companies manufacture multiport serial adapters, which support a wide variety of modem vendor's products. You must supply your own modems.

The other, more costly alternative is to purchase a remote access server. This is an actual computer designed strictly with telecommuting in mind. You install the server, plug in modems, configure the device, and you're ready to go. These devices can support an on-board database of users or they can use separately purchased authentication software that will authenticate users of various NOSs. With some remote access servers you can also obtain add-on packs that allow the server to act as a fax server, dial-out server, or LAN to LAN connector.

These devices can be purchased with asynchronous or ISDN cards or both so that you can support multiple telephony options. Some devices can be purchased equipped with v.34 integrated modems. In most cases you must purchase the modems separately.

Both multiport serial adapters and remote access servers support ISDN. Obviously, provisioning the asynchronous or ISDN phone lines and providing the modems you want to support is your job.

If you are seeking extra speed and multiple NOS support, the remote access server solution is probably the best. If money is an issue, the multiport serial adapters are a more cost-effective solution.

PART VII

Optimizing and Fine-Tuning for Performance

- CHAPTER 24: Ways to Speed Up an Existing Server
- CHAPTER 25: Creating and Using a Network Baseline
- CHAPTER 26: Stress-Testing Techniques

CHAPTER
TWENTY-FOUR

Ways to Speed Up
an Existing Server

- Clone versus name-brand servers

- Adding RAM

- Improving disk performance

- Making Ethernet faster

- Multiple subnets

- Profiling

As a server moves into a production environment, it tends to take on a life of its own. It has good days and bad days. Hopefully your server(s) will have more good days than bad, but you'd be expecting an awful lot if you put up a production server and never anticipated a hiccup or two.

Many things will cause a server to not function as well as anticipated, and the purpose of this chapter is to help you figure out ways to make your server and network perform better. As users begin to use a new server, the load on that server will increase. Additionally, as you add applications to the server, this too will begin to labor it and the network. You'll have to be alert to the signs that your server and network are loaded, and then be proactive, as opposed to reactive, in getting the problem fixed before it becomes a big problem.

Nothing can single-handedly turn off a user to a network faster than poor server performance and poor network bandwidth.

This chapter separates the server and the network into parts that you can specifically look at to determine where the bottleneck is and how to fix the problem.

Clones versus Name-Brand Servers

The question comes up time and time again: Can I use a clone for my server? Let's define first what we mean by clone, at least in networking kinds of terms. A clone is any computer that is not what you might call a *tier one* computer. In the Intel world the tier one computers are:

- IBM
- Compaq
- HP
- Dell

Notice that the tier one computers do not include some that may be your favorites and might include computers that you've had trouble with before. This is not to say that other good computer manufacturers don't exist and that their products aren't very good. These are not official Microsoft guidelines, but they are good guidelines to go by when thinking about servers. These companies engineer their computers from the ground up to be servers and for all the parts in the server to cooperate with one another in the most optimum manner possible. Other computer manufacturers may or may not go to the extensive engineering efforts that these companies do when building servers, and the parts may not be engineered to work together in as cooperative a manner as tier one computers.

You may also find with some tier one computer companies that their gear is *proprietary*, meaning that it is specifically made to work with that computer company's products and nothing else. Proprietary gear tends to be more difficult to troubleshoot and more costly to replace.

Any computers not on the above list, but which have a commonly known brand name, would be considered *tier two* computers. Computers such as Gateway, ALR, and others would fit into this category.

Tier three computers, true clones, are "garage" type computers where the brand is not commonly known and the quality is questionable.

When purchasing servers, even though you can save a little money at purchase time by buying tier two or even tier three computers, my experience has been that you more than make up for it in support calls and poor performance later on. Here are some things to do when determining whether to buy a tier one or tier two computer for a server:

- Call the network operating system (NOS) vendor to see what hardware platforms they recommend (in the case of Microsoft, check the Hardware Compatibility List—discussed below).

- Check Web sites and computer journals for reviews of the various computers.

- Talk to other administrators to see what their experience has been with different computers.

My recommendation would be to *always* purchase tier one computers for servers even though initially you may pay a little more money for the computer. The tier one companies have become aggressive in their pricing structure and you may be surprised to find out how much computer you can purchase for the amount of money you have. If you can't afford to purchase a tier one computer, purchase a tier two. Never, never, *never* purchase a tier three computer for a server—that is, unless you enjoy working on servers at 3:00 A.M.

The Microsoft Hardware Compatibility List (HCL)

Companies such as Microsoft maintain a list of designated computers that the company's software has been certified to be installed on. This list is called the *Hardware Compatibility List* (*HCL*). There is an HCL for NT and one for Windows 95/98. The computer is viewed as a complete entity when being considered for the HCL. In other words, you might think that if you have an HCL-compatible computer you're okay, even if you replace the hard drive in the computer with a non-HCL drive. This is not the case—the computer is considered *in toto* when determining its HCL status.

The purpose of the HCL is to ascertain that the computer meets certain requirements when attempting to run Microsoft software. It's a support issue, both for you and for Microsoft support engineers. If you have a problem with a computer and you call into Microsoft support for help, once the support engineer finds out that your computer isn't on the HCL, there is a certain point to which the engineer will go in providing support and no further. If your computer is indeed on the HCL, the engineer may very well walk you through some diagnostics that point out the brand names and model numbers of the various hardware components of your computer, but that engineer will stick with you through the problem until you've resolved it.

Rule one, then, is to be proactive and purchase known good equipment prior to putting it into production. Don't be stingy when sizing the RAM and disk drives for this new server, either.

TIP   Rule 1: Purchase known good equipment from tier one vendors.

But now let's suppose that you've got a server in production and it's running fine. You've installed various applications on it and now users are beginning to complain about its functionality. It's slow, sometimes dreadfully slow. How do you go about fixing the problem?

Adding RAM

The quickest, cheapest, and best speed improvement you can make on a server is to install more RAM in it.

Today's network operating systems use caching techniques to trick the computer into thinking it has more RAM in it than it actually does. They do this by moving data that is in RAM but hasn't been requested in a while to a hard disk. Disk is much slower than RAM and so the server slows down when requesting cached data from disk. If you notice the hard drive light is on fairly steadily in the course of a day, the server is probably RAM-starved and is caching too much to disk.

By adding RAM to the server, you're giving it more room to cache data to fast memory and hence markedly speed it up. It is absolutely amazing what an addition of, say, a third more RAM to a server can do for its performance.

In the Windows NT 4.0 world you can visually see how much RAM is being used by right-clicking on the Taskbar, selecting Task Manager, and then clicking the Performance tab when the Task Manager comes up. The Performance tab will tell you how much RAM is in the computer and will also show you a real-time graphic of how much RAM is being used at any one time. This way you can get an instant fix on the RAM situation in the computer. Figure 24.1 shows this screen.

FIGURE 24.1:

The Windows NT 4.0 Task Manager showing the Performance tab, measuring RAM and CPU usage

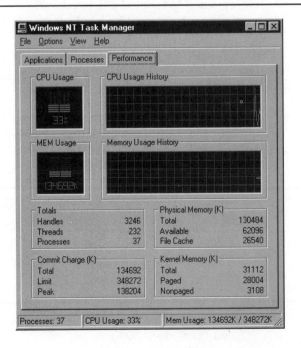

When purchasing RAM you'll have to know the kind of RAM your computer currently has in it. Today there are several different kinds of RAM to choose from—72-pin SIMMS (Single Inline Memory Modules) and EDO DIMMS, for example—so you'll need to know this information. Check the manual that came with the computer for this information.

RAM is installed in special slots that are designed for memory. Usually there are four slots in the computer for RAM, though some computers may have more and some less. You'll need to determine if there are any open slots for you to be able to add RAM to the computer. If you're using SIMMS, you'll generally have to add RAM in pairs. If you're using DIMMS, you can purchase one "stick" of RAM.

If all of the slots are full, consider taking out the RAM currently in them and replacing them with higher capacity RAM. For example, if today you have four slots, each with 8MB of RAM (32MB), consider removing them and replacing them with four 16MB sticks, giving you 64MB. Computers have limitations as to how much RAM can be added, so check the manual that came with your computer to make sure you're not trying to go over!

How much RAM should you purchase? While some people have come up with complicated rules, a good basic rule of thumb is to double the amount of RAM currently in the computer. If it's right now running 128MB of RAM, double it to 256MB. But, if cost is an issue (when is it not?), then you should bump it at least one-third to half again as much as it currently has. Today RAM is cheap and easy to install, so don't waste time scrimping on it!

It should be mentioned here that many people get confused when it comes to processors and RAM. They think that if they buy a computer with the latest high-speed processor in it that their speed problems will be solved. Time after time we've seen people do this and stick with the standard quantity of RAM that ships with the machine, only to find marginal improvements in performance. Do not allow yourself to think this way. It's fine to purchase the latest and greatest high-speed processor, but what you really want to go along with it is more than enough RAM for the computer in the first place. This will require you to think about the kinds of activities the computer will be involved in on a daily basis and to make decisions about it from that perspective.

TIP   Rule 2: Speed issues are *seldom* processor issues. You can almost always solve speed issues with RAM.

A note about processors: Some applications are written in such a way that if they are installed on a dual-processor computer, they will offload parts of their code (called *threads*) to the second processor. Microsoft Exchange Server 5.*x* is a good example of this. The ability of code to separate its operation uniformly onto two or more processors is called *symmetric multiprocessing* (SMP) (as opposed to *asymmetric multiprocessing* where the code is not evenly shared across the processors). If you know that an application is written so that it can run SMP on a multi-processor computer, it may well be worth purchasing a computer capable of this. But this still will not solve speed issues that are RAM-related. To reiterate, don't lull yourself into thinking that running an Exchange server that'll host 1500 users on a dual-processor computer with 64MB of RAM will be adequate. RAM is the key.

One last point about RAM: You can run into compatibility issues when purchasing RAM for a computer, so it's to your benefit to ask the memory vendor if their memory is 100 percent compatible with the type of computer you're installing it in. Get a written, money-back guarantee on this.

Improving Disk Performance

Computers today have the ability to support multiple hard drives. While this isn't a terribly prevalent practice with workstations, you'll often times see more than one hard disk installed on a server. And quite frequently, as an administrator you might make the decision to install even more disk capacity on that server.

The way that the hard drives on servers are configured can have a very direct performance impact and you'll want to take care in planning the configuration of disks on a new server. If the server is already in place, you might want to think about how it's configured today and make decisions about the quality of that configuration—whether to add more disks or change file systems. This section will talk about the things you need to know when determining future server disk capacity and improving existing disk performance.

Adding Another Hard Drive

The first decision you need to make is whether to install an IDE or a SCSI hard disk. If you are in the planning stages with a new server, let me make it very simple for you: Purchase only SCSI hard drives for servers.

TIP

Rule 3: When planning a new server, purchase *only* SCSI hard drives for it.

This will mean that you'll also have to purchase a SCSI adapter for the computer, if it doesn't already have one.

Why only SCSI for servers? For three reasons:

1. The speed and throughput of SCSI drives and adapters (especially ultra-wide SCSI) is so much better than IDE.

2. You can only have a maximum of two devices on an IDE chain and four devices on an EIDE chain. There is clearly not enough room for expansion on a chain of this type. You can hang up to seven devices on a standard SCSI chain and fourteen on wide SCSI, giving you much more flexibility than IDE. Additionally, you don't have to fiddle with the confusing Master/Slave settings for IDE devices. Instead all you'll have to do is be sure you've got the SCSI ID numbers correctly set for each device.

3. If you're considering installing a high-speed redundant array of independent disks (RAID) array controller adapter, the drives that you'll hook to it will have to be SCSI drives. We'll have more on RAID further on in this chapter.

If you already have a server with an IDE hard drive in it and you're considering adding another hard drive, you'd be well advised to add another IDE hard drive rather than installing a SCSI adapter and SCSI drives, or to get rid of the IDE drive and install SCSI. Getting a boot IDE to work with SCSI drives can be a very time-consuming and difficult problem, though it can be done.

TIP

There is a fabulous book available that explains all about SCSI and really should be a part of your collection. It's called *The Book of SCSI* by Peter M. Ridge. It's available from No Starch Press at www.nostarch.com/scsi.htm or 1-800-420-7240.

You'll also want to purchase good quality hard drives. When considering the assembly of a server for an enterprise-computing type of situation, it's to your benefit to consider drives that have a reputation for working well in servers and for not breaking down. Stick with known good vendors of hard drives for servers. Companies such as Quantum, IBM, Maxtor, Fujitsu, and Seagate, among others, all have reputations for manufacturing high quality, high performance hard drives for server-level computing. Many tier one server vendors will have a personal preference for server hard drives. IBM, obviously, will usually ship IBM drives in their servers, while Compaq has standardized on Seagate drives.

The speed of the hard drive is another decision you'll have to make. Today's SCSI hard drives are available in two speeds: 7200 RPM (revolutions per minute) and 10,000 RPM. Seagate has two different hard drives that reflect the differences in speeds: the Barracuda, which runs at 7200 RPM, and the Cheetah that runs at 10,000 RPM—both are solid, reliable hard drives. Other vendors have the same kinds of choices available when determining drive speed.

The type of file system that you intend to install on the hard drive also comes into play when thinking about a drive's performance. Depending on the type of server NOS you're running and the types of file systems supported, you may want to make some determinations about the size and type of drive that you purchase. FAT, for example, cannot work very well with large hard drive spaces, while Windows NT's NTFS can. You may want to purchase a large hard drive and logically split it into a couple of different partitions so that you can support multiple file systems. This is a very common practice in the Microsoft NT world.

Suppose that you have a server that is running very slowly. You've added RAM to it and have also decided to update its hard disk. The current hard disk is a 1.0GB (gigabyte) IDE hard drive and you want to replace it with a 4.3GB SCSI drive. The computer's bus is combination ISA and PCI. You back the computer up across the network. Following are the steps that you'd follow after receiving the hardware and getting ready for the update:

1. Back up the contents of the existing hard drive. Note that you will still have to reinstall the NOS to the new hard drive.

2. Power down the computer and either move to a statically protected work-space or use a static band on your wrist for the work.

3. Remove the IDE hard drive.

4. Install the SCSI adapter. If installing an ISA adapter, you may have to set the IRQ and base address. If PCI, this will probably be handled for you, though you may have to check the decision the system made if you have a lot of devices hanging off of the system.

5. Install the SCSI hard drive, making sure its SCSI ID is set to 0. (Typically the boot disk ID is 0.)

6. Power the computer up, watching carefully for problem BIOS messages. The new SCSI adapter's BIOS should appear on screen right after the POST messages.

NOTE   You may have to make some adjustments to the computer's BIOS so that it knows about the missing IDE drive. Consult your computer's documentation or manufacturer's support for this information.

7. Since you don't have any boot files on drive 0 (your new SCSI drive), the computer will prompt you to insert a boot disk. This is normal.

8. Re-install the operating system for network visibility and then restore your files.

WARNING   If you decide to keep your original disk in the system to boot from and it's a SCSI drive, you need to disable the new adapter's SCSI BIOS or your new hard drives will try to boot instead of the original hard drive. You can have hours of fun with this problem if you don't figure it out right away!

Adding RAID and Disk Striping

If you've set up several hard drives in your computer, you're potentially in a position to take advantage of *RAID*. The concept behind RAID (redundant array of independent disks) is fairly straightforward, and there are a plethora of vendors who are quite familiar with RAID and can help you make decisions about the correct implementation for your site.

The first thing you should know is that there are six levels of RAID:

- RAID0—Writing data in blocks across a group of disks rather than across one disk. This is called *striping* and you would say that the data is written to a *stripe set*. The stripe is written, but there are no redundancy blocks written with it, so if any drive fails, the entire set fails.

- RAID1—Mirroring. The idea is that you have two hard drives and data being written is written to both simultaneously. If one hard drive gives out, the other can act as a backup.

- RAID2—Bit interleaving. Typically used for large computer systems, this system utilizes a method where bits are interleaved across disk arrays. Extra disks are added for *parity*. The idea behind parity is that the system keeps a completely redundant copy of everything, so that if one disk fails, you don't lose anything.

- RAID3—Synchronized spindles. One drive is dedicated to parity. The data is written across the remaining drives in a choice of sizes (bit, byte, block, or other), but each drive holds only a portion of the data. This is good for software systems such as imaging systems.

- RAID4—Block striping with parity. In the case of RAID4 the parity blocks are kept on one dedicated drive. So, if you had five hard drives, for example, you'd dedicate one to be the parity drive and have four left over for your array.

- RAID5—The data and parity blocks are simultaneously written to the drives in a stripe. This creates a highly fault-tolerant fast technology to use.

TIP   A seventh RAID paradigm, often referred to as RAID0+1 or RAID10, is the concept of mirroring two RAID5 stripe sets. This way you get multiple redundancy because you have your data on a RAID5 stripe set with parity and it's being mirrored to a second RAID array.

Of these six levels, you'll probably only be concerned with RAID0, RAID1, and RAID5 (though an imaging system may use RAID3), so we'll limit our conversation to these three.

RAID0, simple striping, is the fastest of the three technologies. If what you're after is a fast array of, say, three drives, then set it up as a simple RAID0 stripe. Remember though that if any one drive fails, you've lost the entire stripe set and you'll have to restore from tape backup after replacing the failed drive and wiping the disks clean. RAID0 is not what we would call fault tolerant, but it is the fastest of the RAID paradigms.

If you're after speed and fault tolerance you'd be wise to consider either *RAID1*, mirroring, or *RAID5*, stripe set with parity. With a RAID1 setup you could even go so far as to install two disk controller cards and two cables leading to two hard drives so that you don't have a single point of failure. If one of the hard drives fails (the mirror cracks), you'll have to break the mirror, replace the drive, and then rebuild the mirror.

RAID5 is the best solution for both speed and fault tolerance, but you have to have at least three (if not more) hard drives. This is because you'll be using $1/n$ of the array for a parity stripe and the setup will not work with less than three hard drives. For example, if you purchase five hard drives with the intent to install a RAID5 array, $1/5$ of the combined disk space will be used up by the parity stripe, leaving you only four hard drives to work with. Thus, with RAID5, the more drives you purchase, the less disk space you wind up dedicating to parity.

All three of the RAID paradigms will assist you in your quest to speed up an existing server, though mirroring is the least speedy of the three.

You still have two choices to make as far as RAID goes. In a Windows NT environment you can choose to implement software RAID or you can choose to install a hardware RAID controller adapter. This may not be such a clear-cut choice with other NOSs, so do some checking. Either way, it is always recommended that you spend the extra money and implement hardware RAID. A good rule of thumb is that users will see a twofold improvement in performance with software RAID and a fourfold improvement with hardware RAID.

TIP   Rule 4: *Always* use hardware RAID as opposed to software RAID.

In software RAID the NOS sees each of the new hard drives as independent entities. You then select the hard drives and instruct the software to format them as a RAID array. In the case of Windows NT, you can choose stripe set without parity, disk mirror, or stripe set with parity. The problem with software RAID is that it is slower than the speeds you can realize with hardware RAID and you have to babysit the array frequently to make sure it's still functional. I've had experiences where Windows NT has logged a drive on a software RAID array offline and I've had to use the disk configuration diskette to get it restored. You don't have these worries with hardware RAID.

Hardware RAID requires the purchase of a fairly expensive RAID array adapter (costing somewhere between $1000 and $2000) and some more installation time. The payoff is well worth it. The RAID array adapter has a processor on board that handles requests from the CPU to write data to disk, thus freeing the CPU for other functions. Because of the array's bus-mastering capabilities, you'll find that your users will see a two- to fourfold increase in speed when you implement a hardware RAID array environment on a server (after having, of course, updated the server's RAM). The hard drives look like one huge glob of disk space to the NOS, and you can partition it any way you like it. You also typically have your choice of installation options, RAID0 through RAID5. Several vendors make good quality RAID array adapters, among them Adaptec, DPT, DAC, and Compaq with its Smart array controller. Included with the hardware RAID array adapter will be some software to install on your NOS so that you can monitor the adapter and perform some diagnostic utilities.

WARNING   If you decide to implement a hardware RAID array adapter in an existing server, please note that you'll have to format the drives so you can initialize the array. You'll do this through the RAID array controller menus. This means that you'll probably be doing this over the weekend, there'll be downtime on the server, you'll need to have good backups of all the data from this server, and you'll want to plan on *plenty* of time to get the adapter installed and functional. This is *not* a trivial undertaking!

Instead of a hardware RAID array controller, you can choose to purchase and install a standalone RAID array cabinet that plugs into your server via a SCSI interconnection. There are several companies that manufacture RAID array cabinets, and they can assemble them according to your specifications. You have your choice of fault tolerance features and drive bays so that your array can go as large as you need it to. Here are some things to think about including when purchasing RAID array cabinets:

- Redundant control panels
- Redundant cooling fans
- Redundant power supplies
- Passive backplane
- Internal or lockable on/off switch
- Ultra wide SCSI
- Support for > 9.0GB drives
- Support for 10,000 RPM drives

Most of these items will make sense to you with the possible exception of the term *passive backplane*. All this really means is that the drives plug into a bus-type backplane instead of utilizing yards of cabling. This is good for lots of reasons, including the fact that throughput is drastically increased since the device links directly to the bus. Also, software can be loaded into backplane firmware, thus eliminating the need to install it on the server.

A RAID cabinet with these kinds of features will cost $30,000 and up, so be prepared to pay the price! Once it is installed, you can use your NOS to chop up the array's disk space into any configuration you like. In one configuration I've seen, 10GB of a 50GB array was used as a Macintosh partition so that Mac users who were graphic artists had a secure place to store their graphics, while the rest of the array was dedicated to regular disk storage.

Making Ethernet Faster

So now you've made sure your server is no longer RAM-starved, you've improved the processing power, and you've beefed up the disk storage. But though users have seen some marginal improvement in the network, it's still not what you'd expected it to be. What to do?

Probably the place where administrators fall down the most easily is in the design and maintenance of their infrastructure. By infrastructure, what we mean is the wiring, connection points, and hubs or switches in your buildings. If you were to visit various sites, more often than not you'd find good quality servers talking to 1980s infrastructure. It's amazing how many administrators are content with 10BaseT hubs that have been in operation for years. Maybe it's because they're not aware that this can be a serious bottleneck for a network. The servers are quick to get the information out there, and then the data swims through the syrup bottle of a network until it hits the user's workstation.

You can make a drastic improvement in your network's operation by considering upgrading your infrastructure. You have two, or possibly three, things to think about:

- The cable plant
- Hubs
- Routers

The Cable Plant

Most pre-1995 buildings that were wired for networks were lucky to be wired for Category 3. You can't run 100BaseT over Category 3 wiring, so if you decide to move into the 100BaseT or 1000BaseT (gigabit over Ethernet) environment and your infrastructure is Category 3, you'll need to upgrade all cabling to Category 5 before you can proceed. This will be a very costly, time-consuming move, so be prepared to do some engineering, cost modeling, and presentation work when getting ready for such an undertaking.

How can you tell what kind of wiring you're looking at? Usually the cabling will be labeled with its rating and will plainly say "CATEGORY 3" or "CAT 3." A company that specializes in network wiring can also tell you.

One word of advice: Unless you've got experience doing network wiring, you're better off hiring a professional to do it. Anyone can buy a crimp gun and RJ-45 connectors, but it takes a pro to understand the differences in stranded vs. unstranded wiring, cable with plenum and cable without (and when to use either), and how to crimp the connections so that they're reliable 100 percent of the time. Also, there are distance limitations with Ethernet, and an inexperienced amateur might end up in trouble when attempting to cable up an office! Pros have LAN meters that can help them determine if there are cable faults and to find out the lengths of cables.

TIP

Rule 5: As often as possible, outsource your infrastructure cable work, or if you have a department in your company that does this work, use them. Include drop cables to workstations in this.

Hubs

Whether you update your cable plant or not, get rid of your hubs and replace them with switches. Why? Because a hub is a dumb passive device whose job is to pass packets and nothing more. There is no intelligence in a hub, and the hub does no decision making. It merely takes in data from your users and MUXes it out to the wire heading to the servers.

The math is simple. If you have a 24-port 10BaseT hub, your users are *sharing* 10 megabits a second between themselves. If only a few users (maybe four users) are online at once, bandwidth is adequate because they each have as much as 25 percent of the available bandwidth at their disposal. A situation where all 24 ports are online and active gives users only 1/24 of the available bandwidth at that time. Let one user perform a huge file transfer or send an e-mail with a large attachment and your other users are toast—bandwidth slows to a crawl. And you have to remember that at least a few of the ports on that hub are probably connected to chatty servers. Throw in some e-mail servers doing RPC, some broadcasts, the fact that Ethernet is a collision-based environment, and well…you get the idea.

Why is it that, as administrators, we won't tolerate outdated workstations very long, but, for some reason, we're just fine with allowing 8- and 10-year-old technology live in our LAN closets?

Switches

A *switch*, on the other hand, has a processor in it that makes decisions about where packets are heading. The processor manages the bandwidth much more effectively, generally granting each user his or her full 10MB. You would say that in this hub-to-switch conversion that you've gone from *shared 10BaseT* to *switched 10BaseT* LAN.

Switches today utilize *virtual LAN (VLAN)* technology that allows the administrator to isolate pockets of users from one another. (Chapter 9 goes into more detail about switches and VLAN technology.) For example, if you have a group of, say, 10 people who are all accountants and they share a switch with 10 engineers, you can set up two VLANs, one for accounting and one for engineering. The switch keeps the traffic for each VLAN isolated so that packets destined from, for example, one engineering computer to another never have to traverse the network and instead only move across the switch fabric.

You can also set up VLANs so that they can occupy ports on more than one switch. For example, suppose that you have three 24-port switches installed in your LAN closet. Your accounting group of 16 people is using some ports off of switch 1 and switch 2. Your engineering group of 10 people is connected entirely to switch 3. Your marketing group of 10 people has some users on switch 2 and switch 3, and your administrative group of 6 people is using only switch 2. You can set up four VLANs. The accounting VLAN will span switch 1 and 2, your marketing VLAN will span switch 2 and 3, and both your engineering and administrative VLANs will only occupy one switch. Figure 24.2 illustrates this scenario.

VLAN technology is all done in the switch software so you don't have to manage anything physically.

FIGURE 24.2:

Three switches sharing VLANs

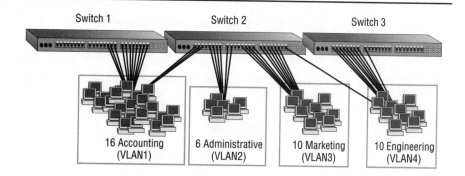

Additionally, another nice feature of switches is that they are usually equipped for Simple Network Management Protocol (SNMP) and can be managed via software such as HP Openview, CA Unicenter, or other network managers. Once you've set up a computer running this software, you have a *Network Monitoring System* (NMS). The switches will report their status and their connected ports' status to the NMS, and you can view from a single computer the status of your entire network. If you move an individual from one VLAN to another, with some types of NMS software all you'll have to do is drag and drop their port in the NMS.

WARNING   A router is required for VLANs to intercommunicate. If there is no router present, a member of the accounting VLAN could not talk to the marketing VLAN. You can buy devices today that perform both switching and routing functions for this purpose. You'll see them referred to as *Layer 3 switches* or *VLAN switches*.

Another nice feature of switches is that they often come equipped with the ability to interconnect to one another using a much faster standard than hubs, such as 100BaseT. This interconnection is called an *uplink*. You've heard the phrase network backbone? Well, this phrase now has some meaning. In Figure 24.3 you see a drawing of a network that has a set of switches in a basement computer room, and then switches on each of the three floors above. The switches are hooked to each other by fast Ethernet ports and Category 5 cabling, and then the users plug into standard 10BaseT ports on the switches (using Category 3 or Category 5 cabling). The servers can be equipped with 100BaseT network cards (or 10/100 sensing) and talk to the switches at 100Mbps (megabits per second). This speed will be maintained throughout the network backbone. When data gets ready to go out a 10BaseT port to a user, it will only be running at 10Mbps at that time. Your recabling efforts are minimized because you only have to make sure Category 5 wiring is run in on the backbone and servers. Your users will see a marked increase in throughput for a minimal investment in infrastructure.

FIGURE 24.3:

A four-floor network with backbone connection

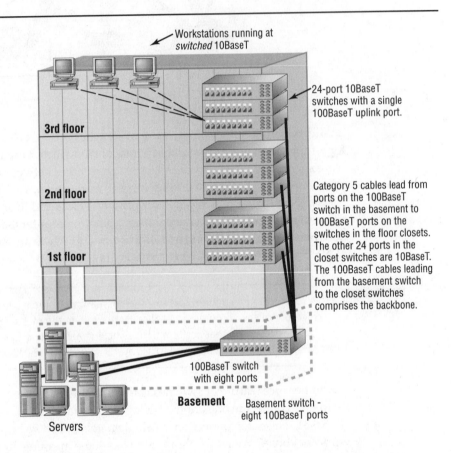

Yet another wonderful feature of switches is what some call *resiliency*. This is the ability to take a port that normally would be dedicated to a user and use it as

NOTE Some switches have a port on the back that allows you to purchase an add-on card for the purpose of creating different kinds of backbones. For example, you can purchase multimode fiber-optic modules that will allow you to connect switches together using fiber-optic cabling.

a fallback uplink to other switches. The speed is reduced because you're using a 10BaseT port instead of a 100BaseT uplink port, but at least the switches can continue talking to each other should the uplink port fail. This is a very nice fault-tolerance feature. Naturally, an NMS system would pick this failure up and alert you.

Even if you cannot afford to re-cable your entire building, upgrading your LAN closets from 10BaseT hubs to 10BaseT switches that are interconnected with 100BaseT will make a highly noticeable difference in the performance of your network.

Lots of times you can find switches that have 10/100BaseT sensing ports that can detect what speed a computer is using to send them data and make adjustments accordingly. Of course, you'll need to have the device's cable run cabled at Category 5 to make this happen.

Many good vendors are in the switch market: 3Com, Intel, Compaq, Bay, Cisco, and so forth. Take your time, go to the vendors' Web sites and get a feel for the kinds of things the switches offer. Then, when you've decided on a vendor, *stick with them*. Don't intermix switches; try to stay brand-loyal once you've decided on a brand.

TIP

Rule 6: Replace *all* your old hubs with switches. Stay brand-loyal once you've made the brand decision. Update the network backbone and server connections to 100BaseT.

The switches will provide you with a serial port, and you can use a laptop to access the switch's software and configure it. Most of today's switches are prepared to pass a variety of protocols and will readily work with TCP/IP or IPX. In some cases you can even key in the IPX network numbers and frame types. And, in this ever-increasing TCP/IP-centric world, you'll have a place to dedicate an IP number, subnet mask, and default gateway.

WARNING

Each switch will require a static IP address, which you should be aware will decrease the number of IP addresses you have to dole out for any one subnet. Make sure that you account for this decrease in the number of available IP addresses. It is not advisable to allow your switches, if they are able, to obtain an IP address from DHCP servers. The day the DHCP scope fills up is the day that you cannot connect with your switches in this case.

If you've configured your switches with an IP address, you can usually use the Telnet program to access the switch over the network and check its status. Or, alternatively, you can use an NMS.

NOTE   Some larger vendors have written their own NMS software. Cisco uses *Ciscoworks* while 3Com has *Transcend*. These provide more functionality than a generic NMS (such as HP Openview) not specifically written for one manufacturer of switch gear. You will still want to be brand-specific in your switch purchase choices.

One last note about switches: Usually they have the ability to allow a variety of different administrators to view them. For example, you could have an administrative account built into the switch that allows full updates to the switch's software. But you also might find that you have a "monitor" account that only allows a person to read the switch information but not change it. And there might also be a "tech" account that gives even more functionality than administrative but is reserved for the times when a technical support person needs to access the device. You may have administrative accounts that fall in between these extremes as well. The point is that each of these accounts has a password, and you will want to change the password on all your switches as soon as they go into production so that it's not easy to hack in to them. A playful hacker gaining Telnet access to a switch could cause some really serious downtime to your network.

WARNING   To prevent unauthorized access, change all administrative passwords on all your switches as you put them into production.

Routers

Implementing a switched environment won't necessarily require you to replace your router, though you may want to take a look at it. Today's routing technology is rapidly heading toward the marriage of layer 2 switches and layer 3 routers, allowing for VLAN routing and vastly higher speeds than was available just a couple of years ago.

In a large network, the upgrade of a router could cost you some serious money. In a smaller network with one or two router ports talking to a couple of subnets, the cost is not overly significant. When making infrastructure determinations, it's to your beneifit to take a close look at the router. Bring in outside consulting help if needed, but figure out if, after speeding up the backbone, you'll have a bottleneck at your router or not.

Multiple Subnets

Perhaps you've heard the phrase "it's an IP-centric world." What is meant by that is that the Internet protocol, TCP/IP, is gaining such notoriety and such worldwide usage that it is incumbent upon you to learn everything you can about it and then to implement it in your network. If you haven't done so already, get started! If you have started, good for you!

TCP/IP brings a host of protocols to the table that give you a functionality that, once you've implemented it, you will ask yourself how you ever got along without it. For example, the Telnet program allows you to access a device, such as a network-type printer or LAN switch, so that you can monitor the device or configure it remotely. FTP allows you to transfer files from one computer to another, and its little brother, TFTP, allows you to download software to LAN equipment from a server.

TCP/IP is a vast, wide learning curve if you haven't worked with it before, so now is the time to get on it. Chapter 3 goes into much more detail on TCP/IP.

TIP   Rule 7: Implement TCP/IP in your network as soon as possible. If at all possible, stop using other network protocols and move to a flat architecture, protocol-wise, on your network.

The basic concept is that you have a grouping of four sets of numbers, called *octets*. Here's an example: 165.127.238.2. It turns out that each of the octets means something, and you have to recognize the numbers. Exactly what the numbers mean and how you can use subnet masks to subdivide and group the numbers you have available are issues that are discussed in Chapter 19. Here we'll just mention some considerations for the speed of your server.

Subnetting groups of users creates a situation where there isn't so much traffic on any one subnet. In other words, you take a large busy subnet, segment it with subnet masking, and you have logically divided the users up into more discrete groups. Since routers (and switches, but *not* hubs) make decisions about where to send a packet based on its address (i.e. is it local or foreign?) and since the majority of traffic is local, user throughput is effectively increased.

You'll have to have a router in the picture to implement subnetting and someone who knows how to program it so that the default gateway is correct for the subnet mask you've chosen. You'll also have to adjust your client computers to point to the new subnet mask and default gateway. Having DHCP running simplifies the operation because you just adjust the DHCP properties to reflect the new changes and then force a lease renewal for everyone.

Keep in mind that any devices with a static IP address will need to have their information changed as well. In the case of printers and things that you normally would Telnet into to configure, it's probably wise to reconfigure the device *before* setting up the subnetting. Otherwise the device's configuration doesn't match the new network, you won't be able reach (or even ping) the device, and you're forced to get out the laptop for reconfiguration or, in the case of a printer card, reset it to factory defaults and let bootp pick it up for reconfiguration. It's a hassle you can avoid simply by reconfiguring your static devices beforehand.

VLAN technology on switches basically accomplishes the same thing as TCP/IP subnetting, without having to go to the trouble of adjusting users' subnet masks.

TIP	There are a variety of good books for learning TCP/IP. Highly recommended is Sybex's *MCSE Guide to TCP/IP for Windows NT 4.0*, written by Todd Lammle. In it you will learn the basics of TCP/IP plus the more technical side of subnetting and the theory about how it's done.

Profiling

The concept behind *profiling* is that you establish a baseline of performance on a specific server and then track its performance over time. You do this by finding out how long it takes for a server to perform different categories of routine operations, thus establishing a characteristic that is measurable over time. Chapter 25 goes into complete detail about how to set up an initial baseline on a server.

Having started a baseline file on a specific server, from time to time you can check it against its baseline. In this manner you can get a feel for the server's "personality"—what loads it down and where its potential bottlenecks may lie. You can then be proactive in updating your server as needed.

For example, if you begin by monitoring the time it takes to copy a large file or group of files to a drive on the server, then routinely monitor an operation such as this, you can find out if disk operations might be a bottleneck for the server. You can then address the problem with an array controller or maybe additional disk controllers. Having a book of numbers that show the disk's performance over a regular interval can illustrate to you how the server is reacting to disk operations and disk loading.

Likewise, if you baseline RAM operations early on and then monitor as applications are loaded and users begin to exercise the server, you can quickly get a feel for what is normal and what is not, and when the server is RAM-starved. Ditto for the CPU.

A network monitoring sniffer, such as the scaled-down version that comes with Windows NT or the full-blown variety that's included with Systems Management Server, can quickly show you the amount of traffic flowing into and out of the server, thus giving you an idea about NIC loading and the potential for bottlenecks. You can outsource sniffing functions as well, should you not have the time or the money to invest in such a product. A second network card in a server, perhaps tied to a different subnet, can, to a certain extent, offload the first NIC and increase performance on the server.

Summary

There are a variety of methods at your disposal for speeding up a slow server or a slow network. Baselining the server (covered in Chapter 25) provides a "situation normal" view for you that you can use later on as the server loads.

In servers, RAM is by far the number one speed culprit. Often times administrators order servers with huge processor speeds but only the standard RAM configuration. They don't bother to buy additional RAM up front and then suffer server slowdown as a result. You can cure a variety of server ills by adding more RAM to the server.

Disk I/O can also be a factor in slow servers. Profiling the server early on can reveal the disk I/O characteristics on a server. A server utilizing IDE technology is already at a disadvantage, and it's wise to upgrade the system to SCSI drives. Even wiser is to purchase servers that are already equipped with SCSI. Throughput is improved and managed better than in IDE-based systems, though you'll incur more costs when setting up SCSI systems.

RAID0, striping without parity, can substantially increase the speed of disk I/O in your server, but you have no redundancy, apart from tape backups, to fall back on. RAID1, mirroring, is a fine fault-tolerance feature and does provide some increase in disk performance. But establishing a RAID5 stripe set with parity, either through software or hardware, can create increased performance and a substantial leap in server fault tolerance. Hardware RAID array controllers are recommended over software RAID. You can purchase RAID array cabinets that hook to a server using SCSI for optimum performance, capacity, and fault tolerance.

Hubs are passive devices that can be replaced by switching technology. Switches, especially when utilized with VLAN technology, can supply an enormous improvement in bandwidth, even on a 10BaseT network. This is because you're moving users from a shared 10BaseT environment, where everybody splits 10Mbps, to a switched 10BaseT setup where the switches manage the bandwidth.

A network backbone can be formed with Category 5 wiring to each switch in the closets. Servers can plug into switches using Category 5 cable and then users can remain on Category 3 wiring, if need be. In this way the costs you incur are minimal, especially for the cable plant, but your overall network performance drastically improves.

Routers can be a serious bottleneck, and it's advisable to look at your router situation and determine whether to upgrade the router, add more memory, or make some other change.

The cable plant (the network infrastructure wiring) can be one of the more costly components to network upgrades. If you're in a Category 3 plant, you don't necessarily have to upgrade the entire plant to Category 5 if you wisely plan out the backbone design and implement switching technology.

Subnetting is a TCP/IP trick that you can use to reduce the number of users in any one subnet. Similar to the concept behind VLAN technology, the idea is to pare down the number of users that talk to each other directly, and thus remove some of the load from the router because users communicate directly with one another in their subnets and are only routed when they need to talk to somebody from another subnet.

CHAPTER

TWENTY-FIVE

Creating and Using a Network Baseline

- What baselines are

- Benefits of baselining

- When baselining should be performed

- How baselining is performed

- The payoff: applying baseline information

N*etwork baselining* is the capturing of pertinent statistical information about network behavior over a period of time. When you set about creating a network baseline, you are creating a history of your network's behavior.

A network baseline should include (but is not limited to) the following information:

- Average and peak network error rates

- Average and peak data throughput (in KB per second)

- Average and peak packets per second

- Average and peak requests being processed

- Average and peak numbers of users

Note the emphasis on determining *averages* (as well as peaks) for each of these different categories of measurement. When you determine an average, you are determining what is *normal* for a given network. Knowing what is normal allows you to easily identify what is *abnormal*. Therefore, one of the key benefits of baselining is your increased ability to spot departures from the normal. Once you know what the normal behavior pattern is for your network, you have more solid criteria to go on than simply "gut feeling" or the number of end-user problem reports when determining whether your network is healthy or is quickly moving towards a minor or major problem scenario.

Of course, this presumes that in creating your baseline, you've sampled your network in a relatively normal or healthy state. Also, because networks tend to be almost constantly changing—adding new users here, a new server there, splitting a segment into multiple segments, and so on—baselining is something that you'll need to do repeatedly in order to keep an updated and more accurate picture of your network's vital statistics.

Certainly, however, that initial baseline is the most important step—it provides you with an initial picture of your network's performance, helps suggest ways you could further refine future baselines to include more details, and helps point out the most heavily used regions of your network (top servers, most active stations, segments with heaviest traffic). Depending on the complexity of your network, these more heavily used areas could warrant their own baselining because such areas may develop their own unique usage patterns.

Benefits of Baselining

We've touched on the most important benefit of network baselining—namely, the ability to know in clear-cut statistics what is normal operational behavior for your network, thereby also giving you the ability to more quickly, accurately, and definitively spot trends away from the normal. Such trends are often either small or large problems in the making, and the sooner you know about them (and what effect they're actually having on the overall network), the sooner you will be able to effectively bring about a resolution. Being able to head off problems before they become noticeable to your network users is an ideal result of baselining.

In addition to being able to spot developing problems, baselining also gives you the ability to plan network upgrades more effectively. By knowing the normal usage patterns for the overall network and each of its segments, you can spot trends of increasing usage over time and project when the more active parts of your network will be nearing their upper capacity limits. This allows you to start developing a more long-term and systematic schedule for upgrading parts of your network, based on genuine needs.

Because good baselining helps spot not only overall trends but trends in each area of your network, you can maximize the effectiveness of your upgrade time and expenses by upgrading only those areas that most need it. Being able to wring optimal performance out of your network by focusing only on improving those specific areas that actually need it is a sure way to ingratiate yourself with your network users (and supervisors), and will certainly make your job more fulfilling and less stressful.

Another benefit of creating and keeping a set of network baselines is that it provides very effective documentation for justifying additional spending for new equipment. When you can show that a utilization trend is quite obviously moving toward needing increased capacity within x number of months, it becomes far easier to get management to approve the additional expenditure. It also makes for smoother long-term budgeting because with a baseline you have more advance warning of what you're moving toward in the future. You may even be able to justify an upgrade that goes a step or two beyond an incremental upgrade by being able to show that the additional expense will meet anticipated growth for a longer (and even identified) time frame.

One other benefit of baselines that is often overlooked is their value in network documentation. For disaster planning and recovery purposes, as well as for day-to-day operational and strategic planning, baseline information fulfills an indispensable role in documenting the past, present, and probable future performance and problem areas of your network.

When Should Baselining Be Performed?

The short version of when it's best to do baselining is: Do it now! Assuming there are no current network "fires" to put out, baselining is something that is important enough to maintaining your network in good operating condition that it should be a high-priority item.

Because a baseline is about spotting what are normal trends on a network, it does little or no good to first go about establishing a baseline once serious problems have surfaced. On the other hand, having performed a network baseline, you are armed with the ability to spot and also resolve problems when, or even before, they occur. So, if you haven't yet created a baseline, there is no time like the present.

Keep in mind that because a baseline is all about creating a statistical history of your network's past and present performance, particularly under average or normal conditions, it is important to include enough sampling time in the baseline to capture the natural ebb and flow—the high and low usage points, high and low error rates, and general traffic patterns, which become clearer over a period of time.

Just as with auto traffic, network traffic in most situations has a "rush hour," or even several such, during the course of a day. Typically, there's a higher volume of traffic near the start and end of each business day, as many users are simultaneously logging in to the network at the start of the day, or reading their e-mail before leaving. Another trend seen at some locations having Internet access is an increased volume of network traffic over lunch hour—as employees are frequently using this time to surf the Web. Even late night can become a "rush hour," for network traffic, as scheduled backups are run simultaneously on multiple servers.

When performing a network baseline, it is not so important to be anticipating these peak periods as it is to simply be aware that such periods exist. You should keep in mind that a good baseline needs to include sufficient time to encompass both the peak and average traffic patterns.

A good baseline period of time to start with is one week. Anything less than a week may leave out certain types of usage patterns that only surface once per week. Perhaps batches of reports are run every Thursday, or intra-network file transfers from remote branches are run only on Fridays. In any case, the point is, again, to make sure that your baselining period includes all of the noteworthy variations in usage that are representative of your network as a whole. Since what is "noteworthy" may not become clear until after the baseline is run, it is best to lean toward the side of excess in selecting a baselining period. But again, one week (including the weekend) is not an unreasonable period of time in most cases.

How Is Baselining Performed?

Network baselining can be performed using any of a variety of network analyzer hardware and/or software. The most common scenario is to simply use Novell's LANalyzer or Microsoft's Performance Monitor and/or Network Monitor applications. The most crucial property needed of any network analyzer for doing baselining is the ability to capture or log the collected information to a file. This means not simply saving a summary screen of averages of various counters, but rather saving an entire set of data points representing the various values at repeated intervals of time. It is only by capturing a large set of individual data points that you can begin to spot trends and compare one set of points to another set (collected later) to detect variations within these trends.

A helpful option offered by many network analyzers is the ability to export the collected data to a comma-delimited text file. This gives you the ability to read the data into any database or spreadsheet program for the purposes of graphing or performing other statistical analysis.

There actually are specialized baselining products starting to appear on the market. One such example is Wandel and Goltermann's DominoWIZARD Baselining System, which combines network analysis and baselining together with built-in graphing and even a troubleshooting wizard.

For the purposes of showing here how to create a network baseline, we'll simply use Microsoft's Performance Monitor, which is installed with every copy of

Windows NT, and is therefore likely to be available even on heterogeneous networks comprised of NetWare, Unix, VINES, or other types of servers in addition to NT (as long as they have an NT server or workstation to monitor from). Later in this chapter, we'll look at some of the most important specific items to log on NetWare 3.*x* and 4.*x* systems, using the MONITOR and SERVMAN tools those systems include.

Baselining with Performance Monitor

Windows NT provides a very useful program called Performance Monitor, which you can use to monitor scores of different counters and settings on the server. Performance Monitor provides four "views," which are different display formats for the data being reported on, ranging from log files to graphical charts. Here's a quick rundown on the four views:

Alert View: Lets you assign a threshold value (maximum or minimum) to a counter. You can specify that exceeding the threshold causes an event to be logged in Performance Monitor's Alert Log, or launches a program the first time (or every time) the event occurs.

TIP   An excellent way to use alerts is by setting a threshold for Requests Failed Total. One potential reason for having a great number of requests failing is corruption and/or configuration errors. Tie this threshold to paging software and have the system page you when it exceeds the set threshold. This, of course, works for a number of other events as well. Be creative and you'll find many reasons for your server to page you. Just be careful, because with too many alerts you might not notice the really important ones.

Log View: Lets you specify counters to be written to a log file at time intervals you specify.

Chart View: Displays your selected counters graphically. You can add as many counters as you like (up to perhaps a dozen or so, at which point the screen is too crowded to view what's going on).

Report View: Like Chart View, displays counters in real time, but without a corresponding chart. (This allows you to fit more counters on the screen.)

Performance Monitor also allows you to monitor counters and values of other NT servers on your network. This allows you to (for example) compare the behavior on two or more different servers over the same time period to see if they are experiencing the same load symptoms, and so on.

Starting Performance Monitor

From any NT server or workstation, Performance Monitor is accessible via the Start menu. To start up Performance Monitor, click the Start button and select Programs ➤ Administrative Tools (Common) ➤ Performance Monitor.

Switch to Log View

To configure Performance Monitor, from the main menu select View ➤ Log. Alternately, you can use the keyboard shortcut of Ctrl+L.

Add Logging Counters

To add counters to be logged, simply click the + toolbar button. An Add to Log dialog box will be displayed. Unlike Chart view, Log view lets you select and add entire categories of counter objects at once. Figure 25.1 shows the Add to Log dialog box.

FIGURE 25.1:

Performance Monitor's Add To Log dialog box lets you add additional counters or counter categories to be displayed or logged, respectively.

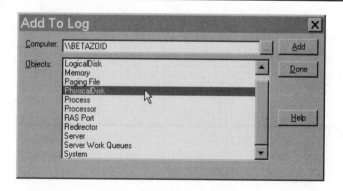

Note that you can select multiple categories at one time by holding down the left mouse button while dragging the mouse pointer through consecutive category items. Click the Add button to add the highlighted entries to the logged objects list.

Depending on the number of protocols installed, whether you are running NT Server or Workstation, and what other server applications are running, you will see probably dozens of counter categories. Table 25.1 lists the counter categories and individual counters that we find the most useful for baselining. If your server application supports NT's Performance Monitor counters, you may see categories that are specific to your server application and are not shown here. However, only categories for currently running server applications will be displayed.

TABLE 25.1: Performance Monitor's Most Important Categories and Counters

Counter Category	Most Important Individual Counters
NetBEUI, NWLink IPX, NWLink NetBIOS, NWLink SPX	Connections Non Retries Connections Open Datagram Bytes Sent/Sec Datagram Bytes Received/Sec Frame Bytes Received/Sec Frame Bytes Sent/Sec Packets Received/Sec Packets Sent/Sec
Network Segment	% Network Utilization
RAS Port (one port) RAS Total (all ports)	Bytes Received/Sec Bytes Transmitted/Sec
Redirector	Bytes Received/Sec Bytes Transmitted/Sec Current Commands File Read Ops/Sec File Write Ops/Sec Read Bytes Cache/Sec Server Disconnects Server Reconnects Server Sessions Server Sessions Hung Write Bytes Cache/Sec
Server	Bytes Received/Sec Bytes Transmitted/Sec Files Open Files Open Total Pool Nonpaged Bytes Pool Paged Bytes Server Sessions

Specify a Log File Name

To specify a file to log to, from the main menu choose Options ➤ Log. (Note that the Log menu option only appears when Performance Monitor is actually in Log mode, which is set via the View ➤ Log menu option).

This will display a Log Options dialog box, as shown in Figure 25.2. Here you can specify a location (drive, directory) as well as a file name for the saved log information. If you specify an existing log file, the new data will simply be appended to the end of the existing file. In the Log Options dialog box you can also specify manual or automatic updates and an update interval. The Start Log/Stop Log button on this dialog is used to start and stop the logging operation.

FIGURE 25.2:

Performance Monitor's Log Options dialog box lets you supply a location and file name for the log file, and you can also specify an update type and interval.

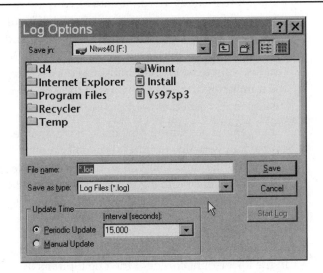

Select an Interval

In the lower-left corner of the Log Options dialog box there is an Update Time option, which lets you specify the update interval, in seconds, for automatic logging. The predefined intervals range from once every second (1), to once every hour (3600), although you can also enter your own number of seconds if you like. The other option provided is to specify Manual Update, in which case nothing is written to the log file until you specifically tell it to record a set of values. This is comparable to taking "snapshots" of your system's state, and can be useful in creating certain types of reports, or in capturing the various counter values as part of documenting a support call. Such snapshots are taken by simply clicking on the toolbar button that displays a small camera icon. For baseline purposes, though, we'll need to use the periodic update.

Generally speaking, the more data points you take in a given time frame, the more complete your trends will be when you go to display them on a graph. On the other hand, the frequent logging of performance information (once every second for example) can itself adversely impact overall performance, to say nothing of the amount of disk space that this would consume. Over the period of a week, if you select a one-minute logging interval, this amounts to 10,080 individual "snapshots" being taken. Selecting just one of the protocol categories of counters adds approximately 1.5KB of data to your log file at each update. Logging only one category once each minute over a week would consume just over 15MB of disk space. This is certainly manageable. Logging the same one category once every second, however, would take around 900MB of disk space. Since you'll usually want to be logging multiple counter categories, you'll need to multiply the number of categories by these figures to get rough estimates of how much disk space is needed to hold the log file.

For general baselining purposes, using an interval of once every minute, or even once every five minutes, is usually more than adequate. Whatever combination of counters and intervals you go with, make sure enough disk space will be available for the entire log file. Also, to avoid adding extra network activity into your measurements, this file should be written to a local hard drive.

Start/End Logging

In the lower-right corner of the Log Options dialog box, just under the Save and Cancel buttons, there's a Start Log button. Once clicked on, this button begins the logging and toggles to a Stop Log button, which you can then click to end the logging process. Note that even for the manual update mode, you will need to use this Start/Stop Log button to actually open and close the log file.

Placing Bookmarks

On Performance Monitor's main dialog box there's a toolbar that includes buttons for changing the view, adding new counter categories, bringing up the options dialog, and so on. Another handy feature is the Bookmark button, which is located on the toolbar just to the right of the manual update (camera) button— it bears an icon resembling an opened book (see Figure 25.3).

FIGURE 25.3:

With the Bookmark button
you can add a bookmark
to your log file for later
reference.

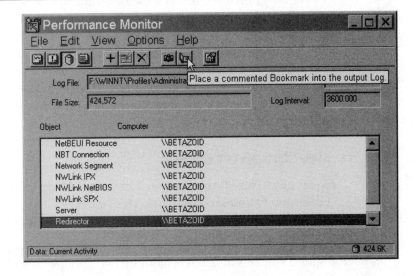

Each time the bookmark button is clicked, it places a time- and date-stamped bookmark into the logging file. This can be very useful for flagging the start or end of some activity during a baselining session that you suspect has an impact on network performance. Later, you can look at the time range surrounding your bookmarks to see what trend changes may have occurred during this time.

Note Taking

If you use the bookmark feature more than a few times during a logging session, you'll want to keep a list of the time/date you made each bookmark, together with a note as to the purpose of each bookmark. One handy way of doing this is simply opening an instance of Notepad and leaving it opened during the logging session. Then, every time you add a bookmark, go to Notepad, press F5 to insert a date/time stamp, and type a line or two of notes about what this bookmark was for (taking care to periodically save this file as well). This is also a good technique for logging network errors or making notes about configurations or anything else that comes to mind. You can store all your Notepad text files in a "notes" folder and use the File Find feature later to search your files for any word or words.

This is a vast improvement over pencil and paper in several ways: The text is probably easier to read, there are no scraps of paper to get lost, the notes are always there to refer to, even months or years later, and it's so simple to do that it seems like less work even than getting out a (paper) notebook and pencil to write on. The only downside is that these notes are only as accessible as the system they're stored on—if the system suddenly fails to boot one day, you may need information from these notes and be unable to get to it. Obviously, in addition to including these notes in your standard backups, you should also periodically print out a paper copy and save them in a binder as a secondary backup system. If you do keep electronic notes in this fashion, don't forget that you can also place these notes into a network-accessible area, so you can reference them from any station you happen to be working at.

View/Graph a Log File

Once you've closed a log file, you can view it at any later point by simply loading it back into Performance Monitor. This is done via the Options ➤ Data From menu option (*not* the File ➤ Open menu option, as you might expect).

Select Options ➤ Data From to bring up the Data From dialog box (shown in Figure 25.4). This dialog box has only two options: Current Activity for charting, reporting, or logging current activity, and Log File for charting or reporting previously logged activity. Choose the latter option and enter or select the name of your saved log file.

FIGURE 25.4:

Performance Monitor's Data From dialog box lets you select a log file to display counters from, rather than using real-time data.

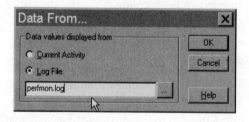

Select a Time "Window"

Having selected an input log file, you must also specify the range of time from that file that you want to view. This is an unnecessary step when all you want to do is view the entire file, but being able to specify a time range is very useful in focusing on a particular period between two bookmarks, for example, or when you want more detail shown for a particular part of the graph.

Figure 25.5 shows the Input Log File Timeframe dialog box. The upper display shows a bar representing the entire log period, and at either end is an area that you can adjust simply by clicking and dragging, to specify the desired start and stop times. If instead you wish to specify a range between two or more bookmarks that you added during the logging phase, the lower half of the dialog box shows a list of all bookmarks in the given log file. Simply select the first one you wish to start viewing from, and click the Set As Start button, located on the right. Then highlight the bookmark you wish to use as the ending time, and click the Set As Stop button, also located on the right.

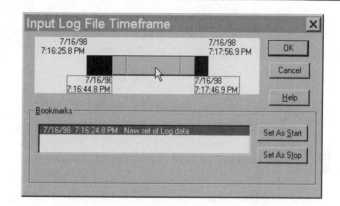

FIGURE 25.5:

Performance Monitor's Input Log File Timeframe dialog box lets you select a range of time to view, which can be specified graphically in the upper view, or by choosing Start and Stop bookmarks in the lower view.

Select Individual Counters to Display

The final step in viewing a saved log file is to select a view (for example, the Chart view) and then add individual counters to this view. Note that while the log file contains all the values for entire categories of counters, here you must select each specific counter you wish to view. To quickly select all counters from a logged category, simply highlight that category and then click and drag the mouse across all the corresponding counters in the counter drop-down list. This step exactly matches how you would go about adding counters to view current activity, the only difference being that the counters are coming from the specified log file, and therefore the list of available counter categories will be limited to only those categories you specified to be logged. Figure 25.6 shows a typical view of several counters being graphed.

FIGURE 25.6:

Performance Monitor in
Chart View mode, display-
ing several counters from a
saved log file

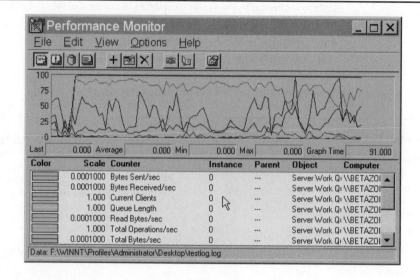

Comparing Multiple Log Files

One thing Performance Monitor itself is currently unable to do is compare two or
more log files simultaneously, within a single view. As a work-around, you can
easily start up multiple instances of Performance Monitor, with a separate file
loaded into each. The only thing this doesn't do for you is automatically synchronize the different Performance Monitor instances to use the same Time Window,
so if you change this in one instance, you'll need to change it for each opened
instance. Fortunately, you can change the time window without having to reselect
the individual counters each time.

Selecting the Best Counters to Log

Because of the way Performance Monitor saves entire categories of counters to
the log file, you do not need to know at logging time exactly which counters are
needed to capture the information you may want later. If in doubt, simply select
additional categories (and allow for the additional disk space needed). However,
beware of skewing your performance results by creating too much disk or network traffic with frequent sampling.

Since you might be using any of a number of logging/baselining packages other than Performance Monitor, though, the following list identifies what you will generally want to include in a baseline report:

- Utilization patterns and types of utilization (logons, file-opens, printing requests, etc.)
- Error rates (peak and average, for frames, packets, connections, etc.)
- Frames and packets per second (peak and average, for each protocol)
- Data throughput (in KB per second), peak and average
- Server activity for most active servers
- User activity for most active users

Again, without logging every detail, erring on the side of selecting slightly too much information helps to avoid the problem of discovering after the fact that your baseline should have included some additional piece of information. In some cases, adding processor, disk, and memory counters (if your software supports them) can provide important clues as to why performance suffers at a particular point during a baseline. When you start hitting upper limits on performance, these additional counters can help identify where the bottleneck lies and what part needs to be upgraded to improve performance.

Monitoring NetWare 3.x and 4.x Systems

For Novell NetWare systems, you'll primarily use the MONITOR tool for baselining. Here are some guidelines for the most important statistics to track.

Monitoring a NetWare 3.x Server

NetWare 3.x is capable of dynamically reallocating memory. It will use all available memory not being used for other things (such as NLMs) for disk cache buffers. Therefore, MONITOR's best indicator of your total memory utilization is the Available Cache Buffers line. The following statistics will help you monitor the performance of your server.

Available Cache Buffers   If the total number of available cache buffers gets too low, it's a signal that almost all the server's memory is in use. Also, the number of disk requests that must be read from disk (rather than from the cache buffers) in memory will increase, slowing the performance of the server. If the available cache buffers number drops below 20 percent, you could experience data loss under some circumstances. This would mean that in a server with 16MB of RAM, only 3MB would be available for cache buffers. You should start planning to increase memory if the available cache buffers percentage drops below 50.

Percentage of Utilization   This statistic shows how much of the total processing power of the CPU is in use. It thus gives you a basic indication of the load on the server. If this number is above 75 percent on a regular basis, you should consider upgrading to a faster processor.

Alloc Short Term Memory   The default size of the pool of Alloc Short Term Memory is 2MB. As the amount in use gets close to 2MB, you should increase the size of the pool with the SET command. Also, you should monitor the resource tags for this memory pool. If you see a module (usually an NLM, or NetWare Loadable Module) using an ever-increasing amount of memory, it's likely there's a problem with that NLM. If unloading and reloading the NLM doesn't fix the problem, see if there's an update or bug fix for the NLM.

Service Processes   The number of service processes indicates outstanding read requests. If an application issues a read request to the server and the disk can't be accessed immediately, a service process is created that will fulfill the request as soon as possible. If there aren't enough cache buffers, the number of service requests will go up, since more requests will need to be serviced from the slower disk instead of memory. Furthermore, the disk can be accessed by only one request at a time, whereas more than one cache buffer can be accessed at once.

If you have enough memory and are still getting service processes, you have a problem either with disk I/O or with packet-receive buffers. You might consider upgrading to an EISA or PCI system and bus-mastering controllers for the hard disks or to a faster CPU, or spreading disk usage out by using multiple hard disk adapters or spanning volumes across multiple disks.

Packet-Receive Buffers   Packet-receive buffers hold packets from workstations until the server can process them and initiate service requests. The default number of buffers is 100. If the number of allocated buffers gets close to 100, increase the number of buffers with this command in STARTUP.NCF:

```
SET PACKET RECEIVE BUFFERS=xx
```

If you have a large number of packet-receive buffers allocated (it could be up to one for every ISA workstation attached to the server or up to 41 per EISA workstation), the requests to the server from the workstations aren't being serviced fast enough.

You can address this problem by increasing the number of service processes, and by increasing disk I/O, either with faster controllers and disks or by increasing the memory available for cache buffering.

Disk-Full Early Warning   You can have NetWare warn you if the available disk space on any partition or volume drops too low by setting the Volume Low Warning Threshold and the Volume Low Warning Reset Threshold. These parameters are specified (with the SET command or in STARTUP.NCF). Specify the number of blocks below which the warning is issued. The default is 256 blocks; with 4KB blocks, the default will warn you when the available space drops below 1MB. You may want to set this to a larger number—1MB of space isn't much any more.

Monitoring a NetWare 4.x Server

NetWare 4.x adds a number of new tools for monitoring the server. In general, the items listed for NetWare 3.x apply to 4.x as well. In addition, NetWare 4.x allows you to monitor the percentage of disk requests that are serviced from cache buffers rather than from the disk. It can also show you the processes currently running and how much of the available processing power they are using, and it can provide early warnings in the event of insufficient memory for cache buffers or full disks. The following are some NetWare 4.x settings to monitor.

Cache Buffer Hits   Rather than simply telling you what percentage of the total server memory is available for cache buffers, NetWare 4.x will allow you to specifically monitor the percentage of disk requests that have been serviced from memory instead of from disk. MONITOR displays the Percentage of Long Term Cache Hits. Keeping the percentage above 90 will result in optimum performance.

Processor Utilization   NetWare 3.*x* displays processor utilization in its main MONITOR display. In addition to this, NetWare 4.*x* has a new menu item in MONITOR, Processor Utilization, that will allow you to track the processes and interrupts (I/O—both disk and LAN cards) that are running on the server and how much of the available processing power they are using.

Cache Buffer Early Warning   You can use SERVMAN to set NetWare 4.*x* to warn you if the number of available cache buffers drops too low. To do so, set the Minimum File Cache Buffer Report Threshold option to 100. This parameter is set in the File Caching submenu of the Console Set Commands menu. It can also be set directly in the STARTUP.NCF file.

Disk-Full Early Warning   You can use SERVMAN to set NetWare 4.*x* to warn you if the available disk space on any volume drops too low by setting the Volume Low Warning Threshold and the Volume Low Warning Reset Threshold options. These parameters are set in the File System submenu of the Console Set Commands menu. They can also be set directly in STARTUP.NCF. Specify the number of blocks. The default is 256 blocks; with 4KB blocks, this setting will warn you when the available space drops below 1MB. You may want to set this to a larger amount, since 1MB of space isn't much.

Using Utilities for Baseline Information

Baselining your network *can* be done with Performance Monitor, FCONSOLE, or MONITOR, although it isn't easy as they do not scale particularly well for larger networks. However, there are many other utilities that will perform monitoring of your network and server. These range from freeware and shareware products available on the Internet or CompuServe to $20,000+ network monitoring systems that run on Unix workstations and will provide full documentation and tracking of every element of a complex, company-wide WAN.

The range and scope of utilities available is enormous. You may not need a high-end system that will provide a complete map of your network, an inventory of the software on every workstation on that network (including operating system and network driver version), and immediate warnings if any of hundreds of problems occur. You may also not have the thousands of dollars in your budget. On the other hand, the administrator of even a small LAN might find it hard to resist a utility that will record and print the configuration of your server, including all the bindery or NDS information, printer setups, and so on, especially if it's free.

The best sources for discovering and evaluating these utilities are the LAN magazines, your local user groups, and the online services. You can download many utilities (freeware and shareware) from the Internet, particularly the Novell Web site.

TIP   As always, if you find a shareware utility useful, please send a check to the programmer. If the program saves you hours of work, the small fee is more than justified. Besides making you feel good, it will help finance updates and bug fixes on the utility and will increase your chances of receiving updates.

Baselining and documenting your network can be a chore, but it could save you in a crisis. Find out what utilities are available (see Appendix B) and use them, or record your configurations manually on paper. Use your server's built-in utilities and even simple devices like the PC transceiver's collision light. Whatever system you use, get a feel for what's normal and what things should look like *before* something goes wrong.

The Payoff: Applying Baseline Information

Once you've recorded a baseline log file, save it. Such baselines will grow in usefulness over time because, as your network grows, comparisons of current or recent baselines with ones taken earlier can shed light on growth patterns—allowing you to more accurately predict future trends and needs, as well as provide feedback on how well an upgrade is handling increased traffic or users.

Once you do a baseline for the network as a whole, each server on a subnet should ideally be baselined separately, in order to give you a clearer picture of where your top network users and most heavily used servers are located. Armed with this information you can address upgrade strategies primarily to those areas that need it, which interestingly enough usually has the effect of helping out the entire network anyway, but without as much expense or hassle as would be involved in upgrading everything.

If you remember the strategies for increasing performance in various parts of your network, baselining will make it that much clearer where to focus your expansion and upgrading efforts for maximal effect.

As we've also mentioned, baselining provides you with a measure of "normalcy" on your network. Armed with a set of logged counters of system activity taken during relatively normal network operation, you can compare these logs with one taken once a problem occurs. This can help you see, in graphical form, where a problem lies, as well as what parts of the network are particularly affected and may need first attention. Comparing baseline information over time can also point out small problems that would otherwise go unnoticed. Since many big problems start out small, this provides you with an early warning system, as well as solid information useful to actually fixing the problem(s).

Summary

We started out this chapter by defining baselining as "the capturing of pertinent statistical information about network behavior over a period of time." We discussed types of information typically included in baselines, such as error rates, data throughput at the byte, frame, and packet levels, numbers of requests made and requests processed, numbers of users, and even system-level information such as memory, disk, and processor usage.

The benefits of baselining are many, and hopefully in this chapter we've given you a good idea not only of what baselining is and how it's done, but also of why it's something your network will really benefit from doing as a regular practice. The payoff comes not only in tracking down problems more effectively (and spotting them before they become larger), but also in being able to plan more efficient upgrades to your network, strategically addressing the most heavily used parts of the network. Baselining provides firm evidence that you can use to justify additional budgeting for network upgrades. Finally, baselining creates a history of your network and should play an essential role in the important and ongoing task of documenting your network.

Our next chapter will look at ways to intentionally place greater stress loads on your network for the purpose of locating network bottlenecks, weak points, and other hidden problem areas. In addition, Chapter 38 provides more information about techniques for disaster prevention.

Stress-Testing Techniques

- What is stress testing?

- Dumb vs. intelligent loads

- Benefits of stress testing

- When stress testing should be performed

- How stress testing is performed

What Is Stress Testing?

Stress testing is when you intentionally cause greater traffic or workloads to be placed on your network, for the purpose of locating bottlenecks, weak points, and other network problem areas. By intentionally pushing your network to the limit, you can spot potential problems before they might otherwise occur, and bolster these areas to handle increased levels of network activity.

Increasing the workload on a network is called loading. By placing a greater load on the network, you find out how your network will respond as usage patterns increase.

Dumb vs. Intelligent Loads

The two types of loads used in network stress testing are *dumb loads* and *intelligent loads*.

Dumb Loads

Dumb loads are simple network traffic that is not addressed to any particular device and doesn't contain any meaningful information. The primary purpose of using dumb loads is to test the cabling system's bandwidth to determine the extent of the load it can carry without significantly degrading network performance.

Intelligent Loads

Intelligent loads are loads that place stress on a particular part of a network or component in order to determine its specific characteristics and capabilities within the context of the surrounding network. Intelligent loads are typically used to test individual servers, server network adapters, routers, or print servers. Intelligent loading involves using network packets that are addressed to a particular node and, in most cases, expect a corresponding reply from the target node.

A typical example of an intelligent load is the testing of a server's network adapter (NIC) by sending it SAP requests. By gradually increasing the number of SAP packets, you can determine the threshold point at which the server adapter is no longer able to keep up. The results of such a test will, of course, differ depending on the speed, buffer size, and bus type of the network adapter targeted, but they provide a good picture of the upper limits that apply to the given network adapter.

Stress testing can also be used to test the effect of individual client applications running on your network. Typical examples include database clients, Web browsers, e-mail clients, and groupware applications, which make greater use of server or network resources.

Benefits of Stress Testing

The benefits of stress testing are similar to those of baselining. Stress testing allows you to determine the weak points in your network, hopefully before those weak points become a real problem for your network users.

By placing excessive loads on the network, you can determine where any network-related bottlenecks exist, such as slower servers, a faulty or damaged cabling system, inefficient server disk configurations, or misconfigured routers.

Stress Testing and Planning for Upgrades

Stress testing allows you to better plan network upgrades that effectively address those areas most needing to be upgraded. Stress testing also is helpful in familiarizing you with the symptoms your network will begin to exhibit with increased usage. Sometimes these symptoms do not show up in the manner you might expect—for example, your users may begin to experience application errors with certain client applications before network usage actually is noticeably affected from the server's vantage point. By familiarizing yourself with these sorts of problems ahead of time, you will be able to respond to these problems much more quickly when they do occur.

You've got a leg up if you already know *why* a problem is occurring when it starts to appear. This saves you from having to start the entire troubleshooting process, often the lengthiest part of resolving any networking problem, once your users are being affected and time is of the essence.

Stress testing also allows you to plan new network segments or other network expansion projects more efficiently and effectively, so that specified hardware requirements will realistically meet the needs of your network environment. Each company, as well as each network, has its own unique combination of servers and cabling topology, protocols, router configurations, database and other server-side software, and mix of client software. There is no way you can be certain whether your expectations of your network's abilities are accurate without actually stressing it and observing the effects.

Stress Testing and Security

Stress testing can even uncover various security flaws. In fact, many of the flaws exploited by hackers on Unix systems are the result of attacks that stress a server to the point where it stops operating normally in some way. SYN or denial-of-services attacks (which we deal with in Chapter 28), achieve their effect by overwhelming the server with TCP/IP packets. Abrupt changes in bandwidth on isolated parts of the network can also signal trouble. In one such case, thanks to proactive performance monitoring, it was discovered that bandwidth on a senior executive's workstation had suddenly increased overnight. At first, a faulty network adapter or cable connection was suspected, but when network monitoring software detected astronomical error rates, the security department was called in. It turned out that a software eavesdropping routine had been installed on the workstation by a junior employee, who had decided to spy on his boss.

NOTE   Continuous bandwidth coming from or going to a particular station can be a key indicator that someone is eavesdropping by monitoring the audio or video port on a computer (this is not uncommon in the biotechnology and aerospace industries, for example).

This is another reason why it is good network administration policy to constantly monitor network utilization via network analyzer software or hardware. Alarms (in the form of event logging, e-mail to an administrator's station, or paging) should be set to trigger when utilization hits unexpectedly high thresholds.

When Should Stress Testing Be Performed?

Unlike baselining, which can be performed continually and should include peak usage periods, stress testing almost by definition is not something you usually want happening during times when normal network usage is taking place.

It is true that sometimes stress testing needs to be done while users are accessing the network "for real," but this should only be done once you've performed general stress testing outside of peak hours and have a good feel for what the various network limits are like. This way, you can make use of user feedback as well as your own observations to determine any detrimental effects caused by the increased load, yet can avoid a gross over-stressing that brings your network completely to its knees.

Therefore, the ideal times for both preliminary and "all-out" stress testing are usually at night or on weekends—or whenever your network's least critical usage time occurs.

In situations where it is crucial that the network be constantly available and responsive to user requests, it may even be necessary to set up a parallel network that mirrors the real one, in order to gather information on how the real network will respond to increased traffic.

Another strategy in such cases is to simply *be gentle*—apply only slightly increased loads, gradually, and carefully watch for the first signs of trouble. By doing this with the assistance of a network analyzer and performance monitoring software, you should be able to quite easily spot performance degradation before it becomes an issue or even is noticeable to your users.

Stress testing is a procedure that you will refine as you become more familiar with your network's strong and weak points. Generally, you want to start out with a broad scope stress test that stresses the entire network, then work your way down to isolating individual network segments. On networks that must be up constantly, though you may need to work in the other direction, testing each segment separately and only finally testing the overall network, and then doing so very cautiously so as not to upset your users.

How Is Stress Testing Performed?

Although more and more specialized products are becoming available to assist in stress testing, much "rough" testing can be accomplished using ordinary tools or applications that are at hand.

Stress testing can be as simple as performing several lengthy, simultaneous file transfers on different client stations and monitoring how transfer time is further impacted by adding more stations.

Simply booting up all the workstations at once (using a circuit breaker or remote administration software) can produce interesting results as all these stations simultaneously connect to the network. While automatic logins aren't normally desirable for security reasons, configuring stations to log on automatically upon booting can allow you to perform a worst-case simultaneous logon scenario, which can uniquely stress the primary domain controller (PDC) or authentication server(s) on your network. This happens, by the way, to be one area that can fail independently of network bandwidth levels.

Many companies are surprised to discover the extent to which simply adding Web browsers to their client stations can impact overall network performance. An interesting test is to ask some or all of your users to simultaneously browse Web pages without stopping to read them. A network that was behaving normally can suddenly slow to an absolute crawl, and you can observe how other types of network activity are adversely affected.

Ideally, you will want to include actual client applications that are typically used by your users as part of a stress-testing procedure, because different applications can cause different traffic types and patterns and may respond in different ways to increased traffic, as well. Programs such as Microsoft Test allow you to record scripts of mouse or keyboard input to "play back" to client software running on individual stations. This allows you to produce very tightly controlled testing, where you can vary the exact number of stations involved, as well as which applications and even which functions of these applications are being used.

Databases—particularly SQL-compliant ones, such as Oracle or SQL Server—can be tested very well by simultaneously starting up SQL scripts on multiple client stations to simulate many simultaneous queries. Be sure to include thorough testing of updates, inserts, deletes, and indexing, as well as record retrieval, because different database servers perform these different types of operations with varying efficiency.

Bridges and routers are good candidates for stress testing. Both of these will at some point start losing (or dropping) frames or packets (respectively) as bandwidth utilization reaches an upper threshold. Normally this limit is far higher than any normal traffic pattern that will exist on a network, but there are exceptions. By gradually increasing the amount of traffic directed to crossing a router or a bridge, you can familiarize yourself with the exact threshold limits involved.

Another strategy especially for testing bridge and router performance is to set up network analyzers on both sides of the bridge or router and compare their statistics to ensure accurate bridged or routed rates, and to detect any bridge- or router-induced errors.

With any benchmarking, careful monitoring of the relevant network statistics, such as increased error rates, packet send-and-receive rates, and bandwidth utilization, is essential. It is preferable to log performance monitoring statistics during the entire process, noting each point at which you increased or adjusted the traffic pattern.

Tools for Stress Testing

An increasing number of tools are appearing on the market that can assist with or further refine the network stress-testing process. To give you some idea of the capabilities involved, we'll look at several of the leading tools here.

Novell's GENLOAD and VARLOAD

GENLOAD and VARLOAD are two of Novell's LANalyzer tools that have been around awhile and still perform useful functions for stress testing. GENLOAD allows you to generate varying amounts of network traffic and view the resulting transmission statistics.

VARLOAD generates a random load between preset utilization limits using preselected packet sizes. The transmit destination address can be set to an invalid address, such as 0x-00-00-00-00-00-00, for dumb loading, or to a specific address for intelligent loading of a particular device or network node.

LoadRunner (Mercury Interactive)

Mercury Interactive's LoadRunner is an integrated client, server, and Web load-testing tool. This product specializes in client/server issues of load testing, and includes support for "virtual users" for testing of text-based and GUI (graphic user interface) applications, as well as database testing and Web browser performance testing. It supports hundreds or even thousands of virtual users, with a single point of control for modifying loads.

This tool supports a wide variety of Unix platforms as well as Windows 95/98 and Windows NT. Database protocols supported include: Oracle OCI, Oracle UPI, Sybase dbLib, Sybase CtLib, Informix I-net, ODBC.

NetBench, ServerBench, and WebBench (Ziff-Davis)

Ziff-Davis has become one of the leading makers of benchmarking software. Initially offering the WinBench benchmarking software as a service to *PC Magazine* subscribers, their benchmarking utilities have increased in sophistication and number, and cover all areas of client, server, and Web benchmarking, including several benchmarking utilities targeted to specific products or platforms (such as JBench for Java and MacBench, for Macintosh computers). What's more, at least some of these are currently free to download (or you can order them on CD-ROM).

NetBench measures the performance of a file server by measuring how well it handles file I/O requests from as many as four different types of clients. Figure 26.1 shows a couple of NetBench screens to give you an idea of what types of things it can do.

ServerBench measures the performance of application servers in a client/server environment by placing automated client loads and measuring the response time of the server.

WebBench measures the performance of various Web servers, in terms of both total Web requests per second and server throughput (measured in bytes per second). Both client and server software is supplied, and a wide variety of clients are supported, including MacOS, Linux, SGI, and Solaris, as well as Windows 95/98 and NT. Servers supported include many Unix flavors, as well as Novell's Intra-NetWare and Microsoft's NT server.

All three of these benchmarks can currently be downloaded at the Ziff-Davis Web site: www.zdnet.com.

FIGURE 26.1:

Ziff-Davis's NetBench

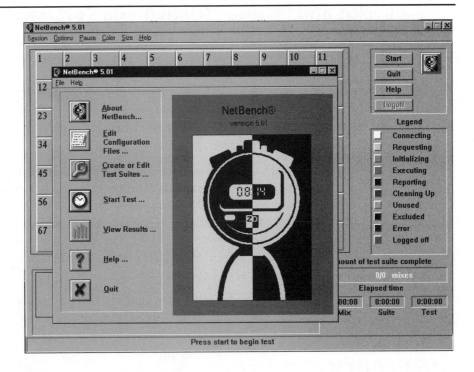

NetTester/1 (Phoenix Software)

Phoenix Software's NetTester/1 tests individual hardware components as well as connectivity and the ability to handle peak loads. Each round-trip packet transaction is analyzed for response time and data integrity, and detailed and summarized reports can be created for either printing or viewing online. NetTester generates both inbound and outbound traffic loads in order to conduct a wider variety of types of load testing.

One nice feature of NetTester is that test sessions can be scheduled for automated load testing any time of the day or night, and remote viewing of real-time testing statistics is possible. This means that you can do load testing of your company's network from home, evenings and weekends—assuming these are times the network is not normally used. Automated stress testing needs to be configured carefully, as you would not want a heavy load test to kick in on a production network just as the workday begins—or even worse, as you're heading off for vacation!

The Phoenix URL is www.phnxsoftware.com.

Chariot and Pegasus (Ganymede Software)

Ganymede Software's first product, Chariot, and their latest, Pegasus, work from the application layer to test a network's response times across the entire network. They support both stress testing and metrics for measuring response time more specifically than simply by frame counts per second, and extensive logging and history views from end-to-end. This innovative approach gives network managers a unique view of their networks. Chariot continues to be the standard for network performance management.

Pegasus is a newer Ganymede offering that builds on Chariot's success and includes the ability to generate data traffic from multiple network systems simultaneously, running packets through all seven layers of the network protocol stack rather than just the network layer. It has sophisticated logging abilities and even outputs test results in the form of HTML files, which can be posted on an intranet and viewed from Web browsers. Their product also handles specialized network stress testing, such as wireless and ATM.

Ganymede Software's URL is `www.ganymedesoftware.com`.

Summary

We began this chapter by defining what stress testing is, and pointed out the difference between dumb and intelligent loads. As is hopefully clear from this chapter, stress testing is one more important part to maintaining a healthy network. It helps you shorten problem response times and decrease after-the-fact troubleshooting projects by acquainting you beforehand with your network's behavior as it approaches the upper limits of utilization. Stress testing in some cases uncovers application software problems resulting from poorly designed software error handling, and can even help tighten up your network's security by indicating security risks or system vulnerabilities that arise under heavy traffic patterns.

In the next chapter, we'll look at specific things you can do to improve your network's security.

PART VIII

Network Security Issues

- CHAPTER 27: Top Ten Things You Can Do to Increase Security
- CHAPTER 28: Internet-Related Security Issues

CHAPTER

TWENTY-SEVEN

Top Ten Things You Can Do to Increase Security

- Implement effective password schemes

- Make default accounts inaccessible

- Assign user and group rights appropriately

- Make e-mail secure from outside attack

- Make e-mail secure from inside attack

- In a peer-to-peer network, use NT Workstation as the default desktop

- Use encryption

- Keep critical network segments segregated

- Use removable disks and drives

- Monitor information access

Good network security requires commitment: commitment from end users, commitment from administration, and a real commitment from top levels of corporate management to make it work. Without the commitment of management, it simply will not work. People, on the whole, hate change. If you come in and start to institute stiff security measures, you are going to rock the end user's world. Whenever worlds get rocked, people complain. Complaints move up the corporate ladder until they find a sympathetic ear, and your security procedures can be overridden. Strong commitment by the very top levels of senior management will prevent that from happening.

Even places like banks, the military, and the government, where security is a fact of life and is taken for granted (to the point that they seem to go overboard with security measures), still get attacked and entered on a routine basis.

Why Network Security?

A story recently circulated through the computer industry of a bet between a security consultant (we'll call him Joe) and an IS Manager (we'll call her Sally). It seems that Sally really felt she had things under control. She was so confident, in fact, that she made a bet with Joe that there was no way into the network. He had just 24 hours to break into the network and to access some vital information with powers to alter or delete it to win the bet.

This was no small company, either. It was a major U.S. corporation, with well-known products. That was the first bit of information Joe needed. He started out with a phone call to the corporate office. The conversation went something like this: "Hi, this is so-and-so out in Everywhere USA. A while ago, one of your sales reps stopped by and wanted to sell me some of your product. At that time, I was not interested in buying anything, but things change, and now I am in desperate need of lots of your stuff. Unfortunately, I have managed to lose the salesperson's card, and have no way of getting in touch with this person. Can you help?"

Now, most companies will bend over backwards to make it easy for people to throw their money at them, and this company was no different. The phone person operator gave Joe the sales rep's name, phone number, pager number, e-mail address—anything and everything necessary for the buyer to get in touch with somebody who would be more than happy to part the buyer from their money. Joe, of course, was taking it all in.

The toughest part of the scam was yet to come. The next phone call would make or break the plan. Joe now called and asked for the IS department. When one of the harried, overworked, and underpaid IS professionals answered the phone, Joe went into his patented song and dance. "Hi, this is INSERT NAME OF SALESPERSON. I am out in the field and I have just done something incredibly stupid. I have deleted all the information I need for calling in and uploading my orders. Can you help me?" Now, all IS people know that sales people are notoriously poor computer users, so this call was not unexpected. As a matter of fact, the IS department had all the information on a single sheet of paper, ready to mail to errant sales people wherever they were. In this case, Joe whined enough that the IS person decided just to fax the material and the fax went to Joe's hotel. Right room number, wrong name; but hotel desk clerks aren't the least bit suspicious. Before Joe hung up, he made sure the IS professional knew how appreciative he was. As a matter of fact, he was so appreciative that he wanted to send a note to the IS person's boss, and that name was?

When our cracker-to-be picked up the fax, he found that it contained all sorts of useful information, including phone numbers of modems, logon IDs and even passwords to access the system. A little reconfiguration of his laptop, and Joe was one step closer to getting into the network. The bet was just about won at this point. All that remained was to access some place vital, so he picked up the phone again and called and asked to talk to someone in Accounts Payable. Now, this is not an unusual request. In most big companies people call every day to complain about their bill, so the folks answering the phone considered it an ordinary call. When the Accounts Payable clerk answered the phone, he gave his name and said "Hello," the standard corporate greeting. At this point, Joe affected the tone and demeanor of the overworked, underpaid IS professional and said something like, "Hi, Clerk's Name, this is INSERT NAME OF IS PROFESSIONAL, we are doing some work on the network, and we need to run a test. You have been chosen at random, and I just need your logon name and password for about 10 minutes to test something out." The clerk, who was somewhat on the ball, was hesitant to give the information out, and was unsure if he should. As a matter of fact, he mentioned he should probably check with someone higher up in IS. "OK," said our consultant, "But he/she is out of town until next week and this project really needs to get done." In the end, the clerk was as harried as the consultant, and just gave Joe the information. The clerk did tell the consultant to call back once the tests were over, so he could change his password.

In the matter of a little more than an hour, with just several phone calls, Joe had the logon name and password of someone who could do damage to the Accounts Payable section of the company's accounting system. The consultant dialed in, connected, logged on as the clerk, and sent an e-mail to the IS manager, letting the manager know that the fool proof, totally secure system was hacked in less than an hour using tools as rare and exotic as the telephone and directory assistance.

Now, let's examine this scenario. Where did the system fail? Can we blame the receptionist for giving out the information on the salesperson? No, not really, some information has got to be public knowledge and certainly the names of sales people would fall under that category.

What about the overworked IS professional? While everyone can make a mistake, this mistake was of a career-limiting proportion—maybe even career-ending. Suppose someone called up and simply asked you, "Gee, I would love to get into your network, can you give me the ability to do that?" You would probably hang the phone up laughing. But just because this person happened to know the name and title of a coworker, everything was OK. This IS person should be given a corrective interview and sentenced to adding paper to printers on the night shift for a couple of months. An IS person should be the last person willing to fax out information on how to access the company's computer network, but too often that is not the case.

What about the clerk who gave out the logon name and password? Should they be the subject of some disciplinary action? It depends. How strongly is security stressed at this organization? What types of policies are in place? Chances are, the security policy is written as part of the Human Resources Policy Manual and forgotten. If it is never enforced, now is a lousy time to start. If anyone should be the subject of a corrective interview, it might be the IS Manager. If the IS Manager had done a better job of stressing security, the clerk would have recognized that this was not a request that should be complied with, and several red flags would have been raised.

How are things like this prevented? Let's get to the top ten things that can be done to help protect your network.

TIP   The goal here is to make it as difficult as possible to crack the security of your system. Network security is like security on your home: You do the best you can, but if someone is determined to break in, chances are they will find a way.

Password Schemes

Starting in Network Administration 101 at the local technical college, would-be system administrators are taught that unique logon names and a strict password policy are the first lines of defense of your corporate network. If these two things are easily compromised, other security measures are not very effective.

Password Basics

If you were *really* concerned about password security, you would have a password policy requiring passwords to be a minimum of 15 random, computer-generated characters, mixing letters, punctuation and numbers. In addition, these passwords would expire on a daily basis, and when the password was changed, it would have to be unique. In addition, the passwords would be checked to make sure no one was playing the sequential game to defeat the password policy. You know the sequential game, since this is the month of June, my password is Earth06. Next month it will be Earth07.

While that policy would be great from an IS point of view, your end users would probably string you up from the nearest server rack.

Let's examine some things that should be in your password policies.

Password Minimum Size

First of all, set a minimum number of characters that should be in the password. All of the major network operating systems allow administrators to do this. Remember, the reason you are setting a minimum is to make it more difficult for someone to guess a password. The more letters you require, the harder it will be to guess; but it will also be harder for users (including you) to enter. So you need to reach a happy medium. You want to have your password minimum set to the maximum number of letters your users can remember *without* writing it down. After all, the worst thing that ever happened to network security was the invention of the Post-It! Many companies feel that 6 or 7 letters in a password seems to be a happy medium.

Password Makeup

Stress to your users that their passwords should contain letters and numbers. Common names should not be allowed. If you really want to be security conscious, find a program that will randomly generate a series of letters and numbers, and have that assign all the passwords. But keep in mind that those passwords would be hard to remember, and many users might resort to Post-Its. You may want to get a copy of some cracking code and run it on your system. The cracking code will go out and test passwords against a dictionary. If it finds a word that it recognizes, it will make a note of that entry.

TIP   Books devoted to network security often contain such code on CD.

User Education

Make sure your users understand that a password is one of the keys to the system. It, along with logon names, opens the door to information. Passwords are to be kept private. Any user caught giving out a password should be subject to some form of disciplinary action. This discipline should be part of the written policy that employees sign when they start working for the company.

You are probably saying to yourself, but what about my system? My users have to remember a logon name and password for the NT domain, a username and password for the Novell system, a password for the mainframe, an e-mail password, a PIN for the voice mail system, and three passwords for individual software accounts. How can you ask them to change these passwords regularly, keep them unique, and still remember them? This really is a tough question. What are you to do? Ultimately, your first responsibility as an IS person is to protect the data on your network. It is up to you to protect the data at all costs. This is why we have things like login names, passwords, file system rights, directory rights, trust assignments and all the rest. The whole system is designed to protect the data. It is true that the user has a lot to remember, and passwords can be an irritant. It is also true that the same user who screams the loudest about having so many passwords to remember is the same end user who can quote the batting average of their favorite baseball player for the last 10 years, remember the exact number of points Michael Jordan scored in each of the championship years, knows which beanie babies are scarce and how much each sold for, or can remember what they planted in the garden last year and what was the final outcome of the crop. Sorry, folks, it is hard to feel sorry for people having to remember 10 extra sequences of numbers and letters when they can already handle this amount of vital information.

Audit the passwords, check them regularly, and police them. Have no sympathy for people who forget and even less for anyone giving out their password or leaving an open computer connection. Some network operating systems have a way to guarantee unique passwords. If a user does forget their password, you may have a set of default passwords to use for the reset. The first reset might be "password," the second might be "password01," the third might be "forgetful," and the fourth might be something stronger.

Different Strokes for Different Folks

Password policies are rather fluid things. Depending on your system, you may have several levels of password security. For example, a clerk in the word processing department may not have the same level of access to sensitive information as the head of the payroll department. In this case, the password restrictions can be set differently for the clerk than for the payroll manager. The clerk may only need a password five characters in length and change it once every 60 days, while the payroll manager may need a password seven characters in length and may need to change it every two weeks.

TIP For an interesting article on passwords, see the 1985 work from the Department of Defense, entitled the *Department of Defense Password Management Guideline,* at `http://www.alw.nih.gov/Security/FIRST/papers/password/dodpwman.txt`.

Remove Default Accounts

For NT there is Administrator, for NetWare 5 there is Admin, and for NetWare 3.*x* there is Supervisor. In each case, there is a default user that has power rights to the entire system. The problem is not that these users exist, the problem is that everyone who has ever worked on a network *knows* they exist. The first line of network defense is the username/password combination. You must match a valid username with a valid password. If someone already knows half of the equation, the second half is easier to break.

Change the Name to Protect the Innocent

Change the name of the administrative user. In NT and in NetWare 4.*x* and 5.*x*, this is not difficult to do. Unfortunately, in NetWare 3.*x*, you cannot rename or remove the Supervisor account; it is there to stay.

NOTE   Before renaming or removing an administrative account, make sure there is another account somewhere in the system with full rights. You want to protect the system, not render it unmanageable!

Supervisor Passwords

Another big issue here is passwords on the administrative account. Of all the accounts on the network, these are often the easiest to crack. Common sense tells you why. How many people are in your IS department with access to the super-user (or equivalent) account? If the number is more than one, we have a communication issue. Typically, the super-user account gets a password during the creation of the system. That password is rarely, if ever, changed, simply because it would involve communicating with too many people. You might forget one, and that one person would be the one who needs it during an emergency. So, to "protect the system" the super-user never has the password changed.

Moreover, it is well known that the most common passwords on administrative accounts are *GOD*, *Supervisor*, and *Administrator*. Short, sweet, and easy to remember. If your password is not one of those, how about the name of the company, the phone number of the company, the address of the company, the name of the company president, or something else common to the entire system? Some of you are probably blushing right now. Gotcha!

If you cannot remove or rename the account, certainly make the password difficult to access. Don't make breaking into your network easier than it needs to be.

Assigning User and Group Rights

You haven't been in networking very long if you haven't heard the horror stories about networks where everyone logging in was given supervisor or administrator rights to everything. When asked why, the IS department said it was easier.

The question begs to be asked, why is the IS department making it easier for people to destroy the data?

User and group rights are a complicated issue, simply because many administrators don't fully understand how they work. In addition, in these days of mixed networks, you not only have to understand how file-system rights work in an NT environment, but also how those rights interact with the NetWare system, the mainframe, and any stray Unix or Mac systems that happen to be floating around. It would be wonderful if these operating systems had at least the same security philosophy, but even that's not true.

For example, the Novell security philosophy has been not to give anyone rights to anything at the outset. When a new user is created in NetWare, that user can usually access some utilities designed for public consumption, but that is about it. The new user has no rights to anything until someone gives them the rights they need.

Microsoft NT, on the other hand, has a different approach: Once a share has been created on the network, everyone has full access to that share until the rights are taken away. Sound confusing? You're right; it can be and in a big hurry.

No matter which network operating system you use, group rights are a key management concept. Effective network management is democratic. Doing unto many rather than doing unto one at a time makes the life of an administrator easier. Whenever possible, use the group function of your NOS. It will make your life that much easier.

File System Rights

Data is placed on a network to share. That is the reason the network was created. Your challenge is to determine, with the help of management, who gets to share what data, and what they can do with the data they have access too.

All popular NOSs basically have the same kinds of rights; they just call them different things and implement them in different ways. For the sake of simplicity, rather than working with any particular NOS, let's just use examples of tasks that need to be completed.

File System Design and Implementation

The first part of assigning file system rights is to design a file system appropriate to your network. Designing a file system is sort of like coming up with a battle plan: It is all-encompassing until the first shot is fired, then you just wing it. At least with a design in place, you have a goal to work for and some policies in place.

When designing your file system, remember the KISS principle and keep it simple, silly—the simpler the better. For example, a server may be designated for file and print services. This machine has a 6GB drive, partitioned into three areas: One area of approximately 1.5GB is labeled System, one area of 2.5GB is labeled Applications, and the remainder of the drive is labeled Data. Pretty standard stuff for most networks.

Basic Rights Assignments

Now that this is accomplished, the drives need to be divided up further. What goes on the System partition? Usually this is reserved for system files, like the NOS, the backup software, and any utilities that need to be added just for management of the system. Who needs access to this partition? Do end users need access, or just administration-level users? Usually this is an area that only the administration users need access to, so that simplifies the assignment of rights. If a user has administration rights, there are no more assignments necessary.

The Applications area is separate from the Data area for several reasons. The most obvious is that we don't want end users messing around in the Applications area. We can segregate this area as much as possible, keeping the rights to the Applications directories as restrictive as possible while still allowing the users to execute the programs. Another reason to separate the two has to do with tape backup programs. Applications are taking up lots of room these days, which means extended time needs to be devoted to backups. Since the Applications area rarely changes, you can feel confident doing an incremental backup, which records only the changes made to the area since the last full backup was made. This should be a relatively quick backup, saving time for the really important stuff, like a full backup of the Data area.

What rights should be assigned to these Application directories? Usually users should be able to execute the program file and that is about it. If there is any writing of files to be done, those files should be designated for the Data directory. For the details of implementing that strategy in any particular NOS or application, check the manual.

So far the assignment of rights has been pretty straightforward, based on common sense and someone else's hard work. The Data directory will change all that.

This is where you have to get creative. The data directory is usually divided into private areas and the shared area. We will discuss the private areas later, but for right now let's concentrate on the shared area.

Data Sharing

The question is not whether we want to share data, it's who you want to share data with. Most networks have a shared area, where anyone and everyone can store and retrieve data. Basically, all users have darn near full rights to these areas. These spots can become the black hole of computer networking. Information gets stored in this area and never, ever comes out. It can stagnate in this area for years. Pity the poor administrator who queries the user about why the preliminary budget spreadsheet for 1992 is still being stored on the network. The answer will always be that the information is vital to the operation of the company and can never ever be deleted, or even moved to offline storage.

So, how does a system administrator handle this problem? Usually, the issue is solved by the creation of workgroups and workgroup storage areas. Let's look at an example. Instead of having just one general shared directory or folder, you create a folder for the accounting group. Inside the accounting group folder, you create folders for Accounts Receivable, Accounts Payable, Budgeting and Management. Some members of the accounting group get access to the Accounts Receivable section, some members may get access to Accounts Payable, some get access to Budgeting, etc. The trick here is that we have broken the responsibilities of the accounting department down and have provided areas for each workgroup to store information.

The most difficult part of this security scheme is trying to figure out who belongs to which workgroup. This is usually a lot more difficult than it sounds at first. The obvious starting point would be to go to the manager and ask which people need access to which area. Don't be surprised if your question is greeted with some form of a blank look. You may have to dig here. Usually there is a department secretary or administrative assistant that has their finger on the pulse of the area. If you can locate this person, you should be in good shape.

As you plan these areas, make plans to have some of the groups overlap. For example, the Budgeting department will probably need to have some idea about how much money is brought in during a certain time period as well as how much money is going out. This will involve read-only access to both the Accounts Receivable and Accounts Payable sections.

It is certainly acceptable for the membership of these groups to overlap. This can get a little tricky, depending on the rights the overlapping groups have. For example, let's look at what happens in an NT environment. In this case, we have a member of Senior Management who oversees both the Accounting Department and the Sales Department. As such, this user is a member of the Accounting group and the Sales group. According to your security plan, the Sales department can read the information in the Accounts Receivable shared area, but it has no access rights to the Accounts Payable section. The Accounting area is broken down into two groups, Receivables and Payables. Each group has full access to their particular area, and the manager is a member of both groups. Because the manager is a member of groups with full access to the two areas, you would expect that the manager would be able to do whatever was necessary in the receivable and payables sections. Unfortunately, that is simply not the case. With NT, if you belong to one group with No Access permissions, you have absolutely no access to the area. You may be able to see that it exists, but you won't be able to access the resources. As an administrator, you have to be aware of the strengths and weaknesses of each NOS.

Different NOS, Different Security

The trick is to know the limitations of the security systems you are working with. You will also be expected to know how the different NOSs work together to give people access to information. No one ever said this job would be easy, just fun!

When instituting a new file-system security plan, it is always a good idea to lay it out on paper. You would be surprised how many holes you can find when you put it in graphical form. You will also be able to spot those areas of overlap where one person should belong to two different groups with opposite needs. You may actually have to create yet another group.

This scheme will also give you the opportunity to test out the effects of your assignments. It is always best to spot problems before they are put into production. For example, the company CEO really doesn't need to know that you almost blocked the visibility to all sales and accounting data. This is an example of what is commonly referred to as a potentially career-limiting mistake!

Unique User Directories

One area where the group concepts definitely will not play is the unique user directory, otherwise called the home directory. Every user gets one, and every user stuffs it full of all sorts of things.

It is a fact of life. Your end users save stuff. Some of the stuff that is saved is private stuff, and it needs to be put into an area where no other user has access. Your end user probably doesn't want to share this stuff, or they would have stored it in a shared area. Since the stuff is not going to be stored in a shared area, we have to make room for the user to store it somewhere else. Hence the use of the Unique User Directories.

Each of the major network operating systems—NetWare, NT, and Unix—has the facility to create a user directory when you create the user. This directory will be a repository for the end user's stuff. The end user will have full access to this directory, but no one else (other than a supervisor-level user) will have access to the area. Usually, these areas are also mapped in some way, so there is a default drive mapping or pointer to this area.

Who Watches the Stuff?

It is up to the end user to police the home directory. The responsibility of the administrator is simply to back the material up, and make sure the area adheres to the corporate disk space management policies. Most such policies say things like, "Every end user can have 10MB of disk space," or "No end user shall back up the local system's hard drive to the network." (Another popular disk space management policy is, "No end user shall use a ZIP utility to zip up the local hard drive and e-mail the results back to another account.")

Information Overload

Seriously, end users should be aware that all information stored on the corporate network is the property of the company, and therefore, management can examine that material at any time. There should also be a written policy in place stating what is and what is not acceptable material that can be stored on the network. Now, we are not just talking about resumes here. If you had $10 for each resume stored on your file server, you would be rich. We are talking about material that is not deemed permissible in the workplace.

This does become an issue, unfortunately, all too often once Internet access is granted. People feel they can go out to the Internet, download information, and save it to their user directories. Some people are shocked to find out that this is not a private area, and that improper use of corporate resources does carry a penalty. Having the written policy in place and signed simplifies many situations.

The information that is not permissible in the workplace can take many forms. Because end users recognize that they can save information to their home directories, you may find a sudden proliferation of games showing up. Some of the games are not a problem, but some games can be networked. All of a sudden, your network performance may take a serious hit.

Unlicensed software tends to magically show up in users' home directories as well. The amazing thing about this phenomenon is that no one is exactly sure how it got there. If you query the person who owns the directory, they will certainly express shock and dismay that such a heinous act has occurred.

The point is that like all network resources, user directories need to be managed. If you set up a routine to examine the contents of the user directories on a regular basis, and take action on what you find, you will discover that the word will spread through the organization and your task will be easier as time goes along. This policing of the user directories can be done in a variety of ways. There is auditing software that can tip you off to irregularities. In some cases, just running a simple batch file that searches for files with an extension of .EXE or .COM will yield remarkable results.

Securing E-Mail

If ever there was an area of network administration that is ripe for misconception, it is e-mail. Much of the confusion comes from the use of the word "mail." Most end users think of snail mail when they see the word mail. As we all know, snail mail is sacred. No one can read your mail; it is a federal offense. In the case of e-mail, this is not the case!

End users also think that the e-mail they receive is always from the person on the "From" line. Unfortunately, that may or may not be true. There are lots of software programs available that will send e-mail and make the recipient think it's from someone else. So, just because that request for an intimate weekend for two comes via e-mail with a return address pointing to your favorite celebrity heartthrob, don't necessarily rush out and buy the tickets. Someone with an odd sense of humor may be having fun with you.

Not only that, when you start talking about securing e-mail, you need to decide exactly what you are planning to secure. Are you planning to secure the system so it can receive encrypted e-mail? Are you going to secure the system so the mail that is sent internally is encrypted? Are you going to protect your system so that it is immune to spamming or spoofing attacks?

When it comes to securing internal electronic mail, the network administrator is also placed between a rock and hard place. On the one hand, the administrator needs to insure that all intra-company communication is secure. People just can't go around reading other people's e-mail. There may be confidential company information in that correspondence, and that needs to be protected at all costs.

On the other hand, the e-mail package is a corporate resource and the courts of the United States have held on more than one occasion that any information transmitted through the e-mail system is the property of the company, and therefore it can be viewed by any authorized representative. What is a system administrator to do?

WARNING

Warning! There is no such thing as a secure e-mail package. While the content of a message can be protected, security of e-mail is notoriously weak. It is not difficult to "forge" a message, making a recipient think the message came from somewhere else. As long as someone can send a message to another person, using a bogus "From" line, e-mail cannot be considered secure.

E-Mail Basics

Whenever you start talking about e-mail, you are suddenly overwhelmed by an avalanche of acronyms. This can quickly become confusing. It would probably help to define some terms, so we know exactly what we are talking about. This will be an e-mail primer. Most of these terms and concepts are discussed further in other chapters, so if you are familiar with them, you can just skip to the next section.

BINHEX: A method conceived for transferring files among Macintosh systems. Files on a Macintosh consist of two parts, the "data fork" and the "resource fork." BINHEX encoding adds a third header part and merges the three parts into a single data stream, which is then slightly compressed and encoded.

Groupware: A type of software to be used in an enterprise environment. Groupware supports more that just e-mail, usually providing resources for communal scheduling, document or forms management, various gateways to other systems, and a common desktop interface that allows for retrieval and management of data.

IMAP4 (Internet Mail Access Protocol Version 4):   IMAP4 is a set of server specifications that deal with how information is stored. Using IMAP4, mail is stored in a single location that is accessible from multiple locations or desktops. Security using IMAP4 is limited to access to the server, meaning that a user must have a valid logon ID and a password to get mail.

LDAP (Lightweight Directory Access Protocol):   LDAP is the "telephone book" of the Internet. It is a listing of users on the Internet, with basic information about the user. LDAP is related to security only in the sense that if you are *not* listed in an LDAP directory, you will be harder to find.

MIME (Multipurpose Internet Mail Extensions):   Before there was MIME, life was really boring: E-mail messages could contain a maximum of 1,000 characters, all the characters had to be ASCII, and no attachments could be added to an e-mail message. Now that MIME is a standard, you can send messages using other character codes besides ASCII, and you can send all sorts of attachments tacked on to e-mail messages.

PGP (Pretty Good Privacy):   Pretty Good Privacy is designed to migrate security to e-mail and data communication. The PGP Business Security Suite offers encryption, decryption, digital signing and verification of e-mail messages and files, 128-bit cryptography, key generation and management tools, and fast search and retrieval of public keys from PGP/Certificate Servers. PGP is one of the two security tools currently being debated for inclusion in e-mail packages. It has the support of some of the Internet's pioneers, including Eudora's e-mail implementation.

POP3 (Post Office Protocol, Version 3):   You will usually hear the terms POP3 and IMAP4 mentioned in the same breath. IMAP4 is the server-side solution, POP3 is the client-side solution. POP3 is used as part of the e-mail client running on the workstation that allows the system to access the Internet mail account. It is not really a part of the e-mail security puzzle.

S/MIME (Secure MIME):   S/MIME is being touted as the answer to e-mail security. It was developed by RSA Data Security and has the support of companies like Microsoft and Lotus to be the foundation of new Internet mail security. Like PGP, S/MIME is an encrypted-key system, in which the sender and the receiver have the key to encode and decode the message. There is currently some discussion about combining the PGP and S/MIME standards together to come up with one (and only one) e-mail security standard.

SMTP (Simple Mail Transfer Protocol):   This is where it all started. SMTP was the beginning standard that specified how e-mail would be addressed, formatted, and sent across the Internet. The original SMTP standard said that all e-mail had to be less than 1,000 characters and formatted using nothing but ASCII characters. There could be no attachments to an e-mail message. This standard was created in 1982 and was revolutionary for the time.

UUEncode (Unix-to-Unix Encode):   A utility that converts a binary file, such as a word-processing file or a program, to text for transmission over a network. UUDecode (Unix-to-Unix Decode) is the utility used to convert the file back to its original state. UUEncode is one of the utilities that allow users to attach documents or other nontext files to e-mail messages.

X.400:   A recommendation developed by a treaty organization of the United Nations, known as the Comite Consultatif International Telegraphique et Telephonic (CCITT). It describes computer-based message handling of electronic messages. The goal of the recommendation is to enable electronic mail users to exchange messages no matter what computer-based messaging system they may use. The foundation for this kind of global messaging requires the ability to transfer messages between different messaging environments that may be operated by different organizations. X.400 is designed to be hardware- and software-independent.

Now that we have defined the basic terms, we can look at the way e-mail is sent internally and then out to the real world.

Internal E-Mail Security

In corporate America today, the three largest-selling LAN/WAN groupware solutions are Microsoft Exchange, Novell's GroupWise, and Lotus Notes/Domino. Since these are the big three, we will concentrate on them.

The three packages have many things in common. Since they are all groupware, you can do more that just send e-mail. Since they are LAN/WAN-based, messages are stored in a central location, called the message store. All of these solutions store the messages in varying type of databases, and the messages (as well as any and all attachments) are encrypted when they are sent and when they are stored. It seems that the sending and storage of messages is relatively secure over the corporate network, so just choosing one of these packages puts you on the right track for securing your internal e-mail.

Each of these packages is made up of a client piece and a server piece. The client piece handles accessing the message store, creating messages, and manipulating data. After the data has been manipulated, it is passed off to the server. It is up to the server-side processes to deliver and store the messages. The major security "holes" come in at the client side of the equation.

Each of the packages has the ability to have a password placed on the e-mail client; in other words, a user cannot access the message store until they enter in the appropriate password. Some of the packages allow this password to be synchronized with the network logon password, allowing the user to access both the network and the e-mail with a single password. This is a two-edged sword. While it is more convenient for the end user, finding one password gives the potential cracker access to the network and e-mail resources of the end user. Administrators may be reluctant to impose yet another password on users; but for at least the most important users, it may be necessary. After all, what if some sly little devil manages to go into the CEO's mail box and read all the mail and (even worse) send out mail to various people within the organization?

Each of the packages also allows for a process called, for the lack of a better name, proxying. A simple example of a proxy would be when a manager allows their administrative assistant access to their mailbox. All the major groupware programs allow the manager to limit what the assistant can do—for example, this person may be able to read incoming e-mail but not to respond. How often managers actually use this feature remains to be seen.

The End User and E-Mail Security

The biggest source of security leaks inside an organization is the end user. End users tend to be really lax when it comes to things like making sure they have closed out of all network sessions before leaving their desks. Many people will fire up their e-mail client when they first get into work in the morning and *never* shut it down completely. It is always there and waiting. This is very convenient for the end user, and also very convenient for someone who wants to access their e-mail account.

External E-Mail Security

This is where life gets a little bit trickier. Internally, pretty much everything is done for the end user, without any thought. The system just automatically keeps information from prying eyes by encrypting it, dividing it up and storing it in a central location. What happens when that message goes out over the Internet to another company?

SMTP/MIME

Messages traveling over the Internet are usually broken down to the "lowest common denominator"—the simplest format—since the client package usually has no idea what type of client is on the other side. That lowest common denominator is usually SMTP/MIME. If you look at the definitions earlier in this section, you will note that SMTP just allows you to send messages in text format, and the MIME portion allows attachments. If your users take no other action than to compose a message and send it over the Internet, that is the form it will take. Is this secure communication? Maybe. This message can be intercepted and read, but this is only going to happen if someone has some very sophisticated equipment and a lot of patience. The greatest risk of Internet mail actually being intercepted and read occurs when the sender addresses the message to the wrong person and sends it out that way. If the message address can be resolved, then the wrong person gets the message. If the message address cannot be resolved, the message is usually stored somewhere on the local mail server in a text-based format, available for people (usually administrators) to read and readdress.

Now, depending on the groupware package you are using, there are some changes to the above scenario. Depending on the configuration of your e-mail system, your client may know that you are going to send this message over the Internet and also that the client on the receiving side has the same package as the sender. In that case, the mail program may decide to "tunnel" the message, meaning that it is encapsulated as normal, sent out over the Internet in encrypted format, and then decrypted by the package on the other side. Again, the end user may not have to do anything special to the message; this will happen as a background process.

Encryption to the Rescue

Most e-mail packages will now allow the sender to decide that the message needs to be encrypted and choose to send it using either PGP or S/MIME. The choice of the protocol is up to the software; the choice to encrypt is up to the end user. When the end user decides to secure the message, this is usually done as an extra step in the usual "send e-mail" process. Before that extra step can be taken, however, a rather complex process must be completed.

First of all, the user must have a digital ID to send or digitally sign an e-mail. These digital IDs come from several different companies, and they depend on the browser you are using. Anyone who uses both Internet Explorer and Netscape Communicator probably has several IDs. You can get users assigned a digital ID for free, and the ID will usually last 60 days. If you want something that will last a little longer, you can pop for around $10 per user and get one that will last for a year. Obtaining the ID is a matter of filling out a form, receiving an e-mail from the security company with the new ID and then installing it by clicking a button. It's not brain surgery, but it's kind of time consuming, and it definitely loses its appeal after the third or fourth time you have to walk a user through the process to renew an ID.

Once the ID is in place, meaning you received it from the security company, the ID has to be attached to the user's Internet mail account. Depending on the POP3 client you are using, this is accomplished in a variety of ways. The company you received your ID from probably has a Web site available that will give you step by step directions.

Once the e-mail account has a digital ID assigned to it, it is up to the end user to share that ID with others. The only way to send encrypted mail to another user is if the recipient has a copy of the digital ID. In this case, the end user sends the intended secure recipient an e-mail, and chooses to digitally sign the e-mail. Once the recipient has received the digitally signed e-mail, they can save the encryption key. Now secure e-mail can be sent from one user to another. This process must be completed every time you want to send another person secured e-mail. Does this become somewhat of a hassle? You bet! Will the e-mail users have to be trained to operate in this mode? Another big yes. Just think of this as job security!

Spamming Protection

What exactly is spamming? *Spam* is defined as junk e-mail. *Spamming*, therefore, is the process of sending out junk e-mail to hundreds or even thousands of users at a crack. How does this affect the computer network in your office?

Most e-mail systems are overworked. Even in brand-new installations, it doesn't take people long to recognize the benefits of e-mail and embrace it fully. Internet e-mail addresses have almost become the 90s version of a social security number. In order to go anywhere or do anything, you have to provide someone somewhere with your e-mail address. These addresses become populated on the Internet, and the companies you have given your address to can now sell that address to other legitimate (and some not-so-legitimate) companies. In addition, many of the online services like America On Line, CompuServe and Prodigy have member directories, with e-mail addresses attached. Getting large groups of e-mail addresses can be tedious, but it is not a difficult process.

Once the e-mail addresses are obtained, it becomes a simple matter for spammers to create a mailing list, devise a sales pitch, and send it to the list. If your company happens to have several hundred (or even several) users on this list, your e-mail subsystem is taking a serious unwanted performance hit delivering messages that the user will probably just delete.

Many Internet service providers, including the online services, have instituted software to deal with spam. Recently, some of the Internet heavy hitters, including Andy Bechtolsheim (a cofounder of Sun Microsystems), Esther Dyson ("the first lady of the Internet"), and Compaq Computer Chairman Ben Rosen, have gotten together to invest venture capital in a San Francisco–based company with the goal of designing software to fight spam.

If you can't find the software to solve the problem, there are other avenues. In some states, spam is illegal. In Washington state, spam became illegal in June, 1998 and Adam Engst and three others from his company TidBits, filed suit against WorldTouch Network, alleging that the company had violated Washington state's law numerous times. WorldTouch sells the "Bull's Eye Gold" e-mail address collection tool for $259, which allows people to harvest e-mail addresses off the Web that they then use to send unsolicited bulk e-mail.

Spoofing

Spoofing became a major topic of conversation after the IP address of a diskless workstation at the San Diego Super Computer center was the target. To give a high-level overview of how spoofing works, someone takes advantages of known holes in the Unix operating system to find a system with a static IP address. The hacker then decides to spam a large number of customers, but they forward spam to the spoofed IP address and send it from there. This way, any attempt to track the source of the e-mail will come up against a perfectly innocent workstation and stop.

The solution to spoofing starts with a firewall. As discussed in Chapter 28, putting a firewall between a corporate network and the Internet makes sense for a number of reasons. In this case, the firewall will redirect any unknown requests and also provide a barrier to mask the IP addresses of the workstations on the network.

NT Workstation

What if your network is not large enough to require a server solution? If you are working in an environment in which workstations are used by multiple people, and information is stored on local hard drives, how do you keep that information safe and secure? One way to insure workstation security is to institute Windows NT Workstation as the default desktop.

NT Workstation becomes, in effect, a very small network. All the security features that you are used to seeing on the big network can be brought down to the workstation. NT Workstation will allow an administrative user to create user accounts on the workstation, create group accounts to share data stored on the local drives, and designate who can access which applications and who can store data in what location on the hard drive.

Advantages of NT Workstation (NTWS)

If configured properly, NTWS allows multiple users to make use of the same computer, while making sure that appropriate applications and data storage areas are shared. It can also allow individual workstations to share data and resources with other stations on the network. In this way, if the NTWS computer has a printer connected, anyone on the network can use the printer.

NTWS is a true 32-bit multitasking operating system. Compared to its cousin, Windows 9x, it does a much better job of segregating open applications and keeping them running in different memory address spaces. This makes the system easier to use for the power user and allows more flexibility.

Many high-end applications are written to take advantage of NT's approach to memory management. Because the OS is so robust, these applications are much better behaved than they would be on Windows 9x.

NT also allows you to dual-boot. If you are using the system as a workstation for tech support, having the ability to switch between a Windows 9x environment and a Windows NT environment can be a useful feature.

NTWS can utilize a variety of different disk formats, including NT File System (NTFS) and the file allocation table (FAT) system familiar from the DOS days.

NTFS allows you to institute permissions at the directory and file levels as well as compress the information on the hard drive, making more drive space available. NTFS also provides faster file access than FAT.

NT uses a technology called the *Hardware Abstraction Layer,* or HAL. This layer sits between the operating system and the hardware. Because of this, you will suffer few hardware lockups that cannot be resolved. If you do suffer a system lockup in an application, chances are the application can be closed using Task Manager, while the functionality of the rest of the computer remains unharmed.

Disadvantages of NTWS

Because NTWS is a true 32-bit multitasking operating system, it requires a powerful hardware platform. Thankfully, the prices of hardware continue to fall. Before making the decision to roll out NTWS to the desktop, be sure to check the NT Compatibility list. Find the system that you want on the list and price out the system. Skimping on hardware (especially memory and disk space) when you are using NTWS is counterproductive in the long run. What you save up front, you will probably spend on tech support or troubleshooting.

NT offers its own unique brand of security. Configuring security for an NT system is not for the faint of heart; making sure it is done properly can be somewhat tricky. Setting up security for a single workstation with multiple users is not much of a hassle, but if you share the workstation on the network, you can have some conflicts. When you share a folder from an NT workstation, the security model says everyone has full rights to the folder. Users must be trained in the use of security before creating shares.

Because NT is the fastest-growing network operating system on the planet, everyone is trying to find ways of hacking it. Unfortunately, it has been found to be somewhat porous. If you do decide to use NT Workstation, make sure that you apply all the current security patches, including those patches meant for Internet Explorer.

NT also is not Plug-and-Play compatible. To install hardware into an NT system requires some knowledge of how the hardware actually works. In today's environment where an entire generation of technicians has grown up around plug and play, this could be a cost factor.

Using Encryption

The world of data encryption is changing. Over 20 years ago, IBM designed the earliest version of what has become known as the Data Encryption Standard, or DES. DES is currently used on all Unix machines for password encryption.

Briefly, here's how it works: DES takes the information and encodes it using a one-way operation called a hash. While a hash is not foolproof, decoding it is a complex task that will eat up resources. For example, it has been estimated that a password can be encoded almost 4,100 different ways. Don't believe me? Here is what the National Institute of Standards and Technology (NIST) has to say in the "Data Encryption Standard (DES)" from the *Federal Information Processing Standards Publication 46-2*, published in 1993:

"The cryptographic algorithm DES transforms a 64-bit binary value into a unique 64-bit binary value based on a 56-bit variable. If the complete 64-bit input is used and if the 56-bit variable is randomly chosen, no techniques other than trying all possible keys using known input and output for the DES will guarantee finding the chosen key. As there are 70,000,000,000,000,000 (70 quadrillion) possible keys of 56 bits, the feasibility of deriving a particular key in this way is extremely unlikely in typical threat environments."

Remember, this was written in 1993. In the late 1990s, computing power has grown and cracking the DES is coming closer and closer to reality. To solve this, the Federal Government and the NIST are now conducting a search for a replacement standard.

Two of the early candidates are Cylink and RSA Data Security. Cylink has proposed the Safer+ algorithm, based on its Safer encryption product, which was unveiled in 1993. Safer+ will operate with 128-bit, 192-bit, and 256-bit key sizes, as well as 128-bit block size, which makes it harder to crack. RSA, which has offered DES alternatives for years, is proposing a solution based on its RC-5 algorithm for high-speed data encryption. This solution also will support a 128-bit block size.

It will take NIST at least two years to evaluate all of the proposals, which means the new standards will be out around the year 2000.

You are probably wondering when and where you will be able to use some of this encryption software. Chances are, you have already experienced the joys of encryption. Both Microsoft and Netscape have recently been given permission to export products with 128-bit encryption for use with banking and financial transactions. Even this is not a first.

Strong 128-bit encryption has been available in browsers for several years and is now standard for both Microsoft Internet Explorer and Netscape Navigator. The algorithms for strong encryption are well known. The most widely accepted is RSA Data Security's encryption scheme using public-key cryptography: Messages are encrypted by the sender using a public key, then decrypted by the recipient using a private key. This is the same type of encryption and decryption that was discussed in the section on e-mail.

Separate Networks

One of the problems of working with Unix networks, mainframe networks, and even Microsoft Windows NT networks is *trust relationships*. A trust relationship is formed when network segments are joined to produce larger, more diverse networks.

This network expansion can be a good thing from the point of administration. If you have one large network, rather than a dozen small networks, it is easier for a centralized group of Information Technology professionals to manage and administer the network.

From a security point of view, bigger is not always better. If a hacker gains access to one section of the interconnected network, the hacker will have access to the entire network. If, however, certain network segments are deemed to be security risks, it might prove to be a wise idea to keep them segregated. You may want to insure that the network segment is self-sufficient, keeping it apart from the rest of the WAN. It will not insure invincibility, but it will eliminate the risk of a network segment being attacked from within.

Removable Disks and Drives

People cannot get access to information that they cannot find, so when in doubt, hide the information. That sounds like a really straightforward solution to the problem, doesn't it?

Typically, with critical special projects, data is stored on some kind of file server. The information is backed up and a copy is kept at a secure off-site location, but the information is still on the file server and susceptible to attack. Recently, there have been advances in hardware that allow for storage of data on removable devices. The removable media can be removed from the system and stored in a safe place, like a locked, fire-proof, heat-resistant safe.

Actually, this capability has been around for years. It was called the floppy disk. Unfortunately, the data explosion has bypassed the traditional floppy disk, with many files or projects growing beyond the 1.44MB a traditional floppy can hold. Technology to the rescue.

Several companies, including Iomega, SyQuest, and others, have come out with removable devices that can store much larger amounts of data. In this case, the end user keeps the sensitive data on a removable device, and then locks up the cartridge at night. Data storage sizes rival traditional disks, the disk speed is usually close to a traditional internal device, and the cost per megabyte is similar.

These devices range in size from approximately 100MB for a ZIP drive to almost 5GB for removable cartridges. Many computer manufacturers are installing these mega-floppies in new computer systems as part of the normal configuration. Having these storage devices installed internally also simplifies making system backups of stand-alone computers.

These devices come in several different flavors: internal or external, parallel or SCSI. Because the devices are simple to install and use mature technology, the external configurations are truly portable. You can carry your data storage with you, and whenever you need more, just access another cartridge. Prices start at around $200.

Monitoring Information Access

Auditing, or logging, is the practice of keeping track of who is doing what where on your network. Auditing programs are designed to track who logged on to the network at what time, how long they stayed on the network, and what they did while they connected.

Most network operating systems support some form of auditing or logging. Both Microsoft Windows NT and Novell NetWare have an auditing or logging function built in. In both cases, the auditing can be customized to track certain events, rather than try to track everything that is happening on the network.

Who Should Audit?

Since auditing is the practice of tracking who is accessing what information, and since the network administrator is the person with the most rights on the network, the designated network auditor should *not* be the system administrator or any member of the IS team. The person put in charge of auditing should have the rights necessary to access any section of the network, but usually, the auditor can just look and not touch. The auditor can track who has accessed a file but cannot see the contents of the file. In this case, the auditor will know that the system administrator was in playing in the payroll data files, but will not have the rights or permissions to read or enter these files. Putting someone with full rights in charge of auditing is kind of like having the fox watch the hen house.

What Should Be Audited?

The network auditor should be instructed to keep track of the data in the sensitive areas of the company, but auditing can involve much more. For example, the auditor may decide to track all system logins between the hours of 5 P.M. and 8 A.M., just to see if there is any strange activity happening during the off hours.

Auditors should also be versed in hacking techniques. It helps if you understand the person who may be trying to access the network. This will let the auditor know to watch out for any accounts where there are repeated refused logins because of bad passwords, or anyone trying to access the /ETC/PASSWRD file on a Unix system.

Auditors should try to track any activity that is not normal. Of course, the definition of *normal* tends to change from company to company. Your auditor has to make that call and stick to it. The auditor should also be aware that doing random checks on random events is probably a wise idea. The fact that random checks may be made should be published so that everyone knows about it. That way, if something does turn up, there will be no surprises. It is also a proactive way of stopping problems before they start.

Auditors should also be involved in software licensing decisions. Most of the auditing programs available include tools for protecting your company against running unlicensed software.

Summary

This chapter covered a lot of ground on security. It is important to keep in mind that the cheapest and easiest form of security is employee education. Any security plan is only as good as the employees carrying it out. If anyone within the organization sees anything suspicious, there should be a reporting method in place, and every report should be taken seriously and handled promptly.

Employees should also know that there are penalties for violating corporate security and that these penalties will be enforced. Too often, threats are made and are proven to be empty. Once that happens, all the policies in the world aren't worth the paper they are written on.

Security is important to your company. Do not assume your network is safe, do not assume that all threats will come from the outside. Make sure you have operational plans in effect before an event occurs, so you know what to do when an attack happens. After all of your data has been compromised is *not* the best time to come up with a security plan.

CHAPTER

TWENTY-EIGHT

Internet-Related Security Issues

- Firewalls and gateways—what's the difference?

- Explore the world of proxy servers

- Is there security with peer-to-peer file sharing?

- Different ways to authenticate users

- VPNs and tunneling—not just for road crews anymore

- Browsers—the way to your computer's heart

- Personal Web servers and FTP servers

- The "Ping of Death"

- Is there security with a Web server?

Some of the topics in this chapter have been discussed briefly in previous sections, but this is the chapter where we take an in-depth look at the security issues surrounding the Internet. There are many ways to protect your network from outside attacks, but it seems that as soon as you do, yet another new threat appears.

Let's start at the outside, and work our way in to the end user.

Firewalls and Gateways

One of the first lines of defense for your network is a firewall. A firewall sits between your network and the outside world, and it helps protect your network by keeping the bad packets out and making sure the good packets go where they are supposed to.

At first glance, firewalls and gateways may seem an odd combination of topics. A firewall brings to mind a rather rigid set of rules and specifications that makes a judgement every time a packet comes through the system. A gateway, on the other hand, brings to mind smoke and mirrors. A gateway is something that translates from one "language" to another, making a mainframe think it's talking to another mainframe when in fact it's talking to a PC.

Firewalls 101

What is a firewall? A *firewall* is any device designed to prevent users outside your network from accessing your network. It is usually a combination of hardware and software, and many firewalls can perform multiple tasks. The first thing to understand about firewalls is why they are necessary; then we'll look at how they work.

In order for your network to connect to the Internet, it must have some sort of router, or *gateway*.

NOTE   This router may be called many things. In fact, Microsoft usually refers to this system as a gateway. For the sake of simplicity, we will stick with *router*.

This router knows where the Internet is, and when it receives a packet destined for the outside world, it passes the packet on. Because this router is a key part of Internet communications, every other workstation must point to it as part of its TCP/IP protocol configuration. Since all these other workstations are going to be looking for the router, it must have a static IP address.

> **NOTE** A *static IP address* is one that never changes. In other words, your router should not receive its IP address from a Dynamic Host Control Protocol (DHCP) server.

Static IP addresses can be wonderful things. When a router is assigned a static IP address, every workstation inside the network can find that address and use that system as a portal to the Internet. Tricky things, portals. Not only do they let things out, they also let things in. Somehow there has to be a method of protecting what comes into the network. That is the job of the firewall.

When packets are sent to and received from the Internet, one of the ways these packets are identified is by the IP address. The IP address acts as a very rudimentary form of authentication on the network. In fact, whenever you access the Internet, you are probably authenticating using your IP address and you don't even realize it. Moreover, many of the Web pages you access will keep track of your IP address as a way to know where to send back information that you request.

Here's what happens. You want to connect to the Internet and get the latest material from www.somewhere.com. When you open your browser, type in the URL, and press Enter, your computer looks at the URL and compares it to information it has locally. Of course, your system probably has no idea that www.somewhere.com is actually at IP address 192.45.16.27. Somehow, your system needs to resolve that information to the IP address. It sends a request to a Domain Name Server (DNS) to provide that information. (Your system knows how to reach the DNS server because that address is part of the TCP/IP configuration.) So your computer puts together a packet with its address, the request for the URL, and the address of the DNS server, and sends it out. When the TCP/IP module gets hold of this packet, the IP module looks at the destination address, realizes that the DNS server is not on the same subnet as your workstation, and forwards the packet to the router or gateway. The router looks at the destination request, figures out a way to get the packet to the address of the DNS server, and sends the packet on its way. When the DNS server receives the request for information about www.somewhere.com, it knows the IP address of the site, so it puts that information into another packet, and sends the packet back to your work-station. When your workstation gets the information, it now knows how to address a packet to get to `www.somewhere.com`, and the communication process contin-ues. Each step along the way, authentication is done through the IP address of the sender.

This is a simple and elegant solution. It is also not very secure. With the addresses of all the workstations on your network flying all over the Internet, anyone could get the address of your computer, and that is the first step to entry. How do you protect against this? One way is to install a firewall.

What Makes Up a Firewall?

The first major component of the really good firewall is planning. There are dozens of firewall packages, some costing tons of money, others available as shareware or with the purchase of hardware. But what really separates one fire-wall from another is the planning that went into the installation and the follow-through after the system has been up and working for a period of time.

Firewall hardware can be just the router. Many routers have advanced security features built in. In other instances, firewalls are hardware and software. Since a firewall is a pass-through mechanism (meaning that packets either pass through the wall or are rejected), the hardware does not need to be state-of-the-art for some implementations. The main thing a fire wall does is accept or reject a packet.

Types of Firewalls

As mentioned above, firewalls come in all shapes and sizes. There are two main implementations of firewalls: a router-based, packet-filtering device and an application-based proxy firewall/gateway.

Router-Based, Packet-Filtering

Router-based, packet-filtering firewalls work at the point of entry into the net-work. The router examines every packet that comes into the network and decides whether to allow the packet access or to discard it. This decision is based on a scheme laid out by the network administrator and is usually based on the source address of the packet.

The router can be configured to allow all packets into the network if they come from a particular network address, thereby disallowing everything else. The flip side of this coin is to allow everything into the network, *unless* it comes from a particular network.

In the first example, imagine you have two offices connected by TCP/IP through a router. In addition, your network has Internet access, but it is through the remote office. Any packet coming into your network must come through the remote office to be valid. In this case, you would configure packet-filtering to allow any packets into the network coming from the remote office. Anything with a source address other than the remote office would be rejected.

In the second example, let's say that your network is hooked to the Internet, and you believe your main competitor may be trying to hack into your network. In this case, you can configure the system to accept all packets unless the packets come from `competitor.com`.

The advantage to a router based firewall is speed and the fact that you will not have to configure another computer to be a firewall. A router-based, packet-filtering system does not do an in-depth check of the packets, it just checks source addresses, so there is no real strain on the system.

While the speed of the system is a benefit, it is also a detriment. Packet-filtering looks at the source address of the packet. The source address of the packet is relatively easy for crackers to fake. In the case of the forged address, the firewall may provide only the illusion of protection. That is why many of the software designers have improved on packet-filtering to take advantage of the other attributes of a packet, filtering things like protocols, ports, and even time of day.

How can you filter protocols? One of the ways that crackers find information about networks is using the simple ping command. For example, if I wanted to try cracking into a particular web site, one of the first pieces of information I would need would be the IP address of the Web server. To find the IP address, I would use any IP-capable machine, with basic IP utilities installed, and type **ping** with the DNS name of the site. In a few seconds, I would receive a message from a particular IP address saying that I had established communication with the server. This communication would take the form of a return IP address with some timing information. I now have one piece of information that I may need to begin my attack on a Web site. What could my potential victims do to prevent this? Filtering a protocol can help. If the firewall was set up to filter the User Datagram Protocol (UDP) piece of the TCP/IP protocol suite, ping attacks would not be allowed to get through.

NOTE This is only a very broad example. Blocking UDP would have wide-ranging effects, including hampering the operation of Domain Name Service (DNS).

How can a firewall improve security by using ports? First of all, you have to understand how a port works. Think of the workstation IP address as the phone number of your company. This is the front desk phone number, the one that rings on the desk of the temp receptionist. Anyway, if someone dialed the main number, the temp answered, and the caller started asking some very specific network-related questions, they probably would not get much information. However, if the caller reached the number of the main desk and asked for your extension, now all the mysteries of the network would be available (assuming you were naïve enough to answer their questions), because you have all the answers at your fingertips. When you think of a port, think of an extension number.

Just like an extension number for an overly chatty employee, a port can be a window through the firewall. At each IP address there are certain default services that use certain ports. For example, port 80 is commonly used by HTTP and ports 20 and 21 are used by File Transfer Protocol (FTP). Telnet uses port 23, Simple Mail Transfer Protocol (SMTP) uses port 25, and Simple Network Management Protocol (SNMP) uses port 161. Each one of these services listens on these ports for messages and then acts on the message. This is kind of like opening a window in your home; it's an easy entry for anyone interested in breaking in. To make matters worse, the ports are even advertised.

TIP   Default port addresses are not difficult to find. As a matter of fact, if you are using a Windows–based system, chances are there is a file called services in the C:\Windows directory. This file lists some of the more common TCP/IP ports. In addition, you can go to the Internet and download a complete list of port addresses by searching for RFC 1700. Consider yourself warned, this is really boring reading!

One way of working around the ports problem is to reassign them, something you as the administrator can do when configuring the firewall. HTTP defaults to port 80, but like most good defaults, it does not have to stay there. You can change the port to whatever you want, as long as your users also know how to make the necessary changes to the browser on their workstations.

Finally, packet-filtering can even be time-sensitive. We mentioned that SMTP, one of the protocols necessary for moving e-mail around the Internet, uses port 25. Suppose that you are managing the firewall, and you leave the default port address at 25 for SMTP. Your boss comes to you and says that too many people are sneaking into work early or staying at work late to send e-mail to their kids. You can put a stop to this, if your firewall will allow it, by simply limiting SMTP access to the network to the hours of 8 A.M. to 5 P.M. As a benefit, you are making sure your fellow employees will not come early or will not stay late. They will love you for it.

There are some other limitations to packet-filtering that you should take into account before choosing this method for your firewall. Remote Procedure Calls (RPCs) form two-way communication between hosts. They are difficult to filter because they negotiate the ports they are going to use. The ports are randomly assigned at system startup. Because this is random, there is no way to filter them effectively without blocking all of UDP. As mentioned in the note above, blocking all of UDP blocks services like DNS.

Application Gateways as Firewalls

Application gateways, as the name implies, are software-based firewalls. They function in a totally different fashion. A gateway is in the business of changing things. It takes a perfectly good piece of data that a PC can understand, and changes it so that a mainframe can chew on it for a while. The gateway may also take that same information and translate it into something only a Mac can deal with.

An application gateway that acts as a firewall works in the same way. It processes each piece of information it deals with. It not only decides whether that piece of information is valid for the network, it also changes it before sending it on to the final destination. This is important because it means the IP packet is not forwarded. As a matter of fact, the IP packet may come out the other side as something completely different, like IPX.

Application gateways have other advantages, too. Since the application gateway is doing so much work to the data already, it really isn't a problem to have the gateway write log files also. These gateways usually come with a rather impressive set of utilities to make the gateway do exactly what you want.

The disadvantages of this type of gateway include its increased work load and corresponding loss of speed. An application gateway usually has to be configured for each type of network service. In addition, since all this work is being done on the packets, you can anticipate that the speed is going to take a major hit. That would be a very safe assumption.

Firewall Issues

After you install a firewall, you shouldn't have any issues, should you? Really, they should all be solved! After all, a firewall is what keeps your network safe from the outside world.

That attitude is one of the biggest fallacies related to firewalls. Too many people take the attitude that once it has been constructed it can be forgotten. That is simply not the case. Firewalls tend to become like living, breathing organisms, needing attention for the first few formative stages of their lives.

Because a firewall is the first line of defense that your network has from the work of the cracker, it must be built strongly and be restrictive. You have to be very careful about what you let into your network. Unfortunately, the more restrictive you become, the more the services that your network provides may suffer. Somewhere there is a fine line, and it usually takes several attempts before the line is drawn.

Since the firewall is the first line of defense in our arsenal, some administrators tend to make it the only line of defense. They spend so much time on the firewall that they forget there are challenges inside the network too. If a firewall is penetrated, on networks like these, it can be almost open season on the data. Again, the best tool you have in constructing a good firewall is planning. That planning should concern all areas of your security scheme: firewall, passwords, logon names, logon times, domain layouts, etc.

What about for those times when even planning isn't going to help? Services on the Internet seem to change weekly, and the protocols that access these services change with them. It's not bad enough that the services change and the protocols change, but sometimes there are different variations to work around. A perfect example would be the recent Microsoft/Sun spat about Java. Sun licensed Java to Microsoft, and Microsoft changed it. Now, there were two "versions" of Java to contend with. If you use an application gateway, that means someone has to write a new application gateway for the different versions. Chances are this will not happen overnight. You, as a network administrator, also have to make a major decision while these applications are being written. Do you open the firewall to take advantage of these nonprotected services, or do you close the firewall to protect the data and have a whole bunch of angry end users? It sort of makes you wonder if this is the reason you make the really big bucks!

Be Alert!

Firewalls fail. It is an unfortunate fact, but they do. The reasons they fail are many, and most involve around-keyboard operation in some way. The firewall may not have been properly installed and configured, or it may not have been properly maintained. Sometimes, however, it's the hardware that fails.

Firewalls are not impenetrable. Hackers and crackers are very good at what they do; otherwise, we wouldn't need this section of the book. There are utilities that will help the hacker/cracker determine what type of firewall you have in place guarding your network. Once that information is known, it is a matter of checking to find out how good the administrator really is. Depending on the platform the firewall runs on, administration may not be an easy job. A firewall running on a Unix box has literally hundreds of applications, protocols, and commands that can point to a hole in the system. After the firewall is in place, be diligent and make sure you continue to tweak it to make sure it operates as advertised. This is done by making sure all the latest patches are applied, and making sure that you keep up to date on the latest types of security attacks. Firewalls do the same types of things; how they do these things depends on the manufacturer. Make sure you read and study the documentation.

Proxy Servers

One step down the security ladder from the firewall implementation is the *proxy server*. The proxy server provides some security, but its primary task is to provide faster access to Web pages by caching information locally instead of making the user go all the way out to Internet to get the information.

Here is how a Web-caching proxy server works. A proxy server, like a firewall, provides a single connection to the Internet. If users want to access information from the Internet, the request is redirected to the proxy server, instead of to the Internet. The proxy server reviews the request and fills it from cache if possible. Otherwise, the proxy server goes out and returns the information the user has requested. Therefore, it is the proxy server's address that is being sent across the Internet, not the individual workstation. When the information is retrieved, it is the proxy server that responds to the local host.

A Web proxy server also keeps track of the Web pages that the users on your network have visited, and it keeps a copy of those pages stored locally. The proxy server then "visits" those Web sites at regular intervals to see if the pages have been changed. If the pages have been altered, the proxy server caches the new copy locally. You can also specify which links (if any) you want brought with the primary Web page. This is a benefit to your users because any time they access a cached Web page, they will receive the page from a local system, rather than having to traverse the Web to locate the material.

The best part of this whole process is that the proxy server does all this work in the background. It can store hundreds of Web pages, so your network is making efficient use of its Internet connection, making sure that your company gets the most for its bandwidth dollar.

There are many proxy cache servers in the marketplace. Three of the most popular are Microsoft's Proxy Server, Netscape's Proxy Server, and C & C Solutions' WinGate. The first two are the most powerful and the most complex. That usually means you will have to dedicate serious resources to the project, in terms of both hardware and money.

Microsoft Proxy Server

Microsoft's Proxy Server is currently at version 2.0 and carries a price tag of around $1,000, with an unlimited number of connections. Proxy Server only runs on an NT server.

Microsoft Proxy Server 2.0 provides distributed Web caching in both a hierarchical and an array-based format. It acts as a gateway with firewall-class security between a LAN and the Internet, and it can block access to undesirable sites. Proxy Server 2.0 is designed to work with existing networks, even IPX networks.

Since the early versions of Proxy Server, Microsoft has improved the product. Besides handling the firewall responsibilities and the proxy-server duties, Proxy Server 2.0 can also be configured to create and manage virtual private networks (VPNs) and an IP/IPX gateway. To make sure you know what is happening with your network, Proxy Server now has built-in event logging.

Microsoft's Proxy Server 2.0 is designed to handle the load for a variety of different-sized businesses. It can handle systems with direct connections to the Internet and can also be configured for dial-up connectivity. In this mode, Proxy Server will dial and connect to the ISP any time there is a request for an IP address that is not on the local network. This is a plus for the business that cannot afford a full-time connection.

Proxy Server provides Web, hierarchical, and reverse caching. To do this, Proxy Server uses its own protocol, Cache Array Routing Protocol, for hierarchical caching. Hierarchical caching using CARP lets you connect multiple proxy servers so they can share their cache information. With proper configuration, you can use this feature for load balancing. In this case, you would configure the proxy server running on the faster, more stable hardware to handle more of the cache requests than a slower or more unstable computer.

Unlike some of its competitors, Microsoft Proxy Server 2.0 provides reverse proxying, a technique used to publish and access internal Web data on the public side of the firewall. In this capacity, Proxy Server 2.0 supports using the HTTP protocol. There is also limited support for the HTTPS protocol.

You can use Proxy Server 2.0 to configure your own virtual private network, or VPN. When you create a VPN, you are basically connecting to your home server from a remote location. Once the connection is established, everything becomes encrypted, and you virtually have a private network. For VPN capabilites, Proxy Server piggybacks onto Windows NT's dial-up capabilities, namely RAS and the Point-to-Point Tunneling Protocol (PPTP). Security is provided using Windows NT RAS usernames and passwords.

Another security feature of Microsoft Proxy Server is built-in local address translation (LAT), which works to "hide" your internal network's physical topology and IP-addressing scheme. In other words, you can make up your own Class A address range for your network, and as long as the proxy server is in place, no one will be the wiser. The proxy server handles all the address translation for you, and you only present one registered IP address to the Internet. The LAT also prevents IP-spoofing attacks against your network. If outsiders cannot see the addresses of the systems inside the firewall, they cannot use them as spoof addresses.

Netscape Proxy Server

Proxy Server is a part of Netscape's SuiteSpot family of servers. The retail price of Proxy Server 3.5 will be around $525, though that is for 100 licenses.

The Netscape Proxy Server is more of a true proxy server than a firewall-wannabe. For example, it lacks the Microsoft Proxy Server's LAT feature.

However, Netscape Proxy Server does provide a robust caching and filtering proxy server. To make up for some of the security shortfalls, Netscape Proxy Server is designed to integrate with some third-party firewall products such as Raptor Systems Inc.'s Eagle and Check Point Software Technologies Inc.'s FireWall-1.

In addition to the integration with the security packages, Netscape's Proxy Server also has a very low-level approach to filtering; its configuration settings allow much more control than the main competition from Microsoft.

What makes Proxy Server 3.5 worth considering is the caching capabilities of the proxy server. You can cache not only the standard Web fare of HTML pages, but you can also cache FTP objects. You can even designate separate Time To Live (TTL) values.

In addition to TTL, you can configure how long the Proxy Server will keep a page cache before it is updated. The caching algorithm even takes into account human nature. The system looks at the date stamp on an HTML document to determine the last time the document was reworked. The age of the document is then multiplied by a "last modified" factor, which is 0.1 by default. The result is the time period that Proxy Server will wait before checking the document to see if it has been updated. Essentially, the idea is that the longer it has been since a Web page has been updated, the less likely it is that the page will be updated any time soon.

Netscape recognizes that Microsoft is here to stay, and if you can't beat them, at least tolerate them. In this case, Netscape also works with CARP for hierarchical cache arrays as well as with the Internet Cache Protocol (ICP). ICP allows the administrator to configure the cache parents and siblings as well as the port numbers, the time-out, and all the default routes.

ICP works like CARP to provide a more robust caching environment. If you have multiple caching servers, you can configure the way each server checks the other servers. For example, assume you have two large offices, each containing multiple proxy servers. In this case, you could configure each building to be a group of caching servers. If a client in the first building makes a request, the caching servers in that building will be polled before going over to the other area. Once in the other area, you can determine which server is polled in which order. There are some limits for those of you working in really large environments. For example, there cannot be more than 62 proxy servers in a group and there cannot be more than two polling rounds.

Netscape is also being proactive in its support for pending specifications. Microsoft Proxy Server 2.0 supports the current version of SOCKS, which is version 4.2.

NOTE   SOCKS is defined as a protocol used for traversing firewalls in a secure and controlled manner. The protocol specifications are made publicly available by the Internet Engineering Task Force (IETF).

Netscape, on the other hand, is providing support for the next iteration of SOCKS, version 5. This specification has not been ratified by the IETF yet, but Proxy 3.5 comes with support written in for the current working draft. The SOCKS 5 proxy standard is also known as authenticated firewall traversal (AFT). It is an open Internet standard and is discussed in RFC 1928. It is designed to perform network proxying at the transport layer of the OSI model. SOCKS 5 handles several issues that SOCKS V4 did not fully address or even omitted, such as:

- Strong authentication
- Authentication method negotiation
- Message integrity and privacy
- Support for UDP applications

Netscape Proxy Server has quite a few parameters that can be set to determine how SOCKS will act. For example, you can determine which ports SOCKS will monitor and whether to allow reverse Domain Name Service (DNS) lookups, and you can define the default routes to other proxy servers. You can also require user authentication for access through the Proxy based on the host subnet mask and port range. Netscape Proxy Server also handles all SOCKS and Winsock traffic with a single proxy engine, while the Microsoft server requires two.

One of the proxy server's basic tasks is filtering. You can control both inbound and outbound traffic by creating URL filters to prevent users from accessing certain Web sites. Proxy Server also integrates with third-party URL filters like CyberPatrol Proxy and SurfWatch.

Netscape's Proxy Server also provides support for reverse proxying. You can have the proxy server redirect Web requests to a Web server inside the proxy and get the benefit of HTML caching for the outbound requests.

Logging is an issue for any network. Netscape's Proxy Server tracks all traffic and activity and sends the information to log files. These files can be viewed raw, or you can use the report generator to view a summarized report. In addition, there are several logging options you can set, and you can also define a custom log file format.

WinGate

WinGate is the least expensive of the three proxy servers discussed in this chapter, and the fact that it can be run on a Windows 95 box implies that the hardware specifications are less stringent than the other systems.

WinGate comes in two flavors, WinGate Pro and WinGate Lite. WinGate Pro is a multiprotocol proxy server that runs on Windows 95, Windows NT Workstation, and Windows NT Server. WinGate Pro comes equipped with all the basics of a good proxy server. It provides a caching proxy service for HTTP, and it has SOCKS support for Version 4 and Version 5 HTTP requests. It also supports File Transfer Protocol (FTP), Internet Relay Chat (IRC), Network News Transfer Protocol (NNTP), Post Office Protocol version 3 (POP3), Real-Audio, and Telnet.

The real strength of WinGate is in its support of dial-up modems, ISDN, and direct LAN Internet connections. This can be the product of the very small office because it is inexpensive, you don't need massive amounts of hardware to run the product, and it can handle dial-up. It can also operate with either static or dynamic IP addresses, so you don't need an ISP account with a fixed IP address. You can just use the plain old $20/month dial-up account with the local ISP. Now, multiple users can access the Internet through that one account.

Wingate Lite lacks some features of the Pro version, such as accounting, auditing, and advanced user control. It also doesn't have support for remote management, and it doesn't support as many protocols as the Pro version.

The WinGate server runs as a background service on Windows NT, Windows NT Workstation, and Windows 95/98. As such, you may not even know it is running.

GateKeeper is the administration portion of WinGate Pro and is used to configure and manage the system. GateKeeper runs as a separate program and is modeled after Microsoft Explorer. With GateKeeper, you can view active connections to the Internet, and the connections list is dynamically updated whenever someone accesses a resource through the proxy server.

Once the initial installation has been completed, you will not be tied down to a single administrative workstation. Using GateKeeper's remote-configuration option will allow you to change the LAN's WinGate configuration or monitor the network from any system on the LAN, or even over the Internet.

For security, the product includes a comprehensive suite of access-control features. Like all proxy servers, it allows you to restrict access by client IP address, by the type of protocol they are using, by the time of day the system is being accessed, by how much traffic is going out over the network, or even by the amount of time the individual end user has spent online. You can also log all this information for retrieval and digestion later.

As mentioned earlier, one of WinGate's strengths is the ability to provide services for the home or small business. It is one of the oldest and most popular modem-sharing applications. While it lacks the modem-teaming capabilities of operating systems like NT, the support for the wide variety of protocols ensures that users will not be complaining because they cannot fully utilize the Internet.

Peer-to-Peer File Sharing and the Internet

Peer-to-peer networking has been around since the early days of computer networks. The names have changed, the procedures have changed, but many of the problems have stayed the same. In a peer-to-peer network, there just is no single point of security administration. Every user who shares resources on their computer has to institute security to protect the information that is already there.

Peer-to-peer networking can be a really wide-open environment, with everybody sharing everything with everyone, simply because it is easier. When you take a network like this and attach it to the Internet, you are now just inviting someone to come in and really clean house.

Peer-to-peer network operating systems take many forms. Your Windows 95/98 computers, your Windows NT workstations, your Unix systems, and even that group in the corner that all use Appletalk to communicate—they all share a type of peer-to-peer network. Having a peer-to-peer network connected to the Internet can be an open invitation, but it is not an invitation to just this small group of systems. In Unix, NT, and AppleTalk, there is the ability to "trust" other networks or domains. As soon as a two-way trust relationship is built up, there is now another portal leading to another area of the network.

Security in an NT Environment

Since NT is the fastest growing network operating system around, let us look at ways to secure a peer-to-peer network consisting of just NT workstations. Security starts with the user account. A user account is created and a password is assigned for that user using the User Manager utility. The information on the user account is stored in the Security Account Manager database, or SAM.

In addition to user accounts, you can also use the User Manager utility to create Local Group accounts. A local group is simply a group of users brought together for a specific purpose. For example, suppose an NT workstation has the company accounting software stored on it. Over the course of a week, five different people may access the computer, but only three of them will need to access the accounting software. In this case, the local administrator can create an accounting group, and give the accounting group permission to use the accounting software and see information stored in the accounting data directory. The computer can be configured so that others using the computer can be excluded from even knowing that the accounting software or data is stored on this computer. If you are a network administrator, think of this workstation as a mini-server.

To ease the burden of trying to figure out when and how to create users and groups, NT has provided you with some defaults. These are shown in Table 28.1.

TABLE 28.1: Default Account Types

Name	Type	Description
Administrator	User	The built-in account for administering the computer
Guest	User	The built-in account for guest access to the computer
Administrators	Group	The local group whose members can administer the computer
Backup Operators	Group	The group whose members can bypass file security to back up files
Guests	Group	The group whose members are granted guest access to the computer or domain
Power Users	Group	The group whose members can share directories or printers
Replicator	Group	The group account that supports file replication in a domain
Users	Group	The group comprising ordinary users

All of these types of users and groups can be configured on a local workstation. That means if you have three people using the same NT 4 workstation, you would need to create accounts for each of these people. What happens to security when we start sharing data?

A user who creates a shared folder will be able to select how many users can access the data and at what time, and that user can assign some permissions to the users coming in to share the information. If the data is stored on a partition that is formatted with NT File System (NTFS), the user will have the ability to assign security at a more granular level.

Folder Security

Folders are shared so that other people on the network can use the information or applications in the folder. For example, you might put a share on the network so that users can access the network version of Excel from *Workstationname*\ Apps\Excel. Another share might point to the *Workstationname*\Shared\ Data\Budgets area.

Just because you have created a folder called Data with a subfolder called Budgets does not mean that anyone else can see the folders. On the contrary, nothing is visible by default. For users to see a directory, the administrator must deliberately share the directory.

Do your users want to remember all those UNC paths? Heck, no. These are the same people who have a difficult time remembering their password—you don't want them to have to remember *Workstationname*\Shared\Data\Budgets. To make sure users can remember where things are, administrators create shares and make them available under a readable share name.

The NT administrator can share any directory (folder) on the computer (that is, the "server"), but only if the user who created the folder has granted the administrator List permission for that folder.

NOTE   If you are not sure what the List permission is or what it is good for, don't worry. A discussion of all permissions comes up next.

How are shares created? Shares can be created using NT Explorer, My Computer, the command prompt, or Server Manager.

As an example, we'll create a share starting from My Computer. Figure 28.1 shows the Properties window for an application folder we're about to share. To access this dialog box, open My Computer from the desktop, browse to a folder, highlight it, right-click, and choose Sharing. Once the Sharing tab is displayed, choose Shared As and enter the share name—in this case, Applications. You can also add a comment so users will know what the share is for, and you can limit the number of users who can hack away on this share. You can allow the Maximum Allowed for the server or set a number of users with which you feel comfortable.

Using NT Explorer or My Computer is probably the most convenient way to create a share, but it is not the only way. You can also create a share using File Manager (if you still use File Manager). If you happen to work in Server Manager, you can also create a share while doing normal management tasks. If you still feel most comfortable at a command prompt, you can use the Net Share utility.

FIGURE 28.1:

Sharing a folder using My Computer

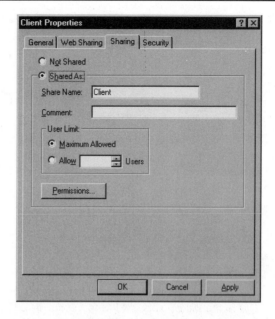

In addition to the shares that the administrator creates, if you are using an NT-based system that has a hard-coded access control list (ACL), you will find that there are at least two hidden shares. These hidden shares are the C$ share, which shares the root computer's C: drive, and the ADMIN$ share, which shares the root of the NT installation. These shares give administrators a path to the \WINNT directory or the operating system directory. Remember that a share name ending in $ results in a hidden or nonvisible share.

Permissions

Now that the share has been set up, you need to make sure those people who need to access it can do so. Figure 28.2 shows a list of permissions that you can grant users or groups at a share point.

Access through share
permissions

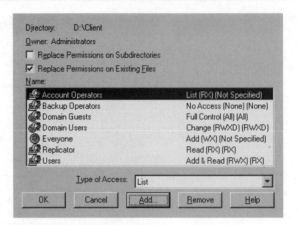

> **NOTE**
>
> It is important to distinguish between share-level permissions and folder- or file-level permissions. Share-level permissions can be granted at any share point, even if the share points to a FAT-formatted device. Folder-level and file-level permissions can only be added to storage devices formatted with NTFS.

Table 28.2 summarizes the four share permissions.

TABLE 28.2: Share Permission Levels

Permission Level	Explanation
Full Control	The user or group can read or see a folder, subfolder, or file; execute an application; write to a closed file; and delete a folder or file. If the share resides on an NTFS partition, the user can also take ownership of the resource and change permissions.
Change	The user or group can read or see a folder, subfolder, or file; execute an application; write to a closed file; and delete a folder or file.
Read	The user or group can read the contents of folders, subfolders, and files in the share and can execute any applications in it.
No Access	Users can connect to the share, but cannot access any resources.

The two most important levels to understand are Full Control and No Access. Full Control means just what it says. The members of the group or the user can do whatever they want to in the share. If you refer back to Figure 28.2, you will see that by default, the Everyone group gets Full Control of a share. No Access will allow a user to connect to the share, but the user will not be able to access any resources associated with the share.

In the Microsoft scheme of security, a good rule of thumb to follow is that the most restrictive permission applies, if you are accessing the data from a share. Thus, if Dawn were a member of two groups, one with Full Control of a share and one with No Access to the same share, Dawn would have No Access to the share.

However, if Dawn were accessing the data by logging on to the computer locally, the opposite is the case: the *least* restrictive permissions apply. To keep this straight, remember this little mnemonic: Share = Most and Locally = Least. Just when you have that down, there is another step to take into consideration. No matter how the user is accessing the data, through a share or locally, if you see No Access, that means No Access.

Set Permissions on NTFS Partitions, Folders, and Files

Shares and permissions assigned to the share affect only remote users—those folks who are attaching to the host computer, rather than logging on to it directly. Any permission granted at the share point is just that, permission to the share point. A user with Change permissions at the share can potentially damage any folder, subfolder, or file that makes up that share.

Security often needs to be more "granular" than that. Regularly, you need to assign a user more rights at the folder level than perhaps they should have at the file level. That is where folder and file permissions enter the picture.

Folder and file permissions are only available if the storage device that hosts them has been formatted using NTFS. If the device is a FAT storage device, there can be no file or folder level permissions applied.

System Actions To do anything, you need permission. Each permission is made up of one or more *system actions*. There are six basic actions, four of which apply for both share and NTFS permissions (see Table 28.3).

TABLE 28.3: System Actions

Permission	Actions
Read (R)	Users can read or see a file. This level is usually used in conjunction with Execute.
Write (W)	Users can add data to a file.
Execute (X)	Users can execute a file. This level is usually used in conjunction with Read.
Delete (D)	Users can delete a file.
Change Permissions (P)	Users can change the access level of other users on this file or folder. This level is granted as part of Full Control if the share is on an NTFS partition.
Take Ownership (O)	Users can claim ownership of a file. This level is granted as part of Full Control if the share is on an NTFS partition.

Given this information, let's reexamine the share-level permissions discussed earlier, to see how they pertain to these actions. Full Control is self-explanatory; it allows all of these actions. By default, when you create a share, the Everyone group has Full Control over the share and its folders, subfolders, and files. The newest user on your network can delete anything on the share. If security is an issue on your network, this could pose a problem.

The Change permission gives the user or group the ability to perform the Read (R), Execute (X), Write (W), and Delete (D) actions . So the user or member of the group can read, execute, write, and delete information in the share.

The share permission Read grants the user or group the ability to read and execute files on the share. It is usually granted to applications and other executable files—files with the extension .EXE or .COM. (You may be asking, What about nonexecutable documents, like text, spreadsheet, and database docs? That would be the Change permission covered in the paragraph above. The share permission Read would only be assigned to a nonexecutable document if no changes were going to be made to it, and that would not be something done at the share point; rather, it would be done at the file level.)

No Access allows the user or members of the group to attach to the share but not to access any information its resources contain.

Directory-Level Permissions What about the NTFS permissions? NTFS permissions are granted to *local* files and directories on a host computer. These permissions can be granted by the owner of the directory or by an administrator. Separate permissions can be granted at the directory and file levels. The directory-level permissions are listed in Table 28.4.

TABLE 28.4: NTFS Directory-Level Permissions

Directory-Level Permission	Permissions Granted
No Access	Users cannot access the directory at all.
List	Users cannot access the directory but can see a listing of its contents.
Read	Users can read data files and execute application files.
Add	Users cannot read any information from the directory or even see the files that are stored in the directory, but they can add data to the directory.
Add and Read	Users can see information in the directory and add information (new files) to the directory. Users cannot modify existing files in the directory.
Change	Users can see files in the directory, add files to the directory, modify files in the directory, and delete files from the directory (or even delete the whole directory). Users can also change the attributes of the directory.
Full Control	Users can do everything they can do with Change, but can also make changes to resources they do not own.

Permissions given to a directory flow down into the directory. If you have given the group EXCEL_Users the Read permission to the folder D:\Applications\ Excel, a member of that group can execute the file EXCEL.EXE.

File-Level Permissions There are times when security needs to be applied at the individual file level. Suppose you have a folder that contains files with the payroll information for the next fiscal year. During the budget process, the payroll file is open so that certain users can make changes. When the payroll process for the year has been finalized, you want those users to be able to read the file but not to make changes to it. Meanwhile, in the same folder, there are files that the management team needs to change. In this case, you would simply change the permissions on the payroll file to allow people to only read the file. When you make the change to just one file, it does not affect any of the other files. See Table 28.5 for an explanation of file-level permissions.

TABLE 28.5: NTFS File-Level Permissions

File-Level Permission	Permissions Granted
No Access	Users cannot access the file at all.
Read	Users can read a data file or execute it if it is an application file.
Change	Users can read, execute, modify, or delete the file.
Full Control	Users can read, execute, write to, or delete the file, and change permissions or take ownership away from the owner of the file.

To set NTFS permissions for a folder or file, highlight that resource, right-click, and select Properties. From the Properties page, select the Security tab and then choose Permissions.

After you've assigned possibly complex permissions to a set of folders and files, what happens if the information is moved? In that case, the information will inherit the permissions of its new home. For example, if Dawn created a file on a share and assigned the Everyone group Read access, and the file was copied to a folder where the Everyone group had Full Control, Everyone would now have Full Control over the file. This is probably not what Dawn wanted to happen.

By the same token, what happens if you are accessing a folder from a share point and the permissions you have been granted to the share point are more generous than the rights you have been assigned to the folder? Remember the basic rule of Microsoft security: if accessing the data through a share, the most restrictive permissions apply.

Peer-to-Peer Review

As you can see, there is a lot involved in peer-to-peer security. This is just Microsoft NT workstation. NT Server becomes more complicated, as you need to take into account domains and trusting remote domains. Security in the world of an Apple network is similar, and Unix is a world all to itself.

The key to peer-to-peer security is making sure that trust relationships are kept to a minimum and that end users actually follow through with the assignment of rights and permissions to shares, folders, and files.

User Authentication

User authentication on a network that is connected to the Internet can be a constant concern. Some network operating systems are more secure than others. This is one of the reasons why a firewall is such an important part of the overall security plan.

In many current books on computer network security you will find references to a couple of dozen programs and utilities designed to hack into a system and break the password codes for user authentication; as noted in Chapter 27, you may even find some of that code on a book's CD. It's a good idea to test it against your own system before somebody else does. User authentication and password schemes have been covered in other sections of this book, including Chapter 27. In this section we will take a look at other areas where you might want to insure that your network is secure, in this case securing the portion of the network that you *want* the outside world to see.

SSL and S-HTTP

Suppose your boss has decided that Web commerce is the way of the future, and your company is going to be at the forefront of this bursting technology. When your boss calls you in to tell you about this great revelation, it is also made clear that the success or failure of this program depends on your keeping the Web site secure, so that customers will feel very comfortable leaving personal information and credit card numbers on the Web.

As you begin to research this material, two acronyms keep popping up, SSL for Secure Socket Layer and Secure Hypertext Transport Protocol (S-HTTP). The two protocols do similar things, but they work with different parts of the standard Internet transactions. SSL is extremely flexible, but not as granular as S-HTTP. SSL provides encryption and user authentication at the OSI transport layer, allowing it to secure not only HTTP messages but also applications such as FTP and Telnet. SSL processes all the data flowing between the applications, not just certain parts. With SSL, you cannot selectively encrypt a field on a form; this may increase processing time. Another SSL shortcoming is that it only authenticates between server applications. In applications that need to authenticate a client, such as online banking, SSL should not be used.

S-HTTP is an extension of the HTTP protocol. By invoking S-HTTP, you can selectively encrypt single fields of data. Unlike SSL, S-HTTP also supports client-to-server authentication, making it ideal for applications that provide access to untrusted sources like the Internet. Because S-HTTP is a derivative of HTTP, however, it can only be used to secure Web transactions; S-HTTP does not work with applications such as FTP and Telnet.

These are two of the technologies that can be used, along with the services of a firewall, to minimize your security risk when deploying Web-to-host solutions to a wide range of users from untrusted networks.

Credit Cards

But what about that credit card thing? How can a user authenticate to your Internet site, give you their credit card number, and know that the transaction is *really* safe? You may have heard the stories about the cracker Kevin Mitnik, who managed to get up to 20,000 credit card numbers from the Internet service provider Netcom. You obviously don't want this happening to your company.

There are basically two ways of taking and clearing credit card transactions over the Internet. The first is the *local-save* scenario and the other is a remote transaction using Common Gateway Interface (CGI) scripts. A CGI script is a program that allows a server to communicate with users on the Internet, using forms. For example, when a user enters information in a form on a Web page, a CGI script interprets the information and communicates it to a database program on the server.

Local Saves   In the local-save scenario, the credit card information is sent from your Web page using a secure, encrypted session. This is where S-HTTP comes into play. As it travels from the client to its final destination, the credit card number goes through several processes. The first step is to verify that it really is a credit card number, and not just a string of numbers that someone typed in trying to get your product for free. To check this information, you would run the number through the same algorithm that is used to generate credit card numbers in the first place. There are two possible outcomes of this process: either the number really is a potential credit card, or it is a fake.

Once the number your system has been given matches the algorithm, you still need to verify that the number really belongs to the applicant. After all, if you can run a number through an algorithm that would check to see if the card meets all the normal specifications, someone else could get their hands on the same algorithm and generate a batch of fake credit card numbers. Once the potentially correct information is received, it is written to a local disk, where it is stored for later verification.

NOTE ISPs are really familiar with the process. People have been using it to get free Internet access. As a matter of fact, there have been utilities available that will automatically register a user for AOL using a bogus credit card number.

Now, if your business is one where you can retrieve the credit card number and run it through your local bank before shipping the product, this is an ideal situation. If, however, you have information that is readily available on the Web for download, you have a period of time where your company could be vulnerable.

Another problem with this approach is that you are storing other people's financial information on your server. Therefore, you are depending on your security plan to be strong enough to protect not only your information, but the information from your customers. If your system is breached, you are putting your most valuable resource at risk for the spending limits of those credit cards. This could be a massive amount.

Banks don't look favorably on money being stolen, and other companies are not particularly enthralled when they end up giving away goods or services. Therefore, investigating agencies become involved, and sooner or later it will come out that some of these stolen credit cards had one thing in common, your server. Once that information is made public, your company attorneys will probably be spending a lot of their time defending lawsuits.

Remote Saves Using CGI Scripts In the case of remote saves using CGI scripts, you company is more or less just the front for the transaction. In other words, your Web site hosts a form provided by a credit card verification service. When the customer fills out the form and sends if off, the information is sent to a remote server at the credit card clearing company for confirmation. Once the number is confirmed, you are free to send out the goods or provide for Web access.

This scenario sounds really good for the selling organization, except that the company will never have any of the credit card information on file about the customer. If ever there was a dispute about the product or the credit card billing, your company would have no local record of the credit card number that the products were charged to. They'd have to obtain, usually for a price, the verification of the transaction from the credit card clearing company.

Virtual Private Networks and Tunneling

One of the problems plaguing companies as their networks continue to grow is how to connect small remote sites to the main corporate computer room without spending thousands of dollars a month on just infrastructure. Sure, it's nice to be able to support a T-1 line for a branch office, but the cost of the service probably isn't justified for an office of 5 or 6 people.

One of the ways of solving this problem is to borrow part of an infrastructure already in place, one that spans the globe and has bandwidth to handle thousands of transactions every second. The best part of this scheme is that you are paying next to nothing in monthly connection fees, and it is all legal.

We've mentioned the virtual private network (VPN) earlier in this chapter, in the context of proxy servers, as well as in the Chapter 22 discussion of telecommuting and remote access. A VPN is really a simple concept. You have a remote user, say a salesperson who operates out of a home-based office. Now, this salesperson needs to connect to the local network every night to download order information, payment instructions, and expense reports. You started out trying a dial-up connection, but since the sales person is located in another state, the long distance bills were killers, and the performance over a 28.8 dial-up session is not something that people want to use as part of an ongoing business relationship.

Someone came up with the bright idea of using the Internet. Heck, for under $100 a month in most locations, you can rent an ISDN line and hook up to the Internet. You still may not be working at T1 speed, but for all intents and purposes, this is a great idea—except that the Internet is not very secure. This is where a VPN comes into play.

With VPN software, when the sales person goes out to the Internet, they connect to the local area network using the Internet as the backbone. When the connection is established, it is encrypted and secure.

How VPNs Work

To make the whole system work, you must do something to guarantee bandwidth and provide as stable a connection as possible. This is usually accomplished by connecting to the Internet via a leased line to a local ISP.

VPN software is available when you purchase a variety of hardware devices, such as a router or a NOS server, or as part of a firewall. Many of the software packages are proprietary; for example, Cisco has a VPN solution with its IOS operating system and NetWare's BorderManager will allow for the creation of a VPN. Another option is to use a VPN service.

NOTE   Standards for virtual private networks are emerging. Standards like IP Security (IPsec) are enacted to guarantee that VPNs can work together, but for stability it is always best to use two of the same devices to connect your network.

As you start to look at various VPN solutions, it's always a good idea to understand some of the underlying VPN technologies. Several VPN products are based on the Point-to-Point Tunneling Protocol (PPTP), the Layer Two Forwarding (L2F) protocol, or the emerging Layer Two Tunneling Protocol (L2TP). These solutions are great for the cost-conscious administrator who is trying to connect a small remote office to the corporate LAN. In this case, you are using the Internet directly rather than a long-distance or toll-free dial-in connection for remote access using a product like Microsoft's Remote Access Service or Symantec's Norton pcANYWHERE. Using some of these products may guarantee the connection but not guarantee the security of the connection.

For security, make sure that you find a product that incorporates the authentication and encryption capabilities defined by the IP Security (IPsec) standards.

VPNs, even IPsec VPNs, do not take the place of corporate network security. Because these systems usually just provide access control to the Network and Transport layers only, your users—or even some of your customers—can have access to the network. Once they are on the network, it is up to you to make sure that access to individual resources is limited based on corporate policy.

Now that you have connected the remote office to the corporate network, what provides the security? Most VPNs are based on the SSL protocol and make use of keys and certificates to verify authenticity. In the case of the remote salesperson, you and the salesperson would have to generate an encrypted key. This key would be exchanged between sites, and whenever communication was established, the key would be used to verify authenticity.

Tunneling

Tunneling is an emerging connection technology. As this is being written, IPsec is in the final stages of being approved by the IETF, but until it is, there is still some confusion about the final outcome.

Tunneling concerns itself with two issues: how to transfer data privately and how to manage the public keys necessary to make the procedure work. Tunneling is the integral part of VPN. You tunnel across the Internet to your local network, creating the VPN.

Encryption

On the encrypting side, IPsec defines two modes, Transport and Tunnel modes. *Tunnel mode* is the more secure because it takes the entire IP packet, including the header, and encrypts it. Then a routing header and a data integrity header are added.

Transport mode, by contrast, encrypts only the original IP packet, leaving the original header in place. This is not as secure as tunneling because anyone with a packet analyzer can read both the source and destination addresses of the packets.

So where does the potential problem lie? The "problem," if you can call it that, is with the security headers. Both modes can use either of two different headers: authentication header (AH) or encapsulated security payload (ESP). When a packet reaches its destination, both security headers check to make sure the data has not been altered. The problem is that only one header is required by IPsec, not both. Since the headers are incompatible, if you were to use one device using the AH and another device using the ESP, the two devices would be incapable of talking to one another.

Encryption Key Management

One thing for the administrator to keep in mind is the automatic regeneration of keys between servers or between clients and the server. Automatic key regeneration simply establishes a new tunnel using a different key. The key, as the name implies, is automatically regenerated without prompting from the administrator. This helps prevent brute-force attacks, because the one thing cracking software programs have going for them is time. The longer the time between key changes, the more chance the key can be broken. If the key is automatically regenerated, the cracker program will not have the time to crack the key.

Setting up two locations to communicate via an IP tunnel is a viable alternative to a VPN. Just be sure that when you do it, you are using the same technology at each side of the tunnel!

Browser Loopholes

It is hard to imagine that less than ten years ago, advertising wasn't even allowed on the Internet! Now, whenever you browse the Internet, your browser is the window to all sorts of glorious things designed to catch and hold your attention.

While the spinning globes, streaming text, and other gizmos make browsing the Web more interesting, they also make individual computers open to attack from unscrupulous Web designers.

Each one of those superwhiz bang gizmos that your browser opens run off of one type of special script or another. All of those scripts run on *your* computer, not on the host of the Web page. It didn't take people long to figure out that if they can make the world turn on your computer, they can also do damage. This section will take a look at some of the differences between the types of scripts. Remember, when in doubt, make sure you spend some time on the Internet, and check the home page of your particular browser. You want to make sure your browser is patched to the latest levels. Some browsers even have an automatic update feature.

Java and JavaScript

These are two completely different things, but the confusion around them runs rampant.

Java

The granddaddy of them all. Java was developed by Sun Microsystems and was truly revolutionary for its time. When an application is developed to run in Java, it is truly platform independent. Now, an application written for Microsoft Windows can also work on a Unix machine without any tweaking.

Java is a great tool, but it has some inherent security holes. These security holes were spotted by various groups, chief among them Princeton University's Department of Computer Science.

Some of the Java holes the research team exposed were:

- The Netscape and HotJava browsers were found to be susceptible to denial-of-service attacks.

- DNS attacks were possible, where the browser's proxies would be knocked out and the system's DNS server could be given a malicious Java applet.

- At least one version of Java-enabled browsers could write to the Windows 95 file system. In most cases, Java applets could take environment variables from the system or actually access data from your local computer.

- Java also had buffer overflow problems.

Because the Java script was coming into the system as part of a requested page from the Web, the applet would be let through the firewall without a problem. It was also shown that some Java applets could actually attack the firewall, opening up security holes in the firewall.

NOTE   Denial-of-service attacks will be discussed later in this chapter.

Since these holes came to light, Sun and JavaSoft have worked hard to plug the gaps. For the average user, a problem with a Java applet will usually be resolved by simply rebooting the computer or shutting down the browser and restarting it. For the administrator, on the other hand, any browser that is Java-enabled is bringing potentially damaging Java applets in through the firewall. While there have not been any recorded instances of Java security breaches causing serious damage, the potential is there.

JavaScript

JavaScript was created by Netscape to use with the Netscape browser. JavaScript is not a compiled programming language, it does not use standard class libraries, and it is usually written in as part of the normal Web page HTML code. JavaScript is easy to learn, even by someone who does not program for a living. It is not as powerful as Java, and therefore is not as much of a security issue.

There are potential problems with JavaScript, but many of these involve poor programming rather than a security attack. For example, a poorly written Java-Script may start eating away at your system memory, requiring you to reboot the machine after it has frozen.

ActiveX

ActiveX was originally designed to be Microsoft's answer to Java. For awhile, there was some really heated competition going on between MS and Sun over which language would be the Internet standard. It didn't take long for the sides to be drawn: Netscape, with JavaScript, went with Java and Microsoft went with Visual Basic, VBScript, and ActiveX . This meant that the Web site you experienced depended a great deal on the browser you were using at that moment. If it was Netscape and the Web site was designed with ActiveX you were out of luck. The same was true with Internet Explorer and Java. How this war of standards will end is anyone's guess. The two browsers are making some effort to be cross-platform compatible, but you will still find Web sites that cater to aficionados of one browser or another.

ActiveX Security Issues

According to the folks at JavaSoft, from the Web site on Java Security Questions and Answers, ActiveX did not get off to a very grand and glorious start. This quote is from an Update on Java security and ActiveX from February, 1997:

"We've received lots of inquiries on the recently publicized Chaos Computer Club's theoretical hack into Microsoft's ActiveX. This well-established hacker organization, headquartered in Hamburg, demonstrated on German television how its members could use an ActiveX control to theoretically electronically transfer funds from an individual's bank account without using a personal identification number or a transaction number."

After a couple of paragraphs touting Java, the report went on to say:

"ActiveX uses a different (security) model. Because it allows arbitrary binary code to be executed, a malicious ActiveX component can be written to remove or alter files on the user's local disk or to make connections to other computers without the knowledge or approval of the user. There is also the risk that a well-behaved ActiveX component could have a virus attached to it. Unfortunately, viruses can be encrypted just as easily as ordinary code."

To solve this problem, Microsoft started pushing for more widespread acceptance of digitally-signed code. If the code is digitally signed, its authenticity can be verified within the program.

ActiveX, by design, has the ability to access certain pieces of your hard drive. It is integrated closely with Visual Basic. There are certain commands in Visual Basic that will let the programmer control a remote computer .

ActiveX works with Object Linking and Embedding (OLE) technology, and OLE is all about linking different types of documents, using different types of data stored on different types of media. In this case, you can pick up your Excel spread sheet and drop it into the middle of a Word report and have it match its original formatting. When you make a change to one document, the other document is changed, only you do not see the change. If ActiveX can masquerade its code as having been spawned by a different application, it can then launch and remotely control the application. Once the ActiveX control has taken over the application there is literally nothing it cannot do.

Is there any solution here? Both Java and ActiveX are so widespread that you can't just tell people to avoid them, can you? Actually, if the security issues we've discussed are important to you and your network, you *can* tell people to avoid them. There *are* administrators who will not allow Java or ActiveX browsers on the network. Basically, if you use Netscape or IE, you are vulnerable.

Ping of Death, Denial-of-Service Attacks, and Other Threats

Throughout this chapter, we have been describing things that can happen. What about things that have happened? This section will deal with some of the better known ways to attack a network.

Each of these attacks causes the attacked system to stop functioning. Whether this cessation of service is caused by the machine being overwhelmed with data it can't handle, or whether the attack goes after a known weakness in the underlying operating system code, the result is the same. The computer that is attacked stops functioning in a normal manner and denies its services to other computers on the network.

Ping of Death

With this little gem, you don't even need any special programs. The simple and common ping utility will do the trick.

In order for the Ping of Death technique to work, you need a Microsoft NT 3.51 server. Send the server an abnormally large ping packet, and when the packet is received (or in some instances when the packet is sent) the server stops working. The server displays the common blue screen of death and quits working. Your server now needs to be restarted.

NetWare 3.12 file servers show some of the same symptoms, but the attack must be a little more refined. In January, 1997 a user in Poland reported that it is possible to abnormally end (abend) a 3.12 fileserver session by sending IPX garbage to socket 4002h. Socket 4002h is an echo port, meaning whatever is sent to that port will be echoed back, and in this case generate an abend.

NOTE   Microsoft has issued a fix for this. For more information see the Web site at www.microsoft.com/kb/articles/q132/4/70.asp.

Syn_Flooder

Syn_Flooder is a utility written in C that, when used against a Unix server, will cause the server to freeze and discontinue operations. It synthetically floods the machine with half-open connection requests. The utility is freely available in Linux code on the Internet. Using the utility is a violation of Federal laws, punishable by imprisonment.

DNSKiller

DNSKiller is another C program that is designed to be run on a Linux platform. It is designed to stop the DNS service on a Windows NT 4.0 Server.

arnudp100.c

Yet another C program. This program is designed to forge the IP address of UDP packets. It can be used to trigger denial of service on UDP ports 7, 13, 19 and 37.

cbcb.c

This is the file name for the Cancelbot utility, which is designed to target Usenet news postings of others. It generates cancel control messages for each message that fits the criteria the cracker designs. This will cause news messages on the Usenet to simply disappear.

Web Server Strategies

Now that you have the perfect Web server up and running the perfect Web page, there are some other security issues we need to take a look at. In this section, we will examine things like access logging, directory-level access, password authentication to the Web page, and obtaining and using authentication certificates.

Access Logging

Most Web pages have some sort of counter attached to them. After all, that is how you know how many people have actually accessed the Web page and perused the Webmaster's creation. That's useful information and provides a form of advertising, but it doesn't tell the site's proprietors *who* has accessed their Web page—for instance, were your business competitors among the visitors? Identifying your viewers is the purpose of access logging.

If you decide that you want to institute access logging, the first question you must answer is where is your Web site located? Control is a wonderful thing. If your Web site is in-house, you pretty much control what your Web server will and will not do. If, on the other hand, your Web site is hosted by an independent ISP, things can get a little more tricky.

Most access logs are generated either by the Web server itself, or for a specific Web page, by a portion of the Web page code called a Server Side Include (SSI) script. Since this script is actually processed by the server, some ISPs prohibit them in hosted Web pages. If your Web page is on a server that you control, then you will not have this problem.

Earlier in this book, back in Chapter 18, we presented a table of different types of Web servers that were available on the market. There were several. The Web server that we'll use in this example is the FastTrack Web Server from Netscape.

FastTrack Log

The process begins by finding how to access your server's current access log. In the case of the FastTrack server, the log file is located in the *servername*\ *volumename*\novonyx\suitespot\admin-serv\logs folder. This file can be viewed using a text editor or by using the Administration utilities as shown in Figure 28.3.

FIGURE 28.3:

Viewing the access log in the SuiteSpot General Administration utility

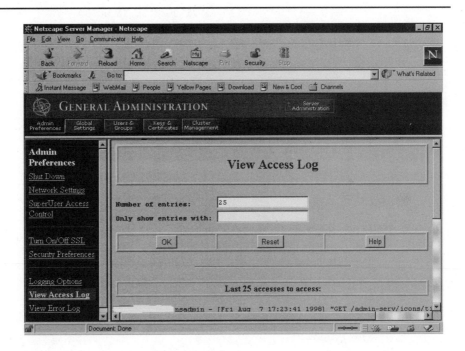

FastTrack, which is one of the free Web servers, does not offer much in the way of reporting capabilities. However, since the access log is stored in a text format, you could import the data into a spreadsheet and sort it.

The access log will tell you the IP address from which a person was accessing the Web site, the time of day the access occurred, and what the user did while accessing the Web site.

As you become more familiar with the Web server, or with the SSI scripts, keep in mind that access logs need to be recycled. If you are going to use them to gather usage information, be sure to archive the logs to a safe spot before the Web server deletes the log and starts a new one.

Here is an example of an access log in the Common Logfile Format:

```
wiley.a.com - - [16/Feb/1996:21:18:26 -0800] "GET / HTTP/1.0" 200 751

wiley.a.com - - [17/Feb/1996:1:04:38 -0800] "GET /docs/grafx/icon.gif
HTTP/1.0" 204 342

wiley.a.com - - [20/Feb/1996:4:36:53 -0800] "GET /help HTTP/1.0" 401
571

arrow.a.com - john [29/Mar/1996:4:36:53 -0800] "GET /help HTTP/1.0" 401
571
```

Table 28.6 describes the last line of the sample access log.

T A B L E 28.6: Sample Access Log

Access Log Field	Example
Hostname or IP Address of Client	Arrow.a.com In this case, the hostname is shown because the Web server's setting for DNS lookups is enabled; if DNS lookups were disabled, the client's IP address would appear.
Field Not Used	None
Username	John The username entered by the client for authentication.
Date/time of Request	29/Mar/1996:4:36:53 -0800
Request	GET /help
Protocol	HTTP/1.0
Status Code	401
Bytes Transferred	571

The Netscape FastTrack Server also offers the option of a flexible logging format, by specifying the way you want your log displayed, or even what information is displayed.

Directory-Level Access

Another way of securing your Web server and your Web site is to limit which directories, files, or file types users can access.

For the FastTrack server, when the Web server gets an incoming request, it determines access based on a set of rules called access control entries (ACEs), and then it determines if the request is allowed or denied. Each ACE determines whether or not the server should continue to the next ACE in the hierarchy. The collection of ACEs is called an access control list (ACL).

When a request comes in to the server, the server looks in the file OBJ.CONF for a reference to an ACL, which is then used to determine access. By default, the server has one ACL file that can contain multiple ACLs.

For example, suppose someone requests the following URL:

```
http://www.psconsulting.com/my_stuff/Web/presentation.html
```

The server would first check the access control list for the entire server. If the ACL for the entire server was set to continue, the server checks to see if there is an ACL for the file type (*.HTML). Then it checks for an ACL for the directory my_stuff. If one exists, it checks the ACE and then moves on to the next subdirectory. The server continues following the URL path either until it reaches an ACL that says to stop or until it reaches the final ACL for the requested URL (in this case, the file PRESENTATION.HTML).

The following example of a FastTrack ACL file shows one way to control access to this server:

```
# File automatically written
#
# You may edit this file by hand
#
version 3.0;
# This ACL allows everyone in the local database or LDAP directory
acl "agents";
authenticate (user,group) {
        prompt = "FastTrack Server";
};
```

```
deny (all)
    user = "anyone";
allow absolute (all)
    user = "all";
# This ACL denies all access to the my_stuff directory
acl "path=C:\Netscape\SuiteSpot\docs\my_stuff";
deny (all)
    user = "anyone";
# This ACL allows access to anyone in the user database
acl "path=C:\Netscape\SuiteSpot\docs\my_stuff\Web";
allow (all)
    user = "anyone";
# This ACL allows access to the file to anyone in the "my_group" group
acl "path=C:\Netscape\SuiteSpot\docs\my_stuff\Web\presentation.html";
allow (all)
    user = "anyone";
    group = "my_group"
# This is the default ACL and denies access to anyone
acl "default";
deny (all)
```

Restricting Access to Files

To restrict user access to specific documents on your Web site, you have to be more granular when using the access control rules. Keep in mind that most access control rules use only a limited set of the available options.

To create an access control rule using the FastTrack Server Manager, do the following:

1. Start FastTrack Server Manager by configuring your Netscape Web browser to point to the Web server, using the port assigned to Server Manager. This is a randomly assigned port that Netscape chooses when it is installed. From FastTrack Server Manager click the name of the Server. This brings up the Server Preferences screen. Choose Restrict Access. The form shown in Figure 28.4 appears. Here you select and edit an existing access control rule or specify a new rule by either choosing the resource you want to apply to the rule (the file, directory, or wildcard pattern you want to control) or typing a name to assign to the ACL.

FIGURE 28.4:

Access Control List
Management

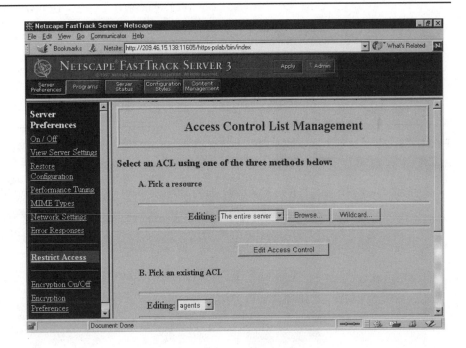

Because the form is longer than the size of the screen, you may need to
scroll to see all three sections of the main form. These sections are:

Pick a resource: This allows you to specify a wildcard pattern for files or
directories to restrict access to (such as *.html) or to specify a directory or
a filename to restrict. You can also browse for a file or directory by clicking
Browse.

Pick an existing ACL: This allows you to select an ACL that you've created from the drop-down list.

Type in the ACL name: This allows you to create named ACLs. Use this
option only if you're familiar with ACL files and the obj.conf configuration file; you'll need to manually edit obj.conf if you want to apply
named ACLs to resources.

2.   In the section you want to modify, from the editing drop-down list select the
part of your Website (the resource) that you want to control. For example,
you can select Entire Server to set up access control for your entire server.

3. Click Edit Access Control. The screen divides into two frames that you use to set the access control rules. If the resource you chose already has access control, the rules will appear.

4. At this point, you should see the Access Control Rules window illustrated in Figure 28.5. Click on New Line. This adds a default ACL rule to the bottom row of the table.

FIGURE 28.5:

Access Control Rules

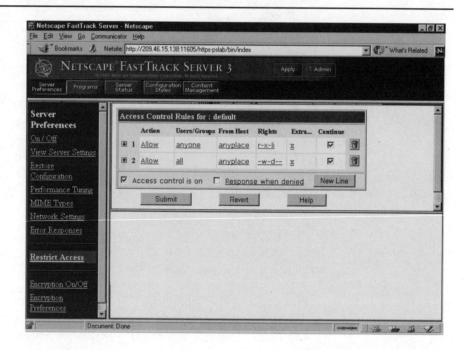

5. Click Deny to select the action you want to apply to the rule. The bottom frame displays a form where you can select whether to allow or deny access to the users, groups, or hosts you'll specify in the following steps. Select the option you want and then click Update.

6. Click on Anyone to specify User-Group authentication, which is listed under the Users/Groups column. The bottom frame displays a form for configuring User-Group authentication. By default, there is no authentication, and so anyone can access the resource.

7. Click on Anyplace to specify the computers you want to include in the rule. The bottom frame displays the From Host form, where you can enter wildcard

patterns of hostnames or IP addresses to allow or deny. Select the options you want and then click Update.

8. Click on All to specify the access rights you want to include in the rule. Check the access rights in the bottom frame and then click Update.

9. Click X under the Extra column to enter a customized ACL entry, if you are familiar with ACL files. This area is useful if you use the access control API to customize ACLs. Click Update.

10. Check the appropriate box in the Continue column if you want the access control rule to continue in a chain. This means that the next line is evaluated before the server determines whether the user is allowed access. When creating multiple lines in an access-control entry, it's best to work from the most general restrictions to the most specific ones.

11. Check the Access Control Is On box.

12. Check Response When Denied if you want the user to be redirected to another URL if their request is denied. Select Respond With The Following URL and type the URL in the field. Click Update.

13. Repeat steps 4 through 10 for each rule you need.

14. Click Submit to store the new access control rules in the ACL file. If you click Revert, the server removes any changes you made to the rules from the time you first opened the two-frame window.

15. Click Save and Apply.

Password Authentication

There is security available with most Web servers to protect parts of your Web site against unauthorized access. As usual, the first line of defense is the username/password combination.

The Netscape FastTrack server is a joint effort between Novell and Netscape, designed to optimize the Netscape servers for NetWare environments. As such, it has the ability to authenticate users with either Lightweight Directory Access Protocol (LDAP) or using Novell Directory Services (NDS). If you choose to use LDAP and if you require users to enter a username and password to get access to the Web site, you store the list of users and groups in an LDAP database. This database is a file stored on the Web server computer.

When users attempt to access a file or directory that requires authentication, the Web browser displays a dialog box asking the user to enter a username and password. The server can get this information in an encrypted format or in plain text, depending on whether encryption is turned on for your server.

After entering the username and password, the user sees either the requested file or directory listing or a message denying access.

Note that if Secure Socket Layer (SSL) encryption is turned off, the username and password are transmitted in plain text. Without encryption someone could intercept the network packets and read the username and password being sent to the Web server. For this reason, password authentication is most effective when combined with SSL encryption, or Host-IP authentication, or both.

Client Certificate Authentication

Another way you can confirm users' identities is with security certificates. Depending on the Web server, you can generate these certificates at the Web server, or you can use certificates generated by a third-party organization. Authentication by certificate can be done in two ways:

- The server can use the information in the certificate as proof of identity.

- The server can verify the certificate itself, provided the certificates are published in an LDAP directory. When a request comes in and you have client authentication on, the server performs these actions in the following order:

    1. When the browser sends the certificate, the server checks if the certificate is from a trusted Certification Authority (CA). If not, the server ends the transaction.

    2. If the certificate is from a trusted CA, the server maps the certificate to a user's entry using the certificate management file. If the certificate maps correctly, then the Web server follows the ACL rule, or command, specified for that user.

The procedures necessary for generating and receiving the public keys necessary for the certificate authentication vary with each Web server. How to generate the key is not as important as insuring that both the Web server and the client have the correct key. Without the right key, authentication cannot occur.

Summary

Using the Internet is a security person's worst nightmare! There are so many ways for the system to be attacked, and even if your network is locked down tightly, something as simple as a browser can cause a firewall to suddenly develop holes. Being diligent is the key. There is new information coming out regularly on security holes that are discovered with all network operating systems, firewalls, browsers and Web servers. Make sure you keep up to date on your reading, and also on your patches!

PART IX

Troubleshooting and Preventive Maintenance

- CHAPTER 29: Basic Elements of Troubleshooting
- CHAPTER 30: Hardware Troubleshooting Tools
- CHAPTER 31: Software Troubleshooting Tools
- CHAPTER 32: Diagnosing Real-World Problems
- CHAPTER 33: Troubleshooting Servers
- CHAPTER 34: Troubleshooting Workstations
- CHAPTER 35: Troubleshooting the Physical Network
- CHAPTER 36: Troubleshooting Network Printing
- CHAPTER 37: Troubleshooting WANs
- CHAPTER 38: A Pound of Prevention

CHAPTER
TWENTY-NINE

Basic Elements of Troubleshooting

- An approach to troubleshooting

- Troubleshooting new and newly upgraded systems

- Troubleshooting existing systems

- Record keeping

- Tools for troubleshooting

- Information resources for troubleshooting

Most businesses have been using PCs for years, usually in the same way that typewriters were used in the past—as individual tools to enhance productivity. Now, of course, many companies are discovering that computers can be networked in local area networks (LANs) and wide area networks (WANs) to increase productivity dramatically. But these resulting networks often are being built piecemeal; first one department networks its computers, then another, and eventually the whole company, but not necessarily according to any overall plan.

Such networks usually consist of several different kinds of workstations—PCs running any of several operating systems, Macintoshes, Unix workstations—all tied together through servers of one sort or another, and perhaps also tied to the old mainframe or minicomputer as well. This is why network operating systems such as NetWare and Windows NT have become so popular—their ability to support multiple different platforms, networking protocols, and networking hardware make them good choices both for smaller networks as well as larger LANs and WANs.

Because the use of networks is growing so rapidly, and because training programs turn out far fewer graduates than are needed, network administrators are in short supply. Often, this has meant that users who know only a little more than their colleagues about computers or networks find themselves pressed into service as administrators. And administrators who began by administering a small departmental network may now find themselves responsible for a half-dozen servers and hundreds of workstations. These people may be able to set up basic configurations of workstations or LANs, but often have little or no formal training or background in troubleshooting. The chapters in this section are intended to help the knowledgeable user understand the principles of troubleshooting, and to apply those principles to fix problems with workstations and networks.

There are many books on troubleshooting that are full of information on what to do in specific situations—if X happens, do Y. There are others that try to present the material contained in the software documentation in a more accessible way. These are useful resources, but the one thing almost never touched on is the *approach* to troubleshooting. The following chapters are not so much about how to get a particular network driver to work with a particular adapter, but rather, they focus on showing you how to isolate the cause of your problem, how to find the information necessary to fix the problem, and then how to apply that knowledge successfully.

An Approach to Troubleshooting

Many people involved with computers and networks of computers regard setting them up initially and fixing them when they stop working as an arcane art. To the average user watching an expert troubleshoot and fix a system, the process might seem like magic. However, whether the expert consciously follows them or not, there are certain basic principles common to all troubleshooting.

The basic process of troubleshooting is simple to state: Determine that there is a problem, isolate the problem, identify the cause of the problem, and fix the problem. The biggest difficulty in applying this relatively simple process to a LAN or WAN, or even to a single workstation or server, is caused by the enormous number of possible combinations of hardware, software, and configurations involved.

Breaking Down the Elements

The simplest approach to this complexity is to break it down: Isolate the WAN into LANs; each LAN into server, workstations, and cabling; each server or workstation into hardware, client operating systems, and networking software; and the physical cabling into segments. Each of these subsystems can be further divided as necessary, until each element can be determined to be the cause of the problem or not.

Often, an experienced troubleshooter will have a seemingly intuitive "feel" for what might be wrong. But what appears to be intuition is usually a rapid process of elimination based on long and often painful previous experience. This experience is useful in rapidly finding and fixing a problem, but it is not essential. Most users, by following a logical and methodical approach, will be able to solve the same problems, although probably not as quickly.

Trying Different Solutions

The optimal approach to becoming a good troubleshooter is to *try things out*. As long as basic precautions are followed to avoid irreparable changes, experimentation is fine. In fact, this is often the way that even a highly experienced troubleshooter will approach a problem: try a few different things until the system is fixed. Experienced troubleshooters simply have a better feel for which things to try first—which "fault points" are the most likely to be broken.

There are a couple of basic ways to determine what things to try first, and how to continue from there. Try the *simple* things first. It's much easier to verify that a PC is plugged in than to disassemble it and check the hard disk to be sure it's receiving power. It's also much more likely that the PC has been accidentally unplugged than that the power connection for the hard disk has failed or worked loose. Also, don't change more than one thing at once; for instance, replacing all the cards in a PC might well fix the problem, but it won't tell you which of the cards has failed. Unless you need to get that PC back online immediately, it's better to remove cards one at a time, putting the old one back if there's no change, until the problem is isolated.

Each chapter in this section will help you determine the most likely failure areas for your particular setup. These vary from system to system, but as you become familiar with the trouble spots for your system, you will be able to rapidly check a few items and often solve your problem within a few minutes. Not only does this save time when irate users are waiting to get back online, it makes you seem like a wizard to your boss.

Two of your best tools for determining likely areas of failure are a well-kept log and a baseline of the system. A *baseline* is a collection of statistics that represent the normal operation of your equipment. These are discussed further in this chapter and in Chapter 25.

Almost all systems that need troubleshooting fall into one of two categories: systems that were working and have failed or new systems that don't work as expected (this includes existing systems that stopped working when something new was added). Each requires a certain basic approach, but the essential underlying principle of all troubleshooting is to eliminate possible causes of the problem until the actual cause is isolated.

Troubleshooting New Systems and Additions to Existing Systems

With a system that is new, or one to which something has been added, the basic approach is to achieve a minimum configuration that works, or return to the configuration that worked before things were changed, and build from there. For instance, a networked workstation will often have a number of cards in it, which might include a network adapter, video display adapter, hard disk controller, mouse, serial/parallel adapter, sound card, internal modem, host adapter, and SCSI controller card. Each of these can potentially interfere with the others.

Stripping Down to the Minimum

To begin with, it's best to fall back to a basic minimum, perhaps only the hard disk controller and video adapter. If the PC will boot with just these cards, then add others until you discover what isn't working, or what is conflicting with the basic system.

With new hardware additions that cause problems, it is unlikely that the new part is defective, so the solution is usually to isolate the conflict between the new item and something in the system. Unless you have specific suspicions about where the conflict may be, the most certain procedure is to remove any extraneous parts from the system. If the new addition works with a basic system, begin adding the remaining components back in until the problem recurs.

Keeping Track of Configuration Details

It is important to keep track of each card in a PC, and what interrupts and memory segments it uses. Actually checking each card's manual and writing down what its configuration is may be the only way you will discover that it is attempting to use the same memory segment as another card. See the "Record Keeping" section later in this chapter for suggestions on how to record data about your system.

You may discover that the default configurations of all the cards in the PC will not work together. In this case, you must determine which cards have alternate configurations and how to set them, and then possibly reset the appropriate software. There are also programs that will help you determine which interrupts and memory segments each card in a system uses. Windows 95 (and Windows 98) is quite helpful in this regard, as long as the problem doesn't prevent the operating system from loading. You can go into the Device Manager (accessible via the Hardware applet in Control Panel, or by right-clicking on My Computer and choosing Properties) and view all the current settings for every installed piece of hardware.

In particular, a helpful and little-known feature of Windows 95/98 Device Manager is that you can simultaneously view *all* IRQs, DMAs, and I/O and memory addresses in use. To do this, open Device Manager, select Computer from the resource list (rather than a specific item under Computer), and click the Properties button. Figure 29.1 shows an example of the resulting window, where we are looking at a machine's IRQ settings. You can also choose the Device Manager's Print option (after highlighting Computer), and get a list of every IRQ, DMA, I/O, and memory address used by everything in the system, broken down by individual devices and by category of resource (IRQ, DMA, etc.) used. A very helpful Print option is to select Print to a File, which gives you all of this information summarized in a handy text file. Needless to say, such text files or printouts can be invaluable when adding new hardware or diagnosing existing hardware conflicts—you may even want to archive a copy of this file for each system on your network (those with varying configurations at least).

FIGURE 29.1:

You can use Device Manager to view all the resource settings for a computer.

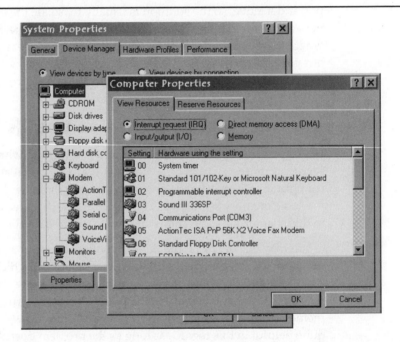

Some network cards, like the NE2000, have more than a dozen possible configurations, but only two or three that are normally used. Unfortunately, the ideal configurations on some cards can be difficult to discover, depending on the quality of the documentation. This is also true in general of all the cards you might find in a PC. Even expensive cards may have terrible documentation; it is one of the few instances where paying more may not necessarily gain you anything.

It is also true that Plug and Play and PCI are not without their problems. Even if all the cards in the system support Plug and Play, and your operating system supports it and has drivers for the cards, things may still not work, or you may find that one card's drivers conflict with those for another card. You should check the documentation and README files on the driver disks that came with the cards to make sure that the drivers are the latest available.

If you cannot find the information you need in the manual for the card, or cannot make sense of what is there, your best bet is to find someone else who has already been through the problem and pick their brain. Possible sources of information include the manufacturer's tech support line or Web site, the dealer you bought the equipment from, your local MIS organization, the Support Alliance, various forums on CompuServe and the Internet, and the local Windows NT or CNA/CNE (Certified NetWare Administrators and Certified NetWare Engineers) user group.

Troubleshooting Existing Systems

With an existing system that was working and has failed, the basic approach is to determine what has changed. This may require a methodical approach at the station level, involving swapping cards or checking connections, or it may be as simple as discovering that a user has added a new piece of software that is incompatible with other software on the system.

Talk to the user(s) experiencing the problem. You might ask these kinds of questions:

- Does the user know of a way to make the problem go away?

- Is there a certain time of day, a particular piece of software, or a certain server associated with the problem?

- Has the user changed the configuration of his or her PC recently?

- What was the user doing when the problem occurred?

NOTE Problems affecting a *group* of users (particularly a group sharing a network segment) almost always point to a different set of issues, which we will deal with later in more detail.

Getting the information from a user can be difficult. Users may not remember the critical change, or may be reluctant to admit having done something that may be causing a problem.

There are a couple of things you can do to make the necessary information easier to find. The first is to keep a record of system configurations on each workstation on your network. This information can be tedious to acquire, although inventory programs can automatically produce most of the information you will want. Another useful approach is to standardize the workstations on your network as much as possible. Make sure that they are all using the same version of the operating system, the same network client software and network adapter, and so on.

Sometimes the change to a system is not intentional. It may be a connection that has worked loose, a corrupted file, or a broken cable. You will still have clues to investigate, but you may need to dig for them. It is still essentially a process of elimination, determined by the various break points of the system. These break points will be covered in detail in the appropriate coming chapters.

Attitude: The Most Important Troubleshooting Tool!

When we meet with other troubleshooters, system engineers, or networking experts, the conversation often turns to troubleshooting, and what makes a good troubleshooter. The consensus is that the single most important ingredient to make a good troubleshooter is not knowledge, or experience, or intelligence. It is *attitude*. A determination to keep trying until you figure out the problem is essential. Any system that worked once can be made to work again. The critical thing is to keep trying until the problem is solved.

The biggest stumbling blocks for most troubleshooters are the mistaken impression that they have "tried everything" and the feeling that the problem is too complex—that they'll never be able to understand the problem. This false first impression is usually caused by looking at the system too quickly, but it may also result from failing to consider the possible effects of elements apparently outside the problem. The feeling of being overwhelmed can be avoided by breaking the problem down into more basic components—break a WAN into LANs, a LAN into server, workstations, and cabling plant, and so on. You can be successful at troubleshooting as long as you are willing to keep trying. You may not be as fast at first as someone with a lot of experience or knowledge of the system, but you can get results. The more familiar you are with your system, of course, the more capable of fixing it you will be. This is one of the functions of performing the baselining and collecting the log sheets for every workstation and server on your network, as explained in the next section.

Record Keeping

It is utterly impossible to overdo documentation of your network. Hours spent collecting information on your network might seem like a waste at the time, particularly to your supervisor, but it could make many, many hours of difference in the time required to get the network running again if there is trouble. Record keeping is cheap insurance.

Record keeping is one of the most useful aids in troubleshooting. It's difficult to isolate what might be causing a problem if you don't know what is in the system. Likewise, if you need to reconfigure a system back to its last working state, it's easier if you don't need to rediscover the settings that got it to work in the first place. Also, your records of similar problems with a similar system and how you got it to work may give you a lead on fixing your current problem.

You should have a record of each system including the date it was installed and the original configuration, the dates and details of each update or addition to hardware or software, and perhaps a printout of the configuration files. Such a record can greatly simplify the problem of isolating the latest change to a system. It will be easier to keep such records if you establish a database or use a standard worksheet when you set up or modify a workstation. Figure 29.2 shows an example of a worksheet for recording server configuration data.

FIGURE 29.2:

An example of a server configuration worksheet

Server Configuration Worksheet
Side One

Name: _Asmodeus_   Location: _Office 1141_   Date: _3/30/96_

Internal IPX Number: _C11412385_   Department: _Marketing_

Brand/Model: _ACMA 150 Mhz Pentium PC1 Tower Award BIOS 6.11_

Support Phone Number: _408 555-1491_   Serial Number: _A11093B31_

Memory Installed: _64 Mb_ Possible: _256 Mb_ Type: _16x32 SIMM_

Board: _LAN Adapter_	**Board**: _LAN Adapter_
Brand: _3Com_	Brand: _3Com_
Support #: _408 764-6399_	Support #: _408 764-6399_
Model #: _36590TP_	Model #: _3C590TP_
I/O Port: _____	I/O Port: _____
Memory Address: _____	Memory Address: _____
Interrupt: _____	Interrupt: _____
DMA: _____	DMA: _____
Slot Number: _3_	Slot Number: _2_
Driver: _3C590.LAN_	Driver: _3C590.LAN_
BIOS Version: _1.21_	BIOS Version: _1.21_
Network Number: _1A114100_	Network Number: _2B114100_
Board: _SVGA_	**Board**: _____
Brand: _On Motherboard_	Brand: _____
Support #: _____	Support #: _____
Model #: _____	Model #: _____
I/O Port: _____	I/O Port: _____
Memory Address: _B000-B7FF_	Memory Address: _____
Interrupt: _____	Interrupt: _____
DMA: _____	DMA: _____
Slot Number: _____	Slot Number: _____
Driver: _____	Driver: _____
BIOS Version: _____	BIOS Version: _____
Network Number: _____	Network Number: _____

Disks - see other side

In addition, an archive of the standard software used on your workstations can make your life much easier. It's far easier and faster to simply copy the files you need from your standard set of floppies or network directory than to copy them from the original floppies or CD-ROM, or to re-create or regenerate them, as required.

FIGURE 29.2:
(cont.)

Server Configuration Worksheet
Side Two — Disks

Controller: _Adaptec 1742B (EISA)_   Int: — DMA: ____ Slot #: _4_
Support #: _510 555-3201_   Driver: _AHA1740.DSK_
Port: — **Mem. Address:** —   BIOS Version: _6.02_

Disk	Size	Heads	Cylinders	Device Code (5-digit)	Logical Device	Physical Partition	Mirrored With
Maxtor PO-125	1 Gb	15	4196	21100	1	0	1
Maxtor PO-125	1 Gb	15	4196	21200	2	1	—

Controller: _Motherboard_   Int: _E_ DMA: ____ Slot #: ____
Support #: _415 555-8195_   Driver: _ISADISK_
Port: _1f0_ **Mem. Address:** ____   BIOS Version: _____

Disk	Size	Heads	Cylinders	Device Code (5-digit)	Logical Device	Physical Partition	Mirrored With
Quantum IDE 105S	100	8	995	11000	1	0	—

A daily log is another useful tool for the network administrator. It can provide a history of a particular problem, making it easier to isolate things that may occur at long or irregular intervals. A good log can make it much easier to justify new purchases or upgrades—particularly if you can show that the same part has failed four times in the last ten months. (And a log will also show your supervisor just what you've been doing with your time.)

Resources for Troubleshooters

Because of the enormous number of possibilities inherent in LANs, no single book can address every possible combination of things that can go wrong. This book, we hope, is a good starting point. Among the additional resources available to you are:

- The network operating system manuals.

- The hardware manufacturer's manuals.

- Third-party books on your network operating system, networking hardware and software, applications you may be using, and so on.

- Trade publications—between the weekly and monthly magazines, there are thousands of pages published every month on hundreds of topics related to networking.

- The Internet and online services—CompuServe, for example, still has a large section on NetWare, and the Internet newsgroups on NT and NetWare (such as `comp.os.netware.misc`) are also extensive. Any question you might have has probably been discussed on one of the forums.

- Your local NT or NetWare user group.

- The local NT user's group or chapter of the Certified NetWare Engineer Professional Association (CNEPA). Even if you're not a member, you can probably get either free advice or professional help through these organizations.

- Your authorized reseller—the dealer you bought NT or NetWare from should have technical support personnel who can help you with your problem.

- Services from Microsoft's and Novell's technical support, including their hotlines (Microsoft: 425-635-7000; NetWare: 800-NETWARE), their Web pages (`www.microsoft.com` and `www.novell.com`), the NT Resource ToolKit, the NetWare Support Encyclopedia, and so on.

- Online or CD-ROM–based collections of information, including *Micro House Technical Library*, *Computer Select*, and the various magazines' CD-ROMs, such as *Byte* on CD-ROM, *LAN Times* CD-ROM, and others.

See Appendix A for more information about the resources available for troubleshooters.

Aids for Troubleshooting

The chapters throughout Part IX provide a number of tools designed to help you implement the approach to problem-solving we've outlined in this chapter. These include troubleshooting hardware and software overviews, fault points that identify where things can go wrong, and examples and real-life stories to help you put the information into context.

The process you should follow to isolate a problem with your LAN is to check the server first, the workstations second, and the physical network third. Your first indication that there is a problem will often be a complaint from a user. The best course is usually to quickly eliminate the most obvious possible causes before doing an in-depth analysis. If a cursory examination shows that the user's workstation seems to be in order, then check to make sure that the server is operational.

Your first check of the server should simply be to see that it is on and responding to the keyboard. If it is, there could still be problems, but it's best to next find out how many workstations are experiencing problems, then do some simple tests to determine whether the physical connections could be causing the problem, before doing a really thorough examination of the server. It's usually faster and less likely to inconvenience lots of users to check a few other workstations than it is to begin working on the server itself.

When multiple users are affected, an effective first strategy is to look for what that group has in common. Perhaps they're all working from the same network drive mapping, or share the same Ethernet hub.

Fault Points for Identifying Problem Areas

Rather than using a typical flowchart, which cannot cover anything close to all the possibilities inherent in a network, we have developed a system that looks at the places where things can go wrong. This approach does require a certain degree of understanding of your system, but is also adaptable to any system. The idea is that there are, within any combination of different types of workstations, network interface cards, network topologies, servers, cabling, software, and so on, a limited number of points where something can go wrong.

For instance, the connection between the network card and the physical wiring is a fault point. Depending on your system, the connector may be any one of a dozen types, each with its own unique way of going bad. Rather than attempt to teach you what all of these are and how to tell if they are the problem, I'll attempt to show you how to isolate your problem to that particular fault point, and leave the rest to you.

The fault points are all the essential links in a network chain. For instance, the workstation hardware and operating system, the software and hardware that allow the workstation to talk over the cabling, the cabling system, and the server itself are all parts of the network chain that connects the user to the server. Other chains may connect the user to the printer or to a modem, from the server to a remote LAN, from the LAN to another LAN, and so on. Each item in the fault-point chain can affect the chain in three ways: it can fail, its links to the previous item can fail, or its links to the next item can fail. For instance, a power cord could be broken, or it could have a faulty connection to the wall socket or to the power supply of the equipment it's attached to.

In every case, the key to finding the fault points and checking them for failure is an understanding of the principles involved in that chain. This does not necessarily mean that you must thoroughly know and understand all the seven levels of the OSI model, for example (although that may help!), but you should at least understand that the network adapter and network driver in a workstation combine to send a message through the wire to the network adapter and network driver in the server. You should also know that, depending on the type of network and whether the packet goes straight to the server or is passed along from one workstation to the next, a missing T-connector at the unused workstation in the next cube might be the problem.

For quick reference, the fault-point chain used in most chapters in Part IX is represented as an illustration like that shown in Figure 29.3.

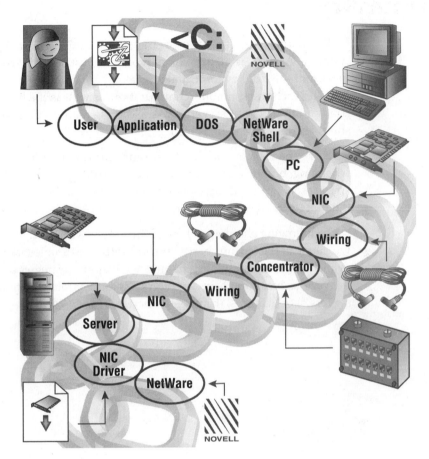

FIGURE 29.3:

The fault-point chain for troubleshooting workstations on a NetWare network

Summary

In this chapter, we've laid the groundwork for this section of chapters on troubleshooting. As we've noted, a key part of being a successful troubleshooter is being persistent. Also of key importance is taking good notes—and this should include notes on each workstation's configuration, as well as the hardware and software configuration of your servers and the cabling plant. A problem and resolution log should certainly be kept as well.

At first glance, network hardware and software problems may seem overwhelming, but the key always is to keep breaking down the problem area into smaller sections until each section can either be ruled out or determined as being the root (or part) of the problem.

The following chapters will begin this process for you. In the next two chapters, we'll look at the various hardware and software troubleshooting tools that are available; then in following chapters we'll apply strategies and tools to diagnose the various breakpoints in a network—with separate chapters on troubleshooting servers, workstations, the physical network, and WANs.

CHAPTER
THIRTY

Hardware
Troubleshooting Tools

- Cable checkers and cable testers

- Handheld diagnostic tools

- Network monitors and network analyzers

- Using network hardware for monitoring

In this chapter we will take a look at some of the testing tools available for ensuring that our network remains healthy. We will start by looking at ways of certifying that our cabling is correct, and work our way up to tools that can monitor and diagnose problems at the Network and Transport layers.

In an attempt to organize this information, we shall break devices up into five categories; they are:

- Basic cable checkers
- Cable testers
- Handheld diagnostic tools
- Network monitoring tools
- Full network analyzers

We will also include a section on collecting diagnostic and performance information from network devices such as switches and routers.

Each one of the listed tools is capable of supplying its own unique body of information regarding your network's health. A well equipped tool kit will contain tools from more than one category. For example, a top-of-the-line network analyzer will not report on the same information as a basic cable checker. There is some information you can collect from a $50 cable checker that a $4,000 analyzer cannot tell you.

Basic Cable Checkers

Basic cable checkers are just that; they do little more than report on whether your cabling can provide basic connectivity. A small voltage is applied to each conductor in the cable. The checker then verifies if the voltage can be detected on the other end. Most checkers will also ensure that this voltage cannot be detected on any other conductors running through the wire. When using a cable checker, you must disconnect the cable from the network prior to testing.

Figure 30.1 shows a basic cable checker. The LEDs provide a pass/fail condition on each of the tests performed. Performing a test requires little more than attaching the cable to the unit and pressing the test button. A good cable checker will have two separate components, one for each end of the cable. This is useful if you need to test cabling that runs through ceilings or walls.

FIGURE 30.1:

A basic cable checker

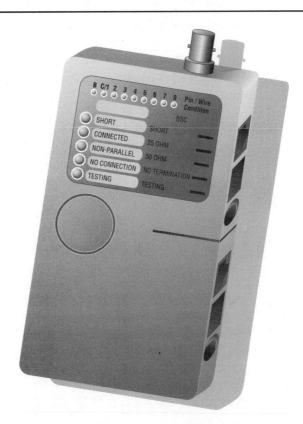

Look for tests that do the following in a thinnet cable checker:

- verify connectivity on the center conductor
- verify connectivity along the shielding
- verify that the conductor and the shield are not shorted together

Look for tests that do the following in a twisted-pair cable checker:

- verify connectivity through each wire

- verify that wires are paired correctly

- verify that wires are not shorted together

- identify when the transmit and receive pairs are not crossed (cross cable)

Most cable checkers light up a series of either four or eight lights when performing these tests.

Topology Wiring Requirements

Each topology uses its own set of wire pair requirements. We covered the pairs required for 10Mb Ethernet back in Chapter 7.

TIP   Good practice is to wire *all* wire pairs, in case a new topology is introduced later which may very well use more wire pairs.

Twisted-pair wiring used by other existing topologies is as follows:

- Ethernet 10BaseT uses pins 1–2, 3–6.

- Ethernet 100BaseTx uses pins 1–2, 3–6.

- Ethernet 100BaseT4 uses pins 1–2, 3–6, 4–5, 7–8.

- Token Ring uses pins 3–6, 4–5.

- 100VG-AnyLAN uses pins 1–2, 3–6, 4–5, 7–8.

- ATM uses pins 1–2, 7–8.

So long as all eight wires (four pairs) are connected, you should be able to operate any of the above topologies.

> **TIP**
>
> Because it uses light as a transmission medium, there are no basic cable checkers for fiber cable. If you have cables that have been previously certified with a tester, and you need a simple tool for testing the path of wire runs, use a pocket flashlight. By shining a flashlight in one end of the cable, you should be able to see the light at the other end.

Cable checkers are fairly inexpensive, ranging in price from $50 to $100. In fact, if you are handy with a soldering iron, it is not all that difficult to build your own cable tester with a peg board and some batteries. While not as pretty as a professional tester, it will do in a pinch if you're tracing a wire fault at 2:00 A.M. on a Sunday morning.

Cable Testers

A *cable tester* will include all of the tests performed by a cable checker, but will also include performance testing to certify a cable's use at a specific topology speed.

Along with checking for shorts and opens, a cable tester will test:

- wire length to ensure that the conductors are not too long

- attenuation or signal loss along the cable

- interference from other conductors known as Near-End Cross Talk (NEXT)

- the impedance (AC resistance) of thinnet terminators

- whether there is active network traffic on the cable

A cable tester will usually have an LCD display for reporting the above information. Some are even capable of storing test results or powering off the unit if it is not used for a specified period of time. Figure 30.2 shows a typical cable tester. Like the cable checker, the better units are two separate components so that new and existing wiring may be tested.

FIGURE 30.2:

A typical cable tester

What distinguishes cable testers is how they check attenuation and NEXT. The Electronic Industry Association and Telecommunications Industry Association (EIA/TIA) is responsible for setting the category standards for cables. In order to certify a cable for CAT3, the attenuation and NEXT tests should be performed from 1MHz to 16MHz in 1MHz steps. Because the level of signal loss or interference can change with frequency, a range of frequencies must be used to certify that the cable is acceptable over the entire range.

In order to certify a cable for CAT5 use, the test frequency range must be extended up to 100MHz. A 1MHz frequency step should still be used. These parameters are important because there is a big difference in frequency range between a CAT3 and a CAT5 tester.

Just because you are using CAT5 cables, connectors, and patch panels, it does not mean that your network will support 100Mb operation per the CAT5 specification. You must actually certify your network for use at this speed with a CAT5 cable tester. Using CAT5 hardware simply gives you the ability to create a 100Mb network.

For example, NEXT is usually caused by crossed or crushed pairs at the connector end of the wire. Because you install most connectors on site while wiring the network, there is no way to detect this condition during the manufacturing process of each individual component. The only way to catch this condition is to perform a CAT5 test on-site, after the wiring is installed.

NOTE   Because NEXT is most likely to occur at the connector, both ends of the cable should be tested. You will need to swap the unit to the other end of the cable when running the second test.

When selecting a twisted-pair cable tester, ensure that it performs attenuation and NEXT testing all the way up to 100MHz if you wish to certify at a CAT5 level. While these units are more expensive than the 16MHz units, it is the only way to ensure that your network is fit for 100Mb operation.

Faulty cables can cause some strange intermittent problems. For example, networks with faulty wiring may function properly 85 percent of the time. During the other 15 percent, during heavy traffic loads, network users may experience problems with connection drops or excessively slow data transfer speeds. An administrator's first reaction, when attempting to diagnose a connectivity problem, is to start checking server settings, driver revision levels, and network cards. It is not until all other options are exhausted that we usually think to check our cables. By certifying the cables beforehand, we can eliminate them as a potential problem area.

Most cable testing is performed with the cable disconnected from any active network devices. Despite this, a good cable tester should have a method of detecting network traffic. This can help when diagnosing a connectivity problem as it gives a quick indication as to whether a network drop is live.

Testing Fiber Cable

Because fiber uses light, not electricity, to conduct network signals, it does not require the same testing parameters as twisted-pair or thinnet. Fiber cable testers come in two varieties, one for checking multimode operation, and one for testing single mode. The multimode version is the most popular, as this is the communication method most widely implemented.

A fiber cable tester will check for signal loss along the length of the cable. This may be indicated with a pass/fail LED, an illuminated bar graph, or an LCD display that provides an absolute numerical value. The bar graph and numerical value are most useful, as they give a quantitative reading.

For example, let's assume you have a fiber cable run that passes through a series of patch panels. When you test the circuit from end to end, you find out it fails. When you test each one of the wire runs individually, you find that each one of them passes.

Obviously you have a connection, somewhere along the run, that is only marginally acceptable. If your tester has a pass/fail LED, you may not be able to isolate the problem. By using a unit that presents an absolute power level, you can determine which connection is causing an unusual amount of signal drop.

Because of the additional features, cable testers are more expensive than cable checkers. Expect to pay $200 to $500 for a CAT3 or fiber cable tester. CAT5 or fiber cable testers run in the $600–$1,200 range.

Handheld Diagnostic Tools

Handheld diagnostic tools can be viewed as crosses between cable testers and network analyzers. They not only include all the features normally associated with cable testers, but they can produce topology information and even a minimal amount of protocol information as well.

Some tools that fall into this category are designed to troubleshoot a specific network environment. For example, one diagnostic tool may check dropped connections and get nearest server requests in a NetWare IPX environment, while an IP diagnostic tool will be able to detect duplicate IP addresses and ping systems by IP address or host name. It is rare to find a tool that can combine these features.

At a minimum, a good handheld diagnostic tool should be able to:

- test connectivity to a remote host by MAC address

- detect transmission errors

- report frames per second and network utilization

- detect which protocols are in use on the network

- report on advertised routing information

- store test results for later retrieval

Figure 30.3 shows the display of a Fluke LANMeter. This unit has the unique ability to be placed in line between a network system and the hub so that communication between the two can be monitored.

FIGURE 30.3:

A display from a Fluke LANMeter

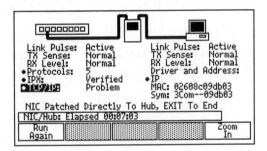

Handheld diagnostic tools tend to be very expensive. A cheap unit will run around $800, while a top-of-the-line model may run closer to $5,000, which is what you would pay for a full network analyzer.

Network Monitoring Tools

Network monitoring tools are used for the day-to-day monitoring of network performance. They are usually implemented as a software product that runs on a standard desktop machine or server. The packet captures that have been presented as figures in several chapters in this section were generated with Novell's LANalyzer product, which is a network monitoring tool. Windows NT comes with a similar program called Network Monitor, or NetMon.

The main focus of a network monitoring tool is the collection of network usage statistics. Unlike a handheld diagnostic tool or a network analyzer that is designed to be used when a problem has been detected, the network monitor is expected to be run continuously, gathering network data. This does not mean that a handheld tool cannot be left turned on to collect statistics or that a network monitor cannot be used to find and fix a problem; it simply means that each tool has its place in the grand scheme of keeping your network operational.

A good network monitor should be able to:

- report frames per second (fps) and network utilization

- graph overall network usage in fps and utilization

- export network usage statistics in a spreadsheet format

- report on network usage on a per station basis

- have some method of assigning station names to MAC addresses

- detect transmission errors

- detect which protocols are in use on the network

- perform and save frame captures

- allow frame captures to be filtered so that specific portions can be analyzed

In short, a network monitoring tool should be able to provide all the required information to plan short- and long-term network design changes.

Network monitors vary widely in price. For example, Microsoft's Network Monitor Tool is included free with Windows NT Server. There are also many shareware or freeware monitoring tools available. In contrast to this, Novell's LANalyzer product sells for a street price between $800 and $1,000.

NOTE   When using a software-based network analyzer, be sure that your NIC card and driver are capable of passing all network frames up through the protocol stack. For example, part of the reason that a 3COM Etherlink III card can communicate so quickly is that it drops all error frames at the Data Link level. This prevents them from being passed up the communication stack and recorded by the network monitor. Your vendor should be able to tell you which NIC cards they have certified for use with their product.

Network Analyzers

Network analyzers are used for troubleshooting network problems that occur between the Data Link and Transport layers. They will not diagnose Physical layer problems. For example, a network analyzer will not tell you that your cable has an attenuation problem or swapped wire pairs. However, a good network analyzer will show you just about everything else that occurs on your network.

Network analyzers are usually implemented as both software and hardware. This is because a network analyzer may be required to capture every frame of data in an extremely busy networking environment, a task that the average NIC card was not specifically designed to do. By designing the network interface to be used for capturing data instead of conducting communications, a vendor can ensure that their analyzer can keep up with even the busiest of networks.

Along with the features provided by a good network monitor, network analyzers will also provide advanced diagnostic features. They will not only report on a problem when it is found, but they will tell you how to fix it.

Figure 30.4 shows the advanced diagnostic ability of the Network General Sniffer. The screen capture indicates that it has detected a delay in transmission between a server and a workstation. It describes what may be causing the problem and possible remedies for resolving it. While most network monitors would be able to document this delayed transmission time, they would not have flagged it as a potential problem.

FIGURE 30.4:

The Network General Sniffer

```
SUMMARY—Delta T—DST————    SRC———
M 1431    0.0034  2F098E0B.1   «14.3Com   D2EDE1  Low throughput = 0 KB/s
                                                  NCP C F=74320600 Burst Wri
   1432    0.0043  2F098E0B.1   «14.3Com   D2EDE1  NCP C F=74320600 Burst Wri
   1433    0.0014  2F098E0B.1   «14.3Com   D2EDE1  NCP C Burst Write 1432 at
                          Application Diagnosis Detail
                    Slow server: 2F098E0B.1 <threshold: 20 %>

  Stations receiving slow response:
EXPERT EXPLAIN
  Diagnosis:  Slow server: 2F098E0B.1 <threshold: 20 %>

  The ratio of slow responses to total responses for a particular station has
  exceeded the "Slow resp %" threshold of 20 percent. A slow response is one
  in which the time between request and response is longer than the "Resp
  time" threshold of 100ms.


  Possible cause:

  This usually means that your server is overloaded. You should examine the
  traffic to your server to see if the traffic is justified. If so, you
  should consider getting a faster server or distributing the load across
  multiple servers.
                          Use ESC to return.
```

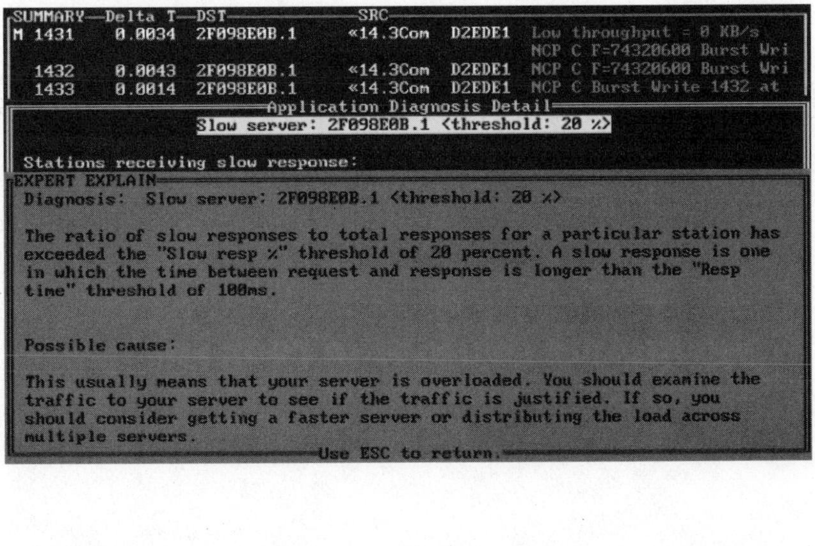

In addition to advanced diagnostics, some analyzers have advanced monitoring abilities as well. ExpertPharaoh from GN NetTest (formally Azure) has the ability to monitor up to eight separate network segments at the same time. These segments can be all the same topology, or a mixture of different LAN and WAN topologies. Figure 30.5 shows a screen capture from the DuoTrack version, which is simultaneously monitoring two different LAN topologies.

FIGURE 30.5:

GN NetTest's ExpertPharaoh monitoring two different topologies

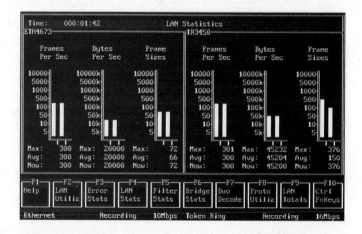

A good network analyzer is the most expensive piece of troubleshooting hardware you can purchase. Depending on the unit's advanced diagnostic abilities, the number of protocols and services it can identify, and the number of segments it can simultaneously monitor, you can expect to pay between $2,000 and $18,000.

Monitoring through Network Hardware

When purchasing network hardware, such as bridges, switches, and routers, one of the features to pay close attention to is the hardware's ability to collect statistics and record network errors. Consider the network design shown in Figure 30.6.

The figure shows a fully switched network. Each server and client has a dedicated connection to the switch. As we discussed in Chapter 9, this dedication creates a separate collision domain off of each port on the switch, which only includes two systems—the switch itself and the attached system.

FIGURE 30.6:

A switched network design

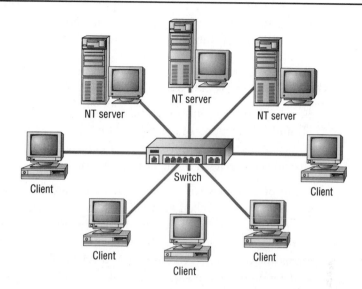

Now, let's assume we go out and spend $12,000 on a shiny new network analyzer. We plug it into the switch and proceed to see nothing, or at least almost nothing. We can monitor network broadcast but cannot see any of the unicast communications. This is because a switch acts as a traffic cop and isolates unicast traffic to the ports that are actually carrying on a conversation. Our analyzer relies on the shared media properties of a LAN topology in order to monitor communications. A switch segregates these communications, so, in effect, our media is no longer shared. We are unable to monitor network traffic with our analyzer.

To remedy this, we could purchase hubs and cascade them off of the switch. This would provide more than one connection to each switch port and give us a place to plug in our network analyzer. The problem with this configuration is that we can only monitor the traffic on the port we are attached to.

Referring back to Figure 30.6, if we plug each of our servers into a separate hub, and then plug each of these hubs into the switch, we can now attach our analyzer to one of the hubs as well in order to monitor traffic. The problem with this configuration is that we can only monitor traffic to one server at a time. While we are monitoring communications to the first server, the second could be overloading from excessive traffic and we would never see it. Also, once we install a hub, we lose the ability to have the servers communicating in full-duplexed mode.

This is why having the switch report on network statistics is so important: It is the central communication point in the network and has the best chance of collecting the most statistics.

Monitoring Features to Look For

So what kind of monitoring ability should you look for in a switch? A switch should collect many of the same statistics that a network monitoring tool does. This will help you to isolate problem areas and determine which collision domains are in need of the most attention.

Figure 30.7 shows a screen capture from a Cisco Catalyst switch. Peak throughput levels are reported on a daily basis. These statistics can help us to monitor traffic patterns to see if this portion of the network can be a potential performance gate for communications. This particular switch has 25 switched 10Mb Ethernet ports and a switched connection to a 100Mb FDDI ring. As you can see, our daily utilization levels have been generally around 11Mbps, peaking only once up to 18Mbps. In other words, this switch is not even breaking a sweat.

FIGURE 30.7:

A Cisco Catalyst switch reporting daily throughput peaks

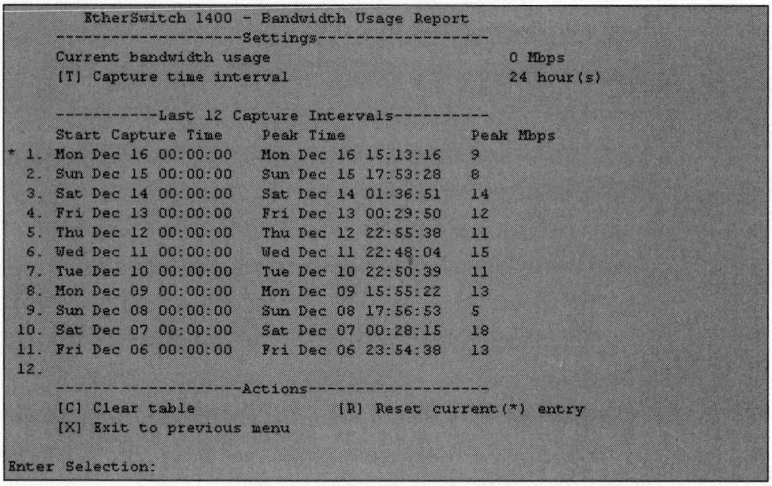

```
        EtherSwitch 1400 - Bandwidth Usage Report
   -------------------Settings-------------------
   Current bandwidth usage                  0 Mbps
   [T] Capture time interval                24 hour(s)

   -----------Last 12 Capture Intervals----------
   Start Capture Time      Peak Time              Peak Mbps
*  1. Mon Dec 16 00:00:00   Mon Dec 16 15:13:16    9
   2. Sun Dec 15 00:00:00   Sun Dec 15 17:53:28    8
   3. Sat Dec 14 00:00:00   Sat Dec 14 01:36:51    14
   4. Fri Dec 13 00:00:00   Fri Dec 13 00:29:50    12
   5. Thu Dec 12 00:00:00   Thu Dec 12 22:55:38    11
   6. Wed Dec 11 00:00:00   Wed Dec 11 22:48:04    15
   7. Tue Dec 10 00:00:00   Tue Dec 10 22:50:39    11
   8. Mon Dec 09 00:00:00   Mon Dec 09 15:55:22    13
   9. Sun Dec 08 00:00:00   Sun Dec 08 17:56:53    5
  10. Sat Dec 07 00:00:00   Sat Dec 07 00:28:15    18
  11. Fri Dec 06 00:00:00   Fri Dec 06 23:54:38    13
  12.

   -------------------Actions-------------------
   [C] Clear table            [R] Reset current (*) entry
   [X] Exit to previous menu

Enter Selection:
```

Figure 30.8 shows the same switch reporting on the number of frames it has processed on a per port basis. The number of frames processed is from the last time the switch was restarted or this statistic screen was reset. This is valuable information, which we can use to load-balance the network and improve overall performance.

FIGURE 30.8:

Per port statistics for the number of frames processed

```
EtherSwitch 1400 - Utilization Statistics Report (Frame counts)

       Receive    Forward    Transmit          Receive    Forward    Transmit
     ---------------------------------          ---------------------------------
 1 :         0          0           0  13:    42256216   42256216    43731720
 2 :         0          0           0  14:     1863506    1863506     4531285
 3 :         0          0           0  15:           0          0           0
 4 :         0          0           0  16:           0          0           0
 5 :         0          0           0  17:      590049     590046     3486334
 6 :         0          0           0  18:    11512665   11512665    12877221
 7 :         0          0           0  19:     2352129    2352129     5439965
 8 :   5310680    5310677     8082272  20:     1588048    1582009     4591431
 9 :  10196001   10192530    13189976  21:           0          0           0
10:    1088154    1088154     4099838  22:    48396860   48396851    49474427
11:          0          0           0  23:     2126872    2126858     5019374
12:   72322740   72322740    88197883  24:           0          0     3047675
                                       25:           0          0           0

A : 235086729*  98289156    88745534*
B :         0          0           0     *FDDI frame counts

Select [R] Reset all statistics, or [X] Exit to previous menu:
```

For example, let's assume that this switch is connected in the configuration shown in Figure 30.9. Our network servers are located on the FDDI ring, and each workstation is cascaded off of a hub that plugs into an Ethernet switch port.

Now that we know what our network looks like, let's refer back to Figure 30.8 and look at the number of frames being processed on each of the Ethernet ports (ports 1–25). According to the report, ports 12, 22, and 13 (in that order) are processing the greatest number of frames. We obviously have some very busy users connected to the hubs off of these ports. Conversely, ports 17, 10, 20, and 14 (in that order) are seeing the least amount of traffic. The ports showing zero traffic are not yet connected to any workstations.

With these statistics in mind, we can now hook up a network monitor or analyzer to the busiest hubs to identify who the heaviest users are. Once these users have been identified, we can move their network connection to one of the quieter hubs.

FIGURE 30.9:

Our switch installed in a
potential network design

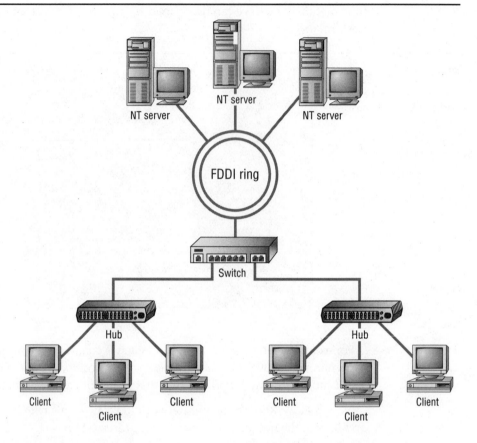

For example, let's assume we hook a network monitor up to the hub off of port 12 for a few days and notice that the users Gretchen and Grendel are each responsible for 25 percent of the traffic being generated off of that port. If we move Gretchen to port 17 and Grendel to port 10, we will reduce the amount of traffic being processed by port 12 to half its current level. While still busy, this brings the amount of transmission down to a level that is more in line with the other ports.

While moving these users will increase the amount of traffic passing through ports 17 and 10, these ports are currently seeing very little traffic. Because users on these ports appear to be only occasional network users, they will probably not even notice the increase in traffic.

Why bother to even collect this information and balance the network load? Each collision domain consists of a shared medium, and only one user can transmit on it at any given time. If you have an imbalance, where some ports are processing more traffic than others, you will have some users that experience sluggish network response while others underutilize the amount of available bandwidth. By balancing the network load, you ensure that all users receive the optimal amount of network bandwidth.

There are other clues as to how our network is performing on this screen. For example, look at the number of frames that the switch has received off of each port and compare this value to the number of frames it has forwarded. You will note that there is a discrepancy in quantity off of ports 8, 9, 20, 22, and 23. There are usually two situations that can cause this.

First, there may be stations that are accessing resources that are located on the same hub. For example, we may have one or more users who have enabled Windows 95 file sharing and have given other users access to their systems. To see if this is the case, we could attach a network monitor or analyzer to the hub and see who is advertising services.

The other situation that can prevent a switch from forwarding frames is when it detects a transmission error. We may have a workstation off one of these ports that is generating frames with a bad FCS (frame check sequence) value. When these errors occur, it is good to have a switch that collects error information as well.

One last note before moving on—you will notice that port 24 has been receiving frames, but has not transmitted any. The Cisco Catalyst has the ability to allow one of the ports to operate as a monitoring port. You can configure any of the available Ethernet ports to monitor one or more of the other ports on the switch. This feature can be extremely useful because it allows you to change the port you are monitoring with a simple configuration change. It also allows you to monitor multiple ports simultaneously.

The monitoring port can also extend the capability of your network monitor. For example, we could choose to monitor the FDDI ring, something that LAN-alyzer is normally incapable of doing because it does not have any supported FDDI drivers. While we will not be able to monitor topology-specific error conditions, we can at least monitor network utilization and capture frames.

Checking For Errors

Figure 30.10 shows a per port error report for our Cisco switch. If we compare this report to the one shown in Figure 30.8, we can see that the frames that were not forwarded on port 22 were in fact due to errors. This lets us know that out of the three ports that were potential problems, we only need to worry about port 22.

FIGURE 30.10:

A per port error report

```
EtherSwitch 1400 - Exception Statistics Report (Frame counts)

        Receive   Transmit   Security         Receive   Transmit   Security
        Errors    Errors     Violations       Errors    Errors     Violations
       ------------------------------------   ------------------------------------
  1 :      0          0           0    13:       1          0           0
  2 :      0          0           0    14:       0          0           0
  3 :      0          0           0    15:       0          0           0
  4 :      0          0           0    16:       0          0           0
  5 :      0          0           0    17:       0          0           0
  6 :      0          0           0    18:       0          0           0
  7 :      0          0           0    19:       0          0           0
  8 :      0          0           0    20:       0          0           0
  9 :      0          0           0    21:       0          0           0
 10:       0          0           0    22:    3231          0           0
 11:       0          0           0    23:       0          0           0
 12:       0          0           0    24:       0          0           0
                                       25:       0          0           0

  A :      0*         0*          0
  B :      0          0           0         *FDDI frame counts

Select [R] Reset all statistics, or [X] Exit to previous menu:
```

You may also notice that there is a discrepancy between the number of errors reported and the number of frames that were not forwarded by this port. This is because each of the statistic screens can be reset separately. The report in Figure 30.10 has been collecting information without being reset for a longer period of time than that shown in Figure 30.8.

So we know we have a problem off of port 22. We now need to determine what that problem is. Fortunately, the switch will report advanced statistics on a per-port basis, as shown in Figure 30.11. According to this report, we have a workstation generating frames with a bad FCS. We now know we need to monitor the stations off of port 22 with our network analyzer and look for the culprit system. Once identified, we can test the NIC and cables to further isolate the problem.

FIGURE 30.11:

Detailed statistics on a Cisco
Catalyst port

```
        EtherSwitch 1400 - Port 22 Statistics Report
    Receive Statistics                Transmit Statistics
--------------------------------  ------------------------------------
Total good frames             48397911  Total frames                49474925
Total octets              >  483677286  Total octets              4030247614
Broadcast/multicast frames      116295  Broadcast/multicast frames   2883748
Broadcast/multicast octets    11874806  Broadcast/multicast octets 416724139
Good frames forwarded         48397902  Deferrals                     160762
Frames filtered                      9  Single collisions              22179
Runt frames                       3195  Multiple collisions            21018
No buffer discards                   0  Excessive collisions               0
                                        Queue full discards                0
Errors:                                 Errors:
  FCS errors                      3231    Late collisions                  0
  Alignment errors                   0    Excessive deferrals              0
  Giant frames                       0    Jabber errors                    0
  Address violations                 0    Other transmit errors            0

Select [A] Port addressing, [C] Configure port,
       [N] Next port, [P] Previous port, [G] Goto port,
       [R] Reset port statistics, or [X] Exit to Main Menu:
```

There are some important lessons here. In a brief session, we have learned the following about our network:

- Three ports are seeing an excessive amount of traffic, compared to the rest of the network.

- Four ports are seeing a small amount of traffic, compared to the rest of the network.

- Off of two of our ports, users are capable of accessing a local resource.

- We have a workstation generating frames with a bad CRC (another way of saying the FCS, or frame check sequence, is bad).

Furthermore, because this particular switch supports Telnet access, all this information could have been collected through a remote dial-in session while sitting home in our fuzzy slippers.

If this switch did not have any of the advanced capabilities described above, we would have been forced to move our network analyzer from port to port manually. Assuming we would want to monitor each port for a minimum of one full work day, what we learned in five minutes would have taken us nearly three weeks to determine.

Because a network device (such as a switch) should always be active while a network is in use, it makes the perfect device for gathering statistics. It is always possible that, when errors occur, your network analyzer may be turned off or be monitoring another segment. By collecting error information from the network hardware itself you can be sure you will always be able to catch errors when they occur.

Monitoring Features to Look For in a Switch

Besides the performance features covered in Chapter 9, a good switch should be able to provide you with the following statistical information and monitoring features:

- overall bandwidth utilization

- utilization on a per port basis

- the number of stations attached to each port

- error reporting on a per port basis that includes collisions

- a diagnostic port for monitoring one or more switch ports

- remote access to the device through telnet or a Web browser

- a system's MAC address, when only one station is attached

Network Monitoring with a Bridge

Because a bridge and a switch are functionally identical (the biggest difference being that a switch has more ports), it is good to look for the same features in a bridge that you do in a switch. With a *bridge*, the ability to collect meaningful statistics becomes a bit less important because a bridge tends to create larger collision domains. This produces less segmentation, and thus fewer points to be monitored.

The network hardware we have discussed so far in this chapter has been used to segment our network into many small collision domains. In fact, the first example used only two devices per collision domain. This gave us many different points that needed to be monitored separately in order to determine the traffic patterns of our entire network.

A bridge, on the other hand, is used to segment the network into larger pieces. Instead of having one system located off of each port, there are more likely to be

25 or more. For example, a single switch installed into a network with 100 devices may create 16 or more collision domains. A bridge installed into the same network is likely to create only two or three. This gives us fewer points that need to be monitored with our analyzer.

At a minimum, you should be able to retrieve the following information from a bridge:

- the number of frames received per port

- the number of frames forwarded per port

- the number and type of errors detected on each port

- the number of collisions detected on each port

This information is a good starting point for determining which areas of the network require the most attention.

Network Monitoring with a Router

Like a bridge, a *router* creates large collision domains, which makes monitoring network activity with a network monitoring tool that much easier. There are actually some things that a router can detect that a network monitor will miss.

Because the router's job is to route network traffic, it is the perfect device for collecting this type of information. The report in Figure 30.12 shows general IP statistics for a Cisco 4000 router. From this screen we can pull some interesting information about the network it is attached to.

FIGURE 30.12:

IP statistics for a Cisco 4000 router

```
IP statistics:
  Rcvd:  82361984 total, 1702782 local destination
         0 format errors, 0 checksum errors, 62 bad hop count
         0 unknown protocol, 6 not a gateway
         0 security failures, 0 bad options
  Frags: 0 reassembled, 0 timeouts, 0 couldn't reassemble
         0 fragmented, 0 couldn't fragment
  Bcast: 1685772 received, 325954 sent
  Mcast: 0 received, 0 sent
  Sent:  356328 generated, 80655134 forwarded
         3979 encapsulation failed, 22 no route
```

First, if we compare the number of frames received (Rcvd) to the number that were addressed to a local destination, we can see that an overwhelming majority of the traffic is being routed. This can be a bad thing, as routers create an inherent delay in packet transmission because they are required to remove the frame header and trailer and then rebuild them upon transmission. Still, there are times when this type of design is desirable—for instance, in separating a slower topology with client systems from servers that are located on a faster backbone. We would need to collect more information to see if the large percentage of frames being routed is something we need to worry about or not.

If we look at the bad hop count value, we can see that we have had a few frames that have exceeded the hop count limit. Sixty-two is not a large number compared to the total quantity received, and they could have been caused by routing loops if another router had unexpectedly dropped offline recently. We want to keep an eye on this statistic to ensure that it does not continue climbing. If it does, we need to review the configuration on each of our routers.

So our router has told us that it has encountered problems with routing frames on the network, something an active network analyzer would catch as well, but a fact that a network monitor might miss completely.

If we look at the broadcast field (`Bcast`), we see that this router has forwarded roughly 20 percent of the broadcasts it has received. Broadcasts that can traverse routers are referred to as *all network broadcasts* and can be a bad thing as they will be propagated throughout our network, affecting every single attached system until the end of the network is reached or the maximum hop count is exceeded. Because they have such wide implications on network performance, we want to limit the number of all network broadcasts as much as possible.

Again, an active network analyzer attached to the network would be able to detect this type of traffic. A simple network monitor would have included this statistic in the general category of *broadcast*.

At a minimum, you should be able to collect the following statistical information from a router:

- the number of frames received per port
- the number of frames forwarded per port
- the number and type of errors detected on each port
- the number of collisions detected on each port
- the number of frames with an excessively high hop count

- the number of frames with no route to host

- the number of broadcasts received and forwarded

If you are using a network monitor to maintain the health of your network, these statistics will help to fill in some of the deficiencies in the network monitor's abilities.

Collecting Statistics with SNMP and RMON

As we discussed in Chapter 3, *SNMP* provides the ability to monitor and control network devices. *RMON* (short for remote monitoring) is similar, except it focuses on the ability to collect statistics from each device.

Using SNMP and RMON, you have the ability to configure a central management station to collect some or all of the statistics discussed in this chapter. From a central console, you can query devices about their health and measured performance levels. Without SNMP and RMON, you must attach to each device through a serial cable or through a Telnet session.

How Important is SNMP and RMON Support?   How important SNMP and RMON should be to your organization depends on the size of your network. If your network is large, spanning many buildings or geographical regions, then the ability to simultaneously monitor multiple network devices should be considered a must. If the collision light is lighting up on a hub in the bowels of some remote basement, it will probably go undetected until there is a major failure.

If your network is relatively small, consisting of only one or two floors of a single building, the additional money spent on devices that include SNMP and RMON support could probably be better spent elsewhere. If you are proactive with monitoring your network's health, you can easily keep up with the statistics generated by a dozen or so devices. It does not take very long to sit down and telnet to each device to ensure that it is functioning properly.

Note that the money you save by refraining from purchasing devices that include SNMP and RMON can easily add up to the purchase price of a good analyzer that will tell you more about your network than SNMP and RMON ever could. Many a network administrator has been talked into buying features that they will never use by a salesperson who knew all the right buzzwords.

Summary

In this chapter, we've looked at a number of hardware tools that are useful for troubleshooting networks. We began with the simplest and least expensive equipment—cable checkers. Cable checkers, and their fancier counterparts, cable testers, are essential for detecting cable and connector damage or breaks. Because problems caused by damaged cables are easy to mistake for other types of problems, it's important to avoid these types of problems right off the bat by testing each cable run (and connector) as it is installed.

Handheld diagnostic tools provide features of cable testers as well as some features found in network analyzers. Good handheld diagnostic tools are able to detect transmission errors, report frames per second and network utilization statistics, detect the protocols used on the network, report advertised routing information, and store these results for later retrieval.

Network monitoring tools perform many of the same checks as handheld diagnostic tools and also sport advanced features, such as per-station reporting, filtered frame capture and logging, and graphing and exporting of test results to a spreadsheet format.

For larger networks, investing in routers, bridges, and other networking equipment that supports remote access through SNMP and RMON can save a tremendous amount of time and allow you to monitor network performance from a central location (or even from home).

In the next chapter, we'll look at software troubleshooting tools, including IntraNetware's LANalyzer and NT's NetMon, plus other command-line and GUI tools that also come in handy when troubleshooting network problems.

CHAPTER

THIRTY-ONE

Software
Troubleshooting Tools

- Novell's LANalyzer

- IntraNetWare tools

- Workstation tools

- NT Server tools

- Unix tools

The preceding chapter discussed the various types of hardware tools available for troubleshooting network problems. In this chapter, we look at the software tools available for network troubleshooting.

We'll begin by looking at Novell's LANalyzer, then move on to the various console and GUI tools that are available on NetWare, Windows NT, and Unix.

Novell's LANalyzer

Novell's *LANalyzer* is a network monitoring tool that is used by many network administrators to monitor the health of their networks. It has a very simple interface that makes gathering statistical information about your network's traffic very easy. It even has some advanced filtering and capturing abilities that make diagnosing network problems that much easier.

LANalyzer is only a single product in a wide range of network monitors and analyzers available from various vendors. While each tool has its own unique screens and procedures for performing specific tasks, they all do basically the same thing—monitor the traffic on your network. The difference is that some do it better than others.

Once you are familiar with one network monitor or analyzer, it is that much easier to sit down in front of another and figure out how to use it. With this in mind, we will focus our discussion here on how to use a network monitor and what type of information it can give us.

Dashboard

The LANalyzer dashboard, as shown in Figure 31.1, is the heart of the LANalyzer program. From here we can view real-time statistics on frames and errors per second, as well as on bandwidth utilization. The gauges give a visual representation of traffic on the network while the numeric value located below each gauge is an absolute value.

NOTE   Like the famous tomato-tomahto debate, there rages an even more complex battle of pronunciations. In fact, it's so savage it's not even about words of the same spelling. These terror-inducing words are *packet* and *frame*. Huh, you say? Yes, frame and packet are exactly the same thing; just different words. It almost entirely depends on which networking protocols you were raised using.

FIGURE 31.1 :

The LANalyzer dashboard

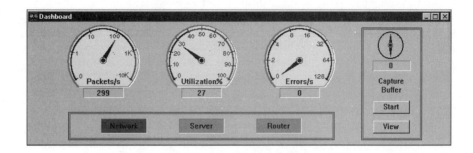

Capture Buffer

The Capture Buffer on the right-hand side of the LANalyzer dashboard allows us to capture frames as they are transmitted on the network. The packet decode figures we have used throughout this section were collected using the Capture Buffer. You have the option to capture all traffic on the network, capture only frames that originate from specific systems, or capture frames that are using certain protocols.

Once a capture session is complete, you can click the View button to observe the results. You can even select from filter criteria to further screen the frames that are presented. For example, you could choose to look only at SPX frames.

At the bottom of the dashboard are three buttons labeled Network, Server, and Router. Each of these buttons is normally colored green. When a problem in one category is detected, the appropriate button will flash and turn red. These are the alarm monitors, and they give a visual indication when a problem has been detected. We are allowed to set minimum thresholds for frame rate, utilization, and number of errors for the network alarm, and whenever one of these thresholds is crossed, it triggers the alarm. The server and router alarms will go off on a per problem basis. You cannot set thresholds for these alarms.

Alarms

When an alarm light turns red, simply double-click on it to produce the alarm dialog box. Figure 31.2 shows the dialog box for Network Alarms. On this screen we can see the date and time the error occurred, as well as which threshold was exceeded.

FIGURE 31.2 :

The Network Alarms
dialog box

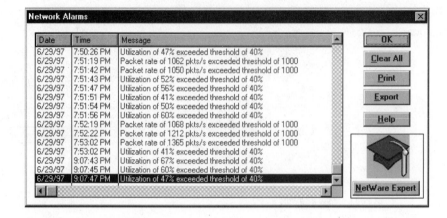

To the right of the screen are buttons that allow us to clear all of these errors from the Network Alarms dialog box, print out the error messages, or export them to a file. We also have a button called NetWare Expert. NetWare Expert allows you to access general information on the error message being highlighted. For example, in the case of high network utilization, the NetWare Expert would tell us that our network may be too busy.

Remember that the errors reported in the Network Alarms dialog box are instantaneous results. This means a very short sample rate (typically one second) is used to determine if a problem has occurred. While this type of measurement is fine when recording errors, it can be an inaccurate picture of network performance. We are less concerned with a momentary spike in traffic than we are with a sustained level of high utilization. To see how our network is doing over a greater period of time, we need to look at detailed statistics and trends.

Detailed Statistics and Trends

The detailed statistics screens will plot frame rate, utilization, or error rate over time. Every five seconds a new data point will be plotted along a 15-minute window. This gives us a more accurate view of actual network utilization than simply looking for the peaks.

Figure 31.3 shows the Detail-Utilization % graph. This graph shows an ideal trend in network utilization. While there are large spikes that show a large amount of data was being transferred on the network, there are also many quiet spots where network activity was at or near zero. The reason this trend is ideal is that it shows that when a station needs to transmit data, it is doing so very quickly. The fact that there are quiet moments on the network tells us that there are plenty of opportunities for other stations to transmit their data as well. If we look at the average utilization level at the bottom of the figure, it only reports 10 percent.

FIGURE 31.3:

A graph of healthy network utilization

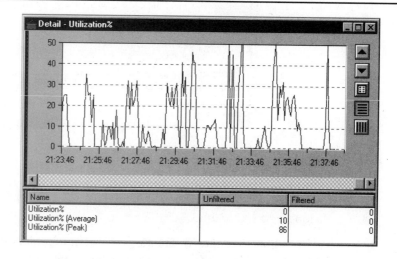

As average utilization levels rise, the chance that a station will need to transmit data while another station is already transmitting increases as well. For example, the network in Figure 31.3 was showing a 10 percent average utilization level. This means that there is a one in ten chance that when a station needs to transmit data, another station is already doing so.

As the average utilization level rises, it becomes more likely that a station will discover the network is busy and have to wait before transmitting data. Figure 31.4 shows a network segment that may soon need attention. The average utilization level is 21 percent. This means that our stations now have a one in five chance of discovering that the network is busy. More importantly, there are no quiet moments on our network. As soon as one station finishes transmitting, another one begins. This network is probably starting to feel a bit sluggish.

FIGURE 31.4:

A network experiencing high utilization

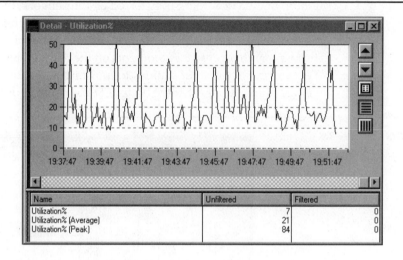

A 15-minute window is still a relatively short period of time. We could have simply had bad timing and measured this network at its all-time worst for the entire year. To get a more accurate picture, we need to monitor performance over a longer period of time.

In addition to detailed statistics, we can monitor long-term trends. The trend graph is identical to the detailed statistics graph except it provides a 12-hour window and can gather statistics for up to six months. It also calculates the sample rate differently. The trend graph will average the results over a 15-minute period of time and then plot a data point. In other words, the average utilization level reported by the detailed statistics graph will create a single data point. This smoothes out all the peaks and valleys and gives us a better idea of the average usage.

If the trend graph shows this 20 percent utilization level to be a momentary spike, then we know our network is probably fine. If, however, it reports that the high utilization level is being maintained for the entire work day, it may be time to start performing some load-balancing before it becomes a serious problem. To do this, we need to check out the station monitor to see who is generating the most traffic.

The Station Monitor

The station monitor, shown in Figure 31.5, allows us to monitor network activity on a per station basis. Normally, MAC addresses are displayed in the station column. This can make it a bit difficult to determine which stations are which. LANalyzer has a feature that allows it to authenticate to one or more NetWare servers and find out which users are logged on from which stations. It will then use the users' logon names to identify each system in the station column.

FIGURE 31.5:

The Station Monitor window

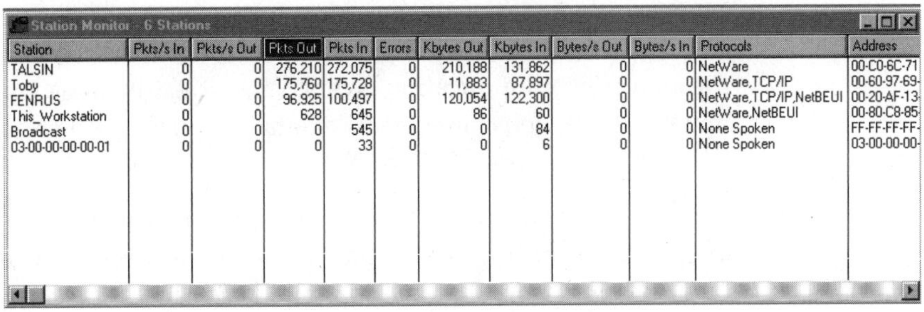

Station	Pkts/s In	Pkts/s Out	Pkts Out	Pkts In	Errors	Kbytes Out	Kbytes In	Bytes/s Out	Bytes/s In	Protocols	Address
TALSIN	0	0	276,210	272,075	0	210,188	131,862	0	0	NetWare	00-C0-6C-71
Toby	0	0	175,760	175,728	0	11,883	87,897	0	0	NetWare,TCP/IP	00-60-97-69-
FENRUS	0	0	96,925	100,497	0	120,054	122,300	0	0	NetWare,TCP/IP,NetBEUI	00-20-AF-13-
This_Workstation	0	0	628	645	0	86	60	0	0	NetWare,NetBEUI	00-80-C8-85-
Broadcast	0	0	0	545	0	0	84	0	0	None Spoken	FF-FF-FF-FF-
03-00-00-00-00-01	0	0	0	33	0	0	6	0	0	None Spoken	03-00-00-00-

This is a feature that is unique to LANalyzer and is extremely useful in a NetWare environment. If LANalyzer cannot identify the station, it allows you to edit a simple text file to add an entry for the system.

Most monitors and analyzers will at least identify the manufacturer associated with the MAC address. While this is helpful if the manufacturer is identified as being Cisco and you only have one Cisco device on your network, it is not very helpful, for example, to see 100 entries identified as 3Com. When choosing a network monitor or analyzer, make sure it has the ability to let you associate real names with MAC addresses.

Our next two columns report packets in and out on a per-second basis. These will show us how many frames a station is sending or receiving at that exact instant in time. The next two columns report the total quantity of frames sent and received since the monitor was restarted. When making long-term plans for network changes, the total quantity of frame transmissions is far more interesting and useful.

Our next column reports on the number of errors transmitted by each station. In an ideal world, this value will remain at zero. If you have a long station list and wish to quickly determine if there are any errors on the network, simply click the title at the top of the column. This will change the sort order so that the station with the greatest number of errors is reported first.

Be very careful in interpreting the results of this column. Much of the information comes secondhand from the receiving station, not just the monitoring tool.

For example, let's assume you sort this list and see that your server has generated 200 errors and you have a list of 30 stations that have error counts ranging from one error to 30 errors. These results do not mean that you may have 31 network cards that are malfunctioning. You may only have one.

If the NIC in the server is going bad, it is entirely possible that it is corrupting frames as they are received, not just when they are being transmitted. If this is the case, the data may be received intact, but will be corrupted before it is sent up through the communication layers. When the transport layer receives the information, it will determine that the data is unusable. The server will then send out a request for a retransmission.

When the network monitor sees the retransmission request, it assumes that the original transmitting system had sent a bad frame—it has no way of knowing that the information became corrupted after it was received by the server. The network monitor would then proceed to incorrectly indicate that the original transmitting station sent a bad frame.

The moral of the story—sometimes it pays to be lazy. Instead of running around trying to fix each station that was indicated as having transmitting errors, focus on the worst offending system and see if the other transmission problems do not go away as well.

After the error column, there is the total KB transmitted and received as well as bytes per second transmitted and received. Like the frame count columns, the total quantities are the most useful.

If we compare the ratio of total KB transmitted to the total frames transmitted, we can get an idea of how efficiently each system is communicating. For example, look at the ratio difference between Toby and Fenrus.

Toby transmitted 175,760 frames to move 11,883KB of data. This means that Toby is communicating with an average frame size of 68 bytes, just barely over our minimum required Ethernet frame size of 64 bytes. Fenrus, on the other hand, transmitted only 96,925 frames while moving 120,054KB of data for an average frame size of 1239 bytes. While not the maximum frame size of 1518 bytes, it is still far more efficient than the transmissions being sent by Toby.

If we focus our attention on Toby and bring this system up to the same level of communication efficiency as Fenrus, we can reduce the number of frames this system generates by nearly 94 percent, while still transferring the data.

NOTE When monitoring average frame size, it is technically impossible to ever achieve an average size equal to the Ethernet maximum of 1518 bytes. This is because workstations send out very small frames when requesting to read or write a file. It is not until data is actually being transferred that the frame size increases to the maximum allowable size. If you can keep the average frame size over 1000 bytes, you are doing extremely well.

So far we have been discussing the LANalyzer product, but the tips and tricks we covered can be applied to any network monitor or analyzer. For example, any monitoring device that displays frames and kilobytes transmitted can be used to calculate the efficiency of your client stations.

In addition to the commercial diagnostic and monitoring tools, such as LANalyzer, most NOSs also include a set of tools for network troubleshooting purposes. None of these tools are capable of retrieving the sheer volume of information that can be recovered by a good network monitor or analyzer. When they are combined, however, they can be used to fill in some of the puzzle pieces as you evaluate how your network is performing.

IntraNetWare

IntraNetWare has both server console and workstation tools that can be used for diagnostic purposes. Each is capable of collecting its own unique pieces of information.

Console Tools

Console tools are designed to be run from the server itself. They can be run directly at the server console or from a remote Rconsole or Telnet session. If you are checking network performance parameters, it's a good idea to work directly from the console. Remote sessions (Rconsole or Telnet) can generate additional traffic and skew diagnostic test results.

Command Line Tools

We will start by looking at tools that are executed directly from the server's command line. Unless otherwise noted, execute the command by typing its name at the server console prompt.

Config

The config command, as shown in Figure 31.6, displays output regarding the configuration of network parameters. Most of this output should look familiar to you because the parameters were covered in Chapter 11. The only new information is the internal network address and the node address at the top of the screen.

FIGURE 31.6:

Output from the config command

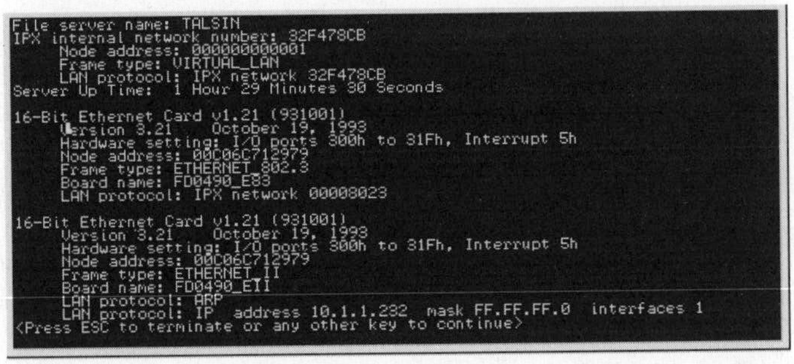

```
File server name: TALSIN
IPX internal network number: 32F478CB
    Node address: 000000000001
    Frame type: VIRTUAL_LAN
    LAN protocol: IPX network 32F478CB
Server Up Time: 1 Hour 29 Minutes 30 Seconds

16-Bit Ethernet Card v1.21 (931001)
    Version 3.21   October 19, 1993
    Hardware setting: I/O ports 300h to 31Fh, Interrupt 5h
    Node address: 00C06C712979
    Frame type: ETHERNET_802.3
    Board name: FD0490_E83
    LAN protocol: IPX network 00008023

16-Bit Ethernet Card v1.21 (931001)
    Version 3.21   October 19, 1993
    Hardware setting: I/O ports 300h to 31Fh, Interrupt 5h
    Node address: 00C06C712979
    Frame type: ETHERNET_II
    Board name: FD0490_EII
    LAN protocol: ARP
    LAN protocol: IP   address 10.1.1.232  mask FF.FF.FF.0  interfaces 1
<Press ESC to terminate or any other key to continue>
```

All NetWare servers use an internal *IPX network address*. This internal address is a communications "backbone" between the different modules that make up the server. For example, when a frame is received by a NIC, the NIC forwards the information onto the internal network just like a router sitting between two logical segments. Because the internal network is treated like any other network, it receives its own address.

The *node address* is the equivalent of a MAC address on a logical network. Each module receives its own node address for communication purposes.

NOTE   The core OS of the server always has a node address of 1.

When reviewing this screen, pay close attention to the line titled LAN Protocol. Sometimes when manually loading and binding a driver, you may misspell a word or use the wrong syntax. If you have a driver loaded but did not successfully execute a binding, this line will change to read, "No LAN protocols are bound to this LAN board."

Display Networks

The display networks command, shown in Figure 31.7, displays all known IPX networks and the metrics required to reach them from the local server. Our first value, 00008023, is the IPX network number. The values 0/1 mean that this network can be reached in zero *hops* and within one *tick*. The zero hop value means that this network is local to the network card. Frames transmitted by the card do not have to cross any routers to reach this network. This could be the network directly attached to the card, or this could be the internal IPX network number. We cannot tell which one it is by using this utility.

FIGURE 31.7:

The display networks command

```
TALSIN:display networks
  00008023  0/1        0A01010A  1/2      32F478CB  0/1
There are 3 known networks.
TALSIN:
```

NOTE   A *tick* is 1/18 of a second or approximately the amount of time required to transmit a frame from one 10Mbps Ethernet segment to another.

Our next entry shows a network that is one hop and two ticks away. This means that it is either another IPX network located on the other side of a router, or the internal IPX network number of another server. We cannot tell which it is by using just this utility.

Our final network is zero hops and one tick. This is either the internal IPX network number for this server or the network directly attached to the network card.

One thing to watch on the display networks screen is the ratio between hops and ticks. If you have a 10Mbps Ethernet network, the number of ticks should always be one more than the number of hops. For example, you should see 0/1, 4/5, or 7/8. If the number of ticks is greater than the number of hops plus one, you have a point of congestion somewhere on your network. This is only applicable if you are using NLSP because RIP simply looks at the hop count and adds one. NLSP actually measures the delay.

Display Servers

The display servers command, shown in Figure 31.8, is similar to the display network command except it reports on known servers. The value listed after the server name is the number of hops that must be traversed to reach this server, measured from the network card.

FIGURE 31.8:

The display servers command

The first two entries, BIRCH_____, are our server advertising the NDS tree name. We know this is the tree name because of the trailing underline. Novell identified trees this way on purpose so they would be easier to spot in a large server list.

So why are we even seeing the tree name in a server list? The display servers command does not identify the physical server(s) themselves, but rather the services being advertised on the network. For example, TALSIN, which is the name of our physical server, is listed three times because it is offering file, print, and NDS services. If we were running a backup server on Talsin, it would appear in this list a fourth time.

All services advertised by the local server should have a hop count of zero. From our list, we see that there is only one server listed with a hop count greater than zero: TOBY.FOOBAR.COM (the COM is truncated on this list). Toby is listed as being one hop away.

Despite what this implies, the server Toby is not sitting on the other side of a physical router. The one hop is listed because NetWare server communications originate from their internal IPX network. The NIC in the server Talsin has to cross the NIC in Toby in order to reach this internal IPX network. Because we experience a network number change when moving from the physical network to the server's internal network, the network card installed in Talsin views Toby as being one hop away.

In short, Toby is actually connected to the same logical network segment as Talsin. If we compare the results of this utility with the results of the display networks command, we can deduce that the remote network listed by display networks must be the internal IPX network number for Toby.

Protocols

Typing the command protocols at the console screen generates a list of protocols loaded on the server. Also shown is the frame type each protocol is using. This command is not as useful as the config command because it does not show you network addresses. It simply gives you a quick list of which protocols are in use.

Packet Burst Statistics Screen

The packet burst statistics screen, shown in Figure 31.9, can look very cryptic indeed to the untrained eye. This screen is actually an excellent resource for monitoring the communication efficiency of each of your clients to ensure they are generating the least possible amount of traffic.

FIGURE 31.9:

The packet burst statistics screen

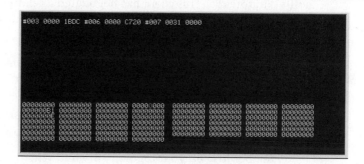

The full command for initializing the packet burst statistic screen is:

```
set enable packet burst statistics screen = on
```

You will then have to change screens (Ctrl+Esc if you are at the console) as the console does not switch to it automatically.

The statistics are listed in groups of three, starting with the connection ID number. Any number that begins with a pound sign (#) identifies the connection ID in a hexadecimal format (yes, decimal form would be much easier, but that would take all the fun out of it). You can compare this number to the connections list on the monitor screen to associate a logon name with a connection number. We talk about the monitor screen later in this section.

So our figure is displaying information for only three connection numbers: 3, 6, and 7. We know this because each one of these values starts with a pound sign. If this was a production server, the first thing we should do is refer back to the monitor screen and see if there are any connections that have not been listed. Only clients that support packet burst are listed on this screen. If a client is not listed, we should find out why it does not support packet burst and upgrade the client's software if possible.

The number listed after the connection ID is the interpacket gap in hexadecimal format. This is not an absolute measurement, but a relative value based on the negotiated gap time. This number represents the gap time that the client associated with this connection ID number has negotiated with the server for burst communications.

For example, connections 3 and 6 are Windows 95 machines using Client32. Both of these clients have negotiated a gap time of zero (meaning "Send me data as fast as you can!"). Connection 7 is using the standard Microsoft client that ships with Windows 95. This client has negotiated a relative gap time of 31. This means that the client is unable to accept frames as fast as the server can dish them out. It has asked that the server pause in between transmissions.

The actual value of the gap time that was negotiated is not as important as how this number equates to other clients on the network. For example, we have two systems that were capable of negotiating a gap of zero while the third client has asked for extremely long pauses between transmissions. We now know we need to look at this third system to determine why it is unable to communicate efficiently.

Remember to keep your topology in mind when you review the negotiated gap time. Clients that are located one or more logical networks away will negotiate a longer gap time due to delays when crossing a router. When comparing these results, make sure you use the same yardstick for all systems.

The third number is a relative value in hexadecimal describing how many burst packets have been negotiated with the client. The higher the number, the more burst packets are transmitted between acknowledgments. For example, connection 3 has negotiated six burst packets per acknowledgment, while connection 6 is using 35.

Do not worry about what value equates to how many burst packets. Like the interpacket gap, use the displayed burst negotiation value as a yardstick to compare like stations. The idea is to identify stations that are unable to communicate as efficiently as others. For example, connection 7 has asked for an acknowledgment for every frame transmitted. We would obviously want to investigate this system first, to find out what the problem is.

The bottom of the screen is debug information and is not very useful for monitoring client communication efficiency. When you have finished your evaluation and wish to close the screen, switch back to the console prompt and type:

```
set enable packet burst statistics screen = off
```

TIP

The packet burst statistic screen uses a lot of CPU overhead. You should not leave this screen enabled all the time. Turn it on when you need to check it, but make sure you disable it when you are done.

reset router

The reset router command clears the router and server table on the server. Initiating this command causes the server to send RIPs and SAPs in order to build a new table. This is useful if you suspect that there may be a routing loop and wish to clear it without downing the server. You can safely run this command with users logged on to the system.

tping

tping is short for *trivial ping*. If you have IP running on your server, this utility allows you to ping a remote host by name or IP address. The syntax is:

```
load tping host
```

where *host* is replaced with the host name or IP address of the remote system with which you wish to check connectivity. tping has no configurable options and reports little more than "host is alive" or "host unreachable." It does not return transmission or round trip time like the ping command discussed below. The fact that you do not have a graphic interface to deal with makes this an easy tool to use if you need to perform a quick connectivity check.

track On

The track on command is used for monitoring RIP and SAP packets on the network. When the command is executed, two separate console screens are started—one for monitoring RIP traffic, and the other for monitoring SAP. Figure 31.10 shows the SAP tracking screen.

FIGURE 31.10:

The SAP tracking screen

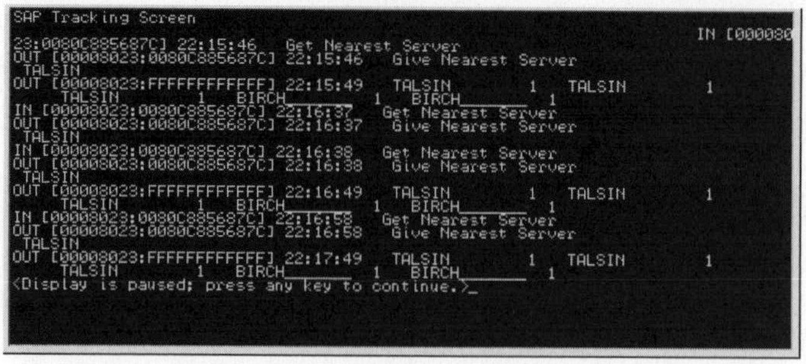

The first line actually starts way off to the right, due to formatting problems with the utility. This line reads:

```
IN [00008023:0080C885687C] 22:15:46   Get Nearest Server
```

The IN means that this is a SAP that the server received from the network; it was not generated internally. The numbers between the brackets list the network number from which the SAP was received, then a colon, then the MAC address of the station that transmitted the SAP. Then there is a time stamp followed by a description of the type of SAP. A Get Nearest Server request is typically sent by a workstation when it begins to initialize its network drivers.

If we look at the next line, it reads:

```
OUT [00008023:0080C885687C] 22:15:46   Give Nearest Server
  TALSIN
```

The OUT means that this SAP was generated by the server. The address within the brackets identifies who the server transmitted the SAP to. We then have another time stamp followed by a description of the SAP. This time the SAP type is identified as being a Give Nearest Server request. The data transmitted was the server's name TALSIN.

This "get" and "give" exchange is how a workstation first finds resources out on the network. Once a workstation receives a Give Nearest Server SAP, it has the resources it needs to find any server on the network. The "give" includes the source network and MAC address for the replying server, so the workstation can now carry on communications with this server directly. Also, because the server maintains a table of all other servers on the network, the workstation can query it for the address of the server it is looking for.

This can be an excellent aid in troubleshooting workstations that are not successfully connecting to the network. If the workstation's MAC address is not seen transmitting a Get Nearest Server request, you know the problem is with the workstations. If you see the workstation transmit a Get Nearest Server request but the server does not reply, it is the server that needs investigation.

As mentioned, `track on` also starts a screen for monitoring RIP traffic. This screen follows the same "in/out" convention that the SAP screen uses. The only difference is that the information displayed deals with routing requests, not server requests.

To shut down the `track on` screens, switch back to a console prompt and enter the command `track off`.

Graphic Tools

NetWare also includes a number of graphical utilities for monitoring network conditions. Each of these tools is started by using the `load` command. The syntax is:

    load *name*

where *name* is replaced with the name of the tool you wish to use.

Many of these tools are console utilities for monitoring a specific type of connection or protocol. All of the console screens are functionally similar. The differences reflect the unique properties of the protocol or connection type it is designed to monitor. Rather than rewrite the network manual on these tools, we will focus on one and give a brief description of the rest.

ipxcon

`ipxcon` is used for monitoring IPX traffic. The main screen, shown in Figure 31.11, gives some general IPX statistics and the Available Options menu has selections for investigating more detail.

The Packets Received and Packets Sent fields show the total number of frames that this system has both sent and received with an IPX header. These fields are important; you can't obtain this information anywhere else. There is a LAN/WAN Information option on the `Monitor` utility, which we discuss later in this section; however, it gives statistics for total traffic, not just for a single protocol.

FIGURE 31.11:

The main screen for the IPX
Console

Packets Forwarded applies when we have two or more NICs in the server and we are routing traffic between two or more logical segments. Because this server is not performing any routing, the value is zero.

If you are routing with the server, you should pay close attention to the ratio between the Packets Received and the Packets Forwarded fields. If the server is routing more than 15 percent of the packets it receives, it may be time to look at relocating users or resources. It is beneficial to do as little routing as possible because this improves server access time.

To the right of this information, we have statistics for circuits, networks, and services. Circuits are the paths the server has available for transferring information. For example, our NIC card is considered a circuit because it provides connectivity to the attached network.

The Networks field identifies how many IPX networks are known to this server. The Services field identifies how many services are available on the network, as known by this server. These two fields report the same information as the display networks and display servers commands covered earlier.

SNMP Access Configuration   The SNMP Access Configuration option allows us to view SNMP settings if IPX is being used as the transfer protocol. The information displayed is identical to what is set using the INETCFG utility we discussed in Chapter 11.

IPX Information   When we select the IPX Information menu option, the IPX Information window appears. This dialog box is shown in Figure 31.12.

FIGURE 31.12:

The IPX Information
dialog box

The first set of statistics is Incoming Packets Received and Incoming Packets Delivered. The first is a count of how many IPX packets were received by the NIC that passed a CRC check. The second shows how many of those packets were forwarded along to the server. These numbers will not necessarily match, as the NIC does not forward every IPX packet it receives to the server. What is important to look for here is the ratio at which the two statistics are climbing.

When it appears that packets are being received faster than they are being forwarded to the server, there is a strong possibility that the server is becoming overwhelmed with the volume of traffic. The No ECB Available statistic within the Monitor utility would let us know for sure (described below).

The Outgoing Requests field indicates the number of frames that the server has attempted to deliver. The Outgoing Packets Sent field indicates how many were successfully transmitted. If you see a large discrepancy between these two numbers, you may have a faulty cable or excessive network traffic.

Detailed IPX Information   If we select the Detailed IPX Information option, the Detailed IPX Information window shown in Figure 31.13 appears. This gives us even further detail as to how our IPX communications are performing.

FIGURE 31.13:

The Detailed IPX Information
window

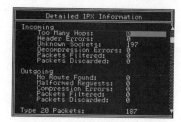

Too Many Hops records how many IPX packets were received wherein the hop count was exceeded. Header Errors records the number of IPX packets received that had incorrect or unreadable information in the IPX, SPX, or NCP header section. Unknown Sockets describes the number of IPX frames received that referenced a socket number the server is not familiar with.

This is more common than you might think. For example, if a *Doom* game is taking place on the locally attached network, the server would be unfamiliar with the socket used by the *Doom* clients and would increment this field. Also, the Microsoft client frequently makes calls to socket numbers that are not used by the network server. If you are using the Microsoft client, you will see this number increment as well.

Decompression errors occur when the server is unable to expand a compressed IPX header. Header compression can be used over a WAN link to reduce bandwidth utilization by reducing the space necessary to store the IPX header. If your server is not directly connected to a WAN, this value should remain zero.

Packets Filtered identifies how many frames have been blocked due to a filter that has been configured with the FILTCFG utility. Filtering is useful in large environments when you wish to reduce broadcast traffic or in environments where it is necessary to connect two logical segments but you wish to filter access from one direction. Whenever an IPX frame is blocked due to a filter setting, this value is incremented by one.

The Packets Discarded field is a catch-all, in that it records the number of frames not delivered for some other reason than the fields listed above. For example, if you are using packet signature and the server detects a spoofed packet, the information would be discarded and this field would be incremented by one.

The Outgoing fields are a mirror of the Incoming fields except that they record errors in transmission. The final field, Type 20 Packets, identifies the number of NetBIOS packets received by this system.

IPX Router Information   If we select IPX Router Information from the main menu, we are given a brief summary of the routing state of the system, including the following information:

- the IPX internal network number
- if RIP is enabled or disabled
- if SAP is enabled or disabled
- if NLSP is enabled or disabled

- if Mobile IPX is enabled or disabled

- the maximum paths that NLSP can load-balance across

- the maximum hop count recognized by this server

NOTE   While it may sound a bit strange to disable RIP or SAP on a server, it can actually be a good way to improve system performance.

Out of the box, NetWare will act as a router. If you install two NICs in the server, it will happily begin routing traffic between each segment. This may not always be necessary, however. For example, consider the network shown in Figure 31.14.

FIGURE 31.14:

A multisegment LAN that does not require routing

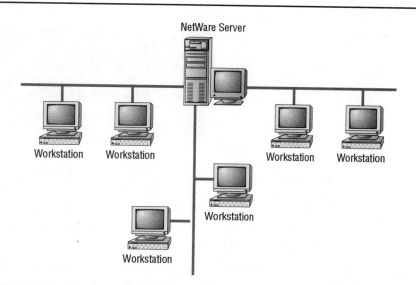

We have three logical segments with workstations attached to each. All work-stations access all of their required network resources directly from the server. Because each user can connect to the server directly from their own logical seg-ment, why bother broadcasting RIP information if nobody is going to use it? By removing routing support from the server (this is done with the INETCFG utility), we free up processor time to perform other tasks as well as reduce the number of broadcasts on our network.

NLSP Information   The NLSP Information screen offers detailed information of the NLSP configuration as well as route information it has discovered. This information was covered in detail in Chapters 2, 3, and 11.

Mobile IPX Information   The Mobile IPX Information option gives detailed information on WAN users using mobile IPX for communications. You can view statistics such as packets sent and received.

Circuits   When the circuits option is selected, the user is allowed to choose from an available circuit (identified by the LAN or WAN card that creates the circuit) in order to view detailed information. Figure 31.15 shows the Circuit Information screen. Much of this information can be found under other options in this utility, or the Monitor utility. The Detailed Circuit Information option at the bottom of the screen provides information that we cannot find elsewhere.

FIGURE 31.15:

The Circuit Information dialog box

Figure 31.16 shows a portion of the Detailed Circuit Information Screen. Here we can see where the server keeps track of how many RIP and SAP frames it is both sending and receiving. Because both of these protocols are broadcast-based, we can use this number to get an idea of how many broadcasts are being transmitted onto the network.

FIGURE 31.16:

The Detailed Circuit Information screen

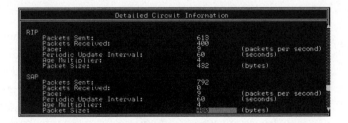

For example, we could record the IPX packet totals shown on the main screen, as well as the quantity of RIP and SAP packets from this screen. We can then record these values again a few hours later. We can now calculate:

- average IPX frames per second

- average RIP and SAP frames per second

- the percentage of total IPX traffic that is broadcast-based

While not quite a network analyzer, this record will at least get you in the ballpark concerning how your network is performing. In fact, we could also record the quantity for total frames sent and received from the `Monitor` screen and add this information into our calculations.

NOTE   Make sure you use a fairly long period of time between measurements when using this method; at least an hour should be fine.

Because you have no way to freeze the values recorded at a certain time, the data will become skewed as you navigate the menus to collect it. Still, if you do not have a proper network monitor or analyzer, this method will at least give you an idea of how much traffic your network is seeing.

Forwarding and Services   Our last two options, Forwarding and Services, report the same information as the `display networks` and `display servers` commands. These menu options simply give you a graphical way of viewing the information.

aiocon

`aiocon` can be used to monitor asynchronous communications across a serial port connection. From this utility you can view the amount of data sent and received.

atcon

`atcon` is the utility for monitoring AppleTalk communications. It is very similar to the `ipxcon` utility, in that it allows you to monitor packet statistics as well as view network and zone information.

atmcon

atmcon is the utility for monitoring ATM connections to your server. From this utility you can view virtual circuit configuration information, send queues, and bytes transmitted and received.

ipxping

ipxping is identical to the IP ping utility, except that, as the name implies, it uses IPX as a transport. This utility allows you to enter the network and node address of a remote host in order to test connectivity.

A useful feature of this utility is that it records the time it takes a packet of data to contact a remote system and then return back to the transmitting station. This is a quick way to be able to check link speed if you suspect that a WAN link may be overloaded. By using this utility during peak and off-peak hours, you can get a good feel for the responsiveness of the connection. It can also help identify trends in bandwidth utilization.

For example, let's assume that every workday you perform a few test pings over a WAN link and record the average results. Over time, you will be able to determine the following:

- what round-trip time correlates to a slow WAN response for users
- whether your bandwidth requirements over the WAN link are increasing, decreasing, or staying the same

This method is by no means as accurate as using an analyzer. If you do not have an analyzer, however, this will at least create some general number for you to gauge WAN performance.

Monitor

Monitor, as the name implies, is the main utility for overseeing the health of your server. It reports on a lot of information regarding every aspect of server performance. For the purpose of this discussion, however, we will focus on the statistics that pertain to network performance. The Monitor General Information screen is shown in Figure 31.17.

FIGURE 31.17:

The Monitor General Information screen

The first statistic of interest on the General Information screen is Packet Receive Buffers. This is the queue available to the server for storing inbound frames. As the NIC receives the frame, it stores it in a packet receive buffer to await processing by the server.

Packet receive buffers have minimum and maximum settings that can be configured directly through Monitor under the Server Parameters menu option. The minimum setting is the number of buffers allocated during system startup. If the server requires more buffers than the minimum value, it is allowed to allocate additional buffers until the maximum is reached.

As frames are stored in the packet receive buffers, the server will begin processing them. If frames are coming in faster than the server can remove them from the packet receive buffer pool, the server may eventually reach a point where the buffer becomes full. It will first try to slow down incoming traffic by transmitting a false collision warning. This gives the server a moment to try to catch up with the contents of the queue. If it continues to have trouble keeping up, it will allocate additional packet receive buffers to queue inbound traffic.

The service processes, Maximum Service Processes and Current Service Processes, also shown on the General Information screen, are responsible for processing the queue. As the NIC places frames into the queue, the service processes are responsible for removing them. If the above described condition occurs where the server is having trouble keeping up with inbound traffic, it will not only allocate additional packet buffers, but additional service processes as well. The more service processes allocated, the faster the packet receive buffer pool can be processed.

Once your server has been in operation for at least a few weeks, record the reported values for the packet receive buffers and the current service processes. Compare these values to the minimum values under the server parameters option. If the values match, you are all set. If the server parameters value is less than the number you recorded from the General Information screen, you should increase the configured minimum value to match the current levels being used.

What you are doing is tuning the server for the next time it is rebooted. By increasing the minimums so that they match current usage levels, the server will not have to reallocate these resources after it is rebooted next time.

Using Figure 31.17 as an example, let's assume our server has already been in use for a month and we wish to tune these parameters. We record the number of packet receive buffers to be 200 and the current service processes to be 15.

Now let's assume that we look under the server parameters option for the minimum settings for these two pools. We note that the minimum packet receive buffers is set at 150 and the minimum service processes is set to 10. This means that over the last month our server has had to allocate 50 new packet receive buffers (for a total of 200) and 5 service processes (for a total of 15).

Unless the last month was exceptionally busy, we can assume that if we need to power down our server again, and it is restored to the original values for these two settings, that the server will again have to allocate 50 new packet receive buffers and 5 service processes. By increasing the minimums to the current usage levels, we can prevent the server from having to go through this a second time.

The reason we wish to avoid having the server allocate its own resources is that it does not do it immediately. It will wait until it is absolutely sure it needs additional resources before it will allocate them. During this time our server performance may appear sluggish. By increasing these values ahead of time, we eliminate this problem.

TIP

These memory resources are normally allocated very slowly. If you ever notice the packet receive buffers climbing rapidly, it may be because of a bad NIC or a buggy NIC driver.

You also want to ensure that these values are not approaching their maximum settings. If the maximums are reached, the server will begin to ignore data requests.

If we press the Tab key we can view the Available Options menu. Besides Server Parameters, the option we are interested in is LAN/WAN Information. Highlight this entry and press Enter.

You will be presented with the Available LAN Drivers dialog box as shown in Figure 31.18. This dialog box is a bit misleading, as it appears you can view different information on a per binding basis. For example, Figure 31.18 shows two options within the box. The truth is, information is presented on a per LAN driver basis. Because our figure shows two protocols bound to the same card, the statistics under each will be identical (except for the report protocol and network address). We can select either driver to view this information.

FIGURE 31.18:

The Available LAN Drivers
dialog box

Figure 31.19 shows the LAN Driver statistics screen. At the top of the screen is the driver version we are using, the node or MAC address of the card, and the protocol and network address for this particular selection. The important information is the Generic Statistics section.

FIGURE 31.19:

The LAN Driver statistics
screen

```
        FD0490_E83 [FD0490 port=300 int=5 frame=ETHERNET_802.3]

Version 3.21
Node address: 00C06C712979
Protocols:
   IPX
      Network address:  00008023

Generic statistics
   Total packets sent:                                 7,693
   Total packets received:                             7,466
   No ECB available count:                                 0
   Send packet too big count:                             0
   Reserved:                                     Not supported
   Receive packet overflow count:                        0
   Receive packet too big count:                         0
   Receive packet too small count:              Not supported
   Send packet miscellaneous errors:                    0
   Receive packet miscellaneous errors:                 0
```

The first three statistics—Total Packets Sent, Total Packets Received, and No ECB Available Count—will be present for any network card. The statistics that follow vary depending on the card's manufacturer.

The values in the Total Packets Sent and Total Packets Received fields include all protocols, not just the protocol listed at the top of the screen. These are the statistics to check if we wish to quantify the amount of traffic on a network segment. If you record these values and measure them over a period of time, you can get a general idea of how much traffic is on your network.

The No ECB Available Count records the number of times the NIC has tried to place a frame into the packet receive buffer pool but there were no buffers available. A high number here is indicative of a server that does not have a high enough minimum setting for the packet receive buffers and the server processes.

Below is a brief description of some of the other statistics you may have listed:

- Send Packet Too Big Count—server transmitted a packet that was too large for the NIC to process
- Receive Packet Overflow Count—indicates an overflow in the adapter's receive buffers
- Receive Packet Too Big Count—received a frame that exceeds topology maximum size
- Receive Packet Too Small Count—received a frame that exceeds topology minimum size
- Send Packet Retry Count—number of transmission failures due to hardware errors
- Checksum Errors—checksum does not match FCS value
- Hardware Receive Mismatch Count—specified packet length does not match actual size
- Total Send OK Byte Count Low—number of bytes transmitted
- Total Send OK Byte Count High—increments by one every time the Total Send OK Byte Count Low reaches 4GB
- Total Receive OK Byte Count Low—number of bytes received
- Total Receive OK Byte Count High—increments by one every time the Total Receive OK Byte Count Low reaches 4GB
- Adapter Reset Count—the number of times the adapter was reset due to an internal failure
- Adapter Queue Depth—indicates an overflow in the adapter's transmit buffers
- Send OK Single Collision Count—single collision with data being sent after recovery
- Send OK Multiple Collision Count—multiple collisions with data being sent after recovery

- Send OK But Deferred—number of delayed transmissions due to heavy network usage

- Send Abort From Late Collision—collision that may be due to excessive cable length

- Send Abort From Excess Collisions—too many collisions detected to transmit

- Send Abort From Carrier Sense—lost contact with the network during transmission

- Send Abort From Excessive Deferral—network too busy for station to transmit

Many of these statistics can give us some great clues as to how our network is performing. For example, if we see the Send OK Multiple Collision Count, or Send OK But Deferred values starting to increment, there is a very good chance that the segment is seeing too much traffic.

ping

`ping` uses the IP protocol to send out a test message to a remote system in order to test connectivity. The settings and uses for ping are identical to `ipxping` except they apply to the IP protocol.

tcpcon

`tcpcon` is the utility for monitoring IP communications. It is very similar to the `ipxcon` utility, in that it allows you to monitor packet statistics as well as view network and routing information.

Workstation Commands

NetWare has only a few workstation commands that are useful for documenting your network and troubleshooting connectivity.

nlist server /a/b

The `nlist server /a/b` command produces a list of known NetWare servers. This command is the equivalent of the command that was available on NetWare 3.1x. If the /b is omitted, only NDS servers are listed.

nlist user /a/b

The nlist user /a/b command produces a list of users who are currently authenticated to the NDS tree. The output also lists the network and MAC address that the user is logged in from.

If you have a network monitor or analyzer that is not capable of collecting NetWare logon names, but the device does allow you to input names from a file, you can use the output from this command to create your list. This is far quicker than having to enter each one manually.

NWD2

NWD2 is a diagnostic utility that is included with the client32 workstation drivers. While this tool does not document or troubleshoot your network, it will identify all the client drivers installed on the workstation.

NWD2 is useful if you are trying to track down a connectivity problem that is related to only one or two workstations. NWD2 documents which drivers and modules are loaded and reports on the revision and date/time stamp of each. This is useful because you can compare the results to a similar workstation that is functioning properly. If you note any variations, you can take steps to upgrade the appropriate drivers.

Windows NT Server

Windows NT does not have a separate console interface as does IntraNetWare. This means that all utilities can be accessed from the server console. We have again divided our utilities into command-line and GUI categories.

Command-Line Networking Tools

The command-line tools should be run from within a Command Prompt box. While they can be executed using Run or Explorer, the utility will close before the results can be reviewed.

arp

The arp command is used to display the entries of the ARP (Address Resolution Protocol) cache. The ARP cache contains a map of IP addresses to MAC addresses for the local segment. In order for the system to communicate with a host on the same logical network, it must create an ARP entry for it first.

This is a useful tool for troubleshooting problems such as duplicate IP addresses. If you know that an IP address is being used that shouldn't be, you can ping the address and check the contents of the ARP cache to find out the MAC address of the machine using the address (the nbtstat utility detailed below may be even more useful in this task).

Available switches are:

- (none): when no switches are used, report the IP address, mask and default gateway
- /all: report on the above as well as which services are available

ipxroute

The ipxroute command is used to collect IPX-related information from the network. In order for this command to collect information, RIP for NWLink and the SAP agent must be loaded.

This command is useful for ensuring that the NT system has connectivity to NetWare servers or remote IPX networks.

Available switches are:

- servers: list known NetWare servers
- stats: identify the number of IPX packets sent and received
- table: display the IPX routing table

nbtstat

nbtstat is used for reporting the NetBIOS names known to this system, or to a remote host. It will also report which systems have been located through network broadcasts or through WINS.

Figure 31.21 shows the nbtstat command using the -r switch. Reported is a list of each system discovered from broadcast packets, and a list of each system discovered through the WINS server. There is no WINS server list in our example because a WINS server is not configured.

FIGURE 31.21:

The nbtstat command using the "-r" switch

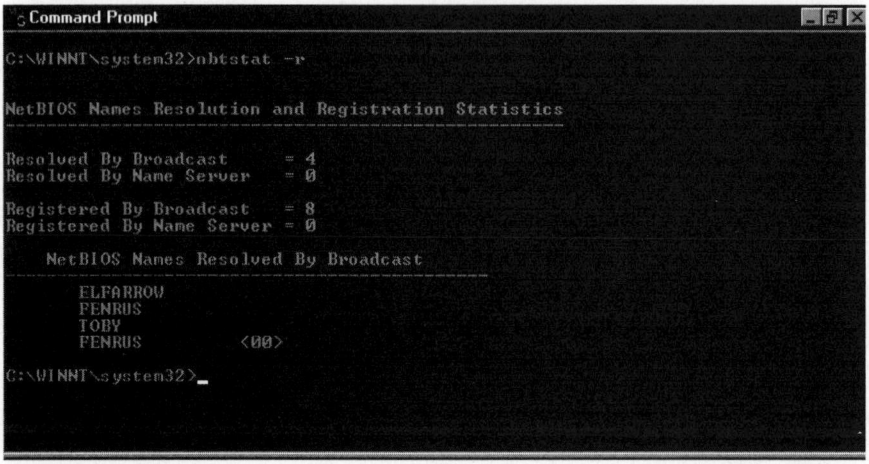

```
Command Prompt                                                            _ □ X

C:\WINNT\system32>nbtstat -r

NetBIOS Names Resolution and Registration Statistics
---------------------------------------------------------------------

Resolved By Broadcast      = 4
Resolved By Name Server    = 0

Registered By Broadcast    = 8
Registered By Name Server  = 0

     NetBIOS Names Resolved By Broadcast
---------------------------------------------------------------------

        ELFARROW
        FENRUS
        TOBY
        FENRUS              <00>

C:\WINNT\system32>_
```

If you have a WINS server configured, you can use the names listed in the Net-BIOS Names Resolved By Broadcast section to determine which systems may need to be reconfigured to use the WINS server.

This can also be a useful utility for resolving IP address conflicts. When used with the -a switch, the utility will display the name table for a remote IP address. The name table includes the local system name as well as the logon name of the local user. This can be valuable information if you are attempting to resolve an IP address conflict.

Available switches are:

- -a *host*: print the name table for the host named *host*

- -a *IP address*: print the name table for the host using the specified IP address

- -c: print the contents of the local name cache

- -n: print the name table for the local system

- -r: report systems discovered through broadcasts and WINS

- -s: display the connect connection table

netstat

netstat reports on IP connection information and LAN card statistics. This utility is useful when you will be offering other IP services besides NetBIOS over IP as all IP sessions are recorded.

As shown in Figure 31.22, this is also a good place to look for general Ethernet statistics. Displayed are total bytes sent and received as well as how much of this traffic was due to broadcast and unicast communications.

FIGURE 31.22:

The netstat command using the "-e" switch

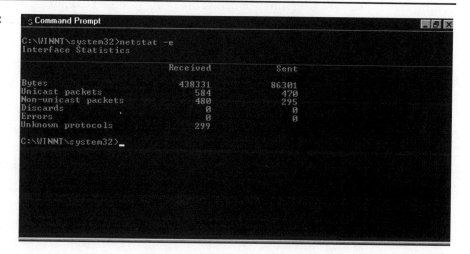

```
Command Prompt

C:\WINNT\system32>netstat -e
Interface Statistics

                           Received            Sent

Bytes                       438331            86301
Unicast packets                584              470
Non-unicast packets            480              295
Discards                         0                0
Errors                           0                0
Unknown protocols              299

C:\WINNT\system32>_
```

If we compare the ratio of broadcast (i.e., "Non-unicast" in the figure) transmissions to unicast, we see that there are almost as many broadcasts being used to transmit information as there are unicasts. Because broadcasts effect all local systems, this is a bad thing. If we were to see a statistic like this in a production environment, we would know it is time to dust off the old network monitor to see who is generating all these broadcasts.

Available switches are:

- -a: list all active connections and ports
- -e: list Ethernet statistics
- -n: same as -a except systems are listed by address, not name
- -r: display the IP routing table

- -s: list statistics on a per port basis

- *NUM*: when a switch is followed by a number, the command is executed at a time interval equal to the numeric value in seconds

nslookup

nslookup is a powerful tool for troubleshooting connectivity problems to determine if they are DNS related. The nslookup tool can be pointed at a specific name server to determine if names are being resolved to an IP address correctly. The best way to understand nslookup is to walk through situations when you may need to use it.

Let's say you are cruising the Web and decide to stop by the Sun Web site to check out their latest product line. You enter the address:

```
http://www.sun.com
```

and attempt to connect to the site. The connection fails, and your browser states that the server could not be contacted. At that moment a friend calls who is all excited about the latest SuperSPARC line. When you complain that you are unable to connect to the Web site, your buddy states that they are on the site as you speak and server response is zippy.

This looks like a job for nslookup. When you launch the utility, the following screen appears:

```
C:\nslookup
Default Server:  clover.sover.net
Address:  204.71.16.10
>
```

Not very exciting, is it? What nslookup is displaying is that it will use the DNS server clover.sover.net to resolve all name queries. The IP address of this system is 204.71.16.10. Your starting server and IP address may vary. This is actually some pretty useful information as we now know who exactly will be responding to our DNS requests. We can also point at other DNS servers on the fly without having to change our system's primary DNS server. (What's that you say? A network change on NT that does not require the system to be rebooted? It's true!)

Our next step would be to enter the host name we wish to resolve. When we do, `nslookup` will produce the following information:

```
> www.sun.com

Server:   clover.sover.net
Address:  204.71.16.10

Non-authoritative answer:
Name:     www.sun.com
Addresses:  192.9.9.100, 192.9.48.5
```

The first line is the address we entered, `www.sun.com`. The rest of the output is produced by `nslookup` in response to that query. The first thing `nslookup` does is remind us which name server we are using. It then proceeds to respond with the requested information.

"Non-authoritative answer" means that `clover.sover.net` is not a DNS server for the host in our query. This lets us know that the information listed was received secondhand from another DNS server.

You will note that the query returned two different IP addresses for this host. Sun is using a DNS feature called "round robin." As users attempt to connect to `www.sun.com`, a different address is handed out each time. This helps to distribute the load across two identical systems. Because we are using `nslookup`, however, we were able to retrieve both addresses.

The next step would be to exit the `nslookup` utility and try pinging each of the two sites. For the purpose of our example we will assume that one server responds while the other one does not.

We now know why our friend was able to connect to Sun's Web site while we were not. They had connected to the functioning system while we happened to connect to the one that was offline.

`nslookup` accepts the following commands, once launched:

```
NAME              - print info about the host/domain NAME using default
                    server
NAME1 NAME2       - as above, but use NAME2 as server
help or ?         - print info on common commands; see nslookup(1) for
                    details
set OPTION        - set an option
    all           - print options, current server and host
    [no]debug     - print debugging information
    [no]d2        - print exhaustive debugging information
```

```
      [no]defname - append domain name to each query
      [no]recurse - ask for recursive answer to query
      [no]vc      - always use a virtual circuit
      domain=NAME - set default domain name to NAME
      srchlist=N1[/N2/.../N6] - set domain to N1 and search list to
N1,N2, etc.
      root=NAME   - set root server to NAME
      retry=X     - set number of retries to X
      timeout=X   - set initial time-out interval to X seconds
      querytype=X - set query type, e.g.,
A,ANY,CNAME,HINFO,MX,PX,NS,PTR,SOA,TXT,WKS,SRV,NAPTR
      port=X      - set port number to send query on
      type=X      - synonym for querytype
      class=X     - set query class to one of IN (Internet), CHAOS,
HESIOD or ANY
server NAME      - set default server to NAME, using current default
server
lserver NAME     - set default server to NAME, using initial server
finger [USER]    - finger the optional USER at the current default host
root             - set current default server to the root
ls [opt] DOMAIN [> FILE] - list addresses in DOMAIN (optional: output
to FILE)

      -a          - list canonical names and aliases
      -h          - list HINFO (CPU type and operating system)
      -s          - list well-known services
      -d          - list all records
      -t TYPE     - list records of the given type (e.g., A,CNAME,MX,
etc.)
view FILE        - sort an 'ls' output file and view it with more
exit             - exit the program, ^D also exits
```

ping

ping on Windows NT is functionally identical to ping on every other platform. ping is used to verify connectivity between two IP hosts and will report the travel time required to echo out the remote host and back again.

Available switches are:

- -n *NUM*: echo the number of times specified by *NUM*

- -l *NUM*: specify the size (in bytes) of the echo packet

- `-r` *NUM*: record the route traveled for the number of hops specified by *NUM*. If more hops are required than the specified value, do not record the remainder of the route.

route

The `route` command was discussed in detail in Chapter 3. Use it to define and display static IP routes to remote network segments.

tracert

The `tracert` command is the Windows NT equivalent of Unix's `traceroute`. It was explained in detail in Chapter 2 (see Figure 2.5).

GUI Networking Tools

The following utilities can be launched directly from the NT desktop or by using the Run command off of the Start menu.

Network Monitoring Tool

We discussed the Network Monitoring Tool earlier, but its functionality is great enough to warrant another mention here. The Network Monitoring Tool provides a similar level of functionality to Novell's LANalyzer, except that only traffic going to or coming from the local system can be monitored. The tool is capable of capturing traffic and performing frame decodes. While the format is slightly different than LANalyzer, the quantity of frame information is the same.

Network Monitoring Tool can be pointed at agents running on other NT servers. You can only view one agent at a time, however, and must manually combine the data to get an overall view of network activity.

NOTE   It is also possible to install and run NetMon on Windows 95. You need to install the Microsoft network monitoring service, in addition to installing the NetMon application, for this to work.

Unlike LANalyzer, which will record trends as well as capture traffic, the Network Monitoring Tool relies on Performance Monitor to record any required trends.

Performance Monitor

The Performance Monitor, as shown in Figure 31.23, allows us to graph multiple performance parameters at the same time. The three listed traces are all network-related; however, we could have chosen to monitor disk or processor utilization as well. This makes it extremely easy to look at the cause and effect relationship between network and other parameters. For example, we can see there is a direct correlation between network utilization and total bytes received while total frames received remains relatively unaffected.

FIGURE 31.23:

Performance Monitor

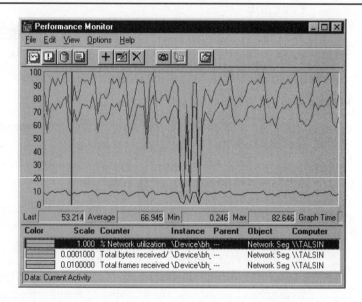

There are some drawbacks to this tool however. The most significant is that we must preset our sample rate to a specific value. Unlike LANalyzer, which collects both trend and detailed statistics at the same time, we can only choose one or the other with Performance Monitor.

Also, our collection of trend data is accomplished by extending the time between which samples are measured. Performance Monitor does not measure a block of results and then average them out like LANalyzer does for long-term trends. Performance Monitor simply takes an instantaneous reading at longer intervals. This means that if the sample rate happens to hit a few bumps or valleys in activity, the entire trend can become skewed. The result is that you lose accuracy as you try to extend the monitoring period.

winmsd

Like the NWD2 utility for NetWare, winmsd can report on driver data and revision information. The difference is that while NWD2 is designed to be run on a workstation, winmsd is used when diagnosing the server.

Figure 31.24 shows the Network tab of the winmsd utility. Reported is not only driver information, but similar statistics to what can be found under the LAN/WAN Driver menu on IntraNetWare. While total bytes sent and received is not shown, these statistics are available from this screen if you scroll down to the bottom.

FIGURE 31.24:

The Network tab of the winmsd utility

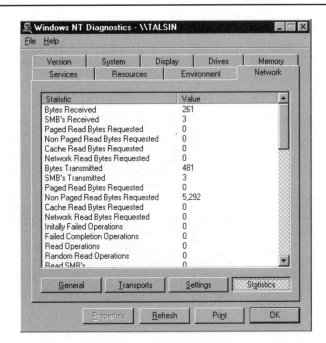

Unix

All of the Unix troubleshooting tools we will cover are command-line utilities. When a tool has been covered in a previous section of this chapter, we will refer you back to the appropriate section.

arp

This command is identical to the arp command under Windows NT. It is used for viewing and modifying the contents of the ARP (Address Resolution Protocol) cache.

ifconfig

ifconfig is normally used to configure a network interface. When used without any switches, it can also be used to report communication information for each network interface.

Figure 31.25 shows the output of the ifconfig utility. The figure shows the IP address as well as transmit and receive errors. If your Unix system is suffering from poor network performance, this is the first place to look to see if any errors are being generated.

FIGURE 31.25:

The ifconfig utility

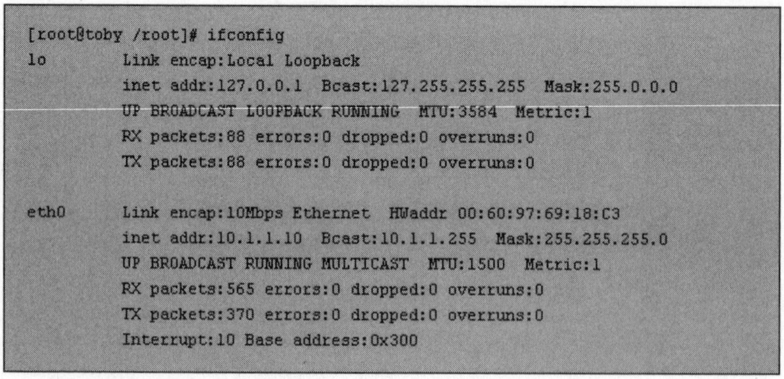

```
[root@toby /root]# ifconfig
lo          Link encap:Local Loopback
            inet addr:127.0.0.1  Bcast:127.255.255.255  Mask:255.0.0.0
            UP BROADCAST LOOPBACK RUNNING  MTU:3584  Metric:1
            RX packets:88 errors:0 dropped:0 overruns:0
            TX packets:88 errors:0 dropped:0 overruns:0

eth0        Link encap:10Mbps Ethernet  HWaddr 00:60:97:69:18:C3
            inet addr:10.1.1.10  Bcast:10.1.1.255  Mask:255.255.255.0
            UP BROADCAST RUNNING MULTICAST  MTU:1500  Metric:1
            RX packets:565 errors:0 dropped:0 overruns:0
            TX packets:370 errors:0 dropped:0 overruns:0
            Interrupt:10 Base address:0x300
```

netstat

netstat is identical to the netstat utility under Windows NT server. netstat is used to monitor the routing table as well as connection and session information.

nslookup

nslookup is used to diagnose problems related to DNS. It is functionally identical to the nslookup utility supplied with Windows NT.

ping

`ping` is used to test IP connectivity between two network hosts. This utility is identical to the `ping` utility supplied with Windows NT.

route

`route` is used to both view and modify the static routing table. It is functionally identical to the Windows NT utility with the same name.

statnet

When `statnet` is executed, it enables the screen shown in Figure 31.26. This utility gives us a snapshot picture as to what type of traffic conditions exist on the network at any given time. All values are dynamic, meaning they will adjust up and down as traffic conditions change. There is no way to produce cumulative or trend data, unfortunately.

FIGURE 31.26:

The `statnet` Network Statistics screen

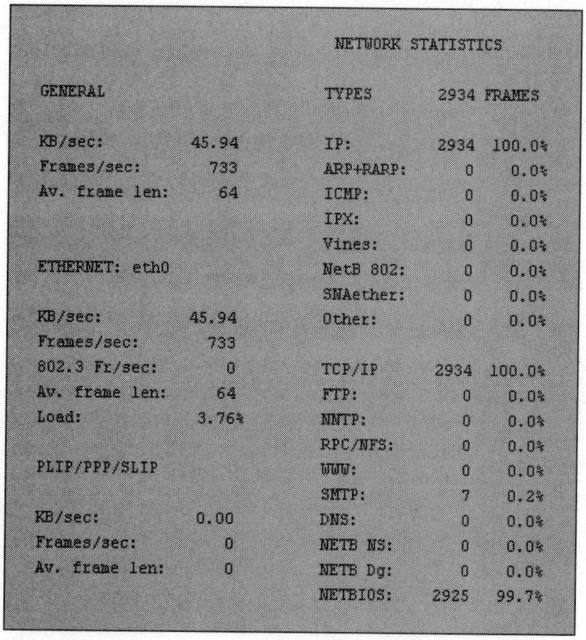

```
                                    NETWORK STATISTICS

          GENERAL                   TYPES        2934 FRAMES

          KB/sec:          45.94    IP:          2934  100.0%
          Frames/sec:        733    ARP+RARP:       0    0.0%
          Av. frame len:      64    ICMP:           0    0.0%
                                    IPX:            0    0.0%
                                    Vines:          0    0.0%
          ETHERNET: eth0            NetB 802:       0    0.0%
                                    SNAether:       0    0.0%
          KB/sec:          45.94    Other:          0    0.0%
          Frames/sec:        733
          802.3 Fr/sec:        0    TCP/IP       2934  100.0%
          Av. frame len:      64    FTP:            0    0.0%
          Load:            3.76%    NNTP:           0    0.0%
                                    RPC/NFS:        0    0.0%
          PLIP/PPP/SLIP            WWW:            0    0.0%
                                    SMTP:           7    0.2%
          KB/sec:           0.00    DNS:            0    0.0%
          Frames/sec:          0    NETB NS:        0    0.0%
          Av. frame len:       0    NETB Dg:        0    0.0%
                                    NETBIOS:     2925   99.7%
```

Because we cannot generate long-term trends, the usefulness of this utility is severely limited. We would need to keep an eagle eye on this screen in order to catch anything out of the ordinary. While this is fine if we know we are currently experiencing a problem, it limits our ability to generate long-term statistics.

Still, the ability to break down network traffic by protocol and service as well as view it in a format that presents this value as a percentage of total bandwidth in use is an alluring feature. Considering the utility is free, we cannot complain too loudly.

tcpdump

`tcpdump` is a frame capture utility that allows you to view the header information of IP frames. A sample of its output is presented in Figure 31.27. From left to right, this utility identifies:

- the time stamp

- the source host and port number

- the destination host and port number

- the flag setting (P=PUSH, S=SYN, F=FIN, R=RST, .=none)

- the start byte:stop byte for packet sequencing

- the amount of data transferred (the number in parentheses)

- the ack means this is an acknowledgment to a data request

- the acknowledgment number (1)

- the data window size (31744)

FIGURE 31.27:

tcpdump recording a Telnet session

```
15:05:46.692522 toby.foobar.com.telnet > ElfArrow.foobar.com.1040: P 8370:8476(106) ack 1 win 31744 (DF)
15:05:46.792522 toby.foobar.com.telnet > ElfArrow.foobar.com.1040: P 8476:8675(199) ack 1 win 31744 (DF)
15:05:46.792522 ElfArrow.foobar.com.1040 > toby.foobar.com.telnet: . ack 8675 win 7845 (DF)
15:05:46.792522 toby.foobar.com.telnet > ElfArrow.foobar.com.1040: P 8675:8781(106) ack 1 win 31744 (DF)
15:05:46.892522 toby.foobar.com.telnet > ElfArrow.foobar.com.1040: P 8781:8980(199) ack 1 win 31744 (DF)
15:05:46.892522 ElfArrow.foobar.com.1040 > toby.foobar.com.telnet: . ack 8980 win 7540 (DF)
15:05:46.892522 toby.foobar.com.telnet > ElfArrow.foobar.com.1040: P 8980:9086(106) ack 1 win 31744 (DF)
15:05:46.992522 toby.foobar.com.telnet > ElfArrow.foobar.com.1040: P 9086:9285(199) ack 1 win 31744 (DF)
15:05:46.992522 ElfArrow.foobar.com.1040 > toby.foobar.com.telnet: . ack 9285 win 8760 (DF)
15:05:46.992522 toby.foobar.com.telnet > ElfArrow.foobar.com.1040: P 9285:9391(106) ack 1 win 31744 (DF)

94 packets received by filter
0 packets dropped by kernel
[root@toby /root]#
```

While not a graphical utility, we do have all the information we require to track communications between systems. `tcpdump` has many available command line switches; some of the most useful are:

- `-e`: print Ethernet header information
- `-i` *INT*: monitor interface *INT*
- `-n`: do not convert host and port numbers to names
- `-q`: reduce the amount of information recorded
- `-S`: absolute instead of relative sequence numbers
- `-t`: do not print the time stamp
- `-v`: more verbose output
- `-vv`: maximum output
- `-w` *FILE*: capture the frames to a file named *FILE*
- `host` *HOSTNAME*: record traffic to and from *HOSTNAME*
- `net` *NETWORK*: record traffic to and from *NETWORK*
- *type*: record traffic of only a certain type. Valid type options are `ether`, `ip`, `arp`, `tcp`, and `udp` (specifying ethernet, IP only, Address Resolution Protocol only, Token Control Protocol only, and Universal Datagram Protocol only, respectively)
- `qualifiers`: `src` (source), `dst` (destination)

Table 31.1 lists some examples of how these switches can be used.

TABLE 31.1 Switch Examples

Command	Effect
`tcpdump -v`	Capture all traffic and report verbose information
`tcpdump -i eth0`	Only monitor the interface Ethernet 0
`tcpdump udp host talsin`	Capture all UDP traffic involving Talsin
`tcpdump dst host talsin port 23`	Capture all traffic headed for port 23 on Talsin
`tcpdump tcp net 10.1.1.0`	Capture all TCP traffic going to and coming from network 10.1.1.0

Telnet

`Telnet` as a troubleshooting tool? It can be, when you use it correctly! `Telnet` can be used to verify that a particular server is accepting connections for a particular service.

For example, let's assume that we wish to set up a Notes server to handle a Notes database replication over the Internet. We believe we have configured the Notes servers correctly and we ensure that each system can ping the other across the Internet. When we initiate the replication, however, the process fails, stating that the remote server could not be reached.

What went wrong? Most likely we have a firewall or router blocking the port that Notes is attempting to communicate on. This is the most likely candidate when one service can reach a remote system (`ping`), but another one cannot (Notes).

To test this theory, enter the following command:

```
telnet notes.foobar.com 1352
```

where `notes.foobar.com` is the name of the remote Notes server we are trying to reach, and 1352 is the TCP port number that Notes uses to communicate.

If we see:

```
trying notes,foobar.com...
telnet: Unable to connect to remote host: Connection refused
```

we know that either port 1352 is blocked between here and the remote Notes system or the system is not configured to accept services on that port.

If we see:

```
trying notes,foobar.com...
Connected to notes.foobar.com.
Escape character is '^]'.
```

we know we have a clear path between here and the remote server on port 1352, and the remote server is accepting services on that port.

While `ping` is fine for testing general connectivity, it does not take into account firewalls or packet filters. These devices are configured to restrict services on certain ports, which will allow some services through but not others.

`Telnet` was not listed under NT because the version included with the operating system has trouble with formatting. If you want to be able to use `Telnet` for testing general connectivity under Windows NT, replace the supplied version with one that has a slightly better VT100 emulation.

traceroute

The `traceroute` command is identical to the Windows NT `tracert` command. This tool is used to record the routers or hops that must be crossed in order to communicate with a remote host.

Summary

This concludes our look at software troubleshooting tools.

We started with Novell's LANalyzer software, which is a good representative of the various network analyzers on the market. It provides detailed network statistics and trends, including average and peak frame rates, peak and average bandwidth utilization, and error rates over time.

We next looked at the console and GUI tools available on the various network operating systems; the primary one of these on NetWare is the `Monitor` application. NetMon, included with NT Server, provides much of the same functionality of LANalyzer, and together with NT's Performance Monitor can provide logging and statistics as well as alarms that are triggered when certain preset thresholds are reached.

Utilities such as `ping`, `arp`, `route`, and `tracert` are great for tracking down address resolution and packet routing problems. `Telnet` is good for verifying that particular IP services are running on a given server.

Now that we know what hardware and software tools we have to work with when diagnosing network problems, it's time to look at some real issues and learn how to apply these tools.

CHAPTER

THIRTY-TWO

Diagnosing Real-World Problems

- Excessive ping activity

- Duplicate IP addresses

- Undeliverable mail

- Connectivity problems after upgrading a server

- Excessive network collisions

We will now apply the troubleshooting tools we've been discussing in previous chapters by looking at some common problems that you are likely to run into from time to time on most networks.

You can rest assured that as a network administrator of a multiprotocol network, you'll be called on to solve a wide range of network-related problems, so in this chapter we've outlined several example troubleshooting cases, each one different in what it requires for troubleshooting.

Ping Strangeness

Our first case involves tracking down unknown traffic on our network. While performing a packet capture with our network monitor, we note the packet exchange recorded in Figure 32.1. We have seven separate hosts that are continually pinging an eighth host, which is our Cisco router. No matter what time of day we perform a capture, this exchange is taking place.

FIGURE 32.1:

Excessive pings on the network

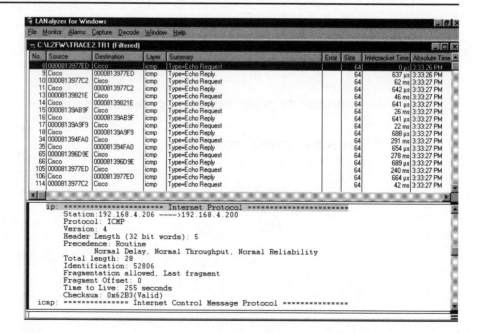

There are two very good reasons why it is worth our time to investigate why this event is taking place.

Security

Excessive pings could be an attempt to probe available network resources, or to perform a denial-of-service attack. Ping is one of those utilities that everyone takes for granted. Because ping is viewed as a simple tool for testing connectivity, most network administrators have no policy in place to control it.

It is for this reason that ping is a very good tool to use when you want to verify the existence of network resources inside a firewall. While administrators may block Telnet or FTP access to their networks, you can usually pass right through many firewalls using ping. This is not to say a firewall cannot block ICMP echo requests; it simply means that many administrators do not configure it to do so.

It is unlikely, however, that this trace is an attacker's probe. A would-be attacker would not be foolish enough to continually check your resources. They would be in and out as quickly as possible.

The other trouble that ping can cause is when it is used with the -f switch. If we use this switch when pinging a host, we tell the ping utility, "Ping the remote host as fast as you possibly can and do not bother waiting for a reply." This causes a flood of ping packets to be sent to the remote system.

Ping is normally used as a means of measuring travel time to a remote host and back again. Because the ability of the remote host to respond to these echo requests can greatly affect the final results, most systems will attempt to reply to a ping echo as quickly as possible.

This is where the trouble starts. If we are sending a flood of ping traffic to a host, it may become so busy trying to respond to the echo requests that performance for other services slows to a crawl. This is referred to as a *denial of service* (*DoS*).

It is unlikely that this trace is an attempt to perform a denial of service, because each host is only pinging the destination system once per second.

Bandwidth

If nothing else, this constant pinging is eating up bandwidth. While it is true that 14fps is not a lot of traffic, it still reduces our potential bandwidth by 20KB. This effect is somewhat cumulative in that the 14 frames are occurring every second of the day. This is not simply a one-time event.

Also, without knowing why this exchange is taking place, we have no way of knowing if the effect will spread to other systems. There could be an error in a configuration file or a script that is causing this to occur.

Looking for Clues

Let's make this interesting and say we do not know who the source IP addresses belong to. We'll assume this is a wild and free environment that allows people to chose IP addresses by counting on their toes or by using Tarot cards.

Our first clue is that the destination system is a router. This implies that the continual pinging may have something to do with the routing table or gateway settings.

Our next clue is that all the systems that are generating the ping requests have the same Ethernet vendor address (000081). This implies that whatever is causing this to occur may be vendor specific. We could then use LANalyzer's Station Monitor to sort on known MAC addresses and verify that every system with this vendor address is generating ping requests.

Let's assume we have verified this. We have seven devices that are using this Ethernet vendor address and each one of them is generating ping requests.

Our next step is to find out which vendor is using that code. By referencing the list in Appendix C, we see that these devices were all manufactured by Synoptic. A quick inventory check verifies that our network is using seven Synoptic manageable hubs for connecting users to network resources.

Our next step is to see if the vendor maintains a support database online, and if so, does it contain any resolutions to this problem. A search of the technical database at Bay Networks (Bay owns Synoptic) reveals that pinging the router is not a bug, but a feature.

The seven hubs support the use of ICMP for dynamically discovering IP routers. The Synoptic Network Management Module (NMM) attempts to discover available routers in order to establish communications with a management station. Because our network does not use a management station, the hubs are still looking for one.

The document states that the NMM will ping the router if:

- It has not detected an ICMP redirect message (pointing it to another router).

- It has not detected an ICMP router advertisement (which are not used in a static route environment).

- It has not received a packet from the router for a specified period of time (in this case that "period of time" is one second, since we already established that the pinging is continual).

In other words, we have three choices:

- Purchase a management station so the hub will stop looking for one.

- Begin broadcasting ICMP router advertisements on our network.

- Disable IP on the hub.

Our first option is expensive and hardly worth the investment to simply reduce this small amount of traffic on our network. Our second would replace 840 unicast frames per minute (total number of ping requests and replies) with one or two routing broadcast frames. Implementing this option would be contingent on what other IP devices are on the network and how this routing information would affect them.

Our third option is clearly the easiest—simply disable IP on each of the hubs. Without an IP address, the hubs have no way to issue ping requests to other IP hosts. One word of caution about removing the IP address, though. If you do not assign an IP address to some network devices, they will automatically begin broadcasting bootp requests once per minute to attempt to get one on their own. Again, this is considered a feature.

If this occurs, you have to decide which is the worst of two evils—a unicast ping echo once a second, or a bootp broadcast once per minute.

Duplicate IP Addresses

A common problem in many networking environments occurs when two machines try to use the same IP address; this can result in intermittent communications. The following series of events is what causes the intermittent communications to occur. Let's assume that host2 and host3 have both been assigned the IP address 10.1.1.10.

- Host1 needs to transmit data to the IP address 10.1.1.10.

- Host1 determines that this is a local address and issues an ARP request.

- Host2 responds to the ARP request with its own MAC address.

- Host1 makes an ARP entry associating the IP address 10.1.1.10 with host2's MAC address.

- Host1 delivers data to host2.

- Host3 responds to the ARP request with its own MAC address.

- Host1 removes the ARP entry for host2 and replaces it by associating the IP address 10.1.1.10 with host3's MAC address.

- Host1 finds it has more data to send to 10.1.1.10.

- Host1 delivers host2's data to host3 per the ARP table entry.

Host2 will eventually time-out the data request as it is no longer able to communicate with host1. When the host3 entry ages out of the ARP cache, the whole process starts over.

NOTE   Information is only cached for a limited period of time. When this time expires and the entry is removed, it is referred to as being aged out.

It's possible that the second time host1 issues an ARP request that host3 will reply first. This will restore connectivity to host2 but interrupt communications with host3. This ping-pong effect will continue until one of the systems powers down or changes its IP address.

So now that we know why duplicate IP addresses are a bad thing, all we need to know is how to identify the offending systems. If you are using either a

Macintosh or Windows 95/98, the machine will send an ARP request during startup to ensure that the address it wishes to use is free. If it's not, the console displays a warning message. While this process will identify one of the two systems, we still have to find the other.

Our best bet is to power down the system we know about and go to a system that does not have an address conflict. From this system, we ping the IP address in question and display the associated MAC address by typing

```
ping ADDR
arp -a ADDR
```

where *ADDR* is the IP address that is in question. You must be on the same logical subnet as the IP address in order for this to work.

We now know the MAC address as well as the illegal IP address the system in question is using. Where we go from here depends on what kind of network environment we are using.

- NetWare—generate a user list and match the MAC address to a logon name

- NT—run NBTSTAT to associate the IP address with a machine name and the name of the local user

- Unix—run who to associate a logon name with the IP address

All of these options assume that the user on the system is logged on to one or more network resources. If they are not accessing network resources, it may be difficult at best to determine who they are. While we could check the Ethernet vendor address to see who made the NIC card for the system, this is not as useful when tracking down a workstation because organizations tend to standardize on only a few network card vendors.

If we have a network monitor or analyzer, we could set the device to capture all traffic exchanged with the system's MAC address. This would let us know exactly what network resources the user is using, and help to simplify the process of tracking them down.

We could also view the decoded data field in each frame. This may yield even more clues as to who this mystery user may be. For example, if while viewing the data we notice that the user in question is accessing the sales database, we can assume that the user works in sales.

Once we have identified the offending system, we can flog the user and assign a legitimate IP address.

Undeliverable Mail

As mail interfaces become more user-friendly, they tend to hide much of the information that can be used for debugging purposes. Most modern mail clients remove the mail header before the message is delivered to the client's mailbox. This "cleans up" the message for users so that their messages only contain pertinent information.

Error messages have also become more generic. When a user receives a bounced mail message that simply states, "Message could not be delivered," what exactly does that mean? There are a number of reasons why a message delivery may fail:

- The post-office-to-SMTP-gateway process does not pick up the message.

- The SMTP gateway is unable to resolve the domain name portion of the destination e-mail address.

- The SMTP gateway is unable to find a mail system for the destination domain.

- The SMTP gateway can find a mail system but cannot find a route to get there, or the connection is down.

- The SMTP gateway connects to the remote mail system but times out due to lack of response.

- The SMTP gateway connects to the remote mail system but the username portion of the e-mail address is rejected.

Each of these issues has a different failure mode and a different method of resolving the problem. As we walk through the process of determining the cause of failure, we will assume that the bounced message contained no usable errors.

Our first step should be to check the error log generated by the SMTP gateway. The gateway should generate a running log of all messages sent and received. It should also indicate when a message delivery failed and why this failure occurred.

But what happens when our error logs do not indicate where the problem lies? When this is the case, we need to emulate a mail system and see what happens during the process of trying to deliver the mail message.

In order to manually test delivery, we will need to perform the following steps:

1. Test local connectivity.

2. Verify that the SMTP mail gateway is working.

3. Find the name server for the remote domain.

4. Find the mail system for the remote domain.

5. Test connectivity to the remote mail system.

6. Verify the recipient's e-mail address.

Our first step is to ensure that we still have a valid connection to the Internet. To do this we can simply try to ping a known host outside of our network. A company's Web server is usually a good bet.

Once we know we still have an Internet connection, we should ensure that the SMTP gateway is still working. We can do this by sending an e-mail to ourselves. If the gateway is capable of processing the address and returning it correctly, it should also be able to perform a delivery outside of the domain.

This assumes that we are dealing with an existing gateway that has been working up until now. If this system has just been configured, this test is not valid because the IP parameters may be set up incorrectly. If this is a new installation, or if we suspect the IP setup, we will need to deliver an e-mail message outside of the domain to verify correct operation of the mail gateway.

Now that we are sure that the mail gateway is working correctly, we can begin the process of emulating mail delivery to see where the problem lies.

Our next step is to find the name server for the remote domain. This can be done by using the whois command or through a search in nslookup. Because the nslookup process is a closer match to the process the mail gateway uses, we will use that method.

So we fire up nslookup and receive our greater-than prompt. The output looks something like the following:

```
Server:   clover.sover.net
Address:  204.71.16.10
>
```

where `clover.sover.net` would be replaced with the name of your local DNS server. We next configure `nslookup` to only show us name servers by typing:

```
>set type = ns
```

Next, we will need to get a list of name servers for the remote domain to which our e-mail message is failing. We do this by typing in the name of the domain. This causes `nslookup` to respond with the following output:

```
> foobar.com

Server:   clover.sover.net
Address:  204.71.16.10

Non-authoritative answer:
foobar.com   nameserver = NS1.FOOBAR.COM
foobar.com   nameserver = NS.FOOBAR.COM
foobar.com   nameserver = NS2.FOOBAR.COM

Authoritative answers can be found from:
NS1.FOOBAR.COM       internet address = 10.50.5.10
NS.FOOBAR.COM        internet address = 10.50.5.5
NS2.FOOBAR.COM       internet address = 10.50.5.20

>
```

We receive a non-authoritative answer. As we discussed in the last chapter, this simply means that this is secondhand information received from another DNS server. To ensure that we receive authoritative answers, we must point `nslookup` at one of the listed name servers by typing:

```
> server ns1.foobar.com

Default Server:  ns1.foobar.com
Address:  10.50.5.10
>
```

We will now receive authoritative answers for any queries regarding `foobar.com`. Next, we need to configure `nslookup` to look only for mail servers. We do this by typing:

```
> set type = mx
```

This tells `nslookup` to only return mail servers in response to all of our queries. Now we simply enter the domain name that we are trying to send mail to, in order to find out which systems it uses to send and receive mail.

```
> foobar.com

Server:  ns1.foobar.com
Address:  10.50.5.10

foobar.com    preference = 10, mail exchanger = ns2.foobar.com
foobar.com    preference = 0, mail exchanger = mail.foobar.com
foobar.com    nameserver = ns1.foobar.com
foobar.com    nameserver = ns2.foobar.com
foobar.com    nameserver = ns.foobar.com
ns2.foobar.com        internet address = 10.50.5.20
mail.foobar.com       internet address = 10.50.5.30
ns1.foobar.com        internet address = 10.50.5.10
ns.foobar.com         internet address = 10.50.5.5
>
```

The mail system with the lowest preference is the preferred mail server. This means that all mail should be delivered to `mail.foobar.com`. If that system is unavailable, mail should be sent to `ns2.foobar.com`. It's a common practice to use one of the name servers as a backup mail system.

We can now record the address information and exit the `nslookup` utility. Next, we need to determine if the mail system is online and accepting e-mail messages. We do this by typing:

```
telnet mail.foobar.com 25
```

This allows us to use Telnet to attempt to deliver a mail message to the remote system. If all goes well, we should see a message similar to the following:

```
$ telnet mail.foobar.com 25
Trying 10.50.5.30...
Connected to mail.foobar.com.
Escape character is '^]'.
220 mail.foobar.com ESMTP Sendmail 8.8.4/8.8.4; Wed, 2 Jul 1997
10:34:02 -0400
```

The first thing to note is the IP address Telnet is *trying*. This should match the IP address we found through `nslookup`. If it does not, the remote mail system may have been moved to a new IP address and our current DNS information is out of date. This can occur when the remote host has a long time to live (TTL) set. When the IP address changes, DNS servers on the Internet will not attempt to reread the IP address (thus finding the new one) until the TTL has expired.

If this is the case, we can force our DNS server to discover the correct IP address by stopping and restarting the DNS service.

If we receive a "connection refused" message instead of the rest of the listed output, we were unable to access mail services on the remote machine. There are four possible causes for not being able to connect to the mail system:

- The Internet connection for the remote domain is down.

- There is a firewall blocking the service.

- The remote mail system is down.

- Mail services are not running on the remote system.

To see what the root cause may be, we could try pinging the remote mail system. If this is successful, we know the remote mail system is online, it is just not accepting any mail messages. If the ping fails, any one of the first three failure modes could be the problem. We could then try pinging other hosts in the domain. If this is successful, we know the remote mail system is down. If we cannot ping any other hosts in the domain, we are left with the possibility that the connection may be down or we have an improperly configured firewall. In either case, there is no way to reach the remote mail system at this time.

Let's assume that we were able to connect to the remote mail system and received the previously listed output. Our next step would be to verify the e-mail address that we were attempting to send the message to. We do this by using the vrfy command. When we attempt to verify the e-mail address, we should receive the following output:

```
vrfy somebody@foobar.com
250 Mary Somebody <somebody@foobar.com>
```

where somebody@foobar.com is replaced with the e-mail address we are testing. If this e-mail address is known to the mail server, it should reply back with the second line shown above, indicating the user's full address, including proper name.

If the mail server reports back

```
vrfy somebody@foobar.com
550 somebody@foobar.com... User unknown
```

we know that the e-mail address is incorrect. This could be due to a spelling error or the user may no longer have a mail account on the system. We can verify which problem is the case by sending mail to `postmaster@foobar.com`. This is a generic mail account that *should* be (operative word being "should") set up on every mail system for reporting e-mail problems. We could send the postmaster an e-mail indicating the e-mail address we are trying to send mail to. The post-master should know if this is an address that was recently removed, or if the spelling is incorrect.

Some mail administrators disable the `vrfy` command because a would-be attacker may try to use it to discover logon names. Some mail systems, like Microsoft Exchange, do not even support this command. If the mail system comes back with

```
vrfy somebody@foobar.com
500 Command unrecognized
```

then `vrfy` has been disabled or is not supported. You are left with contacting the postmaster on the remote mail system to verify the address.

As you can see, there are many places in the e-mail delivery process where the transfer can fail. The trick to resolving e-mail problems is to isolate the failure mode and take appropriate steps to fix it. This is not always possible. For example, if the failure was due to the destination domain's Internet connection being down, there is not a whole lot you can do to help it get back online. At least now you can tell the user who was attempting to send the e-mail message exactly why it did not go through.

Connectivity Problems after a Server Upgrade

In our next case, we upgrade a NetWare file server from version 3.12 to 4.11 and immediately experience a connectivity problem with one of our network devices. Consider the network drawing shown in Figure 32.2. We have two routed segments separated by a network file server. On one of our networks is a Shiva LanRover E, a device which provides dial-in and dial-out connectivity for our network.

FIGURE 32.2:

Our simple two segment network

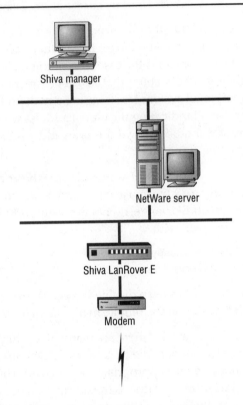

Our network has been functioning just fine, but we have decided to upgrade the NetWare 3.12 server to version 4.11 in order to take advantage of some of the features the NOS can provide. We upgrade the server and verify that workstations located on both segments can log on to the file server and see their files.

All is going well until we power up the LanRover and attempt to connect to it with the management software in order to verify its operation. The management software finds the LanRover, but after a brief period of time the LanRover disappears from the selection screen of the management utility. If we power cycle the device again, it will show up in the management window for about a minute and then disappear.

Figure 32.3 shows a trace of what is occurring. We have set our capture utility to monitor all inbound and outbound communications with the LanRover, and it shows what information is being exchanged just prior to the LanRover dropping offline.

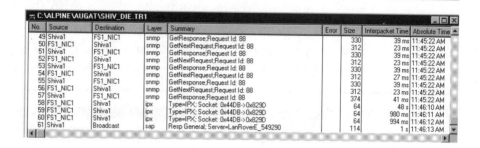

We can see that the LanRover (identified as Shiva1) has been communicating with its management station on the other network, through the NetWare file server (identified as FS1_NIC1). The management station is performing a series of SNMP `get next` commands in order to retrieve the LanRover's configuration information. In this particular case, it is SNMP over IPX (identified in the frame decode, which is not shown). In frame 57 the connection switches over to pure IPX. The management station makes three attempts at an IPX connection, after which the LanRover broadcasts a SAP. It is at this point that the connection dies and no further communication is possible. So what happened to our connection?

First, let's collect our clues and see what we know for sure:

- Workstations connect to the server and never drop offline.

- The management station can initially connect to the LanRover.

- At some point, the connection between the LanRover and the management station falls apart.

- The condition is resolved when the LanRover gets rebooted.

- This condition is repeatable as the connection always drops after a short amount of time.

- This configuration worked when the server was NetWare 3.12.

We can rule out a cabling problem because the LanRover and the management station can actually connect to each other. Also, if it was a cabling problem, rebooting the LanRover would have no effect.

To analyze this complex situation, we need to consider the changes that were made to the way a server communicates, from NetWare 3.12 to NetWare 4.11. One of the biggest was the introduction of the NLSP routing protocol, which is enabled by default with backwards compatibility to RIP/SAP.

Examine Figure 32.4. This is a RIP/SAP server advertising the networks and services that are known to it. Notice that it is sending a RIP and a SAP once per minute, which is being delivered to the broadcast address.

FIGURE 32.4:

A NetWare server using RIP/SAP

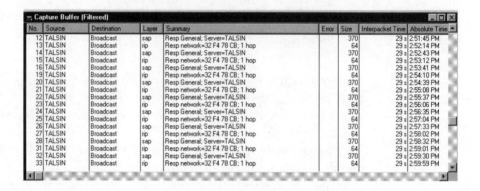

No.	Source	Destination	Layer	Summary	Error	Size	Interpacket Time	Absolute Time
12	TALSIN	Broadcast	sap	Resp General; Server=TALSIN		370	29 s	2:51:45 PM
13	TALSIN	Broadcast	rip	Resp network=32 F4 78 CB; 1 hop		64	29 s	2:52:14 PM
14	TALSIN	Broadcast	sap	Resp General; Server=TALSIN		370	29 s	2:52:43 PM
15	TALSIN	Broadcast	rip	Resp network=32 F4 78 CB; 1 hop		64	29 s	2:53:12 PM
16	TALSIN	Broadcast	sap	Resp General; Server=TALSIN		370	29 s	2:53:41 PM
19	TALSIN	Broadcast	rip	Resp network=32 F4 78 CB; 1 hop		64	29 s	2:54:10 PM
20	TALSIN	Broadcast	sap	Resp General; Server=TALSIN		370	29 s	2:54:39 PM
21	TALSIN	Broadcast	rip	Resp network=32 F4 78 CB; 1 hop		64	29 s	2:55:08 PM
22	TALSIN	Broadcast	sap	Resp General; Server=TALSIN		370	29 s	2:55:37 PM
23	TALSIN	Broadcast	rip	Resp network=32 F4 78 CB; 1 hop		64	29 s	2:56:06 PM
24	TALSIN	Broadcast	sap	Resp General; Server=TALSIN		370	29 s	2:56:35 PM
25	TALSIN	Broadcast	rip	Resp network=32 F4 78 CB; 1 hop		64	29 s	2:57:04 PM
26	TALSIN	Broadcast	sap	Resp General; Server=TALSIN		370	29 s	2:57:33 PM
27	TALSIN	Broadcast	rip	Resp network=32 F4 78 CB; 1 hop		64	29 s	2:58:02 PM
28	TALSIN	Broadcast	sap	Resp General; Server=TALSIN		370	29 s	2:58:32 PM
31	TALSIN	Broadcast	rip	Resp network=32 F4 78 CB; 1 hop		64	29 s	2:59:01 PM
32	TALSIN	Broadcast	sap	Resp General; Server=TALSIN		370	29 s	2:59:30 PM
33	TALSIN	Broadcast	rip	Resp network=32 F4 78 CB; 1 hop		64	29 s	2:59:59 PM

Capture Buffer (Filtered)

Now examine Figure 32.5. This is an NLSP server looking for other NLSP devices. Notice that we are no longer blindly advertising route and service information to anyone who happens to be around. We are specifically looking for other NLSP devices with whom to exchange information.

FIGURE 32.5:

A NetWare server using NLSP

Capture Buffer

No.	Source	Destination	Layer	Summary	Error	Size	Interpacket Time	Absolute Time
217	TALSIN	Broadcast	nlsp	LAN Level 1 NLSP Hello Packet		92	3 s	2:19:09 PM
218	TALSIN	Broadcast	nlsp	LAN Level 1 NLSP Hello Packet		92	8 s	2:19:17 PM
219	TALSIN	Broadcast	nlsp	LAN Level 1 NLSP Hello Packet		92	8 s	2:19:25 PM
220	TALSIN	Broadcast	nlsp	Level 1 Complete Sequence Numbers Packet		116	7 s	2:19:32 PM
221	TALSIN	Broadcast	nlsp	LAN Level 1 NLSP Hello Packet		92	1 s	2:19:33 PM
222	TALSIN	Broadcast	nlsp	LAN Level 1 NLSP Hello Packet		92	8 s	2:19:41 PM
223	TALSIN	Broadcast	nlsp	LAN Level 1 NLSP Hello Packet		92	8 s	2:19:49 PM
224	TALSIN	Broadcast	nlsp	LAN Level 1 NLSP Hello Packet		92	8 s	2:19:57 PM
225	TALSIN	Broadcast	nlsp	Level 1 Complete Sequence Numbers Packet		116	692 ms	2:19:57 PM
226	TALSIN	Broadcast	nlsp	LAN Level 1 NLSP Hello Packet		92	7 s	2:20:05 PM
227	TALSIN	Broadcast	nlsp	LAN Level 1 NLSP Hello Packet		92	8 s	2:20:13 PM
228	TALSIN	Broadcast	nlsp	LAN Level 1 NLSP Hello Packet		92	8 s	2:20:21 PM
229	TALSIN	Broadcast	nlsp	Level 1 Complete Sequence Numbers Packet		116	2 s	2:20:23 PM
230	TALSIN	Broadcast	nlsp	LAN Level 1 NLSP Hello Packet		92	6 s	2:20:29 PM
231	TALSIN	Broadcast	nlsp	LAN Level 1 NLSP Hello Packet		92	8 s	2:20:37 PM
232	TALSIN	Broadcast	nlsp	LAN Level 1 NLSP Hello Packet		92	8 s	2:20:45 PM
233	TALSIN	Broadcast	nlsp	Level 1 Complete Sequence Numbers Packet		116	5 s	2:20:49 PM
234	TALSIN	Broadcast	nlsp	LAN Level 1 NLSP Hello Packet		92	3 s	2:20:52 PM
235	TALSIN	Broadcast	nlsp	LAN Level 1 NLSP Hello Packet		92	8 s	2:21:00 PM
236	TALSIN	Broadcast	nlsp	LAN Level 1 NLSP Hello Packet		92	8 s	2:21:08 PM
237	TALSIN	Broadcast	nlsp	Level 1 Complete Sequence Numbers Packet		116	7 s	2:21:15 PM
238	TALSIN	Broadcast	nlsp	LAN Level 1 NLSP Hello Packet		92	2 s	2:21:17 PM

So what happens when you combine RIP/SAP and NLSP devices on the same network? Examine Figure 32.6. Frame number 410 is Toby, sending out a SAP broadcast. In return, Talsin sends out a SAP as well. In frames 412–415 Talsin has returned to sending out NLSP Hello packets.

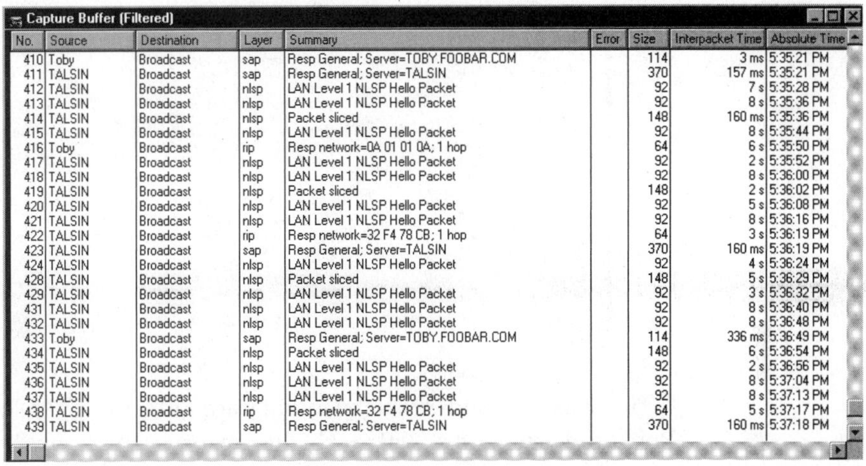

FIGURE 32.6:

A mixed RIP/SAP, NLSP network

No.	Source	Destination	Layer	Summary	Error	Size	Interpacket Time	Absolute Time
410	Toby	Broadcast	sap	Resp General; Server=TOBY.FOOBAR.COM		114	3 ms	5:35:21 PM
411	TALSIN	Broadcast	sap	Resp General; Server=TALSIN		370	157 ms	5:35:21 PM
412	TALSIN	Broadcast	nlsp	LAN Level 1 NLSP Hello Packet		92	7 s	5:35:28 PM
413	TALSIN	Broadcast	nlsp	LAN Level 1 NLSP Hello Packet		92	8 s	5:35:36 PM
414	TALSIN	Broadcast	nlsp	Packet sliced		148	160 ms	5:35:36 PM
415	TALSIN	Broadcast	nlsp	LAN Level 1 NLSP Hello Packet		92	8 s	5:35:44 PM
416	Toby	Broadcast	rip	Resp network=0A 01 01 0A; 1 hop		64	6 s	5:35:50 PM
417	TALSIN	Broadcast	nlsp	LAN Level 1 NLSP Hello Packet		92	2 s	5:35:52 PM
418	TALSIN	Broadcast	nlsp	LAN Level 1 NLSP Hello Packet		92	8 s	5:36:00 PM
419	TALSIN	Broadcast	nlsp	Packet sliced		148	2 s	5:36:02 PM
420	TALSIN	Broadcast	nlsp	LAN Level 1 NLSP Hello Packet		92	5 s	5:36:08 PM
421	TALSIN	Broadcast	nlsp	LAN Level 1 NLSP Hello Packet		92	8 s	5:36:16 PM
422	TALSIN	Broadcast	rip	Resp network=32 F4 78 CB; 1 hop		64	3 s	5:36:19 PM
423	TALSIN	Broadcast	sap	Resp General; Server=TALSIN		370	160 ms	5:36:19 PM
424	TALSIN	Broadcast	nlsp	LAN Level 1 NLSP Hello Packet		92	4 s	5:36:24 PM
428	TALSIN	Broadcast	nlsp	Packet sliced		148	5 s	5:36:29 PM
429	TALSIN	Broadcast	nlsp	LAN Level 1 NLSP Hello Packet		92	3 s	5:36:32 PM
431	TALSIN	Broadcast	nlsp	LAN Level 1 NLSP Hello Packet		92	8 s	5:36:40 PM
432	TALSIN	Broadcast	nlsp	LAN Level 1 NLSP Hello Packet		92	8 s	5:36:48 PM
433	Toby	Broadcast	sap	Resp General; Server=TOBY.FOOBAR.COM		114	336 ms	5:36:49 PM
434	TALSIN	Broadcast	nlsp	Packet sliced		148	6 s	5:36:54 PM
435	TALSIN	Broadcast	nlsp	LAN Level 1 NLSP Hello Packet		92	2 s	5:36:56 PM
436	TALSIN	Broadcast	nlsp	LAN Level 1 NLSP Hello Packet		92	8 s	5:37:04 PM
437	TALSIN	Broadcast	nlsp	LAN Level 1 NLSP Hello Packet		92	8 s	5:37:13 PM
438	TALSIN	Broadcast	rip	Resp network=32 F4 78 CB; 1 hop		64	5 s	5:37:17 PM
439	TALSIN	Broadcast	sap	Resp General; Server=TALSIN		370	160 ms	5:37:18 PM

In frame 416, Toby then sends out a RIP broadcast. At this point, Talsin realizes that there is a RIP/SAP device on the network and that it must switch into RIP/SAP compatibility mode to ensure that information can be exchanged with this system. Once the server sees the RIP packet, it knows that backwards compatibility is required.

So the next time Talsin sends our route and service broadcasts (417–423), it includes a RIP and a SAP broadcast as well. This will continue as long as Talsin thinks there is a device on the network that requires this information.

So what went wrong with our LanRover? If NetWare 4.11 is backwards-compatible, why is it dropping offline? To find out why, examine Figure 32.7.

Our Shiva device (this one is a NetModem E) broadcasts a SAP looking for all local service information. Talsin then responds directly to the NetModem with a unicast reply. Talsin then goes on to transmit NLSP Hello packets, as it did before.

Now, look at frames 42 and 53. Our Shiva device sends out a SAP, but Talsin never replies. There is something else missing from this trace. Our NetModem never sends out a RIP broadcast. It will SAP until the cows come home, but it does not broadcast any RIP information.

FIGURE 32.7:

Shiva modem pool with a NetWare 4.11 server

No.	Source	Destination	Layer	Summary	Error	Size	Interpacket Time	Absolute Time
31	Shiva1	Broadcast	sap	Query General All		64	5 s	5:15:33 PM
32	TALSIN	Shiva1	sap	Resp General; Server=TALSIN		370	780 μs	5:15:33 PM
33	TALSIN	Broadcast	nlsp	LAN Level 1 NLSP Hello Packet		92	3 s	5:15:37 PM
34	TALSIN	Broadcast	nlsp	LAN Level 1 NLSP Hello Packet		92	8 s	5:15:45 PM
35	TALSIN	Broadcast	nlsp	Level 1 Complete Sequence Numbers Packet		116	6 s	5:15:51 PM
36	TALSIN	Broadcast	nlsp	LAN Level 1 NLSP Hello Packet		92	2 s	5:15:53 PM
37	TALSIN	Broadcast	nlsp	LAN Level 1 NLSP Hello Packet		92	8 s	5:16:01 PM
38	TALSIN	Broadcast	nlsp	LAN Level 1 NLSP Hello Packet		92	8 s	5:16:09 PM
39	TALSIN	Broadcast	nlsp	Level 1 Complete Sequence Numbers Packet		116	8 s	5:16:17 PM
40	TALSIN	Broadcast	nlsp	LAN Level 1 NLSP Hello Packet		92	692 ms	5:16:17 PM
41	TALSIN	Broadcast	nlsp	LAN Level 1 NLSP Hello Packet		92	8 s	5:16:26 PM
42	Shiva1	Broadcast	sap	Resp General; Server=NM230A47		114	3 s	5:16:29 PM
43	TALSIN	Broadcast	nlsp	Level 1 Link State Packet		100	964 ms	5:16:30 PM
44	TALSIN	Broadcast	nlsp	LAN Level 1 NLSP Hello Packet		92	4 s	5:16:34 PM
45	TALSIN	Broadcast	nlsp	LAN Level 1 NLSP Hello Packet		92	8 s	5:16:42 PM
46	TALSIN	Broadcast	nlsp	Level 1 Complete Sequence Numbers Packet		132	852 ms	5:16:42 PM
47	TALSIN	Broadcast	nlsp	LAN Level 1 NLSP Hello Packet		92	7 s	5:16:50 PM
48	TALSIN	Broadcast	nlsp	LAN Level 1 NLSP Hello Packet		92	8 s	5:16:58 PM
49	TALSIN	Broadcast	nlsp	LAN Level 1 NLSP Hello Packet		92	8 s	5:17:06 PM
50	TALSIN	Broadcast	nlsp	Level 1 Complete Sequence Numbers Packet		132	2 s	5:17:08 PM
51	TALSIN	Broadcast	nlsp	LAN Level 1 NLSP Hello Packet		92	6 s	5:17:14 PM
52	TALSIN	Broadcast	nlsp	LAN Level 1 NLSP Hello Packet		92	8 s	5:17:22 PM
53	Shiva1	Broadcast	sap	Resp General; Server=NM230A47		114	5 s	5:17:27 PM
54	TALSIN	Broadcast	nlsp	LAN Level 1 NLSP Hello Packet		92	2 s	5:17:30 PM
55	TALSIN	Broadcast	nlsp	Level 1 Complete Sequence Numbers Packet		132	4 s	5:17:34 PM
56	TALSIN	Broadcast	nlsp	LAN Level 1 NLSP Hello Packet		92	4 s	5:17:38 PM
57	TALSIN	Broadcast	nlsp	LAN Level 1 NLSP Hello Packet		92	8 s	5:17:46 PM
58	TALSIN	Broadcast	nlsp	LAN Level 1 NLSP Hello Packet		92	8 s	5:17:54 PM

This was also evident on the initial trace in Figure 32.3. The last thing our Lan-Rover did was send a SAP to which it never received a reply.

As we mentioned in previous chapters, NetWare servers use an internal IPX network number for internal communications. This means that by default, any NetWare server will send both RIP and SAP information. The Shiva devices are not real NetWare servers, and do not have an internal IPX address to broadcast. Because these devices do not RIP, the NetWare server assumes that it does not need to switch to RIP/SAP compatibility mode.

But if the server is not switching to RIP/SAP compatibility mode, how can we communicate at all? The answer lies in the aging time that is used by RIP and NLSP.

If we refer back to Figure 32.7, Talsin responded to the NetModem's initial SAP request. When it did this, the NetModem realized that there was a NetWare server on the wire and created a server and router entry for it. This would allow the device to carry on communications with the server. As we also noted from that figure, the NetModem started sending out SAP broadcasts, to which Talsin never replied. Because the NetModem never received a SAP from Talsin, it assumed that the server must have died a fiery death and removed it from its server and router tables.

So how does this apply to our initial problem? When Shiva1 was first powered up, it would send a SAP query, receive a reply, and create an entry for FS1. If we launch the Shiva Manager just after this occurs, we will be able to connect to the device and exchange information.

Once Shiva1 started sending SAP broadcasts and did not receive a reply from FS1, it assumed that the server was down and that the remote network (where the Shiva Manager was located) was no longer reachable. This interrupted the SNMP transfer in our trace, as Shiva1 would not know how to reach the Shiva Manager to reply to queries. This caused the Shiva Manager to send a few final IPX queries in order to reestablish the connection. Because the device was unable to reply, the manager eventually gave up trying.

We have three possible ways of rectifying this problem:

- Upgrade the Shiva device to support an NLSP protocol.

- Have the Shiva device send RIPs as well as SAPs.

- Switch the NetWare server into RIP/SAP only mode.

Our first option is out of the question. While the vendor may eventually be able to have their devices support NLSP, it is doubtful they can do this by throwing together a patch for you to download. Changing the way a device handles routing information cannot be done as a quick fix.

Our second option has possibilities. As mentioned, the LanRover allows users to dial in and dial out of the network. When a user dials in to the network, they must appear to have a valid network and MAC address in order to communicate.

There are two ways the device could handle the inbound connection. The first would be to have the dial-in connection appear to be directly attached to the network by spoofing a MAC address. When traffic is sent to this spoofed address, the LanRover could act as a proxy and forward the information to the dialed-in user. This would make the user appear to be attached to the existing network.

If the LanRover has the ability to create a virtual IPX network, it can make the user appear to be on this phony network instead of the local network. The Lan-Rover could then act as a router between these two segments, forwarding data to the user as required.

It is this option we are most interested in, because if the device sets up a virtual IPX network, it must advertise it to the rest of the network by sending RIP broadcasts. This would trigger RIP/SAP compatibility mode on our server, which would keep the device from dropping offline.

In order to determine if this latter configuration is possible, we would need to review the device's documentation.

Our third option is probably the easiest to implement. Simply run the INETCFG utility and modify the IPX protocol to use RIP/SAP only. The only drawback with this option is that we would be unable to perform load-balancing on the server. NLSP allows us to install two or more NICs per logical network segment in the server. The benefit of having two or more NICs per segment is that the server will use both cards to transmit data. This doubles the bandwidth potential while the server is transmitting. If we use RIP as our routing protocol, however, we cannot use this feature.

Excessive Network Collisions

Our next case involves a small network with slow connectivity. A diagram of this network is shown in Figure 32.8.

FIGURE 32.8:

A network with slow connectivity

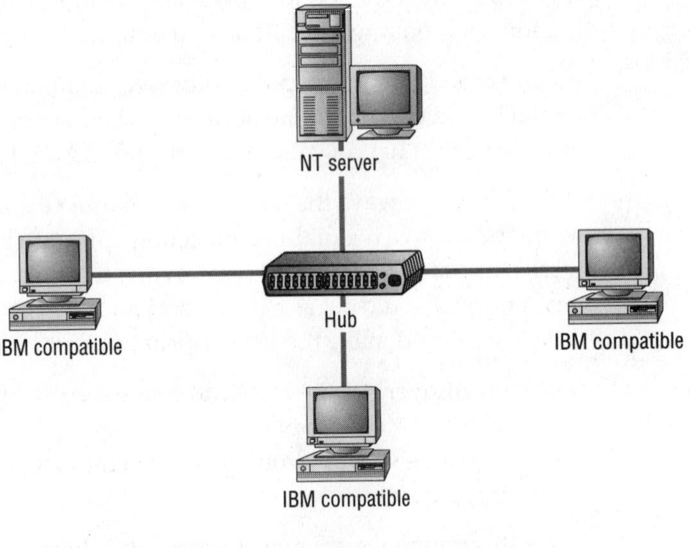

As you can see, our network configuration is not very large. It consists of a single NT server and hub. There are only seven or eight users on the network and all equipment is one year old or less. The topology is 10Mb Ethernet. All cabling is CAT5 twisted-pair and was certified as such after installation.

The problem is that users are experiencing very slow network response. This occurs when communicating with the server, and occasionally when communicating on a peer to peer basis with other Windows 95 workstations. The problem is sporadic; sometimes network response is fine, while at other times it crawls.

Diagnosing the Problem

Our first step should be to check the activity lights on the hub. This is the quickest way to check if our network is seeing an excessive amount of traffic. If the hub has a separate transmit light for each port, we may even be able to isolate the system generating all the traffic.

If we notice a system transmitting frequently, we can trace the drop back to the system to determine whether the user is transferring a lot of information, or if this failure is due to a jabbering network card.

A jabbering network card is a NIC that is stuck in a transmit mode. This will be evident because the transmit light will remain on constantly, indicating that the NIC is always transmitting. This problem can also be caught with a network monitor or analyzer, because the frames the jabbering NIC transmits will produce size errors. If our hub only has a single transmit light, we will need to use a network monitor or analyzer to isolate the offending system.

Let's assume this is not the case. The transmit lights are relatively quiet, but the collision light is flashing just as quickly. We now have a very interesting problem; we are seeing a large number of collisions on our network but there is a relatively small amount of traffic. How can this be?

Working through the Problem Logically

Let's review what we know about collisions. A collision occurs when two or more NICs try to transmit data at the same time. When this happens, the transmissions collide with each other on the wire, making each transmission unusable. If a system detects that it was involved in a collision, it backs off and stops transmitting for a moment.

So in theory, a workstation should never signal a collision unless it has first attempted to transmit data. We already noticed that the collision light is flashing just as often as the transmit lights. This means that one or more of our stations appears to be signaling collisions every time it tries to transmit data. The question is, how can this occur? What would cause a NIC to send a collision signal for every attempt at sending data?

The cabling we are using is twisted-pair. You may remember from our discussion on 10Mb Ethernet that it uses one pair of twisted-pair wires to send data and the other to receive data. This creates two separate circuits for our NIC cards to exchange information. A transmission is considered a collision when the data being transmitted does not match the data being received.

You may also remember that in a full-duplexed environment, a system is told that it is okay to transmit and receive different data at the same time. When only two systems exist on a collision domain, there is no chance of a collision, since each system will be using a different wire pair to transmit (the pair the opposite system uses to receive data). The result is that both systems can transmit simultaneously without fear of causing a collision.

If one of our systems has been incorrectly configured to operate in full-duplex mode, it could be attempting to transmit data even when it detects traffic on the receive pair. While this is fine when we only have two systems and both are configured to operate in full-duplex mode, this can be detrimental to a shared hub environment. Our full-duplex system will continually step on the transmission of other stations, because it doesn't think that it needs to listen prior to transmitting. The result is multiple collisions, and a very high frame error rate. The more data the offending system transmits, the slower our network response becomes, because each of the other NICs detect that multiple collisions are taking place.

So it is possible that we have a NIC that is configured to use full-duplex mode. This would explain why the collision light is flashing just as often as the transmit light. The problem with this theory is that we may expect this condition to exist all the time. As mentioned in the problem description, the problem is sporadic—the offending system may access the network very infrequently, or its NIC may be configured to auto-detect when it can use full-duplex mode.

NOTE
When the NIC is initialized, it will attempt to negotiate a full-duplex connection. If only one other system is detected, and both are capable of full-duplex operation, the operational mode is switched from half-duplex to full-duplex communications.

Because this is a small environment, there is the potential that there may only be two systems active at the same time. If this is the case, what happens then? Unfortunately, many of the earlier NIC cards that were capable of negotiating a full-duplex connection were not able to detect when a hub was between them and the other NIC. The result was that one or both of the two systems would successfully negotiate a full-duplex connection. As other systems would power up, the misconfigured system(s) would interfere with the communications of the other systems.

This problem would be viewed as intermittent, because all that would be required to fix the situation would be to power cycle the systems that negotiated full-duplex communications. This problem would cause network performance to be perceived as sometimes being normal, while other times being slow, even under the same traffic load.

> **NOTE**   To resolve this issue, we need to use the manufacturer's configuration utility that shipped with the NIC cards. By running the utility, you can hard set each NIC to communicate in half-duplex mode only. This will ensure that full-duplex mode is never negotiated.

Summary

One interesting detail to note with the last case is that the main tools we used to resolve this problem were brain power and deduction. The only other aids we used to diagnose the problem were a few blinking lights on the hub. Even a network monitor such as LanAlyzer would have been useless, because it cannot monitor collisions. In short, even our most expensive tool would have been of little help in solving this problem.

The point here is that there is no replacement for understanding how all the pieces of a network fit together in order to communicate. There is no magic or voodoo here, only an intricate web of hardware and software that allows us to send information from point A to point B. A network administrator in a multiprotocol environment must be able to don the detective's cap and analyze this web in order to find the root cause of any given problem.

In the next chapter, we'll focus specifically on troubleshooting network servers themselves.

CHAPTER

THIRTY-THREE

Troubleshooting Servers

■ NT troubleshooting snapshot

■ NetWare troubleshooting snapshot

■ Server fault points

■ Hardware problems

■ Installing NT

■ Installing NetWare

■ Dealing with NetWare Loadable Module (NLM) problems

■ Protecting the server with System Fault Tolerance (SFT)

■ Real-life examples

One of the difficulties of keeping a network operating smoothly is keeping the servers themselves in operation. While network operating systems such as NetWare (IntraNetWare) and Windows NT have made progress in reducing the number of server crashes and in automatically tuning performance, they are both still susceptible to things going wrong.

Perhaps the most crucial problem is when a server simply fails to boot. Typically this happens either when installing a new server operating system and there are still kinks to be worked out between various components in the system, or when a drive goes bad and can't be read at boot time. In this chapter, we'll take a look at various things that can go wrong on a server and discuss how to track down and resolve them.

Snapshot: Troubleshooting Servers

In this section, we look at a "snapshot" you may find handy for diagnosing server problems with Windows NT and NetWare. While we cannot cover every possible scenario that may come up, a number of the more common ones are described here. Just skip down the list of questions until you come to one that describes symptoms similar to what your workstation is experiencing.

NT Server Troubleshooting Snapshot

Is this a new system?

Will the server boot? If yes, skip down to "If the NT system boots successfully…"

Do you get a blue "crash screen" with white text? If so, try rebooting and choosing the VGA Mode NT boot option. This simplifies the bootup process somewhat and may temporarily get around the problem (allowing you to then diagnose and fix the problem once NT is up and running).

Do you get an error message saying the operating system could not be found? If so, and if you have not recently changed drive or partitioning information, then somehow your master boot record (MBR) has gotten replaced. This most often occurs either from a virus or when another OS is installed on the same system, after NT. What you'll need to do in this case is get out your NT emergency repair disk (ERD). This is where you find out the importance of having made, and updated, the ERD whenever you made system changes to hardware or drive partitions. (To make an ERD on a running NT system, simply insert a floppy and run RDISK.EXE.)

You may need to get out your three NT startup floppy disks used to first install NT; if you don't have them or you used a floppyless install, then you may now need to create these floppies using another (working) station—just run WINNT /o to create the set of three floppies. With these floppies, you can boot from the first one (it will prompt for the other two eventually while loading), and you will finally be presented with a list of options, one of which is to "Repair" using your repair disk. If you do not have a repair disk, you may need to actually reinstall NT.

If you choose to reinstall NT to a directory other than the one containing your current (but nonfunctional) NT system, you may actually get a working system that, once the system boot menu appears, allows you to select the original NT boot partition and be back in business.

If you choose to reinstall NT into the same partition and directory occupied by the previous (nonfunctional) NT install, be aware that you will lose all registry settings, including security and user accounts that were configured on that system. Use this only as a last resort, but rest assured this at least will usually succeed in letting you get back at your other files located on the NTFS partitions. (See the following note concerning the NTFSDOS utility.)

Have you lost the administrator password to get onto your system?
Use the procedure described in the preceding question to reinstall NT to the same drive/directory as the current install.

Again, by reinstalling to the same directory, the information on the drive will become available, but the security and all registry information will be reset to default settings. (Be sure to consider the following note about using NTFSDOS first—this might be more useful if you just need to get access to files on a partition.)

If the NT system boots successfully, do you then get errors while NT is loading, or shortly after logging in? Usually by checking the event log, you can determine what device driver or hardware device is not operating properly, and take corrective action. (Such corrective actions might include reinstalling that particular device driver, swapping out the hardware, double-checking IRQ, DMA, and I/O addresses, and removing other hardware one step at a time to isolate the offending piece.)

Note that one error (hardware or software) may cause further errors (possibly hardware errors, but more often software errors) to occur, so look for the first error event for a given boot.

Most often, assuming the system boots properly, the problems you will run into on a server will either be that a network card won't function (due to a misconfiguration or a conflict with another installed network card), or that some other piece of hardware is having a settings conflict. This will usually manifest itself (if it happens at all) immediately or soon after you've upgraded your server by adding new hardware.

To resolve these types of problems, look at the other chapters in this troubleshooting part of the book, and especially at Chapter 30. (Don't skip Chapter 34, which primarily goes into detail about troubleshooting *workstations*, because in many cases workstations have the same hardware problems as servers.)

Does your NT system still have serious driver problems or what appear to be multiple corrupted files? Once more, try using the NT recovery disk first, and if the problem remains, and is serious enough, you may need to reinstall NT, either to a different partition or to existing one, as explained in previous questions.

NOTE   If you're a system or network administrator working with NT workstations or servers, then you will almost certainly be interested in knowing about a very handy program that allows you to read NTFS partitions from DOS. This program is very small (less than 100KB!), so you can place it right on a DOS (or Windows 95/98) boot floppy as a backup way to get to your data. Systems Internals, the company that distributes this (for free!), also sells an expanded version that lets you make changes to the data on an NTFS partition—not all operations are supported, but it provides enough functionality to allow you to edit or remove problem files (driver files, etc.) that may be interfering with the NT boot process. Their URL is `www.sysinternals.com`. Keep this option in mind, in case you ever need to use it.

Is this an existing system?

Do you get an error message saying the operating system could not be found, and you just added or removed a drive (or changed partition information)? If you just changed a drive or the partition information, then the reason NT is not starting up is that the boot loader expected to find NT on a different drive/partition number than it is, and you'll need to temporarily boot into DOS. Use a floppy that has been formatted with system files, and place a copy of ATTRIB.EXE, FDISK.EXE, EDIT.COM, and EDIT.HLP (from a Windows 95 or Windows 98 \Windows\Command directory) onto this floppy. Boot the system using this floppy, then use FDISK to display partition information— use option 4 to view the partitions for the current drive and option 5 to change the current drive. Look for your NTFS partition, and write down both the drive and partition numbers. Next, use ATTRIB to remove the system, hidden, and read-only attributes from the file BOOT.INI, located in the root directory of your system's C: drive (ATTRIB -s -h -r boot.ini).

Then, use EDIT to edit the BOOT.INI file. (First make a backup copy!) If you are certain you know the new disk number and partition number where the existing install of NT is located, change the line looking like multi(0)disk(0)rdisk(2) partition(2)\WINNT= ... so that the correct numbers are in the parentheses following rdisk and partition. If you are not certain where the NT partition is located (if there are multiple NTFS partitions for instance), then duplicate the existing line several times, and make different drive/partition settings for each line. At least this will allow you to repeatedly reboot and choose a different boot menu option, until hopefully you hit on the right combination. As you choose each boot option, remember which one you've selected, in case it works. When you find the correct drive/partition setting, you can go back into the BOOT.INI file and remove the other (incorrect) entries, applying these drive/partition numbers also to the default line (which starts out with default=) as well as to the backup option (the line ending with [VGA MODE]).

Are you running into other problems? With existing servers, you are unlikely to run across configuration errors or interrupt conflicts unless you have just changed something.

The principal problem with existing equipment is failures, either of hardware or software. An exception to this is that some interrupt conflicts may cause intermittent, long-term problems that will only disrupt things occasionally. You may also encounter problems as utilization of the server increases.

The typical solutions here are more memory, more network speed (more or faster NICs), and more hard disk space.

Novell NetWare Troubleshooting Snapshot

Is this a new system?

Will the server boot DOS? If not, review Chapter 30. The section about hardware problems in new servers contains information about the specialized hardware found in servers, such as multiple network adapters and hard disk adapters. For NetWare 2.*x*, it is not strictly necessary that the server boot DOS, but it's a good test—if it won't boot DOS, then NetWare is unlikely to load either. You may need to boot from a floppy, especially with a 2.*x* server.

Will NetWare load? If NetWare won't load, the error messages that appear while it attempts to load are your best clues to the problem. For details on the loading process, see the appropriate section under "NetWare Version-Specific Information," later in this chapter.

If you are running NetWare 2.*x* and using a Novell DCB, you should also check to see if the PROM on the DCB that allows the PC to boot from a SCSI drive has been installed. If the chip has not been installed or has been installed incorrectly, the PC will not recognize the SCSI drive as a bootable disk. Look for bent pins, and make sure that the chip is facing in the correct direction. Be sure to observe static precautions when handling chips and boards! If you aren't familiar with proper static precautions, see Chapter 38 for more details.

Are some devices (such as network cards or disk drives) inaccessible after NetWare loads? This is likely to be a hardware problem. Either a piece of hardware is not functioning correctly or the driver program for that hardware is not functioning correctly. See the "Hardware Problems in New Servers" section, later in this chapter.

Is this an existing system?

Is the server up? If the server is working (the screen is lit, the prompt responds to keyboard input, you can switch to different NLM monitor screens, and so on), then the problem is likely to be in either the workstation or the physical network (the cabling, repeater, MUX, and so on). You can quickly check with MONITOR or FCONSOLE to make sure that all LAN adapters are sending and receiving packets. If they are, then you should next determine how many workstations are experiencing problems. If it is only one, then refer to Chapter 34 for information about troubleshooting workstations. If several or all workstations have similar problems, go to Chapter 35 for information about troubleshooting the physical network. Finally, if the physical network checks out, then you'll need to begin a deeper analysis of the server. This is covered in the "Using SERVMAN, MONITOR, and FCONSOLE" section, later in this chapter.

Can you reboot the server? If the server does not appear to be working—if, for instance, the cursor is frozen, the screen is dark, or it doesn't respond to keyboard input—reboot the server. If the server reboots correctly, then the problem may have been a system error of some sort. Check the error message log to see if there are any unusual error messages. See the "Checking the NetWare System Error Log" section, later in this chapter. You should also make note of any new NLMs or new applications that may have been running on the server; if the problem recurs, they are a good place to start. See the "Troubleshooting NetWare's NLM Problems" section, later in this chapter.

Will the server boot DOS? If the server reboots without error messages but NetWare doesn't load, try just booting DOS. With a NetWare 2.x server, you will need to boot from a floppy. If the server will not boot DOS, then it is likely that the problem is a hardware failure, although it's possible that COMMAND.COM has been corrupted. See the "Hardware Problems in Existing Servers" section, later in this chapter.

Will NetWare load? If NetWare fails to load on a server that was working before, one of two things is likely to have happened: There is a hardware failure, or the NetWare system files may have become corrupted. There are also other possibilities, such as a network "storm" causing so much interference that NetWare cannot function, but the first two possibilities are the most likely.

With NetWare 3.x or 4.x, watch the messages that come up as SERVER.EXE attempts to execute. Usually they will give you the necessary clues to determine what has failed. If you have a backup copy of SERVER.EXE, you can try replacing the one on the boot drive.

With NetWare 2.x, the problem may also be with the DCB or the EPROM on it that allows NetWare to boot from a SCSI drive. If you are using this feature, you should see a message from the BIOS on the DCB that tells you it is making the SCSI drive available as a boot drive. You should keep a backup copy of NET$OS.EXE—it can also become corrupted.

Can you load NetWare but not access some or all server functions?
If the server appears to be functioning but workstations cannot access it, and the physical network appears to be functional, then running MONITOR or FCONSOLE is your first step in isolating the problem. The two most likely areas of failure are the LAN adapters and the disk drive systems. See the "Software Problems in Existing Servers" section, later in this chapter.

Does the server have intermittent problems? Intermittent server failure can be difficult to troubleshoot because there are so many probable causes, including power surges, faulty equipment, or applications running on the server or on a workstation. The important thing to look for to isolate intermittent problems is what changes just before the crash. You will need to investigate by talking to users and researching records and logs. See the "Intermittent Problems with Servers" section, later in this chapter.

A Brief History of NetWare

NetWare began to take over the PC-networking marketplace when it was changed to run on IBM PC compatibles rather than on the original proprietary Motorola 68000-based servers. The first servers were 286-based IBM AT compatibles, and as new chips and capabilities have become available, NetWare has grown to accommodate and make use of the new resources.

As PC-based networks have grown, the demand for more capabilities has also grown to the point that there are now superservers available. These superservers incorporate many of the features of the mainframes they are replacing, such as the ability to replace defective cards or even hard drives without turning the server off, multiple processors, and Error Correction Code (ECC) memory that can self-correct hardware memory errors. Memory and disk storage sizes have expanded by several orders of magnitude, from 640KB of RAM, to 64MB, to 512MB or more, and from 10 or 20MB hard disks, to 2GB (2000MB), to 500GB RAIDs.

As the speed and capabilities of servers have grown, NetWare has also grown in the services it provides. From a relatively simple file- and print-sharing service, NetWare has grown to provide access to other types of computers and computer networks, including Macintoshes, Unix machines, and IBM minicomputers and mainframes. NetWare now supports many network protocols and dozens of network adapters, and can run on hundreds of PC-compatible computers. As its capabilities have grown—or because they have grown—NetWare has become much more complex and difficult to troubleshoot. This chapter will lead you through the troubleshooting process for servers.

In general, the principles of troubleshooting workstations are applicable to servers. In fact, servers are usually more straightforward in basic configuration than workstations because they aren't usually personalized with add-on software. The differences that can make servers a problem to troubleshoot include the high-performance enhancements common to most servers, such as large amounts of RAM, large hard disks, specialized and faster interfaces, and NetWare itself. These differences are covered in this chapter; the basics of getting a workstation to work are covered in Chapter 34.

Fault Points for Servers

Chapter 29 introduced the concept of a chain of fault points as a guide to troubleshooting networks and network components. Within any combination of different types of workstations, network interface cards (NICs), LAN topologies, servers, cabling, software, and so on, there are a limited number of points where problems can occur. Because a conventional flowchart cannot cover anything close to all the possibilities inherent in a network, it makes more sense to look only at those places where things can go wrong.

Figure 33.1 shows the fault chain for troubleshooting NetWare servers. Each item in the chain depends on the previous items for proper operation. For instance, the server will not operate at all without power to the wall socket. A complete fault chain would also include the connection between the wall socket and the power cord, the power cord, and the connection to the power supply. Similarly, the power supply link in the fault chain also includes the connections from the power supply to the motherboard and disk drives. The BIOS controls the motherboard and the beginning of the boot process, and it can cause failures if it isn't recent enough or if its battery power fails. The hardware configuration includes the values stored in the BIOS that tell the PC what type of floppy and hard disk drives it has, as well as the settings on the various cards installed in the server.

FIGURE 33.1:

The fault chain for troubleshooting servers

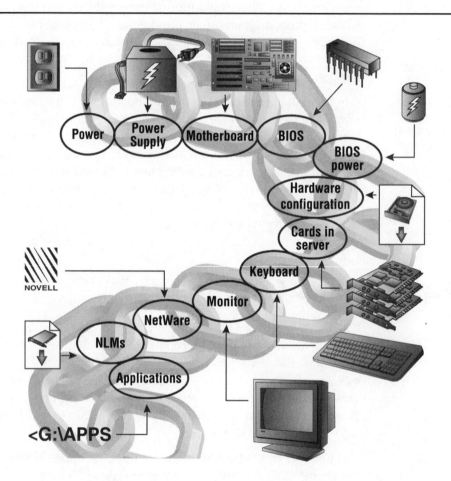

The cards themselves can also fail because of their connection to the motherboard, their connection to whatever device they're attached to, or because of a failure of some component on the card itself. Be aware that many cards now have a BIOS of their own that operates in addition to the BIOS on the motherboard, to add further functionality to the server.

A failure in the keyboard or monitor, or in their cables or connections, may result in a crash, a server that won't boot, or a server that seems dead when it isn't. NetWare, even though it is software, has the same three failure points:

- It can fail in its connection to previous links, such as a driver that accesses the LAN adapter, or in the connection to the next item, which might be a NetWare Loadable Module (NLM) written for a different version of NetWare.

- It can fail internally (crash).

- It can fail because other software fails. NLMs (in NetWare 3.*x* and 4.*x*) or VAPs (Value-Added Processes, in NetWare 2.*x*) add functionality to NetWare, and can fail, usually causing the loss of that functionality, but sometimes causing the whole server to crash. Also, applications running on the server have been known to cause servers to crash if they attempt to access NetWare services with an illegal function call.

NetWare Version-Specific Information

NetWare, as a PC-based network operating system (NOS), has evolved through three major versions. The first PC-based versions of NetWare needed to be generated with all operating system configurations set up in advance. These versions include NetWare 2.0, 2.0a, 2.10, 2.11, 2.12, 2.15, and 2.2, known collectively as 2.*x*. The next evolutionary step for NetWare was 3.0. NetWare 3.0 was the first version of NetWare written for the 80386 processor. It took full advantage of the additional capabilities of the 386 over the 80286, and also allowed reconfiguration of nearly every aspect of the operating system while the server was running. More recently, NetWare 3.10, 3.11, and 3.12 have been released, and all are collectively known as 3.*x*. The third evolutionary step for NetWare is NetWare 4.0. This version adds features specifically designed for large corporate networks. Later versions include 4.01, 4.1, and 4.2, known collectively as 4.*x*.

The biggest difference between the 2.*x*, 3.*x*, and 4.*x* series of NetWare is that the configuration of 2.*x* cannot be changed after the operating system is installed. Versions 3.*x* and 4.*x* can be configured "on the fly," and the configuration can be changed without even bringing the server down, let alone redoing the installation. Version 4.*x* includes additional functionality for large networks, principally the Novell Directory Services (NDS), which allows access to server functions from anywhere on a large internetwork.

NetWare 2.x Operation

If you're new to NetWare, you may wonder why this section is still in here, since 2.x is no longer being shipped by Novell. We have spoken with some poor, benighted souls who are still attempting to run the original NetWare 2.x (from 1987) on the original proprietary Motorola 68000-based servers. We can't be of much help to those people, but there are enough people still using NetWare 2.x (many quite happily!) to make this section worthwhile.

From a floppy, the loading process is this: DOS is loaded from the floppy, then NET$OS.EXE is executed, either manually or from the AUTOEXEC.BAT file. NetWare takes over completely from DOS. When the server boots from a hard disk, it boots from the NetWare cold boot loader, which is written to track 0 of the disk when the hard disk is formatted. The cold boot loader is executed when the server is turned on, and in turn executes NET$OS.EXE, which is the only operating system present—DOS is never loaded. If the server boot drive is a SCSI drive, the PROM (programmable read-only memory) on the DCB (disk coprocessor board), or the BIOS on later model SCSI adapters, is what allows the server to boot from a drive that is not supported by the PC's BIOS.

Commands in the SERVER.CFG and AUTOEXEC.SYS files allow you to automatically run VAPs, set up printers, and execute other commands that add functionality to NetWare in the same manner as an AUTOEXEC.BAT file on a workstation.

Communication buffers are used to hold data packets arriving from workstations. They don't use much memory, so set the number twice as high as you think you'll need. If you set the number too low, it will degrade network performance, because the server will ignore packets it doesn't have room for in the buffers, forcing the workstations to resend the packets. Changing the number requires regenerating the operating system with INSTALL.

NetWare 3.x Operation

The biggest difference between NetWare 2.x and NetWare 3.x is that 3.x can dynamically allocate and deallocate memory as resources or NLMs are loaded or unloaded. Figure 33.2 illustrates the differences in NetWare versions.

FIGURE 33.2:

Differences in NetWare structure from version 2.*x* to versions 3.*x* and 4.*x*

NetWare 2.*x*

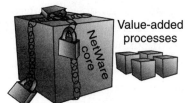

Value-added processes

NetWare 3.*x* and 4.*x*

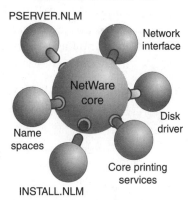

Some resources, such as disk drivers or protocols bound to LAN adapters, are normally loaded permanently, but some may be loaded and unloaded as needed. All remaining free memory is used for file cache buffers, which hold the files last requested, so disk access isn't required if the file is accessed again.

The loading process for NetWare 3.*x* is the same from a floppy or a hard disk. You boot the server with DOS, then run SERVER.EXE. SERVER takes its configuration parameters from the STARTUP.NCF and AUTOEXEC.NCF files. If you will be booting from a DOS partition on the hard disk, it doesn't need to be more than about 2MB, but we recommend at least 4MB. This will give you enough room for a directory where you can place backup copies of SERVER.EXE and STARTUP.NCF, in case those files are corrupted or accidentally changed or removed. It will also give you room to grow if future versions of NetWare require more space for SERVER.EXE or the equivalent.

NetWare 4.*x* Operation

The most complex addition to NetWare 4.*x* is NDS, which uses a distributed NetWare Directory database to manage all services over a large network. A large network is organized logically by country, state, organization, organizational group, organizational role, and so on down the line, rather than according to what hardware is plugged in where. This means that users on a server in one building can access volumes, printers, or other services on servers in other buildings, or even other states or countries, without needing to know the other server's name or going through complex procedures to set things up first.

"Objects" are the basis of NDS; they contain information on various parts of the network, such as drives or printers. Each object contains information about who is allowed to access it, including users and groups, domains or workgroups, titles, and sites. Additional information has been added to many objects' properties to help you further identify items in your network. For example, you can record the telephone numbers and address of each user, or the locations of printers.

User accounts and groups are also set up globally, which means that users can log in to their account on any PC attached to any server and get the same services they would have on their "home" server.

The entire network structure, including servers and their volumes, can be viewed as a tree and browsed by the user. This makes it easier for users in large networks to locate resources without knowing in advance the exact name of the server or device. Files, directory structures, and volumes can be replicated and updated automatically on multiple servers, or at different sites, providing additional fault tolerance and faster access to data (local versus remote).

Other new features include:

- File migration—the ability to automatically move files that aren't being used to other media, such as an optical disk, conserving hard disk space

- Automatic compression and decompression of files

- Suballocation of blocks on a hard disk, which means that on a disk with 4KB blocks, a 512-byte file will no longer use up 4KB

- The beginnings of protected mode operation, that in the future will prevent badly written applications from being able to crash the server

- Additional network management tools to make running the network easier and to allow the remote management of servers and their devices

- SFT Level III—the mirroring of not just disks, but entire servers

These features may make migrating to NetWare 4.x attractive for you, even if you have only one server and a small LAN. The file compression alone could give you another six months to a year before you need to expand your disk drive capacity again. You'll also find that the management tools in NetWare 4.x are much more useful than in previous versions.

The following sections cover troubleshooting new servers and existing servers, including hardware problems and software problems. These will be followed by some further details on special parts of NetWare.

Troubleshooting New Servers

The problems that afflict new servers are conceptually different from those affecting existing servers. You can generally assume that all the hardware in a new server is functional, at least until you have eliminated the other possibilities. The most common problems will be configuration errors, possibly including conflicts between hardware or software settings.

Hardware Problems in New Servers

With NetWare 3.*x* and 4.*x*, the server must be able to boot DOS before you start NetWare. With NetWare 2.*x*, it is not strictly necessary—NetWare boots from the cold boot loader on track 0 of the hard disk. However, if the server will not boot DOS, either from the DOS partition on the hard disk or from a floppy, it probably won't be able to load NetWare either. You can try to boot from a floppy if there is not a bootable hard disk in the server. If you are having problems getting the server to boot DOS, see Chapter 34, which covers troubleshooting workstations. The problems addressed here will be the specialized ones relating to server hardware and getting NetWare running.

The usual differences between a NetWare server and a PC workstation are these: a large hard disk or disks (often with more than one hard disk adapter), lots of RAM, multiple NICs, a faster processor, a faster bus, and of course, the NetWare operating system.

A NetWare server could be anything from a 386 PC with one floppy and a hard drive, one LAN adapter, and a monochrome video adapter to a high-end Pentium MMX or Pentium II PCI bus PC, with 512MB of RAM, an EIDE/Ultra DMA ATAPI disk drive adapter with 3.5- and 5.25-inch floppy drives, the ubiquitous CD-ROM drive, and a hard disk to boot from, two Ultra SCSI 3 fast/wide hard disk adapters with two or more multi-gigabyte hard drives on each adapter, two NICs, and a XVGA monitor and adapter. As your configuration approaches the latter, it can be very difficult to set up.

The following sections describe the most common hardware problem areas.

RAM

These days, adding RAM to a new system is no more complicated than choosing which type of motherboard to get. One type supports standard RAM (i.e., Intel's 44TX/LX) and another type has complete support for PC100 RAM (i.e., Intel's 440BX). RAM upgrades didn't used to be so simple, however, and in the interest of system administrators using older systems, we will first cover legacy RAM situations. Following that we'll discuss more modern approaches to RAM and networking.

Legacy Systems and RAM There are two problems that may occur with large amounts of RAM in legacy systems. The first happens when an additional RAM board is used to add the RAM. The second is simply a function of the way some devices and NetWare itself react when there is more than 16MB of RAM in the system. Most modern systems allow 512MB of RAM to be installed, or even more, but some older PCs will only allow up to 128MB of RAM on the motherboard. There are even older machines still around that may allow only 4MB on the motherboard, and will require additional boards if RAM is to be added. These boards can be difficult to configure; be sure to set the interrupts correctly and to keep the segments of RAM contiguous.

NOTE   Back in the early days of desktop computing, users had to add RAM by using rack mounts for their additional RAM. These racks would allow several RAM cards, typically 1MB or 2MB sticks, to be stacked together, making the system believe that these individual sticks were a single RAM upgrade. They were fussy and often hard to configure, and there were nearly as many variants as there were PC clone vendors at the time.

Additionally, you may need an updated driver for your SCSI adapter or NIC, or you may need to load the driver with a parameter that tells it that your server has more than 16MB of RAM. You may also need to use the REGISTER MEMORY command to tell NetWare that the server has more than 16MB with ISA bus PCs. With EISA bus PCs, you may need to add the following SET command to the AUTOEXEC.NCF file:

```
SET AUTO REGISTER MEMORY ABOVE 16 MB = ON
```

The default setting is ON, but some PCs may not register the memory unless you include the command in AUTOEXEC.NCF.

If you're using a 486 VesaLocal-bus server (or a 586 VesaLocal-bus server, if you can find such a thing), you may experience a driver lockup problem in machines with more than 16MB of memory. This is an acknowledged problem with many cards, including Adaptec VesaLocal-bus SCSI controllers. If you have a situation where your server has grown to the point that you need more than 16MB of RAM, we strongly recommend that you upgrade to either an EISA or a PCI system, which brings us to the modern systems.

Modern Systems and RAM As mentioned above in the section introduction, it is much easier to add RAM to a new or existing server or workstation. Depending on the system, RAM populates slots in a relatively easy fashion, and you even receive bonuses when you populate in bussed pairs, also called interleaving. Windows-based machines now take new RAM easily, making upgrades nearly seamless.

Often, there is a question as to which type of RAM to use. FPM RAM, EDO RAM, BEDO RAM, SDRAM, Async SRAM, SyncBurst SRAM Pipelined, Burst SRAM, and SRAM are all types of RAM that at one time or another have been used as the RAM of choice. Systems developers have narrowed this choice by having the motherboard support a single type of RAM. Common on newer systems is SDRAM.

Despite the apparent diversity, RAM comes in two basic types: Static and Dynamic. Dynamic RAM (DRAM) requires thousands of refresh cycles per second; Static RAM (SRAM) does not. Static RAM is faster, but costs more to manufacture. For this reason SRAM is typically only used as L2 cache memory. DRAM, the slower of the two, is used as the main system memory.

SDRAM (Synchronous DRAM) is capable of handling synchronization with a fast 100MHz system bus, which makes this the RAM of the moment, and you will find it in all current systems. SDRAM will last until bus speeds reach about 200MHz, when a number of other RAM types will come into play.

Type of Bus

A server is a problem to PC designers—a regular PC might have a floppy/hard disk adapter, an I/O board, a modem, a video board, a sound board, and a network adapter. These days, the floppy/hard disk adapter and I/O board are usually combined or integrated onto the motherboard, leaving four boards. A server, on the other hand, could have a floppy/hard disk adapter, an I/O board (also usually on one board or integrated onto the motherboard), a modem, a video board, one or two network adapters, and as many as three SCSI controllers, for a total of seven boards.

Many modern PCI motherboards have three or four PCI slots and three ISA slots. To get high performance for all the network boards and SCSI controllers, it may be necessary to go to either a dual-PCI bus system with seven or eight PCI slots or to an EISA system. The reason that some makers still produce an eight-slot EISA bus system, often with optional additional processors, is to support servers.

EISA has all but disappeared from the PC marketplace but continues to be supported as a server platform because of its board capacity. It is more of a nuisance to configure because it usually requires software, rather than being configured from BIOS as PCI is. However, an eight-slot EISA motherboard is less expensive than a dual-bus PCI motherboard, and EISA network and SCSI adapters have been available for quite a while, are well understood, and have mature drivers. If you are buying a new system, EISA may still be a good choice if you need lots of network and SCSI adapters. Just make sure that you can still get the EISA versions of the cards you want before you buy the PC.

PCI is the wave of the future. It provides a higher potential throughput and it's easier to configure. As time goes on, it will become increasingly more difficult to find EISA cards or systems. Dual-bus PCI systems will become more common and less expensive, and the problems with configuring them will be worked out. When everything works as it should, PCI can be a joy to configure because there are no interrupts to worry about—just plug the cards in and go. Unfortunately, it often isn't that simple. Every BIOS maker seems to handle PCI configuration with different terminology and in different ways, making it difficult to even describe what works. This is a case where the manufacturer's tech support or another administrator who has set up the same configuration may be very helpful.

As manufacturers move toward the Windows 95 Plug and Play model, they seem to be assuming that they no longer need to support anything else, or even document how their cards actually work. You may find, for instance, that interrupt 12 is used by the built-in PS/2 mouse connector on your motherboard, and that it cannot be made available even by disabling the mouse. Similarly, it's now difficult to find a monochrome video board, which is all a server really needs. Many of the new video boards use a number of different areas of memory. If you're running Windows 95, this may not present a problem. However, if you're trying to use a number of other cards under NetWare, you might try using a very basic ISA VGA card (or monochrome, if you can find one) to avoid memory conflicts.

Two good sources of information about potential problems with the cards in your system and what to do about them are the README file on the disk that came with the adapter and online support resources, such as a CompuServe forum or Web page. See Appendix A for more information about resources for troubleshooters.

SCSI Adapters

SCSI stands for Small Computer System Interface. It is most commonly used as a hard disk drive interface, but is also used for many other devices, such as scanners, additional drives such as CD-ROM drives, cartridge drives, tape drives, and so on.

It is common to have two SCSI adapters in the same server to provide for mirrored drives, and possibly a third SCSI adapter for a backup tape drive. It is often the case that SCSI host adapters from different manufacturers will not work in the same PC. For that reason, it is best to use the same manufacturer's cards, and even the same model of card, when more than one adapter is required.

SCSI adapters do not interface with the PC in the same way as IDE and MFM/RLL adapters. If you wish to use a SCSI drive as a boot drive, you may need an additional BIOS, because, even today, some PCs don't know that they should look on the SCSI adapter for a boot drive (typically, this will happen with cheaper systems made by third-tier vendors). The BIOS may be on the SCSI adapter itself, or it may be added to a network adapter to allow this. If you have multiple SCSI adapters, only one should have the BIOS enabled. In addition, you should take care that the interrupt used by a SCSI adapter is not used by other floppy or hard disk adapters, particularly if you have a motherboard with a built-in adapter. With PCI cards, look in the manual to see if the card is a bus-mastering card. If it is, it will need to be in a master slot, not a slave slot. Check your motherboard manual to see which slots are which.

SCSI Devices

The SCSI bus is a daisy chain, with up to seven devices, each connected to the next. Figure 33.3 illustrates the SCSI chain. Each device in the chain has its own unique ID of 0 through 6; the SCSI controller has an ID of 7. If you are having problems with a PC that has more than one SCSI device, make sure that all the devices have unique SCSI IDs. Duplicate IDs will usually cause the server to hang right after the SCSI driver loads. Of course, the method of removing the devices and trying them one at a time to isolate the problem applies here, too.

FIGURE 33.3:

A SCSI chain of devices

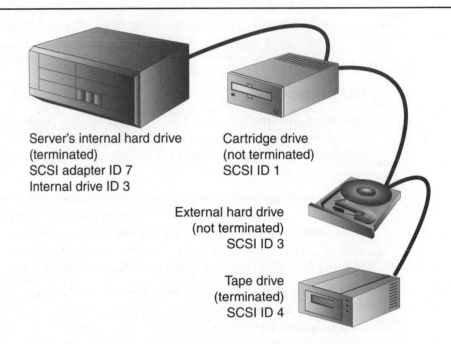

Server's internal hard drive
(terminated)
SCSI adapter ID 7
Internal drive ID 3

Cartridge drive
(not terminated)
SCSI ID 1

External hard drive
(not terminated)
SCSI ID 3

Tape drive
(terminated)
SCSI ID 4

Termination is another major cause of problems with SCSI devices. Often, incorrect termination will cause intermittent problems. Both the first device on the SCSI chain (usually the internal hard disk) and the last device on the chain must be terminated. Problems arise when intermediate devices are terminated or when the first or last drive is not. Some devices have external switches to enable or disable termination and set the SCSI ID; with others, you must move, add, or remove jumpers on the internal printed circuit board. The simplest way to handle termination is to leave the termination jumpers on the internal drive and remove termination from all other devices. Then use an external terminator on the last device. This allows you to add or remove devices easily.

Under no circumstances should you ever disconnect or connect a SCSI device when it is powered up. This can damage not only that device, but any other device in the chain, including the SCSI controller or the PC motherboard. Power everything down before changing connections. This rule also applies to changing termination or manually changing the SCSI ID of a device. Some devices will allow you to change their SCSI ID with software. This, obviously, must be done while everything is on.

RAID Systems

RAID originally stood for redundant array of inexpensive disks. It is usually interpreted now as redundant array of independent disks—the disks in use are not usually inexpensive (though some are, depending on the complexity of the implementation). The original intent was to put a number of small hard disks together in a way that allowed them to imitate one large, more expensive disk. Along the way, users discovered that a RAID system provides more fault tolerance and higher performance than a single drive. Now RAID systems are commonly built with high-end drives, and they may combine 28 or more drives for a 100GB virtual drive.

There are six levels of RAID, as described in detail in Chapter 24. Let's briefly revisit them here:

- Level 0 stripes data across more than one drive.

- Level 1 is essentially disk mirroring.

- Levels 2, 3, and 4 provide variations on how data is placed on several drives.

- Level 5, using at least three drives, reserves one drive as a parity drive, so that if a drive is lost, the data is maintained.

The aspects of a RAID system to be aware of when you are troubleshooting are the SCSI ID number and Logical Unit number (LUN). A single internal RAID controller with seven drives on it must have each drive at a different SCSI address, 0 through 6 (the controller is 7). An external RAID controller looks to the server's internal SCSI controller as if it were a single SCSI device. It has up to seven LUNs (actually SCSI drives) attached to it, but they are all treated as if they were one large disk. You can have up to seven external RAID controllers attached to the internal SCSI controller in the server. See the "RAID for Fault Tolerance" section, in the discussion of system fault tolerance later in this chapter, for more information.

TIP If you want to save money on drives, consider RAID level 5 rather than RAID level 1 (mirroring). Mirroring costs you one additional drive for every drive you install. RAID level 5 can use one drive out of every seven to store the parity information that allows the system to be fault-tolerant.

Hard Drive Preparation

Disk drives to be used with NetWare will not normally need to be formatted before installation, just repartitioned during the NetWare installation.

Mirrored partitions should be the same size—any additional space in the second partition will be unused. There can be multiple partitions on a disk, or a single partition that spans multiple disks. Similarly, all the drives in a RAID system should be the same size. It may not be strictly necessary, depending on the manufacturer, but it's advisable.

WARNING Be careful about creating partitions above 2GB. Some file systems cannot handle more than 2GB in a single partition.

Multiple LAN Adapters

LAN adapters typically use both an interrupt and a memory segment. If you have more than one adapter, the adapters must not use the same interrupt and memory segment. Furthermore, different manufacturers' cards will have different sequences of interrupts and memory segments that they expect to use; thus, it is not always sufficient to set the first adapter to its first configuration and the second adapter to its second configuration. Check the manufacturer's documentation for the usable interrupts and memory segments, and make sure to use different ones for each adapter.

With PCI cards, look in the manual to see if the card is a bus-mastering card. If it is, it will need to be in a master slot, not a slave slot. Check your motherboard manual to see which slots are which.

VGA Adapters

VGA adapters use both an interrupt and a memory segment. This can cause conflicts with network adapters, SCSI adapters, or any other cards in the server that use interrupts or memory segments. Be sure to check the interrupt and memory segment used to ensure that it doesn't conflict with other cards. As mentioned earlier, this information may be difficult to find for Plug-and-Play adapters.

Automatic Loading of BIOS into Upper RAM

Shadow BIOS, or loading the BIOS into the RAM between 640KB and 1MB, is intended to allow BIOS instructions to execute more quickly from the inherently faster 16- or 32-bit RAM instead of from the BIOS. Problems can occur when other hardware (such as a VGA adapter or LAN adapter) or NetWare attempts to access this same area of memory.

Interrupts and EISA or PCI Configuration

Any PC with an ISA bus (or an EISA-bus PC using interrupts) has a limited number of possible interrupts. The problem is that typically there are several cards that want to use interrupts in a particular range. For instance, NICs, mouse adapters, and some display adapters, among other devices, may all want an interrupt between 2 and 5.

Things may be complicated further by cards that limit your choice to one or two of the four possible interrupts. In these cases, careful planning may be required to avoid conflicts. Of course, you should record the interrupts in use for each PC as you configure the cards in it, both to facilitate troubleshooting if it won't boot and to make it easier to add other cards later.

EISA bus PCs in bus-mastering mode no longer have a problem with interrupts. However, in exchange for the old problem, you are now faced with a much more complicated installation procedure. You will need to know the manufacturer of each card, and often the version of the card as well, and what memory, if any, it uses. Then you must run the EISA configuration utility that came with your server to tell it what cards are installed.

You often hear that PCI cards don't use interrupts. This is not really true. They actually use two types of interrupts: the A, B, C, D PCI interrupts and the mapped interrupts determined by BIOS (usually 11, 5, 7, 9). How the BIOS is set up determines whether this happens automatically and how interrupts are mapped. If you have only a couple of PCI cards, you can usually leave things on the AUTO setting and not worry about it. With several cards, especially multiple NICs and SCSI cards, things can get interesting. Be sure to read the manufacturer's documentation on what PCI interrupt you should use and what other settings might need to be changed.

Hardware Security

NetWare and NT both provide several levels of security within the operating system. However, one aspect of security that is rarely mentioned is the security of the physical hardware itself—no software can prevent someone from accidentally unplugging a server or turning it off. We recommend that your server be placed in a lockable room, and that the door be kept locked unless someone is present.

Software Problems in New Servers

No system at all is required (except an NT boot floppy) to begin an NT setup, and only the most basic DOS configuration is needed to set up a NetWare server. Therefore, you shouldn't have too much to worry about in regard to booting your system preparatory to installing the server software. Once setup is initiated, however, it's a different story, as there are myriad options for configuring servers to be used in a network situation. In this section, we'll explore both the NT and NetWare setup processes. The purpose here is not to instruct you in the process of installing a network, but rather to help you debug that process when it fails.

TIP   For boot problems with NT Server and Workstation, please see the procedures contained in the "NT Server Troubleshooting Snapshot" section at the beginning of this chapter. For boot problems with NetWare, see the first few paragraphs of the "NetWare Troubleshooting Snapshot" section, also at the beginning of the chapter. (In regard to NetWare, all you really need to remember is that when NetWare boots, it takes over as the operating system. DOS is not used, and may be removed from memory. Thus, if the server will boot with DOS, nothing further needs to be done before installing NetWare.)

Windows NT Installation

Before beginning an NT Server installation, there are several things you'll want to familiarize yourself with. These include first making sure that all the hardware in your system is included on the Hardware Compatibility List (HCL) for NT (you may succeed in getting NT running on hardware that's not on the list, but because this hardware is not supported by Microsoft, if something goes wrong you'll be left on your own). The HCL typically goes through several revisions each year, so be sure to download the most recent one from Microsoft's Web site. Second, before installing NT, you'll need to decide what role this server will have in relation to other servers on your network. If you do not already have a PDC (primary domain controller), this should be the first server you set up, because you cannot configure a server as a BDC (backup domain controller) without first having a PDC. On the other hand, since it is not possible to downgrade a PDC to a backup domain controller without reinstalling NT, you'll want to be sure it's what you need when you designate a server as a PDC.

Installing NT is pretty straightforward, particularly with relatively newer systems, whose BIOS internally supports large drives. Most network cards are successfully detected during NT installation, although you should still write down any IRQs, DMA channels, and other system resources that are being used by installed hardware components. At the very least, this should help you avoid starting an install with two devices configured to the same IRQ or memory address, and can also be quite helpful later on should you have to install (or reconfigure) device drivers.

To begin an installation of NT, you need to boot into a stripped-down version of NT, although it isn't often described this way. Either you already have some other operating system installed, in which case you can probably access the CD-ROM drive and begin a "floppyless installation," or you will need to perform an initial boot using three floppy disks containing a very minimal NT kernel. The floppyless installation is attractive because it saves time (you will especially appreciate this if you need to start the setup process more than once). The floppyless install essentially copies to the hard drive the same files as are on the NT boot floppies. See our note below, though, about one advantage to doing the floppy-based installation.

To start a floppyless installation, start the WINNT program (for the Intel version, this is located in the \I386 directory of your NT CD-ROM; look in the \ALPHA, \MIPS, or \PPC directory for DEC Alpha, MIPS, or PowerPC systems, respectively). To use the floppyless install option, specify /B on the command line. To specify instead that you want the three boot floppies created, you would use the /OX option.

NOTE In the event you ever need to repair your NT installation, you may need a set of these three boot floppies (also called startup disks). Therefore, it may be worth creating these during your initial install. Be sure to label each of them as requested when the floppies are created.

For most systems equipped with a standard IDE or SCSI CD-ROM drive, the NT stripped-down install kernel will be able to detect the drive and load a driver to allow files to be read directly from the CD-ROM during installation. If you have a slow (2X or even 4X) CD-ROM, or a drive that is not supported by NT during the boot process (or even no CD-ROM drive whatsoever), then you'll need to get all the files in the I386 directory (or corresponding directory for other systems) copied to your hard drive before running the install. This could be done by copying the files from a CD-ROM drive located elsewhere on your network (if you already have a working network and network-aware OS on your system), or by attaching a parallel ZIP drive or other removable media device to your system. These alternatives work, but having a supported CD-ROM drive on your system is far easier and faster. One other observation: If you have plenty of drive space available, then it might be worthwhile to copy the I386 directory to your hard drive, even on CD-ROM equipped systems. There are at least a couple of reasons this could be beneficial. First of all, as fast as CD-ROM drives are becoming, none of them is yet anywhere near as fast as a hard drive, and each time you need to run NT's setup (if you're lucky this will be only once!), you'll appreciate the fact that installing this way runs noticeably faster than using the CD-ROM. Secondly, once you have NT up and running, you will occasionally need to install additional drivers or other NT software, and having NT be able to find and copy these files automatically from the hard drive (instead of prompting you to go find the CD-ROM again and insert it) is a definite plus. The downside is that it does take up additional space (80 to 90MB for NT 4), and it is an additional step to perform the copy the first time around.

To summarize, you can begin an NT install using the three boot floppies (ideal when there is no operating system already installed). Or you can start the NT install process by running WINNT from the \I386 (or corresponding) directory on the CD-ROM. This latter method can also be done after first copying the contents of the \I386 directory into a directory on your hard drive (a good forward-looking step to take if you have sufficient disk space). Finally, WINNT can be used either to initiate the install process, or simply to create the boot floppies. WINNT with the /? parameter causes all the WINNT command-line options to be displayed. For most purposes, the /B (floppyless install) or /OX (create boot floppies) options are appropriate.

However you choose to start the install process, once the initial set of drivers are loaded, you will be presented with a screen that has several options: F1 for Help, R for Repair (this is what you use if you later need to repair damaged system files), Esc key to cancel, or Enter to continue the installation. Press Enter to continue.

Next, a list of all detected SCSI and IDE controllers will be displayed, asking you whether you wish to add to this list. In most cases, especially using newer hardware, you should not need to add anything to this list. There is one case, though, where you might need to alter this list: If you happen to have more recent drivers for your controller than what came with your NT install disc. To add a driver, simply press S and insert the floppy containing the driver when prompted (or choose a driver from the scrolling list). Otherwise press Enter to continue.

Next, the license agreement screen is displayed. You can page down to view this agreement and press F8 to continue. Next, your drive partitions will be examined. If a previous installation of NT is found, you'll be asked whether you wish to upgrade it or install to a new directory.

Incidentally, after you have gotten NT up and running successfully, you may want to repeat this procedure to install a second NT installation to an external drive. This makes a great backup plan in case your main NT installation ever becomes damaged and fails to boot. An option for this second installation gets added to the NT boot menu, and should you ever need to use this backup installation, you would simply connect the external drive, then select the backup installation. (Since this is a totally separate installation, it does not include any security or other system changes added to the other installation, so you may want to update your backup installation every so often to keep it synchronized.) Next, you are asked to verify the computer type, video display, mouse, and keyboard. Generally these settings will be correct, but look carefully and make any corrections as needed. Keep in mind that you can always change the video to a higher resolution (adding more specific video drivers) once NT is up and running. Press Enter to continue.

You are next asked which partition to install NT to, and you can create or remove existing partitions as well. You can choose to install NT to any partition, but you really should allow at least 200MB, and preferably far more, because later when you're installing software on NT, files will often need to be added to the `system` or `system32` directory on this partition. Many install programs also default to using the system partition unless you specify otherwise. Also, NT will initially create a swap file using the system partition. The bottom line is to give the NT system partition as much "breathing space" as you can afford—even 2GB is not grossly overdoing it (it's better to waste some disk space than to run out, perhaps months later, after you have invested lots of time in installing software and configuring your system).

After you highlight the partition you want to install to, you'll need to accept the \WINNT default directory name or else change this (don't change this unless you have good reason to). Press Enter to continue.

At this point, a progress bar will appear, and many files will be copied from the CD-ROM (or hard drive) to a temporary location used during the graphical installation phase. When the copying finishes, you'll be prompted to remove any floppy that may be in the disk drive, and reboot the system. When the system restarts, it should boot into the graphical part of the NT setup, then copy some additional files. Finally a "Welcome to NT Setup" dialog will appear. Choose Next to continue.

The next dialog asks you to choose which licensing mode to use—"per server" is for licensing a given number of concurrent users per server; "per seat" licenses a given number of client stations to access all the servers in the organization. You will have the option to change your mind—once, later, but you should decide at this point what your organization's licensing policy requires and choose accordingly. Click Next to continue.

You will next be presented with a dialog asking for a unique name for this server. This name cannot exceed 15 characters, and must be unique within your entire network. This is followed by a second dialog, which asks you to choose which server type you want. This is where you must specify whether you want a primary domain controller, or a backup domain controller. To choose neither, select the standalone server option.

Next you will be asked for an administrator-level password. This may be left blank for now, but you should definitely change this to a difficult-to-guess (but relatively easy to remember) password at your earliest opportunity later.

The next dialog box allows you to create an Emergency Repair Disk. Unless you don't have a spare floppy handy, you should go ahead and do this.

NOTE   Emergency Repair Disks can be created (or updated) later using the RDISK NT application. It is also helpful to add an RDISK shortcut to your Administrator programs menu, for easy access.

Finally, you will now be given the option of installing several optional components, including Accessibility Options, Accessories, Communications, Games, Microsoft Exchange (client version), and Multimedia. Check or uncheck options as desired and click Next.

This leads us to the networking portion of the NT setup. You will be asked whether this server is going to be connected using a network adapter, modem (dial-up) connection, or both. Most servers will use one or more network adapters, but answer "both" if you intend to use remote access services (RAS). (This can be added later, however.)

Next, you are asked whether this server will be used as an Internet server. If so, you'll check the IIS (Internet Information Server) check box, which installs an FTP and Web server.

Following this, you will be asked to select the appropriate network adapter. The auto-detect feature works well for most cards, but in some cases you'll need to change the settings to match your card.

Now, you need to select which protocols to install. NetBEUI is a good choice for smaller networks, as it has less overhead. Unfortunately it is also not routable, so in many cases you will need either IPX or IP as well. NWLink, which is Microsoft's implementation of IPX/SPX, is good if you need to access NetWare servers. IP, of course, is necessary if you are installing the Internet server software or intend to use this server with the Internet or an intranet. After selecting the protocols needed, click Next to continue to a list of network services. Because the network services (and the protocols) can also be added later, you may wish to keep the number of services initially installed to a minimum, to reduce the chance of having problems with the server's initial boot. Select any services you want installed at this point and click Next.

Based on which (if any) protocols and services you've selected, some settings dialog boxes may appear at this point. Answer each of these as needed.

A bindings dialog box appears next. This lets you modify the order in which multiple protocols are bound to the network adapters. This can also be changed any time later, so we recommend leaving the defaults. The purpose of changing the binding order is to reduce inefficiency by placing the most-used protocol first in the list. Click Next, and a number of files will be copied to your hard drive.

Assuming all went well, the next dialog to appear should ask you for the name of the domain you are creating or joining. If the domain specified cannot be found, you'll get an error message (unless you're creating a new domain, of course). Change this as needed.

If all did not go well, you may be better off going back to an earlier point in the installation and removing one or more options for now. Remember, you can always add options such as protocols and network services later. The other thing that could go wrong is that your network adapter settings don't actually match the card. If this happens, you'll need to change the settings and/or driver to match. If you cannot seem to get the card settings to work, try a different model network adapter—sometimes one card will only support a subset of possible values, and those may already be taken by other hardware in your system.

If you earlier elected to install the IIS (Internet Information Server) option, you'll now be asked for default path locations, a domain name, and related options (including ODBC driver options). Again, we recommend accepting the default choices, as these can be reconfigured later if necessary.

Finally, you are prompted for the correct time zone, time, date, and video driver. An Emergency Repair Disk may also be created at this point. If you chose to install the Microsoft Exchange client, these files will be copied now.

At this point, your NT installation should be complete. After restarting, you can begin configuring security settings and adding users and groups, additional hardware drivers, network protocols, and so on.

NetWare Software Problems

NetWare Installation   The basic process of installing NetWare is a relatively simple one of copying files onto the hard disk of the server. If you have problems, they are likely to be either with the configuration of NetWare after it's installed or with the hardware. SERVER.EXE and NET$OS.EXE are essentially programs like any other. If there are errors in loading them, they will typically be due to memory errors or hardware configuration. With NetWare 2.x, you will get an error when starting NetWare if the LAN adapter or cold boot PROM is defective.

Configuration Files   Although the names of the server configuration files are not the same in different versions of NetWare, they perform the same functions. In NetWare 2.x, the files are SERVER.CFG and AUTOEXEC.SYS; in NetWare 3.x and 4.x, they are AUTOEXEC.NCF and STARTUP.NCF.

Keep a hard copy of these files. It is easy to change a configuration when you are trying to troubleshoot a problem, and then lose track of how it was configured in the first place. If you intend to remove a line in a configuration file for troubleshooting purposes, it may save you headaches to comment it out first, using # (the pound sign). This way, if the problem turns out to be something else, putting the line back in the file is a simple matter of erasing one character, instead of typing in a long string.

It seems ridiculous, but the most common problem with the configuration files is misspellings. Be sure that commands and parameters are spelled correctly and that the values given are within the proper ranges. Case is usually not an issue, but some parameters, especially ones relating to Macintosh or Unix support, may be case-sensitive.

Drive Preparation for NetWare Installation NetWare does not use a standard DOS partition for disk drives. There will be a small DOS partition on the server's boot disk with NetWare 3.*x* or 4.*x*, but the rest of that disk and any others on the system must be partitioned with NetWare partitions. You do this with INSTALL.

You can also choose to do a low-level format and test of the drive with INSTALL under 3.*x* and 4.*x*, or with ZTEST or COMPSURF under 2.*x*. ZTEST reformats track 0, which is used for the cold boot loader. Unless you buy the drive preformatted and certified for NetWare, it is a very good idea to perform a low-level format and test with new systems. It can't hurt (it will destroy any existing data), but it may take some time.

After the drive is formatted and partitioned, a Hot Fix redirection area is set up. This is used if bad blocks are encountered on the disk. The bad blocks are mapped to the redirection blocks, which are then used to replace the bad blocks. If you use MONITOR, you can see the total number of blocks on the drive and the number of redirection blocks. This is normally 2 percent of the total number of blocks. You will also see the number of redirected blocks. This number starts out at zero and, ideally, will never grow.

WARNING   If you notice a large number of redirected blocks, or if the number of redirected blocks is growing regularly, it is a good indication that the disk is deteriorating physically. It's a very good idea to replace such a disk at once. You may wish to try a low-level format, followed by a thorough test of the disk. However, since the cost of a disk is usually much less than the value of the information on it combined with the cost of downtime if the disk quits in the middle of a busy day (you are doing regular backups, aren't you?), it usually pays to just replace the disk.

NetWare lets you create volumes that span multiple partitions and multiple disks. This can allow you to create volumes with very large effective sizes, which can be a problem with some operating systems that may have trouble with partitions over 2 or 2.5GB.

If you set up a volume over 2GB, and you either cannot see the volume or it shows as a different size from a workstation, the problem is not with NetWare, but rather is an inherent limitation of the operating system of the workstation. The only solution is to decrease the size of the volume. Keep in mind that in some cases, the only problem will be that the amount of free space that the operating system shows will be incorrect. The user will still be able to access the volume and perform normal operations.

Device Drivers Each device in a server uses a driver. For example, the driver for a Novell NE2000 card is named NE2000.LAN. Particular care must be used to make sure that the driver is the proper one for the hardware installed, and that it is the version recommended for the version of NetWare you are using. If you don't have the proper driver, you should be able to get it from Novell's Web site at www.novell.com.

Watch the messages as NetWare loads. If the server freezes after a driver is loaded, it may be the wrong driver or an incorrect version of the right driver. If you have two cards of the same type, you must load the device driver twice—once for each card. NetWare will usually give you the message "Driver loaded re-entrantly" or something similar, meaning that it is loading the same code from memory.

Network Address Assignments In a WAN, especially a large one, a common problem is duplicate network addresses. The hexadecimal number used to identify the server must be unique. Fortunately, this is an easy problem to diagnose. A repeating error message will occur at the console on all servers on the LAN, with the text "Router Configuration Error: *Servernumber* is claiming my same Internet address," or something similar. This is another case where having your network well documented comes in handy. All you get on the screen is the server's network number—a long hexadecimal number. If you have those numbers in a list with their corresponding servers, it'll be much easier for you to track down the other server.

Multiple Protocols NetWare 3.11 and higher allow you to run multiple protocols as if they were native. Protocols supported include IPX, SPX, TCP/IP, AppleTalk, NetBIOS, OSI, and SMB. It is possible to have a number of these protocols running on the same NIC. Each protocol must be loaded and bound to the board. The LOAD and BIND commands for each board include certain parameters. If the parameters are not set correctly (if the wrong numbers are used or the spelling is incorrect), the statements may not work for that protocol.

Another possibility is that the LOAD and BIND commands work, but they conflict with other devices on your intranet. This problem occurs more often in a WAN environment than with single LANs. In a single LAN, which isn't connected to anything else, the AppleTalk zone names and zone numbers, the TCP/IP numbers, subnets, and so on, that you specify are not critical. In a WAN environment, or a LAN which may someday be expanded into a WAN, these settings become crucial—they must be coordinated throughout the WAN. It is extremely important to carefully document and structure the AppleTalk zone and TCP/IP setup you use.

If the server boots, and DOS workstations can log in, but Unix or Macintosh workstations cannot see the server, the first place to look is in the INSTALL configurations. Double-check the settings and remember that some items (for instance the Mac zone names) are case-sensitive. For more information about problems with connecting to other systems, see Chapter 37.

NetWare Permissions   There is a saying among system administrators that 90 percent or more of the day-to-day problems that users encounter on a network involve permissions. With permissions for users, permissions for groups, and the task of ensuring that all the proper people are in the proper groups, it's no wonder these issues are complex. They are potentially complicated further by different permissions at different levels of a directory hierarchy and on the files themselves.

One of the best investments you, as a system administrator, can make early on is to study your server's permissions structure until you are thoroughly familiar with it. With NetWare, make sure that you understand completely the difference between the inherited rights and trustee rights and how they combine.

Login Scripts   On NetWare, there are three login scripts that may execute when a user logs in: the default, the user, and the system. The default login script will execute if no system or user login script exists. This script should normally not be used. The system login script executes first, and should contain commands that are necessary to set up all users. The user's login script executes next, and contains the commands that configure the user's environment.

NetWare 4.x adds another login script for groups (called the profile login script), which takes the place of the IF MEMBER OF construction in the system login script under previous versions. This is necessary because groups are global in a network and can be accessed by members from any server. In addition, in NetWare 4.*x*, the system login script is replaced with the container login script, which is executed for members of an organization, rather than on a server-by-server basis, because users are no longer tied to a particular server.

The Dreaded ABEND Message With a new NetWare (or IntraNetWare) installation, an error message beginning with ABEND means that something in your software or hardware configuration is wrong. The first thing to try is rebooting the server.

If the problem recurs, it could be caused by:

- An NLM that is incorrectly configured, corrupted, or simply badly written

- An incorrectly entered SET command

- A printer that is set up incorrectly

- A hardware problem

Try unloading all the NLMs and reloading them one at a time, checking the SET commands in the AUTOEXEC.NCF and STARTUP.NCF files for correct spelling and values within the range allowed (check the System Administration manual for details), and check the setup of all printers configured. Then make sure that the server memory is sufficient for the configuration you are running, and check the server for hardware problems using the procedures listed in the next chapter for workstations.

Troubleshooting Existing Servers

With existing servers, you are unlikely to run across configuration errors or interrupt conflicts, unless you have just changed something.

The principal problem with existing equipment is failures, either of hardware or software. An exception to this is that some interrupt conflicts may cause intermittent, long-term problems that will only disrupt things occasionally.

You may also encounter problems as utilization of the server increases, which can be measured as:

- Traffic on and off the server

- Disk utilization

- Memory utilization, as the number of buffers utilized increases

The typical solutions here are more memory, more network speed (more or faster NICs), and more hard disk space.

Hardware Problems in Existing Servers

Other than problems resulting from changes, which you should troubleshoot using the steps outlined for hardware problems in new servers, the most likely hardware problems are not unique to servers, but are equivalent to workstation problems (see the next chapter for details on troubleshooting workstations). Many hardware problems will produce error messages, either in the system error log or when the system loads, which will make them easy to spot.

Using NT's Event Viewer

NT's event log is an important tool for viewing all errors, warnings, and other information items that have occurred, whether hardware or software (provided the error has not actually caused a system crash).

The Event Viewer operates in one of three modes: System, Security, and Application. In System mode, all system-level events are displayed. If you have enabled security auditing, Security mode will display any security events that have occurred (these include attempted access to restricted folders, printers, or drives, failed logons, and so forth). Application mode allows you to view a list of any events generated by applications or services that support event logging. Note that even Visual Basic provides an easy way for programmers to generate application level events, so the number of applications capable of producing events is likely to increase in the future.

In order to simplify viewing what would otherwise be one long list of events, Event Viewer offers a number of filtering options, including date/time range, computer name and user, source, category, and event ID, as well as restricting the display to informational, warning, or error events. Figure 33.4 shows the Event Viewer with the Filter options dialog box superimposed.

FIGURE 33.4:

NT's Event Monitor, showing the Filter dialog box

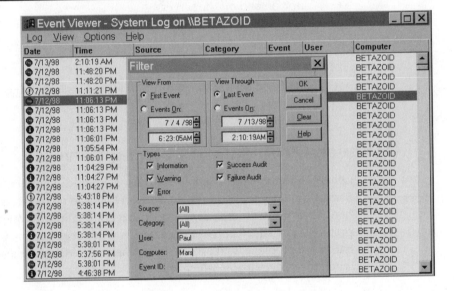

Using NT's Network Monitor

One useful NT tool we've mentioned in earlier chapters is Network Monitor. This application offers several of the same features as Novell's LANalyzer, and can be used to monitor normal network performance (to establish a baseline), to watch for anomalies (excessive network congestion, for example, or multiple logins), and to trigger an event to be recorded in NT's event log.

NOTE   See Chapter 37 for a more complete discussion of NT's Network Monitor and Performance Monitor system tools.

Using NT's Performance Monitor   Another useful tool provided by NT (covered further in Chapter 37) is NT's Performance Monitor. This program lets you monitor all sorts of system-level processes, and again, trigger an event to be recorded in NT's event log whenever a particular process exceeds (in either direction) a preset threshold value. Thus, you can have Performance Monitor keep watch and notify you whenever a server drive fills beyond a certain capacity, or when existing memory is becoming insufficient (as evidenced by excessive page swapping), or when network throughput reaches a certain upper threshold, and so on. The variety of triggers and continuous monitoring possibilities that Network Monitor and Performance Monitor open up is rather amazing—possible uses are limited more by the imagination (or lack thereof) than anything else.

NetWare, of course, also has several tools that you can use to diagnose, and in some cases correct, hardware problems. These tools can also be used to monitor the load on the server and network, and project levels that are too high, so you can upgrade the hardware before critical levels are reached.

Using SERVMAN, MONITOR, and FCONSOLE

SERVMAN (NetWare 4.*x*), MONITOR (NetWare 3.*x*), and FCONSOLE (NetWare 2.*x*) are invaluable tools for deciphering network problems. They will tell you a lot about the normal operation of the server and can help you pinpoint problems that are otherwise difficult to isolate.

For instance, if several workstations are having problems connecting with a 3.*x* server, and the server is running and you can't find any problems with the physical network, choose the LAN Information selection in MONITOR. You will be able to see whether the server is sending and receiving packets, whether there are many bad packets or collisions, and similar information. Likewise, if network performance slows down radically when there are lots of users on a 2.*x* server, and FCONSOLE shows that the Peak Used number of communication buffers is close to or equal to the number of buffers set, you should increase the total number of communication buffers. (This will require regenerating the operating system with INSTALL.)

You should also be aware of the usual state of your server, as shown in MONITOR or FCONSOLE. There are a number of particular things to look for (and record in your log for that server). See the section on baselining in Chapter 25 for details.

Using VREPAIR

VREPAIR is a very useful tool to fix software problems with hard drives. It won't diagnose a problem with the electronics of a drive or tell you about a SCSI conflict or termination problem, but it does a good job of getting the directory entries back in sync with the files they represent.

TIP

The most important thing to know about VREPAIR is that it will handle only one set of problems at a time.

Each time VREPAIR scans a disk, it may find problems, and, if you tell it to, it will fix them. However, the process of fixing one set of problems may uncover further problems, which will require another scan. You should continue running VREPAIR until no errors are reported.

Checking the NetWare System Error Log

The system error log is accessible through SYSCON or NWADMIN from a workstation and from some of the add-on modules in INSTALL.NLM on the server. You should become familiar with typical messages that occur in the log. Then, when problems occur, you will have a better chance of picking out the relevant error message.

Of course, the messages are in chronological order in the log, and if you know when the problem began, this will give you clues regarding which messages you should pay special attention to. Chapter 25 has more information about baselining—accumulating the statistics that your network produces normally and how to use those baseline figures to determine what is wrong.

Software Problems in Existing Servers

With existing software that has been working correctly, there are only a few factors that can cause failure. One is a faulty piece of software that causes problems when it runs, or perhaps only under certain circumstances. This could be an NLM or a user application on someone's workstation.

Another potential cause of failure is increased load on the network that causes the server to overload. This is usually due to running out of memory, which cannot be characterized as a software problem, although you can sometimes fix the problem by reconfiguring the server to allocate less memory in other areas or by unloading unnecessary features. However, software can also cause its own problems under high loads, by not waiting long enough for a response, for instance.

Corrupted SERVER.EXE or NET$OS.EXE Files

It is possible (though unlikely) for SERVER.EXE or NET$OS.EXE to become corrupted, so it is a good idea to back up your file onto a floppy. Then, if you suspect that the file has been corrupted, you can copy it from the floppy onto the server's hard disk, overwriting the existing file. If it won't fit on one floppy, another method is to create a directory on the DOS partition of the server's boot disk, and then place a copy of the NetWare executable file (NET$OS.EXE or SERVER.EXE) in it.

Other than the slight possibility of a corrupted SERVER.EXE file, the software on an existing server is only likely to cause problems if it is changed, or if some other part of your network is changed in a way that conflicts with the configuration of your server. These problems should be treated as changes—see the section about software problems in new installations, earlier in the chapter.

ABEND Messages

You will occasionally see an error message on the server's screen that begins with ABEND. This means that the server software has crashed. (This message appears only on the server's screen.) In an existing system, this is usually a fluke, possibly caused by an application running on the server that is misbehaving, by an NLM that is not functioning correctly, or by a hardware memory error.

The text following the ABEND part of the message will tell you something about the problem. The System Messages manual may be useful in decoding the error message. If the problem recurs, try to find out which applications were running on workstations when the server crashed. If any of them are new applications or new versions, they may be causing problems with the server.

An ABEND message could also be caused by a hardware problem. Make sure that the memory in the server is sufficient for the configuration you are running. If you have recently added new NLMs, disk drives, name spaces on existing drives, or protocol drivers, the server may need more RAM to function correctly. Check the server as a workstation for hardware problems, as described in Chapters 30 and 34.

Running the BINDFIX Utility

BINDFIX is a utility program in NetWare 2.*x* and an NLM in 3.*x* and 4.*x*. It will repair many problems that occur with the binderies. For example, use BINDFIX if a user cannot log in, you can't modify or delete a user account, a password cannot be changed, trustee rights can't be changed, or you get error messages on the console that mention the binderies.

Be sure to have a backup of the bindery files before running BINDFIX. If you do keep separate copies of the bindery files, you may be better off replacing them, rather than using BINDFIX. The names of the files you will need to back up are listed in "Managing the NetWare Binderies or NetWare Directory" section a little later in the chapter.

Using DSTRACE and DSREPAIR

DSTRACE (the Directory Services trace utility) tracks NDS messages between your server and the others in your company. It will allow you to watch all NDS messages on the screen or save them to a log file. It can be very useful for tracing NDS errors.

DSREPAIR is the utility for repairing the NDS database when something goes wrong. Remember that it can be run on only one server's NDS database at a time. Since it also locks the server while it is repairing the database, all users will be unable to use the server. It's not something you normally want to run during working hours, unless you're having serious NDS problems.

Intermittent Problems with Servers

There are many possible causes of intermittent failure of a server, and this can be one of the most frustrating types of troubleshooting to attempt. The causes could be anything from a power surge caused by nearby heavy equipment (or even the power draws from another facility on the same power grid), to faulty equipment, to the applications running on the server or even on a workstation.

To isolate intermittent problems, look for the thing that changes just before the crash. This seems obvious but can be difficult to actually discover. Here are some starting points:

- At what time does the crash occur?

- Do the crashes happen at regular intervals?

- Is there any particular software that is always in use when the crashes occur?

- Which workstations are attached every time the server crashes?

- Are there any unusual error messages in the system error log?

- Do any of the workstations get a message other than "The connection to the file server *myserver* is no longer valid"?

- Are there stages to the problem? If you can isolate events that lead up to the crash, they will give you a clue to the root cause.

Investigating some of these items will take research: talking to the users, discovering what new software has been installed on the server or workstations, finding out who was logged in, and so on. You can simplify this job considerably with the use of network inventory systems, network monitoring equipment, and other software that will help keep track of the various parts of your network and its configuration. You can manually keep track of all installed software and hardware on your server and all the networked workstations, but it's much easier to run a network inventory program regularly to get the information. There is less chance that users will forget to mention that new program they installed, too.

Of course, some problems may be impossible to isolate without some sort of network sniffer. Anyone with an installation that is larger than a couple of servers or that runs more than one or two protocols should consider getting some type of monitoring software and/or hardware, as discussed in the next section.

TIP   The best resources for determining which monitoring system is right for you are the trade magazines, your local NetWare user group, and your authorized reseller.

Using Other Diagnostic Tools

Many levels of diagnostic tools are available to the system administrator. They range from $195 software-only products that will allow you a little more capability than MONITOR, to $50,000+ WAN analyzers that will produce a map of an extended WAN, monitor traffic, inform you if anything unusual happens, and suggest solutions.

Other available software can inventory the software on each workstation on your network, upgrade all workstations on the network with the newest versions of software as they come out, and tell you what hardware is installed in the workstations. There are other programs that enhance the NetWare utilities, producing more detailed reports than MONITOR can, with tracking over time and nice formatting of the printed reports.

Although many of these products can save you time, or be invaluable in a complex WAN environment, you can often produce the same results yourself with a little advance preparation, the tools available to you in NetWare, and some deductive reasoning. For example, a protocol analyzer might be able to monitor network traffic, detect bad packets coming from a server, and notify you of the problem, which server is producing it, and where it is located. However, by assigning network numbers to servers that will allow you to identify them (office number, followed by extension, or something similar), you can get the same information by inspecting the system error logs of your servers regularly. Of course, this is more work, so if you have the money in your budget for a network analyzer, we highly recommend it.

Similarly, the network hardware or software inventory programs are very useful, especially for large networks, but you can gather the same information manually. Appendix C provides forms that you can use to enter inventory information. See Chapters 30 and 31 for more information about diagnostic and network management tools.

Managing the NetWare Binderies or NetWare Directory

The binderies are hidden files that contain all the information you have set up on your users, their passwords, trustee rights, ownership of files, default printers, and so on. SBACKUP, NBACKUP, and other backup programs designed to work with NetWare give you the option to back up the binderies. Be careful—if you restore from an older tape, and restore the binderies, any changes you or the users have made to passwords and the like will revert to what they were as of that backup.

If you wish to back up the binderies manually, they consist of two hidden files, NET$BIND.SYS and NET$BVAL.SYS, in NetWare 2.x, and three files, NET$OBJ.SYS, NET$PROP.SYS, and NET$VAL.SYS, in NetWare 3.x. These files are located in SYS:SYSTEM.

If a user cannot log in, if you can't modify or delete a user account, if a password cannot be changed, if trustee rights can't be changed, or if you get error messages on the console that mention the binderies, try running BINDFIX.

In NetWare 4.x, the bindery is replaced with the NetWare Directory, under NDS. This is a much more capable way of making the services on the server available to clients, and it requires a more extensive database, with many additional properties. NetWare 4.x can be configured to emulate the old style of binderies to maintain compatibility with older servers and workstation shells. The NDS database is in a hidden directory, SYS:_NETWARE, in five files: VALUE.NDS, BLOCK.NDS, PARTITIO.NDS, ENTRY.NDS, and 00006f00.000. This database can and should be replicated on other servers on your network.

Upgrading NetWare

Upgrading NetWare using the UPGRADE utility is usually a relatively pain-free operation. It is well documented, and this book will not go into the details of a normal upgrade. However, even in a straightforward upgrade, there are a number of things that can go wrong. *Never* upgrade without doing a complete backup of your file system first.

The most complicated part of upgrades is the changes in names and structures. In NetWare 2.*x*, SERVER.CFG and AUTOEXEC.SYS are used to run parts of NetWare; in NetWare 3.*x* and 4.*x*, the files are called AUTOEXEC.NCF and STARTUP .NCF. Permission structures—how permissions flow in the directory structure and how users inherit permissions—change considerably from NetWare 2.15 and below, to 2.2 and above, to 3.*x*, and to NetWare 4.*x*. Make sure that you understand the differences before you do an upgrade.

Troubleshooting NetWare's NLM Problems

The installation process for NLMs under NetWare 3.*x* and 4.*x* is fortunately very simple. Just run the INSTALL NLM, and the appropriate files will be put in the proper places on your server. Configuring the NLMs for your particular requirements is another matter. You should also be aware before you upgrade that not all 3.*x* NLMs are compatible with NetWare 4.*x*.

Each NLM comes with appropriate documentation—this book is not intended to replace the user documentation, or even to supplement it. However, the troubleshooting process may certainly be applied to NLMs that you believe are installed correctly but refuse to function for one reason or another.

There are four types of NLMs:

- Disk drivers to allow the use of different types of disk drives (*.DSK).

- LAN drivers for running different protocols on various LAN adapters (*.LAN).

- Name space modules to allow operating systems other than DOS to access and store files on the server. These include modules for Macintosh, NFS (UNIX), and OS/2 (*.NAM).

- Management utilities and server applications, such as MONITOR, INSTALL, and UPS. These allow you to configure and manage the server or add functionality (*.NLM).

If you are having regular abends or problems with server performance, make sure that you have the latest version of all the NLMs you are using. (Updated NLMs and patches are often available on Novell's Web site at www.novell.com.) If necessary, reduce the number of NLMs loaded to the minimum necessary for basic server functions, and add the rest back in, one at a time, until you can determine which one is causing a problem or conflicting with other NLMs.

Using System Fault Tolerance

Novell's NetWare and IntraNetWare use technology called System Fault Tolerance (SFT) to help ensure network reliability in the event of hardware failures. Both Novell's and Microsoft's server products offer effective approaches to increasing the reliability of servers. Data stored on servers is protected through various data redundancy technologies. Both systems support drive duplexing and mirroring (Novell calls this SFT II). Some of these technologies include sufficient redundancy to allow a network server to continue operating (and serving data) even during a hard drive failure.

Keeping a network protected in the event of an entire server failure is a more complex challenge. Novell offers a backup server technology referred to as SFT III. Microsoft is currently testing a similar technology for clustering NT Servers (code-named Wolfpack).

Mirroring and Duplexing

Both mirroring and duplexing are intended to allow the server to continue to provide file services even if a disk fails. With mirroring, all the data on a disk is duplicated on the mirrored disk, and if one disk fails, the other provides continued access to the data. When implemented using two drive controllers (duplexing), these systems also provide the additional advantage of reducing the disk access time by half; the network operating system will read different parts of the data back from both disks simultaneously, allowing twice as much data to be read at a time.

The only drawback to mirroring or duplexing is the added cost. For each volume used, two disks must be purchased; with duplexing, two controllers and two disk enclosures with power supplies are also required. However, given the relatively low cost of disk storage, this is cheap insurance against the lost time a crashed disk will cause on even a small network. Obtaining a new drive and restoring from a backup will take a minimum of hours and perhaps days, and anything on the server that had been changed since the last backup will be lost, as well.

The difference between mirroring and duplexing is the level of duplication of components. Mirroring uses two disks attached to the same controller and usually the same power supply. Duplexing uses separate controllers, disks, and power supplies, providing continuing functionality even if the power supply or controller fails. Figure 33.5 illustrates how mirroring and duplexing work.

FIGURE 33.5:

Mirroring and duplexing

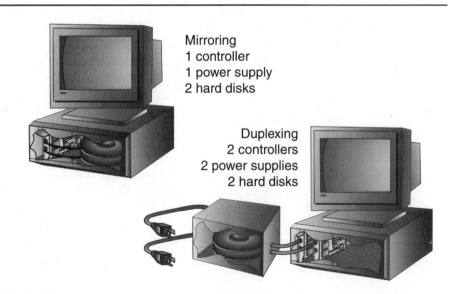

Mirroring
1 controller
1 power supply
2 hard disks

Duplexing
2 controllers
2 power supplies
2 hard disks

RAID for Fault Tolerance

RAID provides more fault tolerance and higher performance than a single drive, and more efficient use of drive space than mirrored drives. RAIDs are commonly built with high-capacity drives, and may combine 28 or more drives to create a much larger "virtual" drive. Figure 33.6 illustrates how a RAID system works.

FIGURE 33.6:

A RAID system uses multiple disks

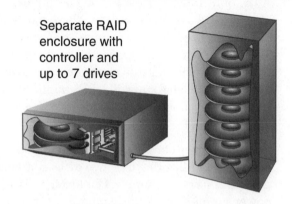

Separate RAID enclosure with controller and up to 7 drives

As explained earlier in the chapter, there are six levels of RAID. The most common is level 5, which uses at least three drives, reserving one drive as a parity drive, so that if a drive is lost, the data is maintained. There can be up to seven drives in a single RAID array. Since RAID level 5 uses a single drive for parity regardless of how many drives are in the array, the most efficient configuration uses seven drives, which results in a total capacity of six drives, with one parity drive.

Because RAID level 5 provides the fault tolerance of mirroring with a much smaller loss of drive space (one drive in three, to one drive in seven, instead of one out of every two drives), it has become very popular. It also offers gains in speed, since data can be pulled off more than one drive at once, better utilizing the performance of the SCSI controller. Finally, as demands for capacity continue to increase, RAID provides an effective way to increase capacity. Drives can be added to a RAID relatively seamlessly, and RAID controllers can be cascaded to a capacity of one or two controllers, each controlling seven controllers attached to seven drives each, for a total capacity of 49 or 98 drives.

NOTE   Windows NT supports the various levels of RAID implemented in hardware, as well as RAID levels 1, 4, and 5 in software. This means you can implement RAID 5 (for example) without any special RAID hardware. (RAID 5 does require a minimum of three hard drives installed.)

SFT Level III

Novell's SFT level III allows you to mirror an entire server, rather than simply the disk drives. This provides a level of fault tolerance previously available only on mainframes and minicomputers. All data written to one server is also written to the second server, which may be in a remote location. If any part of one server fails, the other server takes over. This is particularly important in mission-critical applications where any loss of connectivity might cause extensive business losses, such as in banking or airline applications. Figure 33.7 illustrates how SFT III works.

FIGURE 33.7:

SFT level III

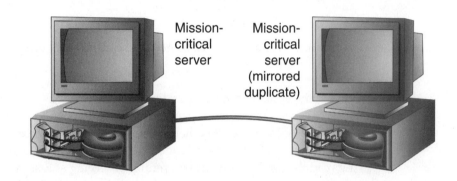

The two servers don't need to be identical, but the lowest configuration will apply to both servers. For instance, if one server has 64MB of RAM and the other 128MB, they will both effectively have 64MB.

Real-Life Stories

This section describes typical problems and how a troubleshooter would go through the process of isolating the fault and fixing it. Two fictional companies and their administrators will be used as examples. They combine the equipment and experience of a number of actual businesses. These two scenarios are intended to show some representative problems often encountered when setting up or troubleshooting a server. Although you may never see these particular problems, they should give you a feel for the process an experienced troubleshooter uses to isolate a problem, determine the solution, and fix the problem.

Scenario One: Installing a New System

The administrator is installing and configuring a new system. He encounters some typical problems associated with late-model servers using large amounts of RAM and more than one hard disk adapter.

Snapshot—Scenario One

Is this a new system?

- Will the server boot DOS?

- Will NetWare load?

- Are some devices (such as network cards or disk drives) inaccessible after NetWare loads?

John, the system administrator for Itsy-Bitsy Inc., has about $25,000 of computer and components sitting in a couple dozen boxes around his office. They are the parts needed to put together the new high-performance server that the Tech Pubs department has been asking for this last year. Being a bright guy, and having read this book before, he is carefully observing anti-static precautions and recording the settings of all the cards, disks, and so forth, as he puts the system together.

The server is a dual Pentium II PCI-bus PC with 128MB of RAM and an internal 4GB IDE hard drive, one 3.5-inch floppy, two serial ports, one parallel port, and VGA support on the motherboard. It supports shadowing the BIOS in RAM. In addition, he has two external enclosures, each with two 3.2GB hard drives, an 8mm SCSI tape drive, two SCSI adapters, and two PCI (32-bit) Ethernet adapters. He will have two drives attached to each SCSI controller, providing full mirroring; controller, disk drives, and power supply will be entirely separate for each set. The tape drive will be added to the daisy chain on the first SCSI controller, the one that the tape drive came with. Of course, the server and enclosures will be plugged into a UPS.

As John installs the boards in the PC, he records the settings of each one on the server configuration form he copied from Appendix C of this book. The first NIC uses interrupt 3 and memory address C000. He sets the second NIC to interrupt 4 and memory address D000. Doing so ensures that there is no interrupt conflict between the cards and makes the LAN configuration easy, too; these are configurations 0 and 1 for the drivers for the NICs.

Next, John installs the two SCSI adapters. He knows that the built-in hard drive adapter uses interrupt 14, so he can choose 10, 11, 12, or 13 for the two cards. He sets them to 10 and 11, records this, and then closes up the server. He next makes sure that only the second of the two SCSI drives in the first enclosure is terminated, and that neither is terminated in the other enclosure. He has terminated the tape drive, which will be the last SCSI device in the chain for that controller.

Finally, everything is ready. He plugs everything into the UPS, attaches and secures all the cables, and crosses his fingers. He turns on the SCSI devices, then flips the main power switch on the PC. Nothing happens. Three hours later, once the UPS's battery has charged, he turns everything on again. This time, assorted fans begin whirring, the PC beeps, and messages begin appearing on the monitor.

John sees several messages, identifying the BIOS, the VGA adapter, and the SCSI adapter. Then DOS is loaded, and he is ready to begin the installation of NetWare. He brings the server up to partition the drives. However, when he starts SERVER.EXE, the SCSI adapter won't load its driver. Belatedly, John remembers seeing in the adapter's documentation that the driver must be loaded with a /v switch if the server contains more than 16MB of RAM. A few minutes later, the driver is loaded with the /v switch and the first SCSI adapter driver loads.

However, once the second driver for the other SCSI adapter loads, John is unable to use INSTALL to partition the drives. In fact, none of the drives show up at all. He begins experimenting. He tries removing one of the cards. The other one works fine and its drives are visible to INSTALL. He reinstalls the first and removes the second. The first one works fine, too. He tries setting the cards to different interrupt settings, thinking that they might not like being on adjacent disk channels. They still won't work when both cards are installed.

Finally, he goes to a higher authority. He calls CompuServe and asks some questions in the NetWare forum. Within a short while, he gets his answer: Those two SCSI adapters just won't work with each other. Maybe in the next version of the driver or ROM...

He decides to put all the drives on the single SCSI adapter that came with the tape drive until he can get another adapter from the same manufacturer. That works fine. He is able to mount all four drives and mirror the first two to the second two. He remembers to remove the termination from the second drive in each enclosure so that the daisy chain of two sets of drives and the tape drive will only be terminated at the end. He also makes sure that the SCSI ID is different for all five SCSI devices.

The drives are mounted and mirrored; now it's time to load the network drivers. John loads the network driver and binds the first protocol to the card. The server hangs. John checks the settings in the LOAD and BIND statements. If the DMA channel or memory segment numbers were wrong, he should get an error message. Instead, the server just freezes. Back to CompuServe. Finally, he discovers that his brand-new NIC should be used with the updated driver supplied on the disk that came with it, rather than with the file with the same name that came with NetWare. After he loads the updated driver and reboots, the NIC works fine.

After a few seconds, the server begins beeping and he sees the message "Router Configuration Error: Marketing is claiming my same Internet address." Then he remembers he has already used his girlfriend's phone number for the Marketing department server's internal network number. He decides to use the system he saw suggested in this book—he uses the number of the office the server is in as the first four digits of the network number, and the extension of the phone in the room as the last four digits. Now, after he has implemented this scheme throughout his company, he'll be able to tell where error messages are coming from without needing to refer to a long list of numbers and the servers they represent, and he will know the phone number of the room the server is in, too.

After the server is operational, he loads MONITOR to check the basic statistics for the server. When he selects Resource Utilization, the first thing he notices is that NetWare is showing total memory as 16MB. He takes the server down and checks the configuration of the server. The BIOS and DOS programs recognize the whole 64MB, but when he starts the server again, it still only shows 16MB. He checks several of the NetWare manuals before he finds the reference to REGISTER MEMORY in the System Administration manual. He enters the command and adds it to AUTOEXEC.NCF, and everything is fine.

Lessons Learned—Scenario One

- Remember to check the termination and ID of SCSI drives. You may not get an outright failure, but instead an intermittent problem that will drive you crazy.

- If you can't figure it out, don't spend huge amounts of time experimenting—try asking someone.

- If you're using more than 16MB of RAM, make sure you know the implications for compatibility with other components and drivers. You may also need to change the default configurations of NetWare to recognize the memory.

- Get adapters from the same manufacturer whenever possible. Even though the standards (Ethernet, SCSI, and so on) are supposed to be the same, they aren't always implemented in quite the same way. Drivers from different manufacturers may conflict with each other, too. If you are having a conflict, you can try using the same driver for both cards. Don't expect this to work, though.

- Make sure your drivers match your devices. Check NetWire or your authorized reseller to see if you have the latest version of the drivers.

- On a multi-server LAN, be sure to have a scheme for coordinating internal network numbers and LAN numbers.

The Fault-Point Chain—Scenario One

In this scenario, there are several chains, from the server to each device, and then on the server itself. The fault points below are for the hard disks. Each problem above has its own chain.

The Disk Drives:

- AC power from the wall.

- The power cord.

- The power supply for the disk drive.

- The power cable from the power supply to the disk drive.

- The disk drive mechanism itself.

- The terminating resistors on the disk drive.

- The data cable from the disk drive to the port on the enclosure.

- The data cable from the enclosure to the controller in the server.

- The terminating resistor on the controller. This chain could also continue instead to an internal SCSI drive in the server.

- The controller (hardware).

- The controller (configuration).
- The disk driver installed in NetWare.

The Server:

- AC power from the wall.
- The power cord.
- The power supply for the server.
- The motherboard.
- The BIOS configuration of the server.
- The configuration of the cards in the server (conflicts).
- Differences in implementations of SCSI on the two controllers.
- DOS.
- NetWare (SERVER.EXE).
- The disk drivers (AHA2740.DSK, OTHER.DSK).
- The formatting and partitioning already on the drives.

NOTE   INSTALL sometimes has problems with drives that were previously formatted with other operating systems. The cure is to format the drives using a DOS formatter, then format them again with NetWare.

Each of these points could have made the disk drives fail to show up as available for partitioning. Some of them can be quickly verified (if the power light on the enclosure is on and you can hear the drive spin up, the first four on that chain are eliminated) before you check the others. In this case, John wasn't initially aware of the possibility that the two controllers might conflict with each other. This may happen to you, too. If you believe you have eliminated all the possibilities, then there is probably something in the chain that you've either overlooked or aren't aware of.

Scenario Two: Maintaining an Existing System

Fran, an administrator for Great Big, Inc., is faced with a server that won't respond to the prompt. She encounters a problem with a faulty NIC and then has trouble with the disk drive, probably caused by the original crash.

Snapshot—Scenario Two

Is this an existing system?

- Is the server up?
- Can you reboot the server?
- Will the server boot DOS?
- Will NetWare load?
- Can you load NetWare but not access some or all server functions?

Fran, the system administrator for Great Big, Inc., comes back to her desk after lunch. There are 15 messages from various users, saying that they can't connect to the server, or that their applications don't work, or that they can't see drive F. Fran notices that all the user complaints are from people with accounts on the Marketing server, so she decides to check that server first, before looking at all the users' workstations. She grabs the data sheet she prepared when she installed the server, which lists its hardware and software configurations, and heads for the office the server is in.

The server is on, and there is text on the monitor (nothing helpful), but the server doesn't respond to the keyboard. Even the CapsLock and NumLock keys don't respond. She checks the connection between the keyboard and CPU and tries again. Still nothing. There is a workstation in the room. She tries to connect to the server and gets the message "Server marketing is unknown at this time."

Fran reboots the server. Both DOS and NetWare load properly and the server is back online. Relieved that another crisis has been averted, she logs in as supervisor from the workstation and begins checking the volumes to make sure that everything is accessible again. After about five minutes, the workstation loses the connection to the server, and on checking, Fran finds that the server has hung again.

After she finishes her primal scream therapy, Fran begins eliminating possible causes. Since the server will boot and load DOS and NetWare, and it has been running fine for quite a while, it's almost certainly not a configuration problem. She is the only one with the supervisor password, and she hasn't changed anything on this server in months, so it shouldn't be a problem with an addition being configured improperly.

She notifies the department members that the server may be down for a while, and then reboots the server again, paying particular attention to the messages from the BIOS, DOS, and NetWare. There are no out-of-the-ordinary messages or errors reported. She logs in again from the workstation and quickly goes to the system error log. At the end are a number of messages relating to Ethernet configuration errors. A clue!

She quickly checks the system error log of another server on the same Ethernet segment, and it does not display the same errors. From this, she deduces that the problem may be related to Ethernet but is probably also unique to this server. She tries to log in again, and the server is down. She turns the server off and replaces the Ethernet card with a spare.

The server comes up, but now it can't mount the second volume. Fran ignores this problem for the moment—it may be the result of the freezes and powering off without shutting down properly. She logs in from the workstation and waits anxiously. Five minutes, then ten, then fifteen pass. There are no new messages in the system error log. It seems that the original problem has been fixed.

Now, it's time to get that second volume mounted again. Fran starts up VREPAIR and begins scanning the unmounted volume for errors. It finds errors and says it's repairing them. When VREPAIR finishes, Fran brings the server down correctly, then restarts it. It still can't mount the second volume. Then Fran remembers that VREPAIR should be run over and over again until it doesn't report any errors.

Unfortunately for Fran, with 20 people clamoring outside the door to know when their server will be back on line, the VREPAIR process is taking about 20 minutes per cycle with this 1.2GB volume. However, on the fourth time through, there are no further errors reported.

When she restarts the server, the volume mounts properly, and everyone is able to log in and get to their files again. Fran reflects that it might have been faster to reformat the drive and restore the disk from last night's backup, but all the work done that day would have been lost. She resolves to talk to her manager about mirroring the drives on the mission-critical servers as insurance against this sort of problem.

Fran then logs the incident in her work log, recording the problems and solutions in case she comes across a similar situation again. She also logs the problems on the data sheet for the server.

Lessons Learned—Scenario Two

- Check to see whether a reported problem is affecting more than one user—it will help you tell whether the problem is with the user's workstation or with the server or cabling.

- Check the server's system error log regularly. Not only will this enable you to distinguish important messages more easily, you may well be able to spot a potential problem before it results in downtime.

- Remember that it may be necessary to run VREPAIR several times before all errors are corrected.

- Mirror the drives on mission-critical servers.

- Keep a log, and keep it updated. It will help you solve the problem the next time. There will be a next time.

The Fault-Point Chain—Scenario Two

There are several fault-point chains in this example. The first one is the original problem with the server.

- AC power from the wall. This includes spikes or brownouts.

- The power cord.

- The power supply for the server.

- The motherboard including RAM.

- The BIOS power. If the batteries wear out, configuration information is lost.

- The BIOS configuration of the server.

- The cards in the server. Each has its own chain of connections, configuration, drivers, and so on.

- The keyboard and its cable.

- The monitor, its power, its cable, and the video adapter.

- NetWare. SERVER.EXE could be corrupted, or could simply have crashed.

- The NLMs loaded when the server crashed.

- Applications running on the users' workstations when the server crashed.

In this case, many of these possibilities are easily eliminated. If there is text on the screen, obviously the server has power and the monitor is working. If the BIOS were configured incorrectly or its batteries worn out, the server wouldn't boot correctly. The keyboard responds after rebooting. Since no one has logged in yet, it couldn't be applications running on the server. This trims the list down to the motherboard, the cards in the server, NetWare itself, and the NLMs. The messages in the system error log pointed the way to the first item to check. But if there hadn't been any messages, the order of things to try (easiest to hardest) might have been this: replacing SERVER.EXE, not loading the NLMs, replacing the cards one at a time, and trying another motherboard.

Summary

In this chapter, we began by looking at an NT troubleshooting snapshot, followed by a similar one for NetWare/IntraNetWare servers. We identified various server fault points and discussed various hardware problems that can affect servers. We looked at the setup procedures for installing NT and NetWare. We discussed system fault tolerance and looked at two real-life examples of troubleshooting server problems.

In the next chapter, we'll discuss the client side of the equation, as we look at the various things than can go wrong with client workstations on a network.

CHAPTER
THIRTY-FOUR

Troubleshooting Workstations

- Snapshot of problem areas

- Workstation fault points

- Troubleshooting Windows and OS/2 clients

- Troubleshooting Macintosh clients

- Troubleshooting Unix clients

- Four troubleshooting scenarios

Workstations tend to be the system administrator's least favorite support area, because a wide variety of things can go wrong and because so many of those things are likely to be noted in less than clear language by multiple users. The worst is that the workstation represents all that is outside of the administrator's direct control. They're thinking, workstation = anarchy. End users make endless adjustments, adjuncts, and end-arounds to their systems in an effort to make them "theirs." In the end, this only serves to fray the nerves of everyone (including the end user, of course, when they find they've created something they can't fix).

In this chapter, we look at various techniques for diagnosing workstation problems. While we cannot cover every possible scenario that may come up, a number of the more common ones are described here.

Snapshot: Troubleshooting Workstations

In this section, we look at a "snapshot" you may find handy for diagnosing workstation problems. While we cannot cover every possible scenario that may come up, a number of the more common ones are described here. Just skip down the list of questions until you come to one that describes symptoms similar to what your workstation is experiencing.

Is This a New PC-Compatible System?

Does the POST (power-on self test) finish without error messages?
If so, go to the next item. If not, the system may be configured incorrectly with the SETUP program, or it may have been assembled incorrectly. Some examples of POST error messages are "RAM configuration error, block 22f," "Kybd Error 301," and "Hard disk not ready." See the section "PC Configuration with the SETUP Program."

Does the workstation boot without error messages?   If so, go to the next item. If not, the error messages should give you a clue as to the problem. Newer video adapters, hard disk adapters, and LAN adapters are examples of possible sources of these messages. See the section "PC Cards and Connections."

Does DOS load without error messages?   If so, go to the next item. If not, try booting from a floppy disk. If this works, replace the COMMAND.COM file on the hard disk. If DOS still won't load correctly, see the section "DOS and Its Configuration."

Do the network drivers load without error messages?   If so, go to the next item. If not, try replacing the network drivers. If this doesn't help, the driver may be configured incorrectly. Check the network adapter version and the version of DOS in use. If everything matches, the NIC may be faulty. See the section "Networking Software."

Can you log in to the server?   If there are no error messages but you cannot see the server, try to log in to another server, if there is one. Also, try to log in from another workstation. If the server is up and more than one workstation cannot log in, the problem is likely to be with the physical network—either the cabling itself, or one of the devices such as a concentrator or repeater. See the section "Troubleshooting Workstations—The Basics" (and also Chapter 35 for details).

Is This an Existing PC-Compatible System?

Is the display readable? Does the cursor respond to the keyboard?   If so, go to the next item. If not, make sure the PC is on. Are there any status lights on? Is the fan running? If the PC is on, but won't respond to keyboard input, it is frozen. Reboot the PC. A simple test to see if the keyboard is functioning is to try the Caps-Lock or NumLock keys—if the indicator lights on the keyboard come on, the keyboard is functioning, whether the screen responds or not. This type of hang is typical of software problems, usually with applications or TSR programs.

The number of possible causes for freezing are practically infinite. If the PC hangs regularly, it could be a hardware problem or a software problem; it could even be both. Check for software problems first. See the section "Troubleshooting PC Software."

If the screen or keyboard still won't respond after rebooting, check their connections to the PC. If they are as they should be, review the hardware configuration to check for interrupt conflicts. See the section "Troubleshooting PC Hardware."

Does the POST (power-on self test) finish without error messages?
If so, go to the next item. If not, the chip that holds the setup data may have lost power, or there may be a hardware failure. Check the configuration with SETUP. See the section "PC Configuration with the SETUP Program." If everything matches your configuration worksheet, see the section "Troubleshooting PC Hardware."

Does the workstation boot without error messages?   If so, go to the next item. If not, the error messages should give you a clue as to the problem. Video adapters, hard disk adapters, and LAN adapters are examples of possible sources of these messages. See the section "PC Cards and Connections."

Does the operating system load without error messages?   If so, go to the next item. If not, try booting from a floppy disk. If this works, replace the COMMAND.COM file on the hard disk with a fresh copy from an installation diskette or CD. If a boot floppy containing DOS (or a Windows 9x boot floppy) still won't load correctly, then the problem may be with some of the items in the AUTOEXEC.BAT or CONFIG.SYS files. See the section "Troubleshooting PC Software."

Does the workstation "see" the server ?   If so, go to the next item. If not, the problem may be in the connection to the physical network, in the physical network itself, or in the server. If the server is working (the screen is on and the console prompt responds), check the connections from the network adapter to the transceiver (if any) and to the physical network. See the section "PC Cards and Connections," and also Chapter 35, which is about troubleshooting the physical network.

Can you log in to the server?   If not, make sure that the user you are attempting to log in as exists, and that the spelling of the username and the password are correct. Try logging in as another user. If this doesn't work, make sure that a station restriction has not been set up for that PC. Also see the section about BINDFIX in Chapter 35. If you are using NDS, be sure that the context is specified correctly.

Does Windows load without errors?   Once the workstation has booted, DOS has loaded, the NetWare shell has loaded, and you can connect with the network, you can be fairly sure that the workstation is functioning correctly. If Windows produces error messages, it is almost certainly because of configuration problems with Windows. See the section "Windows and Networks."

Can Windows attach to the network?   If the workstation can connect to the network under DOS, but not under Windows, this may be caused by a setup problem with Windows. See the section "Windows and Networks."

Is This a Macintosh System?

Does the POST (power-on self test) finish with a tone instead of a chord?   When the POST runs, you will hear a tone when it is completed. If you hear a chord (well, an arpeggio, really: three or more tones one after the other), the POST has failed. If the POST fails, it means you have a hardware problem. Try reseating the cards and memory in the system, and check for loose connections on the power supply, hard disk, floppy drive, and so on. See the section "The Startup Sequence." See the sections under "The Macintosh Client."

Does the workstation boot without error messages and without freezing?   As the Mac boots, you will see icons appear along the bottom of the screen. These icons represent the additional system extensions, Control Panels, or CDEVs (the older term for Control Panels) that are loading. You can usually find the corresponding driver by looking in the System folder, the Extensions folder, or the Control Panels folder for a corresponding icon. (The view must be set to Large Icon.) If there is a problem with a driver, you may get an error message in a window on screen, or the Mac may just freeze. Either way, identify the last icon, reboot with extensions turned off (by holding the Shift key down while the Mac boots), and remove that driver, then reboot. See the sections "The Startup Sequence" and "Problems with the Bootstrapping Sequence."

Do the network drivers load without errors?   The network drivers should load along with the others during the boot process. During a successful bootup, you should be able to see the icons associated with the network drivers, as they appear across the bottom of the screen. The most likely cause of error messages at this point is from faulty configuration information. See the sections under "The Macintosh Client."

Does the workstation see the server in the Chooser?   If not, check to be sure that the Macintosh name space is loaded on the server. If it is, recheck the physical connections and reboot. If it still won't work, try reinstalling the network driver. If that still doesn't work, you may have a faulty network card or LocalTalk adapter.

Summary of Troubleshooting Techniques

PC compatibles can be very difficult to troubleshoot, principally because of their enormous variety. There are at least seven Intel processors in use, at twenty or so different speeds, plus clone processors from other companies such as AMD, IBM, Cyrix, and Thompson. There are many different motherboards and BIOS versions for each processor, hundreds of different hard disks, and thousands of different cards. All this variety can make troubleshooting a maze, especially if you don't have the documentation for the PC. However, if you understand the principles of how the PC loads its BIOS, operating system, network drivers, and other software, you should be able to isolate the cause of any problem and figure out what to do about it.

Most workstations attached to Novell networks are currently IBM-compatible PCs of one type or another. However, there are other possibilities: PS/2s, Macintoshes, and Unix workstations are the most likely. Some of the principles discussed in this chapter apply equally to all sorts of workstations, but some are platform-specific. I'll cover the fault points applicable to all platforms first, then I'll go into the specifics of different platforms: IBM compatibles, Windows clients, OS/2 clients, PS/2 workstations, Macintoshes, and Unix workstations, in that order. The "Real-Life Stories" section at the end of this chapter will lead you through some real problems, showing how they were diagnosed and resolved.

NOTE Troubleshooting servers is covered in Chapter 33. However, if problems with a server occur *before* NetWare loads, you should treat it as a workstation, using the troubleshooting techniques in this chapter.

Fault Points for Workstations

Chapter 33 introduced the concept of *fault points* as an alternative to the more conventional flow charts. The problem with flow charts is that they become too difficult to use with subjects as complex as a network, or even when covering the possible configurations of a workstation.

The basic fault-point chain for a workstation includes the same elements for any type of workstation. If you understand the potential fault points for a workstation, you will be able to isolate any problem to a particular part of the system, then apply the concepts presented in this chapter to figure out how to fix the problem.

Figure 34.1 illustrates a typical fault chain for workstations. Each item in the chain depends on the others, and each item has three parts: the part itself, the connections between it and the preceding part, and the connections between it and the following part. For example, the power at the wall socket can be broken if the power to the socket fails, if the socket itself is faulty, or if the power cord to the PC power supply is defective or not plugged in. Similarly, the power supply itself is connected on the one hand to the wall by means of the power cord and has connections on the other hand to the motherboard, the disk drives, and the fan.

FIGURE 34.1:

The fault-point chain for workstations

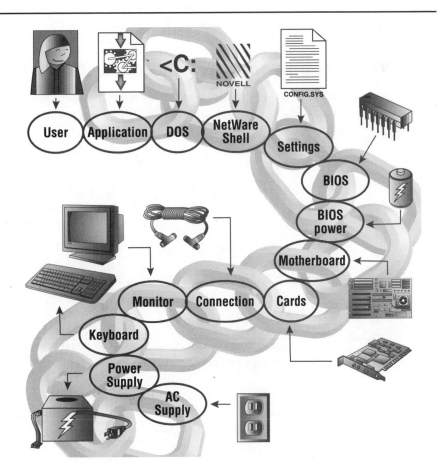

To determine which of the three parts of the chain is causing the problem, you must use deductive logic. If any part of the workstation is receiving power, the power supply and the cable are probably good. If one part of the workstation is not getting power, and the rest are, it's probably the connection for that part to the power supply. If the workstation isn't getting power anywhere, check the power cord and the socket before replacing the power supply.

You might think that the keyboard has only two parts: the keyboard and its connection to the motherboard. However, the third part here is the user. If the wrong keys are pressed, the symptoms may resemble a problem with the keyboard hardware or the connection to the PC. This is also true of the monitor, but it has even more variables: It may be turned off independently of the PC, it has a power connection and a video connection, and it can also be made to seem dead by turning down the contrast and brightness.

Workstation-to-Network Connection Failures

The connection to the network is a common failure point, because of the number of possible fault points and their susceptibility to outside interference. The network connection usually consists of the connection from the NIC in the PC to a transceiver, to a concentrator or hub, or directly to the server, depending on the type of network topology.

For example, take the relatively simple case of a NIC with a thick Ethernet connection, connected to a transceiver that converts the thick Ethernet to 10BaseT, which is connected to a wall jack with a second cable. In this chain, several things can go wrong:

- The thick Ethernet cable can slip from the NIC, can become defective, or can come loose from the transceiver.

- The transceiver can become defective.

- The 10BaseT cable can come out of its socket on the transceiver, can become defective, or can come out of the wall socket.

The network connection fault points are further complicated by the fact that they are often hard to see, difficult to get at, and subject to being kicked by the user or pulled out by a janitor with a vacuum.

PC Card, Motherboard, and BIOS Failures

Each card in the PC has its own fault-point chain, including:

- The connections to the bus and to whatever device it supports
- Its jumper configurations for interrupt, DMA segment, and so forth
- The matching configurations in the setup of the PC, whether in hardware or software

The motherboard has a point of failure where the power supply connects to it, and one for each service it provides, whether on a card, a parallel or serial port, the keyboard interface, the sound interface, or the memory. Each of these can typically be diagnosed by the error messages that appear during the boot sequence, or, as a last resort, by eliminating all other possible causes.

The BIOS, and the associated CMOS, holds configuration information for the PC, including the number and types of floppy and hard drives installed, the number of serial and parallel ports installed, the time, and other information. If the battery that provides power to the BIOS wears out, this information can be lost. If the BIOS is out of date, it may not support new floppy drives or hard drives, or it may cause problems with software, such as Windows not running in the 386-Enhanced mode with an older 386 BIOS.

Operating System and Network Driver Failures

On Systems Running Windows 95 or Windows 98

Compared to a DOS boot (using DOS network requestor software), both Windows 95 and Windows 98 initialize the networking-related drivers later in the OS startup process. Thus, even with a problem network card or incorrect driver setting, normally you will at least see the Desktop screen appear before any errors occur. As a result, it is unlikely you will see a system that fails to boot due to a networking-related problem. One exception to this is if a network adapter happens to have an address conflict, say with an IDE or SCSI interface card, which could directly prevent the system from booting.

One other case where a network card can cause a system to not boot (or appear that it won't boot) is when you've previously had a network adapter installed and the corresponding network adapter drivers installed, and then removed the adapter. If you reboot the machine at this point, what should happen is that Windows 9x simply detects that the card is no longer in the machine. What we have seen happen instead, though, is that in one case the system took a few minutes (with simply a black screen and flashing cursor) before it simply decided to finish booting without the adapter—but with no message indicating that that's what it decided to do. (Of course, the fact that it took so long to boot was indication enough that there was a problem.) To resolve this problem, go into Device Manager (once Windows finally does boot) and either remove the old driver or disable it. (Choose Disable for This Hardware Profile if you envision needing to reinstall the card later.)

Finally, Windows 95 and Windows 98 can be prevented from booting when their MBR (master boot record) gets corrupted (as from a virus) or when a hard drive suddenly dies.

You should always be running a virus checking program, but if you're not, and your MBR ever gets corrupted, it's relatively easy to fix. As long as you have the virus cleaning portion of the virus check program, you should be able to boot using a floppy and then run that program to remove the virus. If you do not have a virus cleaning utility, then follow this procedure:

To remove a virus (or repair the master boot record):

1. Shut off the system.

2. Switch to another system running the same version of the operating system. (Make *sure* it's the same version—it's important.)

3. Create a boot disk containing the *system files*. (Transferring system files is one of the few options offered when you're formatting a floppy).

4. Copy to the floppy the SYS.COM file from the \WINDOWS\SYSTEM directory on the working station.

5. Now, put this floppy into the system that failed to boot, and reboot the system.

6. The system should boot into "DOS", or command-prompt–only Windows 9x. From the command prompt for the floppy drive, type **SYS C:**, which should cause a new MBR to be written over the defective one. (This also transfers system files, such as COMMAND.COM. However, that is not relevant to what we're doing.)

7. Now remove the floppy and attempt to restart the machine.

The system should now restart and boot correctly, unless of course something *else* is causing the problem. If you have any reason to suspect that it was a virus that caused your MBR to get corrupted, the first thing you should really do after fixing the master boot record is run a virus check program.

If your hard drive suddenly dies, first try to restart the system several times. If that doesn't help, it's likely you'll need to have the drive replaced.

If the system stopped working immediately after you added some hardware, then remove it (the hardware itself and/or its expansion card) and see if that resolves the problem. It should, unless you accidentally loosened a card or jarred something in the system in the process of adding this other hardware. Double check that all cables are connected tightly and all expansion cards are seated firmly in the bus. Also check for loose SIMMs or any other signs of loose or disconnected hardware. You should be able to get the system back working again at this point.

If your Windows 9x system does boot, and then displays a driver-related problem or exhibits generally erratic behavior, go into the Device Manager and view the list of all installed devices (drivers, actually). Any detected conflicts should be flagged with a small yellow exclamation mark or red stop sign icon (these are warnings and errors, respectively). Highlight the affected entry and choose Properties to view a brief description of that item's status. In the majority of cases, if there's a resource conflict it will say so. In this case, you can try to reconfigure that driver, or remove or disable the driver (temporarily). Actually resolving a resource conflict requires reconfiguring one or more existing hardware devices to use a different resource, or else removing one of the devices.

On Systems Running NT Workstation or NT Server

Please see Chapter 33 for a troubleshooting snapshot and list of corrective steps for addressing problems related to NT.

If You Happen to Still Be Running DOS/Win3.*x*...

The PC's operating system and the networking software are configured with several files, including AUTOEXEC.BAT, CONFIG.SYS, and, if you're using NetWare, NET.CFG. Each of these files contains statements that must be spelled correctly and must also match the settings on the cards they pertain to.

The network software can fail in its connection with the PC hardware and software, by itself, or in its interface with applications. If the shell isn't configured correctly, it won't match the interrupt and memory address used by the NIC, and some shells work better than others with certain applications.

The version of DOS you use can also cause problems in one of three ways:

- By not working well with the PC hardware (unusual with versions later than 3)

- By not working well with applications

- By not working well with extended memory or other added features

Some applications may require a specific version of DOS. Many versions of DOS provide services such as memory management, networking support, and file compression.

User Failures

Finally, the user is the end point on the workstation fault-point chain. Many of the problems that will be reported to you will not be hardware or software problems, but problems caused by misunderstandings—either misinterpretation of instructions or a lack of knowledge about the software.

As an administrator, the best way to deal with users is to provide some training and to encourage them to acquire training on their own. See Chapter 38, which covers ways to prevent problems, for more information about training users.

Troubleshooting Workstations— The Basics

The basic procedure for troubleshooting workstations follows the approach outlined in Chapter 29: Check the obvious sources of problems first, and get whatever information you can about what went wrong.

All computers work in essentially the same way. This includes PCs, Macintoshes, Unix workstations, minicomputers, and so forth. When you turn the computer on, the system looks in its read-only memory (ROM) for instructions on what to do next. Next, it performs a power-on self test (POST) routine, then reads further instructions from a boot device (usually a hard disk, but it could also be a floppy disk, a tape drive, or even a device on the network). The boot device will load the core operating system into memory, followed by other programs that enhance the operation of the computer. These other programs include network drivers, memory optimization programs, and many, many others. If you understand this process for the computers you deal with, and the messages or indications that go with each stage, you will have a much better chance of understanding what's happening when something goes wrong.

Checking Connections

Often, the only problem with a workstation is a loose or disconnected cable. Never assume that the user has checked seemingly obvious possibilities. Check all the connections, including the keyboard, mouse, monitor, power, and network. The usual workstation has a rat's nest of cables behind it or on the floor under the desk. In some cases, especially with network connections that are relatively sensitive to loose wiring, some connections may appear to be okay—even showing a green attachment light on the transceiver—but still cause problems. The first thing to check with any installed workstation that suddenly begins having problems is that all the connections are solid.

> **TIP**
>
> Unless the workstation is a test or demo machine that is often reconfigured, we strongly recommend that you screw all the connections down tight. It's a pain when you need to replace something, but it lessens the chance of a user kicking something loose or of the janitor pulling out a connection while vacuuming.

Remember that all the connections might not be on the workstation. If the problem is network-related and the connections seem to be okay, check the transceiver or the status light on the network card, if applicable. For example, a LatticeNet transceiver has two lights: SQE Test and Status. If the SQE Test light is out, it indicates that the connection to the PC is out. If the Status light is out and the SQE Test is on, however, it indicates that the connection is broken between the transceiver and the server or concentrator.

The workstation's error message or behavior may not seem to point directly at the problem. For instance, the symptom might be a monitor that is blank or showing a fuzzy or distorted display. These symptoms might be the result of a dead motherboard, a dead display adapter, or an extreme software problem. However, the problem might also be as simple as a video or power cable that has worked loose. Or it could be that another monitor has been placed too close to the first.

Checking for Changes

Troubleshooting workstations is the place to apply the principle of determining what has recently changed. Has the equipment been moved recently? Has anything new been added or removed? If the user says no, check connections anyway—something could have been accidentally kicked loose by the user, or a connector could have gradually worked out of its socket.

You should have a data sheet for the PC. Check it to see if the configuration on it matches the current configuration. Check to see if the fan is running; if not, either the PC is not getting power or the power supply is dead.

Ask the user if he or she knows of any way to make the problem go away. Also ask whether the problem occurs at a particular time or at certain intervals. Find out what software was running when the PC froze, and what the chain of events leading up to the crash were.

Checking New Installations

If you're troubleshooting a new installation, the same principles apply: Check the obvious before trying the obscure. Make sure that the power is on and that the connections are tight before replacing the network cards.

Check the possibilities that cost you the least time or money first. It doesn't cost much to verify a power connection, but rechecking all the wiring of a network is relatively expensive.

Ideally, you should use the same type of workstation throughout the LAN, with the same kind of video adapter, network adapter, and so on. However, in real life this is usually not possible. The next best thing is to standardize on certain brands. If all your network adapters come from the same manufacturer, it will make your life simpler.

Troubleshooting PC-Compatible Stations

PC compatibles, and workstations in general, have a uniform underlying structure. Figure 34.2 illustrates the basic workstation structure.

No matter what components are used, the underlying structure is similar—the motherboard and operating system tie together all the assorted pieces. No matter what the CPU is, how much memory is installed, or what type of display or network adapter is installed, the basic structure remains the same. In terms of the fault-point chain, this is all you need to keep in mind. Similarly, troubleshooting a problem with the display is the same, regardless of whether you have a PC with a monochrome display adapter, a 486 EISA PC with a VESA accelerated XGA (eXtended VGA) adapter, or a dual-Pentium, dual-bus PCI system with lots of cards.

FIGURE 34.2:

Basic workstation structure

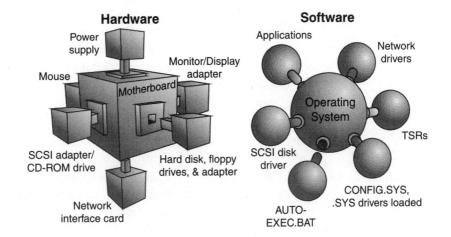

Hardware

Power supply

Monitor/Display adapter

Mouse

Motherboard

SCSI adapter/ CD-ROM drive

Hard disk, floppy drives, & adapter

Network interface card

Software

Applications

Network drivers

Operating System

TSRs

SCSI disk driver

CONFIG.SYS, .SYS drivers loaded

AUTO-EXEC.BAT

Troubleshooting PC Hardware

From a troubleshooter's perspective, PC hardware does not materially change from the first 8088 PC produced in 1983 to the latest dual-processor Pentium II PCI system. There are, of course, vast differences in speed, size, chips, cost, and other features. However, from a functional standpoint, they are very similar: the motherboard holds a CPU chip or two, memory, slots for peripherals, a BIOS chip, a keyboard connector, and some miscellaneous odds and ends. Understand how these pieces work together on any given system, and you can apply that knowledge to any other.

The Boot Sequence

To troubleshoot a PC effectively, you should understand the sequence of events that occur when the machine is turned on. The POST routine will run diagnostic tests on the motherboard, test the memory, and then tell you that the hard disk adapter is working and how many hard disks are connected to it. Then, before DOS begins loading, you may also see messages from some of the cards installed in the PC. Network adapters, SCSI adapters, and video cards are typical examples of cards that produce messages, although not all such cards do.

A missing boot message, or a message like "Error configuring LAN adapter," will give you helpful clues to get a PC working again, but only if you are paying close attention. Often these messages are on the screen for a very short time, and there is usually no way to scroll back up the screen and review them. You may need to reboot the PC several times to get the complete text of a message. This is another time when some advance work will stand you in good stead. If all your PCs have the same configuration, or if you have become familiar with the normal series of messages that appear as each workstation boots, it will be much easier for you to spot anomalies.

Later versions of DOS and Windows 9x make it possible for you to see the messages you normally wouldn't see and choose to load or not load each command in CONFIG.SYS or AUTOEXEC.BAT:

- With DOS, simply press the F8 key when you see the "Loading MS-DOS" message. It will ask you if you want to process CONFIG.SYS. You will then be able to choose to load or not load each command. Then it will ask you if you want to process AUTOEXEC.BAT. If you say yes, you will again be able to choose whether or not to process each command.

- With Windows 95 or 98, holding down the F8 key during the boot process will bring you to a menu that lets you choose to load Windows in safe mode, safe mode with network drivers loaded, or DOS mode. The menu also offers choices for going through each command in sequence, booting in other modes, and for loading normally. See the section about Windows 95 later in this chapter for more information about this type of workstation.

PC Cards and Connections

The power is on, the PC boots reliably, the status light on the transceiver is green, but the workstation won't connect to the network. What's the problem? It may still be a loose connection. Network adapters and transceivers vary considerably in the degree of tolerance they have for loose connections. It is entirely possible for the connection to be solid enough to light the status light on a transceiver, for instance, but still be loose enough to prevent the network adapter from connecting properly. Never depend on the status lights; go ahead and crawl under the desk and check the connections.

WARNING   Always observe static safety precautions. Make sure that you are adequately grounded before handling the internals of any workstation. Your body generates small amounts of static electricity all the time, and walking on carpet generates enough static to destroy any computer component except the power supply. Destroying the parts you are attempting to check is self-defeating to say the least. If you don't have a grounding strap, at least make sure you touch the case of a power supply that's plugged in before handling any cards, memory modules, or the like.

If the external connections are all solid, try reseating the adapter cards. Often the cards are not secured properly and may have worked loose, especially if the connections are changed often. It may also be that the contacts on the edge of the adapter card are somewhat corroded, causing a faulty connection. If this seems to be a possibility, try rubbing the row of connectors at the bottom of the card, gently, with an ink eraser. Be sure not to get rubber shavings in the PC, and wipe the contacts off with a tissue when you're finished. Get a supply of the proper screws and make sure that all cards are screwed down.

If it's a new installation, make sure that the cards are fully seated, and that the connections are fully seated too—it's easy to mistake a good connection for a faulty one in both cases. Install all the supplied screws and cable connectors. This may be a pain initially but the effort will pay off in the long run. Never assume that two cards will work together, especially in their default settings. In fact, some cards may be impossible to use together, because neither will allow a combination of settings that won't interfere with the other.

Cards may also simply be incompatible with each other, either at a hardware level or because the device drivers necessary to access them conflict. In these cases, you should read the documentation for all equipment you plan to install and make sure that compatibility with anything else you plan to install has been established. The most common instance of this sort of problem occurs with SCSI adapters and their drivers. You should not plan to use SCSI adapters from different manufacturers in the same PC.

If you need to ship a workstation, remove the cards and pack them separately. Use original packing if available. Some manufacturers will not honor the warranty if products are not returned in the original shipping containers.

Interrupt Conflicts

Interrupt conflicts are one of the potentially most confusing areas, but also often one of the most straightforward. It's usually just a matter of reading the manuals for the adapters used in the PC (assuming that the interrupts and memory segments are adequately documented). There often seems to be great resistance to reading the manual, but try it. Most manuals will, somewhere, discuss getting the card in question to operate with other cards, sometimes even specifically suggesting alternate settings for use with other specific adapters or certain software.

There are two parts to the settings on ISA cards: the memory address (a segment in RAM) and the IRQ (interrupt). The basic requirement to get cards to work together is to make sure that they use different memory segments and different IRQs.

Interrupt conflicts are primarily an issue in setting up new systems, but sometimes a conflict will produce only intermittent problems. This is especially true when the memory segments used by different cards overlap rather than using all of the same segment. For example, 16-bit video adapters usually use a larger segment than other types of cards, often including memory locations used by Windows. If some software will run but other programs will not, it may be because these programs are attempting to directly address memory in use by an adapter. This can usually be resolved in Windows by using the EMMEXCLUDE command in the SYSTEM.INI file. With other programs, it may be necessary to use a memory manager such as QEMM.

The easiest way to resolve interrupt conflicts is to reduce the number of cards in the PC to the minimum, then add the other cards back in, one at a time, until the conflict is found. Resolving it then becomes a matter of using alternate addresses where possible until the problem is solved.

EISA PCs can avoid interrupt problems entirely by using the enhanced 32-bit bus-mastering mode. However, under certain conditions, such as when the PC needs to have more than 16MB of RAM, all the cards in the system must be EISA-compatible, and EISA drivers must be available for all EISA cards. These cards are often more expensive, but they also provide higher performance.

PCI PCs can also avoid interrupt problems, assuming that there are no ISA cards in the PC and that the cards properly implement the PCI specification. There are issues to be aware of here, too. If the BIOS PCI configuration is set to AUTO, you shouldn't see any problems under normal circumstances. However, if it has been changed to a manual configuration, it is possible to have two cards using PCI interrupt A, B, C or D, or translating to the same ISA interrupt, which can cause problems. Another issue to look at is what version of the PCI specification is supported by the motherboard BIOS and by the cards. If they don't match, you might have problems. Particularly with older systems, you may find an incompatibility problem, such as a high-end graphics card that won't run on a Pentium PC with a 25MHz bus speed.

PC Configuration with the SETUP Program

Depending on the version of the PC, SETUP may be a program that you'll need to run or it may be programmed into the PC's BIOS. See your owner's manual for details if you're not sure how to run it. As an administrator, you should have copies of the SETUP.COM program for every PC that uses it. Be aware that different manufacturers and models will require different versions of the program.

The setup program for most computers can be accessed by pressing the F8, F2, or F10 key immediately after the system starts booting up. There are also a few machines which use the Delete key for this purpose. Usually while booting up, your system will briefly display instructions about which key to press to bring up the internal setup program.

NOTE   On a Windows 95 or Windows 98 system, you may not see the boot instructions for getting into the setup program due to its being hidden by the Windows startup screen. To remove the Windows startup screen, simply press the Esc key and you'll immediately see the typical text-mode boot screen.

Common problems with SETUP include having a device listed incorrectly or omitted from the configuration and losing stored parameters due to a battery failure. The information you set with SETUP is stored in a chip on the motherboard. If the battery that keeps this chip operating fails, the information will be lost. As a result, the PC may be unable to use its floppy and hard drives, may be unable to communicate with its video adapter, or may lose its connection to serial or parallel ports.

The configuration information necessary to use SETUP includes:

- The size and type of floppy drives installed (double-density or high-density, and 3.5-inch or 5.25-inch)
- The type and number of hard drives installed
- The video adapter installed
- The current time and date

The most critical item is the hard drive type. Determine the type of the hard drive(s) installed in the PC and *write it down!* In addition to your log sheet, a label in an inconspicuous place on the outside of the PC is a good idea, but at least put a label on the drive itself. Identifying the drive type incorrectly in SETUP may cause the hard drive to be irretrievably damaged and will certainly cause the information on the drive to become unavailable. If you don't know the drive types for each of your existing PCs, use SETUP to determine them and write them down *before* there is a problem.

NOTE   Almost without exception, newer PCs using IDE drives will automatically detect the type of hard drive installed. When you are configuring a new PC, you will normally enter the BIOS after you have installed the hard drive and choose the Auto Detect Hard Drive option. Depending on the size of the drive, you may have several options on how to configure it, with differing numbers of sectors, heads, and so on. This doesn't mean the drive is variable in this regard, just the translation scheme.

DOS has a limitation of 504MB for direct hard drive support. For drives larger than that, your BIOS and your hard drive adapter must support a translation scheme to fool DOS. This is normally not a problem, but if you configure a drive in the BIOS and see that it is a 1GB hard drive, but FDISK will give you only a 504MB hard drive partition, it means that your hard drive controller doesn't support the Enhanced IDE specification (EIDE), which supports drives over 528MB. You can either replace the controller or run some software, such as DrivePro from Micro House or the Ontrack Disk Manager available with many large IDE drives.

If you are using a SCSI hard drive, you only need to make sure that the SCSI controller's BIOS is enabled. Some controllers' BIOSes will work only when the controller is set to the default memory address (often 330H). This can be a handicap if you are trying to get other cards to work (such as network adapters) that also want the same memory address. The SCSI BIOS does the translation necessary to get drives larger than 504MB to work with DOS.

Plug and Play

The idea behind Plug and Play is to make setting up a PC as simple and easy as setting up a Macintosh. Unfortunately, the execution is not that simple—at least not yet.

In a growing number of cases, you can just put the cards in any available slot, install Windows 95 or Windows 98, and have everything work. In other cases, you may find that the slot you put the card in is not a bus-mastering slot, and that the card needs to be in a bus-mastering slot.

You may also find that the driver that Windows 9x automatically loads when it finds the card is no longer the best driver to use. In this case, you must restart Windows, install a newer driver, then reboot, reconfigure the driver, and then reboot again.

Troubleshooting PC Software

PC software must work on several levels: the basic operating system, extensions and drivers, and application software. This is true of all PC operating systems. It is most straightforward with DOS systems. First, COMMAND.COM loads, which is the basic operating system. It loads the extensions and drivers specified in CONFIG.SYS, then the ones in AUTOEXEC.BAT. Network drivers may be loaded in AUTOEXEC.BAT or in another file, such as NETSTART.BAT, which can be started by AUTOEXEC.BAT. Finally, applications are loaded.

Windows (that is, versions before Windows 95) added another layer between the operating system and the application. Windows loads, and it may load a great many device drivers and extensions, controlled by a number of files including (but not limited to) SYSTEM.INI, WIN.INI, and NETWARE.INI.

Windows 9x, Windows NT, OS/2, and other operating systems, such as Solaris for Intel and NeXTStep for Intel, bypass DOS completely and use their own hardware interface software. The configuration files differ from system to system, but the basic sequence is the same. A small piece of the system, known as the *kernel*, is loaded automatically because it is on track 0 of the hard disk. It then reads other files, which tell it what to load and in what order.

DOS and Its Configuration

The biggest potential problem in troubleshooting workstation software is the wide variety of workstations that are out there. Most workstations combine one or more operating systems, various configuration files, and networking software. With PCs, for example, counting all the licensed versions, there are literally hundreds of versions of DOS; thousands of possible TSR (terminate-and-stay-resident) programs, device drivers, and other add-on enhancements; hundreds of possible configurations of IPX.COM and NETx.COM; and, of course, millions of possible configurations of AUTOEXEC.BAT, CONFIG.SYS, SHELL.CFG, and so on.

There are some basic principles to resolving software problems. If the problem is with an existing system, go back to the last working configuration. Add the new configuration in a piece at a time until you can determine the problem. It may be necessary to comment out the loading of TSRs or drivers in AUTOEXEC.BAT or CONFIG.SYS to discover which is conflicting with the new software you're attempting to install. You can also try pressing the F8 key during the boot process and deciding for each CONFIG.SYS and AUTOEXEC.BAT command whether it should execute or not.

Keeping the old versions of AUTOEXEC.BAT and CONFIG.SYS is not merely a sensible precaution, it's a *necessity*. Reconstructing old versions is time-consuming and may be impossible, depending on standardization, backups, and how well the system is documented. To avoid these problems, simply rename the old versions AUTOEXEC.OLD, CONFIG.BAK, or something similar. Many programs that modify these files use a similar procedure; all should.

Within an existing LAN, it's a good idea to standardize on a basic operating system. Using the same version of DOS, the same AUTOEXEC.BAT and CONFIG.SYS files, the same network drivers (and the same network cards), and the same basic login script will greatly reduce the record keeping necessary to document the network, the software necessary to install a new system or reinstall a faulty one, and the number of possible problems.

WARNING   A workstation with a virus can sometimes be even worse than a server with a virus. Because it might not be backed up, as your server is, the time and effort involved in determining the actual problem with an unprotected workstation that becomes infected can be enormous. Use a virus detection program on every workstation on your network, run a virus scanner on the network itself regularly, and hold occasional sessions to educate your users on viruses. With those precautions, you will probably only be infected once in awhile.

Networking Software

Networking software for a workstation can include NetWare drivers (NETx.COM), ODI (Open Data-link Interface) drivers, or VLMs (Virtual Loadable Modules).

NetWare Drivers (NETx.COM)   Early NetWare drivers were specific to the version of DOS—thus NET2.COM, NET3.COM, and so on, collectively known as NETx.COM. The NETX.COM driver with an actual X is the latest version of the NetWare driver and is the best NetWare driver to use with Windows, as well as being compatible with almost any version of DOS.

It is handy to keep a set of drivers on a floppy for each configuration you use. This will make it easier to configure new systems, as well as to replace drivers that are accidentally erased or corrupted. Use SHELLGEN to create the appropriate IPX for each network adapter in use and run NETX.COM with all of them. If you don't have a copy of NETX.COM, you can download it from NetWire (see Appendix A).

NETx.COM, EMSNETx.COM, and XMSNETx.COM use regular, expanded, and extended memory, respectively. Using expanded or extended memory will give you more free memory in your base 640KB, but may also interfere with Windows or other programs attempting to use these areas of memory.

SHELL.CFG or NET.CFG is the equivalent of CONFIG.SYS for the shell (IPX.COM/NETx.COM). The following are a number of useful settings for specific circumstances:

Local Printers=0	This will keep the workstation from hanging if no ports are captured and the user presses Shift+PrintScreen.
Preferred Server=*servername*	This will ensure that the workstation attaches to the correct server, rather than the one that responds the fastest.
Print Header=255	This will allow PostScript jobs enough header space to configure the printer correctly.

The ODI Drivers   NET.CFG is the configuration file used for RPRINTER on NetWare 2.x- and 3.x-based systems to effect changes to ODI drivers. SHELL.CFG, which utilizes the more capable DOS Requester, is the file that NetWare 4.*x* uses to make changes to the ODI drivers.

The ODI drivers use a different structure than IPX/NETX. ODI is more analogous to the way network drivers are supported on a NetWare server. With the ODI driver, LSL (the Link Support Layer driver) is loaded first. This allows you to load different drivers for each protocol, such as IPX (IPXODI.COM) or TCP/IP (TCPIP.COM).

The ODI drivers are loaded in the following order: LSL.COM, DRIVER.COM (a NIC-specific driver for your card), IPXODI.COM, TCPIP.COM, NETBIOS.COM, or any other protocol-specific drivers, then finally NETX.COM. There must also be an entry in NET.CFG with the following syntax:

```
LINK DRIVER IPXODI
    INT 3
    MEM C800
    PORT 2E0
```

The first line links the proper driver for your protocol to the NIC. The next three lines, which are indented, specify the interrupt, the memory address, and the port address for the card.

The VLMs   The DOS Requester for NetWare uses a group of programs called VLMs (Virtual Loadable Modules), similar to NLMs on a server. VLMs perform the same function as the earlier versions of the *shell*, diverting requests to access network drives or printers from being sent to the local ports, and sending them to the server. VLM.EXE is loaded first, and it then loads a number of other modules, which control the various aspects of attaching to and using the network.

The default sequence of VLMs is as follows:

1. CONN.VLM

2. IPXNCP.VLM

3. TRAN.VLM

4. SECURITY.VLM

5. NDS.VLM

6. BIND.VLM

7. NWP.VLM

8. FIO.VLM

9. GENERAL.VLM

10. REDIR.VLM

11. PRINT.VLM

12. NETX.VLM

The actual VLMs loaded and the order they are loaded in will depend on the network configuration you are using. INSTALL.EXE will automatically determine which VLMs are loaded and in what order, depending on the responses you give during installation.

NOTE   The DOS Requester defaults to Ethernet 802.2, rather than to 802.3 (which was used in previous NetWare versions). If you have a mixed network (that is, with some servers that won't initially be upgraded to 4.x), you should make sure that everything is using the same version, either 802.2 or 802.3.

The DOS Requester does not sit on top of DOS and intercept all disk and port traffic to determine whether it is local or intended for the network. Instead, it works *with* DOS. The principal difference is that the LASTDRIVE entry in CONFIG.SYS should be set to Z:, instead of D: or E:, as is typical with older shells. NetWare and DOS now use the same drive table, which means that rather than needing to know the last drive in the system so it could take the rest, as the older NetWare shells did, the VLMs recognize all the drives in the system and use the rest of the drive letters available. This has the advantage of allowing you to add drives (such as a CD-ROM) without needing to reconfigure the shell.

Windows and Networks

When you're faced with networking Windows workstations, there are three main sets of Windows versions to look at: Windows 3.x (versions 3 through 3.11), Windows 9x (versions 95 and 98), and Windows NT. Each set of versions must be approached differently when you're considering networking them.

Windows 3 through Windows 3.11

Getting Windows 3.x to work can be difficult, particularly with older PCs. Getting it to work on a network can be even more difficult, for several reasons.

Windows normally uses memory in locations that are generally reserved for DOS or hardware, including video and network adapters. As a result, Windows may interfere with the network adapter that's needed to connect to the network. This can be fixed with the EMMEXCLUDE option in the [386Enh] section of the SYSTEM.INI file.

Some older versions of the BIOS in some systems will not run Windows 3.x at all. You can fix this by installing a later version of BIOS, either from the manufacturer or from a supplier such as Phoenix Technologies.

You may also need to update your system to the latest available network driver, a later version of DOS, and perhaps even a newer network card—and that's just to get Windows running on a workstation and able to connect to the network.

NOTE   Windows 3.11 is also known by the name *Windows for Workgroups*.

Here are some general tips for running Windows 3.x with NetWare (or with NT operating as a NetWare server):

- Use Windows 3.11 (Windows for Workgroups) rather than 3.1. In any case, avoid Windows 3, which does not have very much network support.

- Use IPX 3.10 or later, and NETX 3.26 or later, the ODI drivers, or the VLMs.

- Make sure NETWARE.DRV is about 125KB. It often doesn't get uncompressed properly.

- If Windows is not running (or not running properly) in the Enhanced mode, try adding the following statement to the SYSTEM.INI file, under the [386Enh] section:

    ```
    EMMExclude=A000-EFFF
    ```

- If Windows runs with this setting, it means that some card or other program is using memory that Windows wants. If you can discover which part of the memory is the problem (for example C000–C800), change the EMMExclude=A000-EFFF statement to just that segment (EMMExclude=C000-C800).

- You might try two other statements in the [386Enh] section. These statements control the way Windows uses the hard drive and whether or not it accesses a potential problem area in memory:

```
VirtualHDIRQ=FALSE
SystemROMBreakPoint=FALSE
```

- Make sure that the DOS and NetWare environment settings are updated. CONFIG.SYS should have FILES= and BUFFERS= values of at least 30; and STACKS=10 is a good setting. SHELL.CFG (or NET.CFG) should have SPX CONNECTIONS=60, GET LOCAL TARGET STACKS=5 (or 10 if you'll be using IPX/SPX applications regularly), and a FILE HANDLES= setting of at least 80.

- After exiting Windows, you may get a message "Incorrect version of COMMAND.COM—reboot PC." The PC is trying to load DOS from the server, which may have a different version of DOS in the SYS:PUBLIC\ DOS directory than is loaded on the PC. Put the following statement in the user's login script, or make sure that the appropriate version of DOS is loaded on the server (as mentioned earlier, standardizing on one version of DOS for all PCs on your network is a very good idea):

```
COMSPEC=C:\COMMAND.COM
```

- If your network card uses IRQ 2, 9, 10 or higher with Windows 3 or higher, use VPICDA.386, which can be downloaded from NetWire (see Appendix A). Replace the statement DEVICE=VPICDA with DEVICE=VPICDA.386 in your SYSTEM.INI file.

These are only a few of dozens of tips necessary to produce a smoothly running Windows environment in conjunction with NetWare.

NOTE   With these older DOS/Windows 3.x systems in particular, NetWare is by far the most often used networking software. Keep in mind, though, that Windows NT can operate in a NetWare compatibility mode, allowing these older client systems to connect without modifications to an NT server. As far as that goes, even Windows 95 and Window 98 stations can masquerade themselves as a NetWare compatible file and print server simply by installing Microsoft's NetWare file and printer sharing (available under the Services option in the Networking configuration applet in Control Panel).

Windows 95/98

Windows 9*x* provides a number of vastly improved features (vis-à-vis Windows 3.*x*), such as filenames of up to 254 characters, multitasking, and 32-bit support for applications. It also offers much improved peer-to-peer network support and native support for NT and NetWare servers. And although Windows 9*x* includes support for many more network adapter cards than earlier versions, the generic drivers used in many cases are less than optimum; you should check the manufacturer's Web site or bulletin board for updated drivers.

NetWare Clients for Windows 9*x*

From the time Windows 95 first appeared, a number of NetWare client options have been made available for Windows 9*x*, including the built-in Microsoft NetWare client, the built-in Novell NetWare client, the NetWare VLM (Shell 4.*x*), and the Microsoft NDS-compatible Service. Each has advantages and disadvantages.

These NetWare drivers for Windows 9*x* will continue to evolve. See Appendix A for information about where to get the latest versions.

The Microsoft NetWare Client   The basic Microsoft client provides seamless integration with Windows 9*x*, installs automatically during the Windows 9*x* installation, allows the user to set up a single login to both Windows 9*x* and NetWare, and supports 32-bit printing to any network printer. If you are running NetWare 4.*x* (with NDS), be aware that the Microsoft NetWare client for Windows 95 does not include NDS support. Fortunately, Microsoft does include NDS support as an installable service on Windows 98. (See below for a discussion of adding NDS support to Windows 95 stations).

The NetWare VLM Client   Unless you have a specialized need to run the VLM client (in rare cases where it may be needed by older application software), we'd strongly encourage getting away from using VLM drivers and instead use the network drivers and services that are built in to Windows 9*x*. It is much simpler to install and maintain, and in most cases will reduce the potential for network-related connection problems. However, if you do have that rare application that needs the VLM client, here is how to do it.

Using the VLM client requires some finagling: you must remove existing NetWare support in the device manager, then reboot in DOS mode, then install the NetWare Client for DOS/Windows, and then reboot again. You'll see a number of error messages about a missing driver. Ignore them. After Windows 9*x* is up, you'll need to use the Network Control Panel to add a NetWare workstation shell, for versions 4 and above. When you're asked for the locations of the files, they should be in C:\Windows or C:\Nwclient (the default installation locations). Then you'll need to change STARTNET.BAT or add the commands to AUTOEXEC.BAT to go to the login drive, then log in, and then reboot again.

The Novell NetWare Client for Windows 95   If you're running NetWare 4.*x*, it is usually better and easier to use the NetWare Client32 for Windows 95 than to use the NetWare VLM client. You should be able to download it from NetWire, FTP it from `ftp.novell.com`, or use a Web browser to download it from Novell (see Appendix A). Then you'll need to decompress the files and follow the instructions in the README file for installation.

NetWare Client32 fully supports NDS, allowing you to browse the NDS tree from Windows Explorer. It also provides full support for NetWare login scripts and utilities, and it may give you higher performance than the current Microsoft driver. This depends, though, on the size and type of files being accessed on the network. For more on this, see our discussion in Chapter 17, where we compare the NetWare and Microsoft clients in detail.

Microsoft NDS-Compatible Service   Windows 98 supports NDS, but to get the support in Windows 95 you must download the service from a bulletin board or Web server. The latest version available when this was written is 371KB and is installed as a service. (Unlike the Novell Client32, which is a replacement to the existing Microsoft Novell client, the NDS support service that's available for Windows 95 is an addition to the existing Microsoft Novell client.) It adds NDS support, although not to the same level as the Novell client.

The NDS support that is built into Windows 98 is a service that you install from the Networking Control Panel applet. This client provides better NDS support than the service that is available for Windows 95 (and includes some bug fixes). It's a good option if you have servers using NDS and have chosen to go with the Microsoft NetWare client drivers.

Support for Long File names

Windows 9*x* supports long file names, as most other operating systems have done for a long time. However, there are some disadvantages to this support:

- You must enable support for long file names on any and all NetWare servers you are using. Otherwise a mixed network comprised of some servers which support long file names and some which don't will result in file names getting changed when being copied from one server to the other.

- Old DOS or 16-bit Windows applications will not support the long names. (The DOS / command-line version of PKZIP is one example of this!)

- Some backup software may truncate or even drop long file names. Although most newer backup software supports long filenames, be sure you enable this option.

If you're running NetWare 3.11, you should disable the long file name support with Windows for network drives. (To do this, add the line supportLFN=0 to the [NWRedir] section of WIN.INI.) You could also upgrade to a later version of Net-Ware, which is strongly recommended.

Running Other Network Protocols under Windows 9x

One of the great networking benefits of Windows 95 and Windows 98 is their built-in support for running multiple network protocols simultaneously. It is commonplace, for example, for companies to have both NT and NetWare servers, plus in many cases an intranet. Supporting two or three protocols to handle these is as simple as installing each needed protocol from the client's Networking applet in Control Panel.

NOTE   Keep in mind that each additional networking protocol added to a client will increase the throughput overhead on the network, reduce communication speeds (to some extent) and will also increase the amount of RAM used by the system (this last consideration is usually not a major concern for workstations with more than 16MB of RAM installed). If you need the extra protocols, use them; if you don't need them, just be aware that there are overhead penalties to having them installed.

Windows NT

Many of the advantages of Windows 9x are available in Windows NT as well. The most obvious difference is that Windows NT does not support as wide a range of devices. Further, for those devices that NT does support, it doesn't do so as seamlessly as Windows 9x. This is due to its lack of support for Plug and Play. A more subtle difference is that Windows 9x is happiest with at least 16MB of RAM (although it will run with 8MB); NT really needs 32MB for good performance. Also, for many applications, even many 32-bit applications, Windows 9x will yield better performance, at least on many PCs. NT, on the other hand, provides better protection against ill-behaved programs, has a more mature set of drivers, and a more secure file system.

All the caveats mentioned in the Windows 9x section apply here, too. Try before you buy, or at least before you commit to upgrading the whole network.

OS/2 Clients

OS/2 is similar to Windows in that it needs its own network drivers. The only OS/2 issue we'll address here will be getting it to run on your network. To do that, you need the OS/2 Requester program, which is the equivalent of NETx.COM and IPX.COM. This product is furnished with NetWare and is available separately for older networks. Again, you should check to see that you have the latest versions of the drivers (available on NetWire or from the CompuServe NetWare forum; see Appendix A). The Requester files include:

- LSL.SYS
- DDAEMON.EXE
- DRIVER.SYS (such as NE2000.SYS)
- IPX.SYS
- SPX.SYS
- SPDAEMON.EXE
- NWREQ.SYS
- NWDAEMON.EXE
- NWIFS.IFS
- VIPX.SYS
- VSHELL.SYS

You may also be using NMPIPE.SYS, NPSERVER.SYS, NETBIOS.SYS, and NBDAEMON.EXE if you are using named pipes or NetBIOS.

The upgrade to Warp (OS/2 version 3), or even better, Warp Connect, is well worth the cost. You get better network support and increased stability and reliability. If it weren't for IBM's famed ability to turn away developers and discourage customers, OS/2 would probably be posing a big threat to Windows 9x and NT. OS/2 is a stable and mature operating system in its own right. Unfortunately, there aren't many native applications, especially mainstream applications that would also be available on other platforms, and hardware vendors seem to be losing interest as well—fewer support OS/2 than used to.

PS/2 (Micro Channel) Clients

Micro Channel is an essentially obsolete bus developed by IBM in an effort to gain control of the PC hardware specification after the company gave the first version away. Even IBM doesn't make many anymore, and Micro Channel cards are almost impossible to find.

PS/2s using the Micro Channel bus must initially be configured and set up for each card installed, using the supplied installation utility in a manner similar to the EISA setup utility. One valuable benefit of Micro Channel is that, after setup is completed, the problem of interrupts is eliminated. PS/2s use the same software as PC-compatible workstations, described earlier in the chapter.

Macintosh Clients

Macintoshes can be added seamlessly to a NetWare network, either with NetWare for Macintosh or by using MacIPX. In either case, Mac users can access NetWare file server volumes and printers as if they were attached locally. NT Server supports Mac clients as well, with the Apple file and printer sharing services (and optional secure logon client). This section covers the possible problems that might crop up on Mac OS–based systems.

> **NOTE**   System 7 was a major change for Apple's operating system. Mac OS 8.x is yet another very different OS, differing from System 7 in that it adds much-needed interface, speed, and system enhancements—but even with these differences, troubleshooting remains pretty much the same between the two versions.

Macintosh Hardware and Software

Macintosh hardware is in general much easier (and cheaper) to support than hardware for PCs. Apple makes almost all of the system units, and the add-in cards come in a much more tightly controlled specification, which usually doesn't require any physical configuration. The newest Macs use a PCI bus similar to, but not identical with, the PC version. It, too, is easier to install than the PC version.

WARNING   Yes, a PC-oriented PCI card can be put in a Mac. Some of them will even work! However, we don't suggest that you install a PCI card in a Mac unless you have MacOS drivers for it. Otherwise, you could damage your system and/or monitor.

NOTE   For a time in the mid-nineties, Apple allowed other companies to make MacOS-compatible systems. Many of these systems are still available, and some are still new. Although these systems are 100 percent compatible, keep in mind that most of them are based on the PowerPC 603e processor, not exactly a powerhouse in comparison to today's G3 PowerMacs.

Mac system software and applications are generally easier to install and use than their Windows counterparts; the Mac supports most of the major protocols directly, seamlessly, and more or less painlessly. A notable exception to all this is that Macs lack built-in support for Windows Networking, which would allow Macs and PCs to browse and access each other's shared network resources in an integrated fashion (using Chooser or Network Neighborhood). There are, however, many third-party solutions for integrating PCs into a Mac OS network and vice versa, notably PC MacLan, which can be found on the Web at www.miramarsys.com/, and DAVE, which can be found on the Web at www.thursby.com/. If you have a need to more fully integrate PCs into your all-Mac network, keep an eye out for AppleShare IP 6 (which we discussed in Chapter 16). ASIP 6 fully supports Windows Networking, and it can even serve Windows-based workstations without adding special software. (So much for needing NT!)

Unfortunately, since PCs represent a large and growing percent of the market, many developers bring out a PC version first, and then only sometimes port it to the Macintosh, as an afterthought. This, however, is beginning to turn around. As of this writing, Apple has enjoyed three consecutive profitable quarters, has garnered huge interest for the new iMac, is getting the all-important game industry interested in the Mac again, and has Microsoft's Office 98 for the Mac selling like mad.

For the system administrator who's steeped in Windows, however, none of this makes much of a difference, which is unfortunate for them, because their perception of the problematic nature of Mac troubleshooting is out of date. There still remains the one perceived drawback to the Mac: Much of the system-level operation of the Mac is concealed from the user. For example, there is no DOS or equivalent thereof on the Mac OS. When the system is working, this is fine. But when there's a problem, administrators tend to see this as a block against fixing the problem.

Contrary to the prevailing perception, the reality is that troubleshooting the Mac OS is far easier and faster than any DOS-based operating system or even Windows 9x. As of System 7.x the Mac System Folder is laid out in a logical fashion, with the discrete components, called extensions and control panels, in clearly labeled subfolders.

With this in mind, comprehension of Mac OS system basics makes problem-solving quite easy, even for the user (although most administrators try and avoid this like the plague). Understanding the basic operation of the Mac OS System Folder, as outlined here, should make the process of troubleshooting Macintosh clients easier for you.

Understanding the Basics

The most basic components of the Mac OS that are needed to make a bootable system are the *System suitcase* and the *Finder*. These files are located in a folder called System Folder.

The System suitcase holds special files used by the system, such as system sounds and keyboard layout files. The System suitcase can become corrupted, so on occasion, and depending on the thrashing the system has taken from whatever treatment it has received, it will need to be replaced by a clean install.

The Finder is an application whose main function is to provide the GUI (graphical user interface), what is commonly called "the Desktop." From the Finder, users can navigate files on the hard drive and launch other applications, among other things.

Subfolders in the System Folder hold other components that the operating system loads either on startup or as needed. These are called *control panels* and *extensions*, as described here:

- Control panels on a Mac system, like the items you'd find in the Control Panel folder on a Windows 9*x* machine, are actually a group of separate applets (for lack of a better term) that allow control over specific aspects of the system. Examples of these "applets" are Appearance, which defines certain GUI preferences, and AppleTalk, which is used to tell the Mac which port to use for the network connection.

- Extensions, on the other hand, add functionality to the basic system. These are typically enhancements that give new features and capabilities to the basic system feature set. Extensions do not have an interface per se, but they can add menu items, additional options, and/or new interface components to existing system features (i.e., AppleVision adds extended features to the Monitors & Sound CDEV for compatible monitors). Some extensions load code during the startup sequence; others, like Open Transport, are loaded dynamically when they are called on. Control panels can also load code during the startup sequence, if they are true control panels. Extensions and control panels are made active or inactive by what is called the *Extensions Manager* in Mac OS 8.*x*.

Those are the basic elements you need to be aware of before you can even begin to troubleshoot what's going on with most Macs. In the following section we'll present some basic operating principles, with special attention to detailing exactly what goes on during the Mac's startup sequence, and from there touch on standard Mac networking processes. First, though, we thought we'd mention a few pointers about the topics we've just introduced:

- The Finder is a very open system, giving the user a number of different ways to manage his or her files and the launching of applications. As with snowflakes, no two Mac users' Desktops are the same. This seems like it would make it more difficult to solve problems that may crop up with the user's system, but what really counts in such situations—the operating system's hierarchical arrangement of the System Folder—remains the same on all Macs.

- Other than the way they do what they do, there is no real difference between the Windows Control Panel and the Mac Control Panels folder. The Windows Control Panel is a special directory located at the root of the C: drive; it holds special applets that manage and modify certain system options like the display, Internet connection, and the mouse. The Mac Control Panels folder resides in the System Folder, and serves as a repository for the same sort of applets.

- The Mac OS 8 Extensions Manager is really an application. It comes with its own extension that allows the user to activate the Extensions Manager during startup by holding the spacebar until it appears.

The Startup Sequence

The startup sequence is actually pretty easy to understand. Of course, it is a step-by-step procedure:

1. The power is turned on and the ROM polls the system, much like a POST operation in a DOS/Windows PC. The ROMs detect the active system drive, first by looking in the PRAM for a user-designated disk, and then by searching the available devices for an active system folder based on the SCSI bus number. The ROMs then check the Keyboard Activity Cache for any keypress actions. (If the user is holding the C key on a 4MB-ROM PowerMac, then the system will then also poll the CD-ROM drive for an active system folder.) Drivers are activated for all volumes connected to Bus 0, also known as the internal bus.

TIP
There are several user-selectable operations that can be performed during startup by holding certain keys on the keyboard. One of them, mentioned above, instructs the system to use an active system folder on a CD-ROM drive. We list more of these in a sidebar later in this section.

---

2. The system takes over and loads all the basic operational code and begins the "INIT crawl." (Extensions used to be called INITs. Control panels, if you missed it earlier, used to be called CDEVs.) There is a specific sequence of events from this point on. All loads are handled in alphabetical order.

3. First, the system looks in the Extensions folder and loads all INITs that request to be loaded. If the Code Fragment Manager is present (in PowerMacs and on 68k models that use the CFM-68k Extension) then flagged code

fragments are loaded. INITs can cause conflicts, but code fragments usually do not (at least not until the application that uses them is launched).

4. Next comes the Control Panels folder, which is slightly more complicated. CDEVs (the old programmer's name for Control Panel applets) that contain INIT code are loaded first. True CDEVs are loaded next. Control panels that are actually applications (designated by their APPL type code) are only loaded when they are called on, just like a real application.

5. Housekeeping is dealt with by loading all preferences and System Folder items that are required by the system or are specified to be read to RAM at startup. These include port drivers, GUI preferences, and display drivers (such as AppleVision).

NOTE   AppleVision software is loaded in part as an extension, so that white-point color temperatures and gamma curves are set during the startup sequence. You can see this happening when the screen brightness jumps a little.

---

6. Once all this is done, the Finder is loaded. If the Desktop appears as it should, then the startup sequence was fine.

7. Any items located in the Startup Items folder are launched (or opened, depending on what the item is). Many popular objects for Startup Items status are application launchers (DragStrip, Apollo), sounds ("What are you doing, Dave?"), and AppleScripts (Launch VPC).

TIP   Before making any serious changes or complex installations, it is best to load the system with all extensions and control panels off. See the startup options listed in the following sidebar.

Problems with the Bootstrapping Sequence

As with any computer, there are several things that can go wrong with the Mac's startup sequence. With the knowledge of how a Mac typically starts up, we can move on to the task of determining what is wrong if something goes awry. With the Mac there are three distinct potential problem areas: bootstrap, INIT crawl, and the Finder. In this section we'll look at the bootstrap sequence; we'll look at the other two topics in the sections that follow this one.

Special Startup Options

There are a number of special startup operations you can perform during the startup sequence by holding certain keys on the keyboard. Below is a list of common shortcuts that can be helpful in troubleshooting:

1. **To rebuild the Desktop database,** hold the Command (CMD) and Option (OPT) keys any time between startup and when the Finder appears (which signifies that the INIT crawl is over). A dialog will appear asking to confirm the operation. Perform this operation after every major application installation.

2. **To zap the PRAM,** hold down P+R+OPT+CMD as soon as the Mac chimes, and hold these keys down until the machine restarts five times. Do this when you are experiencing inexplicable minor annoyances, random disconnections from the network, and generic icons appearing where custom icons used to be.

3. **To start from a CD-ROM,** hold the C key immediately after the startup chime. This shortcut requires a System 7.5.x or Mac OS 8.x disk and a PowerMac computer. Older systems do not have this command in their ROMs. For non-PowerMac systems, use a boot floppy.

4. **To start without loading extensions, control panels, and startup items,** hold the Shift key. You can depress the Shift key at any time during the startup process to turn off a particular extension, but not all extensions will be turned off. To get all extensions off, hold the Shift key immediately after the startup chime and hold it until the Mac OS splash screen says, "Extensions Disabled."

To begin with, keep in mind that you might get some confused stares from Mac-only users if you refer to the bootstrapping process as a POST; on Macs it's commonly called the "system check." The system check is simply a way for the system to check itself before it starts the operating system. The items checked are:

- ROM self-check
- RAM check (speed, slot position for interleaving, and size)
- SCSI bus 0 and 1 (but see the following note)
- Card bus (NuBus/PDS/PCI)
- CPU type/speed
- Local devices (sound and video subsystem, ports, Ethernet, ADB)

NOTE The SCSI bus test varies from system to system. Some Macs have an Internet IDE bus and an external SCSI bus. Most older PowerBooks, however, have a terminated internal bus and an external SCSI bus for additional hardware.

The problems that might occur during this segment are most commonly related to the ports. These problems are rarely disastrous, but can be extremely annoying. Fortunately, these are easy to diagnose and repair, as it typically only takes a peek at the back to identify which cable is loose. Since tabs on the plastic RJ-45 plugs for Ethernet can break and allow the cable to become disconnected, and ADB mouse plugs that are connected to the back of the keyboard can become loose, these are the first things to look at.

NOTE If an Ethernet-connected workstation starts up without power to the port, the AppleTalk settings will be returned to their default setting, the Printer port. If a user cannot connect to the network at all, check the AppleTalk control panel first.

Beyond the relatively simple problem of loose connections, there are some major problems that can seriously affect startup, namely card and memory problems. If a card is not properly seated, the Mac will know. This doesn't always cause an unrecoverable problem, but can be annoying nevertheless. RAM, on the other hand, if not seated correctly, can cause the Mac to not start up at all. This problem is accompanied by a distinct startup chime, which, depending on the model, can be a car crash sound, the first bars of the theme to *The Twilight Zone*, or variations on the normal startup chime.

NOTE Professional PowerMacs leverage processor card technology so that the processor and its chipsets can easily be upgraded. If the processor card is not installed properly, the system will not do anything at all.

Apple has been making great strides in eliminating many of the problems that can cause a crash in Mac OS 8.*x*, but there's little the OS can do to prevent a poorly installed add-on card. Check all cables, card connections, SCSI connections, and power supply connectors for loosening. If all is well here, startup should proceed as normal.

If, after all manner of checking and reseating, you cannot get the Mac to start as it should, there is most likely a power supply fault. Because of the danger involved in working with power supplies, we recommend that at this point you leave the problem to a certified technician.

Problems with the INIT Crawl and Load Order

As we outlined, extensions to the base operating system, called extensions and control panels, are loaded in a particular order at startup. Problems occurring during startup are commonly caused by a conflict between similar extensions, and may depend on the order in which the extensions are loaded.

> **NOTE**
>
> Mac users tend to use the word *extensions* generically to refer to extensions, control panels, and other INIT crawl items collectively, as there aren't that many situations where you'd have to distinguish between them. In this section, we will occasionally do the same, in keeping with the common parlance.

One sort of extension conflict is the Same Job syndrome. The Mac has inspired many, many dedicated shareware developers to create all sorts of helpful and entertaining additions to the base system extension set. Some, like FinderPOP, give additional functionality to Mac OS 8.*x*'s Contextual Menu extension. One feature of FinderPOP is to allow users to click and hold to get the menu instead of Control-clicking. Another extension, Look Mom, No Hands!, provides exactly the same functionality, and thus, conflicts with FinderPOP. The conflict results in menu redraw errors and, in some cases, hard system crashes. In this case, it is a one-or-the-other proposition. Removing the unwanted extension fixes this problem.

As another example of this sort of conflict, OT/PPP from Apple and FreePPP from RockStar perform the same duties, and both work seamlessly with Open Transport for dial-up connectivity to the Internet. A conflict will arise if the PPP and FreePPP extensions are both loaded in the same session. The conflict symptoms can include unceremonious disconnections, TCP/IP application freezes, and thrashed TCP/IP stack errors (where a dropped connection can still have the port open, requiring a restart).

A second type of conflict, related to the Same Job syndrome, is a problem with the load order. This problem usually requires only a reshuffling of the load order to fix. For example, early versions of the extremely popular ActionFILES from PowerON software, an extension set that adds complete Finder functionality to the Open and Save dialog boxes, had problems with being loaded prior to the Appearance extension. The conflict caused the system to crash at random, and to have severe screen redraw problems. The fix was to place a ~ (a tilde) before the name so the extension was moved to last in the load order. This allowed the Appearance INIT to load before ActionFILES. (Incidentally, the final version of ActionFILES does not conflict with the Appearance extension.)

Modifying the Load Order   Often when there is a problem with the Mac OS, it is labeled as a system corruption problem, and the OS is reinstalled unnecessarily. Because this is usually not the real problem, it gets overlooked, and crops up over and over again. This is one reason why we suggest (a little later in this discussion) that new extensions get installed one at a time. This allows us to examine the system afterwards for any signs of conflict. If a conflict is discovered, then we try to determine what it is the new extension is conflicting with. Here are some questions to ask yourself when tracking it down:

- Does the problem affect the display? Are there places in dialogs where the screen does not get redrawn properly?

- Are there different versions of the same extension for 68k and PPC machines?

- Are there extensions or files that were not included with the installer that are required for the extension to operate properly (i.e., QuickTime, CFM-68k on 68k machines, SOMobjects for Mac OS)?

- Do serial ports report being in use when there is nothing plugged into them (an extremely unlikely occurence)?

- Do previously stable applications now crash at random?

There can be a million other indicators to a problem, as there are millions of possible configurations for a system. An example is older versions of Netscape's Navigator 3.*x* for the Mac. The application would crash at random if QuickTime was not installed. Another is that when PowerMacs first hit the scene, QuickTime was not compatible. Apple engineers created the QuickTime PowerPlug to patch the traps that QuickTime used on 68k machines. The lack of the PowerPlug would make the PowerMac act oddly and crash at times.

As mentioned earlier, other problems were related to the new extension's location in the INIT crawl. When Adobe Type Manager (ATM) was first released it would load first. It was discovered that this caused a number of serious problems.

The fix? Simple. Add a tilde to the name of the extension so the offender would load last (~ATM). The great thing is, you can do the same thing to solve most of your extension problems.

TIP

Some extensions and control panels do not come with handy little installers. Not a problem! The Mac OS is practically an installer in it's own right. Drop your INIT or CDEV on top of a closed System Folder (an inactive System Folder window works, too) and the Finder will determine what it is and put it in the correct folder. Your Mac will even tell you what and how many of each it installed. This can also be done with fonts, Control Strip modules, Contextual Menu extensions, and Preferences.

Of course, you have to discover the conflict in the first place. Not all are as obvious as the above questions would imply. You may get a random crash once a week or so, because a rarely used extension has a bad hair day only periodically. These conflicts are the most difficult to troubleshoot as they are almost hidden from detection. This is the key reason why new extensions should be added one at a time and watched for at least two days of normal operation before being given the green light.

Okay, enough of this. Here are the tips you seek:

1. Open your Extensions and/or Control Panels folder(s).

2. Change the view to List and sort by Name.

3. Locate the offending INIT or CDEV and click on the name once. The name will become highlighted for editing. (NOTE: The whole name is highlighted. If you type any characters while the whole name is highlighted, the original name will be replaced with what you typed. If you make this mistake, you *can* get it back, but only if you immediately hit CMD+Z to undo it.) Press the left arrow key to move the cursor to the front of the text, right arrow key to move to the end.

    • To move the item to the bottom of the list, add a tilde (~) to the front of the name. Adding additional tildes sends it further down the list.

4. Save your changes by hitting the Return key. Watch the item move to its new position without refreshing the display.

The maddening thing is that you can't tell which direction to move the extension in order to solve the problem. If adjusting the load order does not fix the problem, then you'll have to remove the offender or replace it with a newer version from the maker. Of course, it's always a good idea to check the maker's Web site for updates, patches, or new versions.

Not all extensions and control panels receive the INIT crawl treatment. The majority of extensions simply do not appear in the march. This does not mean they are being skipped, it's simply that not all are loaded completely. These types of extensions are first *initialized*; they can load additional code later, if called for. An example of this is Open Transport, which, by default, loads the TCP/IP stack, but only when it is asked to do so. When it's finished (i.e., when the user disconnects), the code is unloaded until the next time.

Recommendations for Fixing Conflicts   To (hopefully) avoid problems and make it easier to identify extension conflicts, follow these guidelines:

- If you are installing a new workstation, use the Custom Install feature of the operating system installer to select and deselect items to be installed. System installer CDs since version 7.5.*x* also run additional installers to install complete Internet connectivity, multimedia support, and multi-processor support, among other things. Install these with caution, for they take up much room and might not support the role envisioned by the IT Director.

- Remove all extensions and control panels that will never be used by the workstation. Not only does this save room, but it also reduces the potential for extension conflict.

It is difficult and time-consuming to go through the same installation procedures for each new workstation in order to meet the IT department's workstation standards plan. You can avoid all the difficulties if you follow this suggestion: Make one workstation meet the standard, remove all unneeded items, arrange folders in the fashion you want, and, when you are done, burn a copy of the drive to a CD-R. Then, whenever a new workstation comes online, you can simply copy the contents of the CD to the new, freshly formatted drive, and *voila!*, you have a new, standards-based workstation ready to go. (Just don't forget to rename the machine in the File Sharing Control Panel.)

- Some applications require several INITs and CDEVs. Microsoft Office for the Mac 4.21 is such an example, installing over a dozen. When this happens it's often difficult to track what is being installed. Your best bet is to become as familiar as possible with the contents of your Extensions folder(s). There are also a number of utilities that aid in the process. Our personal favorite is FileBuddy (best found at www.tucows.com), which, among many other things, can make lists of the same directory at different times and compare them for changes.

TIP

Do you use Word 6 but you're getting a lot of Word 97/98 files from friends and associates? Download the free *Word 97/98 to 6.0/95* converter at the following URL: www.microsoft.com/macoffice/productinfo/98dl/Word_97-98_Converter.hqx.

- On a similar note to the above guideline, do not drop dozens of extensions on the System Folder at one time. Place one, restart, and see what happens before continuing. Not all extensions are stable and network friendly. In a workgroup environment we suggest that you work the new extension through some stress tests before approving it for global use. The moral: Don't be afraid to try something out for several days, even a week or two if you have the opportunity, before loading the next new thing. In the real world, there's no way to fully test a new extension or control panel in a few hours.

TIP

The easiest way to install a new, installer-less extension? Simply drop the item on the closed System Folder or the inactive System Folder window and the system will take over from there, placing the item in the folder it belongs in. The system can recognize extensions, control panels, Contextual Menu items, preferences, fonts, OpenDoc Editors, and Control Strip Modules.

- Avoid allowing users to install non essential extensions. Kaleidoscope, the popular GUI-enhancement extension, is one example of an extension that is, shall we say, not free from trouble, at least in its current version, which can cause random crashes from incomplete or poorly made "Schemes" (interface enhancement files similar to Themes).

TIP

There are two ways to protect your workstation's System Folder from prying fingers or at least from people with a bent for customization. You could install AtEase for Workgroups—and have everyone in the Mac department hate you—or you can set the Protect System Folder check box in the General Controls control panel and then throw the control panel in the trash!

The best tip, of course, is to use common sense and keep mass proliferation of extensions down to a manageable level. If the workstations do need lots of gizmos and doodads, try to locate *applications* that do the same thing, as there are many. Applications tend to cause fewer problems than extensions do. In addition, you might consider that if there *is* no application-based solution, then you probably don't need it.

Problems with the Finder and Startup Items

Once the INIT crawl is over, the screen blanks out, leaving only the Desktop pattern, and the Finder begins to load. If the system crashed, a dialog will appear (that is, if the General Controls control panel is set to display it), telling you the Mac was not shut down properly. If you are rebuilding the Desktop, a dialog will appear asking you to confirm the action. If there is more than one disk mounted locally, it will ask for each disk. Network volumes cannot be rebuilt remotely. If you click Cancel and there are more disks to be rebuilt, it will ask for each one.

When this is done, the Finder loads the Desktop using information stored in various invisible database files located at the root of the hard drive. This information stores data reflecting the location of icons, their label color, whether they are open or not (for folders), how big the window is, and so on. Other files are referenced for how the folders should be viewed, what they contain, and other information helpful to the Finder. Then we get to the more interesting things, like polling the Startup Items folder.

Having trouble keeping all your Macs working the same? No problem. Simply copy the important Mac OS preference files to a diskette or into a special network drive folder and save those on the machines to be updated or repaired. Copying the preferences from a single, easily accessible location allows you to update each machine quickly without having to enter each preference by hand. A popular use for this technique is updating TCP/IP preferences. When DNS server IP numbers change, simply place the new prefs in a public folder and send a notice to everyone, telling them how to install them from the public folder.

Typically, at least one out of every four users launches an application at startup, by dint of having placed it in the Startup folder. This author, for example, has DragStrip, a clean and powerful application launcher, in her Startup folder so that it is launched automatically every time she starts up. Since DragStrip is an application and not an extension, there is little chance for a conflict, but there is at least one possible problem. DragStrip allows the user to switch between active processes by means of a user-defined hotkey set, much as Windows does. There is also an extension, called Program Switcher, that does the same thing. And Microsoft Office for the Mac version 4.2.1 comes with Office Manager, an extension that *also* offers the ability. There is a potential conflict here, as we're sure you can see.

To avoid such potential problems, make sure that there is only one application or extension doing the job, not several. The best way to ensure that your users are not adding these problem creators to your carefully groomed workstations is to maintain an open-door policy: Let them bring you any commercial utilities, shareware, and freeware that they find useful, so that you can test it rigorously to see if you should allow its use on their workstation. If a user finds FinderPOP or ActionFiles to be an essential tool for Mac OS 8 users in the office, they should feel confident that coming to the administrator will result in a carefully tested product, ensuring that, if it's implemented, the utility will not crash their or anyone else's system.

Mounting Remote Volumes

To make sure all workstations are a seamless part of the network, it is important to configure each workstation to automatically mount any remote volumes on startup. To do this, follow these instructions:

1. Ensure that the workstations' AppleTalk or MacIPX control panel is set up correctly. For AppleTalk, set the proper port in the control panel. This is commonly Ethernet; Printer and Modem serial ports are also available. A port will be added to the AppleTalk control panel for each port card added to the system. For MacIPX, select the Network Interface and modify the advanced options as needed.

2. Open the Chooser from the Apple menu and click on AppleShare. On networks with more than one zone, a list will appear in the lower left-hand portion of the dialog. Select a zone, and a list of available servers will appear to the right. Choose the one appropriate for the workstation. Click OK.

3. An authentication dialog appears. Enter your name and password into the correct boxes. If the workstation gets used by a number of people, make sure the Save Name & Password radio button is not active. Click OK.

4. A volume selection dialog appears and offers you the chance to mount whatever volumes are available on that server. Use the Command key to

select multiple volumes. Place an X in the check box after each drive that you want the workstation to mount every time it's started. (If the Save Name & Password option was checked in the previous dialog, then the workstation will not pause during startup to request a username or password. If the Save Name Only option was checked, the workstation will pause to request a password. Otherwise it will ask for a username and password.)

Configuring Open Transport

Open Transport can also cause some problems if you are using TCP/IP for your network protocol, but these problems are typically configuration-related. To configure Open Transport follow these general directions:

1. Open the TCP/IP control panel. Select the transport protocol from the Connect Via pulldown. If there is a dial-up PPP driver installed, it will be available. Otherwise, choose the protocol; the lower section of the control panel will change to give you options related to the protocol.

2. Select the way the workstation is to be configured. For Ethernet the options are Manually, BootP Configuration Server, DHCP Configuration Server, and RARP Configuration Server.

NOTE

At the time of this writing, the current version of Open Transport is 1.3, with 1.5 coming soon (with Mac OS 8.5). OT 1.3 is stable and relatively bug-free, but don't make configuration adjustments while online using a dial-up account (the result is rather unfriendly). The current version can be used on any machine that has 8MB or more of RAM and can run System 7.5 and up. This includes just about every Mac that has ever been built. Not too shabby!

3. Enter all the pertinent information for your network configuration. Keep in mind that there are vastly different levels of complexity here, depending on the User Mode chosen for the workstation. Typically, the Basic Mode is the least problematic, as almost all options are configured automatically. The Administrator Mode allows the administrator to lock out certain fields that require a password to change.

4. For maximum safety, save the settings as a configuration (press CMD+K) and give it an easy-to-remember name. Configurations can be saved for as many as you need. This is helpful if the workstation also needs to utilize dial-up services using PPP.

SCSI Devices for Macintoshes

Although Apple has recently used IDE drives on certain systems, most notably the recent G3 PowerMacs, SCSI was at one time the only hard disk drive interface supported on Macs. The SCSI interface is also used for many other devices, such as scanners and additional drives (such as CD-ROM drives, removable media drives like Zip and SyQuest, and tape-based backup drives).

The SCSI bus is a daisy chain, with up to seven devices, each connected to the next. Figure 34.3 illustrates the SCSI chain for a Macintosh. Each device in the chain has its own unique ID, 0 through 6, with the Mac's motherboard (or the SCSI controller on a PC) having an ID of 7.

FIGURE 34.3:

The SCSI chain for a Macintosh

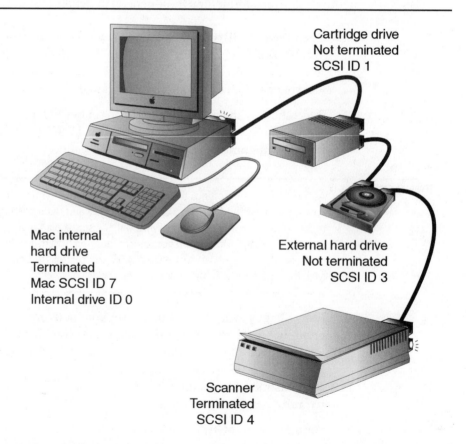

Cartridge drive
Not terminated
SCSI ID 1

Mac internal
hard drive
Terminated
Mac SCSI ID 7
Internal drive ID 0

External hard drive
Not terminated
SCSI ID 3

Scanner
Terminated
SCSI ID 4

Although you can put up to seven devices on a SCSI chain, it is not generally a good idea. The more devices, the greater the chance of problems. Older Power-Books should not be used with more than one or two external SCSI devices. This is because they use a lower-power SCSI bus than is normal, and it doesn't respond well with too many devices. If you are having problems with a Mac that has more than one SCSI device, make sure that all the devices have unique SCSI IDs. Duplicate IDs will usually cause the Mac to hang right after the self-test, or to display the No Valid System Found disk icon with the blinking question mark. Of course, the method of removing the devices and trying them one at a time to isolate the problem applies here, too.

NOTE   All modern Macs, including several pre-PowerMac systems (i.e., Quadra, Centris, and a few Mac IIs) have dual SCSI buses. The main bus, for internal devices, has only two connectors. The external bus, represented as a SCSI port on the back of the machine, is used to add new SCSI devices. This does not, however, mean you can set up two devices on the same ID.

Termination is another major cause of problems with SCSI devices. Often, incorrect termination will cause intermittent problems. Both the first device on the SCSI chain (usually the internal hard disk) and the last device on the chain must be terminated. Problems arise when intermediate devices are terminated, or when the first or last drive is not. Some devices have external switches to enable or disable termination and set the SCSI ID; with others, you must add or remove jumpers on the internal printed circuit board. The simplest way to handle termination is to leave the termination resistors on the internal drive and remove or disable termination from all other devices. Then use an external terminator on the last device. This allows you to add or remove devices easily.

TIP   If you are looking for the perfect device to terminate your lengthy chain, you're in luck. Iomega's Zip drive will have it no other way but to be at the end of the chain. Otherwise, it'll just cause problems and ruin everyone's party. (It's not a bug, it's a feature...yeah, right.)

WARNING   Under no circumstances should you ever disconnect or connect a SCSI device when it is powered up. This can damage not only that device, but any other device in the chain, *including the host computer or SCSI card!*

As the warning points out, power everything down before changing connections. This rule also applies to changing termination or manually changing the SCSI ID of a device. (A few devices will allow you to change their SCSI ID with software, but these are rare. Making changes this way, obviously, requires that everything be on. Even with these rare devices, in most cases you would still be required to restart your Macintosh after making the change.)

Macintosh Printing

Since you know connecting a Mac to a network is as easy as plugging in an Ethernet cable, setting a few control panels, and picking your servers from the Chooser, you now know more than enough about connecting to a printer. Here are the guidelines:

- Keep all printer drivers up to date. If there are several different printers, then simply making sure everyone has the latest drivers for all printers is your safest approach, even if the user never uses that printer. At least it's there.

- Most Mac printer drivers support multiple printers (for example, CSW 4100 and 4500 use the CSW 4000 driver software), so make sure the driver on the workstation is set to send to the correct printer. Otherwise, printing errors can occur, even crashes.

There, that's it! Most printer problems that occur on Macintosh networks are connection related. Check all the configuration basics and then check the printer itself for any errors, jams, or NIC faults.

Unix Workstations

Unix workstations, to an even greater extent than Macintoshes, tend to be simple to troubleshoot from the NetWare administrator's point of view. (That is, when isolating a problem with the NetWare network—Unix itself is *not* simple.) This is because a Unix workstation is usually an integrated package; the hardware, system software, and networking software are usually purchased together and designed to work with each other.

NOTE
Unix configuration and system administration are topics outside the scope of this book. There are many books available on every aspect of this subject.

For the NetWare administrator, there are basically only two questions with a Unix workstation: Can it boot? Can it see the network?

Unix workstations typically have the basic networking software and hardware built in. They usually use the TCP/IP networking protocol, which is supported in NetWare 3.*x* and above. The primary troubleshooting tools are PING, IFCONFIG, and NETSTAT, which all come with the operating system. If you can "ping" the server, you should be able to network with it. IFCONFIG will confirm that the Ethernet adapter itself is performing correctly. NETSTAT will give you information about the TCP/IP portion of your network.

If you are unable to mount network drives but can ping the server, the problem is probably with permissions—either file permissions or the authorizations in the NFS NLM setup. In fact, 90 percent of the problems with Unix probably result from permissions being set incorrectly. These problems are covered in detail in Chapter 13.

Real-Life Stories

These are real-life stories that represent the hard lessons learned by real troubleshooters in the field. The two companies and their administrators are fictional, and are used here only as examples. They combine the equipment and experience of a number of actual businesses. These four scenarios are intended to show some representative problems that might be encountered when setting up or troubleshooting a workstation. You may never see these particular problems, but you should get a feel for the process by which an experienced troubleshooter isolates a problem, determines the solution, and fixes the problem.

Scenario One: Installing a New Workstation

This scenario describes the process of installing and configuring a new high-powered workstation and some typical problems that might be encountered with the installation and configuration.

Snapshot—Scenario One

Is this a new system?

- Does the POST (power-on self test) finish without error messages?

- Does the workstation boot without error messages?

- Does the operating system load without error messages?

- Do the network drivers load without error messages?

- Can you log in to the server?

John, the system administrator for Itsy-Bitsy, Inc., is putting together a new PC for one of his users. The system will need to run Windows 98 as well as standard Office applications, and it's a fairly high-end system. It includes a 266MHz Pentium processor, 32MB of RAM, a 4GB IDE hard drive, a PCI Super VGA adapter and monitor, a bus mouse, a Novell NE2000 Ethernet adapter, 5.25- and 3.5-inch floppy drives, and an IDE CD-ROM drive. The user also needs to have one serial port enabled for an external modem and the parallel port enabled for a printer.

John, being an experienced administrator, doesn't simply load all the cards into the PC and try to boot it. Instead, he adds the accessories incrementally. This takes a little longer, but makes it much easier to discover where the problems are. Of course, since he keeps a log of each system he sets up, he could use the log to determine which settings worked for each card if he had set up a system like this before; however, he hasn't used this combination of cards in the past.

TIP   Try loading new cards into a system one at a time, even if it's a new system. This will make it easier to isolate problems when they occur.

The basic system, just the hard drive and video adapter, boots just fine, so John adds the Ethernet card, being sure to record the settings for the interrupt and memory segment. The PC boots without errors again. After he installs the networking drivers, he tries opening Network Neighborhood to see if the PC can attach to the server. Instead, the PC freezes. After double-checking the settings on the card and the configuration of the driver, he's ready for the last resort. He reads the documentation.

The documentation doesn't appear to be helpful at first, but then John notices that there is a jumper that should be removed if the NE2000 is installed in a PC that uses the Chips and Technologies chip set. Upon checking, he discovers that the PC does in fact use this chip set. Removing the jumper fixes the problem.

He next installs the mouse. It uses one of two IRQs, 2 or 5. Since the LAN adapter uses IRQ 3 in its default setting, either would do. John chooses 5, and notes on the configuration sheet that IRQ 3 (the NIC), IRQ 4 (the COM1 serial port), and IRQ 5 are in use.

The CD-ROM drive is the last item to be added. He makes sure that the CD-ROM drive is connected to the secondary IDE interface, so he can use the Windows 32-bit disk access. After loading the driver, John is able to access the CD-ROM. It looks like the hardware configuration is done. He turns the PC off, makes sure all the screws are tight, puts the case on the machine, tightens all the screws down, reinstalls all the cables in the back, and then restarts the PC. Halfway through the POST routine, the PC hangs. After several resets, it is clear that whatever is happening is no fluke. He sighs and removes the case, then unplugs the CD-ROM, that being the last item installed.

The PC boots properly with the drive unplugged. He checks the orientation of the cable and the power connection to the drive, then restarts the PC. It boots fine. John sits and thinks for a minute. The only other thing that changed was putting the case on and screwing it down.

After some experimenting, John discovers that the PC will boot with the case on, but not when it's seated firmly and screwed down. It can be used temporarily with the case unsecured. He calls the retailer. They've never heard of such a problem but say it might be a short to the chassis somewhere. They say they'll be out to replace the PC within a couple of days.

A few days later, the PC reseller sends a technician out to fix the problem with the case. After swapping the motherboard and hard drive into a new case, the problem goes away.

Lessons Learned—Scenario One

- Keep a log of how each of your PCs is configured. Update it when you change setups. It will pay for itself the first time you are able to check a configuration without needing to take the PC apart and remove boards to verify settings.

- Read the documentation. The least you should do is look for exceptions, which are often set apart in the documentation or even in a README file on the distribution floppy.

- Make sure that neither IRQs (interrupts) nor base I/O memory segments from the different installed devices conflict with each other. Bear in mind that the size of memory used by the I/O segments may vary. Add the size of the segment to the address (remember, the numbers are in hexadecimal) to determine the next safe address to use.

- A freeze might not be caused by a card or configuration error. It can be something as simple as a sloppily manufactured case, a defective power cord, or a card or cable that isn't seated fully.

- Not all IRQs, base I/O addresses, or DMA interrupts are used by cards. For example, the serial ports, which may be on the motherboard, still use IRQs and I/O addresses, and some programs (such as Windows) may access these areas of memory, too.

The Fault-Point Chain—Scenario One

Since the PC itself is running, you might think that none of it would be part of the fault-point chain for this problem. However, there are a number of possibilities. For example, in this case, the motherboard was the actual cause—the NE2000 requires a different setting when used with this type of motherboard. However, other possibilities exist; for example, the problem could be caused by a marginal power supply in an older PC that wouldn't accommodate another board.

The potential faults for the first problem—the PC freezing when network services are accessed—were:

- The power supply to the motherboard: wall socket, power cord, power supply, and connection from the power supply to the motherboard. Faulty power can cause intermittent problems. Although it wouldn't usually become apparent at the same point in a software sequence, this could be the result of the actual activation of the Ethernet interface drawing too much power, or something similar.

- The motherboard, including the BIOS. The BIOS, especially in older PCs, is often the cause of incompatibilities with software, from network drivers to Windows.

- The NIC. This has several aspects, including the seating of the card in the bus, the settings on the card, the card's connection to the network, and the version of ROM (read-only memory) on the card.

- The operating system. Windows (or DOS) will support drivers for various network adapters, but older cards can be harder to configure or have faulty drivers. As a rule of thumb, try not to let the standard version of DOS you use get more than two years old.

Scenario Two: Maintaining an Existing Workstation

In this scenario, the administrator encounters some deceptive symptoms, then finds that an existing server is having problems at the workstation level before NetWare can load.

Snapshot—Scenario Two

Is this an existing system?

- Is the display readable? Does the cursor respond to the keyboard?
- Does the POST (power-on self test) finish without error messages?
- Does the workstation boot without error messages?
- Does the operating system load without error messages?
- Do the network drivers load without errors?
- Does the workstation see the server (in Network Neighborhood)?
- Can you log in to the server?

Fran, the system administrator for Great Big, Inc., gets a call from a user in Accounting. Something is wrong with his workstation; the application is running too slowly. She takes a look at the workstation. The application that's running too slowly is a word processor. She checks, and the file the user is working on is on the file server. She finds out that the user had tried to save changes to the file and the program hasn't responded to anything since. She tries to cancel the save, and eventually, after several mouse clicks, succeeds. She then saves to the local hard disk. This works quickly and normally. She then exits the program and checks the connection to the server. The server doesn't respond.

She finds the server's screen dark. The server's power light is on, and the fan is running, but the screen won't come on and the keyboard doesn't respond, even to the CapsLock or NumLock keys. She quickly checks the other workstations in the department and discovers that none of them can connect to the server. She reboots the server and gets the same result.

She begins eliminating possibilities. The monitor's power light is on, but it could be defective. She pulls a working monitor and video cable off another workstation and tries it. Nothing. She replaces the video card with the good card from the other workstation. Still nothing. In this particular chain of fault points, there is only one link left. The video system consists of the monitor, the cable, the video board, the motherboard, and the PC's power supply. The only one left is the motherboard. She swaps the server's drives and cards into another PC and starts it up. The server is back online.

Later inspection by a technician shows that the motherboard is indeed damaged, probably by a power spike. Fran uses the technician's report to justify UPSs (uninterruptible power supplies) for all servers at the site.

Lessons Learned—Scenario Two

- Workstation symptoms may actually result from network problems, either on the server or the connection to it.

- If you suspect component failure, replace the components in the chain, one at a time, with known good components.

- In an emergency, you can cannibalize one user's workstation (or your own) to replace the parts of a server. No one person's work is more critical than the whole department's. Other resources for quick temporary replacement include renting or leasing through local outlets. See your phone book.

The Fault-Point Chain—Scenario Two

Since all the workstations were unable to connect to the server, the fault chain included the physical network (the cabling plant) as well as the server. However, the server is more likely to fail than the wiring, so Fran checked it first. The dark monitor and lack of response to the keyboard established that the problem was with the server. The fact that the problem repeated when the server was rebooted indicated a hardware problem, unless there had been recent changes to the NetWare configuration.

The potential faults were:

- AC power from the wall.

- The power cord.

- The power supply.

- The power cable from the power supply to the disk drive.

- The disk drives.

- The motherboard.

- The cards in the server.

- The devices connected to the cards (the monitor, the physical wiring, and so on). It's easier to check the connection on the back of a monitor than the electronics inside the monitor, and more likely that the problem is in a loose cable.

- NetWare (changes in configuration, corruption of SERVER.EXE, and so on).

- Outside interference, such as brownouts or a network storm caused by another server or network device overloading the server with bad packets.

Scenario Three: Another Existing Workstation

In this scenario, the administrator encounters a situation similar to the one described in the previous section, but with some critical differences: The administrator listens to a user's diagnosis, jumps to the conclusion that the situation is the same, and doesn't follow some basic precautions.

Snapshot—Scenario Three

Is this an existing system?

- Is the display readable? Does the cursor respond to the keyboard?

- Does the POST (power-on self test) finish without error messages?

- Does the workstation boot without error messages?

- Does the network load without errors?

- Does the workstation see the server?

- Can you log in to the server?

Jethro, Fran's new assistant, gets a call from a user in Accounting. Her connection to the server is down. She informs Jethro that this has happened before—she's sure it's the server. Jethro investigates and discovers that the server is apparently running, but the screen is dark. He reads the log and notes the similarities to the last incident. He decides he should swap the server's drives and cards into the other workstation in the office as quickly as possible to get the server back on line.

He flips the power switch on the server. Within seconds, cries of consternation drift through the doorway of the server room, quickly followed by the users themselves, asking why the server has gone down. Jethro, a cold feeling in his stomach, turns the server back on. The screen lights up with the normal boot messages, and the server begins to boot.

After the server is back online, and he has pacified the users, Jethro makes two discoveries: The screen blanker in MONITOR produces a blank screen in this version of NetWare, rather than the usual bouncing square, and the cable from the first user's NIC to the transceiver has come off at the NIC.

Lessons Learned—Scenario Three

- Don't jump to conclusions and take steps you can't back out of, without trying to confirm your conclusions. If you can't think of some way to confirm your hypothesis, try to at least anticipate what could happen if you're wrong. For instance, Jethro should have checked to see if other users had connections to the server.

- Never take for granted that users know what they're talking about. Listen to them, but confirm what they tell you unless you know from experience that they are knowledgeable about PCs and networking and the setup in their department.

The Fault-Point Chain—Scenario Three

A simplified chain would show the main units that could be responsible for the user's PC not being able to connect to the server:

- The workstation

- The physical network, including the transceiver, the cabling and connectors, the repeater, the concentrator, and the connectors at the server end

- The server itself

Each of these fault points would, of course, have its own fault-point chain. The most likely point of failure is at the workstation. Jethro's biggest mistake was not checking the workstation (either by checking the workstation itself or checking other workstations to see if they were also having problems). He should have checked the fault points in order of likelihood of failure: the workstation first, then the server, then the cabling plant.

Scenario Four: An Existing Macintosh

This scenario covers a common situation encountered with existing Macintosh setups. One of the problems the administrator encounters is in getting reliable information about what the configuration of the system should be, to compare with what it is.

Snapshot—Scenario Four

Is this a Macintosh system?

- Does the POST (power-on self test) finish with a tone instead of a chord?

- Does the workstation boot without error messages and without freezing?

- Do the network drivers load without errors?

- Does the workstation see the server in the Chooser?

When the Art Department calls about a problem with one of the Macs, Fran brings Jethro along because he is familiar with Macs. One of the artists has a Mac that is hanging about halfway through the boot sequence. The user doesn't remember anything in the system that has changed recently.

They reboot the Mac again and watch the series of startup icons carefully. Just before the point at which the Mac freezes, they see an icon that neither of them recognizes. They restart the Mac from a floppy and open the System folder in Icon View. They discover the icon is from a public domain INIT program that is supposed to enhance the usability of the system. The user had forgotten adding it a couple of weeks before.

> **NOTE**   Macs are easy to use, but not necessarily to administer. They often have more add-ons than comparable PCs and hide more of the operating system from the user.

Since the user isn't wedded to the offending INIT, and since its behavior indicates that it may have become corrupted or be interfering with other INITs, they remove it. The system boots properly. Fran makes a note in her log to be on the lookout for this INIT program in other Macs.

But there's one more thing: The user mentions that some of his fonts are no longer available. As long as Fran and Jethro are there, could they help him get them back?

This problem is aggravated by the lack of a standard for the company's Macintosh font manager—something that has been causing Fran trouble for a long time. The Macs used by the Marketing Department mostly use one add-on program to control fonts, the Art Department uses a different program, and other Macs scattered throughout the company may use either, or none.

When Fran checks, she discovers that this Mac is using one of the font control programs to load its fonts. The log for this Mac shows that she installed the latest version of this enhancement program a few days ago. It also shows that this Mac is using the standard set of Art department fonts in the appropriately named folder, that this folder is in the proper place, and that the program is set to open the fonts in that folder.

However, the fonts are not loading at startup. Jethro suggests using the program to load the fonts manually. When they try, they get a message saying that some of the fonts they are trying to load are already loaded. Jethro snaps his fingers—the system may have the same fonts installed in its Fonts folder. They check, and some of the fonts in one of the standard suitcases have also been loaded directly into the system.

After the fonts are removed from the System folder, the conflict goes away and the fonts all load properly. They reboot the Mac to check, and the fonts load automatically. Fran makes another note to check to make sure none of the other Macs she updated have the same fonts in two places.

Lessons Learned—Scenario Four

- When in doubt, return to a basic configuration and add INITs back in one at a time until you discover the conflict. Sometimes, you will be able to tell which INIT, Startup, or CDEV is freezing the Mac by the last icon showing when the Mac freezes during startup. However, this is only one of a pair. The other file contributing to the conflict may be harder to discover, and the one you find may be necessary to the system. You can use special programs that can help you isolate and fix INIT conflicts.

- Try to standardize on utility programs throughout the site. Use the same virus checker, the same font organizer, and so on. Doing so will cut down dramatically on problems in upgrading and supporting systems. This is important in all systems, not just Macs.

The Fault-Point Chain—Scenario Four

Since the Mac was booting at least partway, the indication was that there wasn't any problem with the basic hardware. Furthermore, since the boot sequence from the hard disk was starting, the hard disk and disk driver were probably working correctly. Therefore, the next item to check was the software being loaded during the boot sequence. This is analogous to the AUTOEXEC.BAT and CONFIG.SYS portion of a DOS PC's boot sequence.

The first item (the INIT conflict) had the following fault points:

- The hardware (power supply, motherboard, any additional cards, and so on).
- The hard disk (boot device).
- The system software.
- The extensions being loaded.
- Problems with some of the cards, particularly an EtherTalk adapter. These cards aren't initialized until their extension is loaded, so the problem might appear to be with the extension, when in reality it is a hardware problem with the card.

In this case, because there was a more or less standard set of extensions in use, and because they were familiar with the normal boot sequence for their Macs, Fran and Jethro were able to identify the icon of the offending INIT. However, if this had not been the case, they would have removed all extensions not supplied by Apple, and then rebooted. If the Mac had worked then, they would have added extensions back in until they identified the problem. If the Mac still hadn't booted, they would have reinstalled the system.

Summary

In this chapter, we've looked at a variety of things that can go wrong with workstations. Even aside from the issue of whether the workstation functions properly on the network, there are many things that can go wrong at the workstation level itself, either during the boot process, or with hardware or software conflicts after the operating system has loaded and first attempts to access the hardware.

Most often, the problem will be due to IRQ or DMA conflicts between two or more devices, system files that may be missing or corrupted, or physical damage to the system (due to a power spike, someone tripping on a cable, etc.). The fundamental principle to use in troubleshooting workstations is to isolate which devices or software are most likely to be at fault by simplifying the scenario as far as is practical. When you reach a point where the system begins working, you can then proceed to add back in (one at a time) whatever drivers or devices were removed, deducing the culprit by the process of elimination.

In the next chapter, we'll look at problems that can go wrong with the physical network—cabling, routers, and other types of networking hardware, and discuss ways to troubleshoot and resolve these types of problems.

CHAPTER

THIRTY-FIVE

Troubleshooting the Physical Network

- Snapshot for physical network problems

- Physical network fault points

- Network topologies

- Communications protocols

- Ethernet

- Token Ring

- ARCnet and LocalTalk

- Cabling plant documentation

- Example troubleshooting scenarios

In this chapter, we'll look at different types of problems that appear at the physical layers of a network. We'll discuss problems specific to each of the different network topologies, as well as factors which can impact the various network protocols, then shift attention to the problems endemic to the cabling systems used in these types of networks. As with the preceding chapter, we'll begin by looking at a "snapshot" of various fault points (scan down the list until you reach a matching or similar scenario) to determine where a problem lies, and we'll conclude the chapter with several case examples.

Snapshot: Troubleshooting the Physical Network

Is This a New Network?

How many nodes are affected? Do some of the workstations on the ring or segment work?   The first thing to do is to make sure that the server is running, and that the workstation involved is not having problems. If more than one workstation is involved, and the server is operating correctly, the problem is likely to be in the cabling plant. With a new installation, the first thing to check is that all specified work has been completed. Even with a relatively small network, there may be hundreds of wires, each of which must be properly connected, and dozens of devices which must be set properly, connected, turned on, and so on.

If some workstations are able to connect to the server but more than one cannot, the problem can be physically isolated. What do the working nodes or the non-working nodes have in common? Check to see if a ring is broken, or if all those workstations are on the same card on the concentrator. Bear in mind that it is more likely with new equipment that something has been overlooked rather than that there is an actual failure. Make sure that all equipment is connected and turned on. See the sections "Network Topologies" and "Tracking Down Cabling Plant Problems" later in this chapter.

Is it only one workstation that can't connect?   If only one workstation isn't working, see if it can connect from another location. If so, then the wiring is faulty somewhere between the PC and the server.

There are several ways to isolate the fault in a wiring system without exotic or specialized equipment, although these make testing easier. Visually inspect the wiring: Check that the colors of the insulation on twisted-pair wiring match at both ends of a connection, that the wiring is neat and the connectors are solidly in place, that coaxial cable connectors are solidly crimped, that the connectors are of good quality, and so on. A continuity tester will allow you to check the physical continuity of the wiring. You can make this tester yourself if you are familiar with the basics of electrical work, or buy an inexpensive model from an electronics supplier.

Also make sure that there is adequate cable to reach from where it exits from the wall to any point where the user might place the computer. Users can easily overstretch cable or pull the connector from the socket, trying to move their workstation farther from the wall socket than the cabling allows. See the section "Tracking Down Cabling Plant Problems" later in this chapter.

Is This an Existing Network?

How many nodes are affected? Do some of the workstations on the ring or segment work?   When you know which workstations can connect to the server and which can't, you should be able to find the common point. Are they all on one port of the repeater or one card in the concentrator? Are they all on the same segment or ring? Are they all connecting through a bridge that may have gone down? If there are multiple NICs in the server, are all the workstations that can't see the server on one of the cards? See the sections "Network Topologies" and "Tracking Down Cabling Plant Problems" later in this chapter.

Is it only one workstation that can't connect?   If only one workstation is affected, see if it can connect from another location. If so, then the cabling plant is faulty somewhere between the PC and the server. After you've isolated the problem to one station, you can begin checking the various component parts of the cabling plant between the two points. It may be the wiring, a transceiver, a board in the repeater, a faulty socket in the concentrator, or another problem in the PC-to-server wiring. See the section "Tracking Down Cabling Plant Problems" later in this chapter.

Is the network experiencing intermittent faults and performance problems?   As with other parts of the network, the most difficult problems to isolate are intermittent ones. In the cabling plant, these may be caused by a variety of things, such as cables that run past fluorescent lights and loose connectors or faulty boards in workstations, servers, or other networking hardware (for example, repeaters, concentrators, or hubs). See the section "Tracking Down Cabling Plant Problems," or the section "Patch Panels, Repeaters, and Concentrators," or the section "Routers, Bridges, and Gateways."

As with other intermittent problems, you should discover what parts of the network are affected, what times of day the problems occur, what other events are associated with the problem, and any other information that can tell you what is happening when the problems occur.

The critical aspect to troubleshooting the cabling plant is to first make sure that your problem is not actually being caused by an inoperative or malfunctioning network adapter, server, or PC. Second, you must understand the basics of your network topology. What sort of wiring do you have? What are its maximum lengths of cabling and its requirements for termination and grounds? Will one missing connection take out the whole ring? You should understand the various components that make up your cabling system: transceivers, connectors, wiring, concentrators, repeaters, bridges, and so on.

This chapter describes the aspects of the physical network you should understand, including the various network topologies, data communication protocols, and hardware standards. It also provides suggestions for tracking down cabling plant problems and documenting the cabling plant.

Fault Points for the Physical Network

The approach to troubleshooting introduced in Chapter 1 requires you to identify and isolate the fault points in a system. Using this approach with the physical network can be demanding, because it requires that you understand the basic processes that occur in the system. The possible variations and complexity of the cabling system can make it difficult to approach, but if you take things methodically, one piece at a time, it can be done.

The fault point chain in Figure 35.1 illustrates typical components of the cabling plant. You might not have all of these parts in your system, or you might have others not pictured here. The best way to begin to understand your network is to produce a drawing of a chain like the one in Figure 35.1, but specialized for your network. You should also make a map of the topology of your network, showing each workstation and how it is connected to the server. The various network topologies are discussed in the next section.

FIGURE 35.1:

The fault point chain for
network cabling and
connections

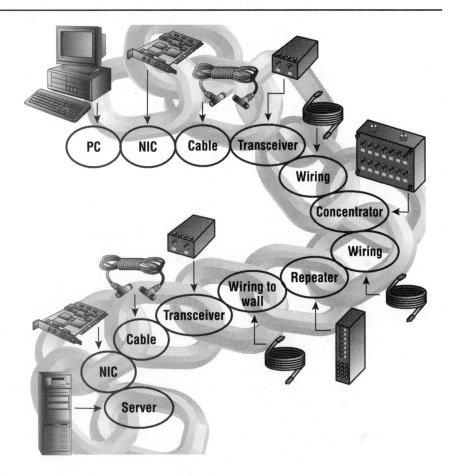

Each link in the chain can fail itself, or it can fail in its connection to a link it is attached to. For example, a cable could break or its connection at either end could fail.

In terms of the physical network, the server's fault points include the network driver for each NIC, the protocol drivers bound to each NIC, and the basic functioning of NetWare itself.

The NIC must be configured correctly, must be seated in the bus connector on the motherboard, and must have a good connection to the network wiring.

There may be one cable directly attaching the workstation to the server, or there may be several lengths of cabling between the two. In every case, the cabling must be connected properly at both ends and must be physically intact. The connectors must be properly attached to the cabling, and, in the case of twisted-pair cabling, the pairs must be connected in the same order at both ends. You must also be careful to make sure that the cabling does not run too close to possible sources of interference, such as fluorescent light ballasts.

Some systems employ *transceivers* to translate between two different physical types of cabling, for instance between the thick Ethernet port on a network card and the 10BaseT jack on the wall. Most transceivers have status lights to allow you to diagnose problems with the connection. If these lights are out, the transceiver is not operating. The connections on both ends of the transceiver must also be solid.

A *repeater* allows you to extend a network beyond the normal limitations of segment lengths. A typical setup provides one port that connects to the server and a number of ports that can be connected to different cable segments (legs). A repeater usually has status lights that show network traffic on each leg, allowing you to determine which legs are performing properly. The repeater can fail at each port connecting to the network cabling and on each internal board that provides a port, or it may fail entirely.

A *concentrator*, or *hub*, is similar to a repeater in its basic concept, which allows the total length of cabling in a network to exceed the maximum length for a single cable. A hub is typical of 10BaseT networks or twisted-pair Token Ring, and will typically have one port that connects directly to the server and one direct connection to each workstation. Depending on the type, it might fail entirely, on one port, or on one board that provides a number of ports. The status lights on the hub can help you determine which (if any) of these has happened, as can switching a problem cable to another port or board.

The workstation and its NIC are the last potential fault points in the fault chain, and they can fail in the same manner as the server and its NIC: the NIC can fail in hardware or be configured incorrectly, or its connection to the bus of the PC or the network cabling can become loose, causing an erratic connection, or its connection may come off entirely.

Network Topologies

Most networks can be categorized into one of three types of physical topology: ring, linear bus, or star. The type of protocol doesn't necessarily indicate the topology. For example, the three most common types of Ethernet, thick (AUI), thin (10Base2), and twisted-pair (10BaseT), use different topologies. Thick Ethernet is typically a linear bus, thin Ethernet is typically a ring, and twisted-pair Ethernet is typically a star. Figure 35.2 illustrates the types of network topologies.

FIGURE 35.2:

Network topologies

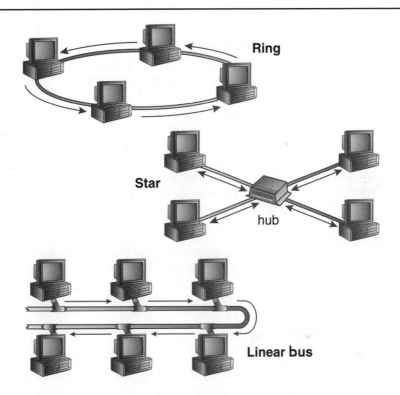

The topology of thin Ethernet can also be described physically as a linear bus because the T-connector that attaches to the workstation functions in the same manner as the drop cable in a thick Ethernet setup. If the T-connector is disconnected from the workstation, only that workstation loses its connection. However, if the cable is detached from the T-connector, every workstation attached to the cable loses its connection. This is true in a thick Ethernet cabling scheme as well, but occurs much less frequently. With thick Ethernet, the drop cable is usually all that the user can reach; they usually don't have physical access to the backbone cable.

Each type of topology has a different fault point chain. A ring is the most susceptible to interruption, because if the physical links are broken anywhere in the ring, the whole ring loses connectivity. To overcome this disadvantage, some ring-type topologies combine star and ring topologies into one.

Along with the network's physical topology, you also need to consider its logical topology. *Physical topology* refers to the way the hardware and wiring are connected. *Logical topology* refers to the way that the information is sent from machine to machine. For example, Token Ring may have a physical star topology, but it is a ring topology logically. This means that you must understand the implications of both the logical and physical topologies in order to isolate the probable cause of problems. For instance, a star topology generally prevents a single break in the cabling from interrupting service to all nodes on the network. However, a Token Ring network, which relies on tokens passed from workstation to workstation around a logical ring, can fail if one connection is broken, even though the physical topology is a star.

NOTE   Be sure you understand the difference between physical and logical topology. A good example is Token Ring, which is physically a star but logically a ring.

Topology is the most important part of your network cabling scheme to understand. If you understand the physical and logical topology, you can isolate the fault points, regardless of the protocol running over the wire.

Ring Topology

In a *ring topology*, either logical or physical, every physical component of the network is typically a fault point for every connection. If one user on a thin Ethernet network (which can be considered a linear bus) disconnects his or her workstation by uncoupling the two wires from the T-connector, rather than the connector from the workstation, every workstation on the network will lose its connection. In practice, networks of this type often consist of several rings connected to a repeater, which is then connected to the server. This arrangement provides some redundancy, in that a failure in the ring usually will affect only the users attached to that port of the repeater.

With Token Ring, the topology is physically a star but logically a ring, in that a token is passed from station to station. If there is any interruption of the ring, the token will not reach the next station, and the network will go down.

The critical thing to know when troubleshooting this type of network is the location of every place where the connection can be broken by human intervention. Aside from mice chewing through the cabling, it isn't likely that the cable itself will fail. The most likely scenario is that someone has removed a connector or kicked wiring under their desk and pulled the cabling out of the jack.

Star Topology

A *star topology* is the most fault-tolerant topology. Each workstation is connected directly to a concentrator, which means that a break in any part of the fault point chain up to the concentrator will affect only one workstation. The two exceptions to this rule are the server and its connection to the concentrator, and the concentrator itself.

10BaseT Ethernet is the most common star topology, and it has become the most common type of network installed because of its fault tolerance and simplicity.

The biggest disadvantage of star topology is that it tends to be more expensive to install. Cabling must be pulled from every workstation to the concentrator or media access unit (MAU); by contrast, a ring network needs cabling only as far as the next workstation. However, the gain in reliability is significant enough that stars have largely displaced the other topologies.

In a star topology, the fault point chain includes only the wiring between that workstation and the concentrator. If more than one workstation is involved, the workstation cabling is unlikely to be the problem. It's most likely that the problem is either with the server, its connection to the concentrator or MAU, or with the concentrator or MAU itself. Of course, this is only true unless the logical topology is a ring.

Linear Bus Topology

In a *linear bus topology*, there are actually two fault chains: the one from each workstation to the bus and the one from the bus to the server. If a workstation connection fails, it will affect only that workstation. An interruption of the bus will cause every connection to the server to fail. In practice, this isn't any different from a star topology if the concentrator fails; however, it is much easier to tell if this is the problem because of the status lights on the concentrator.

Data Communication Protocols

As we've discussed at length in earlier chapters, there are two parts to the method by which computers connect with each other over cabling. The first is the data communication protocol, which specifies how workstations within a network operating system (NOS) communicate. Each protocol is generally associated with a specific NOS, although most NOSs now support most protocols. These protocols divide data to be sent to another computer into small pieces, called *packets*, and add a header and trailer that contain information about the sender, intended recipient, and so on. This process is carried out by the networking software.

The second part is the Physical layer protocol, such as Ethernet, Token Ring, ARCnet, or FDDI. These protocols add further information in a header and trailer that determines which machine gets the packet next. This processing is mostly done by the networking hardware.

The Physical layer protocol surrounds the data communication protocol, which surrounds the data. If a packet is sent from one protocol to another, the surrounding information must be translated. Since the data communication protocols are inside the physical protocols, converting them is more complex, as described later in this chapter, in the section "Routers, Bridges, and Gateways." As an example, Figure 35.3 shows an IPX packet.

FIGURE 35.3:

An IPX packet structure

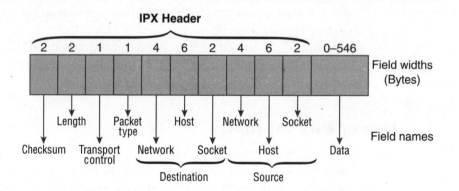

IPX/SPX

The *IPX (Internetwork Packet Exchange)* and *SPX (Sequenced Packet Exchange)* protocols are Novell's native protocols. A node address is a hexadecimal number, up to eight digits long. This number must be unique for each server and workstation.

Each LAN also has an address, called a network address. With the implementation of the worldwide IPX Internet, IPX addresses will be assigned in much the same manner as TCP/IP addresses are for the Unix-based Internet (call 1-800-NETWARE for more information).

IP (TCP/IP)

TCP/IP (Transmission Control Protocol/Internet Protocol) is the standard protocol in the Unix world. It was developed by the Department of Defense and is also the basis of the Internet. Internet addresses are assigned by the InterNIC. If your TCP/IP network is not connected to the Internet, and never will be, you can use any valid range of addresses. However, if there is any chance you will be connected, you should apply for an address.

NOTE A TCP/IP address has the form *xxx.xxx.xxx.xxx*, where each set of *x*'s represents a number from 0 to 128. Depending on how big your company is, you might have an address of 143.*xxx.xxx.xxx*, 143.228.*xxx.xxx*, 143.228.117.*xxx*, or something in between, with the *xxx* representing available addresses for workstations on your network.

NetWare supports TCP/IP as a native protocol and also allows you to run IPX through a TCP/IP network with a process known as *tunneling*, which surrounds an IPX packet with a TCP/IP header and trailer to allow it to be routed from an IPX network, through a TCP/IP network, and back to an IPX network.

Due to security concerns, many businesses no longer have a direct connection to the Internet. It is too great a security risk. They usually have what is known as a *firewall*—a server or router that is between their internal net and the Internet, which only (at least hopefully) allows authorized traffic in or out. With a firewall in place, the internal network numbers can be any valid range of addresses, and only the firewall router needs to have a "proper" authorized Internet number.

NetBEUI

NetBEUI (*NetBIOS Extended User Interface*) is the protocol used by Microsoft's Windows for Workgroups, Windows 95, and Windows NT as their native protocol. It identifies nodes by a unique name of up to 14 alphanumeric characters and divides the network into logical domains. Nodes may contain objects such as printers or disks that have been made available to the network (shared).

NetBIOS

The *NetBIOS* (*Network Basic Input/Output System*) is an application-level interface for networking primarily used by IBM LAN Server and Microsoft LAN Manager networks. NetWare supports NetBIOS. NetBIOS nodes are named with a unique 16-character address.

AppleTalk

AppleTalk can run over Ethernet (either true Ethernet or EtherTalk via Classic Networking), Token Ring (TokenTalk), or LocalTalk (Apple's proprietary cabling). AppleTalk devices include servers, workstations, and printers. AppleTalk Phase 1 allowed for 254 nodes on a network. Phase 2 allows multiple zones, each with 253 nodes.

LocalTalk supports only 230Kbps, Ethernet supports 10Mbps and 100Mbps, EtherTalk supports 10Mbps, and TokenTalk supports 4Mbps. Because of its much higher speed, Open Transport's complete Ethernet implementation is becoming much more prevalent.

> **NOTE**
> Keep in mind that Open Transport supplies the required support for full Ethernet connectivity. Classic networking limits Ethernet access to EtherTalk compatibility, keeping these workstations in the 10BaseT realm.

OSI and the OSI Model

The International Standards Organization (ISO) has developed a standard called *Open Systems Interconnect* (*OSI*). OSI is supposed to resolve the problems existing protocols have with large WANs and high-traffic loads. However, implementation has been slow; existing protocols are deeply entrenched, and most businesses are waiting until the OSI standard catches on before they implement it, which won't happen until more businesses implement the standard.

The *OSI model* describes standards for communication between network nodes at seven levels. The seven levels of OSI are:

- Application
- Presentation
- Session
- Transport
- Network
- Data Link
- Physical

A packet passes through each of these layers on its way from one network device to another. Each layer passes packets to the layer above and below it, but deals with only the information specific to its layer.

A packet arriving at a workstation reaches the Physical layer first. This layer processes the signal sent from another network card, interpreting the voltage changes, number of pulses, and so on to provide bits of information that are then assembled and sent to the Data Link layer.

The Data Link layer is the first layer that handles the packet as such. It may provide error correction to make sure that the packet that is arriving is the same as the one that was sent, discard defective packets, and signal the other workstation to resend the packet if necessary.

The two bottom layers together make up the hardware standards discussed in the next section. The next two layers, the Network and Transport layers, in general comprise the Protocol layer, as discussed earlier.

The Network layer determines the path that a packet takes in going from the sending workstation to the intended recipient. This is the IP part of the TCP/IP protocol, and Novell's IPX also operates at this level.

The next layer, the Transport layer, provides error correction for packet routing in the same way that the Data Link layer provides error correction for the physical transmission. This is the TCP part of TCP/IP.

The four bottom layers of the OSI model are clearly defined and usually have clear analogs in any networking setup. The next three layers are not so clearly defined yet, and they may not correspond with any particular part of your system.

The Session layer deals with making and breaking connections to other systems. Protocols such as SPX and NetBIOS require that a connection to a specific other machine be made at the beginning of a session and broken at the end of the session. Other protocols, known as *connectionless*, don't use this layer.

NOTE Connection-oriented services tend to be used when the order in which packets are received is critical, for instance, in the transmission of real-time data such as video. Connectionless services are used when the packet order is not as critical. Connectionless services provide more flexibility in delivery.

The Presentation and Application layers aren't widely used or well-defined yet. They both deal with further processing such as compression/decompression and file transfer and conversions that are necessary to allow programs to communicate.

An Overview of Hardware Standards

To provide an overview of the basics of hardware standards, the following sections describe Ethernet, Token Ring, LocalTalk, and ARCnet. Each of the standards described here, and the many others not covered, has its own advantages.

The things to consider when evaluating the physical aspects of a new installation are:

- **Cost of installation**—Consider both the wiring required and the hardware, if necessary.

- **Upgradability**—Will you need to rewire your whole building to take advantage of faster technology?

- **Dependability and fault tolerance**—For example, a star topology will cost more for the original installation, but it will pay for itself in increased fault tolerance.

- **Throughput**—The rated speed of a network is not necessarily what you will experience. The load on the network, the quality of the installation, and the protocol will affect throughput. For instance, Token Ring, rated at 4Mbps, may be a better choice than a 10Mbps Ethernet network if heavy loads are anticipated and real-time response (for automation or process control) is necessary.

- **Expandability**—How many more workstations can you add to the network before it chokes or you run out of ports?

- **Standards**—Make sure that what you buy will work with other LANs in your company and with planned future purchases. The best way to ensure this is to make sure that what you buy adheres to a published standard, such as Ethernet (802.2 or 802.3), or a well-established public domain standard, such as ARCnet.

Ethernet

Ethernet is probably the most widely implemented hardware protocol in use for PC-based LANs. It is a broadcast standard, in that each station listens for traffic and transmits if it doesn't hear anything. If two stations transmit at the same time, it produces a collision, and both stations must retransmit. Ethernet is theoretically capable of 10, 100, or 1000Mbps, although that speed is almost never actually achieved under ordinary conditions. In addition to the three most common Ethernet standards, thick (AUI or 10Base5), thin (10Base2), and twisted-pair (10BaseT), there are two major 100Mbps versions, 100BaseTX and 100BaseVG, plus the new 1000BaseTX (which is 1GB Ethernet) implemented over twisted-pair wire. There is also a standard for Ethernet over fiber-optic cable.

The three common types of Ethernet use different topologies. Table 35.1 summarizes the cabling requirements of thick, thin, and 10BaseT (twisted-pair) Ethernet.

TABLE 35.1: Ethernet Cabling Requirements

Requirement	Thick Ethernet (AUI, 10Base5) Coaxial Cable	Thin Ethernet (10Base2) RG-58 Cable	Twisted Pair Ethernet (10Base)
Maximum overall length	2500 meters/ 8200 feet	570 meters/ 3000 feet	Number of segments depends on the concentrator
Maximum segment length	500 meters/ 1625 feet	185 meters/ 600 feet	100 meters/325 feet (from hub to station)
Maximum number of stations	100	30	Limited by the hub; can be from 4 to hundreds

Thick Ethernet

Thick Ethernet is a linear bus. This standard is uncommon, partly because, with the usual installation, the whole network must be brought down to add another station. Thick Ethernet runs over a thick (nearly .25 inch) coaxial cable with up to five trunk segments. It allows runs up to 2500 meters (8200 feet) total, up to 500 meters (1625 feet) per segment, and up to 100 stations per segment.

Thin Ethernet

Thin Ethernet is a linear bus with the vulnerabilities of a ring. Thin Ethernet is common in small installations, because the cabling is simple to install and inexpensive, with no hub required. Thin Ethernet runs over a thinner (about .125 inch) coaxial cable designated RG-58. Thin Ethernet allows a total run of 185 meters (600 feet) per segment, up to 5 segments, and 30 stations per segment. Thick and thin Ethernet allow a maximum of five segments, four repeaters, and three segments with workstations on them on any one LAN. This is known as the 5-4-3 rule.

10BaseT (Twisted-Pair) Ethernet

Twisted-pair Ethernet is a star. For most business installations, it has become the wiring scheme of choice, thanks to its fault tolerance. It does require a hub or concentrator, but the cost of hubs has dropped from more than $100 per port to less than $10 in many cases.

10BaseT (and the faster Ethernet standards) uses twisted-pair wiring like phone wiring, but with four pairs of wires, two pair of which are used for each connection. The maximum run from workstation to hub should not exceed 100 meters (325 feet). The total number of stations is determined by the capacity of the hubs; these may support anywhere from four to hundreds of connections. Although they are expensive, switching hubs can offer substantial performance gains over standard equipment. See the section "Patch Panels, Repeaters, and Concentrators" a little later in the chapter, for more information.

Token Ring

Token Ring is known as an IBM standard, although it was originally developed by another firm. It is usually a star topology physically, but a ring logically. A *token*, a special type of packet, is passed from workstation to workstation around a ring.

Each workstation's location on the ring is a function of when it logged onto the network, relative to the others. A station can only send a packet out when it has the token. After it sends its packet, it releases the token to the next workstation.

Each workstation is usually connected by Type 1, 2, or 3 cable to a MAU, also known as the Multiple Station Access Unit (MSAU). A MAU may have 8, 12, or up to 50 ports plus the ring-in and ring-out ports.

WARNING   Never connect a workstation to the MAU's ring-in or ring-out port. These are only for connecting to another MAU.

Some Token Ring networks are now being implemented over unshielded twisted-pair (UTP) cable, which is much less expensive, although more susceptible to interference. Regardless of the type of wiring, the important thing to understand is that a hardware failure will usually drop a station off the ring, losing only the one connection. However, if a problem occurs that prevents the token from being passed, then the whole ring can fail. This failure can occur if a connection between MAUs is lost, if a LAN adapter fails without dropping its power to the MAU, if electrical interference in the cable distorts signals, and in other similar situations. A simple protocol analyzer can usually tell you where in the ring a break has occurred.

With Type 1 and 2 shielded twisted-pair (STP) cabling, Token Ring supports up to 260 devices, including MAUs and repeaters, although in practice, going much over 100 will cause problems.

Cable lengths from the workstation to MAU can be 300 meters (975 feet) if there is only one MAU, or 100 meters (325 feet) if there are multiple MAUs. MAUs can be up to 200 meters (650 feet) apart. It is wise to keep cable lengths under 100 meters to allow for expansion to multiple MAUs. Both 4 and 16Mbps Token Ring can run on Type 1 and Type 2 cable.

Type 3 cabling (UTP) supports 96 devices maximum per ring. Type 3 supports station-to-MAU cable lengths of 100 meters for single-MAU systems and 45 meters (145 feet) for multiple-MAU systems, with up to 120 meters (390 feet) between MAUs. Type 6 cable is more flexible, and is generally used only for connections from the workstation to a wall jack or in situations where the cable must be routed around tight obstructions.

Table 35.2 summarizes the Token Ring cabling requirements.

TABLE 35.2:   Token Ring Cabling Requirements

Requirement	Type 1 and 2 (Coaxial Cable)	Type 3 (UTP Cable)
Maximum number of devices (including MAUs)	260	96
Maximum cable length (1 MAU), station to MAU	300 meters/975 feet	100 meters/325 feet
Maximum cable length (multiple MAUs), station to MAU	100 meters/325 feet	45 meters/145 feet
Maximum distance between MAUs	200 meters/650 feet	120 meters/390 feet

LocalTalk

Apple was the first personal computer manufacturer to include built-in networking capabilities. This networking protocol, *LocalTalk*, is easy to set up, relatively fault-tolerant, and inexpensive. However, by modern standards, it is very slow at 230Kbps, and under normal conditions, as low as 90Kbps. For networks of more than a few Macs and a printer, this isn't very useful. To meet the needs of modern networks, versions of AppleTalk that run over Ethernet or Token Ring were developed.

Before EtherTalk over 10BaseT Ethernet became common, a number of companies implemented UTP Ethernet on their own. LatticeNet was one of these. Lattice-Net was similar to 10BaseT, but not completely compatible. You were required to either make sure that all your Macs used the same one of the two standards or get a concentrator that could handle both types. LatticeNet, however, is dead. With the advent of standards-based networking for Macintosh systems, this type of workaround is no longer necessary. LocalTalk, on the other hand, is still in use (much less for networking, but still for small workgroup printer sharing).

The theoretical maximum for LocalTalk is about 300 meters (1000 feet) total cabling distance and 32 stations per network. However, if you are anywhere close to this number, you should upgrade to Ethernet or TokenTalk, depending on your topological needs. Cabling specifications and lengths are the same as for Ethernet and Token Ring, as explained in the earlier sections on those standards.

ARCnet

Attached Resource Computer Network (ARCnet) is a standard that actually goes back farther than Ethernet. It is not an IEEE standard, as Token Ring, Ethernet, and FDDI are, but it is widely supported in the industry. Its rated throughput is 2.5Mbps, and it is a star topology, with a token-passing protocol.

One advantage to ARCnet is that, unlike Ethernet, it doesn't require repeaters or relatively expensive concentrators. For larger networks, ARCnet uses a combination of inexpensive passive hubs and active hubs, which are less expensive than similar Ethernet concentrators. Small networks require only the passive hubs. The main difference between active and passive hubs is the length of cable they support.

ARCnet requires RG-62 93-ohm coaxial cable, which is cheaper than the RG-58 cable used for thin Ethernet. It allows 256 stations per LAN, a maximum length of 600 meters (2000 feet) between stations or from station to active hub, and 30 meters (100 feet) between stations and passive hubs. The hub-to-hub distance is 30 meters for passive hub to active hub, 600 meters for active hub to active hub, and up to 6000 meters (20,000 feet) in a segment. Passive hubs can't be connected to other passive hubs.

A new ARCnet specification has been developed that allows 20Mbps. This specification allows ARCnet installations to be upgraded to provide throughput on par with Ethernet or 16Mbps Token Ring. It retains existing wiring but requires new NICs. ARCnet over UTP cable is also possible, but allows only 10 stations per ring, with a maximum distance between them of less than 2 meters (6 feet). This gives 80 stations on an 8-port active hub, with a total maximum wiring length of 120 meters (400 feet).

Here are some tips for ARCnet setups:

- Set the server to station address 255.

- Always terminate unused ports in a passive hub.

- Make sure that a segment doesn't loop back on itself (don't connect hubs in a circle).

- Make sure that no two stations use the same station address.

Table 35.3 summarizes ARCnet cabling requirements.

TABLE 35.3: ARCnet Cabling Requirements

Requirement	Coaxial RG-62 (93-ohm)	UTP Cable
Maximum overall length	6000 meters/20,000 feet	120 meters/400 feet
Maximum number of stations	256	10 per ring; 80 per 8-port active hub
Maximum distance between stations and active hubs	600 meters/2000 feet	6 feet between stations
Maximum distance between stations and active hubs	30 meters/100 feet	N/A
Maximum hub-to-hub spacing	Active-to-active: 600 meters/2000 feet Active-to-passive: 30 meters/100 feet	N/A

Tracking Down Cabling Plant Problems

Cabling for a new network should be installed by professionals. For anything larger than a few workstations, this is almost a necessity. Pulling the wire through the walls; crimping connectors; testing circuits; installing concentrators, patch panels, and punch-down blocks; and so on are all highly specialized tasks best left to experienced professionals. In fact, when you are planning the network, it is best to get bids and input from several vendors. They may even suggest a better way of networking your workstations. If you want to do it yourself, be very sure that you understand fully the limitations on cable lengths for each type of cable you're using, proper methods of termination and grounding, and the setup and configuration of any networking hardware you will be using.

Generally, the company that installs the new cabling will test all the segments for continuity and polarity. They will often warranty their work for 30 to 90 days. In a new installation, the cabling itself is unlikely to cause problems if it is installed correctly. You should check other, more probable causes first. However, if the more likely problems have been eliminated, a basic understanding of your cabling plant will allow you to isolate problems without too much difficulty.

Often, the administrator may have responsibility for all of the hardware that makes up the network, except for the cabling plant. That part of the network may "belong" to facilities, or to corporate MIS. This sort of division of responsibility can make things difficult to resolve. Even when this is not the case, the actual wiring is usually in the walls and cannot be visually inspected. In this sense, the cabling plant is the most obscure part of your network. However, you can usually isolate the problem to one of a very few possibilities without specialized equipment, simply by understanding the topology of your network, analyzing its fault point chain, and checking the break points.

Aside from mice chewing through the cabling, it isn't likely that the cable itself will fail. The most likely cause of a failure in the physical plant is that someone has removed, changed, or broken some part of the cabling plant, or that an electronic part of the plant has failed. Some examples of what can go wrong include:

- Construction workers inadvertently cut cabling.

- Users remove or change connectors without realizing the consequences.

- Someone changes the settings in a router without being sure of all the ramifications.

- There is a hardware failure in a repeater or concentrator.

- The software in a router freezes up.

Check for these sorts of problems before you run continuity checks on all the wiring. Another thing to check is a new source of electromagnetic interference, such as a fluorescent light ballast or an electric motor near a cabling run. This, in particular, is a situation where a map of the physical cabling plant is very useful. See the "Documenting the Cabling Plant" section later in this chapter for details.

Cabling: Lengths, Termination, Grounds, Connectors, and Type

It's been said that 90 percent of all network problems are problems with cabling, particularly with existing networks where nothing has been changed (well, nothing has been changed intentionally). There are three basic things that can give you an edge in tracking down and fixing such problems: understanding your cabling setup, ensuring correct installation of the network hardware, and using quality components such as connectors.

The first is a good understanding of your cabling setup, both physical and logical. This includes the protocol (Ethernet, ARCnet, or Token Ring, for example) and the physical and logical topology (how the signals are routed throughout the network). What are the possible effects of breaking the line? Could a bad network adapter bring down the whole network? You should understand not only how the wires are routed through the walls, but where a packet must travel to reach the server. Does it need to be passed on through several intermediate workstations? Does the connection in the office wall go to the server directly, or does it go to a repeater in a broom closet somewhere?

A recent study suggests that bit errors caused by electromagnetic interference or faulty wiring can cause many thousands of times the performance drain that collisions do. Make sure that twisted-pair cabling has the correct number of twists, that connectors are solidly crimped, that network wiring doesn't run close to other electrical equipment, that the wiring is well grounded, and so on.

TIP   As connectors age, their ability to provide a solid connection may decrease, especially if inexpensive connectors were used in the first place. Be sure to specify high-quality parts, especially in networks where connections might be changed frequently.

Check for the correct types and lengths of cabling. For example, RG-58 may have been switched with RG-62 (the two types of cable are usually marked with their designation along the length of the cable), or RJ-11 (four-pin phone) plugs may have been placed in RJ-45 (eight-pin 10BaseT) jacks. Silver-satin phone cable may have been used for NIC-to-jack connections, instead of Ethernet-rated UTP cable. Are connectors crimped neatly? Are the terminating resistors of the correct ohmage? Make sure that lengths are not over the rated maximums—it's easy to keep adding "just one more" node until you're past the maximum length. Any of these items can contribute to intermittent problems on your network.

Another issue that is becoming a major problem as networks are upgraded is the category of UTP Ethernet cabling. Much of the installed Ethernet UTP cabling is what is known as Category 3 (phone grade). This is not usually a problem for 10BaseT. However, for sites migrating to a 100Mbps standard, the required specification is Category 5. This is a much more stringent specification, which covers the type of cabling, how often the wires are twisted, what connectors are installed, how connectors are installed, and what types of network equipment (such as hubs) are installed. The slightest variations can cause large drops in performance, from the theoretical 100Mbps down to 20Mbps or less. Since this largely negates the expensive migration, it is critical to make sure that the cable installations are done correctly.

Fiber-optic cabling is starting to be seen in even small networks, especially in high-traffic situations or as a "backbone." Troubleshooting tools for optical fiber are not especially complicated, but you need to learn how to use them. A light meter that will read a light source at the other end of a cable and tell you what the transmission efficiency is, and a simple device to ensure that connectors are properly installed are all you will usually need.

One advantage to fiber-optic cable is that once it's configured, it is immune to the electromagnetic interference that can plague copper wire, especially high-performance copper wire. It also tends to be binary in nature; that is, it either works or it doesn't, rather than experiencing some level of performance degradation due to improper installation.

Patch Panels, Repeaters, and Concentrators

Networking hardware should be in a secure area—not just locked up where no one can play with it, but mounted securely and protected from anyone accidentally moving a switch and cutting off 20 users. Don't just put a repeater under a desk and forget about it.

The most important things you can do with a patch panel or punch-down block are to keep it neat and well-documented. It makes it easier to trace or move connections, as well as easier to spot a poorly connected jack.

Repeaters can be thought of as extension cords for networks. If you have, say, 60 workstations on thin Ethernet, spread out over a fairly large area, most cabling cannot connect all of them in one chain—it's simply too many feet of cable, especially if it's run through the walls and up to the ceiling between each office or cube. With a repeater, you can divide the network into several segments, each of which can be 180 meters (600 feet) long. This also gives you some fault tolerance; if one of the segments is broken, it takes down only the workstations on that loop, and the other ports on the repeater aren't affected.

Concentrators, or hubs, come in many varieties and sizes, from a small four-port 10BaseT hub to a $50,000 concentrator that will accept fiber-optic lines to a backbone, provide several hundred 10BaseT ports, and allow remote management through Simple Network Management Protocol (SNMP). With the latter, you can use management software and find out what port on the concentrator has lost its connection or is receiving bad packets, without ever leaving your desk.

The latest developments in Ethernet utilize hubs that are known as switching hubs. They essentially behave as if each PC connected to the hub had its own individual router and the traffic from that PC was sent to only the intended recipient. This greatly reduces the number of packets received by most workstations on the network and increases the total amount of traffic that can be supported on the same network segment. Switching hubs are not cheap, but the performance benefits are great enough that they are rapidly becoming common.

Routers, Bridges, and Gateways

A *bridge* looks at the intended destination of a packet and sends it by the most direct route, using the software or Network layer address. A *router* can route packets for different protocols. A *gateway* converts from one protocol to another. Many of the products on the market today combine parts of all of these functions.

The Novell Multi-Protocol Router allows routing between any protocol supported by NetWare, which is just about everything you might find out there. It can replace dedicated boxes that do only one thing well, and do other things in addition, such as hub management and backups.

All of these devices are fault points in your network. If you find that traffic on one LAN is normal but users can't access services on another LAN, check the router, bridge, or gateway. Remember that a server with two LAN cards is acting as a router between the two LAN segments.

Documenting the Cabling Plant

The cabling company should provide you with a physical map of the wiring the workers have installed, as well as locations of punch-down blocks, repeaters, concentrators, and so on. Familiarize yourself with the locations of all the hardware, and identify the workstations/users on each segment of your network. Doing so will make it much easier to isolate faults. For example, if a certain four users who are all on the same loop complain of network trouble, you immediately know where to start looking.

You should also take the time to make a logical map of your network. Identify how a packet actually is routed to get from a workstation to the server and back. Does it need to pass through each workstation on a loop? Which workstations does it pass through, or is that different, depending on which stations entered the network first?

There are many software packages and software/hardware combinations being marketed to manage your network. Some of them will create and automatically update a logical map of your network. They can tell you when stations go online or offline, if network devices fail, and when and where failures occur. If you have a complex LAN or WAN to look after, these packages can save you many, many hours of time tracing down faults, and they will also greatly increase your response time when failures occur. Not only will they help you find problems, they will usually alert you when a problem occurs, sometimes long before the users become aware of it.

Real-Life Stories

We return to the two fictional companies and their administrators introduced in Chapter 1 to illustrate typical problems with network connections and the process a troubleshooter goes through to isolate and correct those problems.

Scenario One: A New Cabling System

The system administrator encounters some problems typical of a newly installed cabling system and demonstrates some techniques for fault isolation without specialized equipment.

Snapshot—Scenario One

Is this a new network?

- How many nodes are affected? Do some of the workstations on the ring or segment work?

- Is it only one workstation that can't connect?

John, the system administrator for Itsy-Bitsy, Inc., is halfway through a long working weekend. The Marketing department has just moved to a new area, and the cabling contractor finished installing and testing the wiring yesterday. John has gotten the server up and running and is unpacking and connecting the workstations. The network is 10BaseT Ethernet, with a concentrator in a wiring closet and jacks in each work area.

The first few workstations are unpacked and connected to the network with no problems, and they connect to the server without errors. Then John puts his supervisor's PC back together and plugs it in. It boots without error messages, but won't attach to the network. John makes sure that the interrupts are set correctly on the NIC, and then changes the cable from the PC to the wall jack. Still nothing. He goes to the wiring closet and makes sure that the jack for his supervisor's office is active. The connection light is on for that jack. He tries changing the cable to another port, with no improvement. He thinks about changing the jack to another port on the concentrator, but he doesn't have the punch-down tools.

To get some diagnostics, he tries another PC in his supervisor's office, one that was able to connect to the network from another jack. It can't see the server either. He is pretty sure now that there is something wrong, either with the jack, the wiring to the punch-down panel, or that port on the concentrator. He observes that other ports on the same card on the concentrator are working—it's unlikely to be a hardware failure in the concentrator. Next, he gets an Ethernet adapter with an AUI (thick) connector, and a transceiver to 10BaseT. The transceiver has monitor lights for connection, transmit, receive, SQE (heartbeat), and collision. When it's installed and the PC is booted, the connection and SQE come on, and the transmit and receive lights blink on and off, indicating that data is being sent to and from the PC. However, the connection still doesn't work.

There is an electrical connection to the concentrator, and data is being transmitted back and forth. The most likely problem seems to be that the data is being sent but that it's being scrambled somehow. The collision light isn't coming on, and no one is using the network, so traffic is unlikely to be the problem. John concludes that the problem is most likely in the installation of the jack or the punch-down block. He calls the cabling contractor and asks him to come back and recheck this connection, then moves on to the rest of the workstations.

The cabling installer arrives in a couple of hours, grumbling about being called back in. John explains what he has tried, and the installer checks the jack and wiring with a specialized test device. He discovers that two of the wires to the jack have been reversed. He reconnects the wiring to the jack and then tries the PC. It connects to the server with no problem.

Lessons Learned—Scenario One

- If you aren't familiar with the cabling company doing the installation, you may want to have the work double-checked. Don't assume that what the installers say they've checked is perfect—it's very easy to miss a small thing like a polarity error.

- You can isolate seemingly impenetrable problems by taking them step-by-step and eliminating fault points until you have only one or two left.

- There are some areas that can't be resolved without test equipment. However, if the cabling company hadn't been able to resolve this for John, he could have compared the order of the colors of wiring on both ends of the connection to find or eliminate the issue of the cross-connected wires, and he could have punched down the connection on the block again, or replaced the jack, with inexpensive tools. If in doubt, redo it.

The Fault Point Chain—Scenario One

- The driver software in the PC

- The Ethernet transceiver in the PC

- The 10BaseT cable to the wall jack

- The wall jack and its connection

- The cabling from the wall jack to the punch-down panel and its connection

- The wiring from the punch-down panel to the PC's port on the concentrator

- The concentrator

- The wiring from the server's port on the concentrator to the punch-down panel

- The connection at the punch-down block and the cabling from the punch-down panel to the wall jack in the server room

- The wall jack in the server room and its connection

- The cabling from the wall jack to the Ethernet card in the server

- The Ethernet card in the server

- The Ethernet driver software installed in the server operating system

A few minor points, such as the solidity of the connector in the wall jack, could also be included. Many of these can be eliminated immediately. For instance, since other PCs can connect to the server, the last seven items can be disregarded. Furthermore, since the PC can connect from another jack, the first two can be eliminated. Trying another cable eliminates the third item. That only leaves three items, a much easier list to test. Traffic lights on the concentrator and the transceiver show that data is being passed through the cable, which leaves only the connections at the jack and the punch-down block.

Scenario Two: Part of an Existing Network Fails

A portion of an existing network goes down. The administrator follows the process of isolating the problem, determining the cause, and fixing it.

Snapshot—Scenario Two

Is this an existing network?

- How many nodes are affected? Do some of the workstations on the ring or segment work?

Fran, the system administrator for Great Big, Inc., gets a number of calls from users in the Engineering department saying that they aren't able to connect to the server. She checks the server to make sure that it is running. Most of the workstations in the department are still able to connect to the server. The workstations are connected with thin Ethernet, in four segments, or legs, to a multiport repeater, which is in turn connected to the server. Fran looks at the wiring diagram for the department and notices that all the affected workstations are on the same loop. The problem could be either of two things: a break in the loop or a problem with the repeater. Figure 35.4 illustrates this situation.

Fran checks the repeater first, since it is simpler to check than tracing the entire path of the loop, looking for breaks. She finds that the switch that controls the loop in question is turned on. Having found segments switched off by accident before, she had hoped it would be that simple this time, but it isn't. She sighs, then begins tracing the path of the loop, using her network map. The first few connections are all solid and look okay. Then she finds a pair of thin Ethernet cables in an unused cubicle, with no connector connecting them. She finds a spare T-connector, reconnects the two cables, and discovers that the workstations in the loop are back online.

Thin Ethernet LAN using a repeater

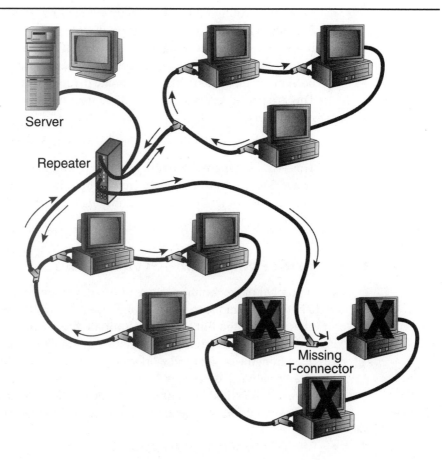

Further research uncovers a user who borrowed the connector, reasoning that since the cube wasn't in use, the connector wasn't doing anything. Fran refrains from strangling him, but sends out a carefully worded cautionary note to all the users on her networks, emphasizing that users who need networking work done should go through her.

Lessons Learned—Scenario Two

- Check the simple things first, but don't be afraid to do some legwork. Even the most daunting task can be handled with a calm and methodical approach.

- Break the problem down by isolating the affected elements. In this case, Fran had a network map and was easily able to determine that all the affected users were on the same leg of the repeater. If she hadn't been able to determine that, her job would have been much harder, since there would have been many more elements to eliminate before the fault point was isolated. This is a perfect example of why documenting your network is a necessity, not a luxury.

- Never underestimate the users' ability to make your life difficult.

- This is a case where a network monitor would have made troubleshooting easier. Some monitors available now would have sent an alarm as soon as the T-connector was removed, identifying the problem and the most probable location of the break.

The Fault Point Chain—Scenario Two

Since a number of workstations were affected, we can eliminate most points of the chain that are unique to individual workstations, such as the network driver and Ethernet adapter. But we can't eliminate the T-connector connecting each card to the cable, because each one has the potential to affect the entire loop. The fault chain from the server to all workstations could also be eliminated, because if the server's network driver, its Ethernet card, the cable to the repeater, or the repeater as a whole had been damaged, none of the workstations on the rest of the network would have been able to log in either. The remaining fault points are:

- The T-connectors on each workstation
- The cabling
- The port on the repeater to which the loop is connected
- The termination on each end of the loop
- The grounding of the loop

Scenario Three: An Existing Token Ring Network

The administrator encounters a problem typical of a Token Ring network. Again, she follows the process of isolating the fault and fixing the problem.

Snapshot—Scenario Three

Is this an existing network?

- How many nodes are affected? Do some of the workstations on the ring or segment work?

The Sales department of Great Big uses Token Ring workstations that access their mainframe through NetWare for SAA. One day, Fran gets a call reporting that no one in the Sales department can access the network. Fran knows that with Token Ring, one workstation can bring down the network if its card fails to pass the token along properly. She checks the server to make sure that nothing is apparently wrong there, then begins checking the workstations. All the workstations reboot without errors and load the Token Ring driver without error messages about the card's configurations. The network doesn't begin to function when any one of the workstations is offline, which tells Fran that none of the workstations is failing to pass the token along; otherwise, the network would function when that workstation was disconnected from the network.

Fran then checks the wiring closet where the MAUs are located. She discovers that the cable leading from the ring-in port on one of the MAUs to the ring-out port on the next MAU is disconnected. She reinserts the connector into the ring-in port, and then checks the network. Everything is running again. Fran asks around to find out if anyone on her staff disconnected the port on purpose, but no one has (or will admit to it).

Lessons Learned—Scenario Three

- Even though Token Ring has a physical star topology, it is logically a ring, which means that one card that doesn't function properly may bring the whole network down. If the PC with the faulty card is powered down, it should remove that station from the network, which will then begin functioning properly again.

- When you have a single device in your cabling system that can affect the entire network—a repeater, concentrator, or MAU—you should check it before initiating a time-consuming process such as checking every workstation on the network.

- Leave checking the continuity of the wiring in the walls for last, but check connections that users (or janitors) can affect first.

- Like the scenario described in the previous section, this is a situation where a network analyzer would have helped. It could have told Fran where the connection was broken and which PCs were acting properly, thus pointing her in the direction of the lost connection between the two MAUs.

The Fault Point Chain—Scenario Three

With Token Ring, a card that goes dead should remove itself from the network. However, a card that remains electrically active but isn't passing the token along properly will halt the entire network. The relevant fault points are these:

- Each card and driver on the ring

- The server, and its card and driver

- The MAU, and the connection between each MAU

The wiring and the connections (at each card, the wall jack, and on the MAU) were not, as a whole, really a factor here. If a link between one PC and the MAU had been broken, either by a faulty connection or a broken wire, it would have deactivated that port on the MAU, and the rest of the network would have been running.

Another possibility in this situation is a source of electromagnetic interference near one cable that garbled the token as it passed through. This could have caused the same sort of problem.

Scenario Four: Caring for a Growing Network

This scenario addresses the problems typical of a network that has been added to, or which has evolved from several small networks. Some basic recommendations are given for revamping such systems and working within a budget.

Snapshot—Scenario Four

Is this an existing network?

- How many nodes are affected? Do some of the workstations on the ring or segment work?

- Is it only one workstation that can't connect?

- Is the network experiencing intermittent faults and performance problems?

Fran has some free time, and since reviews are coming up, she picks an item from her to-do list instead of playing Tetris. The Marketing lab workers have been complaining about the performance of the network in their demo room. It is often slow, and some workstations experience intermittent failures.

Fran begins by inventorying the equipment in the demo room. There are two NetWare servers and about 50 workstations, including PCs, Macs, and Unix workstations, all attached by thin Ethernet or 10BaseT (twisted-pair) Ethernet. The network and servers were all set up by the Marketing people and their system engineer, who quit several months ago and hasn't been replaced. Since then, one of the Marketing staff, who has a fair amount of experience with NetWare and Macs, but almost none with hardware, has been maintaining the network.

After looking at the workstations, Fran inspects the cabling. Some of the workstations have 10BaseT Ethernet adapter cards and are attached to an eight-port 10BaseT mini-hub, which is then attached to another mini-hub, which the server is attached to. Others have a thick Ethernet card (AUI) card, which is then connected to a transceiver that is in turn connected to a 10BaseT cable running to one of the mini-hubs. Others are connected by thin Ethernet to one large segment with about 15 workstations and the other server on it. This situation is illustrated in Figure 35.5.

The thin Ethernet loop is not properly grounded, many of the T-connectors in use are old and obviously low-quality, and some of the cables are ARCnet specification (RG-62, 93-ohm cable) instead of the RG-58A 50-ohm cable required for thin Ethernet. Finally, Fran notices that one of the extra terminators in the box of networking hardware in the room is a 75-ohm terminator, rather than the 50 ohms required for thin Ethernet.

Fran talks with the director of the Marketing department and recommends that they install an all-10BaseT network using two 40-port concentrators. This will let them move connections from one server to the other, allowing for easy reconfiguration of the network as necessary, and it will keep everything in the same topology. She shows the manager how easy it is for things to get out of whack with the current setup, and explains how all the things she found can contribute to poor performance. She adds that the two concentrators would give the lab a much more professional appearance than the haphazard look of the current setup.

FIGURE 35.5:

The Marketing lab topology

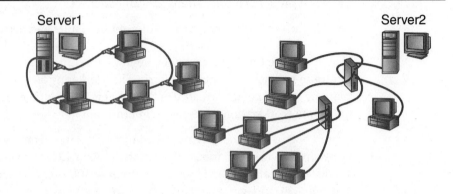

Server1   Server2

The director is unwilling to make the investment, so Fran retreats to her prepared fallback plan: some more 8- or 12-port mini-hubs and the cards or transceivers necessary to get all the workstations running 10BaseT. Even the much more moderate expense represented by three mini-hubs and some new Ethernet adapters is more than the director wants to spend. Finally, Fran shows the director the bottom-dollar plan: upgrade the existing thin Ethernet cable and T-connectors to new, high-quality ones, including extras for reconfiguring the network as necessary, proper grounding, proper terminators, and a few new transceivers and LAN adapters. And one more item—a half-day training course for the lab administrator in proper cabling techniques and troubleshooting.

The director is happy with the low-cost alternative. After a few hours of work the next evening, aided by the newly educated administrator, Fran replaces the thin Ethernet cabling and T-connectors with high-quality ones, grounds the segment, throws away the old stuff to make sure no one will inadvertently add it to the network, and upgrades some of the transceivers and LAN cards on the 10BaseT network. She goes over the procedures for adding workstations to either network with the administrator, and makes sure they have sufficient additional high-quality cable, connectors, and transceivers to allow for normal reconfigurations.

They also make sure that all the workstations are using the same network driver software, and that the Macs are using the same system version and printer driver software. A few days later, Fran checks back with the administrator. Everyone is amazed at the increase in network performance, and the Marketing director is happy with the minimal expense required.

Lessons Learned—Scenario Four

- Don't try to save 25 cents on a connector or a dollar on a cable. It won't be worth it in the long run. This is especially true of the T-connectors used with thin Ethernet. Cheap ones will often become very hard to attach or detach with time, and they can cause nasty intermittent problems.

- Try to avoid letting users set up their own networks. In this case, the systems engineer that did the initial setup knew what he was doing, and the setup was fine, until the administration was handed over to someone who wasn't familiar with cabling.

- Watch out for mismatched equipment. Many connectors and cables look similar and will physically interchange with each other, but impedances and other factors can cause big problems.

- In a lab environment, the simplest solution is the best. In this case, the Marketing personnel sometimes needed to reconfigure the network when the administrator wasn't around. Converting everything to 10BaseT would have substantially reduced the chances of an inexperienced user leaving the ring open or making a connection that didn't completely lock.

- When presenting a plan for an installation to management, try to have more than one scenario: "Plan A will cost more, but will also have the following benefits…. Plan B will sacrifice the following benefits, but reduce costs by this much…"

The Fault Point Chain—Scenario Four

- The network card and network software in each workstation

- The connection from the card to the cable or transceiver

- The transceiver (if applicable)

- The connection from the transceiver to the network cable

- The network cable

- The concentrator (if applicable)

- The connection from the concentrator to the server

- The connection at the server on the thin Ethernet ring

- The LAN adapters and driver software in the servers

Scenario Five: Fun with AppleTalk

This scenario describes a deceptive problem on an AppleTalk network, and how the solution is discovered through observation and deduction.

Snapshot—Scenario Five

Is this an existing network?

- How many nodes are affected? Do some of the workstations on the ring or segment work?

- Is it only one workstation that can't connect?

- Is the network experiencing intermittent faults and performance problems?

Jethro has one of the toughest assignments possible: someone in the Art department is having problems, maybe with a virus. The user's Mac has been intermittently freezing during startup. He grabs his Mac tool kit and starts tracking down the problem. The virus checker on the affected machine is the latest version, and it doesn't report any problems. The user says the problem doesn't seem to occur during any particular type of operation, or when a certain application is open. There aren't any extensions, control panels, or Startup items that Jethro doesn't recognize, but he tries removing all the extraneous extensions. The system still freezes up occasionally. He then tries reinstalling the System Folder from the boot CD-ROM suppled by Apple (7.5.5). There are still intermittent problems.

Another person in the department wanders by and mentions that she is having the same problem. Jethro realizes that the problem must be network-related if it's affecting more than one Mac. He checks, and most of the people in the department had been having problems but hadn't realized they weren't alone.

He begins the tedious process of trying to isolate the common elements of the affected Macs. They aren't all running the same version of the Ethernet driver (ranging from the original EtherTalk to Apple Enet, the new consolidated Ethernet drivers, in MacOS 8.5), they don't all have the same EtherTalk card (most PowerMacs have the built-in AAUI adapter or 10/100base-T ports, but some still need NuBus Ethernet NICs or Fast Ethernet NICs for older PCI-based or new G3 systems installed), and they don't even all use the same System version (most would be using some version of System 7, which could be 7.1.2, 7.5.x, 7.6.x, or 8.x, including MacOS 8.5). Then one of the users asks Jethro to take a look at their printer while he's there—it's been jamming. Jethro figures he might as well take a break from thinking about the other problem, so he shuts down the printer and begins cleaning it thoroughly. After he's been working on the printer for about 20 minutes, one of the users comes over and compliments him on having fixed the problem with her Mac freezing.

A light dawns. He finishes cleaning the printer, then turns it back on. Checking with the affected Macs, he discovers that they are freezing again. It must be the printer. He calls the manufacturer to see if the company know about this. After climbing up the tech support ladder for a while, Jethro is told that yes, they have seen this behavior on some networks, and he is given a long technical reason involving frames and reflection. The tech support individual is helpful and states that they'll have a BIOS upgrade that should fix it within a week or two. Jethro arranges to swap the printer with another PostScript printer currently attached to a parallel port on a PC, which shouldn't be affected by the AppleTalk problem, and takes the offending printer offline. The other PostScript printer is a different brand and works fine.

A couple of months later, the new BIOS arrives, and Jethro upgrades the problematic printer. He reattaches it to the network and holds his breath. As each day passes without freezes, he breathes a little easier.

Lessons Learned—Scenario Five

- Don't assume that a problem is unique to a user who complains. Check around to see if any others are affected. You won't always hear from some users when they have a problem; there is a certain tendency to take some problems for granted. If Jethro had known from the start that more than one user was affected, he could have saved quite a bit of time working on the system and Inits on the individual Mac. A virus would still have been a possibility, of course.

- This is yet another case where a network analyzer would have been very handy. Jethro would most likely have found that some device on the network was sending out bad AppleTalk packets, and he could have at least isolated the cause to AppleTalk hardware or software, and possibly even determined the device causing the problem.

- Don't assume that the computers on your LAN are the only devices that can cause problems. It is common for printers to have networking interfaces built in. Each of these is potentially a problem, too.

- Never assume that the manufacturer of a device did everything right. It is common for PCs to arrive from the factory with configuration errors, devices installed incorrectly, and of course, occasionally with faulty components.

If Jethro had continued with his fault-point analysis, he would eventually have discovered that what all the Macs had in common was the AppleTalk zone that they were on. That would have led to looking at the other devices on that zone: the server and the printer. He might have spent considerable time trying to determine a problem with the server, assuming that it was a result of a configuration error or old driver version, and possibly never even looked at the printer, assuming that it couldn't be causing the problem.

- Never assume that the manufacturer will notify you if something you bought needs to be updated or might cause problems under certain conditions. The best place to hear about this sort of thing is on the forums on CompuServe or at user-group or CNEPA meetings.

- If he hadn't been lucky, the next step for Jethro should have been to try asking around, either within his department or at some of the sources listed in the previous paragraph. He might have found someone else who already had the same problem.

The Fault Point Chain—Scenario Five

Jethro's initial assumption was that the user's problem was unique to that Mac. That was, of course, incorrect. If Jethro hadn't happened to find out that the problem was actually the fault of the printer, he might have replaced every part of the Macintosh, reinstalling its operating system and all the applications. Eventually, with the whole system replaced and the problem still occurring, he would have needed to look at the other factors in the environment that could possibly affect a workstation: the power, electromagnetic interference, and any connection coming into the Mac. The connections might include the keyboard, the printer (network) connection, a serial connection for a modem, and the SCSI port.

Jethro would then have replaced the keyboard and disconnected anything else connected to the Mac. At that point, he would have discovered that the Mac didn't have the problem when not connected to the network. He would then have known that the problem must be caused by something coming from the network rather than anything in the Mac. The fault points are:

- The Mac hardware—motherboard, memory, power supply, disk controller, disks, and ports.

- The MacOS itself.

- The Apple extensions, such as the EtherTalk/Ethernet/Apple Enet driver(s).

- The non-Apple extensions.

- Any applications running when the problem occurred or startup items, like Kodak Digital Science color matching that may be conflicting with Finder-load control panels.

- Other devices on the AppleTalk network—the network driver software for each device on the network. This includes the BIOS in the printer, which was of course the actual problem, and the BIOS in an NT-based server, and the PRAM (zap it) and the desktop DB (rebuild it) on a MacOS-based server.

- The network hardware for each network device. Most PowerMac models have either Apple AUI or 10/100BaseT adapters built-in. For AAUI, the transceiver may be damaged, faulty, or dead.

- The cabling. This could include problems such as lines that run past transformers or fluorescent light ballasts. Checking whether a cable is UTP or not is also a good idea, no matter how crazy it sounds.

- Any other factors in the environment that might interfere with the electronics in the workstation. This could include magnets, power cords that run too close to the CPU, a second workstation, and similar sources of interference.

Summary

In this chapter, we've looked at various things that can go wrong with the physical portion of a network. We started with a snapshot and fault points to help isolate physical network problem areas. We then took a look at both network topologies and network communications protocols, as well as network standards, which include Ethernet, Token Ring, ARCnet, and AppleTalk.

Much of what goes wrong with a network physically can be attributed to cables, connectors, wall jacks, patch cables, and hubs that go bad. While having good troubleshooting skills is essential, it is also good practice to install only high quality cabling and connector equipment, which often outlasts the computers that are connected through it. In most cases, the labor involved in replacing connector equipment outweighs the additional expense.

In the next chapter, we'll shift the focus to troubleshooting network printing—particularly NetWare print servers, which can be scattered throughout a building and involve specialized print server software.

CHAPTER
THIRTY-SIX

Troubleshooting
Network Printing

- Network printing snapshot

- Network printing fault points

- The printing process

- Windows 9x/NT client printer troubleshooting

- Using CAPTURE.EXE

- Postscript printers

- Macintosh and Unix printing

In this chapter, we'll look at various problems that can hinder the ability to print over a network. Windows 9x and Windows NT both include printing locally and across a network as features built into the operating system. NetWare printing, particularly on older systems, uses TSRs (terminate and stay resident programs) for printer handling, printer redirection, and in some cases, printing from remote print servers (where a normal workstation is also configured to act as a print server). Printing from Windows 9x or NT Workstation clients to a print server attached to a NetWare server works as transparently and simply as does printing to an NT Server print server. Nevertheless, problems can still arise.

Snapshot: Troubleshooting Network Printing

Is This a New Printer Setup?

Can you print from any workstations? If you can print from some workstations, go to the next item. If you can't print from any workstations to a particular printer, try other printers, on other servers if available.

With NetWare, can you put print jobs directly into the queue with PCONSOLE? Do they print? If not, go to the next item. If inserting the jobs directly into the queue works, then your problem is likely to be with the capture setup on the workstations, with the print job setup, or with the connection to the server. See the section "The Printing Process" or the section "The Print Server."

Is the queue connected to PSERVER? Use PCONSOLE to see if the queue is attached to PSERVER (the print server software). If it is, make sure that the print server running PSERVER is up and running. See the section "The Printing Process" or the section "PSERVER—Printing Controls." If the print server is running, go to the next item. Otherwise, see Chapter 34 for information about troubleshooting workstations.

Can you print from DOS on the print server? Try printing from DOS on the print server. If the file server is also the print server, you'll need to take the server down first—exiting from NetWare to DOS. Then try printing a DOS file with the command:

```
PRINT FILE.TXT > LPT1:
```
(or whatever port the printer is on)

or

```
DIR C: > LPT1:
```
(or whatever port the printer is on)

If the printer doesn't respond, you have a problem with the printer itself, or with the workstation configuration. If the printer will print from DOS, then PSERVER or some of the associated software is configured incorrectly. See the section "PSERVER—Printing Controls."

Is printing affected on only one workstation or a few workstations? If the problem is with one or a few workstations, but others can print, then you know that the printer itself, the print server, the queues, and so on are operational. Check the workstations that can't print for common items. Are all the workstations that can print using the same print queue or the same print job? Can you print if you log in as a different user? See the section "NetWare Print Queues" and the section "CAPTURE.EXE and Print Jobs—Printing Options."

Can you print from DOS on the workstation? Try printing from DOS on the affected workstation. If you can't print from DOS, check the network connection to make sure you have a connection to the server and try printing a DOS text file from PCONSOLE. If that works, the workstation itself is probably causing the problem, rather than the print setup. See Chapter 34 for information about troubleshooting workstations. Pay particular attention to the printer port configuration, interrupt conflicts, DOS, and the NetWare shell software. Make sure that the print job or capture setup works on other workstations.

If you can print from DOS, it's probably the application. Try printing from other applications. Make sure that the application is set up to print to the proper printer port or queue. If the program is attempting to print to a NetWare queue directly, and you can't find anything wrong, try printing to the LPT1 port and using CAPTURE to redirect the output to the printer. See the section "CAPTURE.EXE and Print Jobs—Printing Options" and the chapters in Part III, which cover network applications.

Is This an Existing Printer Setup?

Is the printer operational? With an existing setup, you can have two major things go wrong: a user becomes unable to print, or no one can access a printer or queue. Isolating the people affected will give you your first clues. One of the first places to check is the printer itself. Printers, more than any other equipment on your network, require maintenance. A large percentage of "printing problems" can be fixed by resetting the printer, cleaning it, installing a new toner cartridge, or adding paper.

If the printer is apparently running, has paper, and is online, go to the next item. If not, see your printer's manual for details on your printer. Check power, cables, connections, and other items that users can get to first. Don't forget to check the paper tray and make sure the cover is closed. See the section "The Printing Process."

Is the print server operational? Next, make sure that the print server is running properly. If you are using NetWare, be aware that some versions of PSERVER.EXE and RPRINTER.EXE are more likely than others to lock up the print server, especially with PostScript printers. See the section "Troubleshooting PostScript Printers."

Check the print server for operation—power on, keyboard responsive, and so on. If the print server is running, go to the next item. If not, troubleshoot the print server as a workstation, as described in Chapter 34.

Can you print from some workstations? If you can print from some workstations, go to the next item. If you can't print from any workstations, try other printers, on other servers if available. If you can print to another printer, queue, or server, the problem is most likely with the setup of the queue or the print server you were attempting to print to, rather than the workstation. See the section "The Printing Process."

(For NetWare) Can you put print jobs directly into the queue with PCONSOLE? **Do they print?** If not, go to the next item. If inserting print jobs directly into the queue works, then your problem is likely to be with the capture setup on the workstations, with the print job setup, or with the connection to the server. See the section "CAPTURE.EXE and Print Jobs—Printing Options."

(For NetWare) Is the queue connected to PSERVER? Use PCONSOLE to see if the queue is attached to PSERVER. If it is, make sure that the print server running PSERVER is up and running. If the print server is running, go to the next item. Otherwise, see Chapter 34 for information about troubleshooting workstations.

(For NetWare) Can you print from DOS on the print server? Try printing from DOS on the print server. If this is the server, you'll need to take down the server first, exiting from NetWare to DOS. Then try printing a DOS file with either of these commands:

`PRINT FILE.TXT > LPT1:` *(or whatever port the printer is on)*

or

`DIR C: > LPT1:` *(or whatever port the printer is on)*

If the printer doesn't respond, you have a problem with the printer itself, or with the workstation configuration. If the printer will print from DOS, then PSERVER or some other part of the print software is incorrectly configured. See the section "PSERVER—Printing Controls."

(For NT/Win9x print servers) Can you print directly from the server station itself? If not, first check the printer itself and its connection to the server. If the cable appears to be connected properly and the printer's "online" light is lit, verify that this is the default or selected printer, and then try to print a test page again.

If you are able to print locally, next verify that the server is actually sharing the printer connection. See if other stations on the network can print to this print server. If so, this indicates there is a configuration problem on the station which isn't printing.

Is printing affected on only one workstation or a few workstations? If the problem is with one or a few workstations, but others can print, then you know that the printer itself, the print server, the queues, and so on are operational. Check the workstations that can't print for common items. Are all the workstations that can print using the same print queue or the same print job? Can you print if you log in as a different user? See the section "The NetWare Print Queue."

Can you print from DOS on the workstation? Try printing from DOS on the affected workstation. If you can't print from DOS, check the network connection to make sure you have a connection to the server. Also recall that printing from DOS requires using either the CAPTURE command from a DOS window (see below), or enabling CAPTURE graphically via the Properties dialog for the printer in question. (Right-click the printer icon in the Printers folder, choose Properties, and click on the Details tab. Click Capture, select a printer port, and click OK.)

For NetWare print servers, try printing a DOS text file from PCONSOLE. If that works, the workstation itself, rather than the print setup, is probably causing the problem. See Chapter 34 for information about troubleshooting workstations. The items to pay particular attention to are the printer port configuration, interrupt conflicts, DOS, and the NetWare shell software. Make sure that the print job or capture setup works on other workstations.

If you can print from DOS, the problem most likely lies with the application. Try printing from other applications. Make sure that the application is set up to print to the proper printer port or queue. If the program is attempting to print to a NetWare queue directly, and you can't find anything wrong, try printing to the LPT1 port and using CAPTURE to redirect the output to the printer. See the section "CAPTURE.EXE and Print Jobs—Printing Options."

Is This a Macintosh Printer Setup?

Is the printer operational? Make sure that the printer itself is operational, has paper and toner, and isn't jammed. Also check to see whether it's only one user who is having a problem printing, or whether several users are having problems. See the section "The Printing Process."

Is the printer connected to the network? With a printer that has been working on a LocalTalk or EtherTalk network, make sure that the connection is firmly seated. If it is, try resetting the printer. If the printer is connected through NetWare for Macintosh and the problem is with the printer, you should see a printer error message in the NetWare for Macintosh screen on the console of the server. The message should give you clues on how to proceed.

Does the printer show up in the correct AppleTalk zone? If the printer is not showing up in the correct AppleTalk zone, it is a configuration problem, either in the configuration of the printer itself if it is attached to an AppleTalk network, or in NetWare for Macintosh. Make sure the zone name is spelled correctly and remember that the spellings are case-sensitive. See the section "Troubleshooting NetWare for Macintosh Printing."

Can you print from some workstations? If you can print from some workstations, make sure that the others are in the same AppleTalk zone. If they are, then see if the ones that can't print are on the same network segment. See Chapter 35 for more information about troubleshooting the physical network. If only one Macintosh can't print, check the network connection. If the connection is solid, try reinstalling the network driver software.

Printing from many workstations to one printer was one of the first uses for PC networks, and printing is still among the most important functions of a network. Network printing services can range from a small piece of hardware that lets a few users share a dot-matrix printer; to a PostScript print server that can service print jobs from DOS, Windows, Macintoshes, or Unix; to a queue that stores a thousand-page print job and prints it in the middle of the night when no one else needs the printer. These printing services all perform similar functions, but they vary widely in cost and complexity.

Printing usually seems to be more maintenance-intensive than other aspects of network technology. NetWare offers a wealth of features, but with those features comes an attendant complexity that many administrators (and users) find daunting. This need not be the case. If you approach setting up and troubleshooting print services in a systematic manner, and with a basic understanding of the process involved, you will find that problems can be resolved in the same manner as any other problems with the network.

Setting up a printer, its queue, its job configuration, the print server, and print server software can be a very complex process. It gets more complicated if you consider PostScript printing, printing to AppleTalk printers, printing to Unix print queues, and other possible variations. This chapter is not intended to lead you through the process of creating your printer setup. The NT, Windows 9x, and NetWare manuals cover the initial setup process well, including some useful troubleshooting hints.

Fault Points for Network Printing

Chapter 35 introduced the concept of a chain of fault points as a guide to troubleshooting networks and network components. Within any combination of different types of workstations, NICs, LAN topologies, servers, cabling, software, and so on, there are a limited number of points where problems can occur.

Because a conventional flowchart cannot cover all the possibilities inherent in a network, it makes more sense to look only at those places where things can go wrong. Figure 36.1 illustrates a typical fault-point chain for network printing.

FIGURE 36.1:

The fault-point chain for network printing

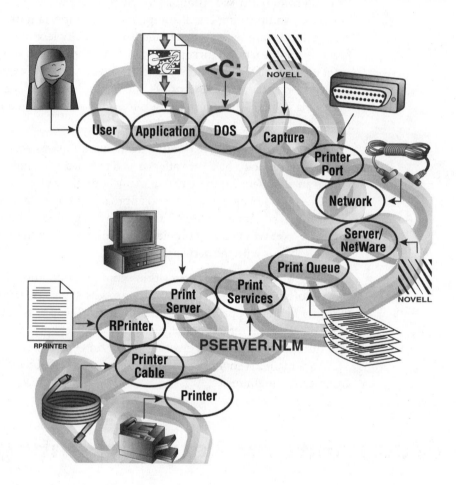

Each of the items in the chain in Figure 36.1 is linked to the preceding and following items. Any one of them can cause the printing process to fail, and if you can determine that the chain works up to any point, all the points before that point are working and can be excluded from the list of potential causes of the problem.

The printer must have power and a solid connection to the cable, and it must be configured to use the correct interface in the correct manner. It must also have toner (or a good ribbon), a supply of paper, and a clear paper path.

The printer cable must be correctly set up to switch the necessary pins to allow both the workstation and the printer to communicate correctly. The cable should also be within the maximum length limits and well insulated, with properly installed connectors. Of course, the connectors should be screwed snugly into the printer port on the PC and the appropriate port on the printer, if the printer is connected to a workstation.

There are four ways a printer can be made accessible to the network:

- Attached to the server directly

- Attached to a PC acting as a dedicated print server

- Attached to an individual's workstation

- Attached directly to the network through an internal or external print server device

On NetWare LANs, RPRINTER.EXE or NPRINTER.EXE may be running, but only if the printer is attached to someone's personal workstation rather than to a dedicated print server or the NetWare server. RPRINTER must be properly configured for the right port on the workstation, and it must be associated with a print queue.

The print server must be properly configured as a workstation to access its drives and NIC. It should also be set up to access the port the printer is attached to, either parallel or serial.

The print server software (PSERVER) provides the connection between print queues and the print server. It must be connected to the print queues with PCONSOLE, and also to the proper print server. PSERVER.EXE can also crash, breaking the connection.

The print queue must be set up and attached to a PSERVER. It must also be able to access the directory on the SYS: volume that actually holds the print jobs until they can be printed.

NetWare must be running properly and must support the PSERVER VAP or NLM. If the printer is set up to print to a PostScript printer or provide print services to Macintosh, Unix, or other operating systems, you will also need to have those services set up properly.

The network connection to the user's workstation must be working correctly and allow the shell to provide the normal NetWare workstation services.

The printer port on the user's workstation can also affect the NetWare printing process. The port doesn't necessarily need to be turned on in the PC's configuration, but if a job is printed to the wrong printer port, NetWare won't properly redirect it to the queue.

CAPTURE.EXE must be set up to print to the proper print queue and use the proper print job. This is one of the easiest places for problems to occur in an existing setup, because it is one of the few parts that the user interacts with.

DOS must be working for the workstation to be able to load the NetWare shell, attach to the network, and access NetWare print services. If the DOS MODE command has been used to change the settings on a serial port and CAPTURE is set to capture from that port, it may affect the capture process.

Some applications access NetWare print services directly, rather than attempting to send the print job to a port, which is then intercepted and sent to the Net-Ware queue. Whether the application does this or not, it can affect the print process if it is configured for the wrong type of printer, or if the print menu misleads the user.

The user is the last (and first) link in the printing process, and not one to be forgotten. Users will tell you that the printer is broken when their CAPTURE statement is sending the job to the wrong printer, or tell you that the print server is down when the printer is out of paper.

NOTE   Users may tell you that the printer doesn't work, or that they can't print, when the only problem is that the printer is out of paper. A system administrator recently reported in a computer publication how he investigated the case of a user who said he couldn't print anymore. After checking a number of possibilities, the administrator discovered that the user couldn't print because the part of the menu that allowed printing wasn't visible on the monitor. After adjusting the display, everything was fine.

The Printing Process

The process described here assumes a very basic setup: a DOS-based print server and a NetWare 3.x server. Note that many old 286 and 386 machines continue to function quite well as NetWare print servers because this is a job that does not require huge amounts of RAM or (usually) high processing speeds. The computer need only be capable of keeping up with the printer, which almost always reads data more slowly than a computer (of whatever speed) can send it.

Using Windows 95, Windows 98, Unix, or NetWare 4.x complicates things somewhat. However, the process is the same conceptually, and if you understand the process, you will be able to follow it through on your system and identify the correct fault point.

Also, in the process described here, the print server may be either a workstation running NT Workstation, Windows 95/98, or DOS NetWare print server software (either RPRINTER.EXE, NPRINTER.EXE, or PSERVER.EXE); or, the print server may be a NetWare or NT server functioning as a print server.

Finally, a third option is a printer attached directly to the LAN, which includes internal software and a controller to make the printer appear and act as a NetWare or other type of print server on the network. In this case, there is no computer to diagnose, so the main things to check are the connection to the LAN and the segment the printer is attached to. You can test such a printer's ability "locally" by temporarily attaching a station directly to the printer and printing a test page.

Otherwise, these different types of print servers make little or no difference in the overall troubleshooting process.

The printing process begins on the workstation, just as it would with a stand-alone PC. The user prints, either from DOS, Windows, or from an application. Instead of the job being sent to the port the printer is on (LPT1, 2, or 3, or COM1 or 2), it is redirected by the Microsoft or NetWare network client software to a file in a queue directory or database on the file server. The print server software checks the queue directory and sends the job to the printer.

Novell's PSERVER may reside on the server as PSERVER.NLM, on a dedicated print server workstation as PSERVER.EXE, or on a router (or NetWare 2.x server) as PSERVER.VAP. RPRINTER.EXE is not a software print server; it allows PSERVER to access a printer connected to a user's workstation as if that printer were attached to the PC on which PSERVER is running. Wherever PSERVER is located, it looks in the appropriate directory (the print queue) in the file server's SYS:/SYSTEM directory. When a file is placed in the print queue directory, PSERVER prints it to the assigned printer.

NetWare 4.*x* uses a different system. PSERVER.NLM handles routing print jobs to a server running NPRINTER.NLM (which can be the same server running PSERVER.NLM). NPRINTER.NLM runs on the server and supports up to 256 printers. NPRINTER.EXE (note that the only difference is the file extension) runs on a workstation and allows network users to print across the network to the printer attached to that workstation. There is no software for configuring a dedicated print server workstation, although you can run NPRINTER.EXE on a workstation that is used only as a print server.

Printers shared on a Windows 9*x* or NT station can be made to appear either as a NetWare print server (using File and Printer Sharing for NetWare) or as a Windows network print server (using File and Printer Sharing for Microsoft Networks). The only necessary step to set up a shared printer is to specify the share name the printer will appear as on the network.

Both Windows and NetWare print servers can also apply restrictions on who uses the printer. This even includes time and day ranges and whether several printers connected to one computer should share the same print queue. In these cases, security is one more place to check. Fortunately it is quite simple to eliminate security restrictions as being the cause of someone's inability to print: Simply try printing using a different logon account.

The "Shell"—(NetWare Printer Redirection)

IPX.COM and NETx.COM, the ODI network drivers (on older print servers), or the VLMs are the first step in the NetWare printing process. When an application attempts to send output to the printer port (LPT1, 2, or 3), the shell intercepts it and sends it as a file to the queue directory on the server instead. This is the same process used to allow users to access drives on the server as if they were local.

TIP   If the application is aware of network print queues, but printing doesn't work when the application tries to insert a print job directly into the queue, try printing to the parallel port (LPT1) and using NetWare's redirection capability instead.

SHELL.CFG is a file in the same directory as NETx.COM (or whatever NetWare shell is loaded) that controls to a degree how the workstation shell is configured. Think of it as the CONFIG.SYS file for the shell. On workstations running RPRINTER, use NET.CFG. There are a number of settings that should be used when configuring printing:

LOCAL PRINTERS = 0	This will keep the workstation from hanging if no ports are captured and the user presses Shift-PrintScreen.
PRINT HEADER = 255	This will make sure PostScript jobs have enough header space to correctly configure the printer.
PRINT TAIL = 255	This will make sure NetWare has enough space in the trailer to the print job to send reset codes to the printer after the job is finished. Use this setting if the printer is being left incorrectly configured after a user finishes printing.
SPX CONNECTIONS = 60	This should be used on dedicated print servers running PSERVER.EXE. It is not necessary on workstations running RPRINTER.

CAPTURE.EXE and Print Jobs—Printing Options

The CAPTURE program is a command-line program that is installed as part of the DOS or Windows 9x NetWare client installation process and allows you to specify many options when printing a document to a print server. For example, to print a PostScript document to a queue called LaserWriterI, your capture statement might be:

```
CAPTURE LPT1 s=Marketing q=LaserWriterI /NB /NT /NFF
```

This captures any text sent to LPT1 and prints it to the queue LaserWriterI on the server Marketing, with no banner page, no tabs, and no form feed. The no-tabs setting is standard when printing from an application that (like most) handles the print formatting, and the no-form-feed option prevents the printer from printing a blank page at the end of a document. The only time you need to add a form feed is if the last page of a print job doesn't print when printing from some applications.

You can also specify these parameters with NPRINT, or by setting up a print job with PRINTCON (or with the NetWare Administrator program in NetWare 4.*x*). Using a print job is a much easier way to set the parameters for complex printing, because it allows you to make choices from menus rather than requiring you to enter the exact spelling and syntax for each setting, as with CAPTURE. PRINTCON allows you to designate a default print job and to set up queues associated with each job. This means that you can switch from printing forms on a line printer, to PostScript on a LaserWriter, and then to text on a Hewlett-Packard printer, with the following simple statements:

```
CAPTURE j=line
CAPTURE j=PS
CAPTURE j=HP
```

Or you can use PRINTCON to change your default print job. Using print jobs makes it much easier for the user to print and for you to troubleshoot the setup.

The NetWare Print Queue

For NetWare, the print queue is actually a directory located in SYS:/SYSTEM with an eight-digit file name that consists of hexadecimal characters (0–9, plus A–F), such as 400000BF. This directory contains any files that have been placed in the queue.

If jobs are being placed in the queue without error messages, and the PCONSOLE Print Queue Status window shows that they are being sent to the printer, but they never print, you should look in the queue directories to see if the files are still there. This will tell you whether the problem is with PSERVER or with the printer:

- If the files are still in the print queue directory, they aren't actually being sent to the printer, and the problem is likely to be with the software.

- If the files are gone, then they are being sent to the printer and aren't printing out, perhaps because of a configuration problem with the print server or the printer.

You should also make sure that when a print queue is selected in the Print Queue Information window of PCONSOLE, the Queue Servers list has at least one PSERVER attached.

The name of the queue in SYS:/SYSTEM usually matches the Print Queue ID entry you will see in PCONSOLE. Under NetWare 4.*x*, this may not be the case if you create the queue in a different container than the one that contains the server running NPRINTER.NLM or PSERVER.NLM.

PSERVER—Printing Controls

PSERVER.NLM, .EXE, or .VAP is the software that controls how the print file is sent from the queue on the NetWare server, and to which printer. PSERVER.NLM runs on the server. PSERVER.VAP may run on a 2.*x* server or on a router. In NetWare 2.*x* and 3.*x*, PSERVER.EXE runs on a dedicated print server workstation.

The version of PSERVER.NLM shipped with NetWare 3.11 has a bug that can cause garbage to be printed if you are using a fast printer and the print server workstation has a small buffer. If the buffer overflows, the job is killed. This can be fixed by upgrading to the latest version of PSERVER.NLM, which can be found on NetWire.

PSERVER.EXE gives you the advantage of off-loading the PSERVER process from the server to a dedicated workstation. The downside is that it requires an additional dedicated workstation. This does have another additional benefit, though. It allows you to lock up your server and still give users easy access to the printers.

Because NPRINTER.NLM supports up to 256 printers, you can offload the print server process from some servers if necessary. This is simpler if the servers are all in the same container. Run PSERVER.NLM on only one server, and NPRINTER.EXE on the workstations with printers attached.

PSERVER creates a directory in SYS:/SYSTEM with a name based on the Print Server ID number assigned to the printer server when it is created (an eight-digit hex number, such as 000A31B4).

The Print Server

The print server can be any of the following:

- A Windows 9*x* or NT station sharing a printer
- A DOS workstation running PSERVER.EXE

- A file server running PSERVER.NLM

- A NetWare 4.*x* server running NPRINTER.NLM and PSERVER.NLM

- A NetWare 4.*x* file server running just NPRINTER.NLM, serving a queue on another 4.*x* server running PSERVER.NLM

In any case, the process of troubleshooting is the same, although it may be easier if the file server and print server are separate workstations. The print server itself can usually be treated as an ordinary workstation. See Chapter 34 for information about troubleshooting workstations.

NetWare Configuration Files or Attributes

Several files (under NetWare 3.*x*) or attributes (under NetWare 4.*x*) can be useful in debugging printing problems:

- The PRINT.*XXX* file is stored in the Print Server directory in SYS:/SYSTEM (for instance, SYS:/SYSTEM/A101B24C) and contains the same information as the Printer Configuration attribute: all the information defined under PCONSOLE in the Printers option.

- The QUEUE.*XXX* file is also in the Print Server directory in SYS:/SYSTEM and contains the same information as the Queue attribute: the queue name and priority.

- The NOTIFY.*XXX* file or Notify attribute lists the user(s) or group specified to be notified when there are problems with print jobs. It's also located in the SYS:/SYSTEM Print Server directory.

Windows 9x/NT Client Printer Troubleshooting

When printing stops working on a Windows 9*x* or NT station or fails to start working on a new station just being added to the network, the following series of steps can assist in getting it up and running, regardless of the type of print *server* being used:

1. Try accessing files or folders located on the server the printer is connected to (if there are any). If this doesn't work, then there's a network connectivity problem to be diagnosed rather than a problem unique to printing.

2. Verify that the printer connection (located in the Printers folder) is actually pointing to the right print server on the network. Right click on the printer, select Properties, Details, and verify that the path to the network printer is correctly specified in the Port drop-down list box. (If it isn't in the list, you may need to click Add Port, Browse, and select the desired network printer.)

3. If you're sure the correct network printer is specified for the network connection you are trying to use, next open the printer connection by double-clicking on that printer in the Printers folder. Then try to print something. Watch carefully to see if your print job appears (even briefly) in the printer window. If the job appears and then leaves (this may happen very quickly or take as long as several minutes for a large print job), then at least the job is leaving the station. Otherwise, this indicates there is still something wrong with the printer configuration, which is preventing the job from being sent to the network.

4. If you find that the print job appears "stuck" in the printer window, try removing and re-adding the printer. First browse for the desired network printer on the network using Explorer, and when you find it, right-click on it and choose Install. This will guide you through the steps again and let you print a sample test page at the end. Again, open the printer icon to see whether your sample page appears and then disappears as the job is sent out to the network.

5. If your print job is now leaving the station, it's time to investigate the server. If possible, test whether another station can successfully print to this printer. If not, check whether the server has a stuck print job which is preventing other jobs from printing. If other stations can print to the printer successfully, but yours cannot, you might try rebooting just to refresh the network and print redirector drivers.

If you have followed this procedure and still have problems, you should at least have isolated the problem to being station-related, network-related, or print-server–related.

In cases where a print server itself is at fault, you next need to try printing locally from that server. If that fails, you may need to diagnose whether the cable, port, or actual printer is at fault. If you can swap the cable out, and then the printer out, you can eliminate those two as possibilities. The other possibility is that there's a parallel or serial interface problem (although this is a rather rare occurrence).

Serial and Parallel Interfaces

PC serial interfaces use the RS-232 interface. This specification is intended to allow a PC to talk to a modem—Data Terminal Equipment (DTE) to Data Communications Equipment (DCE). In the context of printing, however, both the PC and the printer consider themselves to be DTE devices. The means of fixing this problem is to use a special serial cable that "fools" both the printer and PC into thinking that the device on the other end is a DCE. Unfortunately, the way this technique is implemented varies from printer to printer.

The best way to avoid interface problems is to use a parallel connection, if at all possible, because these connections are faster and easier to configure. There may be reasons to use a serial printer, such as a requirement for a longer cable than a parallel connection allows or a printer that has only a serial interface. In that case, you should use a serial cable made as shown in Figure 36.2, rather than a straight-through cable.

FIGURE 36.2:

Serial cable pinouts

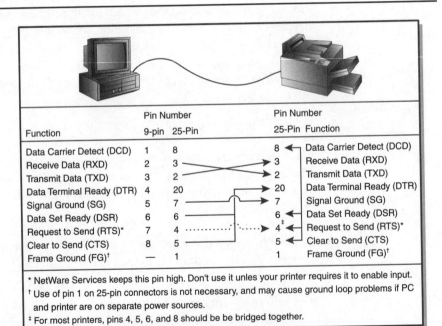

Function	Pin Number 9-pin	25-Pin	25-Pin	Pin Number Function
Data Carrier Detect (DCD)	1	8	8	Data Carrier Detect (DCD)
Receive Data (RXD)	2	3	3	Receive Data (RXD)
Transmit Data (TXD)	3	2	2	Transmit Data (TXD)
Data Terminal Ready (DTR)	4	20	20	Data Terminal Ready (DTR)
Signal Ground (SG)	5	7	7	Signal Ground (SG)
Data Set Ready (DSR)	6	6	6	Data Set Ready (DSR)
Request to Send (RTS)*	7	4	4‡	Request to Send (RTS)*
Clear to Send (CTS)	8	5	5	Clear to Send (CTS)
Frame Ground (FG)†	—	1	1	Frame Ground (FG)†

* NetWare Services keeps this pin high. Don't use it unles your printer requires it to enable input.

† Use of pin 1 on 25-pin connectors is not necessary, and may cause ground loop problems if PC and printer are on separate power sources.

‡ For most printers, pins 4, 5, 6, and 8 should be be bridged together.

> **NOTE**
>
> Serial cables are commercially available. The diagram in Figure 36.2 is just to show you how the signals are switched from PC to printer. This is a sample configuration that will work for many printers; your printer may use different pins. See your printer manual for details, or contact the manufacturer to purchase the necessary cable.

If you use a parallel interface, you may have a problem with interrupts. To avoid interrupt conflicts, you can use a setting when you are configuring the printer. For NetWare, set Use Interrupts to No in the Printer Configuration section of the Print Server Configuration menu of PCONSOLE's Print Server Information. For Windows 9x or NT print servers, you may need to do the following experiment:

Shut down and restart the system, and in the CMOS settings screen (accessed on most systems by hitting the DEL or F10 key during bootup), change the printer port interface type from Enhanced or Bi-Directional to the CMOS settings screen.

Now reboot the system and again attempt to print locally to the printer. If this works, leave the printer setting in CMOS the way you've set it. If this doesn't help, you may want to change the setting back to Enhanced or Bi-Directional, as this mode allows software to communicate better with some newer printers.

The Printer

There is a huge variety of printers available today, ranging from simple dot-matrix printers that haven't changed much in the last 15 years, to laser printers, to dye-sublimation color printers that produce results barely distinguishable from color photographs. In addition to the printers themselves and their hardware interfaces, there is also a control language for each printer. These languages range from relatively simple dot-matrix control codes to the PostScript language, which is as complex and capable as most programming environments. Both the hardware and software aspects of a printer must be taken into account when connecting it to a network.

Printer Hardware

The hardware aspect of the connection to the print server has largely been covered earlier in his chapter. However, you should be aware that most printers have a hardware configuration, which may be set using utility software, with DIP switches inside the printer, or from a front panel display. These will tell the printer what type of connection it has, what protocol and speed to expect over the connection, and so on. See your printer's manual for details. If your print server cannot print at all, even from DOS, it is likely to be a problem with the printer's configuration or its connection.

Printer Software

The other aspect of the printer is the software used to control the printer's actions while printing. In the simplest case, an ASCII-only printer (a daisy-wheel or ball printer) can print only ASCII characters. It may have a few escape codes (so called because they all start with the ASCII character for Esc) to allow bold, italic, and underlined characters. PostScript, at the other end of the spectrum, not only allows any aspect of text to be changed, but prints exceedingly complex graphics as well.

The application from which the user is printing must understand the language of the printer. In addition, the print job or CAPTURE statement must take into account the special requirements of controlling the printer. This is particularly true when printing graphics or PostScript. The flow to the printer must be set to Byte Stream, rather than to Text, when you configure the print job in PRINTCON. This allows the special characters used to control the printer to be sent without being interpreted or removed. The next section offers some tips for troubleshooting PostScript printing.

Troubleshooting PostScript Printers

PostScript is an extremely versatile printer control language developed by Adobe Systems. It allows text to be printed in any size, any weight, any angle, any color, and more. It is also very good at producing graphics. The drawback to this flexibility is the resulting complexity.

NOTE   If you are interested, try printing a word processing file or art file to disk as a Post-Script file, and then open it with a text editor. You will see pages and pages of code describing that document. The PostScript file is actually a program that runs on the controller of a PostScript printer, and tells it how to draw the page. It is not uncommon for a 15KB word processing document to produce a 100KB or larger PostScript file.

PostScript printers have also been associated from the first with the Apple Macintosh. Today, most PostScript printers have Ethernet ports as well as parallel, serial, and AppleTalk ports. You may wish to connect your printer via the Ethernet port; a PostScript printer attached to a print server by an Ethernet port will prove to be quite a bit faster than one connected via a parallel, serial, or AppleTalk port, especially if the Macs are connected to the network with Ethernet cards or adapters.

When printing to a PostScript printer attached to a NetWare print server, you should make sure that the following configuration items have been set:

- Set the print job to Byte Stream Mode with PRINTCON or use the /NT (no tabs) option in your CAPTURE statement.

- Other CAPTURE options you should use are /NFF (no form feeds) and /NB (no banner).

- Set PRINT HEADER = 255 in your SHELL.CFG or NET.CFG file.

- Set PRINT TAIL = 255 in your SHELL.CFG or NET.CFG file if your printer tends to hang after printing a job.

Troubleshooting NetWare for Macintosh Printing

Macintosh printing has become less complex ever since Apple wisely chose to make most PowerMacs with a built-in AAUI or Ethernet port. This does not eliminate them from the troubleshooting chain, however. There are a couple of places to check your configuration of NetWare for Macintosh if you have printing problems.

- If a printer isn't showing up in the AppleTalk zone, or if the AppleTalk screen on the server has error messages like "Can't connect to printer Laser-Writer," make sure that the printer name specified in ATPS.CFG has the name spelled exactly as it appears in the LocalTalk zone, including upper-case and lowercase. If the name seems to be spelled correctly, make sure that there are no leading or trailing spaces in either the configuration file or the name that was given to the printer with the LaserWriter utility.

- If devices are disappearing from zones, or lots of error messages are appearing in the system error log, or if performance is just very slow, make sure that each AppleTalk zone has a unique zone number. Zone number conflicts can cause many types of intermittent conflicts and really slow down AppleTalk performance.

- If a workstation refuses to see the network at all, make sure that Ethernet is selected and active in the AppleTalk Control Panel. AppleTalk defaults to the workstation's printer port if there is no power to the Ethernet connection when the workstation is started up. If you are using a TCP/IP setup with IntraNetWare, make sure that Open Transport is properly configured to use the appropriate server protocol (multiple server configurations can be saved in the OT CDEV by saving the set to a configuration file).

- If you have set up a print job with PRINTCON to print from the PC to an AppleTalk printer, make sure that Mode is *not* set to Reinitialize. This will cause jobs to fail to print.

Troubleshooting Unix Printing

NetWare NFS version 1.2b supports bidirectional printing for Unix printers. This means that PC workstations attached to a NetWare server can print to a printer attached to a Unix workstation, and the Unix workstations can print to the Net-Ware queues. Getting this process to work is more complicated than a standard print server; but approached methodically, it is not any more difficult. The complication is added by the basic difference between the methods of printing on PCs and Unix workstations.

With PCs, the PRINT command in DOS simply sends a stream of data to the parallel or serial port, which is intercepted by NetWare and redirected to a NetWare queue. Unix workstations use a program (called a *daemon*), LPD, to print. LPD is a command that is part of the system software in Unix. It is much more capable than the PRINT command in DOS. It knows what kind of printer it is printing to (for instance, text or PostScript) and where that printer is located, whether on the workstation's printer port or on another workstation. It also knows the name of the queue that it is printing to and where that queue is located. This configuration information is stored in a file called printcap, usually located in the /etc directory.

To set up a Unix workstation to print to a NetWare queue, the printcap file must contain the IP address or hostname of the server and the information on the name of the queue. The manual for NetWare NFS discusses these requirements in detail. For troubleshooting Unix-to-NetWare printing, you should be aware that the following fault points are added to the normal ones for NetWare:

- The LPD daemon. Is it running?

- The printcap file on the Unix side. Is the information about the NetWare server and the queue to print to correct?

- The TCP/IP connection to the server. Can you ping the NetWare server?

- The configuration of NetWare NFS. Is the queue exported? Is it configured correctly?

- The PLPD NLM. Is it loaded and configured properly?

For printing from a NetWare client to a printer on a Unix workstation, the fault chain has the same items, but in reverse order, since the job is going from the NetWare queue to the LPD daemon on the Unix workstation. Additionally, there is a print gateway on the NetWare server that modifies the file after it reaches the print queue, then sends it to the LPD daemon on the Unix host. Of course, in both cases, the normal NetWare printing fault chain also applies, including the workstation-to-printer connection. In the case of NetWare-to-Unix printing, it's a Unix workstation, but you still need to verify that you can print from the workstation to the printer.

Real-Life Stories

This section describes typical network printing problems and how a trouble-shooter would go through the process of isolating the fault and fixing it. The two fictional companies introduced in Chapter 33 and their administrators are again used as examples. They combine the equipment and experience of a number of actual businesses. These five scenarios show some representative problems often encountered when setting up or troubleshooting printers and printing operations. While you may never see these particular problems, they should give you a feel for the process by which an experienced troubleshooter isolates a problem, determines the solution, and fixes the problem.

Scenario One: A New PostScript Printer

The administrators are setting up a new PostScript printer that will be accessible to both Macs and PCs in the marketing department. They'll be attaching it to a dedicated print server.

Snapshot—Scenario One

Is this a new printer setup?

- Can you print from any workstations?
- Can you put print jobs directly into the queue with PCONSOLE? Do they print?
- Is the queue connected to PSERVER?
- Can you print from DOS on the print server?
- Is printing affected only on one workstation or a few workstations?
- Can you print from DOS on the workstation?

  Fran and Jethro are setting up a new PostScript printer for the Marketing department at Great Big, Inc. The printer must be accessible to both Macs and PCs. The server is not physically accessible to the users, so they will be using a PC as a print server. The server is running NetWare 3.12 and NetWare for Macintosh. In earlier versions of NetWare, they would have needed to set the printer up as an AppleTalk printer, and then set up a queue that PCs could use to print to the AppleTalk printer. With this version of NetWare for Macintosh, they can do it the other way: Set up a queue and allow Macintoshes to print to the PC print queue. Another option is to configure AppleTalk to use Ethernet (this requires Open Transport be installed), which will help connect to the PC print server faster.

They set up the workstation that will be the print server. Since it is a dedicated workstation that won't be used for anything else, they use an ancient 286 AT clone that has been sitting around. It has a 20MB hard disk and a Hercules mono-chrome setup, which is fine—it doesn't need color or much disk space to run PSERVER. The only cards in the AT are an NIC and a basics-only video card. The laser printer is attached to the parallel port. The printer is supposed to automatically take input from its serial or parallel port, so there's nothing to configure on the printer.

Before connecting the print server to the network, Fran and Jethro want to check the printer setup on the PC for proper functioning. You can't print from DOS to a PostScript printer, so they load an application that will print PostScript to check the printer. Nothing comes out—the printer's data light doesn't even start blink-ing. After a while, the application shows a message: "Printer unavailable."

Since the application is set to print to LPT1, the problem must be between the application and the printer. The possible fault points are the port, the cable, and the software on both ends to enable the ports. The printer is supposed to deter-mine which port is being used, and the cable is the one that came with the printer, so they check the software on the AT first. After they locate and run SETUP, they discover that the parallel port has been disabled. After they enable it, the applica-tion is able to print to the printer.

Fran and Jethro leave the application on the disk in case any future debugging is required, then take these steps:

- Save the existing AUTOEXEC.BAT and CONFIG.SYS files to .BAK extensions.

- Update the DOS version to the latest.

- Add the latest versions of LSL, NIC driver, IPXODI, and NETX.EXE or VLMs.

- Create a SHELL.CFG or NET.CFG file with the preferred server specified and an SPX CONNECTIONS = 60 entry.

- Load the latest version of PSERVER.EXE onto the disk.

- Set up the AUTOEXEC.BAT file so that it loads IPXODI and NETX or VLMs, then logs in to the network as a user they've created for printing, then loads PSERVER.

This AUTOEXEC.BAT file setup creates a security loophole in that a user could reboot the print server and interrupt the AUTOEXEC.BAT with Ctrl-C after it's logged in, but they've carefully restricted the access for the user. They want the print server to connect automatically to the network so that it can be rebooted or come back up after a power outage, without one of them needing to be there to enter a password. This way, any user can specify the PSERVER to load (they've printed instructions and taped them to the printer). The next step is to set up a print server account and queues, using PCONSOLE and PRINTCON.

Fran and Jethro use PCONSOLE to define a print server. They configure the printer as a remote printer, since it is not on the file server. Then they set up a queue, using the AppleTalk Print Services (ATPS) NLM and configure it to use the printer they've defined. Then they use PRINTCON to set up two print jobs: one for printing PostScript from PCs and one for printing text from PCs (Post-Script printers won't handle text files as HP-compatible printers do). Finally, they reboot the print server, load PSERVER, and start printing test files from several workstations. None of the jobs printed from PCs or Macs come out. Fran and Jethro begin rechecking the configuration.

Oops! "Remote printer" means a printer on a user's workstation attached with RPRINTER. They change the configuration to a local printer on LPT1 and reboot the print server. The jobs that were in the queue begin printing. After the second job prints, the print server hangs. They restart the printer, but the print server still thinks it's offline. They reboot the print server and another job prints, then it hangs again. They look at the configuration of the print server. The Use Interrupts option is set to On, with interrupt 7 specified. That's the correct interrupt, but they decide to try Use Interrupts set to Off. This fixes the problem.

The next job in the queue is a Macintosh job. It prints, but the fonts are all Courier instead of what they should have been. They reread the NetWare for Macintosh documentation and discover that they need to specify a font list for the printer, since it isn't on AppleTalk. They change the configuration of ATPS to look for the font list for the printer in a file instead of through AppleTalk and to download the LaserPrep initialization file with each Macintosh print job, and then reload ATPS. Now the Macintosh jobs are printing with the fonts specified in the document.

Lessons Learned—Scenario One

- Make sure the print server is properly configured with SETUP for the printer. This includes setting the speed, parity, and stop bit if using a serial connection.

- Follow the configuration instructions in the manuals explicitly. Make sure to check the NetWare for Macintosh manual and supplement, if necessary, as well as the print server manual.

- If the print server freezes or you have intermittent problems when jobs are printed to a printer on the parallel port, try setting Use Interrupts to Off.

- If you set up a Macintosh queue to print to a printer that isn't on AppleTalk, you must set up a list that contains the fonts native to the printer. NetWare for Macintosh 3.01 comes with default font lists for the LaserWriter, Laser-Writer Plus, LaserWriter II NT, LaserWriter II NTX, and HP LaserJet with PostScript cartridge. If you have additional fonts, either installed in the printer's ROM or on a hard disk, you can modify the .FNT file to include them. You must also add a -l option to the queue configuration line in the ATPS.CFG file to download LaserPrep with each Mac job.

The Fault-Point Chain—Scenario One

The fault-point chain in this case begins with the users, their applications, and the workstation configurations and connections, but these aren't relevant, because in the first step, none of the workstations can print, indicating a problem with the print server (PSERVER) or printer configuration. Although they are part of the overall fault chain, if the connections from server to workstation, the NIC in the workstation, or the workstation itself isn't working, they should be addressed as discussed in the previous chapters. Therefore, the fault-point chain we consider here is as follows:

- The queue. In this case the queue is set up by the ATPS NLM. A standard queue in a PC-only department wouldn't really be any different; it would just be configured with PCONSOLE instead of the INSTALL NLM.

- The print server attached to the queue. This is a software print server that is configured in PCONSOLE and controls the configuration of the PSERVER version running on the server, a bridge, or the print server workstation.

- The copy of PSERVER. It needs to be loaded and attached to a print server that has been configured with PCONSOLE.

- The physical print server. This may be the file server, a bridge, or a workstation. In this context, it doesn't matter. If the workstation is running properly, the only aspects to look at in this context are whether it is configured for the port the printer is on and whether the DOS and NetWare configuration files are set up properly.

- The connection to the printer. The cable should be appropriate for the type of printer attached, should have solid connections, and so on.

- The printer. It should be properly configured for the type of connection. It should also have paper and a ribbon or toner cartridge, be plugged in, and so on.

Scenario Two: A Router As Print Server

In this scenario, the administrator sets up a NetWare router (in software) to act as a print server. This will allow two physically separated groups to use the same file server and both groups to also have a local printer.

Snapshot—Scenario Two

Is this a new printer setup?

- Can you print from any workstations?
- Can you put print jobs directly into the queue with PCONSOLE? Do they print?
- Is the queue connected to PSERVER?
- Can you print from DOS on the print server?
- Is printing affected on only one workstation or a few workstations?
- Can you print from DOS on the workstation?

John, the administrator for Itsy-Bitsy, has a department that is splitting in two. The Sales department is splitting into Order Entry and Shipping, and the two departments will be in separate locations. The Shipping department needs to take the line printer to print shipping forms, and the Order Entry department is getting a laser printer. The two departments will be separated by several hundred feet, which exceeds the limit for the type of cabling in use for the network. John will either need to add a second server for the Shipping department and move the department's accounts, or put in a bridge, router, or repeater to extend the network.

John decides to locate a router in the Shipping department's new location to handle printing and extend the possible distance from the Sales server by allowing two network segments: one to attach to the server and one for the users in Shipping. This extends the possible distance from the server to the maximum for the type of cabling, since the only things on that segment are the router and the server. It does, of course, also require a second NIC in the server as well as the router, to allow the maximum possible distance between the two machines. Figure 36.3 illustrates this situation.

FIGURE 36.3:

A network connection with two segments and a router

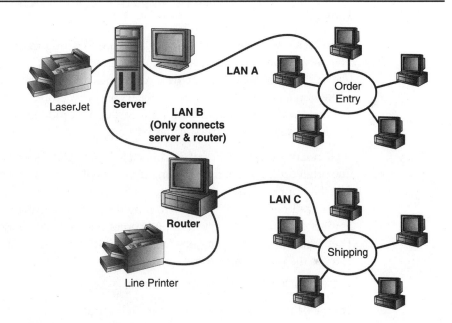

The server is running NetWare 3.12. The router will utilize an old 2.15 server set up to run PSERVER.VAP. The server will run PSERVER NLM. Alternatively, John could add a second server for the Order Entry department, and use a second NIC in both servers to connect the two LANs, but since he already has the old server, he'll use that.

John adds a second NIC to the server to allow the maximum distance between the router and the server, sets up the router, connects the Shipping department's workstations to it, and tests the expanded network. When everything is working, he uses PCONSOLE to set up an additional print queue and print server. He reconfigures the existing queue and print server to use the line printer on the router and sets up new ones for the laser printer on the server.

When the configuration is done, he configures the router with PSERVER.VAP and attaches the printer, then starts PSERVER and tries printing from a workstation in the Shipping department. Nothing comes out of the line printer.

John begins tracing the problem with the CAPTURE statement on the PC he is trying to print from. It's set in the user's AUTOEXEC.BAT file to the old queue. (Nothing came out on that printer either.) He resets CAPTURE to the new print server and queue and tries printing again. Still nothing. Next, he tries inserting a job directly into the queue. Nothing comes out of the printer. He reboots the PC running PSERVER as a workstation and tries to print a DOS file to the COM1 port. Nothing.

He uses the SETUP program to see if the PC is configured to use COM1. It is. The only remaining item is the cable. The line printer is serial-only, and the server uses a 25-pin serial cable; the new router has a 9-pin serial port, so John had picked up a new serial cable at the local computer store. On investigation, it turns out that they have sold him a straight-through, or modem cable. He gets a serial printer cable and hooks the printer back up.

He can print from DOS to the printer. He loads PSERVER and tries printing to the line printer from one of the Shipping department workstations. Success! John knows that the print job configuration is stored in a file in the user's SYS:MAIL/ID# directory, so rather than use PRINTCON to copy the print jobs to every user, he creates the new set of print jobs for one user and copies the file to everyone's mail directory. Then he creates two groups, one for Order Entry and one for Shipping, and adds an entry to the system login script for each group:

```
IF MEMBER OF SHIPPING THEN CAPTURE J=LINE
```

This sets the default job correctly for each group.

Then he changes the printer configuration for the Order Entry department's print server to match the new laser printer. He leaves the queue alone—there shouldn't be any problem there. Testing the printer, he finds no problems from any of several workstations.

Lessons Learned—Scenario Two

- Most of the printing problems you will encounter are the results of incorrect setup of the printer, workstation, print server, or queue. Double-check all configuration items before you go to the next step.

- Make sure that cabling, interrupts, and printer configurations are correctly set and match the corresponding settings in the workstation.

- Take the troubleshooting process systematically; it's complex, but can be resolved if you take it one step at a time.

The Fault-Point Chain—Scenario Two

- The workstation shell and CAPTURE setup

- The queue on the server

- The print server attached to the queue

- The server or router on which PSERVER is running

- The configuration of the PC

- The connection to the printer

- The printer's configuration

- The printer hardware

Scenario Three: Remote Printing with NetWare 4.x

This scenario is similar to the one described in the previous section, but the administrator sets up a printer on a hardware printer server and plans to make the printer available in two different containers under NetWare 4.x. This will allow different groups to use the same printer. In fact, one of the groups has people in two locations, one out of state. They will still be able to print to this printer, which will usually be cheaper and faster than faxing.

Snapshot—Scenario Three

Is this a new printer setup?

- Can you print from any workstations?

- Can you put print jobs directly into the queue with PCONSOLE? Do they print?

- Is the queue connected to PSERVER?

- Can you print a test page on the print server?

- Is printing affected on only one workstation or a few workstations?

- Can you print from DOS on the workstation?

John, the administrator for Itsy-Bitsy, has two departments using NetWare 4.01. They both need the use of a high-speed laser printer, but neither can really justify it by themselves. They decide to pool resources, since they are not far apart physically. John will attach the printer to a direct-connect Ethernet print server and put the print queue in both containers. The out-of-state users will also be able to print to the printer, since they're in the same departmental container as one of the local groups.

John sets up and configures the printer and the Ethernet print server box. He loads the printer server installation software on a convenient PC and sets up the print server. The print server can be printed to directly, without requiring a queue on the server, which reduces overhead on the server. He prints a test job to the printer, and it works. He then makes the printer available to the two containers, checks the permissions, and goes home, feeling the satisfaction of a job well done.

The next day when he comes in, one of the department supervisors comments that they had expected to be able to print to the printer, since it was all set up. He feels that old familiar sinking feeling—they should be able to. He looks on their PC first. The printer doesn't show up in the list of available printers. They are using Windows 98 and the Microsoft 32-bit client with NDS support, but when he browses both containers, the printer doesn't show up. He checks on another PC, and it's not there either. He retreats to his office and brings up NWADMIN, thinking that it may be a permissions problem.

The printer shows up from his system, which is to be expected, since he is the user ADMIN, with rights to everything. He logs in as his test user, with fairly limited rights. He can still see the printer, so he tries printing to it. No problem. He goes back to the PC he configured the print server from and checks the print server configuration. He can't see anything wrong there.

Then it hits him: Both his office PC and the one he used to configure the print server are running Windows 95, and the two that can't see the printer are running Windows 98. He goes back to the documentation to see if there are any considerations when running Windows 95. He is chagrined to find that neither the printed documentation nor the Help files on the installation disks mention Windows 98! The latest dates on the files on the disks are from December 1996.

He goes back to his office and logs onto the print server manufacturer's Web page. Sure enough, there are specific printer drivers that need to be loaded to support the print server. He downloads them and installs them on one of the Windows 98 PCs. No problems. He then installs the drivers on the rest of the Windows 98 PCs, and everyone is happy.

NOTE   We are not aware of any printer driver which worked under Windows 95 failing to work under Windows 98, however it is conceivable because the Windows 98 driver model has been changed in several areas to be compatible with drivers designed for NT.

Lessons Learned—Scenario Three

- Don't assume that because it works on one PC that it will work on all PCs, especially if they're running different operating systems.

- Don't assume that because you just bought the thing, and the system you want to run it on has been out for months, that it's supported. It could be an old copy of the software that's been sitting in a warehouse for months, or it might be that the vendor hasn't gotten around to the update yet.

- Remember that bulletin boards, CompuServe forums, and especially Web pages are great resources for not only finding problems, but getting the updated drivers necessary to fix some of them, as well as the experiences of others who have already done it.

The Fault-Point Chain—Scenario Three

- The application being printed from.

- The operating system printing setup. This could be anything from CAPTURE on a DOS 3.3 or later system to Windows 95, OS/2, or Unix printer drivers.

- The configuration of the print server.

- The connection to the printer.

- The printer's configuration.

- The printer hardware.

Scenario Four: A Single Workstation That Can't Print

The administrator encounters a problem with a user who can't print any more. She isolates the problem to a single workstation, then finds the problem on that workstation and fixes it.

Snapshot—Scenario Four

Is this an existing printer setup?

- Is the printer operational?
- Is the print server operational?
- Can you print from some workstations?
- Can you put print jobs directly into the queue with PCONSOLE? Do they print?
- Is the queue connected to PSERVER?
- Can you print from DOS on the print server?
- Is printing affected on only one workstation or a few workstations?
- Can you print from DOS on the workstation?

Fran receives a call that one of the printers in Great Big's Marketing department is not working. When she arrives, she checks with the user first to find out exactly what the problem is. The user says that an application won't print to the Post-Script printer anymore. Fran begins by checking the printer and print server. The printer is online and has paper, and the print server is operational. She checks around and finds that other people on the network can print, both from a DOS prompt and from the application the user is trying to print from. Fran tries inserting a print job with PCONSOLE. It prints fine. She then tries printing from DOS. The job prints to the other printer in the department.

A light dawns. She types CAPTURE and finds that the default is to the wrong printer. The system login script is set up so that the default printer is the text printer. If the user is using a program that needs PostScript, she puts them in a group called PostScript, which uses a line in the system login script like the following:

```
IF MEMBER OF GROUP POSTSCRIPT THEN CAPTURE J=LASERWRITER
```

However, this user has a line in their AUTOEXEC.BAT file that sets CAPTURE J=HP (for the Hewlett-Packard LaserJet), which executes after the user logs in to the network. She looks at the date on the AUTOEXEC.BAT and finds it is more than two years old, dating back to before they had a PostScript printer.

Further research shows that the user had been playing with his AUTOEXEC .BAT and accidentally deleted it, then copied an old version off a backup floppy they had kept from long ago. Fran copies the standard AUTOEXEC.BAT file she has created and stored in the SYS:PUBLIC directory onto the PC, and then modifies it slightly for that particular user. She reboots the PC, and everything works as it should.

Lessons Learned—Scenario Four

- Ask the user if he or she changed anything on the system recently. Fran might have been able to save herself some time by discovering first that the user had changed his AUTOEXEC.BAT file. Again, if you don't need to count on the user for information, your life will be easier. If Fran had a configuration worksheet for the user's workstation, she might have noticed right away that the date and size of the AUTOEXEC.BAT file didn't match the standard.

- No matter how much time and effort you spend making sure that every user is set up properly, there will always be some way the user can mess things up. Be on the lookout for the things that the user can affect, including a personal login script, the configuration files on a PC, the default print job as set in PRINTCON, and so on.

- If you have a standard operating system, set of network drivers, configuration files, and so on, you can make your life easier. For example, in this case, Fran noticed that the AUTOEXEC.BAT file had a date that was older than it should have been. If she hadn't been aware of this, she would have needed to reboot the PC and look at the messages on the screen as it booted and the user logged in, or opened the file with a text editor to find the problem.

The Fault-Point Chain—Scenario Four

- The workstation shell and CAPTURE setup

- The queue on the server

- The print server attached to the queue

- The server or router PSERVER is running on
- The configuration of the PC
- The connection to the printer
- The printer's configuration
- The printer hardware

Scenario Five: Macintosh Printing Problems

The administrator deals with a problem typical of AppleTalk networks, especially ones with a mixed LocalTalk and Ethernet environment.

Snapshot—Scenario Five

Is this an existing printer setup?

- Is the printer operational?
- Is the printer connected to the network?
- Does the printer show up in the correct AppleTalk zone?
- Can you print from some workstations?

Jethro receives a call that one of the Mac users can't see her printer in the Chooser any more. He arrives, and after assuring himself that the Chooser is set to the correct AppleTalk zone and that the AppleTalk Control Panel is properly set to Ethernet, begins to track down the problem. The Mac's Chooser does list the correct number of zones and shows the server under File Sharing, so Jethro assumes that the Mac's connection to the network is working. He checks on another Mac, and the printer isn't visible there, either. Since the printer is supposed to be available (although, if you wish, you can hide the actual printer from the Chooser and make only the NetWare queue available), Jethro assumes that the problem isn't related to the queue or printer server.

He then takes a quick look at the printer itself. It's turned on and seems to be working correctly—no error lights, the cover is closed, and so on. Jethro resets the printer just to make sure, and rechecks the Chooser. Still nothing. Then he remembers that the Macs are all connected with AppleTalk, not LocalTalk. That means that the LaserWriter must either be connected to the server with an Ethernet card or, if it's an older printer, have an AppleTalk interface, which requires an AppleTalk Ethernet adapter.

The printer turns out to need an adapter, which he finds in the morass of wiring under the printer. He powers it off and on again, hoping to reset it. When he checks the Chooser on the workstation, the printer icon appears as it should. Problem solved.

Lessons Learned—Scenario Five

- Macintosh networks are once again the simple creatures they were before MacTCP, EtherTalk adapters, and slow LocalTalk connections. Since Apple integrated industry-standard Ethernet capabilities (AAUI in first-generation PowerMacs and a few '040 systems, 10BaseT in second- and third-generation PowerMacs, and 10/100BaseT adapters in G3 Power-Macs), it has been extrodinarily easy to set up, manage, and troubleshoot Mac networks. Still, older equipment is not gone, just relegated to simpler tasks. AppleTalk and Open Transport fully support Ethernet, so if there is a problem, check the AppleTalk Control Panel to make sure it's switched to Ethernet, or you won't see a thing on the network.

- Just because the lights are on doesn't mean a device is functioning correctly. It is difficult to tell the status of a laser printer, especially with LaserWriters, which do not have a status display. MacOS-based systems, however, have comprehensive reporting built into the printer software, so an error on a printer will ususally be reflected in a clearly stated alert dialog which explains the problem in plain English, not some cryptic code that must be looked up.

- With printing problems, one of the first things you should do is find out how many users are affected. This will keep you from wasting time checking a workstation's connections and networking software when the problem is actually with the printer or print server. Another way to approach this is to see if the workstation's network connection is still working. Is the file server still available? If it is, then the problem is not likely to be related to the connection.

The Fault-Point Chain—Scenario Five

- The Macintosh AppleTalk and Open Transport software

- The Mac's connection to the network, including NIC and connections

- The adapter from the print server to the Ethernet printer

- The printer

In this case, the queue and print server are not part of the fault chain, because the Macintoshes were printing directly to the LaserWriter rather than to the queue. If NetWare for Macintosh had been set up so that only the queue was available in the Chooser, and the printer itself hidden, then it would have been necessary to include the queue and printer server in the troubleshooting process, as it would have been if a similar problem had occurred with PCs.

Summary

In this chapter, we first looked at network printing snapshots and fault points to identify areas where printing problems can occur. We described the network printing process, which includes software intercepting the print job from a workstation (which may "think" it is simply printing to a local printer) and redirecting that job to a remote printer (print server) located elsewhere on the network. We discussed using the CAPTURE statement and outlined a procedure for troubleshooting printing from Windows 9x/NT stations. We also looked at potential problems with Macintosh and Unix printing, and followed this with a set of four printing trouble scenarios and their steps for troubleshooting and resolution.

In the next chapter, we'll discuss potential problems with WANs (wide area networks) and ways of resolving these.

CHAPTER
THIRTY-SEVEN

Troubleshooting WANs

- Review of WANs (wide area networks)

- Additional fault points for WANs

- WAN-related problems

- Network management and diagnostic tools

- Services across WANs

- Novell Directory Services

Many companies are no longer limited to single LANs, but have multiple LANs connected to form *WANs* (*wide area networks*), or *internetworks*. As you would expect, it is more difficult to isolate problems when internetwork connections are involved. Your system may consist of multiple LANs within a single building or campus, or WANs over multiple sites, which may span a city, a continent, or the entire globe.

In your role as network administrator, you may be called on to troubleshoot a WAN connection. Suppose one of your users is trying to download files from a server in another state. Does the problem arise from permissions on the far end? The router? The Internet service provider? User error? This chapter will help you determine where the problem lies. It will not cover how to set up WANs and every possible variation used to connect LANs. Instead, it provides the basic principles of connecting and troubleshooting WANs; these principles will be applicable no matter which specific hardware or topology you use.

This chapter will discuss how LANs are interconnected, troubleshooting methods and tools, and user services. We'll begin with a review of WANs.

How LANs Are Connected to Form WANs

To help you understand the process that you are troubleshooting, let's review the various methods of connecting LANs. A basic definition of a LAN is a group of workstations connected to a server with a single type of topology. This can be as simple as a few PCs connected by Token Ring to a server, or as complex as PCs running Windows 95, Windows 98, and OS/2 connecting with IPX/SPX, TCP/IP, NetBIOS, and NetBEUI; Macintoshes using EtherTalk; and Unix workstations using TCP/IP; all connected by Ethernet to a server. As long as there is only one network number and one server, it is still one LAN.

Another network size classification is *metropolitan area network* (*MAN*). A MAN is a network linking more than one site, but limited to a metropolitan area. (In cases such as Los Angeles or New York, these can, of course, be quite extensive.) Generally, a MAN offers wider access and high performance (100Mbps or greater).

NOTE   If you need detailed help with creating or maintaining a WAN, there are many good books and other network resources to which you can refer (see Appendix A). If you're not familiar with some of the standards and acronyms used in WAN technology, see the glossary (Appendix D) at the end of the book.

The simplest method of connecting two existing networks is to put two NICs in a single server and connect each of the existing networks to one of the NICs. In this case, the server with two network cards is acting as a router. From this simple example you can go all the way to multiple LANs connected via high-speed leased lines, or even through satellite connections.

Connecting Multiple LANs at One Site

There are several reasons you may have multiple LANs at one site, such as:

- The LANs were created separately and at different times, in response to the varying needs of different departments. Later, they were hooked together to form an internetwork. In fact, this is typical of the development of networking at many companies.

- Different departments are using different types of LANs. For example, the Engineering department might be using Token Ring, the Accounting department Ethernet, and the Marketing and Art departments LocalTalk.

- You needed to reduce network traffic or provide more services than a single server could handle. Too many workstations on a single LAN, or too many users on a single server, can cause the entire network to bog down. Splitting the network into several LANs reduces traffic and server overhead, improving performance for everyone.

Depending on the setup at your site, the LANs may be connected with bridges, routers, or gateways, as explained in the following sections.

Bridges

Bridges are the least complex method of connecting two LANs (although once they are connected, they are actually one LAN, with one network number). A bridge generally connects similar types of networks, such as Token Ring to Token Ring, but it can connect different types of cabling, such as thick Ethernet to 10BaseT. A bridge can be used to divide a LAN with too much traffic into several segments. Because only the packets that are destined for the segment on the other side pass through the bridge, it can substantially reduce traffic on both parts of the LAN.

NOTE Versions of NetWare before 3.*x* called the function built into NetWare a bridge. Actually, the NetWare product has attributes of both a bridge and a *router*. In later versions of NetWare, it is referred to as a router. NT's routing feature is usually referred to as *packet forwarding*, or simply *routing*. These software routing solutions offer convenience but are not necessarily as robust or as fast as are dedicated hardware routers and bridges.

Bridges are designed to handle specific protocols, such as IPX/SPX, Apple-Talk, TCP/IP, and so on. A bridge looks at the hardware address of each packet and sends it to the other side if the address is on that side. Since the hardware address is always in the same place in a packet, the function of a bridge is relatively simple, and bridges are generally the fastest type of connection between two LANs (for a given cost or speed of processor). A bridge generally learns the addresses of all the workstations on either side by occasionally polling them for this information.

Routers

A *router* differs from a bridge in that it can handle multiple protocols. Also, the network on each side of a router is actually a different LAN, with different network numbers. A router doesn't just read the destination hardware address; it can read the packet to find out its eventual destination, rather than just the next one identified by the destination hardware address. A router can add further information to a packet to enable it to go through a LAN that uses a different hardware standard, such as Ethernet to Token Ring, or take that information off a packet it receives from the other side of such a LAN.

Another difference is that routers don't handle every packet on the LAN (they aren't "transparent"). Instead, a packet that is to be passed through the router must be addressed to it. NetWare handles this automatically, but some protocols (TCP/IP, for instance) require you to tell a workstation the address of the router to which it should send packets for forwarding.

A router is more capable than a bridge but requires more processing, which, all other things being equal, makes a router either slower or more expensive than a bridge. There is also an in-between class of devices called *brouters*, which combine the functionality of bridges and routers, generally by examining every packet on the LAN (transparency) but only being able to handle some protocols.

Gateways

A *gateway* is the most complex type of device for connecting LANs, and it is typically very specialized. It doesn't just transfer packets from one LAN or one protocol to another; it usually translates between two dissimilar standards. For example, a gateway might act as a file translator, to allow your Macintoshes to access files on a Unix server, or as a mail gateway, translating between the Net-Ware mail protocol MHS and another, such as X.400.

Gateways are typically complex to configure. You should understand the basics of configuring both sides of the gateway. For instance, for a file-and-print-services gateway that translates between AppleTalk and Unix (TCP/IP), you should understand how to configure both AppleTalk and TCP/IP.

Connecting LANs between Buildings

LANs in buildings that are close enough together to be linked with a cable or by a beam of light can be connected by either repeaters or bridges (discussed below), depending on the requirements of the network. Buildings can be connected with wire or fiber-optic cable, or linked with wireless means, such as an infrared laser or a pair of radio transceivers.

Repeaters

A *repeater* is a device that simply passes everything it sees to every segment hooked up to it. It may support several types of cable—for instance, thick, thin, twisted-pair, and fiber-optic Ethernet—and is primarily used to extend the maximum length of cable. The primary disadvantage to a repeater is that it passes everything through; this can make for a very high-traffic load if too many workstations are connected.

There are two basic types of repeaters, single-port and multiport. A *single-port* repeater is used simply to extend the possible length of cabling for a network segment. A *multiport* repeater allows several "legs" on the same segment. A repeater with many ports may also be known as a *hub* or a *concentrator*. Repeaters are relatively inexpensive and easy to set up.

Bridges

A *bridge* provides the same type of extension as a repeater, with the added benefit of traffic isolation, since only the traffic destined for the other building is passed across. Bridges do cost more and require software configuration, but they are also much more flexible.

Connecting LANs across Long Distances

Once you go beyond the connection range that can be spanned by physical cabling, your options become much more limited. You can set up a satellite or microwave link, lay your own long-distance cable, or use the facilities provided by your local telephone company.

Telephone Company Services

Transmitting data over a phone line intended for voice has its limitations. Because the line is engineered for voice communications, it will support a maximum data communications rate of only about 33,600bps (bits per second), or 230,400bps with data compression. 56K modems can achieve compressed throughput of 340,000bps, although these rates are typically unattainable due to inherent line noise.

The basic divisions between the types of services are:

- Dial-up connections that can connect to any other phone line versus leased lines that connect two specific sites

- Analog connections versus digital connections, which can allow speeds of up to 622Mbps (million bits per second) or more

Where there were once no competitors to the phone companies, there are now many. The service of providing a long-distance connection, say between an office in San Francisco and one in New York, can be broken into three parts: the connection from your building to the local branch office of the local phone company at each end, plus the carrier between the two phone company offices. You may find several companies that can provide the long-distance service—AT&T, Sprint, MCI, and WillTel to name a few.

NOTE   It may still be difficult to find more than one local service in many areas, but that will probably change in the near future. The upshot of the competition is that prices are dropping every year, and what was once an economic impossibility is now feasible, and will soon be taken for granted.

Improvements in switched digital circuits and decreases in connect times (the time required to initiate a connection between sites) are making dial-up digital connections a reasonable alternative for WAN links that don't need to be up all the time. How often do you need to be able to print to a remote site? Is a two-second delay acceptable? Call your local carrier and the long-distance companies if you're not sure what alternatives are feasible in your area.

Analog Dial-Up Connections   Almost all dial-up connections use analog service, which is slower than digital but offers the flexibility to connect to anyone with a phone. The typical problems associated with analog dial-up connections are:

- The limited speed available through lines intended for voice

- The relatively high levels of line noise

- The rates charged for standard phone service

Leased Analog Connections   If you are using a dial-up line to connect regularly with another site, you may save money by leasing an analog connection. This won't typically offer higher speed, but it can give you a cleaner, more reliable connection. If the connection is used frequently, a leased line will be less expensive than making standard connections.

Digital Dial-Up Connections   As the phone companies convert from equipment intended only for voice transmission to digitally-based equipment designed to also handle data and even video, they are making high-speed dial-up connections available. These range in speed from 56Kbps (kilobits per second) to 100Mbps or more.

The typical problems associated with digital dial-up connections are:

- These services are currently available only within metropolitan areas, and then only in some areas.

- A dial-up connection that is used more than a few minutes a day may end up costing more than a higher-speed leased line.

- Digital connections generally require equipment much more expensive than a simple modem, although you can find ISDN (Integrated Services Digital Network) adapters for under a few hundred dollars.

The areas served by all-digital services will expand, and eventually you will be able to get a dial-up digital connection anywhere that you can now reach with a standard phone line. Check with your local phone company for availability. The equipment you will need depends on the type of connection. When contacting vendors such as MCI or your local Bell, ask them what type of equipment they recommend and support.

Leased Digital Connections   If you need a connection with a throughput of over 64Kbps, you will probably need to lease a digital line. Digital services that may be available to you include:

- Leased ISDN at 64Kbps and up. *ISDN* is an international standard for telecommunications developed by the CCITT. It can handle voice, video, and data over one digital line. It generally provides 64 or 128Kbps. *Broadband ISDN (B/ISDN)*, which will soon be available, uses broadband transmission and fiber-optic cables to provide speeds up to 150Mbps.

- FDDI at 100Mbps. *FDDI (Fiber Data Distribution Interface)* is an ANSI standard for fiber-optic networks.

- ATM, which can provide 622Mbps or more. *ATM (asynchronous transfer mode)* is a protocol designed to send parts of a transmission over different routes as they become available. It works well with mixed video and data transmissions.

CCITT stands for Consultative Committee for International Telephony and Telegraphy. It is an international organization based in Geneva that sets telecommunications standards, including X.25, V.22, V.32, V.42, X.400, and X.500. ANSI stands for American National Standards Institute. It is an American body that sets standards, and is a voting member of ISO (the International Standards Organization, a standards organization with over 75 member countries).

These types of services tend to become more expensive as the distance between sites increases. There are also services called *fractional T1* and *fractional T3*, which divide the channel into several subchannels at a reduced cost and speed. Your local service provider's representatives can quote rates. As with digital dial-up connections, you will need special equipment to access these services.

Where the only option was once to lease a dedicated line from one site to another, there is now an alternative that is expanding very rapidly, due to its relative economy. This alternative is Frame Relay, which provides a structure similar to X.25, but at T1 or even T3 speeds. Frame Relay and X.25 are described in the "Connecting LANs around the World" section later in this chapter.

Other Options

Other options for connecting LANs include satellite communications, microwave relays, and independent providers of services similar to those available from the phone companies.

Satellite services can provide widespread communications for organizations with many sites across a continent. However, the drawback is that satellite communications are more expensive than leased lines for distances of less than a thousand miles or so. They also tend to be slower than land-based communications, at least unless large, expensive antennas are installed rather than the usual six-foot dish.

Microwave relays can provide high-speed, secure communications between sites, but are generally so expensive that they are reserved for highly specialized applications and those with unlimited budgets (like the government). Some organizations such as railroads, television networks, or cellular phone companies may lease some of their extra capacity. Within limited ranges (three to five miles), inexpensive microwave equipment can provide 1.5Mbps connectivity to a large number of sites for a one-time investment with no monthly fees. The drawbacks are that the range is limited, and all sites to be connected must be in line-of-sight.

Connecting LANs around the World

Beyond WANs and MANs are the worldwide networks. Depending on the country you need to connect to, you may find that standard services range from some that are more sophisticated than U.S. services, to some that are barely above the level of carrier pigeons. Western Europe, for example, has large areas already networked with ISDN and ATM, and Eastern Europe has areas in which the line quality is so bad that special modems are required to support any speed over 300bps.

Cost can also be a major factor. A leased line that costs $1200 per month to connect San Francisco to New York could cost $3600 a month to London, and $5000 a month to Tokyo.

X.25

X.25 is the CCITT standard for a terminal interfacing with a packet-switching network. It is implemented worldwide in many public and private networks.

Illustrations of X.25 typically show a number of different types of installations, all with lines ending in a cloud in the center of the picture. This is meant to illustrate the wide variety of ways that users can access X.25 services, and the large number of possible routes that the data can take from one end to the other.

X.25 services can be accessed by dial-up lines or leased lines, at speeds from 1200bps to 1.544Mbps or higher. The primary advantage to this type of service is that it is very widespread and is widely supported by many vendors. The biggest disadvantage is that it is relatively slow. It is an excellent way of forwarding e-mail between LANs, but would not be appropriate for a regularly used data connection.

Frame Relay

Frame Relay is similar to X.25 in that it is often pictured on network diagrams as a cloud. However, it can provide speeds of T1 (1.5Mbps) or T3 (45Mbps). Charges are based on the local-access charge at each end, plus a set fee for the long-distance connection. It can provide a very cost-effective method of connecting remote sites. Frame Relay service is expanding rapidly because the overall cost can be much lower than for dedicated lines.

The problem with Frame Relay is that all the traffic from all customers goes through the same public network. This means that unless you pay for guaranteed access speeds, you may experience delays if there are lots of other people using the network, too.

Leased Lines

Typically, any service that can be had across town can be had around the world, but the cost will be much higher. For instance, T1 lines typically double in cost as distances increase from 500 miles to 2000 miles, so connecting New York to Japan will increase the cost considerably. Where a 1000-mile T1 (1.544Mbps) line might cost $10,000 per month, a T3 (45Mbps) line might cost $100,000 per month. For longer distances, especially overseas, these prices go much higher.

Other Options

As distances increase, satellite communications may become more practical. If you have heavy traffic between LANs on different continents, a satellite link can provide reliable, relatively inexpensive high-speed throughput. The initial installation can be expensive, but with enough use, it can save you money over a leased line that continues to cost you money every month.

Additional Fault Points of WANs

As is sometimes the case within buildings, the actual hardware and wiring used to connect your LANs will seldom belong to you or be under your control. The positive side of this is that the service provider is responsible for maintaining, troubleshooting, and upgrading this hardware. The down side is that it can be difficult to get a response from some companies as quickly as you would like in an emergency. Although you won't deal with equipment that is typically outside your jurisdiction, you will need to be able to determine whether it's your equipment or the phone company's that is causing the problem.

Of course, the basic principles of troubleshooting apply to WAN equipment as well. If your problem is with an existing installation, determine what has changed. One item that makes routers and bridges different from most of the equipment you'll deal with is that they add items on their own. They build lists of the equipment and networks they know about. If a workstation with the wrong address comes up on the network, the router could add the address, then become confused about the services it's supposed to provide. You can usually reboot the router and get back to the default routing table.

If it's a new installation, get the most basic configuration possible working first, then add the additional features in. This might mean concentrating on IPX first, then other protocols, or even following the boot process, as you might with a PC, to see if the router is operating correctly.

Another item to look at is the scope of the problem. Is every group in the building affected? If you can isolate the groups having problems, you can get an idea of what they have in common.

Troubleshooting WAN Hardware

The basic WAN hardware is a device that sends traffic from your LAN to another LAN. This may be as simple as a repeater on either end of a few hundred feet of coaxial cable linking two buildings, or as complex as a T1 bridge connected to a CSU/DSU, attached to a leased line that connects two sites in different states.

From a troubleshooting standpoint, there is very little difference in the basic approach to either of the extremes. First determine whether traffic is getting to the WAN link device, then whether the device is operating correctly, and finally whether the device is able to read signals coming or going on the link. If these conditions are all met, the problem is probably elsewhere. Of course, determining these items can be difficult, especially without a LAN analyzer or similar equipment. The simplest test is to see whether you can get to any devices on the other end of the connection.

Problems with Repeaters

Repeaters are the simplest type of device used to link LANs. Depending on the distance, you could use a repeater to link two buildings with either thin or thick Ethernet, or with a fiber-optic connection. Thin Ethernet allows a maximum distance of 185 meters (about 600 feet), and thick Ethernet allows 500 meters (more than 1600 feet). A fiber-optic connection can be up to several miles.

It is relatively simple to tell whether most repeaters are operating. If the activity lights on the front are blinking, the device is probably working. Also, if a device on one side of the repeater can see devices on the other side, the connection is working. The additional fault points for this type of setup include the repeater at each end of the long cable and the long cable itself. With a multiport repeater, the separate ports can be isolated, usually with switches. This can make isolating parts of the network for troubleshooting easier, but it can also cause problems if a port is shut off accidentally.

Problems with Bridges

A bridge can be used for something as simple as a few hundred feet of cable linking two buildings or for an application as complex as a T1 leased line linking a New York office to a Los Angeles office. As with any other network connection device, the elements for troubleshooting are to determine whether the traffic is getting to the bridge, whether the bridge is operational, and whether the traffic is getting from the bridge to the other side of the link.

Bridges, routers, and gateways usually can be accessed through remote management or monitoring software, which means you can make sure that the device is operational without needing to physically go to it and use its console. You should also be able to examine the routing table to determine what network devices the bridge knows about.

A simple way to isolate a bridge as a break point is to try to attach to a server that is on the other side of the bridge. If you know that the server is up (if workstations on that side of the bridge can attach to it), but you can't reach it from the far side of the bridge, you have isolated the break point to the bridge or to the physical connections attached to the bridge.

Problems with Routers

A router may be internal to a server (a server with two NICs that routes between the two LANs), or it may be a stand-alone product, running either proprietary software on proprietary hardware or generic software on a PC platform. Novell has two products: the standard router included with NetWare and the Multi-Protocol Router (MPR), both of which run on a standard PC platform.

The troubleshooting process described above for bridges applies equally well to routers. The biggest difference is that because routers handle multiple protocols, a router may be routing one protocol (perhaps IPX) correctly, but not another (such as TCP/IP). To isolate such problems, you will need to check each protocol to see if it is being forwarded through the router.

Problems with Gateways

Gateways can be more difficult to troubleshoot because they generally involve a service as well as protocol translation. For instance, a gateway that allows Macintoshes to print to a Unix printer might seem to be inoperative even if the actual problem is that the LPD daemon on the Unix host isn't working. To troubleshoot gateways, you must understand the process on both sides of the device. Whether file, print, or mail services are involved, you should be able to determine that the process is functioning properly on both sides of the gateway. The starting point here is to make sure that the service can be used from the near side first.

For instance, if you are trying to determine if a gateway is causing the printing problem in which Macintoshes on one network can't print to a printer on a Unix system on the other side of a gateway, try printing from the Unix system first. If that works, try printing from another Unix system. If that also works, then you can safely assume that the physical process of printing is okay. However, one user might be able to print and another not, depending on how access to the queue is set up. You should be sure that the Macintosh user is set up as a user on the Unix system, or that the permissions will allow anyone to use the queue. If it all works, then you can move on to testing the gateway.

Problems with Dial-In/Dial-Out Servers

With more and more services accessible through modems, *dial-in* and *dial-out servers* are allowing users to connect with a network from home or a portable computer, or to dial out to a service from their office, without needing to have a modem for each workstation on the LAN. One such server, with up to 16 modems, can serve the needs of dozens of users at a much lower cost than a modem for each workstation. Consolidating the modems on a network in this way can also enhance security and make upgrades to hardware and software much easier. Some network modems also provide fax services. As ISDN becomes more available, servers are beginning to support ISDN modems as well.

Telecommunications Standards   The biggest difficulty in troubleshooting dial-in and dial-out connections lies in the lack of standardization in the telecommunications world. There are many protocols and standards, such as V.32, V.32bis, V.42, V.90, Hayes-compatible, and so on. The problem is that different manufacturers do not always implement these standards in exactly the same way. Even modems that claim to be Hayes-compatible may have different default command sets than other modems that also claim Hayes compatibility. The modem world very much resembles the PC world before the IBM PC became the dominant standard. There are many manufacturers offering enhanced performance, but their equipment may only work with the same modem on the other end.

There is also no set standard for communication protocols. The simplest protocols specify data bits (7 or 8), parity (odd, even, or none), stop bits (1, 1.5, or 2), and speed (50–57,600 baud). There are also several data-compression schemes, some "standard" and some proprietary. Furthermore, the serial port that connects the modem to the server may be a standard COM port or an enhanced port using the 16550 UART chip or the one offered by the Novell WNIM+ adapter. The only way to ensure that these settings match is to speak with the users on the other end and ascertain what settings they are using. One can rather easily assume that 16,550 UARTs are being employed unless the units in question are pre-80486 DX/2 66 Intel-based systems, but it is still smart to check.

NOTE
Baud is the number of transitions per second in a signal on a line. It is commonly, but not always accurately, equated with bits per second. For instance, 9600 baud with compression can produce 19,200bps or more.

Communications Settings   Setting up the server itself will not require that you confirm that both sides of a connection are using the same speed, protocol, and so on, but you cannot troubleshoot problems with such connections without understanding the settings. There are several parts to a dial-in/dial-out server. The easy parts are the ones that are the same on any server: the workstation, NIC, COM port or WNIM+ adapter, operating system software, and server software. You may also need to troubleshoot the user's software that is accessing the server. The hard part comes when everything up to the modem is working correctly.

The great number of possible settings makes it imperative that you know exactly what both sides of the connection you are trying to set up expect. Dial-in/dial-out servers include software for the workstation that allows the user to configure the modem for the protocol that is used on the other end. Many modems will negotiate automatically with the modem on the other end until they determine a common setting that they both understand. Unfortunately, this may be much slower than what could be achieved if the modems were both set properly to begin with. This can mean the difference between requiring a few minutes to send a file of several hundred kilobytes or a few hours to send the same file.

Line Quality   Another factor in the smooth operation of a dial-in/dial-out server is the line quality. You will probably want to use a line that doesn't pass through your PBX system. Check with your phone company for other options that may be available. You may already have such a line for your fax machine.

ISDN connections are both simpler and more difficult. The morass of protocols and standards goes away. Getting two ISDN modems to connect to each other is much simpler and faster than with analog modems. The more difficult part is getting the phone company to connect a line for you, and figuring out what it costs. Also, there are two basic types of ISDN services. They are Basic Rate Interface (BRI), which provides two 64Kbps channels plus a control channel, and Primary Rate Interface (PRI), which provides thirteen 64Kbps channels plus a control channel. You may want a BRI at each remote site, and a PRI at your main office.

Dealing with Telecommunications Service Providers

In general, you will not be able to troubleshoot the problems that originate with your telecommunications service provider. However, you will get faster service if you do your best to eliminate all other possibilities before contacting the provider. If you have a good idea of the topology of your network, you should be able to isolate the problem to one side or the other side of the interface with the telecommunications network.

For example, if the workers in the other office can ping their router but nothing past it, and you have the same experience, and the routers were working before, you probably have a bad connection. You should try at least this much fault isolation before calling the service provider.

TIP Try to establish a relationship with a particular customer representative. Once you've established mutual trust, you won't need to prove to the telecommunications service company that you know what you're doing every time you call.

Troubleshooting WAN Software

There are two typical problems with software on a WAN:

- Incorrect configuration, which is symptomatic of a lack of planning or management on a WAN. This kind of problem is usually caused by two workstations or servers using the same address or network number, or two servers on the same cable segment not having the same number for that cable. In either case, the ultimate cause is a lack of documentation or standards for that network.

- Corruption of files or software freezes, which can be caused by many different things, such as hardware problems, user errors, bugs in the software, or configuration problems.

Most routers can be upgraded via software and run proprietary code to route between sites. This code may be updated regularly, and the updates may fix one problem while breaking something else. There are several things you can do about this. One is to retain the old versions—better the devil you know than the one you don't. Also, develop a relationship with the vendor's tech support. If they know you, they'll not only respond better, but they may make early releases available or be more honest about problems. Don't jump on a new release right away if what you have is working. Some of this software is so complex that it may seem that there's no way to make everything work—something will always be broken.

Software Planning and Management

At a minimum, you need to coordinate the internal network numbers, IPX numbers, and similar configuration settings for other protocols, such as TCP/IP. You may need to coordinate these numbers with an outside agency. TCP/IP, for example, is regulated by the Defense Data Network's Network Information Center. If you have a site that is not connected to the Internet, and never will be, you can use any numbers that are valid. If you want to be able to connect to the rest of the world, you must have an assigned address. The same will shortly be true of IPX addresses.

Network Addresses   Management software will quickly compile and display all the addresses in use on your network. This not only ensures that you won't have address conflicts, but it will also make troubleshooting easier when you receive a message like: "Node at 140.11.138.244 has caused a bindery error." Another alternative is to use a service that provides addresses when PCs boot. There are several for TCP/IP, including bootp and DHCP.

Configuration Utilities   Bridges, routers, and gateways come with some sort of configuration utility. This utility will usually allow you to monitor and troubleshoot the device as well as establish the initial configuration.

If you have a NetWare server that is also acting as a router, you can use NetWare utilities to monitor the router. Utilities such as MONITOR, FCONSOLE, and TCPCON enable you to track packets sent and received and monitor other device information. NT Server (and also Workstation) can also act as routers, and the Network Monitor and Performance Monitor utilities perform similar monitoring services.

With both stand-alone devices and servers, you should have some idea of what the normal traffic looks like and what the normal statistics are for the device. If nothing more, occasionally open the device with the configuration utility and look at the information, just to familiarize yourself with what things should look like. Unless you know this, you won't know what is out of whack when you're trying to troubleshoot the device.

Baselining, as discussed throughout this book, is one of the cornerstones of troubleshooting. It is very difficult to know if something is wrong unless you know what it should look like. The items to look for at the most basic level will tell you that traffic is moving in and out of your device. The specifics will vary with the type of device, the protocol, and so on, but you should see information about the number of packets received, number of packets sent, and the number of bad packets (often subdivided into different types of bad packets, depending again on the type of protocol).

For example, if you have been monitoring the packet information and know that you are usually receiving about 10,000 packets a day, and the number drops to 100 or jumps to 100,000, you will have a start on finding the problem. If you are receiving a larger number than you are sending, this may also indicate a problem. Of course, large or steadily increasing numbers of bad packets also indicate a problem. The NetWare System Administration manual discusses the statistics that MONITOR tracks, and the manual for your device or monitoring software may also describe which items you should check.

TIP
The causes of bad packets, and how to isolate and fix the problem(s), are the subject of numerous books. LANalyzer for Windows offers a distinct advantage in this area; it has a help facility called Network Advisor that will tell you not only that bad packets are being received, but also what typically causes that sort of error and where it is coming from. We highly recommend this product or something similar for anyone with a large LAN or multiple LANs. The LANalyzer for Windows package also includes a very good book on the subject, *Novell's Guide to NetWare LAN Analysis*, by Laura Chappell, which covers using LANalyzer for Windows to diagnose problems on Ethernet.

Software Configuration

Once you get a configuration that works for a network device, server, or whatever, record it! Keep copies of the information with the machine, in a central area, and at home. It will be useful in reconstructing a device after the configuration is lost, in identifying conflicts with other devices, and in determining the best settings for new devices.

If you have your configurations documented, you can also avoid discovering conflicts after they have caused every server on your network to crash or caused a "Router Configuration Error" message. Solving a conflict problem quickly won't make you look good if you could have avoided it in the first place. Also, since routers may add to their configuration tables automatically, you should have a base configuration that you can return to if there are problems.

Address Conflicts

A major problem with LANs is also one of their benefits. They are not terribly complex (compared with a mainframe) and can be administered by local personnel, rather than requiring a centralized IS department. However, as companies and their networks grow, some level of coordination becomes critical. With two or three servers, the chances that two will use the same internal IPX number seem minuscule, but that's exactly the time to begin coordinating information, not when there are 50 servers.

With an IPX address conflict, you will get a "Router Configuration Error" and an annoying beep on the server's console. With a TCP/IP address conflict, you may have every workstation on your network crash. The only way to avoid address conflicts is to document configurations and coordinate with other administrators.

Network Management Tools

As networks grow in complexity, the need for management and diagnostic software becomes greater. With a single LAN, it's relatively easy to determine whether network traffic is getting to a device or not. Once you have several LANs, perhaps running different or multiple protocols, diagnosing problems becomes much more difficult. Fortunately, the software necessary to help you determine and fix problems is becoming less expensive and more capable all the time. For example, the original Novell LANalyzer product retailed for around $15,000. LANalyzer for Windows offers 90 percent of the functionality, plus some great features the original product lacks, and has a street price of under $1000.

If you have a WAN, or even multiple LANs at a single site, you should have some level of network monitoring capability. You can usually diagnose most WAN problems without such capability—eventually. Given the cost of having dozens or hundreds of users offline for hours while you track down what went wrong, the software will quickly pay for itself.

What's Available

There are network management and/or analysis products ranging in price from less than $100 to about $100,000. The capabilities you need depend on the complexity of your network. The basic, bottom-line capability is to track the packets flowing on your network. How much the program can tell about the packets and what other diagnostic tools are included will depend on the product.

Most products can cover only one LAN. You will need a basic tool for each LAN segment, or a more capable (and expensive) product that can cover the WAN. Top-of-the-line packages include a workstation (usually a Unix workstation) and may offer services such as network mapping that will alert you if any configuration on your WAN changes.

It can be difficult to justify spending money on preventive measures and "conveniences." However, you can estimate the cost of downtime per hour on your LAN, and then measure that against the cost of a tool that could save you hours in getting your network fixed and back online. The larger your network or internetwork, the easier it is to justify management and diagnostic tools, and the more you need such tools.

Features to Look For

The following sections describe some of the basic features that you may want in your network management package. You can then use the information resources listed in Appendix A to determine the best program for you. Appendix B lists some of the software available.

Packet Monitoring

You should be able to see information on the various types of packets moving on the network, including numbers of good and bad packets and their sources. Packet-monitoring facilities may also include the ability to look at the header information for each packet, or to decode the packet completely and look at the contents. You will usually be able to set thresholds for certain types of events, and the software will then notify you if the limits you set are exceeded.

Trend Analysis

Some programs allow you to save information about your network's normal traffic and establish trends over time. This can be enormously helpful in both identifying problems and upgrading your network before performance degrades significantly.

Online Help

You can have megabytes of decoded packets, but unless you understand what the information in the packet header means, the data won't do you much good. You can have an alarm that tells you that your Token Ring network is beaconing, but unless you know what beaconing is and what the likely source of the problem is, there isn't much you can do with the information. You can learn this information by taking a course, such as the Basic and Advanced LANalyzer classes available through Novell Authorized Education Centers, or you can get a book on the subject and learn the information yourself, or you can get a program that will help you figure it out. (The Network Advisor in LANalyzer for Windows is a great example of how such built-in help should work.)

SNMP Management

The Simple Network Management Protocol (SNMP) is a standard for managing networking devices that many manufacturers incorporate into their software and hardware. If your management software and your network devices support SNMP, you will be able to manage many different devices, from different manufacturers, with one management tool.

Network Mapping

Management programs offer many levels of network mapping. Some produce simple logical maps of your network that tell you how many workstations are on each segment and provide some basic information about them. Other programs can keep track of data on device locations, distance between devices, types of connections, and so on, and can then help you isolate faults caused by changes in the physical network.

Network Inventory

Network inventory programs also span a wide range of functionality. Simpler applications can tell you what kind of workstation is at each network address. Other programs can tell you all the software on every workstation's disk, the operating system version, the contents of the AUTOEXEC.BAT and CONFIG.SYS files, and more. You can even find programs that allow you to track usage of applications, determine how many valid copies of each you have, and update software remotely on every workstation.

Server Management

NetWare provides some basic tools for managing your server, keeping track of users, and so on, but these tools are limited. There are a number of companies offering extensions to NetWare. These products allow you to print reports of all users and the files and directories they own and have trustee rights to; the setups of printers, print servers, and print queues; the basic configuration files and the ones for any additional NLMs you may have installed; and other aspects of your server. If you have more than one server, or even one that has a lot of disk space or many users, this sort of utility can make your documentation chores much easier. Some programs will even monitor CPU utilization, disk access, and memory usage and alert you if you need to upgrade your processor, NIC, or disk system.

Diagnostic Tools

Diagnostic tools range from a simple voltmeter or continuity checker to a $100,000 package, preinstalled on a Unix workstation, that can monitor your entire WAN and alert you if problems arise or are about to arise. The two basic categories are hardware-based products and software-only products. Hardware-based tools are generally faster, and often more capable than software-only tools—and usually more expensive, as well.

Many diagnostic tools include management functions, and some management tools can be used for diagnostic purposes—it depends as much on how you are using the tool as what it is intended for. The two functions should be tightly integrated: If you manage and document your network well, you will often be able to avoid problems before they arise.

The larger your network, the more you should have some kind of diagnostic tools. There are many multisite networking problems that cannot be diagnosed without the right tools, or at least will take much longer to figure out. Some networking errors are quite deceptive. For example, a bad routing table can produce errors that are similar to other types of problems.

Hardware-Based Products

Most hardware-based tools for WAN troubleshooting include protocol analysis. They may be referred to as sniffers, protocol analyzers, or packet decoders. These are all descriptions of the same basic function: intercepting the packets flowing through your network and gathering information about them. The differences between products lie in how much they will do with the packets and how much information they can collect, sort, generate reports on, and watch over a period of time to establish trends.

If you have a large internetwork or very high levels of traffic, the hardware-based products can still provide an advantage. At the high end of the scale, products are available that do much more than capture and decode packets. They may be able to monitor every device on your network at once, build both physical and logical maps of your network, or even allow you to simulate different network configurations so you can plan upgrades in advance.

Protocol Analyzers

A *protocol analyzer* consists of two parts: the hardware that collects the packets that are traveling along the wires of your network, and the software that provides you with information about those packets. The hardware may be a special NIC for your workstation or a complete (sometimes portable) workstation. The need for dedicated hardware is decreasing as LAN adapters grow in power. Many modern LAN adapters include a CPU with more power than PCs had a few years ago, as well as on-board RAM.

There are problems that simply can't be solved without a protocol analyzer, and many others that will take much longer to diagnose without one. For instance, if all the packets from another site are arriving but have been mangled by the router, all the connection lights will be on, and everything will appear to be working, but you won't be able to communicate. A protocol analyzer is the only way to see a problem like this directly, although you might get a clue from your server showing that all the packets from a certain address are bad.

Hardware-based protocol analyzers range in price from a few hundred dollars to $50,000 or more for some workstation-based integrated network management and analysis tools. The level of capability you want (or need) will depend on the complexity of your internetwork and its stability. If you seldom or never have new networks or servers added to your network, you may not need much management capability at all. If you have a dynamic, growing internetwork, or are supporting hardware or software development, for instance, you will probably want more capability.

The basic questions you should consider in a protocol analyzer include:

- What protocols are supported? Even if you are only using one protocol now, you may want to leave room for expansion or upgrades in the future.

- How much information will the product gather? This may range from simply telling you how many packets of each type are coming through the network to providing specific information such as the original sender of the packet, its intended recipient, the purpose of the data in the packet, and the contents of the data part of the packet. Some products may allow trend analysis over periods from days to years.

- Can it save your network information in a spreadsheet or database format? You should look at what data formats the product will export to.

- Can the product simulate network traffic levels (loads)? One of the problems that you will face in trying to troubleshoot WAN problems is that some of them will occur sporadically or periodically. Some protocol analyzers will also allow you to simulate a number of users producing various levels of traffic to stress the network, hopefully reproducing the conditions that caused your problem.

- Can the product gather information about the networking devices that connect your LANs? Some products are limited to gathering information about the single LAN segment they are attached to.

- Does the product support SNMP or CMIP (Common Management Information Protocol)? If so, you will be able to remotely manage any devices that also support these protocols.

- How portable is the product? Many protocol analyzers can only see the LAN segment they are attached to. If you have to carry the machine from segment to segment, it's nice to have a fairly small package.

- Does the product include time-domain reflectometry (TDR)? This allows you to isolate cable breaks to a particular distance from your location or the nearest node. TDR can be invaluable in tracing cabling problems.

- Does the product include packet filtering? This allows you to select packets that fit certain parameters; for instance, you could select only the packets being sent by a certain workstation or server. You might consider the number of filters a product has, the degree of flexibility in combining filters to provide Boolean searches, and whether it allows you to create your own filters.

Other Hardware Tools

Other types of diagnostic tools serve specialized functions. Some examples are:

- Stand-alone products that perform the TDR function mentioned in the previous section to determine the location of breaks in your cabling

- Continuity testers, which can check cabling for breaks, and in some cases also check polarity to make sure that the two wires in a twisted-pair connection haven't been crossed

- Voltage checkers, which can help diagnose a LAN adapter that is defective and unable to maintain the proper voltage

Software-Only Products

The only real difference between hardware-based products and software-only products is that the latter rely on the standard networking hardware already installed on your workstation to gather the packets off the wire. These products will usually require a special LAN driver for your card, and they may not support all NICs. Software-only products are usually much less expensive than hardware-based products, but may be less capable or slower.

Tools in Windows NT

Two tools that are included with NT and which should be considered indispensable by anyone administering a network comprised of NT Servers are Network Monitor (NETMON.EXE) and Performance Monitor (PERFMON.EXE).

Network Monitor   Network Monitor (also referred to as NetMon) is a very useful tool for analyzing network traffic at the packet level for IPX, TCP/IP, NetBEUI, and other installed protocols. For more coverage of this tool, see Chapter 33.

Performance Monitor   Performance Monitor (discussed in greater detail in Chapter 33) includes the ability to monitor just about any imaginable aspect of an NT system, including network, processor, disk, modem connection, and RAM. You can view and monitor many details for any running process (some applications or DLLs have many processes), and below that, you can even monitor many details on a per thread basis for any given thread running anywhere in the entire system! And for any property, or any combination of properties you select, you can use one of four different monitoring modes: Chart, Alert, Log, and Report. Following are some typical uses for troubleshooting using Performance Monitor:

- Use a combination of Cache, Physical Disk, Memory, and Processor properties to determine whether a sluggish system needs more disk space, memory, or a faster (or an additional) processor.

- Use the Server properties for security-related issues—to monitor failed logons, unsuccessful attempts to access secured network resources (files, disks, printers, etc.), or to view how many users have logged in or are currently logged in. You may even want to send system alerts to a different machine to be immediately apprised of certain security-related events.

- Use the Server, Server Work Queues, and protocol-level properties to determine how much server activity is occurring on a given server. Too much activity would indicate a need for another network card or another server to better handle the network requests.

Three more points to keep in mind with Performance Monitor: First, you can run Performance Monitor on one station or server to monitor events or properties on another server. This even works over a RAS dial-up session (in the event you need to check on a network while you're at home, or when monitoring a network remotely for a client). The only proviso in doing this is to take into account this added network traffic when you're trying to monitor network performance-related properties. Second, don't forget that you can run multiple instances of Performance Monitor simultaneously. This is helpful in cases where you may want to combine the abilities of two or more modes—logging some events, triggering events on others, and visually monitoring still others. Third, once you get Performance Monitor configured in a helpful way, save that configuration. Over time you will accumulate a good collection of different views, and chances are that if they helped in one case, you (or others) may find them helpful again in the future.

Finally, additional categories of application-level monitoring properties can be added by applications that supply their own counters. Some server application examples of this are Microsoft's Exchange Server, IIS (Web Server), and SQL (Database) Server.

NOTE

Application-level monitoring properties show up as more categories of selectable monitor properties in Performance Monitor (for any applications that support this feature and are installed). These additional monitoring properties, however, are only visible in Performance Monitor when the application(s) that provide these properties are actually running.

Tools in NetWare

NetWare comes with some basic tools that can be used for diagnosing problems on your networks, and these should not be underestimated. Using MONITOR, FCONSOLE, or TCPCON, you can determine traffic flows for each of the LAN cards in your server, and you can monitor some common problems, such as packets that are outside the normal size or improperly formatted. The only problem with these tools is that they have no data-gathering or reporting features. The numbers are reset every time you bring the server up or down, and there is no easy way of printing the information.

There are a number of inexpensive programs, some created but not supported by Novell, that can provide you with the ability to save these statistics and format them nicely for printed reports. If you can't fit anything more into your budget, at least get one of these reporting programs. Most are available as shareware from NetWire. (See Appendix B for a listing of some of the programs available and their sources.)

LANalyzer for Windows

One software product that is highly recommended for anyone managing more than two small LANs is LANalyzer for Windows. This extremely capable package not only has the advantage of being a Novell product (designed to work well with NetWare), but it also includes almost all of the features listed above for hardware-based products, as well as the Network Advisor, a tool that is a highly useful product in itself. It can not only recommend actions for any problem you are likely to run across, it can explain the underlying principles of networking involved and teach you the specialized terminology and concepts you need to know to really understand your network.

Other Software Products

There are many other software-only products available, designed to support various combinations of software platforms and many different LAN adapters, and offering widely varying capabilities. Most of the features in the list for hardware-based products are available, with the possible exceptions of load simulation and TDR. There may even be software-only products with these features coming soon. Use the sources listed in Appendix A to determine what's available and what will suit your needs. Your fellow administrators will generally be happy to tell you about their experiences with products they've used (sometimes in greater detail than you want).

Managing without Diagnostic Equipment

All of the products described so far can make your life easier, greatly speed up the process of finding and resolving problems, and enable you to manage larger networks with fewer network administrators. However, it is very rare that a problem will be unsolvable without such equipment. If you have the problem now and don't have the equipment, you will simply need to follow the basic principles of troubleshooting: Identify the fault points, check them one at a time, and approach the problem systematically.

For example, if you have a problem with a network card that has gone bad, it may be *jabbering*, or sending out large numbers of bad packets. This may not only affect network performance in general, it may cause servers or workstations to freeze. In this case, something like LANalyzer for Windows could identify the problem in seconds. However, you could identify and isolate the problem without special tools by following a procedure like this:

- Check the LANs with NetMon (on NT) or MONITOR (on NetWare), looking for a large number of bad packets.

- Isolate each LAN until you find the one that is producing the faulty packets.

- Take workstations offline one at a time until you find the one that has the faulty NIC.

You might not be able to identify the NIC as the problem immediately, but you can isolate the problem to the workstation, which will then give you a limited number of fault points to check: the motherboard, the operating system, the LAN driver, the NIC, and the transceiver (if installed).

Services across WANs

WANs were originally conceived of as a way to share resources, such as files, printers, and modems, within a department. Providing these services to many users across multiple LANs is a growing concern as companies grow or replace mainframes with LANs (commonly known as *downsizing* or *rightsizing*). Setting up, maintaining, and troubleshooting a print queue can be complex on a single LAN with a few dozen users. Trying to give users on other servers or at other sites access to your printer can become an enormous headache. These issues have become enough of a concern that NetWare 4.*x* contains many new features specifically designed to address the needs of users across WANs. These services are known collectively as Novell Directory Services, or NDS, and are discussed a little later in this chapter.

Printing on WANs

Giving users outside your LAN access to your printer can be relatively simple. Just give the user Guest and/or the group Everyone access to the print queue. However, a user in another state who needs to print a document to your printer (saving considerable time over mailing the printout) will need to know the exact name of your server, how to attach to it, the exact name of the print queue and print job, if any, and (for DOS applications) how to set up CAPTURE to print to that queue. They may also need other information if the printer is specialized (Post-Script, a color printer, or the like).

Things can be further complicated if you need to restrict use of the printer and cannot grant Guest or Everyone access to the queue. In this case, you may need to create a special user with access to the queue.

If you must coordinate the details of WAN printing, the first step is to document your configuration, including the configuration of the printer, print server, and print queue. As we have said many times before, you cannot overdo documentation. In this case, it is especially true. If a user in another state is on the phone waiting for the information necessary to print to your printer, it will be much faster to open a binder and read the information off than to log in, run three or more different programs to obtain the configuration information, and try to present it in an orderly manner. If this is a frequent request, you might want to prepare instructions on how to accomplish the process, which would also be very useful as part of a manual for new users on your LAN.

Another thing that will make your life easier for NetWare printing is to take the time to set up print jobs and become familiar with the NetWare print utilities (PRINTCON, PCONSOLE, and CAPTURE). Use PRINTCON to define print jobs, rather than depending on long CAPTURE statements. It is much easier to explain (and document) CAPTURE J=LW than CAPTURE Q=PostScript F=1 NB NFF K. Similarly, you can set up a print job as the default job for the GUEST account, allowing anyone logging in as GUEST to print without further effort.

You can also set up queues on other servers that print to the print server on your LAN. If you have users on other servers who regularly send jobs to your printer, you may want to consider this. Keep in mind that this approach requires coordination between the supervisors of both servers, because you must be SUPERVISOR to create the queues, and SUPERVISOR on the other server to attach the queue to that server's print server.

Managing Multiple Logins

Some of your users may need to attach to more than one server. With NetWare 2.*x* and 3.*x*, you can log in to only one server at a time. If you need to connect to more servers, you must use ATTACH, which does not execute a login script. This means that users attaching to multiple servers must manually execute the additional commands to map drives, set up default print queues, and so on.

Fortunately, NetWare 4.*x* fixed these problems by having one login for the entire network. However, you can make life easier for users by putting a batch file in the login directory that will execute the appropriate MAP and CAPTURE statements.

Novell Directory Services and WANs

NetWare 4.0 is the first version of NetWare designed specifically with the needs of large company-wide WANs in mind. Its principal new feature is the *NDS (Novell Directory Services)* database, which is the equivalent of a network-wide bindery that encompasses all the servers on your network. You can organize your network by logical groups, since you are no longer confined by the physical structure of your system. Although NT does not yet have anything like NDS (although you can install NDS on it), NT 5.0 is rumored to be including this support with a new enterprise-wide network management directory structure.

The New Structure of NetWare 4.*x*

NDS uses a completely new paradigm for network structure. Instead of a group of servers, each with its own bindery containing information on the users, printers, volumes, and so on for that server only, there is a single distributed directory, with multiple copies replicated throughout the network, which contains information on all the resources, users, groups, and so on, on that network. Users, resources, and rights to those resources are managed on a network-wide basis, rather than by individual servers. Each user has one login, and can log in from any workstation on any LAN and have the same access to resources that the user would have on his or her own workstation.

The NDS Tree

A company-wide internetwork is organized in a tree-like structure, as illustrated in Figure 37.1. The root is the total directory that encompasses the entire company. It is divided into *containers*, which are logical units such as divisions, organizations, workgroups, and so on. Containers may contain other containers. Each container contains *leaf objects*, which are entities such as users, printers, print queues, volumes, etc. Leaf objects do not contain other objects. For example, you might be a user Admin, in a container Traps (Organizational Unit), in a container Explosives (Organizational Unit), in a container Engineering (Organization), in a company Acme (Root).

Every container and leaf in the database has properties, which hold the information about the object. These include, for example, login name, phone number, and address for a user object, or printer type, print queue, and Access Control List for a printer object. An Access Control List is associated with each object, and it lists which users have access to that object.

NDS Objects

Every part of the network, whether container or leaf, is an object. There are essentially three types of objects: the root object, container objects, and leaf objects. There can be only one root object in a tree structure.

FIGURE 37.1:

An example of a NetWare
4.*x* NDS tree

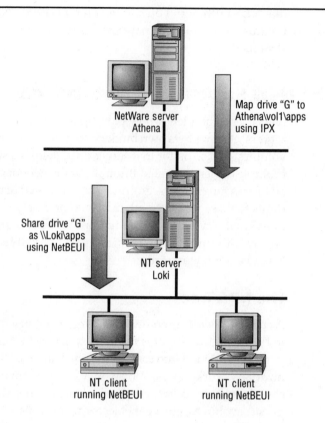

NetWare server
Athena

Map drive "G" to
Athena\vol1\apps
using IPX

Share drive "G"
as \\Loki\apps
using NetBEUI

NT server
Loki

NT client
running NetBEUI

NT client
running NetBEUI

WARNING If you have two organizations and you make each a separate tree with its own root, you can have great difficulty later merging the two trees into one. NetWare 4.1 provides a tool for merging trees, but you may find that usernames or other items are duplicated, and you will need to rename resources. It is also painful to change the names of existing Organization (container) objects. For these reasons, you should consider very carefully both your existing organization and possible growth or changes in structure before planning your network. Before planning a NetWare 4.*x* network, read the April 1993 issue of Novell's *AppNotes* publication (you can read it online at `developer.novell.-com/research/appnotes.htm`), Novell's Quick-Path to NetWare 4.1 Networks, or the NDS booklet provided with each copy of Net-Ware 4.1.

There are two types of container objects you will usually see: Organization and Organizational Unit (OU). Each allows you to set defaults for a user, and to set up a login script for every user in that container. Each user can have only one container login script. Thus, you can give every member of a department access to the same resources, whether they are attached to the same server or located in different states.

There are many different leaf objects, organized into user-related objects, server-related objects, printer-related objects, informational objects, and miscellaneous objects. *User-related objects* include users, groups, organizational roles, and profiles. An organizational role is a set of rights that can be assigned to different users. For instance, if the manager of a group changes, you would disassociate the former manager as a user from the Manager organizational role object and associate the new manager with that object. A profile is a type of login script that can be associated with a group of users who may not all be in the same Organizational Unit. Login scripts are executed in the following order: container login script (associated with the Organization or Organizational Unit), profile, and then user login script.

Server-related objects include servers, volumes, and directory maps. Servers and volumes are what you would expect. Directory maps can be thought of as aliases for a directory. If you map a search drive to a directory in your user's login scripts, and then later change the name of the directory, you will then need to change each login script. With a directory map, you can map the search drive to the directory map in the login scripts. Then if the name of the directory changes, you can modify the directory map and leave the login scripts as they are.

Printer-related objects include print queues, print servers, and printers. These are handled in the same manner as with previous versions of NetWare, but can be managed through the NDS system as well. Informational objects include AFP servers and computers. AFP servers are separate objects holding information on servers running the AppleTalk Filing Protocol. These may include NetWare servers represented by server objects. They will need a separate AFP server object to describe their AFP-related information. Computer objects store information about the computers on your network. They are not required, but are an easy way to store, maintain, and access the information you should have about the workstations on your network.

Miscellaneous objects include aliases, bindery objects, bindery queues, and unknown objects. Aliases are pointers to other objects in the NDS. They make it appear as if the object referred to is located where the alias is stored. Aliases are a simple way to give users in one container access to resources in another container. Bindery objects and bindery queues are used to provide backward-compatibility with previous versions of NetWare. They represent resources that are to be made available to users with previous versions of NetWare. Unknown objects are objects that cannot be classified as a known type of object.

NWADMIN: The New Management Tool

The most welcome addition to the management tools provided with NetWare in version 4.*x* is NWADMIN. This is a graphical user interface utility that runs under Windows.

NWADMIN can show you the entire network (if you have the rights to view the whole network) and allow you to inspect, modify, create, or delete objects on any part of the network (if you have those rights). It allows you to perform tasks that previously required switching between a half-dozen different programs, such as SYSCON, FILER, PCONSOLE, PRINTCON, and PRINTDEF.

Troubleshooting NDS

NetWare 4.*x* can be harder to troubleshoot than older versions of NetWare, simply because it allows a more complex structure to be built. Some things to watch for:

- Make your directory structure as flat as possible. Try not to have more than three levels of organization—four at most.

- Don't have too many copies of the directory. The directory is updated regularly, and every copy is also updated. If there are too many copies, your network traffic may become unmanageable.

- Remember to think globally. Don't have more than one account per user. Similarly, login scripts from multiple accounts on prior versions of NetWare must be consolidated. Be sure that you resolve any potential conflicts in the new scripts.

- You may find that you will have different Everyone groups and Guest accounts in different partitions. This can happen if you use the server upgrade system to upgrade to NetWare 4.*x*. Each server has a different membership for Everyone, and this forces the creation of a new group.

- The biggest problem for users with NDS will be in understanding the new structure, especially contexts. Make certain you understand the contexts on your network completely. We recommend setting the user's context at login to their usual work area. This will allow them to type:

  ```
  login username
  ```

  instead of:

  ```
  login .cn=username.ou=widgets.o=marketing
  ```

In general, the differences between NetWare 4.*x* and NetWare 3.*x* are in the organizational structures allowed rather than in the underlying protocols used. Making the switch to NDS (or to NT 5's upcoming enterprise directory services) significantly reduces the complexity involved in administering and accessing a large network's many shared resources, yet it permits the building of even larger networks, which can add to the overall complexity and increase the number of LAN or WAN fault points.

The crucial strategy is to treat each subnetwork, as well as the WAN links themselves, as separate fault points, each of which needs to be eliminated independently from your list of suspects when troubleshooting the cause of a WAN problem.

Summary

In this chapter, we began by reviewing how networks are interconnected to form MANs (metropolitan area networks) as well as WANs, and the ways this adds to what can go wrong as well as increases the complexity of determining where a problem lies. We looked at network management and diagnostic tools that are available and discussed network services that are made available across WAN connections. We ended with a discussion of Novell Directory Services (NDS), and listed a number of things to do to help reduce the chance of problems occurring when using NDS.

In the following chapter, we'll look at ways to prevent network-related problems from occurring in the first place. When it comes to dealing with network problems, a good defense (prevention) is at least as important as a good offense (troubleshooting).

CHAPTER

THIRTY-EIGHT

38

A Pound of Prevention

- Backup systems

- Protection against power failures

- Equipment quality

- Preventive maintenance and other precautions

- Fault tolerance

- Network plans and logs

- User training

- Virus protection

- Security measures

- Disaster recovery—in advance

As administrator of even a small network, you can spend most of your time putting out fires—reacting to problems rather than planning for them. Prevention is a difficult area for most administrators. The time and expense involved are difficult to justify, because if you do it correctly, the problems you prevent will never show up; and it can be hard to convince your supervisors to spend money on something that might never occur.

Some preventive measures are becoming easier to justify. For example, when PC-based networks first began cropping up, backup systems were not always included as a matter of course. Now, it would (or at least should) be highly unusual to see more than three or four PCs networked without some type of backup system in place. UPSs (uninterruptible power supplies) are becoming equally common, at least on servers.

Other types of prevention and preventive maintenance will be more difficult to justify. One plan of attack is to begin small and document the results. The difference between a network with no downtime during business hours in the course of a year and one in which several failures interrupt business for hours or even days is not hard to quantify. If you can improve your uptime by some quantifiable amount, and show where other preventive measures would have reduced or eliminated downtime, you will have less trouble justifying future requests.

Another area to look at is tracking the growth of your LAN, and planning for the future. It may seem that the new high-powered server you just installed should last for a good while, but suppose the department has also grown by 20 workstations, and that the average load per workstation has increased by a factor of four as users begin to be accustomed to their new PCs. Tracking this sort of growth will enable you to justify and install upgrades or additional equipment as necessary to meet the growing needs of your users.

Finally, you should plan for problems beyond the scope of a disk drive crash or lost files disasters. If you don't plan for disaster, and it occurs, it isn't just a question of interruption of business.

NOTE   A recent study showed that of all the businesses whose networks were struck by disasters such as floods, thefts, lightning, earthquakes, or viruses wiping out their data, most of those that had disaster-recovery plans are still in business. Important: More than 90 percent of those who didn't have plans were *out of business* within two years.

Managing Backup Systems

Every network that does more than allow printer sharing should have a backup system. You *will* need backups. Eventually, any LAN administrator who doesn't have a verified backup plan working will regret it. Even mirroring disks is not a substitute for a good backup procedure.

Backups are not only for restoring a drive that breaks. You'll find that users will occasionally delete files that are still needed. If a server's drive is close to full, the NetWare Salvage utility, or similar utilities from other vendors, may not be able to recover a deleted file, depending on how long it's been since the file was deleted.

Every server, no matter how small it is or how little data it stores, should be backed up. Backup drives are available in a price range from a few hundred dollars to many thousands. Even a server being used solely as a print server, with little or no data on it, should be backed up. For one thing, there are probably mail directories on the server that users would be very unhappy about losing; and for another, restoring from an inexpensive 2GB tape is a lot faster than reinstalling NT, Mac OS, Unix, or NetWare from scratch.

If you don't have backups of your server, you will wish you had. Eventually, you *will* need a backup, either to restore the server after a disaster, or to recover files that a user has inadvertently deleted. Fast, reliable, and convenient backups are available in capacities from 20MB to 10GB and more, and in price ranges from a few hundred dollars to many thousands. There is no excuse for not having backups. The cost is much less than the cost of reconstructing the data on even a small hard disk.

WARNING   Back up your server. Back up your server. *Back up your server*. This can't be stressed enough. There is nothing more important to surviving a disaster than having backups. And once you have made backups, *test them*.

Be sure of the integrity of your backups. Many backup programs do not adequately warn you if a backup didn't completely finish, or if there were bad blocks on your tape. At a minimum, you should back up your entire system and then restore at least some of the files to test the backup when you install the server and backup device, and also whenever you make major changes in the server, such as upgrades. Depending on the nature of the data on your server, you may need to do full backups every night, or incremental backups may fill your needs.

Thanks to the growing awareness that backups are not a luxury but a necessity, there are numerous backup systems available from many manufacturers. There are several varieties, most of which are tape-based, including several cassette formats, 8mm and 4mm (DAT), and even systems that use video cassettes (uncommon because of its failure rate). Usually only a few companies make the actual mechanisms, which are then packaged with different software and sold under brand names. The software is a major part of the difference between different brands, and much more important than a slight difference in speed or transfer rate.

Evaluating Backup Systems

The PC and LAN magazines probably publish half a dozen backup-unit evaluations a year. Read the latest articles to gain an idea of what's available. You will usually also learn which units to avoid, and why, and which variety of tape is currently considered the best.

NOTE With prices on CDRW (CD-ROM Read/Writable) systems plummeting, CD-ROM is fast becoming an interesting alternative for backing up smaller (650 megs or less) partitions. A similar point can be made about less ubiquitous but still common alternative technologies such as Syquest Sparq and Iomega Jaz removable drives. Look for DVD-ROM, with its far greater capacity, to become a very attractive backup medium once writable drives and media become widely available.

When evaluating a backup system, there are a number of factors to consider:

- Capacity
- Speed
- Software
- Cost of the media
- Cost of the unit
- Reliability of the drive

- Operating systems supported

- Support from the manufacturer

- NDS backups (for NetWare 4.*x*)

- Support for other file systems

These factors are described in the following sections.

Backup System Capacity

What is the capacity of the tape drive? It should be enough to support your current configuration, and at least double your current disk drive capacity. Don't buy a 4GB tape system if you have a 4GB hard drive—in a year you will probably have 8GB of hard disk space. Besides, the difference in price between a 4GB tape drive and an 8GB (or larger) tape drive is relatively small.

If your backup capacity is limited, back up data first, applications second. Applications, and the network server software which can be reinstalled and usually doesn't change after installation, can be backed up once in a while, when new versions are installed. Data, on the other hand, should be backed up regularly—nightly if possible. If backup capacity is an issue, nightly incremental backups of data are better than weekly full backups.

Backup System Speed

Speed is an issue, not because you will be sitting and watching the backup (the software should allow *unattended* backups), but because you need to schedule the backup for a time of day when nobody will be using the network, and that time may be limited.

If you designate 2:00 A.M. to 6:00 A.M. as the time when no one will be using the system, your tape drive should be able to back up your system in less than four hours. You can estimate this by dividing the number of megabytes on the server by the rated speed of the tape drive (for example, 500MB divided by 10MB per minute equals 50 minutes).

Backup Software

The most important thing to evaluate in choosing a tape drive is the software provided with it. This may range from no software at all to a versatile suite of programs that will not only do your backups at 2:00 AM for you, but verify the tape and inform you of any errors.

This software may seem expensive, and it can cost considerably more than the tape drive. Some versions cost more depending on how many clients your server software supports. But keep in mind that if the software provides consistent, reliable backups and works with everything on your network, it's worth the expense—how much is your data worth?

Cost of the Backup Media

If you use 20 tapes for your incremental backups and two tapes a month for full backups that are then stored off site, you will use about 50 tapes a year. In two years, this expense could be more than the cost of the drive.

NOTE   The cost of the media your backup system uses will be more important in the long run than the cost of the drive.

In some cases, lower-cost alternatives exist. For example, in an 8mm tape drive, you can use 8mm video tape instead of data-certified tapes, reducing your costs by about half. However, unless your software verifies the backup every time it is made, and is capable of bypassing a bad block on the tape, you may get backups that can't be restored from, and you may not know this until you need to restore that backup. The few hundred dollars a year you save aren't worth it if you can't restore from the tapes.

Cost of the Backup Unit

Tape backup units range in price from a couple of hundred dollars for a 2GB unit to thousands of dollars for a unit that will do a month's worth of unattended backups on a multi-gigabyte system. Within any standard (such as 4mm DAT), the mechanisms are often similar or the same. What you'll pay for is the software and support. Determine what capacity you need, double it, and then buy the best software you can afford.

NOTE   Remember, your server's disk contains hundreds or thousands of hours of work, at many dollars an hour. Don't skimp on the backup system.

Backup System Reliability

It does no good to have an extensive backup system in place, and then discover that the tape drive has failed or that the software didn't inform you that the backup tapes had bad blocks and your backups can't be used. Read the magazines for impressions of the internal mechanisms and the various companies that package them. Before you buy a unit, you might also want to ask about it on CompuServe, the news group on the Internet, or at your local CNEPA chapter or NT or Novell user group meeting.

Make sure to test whatever backup system you have in place. After the hard disk has disintegrated is no time to discover that those backup tapes you've been making for the last year can only produce an "Error reading from tape" message.

Backup System Support

Support for your backup system can be difficult to evaluate in advance, except by learning what experiences others have had with the company. Ask the company for names of users in your area. Read the reviews to see if the reviewers tried to access the tech support or had hardware or setup problems.

NOTE   You might also try placing a test call to the backup system manufacturer's support line to see how easy or difficult it may be to get help when you actually need it, and to get first-hand experience in the support process for the device.

NDS Backups

If you are running NetWare 4.*x*, your backup software should be able to back up and restore the Novell Directory Services database. This can be critical, because if your Directory database is corrupted, not merely the one server, but all services on your entire network could be inaccessible.

Backups for Other File Systems

If you have clients other than DOS/Windows 3.*x* (and who doesn't?), you will need to consider the backup software's support for other *name spaces*. This includes Windows 95/98, OS/2, Macintosh, and NFS (Unix) systems, which support longer file names and therefore have different file allocation table and permission structures than DOS. For example, although NetWare supports the name spaces on the server's hard disks, if the backup software doesn't support them, when you restore files, you'll get file names truncated to the DOS "eight-dot-three" format.

Developing a Backup Plan

Your backup strategy will depend on your users' needs. There are many possible strategies, ranging from a full backup of all files daily to an incremental backup that only adds files that have changed since the last backup. Each strategy has advantages and disadvantages. A daily full backup provides the maximum possible level of recoverability, but uses a very large number of tapes; the incremental systems use fewer tapes, but take more effort to recover complete file systems.

If you don't want to do a full backup nightly, we recommend that you do an incremental backup nightly, and a full backup either weekly or monthly. The full backups should be stored in a secure area either on or off site, for at least a year. This gives you insurance against accidentally deleted files that aren't noticed for a while, as well as against a virus infecting your recent backups.

NOTE   If you are using incremental backups, be sure that you know the order in which the tapes were made.

You will usually restore first from the last full backup, and then from each incremental tape. If you get one of the incremental tapes out of order, you can overwrite recent files with older versions. Label the tapes clearly, both on the case and the tape cartridge itself. It is a very good idea to have your backup schedule documented and posted. This can ease the headache if a problem occurs when you are off site. Do you want to fly back a week early from your first vacation in two years to restore some data? Print a schedule that shows the rotation of the numbered incremental tapes, and what dates they will be used.

You may also wish to use an off-site storage service for some or all of your backups. This is a typical part of most disaster-recovery plans. It allows a business to restore working files to new servers after fire, earthquake, theft, or other disasters that could affect any backups stored near the original server.

Backing Up Workstation Data

We strongly recommend that you confine the data on workstations to the operating system and applications. Instruct your users to store their data on the file server. This will ensure that the data is included in the regularly scheduled backups. In almost every case, if the application is on the local drive and the data is on the server, users will not notice any degradation in performance.

Unfortunately, with most operating systems, there is no way to prevent the user from storing data on the local hard drive (Unix is a notable exception). The only way to deal with this problem is education and periodic reminders. (Well, diskless workstations are also a possibility!)

NOTE   There is a third-party product available, AtEase for Workgroups, (for Apple users only, unfortunately) which offers the ability to restrict disk access privileges even for local drives–including floppies and CD-ROMs. Windows 9x stations can be configured to restrict access to the control panel, Registry settings, and even lock desktop icons in place, but users are not prevented from accessing (and therefore possibly damaging) the files on their local drive.

If your users absolutely must store data on their workstations, you might want to install a backup tape device in each workstation, and automatically back up each machine every night. Low-capacity tape backup drives are very inexpensive (often less than $150).

There are several other solutions to the problem of backing up workstations. You can create a backup volume on a server, and create batch files or scripts that log in and copy everything on a workstation hard drive to that area temporarily. In this rotating system, each day's backup can be deleted from the server after the volume has been backed up to tape, to make room for the next workstation backup. For example, if you have 20 users on your network, each with a hard disk of 400MB, this system would back up every workstation once every 20 days and use 400MB of disk space on the server.

Another approach is to get a small portable tape drive that attaches to a workstation's parallel port (or a Mac's SCSI or serial port). You can then back up each workstation in rotation with this device. If, as suggested, the workstation has only the operating system and applications, this sort of backup will be necessary only when a system is first configured, and then when significant changes have been made, such as the installation or upgrading of applications or the operating system.

There is also software available that allows workstations to back up to a networked tape drive. This system uses a TSR program or script that runs on each workstation and sends the files to be backed up to a network backup server. This is a fairly inexpensive way to back up workstations, but there are a couple of caveats: all workstations must be left on, and you need to buy and set up a network backup server. Also, if you back up all the data on each workstation, it can take quite a long time. If you back up only specified directories, anything the user puts anywhere else won't be backed up. Some software will let you back up everything except specified directories.

> **NOTE**   If a client-side backup solution interests you, then by all means check out Picture Taker (from Lanovation) and Ghost (from Binary Research International). Ghost lets you backup and restore entire client hard drives across a network (even with no OS already installed on the client). Picture Taker offers the ability to take incremental snapshots (or "pictures") of a system, thereby allowing you to rollback to any previous snapshot, as well as add any existing snapshot to another similar client station (which can tremendously simplify installation of several software packages simultaneously for instance).

Managing Power Protection

Given the number of problems that can follow power loss or fluctuation, a good UPS, SPS (standby power supply), or at least a surge protector is a very cheap investment. It doesn't take a lightning storm to damage computer equipment; the spikes caused by some appliances being turned on or off, static discharges from a variety of sources (including users), and older power company equipment may cause enough variation in power to damage systems.

Evaluating Power Protection Systems

There are several levels of protection against faulty power. The first level is a *surge protector*, which will screen out harmful over-voltages, surges, and spikes. It will not protect your system if the power goes off. The second level of protection is an SPS. It switches to a battery-powered power supply if it detects problems with your power. It will provide protection against brown-outs and power outages. The third level of protection is a UPS. This type of protection is the ultimate—your computer is always powered by the battery-powered power supply, which is constantly being recharged by your normal AC power. This means that there is no direct connection between your power line and the computer. There is also no switchover time as with an SPS.

There are several items to check before buying power protection:

- Look at the manufacturer's warranty. Some manufacturers will replace any equipment damaged by power variations while connected to their system.

- Check carefully whether a battery-powered unit is an SPS or a true UPS. UPSs tend to be a little more expensive, although both types are much less expensive than they were a few years ago.

- See if the power supplied from the battery is true sine wave. Some units simulate sine wave power, which can provide slightly different results that very sensitive equipment might not like.

TIP   Both the simulated sine wave power supplies and SPS devices have come a long way in the last few years. It is now difficult to say that a UPS is distinctly better than an SPS, or that true sine wave is better than simulated. However, with prices on even the best units dropping as they are, UPSes, true sine wave power supplies, and the premium surge protection systems are the best bets. See the latest reviews in your favorite PC and LAN magazines or on the Internet.

Another issue for the server is the UPS interface. Most UPS and SPS devices provide a serial connection or a card for the server that will allow the server to detect a power outage and shut down properly if necessary before the battery power runs down. This prevents disk corruption that would be caused by powering off the server without taking it down first. This type of interface is highly recommended for server UPS systems.

A reasonable balance of protection and cost is to put a surge protector on every computer and a UPS on each server. Modems and fax machines should also be protected. Phone lines can also transmit potentially harmful variations in current, and surge protectors with phone line filtering capability are available. If cost is not a large factor, or if some workstations are mission-critical, consider using UPSs on workstations as well.

Evaluating System Power Requirements

Evaluating the power requirements of your computer system is fairly simple. Look on the power supply of each unit that will be attached (system unit, monitor, external disk drive, and so on). Each power supply should have a rated capacity in amps. Usual figures are in the neighborhood of 5 to 7 amps for the CPU, 1.5 to 2 for small monitors, 5 to 10 for large monitors, 2 for external hard disks, and the like. Whatever the amps capacity, multiply that number by the voltage of your system (110 in the US, 220 or 240 most other places). For example, if the total needed is 10 amps, multiply that by 110 (in the U.S.). The total figure, 1100, is the maximum number of volt-amps (VA) your system can use.

For a workstation with a small (14-inch) monitor, a 400 VA power supply will probably provide 10 to 20 minutes of backup. For a workstation with a large monitor, you might need 600 to 800 VA. A server with a couple of external hard drive subsystems should probably have 800 to 1200 VA for a reasonably long duration if the power goes off.

NOTE   You may wish to put only the computer and drives onto the UPS, connecting the monitor and other external peripherals instead to normal AC, to increase the backup time provided by the UPS system. There is one benefit, though, to connecting these other peripherals to the UPS: The power is conditioned at a steadier and more consistent rate and therefore is gentler on all connected electronic equipment. Surges and sudden drops in current can sometimes cause serious damage, and a UPS helps address this concern as well. Just remember to take into account all such devices when calculating the necessary power rating of your UPS.

The Quality of Your Equipment

The difference in price between an inexpensive PC clone server and a high-performance, brand-name server can be double or more. However, eight hours of downtime for a department of 20 users can cause a loss of far more money than what you saved on a lower-cost server—not counting the possibility of deadlines missed, extra costs to rush jobs through, overtime, repairs to the downed equipment, and so on.

This is not to say that even the most expensive equipment will not break down occasionally, but it should be less likely to do so. The service providers should be more responsive as well, and it's easier to find replacement parts for brand-name equipment. But keep in mind that some major brands tend to use proprietary parts, which can mean that replacements can be obtained only from the original vendor, at rather high prices.

Many computer manufacturers and retailers are sensitive to the special requirements of servers. In addition to bigger PCs with extra-high-speed interfaces and more drive slots, they may offer added features to make their equipment more reliable and service programs that guarantee repair or replacement of defective parts within a matter of hours. The added features may include redundant power supplies or special bus slots that allow swapping cards in and out with the PC still running.

Again, even the most expensive, best-rated equipment can break down. In the case of mission-critical equipment, it's not a bad idea to have a replacement machine, fully configured, ready to replace an existing machine if necessary. The investment can readily be recouped by avoiding the delay necessary to buy new equipment if the existing setup goes down, especially in cases where equipment orders must be processed by another part of the company, such as a purchasing department. In a large WAN, having a standard server configuration can make it much easier to provide parts, and of course will also make it easier for the corporate MIS department to support the platform.

Fault tolerance systems provide another way to protect your server, as discussed later in this chapter.

Preventive Maintenance and Other Precautions

Regular maintenance is often omitted, either because it isn't seen as a high enough priority to justify the time spent or simply because it can be a chore. However, preventive maintenance can save the administrator considerable trouble. It is much easier to fix something before it becomes a problem than to wait until it interferes with a user's work, requires the administrator's time for emergency repairs, and costs money to replace parts that might have lasted much longer with good maintenance.

Getting Rid of Dust and Other Contaminants

It is impossible to prevent dust from getting into equipment, and too much dust can have unfortunate consequences. To minimize dust, make sure that slot covers are replaced if cards are removed from a PC, and that the case is completely closed. This can also prevent bugs in the machinery—literally! Insects of many types and even mice have been known to take up lodgings inside computers, often with very strange results. In commercial settings, the normal dust can have a fairly high metallic content, and too thick an accumulation can cause electrical shorts. It can also interfere with ventilation, causing overheating and shortening the life of equipment as well as causing failures. Regular vacuuming and adequate ventilation can extend the life of equipment.

Keyboards are also susceptible to dust and many other forms of contamination, from food to eraser shavings. Again, regular vacuuming is a simple way to prevent failures. Keeping monitor screens clean may not increase the life of the monitor, but it will definitely reduce eyestrain among users. The static charge that normally builds up on most monitors collects dust and other airborne particles like a magnet. Mouse devices will also last longer and function better if they are cleaned regularly.

Checking Connections

There are no perfect connections. It is a good idea to schedule some time every six months or so to check all the computers on a LAN for loose connections. Take a look at the power cords, the monitor, network, serial, and parallel cables, and the cards.

A power cord that is loose in the power supply receptacle can cause arcing, which cannot only cause the eventual failure of the power supply, but can generate interference with the electronics in the PC. Likewise, a network connection that is not fully seated may not simply fail, but instead produce intermittent problems that are difficult to trace. Make sure that all fasteners are screwed down snugly and that everything is seated properly. At the very least, check all the connections whenever you have occasion to work on a PC.

Taking Anti-Static Precautions

Believe it or not, simply walking across a carpeted room can build up a 50,000 volt charge in your body. Discharging this voltage into electronic equipment designed to deal with a maximum of 12 volts can instantly destroy it. Newer electronics, with their tighter tolerances and lower power requirements, are even more susceptible to static than older equipment. An anti-static mat and a professional-quality grounding strap are quite inexpensive (often around $12–30)—some hardware maintenance courses include a set as part of the cost of the course. In any case, the investment is much less than almost any circuit board.

Not following anti-static precautions may not result in dead equipment but can still incur high costs. Static can cause cumulative, nonfatal damage that has the effect of drastically shortening the life of electronics.

WARNING You can "kill" electronic parts just by holding them in your hand and walking across a carpet floor. Be sure that the parts are protected in an anti-static bag, or that you are grounded before touching them.

When working on a PC, you should always have a grounding strap attached to a good ground before you open the PC. That said, however, you can ensure generally adequate protection of the PC's components by leaving it plugged in and touching the power supply or frame before handling any components. This field expedient is much better than nothing. Of course, working inside a system that is still plugged in presents another type of danger—electrical shock, so only do this if you really know what you're doing. We've received several shocks from systems that were turned off, and even unplugged, but still had charges stored in the capacitors on the motherboard. To *really* be safe, you should unplug a system and give it some time to drain out these charges (30 minutes should be sufficient).

If you remove parts from a PC, you should always transport them in a static-safe bag. Just walking across a room holding a PC board could damage the board. Be sure the bag is an anti-static bag (the silvery mylar type) rather than a plain plastic bag—some plastic bags can generate enough static to damage the cards by themselves. Save the anti-static bags that most cards come in and reuse them when you need to transport parts.

Following Manufacturer's Directions

Another type of precaution you should take is to follow the manufacturer's directions when dealing with hardware or software. For example, most programs should be exited before the workstation is turned off. This is also true of most operating systems these days—Windows 95/98, NT Workstation, OS/2, the Mac OS, most varieties of Unix, Windows NT, and of course NetWare should all be shut down before powering off the system.

Make sure that an SVGA monitor and the graphics card it's attached to both support the same resolutions; you can damage a monitor by trying to run it at too high a refresh rate or resolution.

If you're dealing with a Macintosh, it is recommended that you wait five minutes after it has been turned off before removing or adding cards.

Maintaining a Return Path

Under Windows 95, export the Registry to a text file. If the Registry and its backup copy both become corrupted (an unfortunately common occurrence), you can import the text file back into the Registry and reboot. Use the Registry Editor (REGEDIT.EXE) to export the Registry. Be sure to export the *entire* Registry, not just one branch.

NOTE Another precaution that takes a little extra trouble, but can make the administrator's life much easier, is to provide a simple return path to the old version of anything being changed or upgraded. Rename AUTOEXEC.BAT files to AUTOEXEC.OLD, and save old versions of applications, drivers, and so on.

TIP In addition to backing up the Registry as a text file, you may also want to back up the actual Registry files themselves. Look for two hidden files in the \WINDOWS\SYSTEM directory called USER.DAT and SYSTEM.DAT. Copy both of these to a different backup directory before making major changes to hardware or software that may affect the Registry. You may also want to back up the pair of files with similar names but having .DA0 extensions—these are actually a set of backup files containing a copy one generation prior to the current .DAT files. Having these Registry files backed up gives you added insurance in the event the Registry gets so hosed that the system fails to start. In order to copy or replace these files, use the ATTRIB command with the -r, -s, and -h parameters, to remove read-only, system, and hidden file attributes, respectively.

It's much easier to make sure that you have a good copy of a setup that works than to try to re-create a configuration from memory or track down and reload an application, its updates, new version of printer drivers, and the like, all of which may be in different locations.

Similarly, when upgrading hardware, don't rush to throw the old equipment out. For example, if a new video card fails, it's much better to be able to get a workstation running again with a monochrome monitor and have at least partial functionality than to have to first rush out and buy another VGA card or, worse, to wait for the purchasing department to buy one and forward it to you.

TIP   One final tip: When installing your server software, consider running the install a second time to an external SCSI (or removable) drive. In the event of a catastrophic boot disk failure, this strategy allows you to swap in a new boot drive quickly and get the network operational again. Keep in mind this approach involves an entirely different install, however, so information such as user accounts would need to be added to this backup system prior to use.

Maintaining Fault Tolerance

In the old days of mainframes and terminals, everything had a backup. There was a generator that took over if power failed, and most parts that might fail in the mainframe had a backup part that took over without interrupting service. As PC networks have begun to be used for the same sorts of things that mainframes were used for—namely, applications in which a few hours without service could literally ruin a company—manufacturers have begun to provide the same sorts of redundancy and fault tolerance. Novell has led the way in providing *SFT* (*System Fault Tolerance*) as a part of NetWare. Chapter 33, which covers troubleshooting servers, describes in detail the SFT levels and how they work. Here is a brief review of SFT functions and their benefits.

The first level of SFT provides protection from disk drive failure in several ways. First, it performs read-after-write verification. Data written to disk is read immediately and compared with the data still in memory. If there is a difference, the block on the disk that was written to is marked as bad. The Hot Fix Redirection area is that part of the disk that is used to provide substitute blocks for any blocks on the disk that fail. If your Hot Fix Redirection area starts getting full, it is a sign that the disk is failing.

Next, SFT allows duplexed and mirrored drives. With both techniques, each logical drive is actually two physical drives—data written to a drive is actually written to two different mirrored drives. This has two benefits: It is a highly effective precaution against drive failure, and it effectively reduces the access time of any physical drive by 50 percent. Technically, the difference between these methods is that a mirrored drive may have two drives connected to the same controller and power supply; a duplexed drive has separate power supplies and controllers, so that no one failure will result in a loss of data or of access to data.

Mirroring doubles the cost of data storage, but in mission-critical areas, it can prevent a much more costly loss of time, productivity, and data. If a drive fails in a mirrored system, the users won't even notice. The administrator is notified and can replace the defective drive when it won't disrupt the network.

The next level, SFT III, provides complete protection against any failure of any component in a server—the whole server is duplicated. All functions of the main server are duplicated on the mirror server. If anything happens to the first server, the second server takes over and service is not interrupted. The servers can even monitor each other for hardware problems and take over if a fault is causing a slowdown in networking capability.

The cost involved will be double that of a single server, but in mission-critical circumstances, this technique will ensure that no single equipment failure can bring down the network. Moreover, because the two servers don't need to be right next to each other, it can also provide insurance against theft, fire, or other catastrophes that can destroy all networking capability.

In addition to the SFT III package offered by Novell, another option at the drive level which is certainly worth considering is RAID 5. Unlike lesser RAID levels 1 to 4, RAID level 5 combines redundancy with increased reading speed because data is stored across three or more drives (and with the right hardware, hardware reads from each drive can occur simultaneously). RAID 5 is available as a hardware solution (more expensive), but Windows NT offers software RAID 5 support built-in (available if you have three or more partitions).

Microsoft's Wolfpack (clustering) technology may be available by the time you are reading this, and it promises to add automatic fail-over protection as does SFT III by using a number of interconnected NT servers. There are also other alternatives offered by other vendors. These may offer advantages such as not requiring the high-performance (expensive) connections between servers that SFT III requires, or not requiring that backup servers be identically configured. As with other network components, your best sources of information about the other fault-tolerance system products are magazine reviews, online sources, and user groups. See Appendix A for more information about such resources.

Keeping Network Plans and Logs

Keep a record of existing configurations. This not only makes it easier to plan upgrades and determine possible causes without opening PCs, it provides a place to return to if an upgrade or new configuration doesn't work. If you include serial numbers in your log, it will make dealing with most technical support departments much easier. Instead of needing to trot down the aisle, open a PC, and pull a card to get the serial number, you will have it on record, easily accessible when calling tech support.

Documenting the Network

The level of documentation that you have for your network will *directly* affect the time it takes to recover from a disaster. Ideally, you should document all of the following:

- Each server and workstation's hardware configuration. This includes processor, memory, floppy and hard disk types, installed cards and their settings, and any other hardware additions.

- The software configuration of each workstation. This includes the operating system version; printouts and/or backup copies of configuration files such as AUTOEXEC.BAT, CONFIG.SYS, SHELL.CFG, WIN.INI, and SYSTEM.INI; Windows 95/98 System Registries; a printout of the directory structure; a list of applications, including version and license number (if applicable); and any other specialized software such as device drivers.

- The software configuration for the server. You do have printouts of your AUTOEXEC.NCF and STARTUP.NCF files, don't you? How long would it take you to re-create them if they were lost? Even if you have good backups, you may wish you had a map of the directory structure on all volumes of your server and copies of NET$OS.EXE or SERVER.EXE, the other .DSK and .LAN drivers necessary to boot the server, and any other configuration files or drivers stored in the DOS partition of the boot drive.

- Maps of the physical and the logical structure of your LAN. The physical map will help you with problems in the cabling plant, and the logical map will help you to conceptually isolate the fault points involved in any particular problem.

- The backup plan. What tapes are used in what rotation? How often are full backups made, and where are they stored? Remember, your assistant might be the one guessing which tape to restore from.

- Procedures to follow in case you aren't there. What do the users do if a print server hangs the day after you leave for a two-week training seminar? (You may also need a quick reminder yourself if it's something you haven't dealt with for a while.)

TIP   After backups, the next most important thing you can do to survive a disaster is to document everything, and keep a copy of the documentation and backups off site.

All this information can be collected manually, and should be, if there's no other alternative. However, there are programs that will do all the data collection for you, nicely format the reports, and update the information automatically each time a workstation is logged on to the network. See Appendix B for information about some of the products available.

Using a network analyzer or a statistics program such as `FConsole` or `Monitor` to get an idea of normal traffic on your network will make it much easier to isolate problems caused by abnormal traffic. See Chapter 25 for information about baselining your network.

Logging Network Events

Keeping a log or diary of changes to the LAN, as well as problems that have come up and the solutions, will also save you a good deal of time. Re-creating a solution that took 20 hours of work to discover the first time doesn't make sense, especially when a few minutes spent logging the problem and solution can prevent the necessity.

A log can also be useful in other ways. It can allow you to establish trends with problem equipment, situations, or users. It is much easier to justify a more reliable (and more expensive) server if you have documented how many times the current model has failed in the last year. A log can also provide documentation of how you spend your time. Many managers want regular status reports; a well-kept log can provide the basis for your reports, or may even be copied and pasted into a template status report. Even if a regular status report is not required, a log can make justifying a promotion or getting additional personnel much easier.

Training the Users

Much of your time as an administrator will probably be used to support users. Most of the problems your users have will not be related to hardware or software failure, but to failures in understanding. From the apocryphal user who can't find the "Any" key ("Press any key to continue") to the one whose document won't print because there's no paper in the printer, these people have problems that they could probably solve themselves with a bit of encouragement and a little training.

There are several methods you can use to train your users and to encourage them to acquire training on their own, without being perceived as unresponsive or condescending. For example, try to put a little time between a user's request for help and your response. Don't delay, obviously, just finish what you're working on first. Not only does this improve your chances of completing your regular tasks, but it increases the chances that your help won't be needed; users left to themselves for a while will sometimes be able to solve the problem on their own. If your users get accustomed to your leading them by the hand through every unfamiliar process (and some familiar ones), they will always expect this of you. As a result, you will spend more and more time on these tasks instead of administering your network, let alone planning for the coming requirements for your organization.

Without making users feel stupid, you can also encourage them to read the manual or help system. Rather than jumping up from the dead PC you're working on and showing someone how to print from within his application, tell him you can't get away right now, but the information he needs is in the online help. On the other hand, oftentimes users are not going to have access to hard-copy manuals, and the effectiveness of online help systems can vary widely. Particularly with more flexible and highly configurable types of software, online help may simply not address the particular needs your users may run into.

The biggest hurdle you may face in training your users and getting them to be more self-sufficient will be in obtaining support from management. The best approach to take with your supervisor is to document how you spend your time, what support requests you receive, and your proposed future projects. Let your bosses tell you that they would rather have you working on optimizing network performance than reading an application's manual to a user.

Let's certainly not, on the other hand, belittle the important role of training. While it may be said that software is in some ways becoming simpler, it is also true that ever more sophisticated office, e-mail, and groupware packages, as well as more specialized software products, are creating learning curves which can understandably frustrate and intimidate users—and reduce their productivity. More and more now, new technologies roll out faster than users can really become familiar with them. While training per se is not usually part of a network administrator's duties, suggesting, recommending, and campaigning for it may be. Your access to performance and support-call statistics can give you a unique view which could help convince management of the benefits of increased user training, whether it be generally speaking or in some particular areas. A simple check of local computer newspapers or the Yellow Pages yields an ever-growing list of companies that specialize in offering on- or off-site training for any conceivable software package or suite of products, and specialized training packages can also frequently be arranged.

Protecting Your Network against Viruses

You've documented everything in sight, you have a UPS on every workstation, you've just finished mirroring the server with SFT III, and you have a thoroughly tested backup system and the best equipment available. Then, one day, a user brings in a disk from home, loads a program onto their PC, and a short while later, your entire network is out of commission. And since the virus was replicated in several days of backups, it turns out that you've permanently lost 10 days of work. Sound far-fetched? It has happened. It put a flourishing British investment firm into receivership. Don't take chances. Use a network virus-scanning system on your server, and equip every workstation with scanning software.

There are virus checkers that check for more than 2000 viruses. Some virus scanners run as NetWare NLMs, some as device drivers on workstations, and others as stand-alone programs that will scan local and network drives. Many are free or low cost, and all are less expensive than re-creating all your data and reinstalling all your applications, to say nothing of trying to figure out what has been scrambled and what hasn't, and what to do about that.

Keep the scanners updated. With the rate at which nasty people are creating new viruses, a current version of virus software probably won't be providing good protection for more than a month or two.

> **NOTE** We had a user bypass the virus-scanning system on a PC and infect the network. Her reason? The virus scanner on her PC in the other building had "passed" the disk, and she knew therefore that the disk couldn't be infected. It turned out that her scanning software was over a year old!

Software developers are constantly making advances in virus detection and prevention. There are network virus scanners that monitor suspicious activity on the network, and hardware add-ons that should prevent viruses from gaining access to the PC. However, the only constant in virus detection is that the virus creators will eventually figure out a way to bypass anything that comes along on the preventive side. Stay abreast of the technology. See Appendices A and B for some suppliers of virus-detection software and resources for learning more about virus detectors.

The threat of your network being infected by viruses is another reason for maintaining good backups. Unfortunately several backups may take place before a virus is detected, so it is important to maintain several sets of backups going back several weeks, in addition to keeping frequent (ideally daily) backups. Keep on hand spare boot floppies that are known to be uninfected, so you can be sure to be able to boot up a station virus-free long enough to purge any virus residing on the drive.

While server operating systems such as NetWare and NT are less prone to infection from viruses, this tends to make it all the more serious if a problem should ever occur. Be extremely careful, for instance, when booting a server temporarily from any floppy disk; because of the different way servers access the hard disk partitions for instance, a virus which manages to get onto a server drive can be far more crippling. Removing such a virus may require reformatting and reinstalling the server OS—not a happy prospect to be sure.

> **TIP** Keeping a spare server boot drive on hand provides you with an additional weapon to combat viruses. Should one ever infect a server boot partition, simply shut down the system, then attach the alternate boot drive (again, an external SCSI or removable drive is best for this), and boot using the alternate system. Once this is up and running, you should be able to run virus scanning software against the infected partition(s) and thus eliminate the virus.

Elements of Network Security

It does no good to protect your network against every sort of problem you can imagine, only to have a disgruntled employee or hacker reformat your hard disk or worse. There are several elements to security, including physical security, login security, user access rights, and dial-in access. The chapters in Part VIII discuss these issues in depth; here's a quick summary.

Physical Security

Your server should be *physically secured*. This can be difficult, especially if it is used as a print server and has printers directly connected to it. At least, lock the console on NetWare 3.*x* and 4.*x* servers, use good password security on NT servers, and use the dedicated mode routers. You may want to use the secure console command on NetWare servers, as well. This prevents the loading of unauthorized NLMs designed to bypass security, and it unloads DOS so that no one can take the server down and run a DOS program to alter data or bypass security. Once DOS is unloaded, the server must be powered down and back up to reload DOS.

With Windows NT (or any server software), guard administrator account passwords carefully, and consider adding event logging to adminstrator-privileged activities on the server.

It is still possible to reboot a server from a floppy and load SERVER.EXE or a DOS program designed to bypass NetWare security, then access the server. A similar utility exists for reading NT's NTFS partitions from DOS. If this kind of access is a concern, you can disable or even remove the floppy drives, or you can install a hardware password, if your server's BIOS permits it. Most PCs allow this.

Another aspect of physical security involves every workstation on your network. A hacker, given access to users' PCs and desks, can often break into their accounts, or even the supervisor's account. You can limit the workstations from which the supervisor can log in to yours, and lock it up. But the best idea is to arrange for a guard to walk through the building, and make sure all users monitor unauthorized access to other PCs in their area. Other physical security techniques are anti-theft registration stickers, cables that secure the server to something immobile, and video surveillance. For those with special needs, there are even gunshot-secure, self-contained, air-conditioned locking cabinets for large RAIDs; server racks; and even rack-mounted consoles, complete with slideout keyboards. Some are cheap, others are very expensive, but most are quite effective in limiting access to servers and server consoles.

Password and Login Security

Companies that hire outside consultants to check their security are often astounded at the ease with which the consultants acquire access to their networks. Many users choose passwords that can be guessed easily, or even write the passwords down and "hide" them on the bottoms of drawers and similar obvious places. When you set up a user's account, you can set the password and keep the user from changing it, set a minimum password length, or force password changes at specified intervals and require that new passwords be unique, which prevents users from using the same password they had before.

Other programs will produce passwords that are not in any dictionary, yet are easy to remember. If this kind of security is a serious consideration for you, you might consider using this sort of program to issue passwords, and lock the passwords so the users can't change them.

The supervisor password should be known only to you and a designated backup person as may be required by company policy. If other users need to have access to supervisor privileges, create a supervisor-equivalent account. This prevents someone else from logging in as supervisor and changing the supervisor password. If someone changes the password on the supervisor-equivalent account, you can fix that by logging in as supervisor and changing the password or even deleting the account. Just remember that there's only one supervisor account, and if you're locked out of it, regaining access to the server can be a major problem.

> **NOTE** If you do have the misfortune of being locked out of the supervisor account, you can sometimes fix it, but it will generally require taking down the server and playing games with the binderies or the NDS database—not for the faint of heart. There is always the possibility that you will need to re-create the binderies or NDS database by hand from your documentation if something goes wrong, too... You do have your bindery or NDS database information documented by now, don't you?

Many users have their login name in their AUTOEXEC.BAT file, as in:

```
LOGIN SERVERNAME\LOGINNAME
```

This means they don't need to type their login name at the login prompt, but it also provides a would-be break-in artist with half of the combination to their workstation. If security is a major consideration for you, you may wish to leave this line out of the AUTOEXEC.BAT file.

Trustee and File Rights

If someone bypasses the physical security and the login security, and is able to log in as a user, you can still limit his or her ability to wreak havoc on the network by setting trustee and file rights correctly. *Trustee rights* apply to individual users and define their access to directories and files; *file rights* apply to the files or directories themselves and define all users' access to those files. These two types of rights can aid you in preventing unauthorized modification or deletion of critical files.

For instance, the files in SYS:PUBLIC and SYS:SYSTEM are normally set read-only, so no one can change or delete them. When updating some files in these directories, some administrators simply change all files in the directory to read/write. Failure to change them back to read-only afterwards allows anyone to delete or modify the files.

You should also set rights carefully on applications and data files on the server. Most applications require only read rights to use them. However, some applications require that users be able to modify some files. You can often have separate copies of these files in each user's directory. At least make sure that all the other files in the application's directory are write-protected.

Dial-In Access Security

As telecommuting becomes a reality for more workers, network administrators are increasingly faced with security problems related to dial-in access. Having an access server on your network is equivalent to having a workstation plugged in at a park bench somewhere, where absolutely anyone in the world can attempt to log in.

To provide *dial-in access security*, you can restrict the number of login attempts allowed during any dial-in session. This prevents hackers from dialing in and trying thousands of logins or passwords. You can also use dial-back systems. These range from a (not very secure) system that calls the user back at a number entered during the login attempt to a system with separate lines for dialing in and dialing out, which won't even allow dialing in on the lines that dial users back.

In addition to the access server, you may have some users with modems on their workstations. If they routinely leave these on, a hacker could gain access to the PC, load a remote control program onto the PC, and use that to attempt to log in to the server. You can address this by preventing logins from that workstation during off hours (of course, this won't work if the user needs to be able to access the network during those hours). Or, even better, eliminate individual modems altogether. You should at least make sure that the workstation's AUTOEXEC.BAT file doesn't include the user's login name or password. The important thing is to be aware of the potential hole in your security.

Other Access Security

There are other possibilities that a hacker could use to gain access to your system. For instance, if you have NFS support on your server, a user with a Unix workstation could mount the drives on your server that have been exported, and possibly bypass your security. You can fix this by setting up the NFS NLM correctly. Keep in mind that some add-ons may cause potential holes in your system, so you need to look for them and find ways to prevent them.

The only constant in security systems is that anything that someone creates as the ultimate, undefeatable security system, someone else will eventually circumvent. You should make a regular effort to learn about new advances in security (and virus detection), and keep your system updated.

Recovering from Disaster—in Advance

The preventive measures discussed in this chapter can save you from many kinds of problems. However, you should be prepared to recover from fires, floods, and other kinds of disasters that you cannot avoid. Having a plan gives you a sense of direction after a problem occurs. Creating the plan forces you to consider possible problems and prepare for them, which can prevent serious losses after disaster strikes.

The Recovery Plan

Most areas of the country have their regional disasters. Earthquakes, cyclones or hurricanes, floods, blizzards—they all have potential ramifications to your network. Although you can't constantly worry about what might happen, you should consider the possibilities and how you would deal with them.

Your plan may be as simple as storing your backup tapes and copies of your network documentation in a different room from the server, or as extensive as detailed lists of what steps you would take, who you would talk to (with their phone numbers and addresses), what services or equipment you would request, and what these items would cost. The scope of your recovery plan will depend on the complexity of your network and on how soon it must be working after a problem.

Data Recovery in Advance

There are programs available for both PCs and Macs that will (sometimes) recover deleted files or data from drives that crash or are accidentally formatted. Most of these programs have a utility that should be loaded on the workstation ahead of time. This utility will keep track of files after they have been deleted, significantly improving the recovery program's chances of getting your data back. You should consider a utility of this type for all your network workstations.

Recovery Services in Advance

Many companies offer troubleshooting and disaster-recovery services. These companies range from large national organizations, such as TRW and Wang, to local businesses, to freelancers, to companies that specialize in recovering as much as possible from fire- or flood-damaged systems. The services they provide range from network analysis using LANalyzer or another protocol analyzer to hard disk recovery.

You should develop a disaster-recovery plan and set up relationships with these services in advance. It will not make things easier for you if you must spend two days after the disaster setting up an account and authorizing payment before the service will begin fixing your problems.

Summary

This wraps up our final chapter—avoiding catastrophes with a "pound" of prevention. If you do nothing else, *at least do backups*. Ideally, this includes paper backups (notes in printed form) of workstation and server configurations, directory structures, cable layout, and other important details you can envision needing.

Preventive maintenance, backup power supplies, anti-virus software on both the server and workstations, and physically securing your server(s) are also important precautions.

Training your users (and for that matter, also your networking assistants) will always pay off in fewer support calls and more problem-free, effective use of the network resources you work at so earnestly to keep operational.

APPENDICES

■ APPENDIX A: Information Resources

■ APPENDIX B: Vendor Web Sites

■ APPENDIX C: Manufacturer's Ethernet Identifiers

■ APPENDIX D: Glossary

APPENDIX

A

Information Resources

- Networking-related books by SYBEX

- Magazines

- Internet newsgroups

- Standards organizations

- Related Web sites

- Certification programs

This appendix contains a collection of helpful sources of information on networking-related topics.

Books

See www.sybex.com for an online catalog, ordering information, and support. Here are just some of the networking-related titles published by SYBEX.

Network Administration

Mastering Microsoft Exchange Server 5.5, 3rd Ed.

by Barry Gerber

ISBN 0-7821-2237-X

Mastering Windows NT Server 4, 5th Ed.

by Mark Minasi

ISBN 0-7821-2163-2

NT Enterprise Network Design

by Morgan Stern, Gary Monti, and Vahan Bachmann

ISBN 0-7821-2156-X

Mastering TCP/IP for NT Server

by Mark Minasi and Todd Lammle with Monica Lammle

ISBN 0-7821-2123-3

Mastering Netscape SuiteSpot 3 Servers

by Robert P. Lipschutz, Len Gilbert, Kevin Heard, Julie A. Kent, Mitchell Nguyen, Keith Smith, and Adil Soofi

ISBN 0-7821-2104-7

Introduction to Local Area Networks, 2nd Ed.

by Robert M. Thomas

ISBN 0-7821-2099-7

Extranet Design and Implementation

by Peter Loshin

ISBN 0-7821-2091-2

Multiprotocol Network Design and Troubleshooting

by Chris Brenton

ISBN 0-7821-2082-2

Mastering Microsoft Internet Information Server 4

by Peter Dyson

ISBN 0-7821-2080-6

Mastering Microsoft Exchange Server 5, 2nd Ed.

by Barry Gerber

ISBN 0-7821-2053-9

GroupWise 5.2 Administrator's Guide

by Richard Beels, Danita Zanrè, and Scott Kunau

ISBN 0-7821-1993-X

Mastering Netscape SuiteSpot Servers

by Robert P. Lipschutz, John Garris, and Adil Soofi

ISBN 0-7821-1976-X

Mastering Microsoft Internet Information Server

by Peter Dyson

ISBN 0-7821-1899-2

Lotus Notes 4.5 Administrator's Guide

by Bret Swedeen

ISBN 0-7821-1841-0

Networking the Small Office

by Patrick Campbell

ISBN 0-7821-1790-2

Intranets

The ABCs of Intranets

by Peter Dyson, Pat Coleman, and Len Gilbert

ISBN 0-7821-2064-4

Mastering Intranets: The Windows 95/NT Edition

by Pat Coleman and Peter Dyson

ISBN 0-7821-1991-3

Introduction to Local Area Networks

by Robert M. Thomas

ISBN 0-7821-1814-3

IntraNetWare/NetWare

Mastering Novell NetWare

by Cheryl C. Currid and Craig A. Gillett

ISBN 0-89588-630-8

Mastering NetWare 5

by James E. Gaskin

ISBN 0-7821-2268-X

IntranetWare BorderManager

by James E. Gaskin

ISBN 0-7821-2138-1

CNA (SM) Study Guide for IntranetWare, 2nd Ed.

by Michael Moncur and James Chellis

ISBN 0-7821-2098-9

CNE Study Guide for IntranetWare

by Michael Moncur, James Chellis, Richard Easlick, and Amy Olsen

ISBN 0-7821-2090-3

CNE Testing Guide for IntranetWare

by Frank Cabiroy

ISBN 0-7821-2048-2

Building Intranets on NT, NetWare, and Solaris: An Administrator's Guide

by Morgan Stern and Tom Rasmussen

ISBN 0-7821-2002-4

Managing Small NetWare 4.11 Networks

by Douglas Wade Jones

ISBN 0-7821-1963-8

The Network Press Administrator's Handbook to NetWare 4.11/IntranetWare

by Michael G. Moncur

ISBN 0-7821-1949-2

The Complete Guide to NetWare 4.11/IntranetWare

by James E. Gaskin

ISBN 0-7821-1931-X

The NetWare 3.12 Administrator's Handbook, 2nd Ed.

by Kelley J.P. Lindberg

ISBN 0-7821-1905-0

Troubleshooting NetWare Systems, 2nd Ed.

by Logan G. Harbaugh

ISBN 0-7821-1904-2

The Complete Guide to NetWare LAN Analysis, 3rd Ed.

by Laura Chappell and Dan E. Hakes

ISBN 0-7821-1903-4

Migrating from NetWare to Windows NT

by Michael Joseph Miller

ISBN 0-7821-1898-4

The Network Press QuickPath to NetWare 4.11 Networks, 2nd Ed.

by Jeffrey Hughes and Blair Thomas

ISBN 0-7821-1883-6

The CNA (SM) Study Guide for NetWare 4

by James Chellis and Michael Moncur with James Chavez

ISBN 0-7821-1882-8

The CNA (CLM) Study Guide, 2nd Ed.

by David James Clarke, IV

ISBN 0-7821-1819-4

The CNE Update to NetWare 4.1

by Michael G. Moncur with James Chellis and Ralph Edwards

ISBN 0-7821-1812-7

Novell's Guide to NetWare 3.12 Networks

by Cheryl Currid and Company

ISBN 0-7821-1093-2

Reference

The Encyclopedia of Networking, 2nd Ed.

by Werner Feibel

ISBN 0-7821-1829-1

The Complete Guide to Novell Directory Services

by David Kearns and Brian Iverson

ISBN 0-7821-1823-2

The Network Press Dictionary of Networking, 2nd Ed.

by Peter Dyson

ISBN 0-7821-1818-6

Novell's Dictionary of Networking

by Peter Dyson

ISBN 0-7821-1494-6

Windows NT

Windows NT 4 Complete, 2nd Ed.

by Mark Minasi

ISBN 0-7821-2218-3

Mastering Windows NT Server 4, 5th Ed.

by Mark Minasi

ISBN 0-7821-2163-2

NT Enterprise Network Design

by Morgan Stern, Gary Monti, and Vahan Bachmann

ISBN 0-7821-2156-X

Mastering TCP/IP for NT Server

by Mark Minasi and Todd Lammle with Monica Lammle

ISBN 0-7821-2123-3

Windows NT Server 4: No experience required.

by Robert Cowart and Boyd Waters

ISBN 0-7821-2081-4

Windows NT 4 Complete: Box set

by Mark Minasi

ISBN 0-7821-2045-8

NT Network Security

by Matthew Strebe, Charles Perkins, and Michael G. Moncur

ISBN 0-7821-2006-7

The ABCs of Windows NT Workstation 4

by Charlie Russel

ISBN 0-7821-1999-9

Fast Track to NT Server 4

by Robert Cowart and Boyd Waters

ISBN 0-7821-1982-4

NT 4/Windows 95 Developer's Handbook

by Ben Ezzell with Jim Blaney

ISBN 0-7821-1945-X

Mastering Windows NT Server 4, 3rd Ed.

by Mark Minasi, Christa Andersen, and Elizabeth Creegan

ISBN 0-7821-1920-4

Migrating from NetWare to Windows NT

by Michael Joseph Miller

ISBN 0-7821-1898-4

Mastering Windows NT Workstation 4

by Mark Minasi and Patrick T. Campbell

ISBN 0-7821-1888-7

Mastering Windows NT Server 3.51, 2nd Ed.

by Mark Minasi, Christa Anderson, and Elizabeth Creegan

ISBN 0-7821-1874-7

Unix/Linux

The Complete Linux Kit

Compiled by Daniel A. Tauber

ISBN 0-7821-1669-8

The Unix Desk Reference

by Peter Dyson

ISBN 0-7821-1658-2

Understanding Unix, 2nd Ed.

by Stan Kelly-Bootle

ISBN 0-7821-1499-7

Security

NT Network Security

by Matthew Strebe, Charles Perkins, and Michael G. Moncur

ISBN 0-7821-2006-7

Online Magazines

Data Communications

www.data.com

InfoWorld

www.infoworld.com

Information Week Online

www.informationweek.com

Internet Telephony

www.internettelephony.com

Internet Week

pubs.cmpnet.com/internetwk

LAN Times Online

www.lantimes.com

Linux Gazette

www.ssc.com/lg

Linux Journal

www.ssc.com/lj/index.html

Mac Week

macweek.zdnet.com

NetWare Connection

www.novell.com/nwc

PC Magazine Online

www.zdnet.com/pcmag

PC Week

www.zdnet.com/pcweek

Products (Ziff-Davis reviews of computer and networking products)

www.zdnet.com/products

TechWeb (technology news)

www.techweb.com

tele.com

www.teledotcom.com

Unix Review's Performance Computing

www.performancecomputing.com

Win98 Magazine

www.win98mag.com/current/cover.html

Windows NT Magazine

www.winntmag.com

Windows Sources

www.zdnet.com/wsources

ZDNet's e-business (Internet commerce and communication)

`www.zdnet.com/icom/e-business/index.html`

Internet Newsgroups

This is, of course, only a partial listing. New newsgroups are constantly being added, but these are currently the main newsgroups for networking issues covered in this book.

MS Windows/Windows NT

```
comp.os.ms-windows.networking.misc
comp.os.ms-windows.networking.ras
comp.os.ms-windows.networking.tcp-ip
comp.os.ms-windows.networking.win95
comp.os.ms-windows.networking.windows
comp.os.ms-windows.nt.admin.networking
microsoft.public.win95.networking
microsoft.public.winnt50.beta.networking
```

Novell IntraNetWare/NetWare

```
comp.os.netware.announce
comp.os.netware.connectivity
comp.os.netware.misc
comp.os.netware.security
microsoft.public.winnt50.beta.netware.interop
```

Linux

```
alt.os.linux
alt.linux.slakware
alt.os.linux.caldera
alt.os.linux.slackware
```

```
comp.os.linux.announce
comp.os.linux.answers
comp.os.linux.hardware
comp.os.linux.networking
comp.os.linux.setup
```

Unix

```
alt.unix.wizards
cern.security.unix
comp.security.unix
comp.sources.unix
comp.unix.admin
comp.unix.questions
```

Miscellaneous

```
comp.sys.ibm.pc.hardware.networking
cuug.networking
```

Standards Organizations

American National Standards Institute (ANSI) has served as administrator and coordinator of the United States private sector voluntary standardization system for over 80 years. Standards are developed by establishing consensus among numerous qualified private- and public-sector organizations. Find them on the Web at web.ansi.org.

The **Institute of Electrical and Electronic Engineers Standards Association (IEEE-SA)** is a major standards body for all the IEEE societies and their representative electrotechnological industries. IEEE itself has been around a number of years and was already involved in developing and promulgating the IEEE networking standards. More recently, at the end of 1996, a new IEEE "spin-off" was formed—the IEEE Standards Association. Anyone interested can join the IEEE and IEEE-SA and participate in standards activity. Find them on the Web at standards.ieee.org.

The **Internet Engineering Task Force (IETF)** is a large, open, international community of network designers, engineers, users, administrators, vendors, and researchers, dedicated to furthering the development and smooth operation of the Internet. Find them on the Web at www.ietf.cnri.reston.va.us.

The **International Organization for Standards (ISO)** is headquarted in Geneva, Switzerland, and is a worldwide federation of national standards bodies from over 130 different countries. Note the abbreviation ISO is not directly an acronym (or it would be IOS). "ISO" comes from a Greek prefix meaning "equal" or "standard." Find them on the Web at www.iso.ch.

Web Pages

Interoperability Labs Tutorials

www.iol.unh.edu/training

This is a collection of online course material covering a wide variety of networking related issues, including network topologies, protocols, and programming.

DevCentral Learning Center

www.iftech.com/learning/tutorials

Online course material from Interface Technologies. Covers everything from Web Development to NT.

Charles Spurgeon's Ethernet Web Site

www.ots.utexas.edu:8080/ethernet

Provides extensive coverage of Ethernet technology, including the new Gigabit Ethernet (802.3z).

RFC Search Index

www.nexor.com/public/rfc/index/rfc.html

This site lets you perform searches for various RFCs (request for comments) on Internet technologies.

SAMBA

`samba.anu.edu.au`

Information on various topics from Unix to PC networking.

Linux Online

`www.linux.org`

All sorts of information on Linux, including where to obtain it and how to install and use it.

WinFiles.com

`www.winfiles.com`

Huge collection of Windows tools and shareware, including software for Windows NT and Windows CE as well as Windows 95 and Windows 98.

World Wide Web Consortium

`www.w3.org`

W3C's Web site has, among other things, a great wealth of information about the World Wide Web for developers and users, reference code implementations to embody and promote standards, and various prototype and sample applications to demonstrate uses of new technologies. Anyone who is interested in Internet-based development (or needs to follow it) should periodically check the announcements on this site.

Certification Programs

Certification programs offered by various networking software vendors are a great way to increase your knowledge and skills in a measured fashion—and they're great resume enhancers as well.

CNA, CNE

Novell's Certified Netware Administrator (CNA) and Certified NetWare Engineer (CNE) are recognized credentials for NetWare LAN administrators and engineers.

Novell Education

education.novell.com

Novell Certification

education.novell.com/certinfo/index.htm

MCSE

Microsoft Certified Systems Engineers have a demonstrated proficiency with Windows and Windows NT networking products, and the already high demand for certified networking professionals is constantly increasing.

Microsoft Training and Education

www.microsoft.com/train_cert and

www.microsoft.com/mcp/mktg/choices.htm

Microsoft Certified Professional Magazine Online

www.mcpmag.com

APPENDIX

B

Vendor Web Sites

- Networking hardware companies

- Cables/connectors companies

- Networking software companies

- Networking mail-order companies

Hardware

3Com (network adapters, etc.)

www.3com.com/products

Acclaim Inc. (Frame Relay, switches, etc.)

www.acclaiminc.com/product.htm

Accton (various networking products)

www.accton.com

ADAX Inc. (ISDN, WAN, and LAN products)

www.adax.com

Ancor Communications (Gig Ethernet, FDDI products, etc.)

www.ancor.com

Asante Technologies (Fast Ethernet, etc.)

www.asante.com

Ascend (WAN, routers, switches, software, etc.)

www.ascend.com

Bay Networks (network adapters, etc.)

www.baynetworks.com

Cisco Systems (routers, bridges, etc.)

www.cisco.com

Connect-tek (switches, server racks, furniture)

www.connect-tek.com

D-Link Systems (hubs, etc.)

www.dlink.com

Develcon (bridges, routers, etc.)

www.develcon.com

Digilog Network (network analysis tools)

www.digilog.com

ECI Telematics (WAN voice and data technology)

www.telematics.com

Edimax Computer (hubs, switches, etc.)

www.edimax.com

Eicon Technologies (various networking products)

www.eicon.com

Emulex (servers, LAN/WAN equipment)

www.emulex.com

Equinox (networking equipment)

www.equinox.com

Farallon (Mac and Windows networking products)

www.farallon.com

FastComm (routers, test equipment, Frame Relay, etc.)

www.fastcomm.com

Hewlett-Packard (routers, bridges, print server products, etc.)

www.hewlett-packard.com

HT Communications (Frame Relay, T1, ISDN, etc.)

www.htcomm.com

Intel (various networking products)

www.intel.com

LANart (hubs, switches, fiber-optic network products)

www.lanart.com

Lantronix (network equipment)

www.lantronix.com

Linksys (network adapters, hubs, etc.)

www.linksys.com

Maxtech (network adapters, etc.)

www.maxtech.com

Memotec (Frame Relay, voice, etc.)

www.memotec.com

Motorola (routers, bridges, etc.)

www.motorola.com

National Semiconductor (various networking products)

www.national.com

Nbase Communications (Gig Ethernet, extranet equipment)

www.nbase.com

Netgear (network adapters, hubs, etc.)

www.netgear.com

Netrix (voice-over data products)

www.netrix.com

Newbridge (network management solutions)

www.wtl.co.uk

Olicom (switches, ATM, Token Ring, etc.)

www.olicom.com

Perle Systems (dial-up and remote access products)

www.perle.com

Plaintree Systems (Gig Ethernet switches, etc.)

www.plaintree.com

Proteon (bridges, routers, etc.)

www.proteon.com

Racal (Frame Relay, data and telecom products)

www.racal.com

RAD Data Comm. (packet switches, WAN and LAN equipment)

www.rad.com

Samsung (ATM and other networking products)

www.samsungtelecom.com

SMC (network adapters, hubs, etc.)

www.smc.com

SVEC Computer Systems (Fast Ethernet, switches, hubs, adapters, etc.)

www.svec.com

TDK Systems (network adapters, mobile computing technology)

www.tdksystems.com

TRENDware (Fast Ethernet and other networking equipment)

www.trendware.com

Wisecom (network adapters, hubs, etc.)

www.wisecominc.com

Xircom (network adapters, mobile networking products)

www.xircom.com

Xylan Networking (switched network equipment)

www.xylan.com

Cables/Connectors

Belkin (networking and cables)

www.belkin.com

Cabletron Systems (routers, bridges, etc.)

www.cabletron.com

StarTech (varied networking equipment)

www.startechcomp.com

Software

Artisoft (LANtastic software, telephony products)

www.artisoft.com

Banyan Systems (VINES, StreetTalk server software, and other networking products)

www.banyan.com

IBM (hardware, software, mainframe connectivity products)

www.ibm.com

Miramar Systems (Apple to Windows networking solutions)

www.miramarsys.com

Novell (server and diagnostic software and hardware)

www.novell.com

Microsoft

www.microsoft.com

Mail-Order Networking Equipment Suppliers

Belkin (networking and cables)

www.belkin.com

Black Box (networking connectivity and cables)

www.blackbox.com

CABLExpress (networking and cables)

www.cablexpress.com

Comark (computers and equipment)

www.comark.com

APPENDIX

C

Manufacturer's Ethernet Identifiers

The following is a list of the most common Manufacturer's Ethernet Identifier (MEI) numbers in use today. You may note a preponderance of Cisco entries. This is a strong indicator of their position in the networking market. This is not, however, all there are. In fact, there are hundreds more. Michael A. Patton, with contributions from the Internet community, has compiled and organized a complete list of MEIs; the list is frequently updated. You can find it on the Web at `www.cavebear.com/CaveBear/Ethernet/vendor.html`.

The identifier is the first six bytes of the MAC address assigned to every Ethernet networking device. This ID number can be used to identify the manufacturer of a specific device (or at least the Ethernet interface). Note that some manufacturers have multiple ID numbers. Some of these become a vendor's MEI through buyouts and mergers. Check the Web site for a short history of each MEI if you are having trouble locating device-specific information.

Identifier	Manufacturer	Notes/Devices, Specifics
000000	Synoptic	
00000C	Cisco	
000011	Tektronix	
00001C	JDR Microdevices	Generic, NE2000 drivers
00002A	TRW	
00003D	AT&T	
00004C	NEC Corporation	
000055	AT&T	
000063	Hewlett-Packard	LanProbe
00006B	MIPS	
00007D	Cray Research Super-servers, Inc.	
00007F	Linotype-Hell AG	Linotronic typesetters
000080	Cray Communications (formerly Dowty Network Services)	

000081	Synoptic	
000094	Asante	MAC
0000AA	Xerox	Xerox machines
0000C5	Farallon Computing, Inc.	
0000D1	Adaptec, Inc.	"Nodem" product
0000D3	Wang Labs	
0000F8	DEC	
000143	IEEE 802	
000204	Novell NE3200	
000400	Lexmark (Print Server)	
0004AC	IBM	PCMCIA Ethernet adapter
000502	Apple (PCI bus Macs)	
00060D	Hewlett-Packard	JetDirect Token Ring interfaces
000629	IBM RISC6000 system	
00067C	Cisco	
0006C1	Cisco	
00070D	Cisco	2511 Token Ring
000855	Fermilab	
0008C7	Compaq	
001011	Cisco Systems	Cisco 75xx
00101F	Cisco	
00102F	Cisco	Cisco 5000
00104B	3Com	3C905-TX PCI
001079	Cisco	5500 Router
00107A	Ambicom	
0010F6	Cisco	

002000	Lexmark (Print Server)	
002035	IBM (International Business Machines)	Mainframes, Etherjet printers
0020AF	3COM Corporation	
0020B9	Metricom, Inc.	
0020C5	Eagle NE2000	
00400B	Crescendo (now owned by Cisco)	
004010	Sonic	Mac Ethernet interfaces
0040A6	Cray Research Inc.	
006008	3Com	Found in a 3Com PCI form factor 3C905 TX board
006009	Cisco	Catalyst 5000 Ethernet switch
00602F	Cisco	
00603E	Cisco	100Mbps interface
006047	Cisco	
00605C	Cisco	
006070	Cisco	Routers (2524 and 4500)
006083	Cisco Systems, Inc.	Routers (3620/3640)
00608C	3Com (1990 onwards)	
006097	3Com	
0060B0	Hewlett-Packard	
00801A	Bell Atlantic	
00801C	Cisco	
008037	Ericsson Business Communications	
0080A3	Lantronix	

0080C2	IEEE	802.1 Committee
0080D3	Shiva	Appletalk-Ethernet interface
0080D6	Apple Mac Portable	
00A000	Bay Networks	Ethernet switch
00A0D1	National Semiconductor	COMPAQ Docking Station
00A040	Apple (PCI Mac)	
00A0C9	Intel (PRO100B cards)	
00AA00	Intel	
00C049	US Robotics Total Control™ NETServer Card	
00C087	UUNET Technologies, Inc.	COMPAQ Docking Station
00DD00	Ungermann-Bass	IBM RT
00DD01	Ungermann-Bass	
00DD08	Ungermann-Bass	
00E014	Cisco	Ethernet switch
00E01E	Cisco	Lightstream 1010
00E034	Cisco	
00E04F	Cisco	
00E08F	Cisco Systems	Catalyst 2900
00E0A3	Cisco	
00E0B0	Cisco Systems	Catalyst 2900/5000
00E0F7	Cisco	
00E0F9	Cisco	
00E0FE	Cisco	
026060	3Com	

02608C	3Com	IBM PC; Imagen; Valid; Cisco; Macintosh
080002	3Com (formerly Bridge)	
080007	Apple	
080009	Hewlett-Packard	
080011	Tektronix, Inc.	
080017	National Semiconductor Corp. (used to have Network System Corp., wrong NSC)	
080020	Sun	
080028	TI	Explorer
08002B	DEC	
080030	CERN	
08003E	Motorola	VME bus processor modules
08005A	IBM	
080069	Silicon Graphics	
080079	Silicon Graphics	
09006A	AT&T	
10005A	IBM	
1000D4	DEC	
1000E0	Apple A/UX	
3C0000	3Com	Dual-function (V.34 modem + Ethernet) card
400003	NetWare	
444553	Microsoft	Windows 95/98 internal "adapters"
52544C	Novell 2000	

| AA0003 | DEC | Global physical address for some DEC machines |
| AA0004 | DEC | Local logical address for DECNET systems |

APPENDIX D

D

Glossary

10Base2   A standard for transmitting Ethernet over thinnet (RG-58) cable.

10Base5   A standard for transmitting Ethernet over thicknet (1/2-inch round, 50-ohm coaxial) cable.

10BaseT   A standard for transmitting Ethernet over twisted-pair cable.

10BaseFL   A standard for transmitting Ethernet over fiber-optic cable.

access permissions   A network security model in which rights to access network resources are determined on the basis of security policies stored in a user-access database on a server. A user logs on to a network. After that user has been allowed onto the network, the network security system determines access privileges in accordance with the security policies stored in the user-access database.

active hub   A hub that amplifies transmission signals and sends them to all the computers connected to it. This type of hub is often called a *multiport repeater.*

active monitor   A device on a Token Ring network (usually the device that has been operating on the network for the longest time) that periodically checks the status of the network and monitors for network errors.

adapter   Any hardware device that allows communications to occur through physically dissimilar systems. This term usually refers to peripheral cards permanently mounted inside a computer that provide an interface from the computer's bus to another media such as a hard disk or a network.

adaptive speed leveling   A modem technology that allows modems to attempt a change in the bit rate at which data is transmitted to optimize for changing telephone line conditions. For instance, a connection initially made at 33.6 might drop to 28.8 if the error rate exceeds a certain threshold that indicates a transient line problem.

Address Resolution Protocol (ARP)   An Internet protocol for resolving an IP address into a Physical layer address (such as an Ethernet media access controller address).

amplifier   A type of repeater that simply amplifies the entire incoming signal. Unfortunately, it amplifies both the signal and the noise.

amplitude   In communications, the distance between the highest and lowest points in a wave. The amplitude controls the strength, or volume, of the signal.

analog data   Data that has an infinite number of possible states, rather than the simple 1's and 0's of a digital signal. Audio, video, and voice telephone signals, for example, can all be represented using analog signals.

applet   A small application (typically written in Java) that runs inside another application, such as a Web browser.

AppleTalk   A networking system developed by Apple for use with Macintosh computers. The software for AppleTalk connectivity is built in to the Macintosh operating system (Mac OS 8.*x* and System 7.*x*).

Application layer   The layer of the OSI model that interfaces with user-mode programs called applications by providing high-level network services based upon lower-level network layers. Network file systems like named pipes are an example of Application layer software.

ARCnet   A network topology, created by Datapoint Corporation in 1977, that can connect up to 255 nodes on coaxial, twisted-pair, or fiber-optic. ARCnet uses a token-passing scheme and typically reaches speeds up to 2.5Mbps. Some newer generations of ARCnet can reach a speed of 100Mbps.

asynchronous   A type of communication that sends data using flow control rather than a clock to synchronize data between the source and destination.

asynchronous transfer mode (ATM)   A network transfer method that transmits data in 53-byte packets, called *cells*. ATM is most frequently used on WANs but is sometimes used for LANs and MANs. ATM can reach speeds of up to 2.488Gbps. ATM is frequently called *cell relay*.

Attachment User Interface (AUI)   AUI specifies how a transceiver is attached to an Ethernet device.

attenuation   A communications term referring to a signal decreasing in volume (and amplitude) over a distance. The length of the cable and its resistance can affect the amount of attenuation.

back end   The server component of a client-server system. It provides services to the front end (the client component).

bandwidth   In network communications, the amount of data that can be sent across a wire in a given time. Each communication that passes along the wire decreases the amount of available bandwidth.

baseband   A transmission technique in which the signal uses the entire bandwidth of a transmission medium. Computers can transmit across the medium only when the channel is not busy.

baseline   A snapshot of a computer's current performance statistics that can be used for analysis and planning purposes. Analysis and scaling decisions should be based on the mean performance values of baseline and several samplings taken at peak and low times of network activity.

Basic Input/Output System (BIOS)   A set of routines in firmware that provides the most basic software interface drivers for hardware attached to the computer. The BIOS contains the bootstrap routine.

baud rate   The per-second rate of state transitions (that is, from 1 to 0 and vice versa) of a signal. Baud rates of modems define the speed at which they make state transitions. Because state transitions can represent more than a single bit each, this rate is different from the BPS rate.

beaconing   The process on a Token Ring network by which a device, in the event of a cable fault, determines the state of the network and the location of the fault.

binary   The numbering system used in computer memory and in digital communication. All characters are represented as a series of 1's and 0's. For example, the letter *A* might be represented in a translation code as 01000001.

binding   The process of linking a protocol to a network interface card or device driver.

bits   In binary data, each unit of data is a bit. Each bit is represented by either 0 or 1 and is stored in memory as an on or off state.

bits per second (bps)   The amount of data transferred in a second.

border   A security perimeter formed by natural or logical boundaries that can only be passed at defined locations called border gateways.

border gateways   Routers that attach a private network to the Internet. They are usually used in a system as security checkpoints that force all traffic into and out of a secured system through a single point of access control. Traffic passing through the border gateways is security tested before being passed through to the secure system. Firewalls are an example of border gateways.

bottleneck   A condition in which network data transfer is slowed significantly because of a problem with a network device.

bridge   A network interconnectivity device that selectively determines the appropriate segment to which it should pass a signal. Through address filtering, bridges can divide busy networks into segments and reduce network traffic.

broadband   A network transmission method in which a single transmission medium is divided and shared simultaneously.

broadcast storm   A network condition in which a malfunctioning network card or some other problem overwhelms a network with message broadcasts. You can use routers to limit broadcast storms.

brouter   A network interconnectivity device that can provide both bridge and router services.

brownout   A temporary decrease in the voltage level of power supplied to network devices. Brownouts are frequently called *sags*.

buffer   In communications, an area of memory used as temporary storage for data being sent or received. The term *buffer* can refer to any area of memory in a computer.

bus (linear bus)   A network topology in which all computers are connected by a single length of cabling with a terminator at each end. The bus is the simplest and most widely used network design.

byte   The unit of data storage and communication in computers. In PC systems a byte is usually eight bits, or an eight-digit binary number. A single byte can represent numbers between 0 and 255.

carrier sense multiple access with collision detection (CSMA/CD)   This is the protocol by which Ethernet devices share access to an Ethernet network.

cells   The data blocks used by ATM. Cells are exactly 53 octets long.

certificates   Encrypted electronic documents that attest to the authenticity of a service, provider, or vendor of a product. Forgery of certificates is not feasible, so the information they contain may be trusted. To require connection using secure socket layer, a key with a valid certificate must be installed.

channel service units/digital service units (CSUs/DSUs)   Network interconnectivity devices that connect a network to the public telephone network. CSUs/DSUs translate signals and shield networks from noise and high voltage on the public network.

chip creep   A situation in which integrated circuits gradually lose contact with their sockets because of temperature changes.

circuit   A communications channel established between two network devices.

circuit switching   A type of data transmission in which a circuit is established between endpoints and data is sent in a stream through a network.

cladding   In fiber-optic cabling, a layer of glass that surrounds the inner core and reflects light back into the core.

Class A domain   Large networks on which the first byte specifies the network number, and the last three bytes specify the local addresses.

Class B domain   Medium networks on which the first two bytes specify the network number, and the last two bytes specify the local addresses.

Class C domain   Small networks on which the first three bytes specify the network number, and the last byte specifies the local address.

classless addressing   A subnet mask that splits the network number and the host number without regard for byte boundaries.

client-server architecture   A network architecture in which clients request data, programs, and services from servers. The servers then provide the data, programs, and services to the clients. Applications written for the client-server architecture typically have different components for the server and for the client. Client-server architecture allows clients to exploit the processing power of the server.

client-server network   A server-centric network in which some network resources are stored on a file server, while processing power is distributed among workstations and the file server.

coaxial cable   One type of cable used in network wiring. Typical coax types include RG-58 and RG-62. The 10Base2 system of Ethernet networking uses coaxial cable. Coaxial cable is usually shielded. The thicknet system uses a thicker coaxial cable.

collision   A situation that occurs when two or more network devices transmit at the same time, through the same channel. The two signals transmitted meet and cause data to be destroyed.

COM Port Communications port. A serial hardware interface conforming to the RS-232 standard for low-speed serial communications.

concentrator *See* hub.

congestion A condition in which a network transmission medium is overwhelmed with network traffic, causing network performance to decline.

crosstalk Interference, or noise, created on a network transmission medium by another physically adjacent medium. This interference can corrupt data.

Data Link Control (DLC) An obsolete network transport protocol that allows PCs to connect to older IBM mainframes and HP printers. *See* TCP/IP.

Data Link A hardware protocol used to connect computers. Usually Ethernet in local area networks or Frame Relay in leased telephone line connections.

Data Link layer In the OSI model, the layer that provides the digital interconnection of network devices and the software that directly operates those devices, such as network interface adapters. *See* Network layer, OSI model.

datagram packet-switched network A type of network on which messages are divided into a stream of separately addressed packets. Each packet is routed independently. The packets are reassembled at the destination address.

decoding The process of translating a message from a transmittable standard form to the native form of the recipient.

decryption The opposite of *encryption.*

dedicated line A transmission medium that is used exclusively between two locations. Dedicated lines are also known as leased lines or private lines.

dedicated server A computer that functions only as a server and is not used as a client or workstation.

demarcation point The point inside your building (or on the premises) at which the phone company (or other service provider) is no longer responsible for network cabling or service.

dial-up connections Data Link layer digital connections made via modems over regular telephone lines, thus providing network connections (analog or digital) that can be made to any receiving station in the world by specifying (dialing) the receiver's unique address. The term *dial-up* refers to temporary digital connections, as opposed to leased telephone lines that provide permanent connections.

digital data Data that uses 1's and 0's to store information.

Digital Intel Xerox (DIX) Another term for the AUI connector.

digital line A data or voice network interconnectivity medium that supports digital signaling.

digital signaling   Data transmission in the form of discrete units (on or off, 1 or 0, and so on).

disk duplexing   A type of disk mirroring that uses multiple disk controllers along with multiple drives, providing for increased security.

disk mirroring   The process of creating one volume that stores the same data on two partitions on separate drives. If one drive fails, the volume contents can be read from the surviving drive.

disk striping   Data that is stored across partitions of identical size on different drives. Also referred to as RAID 0.

disk striping with parity   Disk striping with redundant parity information distributed across the stripe set that can be used to regenerate the contents of any one missing disk. Also referred to as RAID 5.

distance-vector routing   A method of route discovery in which each router on the network broadcasts the information contained in its routing table. The other routers then update their routing tables with the broadcast information they receive.

domain   In Windows NT Server, a group of computers that share the same security and logon authentication database.

domain controllers   Servers that authenticate workstation network logon requests by comparing a user name and password against account information stored in the user accounts database. A user cannot access a domain without authentication from a domain controller.

domain name   The textual identifier of a specific Internet host. Domain names are in the form of: *server.organization.type* (as in `www.sybex.com`) and are resolved to Internet addresses by domain name servers.

domain name server   An Internet host dedicated to the function of translating fully qualified domain names into IP addresses. *See* domain name.

Domain Name Service (DNS)   The TCP/IP network service that translates textual Internet network addresses into numerical Internet network addresses. *See* domain name, TCP/IP.

duplexing   A method of using a second hard drive with a second hard drive controller to provide fault tolerance.

dynamic route selection   Uses the cost information that is continually being generated by routing algorithms and placed in routing tables to select the best route for each packet. As network conditions change, the router can select the best path.

electromagnetic interference (EMI)   A type of low-voltage, low-current, high-frequency signal that interferes with normal network transmission. EMI is typically caused by improper insulation or insufficient grounding.

electrostatic discharge (ESD)   An electric shock created by a buildup of static electricity. ESD frequently damages computer components.

encoding   The process of translating a message from the native form of the sender to a transmittable standard form.

encryption   The process of obscuring information by modifying it according to a mathematical function known only to the intended recipient. Encryption secures information being transmitted over nonsecure or untrusted media. The process of turning a plaintext into a ciphertext using a cipher and a key.

Ethernet   The most popular network specification. Developed by Xerox in 1976, Ethernet offers a transfer rate of 10Mbps. Ethernet uses a bus topology and thick or thin coaxial, fiber-optic, or twisted-pair cabling.

Explorer   The default shell for Windows 95/98 and Windows NT 4. Explorer implements the more flexible Desktop objects paradigm rather than the Program Manager paradigm used in earlier versions of Windows.

fax modem   A special modem that includes hardware to allow the transmission and reception of facsimiles.

Fiber Distributed Data Interface (FDDI)
A network specification that defines the transmission of information packets using light produced by a laser or light-emitting diode (LED). FDDI uses fiber-optic cable and equipment to transmit data packets. It has a data rate of up to 100Mbps and allows very long cable distances.

fiber-optics   One medium type used for network communications. Fiber-optics uses a tiny glass or plastic fiber and sends a light signal through it.

File Transfer Protocol (FTP)   A TCP/IP protocol that permits the transferring of files between computer systems. Because FTP has been implemented on numerous types of computer systems, file transfers can be done between different computer systems (for example, a personal computer and a minicomputer).

firewall   A security control device that connects two networks and determines which traffic should be allowed to pass between them. Usually implemented as a dual-homed computer attached to both the Internet and an intranet that protects the computers on the intranet from intrusion by blocking connections from untrusted sources and on specific protocols. Firewalls are the strongest form of Internet security yet implemented. Firewalls incorporate the functions of packet filtering, IP masquerading, and application proxy to perform their function.

frame   A unit of data, often called a *packet* or *block*, that can be transmitted across a network or internetwork. The term *frame* is most frequently used regarding Ethernet networks.

Frame Relay   A telephony protocol that routes digital trunk circuit data over the telephone network in a manner similar to packet-switched networks like IP. Frame Relay simply provides for virtual permanent circuits with various levels of guaranteed service referred to as *Committed Information Rates (CIRs)*.

frequency   The repetition rate, usually of a signal, usually reported in cycles per second, or Hz.

front end   The client component of a client-server system. A front-end application works with a back-end component stored on a server.

gateway   A network interconnectivity device that translates communications protocols.

Gopher   An Internet service that provides text and links to other Gopher sites. Gopher predates HTTP by about a year, but has been made obsolete by the richer format provided by HTTP.

groupware   Applications that involve group interaction across a network (excepting simple e-mail). Lotus Notes and Microsoft Exchange are two popular groupware packages.

guaranteed state changes   A type of synchronous timing coordination, used by synchronous modems, in which the clock information is embedded in the data signal.

handshaking   The exchange of codes between two devices in order to negotiate the transmission and reception of data.

hop   In routing, a server or router that is counted in a hop count.

hop count   The number of routers a message must pass through to reach its destination. You use hop counts to determine the most efficient network route.

hub   A network connectivity device that brings media segments together in a central location. The hub is the central controlling device in some star networks. The two main types are active hubs and passive hubs. *See also* active hub, intelligent hub, passive hub.

hunt   In network jargon, "hunting to" a remote device encompasses the stages of looking for, validating, and connecting to that device. This can apply to many paradigms in networking.

Hypertext Markup Language (HTML)
A textual data format that identifies sections of a document as headers, lists, hypertext links, etc. HTML is the data format used on the World Wide Web for the publication of Web pages.

Hypertext Transfer Protocol (HTTP)
An Internet protocol that transfers HTML documents over the Internet and responds to context changes that happen when a user clicks on a hypertext link.

Integrated Services Digital Network (ISDN)   A CCITT standard for digital communications. ISDN lines allow voice, video, and data transfer all on the same line.

intelligent hub   A hub that provides network management and intelligent path selection in addition to signal regeneration.

interconnectivity devices   Devices that connect independent networks. They include routers, brouters, gateways, and CSUs/DSUs.

Internet Protocol (IP)   The Network layer protocol upon which the Internet is based. IP provides a simple connectionless packet exchange. Other protocols such as UDP or TCP use IP to perform their connection-oriented or guaranteed delivery services.

internetwork   Two or more independent networks that are connected and yet maintain independent identities. Internetworks are joined by interconnectivity devices.

interrupts   Inputs to the CPU in a PC that allow devices to get its attention—to interrupt it—if it is performing another task. Interrupts are also called *IRQs* (for interrupt requests).

intranet   A privately owned network based on the TCP/IP protocol suite. *See* TCP/IP.

IP address   A four-byte number that uniquely identifies a computer on an IP internetwork. InterNIC assigns the first bytes of Internet IP addresses and administers them in hierarchies. Huge organizations like the government or top-level ISPs have class A addresses, large organizations and most ISPs have class B addresses, and small companies have class C addresses. In a class A address, InterNIC assigns the first byte, and the owning organization assigns the remaining three bytes. In a class B address, InterNIC or the higher-level ISP assigns the first two bytes, and the organization assigns the remaining two bytes. In a class C address, InterNIC or the higher-level ISP assigns the first three bytes, and the organization assigns the remaining byte. Organizations not attached to the Internet are free to assign IP addresses as they please.

ISDN modem   An interconnectivity device that connects a computer to an ISDN line.

Kerberos   The basis for the new security features that will be available with Windows NT 5. Like the Windows NT domain model, Kerberos is a trusted authentication system for large-scale networks. Kerberos keeps a database of the private keys of its users and network services.

leased line   A communications circuit permanently established for a single customer. Also called a *private line*.

Lightweight Directory Access Protocol (LDAP)   An open standard for storing user and group information independent of the operating system that hosts the WWW service.

link-state routing   A type of routing in which routers broadcast their complete routing tables only at startup and infrequent intervals.

local area network (LAN)   A network of computers operating on the same high-speed, shared media network Data Link layer. The size of a local area network is defined by the limitations of high-speed shared media networks to generally less than one kilometer in overall span. Some LAN backbone data link protocols, such as FDDI, can create larger LANs called *metropolitan* or *medium area networks (MANs)*.

media access protocol   A specification for arbitrating access to physical network media among all devices that wish to transmit on the network. CSMA/CD is a media access protocol.

message switching   The process of transmitting messages over a network, where each message is routed through the network independently.

metropolitan area network (MAN)

A network larger than a local area network (LAN) but smaller than a wide area network (WAN). MANs span a single city or metropolitan area.

microwaves

A type of unbounded network transmission medium. Microwaves are most often used to transmit data across satellite links and between earth-based equipment, such as telephone relay towers. Microwave transmission is commonly used to transmit signals when bounded media, such as cable, cannot be used.

mirroring

The process of keeping a constant backup of the server data on another server. Every change to the data made to the primary server is immediately communicated to the backup mirror server so that if the primary server fails for any reason, the mirror can take over instantly.

modem

A device that converts the digital communications of a computer into analog signals that can be carried over a regular telephone line.

modulation

The process of modifying a carrier signal to transmit information.

Multimedia Internet Mail Extensions (MIME)

A specification for the content types of files transmitted over the Internet. Web servers identify the type of file being sent to Web browsers using MIME types.

multiplexer

A device that multiplexes signals for transmission over a segment and reverses this process for multiplexed signals coming in from the segment. Frequently shortened to *mux*.

Multiple Station Access Unit (MSAU)

The hub in a Token Ring network.

multiplexing

A method of sharing a single medium segment by combining several channels for transmission over that segment using a multiplexer. Multiplexed signals are later separated at the receiving end in a process called *demultiplexing*.

multiport repeater

See active hub.

mux

See multiplexer.

NetBIOS Extended User Interface (NetBEUI)

A simple Network layer transport developed to support NetBIOS installations. NetBEUI is not routable, and so it is not appropriate for larger networks. NetBEUI is the fastest transport protocol available for Windows NT.

NetBIOS gateway

A service provided by RAS that allows NetBIOS requests to be forwarded independent of transport protocol. For example, NetBIOS requests from a remote computer connected via NetBEUI can be sent over the network via NWLink.

NetWare

A popular network operating system developed by Novell in the early 1980s. NetWare is a cooperative multitasking, highly optimized, dedicated-server network operating system that has client support for most major operating systems. Recent versions of NetWare include graphical client tools for management from client stations. At one time, NetWare accounted for more than 70 percent of the network operating system market.

Novell Directory Services (NDS) In NetWare, a distributed hierarchy of network services such as servers, shared volumes, and printers. NetWare implements NDS as a directory structure having elaborate security and administration mechanisms. The CSNW provided in Windows NT 4 supports the NDS tree. *See* NetWare.

NetWare Link (NWLink) A Windows NT transport protocol that implements Novell's IPX. NWLink is useful as a general purpose transport for Windows NT and for connecting to NetWare file servers through CSNW.

NetWare NetBIOS Link (NWNBLink) NetBIOS implemented over NWLink. *See* Network Basic Input/Output System (NetBIOS), NetWare Link (NWLink).

network A group of computers and various devices (such as printers and routers) that are joined together on a common network transmission medium.

network address A unique address that identifies each node, or device, on the network. The network address is generally hardcoded into the network card on both the workstation and server. Some network cards allow you to change this address, but there is seldom a reason to do so.

Network Basic Input/Output System (NetBIOS) A client-server interprocess communication service developed by IBM in the early 1980s. NetBIOS presents a relatively primitive mechanism for communication in client-server applications, but its widespread acceptance and availability across most operating systems make it a logical choice for simple network applications.

network connectivity Linking of segments of a single network.

Network Interface Card (NIC) A Physical layer adapter device that allows a computer to connect to and communicate over a local area network.

Network layer The layer of the OSI model that creates a communication path between two computers via routed packets. Transport protocols implement both the Network layer and the Transport layer of the OSI stack. IP is a Network layer service.

Network News Transfer Protocol (NNTP) A protocol for the transmission of a database of topical message threads between news servers and newsreader clients.

network operating system A computer operating system specifically designed to optimize a computer's ability to respond to service requests. Servers run network operating systems. Windows NT Server and NetWare are both network operating systems.

network printer A network printer can use physical or logical ports. By defining a printer as a network printer, you make the printer available to local and network users.

node Any network device (such as a server, workstation, or router) that can communicate across the network.

noise   A low-voltage, low-current, high-frequency signal that interferes with normal network transmissions, often corrupting data.

octet   Exactly eight bits of data. Bytes are usually, but not always, eight bits. Octets are always eight bits.

OSI (Open System Interconnection) model   A model defined by the International Standards Organization (ISO) to conceptually organize the process of communication between computers in terms of seven layers, called *protocol stacks*. The seven layers of the OSI model provide a way for you to understand how communications across various protocols take place.

optical fiber   Glass filament cable that conveys signals using light rather than electricity.

Operating System 2 (OS/2)   A 16-bit (and later, 32-bit) operating system developed jointly by Microsoft and IBM as a successor to MS-DOS. Microsoft bowed out of the 32-bit development effort and produced its own product, Windows NT, as a competitor to OS/2. OS/2 is now a preemptive multitasking 32-bit operating system with strong support for networking and the ability to run MS-DOS and Win16 applications, but IBM has been unable to entice a large number of developers to produce software that runs natively under OS/2.

oversampling   A type of synchronous communication in which the receiver samples the signal at ten times the data rate. One of the ten samples provides the data; the other nine provide clocking information.

packet   The basic division of data sent over a network. Each packet contains a set amount of data along with a header containing information about the type of packet and the network address to which it is being sent. The size and format of a packet depend on the protocol and frame types used.

packet switching   A type of data transmission in which data is divided into packets, each of which has a destination address. Each packet is then routed optimally across a network. An addressed packet may travel a different route than packets related to it. Packet sequence numbers are used at the destination node to reassemble related packets.

parity checking   A simple form of error checking employed by asynchronous modems. Extra bits added to data words can indicate when data transmission has been flawed.

passive hub   A hub that simply combines the signals of network segments, with no signal processing or regeneration.

password-protected shares   A network security model in which passwords are required for gaining access to each shared resource on a network.

peer   A networked computer that both shares resources with other computers and accesses the shared resources of other computers. A non-dedicated server.

peer-to-peer network   A local area network in which network resources are shared among workstations, without a file server.

permissions   Assignments of levels of access to a resource, made to groups or users. Security constructs used to regulate access to resources by user name or group affiliation. Permissions can be assigned by administrators to allow any level of access, such as read only, read/write, delete, etc., by controlling the ability of users to initiate object services. Security is implemented by checking the user's security identifier against each object's access control list.

phase   The amplitude of a cyclic signal at a specific point in time.

ping   A protocol used to check the connected route between two systems on an IP network. Also the name of the utility used to generate ping traffic.

plant   The wires that connect computers together in a LAN.

plenum   The space between the ceiling of an office and the floor above. Usually, fire codes require that only special, plenum-grade cable be used in this space.

point-to-point   Network communication in which two devices have exclusive access to a network medium. For example, a printer connected to only one workstation would be using a point-to-point connection.

Point-to-Point Protocol (PPP)   Allows the sending of IP packets on a dial-up (serial) connection. It supports compression and IP address negotiation.

Presentation layer   That layer of the OSI model that converts and translates (if necessary) information between the Session and Application layers.

print server   Print servers are the computers to which shared printers are attached. Print servers queue print jobs coming in from clients on the network and print them sequentially.

proprietary   Describes a system that is defined by one vendor and typically not supported by others. ARCnet started as a proprietary protocol, as did Token Ring.

protocol analyzer   A device that monitors network activity, providing statistics you can use in determining baseline and optimum performance.

protocols   The specifications that define procedures used by computers when they transmit and receive data. In other words, the rules by which computers communicate.

protocol stack (suite)   A collection of protocols that are associated with and implement a particular communication model (such as the DOD networking model or the OSI reference model).

proxy server   A server dedicated to the function of receiving Internet Web requests for clients, retrieving the requested pages, and forwarding them to clients. Proxy servers cache retrieved Web pages to improve performance and reduce bandwidth, and also serve the security function of protecting the identity of internal clients.

public switched telephone network (PSTN)   A term that includes the network used to make ordinary telephone calls and modem communications, as well as dedicated lines that are leased by customers for private, exclusive use. Commercial service providers offer numerous services that facilitate computer communication across PSTN.

radio frequency interference (RFI)
Noise created in the radio-frequency range.

redirector   Software loaded onto a workstation that can forward or redirect requests away from the local bus of the computer onto a network. These requests are then handled by a server. This type of software is often called a *shell*, *requester*, or *client*.

Redundant Arrays of Independent/ Inexpensive Disks (RAID)   A technique for achieving fault tolerance on a network by using several hard disks. If one or more drives fail, network data can be saved.

relative expense   A measure of the actual monetary cost when a given link is used during routing.

repeater   A network connectivity device that amplifies network signals to extend the distance they can travel.

requester   *See* redirector.

Remote Access Service (RAS)   A service that allows network connections to be established over PSTN lines with modems. The computer initiating the connection is called the RAS client; the answering computer is called the RAS host.

remote procedure call (RPC)   A network interprocess communication mechanism that allows an application to be distributed among many computers on the same network.

ring   A network topology in which computers are arranged in a circle. Data travels around the ring in one direction, with each device on the ring acting as a repeater. Ring networks typically use a token-passing protocol.

routable protocols   Protocols that support internetwork communication.

route discovery   The process a router uses to find the possible routes through the internetwork and then build routing tables to store that information.

router   An intelligent internetwork connectivity device that routes using logical and physical addressing to connect two or more logically separate networks. Routers use algorithms to determine the best path by which to send a packet.

RS-232   The most common serial communications system in use.

sag   *See* brownout.

segmentation   The process of splitting a larger network into two or more segments linked by bridges or routers.

separate clock signal   A method of synchronous communication in which a separate channel carries clocking information.

Serial Line Internet Protocol (SLIP)   A protocol that permits the sending of IP packets on a dial-up (serial) connection. It does not by itself provide support for compression or for IP address negotiation.

server   A computer dedicated to servicing requests for resources from other computers on a network. Servers typically run network operating systems such as Windows NT Server or NetWare. *See* NetWare, Windows NT.

server-based network   A network that uses one or more central, dedicated server. Also referred to as a client-server network. The Windows NT domain model is server-based.

Session layer   The layer of the OSI model dedicated to maintaining a bidirectional communication connection between two computers. The Session layer uses the services of the Transport layer to provide this service. *See* OSI model.

shielded twisted-pair   A type of wiring that includes a pair of conductors inside a metal or foil shield. This type of medium can support faster speeds than non-shielded wiring. *See also* twisted-pair.

signaling   The process of sending information over media.

signal-regenerating repeaters   A type of repeater that eliminates noise by creating an exact duplicate of incoming data, identifying it amidst the noise, reconstructing it, and retransmitting only the desired information.

Simple Mail Transfer Protocol (SMTP)   An Internet protocol for transferring mail between Internet hosts. SMTP is often used to upload mail directly from the client to an intermediate host, but can only be used to receive mail by computers constantly connected to the Internet.

Simple Network Management Protocol (SNMP)   An Internet protocol that manages network hardware such as routers, switches, servers, and clients from a single client on the network.

source-routing bridge   A type of bridge that requires a predefined route to be included with the addresses of signals it receives. IBM Token Ring networks use this type of bridge.

spike   *See* transient.

spooler   A software program that stores documents until they can be printed and coordinates how print jobs are sent to a printer.

stand-alone environment   Computers operating without connection to a network.

standby monitor   A device on a Token Ring network that monitors the network status and may become the active monitor in the case of failure of the active monitor.

star   A network topology in which all the cables run from the computers to a central location, where they are connected by a hub.

start bit   A bit that is sent as part of a serial communication stream to signal the beginning of a byte or packet.

static route selection   A type of routing in which the data path is determined in advance rather than on-the-fly by the router.

stop bit   A bit that is sent as part of a serial communications stream to signal the end of a byte or packet.

subnets (subnetworks)   Routers organize networks in logical network segments, known as subnets or subnetworks, to facilitate internetwork packet transmission. Each subnet or subnetwork is given a logical address.

switching   In a LAN environment, switching provides each network transmission with an independent path through the network free of collisions with other network transmissions.

synchronous modem   A connectivity device that uses careful timing and coordination between modems to send large blocks of data without start and stop bits.

synchronous transmission   A type of transmission that uses a clock to control the timing of bits being sent.

T-carrier   A type of multiplexed, high-speed, leased line. T-carrier service levels include T1, T2, T3, and T4. T-carriers offer transmission rates of up to 274Mbps.

TCP/IP   Transmission Control Protocol/Internet Protocol. Generally used as shorthand for the phrase *TCP/IP protocol suite.*

terminator   A device at the end of a cable segment that indicates that the last node has been reached. In the case of Ethernet cable, a 50-ohm resistor (a terminator) at both ends of the cable prevents signals from reflecting back through the cable.

throughput   The amount of data that has been sent over a given time. For example, 10BaseT Ethernet has a theoretical maximum throughput of 10Mbps. In practice, the throughput depends on the quality and length of wiring and is usually slightly less than 10Mbps.

tick count   A term used to quantify routing costs. A tick count refers to the amount of time required for a message to reach its destination.

time-division multiplexing (TDM)   A type of multiplexing in which a channel is divided into time slots that are allocated to each communicating device.

token passing   A network access method used by FDDI, Token Ring, and Token Bus networks. A short message (token) is passed around the ring. To transmit, a node must be in possession of a token. This prevents multiple nodes from transmitting simultaneously and creating collisions.

Token Ring   A network that uses a token-passing protocol in a logical ring. A token is a small frame with a special format that designates that its holder (a network device) may transmit. When a node needs to transmit, it captures a token and attaches a message to it, along with addressing information. Token Ring transmits at 4- or 16Mbps.

topology   A type of network connection or cabling system. Networks are usually configured in a bus, ring, star, or mesh topology.

transceiver   The device that performs both the transmission and reception of signals on a given medium.

transient   A high-voltage burst of electric current, usually lasting less than one second, occurring randomly. Transients are often referred to as *spikes*.

transparent bridge   A type of bridge that determines where to send data based on a table of addresses stored in memory.

Trojan horse   A dangerous or destructive program that is designed to disguise itself as something harmless.

twisted-pair   A type of wiring used for network communications that uses copper wires twisted into pairs.

Unix   A multitasking, kernel-based operating system developed at AT&T in the early 1970s and provided (originally) free to universities as a research operating system. Because of its availability and ability to scale down to microprocessor-based computers, Unix became the standard operating system of the Internet and its attendant network protocols and is the closest approximation to a universal operating system that exists. Most computers can run some variant of the Unix operating system.

unshielded twisted-pair   A type of cable usually containing four pairs of wire, each pair twisted to reduce interference. Commonly used in telephone and LAN cabling.

vampire tap   A specific type of Ethernet transceiver on a thicknet network. The vampire tap does not break the thicknet cable, but instead pierces the jacket of the cable to contact the center conductor.

virtual circuit   A logical connection made between two devices across a shared communications path. There is no dedicated physical circuit between the devices, even though they are acting as though there is one.

virtual circuit packet switching   An internetwork transmission technique in which all packets travel through a logical connection established between the sending device and the receiving device.

virtual server   A set of directories that simulate the functionality of a WWWROOT directory in that they appear to be Web servers unto themselves. IP addresses are unique to each virtual server and serve as the selection factor between them on the same machine. One actual server can embody many virtual servers.

virus   A dangerous or destructive program that alters stored files or system configuration and copies itself onto external disks or other computers.

Web browser   An application that makes HTTP requests and formats the resulting HTML documents for users. The preeminent Internet client, most Web browsers understand all standard Internet protocols and scripting languages.

Web page   Any HTML document on an HTTP server. *See* Hypertext Markup Language, Hypertext Transfer Protocol.

Webmaster   The administrator of a Web site.

wide area network (WAN)   A network typically spanning multiple cities.

Windows 3.11 for Workgroups   The current 16-bit version of Windows for less-powerful, Intel-based personal computers; this system includes peer networking services.

Windows 95/98   The current 32-bit version of Microsoft Windows for medium-range, Intel-based personal computers; this system includes peer networking services, Internet support, and strong support for older DOS applications and peripherals.

Windows Internet Name Service (WINS)   A network service for Microsoft networks that provides Windows computers with Internet numbers for specified NetBIOS names, facilitating browsing and intercommunication over TCP/IP networks.

Windows NT   The current 32-bit version of Microsoft Windows for powerful Intel, Alpha, PowerPC, or MIPS-based computers; the system includes peer networking services, server networking services, Internet client and server services, and a broad range of utilities.

Windows Sockets   An interprocess communications protocol that delivers connection-oriented data streams used by Internet software and software ported from Unix environments.

word   The standard unit of data manipulated by a computer. A word typically consists of 8, 16, 32, or 64 bits.

workgroup   A group of computers linked together to share resources. A workgroup is less sophisticated than a domain in that workgroups lack the central administrative capacities of a domain.

workstation   A powerful personal computer, usually running a preemptive, multitasking operating system like Unix or Windows NT.

World Wide Web (WWW)   The collection of computers on the Internet running HTTP (Hypertext Transfer Protocol) servers. The WWW allows for text and graphics to have hyperlinks connecting users to other servers. By using a Web browser, such as Netscape Navigator or Internet Explorer, a user can cross-link from one server to another at the click of a button.

worm   A destructive or dangerous program that can spawn another fully working version of itself.

write-back caching   A caching optimization wherein data written to the slow store is cached until the cache is full or until a subsequent write operation overwrites the cached data. Write-back caching can significantly reduce the write operations to a slow store because many write operations are subsequently obviated by new information. Data in the write-back cache is also available for subsequent reads. If something happens to prevent the cache from writing data to the slow store, the cache data will be lost. *See* write-through caching.

write-through caching   A caching optimization wherein data written to a slow store is kept in a cache for subsequent rereading. Unlike write-back caching, write-through caching immediately writes the data to the slow store and is therefore less optimal but more secure.

X.25   A telephony protocol that routes digital trunk circuit data over the telephone network in a manner similar to packet-switched networks like IP. X.25 is a more robust, older protocol than Frame Relay and provides more error correction and addressing for the establishment of temporary circuits.

zone transfer   Transferring a block of DNS data (typically an entire IP subnet) from one DNS server to another.

INDEX

Note to the Reader: Page numbers in **bold** indicate the principal discussion of a topic or the definition of a term. Page numbers in *italic* indicate illustrations.

NUMBERS

1Gbps Ethernet topology, 229–231

3Com AccessBuilder 4000 remote access server, 891–894, *891, 893*

10BaseT (twisted-pair) Ethernet standard, 1292, 1464

10Mb Ethernet topology, 221–225

100VG-AnyLAN topology, 231–235, 1062

127.0.0.1 loopback address, 88–89, 756

802.*x* IEEE standards, 172–173

A

A class IP addresses, 84–88, *86, 87*, 757–758, 1467

AARP (AppleTalk Address Resolution Protocol), **161**

ABENDs or abnormal ends in NetWare, 406–407, *407*, 1188, 1193

AC circuits, **276–278**, *277*

ACAP (Application Configuration Access Protocol), **122**

Access Control Lists (ACLs) in Lotus Notes, 565–567

access logging in Web servers, 1028–1031, *1029*

access network design, 829–830

access rights. *See* permissions; rights

AccessBuilder 4000 remote access server, 891–894, *891, 893*

accessing

    shared resources in OS/2 Warp, 585–586

    shares with SAMBA in Linux, 541–544

account administration

    in Linux, 516, *516*

    in Lotus Notes, 561, *561*

    in NetWare, 410

    in Windows NT, 465–468, *468*

ACLs (Access Control Lists) in Lotus Notes, 565–567

active monitors (AMs), **195–196**, *197*, **1464**

ActiveX programs for Web browsers, **724–725**, **1025–1026**

Adapters tab in Windows NT Network Properties window, 495–496, *496*

adding

    content to intranets, 767–768

    hard disk drives to servers, 907–910

    protocols to Windows NT, 489, *489*

    RAID and disk striping to servers, 910–914, 1469

    RAM to servers, 904–907, *905*

    services to Windows NT, 475–476, *475, 476*

additions to systems, troubleshooting, **1044–1047**

addresses

    address conflicts in wide area networks, 1375

    Address Resolution Protocol (ARP) frames, 220

    AppleTalk address space, **159–162**

        AARP (AppleTalk Address Resolution Protocol), 161

        AMTs (Address Mapping Tables), 161

        local frame delivery, 161

        NBP (Name Binding Protocol), 162

        network numbers, 159–160

overview of, 159–161

seeding and nonseeding nodes, 160

ZIP (Zone Information Protocol), 162

zones, 42, 162

base I/O port address settings, 1045–1046, *1046*

functional addresses for Token Ring stations, 194–195

host addresses, **42, 761–762**

internal IPX network addresses, 1094

IP addresses, **42, 79–103, 753–765**

127.0.0.1 loopback address, 88–89, 756

address classes, 84–88, *86, 87,* 757–758, 1467

address conventions, 79–80

Advanced IP Addressing dialog box in Windows NT, 493, *493*

ARP (Address Resolution Protocol), 102–103, 1464

assigning, 763–765

broadcast addresses, 89, 91–93, 219

determining network and host addresses, 761–762

DHCP (Dynamic Host Configuration Protocol) and, 763–765

DNS (Domain Name Service) and, 102–103

lost address spaces, 101, *102*

multicast addresses, 90–93, *91*

network address translation (NAT) devices and, 94, 709–710

network and host addresses, 42, 761–762

nonstandard subnet masks, 94–100, *95, 97, 100*

optimizing servers with multiple subnets, **921–922**

registered IP addresses, 83–88, *86, 87*

reserved address ranges, 93–94

standard subnet masks, 42, 80–83, *82,* 758–761

switches and, 919

troubleshooting duplicate IP addresses, **1136–1138**

unicast addresses, 80, 91

zeros in, 83

IPX addresses, 132–134, *132, 133*

loopback addresses, **88–89, 756**

MAC (media access control) addresses, **7,** 218–219, *220*

NetBIOS addresses, **149–152**

node types, 150–152, *150,* 154

overview of, 149–150

network addresses

assigning to NetWare servers, 1186

defined, **42, 761–762, 1474**

IPX network addresses, 132–134, *132, 133,* 1094

wide area network address problems, 1373

node addresses, 218, 1094

administration

administration books, 1426–1428

in AppleShare protocol, 622–623, 626

Administrative Wizard in Windows NT, 468, *468*

administrator passwords, 970

ADSL (Asymmetric DSL), 397–398

ADSP (AppleTalk Data Stream Protocol), **616**

Advanced IP Addressing dialog box in Windows NT, 493, *493*

Advanced Login tab in Novell IntraNetWare Client Services Configuration window, 652–653, *653*

AEP (AppleTalk Echo Protocol), **617–618**

AFP (AppleTalk Filing Protocol), **165–167, 618, 621**

aiocon tool in NetWare, 1107

alarms in LANalyzer, 1087–1088, *1088*

Alert Beep option for Client32 drivers, 655

Alert view in Windows NT Performance Monitor, 932

all network broadcasts, **89**

alternating current, **276–278,** *277*

Amaya Web browser, **725**

amplitude, **270–271,** *271,* **1464**

AMs (active monitors), **195–196,** *197,* **1464**

AMTs (Address Mapping Tables), **161**

analog communications, **5–6, 270–272.** *See also* digital communications

amplitude and, 270–271, *271,* 1464

analog dial-up connections, 249–251, 1363

cabling and, 279

communication synchronization and, 278–279

frequency and, 270–272

noise and, 272, *273*

remote access connections using analog lines, 254–255

analyzers

  network analyzers, 1069–1070, *1069, 1070*

  protocol analyzers, 1379–1381, 1476

anti-static precautions, 1406–1407

anti-virus procedures, **1222–1223, 1414–1415, 1480**

Apache Web servers, **718–719**

Apple Computer. *See* Macintosh computers

AppleShare protocol, **166–168, 619–627**

  AppleShare 5 features, **620–627**

    administration, 622–623, 626

    CGI (Common Gateway Interface) support, 623

    HTTP logging, 623

    IMAP (Internet Message Access Protocol) support, 624

    mail server, 623–624

    overview of, 620–621

    print server, 625

    security, 622–623

    TCP/IP over AFP, 621

    Viacom Internet Gateway, 627

    Web and File Server, 621–622

    ASIP (AppleShare IP), **166–168, 620**

    OpenDoc format and, 626–627

    Windows networking and, 700

  history of, 619–620

AppleTalk protocol, **18–19, 61, 73, 158–158, 610–618, 1288, 1464.**
  See also Macintosh computers

  address space, **159–162**

    AARP (AppleTalk Address Resolution Protocol), 161

    AMTs (Address Mapping Tables), 161

    local frame delivery, 161

    NBP (Name Binding Protocol), 162

    network numbers, 159–160

    overview of, 159–161

    seeding and nonseeding nodes, 160

    ZIP (Zone Information Protocol), 162

    zones, 42, 162

  ADSP (AppleTalk Data Stream Protocol), 616

  AEP (AppleTalk Echo Protocol), 617–618

  AppleTalk routing, **163–164,** *164*

  DDP (Datagram Delivery Protocol), 616

  EtherTalk, **614–615**

    ELAP (EtherTalk Link Access Protocol), 614

    extended versus non-extended networks, 615

    zones, 614–615

  flags, **61**

  in Linux, 522, 532

  LocalTalk, **611–614, 1294–1295**

    CSMA/CA (carrier sense multiple access with collision avoidance), 612–613

    dynamic node assignment, 613–614

    LLAP (LocalTalk Link Access Protocol), 612

  Microsoft AppleTalk Protocol Properties dialog box, 486, *487*

  in NetWare

    binding AppleTalk protocol to network interface cards, 423

    configuring AppleTalk with INETCFG.NLM, 440–441

    configuring LAN interfaces to use AppleTalk, 443–444

    loading APPLETALK.NLM, 419–421

  Network layer services, **162–163**

  OSI model and, 159, *159*

  overview of, 18–19

  RTMP (Routing Table Maintenance Protocol), 163–164, *163,* 617

  sockets, **73**

  TokenTalk, **615**

  Transport and Session layer services, **164–165**

    ASP (AppleTalk Session Protocol), 165, 616

    ATP (AppleTalk Transaction Protocol), 164–165, *164,* 617

    PAP (Printer Access Protocol), 165, 618

  troubleshooting, **1312–1315**

  upper layer services, **165–168**

    AFP (AppleTalk Filing Protocol), 165–167, 618, 621

    ASIP (AppleShare IP), 166–168, 620, 626–627, 700

  zones

    in AppleTalk, 42, 162

    in EtherTalk, 614–615

    ZIP (Zone Information Protocol), 162

Application Configuration Access Protocol (ACAP), **122**

application gateways, **751–753**

Application Launcher (NAL) in NetWare, 411

Application layer

    IPX Application layer services, **147–148**

    in OSI model, **37**, 38, 41, 64, 74, **1290**, **1465**

    TCP/IP Application layer services, **111–131**. *See also* DHCP; Domain Name Service; Network File System; SNMP

        ACAP (Application Configuration Access Protocol), 122

        bootp (Boot Protocol), 111, 112, 415

        FTP (File Transfer Protocol), **116–118**, *116*, *117*, 415, 523–524, **1470**

        Gopher, 119, 524, 1471

        HTTP (Hypertext Transfer Protocol), **119–120**, 214, 524, 623

        IMAP4 (Internet Message Access Protocol, Version 4), **120–122**, 524, 624, 978

        MIME (Multimedia Internet Mail Extensions), **119**, 127, 978, 981

        NetBIOS over IP, **124**, 154–156, *155*

        NNTP (Network News Transfer Protocol), 123–124, 1474

        Passive FTP (PASV FTP), 117–118

        POP (Post Office Protocol), 120–121, **125–127**, 524, **978**

        SMTP (Simple Mail Transfer Protocol), 127, 979, 981, 1478

        Telnet, **61–64**, *63*, 73, *74*, **129**, 525, 1128–1129

        WHOIS, 129–131

application section of extranets, 827

application servers, **390–391**

applications

    application-based e-mail systems, 391

    extranet application architectures, 787

    network aware applications, 389–390

    port numbers and, 69–70

applying baseline information, **945–946**

ARCnet networks, **1295–1296**, **1465**

arnudp100.c attacks, **1028**

ARP (Address Resolution Protocol), **102–103**, **1464**

ARP (Address Resolution Protocol) frames, 220

arp command

    in Unix, 1124

    in Windows NT, 1114–1115

Artisoft. *See* LANtastic

AS (autonomous systems), **107–108**, *108*

ASIP (AppleShare IP), **166–168**, 620

    OpenDoc format and, 626–627

    Windows networking and, 700

ASP (AppleTalk Session Protocol), **165**, **616**

assigning

    IP addresses, 763–765

    user and group rights, 970–976

Asymmetric DSL (ADSL), 397–398

asynchronous transfer mode (ATM) networks, 242–246, *244*, 1062, 1465

AT&T 285A standard for twisted-pair connectors, 293–295

atcon tool in NetWare, 1107

ATM (asynchronous transfer mode) networks, 242–246, *244*, 1062, 1465

ATM Cell Switching Internet connections, **715**

atmcon tool in NetWare, 1108

ATP (AppleTalk Transaction Protocol), 164–165, *164*, **617**

Attached Resource Computer Network (ARCnet), **1295–1296**, **1465**

attitude, **1048–1049**

auditing

    Auditcon utility in NetWare, 412–413

    information access, 988–989

    in Windows NT, 469–470

authentication, **467**, **472**, **1017–1020**, **1035–1036**

    credit card transactions and, 1018–1020

    password authentication in Web servers, 1035–1036

    S-HTTP (Secure HTTP), 1017–1018

    SSL (Secure Sockets Layer) and, 472, 1017–1018

    in Windows NT, 467

Author access in Lotus Notes, 566

Auto Reconnect Level option for Client32 drivers, 655

automatic loading of BIOS into upper memory, 1177

autonomous systems (AS), **107–108**, *108*

Azure ExpertPharaoh software, 1070, *1070*

B

B class IP addresses, 84–88, *86, 87*, 757–758, 1467

backbone connections for stackable hubs, 341

backbone networks, **831–832**, *831*

backbone section of extranets, 828–829, *828*

background processes in Linux, 511–513, *512, 513*

Backup Call Associations options in INETCFG.NLM, 435–436, *436*

backup domain controllers (BDCs), **466–467**

backup systems, **1395–1402**

    backing up workstation data, 1401–1402

    backup plans, 1400

    backup software, 1397–1398

    capacity of, 1397

    cost of backup media, 1398

    cost of tape drives, 1398

    evaluating, 1396–1397

    file system backups, 1399–1400

    NDS backups, 1399

    reliability of, 1399

    speed of, 1397

    support for, 1399

balancing traffic segmentation and bridge latency, 348–349

bandwidth

    bandwidth on demand WAN connections, 57, 256

    bandwidth problems in internetworking, 784

    defined, **1465**

    excessive pings and, 1134

    fiber-optic cable and, 302, 306

    and selecting cabling, 280

    twisted-pair cable and, 297

Banyan VINES, **18, 486, 586–597**

    creating File Services and Print Services, 596–597

    creating users, groups, and organizations, 596, *596*

    installing Banyan Enterprise Client, 592–594

    logging in to, 596

    naming conventions, 595, *595*

RPC Support for Banyan service in Windows NT, 486

StreetTalk, **587–595**

    installing StreetTalk Explorer for Windows NT, 594

    installing StreetTalk for Windows NT, 588–592, *589, 590*

    naming conventions, 595, *595*

    Network Communications dialog box, 589–591, *590*

base I/O port address settings, 1045–1046, *1046*

baselining, **928–946, 1465**

    advantages of, 929–930

    applying baseline information, **945–946**

    how to perform, 931–932

    when to perform, 930–931

    in wide area networks, 1374

    with Windows NT Performance Monitor, **932–945, 1122, 1190–1191**

        adding logging counters, 933–934, *933*

        comparing log files, 940

        monitoring NetWare 3.*x* servers, **941–943**

        monitoring NetWare 4.*x* servers, **943–944**

        placing bookmarks, 936–937, *937*

        selecting counters to display, 939, *940*

        selecting counters to log, 940–941

        selecting log files, 935, *935*

        selecting time intervals, 935–936

        selecting time ranges, 938–939, *939*

        starting Performance Monitor, 933

        starting and stopping logging, 936

        switching to Log view, 933

        taking notes, 937–938

        troubleshooting servers, 1190–1191

        using other utilities, 944–945

        viewing or graphing log files, 938, *938*

        views, 932–933

basic cable checkers, **1060–1063**, *1061*

baud rate, 393, 869–870, 1465

BDCs (backup domain controllers), **466–467**

beacon frames in FDDI networks, 237–239, *239*

beaconing in Token Ring networks, **201–202, 1465**

benchmarking. *See* baselining

BGP (Border Gateway Protocol), **109–110**

bidirectional cable modems, 397

binderies in NetWare, 1196

binding

    Bindings tab in Windows NT Network Properties window, 496, *497*

    defined, **1466**

    in NetWare

        bind command, 105

        BINDFIX utility, 1193–1194

        binding AppleTalk protocol to network interface cards, 423

        binding IPX protocol to network interface cards, 422–423

        binding TCP/IP protocol to network interface cards, 423–424

        Bindings option in INETCFG.NLM, 442–445

Binhex encoding, 127, 977

BIOS

    automatic loading into upper memory, 1177

    BIOS failures, 1221

    defined, **1465**

bits, **6, 30, 1466**

bits per second (bps), 393, 869–870, 1466

block suballocation in NetWare, 408

blocking broadcasts with routers, 374

BNC connectors, **284–285**, *285*, 327

b-nodes in NetBIOS addresses, 150–151, *150*

Boards option in INETCFG.NLM, 427–430, *427, 428*

bookmarks in Windows NT Performance Monitor, 936–937, *937*

books, **1426–1435**. *See also* information resources

    intranets, 1428–1429

    NetWare, 1429–1432

    network administration, 1426–1428

    reference, 1432

    security, 1435

    Unix/Linux, 1435

    Windows NT, 1432–1434

boot manager in Linux, 537

boot PROM chips, **386–387**

boot sequence

    in Macintosh workstations, 1249–1252

    in PC computers, 1227–1228

bootp (Boot Protocol), **111, 112**

    Linux bootp server, 523

    NetWare bootp support, 415

Border Gateway Protocol (BGP), **109–110**

bps (bits per second), 393, 869–870, 1466

bridges, **16, 345–359, 1300, 1466**

    balancing traffic segmentation and bridge latency, 348–349

    Bridge Protocol Data Units (BPDUs), 353

    bridge tables, **16**

    brouters, **16, 380, 1466**

    and connecting LANs at a site, 1359–1360

    and connecting LANs between buildings, 1362

    cyclic redundancy checks (CRCs) and, 350

    defined, **16, 345**, *345*, **1300, 1466**

    examples, 345–348, *346, 347, 348*

    and finding cable plant problems, 1300

    frame check sequence (FCS) and, 350

    ID numbers, 353

    and monitoring networks, 358–359

    monitoring tools in network hardware, **1070–1081**

        in bridges, 1078–1079

        error reports, 1076–1078, *1076, 1077*

        features to look for, 1072–1075, *1072, 1073, 1074*

        in routers, 1079–1081, *1079*

        SNMP and RMON (remote monitoring) support, 1081

        in switches, 1078

    protocol independence of, 349–350

    versus routers, 375

    segmenting traffic with, 353–358, *354*

    Spanning Tree protocol, **350–353**

        bridge looping and, 351–354, *351*

    wide area network problems and, 1368–1369

broadcasts

    all network broadcasts, 89

blocking with routers, 374

broadcast addresses, 89, 91–93, 219

brouters, **16, 380, 1466**

browsers, **721–726, 730, 1023–1026, 1480**

    Amaya, 725

    browser security, 736–737

    Cyberdog, 725–726

    defined, **1480**

    HotJava, 726

    implementing, 724, 730

    Internet Explorer versus Netscape, 721–725

    loopholes, **1023–1026**

        ActiveX, 1025–1026

        Java, 1024

        JavaScript, 1025

    Mosaic, 726

    Opera, 726

    plug-ins and ActiveX programs, 724–725, 1025–1026

burst mode in NCP (NetWare Core Protocol), 144–147, *145, 146*

Burst Mode option for Client32 drivers, 656

bus architectures, **324–326**

    EISA (Extended Industry Standard Architecture), 325, 1177

    ISA (Industry Standard Architecture), 324–325

    Micro Channel, 325, 1244

    for multiport serial adapters, 882

    NU-Bus, 325

    PCI (Peripheral Component Interconnect), 325–326, 1172, 1177

    S-Bus, 325

    and troubleshooting NetWare servers, 1171–1173

    VESA local bus, 325

bus topology, **208**, *209*

    linear bus topology, **1285, 1466**

    thin Ethernet (thinnet) cabling and, 13

business relationships, extranets and, 800

bytes, **6, 30, 1466**

C

C2 security certification in NetWare, 411

C class IP addresses, 84–88, *86, 87*, 757–758, 1467

cable modems, **396–397**

cabling, **280–308**. *See also* connectors; transmission media

    analog and digital communications and, 279

    ARCnet cabling requirements, **1296**

    basic cable checkers, **1060–1063**, *1061*

    cable testers, **1063–1066**, *1064*

    coaxial cables

        defined, **13, 1467**

        for Ethernet networks, **180–181**, *181*

    defined, **13–14**

    Ethernet cabling requirements, **1062, 1291**

    fiber-optic cable, **14, 299–308, 1299, 1470**

        advantages and disadvantages, 301, 303, 305–307

        bandwidth and, 302, 306

        cable properties, 299–305, *300, 303, 304*

        connectors, 305, *306*

        cost, 307

        fiber cable testers, **1063, 1066**

        installing, 307

        light dispersion and, 301

        multimode cable, 301–302

        noise and, 306

        protocols and, 305

        Rx versus Tx connections, 303–304

        security and, 306

        single-mode cable, 301

        specifications, 308

        switching time, 302

        topologies and, 304, *304*

        uses for, 307–308

    finding cable plant problems, **914–915, 1296–1301**

        cable, terminator, ground, and connector problems, 1297–1299 documenting cable plants, 1300–1301

overview of, 1296–1297

patch panel, repeater, and hub problems, 1299–1300

router, bridge, and gateway problems, 1300

media converters, **15**, **330–332**, *331*

multiport serial adapter problems, 886

network interface cards and, 326–327, *327*

noise

analog communications and, 272, *273*

defined, **272**, **1474**

digital communications and, 30, 273–274, *274*, *275*

electromagnetic interference (EMI), **13**, **276–278**, *277*, **1469**

fiber-optic cable and, 306

radio frequency interference (RFI), **13**, **278**, **1477**

thin Ethernet (thinnet) cabling and, 286

twisted-pair cable and, 298

plenum cable, 297, 1476

propagation delay, **226–228**, *227*

punch-down panels, **15**, **328–330**, **1299**

selecting, **280–282**, **312–315**

analog and digital communications and, 280

for campus networks, 314–315

cost and, 281–282

and distances between computer systems, 281

environments and, 281

fault tolerance and, 281

future growth and, 280

for medium-size networks, 313–314

for small remote offices, 313

user and application bandwidth demands and, 280

thick Ethernet (thicknet) cabling, **14**, **180–181**, *181*, **1292**

thin Ethernet (thinnet) cabling, **13–14**, **180–181**, **282–289**, **1292**

advantages and disadvantages, 286–288

bus topology and, 13

cable properties, 282–284, *283*

connectors, 284–285, *284*, *285*

cost, 286

fault resistance, 287–288

noise and, 286

scalability and, 287

shielding and, 286

specifications, 288–289

terminators, 180, 284–285, *285*, 1479

topology support, 288

uses for, 288

Token Ring cabling requirements, **1062**, **1293–1294**

troubleshooting new cabling systems, **1301–1304**

twisted-pair cable, **192**, **289–299**, **1292**, **1480**

10BaseT (twisted-pair) Ethernet standard, 1292, 1464

advantages and disadvantages, 296–298

AT&T 285A standard for connectors, 293–295

bandwidth and, 297

cable properties, 289–291, *290*, *292*

categories of, 290–291

color-coding for connectors, 293–295

connectors, 293–295, *294*, *295*

cost, 297

cross cables, 295

EIA standard for connectors, 293, 295

fault tolerance and, 297

full duplex communications, 292–293

installing, 296

length limits, 298

noise and, 298

shielded twisted-pair (STP) cabling, 192, 1478

specifications, 299

splicing, 329

straight-through cables, 295

topology wiring requirements, **1062**

uses for, 298

unshielded twisted-pair (UTP) cabling

CAT3 (Category 3) cable, 226, 234, 328, 329, 1298–1299

CAT5 (Category 5) cable, 14, 328, 329, 1298–1299

in Ethernet networks, 181–182, *182*, 1298–1299

hubs and, 338

star topology and, 14

in Token Ring networks, 192

Web sites for cable vendors, 1451

cache buffer statistics in Windows NT Performance Monitor, 942, 943, 944

Cache NetWare Password option for Client32 drivers, 656

Cache Writes option for Client32 drivers, 656

campus networks, 314–315

Capture Buffer option in LANalyzer, 1087

CAPTURE program in NetWare, 1326, 1329–1330, 1385, 1386

Carbon Copy software, **849–850**

carrier sense multiple access with collision avoidance (CSMA/CA), **612–613**

carrier sense multiple access with collision detection. *See* CSMA/CD

CAT3 (Category 3) UTP cable, 226, 234, 328, 329, 1298–1299

CAT5 (Category 5) UTP cable, **14**, 328, 329, 1298–1299

CAUs (controlled access units), **192**

cbcb.c attacks, **1028**

cells in ATM networks, **243**

certificates

client certificate authentication, **1036**

defined, **1467**

in Lotus Notes, **563–564**

certification programs, **1442**

Certified NetWare Administrator (CNA) and Certified NetWare Engineer (CNE) programs, **1442**

CGI (Common Gateway Interface), 623

changing administrator names, 970

channel aggregation in Windows NT, 471

channel binding, **393–394**

CHAP (Challenge Handshake Authentication Protocol), 435, 493

Chariot utility, 958

Chart view in Windows NT Performance Monitor, 932

chassis hubs, **15**, **338–340**

check valves in network interface cards, **326**

Checksum option for Client32 drivers, 656–657

CIR (committed information rate), **263**

circuit switching, **212–213**, *213*, **1467**

circuits options in NetWare IPX Console, 1106–1107, *1106*

Citrix WinFrame software, **387**

Client32 drivers in NetWare, **633–683**

Advanced Settings tab and NET.CFG settings, **655–669**

Alert Beep option, 655

Auto Reconnect Level option, 655

Burst Mode option, 656

Cache NetWare Password option, 656

Cache Writes option, 656

Checksum option, 656–657

Close Behind Ticks option, 657

Delay Writes option, 657

DOS Name option, 657–658

Environment Pad option, 658

File Cache Level option, 658–659

Force First Network Drive option, 659

Handle Net Error option, 659

Hold Files option, 659

Ignore Below 16meg Memory Allocate Flag option, 659–660

Large Internet Packet Start Size option, 660

Large Internet Packets option, 660

Link Support Layer Max Buffer Size option, 660

Lock Delay option, 660–661

Lock Retries option, 661

Log File option, 661

Log File Size option, 661

Long Machine Type option, 661

Max Cache Size option, 661–662

Max Cur Dir Length option, 662

Max Read Burst Size option, 662

Max Write Burst Size option, 662

Mem Pool Size option, 662

Message Timeout option, 663

Minimum Time To Net option, 663

Name Context option, 663

NCP Max Timeout option, 663

Net Status Busy Timeout option, 664

Net Status Timeout option, 664

NetWare Protocol option, 663

Network Printers option, 664

NWLanguage option, 664–665

Opportunistic Locking option, 665

Packet Burst option, 665

Packet Burst Read Window Size option, 665

Packet Burst Write Window Size option, 665

Preferred Server option, 666

Preferred Tree option, 666

Print Header option, 666

Print Tail option, 666

Read Only Compatibility option, 666

Search Dirs First option, 667

Search Mode option, 667–668

Set Station Time option, 668

Short Machine Type option, 668

Show Dots option, 668

Signature Level option, 668–669

True Commit option, 669

Use Video BIOS option, 669

advantages of, **636–637**

Client32 for DOS/Windows 3.1x, **637–642**

  configuring networking with NET.CFG file, 642

  installing, 637–640, *638*

  startnet.bat file, 639–641

Client32 for Windows 95/98, **642–650, 654–669**

  Advanced Settings tab options, 654–669

  configuring, 644–650, *644*

  installing, 642–644, *643*

communicating with other operating systems, 634–635

IntraNetWare client for Windows NT, **650–669**

  Advanced Settings tab options, 654–669

  configuring, 651–654, *651*

  installing, 650–651, *651*

legacy drivers, 635–636

versus Microsoft client drivers for NetWare, **673–681**

NetWare Client32 Properties window for Windows 95/98, **644–650, 655–669**

  Advanced Settings tab, 649–650, *649*, 655–669

  Client32 tab, 645, *645*

  Default Capture tab, 647–649, *647*

  Login tab, 645–647, *646*

  opening, 644, *644*

Novell IntraNetWare Client Services Configuration window for Windows NT, **651–669**

  Advanced Login tab, 652–653, *653*

  Advanced Settings tab, 654–659

  Client tab, 652, *652*

  Login tab, 652

  Novell Workstation Manager tab, 653–654, *654*

  opening, 651, *651*

client communications, **634–703**. *See also* Network File System

  communications between operating systems, **634–635**

  with FTP servers or Web servers, **700–703**

    in Macintosh environments, 701

    overview of, 700

    in Unix or Linux, 703

    in Windows 3.1x, 701

    in Windows 95/98 or NT Workstation, 702

    in Windows NT Server, 702

  in Macintosh environments, **697–700**

    with FTP servers or Web servers, 701

    NetWare support, 697–698

    peer-to-peer networking with Macintosh, Windows 95/98, and Windows NT, 700

    Windows NT support, 698–699

  Microsoft client drivers for NetWare, **670–681**

    versus Client32 drivers, **673–681**

    configuring, 671–672, *672*

    installing and configuring Microsoft NDS client, 672–673, *673*, 1241

    installing in Windows 95/98, 670–671, *670*, *671*

    Microsoft Client for NetWare Networks Properties window, 671–672, *672*

  NetWare IP, **681–683**, *682*

client communications in Windows NT environments, **477–479**, **683–691**

  Client for Microsoft Networks Properties window, **685–691**

  configuring TCP/IP, 686–691

  enabling Windows NT domain logons, 685

  Logon Validation options, 685–686

  quick logon option, 685–686

  configuring Windows NT Workstation, 691, *692*

  Gateway (and Client) Services for NetWare in Windows NT, 477–479, *478, 479*

  installing TCP/IP support, 684, *684*

  Microsoft clients on Windows 95/98, **683–691**

  configuring, 685–691, *685, 687, 688, 690*

  installing, 683–684

  TCP/IP Properties dialog box, **686–691**

  Advanced tab, 691

  Bindings tab, 690

  DNS Configuration tab, 687–689, *688*

  Gateway tab, 689

  IP Address tab, 686–687, *687*

  NetBIOS tab, 689

  WINS Configuration tab, 689–690, *690*

client/server applications

  defined, **1467**

  Lotus Notes client software, 555, 568–569

clients. *See also* servers; troubleshooting workstations; workstations

  Banyan Enterprise Client, 592–594

  client certificate authentication, **1036**

  connecting to in LANtastic, 599–600, *600*

  defined, **391**

  Gateway (and Client) Services for NetWare in Windows NT, 477–479, *478, 479*

  Lotus Notes client software, 555, 559–560, 568–569

  PS/2 (Micro Channel) clients, 1244

  thin clients, **386–388**

clone servers, **902–903**

Close Behind Ticks option for Client32 drivers, 657

cluster size in Windows NT, 464–465

CNA (Certified NetWare Administrator) programs, **1442**

CNE (Certified NetWare Engineer) programs, **1442**

coaxial cables. *See also* thin Ethernet (thinnet) cabling

  defined, **13**, **1467**

  for Ethernet networks, **180–181**, *181*

codexes, **394–395**

collision domains, **347**, *348*

collisions. *See also* CSMA/CA; CSMA/CD

  CSMA/CA (carrier sense multiple access with collision avoidance), **612–613**

  CSMA/CD (carrier sense multiple access with collision detection)

  defined, **11**, **175**, **216–218**, *217*, **1466**

  receiving frames, 177–179, *178*

  transmitting frames, 175–177, *176*

  defined, **8**, **11**, **176**, **1467**

  troubleshooting excessive network collisions, **1150–1153**, *1150*

color-coding for twisted-pair connectors, 293–295

combo network interface cards, **327**

command-line interface in Linux, 510

command-line tools

  in NetWare, **1094–1101**

  config, 1094–1095, *1094*

  display networks, 1095, *1095*

  display servers, 1096, *1096*

  packet burst statistics screen, 1097–1099, *1097*

  protocols, 1097

  reset router, 1099

  tping, 1099

  track on, 1099–1101, *1100*

  in Windows NT, **1114–1121**

  arp, 1114–1115

  ipxroute, 1115

  nbtstat, 1115–1116, *1116*

  netstat, 1117–1118, *1117*

  nslookup, 1118–1120

  ping, 1120–1121

  route, 1121

  tracert, 1121

commands
    bind command in NetWare, 105
    route, 105–106
    traceroute, 43–45, *43*, *45*
commerce. *See* e-commerce
committed information rate (CIR), **263**
Common Gateway Interface (CGI), 623
Common Object Model (COM), **795**
Common Object Request Broker Architecture (CORBA), **795**
communication synchronization, **278–279**
Compaq Carbon Copy, **849–850**
compiling Linux kernel, 537
compression
    in analog communications, 250
    in NetWare, 409
    in Windows NT, 464
Computer Browser service in Windows NT, 476
computers. *See* clients; Macintosh computers; PC computers; servers; workstations
concentrators. *See* hubs
config command in NetWare, 1094–1095, *1094*
configuration report servers (CRSes), **198**
configuring. *See also* client communications
    copying workstation configurations, 385–386
    IntraNetWare client for Windows NT, 651–654, *651*
    LANtastic, 599, *599*
    Linux kernel, **527–537**
        cleaning up the work space, 536
        compiling the kernel, 537
        configuration options, 528–536
        configuring the boot manager, 537
        overview of, 527–528, *528*, *529*
        performing dependency checks, 536
    Lotus Notes, 555–556, *556*
    Microsoft client drivers for NetWare, 671–672, *672*
    Microsoft NDS client, 672–673, *673*, 1241
    modems, 871
    NetWare networking from the command line, **418–425**

        binding AppleTalk protocol to network interface cards, 423
        binding IPX protocol to network interface cards, 422–423
        binding TCP/IP protocol to network interface cards, 423–424
        loading APPLETALK.NLM, 419–421
        loading LAN drivers, 421–422
        loading TCPIP.NLM, 418–419
        running network commands during startup, 424–425, *425*
    NetWare networking with INETCFG.NLM, **426–451**
        Backup Call Associations options, 435–436, *436*
        Bindings option, 442–445
        Boards option, 427–430, *427*, *428*
        Configure Remote Access To This Server option, 447–449, *447*
        configuring AppleTalk protocol, 440–441
        configuring IPX protocol, 437–440
        configuring LAN interfaces to use AppleTalk, 443–444
        configuring LAN interfaces to use IPX, 442–443
        configuring LAN interfaces to use TCP/IP, 444
        configuring network drivers, 427–429, *428*
        configuring SNMP, 446
        configuring TCP/IP protocol, 441–442
        configuring WAN groups to use TCP/IP, 444–445, *445*
        Edit AUTOEXEC.NCF option, 449
        Export Configuration option, 446–447
        Go To Fast Setup option, 451
        Import Configuration option, 447
        Manage Configuration option, 446–449, *446*
        Network Interface option, 430–432, *430*, *431*
        PPP Network Interface Configuration window, 430–432, *431*
        Protocols option, 437–442, *437*
        Reinitialize System option, 450–451
        View Configuration option, 449–450, *450*
        WAN Call Directory option, 432–435, *433*
    network access in Linux, **526–540**
        AppleTalk support, 532
        changing network driver settings, 537–538, *538*
        configuring the kernel, **527–537**

configuring routing, 539–540, *540*

Ethernet support, 534

firewall options, 530

IP tunneling, 531

IPX support, 532

Kernel Configurator window, 537–538, *538*

Network Configurator window, 539–540, *540*

network interface card configuration, 534–535, 536

PPP support, 533, 535–536

radio network support, 534

Set Module Options dialog box, 538, *538*

SLIP support, 533

starting network services, 538–539

TCP/IP support, 517, 523–525, 530–532, 549

network access in Lotus Notes, **570–573**, *570*, *571*

Open Transport in Macintosh workstations, 1259

OS/2 Warp, 578–583, *582*

SNMP in NetWare, 446, 1102

TCP/IP services in Linux, 549

TCP/IP services in Windows NT, 686–691

tracking configurations, **1045–1047**, *1046*

Windows NT with Network Properties window, **473–497**

  Adapters tab, 495–496, *496*

  Advanced IP Addressing dialog box, 493, *493*

  Bindings tab, 496, *497*

  Configure Gateway dialog box, 479, *479*

  configuring network interface cards, 495–496, *496*

  Identification tab, 473–474, *474*

  Microsoft AppleTalk Protocol Properties dialog box, 486, *487*

  Microsoft TCP/IP Properties dialog box, 494–495, *494*

  Network Access Order dialog box, 478–479, *478*

  Network Configuration dialog box, 483, *483*

  Network Services tab, 474–488, *475*, *476*

  New Profile dialog box, 484, *484*

  New Remoteboot Workstation dialog box, 484–485, *485*

  NWLink IPX/SPX Properties dialog box, 491, *491*

  PPTP Configuration dialog box, 491–492, *492*

  Printer Ports dialog box, 490, *490*

  Protocols tab, 488–495, *489*

  Remote Access Setup dialog box, 482–483, *483*, 492, *492*

  Remoteboot Manager, 484, *484*

  saving changes, 497

  setting protocol binding order, 496, *497*

  Windows NT Remote Access Service (RAS), **861–869**

    configuring communications, 861–863, *862*

    configuring Dial-Up Networking clients, 868

    configuring protocols, 863–865, *864*, *865*

    configuring security, 865–867, *866*, *867*

    disadvantages of RAS, 868–869

  Windows NT Workstation for client communications, 691, *692*

conflicts

  address conflicts in wide area networks, 1375

  extension conflicts, 1255–1257

  interrupt conflicts in PC computers, 1230–1231

connection control fields in IPX protocol, **61**

connection jumping, **412**

connectionless communications, **64–68**, *65*, **1290**

connection-oriented communications, **61–64**, *63*, **1290**

connectors. *See also* cabling

  BNC connectors, 284–285, *285*, 327

  DB connectors, 193, 880, *880*

  FDDI connectors, 305

  for fiber-optic cable, 305, *306*

  and finding cable plant problems, 1297–1299

  IBM connectors, 193

  RJ-11 connectors, 293, *294*, 328

  RJ-45 connectors, **193**, **293**, *294*

    hubs and, 338, 342

    for network interface cards, 323, 327

  SMA connectors, 305, 328

  T-connectors, 180

  for thin Ethernet (thinnet) cabling, 284–285, *284*, *285*

  in Token Ring networks, 193

  for twisted-pair cable, 293–295, *294*, *295*

  Web sites for connector vendors, 1451

console tools in NetWare, **1093–1101**

container objects in Novell Directory Services, 1387–1389

contaminants, 1406

control of extranets, 818, 820

control panels in Macintosh workstations, 1247, 1252–1257

controlled access units (CAUs), **192**

convergence time in link-state routing, 58, 59–60

copying workstation configurations, 385–386

copyleft software, **505**

CORBA (Common Object Request Broker Architecture), **795**

corrupted SERVER.EXE or NET$OS.EXE files in NetWare,
    1192–1193

cost
    of backup media, 1398
    of cabling, 281–282
    of chassis hubs, 340
    of fiber-optic cable, 307
    of firewalls, 711
    of Internet access, 715–716, 729
    of multiport serial adapters, 890
    of remote access servers, 895
    in routing, 58–59
    of tape drives, 1398
    of telecommuting, 840–841, 842
    of telecommuting via remote control, 848
    of thin Ethernet (thinnet) cabling, 286
    of twisted-pair cable, 297

counting to infinity in distance-vector routing, **55**

CPUs support in Windows NT, 462, 463

CRCs. *See* cyclic redundancy checks

creating
    File Services and Print Services in Banyan VINES, 596–597
    hunt groups for modem pools, 253–254
    Linux shares with SAMBA, 545–548
    NetWare shares with SAMBA, 451–454, *455*
    users, groups, and organizations in Banyan VINES, 596, *596*

credit card transactions, 1018–1020

cross cables, **295**

cross-certification in Lotus Notes, **564**

CRSes (configuration report servers), **198**

CSMA/CA (carrier sense multiple access with collision avoid-
    ance), **612–613**

CSMA/CD (carrier sense multiple access with collision detection)
    defined, **11**, **175**, **216–218**, *217*, **1466**
    receiving frames, 177–179, *178*
    transmitting frames, 175–177, *176*

CSU/DSUs (channel service unit/data service unit), **398**, *398*

CSUs (channel service units), **399**

customer support hotlines, **1052**

cut-through mode switches, **361–362**

Cyberdog Web browser, **725–726**

cyclic redundancy checks (CRCs), **174–175**
    bridges and, 350
    routers and, 373–374

D

DAC (dual-attach concentrators) in FDDI networks, 240, *241*

DAS (dual-attach stations) in FDDI networks, 237, *238*, 240, *241*

dashboard in LANalyzer, 1086, *1087*

data communication protocols, **1286**, *1286*

Data Link Control (DLC) protocol, 490, *490*, 1468

Data Link layer
    Linux Data Link layer support, 519
    in OSI model, **36**, 39, 40, 46, 64, **1289**, **1468**

data migration in NetWare, 409–410

data section of Ethernet frames, 174

data sharing, 973–974

Datagram Delivery Protocol (DDP), **616**

datagram packet switching networks, **214–215**, *215*, 261–262, **1468**

datagram service in NetBIOS protocol, 156–157

DB connectors, **193**, **880**, *880*

DC circuits, **276**

DCOM (Distributed Common Object Model), **795**

DDP (Datagram Delivery Protocol), **616**

de facto standards, **70**

default accounts in Windows NT Workstation, 1008–1009

Default Capture tab in NetWare Client32 Properties window, 647–649, *647*

Delay Writes option for Client32 drivers, 657

deleting

    default accounts, 969–970

    protocols in Windows NT, 489, *489*

    recovering deleted files in Windows NT, 465

    services from Windows NT, 475–476, *475, 476*

demand priority in 100VG-AnyLAN topology, **231–232**

demarcation points, **248, 1468**

denial-of-service (DoS) attacks, **827**, 1024, 1028

dependency checks in Linux, 536

Depositor access in Lotus Notes, 566

Designer access in Lotus Notes, 566

designing

    extranets, **827–832**

        access network design, 829–830

        backbone networks, 831–832, *831*

        backbone section, 828–829, *828*

        end-user or application section, 827

        full-mesh networks, 830, *830*

        Internet 2 project, 809

        network section, 828

        partial-mesh networks, 830–831, *831*

    file systems, 971–972

    firewalls, 709–710, *710*

Detailed IPX Information option in NetWare IPX Console, 1103–1104, *1103*

device drivers. *See* drivers

DHCP (Dynamic Host Configuration Protocol), **112**

    and assigning IP addresses, 763–765

    DHCP Relay agent in Windows NT, 476–477

    DHCP server in NetWare, 415

    IP addresses and, 763–7653

    Microsoft DHCP Server, 479–480

diagnostic tools, **1066–1067**. *See also* troubleshooting

    handheld diagnostic tools for troubleshooting hardware, 1066–1067, *1067*

    for troubleshooting servers, 1195–1196

    for troubleshooting wide area networks, **1378–1384**

        doing without, 1384

        hardware-based products, 1379–1381

        LANalyzer, 1086–1093, 1383

        in NetWare, 1383

        protocol analyzers, 1379–1381, 1476

        software-only products, 1381–1384

        Windows NT Network Monitor, 481–482, *482*, 1121, 1190, 1381

        Windows NT Performance Monitor, 1382–1383

dial-in access security, **1418–1419**

dial-in/dial-out servers, 1370–1371

dial-up connections

    defined, **1468**

    dial-up analog connections, **249–251**

    to local ISPs, 714

digital communications. *See also* analog communications

    cabling and, 279

    communication synchronization and, 278–279

    defined, **5–6**, **272–276**, *274, 275*

digital dial-up LAN connections, 1363–1364

digital leased lines, **258–259, 1468**

Digital Network Architecture (DNA), **32**

Digital Subscriber Lines (DSLs), **397–398, 888–889**

direct current, **276**

directories. *See also* NDS (Novell Directory Services)

    directory replication in Windows NT, 465

    directory-level access in Web servers, 1031–1035, *1033, 1034*

    directory-level permissions in Windows NT Workstation, 1015

    folder security in Windows NT Workstation, 1009–1011, *1011*

    user or home directories, 974–976

Directory Services in Windows NT, 465

disaster recovery, **1419–1421**

disk mirroring and duplexing, **910–911**, **1198–1199**, *1199*, **1469**

disk striping, **910–912**, **1469**

disks. *See* hard disk drives

display networks command in NetWare, 1095, *1095*

display servers command in NetWare, 1096, *1096*

distance-vector routing, **49–56**, **1469**. *See also* routing

    counting to infinity in, 55

    limitations of, 53–56, *54*, *55*

    propagating network information with, 49–53, *50*

Distributed Common Object Model (DCOM), **795**

distributed objects, **794–795**

distributing Linux, 505

DLC (Data Link Control) protocol, 490, *490*, 1468

DMA channel settings, 1045–1046, *1046*

DNA (Digital Network Architecture), **32**

document databases in Lotus Notes, 554

documentation

    documenting cable plants, 1300–1301

    documenting networks, 1049–1051, *1050*, *1051*, 1411–1412

domain controllers in Windows NT, **466–467**

Domain Name Service (DNS)

    defined, **112–116**, *113*, **1469**

    DNS server in NetWare, 415

    DNSKiller attacks, 1027

    IP addresses and, 102–103

    Linux DNS server, 523

    Microsoft DNS Server, 473, 480

    WINS (Windows Internet Name Service) and, 480

domains in Windows NT, 465–466, 469, 1469

Domino software, **569–570**

DOS. *See also* PC computers

    Client32 for DOS, **637–642**

        configuring networking with NET.CFG file, 642

        installing, 637–640, *638*

        startnet.bat file, 639–641

    DOS file servers, 389

DOS Name option for Client32 drivers, 657–658

    operating system and network driver failures, 1223–1224

    troubleshooting problems, 1234

DoS (denial-of-service) attacks, **827**, 1024, 1028

downloading

    Linux installation files, 504, 506

    SAMBA files for NetWare, 452

downstream neighbors of Token Ring stations, 188

drivers. *See also* Client32 drivers

    changing network driver settings in Linux, 537–538, *538*

    in NetWare

        configuring with INETCFG.NLM, 427–429, *428*

        legacy drivers for clients, 635–636

        loading LAN drivers, 421–422

        in NetWare servers, 1186

        troubleshooting, 1235–1236

    network driver failures

        in DOS and Windows 3.*x*, 1223–1224

        in Windows 95/98, 1221–1223

        in Windows NT, 1223

    ODI drivers, 635–636, 1235–1236

drives. *See* hard disk drives

drops, **328**, 329

DSLs (Digital Subscriber Lines), **397–398**, **888–889**

DSMigrate utility in NetWare, 404–405

DSTRACE and DSREPAIR software in NetWare servers, 1194

DSUs (data service units), **398–399**

dual-attach concentrators (DAC) in FDDI networks, 240, *241*

dual-attach stations (DAS) in FDDI networks, 237, *238*, 240, *241*

dumb loads, **950**

duplexing disks, 910–911, 1198–1199, *1199*, 1469

dust, 1406

Dynamic Host Configuration Protocol. *See* DHCP

dynamic node assignment in LocalTalk, 613–614

dynamic packet-filtering firewalls, 67–68

dynamic routing, **106–110**, **1469**

E

E2 security certification in NetWare, 411

EBGP (External Border Gateway Protocol), 109–110

e-commerce, 785, 800–801, 817

EDI (Electronic Data Interchange) vendors, **822**

Edit AUTOEXEC.NCF option in INETCFG.NLM, 449

Editor access in Lotus Notes, 566

educating users, 1413–1414

EGP (Exterior Gateway Protocol), **107–109**, *108*

EIA standard for twisted-pair connectors, 293, 295

EISA (Extended Industry Standard Architecture) bus, **325**, 1177

ELAP (EtherTalk Link Access Protocol), **614**

electromagnetic interference (EMI), **13**, **276–278**, *277*, **1469**

Electronic Data Interchange (EDI) vendors, **822**

e-mail

    AppleShare 5 mail server, 623–624

    file-based versus application-based e-mail systems, **391**

    Linux Mail server, 524

    in Lotus Notes, 560–561

    security, **976–983**

        encryption, 981–982

        external security, 980–983

        internal security, 979–980

        overview of, 976–977

        SMTP and MIME and, 981

        spamming protection, 982–983

        spoofing, 983

        terms defined, 977–979

    testing e-mail delivery, 1139–1143

    troubleshooting undeliverable e-mail, **1138–1143**

encryption

    defined, **1470**

    guidelines, 981–982, 986–987, 1022–1023

    in Lotus Notes, 74, 564–565

end-user section of extranets, 827

Environment Pad option for Client32 drivers, 658

error reports in network hardware monitoring tools, 1076–1078, *1076*, *1077*

Ethernet networks, 8, **11**, **172–185**, **216–221**, **1291–1292**, **1456–1461**, **1470**. *See also* networks; troubleshooting physical networks

    1Gbps Ethernet topology, 229–231

    10Mb Ethernet topology, 221–225

    100Mb Ethernet topology, 225–229

    advantages and disadvantages, **183–184**

    cabling requirements, **1062**, **1291**

    coaxial cables, **180–181**, *181*

    CSMA/CD (carrier sense multiple access with collision detection), **11**, **175–179**, **216–218**, **1466**

        defined, **11**, **175**, **216–218**, *217*, **1466**

        receiving frames, 177–179, *178*

        transmitting frames, 175–177, *176*

    frames, **173–179**, **218–221**

        Address Resolution Protocol (ARP) frames, 220

        broadcast addresses and, 219

        CRCs (cyclic redundancy checks), 174–175

        data section, 174

        frame check sequence (FCS), 174–175

        header section, 174, 218–221

        MAC (media access control) addresses and, 218–219, *220*

        node addresses and, 218, 1094

        preamble section, 173

        receiving with CSMA/CD, 177–179, *178*

        transmitting with CSMA/CD, 175–177, *176*

    IEEE 802.*x* standards, **172–173**

    improving Ethernet performance, **914–921**

        with cable plants, 914–915

        with hubs, 915–916

        with routers, 920–921

        with switches, 916–920, *917*, *918*

    Linux Ethernet support, 534

    Manufacturer's Ethernet Identifier (MEI) numbers, **1456–1461**

    T-connectors, **180**

    thick Ethernet (thicknet) cabling, **14**, **180–181**, *181*, **1292** thin Ethernet (thinnet) cabling, **13–14**, **180–181**, **282–289**, **1292**

  advantages and disadvantages, 286–288

  bus topology and, 13

  cable properties, 282–284, *283*

  connectors, 284–285, *284*, *285*

  cost, 286

  fault resistance, 287–288

  noise and, 286

  scalability and, 287

  shielding and, 286

  specifications, 288–289

  terminators, 180, 284–285, *285*, 1479

  topologies and, 288

  uses for, 288

troubleshooting, **1304–1306**, *1305*

unshielded twisted-pair (UTP) cabling, **181–182**, *182*, 1298–1299

EtherTalk protocol, **614–615**

  ELAP (EtherTalk Link Access Protocol), 614

  extended versus non-extended networks, 615

  zones, 614–615

evaluating

  backup systems, 1396–1397

  power needs, 1404

  power protection systems, 1402–1403

Event Viewer in Windows NT, 1189–1190, *1190*

excessive network collisions, **1150–1153**, *1150*

exchange carriers, **248–249**, *249*

ExpertPharaoh software, 1070, *1070*

Export Configuration option in INETCFG.NLM, 446–447

Extended Industry Standard Architecture (EISA) bus, **325**, 1177

extended networks, **615**

extensions in Macintosh workstations, 1247, 1252–1257

Exterior Gateway Protocol (EGP), **107–109**, *108*

External Border Gateway Protocol (EBGP), 109–110

external e-mail security, 980–983

external port connections for network interface cards, 320, 321–322, *322*

extranets, **20**, **781–783**, **786–833**. *See also* extranets; internetworking; intranets

  adding value with, 801

  advantages of, 820

  application architectures, 787

  business relationships and, 800

  control of, 818, 820

  designing, **827–832**

    access network design, 829–830

    backbone networks, 831–832, *831*

    backbone section, 828–829, *828*

    end-user or application section, 827

    full-mesh networks, 830, *830*

    Internet 2 project, 809

    network section, 828

    partial-mesh networks, 830–831, *831*

  distributed objects and, 794–795

  Electronic Data Interchange (EDI) vendors, 822

  expanding intranet borders with, 799–800

  as extended intranets, 790–793, *791*, *792*

  extending intranet functionality with, 798–800

  as external intranets, 787–789, *789*, *790*

  extranet phase of internetworking history, 781–783, *783*

  extranet service providers, 814, 821–822

  hybrid extranets, **812**, **821**

  Internet 2 project example, **807–811**

    architecture of, 810, *811*

    design principles, 809

    organizational cooperation, 809–810

    overview of, 807–808

  Internet commerce and, 800–801, 817

  internetworking and, 781–783, *783*, 786–787, 795–797

  interoperability and, 794, 796

  as interorganizational internetworks, **807**

  open extranets, **815–820**

    advantages and disadvantages, 818–819, *818*, 820

    control of, 818, 820

    implementing, 819–820

overview of, 802, 806, 832–833

platform independence and, 796–797

private extranets, **812–815**

    advantages and disadvantages, 814–815

    implementing, 815

    versus the Internet, 812–813, *813*

topologies of, **811–812**

value-added networks (VANs) and, 821, 822

virtual private networks (VPNs), **21, 789, 823–827**

    Alta Vista Tunnel, **823–826**, *824*

    denial-of-service (DoS) attacks, 827, 1024, 1028

    how VPNs work, 824–826, *824*, *825*

    Internet security and, 1020–1022

    PPTP (Point-to-Point Tunneling Protocol) and, 826

    security systems, 826–827

    tunneling versus firewall gateway VPNs, 823–824

F

Fast Setup in INETCFG.NLM, 451

FAT file system in Windows NT, **464–465**

fault points. *See also* troubleshooting

    defined, **1053–1054**, *1055*

    for network printing, **1323–1326**, *1324*

    for physical networks, **1280–1282**, *1281*

    for servers, 1163–1165, *1164*

    of wide area networks, **1367–1375**

        address conflicts, 1375

        baselining, 1374

        bridge problems, 1368–1369

        configuration utilities and, 1373–1374

        dial-in/dial-out server problems, 1370–1371

        gateway problems, 1369–1370

        network address problems, 1373

        repeater problems, 1368

        router problems, 1369

        software configuration problems, 1374–1375

        telecommunications service provider problems, 1372

        troubleshooting WAN hardware, **1368–1371**

        troubleshooting WAN software, **1372–1375**

    for workstations, **1218–1224**

        DOS/Windows 3.*x* system and network driver failures, 1223–1224

        PC Card, motherboard, or BIOS failures, 1221

        user failures, 1224

        Windows 95/98 system and network driver failures, 1221–1223

        Windows NT system and network driver failures, 1223

        workstation-to-network connection failures, 1220

fault tolerance

    defined, **281, 1409–1410**

    NetWare System Fault Tolerance (SFT), **1198–1201**

        mirroring and duplexing, 910–911, 1198–1199, *1199*, 1469

        RAID and, 1199–1200, *1200*

        SFT level III, 1201, *1201*, 1410

    and selecting cabling, 281

    twisted-pair cable and, 297

FCONSOLE utility in NetWare, 1191

FCS (frame check sequence)

    bridges and, 350

    Ethernet frames and, 174–175

FDDI connectors, **305**

FDDI networks, **14, 235–242, 1470**

    beacon frames, 237–239, *239*

    cables, **14**

    dual-attach concentrators (DAC), 240, *241*

    dual-attach stations (DAS), 237, *238*, 240, *241*

    single-attach stations (SAS), 240, *241*

    tokens in, 236–237

    topology rules, 242

    uses for, 241

fiber-optic cable, **14, 299–308, 1299, 1470**. *See also* cabling

    advantages and disadvantages, 301, 303, 305–307

    bandwidth and, 302, 306

    cable properties, 299–305, *300*, *303*, *304*

    connectors, 305, *306*

cost, 307

fiber cable testers, **1063**, **1066**

installing, 307

light dispersion and, 301

multimode cable, 301–302

noise and, 306

protocols and, 305

Rx versus Tx connections, 303–304

security and, 306

single-mode cable, 301

specifications, 308

switching time, 302

topologies and, 304, *304*

uses for, 307–308

File Cache Level option for Client32 drivers, 658–659

file compression

    in analog communications, 250

    in NetWare, 409

    in Windows NT, 464

file permissions. *See* permissions; rights

file servers, **388–389**

    AppleShare 5 Web and File Server, 621–622

    Windows file servers, 389

File Services in Banyan VINES, 596–597

file systems

    backing up, 1399–1400

    designing and implementing, 971–972

    file system rights, **971–974**

    in Linux, 514–515, *515*

    NetWare file system, **408–410**

        data migration, 409–410

        disk suballocation, 408

        file compression, 409

    security and, 971–972

    in Windows NT, 464–465

File Transfer Protocol. *See* FTP

file-based e-mail systems, 391

file-level permissions in Windows NT Workstation, 1015–1016

files

    recovering deleted files in Windows NT, 465

    service files, 68–69

    uuencoding and uudecoding, 127, 979

filtering

    packets in Windows NT, 471–472

    traffic with routers, 375

Finder application in Macintosh workstations, 1246, 1247, 1257–1258

finding cable plant problems, **914–915**, **1296–1301**

    cable, terminator, ground, and connector problems, 1297–1299

    documenting cable plants, 1300–1301

    overview of, 1296–1297

    patch panel, repeater, and hub problems, 1299–1300

    router, bridge, and gateway problems, 1300

Finger server in Linux, 523

firewalls, **709–712**, **747–753**, **994–1001**, **1470**. *See also* Internet access; intranets; security

    additional benefits, 711

    application gateways as firewalls, 751–753, 999

    connectionless communications and, 67–68

    cost of, 711

    designing, 709–710, *710*

    failures, **1001**

    firewall gateway virtual private networks, 823–824

    versus gateways, **994–996**

    guidelines, **1000**

    in Linux, 530

    Network Address Translation (NAT) and, 94, 709–710

    packet inspection firewalls, 752–753

    packet-filtering firewalls, 67–68, 749–750, 752–753, 996–999

    planning, 996

    proxy servers and, 751

    routers or gateways and, 994–996

    security and, 710–711

    selecting for intranets, 748–749

    sexual harrassment and, 712

spoofing and, 983

Windows NT and, 472

fixed-frequency signals, **310**

flags, **61**

flow charts. *See* fault points

Fluke LANMeter, 1067, *1067*

folders. *See* directories

Force First Network Drive option for Client32 drivers, 659

Forwarding and Services option in NetWare IPX Console, 1107

fractional T1 and T3 lines, **261**, **1364–1365**

fragments, **177**

Frame Relay networks, **261–264**, *262*, **714**, **1366**, **1470**

frames. *See also* packets

beacon frames in FDDI networks, 237–239, *239*

defined, **7**, **30**, **1470**

Ethernet frames, **173–179**, **218–221**

Address Resolution Protocol (ARP) frames, 220

broadcast addresses and, 219

CRCs (cyclic redundancy checks), 174–175

data section, 174

frame check sequence (FCS), 174–175

header section, 174, 218–221

MAC (media access control) addresses and, 218–219, *220*

node addresses and, 218, 1094

preamble section, 173

receiving with CSMA/CD, 177–179, *178*

transmitting with CSMA/CD, 175–177, *176*

fragments, 177

frame check sequence (FCS)

bridges and, 350

Ethernet frames and, 174–175

frame rates, 222

frame types supported in NetWare, 416–418

Link State Protocol (LSP) frames, 57

local frame delivery in AppleTalk, 161

in NCP (NetWare Core Protocol), 142–144, *143*

versus packets, 37

SAP frames, 148

transmitting in Token Ring networks, 189–190

frequency

defined, **270–272**, **1470**

microwave signals and, 310

frequency shifting in analog communications, 250

FTP (File Transfer Protocol)

defined, **116–118**, *116*, *117*, **1470**

Linux FTP server, 523–524

NetWare FTP server, 415

Passive FTP (PASV FTP), 117–118

FTP servers, **700–703**

in Macintosh environments, 701

overview of, 700

in Unix or Linux, 703

in Windows 3.1x, 701

in Windows 95/98 or NT Workstation, 702

in Windows NT Server, 702

full duplex communications, 292–293

switches and, 360–361

full-mesh networks, **830**, *830*

function code fields in NCP (NetWare Core Protocol), 143

functional addresses for Token Ring stations, 194–195

G

Ganymede Software Chariot and Pegasus utilities, 958

garbage collection in NetWare, 408

Gateway (and Client) Services for NetWare in Windows NT, 477–479, *478*, *479*

gateways

application gateways as firewalls, 751–753, 999

connecting LANs at a site, 1361

defined, **709**, **1300**, **1471**

and finding cable plant problems, 1300

firewall gateway virtual private networks, 823–824

versus firewalls, **994–996**

IPX-to-IP gateway in NetWare, 414

versus routers, 43

Viacom Internet Gateway in AppleShare 5, 627

and wide area network problems, 1369–1370

GENLOAD utility, 955

GN NetTest ExpertPharaoh software, 1070, *1070*

Go To Fast Setup option in INETCFG.NLM, 451

Gopher servers

defined, **119, 1471**

Linux Gopher server, 524

graphing in Windows NT Performance Monitor, 938, *938*

groups

in Banyan VINES, 596, *596*

group rights, 970–976

in Linux, 516, *516*

in Windows NT, 469

groupware, **977, 1471**

H

half duplex communications, **292–293**

handheld diagnostic tools, **1066–1067**, *1067*

Handle Net Error option for Client32 drivers, 659

handshaking, **61–64**, *63*, **1471**

hard disk drives

adding to servers, 907–910

connecting to remote drives in LANtastic, 600–602, *600, 601*

disk suballocation in NetWare, 408

mirroring and duplexing disks, **910–911, 1198–1199**, *1199*, **1469**

preparing for NetWare installation, 1185–1186

removable disks and drives, 987–988

sharing in LANtastic, 602

and troubleshooting NetWare servers, 1176

hardware. *See also* remote access

Hardware Compatibility List (HCL), 904

hardware troubleshooting tools, **1060–1082**

basic cable checkers, 1060–1063, *1061*

cable testers, 1063–1066, *1064*

fiber cable testers, 1063, 1066

handheld diagnostic tools, 1066–1067, *1067*

network analyzers, 1069–1070, *1069, 1070*

network monitoring tools, 1067–1068

hardware-based diagnostic tools for wide area networks, 1379–1381

Internet access requirements, 727–728, *728*

monitoring tools in network hardware, **1070–1081**

in bridges, 1078–1079

error reports, 1076–1078, *1076, 1077*

features to look for, 1072–1075, *1072, 1073, 1074*

in routers, 1079–1081, *1079*

SNMP and RMON (remote monitoring) support, 1081

in switches, 1078

quality of, **1404–1405**

Token Ring hardware, **191–193**

CAUs (controlled access units), 192

connectors, 193

LAMs (lobe attachment modules), 192

lobes, 192

loopback mode lobes, 193

MSAUs (multi-station access units), 191, 192, 1293

network interface cards, 192

overview of, 191, *191*

phantom charges applied to lobes, 193

relay switches, 191, 193

shielded and unshielded twisted-pair cables, 192

Web sites for hardware vendors, 1446–1451

hardware problems in existing servers, **1188–1192**

NetWare troubleshooting tools

MONITOR, 481–482, *482*, 1121, 1191

SERVMAN and FCONSOLE, 1191

system logs, 1192

VREPAIR, 1191–1192

Windows NT troubleshooting tools

Event Viewer, 1189–1190, *1190*

Network Monitor, 481–482, *482*, 1121, 1190, 1381

Performance Monitor, 1190–1191

hardware problems in new NetWare servers, **1169–1178**

    automatic loading of BIOS into upper memory, 1177

    bus architecture, 1171–1173

    hard disk drives, 1176

    interrupts and EISA or PCI configurations, 1172, 1177

    multiple network interface cards, 1176

    overview of, 1169

    RAID systems, 1175–1176

    RAM, 1170–1171

    SCSI adapters and devices, 1173–1175, *1175*

    security, 1178

    VGA adapters, 1176–1177

HDSL (Highspeed DSL), 397–398

header section of Ethernet frames, **174, 218–221**

hello packets, **56**

Help

    online Help, 1377

    resources for troubleshooting, 1052

Highspeed DSL (HDSL), 397–398

high-speed remote access, **874–875**

h-nodes in NetBIOS addresses, 152, 154

Hold Files option for Client32 drivers, 659

home directories, 974–976

hops, **43, 1471**

host addresses, **42, 761–762**

HotJava Web browser, **726**

hotlines for technical support, **1052**

HTTP (Hypertext Transfer Protocol)

    defined, **119–120, 214, 1471**

    HTTP logging in AppleShare 5, 623

    Linux HTTP server, 524

    S-HTTP (Secure HTTP), 1017–1018

hubs, **15, 291, 338–342, 1282, 1299–1300, 1471**

    chassis hubs, **15, 338–340**

    and finding cable plant problems, 1299–1300

    optimizing servers with, **915–916**

    port density of, 338

    stackable hubs, **15, 340–342**

        backbone connections, 341

        managed or intelligent stackable hubs, 15, 340–341, 1471

        unmanaged stackable hubs, 15, 341

        uplink port connections, 15, 342, *342*

    virtual hubs, 339

hunt groups for modem pools, **253–254**

hybrid extranets, **812, 821**

I

I/O port address settings, 1045–1046, *1046*

IBGP (Internal Border Gateway Protocol), 109–110

IBM

    IBM connectors, **193**

    LAN Manager, **576–577**

    OS/2 Warp, **18, 576–586**

        accessing shared resources, 585–586

        history of, 576–577

        installing and configuring, 578–583, *582*

        sharing resources, 583–585, *584*

ID numbers for bridges, 353

Identification tab in Windows NT Network Properties window, 473–474, *474*

IEEE 802.*x* standards, **172–173**

ifconfig command in Unix, 1124, *1124*

Ignore Below 16meg Memory Allocate Flag option for Client32 drivers, 659–660

IIS (Internet Information Server) in Windows NT, 472, 480–481, 719

IMAP4 (Internet Message Access Protocol, Version 4)

    AppleShare 5 IMAP support, 624

    defined, **120–122, 978**

    Linux IMAP server, 524

implementing

    file systems, 971–972

    open extranets, 819–820

private extranets, 815

Web browsers, 724, 730

Import Configuration option in INETCFG.NLM, 447

index servers in Windows NT, 473

Industry Standard Architecture (ISA) bus, **324–325**

INETCFG.NLM utility, **426–451**. *See also* NetWare

    Backup Call Associations options, 435–436, *436*

    Bindings option, 442–445

    Boards option, 427–430, *427*, *428*

    Configure Remote Access To This Server option, 447–449, *447*

    configuring AppleTalk protocol, 440–441

    configuring IPX protocol, 437–440

    configuring LAN interfaces to use AppleTalk, 443–444

    configuring LAN interfaces to use IPX, 442–443

    configuring LAN interfaces to use TCP/IP, 444

    configuring network drivers, 427–429, *428*

    configuring SNMP, 446

    configuring TCP/IP protocol, 441–442

    configuring WAN groups to use TCP/IP, 444–445, *445*

    defined, **426**, *426*

    Edit AUTOEXEC.NCF option, 449

    Export Configuration option, 446–447

    Go To Fast Setup option, 451

    Import Configuration option, 447

    Manage Configuration option, 446–449, *446*

    Network Interface option, 430–432, *430*, *431*

    PPP Network Interface Configuration window, 430–432, *431*

    Protocols option, 437–442, *437*

    Reinitialize System option, 450–451

    View Configuration option, 449–450, *450*

    WAN Call Directory option, 432–435, *433*

information resources, **1426–1442**

    books, **1426–1435**

        intranets, 1428–1429

        NetWare, 1429–1432

        network administration, 1426–1428

        reference, 1432

        security, 1435

        Unix/Linux, 1435

        Windows NT, 1432–1434

    certification programs, **1442**

    newsgroups, **1438–1439**

        Linux, 1438–1439

        NetWare, 1438

        Unix, 1439

        Windows/Windows NT, 1438

    online magazines, **1435–1438**

    standards organizations, **1439–1440**

    Web sites, **1440–1441**

inherent rights masks in NetWare, 412

INIT crawl problems in Macintosh workstations, 1252–1257

initializing Token Ring stations, 199–200

installing. *See also* migrating; upgrading

    Banyan Enterprise Client, 592–594

    Compaq Carbon Copy, 849

    fiber-optic cable, 307

    IntraNetWare client for Windows NT, 650–651, *651*

    LANtastic on Windows NT, 597–598

    Linux, 504, 506–509, *507*, *508*

    Lotus Notes, 555

    Microsoft client drivers for NetWare in Windows 95/98, 670–671, *670*, *671*

    Microsoft NDS client, 672–673, *673*, 1241

    modems, 871–873, *872*

    multiport serial adapters, 884–885

    NetWare, 404–405, 1184, 1185–1186

    OS/2 Warp, 578–583, *582*

    servers, 1202–1207

    StreetTalk Explorer for Windows NT, 594

    StreetTalk for Windows NT, 588–592, *589*, *590*

    TCP/IP support in Windows NT, 684, *684*

    Timbuktu Pro, 847, 858–859

    troubleshooting new systems and additions to systems, **1044–1047**

    twisted-pair cable, 296

    Windows NT, 460–462

Windows NT Remote Access Service (RAS), **861–869**

configuring communications, 861–863, *862*

configuring Dial-Up Networking clients, 868

configuring protocols, 863–865, *864*, *865*

configuring security, 865–867, *866*, *867*

disadvantages of RAS, 868–869

Windows NT Server, 460–462, 1178–1184

workstations, 1263–1267

intelligent loads, **950–951**

intelligent stackable hubs, **15**, **340–341**, **1471**

interference, **272**

analog communications and, 272, *273*

digital communications and, 30, 273–274, *274*, *275*

electromagnetic interference (EMI), **13**, **276–278**, *277*, **1469**

fiber-optic cable and, 306

radio frequency interference (RFI), **13**, **278**, **1477**

thin Ethernet (thinnet) cabling and, 286

twisted-pair cable and, 298

intermittent server problems, **1194–1195**

Internal Border Gateway Protocol (IBGP), 109–110

internal e-mail security, 979–980

internal IPX network addresses, 1094

internal network interface cards, **321**, **324–326**, *324*

Internet. *See also* extranets; internetworking; intranets

Domino software and Internet access, 569–570

Internet phase of internetworking history, 774–779, *774*, *775*, *779*

LIP (Large Internet Protocol), **144**

versus private extranets, 812–813, *813*

Viacom Internet Gateway in AppleShare 5, 627

Internet 2 project. *See* extranets

Internet access, **708–738**. *See also* firewalls

ATM Cell Switching connections, 715

browsers, **721–726**, **730**, **1480**

ActiveX loopholes, 1025–1026

Amaya, 725

browser security, 736–737

Cyberdog, 725–726

defined, **1480**

HotJava, 726

implementing, 724, 730

Internet Explorer versus Netscape, 721–725

Java loopholes, 1024

JavaScript loopholes, 1025

Mosaic, 726

Opera, 726

plug-ins and ActiveX programs, 724–725, 1025–1026

security loopholes, 1023–1026

cost of, 715–716, 729

dial-up connections to local ISPs, 714

hardware requirements, **727–728**, *728*

ISDN connections, 255–258, 714, 874, 888, 1471, 1472

modems and, 727

overview of, 708–709

routers and, 727

security, **730–737**

SMDS (Switched Multimegabit Data Service) connections, 715

T1 and T3 connections, 261, 715, 1364–1365

types of connections, 712–716

Web servers, **700–703**, **717–721**

Apache servers, 718–719

AppleShare 5 Web and File Server, 621–622

in Macintosh environments, 701

Microsoft Internet Information Server (IIS), 472, 480–481, 719

NCSA httpd servers, 718

Netscape servers, 719

in NetWare, 415–416

operating systems for, 720–721

overview of, 700

in Unix or Linux, 703

in Windows 3.1x, 701

in Windows 95/98 or NT Workstation, 702

in Windows NT Server, 702

X.25 and Frame Relay connections, 261–264, *262*, 714, 1366, 1470, 1482

Internet commerce, 785, 800–801, 817

Internet Explorer, **721–725**

Internet Information Server (IIS) in Windows NT, 472, 480–481, 719

Internet Message Access Protocol, Version 4. *See* IMAP4

Internet Protocol suite. *See* TCP/IP protocol suite

Internet Relay Chat (IRC) in Linux, 524

Internet security, **709–712**, **747–753**, **994–1037**. *See also* security

  browser loopholes, **1023–1026**

    ActiveX, 1025–1026

    Java, 1024

    JavaScript, 1025

  denial-of-service (DoS) attacks, **827**, 1024, 1028

  encryption, 981–982, 986–987, 1022–1023, 1470

  firewalls, **709–712**, **747–753**, **994–1001**, **1470**

    additional benefits, 711

    application gateways as firewalls, 751–753, 999

    connectionless communications and, 67–68

    cost of, 711

    designing, 709–710, *710*

    dynamic packet-filtering firewalls, 67–68

    failures, **1001**

    firewall gateway virtual private networks, 823–824

    versus gateways, **994–996**

    guidelines, **1000**

    in Linux, 530

    Network Address Translation (NAT) and, 94, 709–710

    packet inspection firewalls, 752–753

    packet-filtering firewalls, 67–68, 749–750, 752–753, 996–999

    planning, 996

    proxy servers and, 751

    routers or gateways and, 994–996

    security and, 710–711

    selecting for intranets, 748–749

    sexual harrassment and, 712

    spoofing and, 983

    Windows NT and, 472

  peer-to-peer networking in Windows NT Workstation, **1007–1017**

    default accounts, 1008–1009

    directory-level permissions, 1015

    file-level permissions, 1015–1016

    folder security, 1009–1011, *1011*

    overview of, 1007–1009, 1016–1017

    permissions, 1011–1016, *1012*

    system actions, 1013–1014

  proxy servers, **751**, **951**, **1001–1007**

    firewalls and, 751

    Microsoft Proxy Server, 1002–1003

    Netscape Proxy Server, 1003–1006

    WinGate, 1006–1007

  threats, **1026–1028**

    arnudp100.c, 1028

    cbcb.c, 1028

    DNSKiller, 1027

    Ping of Death, 1027

    Syn_Flooder, 1027

  tunneling and, 1022–1023

  user authentication, **467**, **472**, **1017–1020**, **1035–1036**

    credit card transactions and, 1018–1020

    password authentication in Web servers, 1035–1036

    S-HTTP (Secure HTTP), 1017–1018

    SSL (Secure Sockets Layer) and, 472, 1017–1018

    in Windows NT, 467

  virtual private networks (VPNs) and, 1020–1022

  Web server security, **1028–1036**

    access logging, 1028–1031, *1029*

    client certificate authentication, 1036

    directory-level access, 1031–1035, *1033*, *1034*

    in Netscape FastTrack Server, 1029–1036, *1029*

    password authentication, 1035–1036

Internet service providers (ISPs), 84, 714

InterNetNews daemon in Linux, 525

Internetwork Packet Exchange. *See* IPX

internetworking, **772–785**, **1472**. *See also* extranets; Internet; intranets; virtual private networks

  bandwidth problems, 784

  extranets and, 781–783, *783*, 786–787

extranets as interorganizational internetworks, **807**

future of, 783–785

history of, **774–783**

    extranets phase, 781–783, *783*

    Internet phase, 774–779, *774, 775, 779*

    intranet phase, 780–781, *781*

Internet commerce and, 785

interoperability and, 786

overview of, 772–774

portability and, 786–787

scalability and, 776

InterNIC, 83–84, 93–94

interoperability

extranets and, 794, 796

internetworking and, 786

interpacket gap in NCP (NetWare Core Protocol), 144

interrupts

defined, **1472**

interrupt conflicts in PC computers, 1230–1231

interrupt settings for network interface cards, 1045–1046, *1046*

in NetWare servers, 1172, 1177

intranets, **20**, **716–717**, **742–768**, **788**, **1472**. *See also* extranets; firewalls; internetworking; virtual private networks

adding and maintaining content, 767–768

advantages and disadvantages, **743–746**

books about, 1428–1429

extranets and

    expanding intranet borders with extranets, 799–800

    extending intranet functionality with extranets, 798–800

    extranets as extended intranets, 790–793, *791, 792*

    extranets as external intranets, 787–789, *789, 790*

intranet phase of internetworking history, 780–781, *781*

IP addresses and, **753–765**

    assigning IP addresses, 763–765

    determining network and host addresses, 761–762

    DHCP and, 763–765

    subnet masks, 758–761

security, **765–766**

selecting Web servers, 766–767

IntraNetWare. *See* NetWare

IP addresses, **42**, **79–103**, **753–765**, **1472**. *See also* TCP/IP protocol suite

127.0.0.1 loopback address, 88–89, 756

address classes, 84–88, *86, 87*, 757–758, 1467

address conventions, 79–80

Advanced IP Addressing dialog box in Windows NT, 493, *493*

ARP (Address Resolution Protocol), 102–103, 1464

broadcast addresses, 89, 91–93, 219

DNS (Domain Name Service) and, 102–103

intranets and, **753–765**

    assigning, 763–765

    determining network and host addresses, 42, 761–762

    DHCP and, 763–765

    subnet masks, 758–761

IP version 6 (IPv6), 759

lost address spaces, 101, *102*

multicast addresses, 90–93, *91*

network address translation (NAT) devices and, 94, 709–710

registered IP addresses, 83–88, *86, 87*, 755–756

reserved address ranges, 93–94

subnet masks

    defined, **42**, **758–761**

    nonstandard subnet masks, 94–100, *95, 97, 100*

    optimizing servers with multiple subnets, **921–922**

    standard subnet masks, 42, 80–83, *82*

switches and, 919

troubleshooting duplicate IP addresses, **1136–1138**

unicast addresses, 80, 91

zeros in, 83

IP routing, **103–110**

BGP (Border Gateway Protocol), 109–110

dynamic routing, 106–110, 1469

EGP (Exterior Gateway Protocol), 107–109, *108*

OSPF (Open Shortest Path First), 109

RIP (Routing Information Protocol)

    defined, **43**, **106–107**, **134**

    RIP for Internet Protocol service in Windows NT, 485, 494

route command, 105–106

static routing, 46–49, *47*, *48*, 103–106, *104*

traceroute command, 43–45, *43*, *45*

IP tunneling in Linux, 531

IPX Console in NetWare, **1101–1107**

circuits options, 1106–1107, *1106*

Detailed IPX Information option, 1103–1104, *1103*

Forwarding and Services option, 1107

IPX Information option, 1102–1103, *1103*

IPX Router Information option, 1104–1105, *1105*

load command and, 1101

Mobile IPX Information option, 1106

NLSP Information screen, 1106

SNMP Access Configuration option, 1102

IPX (Internetwork Packet Exchange) protocol, **61**, **73**, **131–148**, **1287**

Application layer services, **147–148**

connection control fields, **61**

IPX network addresses, 132–134, *132*, *133*, 1094

IPX packet structure, 1286, *1286*

IPX routing, **134–135**

NLSP (NetWare Link State Protocol), 60, 134–135, 1106

RIP (Routing Information Protocol), 43, 106–107, 134

Linux IPX support, 532

NetBIOS over IPX, 153–154, *153*

in NetWare

binding IPX protocol to network interface cards, 422–423

configuring IPX protocol with INETCFG.NLM, 437–440

configuring LAN interfaces to use IPX, 442–443

IPX-to-IP gateway, 414

NWLink protocol

defined, **479**, **490–491**, *491*, **1474**

RIP for NWLINK service in Windows NT, 485

OSI model and, 131, *131*

SAP (Service Advertising Protocol)

SAP agent in Windows NT, 486

SAP frames, 148

sockets, **73**, **147**

Transport layer services, **135–147**. *See also* NCP

IPX (Internetwork Packet Exchange) protocol, 136–137, *137*

LIP (Large Internet Protocol), 144

SPX (Sequence Packet Exchange) protocol, 137–139, *138*, *139*, 1287

SPX I (Sequence Packet Exchange) protocol, 139–141, *140*

SPX II (Sequence Packet Exchange) protocol, 141

ipxping tool in NetWare, 1108

ipxroute command in Windows NT, 1115

IRC (Internet Relay Chat) in Linux, 524

IRQs

defined, **1472**

interrupt conflicts in PC computers, 1230–1231

IRQ settings for network interface cards, 1045–1046, *1046*

in NetWare servers, 1172, 1177

ISA (Industry Standard Architecture) bus, **324–325**

ISDN lines, **255–258**, **714**, **874**, **888**, **1471**

ISDN modems, **395–396**, **1472**

ISPs (Internet service providers), 84, 714

J

Java loopholes, 1024

JavaScript loopholes, 1025

K

keeping records, 1049–1051, *1050*, *1051*

kernel

in Linux, **527–538**

cleaning up the work space, 536

compiling the kernel, 537

configuration options, 528–536

configuring the boot manager, 537

Kernel Configurator window, 537–538, *538*

overview of, 527–528, *528*, *529*

performing dependency checks, 536

in NetWare, 405

L

labeling ports for multiport serial adapters, 886

LAMs (lobe attachment modules), **192**

LAN cards. *See* network interface cards

LAN Manager, **576–577**

LANalyzer, **1086–1093**, **1383**

alarms, 1087–1088, *1088*

Capture Buffer option, 1087

dashboard, 1086, *1087*

station monitors, 1090–1093, *1091*

and troubleshooting wide area networks, 1383

utilization statistics, 1088–1090, *1089*, *1090*

LanRover E/T/Plus remote access server, 894–895, 1144–1150, *1144*

LANs. *See* local area networks

LANtastic, **18**, **597–605**

configuring, 599, *599*

connecting to computers, 599–600, *600*

connecting to remote drives and printers, 600–602, *600*, *601*

installing on Windows NT, 597–598

LANtastic Custom Control Panel, **599–605**

Manage Servers tab, 602–605

Online Information tab, 599, *599*

Preferred Servers button on Use Network tab, 602

Use Network tab, 599–602

managing accounts, 602–604, *603*

optimizing LANtastic server performance, 604–605, *605*

sharing drives and printers, 602

Large Internet Packet options for Client32 drivers, 660

Large Internet Protocol (LIP), **144**

lasers, 309–310

latency

bridge latency, 348–349

defined, **332**

leaf objects in Novell Directory Services, 1387

lease periods in DHCP, 112

leased analog LAN connections, 1363

leased digital LAN connections, 1364–1365

leased lines, **258–259**, 1366–1367, **1468**, **1472**

LEDs (light-emitting diodes), **300–301**

legacy drivers for NetWare clients, 635–636

light dispersion, 301

light transmission media, **309–310**

light-emitting diodes (LEDs), **300–301**

Line Printer Daemon (LPD) printers, **481**

link speeds, 58–59, *59*

Link State Protocol (LSP) frames, 57

Link Support Layer Max Buffer Size option for Client32 drivers, 660

link-state routers, **56**

link-state routing, **56–60**, **1472**. *See also* routing

convergence time and, 58, 59–60

load balancing, 58–60, *59*, 212

propagating network information, 56–58

and recovering from router failure, 60

Linux, **17–18**, **503–550**. *See also* Network File System; Unix

account administration, 516, *516*

books about, 1435

client communications with FTP servers or Web servers, 703

configuring the kernel, **527–538**

cleaning up the work space, 536

compiling the kernel, 537

configuration options, 528–536

configuring the boot manager, 537

Kernel Configurator window, 537–538, *538*

overview of, 527–528, *528*, *529*

performing dependency checks, 536

configuring network access, **526–540**

AppleTalk support, 522, 532

changing network driver settings, 537–538, *538*

configuring the kernel, **527–537**

configuring routing, 539–540, *540*

Ethernet support, 534

firewall options, 530

IP tunneling, 531

IPX support, 532

Kernel Configurator window, 537–538, *538*

Network Configurator window, 539–540, *540*

network interface card configuration, 534–535, 536

PPP support, 533, 535–536

radio network support, 534

Set Module Options dialog box, 538, *538*

SLIP support, 533

starting network services, 538–539

TCP/IP support, 517, 523–525, 530–532, 549

configuring TCP/IP services, **549**

as copyleft software, 505

core operating system, **509–514**

background processes, 511–513, *512, 513*

command-line and X-Windows interfaces, 510

memory and, 510, 529

as a multiuser system, 510–511

Performance Monitor, 514

portability of, 509

Service Manager, 514

virtual memory, 510

distributing, 505

DNSKiller attacks, 1027

downloading installation files, 504, 506

features, 505–506

file permissions, 517–518

file system, 514–515, *515*

future of, 550

history of, 504–505

installing, **504**, **506–509**, *507, 508*

Linux newsgroups, 1438–1439

MAKE files, 527–528, *528*, 536–537

mount points, 515

networking features, **518–522**

AppleTalk networking, 522, 532

IP networking support, 519–511, *520*, 530–532, 549

NCP (NetWare Core Protocol) support, 521–522

NetBEUI networking, 522

OSI Data Link layer support, 519

routing support, 522, 539–540, *540*

SAMBA suite, **541–549**

accessing shares, 541–544

creating shares, 545–548

global settings, 546–547

nmbd tool, 545

smb.conf tool, 546–548, *548*

smbclient tool, 541–543

smbd tool, 545–546

smbmount tool, 543

smbumount tool, 543

uses for, 549

security tools, **517–518**, 532

shadow passwords, 517

TCP Wrapper program, 517

TCP/IP applications, **523–525**

bootp server, 523

DNS server, 523

Finger server, 523

FTP server, 523–524

Gopher server, 524

HTTP server, 524

IMAP server, 524

Internet Relay Chat (IRC), 524

InterNetNews daemon, 525

Mail server, 524

NFS server, 525

NTP (network time protocol), 525

POP3 server, 524

SNMP Manager, 525

Talk, 525

Telnet server, 525

users and groups, 516, *516*

LIP (Large Internet Protocol), **144**

LLAP (LocalTalk Link Access Protocol), **612**

load balancing

in link-state routing, **58–60**, *59*

logical topologies and, 212

load command in NetWare, 1101

load order in Macintosh workstations, 1253–1255

LoadRunner utility, 956

lobe attachment modules (LAMs), **192**

lobes in Token Ring networks, **192**

local area networks (LANs), 30, **221–246**, **1358**, **1359–1367**, **1472**.
   See also wide area networks

connecting LANs across long distances, **1362–1365**

analog dial-up connections, 1363

digital dial-up connections, 1363–1364

leased analog connections, 1363

leased digital connections, 1364–1365

with microwave relays, 1365

with satellite services, 1365

with telephone company services, 1362–1365

connecting LANs around the world, **1365–1367**

with Frame Relay and X.25 connections, 1366

with leased lines, 1366–1367

with satellite services, 1367

connecting LANs at a site, **1359–1361**

with bridges, 1359–1360

with gateways, 1361

with routers, 1360–1361

connecting LANs between buildings, **1361–1362**

with bridges, 1362

with repeaters, 1361–1362

defined, **1472**

LAN topologies, 30, **221–246**, **1358**

1Gbps Ethernet topology, 229–231

10Mb Ethernet topology, 221–225

100Mb Ethernet topology, 225–229

100VG-AnyLAN topology, 231–235, 1062

ATM (asynchronous transfer mode), 242–246, *244*, 1062, 1465

FDDI, 14, 235–242, *236*, *238*, *239*, *241*

local bus, **325**

local exchange carriers, **248–249**, *249*

local frame delivery in AppleTalk, 161

local-save user authentication, 1018–1019

LocalTalk protocol, **611–614**, **1294–1295**

CSMA/CA (carrier sense multiple access with collision avoidance), 612–613

dynamic node assignment, 613–614

LLAP (LocalTalk Link Access Protocol), 612

Lock Delay option for Client32 drivers, 660–661

Lock Retries option for Client32 drivers, 661

log files. *See also* Performance Monitor in Windows NT

for Client32 drivers, 661

system logs in NetWare, 1192

Log view in Windows NT Performance Monitor, 933

logging

information access, 988–989

network events, 1412–1413

Web server access, 1028–1031, *1029*

logging in to Banyan VINES, 596

logical networks, **42**

logical topologies, **211–212**

login scripts in NetWare, 1187–1188

login security, 1417–1418

Login tab

in NetWare Client32 Properties window for Windows 95/98, 645–647, *646*

in Novell IntraNetWare Client Services Configuration window for Windows NT, 652

Logon Validation options in Client for Microsoft Networks Properties window, 685–686

long filename support

in NetWare, 408

in Windows 95/98 workstations, 1241–1242

Long Machine Type option for Client32 drivers, 661

loopback addresses, **88–89, 756**

loopback mode lobes, **193**

loopback multiport serial adapters, 883

lost address spaces, **101**, *102*

Lotus Notes, **18, 74, 554–573**

    account administration, 561, *561*

    as a client/server application, 559–560

    communications with other operating systems, **634–635**

    configuring, 555–556, *556*

    configuring network access, **570–573**, *570, 571*

    document databases, 554

    Domino software and Internet access, **569–570**

    e-mail features, 560–561

    installing, **555**

    Lotus Notes client software, 555, **568–569**

    Lotus Script, 560

    networking features, **567–568**

    operating systems and, 555

    optimizing Windows NT for, 556, *557*

    protocol support, 567

    remote dial-up connections, 568

    replication, 557–559, *558*, 568

    security, **562–567**

        Access Control Lists (ACLs), **565–567**

        Author access, 566

        certificates, **563–564**

        Depositor access, 566

        Designer access, 566

        Editor access, 566

        encryption, **74, 564–565**

        Manager access, 565

        No Access access, 566

        Reader access, 566

        User ID files, **562–563**

    TCPIP Port Status dialog box, 571–573, *571*

    User Preferences window, 570–571, *570*

    Windows NT and, 556, *557*, 561, *561*

LPD (Line Printer Daemon) printers, **481**

LSP (Link State Protocol) frames, 57

M

MAC (media access control) addresses, 7

    Ethernet frames and, 218–219, *220*

Macintosh computers. *See also* AppleTalk protocol

    Binhex encoding, 127, 977

    client communications, **697–700**

        with FTP servers or Web servers, 701

        NetWare support, 697–698

        peer-to-peer networking with Macintosh, Windows 95/98, and Windows NT, 700

        Windows NT support, 698–699

    Cyberdog Web browser, 725–726

    Macintosh file servers, 389

    Services for Macintosh in Windows NT, 486, *487*

    troubleshooting Macintosh printers, 1262, 1322–1323, 1337–1338, 1352–1354

    troubleshooting Macintosh workstations, **1217–1218, 1244–1262**

        bootstrap sequence, 1249–1252

        configuring Open Transport, 1259

        control panels and extensions, 1247, 1252–1257

        example, 1271–1274

        Finder application, 1246, 1247, 1257–1258

        fixing extension conflicts, 1255–1257

        INIT crawl problems, 1252–1257

        modifying load order, 1253–1255

        mounting remote volumes, 1258–1259

        overview of, **1217–1218, 1244–1248**

        printing, 1262

        SCSI devices, 1260–1262, *1260*

        startup sequence, 1248–1258

        System suitcase, 1246

magazines online, **1435–1438**

mail-order hardware vendor Web sites, 1452–1453

MAKE files in Linux, 527–528, *528*, 536–537

Manage Configuration option in INETCFG.NLM, 446–449, *446*

Manage Servers tab in LANtastic Custom Control Panel, 602–605

managed stackable hubs, **15**, **340–341**

Manager access in Lotus Notes, 565

ManageWise utility in NetWare, 411

managing accounts in LANtastic, 602–604, *603*

MANs (metropolitan area networks), **1358**, **1473**

Manufacturer's Ethernet Identifier (MEI) numbers, **1456–1461**

mapping networks, 1377

Max Cache Size option for Client32 drivers, 661–662

Max Cur Dir Length option for Client32 drivers, 662

Max Read Burst Size option for Client32 drivers, 662

Max Write Burst Size option for Client32 drivers, 662

MCSE (Microsoft Certified Systems Engineer) programs, **1442**

media access control (MAC) addresses, 7

    Ethernet frames and, 218–219, *220*

media converters, **15**, **330–332**, *331*

medium-size networks, 313–314

MEI (Manufacturer's Ethernet Identifier) numbers, **1456–1461**

Mem Pool Size option for Client32 drivers, 662

memory

    adding RAM to servers, 904–907, *905*

    automatic loading of BIOS into upper memory, 1177

    Linux and, 510, 529

    memory address settings, 1045–1046, *1046*

    memory statistics in Windows NT Performance Monitor, 942

    NetWare and, 405–406

    in NetWare servers, 1170–1171

    RAM problems in new NetWare servers, 1170–1171

    virtual memory

        in Linux, 510

        in Windows NT, 463

    Windows NT and, 463

Mercury Interactive LoadRunner utility, 956

message switching, **213–214**, *214*, **1472**

Message Timeout option for Client32 drivers, 663

metropolitan area networks (MANs), **1358**, **1473**

Micro Channel bus, **325**

Micro Channel clients, 1244

microprocessor support in Windows NT, 462, 463

Microsoft Certified Systems Engineer (MCSE) programs, **1442**

Microsoft Hardware Compatibility List (HCL), 904

Microsoft Internet Explorer, **721–725**

Microsoft NDS Service, 672–673, *673*, 1241

Microsoft NetWare Client, 1240

Microsoft Object Linking and Embedding (OLE), **795**

Microsoft Proxy Server, 1002–1003

Microsoft technical support hotlines, **1052**

Microsoft Windows 3.*x*

    Client32 for DOS/Windows 3.1x, **637–642**

        configuring networking with NET.CFG file, 642

        installing, 637–640, *638*

        startnet.bat file, 639–641

    client communications with FTP servers or Web servers, 701

    defined, **1481**

    troubleshooting Windows 3.*x* workstations, 1238–1239

    Windows newsgroups, 1438

Microsoft Windows 95/98, **642–650**, **654–681**, **1481**

    client communications with FTP servers or Web servers, 702

    defined, **1481**

    Microsoft client drivers for NetWare, **670–681**

        versus Client32 drivers, **673–681**

        configuring, 671–672, *672*

        installing, 670–671, *670*, *671*

        installing and configuring Microsoft NDS client, 672–673, *673*, 1241

        Microsoft Client for NetWare Networks Properties window, 671–672, *672*

    NetWare Client32 Properties window, **644–650**, **655–669**

        Advanced Settings tab, 649–650, *649*, 655–669

        Client32 tab, 645, *645*

        Default Capture tab, 647–649, *647*

        Login tab, 645–647, *646*

        opening, 644, *644*

NetWare Client32 for Windows 95/98, **642–650, 654–669**

    Advanced Settings tab options, 654–669

    configuring, 644–650, *644*

    installing, 642–644, *643*

Novell NetWare Client for Windows 95, 1241

operating system and network driver failures, 1221–1223

peer-to-peer networking with Macintosh, Windows 95/98, and Windows NT, 700

Registry, 1408

troubleshooting workstations, **1240–1242**

    long filename support, 1241–1242

    Microsoft NDS Service, 672–673, *673*, 1241

    Microsoft NetWare Client, 1240

    NetWare VLM client, 1240–1241

    Novell NetWare Client for Windows 95, 1241

    protocol support, 1242

Windows newsgroups, 1438

Microsoft Windows NT Server, **17, 460–499, 1481**. *See also* troubleshooting

account administration, 465–468, *468*

Administrative Wizard, 468, *468*

auditing, 469–470

backup domain controllers (BDCs), 466–467

books about, 1432–1434

channel aggregation, 471

client communications, **477–479, 683–691**

cluster size and, 464–465

command-line tools, **1114–1121**

    arp, 1114–1115

    ipxroute, 1115

    nbtstat, 1115–1116, *1116*

    netstat, 1117–1118, *1117*

    nslookup, 1118–1120

    ping, 1120–1121

    route, 1121

    tracert, 1121

communications with other operating systems, **634–635**

core operating system, **462–463**

directory replication, 465

Directory Services, 465

domains, **465–466, 469, 1469**

FAT and NTFS file systems, 464–465

file compression, 464

firewalls and, 472

graphical troubleshooting tools, **1121–1123**

    Network Monitor, 481–482, *482*, 1121, 1190, 1381

    Performance Monitor, 1122, *1122*

    winmsd utility, 1123, *1123*

index servers, 473

installing, **460–462, 1178–1184**

IntraNetWare client for Windows NT, **650–669**

    Advanced Settings tab options, 654–669

    configuring, 651–654, *651*

    installing, 650–651, *651*

LAN Manager and, 577

LANtastic installation on Windows NT, 597–598

Lotus Notes and, 556, *557*, 561, *561*

Macintosh Windows NT support, **698–699**

memory and, 463

Microsoft client drivers for NetWare, **670–681**

    versus Client32 drivers, **673–681**

    configuring, 671–672, *672*

    installing and configuring Microsoft NDS client, 672–673, *673*, 1241

    Microsoft Client for NetWare Networks Properties window, 671–672, *672*

migrating to from NetWare, 461–462

Network Properties window, **473–497**

    Adapters tab, 495–496, *496*

    Advanced IP Addressing dialog box, 493, *493*

    Bindings tab, 496, *497*

    Configure Gateway dialog box, 479, *479*

    configuring network interface cards, 495–496, *496*

    Identification tab, 473–474, *474*

    Microsoft AppleTalk Protocol Properties dialog box, 486, *487*

    Microsoft TCP/IP Properties dialog box, 494–495, *494*

    Network Access Order dialog box, 478–479, *478*

Network Configuration dialog box, 483, *483*

Network Services tab, 474–488, *475, 476*

New Profile dialog box, 484, *484*

New Remoteboot Workstation dialog box, 484–485, *485*

NWLink IPX/SPX Properties dialog box, 491, *491*

PPTP Configuration dialog box, 491–492, *492*

Printer Ports dialog box, 490, *490*

Protocols tab, 488–495, *489*

Remote Access Setup dialog box, 482–483, *483*, 492, *492*

Remoteboot Manager, 484, *484*

saving changes, 497

setting protocol binding order, 496, *497*

Novell IntraNetWare Client Services Configuration window, **651–669**

Advanced Login tab, 652–653, *653*

Advanced Settings tab, 654–659

Client tab, 652, *652*

Login tab, 652

Novell Workstation Manager tab, 653–654, *654*

opening, 651, *651*

operating system and network driver failures, 1223

optimizing for Lotus Notes, 556, *557*

packet filtering, 471–472

peer-to-peer networking with Macintosh, Windows 95/98, and Windows NT, 700

Performance Monitor, **932–945, 1122, 1190–1191, 1382–1383**

adding logging counters, 933–934, *933*

comparing log files, 940

monitoring NetWare 3.*x* servers, **941–943**

monitoring NetWare 4.*x* servers, **943–944**

placing bookmarks, 936–937, *937*

selecting counters to display, 939, *940*

selecting counters to log, 940–941

selecting log files, 935, *935*

selecting time intervals, 935–936

selecting time ranges, 938–939, *939*

starting Performance Monitor, 933

starting and stopping logging, 936

switching to Log view, 933

taking notes, 937–938

troubleshooting servers, 1190–1191

troubleshooting wide area networks, 1382–1383

using other utilities, 944–945

viewing or graphing log files, 938, *938*

views, 932–933

Ping of Death attacks, 1027

policies, 467

primary domain controllers (PDCs), 466–467

processor support, 462, *463*

protocol support, **470, 471, 475, 488–495**. *See also* TCP/IP support

adding or deleting protocols, 489, *489*

configuring protocols, 488–489, *489*

DLC (Data Link Control), 490, *490*, 1468

NetBEUI, 490

NWLink, 479, 490–491, *491*, 1474

NWLink NetBIOS, 491

overview of, 470, *471*

PPTP (Point-to-Point Tunneling Protocol), 471, 491–493, *492, 493*, 826

services and, 475

setting protocol binding order, 496, *497*

Streams option, 494

rebooting, 472

recovering deleted files, 465

Remote Access Service (RAS), **471, 482–484, 491–492, 861–869, 1477**

configuring communications, 861–863, *862*

configuring Dial-Up Networking clients, 868

configuring protocols, 863–865, *864, 865*

configuring security, 865–867, *866, 867*

disadvantages of, 868–869

PPTP (Point-to-Point Tunneling Protocol) and, 491–493

Remote Access Setup dialog box, 482–483, *483*, 492, *492*

remote-control features, 463

RISC processors and, 462

routing, 470, 471

SAMBA and, 124, 152

security, **469–470**

services, **475–488**. *See also* remote access

adding or deleting, 475–476, *475*, *476*

Computer Browser, 476

DHCP Relay agent, 476–477

Gateway (and Client) Services for NetWare, 477–479, *478*, *479*

Microsoft DHCP Server, 479–480

Microsoft DNS Server, 473, 480

Microsoft Internet Information Server (IIS), 472, 480–481, 719

Microsoft TCP/IP Printing, 481, *481*

Network Monitor agent, 481

Network Monitor tools and agent, 481–482, *482*

protocol support and, 475

Remoteboot, 484–485, *484*, *485*

RIP for Internet Protocol, 485, 494

RIP for NWLINK, 485

RPC Configuration, 486

RPC Support for Banyan, 486

SAP agent, 486

Server service, 486

Services for Macintosh, 486, *487*

Simple TCP/IP Services, 487

SNMP service, 487–488

WINS (Windows Internet Name Service), 152, 154–156, *155*, 473, 480, 488, 1481

Workstation service, 488

shares, 389

SSL (Secure Sockets Layer) and, 472, 1017–1018

StreetTalk Explorer for Windows NT, 594

StreetTalk for Windows NT, 588–592, *589*, *590*

TCP/IP support

configuring, 494–495, *494*, 686–691

installing, 684, *684*

Microsoft TCP/IP Printing, 481, *481*

RIP for Internet Protocol service, 485, 494

Simple TCP/IP Services, 487

TCP/IP applications, 472–473, 497

telecommuting via remote access, 861

topologies supported, 470

troubleshooting workstations, 1242–1243

trust relationships, 466

trustee rights, 470, 1418

UNC (universal naming convention), 389

upgrading, 461–462

user authentication, 467

users and groups, 469

virtual memory, 463

Windows file servers, 389

Windows NT newsgroups, 1438

Windows NT Server 5 features, 498

workstations and, 463, 488

Microsoft Windows NT Server client communications, **477–479**, **683–691**

Client for Microsoft Networks Properties window, **685–691**

configuring TCP/IP, 686–691

enabling Windows NT domain logons, 685

Logon Validation options, 685–686

quick logon option, 685–686

with FTP servers or Web servers, 702

Gateway (and Client) Services for NetWare in Windows NT, 477–479, *478*, *479*

installing TCP/IP support, 684, *684*

Microsoft clients on Windows 95/98, **683–691**

configuring, 685–691, *685*, *687*, *688*, *690*

installing, 683–684

TCP/IP Properties dialog box, **686–691**

Advanced tab, 691

Bindings tab, 690

DNS Configuration tab, 687–689, *688*

Gateway tab, 689

IP Address tab, 686–687, *687*

NetBIOS tab, 689

WINS Configuration tab, 689–690, *690*

Microsoft Windows NT Workstation

client communications with FTP servers or Web servers, 702

configuring, 691, *692*

peer-to-peer networking, **1007–1017**

  default accounts, 1008–1009

  directory-level permissions, 1015

  file-level permissions, 1015–1016

  folder security, 1009–1011, *1011*

  overview of, 1007–1009, 1016–1017

  permissions, 1011–1016, *1012*

  system actions, 1013–1014

  security, 984–985

microwave networks, 310, 1365

migrating. *See also* upgrading

  data in NetWare, 409–410

  to Windows NT from NetWare, 461–462

MIME (Multimedia Internet Mail Extensions), **119**, **127**, **978**, 981

Minimum Time To Net option for Client32 drivers, 663

mirroring disks, **910–911**, **1198–1199**, *1199*, **1469**

miscellaneous objects in Novell Directory Services, 1390

m-nodes in NetBIOS addresses, 152

Mobile IPX Information option in NetWare IPX Console, 1106

modems, **393–398**, **869–875**. *See also* telecommuting

  baud rate versus bits per second (bps), 393, 869–870, 1465, 1466

  cable modems, 396–397

  versus codexes, 394–395

  configuring, 871

  creating hunt groups for modem pools, 253–254

  DSLs (Digital Subscriber Lines), 397–398

  installing, 871–873, *872*

  Internet access and, 727

  ISDN modems, 395–396, 1472

  modem channel binding, 393–394

  multiport serial adapters and, 883

  optimizing modem use, 873

  overview of, **869–870**

  power cycling, 254

  UART chips and, 870

monitor contention, **195**, **200**

MONITOR utility in NetWare, 1108–1113, *1109*, *1111*, 1191

monitoring

  monitoring tools in network hardware, **1070–1081**

    in bridges, 1078–1079

    error reports, 1076–1078, *1076*, *1077*

    features to look for, 1072–1075, *1072*, *1073*, *1074*

    in routers, 1079–1081, *1079*

    SNMP and RMON (remote monitoring) support, 1081

    in switches, 1078

  NetWare 3.*x* servers with Windows NT Performance Monitor, 941–943

  network monitoring tools, **1067–1068**

  networks, 358–359

Mosaic Web browser, **726**

motherboard failures, 1221

mount points in Linux, **515**

mounting remote volumes for Macintosh workstations, 1258–1259

MPR (Multi-Protocol Router) in NetWare, 413

MSAUs (multi-station access units), **191**, **192**, **1293**

multicast addresses, **90–93**, *91*

multihoming support in NetWare, 415–416

Multimedia Internet Mail Extensions (MIME), **119**, **127**, **978**, 981

multimode fiber-optic cable, **301–302**

multiple collision, **217**

multiple network interface cards in NetWare servers, 1176

multiple protocols in NetWare, 1186–1187

multiport serial adapters, **880–890**. *See also* remote access

  bus architectures, 882

  cable problems, 886

  cost of, 890

  DB-9 and DB-25 connectors, 880, *880*

  DSL (Digital Subscriber Lines) and, 888–889

  installing, 884–885

  ISDN lines and, 888

  labeling ports, 886

  loopback adapters, 883

  modems and, 883

  phone lines and, 883, 888–889

  versus remote access servers, 895–896

testing, 887

types of, 880–883, *880, 882*

UART chips and, 883–884

Multi-Protocol Router (MPR) in NetWare, 413

multi-station access units (MSAUs), **191, 192, 1293**

multiuser system, Linux as, 510–511

N

NAL (Novell Application Launcher), 411

Name Binding Protocol (NBP), **162**

Name Context option for Client32 drivers, 663

name-brand servers, **902–903**

naming conventions in Banyan VINES and StreetTalk, 595, *595*

NAT (Network Address Translation), **94, 709–710**

NBNS (NetBIOS Name Server), **151–152**

NBP (Name Binding Protocol), **162**

nbtstat command in Windows NT, 1115–1116, *1116*

NCP (NetWare Core Protocol), **141–147**

burst mode, 144–147, *145, 146*

frames, 142–144, *143*

function code fields, 143

interpacket gap, 144

Linux NCP support, 521–522

LIP (Large Internet Protocol), 144

NCP Max Timeout option for Client32 drivers, 663

NCSA httpd Web servers, **718**

NDS (Novell Directory Services), **410, 672–673, 1196, 1241, 1386–1391, 1474**. *See also* NetWare

backing up, 1399

container objects, 1387–1389

installing and configuring Microsoft NDS client, 672–673, *673*, 1241

leaf objects, 1387

managing, 1196

miscellaneous objects, 1390

NDS objects, 1387–1390, *1388*

NDS trees, 1387

NetWare Administrator (NWADMIN), 1390

Organization and Organizational Unit (OU) objects, 1389

printer-related objects, 1389

server-related objects, 1389

troubleshooting, 1390–1391

user-related objects, 1389

NET$OS.EXE file in NetWare, 1192–1193

NET.CFG file. *See* Client32 drivers

Net Status Busy Timeout option for Client32 drivers, 664

Net Status Timeout option for Client32 drivers, 664

NetBench utility, 956, *957*

NetBEUI protocol, **43, 157–158, 1288, 1473**

in Linux, 522

in Windows NT, 490

NetBIOS protocol, **43, 148–157, 1288, 1473, 1474**

datagram service, 156–157

NetBIOS addresses, **149–152**

node types, 150–152, *150*, 154

overview of, 149–150

NetBIOS gateways, **1473**

NetBIOS Name Server (NBNS), 151–152

NetBIOS routing, **153–156**

NetBIOS over IP, 124, 154–156, *155*

NetBIOS over IPX, 153–154, *153*

Network layer and, 43

NWLink NetBIOS protocol, 491

OSI model and, 148, *149*

peer-to-peer networking and, 149

session service, 157

Session and Transport layer services, **156–157**

WINS (Windows Internet Name Service) and, 152, 154–156, *155*, 473

Netscape FastTrack Server, 1029–1036, *1029*

Netscape Navigator, **721–725**

Netscape Proxy Server, 1003–1006

Netscape Web servers, **719**

netstat command

in Unix, 1124

in Windows NT, 1117–1118, *1117*

NetTester/1 utility, 957

NetWare, **17**, **141–147**, **403–456**, **1473**. *See also* Client32 drivers

ABENDs or abnormal ends, 406–407, *407*, 1188, 1193

account administration, 410

bind command, 105

books about, 1429–1432

communications with other operating systems, **634–635**

configuration files, 1184–1185

configuring networking from the command line, **418–425**

binding AppleTalk protocol to network interface cards, 423

binding IPX protocol to network interface cards, 422–423

binding TCP/IP protocol to network interface cards, 423–424

loading APPLETALK.NLM, 419–421

loading LAN drivers, 421–422

loading TCPIP.NLM, 418–419

running network commands during startup, 424–425, *425*

configuring networking with INETCFG.NLM, **426–451**

Backup Call Associations options, 435–436, *436*

Bindings option, 442–445

Boards option, 427–430, *427*, *428*

Configure Remote Access To This Server option, 447–449, *447*

configuring AppleTalk protocol, 440–441

configuring IPX protocol, 437–440

configuring LAN interfaces to use AppleTalk, 443–444

configuring LAN interfaces to use IPX, 442–443

configuring LAN interfaces to use TCP/IP, 444

configuring network drivers, 427–429, *428*

configuring SNMP, 446

configuring TCP/IP protocol, 441–442

configuring WAN groups to use TCP/IP, 444–445, *445*

Edit AUTOEXEC.NCF option, 449

Export Configuration option, 446–447

Go To Fast Setup option, 451

Import Configuration option, 447

Manage Configuration option, 446–449, *446*

Network Interface option, 430–432, *430*, *431*

PPP Network Interface Configuration window, 430–432, *431*

Protocols option, 437–442, *437*

Reinitialize System option, 450–451

View Configuration option, 449–450, *450*

WAN Call Directory option, 432–435, *433*

DOS Requester and VLMs, **1236–1237**

drivers

configuring with INETCFG.NLM, 427–429, *428*

legacy drivers for clients, 635–636

loading LAN drivers, 421–422

in NetWare servers, 1186

troubleshooting, 1235–1236

DSMigrate utility, 404–405

file system, **408–410**

data migration, 409–410

disk suballocation, 408

file compression, 409

frame types supported, 416–418

garbage collection, 408

Gateway (and Client) Services for NetWare in Windows NT, 477–479, *478*, *479*

GENLOAD and VARLOAD stress testing utilities, 955

history of, **1162–1163**

installing, **404–405**, 1184, 1185–1186

IPX-to-IP gateway, 414

kernel, 405

login scripts, 1187–1188

long filename support, 408

Macintosh NetWare support, **697–698**

ManageWise utility, 411

memory and, 405–406

Microsoft client drivers for NetWare, **670–681**

versus Client32 drivers, **673–681**

configuring, 671–672, *672*

installing and configuring Microsoft NDS client, 672–673, *673*, 1241

installing in Windows 95/98, 670–671, *670, 671*

Microsoft Client for NetWare Networks Properties window, 671–672, *672*

Microsoft NetWare Client, 1240

migrating to Windows NT from, 461–462

MONITOR utility, 1108–1113, *1109, 1111*, 1191

monitoring NetWare 3.*x* servers with Windows NT Performance Monitor, 941–943

monitoring NetWare 4.*x* servers with Windows NT Performance Monitor, 943–944

multiple protocols in, 1186–1187

Multi-Protocol Router (MPR), 413

NCP (NetWare Core Protocol), **141–147**

    burst mode, 144–147, *145, 146*

    frames, 142–144, *143*

    function code fields, 143

    interpacket gap, 144

    Linux NCP support, 521–522

    LIP (Large Internet Protocol), 144

    NCP Max Timeout option for Client32 drivers, 663

NetWare 5 features, 455–456

NetWare IP, **681–683**, *682*

NetWare newsgroups, 1438

NetWare VLM client, 1240–1241

NLSP (NetWare Link State Protocol), 60, 134–135, 1106

Novell Application Launcher (NAL), 411

Novell Directory Services (NDS), **410**, **672–673**, **1196**, **1241**, **1386–1391**, **1474**

    backing up, 1399

    container objects, 1387–1389

    installing and configuring Microsoft NDS client, 672–673, *673*, 1241

    leaf objects, 1387

    managing, 1196

    NDS objects, 1387–1390, *1388*

    NDS trees, 1387

    NetWare Administrator (NWADMIN), 1390

    Organization and Organizational Unit (OU) objects, 1389

    printer-related objects, 1389

    server-related objects, 1389

    troubleshooting, 1390–1391

    user-related objects, 1389

Novell NetWare Client for Windows 95, 1241

ODI (Open Datalink Interface), **635–636**, **1235–1236**

Ping of Death attacks, 1027

printing, **1325–1333**, **1337–1338**

    CAPTURE program, 1326, 1329–1330, 1385, 1386

    configuration files, 1332

    NetWare for Macintosh printing, 1337–1338

    NPRINT program, 1330

    NPRINTER.NLM, 1328, 1331

    overview of, 1325–1328

    PCONSOLE, 1330–1331

    PRINT JOBS, 1329–1330

    print queues, 1330–1331

    print servers, 1331–1332

    PRINTCON program, 1330, 1386

    PSERVER.NLM and, 1325–1326, 1327–1328, 1331

    RPRINTER, 1329

    SHELL.CFG and, 1328–1329

    troubleshooting Windows 95/9/NT client printers, 1332–1333

protocol support, 413–414, 416–417

routing, 413–414

SAMBA tools, **451–454**, **541**

    copying files to correct locations, 454

    creating shares with SAMBA, 451–454, *455*

    downloading SAMBA files, 452

    preparing NetWare, 453

    starting SAMBA, 454, *455*

security, **411–413**, **1178**

    Auditcon utility, 412–413

    C2 and E2 certifications, 411

    connection jumping, 412

    inherent rights masks, 412

    packet signatures, 412

permissions, 1187

SECURE.NCF script, 413

in servers, 1178

SERVMAN and FCONSOLE utilities, 1191

stress testing utilities, 955

System Fault Tolerance (SFT), **1198–1201**

mirroring and duplexing, 910–911, 1198–1199, *1199*, 1469

RAID and, 1199–1200, *1200*

SFT level III, 1201, *1201*, 1410

TCP/IP applications, **414–416**

bootp support, 415

DHCP server, 415

DNS server, 415

FTP server, 415

multihoming support, 415–416

Web servers, 415–416

technical support hotlines, **1052**

telecommuting via remote access, 861

topologies supported, 413

upgrading, 404–405, 1197

NetWare Protocol option for Client32 drivers, 663

NetWare troubleshooting tools, **1093–1114**

command line tools, **1094–1101**

config, 1094–1095, *1094*

display networks, 1095, *1095*

display servers, 1096, *1096*

packet burst statistics screen, 1097–1099, *1097*

protocols, 1097

reset router, 1099

tping, 1099

track on, 1099–1101, *1100*

console tools, **1093–1101**

graphical tools, **1101–1113**

aiocon, 1107

atcon, 1107

atmcon, 1108

IPX Console, 1101–1107

ipxping, 1108

Monitor, 1108–1113, *1109*, *1111*, 1191

ping, 1113

tcpcon, 1113

IPX Console, **1101–1107**

circuits options, 1106–1107, *1106*

Detailed IPX Information option, 1103–1104, *1103*

Forwarding and Services option, 1107

IPX Information option, 1102–1103, *1103*

IPX Router Information option, 1104–1105, *1105*

load command and, 1101

Mobile IPX Information option, 1106

NLSP Information screen, 1106

SNMP Access Configuration option, 1102

LANalyzer, **1086–1093**, **1383**

alarms, 1087–1088, *1088*

Capture Buffer option, 1087

dashboard, 1086, *1087*

station monitors, 1090–1093, *1091*

and troubleshooting wide area networks, 1383

utilization statistics, 1088–1090, *1089*, *1090*

workstation commands, **1113–1114**

Network Access Order dialog box in Windows NT, 478–479, *478*

Network Address Translation (NAT), **94**, **709–710**

network addresses, **42**, **761–762**, **1474**

assigning to NetWare servers, 1186

IPX network addresses, 132–134, *132*, *133*, 1094

wide area network address problems, 1373

network administration books, 1426–1428

network analyzers, **1069–1070**, *1069*, *1070*

network aware applications, **389–390**

network baselining. *See* baselining

Network Communications dialog box in StreetTalk, 589–591, *590*

Network Configuration dialog box in Windows NT, 483, *483*

Network Configurator window in Linux, 539–540, *540*

Network File System (NFS) protocol, **64**, **122–123**, **525**, **634–635**, **692–697**. *See also* Linux; Unix

and communicating with other operating systems, 634–635

configuring NFS clients, **695–697**

configuring fstab files, 696, *696*

mounting remote file system, 696–697

overview of, 695

configuring NFS servers, **692–695**

configuring file systems for export, 693

editing exports files, 693–695

exporting file systems, 695

overview of, 692–693

connectionless communications and, 64, *65*

Linux NFS server, 525

network frames. *See* frames

Network General Sniffer software, 1069, *1069*

network interface cards (NICs), **192, 320–327, 1474**

Boards option in INETCFG.NLM, 427–430, *427, 428*

boot PROM chips, **386–387**

cabling support, 326–327, *327*

check valves, 326

combo cards, 327

configuring in Linux, 534–535, *536*

configuring in Windows NT, 495–496, *496*

external port connections, 320, 321–322, *322*

internal network cards, 321, 324–326, *324*

IRQs, DMAs, I/O port and memory address settings, 1045–1046, *1046*

multiple network interface cards in NetWare servers, 1176

network driver failures

in DOS and Windows 3.*x*, 1223–1224

in Windows 95/98, 1221–1223

in Windows NT, 1223

parallel port network cards, 321–322, *322*

PC-card connections, 320, 322–323, *323*

in Token Ring networks, 192

topology support, 324–327, *327*

transceivers, 327, *327*, 1282, 1479

Network Interface option in INETCFG.NLM, 430–432, *430, 431*

Network layer

Network layer services in AppleTalk, **162–163**

in OSI model, **36**, 38, 40, 42, **1289, 1474**

Network Management Module (NMM), 1135

network management tools, **1375–1378**

features to look for, 1376–1378

network inventory, 1377–1378

network mapping, 1377

online Help, 1377

packet monitoring, 1376

server management, 1378

SNMP management, 1377

trend analysis, 1376–1377

Network Monitor in Windows NT, 481–482, *482*, 1121, 1190

network monitoring tools in network hardware, 1067–1068

Network News Transfer Protocol (NNTP), **123–124, 1474**

network numbers in AppleTalk, 159–160

Network Printers option for Client32 drivers, 664

Network Properties window in Windows NT, **473–497**

Adapters tab, 495–496, *496*

Advanced IP Addressing dialog box, 493, *493*

Bindings tab, 496, *497*

Configure Gateway dialog box, 479, *479*

configuring network interface cards, 495–496, *496*

Identification tab, 473–474, *474*

Microsoft AppleTalk Protocol Properties dialog box, 486, *487*

Microsoft TCP/IP Properties dialog box, 494–495, *494*

Network Access Order dialog box, 478–479, *478*

Network Configuration dialog box, 483, *483*

Network Services tab, 474–488, *475, 476*

New Profile dialog box, 484, *484*

New Remoteboot Workstation dialog box, 484–485, *485*

NWLink IPX/SPX Properties dialog box, 491, *491*

PPTP Configuration dialog box, 491–492, *492*

Printer Ports dialog box, 490, *490*

Protocols tab, 488–495, *489*

Remote Access Setup dialog box, 482–483, *483*, 492, *492*

Remoteboot Manager, 484, *484*

saving changes, 497

setting protocol binding order, 496, *497*

network section of extranets, 828

network services. *See* services

network time protocol (NTP) in Linux, 525

networking standards, **6–9**

networks. *See also* Ethernet; peer-to-peer networking; Token Ring; topologies; troubleshooting physical networks

   access network design, 829–830

   ARCnet networks, **1295–1296**, **1465**

   backbone networks, **831–832**, *831*

   bridges and monitoring networks, 358–359

   campus networks, **314–315**

   datagram packet switching networks, **214–215**, *215*, 261–262, **1468**

   defined, **1474**

   documenting, **1049–1051**, *1050*, *1051*, **1411–1412**

   extended versus non-extended networks, 615

   full-mesh networks, **830**, *830*

   logical networks, **42**

   mapping, 1377

   medium-size networks, 313–314

   microwave networks, 310, 1365

   partial-mesh networks, **830–831**, *831*

   segmenting

      balancing traffic segmentation and bridge latency, 348–349

      with bridges, 353–358, *354*

      defined, **8**, **16**, **343–344**, **1477**

      populated versus unpopulated segments, 289

      repeated segments, 289

      routers and, 344

      segment congestion, 58–59, *59*

   X.25 networks, **261–264**, *262*, **714**, **1366**, **1482**

New Profile dialog box in Windows NT, 484, *484*

New Remoteboot Workstation dialog box in Windows NT, 484–485, *485*

newsgroups, **1438–1439**. *See also* information resources

   InterNetNews daemon in Linux, 525

   Linux, 1438–1439

   NetWare, 1438

   NNTP (Network News Transfer Protocol) and, 123–124, 1474

   spamming in, 124

   Unix, 1439

   Windows/Windows NT, 1438

NFS. *See* Network File System

NICs. *See* network interface cards

nlist user command in NetWare, 1114

NLSP (NetWare Link State Protocol), **60**, **134–135**, 1106

nmbd SAMBA tool in Linux, 545

NMM (Network Management Module), 1135

NNTP (Network News Transfer Protocol), **123–124**, **1474**

No Access access in Lotus Notes, 566

nodes

   defined, **1474**

   dynamic node assignment in LocalTalk, 613–614

   node addresses, 218, 1094

   node types in NetBIOS addresses, 150–152, *150*, 154

   seeding and nonseeding nodes in AppleTalk, 160

noise

   analog communications and, 272, *273*

   defined, **272**, **1474**

   digital communications and, 30, 273–274, *274*, *275*

   electromagnetic interference (EMI), **13**, **276–278**, *277*, **1469**

   fiber-optic cable and, 306

   radio frequency interference (RFI), **13**, **278**, **1477**

   thin Ethernet (thinnet) cabling and, 286

   twisted-pair cable and, 298

non-extended networks, **615**

nonseeding nodes in AppleTalk, **160**

nonstandard subnet masks, **94–100**, *95*, *97*, *100*

Notes. *See* Lotus Notes

Novell. *See* NetWare

NPRINT program in NetWare, 1330

NPRINTER.NLM in NetWare, 1328, 1331

nslookup command

   in Unix, 1124

   in Windows NT, 1118–1120

NTFS file system in Windows NT, **464–465**

NTP (network time protocol) in Linux, 525

NU-Bus architectures, **325**

numbering of layers in OSI model, 38

NWADMIN (NetWare Administrator), 1390

NWD2 command in NetWare, 1114

NWLanguage option for Client32 drivers, 664–665

NWLink protocol

    defined, **479**, **490–491**, *491*, **1474**

    NWLink IPX/SPX Properties dialog box in Windows NT, 491, *491*

    NWLink NetBIOS protocol, 491

    RIP for NWLINK service in Windows NT, 485

0

Object Linking and Embedding (OLE), **795**

objects, distributed objects, **794–795**

ODI (Open Datalink Interface), **635–636**, **1235–1236**

online Help, 1377

Online Information tab in LANtastic Custom Control Panel, 599, *599*

online magazines, **1435–1438**

Open Datalink Interface (ODI), **635–636**, **1235–1236**

open extranets, **815–820**. *See also* extranets

    advantages and disadvantages, 818–819, *818*, 820

    control of, 818, 820

    implementing, 819–820

Open Shortest Path First (OSPF) protocol, **109**

Open Transport in Macintosh workstations, 1259

OpenDoc format, **626–627**

opening

    NetWare Client32 Properties window for Windows 95/98, 644, *644*

    Novell IntraNetWare Client Services Configuration window for Windows NT, 651, *651*

Opera Web browser, **726**

Opportunistic Locking option for Client32 drivers, 665

optimizing

    Ethernet networks, **914–921**

    with cable plants, 914–915

    with hubs, 915–916

    with routers, 920–921

    with switches, 916–920, *917*, *918*

    LANtastic server performance, 604–605, *605*

    modem use, 873

    servers, **904–924**

        adding hard disk drives, 907–910

        adding RAID and disk striping, 910–914, 1469

        adding RAM, 904–907, *905*

        with cable plants, 914–915

        with hubs, 915–916

        improving disk performance, **907–914**

        improving Ethernet performance, **914–921**

        LANtastic server performance, 604–605, *605*

        with multiple subnets, **921–922**

        with profiling, **922–923**

        with routers, 920–921

        with switches, 916–920, *917*, *918*

    Windows NT for Lotus Notes, 556, *557*

Organization and Organizational Unit (OU) objects in Novell Directory Services, 1389

organizations in Banyan VINES, 596, *596*

OS/2 Warp, **18**, **576–586**, **1243–1244**, **1475**

    accessing shared resources, 585–586

    history of, 576–577

    installing and configuring, 578–583, *582*

    sharing resources, 583–585, *584*

    troubleshooting OS/2 clients, 1243–1244

OSI (Open Systems Interconnection) model, **9–10**, **33–43**, **1288–1290**, **1475**. *See also entries for specific layers*

    AppleTalk protocol and, 159, *159*

    Application layer, **37**, 38, 41, 64, 74, **1290**, 1290, **1465**

    Data Link layer, **36**, 39, 40, 46, 64, **1289**, **1468**

        support for in Linux, 519

    how OSI works, **38–42**

        receiving data, 40–42, *41*

        requesting file information, 38–40, *39*

    IPX protocol and, 131, *131*

NetBIOS protocol and, 148, *149*

Network layer, **36**, 38, 40, 42, **1289**, **1474**

numbering of layers, 38

Physical layer, **34**, 40, 64, 1289

Presentation layer, **37**, 38, 41, 74, **1290**, **1476**

Session layer, **37**, 38, 41, 68, **1290**, **1478**

TCP/IP protocol suite and, 78, *79*

Transport layer, **36**, 38, 40, 61–62, 64, 1289

OSPF (Open Shortest Path First) protocol, **109**

overhead in digital communications, **275**

overloading switches, 363–364

P

Packet Burst option for Client32 drivers, 665

Packet Burst Read Window Size option for Client32 drivers, 665

packet burst statistics screen in NetWare, 1097–1099, *1097*

Packet Burst Write Window Size option for Client32 drivers, 665

packet inspection firewalls, **752–753**

packet signatures in NetWare, 412

packet switching, **214–215**, *215*, 261–262, **1468**, **1475**

packet-filtering firewalls, **67–68**, **749–750**, **752–753**, **996–999**

packet-receive buffer statistics in Windows NT Performance Monitor, 942–943

packets. *See also* frames

    defined, **7**, **374**, **1475**

    dynamic packet-filtering firewalls, 67–68

    versus frames, 37

    hello packets, **56**

    IPX packet structure, 1286, *1286*

    packet filtering in Windows NT, 471–472

    packet monitoring, 1376

PAP (Password Authentication Protocol), 435, 493

PAP (Printer Access Protocol) in AppleTalk, **165**, **618**

parallel port network interface cards, **321–322**, *322*

partial-mesh networks, **830–831**, *831*

Passive FTP (PASV FTP), **117–118**

passwords. *See also* security

    administrator passwords, 970

    login security and, 1417–1418

    Password Authentication Protocol (PAP), 435

    password authentication in Web servers, 1035–1036

    password policies, **967–969**

    shadow passwords in Linux, 517

patch panels, **1299–1300**

PC Cards

    PC Card connections for network interface cards, 320, 322–323, *323*

    PC Card failures, 1221

    troubleshooting, 1228–1230

PC computers, **1214–1217**, **1218**, **1226–1237**. *See also* DOS

    troubleshooting hardware problems, **1226–1233**

        boot sequence, 1227–1228

        interrupt conflicts, 1230–1231

        overview of, **1214–1217**, **1218**, **1226–1227**, *1227*

        PC Cards and connections, 1228–1230

        Plug and Play devices, 1233

        SETUP configuration problems, 1231–1233

    troubleshooting software problems, **1214–1217**, **1218**, **1226–1227**, **1233–1237**

        DOS, 1234

        NetWare DOS Requester and VLMs, 1236–1237

        NetWare drivers, 1235–1236

        ODI drivers, 635–636, 1235–1236

        overview of, **1214–1217**, **1218**, **1226–1227**, *1227*

pcANYWHERE, **850–858**

    features, 858

    host installation, 851–856, *852*

    operating system support, 850

    remote client installation, 856–857, *857*

PCI (Peripheral Component Interconnect) bus, **325–326**, 1172, 1177

PCONSOLE program in NetWare, 1330–1331

PDCs (primary domain controllers), **466–467**

peer-to-peer networking

    defined, **1007–1008**, **1475**

    NetBIOS protocol and, 149

in Windows NT Workstation, **1007–1017**

    default accounts, 1008–1009

    directory-level permissions, 1015

    file-level permissions, 1015–1016

    folder security, 1009–1011, *1011*

    overview of, 1007–1009, 1016–1017

    permissions, 1011–1016, *1012*

    system actions, 1013–1014

Pegasus utility, 958

performance. *See* optimizing

Performance Monitor in Linux, 514

Performance Monitor in Windows NT, **932–945**, **1122**, **1190–1191**, **1382–1383**

    adding logging counters, 933–934, *933*

    comparing log files, 940

    monitoring NetWare 3.*x* servers, **941–943**

    monitoring NetWare 4.*x* servers, **943–944**

    placing bookmarks, 936–937, *937*

    selecting counters to display, 939, *940*

    selecting counters to log, 940–941

    selecting log files, 935, *935*

    selecting time intervals, 935–936

    selecting time ranges, 938–939, *939*

    starting Performance Monitor, 933

    starting and stopping logging, 936

    switching to Log view, 933

    taking notes, 937–938

    troubleshooting servers, 1190–1191

    troubleshooting wide area networks, 1382–1383

    using other utilities, 944–945

    viewing or graphing log files, 938, *938*

    views, 932–933

Peripheral Component Interconnect (PCI) bus, **325–326**, 1172, 1177

permanent virtual circuits (PVCs), **262**

permissions. *See also* rights

    defined, **1464**, **1476**

    in Linux, 517–518

    in NetWare, 1187

in Windows NT Workstation, **1011–1016**

    directory-level permissions, 1015

    file-level permissions, 1015–1016

    overview of, 1011–1013, *1012*

    system actions, 1013–1014

PGP (Pretty Good Privacy), **978**

phantom charges, **193**

phase shifting in analog communications, 250

Phoenix Software NetTester/1 utility, 957

Physical layer

    in OSI model, **34**, **40**, **64**, **1289**

    Physical layer protocols, 1286, *1286*

physical security, **1416–1417**

physical topologies, **208**, **211**

ping command

    defined, **1476**

    in NetWare, 1113

    Ping of Death attacks, **1027**

    in Unix, 1125

    in Windows NT, 1120–1121

plain old telephone services (POTS), **249–250**

planning. *See* designing

platform independence of extranets, 796–797

plenum cable, **297**, **1476**

Plug and Play devices, 1233

plug-ins for Web browsers, **724–725**

p-nodes in NetBIOS addresses, 151–152, 154

point of presence (POP) locations, **248**

Point-to-Point Protocol (PPP)

    defined, **1476**

    Linux PPP support, 533, 535–536

    PPP Network Interface Configuration window in Windows NT, 430–432, *431*

point-to-point topologies, **247**, *247*

Point-to-Point Tunneling Protocol (PPTP), 471, 491–493, *492*, *493*, 826

policies in Windows NT, **467**

polling servers in AppleTalk Filing Protocol, 166–167

POP (point of presence) locations, **248**

POP (Post Office Protocol), **125–127, 978**

  IMAP4 (Internet Message Access Protocol, Version 4) and, 120–121, 524, 624, 978

  Linux POP3 server, 524

populated segments, **289**

portability 74

  internetworking and, 786–787

  of Linux, 509

ports

  base I/O port address settings, 1045–1046, *1046*

  data ports, 116

  external port connections for network interface cards, 320, 321–322, *322*

  FTP and, 116

  Lotus Notes TCPIP Port Status dialog box, 571–573, *571*

  for multiport serial adapters, 886

  network services and port numbers, 68–73, *74*

  parallel port network interface cards, 321–322, *322*

  port density of hubs, 338

  Printer Ports dialog box in Windows NT, 490, *490*

  uplink port connections for stackable hubs, 15, 342, *342*

  upper port numbers, 70–71

  URLs and port numbers, 71

  well-known ports, 70–71

PostScript printers, **1336–1337, 1340–1344**

POTS (plain old telephone services), **249–250**

power cycling modems, 254

power protection, **1402–1404**

  evaluating power needs, 1404

  evaluating systems, 1402–1403

  standby power supplies (SPSs), 1403

  surge protectors, 1402–1403

  uninterruptible power supplies (UPSs), 1403

PPP (Point-to-Point Protocol)

  defined, **1476**

  Linux PPP support, 533, 535–536

  PPP Network Interface Configuration window in Windows NT, 430–432, *431*

PPTP (Point-to-Point Tunneling Protocol), 471, 491–493, *492, 493*, 826

preamble section of Ethernet frames, **173**

Preferred Server option for Client32 drivers, 666

Preferred Servers button in LANtastic Custom Control Panel, 602

Preferred Tree option for Client32 drivers, 666

Presentation layer in OSI model, 37, 38, 41, 74, **1290, 1476**

Pretty Good Privacy (PGP), **978**

preventive maintenance, **1405–1409**

  anti-static precautions, 1406–1407

  checking connections, 1406

  dust and contaminants, 1406

  following manufacturer's directions, 1407–1408

  maintaining return paths, 1408–1409

primary domain controllers (PDCs), **466–467**

primary zones in AppleTalk protocol, 162

Print Header option for Client32 drivers, 666

print jobs in NetWare, 1329–1330

print queues, **390**

  in NetWare, 1330–1331

print servers

  in AppleShare 5, 625

  defined, **389–390, 1476**

  in NetWare, 1331–1332

  routers as, 1344–1347, *1345*

Print Services in Banyan VINES, 596–597

Print Tail option for Client32 drivers, 666

printers, **1335–1336**

  AppleTalk PAP (Printer Access Protocol), **165, 618**

  connecting to in LANtastic, 600–602, *600, 601*

  Line Printer Daemon (LPD) printers, 481

  Printer Ports dialog box in Windows NT, 490, *490*

  printer software, 1336

  printer-related objects in Novell Directory Services, 1389

  sharing in LANtastic, 602

  troubleshooting PostScript printers, **1336–1337**

printing

  Microsoft TCP/IP Printing service, 481, *481*

  in NetWare, **1325–1333, 1337–1338**

    CAPTURE program, 1326, 1329–1330, 1385, 1386

    configuration files, 1332

NetWare for Macintosh printing, 1337–1338

NPRINT program, 1330

NPRINTER.NLM, 1328, 1331

overview of, 1325–1328

PCONSOLE, 1330–1331

print jobs, 1329–1330

print queues, 1330–1331

print servers, 1331–1332

PRINTCON program, 1330, 1386

PSERVER.NLM and, 1325–1326, 1327–1328, 1331

RPRINTER, 1329

SHELL.CFG and, 1328–1329

troubleshooting Windows 95/9/NT client printers, 1332–1333

serial versus parallel interfaces, 1334–1335, *1334*

troubleshooting, **1318–1323, 1336–1354**

examples, **1340–1354**

fault points for network printing, **1323–1326**, *1324*

Macintosh printers, 1262, 1322–1323, 1337–1338, 1352–1354

NetWare for Macintosh printing, 1337–1338

overview of, **1318–1323**

PostScript printers, 1336–1337, 1340–1344

remote printing with NetWare 4.*x*, 1347–1349

routers as print servers, 1344–1347, *1345*

troubleshooting Windows 95/9/NT client printers in NetWare, 1332–1333

Unix printing, 1338–1339

workstation printing problems, 1350–1352

private extranets, **812–815**. *See also* extranets

advantages and disadvantages, 814–815

implementing, 815

versus the Internet, 812–813, *813*

privileges. *See* permissions; rights

processes in Token Ring networks, **199–202**

beaconing, 201–202, 1465

initializing stations, 199–200

monitor contention, 195, 200

ring polling, 195, 200

ring purging, 200

processor support in Windows NT, 462, 463

profiling, **922–923**

promiscuous mode systems, **218**

propagation delay, **226–228**, *227*

proprietary systems, **32, 1476**

protocols. *See also* AppleShare; AppleTalk; IPX; NetBIOS; TCP/IP

bridges and, 349–350

CHAP (Challenge Handshake Authentication Protocol), 435, 493

connectionless protocols, **64–68**, *65*, **1290**

connection-oriented protocols, **61–64**, *63*, **1290**

CSMA/CA (carrier sense multiple access with collision avoidance), **612–613**

CSMA/CD (carrier sense multiple access with collision detection), **11, 175–179, 216–218, 1466**

receiving frames, 177–179, *178*

transmitting frames, 175–177, *176*

data communication protocols, **1286**, *1286*

defined, **10–11, 31, 371, 1476**

DLC (Data Link Control), 490, *490*, 1468

EBGP (External Border Gateway Protocol), 109–110

fiber-optic cable and, 305

IBGP (Internal Border Gateway Protocol), 109–110

Lotus Notes protocol support, 567

LSPs (link state protocols), 57

multiple protocols in NetWare, 1186–1187

NCP (NetWare Core Protocol), Linux NCP support, 521–522

NetBEUI

defined, **43, 157–158, 1288, 1473**

in Linux, 522

in Windows NT, 490

NetWare protocol support, 413–414, 416–417

network addresses and, 42

NTP (network time protocol), 525

NWLink

defined, **479, 490–491**, *491*, **1474**

NWLink IPX/SPX Properties dialog box in Windows NT, 491, *491*

NWLink NetBIOS protocol, 491

RIP for NWLINK service in Windows NT, 485

ODI (Open Datalink Interface) and, 635–636

PAP (Password Authentication Protocol), 435, 493

PPP (Point-to-Point Protocol)

  defined, **1476**

  Linux PPP support, 533, 535–536

  PPP Network Interface Configuration window in Windows NT, 430–432, *431*

protocol analyzers, **1379–1381**, **1476**

protocols command in NetWare, 1097

Protocols option in NetWare's INETCFG.NLM, 437–442, *437*

  routers and, 371–372, 374–375, 376

Spanning Tree protocol, **350–353**

  bridge looping and, 351–354, *351*

tunneling protocols

  defined, **21**

  PPTP (Point-to-Point Tunneling Protocol), 471, 491–493, *492, 493*, 826

Windows 95/98 workstation protocol support, 1242

Windows NT protocol support, **470, 471, 475, 488–495**

  adding or deleting protocols, 489, *489*

  configuring protocols, 488–489, *489*

  DLC (Data Link Control), 490, *490*, 1468

  NetBEUI, 490

  NWLink, 479, 490–491, *491*, 1474

  NWLink NetBIOS, 491

  overview of, 470, 471

  PPTP (Point-to-Point Tunneling Protocol), 471, 491–493, *492, 493*, 826

  services and, 475

  setting protocol binding order, 496, *497*

  Streams option, 494

  TCP/IP, 494–495, *494*

  X.400, 979

proxy servers, **751, 1001–1007, 1476**

  firewalls and, 751

  Microsoft Proxy Server, 1002–1003

  Netscape Proxy Server, 1003–1006

  WinGate, 1006–1007

PS/2 (Micro Channel) clients, 1244

PSERVER.NLM in NetWare, 1325–1326, 1327–1328, 1331

punch-down panels, **15, 328–330, 1299**

  labeling schemes, 330

Q

quality of service in 100VG-AnyLAN topology, **231–232**

quick logon option in Client for Microsoft Networks Properties window, 685–686

R

radio frequency interference (RFI), **13, 278, 1477**

radio wave transmission, **310–312, 534**

  fixed-frequency versus spread-spectrum signals, 310

  Linux radio network support, 534

  microwave signals, 310, 1365

  space-based transmissions, 311–312

  terrestrial transmissions, 310–311

RAID (redundant array of redundant disks)

  defined, **910–914, 1477**

  NetWare System Fault Tolerance and, 1199–1200, *1200*

  and troubleshooting NetWare servers, 1175–1176

RAM. *See also* memory

  adding to servers, 904–907, *905*

  RAM problems in new NetWare servers, 1170–1171

RAS. *See* remote access

Read Only Compatibility option for Client32 drivers, 666

Reader access in Lotus Notes, 566

rebooting Windows NT, 472

receiving Ethernet frames with CSMA/CD, 177–179, *178*

record keeping, 1049–1051, *1050, 1051*

recovering

  deleted files in Windows NT, 465

  from disaster, 1419–1421

  from router failure, 60

Red Hat Linux. *See* Linux

redundant routes, **48–49**, *48*

reference books, 1432

reflection, **278**

registered IP addresses, **83–88**, *86, 87*

Registry in Windows 95/98, 1408

Reinitialize System option in INETCFG.NLM, 450–451

relay switches, **191, 193**

reliability of backup systems, 1399

remote access, **880–896**. *See also* telecommuting

    multiport serial adapters, **880–890**

        bus architectures, 882

        cable problems, 886

        cost of, 890

        DB-9 and DB-25 connectors, 880, *880*

        DSL (Digital Subscriber Lines) and, 888–889

        installing, 884–885

        ISDN lines and, 888

        labeling ports, 886

        loopback adapters, 883

        modems and, 883

        phone lines and, 883

        versus remote access servers, 895–896

        testing, 887

        types of, 880–883, *880, 882*

        UART chips and, 883–884

    remote access connections using analog lines, 254–255

    remote access servers, **890–895**

        3Com AccessBuilder 4000, 891–894, *891, 893*

        cost of, 895

        versus multiport serial adapters, 895–896

        Shiva LanRover E/T/Plus, 894–895, 1144–1150, *1144*

    Remote Access Service (RAS) in Windows NT, **471**, **482–484**, **491–492**, **861–869**, **1477**

        configuring communications, 861–863, *862*

        configuring Dial-Up Networking clients, 868

        configuring protocols, 863–865, *864, 865*

        configuring security, 865–867, *866, 867*

        defined, **471, 482–484**, *483*, **878–879, 1477**

        disadvantages of, 868–869

        PPTP (Point-to-Point Tunneling Protocol) and, 491–493

        Remote Access Setup dialog box, 482–483, *483*, 492, *492*

    remote dial-up connections in Lotus Notes, 568

    telecommuting via remote access, **859–869**

        advantages of, 860

        in NetWare versus Windows NT, 861

        in Unix, 861

remote control

    remote control dial-in connections, **251–252**

    telecommuting via remote control, **846–859**

        advantages and disadvantages, 847–849

        Compaq Carbon Copy, 849–850

        cost, 848

        pcANYWHERE, 850–858

        security, 848

        Timbuktu Pro, 847, 858–859

    in Windows NT, 463

remote drives, connecting to in LANtastic, 600–602, *600, 601*

remote monitoring (RMON), **1081**

remote node connections, **252–253**

remote printing with NetWare 4.*x*, 1347–1349

remote procedure calls (RPCs)

    defined, **1477**

    RPC Configuration service in Windows NT, 486

remote saves using CGI scripts, 1019–1020

remote volumes

    in AppleTalk Filing Protocol, 167

    in Macintosh workstations, 1258–1259

Remoteboot service in Windows NT, 484–485, *484, 485*

removable disks and drives, 987–988

REMs (ring error monitors), **198**

repeated segments, **289**

repeaters, **15**, **336–337**, *337*, **1282, 1477**

    cable plant problems and, 1299

    connecting LANs between buildings, 1361–1362

    wide area network problems, 1368

replicating directories in Windows NT, 465

replication in Lotus Notes, 557–559, *558*, 568

reply type fields in NCP (NetWare Core Protocol), 142

Report view in Windows NT Performance Monitor, 932

request type fields in NCP (NetWare Core Protocol), 142

reserved IP address ranges, **93–94**

reset router command in NetWare, 1099

return paths, 1408–1409

RFI (radio frequency interference), **13**, **278**, **1477**

rights, **470**, **970–976**, **1418**. *See also* permissions; security

    assigning, 972–973

    and data sharing, 973–974

    file rights, 1418

    file system rights, 971–972

    trustee rights in Windows NT, 470, 1418

    user directories and, 974–976

    user and group rights, 970–971

ring error monitors (REMs), **198**

ring parameter servers (RPSes), **197–198**

ring polling, **195**, **200**

ring purging, **200**

ring topology, **210**, *210*, **1284–1285**, **1477**

RIP (Routing Information Protocol)

    defined, **43**, **106–107**, **134**

    RIP for Internet Protocol service in Windows NT, 485, 494

RISC processors, 462

RJ-11 connectors, **293**, *294*, 328

RJ-45 connectors

    defined, **193**, **293**, *294*

    hubs and, 338, 342

    for network interface cards, 323, 327

    switches and, 359

RMON (remote monitoring), **1081**

root name servers in Domain Name Service, **113–114**

route command

    in Unix, 1125

    in Windows NT, 1121

routers, **16**, **43**, **56**, **60**, **371–379**, **1300**, **1477**

    blocking broadcasts, 374

    versus bridges, 375

    brouters, **16**, **380**, **1466**

    connecting LANs at a site, 1360–1361

    cyclic redundancy checks (CRCs) and, 373–374

    examples, 372–374, *372*, 376–378, *377*

    filtering traffic, 375

    and finding cable plant problems, 1300

    firewalls and, 994–996

    versus gateways, 43

    hops, **43**, **1471**

    Internet access and, 727

    IPX Router Information option in NetWare IPX Console, 1104–1105, *1105*

    link-state routers, **56**

    monitoring tools in network hardware, **1070–1081**

        in bridges, 1078–1079

        error reports, 1076–1078, *1076*, *1077*

        features to look for, 1072–1075, *1072*, *1073*, *1074*

        in routers, 1079–1081, *1079*

        SNMP and RMON (remote monitoring) support, 1081

        in switches, 1078

    optimizing servers with, **920–921**

    as print servers, 1344–1347, *1345*

    protocols and, 371–372, 374–375, 376

    recovering from router failure, 60

    switch routers, **379**

    VLAN (virtual local area network) switches and, 917

    when to use, 376–378, *377*

    wide area network problems, 1369

routing, **43–60**

    AppleTalk routing, **163–164**, *164*

    cost, 58–59

    distance-vector routing, **49–56**, **1469**

        counting to infinity in, 55

        limitations of, 53–56, *54*, *55*

        propagating network information with, 49–53, *50*

    IP routing, **103–110**

        BGP (Border Gateway Protocol), 109–110

dynamic routing, 106–110, 1469

EGP (Exterior Gateway Protocol), 107–109, *108*

OSPF (Open Shortest Path First), 109

RIP (Routing Information Protocol), 43, 106–107, 134, 485, 494

route command, 105–106

static routing, 46–49, *47*, *48*, 103–106, *104*

traceroute command, 43–45, *43*, *45*

IPX routing, **134–135**

NLSP (NetWare Link State Protocol), 60, 134–135, 1106

RIP (Routing Information Protocol), 43, 106–107, 134, 485

link-state routing, **56–60**, **1472**

convergence time and, 58, 59–60

load balancing, 58–60, *59*, 212

propagating network information, 56–58

and recovering from router failure, 60

in Linux, 522, 539–540, *540*

NetBIOS routing, **153–156**

NetBIOS over IP, 124, 154–156, *155*

NetBIOS over IPX, 153–154, *153*

in NetWare, 413–414

redundant routes, 48–49, *48*

routing loops, **56**

routing tables, **43**, **45–46**

RTMP (Routing Table Maintenance Protocol), 163–164, *163*, 617

static routing, 46–49, *47*, *48*, 103–106, *104*

traceroute command and, 43–45, *43*, *45*

in Windows NT, 470, 471

RPCs (remote procedure calls)

defined, **1477**

RPC Configuration service in Windows NT, 486

RPRINTER program in NetWare, 1329

RPSes (ring parameter servers), 197–198

RTMP (Routing Table Maintenance Protocol), **163–164**, *163*, **617**

Rx fiber-optic connections, 303–304

S

S/MIME (Secure MIME), **978**

SAMBA tools, **124**, **451–452**

in Linux, **541–549**

accessing shares, 541–544

creating shares, 545–548

global settings, 546–547

nmbd tool, 545

smb.conf tool, 546–548, *548*

smbclient tool, 541–543

smbd tool, 545–546

smbmount tool, 543

smbumount tool, 543

uses for, 549

in NetWare, **451–454**, **541**

copying files to correct locations, 454

downloading SAMBA files, 452

preparing NetWare, 453

starting SAMBA, 454, *455*

in Windows, 152

Windows NT and, 124, 152

sample rate in leased lines, **260**

SAP (Service Advertising Protocol)

SAP agent in Windows NT, 486

SAP frames, 148

satellite services

connecting LANs across long distances, 1365

connecting LANs around the world, 1367

saving

changes in Windows NT Network Properties window, 497

local-save user authentication, 1018–1019

remote saves using CGI scripts, 1019–1020

S-Bus architectures, **325**

scalability

internetworking and, 776

of thin Ethernet (thinnet) cabling, 287

SCSI devices, **1173–1175**, *1175*

    in Macintosh workstations, 1260–1262, *1260*

SDSL (Symmetric DSL), 397–398

seamless interoperability of extranets, 794, 796

Search Dirs First option for Client32 drivers, 667

Search Mode option for Client32 drivers, 667–668

searching. *See* finding

secondary zones in AppleTalk protocol, 162

Secure HTTP (S-HTTP), 1017–1018

Secure MIME (S/MIME), **978**

security, **1416–1419**. *See also* Internet security

    AppleShare 5 security, **622–623**

    books about, 1435

    certificates

        client certificate authentication, **1036**

        defined, **1467**

        in Lotus Notes, **563–564**

    denial-of-service (DoS) attacks, **827**, 1024, 1028

    dial-in access security, **1418–1419**

    e-mail security, **976–983**

        encryption, 981–982

        external security, 980–983

        internal security, 979–980

        overview of, 976–977

        SMTP and MIME and, 981

        spamming protection, 982–983

        spoofing, 983

        terms defined, 977–979

    encryption

        defined, **1470**

        guidelines, 981–982, 986–987, 1022–1023

        in Lotus Notes, 74, 564–565

    fiber-optic cable and, 306

    firewalls, **709–712**, **747–753**, **994–1001**, **1470**

        additional benefits, 711

        application gateways and, 751–753

        application gateways as firewalls, 751–753, 999

        connectionless communications and, 67–68

        cost of, 711

        designing, 709–710, *710*

        dynamic packet-filtering firewalls, 67–68

        failures, **1001**

        firewall gateway virtual private networks, 823–824

        versus gateways, **994–996**

        guidelines, **1000**

        in Linux, 530

        Network Address Translation (NAT) and, 709–710

        packet inspection firewalls, 752–753

        packet-filtering firewalls, 67–68, 749–750, 752–753, 996–999

        planning, 996

        proxy servers and, 751

        routers or gateways and, 994–996

        security and, 710–711

        selecting for intranets, 748–749

        sexual harrassment and, 712

        spoofing and, 983

        Windows NT and, 472

    hacker break-in example, **964–966**

    Internet security, **730–737**

    intranet security, **765–766**

    Linux security tools, 517–518, 532

    login security, **1417–1418**

    Lotus Notes security, **562–567**

        Access Control Lists (ACLs), **565–567**

        Author access, 566

        certificates, **563–564**

        Depositor access, 566

        Designer access, 566

        Editor access, 566

        encryption, **564–565**

        Manager access, 565

        No Access access, 566

        Reader access, 566

        User ID files, **562–563**

NetWare security, **411–413, 1178**

    Auditcon utility, 412–413

    C2 and E2 certifications, 411

    connection jumping, 412

    inherent rights masks, 412

    in NetWare servers, 1178

    packet signatures, 412

    permissions, 1187

    SECURE.NCF script, 413

passwords

    administrator passwords, 970

    login security and, 1417–1418

    Password Authentication Protocol (PAP), 435

    password authentication in Web servers, 1035–1036

    password policies, **967–969**

    shadow passwords in Linux, 517

PGP (Pretty Good Privacy), **978**

physical security, 1416–1417

security guidelines, **964–990**

    administrator passwords, 970

    assigning user and group rights, **970–976**

    auditing or logging information access, 988–989

    changing administrator names, 970

    data sharing, 973–974

    deleting default accounts, 969–970

    encryption, 981–982, 986–987, 1022–1023, 1470

    file system design and implementation, 971–972

    file system rights, 971–974

    network size and, 987

    operating system interactions, 974

    password policies, 967–969

    removable disks and drives, 987–988

    trust relationships and, 987

    user or home directories, 974–976

    Windows NT Workstation security, 984–985

stress testing and, 952

of telecommuting via remote control, 848

virtual private network security, **826–827**

Web browser security, **736–737**

Windows NT security, **469–470**

seeding nodes in AppleTalk, **160**

segmenting networks

    balancing traffic segmentation and bridge latency, 348–349

    with bridges, 353–358, *354*

    defined, **8, 16, 343–344, 1477**

    populated versus unpopulated segments, 289

    repeated segments, 289

    routers and, 344

    segment congestion, 58–59, *59*

selecting

    cabling, **280–282, 312–315**

        analog and digital communications and, 280

        for campus networks, 314–315

        cost and, 281–282

        and distances between computer systems, 281

        environments and, 281

        fault tolerance and, 281

        future growth and, 280

        for medium-size networks, 313–314

        for small remote offices, 313

        user and application bandwidth demands and, 280

    firewalls for intranets, 748–749

    repeaters, 337, *337*

    Web servers for intranets, 766–767

Sequence Packet Exchange. *See* SPX

server-related objects in Novell Directory Services, 1389

servers, **113–114, 119, 166–167, 388–392, 1478**. *See also* baselining; clients; troubleshooting servers; workstations

    application servers, **390–391**

    clones versus name-brand servers, **902–903**

    defined, **1478**

    DHCP server in NetWare, 415

    dial-in/dial-out servers, 1370–1371

    file servers, **388–389**

        AppleShare 5 Web and File Server, 621–622

        Windows file servers, 389

FTP servers, **700–703**

  in Macintosh environments, 701

  overview of, 700

  in Unix or Linux, 703

  in Windows 3.1x, 701

  in Windows 95/98 or NT Workstation, 702

  in Windows NT Server, 702

Gopher servers, **119**, 524, **1471**

installing, 1202–1207

in Linux, **523–525**

  bootp server, 523

  DNS server, 523

  Finger server, 523

  FTP server, 523–524

  Gopher server, 524

  HTTP server, 524

  IMAP server, 524

  Mail server, 524

  NFS server, 525

  POP3 server, 524

  Telnet server, 525

mail server in AppleShare 5, 623–624

Manage Servers tab in LANtastic Custom Control Panel, 602–605

Microsoft DHCP Server, 479–480

Microsoft DNS Server, 473, 480

Microsoft Hardware Compatibility List (HCL) and, 904

optimizing, **904–924**

  adding hard disk drives, 907–910

  adding RAID and disk striping, 910–914, 1469

  adding RAM, 904–907, *905*

  with cable plants, 914–915

  with hubs, 915–916

  improving disk performance, **907–914**

  improving Ethernet performance, **914–921**

  LANtastic server performance, 604–605, *605*

  with multiple subnets, **921–922**

  with profiling, **922–923**

  with routers, 920–921

  with switches, 916–920, *917*, *918*

Preferred Servers button in LANtastic Custom Control Panel, 602

print servers

  in AppleShare 5, 625

  defined, **389–390**, **1476**

  in NetWare, 1331–1332

  routers as, 1344–1347, *1345*

proxy servers, **751**, **1001–1007**, **1476**

  firewalls and, 751

  Microsoft Proxy Server, 1002–1003

  Netscape Proxy Server, 1003–1006

  WinGate, 1006–1007

remote access servers, **890–895**

  3Com AccessBuilder 4000, 891–894, *891*, *893*

  cost of, 895

  versus multiport serial adapters, 895–896

  Shiva LanRover E/T/Plus, 894–895, 1144–1150, *1144*

root name servers in Domain Name Service, **113–114**

server polling in AppleTalk Filing Protocol, 166–167

Server service in Windows NT, 486

ServerBench utility, 956, *957*

troubleshooting server upgrades, **1143–1150**, *1144*, 1197

Web server security, **1028–1036**

  access logging, 1028–1031, *1029*

  client certificate authentication, 1036

  directory-level access, 1031–1035, *1033*, *1034*

  in Netscape FastTrack Server, 1029–1036, *1029*

  password authentication, 1035–1036

Web servers, **700–703**, **717–721**

  Apache servers, 718–719

  AppleShare 5 Web and File Server, 621–622

  in Macintosh environments, 701

  Microsoft Internet Information Server (IIS), 472, 480–481, 719

  NCSA httpd servers, 718

  Netscape servers, 719

  in NetWare, 415–416

operating systems for, 720–721

overview of, 700

selecting for intranets, 766–767

in Unix or Linux, 703

in Windows 3.1x, 701

in Windows 95/98 or NT Workstation, 702

in Windows NT Server, 702

versus workstations, **391–392**

service files, 68–69

Service Manager in Linux, 514

services

across wide area networks, **1385–1386**

managing multiple logins, 1386

printing, 1385–1386

defined, **68–73**, *74*, **388**, **474–475**

in Windows NT, **475–488**. *See also* remote access

adding or deleting, 475–476, *475, 476*

Computer Browser, 476

DHCP Relay agent, 476–477

Gateway (and Client) Services for NetWare, 477–479, *478, 479*

Microsoft DHCP Server, 479–480

Microsoft DNS Server, 473, 480

Microsoft Internet Information Server (IIS), 472, 480–481, 719

Microsoft TCP/IP Printing, 481, *481*

Network Monitor agent, 481

Network Monitor tools and agent, 481–482, *482*, 1121, 1190, 1381

protocol support and, 475

Remoteboot, 484–485, *484, 485*

RIP for Internet Protocol, 485, 494

RIP for NWLINK, 485

RPC Configuration, 486

RPC Support for Banyan, 486

SAP agent, 486

Server service, 486

Services for Macintosh, 486, *487*

Simple TCP/IP Services, 487

SNMP service, 487–488

Windows Internet Name Service (WINS), 152, 154–156, *155*, 473, 480, 488, 1481

Workstation service, 488

SERVMAN utility in NetWare, 1191

Session layer

in OSI model, **37**, 38, 41, 68, **1290**, **1478**

Session layer services in AppleTalk

ASP (AppleTalk Session Protocol), 165, 616

PAP (Printer Access Protocol), 165, 618

Session layer services in NetBIOS, **156–157**

session service in NetBIOS protocol, 157

Set Module Options dialog box in Linux, 538, *538*

Set Station Time option for Client32 drivers, 668

setting protocol binding order in Windows NT, 496, *497*

SETUP program problems, 1231–1233

sexual harrassment, 712

SFT. *See* System Fault Tolerance

shadow passwords in Linux, 517

shared resources

in OS/2 Warp

accessing, 585–586

sharing resources, 583–585, *584*

sharing data, 973–974

sharing drives and printers in LANtastic, 602

shares

creating NetWare shares with SAMBA, 451–454, *455*

defined, **389**

in Linux

accessing, 541–544

creating, 545–548

in Windows NT, 389

SHELL.CFG file in NetWare, 1328–1329

shielded twisted-pair (STP) cabling. *See also* twisted-pair cable

defined, **1478**

in Token Ring networks, 192

Shiva LanRover E/T/Plus remote access server, 894–895, 1144–1150, *1144*

Short Machine Type option for Client32 drivers, 668

Show Dots option for Client32 drivers, 668

S-HTTP (Secure HTTP), **1017–1018**

Signature Level option for Client32 drivers, 668–669

Simple Mail Transfer Protocol (SMTP), **127**, 979, 981, **1478**

Simple Network Management Protocol. *See* SNMP

Simple TCP/IP Services in Windows NT, 487

single-mode fiber-optic cable, **301**

SLIP (Serial Line Internet Protocol)

>defined, **1477–1478**

>Linux SLIP support, 533

SMA connectors, **305**, 328

smb.conf SAMBA tool in Linux, 546–548, *548*

smbclient SAMBA tool in Linux, 541–543

smbd SAMBA tool in Linux, 545–546

smbmount SAMBA tool in Linux, 543

smbumount SAMBA tool in Linux, 543

SMDS (Switched Multimegabit Data Service) Internet connections, **715**

SMs (standby monitors), **197**, **1478**

SMTP (Simple Mail Transfer Protocol), **127**, 979, 981, **1478**

SNA (System Network Architecture), **32**

SNMP (Simple Network Management Protocol)

>configuring in NetWare, 446, 1102

>defined, **128–129**, **1478**

>Linux SNMP Manager, 525

>SNMP Access Configuration option in NetWare IPX Console, 1102

>SNMP service in Windows NT, 487–488

>support for in network hardware monitoring tools, 1081

>switches and, 917

>wide area networks and, 1377

sockets

>in AppleTalk protocol, **73**

>in IPX protocol, **73**, **147**

software problems

>in existing NetWare servers, **1192–1194**

>>ABEND messages, 406–407, *407*, 1188, 1193

>>with BINDFIX, 1193–1194

>>corrupted SERVER.EXE or NET$OS.EXE files, 1192–1193

>>with DSTRACE or DSREPAIR, 1194

>in new servers, **1178–1188**

>>NetWare servers, 1184–1188

>>Windows NT servers, 1178–1184

software troubleshooting tools, **1086–1129**

>Unix commands, **1123–1129**

>>arp, 1124

>>ifconfig, 1124, *1124*

>>netstat, 1124

>>nslookup, 1124

>>ping, 1125

>>route, 1125

>>statnet, 1125–1126, *1125*

>>tcpdump, 1126–1127, *1126*

>>Telnet, 1128–1129

>>traceroute, 1129

>Windows NT Server command-line tools, **1114–1121**

>>arp, 1114–1115

>>ipxroute, 1115

>>nbtstat, 1115–1116, *1116*

>>netstat, 1117–1118, *1117*

>>nslookup, 1118–1120

>>ping, 1120–1121

>>route, 1121

>>tracert, 1121

>Windows NT Server graphical tools, **1121–1123**

>>Network Monitor, 481–482, *482*, 1121, 1190, 1381

>>Performance Monitor, 1122, *1122*

>>winmsd utility, 1123, *1123*

software troubleshooting tools in NetWare, **1093–1114**

>command line tools, **1094–1101**

>>config, 1094–1095, *1094*

>>display networks, 1095, *1095*

>>display servers, 1096, *1096*

>>packet burst statistics screen, 1097–1099, *1097*

>>protocols, 1097

>>reset router, 1099

tping, 1099

track on, 1099–1101, *1100*

console tools, **1093–1101**

graphical tools, **1101–1113**

aiocon, 1107

atcon, 1107

atmcon, 1108

IPX Console, 1101–1107

ipxping, 1108

Monitor, 1108–1113, *1109, 1111*

ping, 1113

tcpcon, 1113

IPX Console, **1101–1107**

circuits options, 1106–1107, *1106*

Detailed IPX Information option, 1103–1104, *1103*

Forwarding and Services option, 1107

IPX Information option, 1102–1103, *1103*

IPX Router Information option, 1104–1105, *1105*

load command and, 1101

Mobile IPX Information option, 1106

NLSP Information screen, 1106

SNMP Access Configuration option, 1102

LANalyzer, **1086–1093, 1383**

alarms, 1087–1088, *1088*

Capture Buffer option, 1087

dashboard, 1086, *1087*

station monitors, 1090–1093, *1091*

and troubleshooting wide area networks, 1383

utilization statistics, 1088–1090, *1089, 1090*

workstation commands, **1113–1114**

software vendor Web sites, 1452

software-only diagnostic tools for wide area networks, 1381–1384

SONET (synchronous optical network), **264–265**

space-based radio wave transmission, **311–312**

spamming, **124, 982–983**

Spanning Tree protocol, **350–353**

bridge looping and, 351–354, *351*

speed of backup systems, 1397

splicing twisted-pair cable, 329

spoofing, **983**

spread-spectrum signals, **310**

SPSes (standby power supplies), 1403

SPX (Sequence Packet Exchange) protocol, **137–139**, *138, 139*, **1287**

SPX I (Sequence Packet Exchange) protocol, **139–141**, *140*

SPX II (Sequence Packet Exchange) protocol, **141**

SSL (Secure Sockets Layer), 472, 1017–1018

stackable hubs, **15, 340–342**. *See also* hubs

backbone connections, 341

managed or intelligent stackable hubs, 15, 340–341, 1471

unmanaged stackable hubs, 15, 341

uplink port connections, 15, 342, *342*

standard subnet masks, **42, 80–83**, *82*, **758–761**

standards

de facto standards, **70**

network standards, **6–9**

standards organizations, **1439–1440**

standby monitors (SMs), **197, 1478**

standby power supplies (SPSes), 1403

star topology, **209**, *209*, **1478**

unshielded twisted-pair (UTP) cabling and, 14

starting

logging in Windows NT Performance Monitor, 936

network services in Linux, 538–539

SAMBA for NetWare, 454, *455*

Windows NT Performance Monitor, 933

startup sequence in Macintosh workstations, 1248–1258

static routing, **46–49**, *47, 48*, **103–106**, *104*

station monitors in LANalyzer, 1090–1093, *1091*

statnet command in Unix, 1125–1126, *1125*

stopping logging in Windows NT Performance Monitor, 936

store-and-forward connections, **213**

store-and-forward mode switches, 362

STP (shielded twisted-pair) cabling. *See also* twisted-pair cable

defined, **1478**

in Token Ring networks, 192

straight-through cables, **295**

Streams option in Windows NT, 494

StreetTalk

   defined, **587**

   installing StreetTalk Explorer for Windows NT, 594

   installing StreetTalk for Windows NT, 588–592, *589, 590*

   naming conventions, 595, *595*

   Network Communications dialog box, 589–591, *590*

stress testing, **950–958**

   benefits of, 951–952

   dumb loads, 950

   how to perfom, 954–955

   intelligent loads, 950–951

   security and, 952

   tools, **955–958**

      Ganymede Software Chariot and Pegasus, 958

      Mercury Interactive LoadRunner, 956

      Novell GENLOAD and VARLOAD, 955

      Phoenix Software NetTester/1, 957

      Ziff-Davis NetBench, ServerBench, and WebBench, 956, *957*

   upgrades and, 951–952

   when to perform, 953

striping, **910–912, 1469**

suballocating disks in NetWare, 408

subfunction code fields in NCP (NetWare Core Protocol), 143

subnet masks

   defined, **42, 758–761, 1479**

   nonstandard subnet masks, 94–100, *95, 97, 100*

   optimizing servers with multiple subnets, 921–922

   standard subnet masks, 42, 80–83, *82*

support hotlines, **1052**

surge protectors, 1402–1403

switch routers, **379**

Switched Multimegabit Data Service (SMDS) Internet connections, **715**

switches, **291, 359–371**

   cut-through mode, 361–362

   full duplex operations, 360–361

   IP addresses and, 919

monitoring tools in network hardware, **1070–1081**

   in bridges, 1078–1079

   error reports, 1076–1078, *1076, 1077*

   features to look for, 1072–1075, *1072, 1073, 1074*

   in routers, 1079–1081, *1079*

   SNMP and RMON (remote monitoring) support, 1081

   in switches, 1078

optimizing servers with, **916–920**, *917, 918*

SNMP (Simple Network Management Protocol) and, 917

store-and-forward mode, 362

switch overload, 363–364

VLAN (virtual local area network) technology, **364–368, 916**

   examples, 364–367, *365, 366, 367*

   limitations of, 367–368

   routers and, 917

   when to use, 368–371, *369, 370*

switching, **212–215, 1479**

   ATM Cell Switching Internet connections, 715

   circuit switching, 212–213, *213*, 1467

   defined, **1479**

   message switching, 213–214, *214*, 1472

   packet switching, 214–215, *215*, 261–262, 1468, 1475

   switching time in fiber-optic cable, **302**

Symmetric DSL (SDSL), 397–398

synchronizing communications, **278–279**

synchronous optical network (SONET), **264–265**

Syn_Flooder attacks, **1027**

Synoptic Network Management Module (NMM), 1135

system actions in Windows NT Workstation, **1013–1014**

System Fault Tolerance (SFT) in NetWare, **1198–1201**. *See also* fault tolerance

   mirroring and duplexing, 910–911, 1198–1199, *1199*, 1469

   RAID and, 1199–1200, *1200*

   SFT level III, 1201, *1201*, 1410

system logs in NetWare, 1192

System Network Architecture (SNA), 32

System suitcase in Macintosh workstations, 1246

T

T1 lines, **259–261**, **715**, **1364–1365**

T3 lines, **715**, **1364–1365**

Talk program in Linux, 525

tape backup systems. *See* backup systems

T-connectors, **180**

TCP/IP protocol suite, **61**, **78–131**, **1287**, **1479**

　AppleShare 5 TCP/IP over AFP protocol, 621

　AppleShare IP (ASIP), **166–168**, **620**

　　OpenDoc format and, 626–627

　　Windows networking and, 700

　Application layer services, **111–131**. *See also* DHCP; Domain Name Service; Network File System; SNMP

　　ACAP (Application Configuration Access Protocol), 122

　　bootp (Boot Protocol), 111, 112, 415

　　FTP (File Transfer Protocol), **116–118**, *116*, *117*, 415, 523–524, **1470**

　　Gopher, 119, 524, 1471

　　HTTP (Hypertext Transfer Protocol), 119–120, 214, 524, 623

　　IMAP4 (Internet Message Access Protocol, Version 4), 120–122, 524, 624, 978

　　MIME (Multimedia Internet Mail Extensions), 119, 127, 978, 981

　　NetBIOS over IP, 124, 154–156, *155*

　　NNTP (Network News Transfer Protocol), 123–124, 1474

　　Passive FTP (PASV FTP), 117–118

　　POP (Post Office Protocol), 120–121, **125–127**, 524, **978**

　　SMTP (Simple Mail Transfer Protocol), 127, 979, 981, 1478

　　Telnet, 61–64, *63*, 73, 74, **129**, 525, 1128–1129

　　WHOIS, 129–131

　flags, **61**

　IP addresses, **42**, **79–103**, **753–765**

　　127.0.0.1 loopback address, 88–89, 756

　　address classes, 84–88, *86*, *87*, 757–758, 1467

　　address conventions, 79–80

　　Advanced IP Addressing dialog box in Windows NT, 493, *493*

　　ARP (Address Resolution Protocol), 102–103, 1464

　　assigning, 763–765

　　broadcast addresses, 89, 91–93, 219

　　determining network and host addresses, 761–762

　　DHCP (Dynamic Host Configuration Protocol) and, 763–765

　　DNS (Domain Name Service) and, 102–103

　　lost address spaces, 101, *102*

　　multicast addresses, 90–93, *91*

　　network address translation (NAT) devices and, 94

　　network and host addresses, 42, 761–762

　　nonstandard subnet masks, 94–100, *95*, *97*, *100*

　　optimizing servers with multiple subnets, **921–922**

　　registered IP addresses, 83–88, *86*, *87*

　　reserved address ranges, 93–94

　　standard subnet masks, 42, 80–83, *82*, 758–761

　　switches and, 919

　　troubleshooting duplicate IP addresses, **1136–1138**

　　unicast addresses, 80, 91

　　zeros in, 83

　IP routing, **103–110**

　　BGP (Border Gateway Protocol), 109–110

　　dynamic routing, 106–110, 1469

　　EGP (Exterior Gateway Protocol), 107–109, *108*

　　OSPF (Open Shortest Path First), 109

　　RIP (Routing Information Protocol), 43, 106–107, 134, 485, 494

　　route command, 105–106

　　static routing, 46–49, *47*, *48*, 103–106, *104*

　　traceroute command, 43–45, *43*, *45*

　IP tunneling in Linux, 531

　IPX-to-IP gateway in NetWare, 414

　Linux TCP/IP applications, **523–525**

　　bootp server, 523

　　DNS server, 523

　　Finger server, 523

　　FTP server, 523–524

　　Gopher server, 524

　　HTTP server, 524

IMAP server, 524

Internet Relay Chat (IRC), 524

InterNetNews daemon, 525

Mail server, 524

NFS server, 525

NTP (network time protocol), 525

POP3 server, 524

SNMP Manager, 525

Talk, 525

Telnet server, 525

Linux TCP/IP support, 517, 519–511, *520*, 523–525,
    530–532, 549

Lotus Notes TCPIP Port Status dialog box, 571–573, *571*

Microsoft TCP/IP Printing service, 481, *481*

Microsoft TCP/IP Properties dialog box, 494–495, *494*

in NetWare

    binding TCP/IP protocol to network interface cards,
        423–424

    configuring LAN interfaces to use TCP/IP, 444

    configuring TCP/IP, 441–442

    configuring WAN groups to use TCP/IP, 444–445, *445*

    loading TCPIP.NLM, 418–419

NetWare IP, **681–683**, *682*

NetWare TCP/IP applications, **414–416**

    bootp support, 415

    DHCP server, 415

    DNS server, 415

    FTP server, 415

    multihoming support, 415–416

    Web servers, 415–416

OSI model and, 78, *79*

TCP (Transmission Control Protocol), 110

TCP Wrapper program in Linux, 517

Transport layer services, **110**

UDP (User Datagram Protocol), 64, 67–68, 110, 112

Windows NT TCP/IP support

    configuring, 494–495, *494*, 686–691

    installing, 684, *684*

    Microsoft TCP/IP Printing, 481, *481*

RIP for Internet Protocol service, 485, 494

Simple TCP/IP Services, 487

TCP/IP applications, 472–473, 497

tcpcon tool in NetWare, 1113

technical support hotlines, **1052**

telecommunications service providers, 1372

telecommuting, **838–875**. *See also* remote access

    advantages of for employees, **843–844**

        flexibility, 843

        morale, 843

        taxes, 843–844

    advantages of for employers, **839–843**

        absenteeism, 842–843

        corporate citizenship, 84

        corporate expansion, 842

        costs, 840–841, 842

        disaster recovery, 842

        insurance costs, 842

        overview of, 839–840

        productivity, 841

        recruitment, 842

    disadvantages of, **844–846**

    high-speed remote access, **874–875**

    ISDN lines and, 874

    modems, **393–398**, **869–875**

        baud rate versus bits per second (bps), 393, 869–870,
            1465, 1466

        cable modems, 396–397

        versus codexes, 394–395

        configuring, 871

        creating hunt groups for modem pools, 253–254

        DSLs (Digital Subscriber Lines), 397–398

        installing, 871–873, *872*

        Internet access and, 727

        ISDN modems, 395–396

        modem channel binding, 393–394

        multiport serial adapters and, 883

        optimizing modem use, 873

TOKEN RING

overvie...
power c...
UART c...
via remote c...
advanta...
Compac...
cost, 848
pcANY...
security,
Timbuktu Pro, 847, 858–859
tunneling and, **874–875**
when to implement, 839
telecommuting via remote access, **859–869**. *See also* remote access
advantages of, 860
installing Windows NT Remote Access Service (RAS), **861–869**
configuring communications, 861–863, *862*
configuring Dial-Up Networking clients, 868
configuring protocols, 863–865, *864*, *865*
configuring security, 865–867, *866*, *867*
disadvantages of RAS, 868–869
in NetWare versus Windows NT, 861
in Unix, 861
Telnet
connection-oriented communications and, 61–64, *63*
defined, **129**
Linux Telnet server, 525
port numbers and, 73, *74*
Telnet command in Unix, 1128–1129
10BaseT (twisted-pair) Ethernet standard, **1292**, **1464**
10Mb Ethernet topology, 221–225
terminators
defined, **1479**
in Ethernet networks, 180, 284–285, *285*
and finding cable plant problems, 1297–1299
terrestrial radio wave transmission, **310–311**
testing. *See also* stress testing
e-mail delivery, 1139–1143
multiport serial adapters, 887

thick Ethernet (thicknet) cabling, **14**, **180–181**, *181*, **1292**
thin clients, **386–388**
thin Ethernet (thinnet) cabling, **13–14**, **180–181**, **282–289**, **1292**
advantages and disadvantages, 286–288
bus topology and, 13
cable properties, 282–284, *283*
connectors, 284–285, *284*, *285*
cost, 286
fault resistance, 287–288
noise and, 286
scalability and, 287
shielding and, 286
specifications, 288–289
terminators, 180, 284–285, *285*, 1479
topology support, 288
uses for, 288
Timbuktu Pro software, **847**, **858–859**
time division in leased lines, **259–260**
time settings in Windows NT Performance Monitor, 935–936, 938–939, *939*
TLAP (TokenTalk Link Access Protocol), **615**
Token Ring networks, **8**, **11**, **188–204**, **1292–1294**, **1479**. *See also* networks; troubleshooting physical networks
advantages and disadvantages, **202–203**
cabling requirements, **1062**, **1293–1294**
hardware, **191–193**
CAUs (controlled access units), 192
connectors, 193
LAMs (lobe attachment modules), 192
lobes, 192
loopback mode lobes, 193
MSAUs (multi-station access units), 191, 192, 1293
network interface cards, 192
overview of, 191, *191*
phantom charges applied to lobes, 193
relay switches, 191, 193
shielded and unshielded twisted-pair cables, 192
Token Ring processes, **199–202**
beaconing, 201–202, 1465

initializing stations, 199–200

monitor contention, 195, 200

ring polling, 195, 200

ring purging, 200

Token Ring stations, **188–190**, **193–200**

active monitors (AMs), 195–196, *197*, 1464

configuration report servers (CRSs), 198

functional addresses, 194–195

and how Token Ring works, **188–190**, *189*

initializing, 199–200

ring error monitors (REMs), 198

ring parameter servers (RPSs), 197–198

standby monitors (SMs), 197, 1478

transmitting frames, 189–190

upstream and downstream neighbors, 188

tokens, 8, **11**, 195, **1292–1293**

troubleshooting, **1306–1308**

tokens

in FDDI networks, 236–237

in Token Ring networks, 8, 11, 195, 1292–1293

TokenTalk protocol, **615**

tools. *See* troubleshooting tools

topologies, **7–8**, **12**, **30**, **208–265**, **1282–1285**, **1479**. *See also* Ethernet; networks; Token Ring

bus topology

defined, **208**, *209*

linear bus topology, **1285**, **1466**

thin Ethernet (thinnet) cabling and, 13

connection types, **212–215**

circuit switching, 212–213, *213*, 1467

message switching, 213–214, *214*, 1472

packet switching, 214–215, *215*, 261–262, 1468, 1475

fiber-optic cable and, 304, *304*

local area network (LAN) topologies, **30**, **221–246**

1Gbps Ethernet topology, 229–231

10Mb Ethernet topology, 221–225

100Mb Ethernet topology, 225–229

100VG-AnyLAN topology, 231–235, 1062

ATM (asynchronous transfer mode), 242–246, *244*, 1062, 1465

FDDI, 14, 235–242, *236*, *238*, *239*, *241*

logical topologies, **211–212**, **1284**

NetWare topology support, 413

network interface cards and, 324–327, *327*

physical topologies, **208**, **211**, **1284**

ring topology, **210**, *210*, **1284–1285**, **1477**

star topology

defined, **209**, *209*, **1285**, **1478**

unshielded twisted-pair (UTP) cabling and, 14

thin Ethernet (thinnet) cabling and, 288

wide area network (WAN) topologies, **30**, **246–265**

bandwidth on demand connections, 57, 256

creating hunt groups for modem pools, 253–254

demarcation points, 248, 1468

dial-up analog connections, 249–251

Frame Relay and X.25 technologies, 261–264, *262*, 714, 1366, 1470, 1482

ISDN lines, 255–258, 714, 874, 888, 1471, 1472

leased lines, 258–259, 1366–1367, 1468, 1472

local exchange carriers, 248–249, *249*

plain old telephone services (POTs), 249–250

point of presence (POP) locations, 248

as point-to-point topologies, **247**, *247*

remote access connections using analog lines, 254–255

remote control dial-in connections, 251–252

remote node connections, 252–253

SONET (synchronous optical network), 264–265

T1 lines, 259–261, 715, 1364–1365

Windows NT topology support, 470

tping command in NetWare, 1099

traceroute command, 43–45, *43*, *45*

tracert command in Windows NT, 1121

track on command in NetWare, 1099–1101, *1100*

tracking configurations, 1045–1047, *1046*

training users, 1413–1414

transceivers, **327**, *327*, **1282**, **1479**

Transmission Control Protocol (TCP), **110**

transmission media, **270–279**, **309–315**. *See also* cabling
  analog transmissions, **5–6**, **270–272**
    amplitude and, 270–271, *271*, 1464
    analog dial-up connections, 249–251
    cabling and, 279
    communication synchronization and, 278–279
    frequency and, 270–272
    noise and, 272, *273*
    remote access connections using analog lines, 254–255
  communication synchronization and, **278–279**
  digital transmissions
    cabling and, 279
    communication synchronization and, 278–279
    defined, **5–6**, **272–276**, *274*, *275*
  light transmission, 309–310
  noise
    analog communications and, 272, *273*
    defined, **272**
    digital communications and, 30, 273–274, *274*, *275*
    electromagnetic interference (EMI), **13**, **276–278**, *277*, **1469**
    fiber-optic cable and, 306
    radio frequency interference (RFI), **13**, **278**, **1477**
    thin Ethernet (thinnet) cabling and, 286
    twisted-pair cable and, 298
  radio wave transmission, **310–312**, **534**
    fixed-frequency versus spread-spectrum signals, 310
    Linux radio network support, 534
    microwave signals, 310, 1365
    space-based transmissions, 311–312
    terrestrial transmissions, 310–311
  selecting, **280–282**, **312–315**
    analog and digital communications and, 280
    for campus networks, 314–315
    cost and, 281–282
    and distances between computer systems, 281
    environments and, 281
    fault tolerance and, 281
    future growth and, 280

    for medium-size networks, 313–314
    for small remote offices, 313
    user and application bandwidth demands and, 280
transmitting
  Ethernet frames with CSMA/CD, 175–177, *176*
  frames in Token Ring networks, 189–190
Transport layer
  ATP (AppleTalk Transaction Protocol) and, 164–165, *164*, 617
  in OSI model, **36**, 38, 40, 61–62, 64, **1289**
Transport layer services
  in AppleTalk, 164–165
  in NetBIOS, 156–157
  in TCP/IP, 110
Transport layer services in IPX, **135–147**. *See also* NCP
  IPX (Internetwork Packet Exchange) protocol, 136–137, *137*
  LIP (Large Internet Protocol), 144
  SPX (Sequence Packet Exchange), 137–139, *138*, *139*, 1287
  SPX I (Sequence Packet Exchange), 139–141, *140*
  SPX II (Sequence Packet Exchange), 141
traps in SNMP, 129
trend analysis, 1376–1377
troubleshooting, **24–26**, **1042–1391**
  breaking down the elements, 1043
  documentation and, 1049–1051, *1050*, *1051*
  duplicate IP addresses, **1136–1138**
  excessive network collisions, **1150–1153**, *1150*
  excessive pings, **1132–1135**, *1132*
  existing systems, **1047–1048**
  with fault points, **1053–1054**, *1055*, **1163–1165**, *1164*
  Help resources for, **1052**
  importance of attitude, **1048–1049**
  and keeping records, 1049–1051, *1050*, *1051*
  new systems and additions to systems, **1044–1047**
  Novell Directory Services, 1390–1391
  overview of, 24–26, 1042
  server upgrades, **1143–1150**, *1144*, 1197
  strategies for, **1042–1044**, **1053**

stripping down to the minimum, 1045

tracking configurations, 1045–1047, *1046*

trying different solutions, 1043–1044

undeliverable e-mail, **1138–1143**

worksheets for, 1049–1051, *1050, 1051*

troubleshooting physical networks, **1278–1282, 1296–1315**

  examples, **1301–1315**

    AppleTalk networks, 1312–1315

    existing Ethernet networks, 1304–1306, *1305*

    existing Token Ring networks, 1306–1308

    growing networks, 1308–1311, *1310*

    new cabling systems, 1301–1304

  fault points for physical networks, **1280–1282,** *1281*

  finding cable plant problems, **914–915, 1296–1301**

    cable, terminator, ground, and connector problems, 1297–1299

    documenting cable plants, 1300–1301

    overview of, 1296–1297

    patch panel, repeater, and hub problems, 1299–1300

    router, bridge, and gateway problems, 1300

  overview of, **1278–1280**

troubleshooting printing, **1318–1323, 1336–1354**

  examples, **1340–1354**

    Macintosh printing problems, 1352–1354

    PostScript printers, 1340–1344

    remote printing with NetWare 4.*x*, 1347–1349

    routers as print servers, 1344–1347, *1345*

    workstation printing problems, 1350–1352

  fault points for network printing, **1323–1326,** *1324*

  Macintosh printers, 1262, 1322–1323, 1337–1338, 1352–1354

  NetWare for Macintosh printing, 1337–1338

  overview of, **1318–1323**

  PostScript printers, 1336–1337, 1340–1344

  troubleshooting Windows 95/9/NT client printers in NetWare, 1332–1333

  Unix printing, 1338–1339

troubleshooting servers, **1156–1210.** *See also* servers

  diagnostic tools, 1195–1196

  examples, **1201–1210**

  installing servers, 1202–1207

  maintaining existing systems, 1207–1210

  with fault points, 1053–1054, *1055,* 1163–1165, *1164*

  hardware problems in existing servers, **1188–1192**

    with NetWare MONITOR, 481–482, *482,* 1121, 1191

    with NetWare SERVMAN and FCONSOLE, 1191

    with NetWare system logs, 1192

    with NetWare VREPAIR, 1191–1192

    with Windows NT Event Viewer, 1189–1190, *1190*

    with Windows NT Network Monitor, 481–482, *482,* 1121, 1190, 1381

    with Windows NT Performance Monitor, 1190–1191

  hardware problems in new NetWare servers, **1169–1178**

    automatic loading of BIOS into upper memory, 1177

    bus architecture, 1171–1173

    hard disk drives, 1176

    interrupts and EISA or PCI configurations, 1172, 1177

    multiple network interface cards, 1176

    overview of, 1169

    RAID systems, 1175–1176

    RAM, 1170–1171

    SCSI adapters and devices, 1173–1175, *1175*

    security, 1178

    VGA adapters, 1176–1177

  intermittent problems, **1194–1195**

  NetWare servers

    ABEND messages, 406–407, *407,* 1188, 1193

    configuration files, 1184–1185

    drivers, 1186

    with fault points, 1053–1054, *1055,* 1163–1165, *1164*

    installations, 1184

    login scripts, 1187–1188

    managing binderies or Novell Directory Services (NDS), 1196

    multiple protocols, 1186–1187

    NetWare 2.*x* servers, 1166

    NetWare 3.*x* servers, 1166–1167, *1167*

    NetWare 4.*x* servers, 1167–1169, *1167*

    network address assignments, 1186

NLM problems, 1197–1198

overview of, **1160–1162**

permissions, 1187

preparing hard disk drives for NetWare installation, 1185–1186

upgrading NetWare, 1197

NetWare System Fault Tolerance (SFT), **1198–1201**

mirroring and duplexing, 910–911, 1198–1199, *1199*, 1469

RAID and, 1199–1200, *1200*

SFT level III, 1201, *1201*, 1410

software problems in existing NetWare servers, **1192–1194**

ABEND messages, 406–407, *407*, 1188, 1193

with BINDFIX, 1193–1194

corrupted SERVER.EXE or NET$OS.EXE files, 1192–1193

with DSTRACE or DSREPAIR, 1194

software problems in new servers, **1178–1188**

NetWare servers, 1184–1188

Windows NT servers, 1178–1184

Windows NT servers, **1156–1160, 1178–1184, 1189–1191**

with Event Viewer, 1189–1190, *1190*

installation process, 1178–1184

with Network Monitor, 481–482, *482*, 1121, 1190, 1381

overview of, **1156–1160**

with Performance Monitor, 1190–1191

troubleshooting tools (hardware), **1060–1082**

basic cable checkers, 1060–1063, *1061*

cable testers, 1063–1066, *1064*

fiber cable testers, 1063, 1066

handheld diagnostic tools, 1066–1067, *1067*

monitoring tools in network hardware, **1070–1081**

in bridges, 1078–1079

error reports, 1076–1078, *1076*, *1077*

features to look for, 1072–1075, *1072*, *1073*, *1074*

in routers, 1079–1081, *1079*

SNMP and RMON (remote monitoring) support, 1081

in switches, 1078

network analyzers, 1069–1070, *1069*, *1070*

network monitoring tools, 1067–1068

troubleshooting tools (software), **1086–1129**

Unix commands, **1123–1129**

arp, 1124

ifconfig, 1124, *1124*

netstat, 1124

nslookup, 1124

ping, 1125

route, 1125

statnet, 1125–1126, *1125*

tcpdump, 1126–1127, *1126*

Telnet, 1128–1129

traceroute, 1129

Windows NT Server command-line tools, **1114–1121**

arp, 1114–1115

ipxroute, 1115

nbtstat, 1115–1116, *1116*

netstat, 1117–1118, *1117*

nslookup, 1118–1120

ping, 1120–1121

route, 1121

tracert, 1121

Windows NT Server graphical tools, **1121–1123**

Network Monitor, 481–482, *482*, 1121, 1191, 1381

Performance Monitor, 1122, *1122*

winmsd utility, 1123, *1123*

troubleshooting tools (software) in NetWare, **1093–1114**

command line tools, **1094–1101**

config, 1094–1095, *1094*

display networks, 1095, *1095*

display servers, 1096, *1096*

packet burst statistics screen, 1097–1099, *1097*

protocols, 1097

reset router, 1099

tping, 1099

track on, 1099–1101, *1100*

console tools, **1093–1101**

graphical tools, **1101–1113**

aiocon, 1107

atcon, 1107

atmcon, 1108

IPX Console, 1101–1107

ipxping, 1108

Monitor, 1108–1113, *1109*, *1111*, 1191

ping, 1113

tcpcon, 1113

IPX Console, **1101–1107**

circuits options, 1106–1107, *1106*

Detailed IPX Information option, 1103–1104, *1103*

Forwarding and Services option, 1107

IPX Information option, 1102–1103, *1103*

IPX Router Information option, 1104–1105, *1105*

load command and, 1101

Mobile IPX Information option, 1106

NLSP Information screen, 1106

SNMP Access Configuration option, 1102

LANalyzer, **1086–1093**, **1383**

alarms, 1087–1088, *1088*

Capture Buffer option, 1087

dashboard, 1086, *1087*

station monitors, 1090–1093, *1091*

and troubleshooting wide area networks, 1383

utilization statistics, 1088–1090, *1089*, *1090*

workstation commands, **1113–1114**

troubleshooting wide area networks, **1367–1386**. *See also* wide area networks

diagnostic tools, **1378–1384**

doing without, 1384

hardware-based products, 1379–1381

LANalyzer, 1086–1093, 1383

in NetWare, 1383

protocol analyzers, 1379–1381, 1476

software-only products, 1381–1384

Windows NT Network Monitor, 481–482, *482*, 1121, 1191, 1381

Windows NT Performance Monitor, 1382–1383

fault points of WANs, **1367–1375**

address conflicts, 1375

baselining, 1374

bridge problems, 1368–1369

configuration utilities and, 1373–1374

dial-in/dial-out server problems, 1370–1371

gateway problems, 1369–1370

network address problems, 1373

repeater problems, 1368

router problems, 1369

software configuration problems, 1374–1375

telecommunications service provider problems, 1372

troubleshooting WAN hardware, **1368–1371**

troubleshooting WAN software, **1372–1375**

network management tools, **1375–1378**

features to look for, 1376–1378

network inventory, 1377–1378

network mapping, 1377

online Help, 1377

overview of, 1376–1377

packet monitoring, 1376

server management, 1378

SNMP management, 1377

trend analysis, 1376–1377

services across WANs, **1385–1386**

managing multiple logins, 1386

printing, 1385–1386

troubleshooting workstations, **1213–1274**. *See also* workstations

checking connections, changes, and new installations, 1225–1226

examples, **1263–1274**

existing Macintosh workstations, 1271–1274

existing workstations, 1269–1271

installing workstations, 1263–1267

maintaining workstations, 1267–1269

fault points for workstations, **1218–1224**

DOS/Windows 3.*x* system and network driver failures, 1223–1224

PC Card, motherboard, or BIOS failures, 1221

user failures, 1224

Windows 95/98 system and network driver failures, 1221–1223

Windows NT system and network driver failures, 1223

workstation-to-network connection failures, 1220

Macintosh workstations, **1217–1218**, **1244–1262**

bootstrap sequence, 1249–1252

configuring Open Transport, 1259

control panels and extensions, 1247, 1252–1257

example, 1271–1274

Finder application, 1246, 1247, 1257–1258

fixing extension conflicts, 1255–1257

INIT crawl problems, 1252–1257

modifying load order, 1253–1255

mounting remote volumes, 1258–1259

overview of, **1217–1218**, **1244–1248**

printing, 1262

SCSI devices, 1260–1262, *1260*

startup sequence, 1248–1258

System suitcase, 1246

OS/2 clients, **1243–1244**

overview of, **1224–1226**

PC hardware problems, **1226–1233**

boot sequence, 1227–1228

interrupt conflicts, 1230–1231

overview of, **1214–1217**, **1218**, **1226–1227**, *1227*

PC Cards and connections, 1228–1230

Plug and Play devices, 1233

SETUP configuration problems, 1231–1233

PC software problems, **1214–1217**, **1218**, **1226–1227**, **1233–1237**

DOS, 1234

NetWare DOS Requester and VLMs, 1236–1237

NetWare drivers, 1235–1236

ODI drivers, 1235–1236

overview of, **1214–1217**, **1218**, **1226–1227**, *1227*

PS/2 (Micro Channel) clients, 1244

Unix workstations, **1262–1263**

Windows workstations, **1237–1243**

long filename support, 1241–1242

Microsoft NDS Service, 672–673, *673*, 1241

Microsoft NetWare Client, 1240

NetWare VLM client, 1240–1241

Novell NetWare Client for Windows 95, 1241

protocol support, 1242

Windows 3.*x*, 1238–1239

Windows 95/98, 1240–1242

Windows NT, 1242–1243

True Commit option for Client32 drivers, 669

trust relationships, 466, 987

trustee rights in Windows NT, **470**, **1418**

tunneling

encryption and encryption key management, 1022–1023

Internet security and, 1022–1023

IP tunneling in Linux, 531

PPTP (Point-to-Point Tunneling Protocol), 471, 491–493, *492*, *493*, 826

telecommuting and, 874–875

tunneling protocols, **21**

tunneling virtual private networks, 823–824

twisted-pair cable, **192**, **289–299**, **1292**, **1480**. *See also* cabling

10BaseT (twisted-pair) Ethernet standard, 1292, 1464

advantages and disadvantages, 296–298

AT&T 285A standard for connectors, 293–295

bandwidth and, 297

cable properties, 289–291, *290*, *292*

categories of, 290–291

color-coding for connectors, 293–295

connectors, 293–295, *294*, *295*

cost, 297

cross cables, 295

EIA standard for connectors, 293, 295

fault tolerance and, 297

full duplex communications, 292–293

installing, 296

length limits, 298

noise and, 298

shielded twisted-pair (STP) cabling, 192, 1478

specifications, 299

splicing, 329

straight-through cables, 295

topology wiring requirements, **1062**

unshielded twisted-pair (UTP) cabling

CAT3 (Category 3) cable, 226, 234, 328, 329, 1298–1299

CAT5 (Category 5) cable, 14, 328, 329, 1298–1299

in Ethernet networks, 181–182, *182*, 1298–1299

hubs and, 338

star topology and, 14

in Token Ring networks, 192

uses for, 298

Tx fiber-optic connections, 303–304

type 20 propagation, 153

U

UART chips, 870, 883–884

UDP (User Datagram Protocol), 64, 67–68, 110, 112

UNC (universal naming convention), **389**

undeliverable e-mail, **1138–1143**

unicast addresses, 80, 91

unidirectional cable modems, 396–397

uninterruptible power supplies (UPSs), 1403

Unix. *See also* Linux; Network File System

Apache Web servers, 718–719

books about, 1435

client communications with FTP servers or Web servers, 703

communications with other operating systems, **634–635**

defined, **17–18**, **502–503**, **1480**

DNSKiller attacks, 1027

history of, 502–503

MAKE files, **503**

software troubleshooting tools, **1123–1129**

arp, 1124

ifconfig, 1124, *1124*

netstat, 1124

nslookup, 1124

ping, 1125

route, 1125

statnet, 1125–1126, *1125*

tcpdump, 1126–1127, *1126*

Telnet, 1128–1129

traceroute, 1129

Syn_Flooder attacks, 1027

telecommuting via remote access, 861

troubleshooting printing, **1338–1339**

troubleshooting Unix workstations, **1262–1263**

Unix file servers, 389

Unix newsgroups, 1439

versions of, 503–504

unmanaged stackable hubs, **15**, **341**

unpopulated segments, **289**

unshielded twisted-pair (UTP) cabling. *See also* twisted-pair cable

CAT3 (Category 3) cable, 226, 234, 328, 329, 1298–1299

CAT5 (Category 5) cable, 14, 328, 329, 1298–1299

in Ethernet networks, 181–182, *182*, 1298–1299

hubs and, 338

star topology and, 14

in Token Ring networks, 192

upgrading. *See also* installing; migrating

NetWare, 404–405, 1197

stress testing and, 951–952

troubleshooting server upgrades, 1143–1150, *1144*, 1197

Windows NT, 461–462

uplink port connections for stackable hubs, **15**, **342**, *342*

upper layer services in AppleTalk, **165–168**

AFP (AppleTalk Filing Protocol), 165–167, 618, 621

ASIP (AppleShare IP), 166–168, 620, 626–627, 700

upper port numbers, **70–71**

upper-layer communications, **74**

upstream neighbors of Token Ring stations, 188

URLs (universal resource locators), port numbers and, 71

Use Network tab in LANtastic Custom Control Panel, 599–602

Use Video BIOS option for Client32 drivers, 669

user authentication, **467**, **472**, **1017–1020**, **1035–1036**
credit card transactions and, 1018–1020
password authentication in Web servers, 1035–1036
S-HTTP (Secure HTTP), 1017–1018
SSL (Secure Sockets Layer) and, 472, 1017–1018
in Windows NT, 467
user failures, 1224
User ID files in Lotus Notes, **562–563**
User Preferences window in Lotus Notes, 570–571, *570*
users
in Banyan VINES, 596, *596*
in Linux, 516, *516*
training, 1413–1414
user authentication in Windows NT, 467
user or home directories, 974–976
user rights, 970–976
user-related objects in Novell Directory Services, 1389
in Windows NT, 469
utilities. *See* troubleshooting tools
utilization rates, **222**
utilization statistics
in LANalyzer, 1088–1090, *1089*, *1090*
in Windows NT Performance Monitor, 942, 944
uuencoding and uudecoding files, 127, 979

virtual memory
in Linux, 510
in Windows NT, 463
virtual path identifiers (VPIs) in ATM networks, **244**
virtual private networks (VPNs), **21**, **789**, **823–827**. *See also*
extranets; intranets
denial-of-service (DoS) attacks, 827, 1024, 1028
how VPNs work, 824–826, *824*, *825*
Internet security and, 1020–1022
PPTP (Point-to-Point Tunneling Protocol) and, 826
security, 826–827
tunneling versus firewall gateway VPNs, 823–824
viruses, **1222–1223**, **1414–1415**, **1480**
VLAN (virtual local area network) switches, **364–368**, **916**
examples, 364–367, *365*, *366*, *367*
limitations of, 367–368
routers and, 917
VLMs (Virtual Loadable Modules) in NetWare
defined, **1236–1237**
NetWare VLM client, 1240–1241
volumes
mounting remote volumes for Macintosh workstations,
1258–1259
remote volumes in AppleTalk Filing Protocol, 167
VREPAIR utility in NetWare, 1191–1192

V

VARLOAD utility, 955
Very high rate DSL (VDSL), 397–398
VESA local bus, **325**
VGA adapters, 1176–1177
Viacom Internet Gateway in AppleShare 5, 627
View Configuration option in INETCFG.NLM, 449–450, *450*
views in Windows NT Performance Monitor, 932–933
VINES. *See* Banyan VINES
virtual hubs, **339**

W

WANs. *See* wide area networks
Wavelet DSL (WDSL), 397–398
Web browsers, **721–726**, **730**, **1023–1026**, **1480**
Amaya, 725
browser security, 736–737
Cyberdog, 725–726
defined, **1480**
HotJava, 726

implementing, 724, 730

Internet Explorer versus Netscape, 721–725

loopholes, **1023–1026**

    ActiveX, 1025–1026

    Java, 1024

    JavaScript, 1025

Mosaic, 726

Opera, 726

plug-ins and ActiveX programs, 724–725, 1025–1026

Web proxy servers, **751**, **1001–1007**

    firewalls and, 751

    Microsoft Proxy Server, 1002–1003

    Netscape Proxy Server, 1003–1006

    WinGate, 1006–1007

Web servers, **700–703**, **717–721**. *See also* Internet access; servers

    Apache servers, 718–719

    AppleShare 5 Web and File Server, 621–622

    in Macintosh environments, 701

    Microsoft Internet Information Server (IIS), 472, 480–481, 719

    NCSA httpd servers, 718

    Netscape servers, 719

    in NetWare, 415–416

    operating systems for, 720–721

    overview of, 700

    security, **1028–1036**

        access logging, 1028–1031, *1029*

        client certificate authentication, 1036

        directory-level access, 1031–1035, *1033*, *1034*

        in Netscape FastTrack Server, 1029–1036, *1029*

        password authentication, 1035–1036

    selecting for intranets, 766–767

    in Unix or Linux, 703

    in Windows 3.1x, 701

    in Windows 95/98 or NT Workstation, 702

    in Windows NT Server, 702

Web sites, **1052**, **1440–1441**, **1446–1453**, **1480**

    for cable and connector vendors, 1451

    defined, **1480**

    for hardware vendors, 1446–1451

    for Help with troubleshooting, 1052

    listed, **1440–1441**

    for mail-order hardware vendors, 1452–1453

    for software vendors, 1452

WebBench utility, 956, *957*

well-known ports, **70–71**

WHOIS utility, **129–131**

wide area networks (WANs), **1358–1391**, **1480**

    configuring WAN groups to use TCP/IP in NetWare, 444–445, *445*

    connecting LANs across long distances, **1362–1365**

        analog dial-up connections, 1363

        digital dial-up connections, 1363–1364

        leased analog connections, 1363

        leased digital connections, 1364–1365

        with microwave relays, 1365

        with satellite services, 1365

        with telephone company services, 1362–1365

    connecting LANs around the world, **1365–1367**

        with Frame Relay protocol, 1366

        with Frame Relay and X.25 connections, 1366

        with leased lines, 258–259, 1366–1367, 1468, 1472

        with satellite services, 1367

    connecting LANs at a site, **1359–1361**

        with bridges, 1359–1360

        with gateways, 1361

        with routers, 1360–1361

    connecting LANs between buildings, **1361–1362**

        with bridges, 1362

        with repeaters, 1361–1362

    defined, **1480**

    diagnostic tools, **1378–1384**

        doing without, 1384

        hardware-based products, 1379–1381

        LANalyzer, 1086–1093, 1383

        in NetWare, 1383

        protocol analyzers, 1379–1381, 1476

software-only products, 1381–1384

Windows NT Network Monitor, 481–482, *482*, 1121, 1191, 1381

Windows NT Performance Monitor, 1382–1383

fault points of WANs, **1367–1375**

   address conflicts, 1375

   baselining, 1374

   bridge problems, 1368–1369

   configuration utilities and, 1373–1374

   dial-in/dial-out server problems, 1370–1371

   gateway problems, 1369–1370

   network address problems, 1373

   repeater problems, 1368

   router problems, 1369

   software configuration problems, 1374–1375

   telecommunications service provider problems, 1372

   troubleshooting WAN hardware, **1368–1371**

   troubleshooting WAN software, **1372–1375**

network management tools, **1375–1378**

   features to look for, 1376–1378

   network inventory, 1377–1378

   network mapping, 1377

   online Help, 1377

   overview of, 1376–1377

   packet monitoring, 1376

   server management, 1378

   SNMP management, 1377

   trend analysis, 1376–1377

Novell Directory Services (NDS), **410, 672–673, 1196, 1241, 1386–1391, 1474**

   backing up, 1399

   container objects, 1387–1389

   installing and configuring Microsoft NDS client, 672–673, *673*, 1241

   leaf objects, 1387

   managing, 1196

   miscellaneous objects, 1390

   NDS objects, 1387–1390, *1388*

   NDS trees, 1387

NetWare Administrator (NWADMIN), 1390

   Organization and Organizational Unit (OU) objects, 1389

   printer-related objects, 1389

   server-related objects, 1389

   troubleshooting, 1390–1391

   user-related objects, 1389

services across WANs, **1385–1386**

   managing multiple logins, 1386

   printing, 1385–1386

WAN Call Directory option in INETCFG.NLM, 432–435, *433*

WAN topologies, **30, 246–265**

   bandwidth on demand connections, 57, 256

   creating hunt groups for modem pools, 253–254

   demarcation points, 248, 1468

   dial-up analog connections, 249–251

   Frame Relay and X.25 technologies, 261–264, *262*, 714, 1366, 1470, 1482

   ISDN lines, 255–258, 714, 874, 888, 1471, 1472

   leased lines, 258–259, 1366–1367, 1468, 1472

   local exchange carriers, 248–249, *249*

   plain old telephone services (POTS), 249–250

   point of presence (POP) locations, 248

   as point-to-point topologies, **247**, *247*

   remote access connections using analog lines, 254–255

   remote control dial-in connections, 251–252

   remote node connections, 252–253

   SONET (synchronous optical network), 264–265

   T1 lines, 259–261, 715, 1364–1365

Windows. *See* Microsoft Windows

WinFrame software, **387**

WinGate proxy servers, 1006–1007

winmsd utility in Windows NT, 1123, *1123*

WINS (Windows Internet Name Service)

   defined, **488, 1481**

   Domain Name Service and, 480

   NetBIOS and, 152, 154–156, *155*, 473

Wizards, Administrative Wizard in Windows NT, 468, *468*

worksheets for troubleshooting, **1049–1051**, *1050, 1051*

workstations, **384–388**, **1481**. *See also* clients; servers; troubleshooting workstations
    backing up workstation data, 1401–1402
    boot PROM chips, 386–387
    installing, 1263–1267
    maintaining, 1267–1269
    versus servers, 391–392
    thin clients, **386–388**
    troubleshooting printing problems, 1350–1352
    Windows NT and, 463, 488
    workstation commands in NetWare, **1113–1114**
    workstation images, 385–386
    Workstation service in Windows NT, 488

X

X.25 networks, **261–264**, *262*, **714**, **1366**, **1482**
X.400 protocol, **979**
xDSL, 397–398
X-Windows interface in Linux, 510

Z

zeros in IP addresses, 83
Ziff-Davis NetBench, ServerBench, and WebBench utilities, 956, *957*
zones
    in AppleTalk, 42, 162
    in EtherTalk, 614–615
    ZIP (Zone Information Protocol), 162

From the Experts...

Who bring you Mark Minasi's #1 best-selling *Complete PC Upgrade & Maintenance Guide*, Sybex now presents...

Nearly a million copies sold!

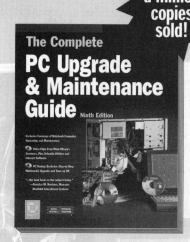

The Complete Network Upgrade & Maintenance Guide

BY MARK MINASI, JIM BLANEY, CHRIS BRENTON

The Ultimate Networking Reference—this book is a practical and comprehensive guide to implementing, upgrading, and maintaining networks, from small office LANs to enterprise-scale WANs and beyond.

ISBN: 0-7821-2259-0
1536 pp., $69.99

The Complete Website Upgrade & Maintenance Guide

BY LISA SCHMEISER

Destined to be the industry's ultimate Website reference, this book is the most comprehensive and broad-reaching tome, created to help you turn an existing site into a long-lasting sophisticated, dynamic, effective tool.

ISBN: 0-7821-2315-5
912 pp., $49.99

The Complete PC Upgrade & Maintenance Guide, 9th edition

BY MARK MINASI

After selling nearly <u>one million copies</u> of its previous editions, the 9th edition carries on the tradition with detailed troubleshooting for the latest motherboards, sound cards, video boards, CD-ROM drives, and all other multimedia devices.

ISBN: 0-7821-2357-0
1600 pp., $59.99

SYBEX BOOKS ON THE WEB

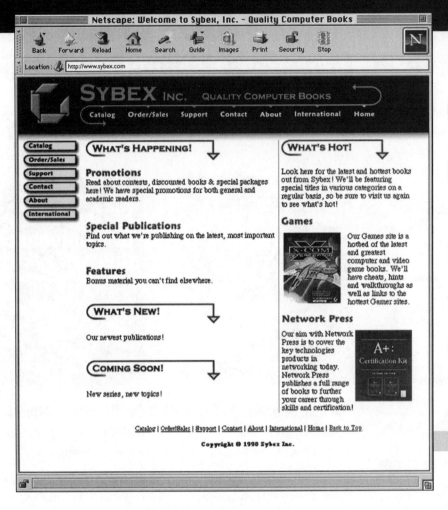

At the dynamic and informative Sybex Web site, you can:

- view our complete online catalog
- preview a book you're interested in
- access special book content
- order books online at special discount prices
- learn about Sybex

www.sybex.com

SYBEX Inc. • 1151 Marina Village Parkway, Alameda, CA 94501 • 510-523-8233

The CD-ROM for *The Complete Network Upgrade and Maintenance Guide*

This CD-ROM provides value-added features to *The Complete Network Upgrade and Maintenance Guide*:

On this CD you'll find a wide assortment of networking tools and utilities, from simple messaging utilities (*WinPop Plus*) to comprehensive enterprise network management and diagnostic software (Mission Critical Software's *Enterprise Administrator*, an advanced, rules-based administrative environment for large-scale Windows NT networks; and *Enterprise Event Manager*, a leading Windows NT enterprise event management tool). Some of the tools included here are shareware versions; be sure to register them if you find them useful.

We've also included an electronic version of this book, containing the complete text and graphics of the book chapters in an Adobe™ Acrobat™ PDF file format. (Of course, we've included the Adobe Acrobat Reader on the CD-ROM. Install it by running the ACROREAD.EXE file in the Acrobat folder.)

> **NOTE**
>
> Acrobat and Acrobat Reader © 1987–1997 Adobe Systems Incorporated. All rights reserved. Adobe, Acrobat, and the Acrobat logo are trademarks of Adobe Systems Incorporated which may be registered in certain jurisdictions.

Products Included on this CD-ROM:

Adobe Acrobat Reader

aVirt Gateway Server

Emergency Messaging System 2.0

GetTime Time Synchronization Software

GnatBox Light, version 2.1.0

LANCharge

Mission Critical Software's Enterprise Administrator and Enterprise Event Manager

NDS List, Version 1.1

NetConnect

NetHelper 2.0

Net Sentry Version 1.00

PingGraph version 1.0.2

WinPop Plus

To install any of the products from this CD, simply run the appropriate .EXE file as found in the product's folder. (Most of the folders contain a SETUP.EXE file; some, however, have an .EXE file named after the product.) Please note that although some of the programs included here may run on multiple platforms, Sybex has tested them only on Windows 95 and Windows NT 4, and so makes no warranty concerning their effectiveness on other platforms.

> **NOTE**
>
> Check out the README.TXT file in the root folder of the CD-ROM for individual program descriptions and installation instructions. In addition, please be sure to check out each product's "readme" file (look for TXT, DOC, or PDF files in the product folder) for further information about the program—including information concerning how to register it for your use. In some cases, the product is intended only as a demonstration of what the full, registered version can do for you, and the version on this CD-ROM may be designed to stop working after a certain number of days.